# CLAT & AILET

## Chapter-Wise
## SOLVED PAPERS
## 2008-2017

*Includes*

**4 Model Papers &**
**CLAT & AILET Solved Papers 2018**

*by*

**Gautam Puri**
(Alumnus IIM Bangalore)

**CL MEDIA (P) LTD.**

**Edition : 2018**



**Typeset by :** *CL Media DTP Unit*

**Administrative and Production Offices**

**Published by :** **CL Media (P) Ltd.**
A-41, Lower Ground Floor,
Espire Building,
Mohan Cooperative Industrial Area,
Main Mathura Road,
New Delhi - 110044

**Marketed by :** **G.K. Publications (P) Ltd.**
A-41, Lower Ground Floor,
Espire Building,
Mohan Cooperative Industrial Area,
Main Mathura Road,
New Delhi - 110044

For product information :
Visit ***www.gkpublications.com*** or email to ***gkp@gkpublications.com***

# Preface

*'Even when laws have been written down, they ought not always to remain unaltered.'* Aristotle in his famous quote has rightly captured the essence of pursuing law. Law as a career option is drawing in large numbers, and rightly so. Great demand in government as well as corporate arena has further cemented the position that law as a career has enjoyed over the years. The profession has seen a paradigm shift; crisp business suits have replaced black robes and fancy corporate offices have filled in for dull courtrooms.

Common Law Admission Test (CLAT) is one entrance that almost every law aspirant sits for. CLAT is an all India entrance exam conducted by 14 National Law Schools/Universities on a rotational basis. Apart from these prestigious universities, there are some other institutes too that accept CLAT scores for admission to their under-graduate/post graduate programs. National Law University, Delhi (NLUD) is the only other National Law University that doesn't accept CLAT scores and conducts its own entrance examination.

Naturally, cracking such coveted and highly competitive examinations is no cake walk. However, you can certainly guarantee yourself a smooth journey if you start early and plan it well. Like any other competitive exam, law school tests aim at assessing your language, logical reasoning and decision making skills. Still, what makes these exams different from the rest is the relatively greater stress that is placed on gauging the reasoning skills of the aspirants, a must-have for any potential lawyer. Regular practice coupled with a balanced approach shall see you through the exams.

After you are well acquainted with the basics, the best idea is to solve past year papers. They not only help in building concepts but also give an insight into the paper. This will help you strategize well according to the exam and familiarize you with the pattern.

This book consists of solved past year papers for both CLAT and NLU-D. The questions of the same type from various years have been grouped together for your convenience. This will enable you practice them topic wise, ensuring you do not skip anything in the process. Detailed solutions have been provided for all questions making sure you don't have an iota of doubt.

**English :**

A word about the English section- CLAT and NLUD like to throw surprises, leaving students bewildered in the examination halls. CLAT-2011, for example, had four RCs leaving out grammar and vocabulary questions, which are famously part of the paper otherwise. Thus, it's always better to go with an open mind, ready to field the googlies.

Many students tend to fumble when they're answering the Reading Comprehension (RC) section. This can be attributed to the fact that many students do not enjoy reading. Often the topics covered in the CLAT and other law entrance tests are dry and not of any great interest to the student. Also, since they require a close reading of the passage, students fear that they are wasting too much time and end up making mistakes. However, what they don't realize is that it can also be used to their advantage. The answers are all in front of them; all they have to do is read and find them. With the right technique, this can become a very scoring area.

The right RC strategy - i) Read the passage once quickly in order to understand the central idea. In case certain areas of the passage elude your understanding at first, do not worry. Now read the questions and come back to the relevant portion of the passage in order to eliminate options. Look for key words in the question stem in order to identify the part of the passage where you are most likely to find the answer. ii) Some students prefer to read the passage first and then go to the questions while some tend to read the questions and scan the passage for answers. This might work with questions that are factual. For inference based questions this may prove fatal as you need understanding of the entire passage. While there is no right strategy, your modus operandi can be the one that works better (and faster) for you. Solve plenty of questions to know what yields the best results so that you're all set for the actual Test.

Para jumbles can be very scoring if attempted correctly. In these questions, you must try and look for keywords that help you make pairs in the given sentences. Find words that show comparison or contrast. Words like 'hence' and 'therefore' show consequence whereas 'but', 'rather', 'nevertheless' show contrast. Some other words like 'furthermore' and 'along with' are a dead give-away when it comes to furthering an argument. You can use these key words to determine which sentence will come next.

## Analytical Reasoning and Quantitative Ability :

Analytical Reasoning and Quantitative ability questions are based on basic common sense and logic. They can be easily attempted even by students who have given up Mathematics after Class X. When you're in the practicing stage, mark the questions that you can't solve in the first attempt with an asterisk (*). This will make things easier for you when you go back to revise that particular topic. When you're short on time, there is no point in revising each and every question; especially those which you have been able to crack easily.

## Legal Aptitude :

Legal Aptitude section carries the highest weight in Law entrance papers and hence you need to be rock solid in this area. This section can be broadly categorized into:

1. Legal Knowledge.
2. Legal Reasoning.

For solving a legal knowledge question you must be well versed with the basics of law. This, to a certain extent, requires reading relevant and authentic text at a consistent pace throughout your preparatory period. Along with this, keep a regular watch on day to day happenings around the world in the legal arena. Make sure that you have a study plan enabling you to cover the entire syllabus and allowing you to read and re-read the subjects. Don't read just anything and everything. Choose your study material and mock questions very carefully.

Legal reasoning is simply an extension of critical reasoning. Knowledge of law is never required to solve a legal reasoning question. In fact, unnecessary knowledge of law generally becomes misleading. A good lawyer is one who can analyze and reason out a solution to the problem. Knowledge of law comes next. To solve a legal reasoning question, emphasis should be given on understanding the principle clearly and applying that principle over the given factual situation. Law is logic, so stick to the principle of law and answer the question based on the applicable principle. Solving a legal reasoning question requires an intense amount of practice. Therefore, practice the tests keeping the time frame in mind so that you get used to it. This, in turn, lets you wrap up the test conveniently in the actual examination. Besides this, make sure that the practice questions are authentic, correct and meet the standards of law entrance examinations.

Towards the preparation of Legal Aptitude section, 'practice' is the keyword; practice tests will prepare you fast and will ensure that you are on the right way. Also make sure that not only are you able to solve the questions, but also are able to solve them in the set time frame.

## General Knowledge :

General Knowledge today is one of the standard aspects of every competitive exam. This particular section exists primarily to assess whether a candidate keeps himself aware of the latest happenings and has a learning aptitude displayed by his knowledge of basic social and everyday science. Learning aptitude here means something that a successful undergraduate student, aspiring to get admission in a premiere law school, must have in order to qualify. The general knowledge preparation requires constant updating of all the spheres of society, be it economic or social. For starters, one can take up reading a good newspaper (preferably The Hindu and Economic Times). The preparation strategy here will count on the understanding of two parts of General Studies, viz. Current G.K. and Static G.K.

For Static G.K., a candidate must keep himself/herself aware about basic History, Geography, Civics and Science studied till 10th standard in school.

For Current G.K., a candidate must subscribe to a national daily (preferably one in English language) and shall go through monthly magazines in order to consolidate all the information. The candidate should try to cover at least up to 9 months before the exam to have an appreciable grip of this section.

Lastly, one should always cultivate a habit of reading reputed newspaper dailies and magazines as reading a good newspaper will help you further your understanding in English Vocabulary and will also enhance your reading pace.

All the best....!

# About the Exam

## About AILET

All India Law Entrance Test (AILET) is conducted to take admission into undergraduate and postgraduate courses in law offered by National Law University (NLU), Delhi. Candidates who aspire to pursue post graduate level legal courses must have to appear for All India Law Entrance Test (AILET). The National Law University, Delhi was established in 2008 by Act No. 1 of 2008 is premier Law University established in the capital city of India.

The total number of seats for this course is 80 out of which 10 seats are for foreign nationals.

### Eligibility

One has to be less than 21 years of age (23 for SC/ST) on the first day of July of the year of admission and should have passed the Higher Secondary School Examination (10+2) system or an equivalent exam with at least 50% marks. Candidates awaiting results of the qualifying examination can also appear for the test on condition that they produce proof of having passed the qualifying examination with the prescribed marks at the time of interview.

### Subject areas with Weightage:

AILET contains 150 multiple choice questions for 150 marks. Duration of the exam would be 1.5 hours. The sections and the marks allotted to them are:

| Sl.No. | Subjects | Weightage |
|---|---|---|
| 1 | English | 35 Marks |
| 2 | General Knowledge including current affairs, General Science, History, Geography, Economics, Civics | 35 Marks |
| 3 | Legal Aptitude | 35 Marks |
| 4 | Logical Reasoning | 35 Marks |
| 5 | Elementary Mathematics (Numerical Ability) | 10 Marks |

There is no negative marking for incorrect answers.

## About CLAT

The Common Law Admission Test (CLAT) is an all India entrance examination conducted by 14 National Law Schools/ Universities for admissions to their under-graduate degree programme (B.A.LL.B). The 14 participating NLUs in the order of their establishment are:

1. National Law School of India University, Bangalore (NLSIU)
2. NALSAR University of Law, Hyderabad (NALSAR)
3. National Law Institute University, Bhopal (NLIU)
4. The West Bengal National University of Juridical Sciences, Kolkata (WBNUJS)
5. National Law University, Jodhpur (NLUJ)
6. Hidayatullah National Law University, Raipur (HNLU)
7. Gujarat National Law University, Gandhinagar (GNLU)
8. Dr. Ram Manohar Lohiya National Law University, Lucknow (RMLNLU)
9. Rajiv Gandhi National University of Law, Patiala (RGNUL)
10. Chanakya National Law University, Patna (CNLU)
11. National University of Advanced Legal Studies, Kochi (NUALS)
12. National Law University, Orissa (NLUO)
13. National University of Study & Research in Law, Ranchi (NUSRL)
14. National Law University & Judicial Academy, Assam (NLUJA)

The first CLAT Committee (consisting of Vice-Chancellors of the participating institutes) decided that the test should be conducted by rotation in the order of their establishment. Accordingly CLAT-2008 (NLSIU, Bangalore), CLAT-2009 (NALSAR, Hyderabad), CLAT-2010 (NLIU, Bhopal) and CLAT 2011 (WBNUJS, Kolkata) were conducted. The CLAT-2012 was conducted by National Law University, Jodhpur (NLU, Jodhpur), CLAT 2013 was conducted by Hidayatullah National Law University (HNLU), Raipur and CLAT 2014 was conducted by Gujarat National Law University, Gandhinagar.

**Eligibility**

Eligibility for Under-Graduate Programme:

To be eligible to appear in CLAT for under Graduate programme (B.A.LL.B.) a candidate should have obtained a Senior Secondary School/Intermediate (10+2) or its equivalent qualification from a recognized Board with not less than 50% marks in aggregate (45% in case of SC/ST/OBC and PWD)**. Candidates who have appeared in the 10+2 examination and are awaiting results are also eligible to appear in the test. Age of candidate should not be more than 20 years in case of General/OBC candidates (22 years in case of SC/ST and persons with Disability)** as on 1st July, of the year.

The candidate must have passed the qualifying examination at the time of his/her admission and be able to submit its proof.

** Subject to State reservation at the University concerned.

| | |
|---|---|
| Total Marks | 200 |
| Total number of multiple-choice questions of one mark each | 200 |
| Duration of examination | Two Hours |

**Subject areas with Weightage**

| Sl. No. | Subject | Weightage |
|---|---|---|
| 1 | English including Comprehension | 40 Marks |
| 2 | General Knowledge/ Current Affairs | 50 Marks |
| 3 | Elementary Mathematics (Numerical Ability) | 20 Marks |
| 4 | Legal Aptitude | 50 Marks |
| 5 | Logical Reasoning | 40 Marks |

There is no negative marking for incorrect answers.

# CONTENTS

## English



## Reasoning



## Quantitative Aptitude



## Legal Aptitude



## General Knowledge

## Chapter-Wise Solved Papers



## Model Papers



## Solved Papers

# ENGLISH

# 1

# VOCABULARY

## ANTONYMS

**Directions for questions 1 to 13:** Choose the word which is most nearly the OPPOSITE in meaning to the **bold** word from the given options.

**1. Equanimity**

(*a*) Resentment (*b*) Dubiousness
(c) Duplicity (*d*) Excitement

**(AILET, 2008)**

**2. Palliate**

(*a*) Apologise (*b*) Hesitate
(c) Wait impatiently (*d*) Cure completely

**(AILET, 2008)**

**3. Obsequious**

(*a*) Brusque
(*b*) Quick-witted
(c) Sharp-tongued
(*d*) Luxurious

**(AILET, 2008)**

**4. Obstreperous**

(*a*) Critical (*b*) Unruly
(c) Unpleasing (*d*) Weak **(AILET, 2008)**

**5. Endemic**

(*a*) Decorative (*b*) Frustrating
(c) Terrorising (*d*) Universal

**(AILET, 2008)**

**6. Ductile**

(*a*) virtuous (*b*) grotesque
(c) contentious (*d*) stubborn

**(AILET, 2009)**

**7.** The Prime Minister's radio broadcast **galvanised** the people's spirit

(*a*) destructed
(*b*) frightened
(c) distracted
(*d*) dampened

**(AILET, 2009)**

**8. Perennial**

(*a*) Frequent (*b*) Regular
(c) Lasting (*d*) Rare **(AILET, 2012)**

**9.** My first speech was a **fiasco.**

(*a*) success (*b*) disaster
(c) fun (*d*) joy **(AILET, 2012)**

**10. Protean**

(*a*) Versatile (*b*) Amateur
(c) Dull (*d*) Cautious

**(AILET, 2013)**

**11. Predilection**

(*a*) Antipathy (*b*) Ignorance
(c) Dissonance (*d*) Disharmony

**(AILET, 2013)**

**12. Impalpable**

(*a*) Visible (*b*) Audible
(c) Tangible (*d*) Fearless

**(AILET, 2013)**

**13. Parochial**

(*a*) Dogmatic (*b*) Dominant
(c) Cosmopolitan (*d*) Niggardly

**(AILET, 2013)**

**Directions (Q. 14 - 17) :** In the following questions, choose the word which is most nearly the OPPOSITE in meaning to the **bold** word and mark it in the Answer Sheet. **(AILET 2014)**

**14. Ambiguity**

(*a*) lucidity (*b*) basal
(c) dull (*d*) necessity

**15. Antidote**

(*a*) medicine (*b*) poison
(c) anodyne (*d*) amity

**16.** Which is NOT a synonym for **'accumulation'?**

(*a*) collection (*b*) conglomeration
(c) assemblage (*d*) collagen

**17.** Which is NOT a synonym for **'incline'?**

(*a*) trenchant (*b*) slope
(c) acclivity (*d*) gradient

## Solutions

**1.** d 'Equanimity' means 'composure'. 'Excitement' is the correct antonym for it.

**2.** * 'Palliate' as a verb is to reduce or to mitigate. None of the given options are correct antonyms.

**3.** c 'Obsequious' means to try too hard to please somebody, especially somebody who is important, by being excessively compliant and flattering. 'Sharp-tongued' is the correct choice which means being critical and nasty.

**4.** d 'Obstreperous' is something marked by unruly and aggressive noisiness. 'Weak' is most nearly the opposite in meaning.

**5.** d 'Endemic' refers to something that is local or native of a place. Universal is the correct opposite to it.

**6.** d 'Ductile' means easily influenced. So, 'stubborn' is an opposite of 'ductile'.

**7.** d 'Galvanize' means to arouse or stimulate awareness or action. 'Dampen', meaning to diminish the activity or vigor of something, is the best antonym for it.

**8.** d 'Perennial' means perpetual or continuous. Rare is opposite in meaning to it and hence the correct choice.

**9.** a 'Fiasco' means a disaster or failure. Success is the correct antonym.

**10.** c 'Protean' means 'able to change quickly and easily'. Option (*a*), 'versatile', means 'changing or fluctuating readily', so option (*a*) is not the correct answer. Option (*c*), 'dull', means 'not interesting or exciting'. It forms the closest antonyms among the given options. Hence, option (c) is the correct answer.

**11.** a 'Predilection' means 'an established preference for something'. Option (*b*) is clearly not the correct answer. Option (*c*), 'dissonance' means 'lack of agreement' and thus is not the correct answer. Option (*d*) is also not the correct answer. Option (*a*), 'antipathy', means 'hostility' which is most nearly the opposite of predilection. Hence, option (*a*) is the correct answer.

**12.** c 'Impalpable' means something that cannot be felt physically. Option (*c*), 'tangible', means something that can be clearly seen to exist. Thus, option (c) is most nearly the opposite of impalpable. Hence, option (c) is the correct answer.

**13.** c 'Parochial' means 'only concerned with small issues that happen in your local area and not interested in more important things; of or relating to a church parish'. Option (*a*), 'dogmatic', means 'characterized by or given to the expression of opinions very strongly or positively as if they were facts'. Thus, option (*a*) is not the correct answer. Option (*d*), niggardly, means 'unwilling to be generous with money, time, etc.' Thus, option (*d*) is also not the correct answer. Option (*c*), 'cosmopolitan' means 'containing people of different types or from different countries, and influenced by their culture'. Thus, option (c) is most nearly the opposite of parochial. Hence, option (c) is the correct answer.

**14.** a 'Ambiguity' means something that does not have a single clear meaning. 'Lucidity' means clearness of thought. Hence, option (*a*) is the correct answer. 'Basal' means fundamental.

**15.** b 'Antidote' is something that corrects or improves the bad effects of something. 'Poison' is something (such as an idea, emotion, or situation) that is very harmful or unpleasant. Hence, option (*b*) is the correct answer. 'Anodyne' is something that is not likely to offend or upset anyone. 'Amity' refers to a feeling of friendship.

**16.** d 'Accumulation' means collection. 'Conglomeration' is a group or mixture of different things. 'Collagen' is a substance that occurs naturally in the bodies of people and animals and is often put into creams and other products that are sold to make a person's skin smoother and less wrinkled. Hence, option (*d*) is the correct answer.

**17.** a 'Incline' means to lean or slope. 'Acclivity' is an ascending slope. 'Gradient' is a place where ground slopes up or down. 'Trenchant' refers to something that is very strong, clear and effective. Hence, option (*a*) is the correct answer.

## SYNONYMS

**Directions (Q. 1 - 21) :** Choose the word which is most nearly the SAME in meaning to the **bold** word from the given options.

**1. Charlatan**

(*a*) Monster
(*b*) Pre-historic man
(c) Quack
(*d*) An ex-convict **(AILET, 2008)**

**2. Cavil**

(*a*) Frivolous objection
(*b*) To criticize sharply; reprove
(c) Moving away from centre
(*d*) Working of brain; thought process

**(AILET, 2008)**

**3. Cynosure**

(*a*) Able to coexist (*b*) Brief
(c) Centre of attention (*d*) Abridgement

**(AILET, 2008)**

**4. Consummate**
(*a*) One of zenith of perfection
(*b*) Existing from birth
(c) Constant; always present
(*d*) A history **(AILET, 2008)**

**5. Obsequious**
(*a*) poor (*b*) cheerful
(c) servile (*d*) sullen
**(AILET, 2009)**

**6. Dialectic**
(*a*) argumentative (*b*) instructive
(c) constructive (c) destructive
**(AILET, 2009)**

7. You may think at first that it is **queer** to talk of having too much paper money and that money is so nice and useful that you cannot have too much of it.
(*a*) Ridiculous (*b*) Absurd
(c) Anomalous (*d*) Odd **(AILET, 2010)**

8. The government is under no obligation to offer contracts to companies which choose to **flout** guidelines.
(*a*) Condemn (*b*) Ignore
(c) Defy (*d*) Neglect **(AILET, 2010)**

9. Indians exhibited a remarkable **solidarity** at the time of war.
(*a*) Coalition (*b*) Co-operation
(c) Unification (*d*) Unity **(AILET, 2010)**

10. His **impeccable** style caught the attention of all critics.
(*a*) Faultless (*b*) Inoffensive
(c) Upright (*d*) Harmless
**(AILET, 2010)**

11. The inspector was a **vigilant** young man.
(*a*) Intelligent (*b*) Ambitious
(c) Watchful (*d*) Smart **(AILET, 2010)**

12. The young is quite **sanguine** about the result of his competitive examination.
(*a*) Depressed (*b*) Pessimistic
(c) Anxious (*d*) Optimistic
**(AILET, 2010)**

13. It was a **scurrilous** attack on him.
(*a*) Serious (*b*) Unjustified
(c) Insulting (*d*) Justified
**(AILET, 2010)**

14. Both parties were **amenable** to a peaceful settlement of the land dispute.
(*a*) Unresponsive (*b*) Responsive
(c) Unwilling (*d*) Doubtful
**(AILET, 2010)**

**15. Lynch**
(*a*) Hang (*b*) Madden
(c) Killed (*d*) Shoot **(AILET, 2012)**

16. His speech was nothing but a string of **platitudes**.
(*a*) grand statements
(*b*) stereo-typed statements
(c) noble sentiments
(*d*) humorous anecdotes **(AILET, 2012)**

**17. Lethargy**
(*a*) Serenity (*b*) listlessness
(c) impassivity (*d*) laxity **(CLAT 2012)**

**18. Emaciated**
(*a*) tall (*b*) languid
(c) very thin (*d*) wise **(CLAT 2012)**

**19. Latent**
(*a*) concealed (*b*) apparent
(c) lethargic (*d*) prompt **(CLAT 2012)**

**20. Sporadic**
(*a*) epidemic (*b*) whirling
(c) occasional (*d*) stagnant **(CLAT 2012)**

**21. Compendium**
(*a*) summary (*b*) index
(c) reference (*d*) collection **(CLAT 2012)**

**Directions (Q. 22 - 26) :** Select the correct meanings of the word in **bold**. **(CLAT 2010)**

**22. Lexicon**
(*a*) number (*b*) legal document
(c) dictionary (*d*) captain's dog

**23. Hex**
(*a*) crude person (*b*) herb
(c) parrot (*d*) evil spell

**24. Seminary**
(*a*) chapel (*b*) college
(c) convocation hail (*d*) hostel

**25. Litergy**
(*a*) prayer (*b*) priest
(c) ritual (*d*) church

**26. Laity**
(*a*) church members not baptized
(*b*) church members baptized
(*c*) priests
(*d*) church members who are not ordained priests

**Direction (Q. 27 - 30) :** In the following questions, choose the word which is most nearly the **same** in meaning to the **bold** word and mark it in the Answer Sheet.

**27. Aberration**

(*a*) Deviation (*b*) Embarrassment
(c) Abhorrence (*d*) Absence **(AILET 2013)**

**28. Potpourri**

(*a*) Medley (*b*) Dose
(*c*) Weird (*d*) Overabundance
**(AILET 2013)**

**29. Imposture**

(*a*) Claim (*b*) Status
(*c*) Destruction (*d*) Deception
**(AILET 2013)**

**30. Parley**

(*a*)Discuss (*b*) Deliver
(*c*) Sweeten (*d*) Race **(AILET 2013)**

**Directions (Q. 31 - 34) :** In the following questions, choose the word which is most nearly the SAME in meaning to the **bold** word and mark it in the Answer Sheet. **(AILET 2014)**

**31. Aphorism**

(*a*) prune (*b*) wither
(*c*) aphis (*d*) proverb

**32. Passe**

(*a*) rude (*b*) old - fashioned
(*c*) modern (*d*) chic

**33. Vituperation**

(*a*) moisture (*b*) parallel
(*c*) malediction (*d*) recover

**34. Qualm**

(*a*) concavity (*b*) amplitude
(*c*) misgiving (*d*) repute

**Solutions**

**1.** c The word 'charlatan' means a cheat or a quack.

**2.** a 'To cavil' is to find fault unnecessarily. Hence, option (*a*), frivolous objection, is correct.

**3.** c 'Cynosure' is the centre or focus of attention and admiration. Abridgement means to reduce or cut short.

**4.** a 'Consummate', as an adjective, means complete or perfect in every sense.

**5.** c 'Obsequious' is being obedient or compliant. Servile is the correct word which means the same.

**6.** a 'Dialectic' is the art or practice of arriving at the truth by the exchange of logical arguments. Argumentative is the correct word.

**7.** b 'Queer' means deviating from normal or expected. Absurd is the closest synonym.

**8.** c 'Flout' means to disregard, show disdain. Defy is the closest synonym.

**9.** d 'Solidarity' means unity.

**10.** a 'Impeccable' means flawless, faultless.

**11.** c 'Vigilant' means keenly watchful to detect danger.

**12.** d 'Sanguine' means cheerfully optimistic.

**13.** c 'Scurrilous' means grossly or obscenely abusive, insulting.

**14.** b 'Amenable' means ready or willing to answer, responsive.

**15.** c 'Lynch' means to kill by hanging. Hence, option (c) is the correct answer.

**16.** b 'Platitude' refers to a statement that has been used too often to be interesting or thoughtful. 'Stereo-typed statements' fits the bill perfectly making option (*b*) the correct choice.

**17.** d 'Lethargy' means a state of sluggishness or drowsiness. Though the answer is given as option (*d*), 'laxity', the correct answer should be listlessness. 'Listlessness' means lack of spirit, energy which is a synonym of lethargy. 'Laxity' means deficient in firmness; loose. 'Serenity' means calmness or peace. 'Impassivity' is being unsusceptible to physical feeling. Hence, the correct answer is listlessness.

**18.** c 'Emaciated' means losing flesh so as to become very thin. Thus, the correct choice is option (*c*). 'Languid' means sluggish in character, or lacking force and quickness in movement.

**19.** a 'Latent' means something that is hidden. 'Concealed' is the correct synonym. Hence, option (*a*) is correct.

**20.** c 'Sporadic' is something that occurs irregularly or randomly. 'Occasional' is the correct synonym for the same. 'Epidemic' is something that spreads very fast. 'Whirling' refers to moving in a circular motion with force. 'Stagnant' means something that doesn't advance or develop.

**21.** d 'Compendium' is a list or collection of a number of items. For example, *'He published a compendium of folk tales'*. 'Collection' is the correct synonym. 'Summary' is a brief account of something. 'Index' is an alphabetical list of items with reference to where they occur, typically found at the end of a book. 'Reference' means the act of mentioning or hinting at something. Hence, option (*d*) is correct.

**22.** c 'Lexicon' is a dictionary, especially Greek, Hebrew, Arabic etc.

**23.** d 'Hex' is a cast or spell, a curse.

**24.** b 'Seminary' is a college that prepares students to be priests, ministers etc.

**25.** c 'Litergy' (also spelt as liturgy) is a form of religious rite prescribed for public worship.

**26.** d 'Laity' refers to lay people i.e. ordinary people, different from the clergy. Thus, church members who are not ordained priests (clergy) constitute the laity.

**27.** a 'Aberration' means 'the fact or an instance of deviating'. Thus, option (*a*) is correct. Option (*c*), 'abhorrence', means 'a feeling of strong hatred, especially for moral reasons'.

**28.** a 'Potpourri' means 'a miscellaneous collection or a mixture of various things that were not originally intended to form a group'. Option (*a*), 'medley', means 'a mixture of people or things of different kinds'. Hence, option (*a*) is the correct answer.

**29.** d 'Imposture' means 'an act of tricking people deliberately by pretending to be somebody else'. Option (*d*), 'deception', means 'the act of deliberately making somebody believe something that is not true'. Hence, option (*d*) is the correct answer.

**30.** a 'Parley' means 'to speak with another, to confer, that is a discussion between enemies or people who disagree'. Option (*a*), 'discuss' means 'to talk about'. Hence, option (*a*) is the correct answer.

**31.** d 'Aphorism' is a short phrase that expresses a true or wise idea. 'Proverb' is a brief popular saying that expresses a belief that is generally thought to be true. Hence, option (*d*) is the correct answer. 'Prune' is to reduce (something) by removing parts that are not necessary or wanted. 'Wither' means to become weak or dry. 'Aphis' is an animal that constitutes the genus.

**32.** b 'Passe' refers to something that is no longer fashionable or popular. Hence, option (*b*) is the correct answer.

**33.** c 'Vituperation' refers to harsh or angry criticism. 'Malediction' means curse. Hence, option (*c*) is the correct answer.

**34.** c 'Qualm' is a feeling of doubt or uncertainty about whether you are doing the right thing. 'Misgiving' is a feeling that something might not be right or might not work as planned. Hence, option (*c*) is the correct answer. 'Concavity' is the quality or state of being concave. 'Amplitude' is a measurement that indicates the movement or vibration of something.

## IDIOMS/PHRASES

**Directions for questions 1 to 18:** In the following questions, four alternatives are given for the idiom/phrase marked in **bold**. Choose the alternative which best expresses the meaning of the idiom/phrase from the options given.

**1.** The neighbour had to **pay through his nose** for a brand new car.

(*a*) Take huge loans
(*b*) Pay a reasonable price
(c) Pay an extremely high price
(*d*) Make a quick buck **(AILET, 2010)**

**2.** If he phones again, I am going to give him a **piece of my mind.**

(*a*) To be nice to him
(*b*) To take advantage of him
(c) To reprimand
(*d*) To support him **(AILET, 2010)**

**3. To give the game away**

(*a*) To lose the game
(*b*) To give a walk-over in a game
(c) To reveal the secret
(*d*) To play the game badly **(CLAT 2009)**

**4. To cool one's heels**

(*a*) To close the chapter
(*b*) To walk on the heels
(c) To kick someone with the heels
(*d*) To wait and rest for some time **(CLAT 2009)**

**5. To bury the hatchet**

(*a*) To fight with the hatchet
(*b*) To forget the enmity
(c) To bury the treasure under ground
(*d*) To pick up enmity **(CLAT 2009)**

**6. Gift of the gab**

(*a*) Gift for hard work
(*b*) Gift undeserved
(c) Gift of being a good conversationalist
(*d*) Gift from unknown person **(CLAT 2009)**

**7. To smell a rat**

(*a*) To suspect a trick
(*b*) To detect a foul smell
(c) To behave like a rat
(*d*) To trust blindly **(CLAT 2009)**

**8.** I have **hit upon** a good plan to get rid of him.

(*a*) found (*b*) chanced upon
(c) decided to beat him (*d*) borrowed **(CLAT 2010)**

9. He is **sticking out for better** terms.
(*a*) threatens to take action
(*b*) insists on using the force
(*c*) decides to give concessions
(*d*) persists in demanding **(CLAT 2010)**

10. He **broke off** in the middle of the story.
(*a*) failed (*b*) began crying
(c) stopped suddenly (*d*) felt uneasy
**(CLAT 2010)**

11. He refused to be **led by the nose**.
(*a*) to follow like an animal
(*b*) to be treated as a fool
(*c*) to follow submissively
(*d*) to be treated violently **(CLAT 2010)**

12. The new cotton mill is mortgaged **up to the eye**.
(*a*) apparently (*b*) completely
(c) deceptively (*d*) actually **(CLAT 2012)**

13. When they embraced a new religion, it is safe to say they did it for **loaves and fishes**.
(*a*) selflessly (*b*) honest reasons
(c) material benefits (*d*) because of fear
**(CLAT 2010)**

14. He **burnt his fingers** by interfering in his neighbor's affair.
(*a*) got himself into trouble
(*b*) burnt himself
(c) got himself insulted
(*d*) got rebuked **(CLAT 2012)**

15. Mr. Gupta, who is one of the trustees of a big charity, is suspected of **feathering his own nest**.
(*a*) being lazy in doing his work
(*b*) being too generous
(c) neglecting his job
(*d*) making money unfairly **(CLAT 2012)**

16. Mrs. Hashmi has been **in the blues** for the last several weeks.
(*a*) abroad (*b*) unwell
(c) depressed (*d*) penniless **(CLAT 2012)**

17. For the first week, the apprentice felt like **a fish out of water**.
(*a*) frustrated (*b*) homeless
(c) disappointed (*d*) uncomfortable
**(CLAT 2012)**

18. His friends failed to see why he should **ride the high horse** just because he had won an election.
(*a*) become abnormal (*b*) appear arrogant
(c) indulge in dreams (*d*) hate others
**(CLAT 2012)**

**Directions (Q. 19 – 23):** *Given below are a few foreign language phrases which are commonly used. Choose the correct meaning for each of the phrases and shade the appropriate answer in the space provided for it in the OMR sheet.* **(CLAT 2013)**

19. El Dorado
(*a*) An imaginary place
(*b*) High altitude
(*c*) A literary man
(*d*) A country full of gold and precious stones

20. quantum ramifactus
(*a*) The amount of damage suffered
(*b*) The amount of damage caused
(*c*) The amount of damage paid
(*d*) The amount of damage received

21. Corpus delicti
(*a*) Fake evidence of an offence
(*b*) Hearsay evidence of an offence
(*c*) Lack of evidence of an offence
(*d*) An evidence which constitute an offence

22. Vis-a-vis
(*a*) Direct (*b*) Opposite
(c) Face to face (*d*) Agree

23. Carte blanche
(*a*) Complete authority (*b*) Issue the warrant
(*c*) No authority (*d*) Lack of authority

**Directions (Q. 24 – 28) :** *Choose the explanation that catches the spirit of the idiom given in each question.* **(CLAT 2013)**

24. To blaze a trail:
(*a*) To set on fire
(*b*) To blow the trumpet
(*c*) To initiate work in a movement
(*d*) To be hopeful

25. A snake in the grass:
(*a*) A secret or hidden enemy
(*b*) An unreliable person
(*c*) Unforeseen happening
(*d*) A dangerous enemy

26. Have too many irons in the fire:
(*a*) Engaged in too many enterprises at the same time
(*b*) Facing too many problems at the same time
(*c*) Said or done too many things at the same time
(*d*) To incite the feeling amongst the people

27. A fair weather friend:
(*a*) A friend who is fair to us at all the times
(*b*) A friend who deserts us in difficulties
(*c*) A friend whom we love the most
(*d*) A friend who loves us the most

**28.** A Panacea:
(*a*) An injection that serves as a life line
(*b*) A lecture full of precepts
(*c*) A strong drug that induces sleep
(*d*) A single cure for all diseases or troubles

**Directions (Q. 29 - 30) :** Choose the exact meaning of the idioms/phrases. **(AILET 2014)**

**29.** She exhibited remarkable *sang froid* during the crisis.
(*a*) temper (*b*) irritation
(*c*) composure (*d*) anger

**30.** The co-operation and *esprit de corps* between the soldiers and the officers was directly responsible for their victory.
(*a*) bravery (*b*) loyalty
(*c*) subordination (*d*) unity

**Directions (Q. 31 to 35) :** Choose the explanation that best reflects the spirit of the idiom/proverb/phrase given in each question.

**31.** To make clean breast of: **(CLAT 2014)**
(*a*) To tell the truth about something
(*b*) To gain prominence
(*c*) To destroy before it blooms
(*d*) To praise oneself

**32.** A man of straw: **(CLAT 2014)**
(*a*) A creditable man
(*b*) A very active man
(*c*) A man of no or little substance
(*d*) An unreasonable man

**33.** A wild-goose chase: **(CLAT 2014)**
(*a*) A wise search (*b*) A fruitful search
(*c*) A worthwhile hunt (*d*) A futile pursuit

**34.** Put on the market: **(CLAT 2014)**
(*a*) To offer for sale (*b*) Alongside the market
(*c*) Already purchased (*d*) None of the above

**35.** To meet someone halfway: **(CLAT 2014)**
(*a*) To show that you are prepared to strain your relationship with someone
(*b*) To compromise with someone
(*c*) Confrontation
(*d*) Incongruity

## Solutions

**1.** c 'To pay through the nose' means to pay too much for something.

**2.** c 'To give someone a piece of mind' means to speak angrily to someone because they have done something wrong.

**3.** c 'To give away the game' means to reveal a secret.

**4.** d 'To cool one's heels' means to rest for some time.

**5.** b 'To bury the hatchet' means to forget the enmity.

**6.** c 'Gift of the gab' means to be a glib talker or a good conservationalist.

**7.** a 'To smell a rat' means to suspect a trick or a foul play.

**8.** b 'Hit upon' means to find something by chance. 'Chanced upon' is the closest in meaning to this.

**9.** d 'Sticking out' means to continue to endure something unpleasant for a long time waiting for the things to become better. Option (*d*), persistent in demanding, is the correct choice.

**10.** c To 'break off' is to stop talking, take a pause. 'Break down' is to start crying.

**11.** c 'To lead someone by the nose' is to control someone and to make them do exactly what you want them to do. Thus, option (*c*), 'to follow submissively', is the best choice.

**12.** b 'Up to the eye' means to the extreme, completely, or to have too much of something. 'Completely' is the correct choice, i.e. the mill has been mortgaged to the last penny.

**13.** c 'Loaves and fishes' is an idiom for a miracle of Jesus Christ wherein He provided food to the poor and hungry from only five loaves of bread and two fishes. After feeding thousands of men, a lot of food was still left. Thus, 'loaves and fishes' here refer to the material benefits that people seek to get from God.

**14.** a 'Burning one's fingers' means getting into trouble as a result of being a part of something. Hence, option (*a*) is the correct choice.

**15.** d 'Feathering your own nest' means to make a profit for oneself especially by taking advantage of one's position. Thus, option (*d*) is the correct choice.

**16.** c 'In the blues' refers to being sad or depressed. Hence, depressed is the right choice for the same.

**17.** d 'Like a fish out of water' means to be uncomfortable or restless. Option (*d*) is the correct choice.

**18.** b 'Riding a high horse' means behaving in a way as if he/she is better than everyone else. Thus, riding a high horse means to appear proud and arrogant. Thus, option (*b*) is correct.

**19.** a 'El Dorado' refers to a place of great wealth which the 16th century explorers believed to exist in South America. Hence, we can say that it is an imaginary place, making option (A) the correct answer.

**20.** a The phrase could not be located anywhere. Therefore, collaborating the meanings of 'quantum' and 'ramification' individually can lead to the correct answer . 'Quantum' means the smallest amount of something. 'Ramification' is the result of an action, decision, etc. Therefore, it can be conclude that 'quantum ramifactus' means the amount of damage suffered. There is another phrase 'quantum damnificatus', which means an issue directed by a court of equity to be tried in a court of law, to ascertain by a trial before a jury, the amount of damages suffered by the non-performance of some collateral undertaking which a penalty has been given to secure. When such damages have thus been ascertained the court grants relief upon their payment. In case the intended phrase is 'quantum damnificatus' and not 'quantum ramifactus', the answer still remains option (A).

**21.** d 'Corpus delicti' refers to the material evidence upon which a crime has been committed or evidence that can be seen, for example a dead body. Hence, option (D) is the correct answer.

**22.** c 'Vis-a-vis' is a French word that literally translates to face-to-face. Hence, option (C) is the correct answer.

**23.** a 'Carte blanche' is a French word, which means to give complete authority. Hence, option (A) is the correct answer.

**24.** c 'To blaze a trail' means to be the first to do or to discover something that others follow. Hence, option (C) is the correct answer.

**25.** a 'A snake in the grass' refers to a person who pretends to be your friend but who cannot be trusted. Hence, option (A) is the correct answer. Option (B) is incorrect because an unreliable person is someone who cannot be trusted. He may or may not pretend to be a friend.

**26.** a 'Have too many irons in the fire' means to do too many things at once. Hence, option (A) is the correct answer.

**27.** b 'A fair weather friend' is a friend whose friendship cannot be relied on in times of difficulty. Hence, option (B) is the correct answer.

**28.** d 'A panacea' is a solution or remedy for all difficulties or diseases. Hence, option (D) is the correct answer.

**29.** c The phrase 'sang froid' refers to the ability to stay calm in difficult or dangerous situations. Hence, option (*c*) is the correct answer.

**30.** d The phrase 'esprit de corps' refers to a common spirit of comradeship, enthusiasm and devotion to a cause among the members of a group. Hence, option (*d*),unity, is the correct answer.

**31.** a 'To make clean breast of' means 'to tell the truth about something so that you no longer feel guilty'. Hence, option (*a*) is the correct answer.

**32.** c 'A man of straw' means 'a person of little substance'. Hence, option (*c*) is the correct answer.

**33.** d 'A wild-goose chase' means 'a search for something that is impossible for you to find or that does not exist and which makes you waste a lot of time'. Hence, option (*d*) is the correct answer.

**34.** a 'Put on the market' means 'to offer for sale'. Hence, option (*a*) is the correct answer.

**35.** b 'To meet someone halfway' means 'to reach an agreement with somebody by giving them part of what they want'. Hence, option (*b*) is the correct answer.

## FILL IN THE BLANKS

**Directions for questions 1 to 11:** Fill in the blanks with the most appropriate word from the options given.

**1.** Judicial decrees may not change the heart, but they can __________ the heartless.

(*a*) Transform (*b*) Subdue
(c) Diarm (*d*) Regulate

**(AILET, 2008)**

**2.** He is __________ of spelling reforms.

(*a*) a protagonist (*b*) an advocate
(c) an envoy (*d*) a champion

**(AILET, 2009)**

**3.** If I __________his address, I could write to him.

(*a*) knew (*b*) had known
(c) know (*d*) will know

**(AILET, 2012)**

**4.** When the morning ______, murder was discovered.

(*a*) occurred (*b*) arrived
(c) came (*d*) happened

**(AILET, 2012)**

**5.** I______a car to be absolutely necessary these days.

(*a*) consider (*b*) regard
(c) think (*d*) agree **(AILET, 2012)**

**6.** Do not intrude, they are talking _____ a confidential matter.

(*a*) on (*b*) for
(c) over (*d*) in **(AILET, 2012)**

**7.** I slept after lunch__________ armed chair.

(*a*) over (*b*) into
(c) in (*d*) on **(AILET, 2012)**

**8.** He is so __________ that he immediately believed my story of ghosts.

(*a*) innocent (*b*) credulous
(c) vociferous (*d*) credible **(AILET, 2012)**

**9.** I will help only __________.
(*a*) if I shall have time (*b*) if I would have time
(c) if I had time (*d*) if I have time
**(AILET, 2012)**

**10.** He doesn't work with hands, he works __________ the machine.
(*a*) with (*b*) by
(c) at (*d*) on **(AILET, 2012)**

**11.** Every Shakespearean hero has an internal __________ in his character.
(*a*) defect (*b*) weakness
(c) fault (*d*) flaw **(AILET, 2012)**

**12.** Her true feelings manifested themselves in her sarcastic asides; only then was her _____revealed.
(*a*) sweetness (*b*) bitterness
(*c*) anxiety (*d*) charm **(AILET, 2013)**

**13.** The tapeworm is an example of _______organism, one that lives within or on another creature, deriving some or all its nutrients from its host.
(*a*) a protozoan (b) a parasite
(*c*) a hospitable (*d*) an autonomous
**(AILET, 2013)**

**14.** While the disease is in a latent state it is almost impossible to determine its existence by
(*a*)observation (*b*) analysis
(*c*) examination (*d*) estimate
**(AILET, 2013)**

**15.** Language, culture and personality may be considered independently of each other in thought, but they are ________ in fact.
(*a*) pervasive (*b*) inseparable
(*c*) autonomous (*d*) immutable
**(AILET, 2013)**

**Directions (Q. 16 – 17):** *Select the best option from the four alternatives given below and shade the appropriate answer in the space provided for it in the OMR answer sheet.* **(CLAT 2013)**

**16.** He spoke _________ about his prospects.
(*a*) Confidentially (*b*) Consciously
(*c*) Confidently (*d*) Conscientiously

**17.** Known as devout and serious person, she also has ______ sense of humour.
(*a*) Better (*b*) Quick
(*c*) Good (*d*) Beautiful

## Solutions

**1.** d The sentence tells us what judicial decrees cannot achieve- they cannot change somebody's heart. The second part is about what these decrees can achieve. In such a context 'regulate' is the best option as it goes along with the idea of preserving law and order. 'Subdue', meaning to bring under control, is too extreme. 'Transform' means to change completely. It does not go with the meaning of the sentence. 'Diarm' is no word in the dictionary. Hence, option (*d*) is the best choice.

**2.** b 'An advocate', meaning a person who publicly supports or recommends a particular cause or policy, is the best word to complete the sentence.

**3.** a Some clauses with *if* are like hypotheses so we use **past tense** forms to talk about the present and future. The correct statement should therefore use 'knew'.

**4.** b The sentence requires past perfect tense which is there only in option (*b*). Hence, "arrived" is the correct choice.

**5.** a In this question the person making the statement is giving an opinion about the car. We need a word that means 'to think of something in a particular way'. Hence 'consider' is the right choice.

**6.** c 'Over' is used when referring to a cause of interest or discussion.

**7.** c The correct statement should be "in an armed chair". 'into' is used to show movement or transition, as in "into the water".

**8.** b The statement requires a word that indicates naivety and artlessness. Hence, 'credulous' is the right fit.

**9.** d For situations in the present or future where we are describing what hasn't happened yet but we can easily imagine it happening, we use present tense in the conditional clause and will + verb in the main clause.

**10.** c The correct preposition is 'at'. 'At' is used as a preposition of place where you are to do something typical (study, watch a film, work).

**11.** d Defect is the general word for any kind of shortcoming or imperfection, whether literal or figurative: a defect in eyesight, in a plan. Weakness can refer to a quality regarded as a disadvantage. Fault is an error or a mistake. Flaw refers to a feature that mars the perfection of something. Flaw is the right word here; an otherwise perfect hero may have an internal flaw.

**12.** b The word 'sarcastic' in the first part of the sentence implies that the subject is using sarcasm. Sarcasm means 'a way of using words that are the opposite of what you mean in order to be unpleasant to somebody or to make fun of them'. Option (*b*), bitterness means 'feeling unhappy or angry because you feel that you have been treated unfair'. Option (*b*) clearly implies unpleasant feelings of the subject in the given context. Hence, option (*b*) is correct.

**13.** b The definition given in the sentence is that of a parasite, hence option (*b*) is the correct answer.

**14.** a Option (*b*), 'analysis' means 'the separation of a substance into its constituent elements, usually by chemical means, for the study and identification of each component'. Hence, option (*b*)incorrect in the given context. Option (*c*), 'examination' means 'the act of examining something closely (as for mistakes) as well as examination also means 'a set of questions or exercises evaluating skill or knowledge'; hence, incorrect in the given context. Option (*d*), 'estimate' means 'a judgement that you make without having the exact details or figures about the size'. Hence, it is incorrect in the given context. Option (*a*), 'observation' means 'an act or instance of watching or noting something for a scientific or other special purpose'. Hence, option (*a*) is correct.

**15.** b Option (*a*), 'pervasive' means 'spreading gradually to affect all parts of a place or thing'. Hence, it is not appropriate in the given context. Option (*c*), 'autonomous' means 'able to govern itself or control its own affairs, existing or capable of existing independently', which is wrong in the given context. Option (*d*), 'immutable' means 'that cannot be changed; that will never change', hence it is incorrect. Option (*b*), 'inseparable' clearly explains the meaning that although language, culture and personality are independent of each other, yet they cannot be separated in functional form. Hence, option (*b*) is correct.

**16.** c Grammatically, all the options are correct. However, logically, only option (C) fits in best because one is likely to be confident while speaking about his prospects. 'Confidentially' (secretively and with trust), 'consciously' (knowingly) and 'conscientiously' (carefully) do not fit in the context better than confidently. Hence, option (C) is the correct answer.

**17.** c Sense of humour cannot be 'quick' or 'beautiful'. Therefore, options (B) and (D) are incorrect. 'Better', being a comparative adjective is incorrect in this context because the statement shows no comparison. Hence, the correct answer is option (C).

## FOREIGN WORDS

**Directions for questions 1 to 15:** Given below in **bold** are a few foreign language phrases that are commonly used. Choose the correct meaning for each of the phrases.

**1. Prima facie** **(CLAT 2008)**

(*a*)the most important (*b*) that which comes first
(c) at first view (*d*) the face that is young

**2. Sine die**

(*a*) without setting a fixed day
(*b*) by voice vote
(*b*) applying mathematical concepts to solve a difficult problem
(*d*) signing legal documents before death

**(CLAT 2008)**

**3. Bona fide**

(*a*) identification card
(*b*) without doubt
(c) in good faith
(*d*) indispensable condition **(CLAT 2008)**

**4. Status quo**

(*a*) legally valid (*b*) present condition
(c) social position (*d*) side remarks

**(CLAT 2008)**

**5. De jure**

(*a*) here and there (*b*) as per law
(c) small details (*d*) in the same place

**(CLAT 2008)**

**6. Mala fide**

(*a*) in good faith (*b*) in bad faith
(c) without any faith (*d*) with full faith

**(CLAT 2009)**

**7. Pro rata**

(*a*) at the rate of (*b*) at quoted rate
(c) in proportion (*d*) beyond all proportion

**(CLAT 2009)**

**8. Vice versa** **(CLAT 2009)**

(*a*) in verse (*b*) versatile verse
(c) in consonance with (*d*) the other way round

**9. Ab initio**

(*a*) from the very beginning
(*b*) high initiative
(c) thing done later
(*d*) without initiative **(CLAT 2009)**

**10. Alibi**

(*a*) every where (*b*) else where
(c) no where (*d*) without any excuse

**(CLAT 2009)**

**11. Mala fide**

(*a*) generous (*b*) bad intention
(c) trustworthy (*d*) genuine **(CLAT 2012)**

**12. Tabula rasa**

(*a*) clean slate (*b*) agitated
(c) deprived (*d*) creative **(CLAT 2012)**

**13. Carte blanche**
(*a*) slavery (*b*) complete discretion
(c) anarchy (*d*) dependent
**(CLAT 2012)**

**14. De jure**
(*a*) illegal (*b*) heir
(c) concerning law (*d*) forbidden
**(CLAT 2012)**

**15. Raison d'etre**
(*a*) logical conclusion (*b*) reason for existence
(c) free choice (*d*) dubious argument
**(CLAT 2012)**

**Directions (Q. 16 - 20) :** Given below are a few foreign language phrases which are commonly used. Choose the correct meaning for each of the phrases.

**16.** *Ex officio* **(CLAT 2014)**
(*a*) By virtue of previously held position
(*b*) Former official
(*c*) By virtue of office
(*d*) Outside the office

**17.** *Ultra Vires* **(CLAT 2014)**
(*a*) Within powers (*b*) Full powers
(*c*) Near powers (*d*) Beyond powers

**18.** *Quid pro quo* **(CLAT 2014)**
(*a*) Something for nothing
(*b*) Something for something
(*c*) Everything for something
(*d*) Something for everything

**19.** *Inter vivos* **(CLAT 2014)**
(*a*) between the living
(*b*) among the living and the dead
(*c*) between the dead
(*d*) among the dead and the living

**20.** *Corpus juris* **(CLAT 2014)**
(*a*) body of judges (*b*) group of jurists
(*c*) body of law (*d*) knowledge of law

## Solutions

**1.** c The correct meaning is 'at first view'.
**2.** a The correct meaning is 'without setting a fixed day'.
**3.** c The correct meaning is 'in good faith'.
**4.** b The correct meaning is 'present condition'.
**5.** b The correct meaning is 'as per law'.
**6.** b 'Mala Fide' means in bad faith.
**7.** c 'Pro rata' means in proportion of something.
**8.** d 'Vice versa' means the other way round.
**9.** a 'Ab initio' means from the beginning.
**10.** b 'Alibi' is a claim or piece of evidence that one was elsewhere when an act, typically a criminal one, is alleged to have taken place. Thus, option (*b*) is the correct choice.
**11.** b 'Mala fide' means in bad faith. Hence, option (*b*) is the correct choice. Bona fide means in good faith.
**12.** a 'Tabula Rasa' refers to absence of any preconceived notions, a clean slate. Option (*a*) is the correct choice.
**13.** b 'Carte Blanche' means having complete freedom to act as one wishes. Option (*b*), complete discretion, is the correct answer.
**14.** c 'De jure' means 'legally' or by right. Option (*c*), by law, is the correct answer.
**15.** b 'Raison d'etre' is a French phrase which means reason for being. Option (*b*), reason for existence, is correct.
**16.** c 'Ex officio' means by virtue of one's position or status.
**17.** d 'Ultra Vires' means beyond one's legal power or authority.
**18.** b 'Quid pro quo' means a favour or advantage granted in return for something.
**19.** a 'Inter vivos' means between living people.
**20.** c 'Corpus juris' means a body of law, especially the laws of a nation or state.

## SPELLING

**Directions(Q. 1 - 15) :** Three of the four words given below are spelt wrongly. Select the word that is spelt correctly.

**1.** (*a*) acquintence (*b*) acquaintence
(c) acquaintance (*d*) acquintance
**(CLAT 2008)**

**2.** (*a*) neglegense (*b*) negligence
(c) negligance (*d*) negligence
**(CLAT 2008)**

**3.** (*a*) grevance (*b*) greivance
(c) grievance (*d*) grievence
**(CLAT 2008)**

**4.** (*a*) heirarchical (*b*) hierarchical
(c) hiererchical (*d*) heirerchical
**(CLAT 2008)**

**5.** (*a*) garanter (*b*) garantor
(c) guaranter (*d*) guarantor **(CLAT 2008)**

**6.** (*a*) renaissance (*b*) renaisance
(c) renaissence (*d*) renaisence
**(CLAT 2009)**

**7.** (*a*) malaese (*b*) melaize
(c) melaise (*d*) malaise **(CLAT 2009)**

**8.** (*a*) irelevant (*b*) itrelevent
(c) irrelevant (*d*) irrellevant
**(CLAT 2009)**

**9.** (*a*) survilance (*b*) surveillance
(c) surveiliance (*d*) surveilliance
**(CLAT 2009)**

**10.** (*a*) gaiety (*b*) gaietty
(c) gaeity (*d*) gaitty **(CLAT 2009)**

**11.** (*a*) Misogynists (*b*) Mysogynists
(c) Mysoginists (*d*) Mysagynists
**(CLAT 2010)**

**12.** (*a*) Aracnophobia (*b*) Aranchophobia
(c) Arochnophobia (*d*) Arachnophobia
**(CLAT 2010)**

**13.** (*a*) Cmamon (*b*) Cinnamon
(c) Cinnaman (*d*) Cinaman
**(CLAT 2010)**

**14.** (*a*) Alcohol (*b*) Aichohol
(c) Aichohal (*d*) Aichohel
**(CLAT 2010)**

**15.** (*a*) Bioclymatalogy (*b*) Bioclimatalogy
(c) Bioclimatology (*d*) Bioclimatelogy
**(CLAT 2010)**

**Directions (Q. 16 - 20) :** *Select the word that is spelt correctly* **(CLAT 2013)**

**16.** (*a*) paraphernalia (*b*) paraphrenalia
(c) parapherenalia (*d*) paraphrennalia

**17.** (*a*) enterprenuer (*b*) entrepreneur
(c) entrepenur (*d*) enteruepeur

**18.** (*a*) onomaetopoeia (*b*) onomoatopoeia
(c) onomatopoeia (*d*) onomatopoeia

**19.** (*a*) hemorhage (*b*) haemorhhage
(c) haemorrhage (*d*) hemoorhage

**20.** (*a*) dylexsia (*b*) dyslexia
(c) dislexia (*d*) dislecsia

**Directions (Q. 21 - 25) :** Select the word that is spelt CORRECTLY.

**21.** Which of the following spellings is correct? **(CLAT 2014)**
(*a*) Concensus (*b*) Consencus
(*c*) Consenssus (*d*) Consensus

**22.** Which of the following spellings is correct? **(CLAT 2014)**
(*a*) Procede (*b*) Proceed
(*c*) Proceede (*d*) Proced

**23.** Which of the following spellings is correct? **(CLAT 2014)**
(*a*) Accommodate (*b*) Acommodate
(*c*) Accomodate (*d*) Acomodate

**24.** Which of the following spellings is correct 'for a page at the beginning of a book'? **(CLAT 2014)**
(*a*) Foreward (*b*) Forword
(*c*) Forworde (*d*) Foreword

**25.** Which of the following spellings is correct? **(CLAT 2014)**
(*a*) Arguement (*b*) Argument
(*c*) Arguemant (*d*) Arguemint

## Solutions

**1.** c The right spelling is 'acquaintance', which means 'a person known to one, but usually not a close friend'.

**2.** b,dBoth the options show the same spelling, hence both of them can be considered to be the right answer. 'negligence' means 'the quality of being negligent'.

**3.** c The right spelling is 'grievance', which means 'a wrong considered as grounds for complaint'.

**4.** b The correct spelling is 'hierarchical', which means 'belonging to a hierarchy'.

**5.** d The correct spelling is 'guarantor', which means 'a person or group that guarantees'.

**6.** a Option (*a*) has the correct spelling, 'renaissance'.

**7.** d Option (*d*) has the correct spelling, 'malaise'.

**7.** c 'Irrelevant' is the correct spelling.

**9.** b 'Surveillance' is the correct spelling.

**10.** a 'Gaiety' is the correct spelling.

**11.** a Option (*a*) gives the correct spellings.

**12.** d Option (*d*) gives the correct spellings.

**13.** b Option (*b*) gives the correct spellings.

**14.** a Option (*a*) gives the correct spellings.

**15.** c Option (c) gives the correct spellings.

**16.** a The correct spelling is "paraphernalia". Hence, the correct answer is option (A).

**17.** b The correct spelling is "entrepreneur". Hence, the correct answer is option (B).

**18.** c,d The correct spelling is "onomatopoeia". Hence, the correct answer can be both option (C) and option (D) as they contain the same spellings.

**19.** c The correct spelling is "haemorrhage". Hence, the correct answer is option (C).

**20.** b The correct spelling is "dyslexia". Hencė, the correct answer is option (B).

**21.** d The correct spelling of the word is 'Consensus'.

**22.** b The correct spelling of the word is 'Proceed'.

**23.** a The correct spelling of the word is 'Accommodate'.

**24.** d The correct spelling of the word is 'Foreword'.

**25.** b The correct spelling of the word is 'Argument'.

■■

# 2

# GRAMMAR

### SPOT ERROR

**Directions for questions 1 to 20:** Some of the sentences given below have errors and some have none. Find out which part of the sentence has an error.

**1.** He returned back (*a*)/ when he sensed (*b*)/ that there was danger. (c)/ No error (*d*) **(AILET, 2008)**

**2.** The progress of those plants (*a*)/ is not being very encouraging (*b*)/ and they are in various stage of decay. (*c*)/ No error. (*d*) **(AILET, 2008)**

**3.** Not only the bandits robbed (*a*)/ the traveller of his purse (*b*)/ but also wounded him grievously. (*c*)/ No error. (*d*) **(AILET, 2008)**

**4.** No less than twenty persons (*a*)/ were killed in (*b*)/ the air crash. (c)/ No error. (*d*) **(AILET, 2008)**

**5.** The police went through the building (*a*)/ with fine toothcombs (*b*)/ but they found no evidence (*c*)/ No error. (*d*) **(AILET, 2008)**

**6.** He not only denied (*a*)/ having borrowed money from me, (*b*)/ but also having ever met me. (c)/ No error. (*d*) **(AILET, 2009)**

**7.** The running party stood (*a*)/ for implementation of the Bill (*b*)/ and was ready to stake their political existence. (c)/ No error. (*d*) **(AILET, 2009)**

**8.** If I were he, (*a*) / I should not (*b*)/ accept the post. (c)/ No error (*d*) **(AILET, 2009)**

**9.** Men are apt to (*a*)/ pick up holes (*b*)/ in the views of those whom they do not like. (c)/ No error (*d*) **(AILET, 2011)**

**10.** The myth that some races (*a*) /are naturally superior than others (*b*)/has now been fully demolished. (c)/ No error (*d*) **(AILET, 2011)**

**11.** The steep rise in the price of petroleum products (*a*)/ have affected (*b*)/ the economic development of the developing nations. (c)/ No error (*d*) **(AILET, 2011)**

**12.** Kiran as well as Kamal (*a*)/ are leaving (*b*)/ for Mumbai. (c)/ No error (*d*) **(AILET, 2011)**

**13.** Much water (*a*)/ has flown (*b*)/ under the bridge since then. (c)/ No error (*d*) **(AILET, 2011)**

**14.** Everyone of the men present here (*a*) / has given a day's pay (*b*)/ as their contribution to the fund (c)/ No error (*d*) **(AILET, 2011)**

**15.** Found guilty (*a*)/ on murder (*b*)/ the accused was sentenced to death. (c)/ No error (*d*) **(AILET, 2011)**

**16.** The number of marks carried by each question (*a*)/ are indicated (*b*)/ at the end of the Question. (c)/ No error. (*d*) **(AILET, 2012)**

**17.** As much as I admire him for his sterling qualities (*a*)/ I cannot excuse him for (*b*)/ being unfair to his friends. (c)/ No error. (*d*) **(AILET, 2012)**

**18.** Many times the news has been published (*a*)/ in the papers that the end of the world will be certain (*b*)/ if a nuclear war breaks out. (c)/ No error. (*d*) **(AILET, 2012)**

**19.** She reluctantly said that (*a*)/ if nobody else was doing it (*b*)/ she will do it. (c)/ No error (*d*) **(AILET, 2012)**

**20.** Though child marriage (*a*) /has been banned, (*b*) the custom still prevailed among some groups in India. (c)/ No error. (*d*) **(AILET, 2012)**

**Directions (Q. 21 - 24) :** Each of the following sentences contain four parts, marked a, b, c, and d. One of these parts is incorrect. Indicate the letter of the incorrect part.

**21.** The Baby showed a noticeable (*a*)/ distaste for (*b*)/ these kind (c)/ of prepared baby food. (*d*) **(NULD 2011)**

**22.** They cannot go camping right now (*a*)/ because (*b*)/ they are taking care of (c)/ a three-weeks-old baby. (*d*) **(NULD 2011)**

**23.** If it (*a*)/ will rain (*b*)/ this afternoon, we will have (c)/ to cancel the picnic. (*d*) **(NULD 2011)**

**24.** Are (*a*)/ you familiar of(*b*)/ the latest (c)/ scientific developments in the field? (*d*) **(NULD 2011)**

## Solutions

**1.** a This is a classic case of redundancy – 'back' is not required when 'returned' has already been used.

**2.** c We require the plural 'stages' after 'various'.

**3.** a The modifier 'not only' has been placed incorrectly; it should have been 'The bandits not only robbed..'

**4.** a It should have been 'No less than twenty people (not persons)'

**5.** b Part (*b*) should have been something like 'with a fine-tooth (or fine-toothed) comb'. 'Fine' modifies tooth not toothcomb.

**6.** a The modifier 'not only' must be placed after 'denied'. The sentence talks of 'he' denying two things- not only having borrowed money but also having ever met me.

**7.** c 'Their' is an incorrect pronoun for 'party'. The correct pronoun should be 'its'.

**8.** b The sentence talks of something that is/cannot be true. 'Would' in place of 'should' must be used to talk of ideas like hypothesis.

**9.** b 'Pick up holes' is grammatically incorrect. 'Pick holes' is the correct phrase. It means to find mistakes in something someone has done or said, to show that it is not good or not correct. For example: The lawyer did her best to pick holes in the witness's statement.

**10.** b With the words superior, inferior, anterior, posterior 'than' is not used. 'Superior to' is the correct phrase.

**11.** b The subject of the sentence is 'the steep rise' which is singular in number. So, 'have' is incorrect. 'has affected' is the correct phrase.

**12.** b With the words 'with', 'together with', 'along with', 'as well as', the subject should follow the first subject. Since the first subject is singular in number (Kiran), so the verb should be 'is'.

**13.** b 'Much water has passed/flowed under the bridge' is the correct phrase. It means that something is in the past and no longer important.

**14.** c With the words 'each' and 'every', the verb as well as the pronoun should be singular in number. So, usage of the pronoun 'their' is incorrect.

**15.** b 'on murder' is incorrect because of the preposition 'on'. 'Found guilty of murder' is the correct phrase.

**16.** b Part (*b*) is incorrect as it has 'subject verb agreement' error. The subject here is 'number' and not 'marks', and since it is singular, the correct verb should be 'is' not 'are'.

**17.** a Since part (*b*) forms the beginning of another clause after part (*a*), there should be a comma at the end of part (*a*).

**18.** d The sentence is correct in its given form.

**19.** c The modal verb "would" is used in a conditional sense (or in a hypothetical/theoretical situation). "Will" is used when something is going to be done, not just hypothetically/conditionally. The correct sentence should be, "She would do it".

**20.** c 'Prevailed' is incorrect as the sentence is in present tense. It talks about the custom being 'still prevalent'. Hence, the correct usage should be 'the custom prevails'. Option (c) is the correct choice.

**21.** c As the word 'these' is used to denote plural number, so 'these kind' is incorrect. 'these kinds' is the correct phrase.

**22.** d 'Three-weeks-old; is incorrect. The correct phrase should have been 'three-week old baby'. Three-week is a chunk of time that is expressed as a single unit and is thus singular.

**23.** b 'Will rain' is incorrect. The correct phrase should be 'If it rains this afternoon'.

**24.** b The preposition 'of' is inappropriate with the word 'familiar'. 'familiar with' is the grammatically correct phrase.

## FILL IN THE BLANKS

**Directions (Q. 1 - 55) :** Choose the word or phrase that best completes the sentence from the given alternatives.

**1.** I was surprised ________.

(*a*) at his letting out the secret

(*b*) why he let out the secret

(c) that he let out the secret

(*d*) by his letting out the secret **(AILET, 2008)**

**2.** It is not possible to ________.

(*a*) mix oil in water (*b*) mix oil into water

(c) mix oil with water (*d*) mix oil by water

**(AILET, 2008)**

**3.** He ________ and escaped.

(*a*) forced the door open

(*b*) forced open the door

(c) open forced the door

(*d*) the door forced open **(AILET, 2008)**

**4.** Let________ finish this work as soon as possible.

(*a*) you and I (*b*) you and me

(c) I and you (*d*) me and you

**(AILET, 2008)**

5. ______ the room, the door hit him on the brow.
(a) While entering (b) As he entered
(b) On entering (d) On having entered
**(AILET, 2008)**

6. To answer accurately is more important than ________.
(a) quick finish (b) finish quickly
(c) finishing quickly (d) you finish quickly
**(AILET, 2010)**

7. Professional people now-a-days appreciate _____ when it is necessary to cancel an appointment.
(a) your calling them
(b) that you would call them
(c) you to call them
(d) you are calling them **(AILET, 2010)**

8. Who will ______ the children when their mother is in the hospital?
(a) look after (b) look for
(c) look up (d) look about
**(AILET, 2010)**

9. The teacher gives many examples to ________ the idea contained in the poem.
(a) bring about (b) bring in
(c) bring forth (d) bring out
**(AILET, 2010)**

10. That magnificent ________ temple was constructed by the Chinese.
(a) eight -centuries-old
(b) eight-century' s-old
(c) old-eight-centuries
(d) eight-century-old **(AILET, 2010)**

11. Wheat is not native to India and Barley ________.
(a) isn't either (b) is either
(c) is neither (d) isn't neither
**(AILET, 2010)**

12. Encounters between people from different countries can results in misunderstandings ____ different concepts about space.
(a) because they (b) is because they
(c) is because their (d) because of their
**(AILET, 2010)**

13. I saw _____ movie last night.
(a) the (b) a
(c) an (d) one
**(AILET, 2011)**

14. The RBI in consultation with Government of India has _____ working group to suggest measures for revival of weak public sector banks.
(a) appointed (b) constituted
(c) devolved (d) none of these
**(AILET, 2011)**

15. He stepped out and began to walk _____.
(a) behind (b) around
(c) besides (d) none of these
**(AILET, 2011)**

16. The lady received quick promotions when they saw how ______ she was.
(a) lethargic (b) hostile
(c) correct (d) hard working
**(AILET, 2011)**

17. The shower in the bathroom needs mending as it has started ______.
(a) trickling (b) soaking
(c) dripping (d) overflowing
**(AILET, 2011)**

18. The person who is looking for sympathy talks _____.
(a) petulantly (b) despicably
(c) plaintively (d) deftly **(AILET, 2011)**

19. The very nature of society is inimical ____ freedom.
(a) of (b) to
(c) with (d) on **(AILET, 2011)**

20. Wilbur Wright flew his airplane _____ France in 1909.
(a) on (b) upon
(c) until (d) over **(AILET, 2011)**

21. They live on a busy road. ___ a lot of noise from the traffic.
(a) It must be (b) It must have
(c) There must have (d) There must be
**(CLAT 2008)**

22. The more electricity you use, _____.
(a) your bill will be higher
(b) will be higher your bill
(c) the higher your bill will be
(d) higher your bill will be **(CLAT 2008)**

23. Ben likes walking. _______.
(a) Every morning he walks to work
(b) He walks to work every morning
(b) He walks every morning to work
(d) He every morning walks to work **(CLAT 2008)**

**24.** It's two years ______ Sophy.
(*a*) that I don't see (*b*) that I haven't seen
(c) since I didn't see (*d*) since I last saw
**(CLAT 2008)**

**25.** What was the problems? Why ______ leave early?
(*a*) have you to (*b*) did you have to
(c) must you (*d*) you had to
**(CLAT 2008)**

**26.** Nobody believed Arun at first, but he ______ to be right.
(*a*) worked out (*b*) came out
(c) found out (*d*) turned out
**(CLAT 2008)**

**27.** We can't ______ making a decision. We have to decide now.
(*a*) put away (*b*) put over
(c) put off (*d*) put out **(CLAT 2008)**

**28.** The accident was my fault, so I had to pay for the damage ______ the other car.
(*a*) of (*b*) for
(c) to (*d*) on **(CLAT 2008)**

**29.** I really object ______ people smoking in my house.
(*a*) to (*b*) about
(c) for (*d*) on **(CLAT 2008)**

**30.** A contract may be ______ if the court finds there has been misinterpretation of the facts.
(*a*) restrained (*b*) rescinded
(c) compelled (*d*) conferred **(CLAT 2008)**

**31.** Some people believe that in emotional maturity men are inferior ______ women.
(*a*) than (*b*) to
(c) from (*d*) against **(CLAT 2009)**

**32.** My father was annoyed ______ me.
(*a*) towards (*b*) against
(c) with (*d*) upon **(CLAT 2009)**

**33.** Some orthodox persons are averse ______ drinking liquor.
(*a*) against (*b*) for
(c) towards (*d*) to **(CLAT 2009)**

**34.** The Cinema Hall was on fire and the Cinema owner had to send ______ the Fire Brigade.
(*a*) for (*b*) through
(c) off (*d*) in **(CLAT 2009)**

**35.** He was not listening ______ I was saying.
(*a*) that (*b*) which
(c) to what (*d*) what **(CLAT 2009)**

**36.** Drinking country liquor at marriage is a custom ______ certain tribes.
(*a*) in (*b*) among
(c) between (*d*) with **(CLAT 2009)**

**37.** The struggle for justice brings ______ the best of moral qualities of men.
(*a*) forward (*b*) about
(c) in (*d*) out **(CLAT 2009)**

**38.** If he ______ a horse he would fly.
(*a*) was (*b*) were
(c) is (*d*) goes **(CLAT 2009)**

**39.** Mohan has a bad habit of ______ at on odd hour.
(*a*) turning up (*b*) turning in
(c) turning over (*d*) turning Off
**(CLAT 2009)**

**40.** He must refrain ______ immoral conducts.
(*a*) off (*b*) through
(c) from (*d*) against **(CLAT 2009)**

**41.** Slavery was not done away ______ until the last century.
(*a*) with (*b*) for
(c) to (*d*) off **(CLAT 2010)**

**42.** Does he not take ______ his father?
(*a*) before (*b*) for
(c) after (*d*) like **(CLAT 2010)**

**43.** We will have to take ______ more staff if we're to take on more work.
(*a*) up (*b*) onto
(c) into (*d*) on **(CLAT 2010)**

**44.** Mother takes everything in her ______.
(*a*) steps (*b*) face
(c) stride (*d*) work **(CLAT 2010)**

**45.** Sale have really taken ______ now.
(*a*) up (*b*) on
(c) of (*d*) off **(CLAT 2010)**

**46.** Give an example pertinent ______ the case.
(*a*) with (*b*) on
(c) for (*d*) to **(CLAT 2012)**

**47.** My voice reverberated ______ the walls of the castle.
(*a*) with (*b*) from
(c) in (*d*) on **(CLAT 2012)**

**48.** The reward was not commensurate ______ the work done by us.
(*a*) for (*b*) on
(c) with (*d*) order **(CLAT 2012)**

**49.** Our tragic experience in the recent past provides an index ______ the state of lawlessness in this region.

(*a*) of (*b*) in
(c) at (*d*) by **(CLAT 2012)**

**50.** Your conduct smacks ______ recklessness.

(*a*) of (*b*) with
(c) from (*d*) in **(CLAT 2012)**

**51.** A good judge never gropes ______ the conclusion.

(*a*) to (*b*) at
(c) on (*d*) for **(CLAT 2012)**

**52.** Nobody in our group is a genius ______ winning friends and in convincing people.

(*a*) for (*b*) in
(c) of (*d*) at **(CLAT 2012)**

**53.** If you are averse ______ recommending my name, you should not hesitate to admit it.

(*a*) about (*b*) for
(c) to (*d*) against **(CLAT 2012)**

**54.** Religious leaders should not delve ______ politics.

(*a*) in (*b*) with
(c) at (*d*) into **(CLAT 2012)**

**55.** What you say has hardly any bearing ______ the lives of tribals.

(*a*) about (*b*) for
(c) on (*d*) with **(CLAT 2012)**

**56.** The event passed ______ without any untoward incident.

(*a*) of (*b*) on
(*c*) off (*d*) away **(AILET 2013)**

**57.** Please give me ______ to drink.

(*a*) little water (*b*) a little water
(*c*) any water (*d*) some water
**(AILET 2013)**

**58.** The country is ushering ______ a new era.

(*a*) into (*b*) in
(*c*) of (*d*) over **(AILET 2013)**

**59.** He is a traitor ______ the country.

(*a*) for (*b*) to
(*c*) in (*d*) of **(AILET 2013)**

**60.** There is no culture in the world ______ absolutely pure.

(*a*) that which is into (*b*) that be
(*c*) that is (*d*) that what is
**(AILET 2013)**

**61.** He led me ______ the green lawn to the palatial building.

(*a*) upon (*b*) across
(*c*) along (*d*) on **(AILET 2013)**

**62.** The lease of our premises has ______ and we have to vacate it.

(*a*) run out (*b*) run off
(*c*) run over (*d*) run down **(AILET 2013)**

**63.** His boss ______ an explanation of his conduct with his colleagues.

(*a*) called up (*b*) called upon
(*c*) called for (*d*) called off **(AILET 2013)**

**64.** He ______ his departure for a week as his mother was not well.

(*a*) put off (*b*) put up
(*c*) put out (*d*) put aside **(AILET 2013)**

**Directions for (Q. 65 - 72):** *Select the best option from the four alternatives given below and shade the appropriate answer in the space provided for it in the OMR answer sheet.* **(CLAT 2013)**

**65.** Unless he ______ this office, I will not say anything.

(*a*) Left (*b*) Did not leave
(*c*) Leaves (*d*) Had left

**66.** ______, I would help all the poor people.

(*a*) If I am rich (*b*) If I was rich
(*c*) If I were rich (*d*) In case I am rich

**67.** I ______ the news an hour ago.

(*a*) Have heard (*b*) Heard
(*c*) Was hearing (*d*) Have been hearing

**68.** The boy is not interested in playing, ______ ?

(*a*) Doesn't he? (*b*) Isn't he?
(*c*) Didn't he? (*d*) Is he?

**69.** He told us that we should never live beyond ______ means.

(*a*) His (*b*) Their
(*c*) Our (*d*) Her

**70.** May I request ______ you again to consider my case favourably.

(*a*) To (*b*) Onto
(*c*) Of (*d*) Noproposition required

**71.** Galileo said, "The Earth ______ around the sun".

(*a*) Revolved (*b*) Is revolving
(*c*) Revolves (*d*) Is revolved

**72.** We ______ our work before the guests arrived at our house.

(*a*) Shall finish (*b*) Have finished
(*c*) Had finished (*d*) Shall have finished

**Directions (Q. 73 - 82) :** Fill in the blank by choosing the most appropriate option.

**73.** A vote of ................ proposed at the end of the meeting. **(CLAT 2014)**

(*a*) thanks were (*b*) thank was

(*c*) thanks had been (*d*) thanks was

**74.** During the recession many companies will................lay off workers. **(CLAT 2014)**

(*a*) be forced to (*b*) have the force to

(*c*) forcefully (*d*) be forced into

**75.** She has good................over the famous foreign languages. **(CLAT 2014)**

(*a*) expertise (*b*) command

(*c*) control (*d*) authority

**76.** The Chairman pointed out in favour of the manager that the profitability of the industrial plant had ............ since he took over the administration. **(CLAT 2014)**

(*a*) arisen (*b*) declined

(*c*) added (*d*) increased

**77.** When the examinations were over,...............went to Paris. **(CLAT 2014)**

(*a*) me and Rohan (*b*) I and Rohan

(*c*) Rohan and me (*d*) Rohan and I

**78.** Let's go for a walk,................ ? **(CLAT 2014)**

(*a*) can we (*b*) shall we

(*c*) cant' we (*d*) shouldn't we

**79.** Had Anil been on time, he.......... missed the train.

(*a*) would not have been (*b*) had not **(CLAT 2014)**

(*c*) will not have (*d*) would not have

**80.** The most alarming fact is that infection is spreading......................the state and reaching villages and small towns. **(CLAT 2014)**

(*a*) over (*b*) across

(*c*) far (*d*) from

**81.** In big cities people are cut.............. from nature.

(*a*) off (*b*) down **(CLAT 2014)**

(*c*) away (*d*) out

**82.** The dissidents............a great problem in every political party. **(CLAT 2014)**

(*a*) give (*b*) cause

(*c*) pose (*d*) hold

## Solutions

**1.** a. The best answer is option (*a*). 'To express surprise at...' is an idiomatic expression.

**2.** c. The answer is option (*c*). We require the preposition 'with' here as the two components - water and oil-are complementary to each other and one is not given importance over the other.

**3.** a The correct answer is option (*a*). Only this option uses the correct sequence of words. 'Open' is the modifier that must be placed after 'door' since it modifies it.

**4.** b This is an imperative sentence where the subject is understood. The pronoun 'you and me' are both objects of the verb 'let' and should be used in the objective case.

**5.** a The best answer is option (*a*). The conjunction 'while' best brings out the meaning that the person was hit when he was entering the room.

**6.** b Correct form of adverb 'quick' should be used (quickly) for maintaining parallelism. Also, the sentence has an error- preposition 'to' is required after 'than'. Option (*b*) 'finish quickly' is the right option.

**7.** a 'They' appreciate your action of calling, not 'you', hence option (*a*) is correct. Moreover, an object should follow the verb 'appreciate'. Only the phrase in option (*a*) can be used as a noun phrase, hence as an object.

**8.** a 'look after' is the correct idiomatic expression. It means to take care of.

**9.** d 'bring out' is the correct idiomatic expression. It means to reveal/expose.

**10.** d 'eight century old' is used as an adjective to the noun 'temple', hence it is not used as plural. Thus, 'eight centuries old' will not be used.

**11.** a Two simple sentences are joined by a conjunction; so they must be in parallel form. 'is not' should be followed by 'is not either'.

**12.** d Two different parts of the sentence (before and after the blank) must be joined by a conjunction (in this case because). So options (c) and (*d*)are eliminated. 'because they different concepts' doesn't make sense; it should be 'because they differ about..', hence option (*a*) is wrong. Only option (*d*) is correct.

**13.** b Since the word 'movie' is a countable noun, it should be preceded by an article 'a'.

**14.** a 'Appointed' in the correct word. The sentence has an error- an article 'a' is required before the countable noun 'working group'.

**15.** b 'walk around' is the correct phrase. It means to walk with no particular goal. It also means to behave in a certain manner or have certain properties; for example: He walks around with his nose in the air.

**16.** d Hard-working is both logically as well as grammatically correct in the given context. Lethargic and hostile are not positive traits and are logically incorrect in the context of promotions.

**17.** c The word 'dripping' is logically correct here.

**18.** c 'Plaintive' means sounding sad, especially in a weak complaining way; mournful. For example: a plaintive cry/voice. Thus, the adverb 'plaintively' is correct here.

**19.** b The preposition 'to' is appropriate with the word 'inimical'.

**20.** d 'Over' is the correct preposition in the given context.

**21.** d The right answer is option (*d*) because the sentence refers to a place where there is noise.

**22.** c The consistency in the sentence can be maintained through option (*c*), as the sentence indicates the comparative degree of adjective.

**23.** b The sentence is talking of Ben in Active Voice, to refer to the same idea in continuation, the next following sentence should be 'he walks to work...'

**24.** d The sentence is in simple past tense and hence the answer is option (*d*).

**25.** b The correct usage of interrogative simple past tense is 'why did you have to...?'

**26.** d 'turned out' is the correct phrase to be used in the sentence.

**27.** c 'put off' is the right phrase for the sentence.

**28.** c The damage was caused 'to' the other car.

**29.** a One objects 'to' something or some clause.

**30.** b Restrained – to hold back

Rescinded – to make void or annul

Compelled – to force or drive to a course of action

Conferred – to consult together

'Rescinded' is the correct choice.

**31.** b 'Inferior' and 'superior' are idiomatically followed by 'to' in typical constructions like the one given.

**32.** c 'Annoyed' must be followed by 'with'. One gets annoyed 'with' something/someone, not 'against', 'towards' or 'upon'.

**33.** d Certain words are followed by particular prepositions only. 'Averse' is always followed by 'to'. Other words of this type are 'conform to', 'comply with', 'absolve from' etc.

**34.** a To send 'for' someone/something is to call that person/thing. To send 'in' is to cause (someone) to arrive in or become involved in a particular place or situation. Both the options are correct here but option (*d*) makes more sense in the context of the statement.

**35.** c 'to what' is the correct choice. 'listening' should be followed by 'to'.

**36.** b 'Among' is used when talking about things that are not distinct items or individuals. 'Between' is used when talking about distinct individuals or items even if they are more than two. Since, the sentence here talks about 'certain tribes' which are similar entities, 'among' is the correct choice.

**37.** d 'To bring out' means to uncover or make visible something that was previously hidden/not visible.

**38.** b For constructions like the one given in this sentence, where the author talks about things which he wants to happen, anticipates will happen or imagines happening, we use 'were' instead of was.

**39.** a 'Turn up' means to make an appearance, arrive. The correct choice is option (*a*).

**40.** c 'from' here is the correct choice. It is used to indicate separation, exclusion or removal.

**41.** a 'with' is the correct preposition. 'done away with' is a phrasal verb which means to discard something, stop doing something.

**42.** c 'take after' someone, meaning to look or behave like someone is the correct phrasal verb.

**43.** d The first 'take on' means hire; the second 'take on' means to undertake.

**44.** c 'To take something in stride' means to cope up with something calmly; without disrupting one's normal routine.

**45.** d 'take off' is to achieve wide use or popularity.

**46.** d Pertinent means having a clear and definite relevance to the matter at hand. The correct preposition used with pertinent is 'to'. Hence, option (*d*) is correct.

**47.** b Reverberate means 'to echo'. The voice would reflect 'from' the walls to give rise to an echo or reverberation. Hence, 'from' is the correct preposition.

**48.** c Commensurate refers to a correct or suitable amount when compared with something. Hence, rewards are commensurate 'with' the work. Thus, option (c) is correct.

**49.** a The correct preposition used with index is 'of'. Index is a list 'of' items. Hence, option (*a*) is correct.

**50.** a 'Smacks of' is a phrasal verb meaning something having an unpleasant quality. If something 'smacks of' something, it means it has that unpleasant quality. 'Your conduct smacks of recklessness' means your conduct is reckless.

**51.** d Grope means trying to feel something with hands when you can't see it with your eyes. 'Gropes for' is a phrasal verb that means to try to look for the right answer, the right word for something. 'A good judge will never 'grope for' the conclusion' means he won't consciously look for a correct conclusion rather he would naturally arrive at one.

**52.** d Genius is a very rare, exceptionally brilliant skill. A person is called a genius when he is exceptionally brilliant at something. The correct preposition used here should be 'at' which refers to a general area of proficiency. Genius is followed by 'at'. Good can be followed by both 'at' and 'in'. 'in' is more specific; for example, we use 'in' for school subjects. *"I am good in math"* and *"I am good at basketball"*.

**53.** c Averse refers to a strong dislike for something. The correct preposition for averse is 'to'. For example, *"I am averse to spiders"* means that I dislike spiders. Hence, option (c) is correct.

**54.** d Delve means to carefully research something or examine in detail. But delve is an intransitive verb and can't have a direct object. For example, *"The philosopher delves **into** his book for insights"*. Hence, option (*d*) is correct.

**55.** c Bearing means to have an effect on something. Hence option (*c*), 'on', is the correct preposition for bearing.

**56.** c Option (*a*), pass of, is incorrect usage. Option (*b*), 'pass on', means 'to place into the hands or custody of'. Option (*d*), 'passed away' means 'to die', hence incorrect. Option (*c*), 'passed off' means 'to continue to completion, to occur'. Hence, option (c) is correct.

**57.** b Option (*a*), usage of 'little' implies 'negligible, none'. Hence, it is incorrect. Options (c) and (*d*) are incorrect as 'any' and 'some' are used when the speaker cannot specify or does not need/want to specify a number or an exact amount. Usage of 'a little' implies 'a positive idea along with an uncountable noun'. Option (*b*), 'a little', implies 'a small quantity' (of water in the given context). Hence, option (*b*) is correct.

**58.** b Option (*a*), 'into' is used to denote 'to the inside or interior of, for example: *went into the house'*. Hence, it is incorrect. Options (c) and (*d*) are also inappropriate usages. Option (*c*), 'in' is used to indicate inclusion within or occurrence during a period or limit of time. 'Era' denotes a period of time. Hence, option (*b*) is correct.

**59.** b Option b, 'to', is correct as preposition 'to' is used to show that two things are attached or connected. Hence, option (*b*) is the correct answer in the given usage.

**60.** c Option (c) is correct as 'that' is used for referring to somebody/something that has already been mentioned or is already known about. Hence, here in the given context, 'that is' the correct answer.

**61.** b Option (*b*) is correct as 'across' is used to represent from one side to the other side.

**62.** a Option (*a*), 'run out' is an intransitive verb, which is used to denote 'to come to an end, expire'. Hence, option (*a*) is correct.

**63.** c Option (*c*), 'called for' is used to denote 'to need something'. In the given context, the boss needs an explanation. Hence, option (c) is correct.

**64.** a 'To put something up' means 'to raise something or put it in a higher position', hence option (*b*) is incorrect in the given context. 'To put somebody out' means 'to be upset or offended'; hence option (c) is incorrect in the given context. 'To put aside' means 'to ignore or forget something, usually a feeling or difference of opinion'. Thus, option (*d*) is incorrect. Option (*a*), 'put off' means 'to hold back to a later time'. In the given context, the subject delayed his departure- "He put off his departure for a week as his mother was not well." Hence, option (*a*) is correct.

**65.** c If the clause, other than the one containing 'if' or 'unless', contains 'will +verb form 1', the conditional clause should be in simple present tense. For example, if you do your work in time, I will take you to the zoo. All other options are incorrect due to the same reason.

**66.** c Some clauses containing 'if' are like hypothesis, suppositions or desires and in such cases, we use past tense forms to talk about present and future. In such cases, if the verb is a form of 'be' in the conditional clause, the form of 'be' to be used is 'were' irrespective of the subject. For example, if she were not a writer, she would be an actress. Therefore, the correct sentence will be 'If I were rich, I would help all the poor people'. Hence, the correct answer is option (C).

**67.** b The blank will take a verb that is in simple past tense since the statement contains a specific time reference. This renders option (A) incorrect since 'have heard' suggests that the news was heard at an unknown time. Option (C) and (D) are incorrect because 'hear' belongs to the category of verbs that generally are not used in their 'ing' verb forms like see, love, remember, etc. Had option (C) been 'was listening to', it would have been correct. Hence, option (B) is the correct answer.

**68.** d If a statement is negative, then the question tag (short questions that we put at the end of sentences) is positive and vice-versa. Also, the question tag takes the same verb as used in the preceding part of the statement. For example: He <u>did</u> his homework, <u>didn't</u> he? Similarly, in the given sentence, the verb is 'is not'. Therefore, the correct question tag would be 'is he'. Hence, option (D) is the correct answer.

**69.** c 'We' is the subject in the phrase 'we should never.means'. Therefore, the personal possessive pronoun will be in accordance with 'we'. Hence, option (C) is the correct answer.

**70.** d Option (D) is the correct answer because the correct usage is 'to request someone', not 'request to/onto/ of someone' (to do something) . Therefore, option (C) is incorrect.

**71.** c The statement quoted is a universal fact and should therefore be written in simple present tense. Hence, option (C) is correct.

**72.** c The statement before the conjunction 'before' should be in past perfect tense because the task of doing the work had already finished before the guests arrived. Past Perfect is used to express that an action occurred before another action in the past. For example, I had never seen such a beautiful beach before I went to Kauai. Hence, option (C) is the correct answer.

**73.** d Since the sentence states that the action of 'proposing a vote for thanks' was done at some point of time (at the end of the meeting) in the past, we will use the simple past tense. Hence, option (*d*) is the correct answer. Option (*a*) is incorrect because the subject 'vote' is singular and so it should not be followed by a plural verb 'were'. Option (*b*) is incorrect because the correct phrase is 'vote of thanks', which refers to an informal vote to thank some chairman or other officer of an organization for the work he has done on the organization's behalf. Option (*c*) is incorrect because the action (proposing a vote for thanks) did not happen at some point in the past before some action or time in the past (as it happens in the case of simple past tense).

**74.** a According to the sentence, recession will force companies to lay off/dismiss their workers or the companies will be forced/compelled to lay off their workers. Hence, option (*a*) is the correct answer. Option (*b*) is incorrect because the phrase 'will have the force to' is grammatically incorrect in the given context. Option (*c*) is incorrect because the sentence does not mean that the companies will dismiss its employees willingly but that recession will force the companies into doing it. Option (*d*) is incorrect because the correct phrase would have been "companies will be forced into laying off workers".

**75.** b Option (*b*) is the correct answer because 'to have good command over a language' means to have good amount of knowledge to use that language. Option (*a*) is incorrect because 'expertise' is not followed by 'over' but 'in'. Options (*c*) and (*d*) are incorrect because it is incorrect to say that one has 'control/authority' over language to mean that one has good knowledge of some language.

**76.** d Option (*d*) is the correct answer because the profitability of the industrial plant is likely to have increased (after the manager took over the administration) as the Chairman spoke in 'favour' of the manager. Option (*b*) is logically incorrect due to the same reason. Option (*a*) is incorrect because an industrial plant can start to make profit but we can't say that its 'profitability has arisen'. Option (*c*) is inappropriate because 'added' cannot be used in this context to mean 'increased'.

**77.** d In positive and neutral contexts, the correct placement of pronouns in a statement is in the following order :

2nd person pronoun → 3rd person pronoun → 1st person pronoun.

For example - You, he (any name) and I will be responsible for the decorations. Also, in this context, 'Rohan and I' are subjects who performed the action of 'going to Paris' not objects on whom the action was performed, so 'I' (used for subjects) and not 'me' (used for objects) is appropriate here. Hence, option (*d*) is the correct answer and all other options are incorrect.

**78.** b 'Shall' is the helping verb (generally used with first person pronouns like 'I' and 'We') in question tags to politely seek permission. For example - I was thinking of borrowing your dress, shall I/ may I? Hence, option (*b*) is the correct answer. Option (*a*) would have been correct if the sentence were to be - 'We can't go for a walk, can we?' Option (*c*) would have been correct if the sentence were to be - 'We can go for a walk, can't we?' Option (*d*) would have been correct if the sentence were to be 'We should go for a walk, shouldn't we?'

**79.** d In case of conditional sentences of the type 'If X had existed (or Had X existed), Y would have happened', we use:

'had + verb form 3' (had existed) in the conditional phrase and 'would have + verb form 3' (could have happened) in the other phrase.

For example - had I / If I had owned a house in Delhi, I would not have stayed at my Uncle's house last week. Hence, option (*d*) is the correct answer. Option (*a*) is incorrect because 'been', which is generally followed by 'verb form 1 + ing', is inept in this context. Here, the action of Anil having 'missed the train' is not a continuous action. Option (*b*) is incorrect because 'had not' does not connote 'past possibility'. Option (*c*) is incorrect because the action would have happened in the past while 'will' suggests future.

**80.** b Option (*b*) is the correct answer because an infection can spread 'across/throughout' the state. Option (*a*) is incorrect because 'over' which means 'at a position above or higher than' is logically inept in this context. Option (*c*) is incorrect because an infection cannot spread 'far the state'. Option (*d*) is incorrect because the sentence does not mean that the state is the place from where the infection is spreading to villages. Also, 'something spreads from somewhere to/till some other place'.

**81.** a Option (*a*) is the correct answer because 'cut off', which means separated is logically correct in this context. 'Cut down' means to make something fall down by cutting it at the base; 'cut away' means to remove something from something by cutting and 'cut out' means to remove something from something larger by cutting, usually with scissors.

**82.** b Options (*b*) and (*c*) are equally good because dissidents by virtue of holding different opinions can both 'cause' and 'pose' (be a great problem themselves) a great problem in every political party. So, although according to the answer key released by CLAT, option (*b*) is the correct answer but there is no reason to negate option (*c*) and choose (*b*) over it. Option (*a*) is incorrect because one can get rid of one's problems by giving them to somebody else but we cannot use 'give' in this context to express 'cause'. Option (*d*) is incorrect because it is meaningless to say that dissidents 'hold' great problems in parties.

## CLOZE TEST

**Directions for questions 1 to 34 :** In each of the following passages, every blank is numbered distinctly and options for the blanks are given against corresponding numbers. Fill in the blanks with the most appropriate word from the options given.

__ 1 __ evening we decided to ____ 2 ____camp as the weather was not encouraging. The wind was high and ____ 3 ____ storm clouds ____ 4 ____ a wild wet night. Moreover we ____ 5 ____ at a spot which looked ____ 6 ____ for a camp. A level ____ 7 ____ in the lee of a high hill ____ 8 ____some shelter from the wind; fresh water was near ____ 9 ____ in a storm which flowed across the plain; a ____ 10 ____ of trees provided adequate supplies of fuel; and the dry grass which ____ 11 ____ on the hill side would enhance the comfort of our beds. Each member of the part ____ 12 ____ a task. Some erected the tens; others prepared a scanty meal; yet others ____ 13 ____ to the needs of the ponies, now exhausted after a very strenuous day. As the angry sun sank, the bustle of activity was hushed into silence and each man ____ 14 ____ down to sleep. **(AILET, 2009)**

**1.** (*a*) a the (*b*) after the
(c) in the (*d*) before

**2.** (*a*) dig (*b*) fixed
(c) plant (*d*) pitch

**3.** (*a*) collecting (*b*) gathering
(c) accumulating (*d*) moving

**4.** (*a*) preceded (*b*) proceeded
(c) predicted (*d*) proved

**5.** (*a*) arrived (*b*) have arrived
(c) would arrive (*d*) had arrived

**6.** (*a*) promise (*b*) promiseful
(c) promising (*d*) prosperous

**7.** (*a*) expense (*b*) land
(c) expanse (*d*) piece of land

**8.** (*a*) gave (*b*) afforded
(c) supplied (*d*) cast

**9.** (*a*) in hand (*b*) on hand
(c) at hand (*d*) of hand

**10.** (*a*) group (*b*) cluster
(c) collection (*d*) grove

**11.** (*a*) abundant (*b*) luxuriant
(c) abounded (*d*) abounded in

**12.** (*a*) allotted (*b*) was allotted
(c) had allotted (*d*) has allotted

**13.** (*a*) will attend (*b*) had attended
(c) attended (*d*) would have attended

**14.** (*a*) settled (*b*) settles
(c) laid (*d*) lay

If you look very closely at a newspaper photograph you will see that the grey areas are made up of black dots of various sizes. The lighter the shades of grey, the smaller the dots. In ___15___ area the dots are larger. The process by which this ___16___ is achieved is called half-tone screening. First of all a negative ___17___ is made of the picture. That is, the light and dark areas are ___18___ so that white becomes ___19___ and black becomes white. This picture is projected ___20___ a special screen. The screen is made of glass and has lines ___21___ on it both vertically and horizontally. So the screen is divided up ___22___ tiny squares rather like graph paper. When the light ___23___ the negative is shone through this ___24___ it is broken up into dots. This light lands on a metal plate that is coated with chemicals. **(AILET, 2011)**

15. (*a*) smaller (*b*) darker (c) lighter (*d*) small
16. (*a*) effect (*b*) colour (c) tone (*d*) affect
17. (*a*) photograph (*b*) print (c) copy (*d*) paint
18. (*a*) reversed (*b*) removed (c) coloured (*d*) darkened
19. (*a*) dark (*b*) dotted (c) black (*d*) white
20. (*a*) into (*b*) above (c) through (*d*) on
21. (*a*) ruled (*b*) cut (c) reflected (*d*) deflected
22. (*a*) from (*b*) into (c) like (*d*) in
23. (*a*) from (*b*) of (c) on (*d*) at
24. (*a*) graph paper (*b*) framework (c) screen (*d*) paper

The Ganga is ___25___ they said, in her giving and her taking away. If you ask her for anything she ___26___ it gently. A calm and slow oblivion in ___27___ ever-flowing waves. Mridula hoped it was true. She sat on the stone steps of the Kedar Ghat, ___28___ the first rays of the Sun touch the ripples on the river with ___29___ of metallic gold. Ganga *paschim vahini* – the east flowing river ___30___ west at Varanasi like a moody woman. People bathed, said prayers standing chest ___31___ in her water, muttering ___32___ to her and to the rising sun, repeating endlessly the ___33___ of prayer pouring water through their finger in habits for which may be they never ___34___ the meaning. **(AILET, 2012)**

25. (*a*) kind (*b*) name (c) flow (*d*) cruel
26. (*a*) takes (*b*) refuse (c) ignore (*d*) gives
27. (*a*) their (*b*) her (c) any (*d*) only
28. (*a*) counting (*b*) persuing (c) dotting (*d*) watching
29. (*a*) dullness (*b*) dampness (c) glints (*d*) splint
30. (*a*) steers (*b*) hears (c) looks (*d*) turns
31. (*a*) deep (*b*) down (c) up (*d*) fallen
32. (*a*) appeals (*b*) pleas (c) invocations (*d*) considerations
33. (*a*) culture (*b*) rituals (c) works (*d*) deed
34. (*a*) mentioned (*b*) heard (c) conceived (*d*) knew

**Directions (Q. 35 - 43) :** Fill in the blanks with the best alternative among the four options:

Around the world, forests are being destroyed at a rate of about thirteen million hectares a year and deforestation accounts for an estimated 17% - 20% of all global emissions. In addition, forests and other terrestrial carbon sinks play a **....(35)....** role in preventing runaway climate change, soaking up a full 2.6 Gt of atmospheric carbon every year. The destruction of forests, therefore, not only emits carbon — a staggering 1.6 Gt a year, which severely **..(36)....** forests' capacity to absorb emissions from other sources - but also drastically**....(37)....** the amount of forested land available to act as a carbon sink in the future.

However, the effects of deforestation extend beyond carbon. Rainforests **....(38)....** a wide variety of ecosystems services, from regulating rainfall to purifying groundwater and keeping fertile soil from **....(39)....**; deforestation in one area can seriously damage food production and **....(40)....** to clean water in an entire region. The value of global ecosystem services has been estimated at 33 trillion USD each year (almost half of global GDP), but these services have been taken for granted without a mechanism to make the market reflect their value. Rainforests are also a home and **....(41)....** of income for a huge number of people in Africa, Asia, and South America

...(42).... this, economic pressures frequently drive both local communities and national governments in the developing world to ....(43).... these forests in ways that are unsustainable, clear-cutting vast areas for fuel, timber, mining, or agricultural land. **(AILET 2014)**

**35.** (*a*) tough (*b*) important (*c*) vital (*d*) biggest

**36.** (*a*) affect (*b*) diminish (*c*) increases (*d*) impairs

**37.** (*a*) plagues (*b*) develops (*c*) reduces (*d*) shortens

**38.** (*a*) sell (*b*) offer (*c*) give (*d*) provide

**39.** (*a*) transforming (*b*) decoding (*c*) erupting (*d*) eroding

**40.** (*a*) handiness (*b*) excess (*c*) availability (*d*) access

**41.** (*a*) beginning (*b*) source (*c*) ways (*d*) reference

**42.** (*a*) despite (*b*) also (*c*) in spite (*d*) apart

**43.** (*a*) exploit (*b*) encompass (*c*) nurture (*d*) work

## Solutions

**1.** c 'In the' is the correct usage, since 'evening' is the time when the decision was taken.

**2.** d 'Pitch' camp means to set up a campsite.

**3.** b The correct adjective for clouds here is 'gathering'.

**4.** a 'Preceded', meaning to come before something, is the logical word to fill in the blank.

**5.** a The passage is in simple past tense, thus, 'arrived' is the correct choice.

**6.** c 'Promising', meaning 'likely to develop in a desirable manner', is the correct word to fill in the blank.

**7.** c 'Expanse' is the correct choice. It means a wide and open extent, as of surface, land or sky.

**8.** a 'Gave' is the correct word. Shelter is always given, not supplied, afforded or cast.

**9.** c 'At hand', meaning near in time or place or within reach, is the correct phrase.

**10.** d 'Grove' of trees,' meaning a group of trees, is the correct usage.

**11.** c 'Abounded' is the past tense of 'abound' which means to exist in large numbers.

**12.** b Since each member was given a task, 'was allotted' is the correct choice. 'Allotted', 'had allotted' and 'has allotted' are incorrect because they give the sense that the members gave the tasks to someone else whereas the passage states that they were given the tasks.

**13.** c 'Attended' must be used to maintain consistency of tense in the sentence.

**14.** d 'Lay' is used both in past and present tense but its meaning is different in both the cases. In present tense 'lay' needs an object to it, as in *"I lay the book on the table"* which means to put something down. Its past tense is 'laid', as in *"I laid the book on the table"*. 'Lay' is also used as past tense of 'lie' meaning to recline. *"He lay down early for sleep yesterday"*. Here, 'lay', the past tense of 'lie', is the correct choice since the passage is in simple past tense.

**15.** b The previous sentence talks about the size of dots when the color of the dots is on the lighter side of grey. The next sentence that talks about larger dots should logically refer to darker areas. Hence, option (*b*), 'darker', is the correct choice.

**16.** c The reference to half-tone and the technical nature of the paragraph suggests that 'tone' would be the most suitable word for the given blank.

**17.** b Since the initial step cannot logically be a copy, option (c) is negated. 'Print' is the most suitable word as per the context.

**18.** a The reversal of light areas and dark areas so that black becomes white is the only logically correct idea. Hence, 'reversed' is the correct choice.

**19.** c As black becomes white, so white should become 'black'. Hence, option (c) is the correct choice.

**20.** d The picture is projected on the screen. 'On' is the correct preposition.

**21.** a The verb 'ruled' which means arranged is the correct choice.

**22.** b The preposition 'into' is the correct choice.

**23.** a 'Light from the negative' is the correct phrase.

**24.** c The paragraph mentions the screen and the former sentence also talks about the picture being projected on the screen. This makes 'screen' the correct word for the given blank.

**25.** a 'Kind' is the correct adjective since the sentence talks about Ganga's qualities of giving and taking away.

**26.** d The Ganga 'gives' anything that we 'ask' for, hence option (*d*) fills the blank correctly. 'Refuse', 'take' and 'ignore' do not fit in the context here.

**27.** b The Ganga is referred to as 'her' in the sentences above. Same pronoun follows here. 'Only' and 'any' do not make sense in the context of the passage. Hence, option (*b*) is correct.

**28.** d One cannot 'count', 'dot' or 'pursue' the rays of the sun. The correct verb here is 'watching'.

**29.** c Gold shines or 'glints'. Hence, 'glints' is the correct adjective for metallic gold.

**30.** d The sentence talks about the river changing its direction. Hence, 'turn' is the correct choice here.

**31.** a The correct word is 'deep'. People stand 'chest deep' in water which means that they are submerged in water chest down.

**32.** c Invocations meaning 'spoken words that are believed to have magical powers' is the right option.

**33.** b Pouring water through their fingers is a ritual that people do while bathing in Ganga. Hence, option (*b*) is correct.

**34.** d 'Knew' is the right word. Heard, mentioned and conceived are incorrect in the context of the passage.

**35.** c Forests and other terrestrial carbon sinks cannot play 'tough' or 'biggest' role in preventing climate change. They can only play a vital or an important role. Therefore, options (*a*) and (*d*) are incorrect. Option (*b*) is incorrect because 'important' will take the article 'an' and not 'a' before it. Hence, option (*c*) is the correct answer.

**36.** d Option (*c*) is incorrect because destruction of forests cannot have a positive effect onforests capacity to absorb emissions. It will only adversely affect the forests capacity. Moreover, 'severely' means very badly or unpleasantly. So, in this context, we cannot use 'increase' with it. Options (*a*) and (*b*) are incorrect because 'affect' and 'diminish' are plural verbs but the blank requires a singular verb. Only option (*d*) is grammatically and logically correct and hence, is the answer.

**37.** c Option (*c*) is the correct answer because the destruction of forests will reduce/decrease the amount of forested land that can act as carbon sink. Other options are incorrect because the destruction of forests will not 'plague', 'shorten' or 'develop' forest land in this context.

**38.** d The correct answer is option (*d*), 'provide'. However, according to the answer key released by NLUD, the answer for this question is option (*b*). When someone or something offers something, you can either take it or turn it down. But if someone or something provides you something, he is making something available to you. You don't have an option of turning it down. The services provided by eco-system cannot be turned down. Therefore, the blank will take option (*d*) as the correct answer.

**39.** d Option (*d*) is the correct answer because the rainforests will prevent the fertile soil from 'eroding'. Other options are incorrect because fertile soil cannot be 'transformed', 'decoded' or erupted'.

**40.** d Options (*a*) and (*b*) are incorrect because they render the sentence meaningless. 'Availability' will not take the preposition 'to' but 'of' after it and therefore, it is incorrect. 'Access' means a way of getting near, at, or to something or someone. Hence, option (*d*) is the correct answer.

**41.** b 'Source' means cause of something. Hence, option (*b*) is the correct answer. Options (*a*), (*c*) and (*d*) will render the sentence incorrect.

**42.** a 'Apart' and 'also' will not take the word 'this' immediately after them. Therefore, options (*b*) and (*d*) are incorrect. Option (*c*) is incorrect since 'in spite' always takes the preposition 'of' after it. Only 'despite' fits in the meaning of the sentence and therefore, is the correct answer.

**43.** a 'Nurture' is incorrect since the sentence says that the methods used by them are unsustainable. Only option (*a*) fits in the meaning of the sentence, which means that economic pressures force communities and governments to exploit forests in unsustainable ways.

## TENSES

**Directions (Q. 1 - 10) :** Complete the sentences by filling in the blanks with the correct tenses from the given choices.

**1.** I wish you ____ louder as I can't hear what you say.

(*a*) were speaking (*b*) spoke
(c) would speak (*d*) speak **(AILET, 2010)**

**2.** The audience ________ to take their seats please.

(*a*) is requested (*b*) have requested
(c) may request (*d*) are requested

**(AILET, 2010)**

**3.** It ________all day yesterday before the garden wall collapsed.

(*a*) rained (*b*) has been raining
(c) had rained (*d*) was raining

**(AILET, 2010)**

**4.** Each member of this group ________ guilty.

(*a*) is (*b*) are
(c) is being (*d*) were **(AILET, 2010)**

**5.** The Prime Minister ____ to visit the hospital tomorrow.

(*a*) will (*b*) is
(c) must (*d*) have **(AILET, 2010)**

**6.** Last night the radio said that the volcano, Etna, in Sicily ________

(*a*) will erupt (*b*) is erupting

(c) erupts (*d*) has to erupt

**(AILET, 2010)**

**7.** They say that the Princess ________ incognito at the Sheraton.

(*a*) have stayed (*b*) is staying

(c) stay (*d*) will have been staying

**(AILET, 2010)**

**8.** She ____ in Calcutta for a quarter of a century now.

(*a*) will live (*b*) lived

(c) has been living (*d*) had been living

**(AILET, 2010)**

**9.** When we went to their home, Sushma ________ some fresh coffee for us.

(*a*) made (*b*) has made

(c) will make (*d*) is making

**(AILET, 2010)**

**10.** Evidence shows that Jackson ________inside the house at the time of the murder.

(*a*) was (*b*) is

(c) will be (*d*) has been

**(AILET, 2010)**

## Solutions

**1.** b Whenever, we use 'I wish', past subjunctive must follow (here in this case 'spoke' not 'speak').

**2.** d 'Audience' is a collective noun which is considered singular or plural depending on the context in which it is used. When it refers to the group of people comprising the audience as one entity, as a whole, then it is considered as singular. For example- *"The audience is enjoying the performance."* However, when we talk of people in the audience as separate individuals, it is considered as a plural noun. In the given sentence, audience refers to separate individuals who are requested to take their respective seats. Thus, here 'audience' is a plural noun that must take a plural verb 'are'.

**3.** c Since the event of 'raining' has happened before that of 'wall collapsed', past perfect must be used.

**4.** a The subject in the given sentence is 'Each member' which is singular, so singular verb must be used.

**5.** b Since 'The Prime Minister' is singular, 'have' can't be used, and of the other given options, only 'is' fits in the sentence.

**6.** b Among the given option, only option (*b*) best fills the blank. Option (*a*) is incorrect as we can't predict beforehand that the volcano is going to erupt. Thus, option (*a*) makes the sentence logically incorrect. Option (c) doesn't fit in grammatically. Option (*d*) is incorrect since we can't make such a definitive statement (has to erupt) about a volcano. Option (*b*) logically and grammatically completes the sentence and thus, is the right choice.

**7.** b Options (*a*) and (c) are wrong because they don't agree with the singular subject. 'The Princess' 'will have been staying' is wrong. Only option (*b*) is correct.

**8.** c An action that started in the past is still going on, so present perfect continuous must be used.

**9.** a Sentence started with the past tense. Simple past must follow.

**10.** a Sentence talks about a past event. Simple past must follow.

## WORD COMBINATION

**Directions (Q. 1 - 5) :** Given below are five list of words followed by some choices. In each case, choose the alternative that you can combine with every word in that particular list to form a familiar word phrase.

**1.** Down, aside, about, forth

(*a*) set (*b*) fly

(c) burn (*d*) take **(CLAT 2008)**

**2.** Over, about, after, at

(*a*) cross (*b*) lay

(c) here (*d*) go **(CLAT 2008)**

**3.** Forward, across, around, upon

(*a*) straight (*b*) come

(c) fast (*d*) mark **(CLAT 2008)**

**4.** In, down, for, out

(*a*) pray

(*b*) try

(c) grow

(*d*) stand **(CLAT 2008)**

**5.** Away, through, up, down

(*a*) stray (*b*) come

(c) break (*d*) speak **(CLAT 2008)**

## Solutions

**1.** a Set down – to put in a particular place

Set aside – for a particular purpose

Set about – to start

Set forth – to give an account of

**2.** d Go over – to repeat or review

Go about – to perform

Go after – to strive for

Go at - attack

3. b Come forward – to offer one's service
Come across – to find or encounter
Come around – to recover consciousness
Come upon – to meet unexpectedly

4. d Stand in – to act as a stand-in
Stand down – to withdraw
Stand for – to represent
Stand out – to project

5. b Come away – to leave in a certain condition
Come through – to finish successfully
Come up – to arise
Come down – to lose wealth or rank

## PARTS OF SPEECH

**Directions (Q. 1 - 3) :** Identify the part of speech of the underlined words in the given sentences.

1. I must perfect the operation to make the perfect robot.
(*a*) verb (*b*) adverb
(c) adjective (*d*) noun **(CLAT 2010)**

2. A kindly person is one who behaves kindly.
(*a*) noun (*b*) preposition
(c) adverb (*d*) verb **(CLAT 2010)**

3. He is not normally a very fast runner, but he runs fast in major events.
(*a*) adverb (*b*) adjective
(c) verb (*d*) noun **(CLAT 2010)**

### Solutions

1. a 'Perfect' here is a verb which means to make something completely free from faults and defects.
2. c 'Kindly' here is an adverb (of manner) which means 'in a kind manner'.
3. a 'Very' is used here for emphasis which modifies 'fast', the adjective. Thus, it is an adverb.

## PHRASE REPLACEMENT

**Directions (Q. 1 - 3) :** In the following sentences, substitute the underlined phrases with any of the given choices to express the opposite meaning.

1. She always praises everything I say.
(*a*) picks holes in (*b*) dislikes
(c) rebukes (*d*) picks holes to
**(CLAT 2010)**

2. He often says how wonderful his school is.
(*a*) says he is unworthy (*b*) appreciates
(c) runs up (*d*) runs down
**(CLAT 2010)**

3. She said I was the best boss they'd ever had. It was obvious she was praising me sincerely.
(*a*) not appreciating me
(*b*) befooling me
(*c*) buttering me up
(*d*) disliking me **(CLAT 2010)**

### Solutions

1. a 'Pick holes in' means to find faults.
2. d The word 'run down' is opposite to the underlined phrase in meaning . [ However, if we substitute the phrase in the sentence by run down, sentence sounds awkward. Other options do not fit in at all.]
3. c 'Buttering up' means to praise insincerely.

## SENTENCE CORRECTION

**Directions (Q. 1 - 5):** In the following questions, a group of sentences about a single topic are given. One or more of the sentence(s) is/are **grammatically incorrect.** You have to identify the incorrect sentence(s). **(AILET, 2013)**

1. I. It began with acquisitions in information technology and related services sector.
II. In pharmaceuticals, Wockhardt has bought C.P. Pharma of the United Kingdom for $ 10.85 million.
III. Tata Tea has taken over Tetley of the UK, the world's biggest tea bag maker, for $ 430 million.
IV. With the processes, it has become the world's second largest tea company.
(*a*) II and IV (*b*) IV only
(c) II and III (*d*) I, II and IV

2. I. There are two main reasons for that predatory mood.
II. Having established a domestic presence, the component makers are now looking for an international presence.
III. Second, having improved their productivity, quality and reliability, Indian companies feel more confident about spreading their wings abroad.
IV. Various other factors are being attributed to this Indian penchant for the takeover game in all sectors.
(*a*) I only (*b*) I and II
(c) II only (*d*) III and IV

3. I. Moving one by one step away from the expected with the graphics and photography can also create reader's interest.
II. Try using a conceptual image or photo to highlight your main message versus very first thing to come to mind when thinking about your product or services.

III. Another form of contrast is in the actual design.

IV. An unusual fold in a brochure or direct mail piece can add excitement.

(*a*) I and II (*b*) II and III

(*c*) I and IV (*d*) No error

**4.** I. The typeface that you choose for your print project is an important piece of the foremost overall design process.

II. First, narrow down your choice by selecting the tone you want to present.

III. Typefaces can convey personality.

IV. For instance, if you are in the banking industry you might choose a classic serif font, such as Garamond, to convey dependability.

(*a*) I only (*b*) II only

(*c*) III only (*d*) IV only

**5.** I. Readability is crucial.

II. Be sure of the font we choose is legible and logical.

III. With all of the newest and interesting typefaces available today, it is tempting to pick one that you think looks "cool".

IV. This can work if you are going for an edgy look that will appeal to a young audience, but your copy still needs to be easily understood.

(*a*) I and IV (*b*) II only

(*c*) III only (*d*) II and III

### Solutions

**1.** b 'With the processes' is grammatically incorrect. The correct sentence should be "In the process, it has become tea company." Remaining sentences are grammatically correct. Hence, option (*b*) is correct.

**2.** a Since the directions clearly spell that the sentences are about a single topic, it can be inferred that the "predatory mood" talked about in sentence I refers to the acquisitions talked about in the previous question. Thus, the correct pronoun for "predatory mood" here is 'this'. All other sentences are grammatically correct. Hence, option (*a*) is correct.

**3.** a In sentence I, the correct phrase should be "step by step". In sentence II articles 'a' and 'the' are missing. Also, instead of 'to', 'that' is the correct usage. 'That' is used for referring to somebody/something that has already been mentioned or is already known about. The correct sentence should be "Try using a conceptual image or ***a*** photo to highlight your main message versus ***the*** very first thing ***that comes*** to mind when thinking about your product or service." Hence, option (*a*) is correct.

**4.** a Usage of the word 'foremost' with 'overall is incorrect. Foremost means: the most important or famous; in a position at the front. In the given context, foremost is laying emphasis which is already explained by the phrase, 'is an important piece of the..' Correct sentence is: "The typeface that you choose for your print project is an important piece of the overall design process". Hence, option (*a*) is correct.

**5.** d Sentence II is incorrect as instead of 'of', 'that' is the correct usage. The correct sentence should be "Be sure *that* the font we choose is legible and logical". 'That' is used for referring to somebody/something that has already been mentioned or is already known about. 'That' refers to 'readability' mentioned in sentence I. In sentence III, the usage of "newest" is incorrect. The sentence is not parallel as both the adjectives are not in the same form (newest is superlative, interesting is positive). The correct sentence should be "With all of the new and interesting.".Hence, option (*d*) is correct.

## SPOT THE CORRECT SENTENCE

**Directions (Q. 18 - 19) :** Answer the questions based on the following information. **(AILET 2014)**

*In each of the question below, four different ways of writing a sentence are indicated. Choose the best way of writing the sentence.*

**1.** (*a*) The main problem with the notion of price discrimination is that it is not always a bad thing, but that it is the monopolist who has the power to decide who is charged what price.

(*b*) The main problem with the notion of price discrimination is not that it is always a bad thing, it is the monopolist who has the power to decide who is charged what price.

(*c*) The main problem with the notion of price discrimination is not that it is always a bad thing, but that it is the monopolist who has the power to decide who is charged what price.

(*d*) The main problem with the notion of price discrimination is not it is always a bad thing, but that it is the monopolist who has the power to decide who is charged what price.

**2.** (*a*) A symbiotic relationship develops among the contractors, bureaucracy and the politicians, and by a large number of devices, costs are artificially escalated and black money is generated by underhand deals.

(*b*) A symbiotic relationship develops among contractors, bureaucracy and politicians, and costs are artificially escalated with a large number of devices and black money is generated through underhand deals.

(*c*) A symbiotic relationship develops among contractors, bureaucracy and the politicians, and by a large number of devices costs are artificially escalated and black money is generated on underhand deals.

(*d*) A symbiotic relationship develops among the contractors, bureaucracy and politicians, and by large number of devices costs are artificially escalated and black money is generated by underhand deals.

### Solutions

**1.** c Option (*a*) is logically incorrect because the problem with price discrimination cannot be that 'price discrimination is not always a bad thing'. Option (*b*) is incorrect because the change in the direction of the argument should be marked by a conjunction 'but' and not a comma. The grammatical error in option (*d*) is in the phrase 'is not it is always'. Had it been 'is not that it is always', it would have been correct. Only option (*c*) is grammatically correct and hence, is the answer.

**2.** b There is a parallelism error in option (*a*). Since all the them, 'contractors ', 'politicians'and 'bureaucracy' are the three subjects in the statement, either all of them or none of them should be preceded by the article 'the'. Options (*c*) and (*d*) are also incorrect due to the same reason. Also, there is a modifier error in options (*a*), (*c*) and (*d*). The correct phrase should be "costs are artificially escalated by/with a large number of devices". Only option (*b*) is grammatically correct and hence, is the answer.

## WORD USAGE

**Directions (Q. 1 - 3) :** In the following questions, the word at the top is used in four different ways. Choose the option in which the usage of the word is INCORRECT or INAPPROPRIATE. **(AILET 2014)**

**1. Passing**

(*a*) She did not have passing marks in mathematics.

(*b*) The mad woman was cursing everybody passing her on the road.

(*c*) At the birthday party, all the children enjoyed a game of passing the parcel.

(*d*) A passing taxi was stopped to rush the accident victim to the hospital.

**2. Bolt**

(*a*) The shopkeeper showed us a bolt of fine silk.

(*b*) As he could not move, he made a bolt for the gate.

(*c*) Could you please bolt the door?

(*d*) The thief was arrested before he could bolt from the scene of the crime.

**3. Fallout**

(*a*) Nagasaki suffered from the fallout of nuclear radiation.

(*b*) People believed that the political fallout of the scandal would be insignificant.

(*c*) Who can predict the environmental fallout of the WTO agreements?

(*d*) The Headmaster could not understand the fallout of several of his good students at the public examination

### Solutions

**1.** a Option (*a*) is incorrect. The correct sentence is 'She did not have pass marks in mathematics.' 'Passing' in options (*b*) and (*d*) means going by or past. 'Passing the parcel', as used in option (*c*), is a game in which something, such as a bowl, is passed to the other players.

**2.** b 'Bolt', as used in option (*a*), refers to a long piece of cloth wound in a roll around a piece of cardboard. In option (*c*), bolt refers to a long, narrow piece of metal that you slide across the inside of a door or window in order to lock it. In option (*d*) it means to dart off. The usage of the word is logically inappropriate in option (*b*). The person cannot make a bolt for the gate as the first part of the sentence states that he could not move. Hence, option (*b*) is the correct answer.

**3.** d In option (*a*), fallout refers to the radioactive particles that are produced by a nuclear explosion and that fall through the atmosphere. In options (*b*) and (*c*) it means bad effect. Option (*d*) is grammatically incorrect as the use of the word 'fallout' does not make sense.

■■

# 3

# READING COMPREHENSION

**Directions (Q. 1 - 112) :** Each set of questions in this section is based on a passage. The questions are to be answered on the basis of what is **stated** or **implied** in the corresponding passage. For some of the questions, more than one of the choices could conceivably answer the question. However, you are to choose the **best** answer; that is, the response that most accurately and completely answers the questions.

**Passage for questions 1 to 5:**

One of the most prolific authors of all time, Isaac Asimov was influential both in science fiction and in the popularization of science during the twentieth century, but he is also justly famous for the scope of his interests. Although the common claim that Asimov is the only author to have written a book in every category of the Dewey decimal system is untrue, its spirit provides an accurate picture of the man: a dedicated humanist who lauded the far-reaching power of reason. His most famous work, the *Foundation* trilogy, can be read as an illustration of Asimov's belief in reason and science, but even while he expressed that belief, science itself was calling it into question.

*Foundation* describes a time in which a vast Empire spanning the galaxy is on the verge of collapse. Its inevitable doom is a consequence not of its size, but of the shortsightedness of its leaders. In this environment, a scientist named Hari Seldon devises an all encompassing plan to help human civilization recover from the trauma of the Empire's coming collapse. Using mathematics, Seldon is able to predict the future course of history for thousands of years, and he takes steps that are geared toward guiding that future in a beneficial direction. The trope of the benevolent and paternalistic scientist shaping existence from behind the scenes, present in much of Asimov's fiction, is never more explicit than in the *Foundation* series, which describes with an epic sweep the course and progress of the Seldon Plan.

As naive and, perhaps, self-serving as the conceit of *Foundation* may seem to contemporary readers, it retains to some degree its ability of comfort by offering an antidote to the complex and unpredictable nature of experience. Science in Asimov's time was, in popular conceptions, engaged in just this pursuit: discerning immutable laws that operate beneath a surface appearance of contingency, inexplicability, and change. But even while Asimov wrote, science itself was changing. In Physics, the study of matter at the subatomic level showed that indeterminacy was not a transitory difficulty to be overcome, but an essential physical principle. In Biology, the sense of evolution as a steady progress toward better adapted forms was being disturbed by proof of a past large-scale evolution taking place in brief explosions, of frantic change. At the time of Asimov's death, even Mathematics was gaining popular notice for its interest in chaos and inexplicability. Usually summarized in terms of the so-called 'butterfly effect', chaos theory showed that perfect prediction could take place only on the basis of perfect information, which was by nature impossible to obtain. Science had dispensed with the very assumptions that motivated Asimov's idealization of it in the Seldon Plan. Indeed, it was possible to see chaos at work in *Foundation* itself: as sequels multiplied and began to be tied into narrative threads from Asimov's other novels, the urge to weave one grand narrative spawned myriad internal inconsistencies that were never resolved.

**(AILET, 2008)**

1. Which one of the following most accurately expresses the main point of the passage?
   (*a*) Isaac Asimov's greatest work, the *Foundation* trilogy, is an expression of the common trope of the benevolent and paternalistic scientist
   (*b*) Popularizations of science are always to some degree dependent idealizations and simplifications of that science, as Isaac Asimov's work demonstrates
   (c) The impossibility of the conceit on which Isaac Asimov's *Foundation* trilogy is based demonstrates that Asimov's fiction was based on imperfect understandings of science.
   (*d*) Isaac Asimov's idealization of science as revealed in his *Foundation* series was called into question by the science of his time, which was increasingly focused on Chaos and indeterminacy

**2.** Which one of the following statements most accurately expresses the purpose of the final paragraph?

(*a*) The ultimate failure of the *Foundation* series as a coherent scientific narrative is discussed

(*b*) A claim is made about the purpose of Asimov's writing and then is finally rejected

(*c*) A key theme of Asimov's *Foundation* series is described and discoveries in science that seem contrary to that theme are outlined

(*d*) The history of science is used to demonstrate the falsity of a widely believed claim about the power of human reason

**3.** The author's reference to a common claim made about Isaac Asimov, serves to

(*a*) Demonstrate that many untrue beliefs are held about him

(*b*) Illustrate the broad scope of his interests and writings

(c) Undermine the claim that he was prolific writer

(*d*) Substantiate his belief in the power of human reason

**4.** With respect of the Seldon Plan, the author's attitude can most properly be described as

(*a*) Amused at the naive conception of history it implies

(*b*) Uncertain of the practical impossibility of its application

(c) Ambivalent because of the reliance on human reason it requires

(*d*) Convinced that it illustrates Asimov's attitude toward science

**5.** Which one of the following statements best illustrates the "butterfly effect" as it is described in the passage's third paragraph?

(*a*) A system implemented to predict the weather worldwide for the next century is soon found to be inaccurate because it was supplied with the incomplete data

(*b*) Efforts to predict the result of a nuclear reaction fail because of indeterminacy inherent in the behavior of subatomic particles

(c) The fossil record indicates that certain adaptations found in many organisms appeared soon after a past catastrophic event

(*d*) Scientific predictions about the future course of human history are found to be reasonably accurate once existing social theories are reconciled.

**Passage for questions 6 to 13:**

Most people acknowledge that not all governments have a moral right to govern and that there are sometimes morally legitimate reasons for disobeying the law, as when a particular law prescribes behaviour that is clearly immoral. It is also commonly supposed that such cases are special exceptions and that, in general, the fact that something is against the law counts as a moral, as well as legal, ground for not doing it; i.e. we generally have a moral duty to obey a law simply because it is the law. But the theory known as philosophical anarchism denies this view, arguing instead that people who live under the jurisdiction of governments have no moral duty to those government to obey their laws. Some commentators have rejected this position because of what they take to be its highly counter intuitive implications:(*a*) that no existing government is morally better than any other (since all are , in a sense, equally illegitimate), and (2) that, lacking any moral obligation to obey any laws people may do as they please without scruple. In fact, however, philosophical anarchism does not entail these claims.

First, the conclusion that no government is morally better than any other does not follow from the claim that nobody owes moral obedience to any government. Even if one denies that there is a moral obligation to follow the laws of any government, one can still evaluate the morality of the policies and actions of various governments. Some governments do more good than harm, and others more harm than good, to their subjects. Some violate the moral rights of individuals more regularly, systematically, and seriously than others. In short, it is perfectly consistent with philosophical anarchism to hold that governments vary widely in their moral stature.

Second, philosophical anarchists maintain that all individuals have basic, non-legal moral duties to one another-duties not to harm others in their lives, liberty, health, or goods. Even if governmental laws have no moral force, individuals still have duties to refrain from those actions that constitute crimes in the majority of legal systems (such as murder, assault, theft, and fraud). Moreover, philosophical anarchists hold that people have a positive moral obligation to care for one another, a moral obligation that they might even choose to discharge by supporting cooperative efforts by governments to help those in need. And where others are abiding by established laws, even those laws derived from mere conventions, individuals are morally bound not to violate those laws when doing so would endanger others. Thus, if others obey the law and drive their vehicles on the right, one must not endanger them by driving on the left for , even though driving on the left is not inherently immoral, it is morally wrong to deliberately harm the innocent. **(AILET, 2009)**

**6.** Which one of the following most accurately expresses the main point of the passage?

(*a*) Some views that certain commentators consider to be implications of philosophical anarchism are highly counter-intuitive.

(*b*) Contrary to what philosophical anarchists claim, some governments are morally superior to others and citizens under legitimate governments have moral obligations to one another.

(*c*) It does not follow logically from philosophical anarchism that no government is morally better than any other or that people have no moral duties toward one another.

(*d*) Even if as certain philosophical anarchists claim, governmental laws lack moral force, people still have moral obligation to refrain from harming one another.

**7.** The author identifies which one of the following as a commonly held belief?

(*a*) In most cases we are morally obligated to obey the law simply because it is the law.

(*b*) All governments are in essence morally equal.

(*c*) We are morally bound to obey only those laws we participate in establishing.

(*d*) Most crimes are morally neutral, even though they are illegal.

**8.** The author's stance regarding the theory of philosophical anarchism can most accurately be described as one of

(*a*) ardent approval of most aspects of the theory.

(*b*) apparent acceptance of some of the basic positions of the theory

(*c*) concerned pessimism about the theory's ability to avoid certain extreme views

(*d*) hesitant rejection of some of the central features of the theory

**9.** By attributing to commentators, the view that philosophical anarchism has implications that are "counter-intuitive", the author most likely means that the commentators believe that

(*a*) the implications conflict with some commonly held beliefs.

(*b*) there is little empirical evidence that the implications are actually true.

(*c*) common sense indicates that philosophical anarchism does not have such implications.

(*d*) the implications appear to be incompatible with each other.

**10.** Which one of the following scenarios most completely conforms to the view attributed to philosophical anarchists in third paragraph?

(*a*) A member of a political party that is illegal in a particular country divulges the names of other members because he fears legal penalties.

(*b*) A corporate executive choose to discontinue illegally when she learns that the chemicals are contaminating the water supply.

(*c*) A person who knows that a co-worker has stolen funds from their employer decided to do nothing because the co-worker is widely admired.

(*d*) A person neglects to pay her taxes, even though it is likely that she will suffer severe legal penalties as a consequence, because she wants to use the money to finance a new business.

**11.** It can be inferred that the author would be most likely to agree that

(*a*) people are subject to more moral obligations than is generally held to be the case

(*b*) government that are morally superior recognize that their citizens are not morally bound to obey their laws.

(*c*) one may have good reason to support the efforts of one's government even if one has no moral duty to obey its laws.

(*d*) there are some sound arguments for claiming that most governments have a moral right to require obedience to their laws.

**12.** The author's discussion of people's positive moral duty to care for one another functions primarily to

(*a*) demonstrate that governmental efforts to help those in need are superfluous.

(*b*) suggest that philosophical anarchists maintain that law that foster the common good are extremely rare.

(*c*) imply that the theoretical under-pinnings of philosophical anarchism are inconsistent with certain widely held moral truths.

(*d*) indicate that philosophical anarchists recognise that people are subject to substantial moral obligations.

**13.** In the passage, the author seeks primarily to

(*a*) describe the development and theoretical under-pinnings of a particular theory.

(*b*) establish that a particular theory conforms to the dictates of common sense.

(*c*) argue that two necessary implications of a particular theory are morally acceptable.

(*d*) defend a particular theory against its critics by showing that their arguments are mistaken.

**Passage for questions 14 to 21:**

Artists should treat their art as art and take the process of making it as seriously as anyone takes their chosen profession. Great skill and insight are required in order to create truly original art. Transforming an idea or concept into a technically thought- provoking or emotion-arousing work of art in any medium is a talent that few people possess. And there you have the "purist's vision."

Now if an artist wants to create art and never sell it, then he or she never has to worry about how to price it. That artist can afford to be a "purist," as you put it, produce art free of any encumbrances or concerns about what the art world or anyone else might think, and avoid "prostituting" or "debasing" that art by placing dollar values on it. But if you're an artist who wants to sell your art or who has to sell it in order to survive as an artist, you must use whatever tools are available to figure out how much it's worth and how best to sell it.

Let's say you're just starting out as an artist, you have little or no experience showing or selling your work, and in a period of two minutes, you produce a pencil drawing on a piece of paper. You view this drawing as highly significant in your evolution as an artist and rank its creation as the single most important creative moment of your life. Consequently, you put a price of $20,000 on it because only for that amount of money will you agree to part with such an important work of art. This is a "purist's vision" approach to pricing as opposed to a "realities of the marketplace" approach.

From a business standpoint, you'll have an extremely difficult time selling your drawing, as you won't be able to justify the $20,000 price to real art buyers in the real art world. You have no track record of selling art in that price range, and you have few or no shows, critical reviews, or supporting data from outside sources indicating that your art has that kind of value or collectibility in the marketplace. The overwhelming majority of art buyers who have $20,000 to spend look for works of art by established artists with documented track records of showing and selling art in that price range.Your drawing is still highly significant to you, but what someone is willing to pay for it on the open market is a matter for art buyers to decide. You can price it however you wish, but you can never force anyone to buy it. That's the way the art business works. So if you want to sell it, you have to figure out what dollar amount someone is likely to pay for it on the open market and then price it at that amount. But the tale of your drawing does not end here.

The art world may, one agree with you that the product of your two-minute moment precipitates a major transformational turning point in your career, and is well worth a $20,000 asking price, but you're going to have to prove first. Aspects of that drawing will have to be reflected in your art from the moment you created it onwards, the art world will have to recognize your art both critically and from the marketing standpoints, and you'll have to successfully produce, show, and sell for many years. Then one day, when your first retrospective exhibition opens at the Four-Star Museum of Art, that drawing will hang framed and captioned as the first inspiration for all subsequent work. The art world will then understand and respect its significance, and a serious collector may well be willing to pay an extraordinary price to own this historically important document of your career.

Returning for a moment to the concept of a purist artist who creates art and never sells it, sooner or later (hopefully later), that purist will pass on and leave behind a body of work. Unless that artist leaves specific instructions in his or her will for that body of work to be destroyed, it will become subject to those market forces that the artist strived for a lifetime to avoid. At the very least, it'll have to be appraised for tax, donation, or inheritance purposes. In most cases, it eventually comes onto the market either through a probable sale, an auction, or as represented by a dealer, gallery, or family member. The moral of the story is that one way or another, someone somewhere at some point in time will use tried and true methods to realistically price and either sell, donate, trade or otherwise transact any work of art that comes onto the market in any way, shape, or form. I hope that that person will be you, the artist, and that you'll price your art according to what the market will bear, sell plenty of it, and have a long and rewarding career.

**(AILET, 2010)**

Answer the following questions indicating your option for each question:

**14.** The purist's art is

(*a*) one that arouses emotions.

(*b*) thought-provoking.

(c) technically sound.

(*d*) free from any encumbrances or concerns about what the world or anyone else might think of it.

**15.** The "realities of the marketplace" approach entails:

a. "prostituting" one's art by putting a dollar price on it.

b. gauging the market value of one's art and then putting a price on it.

c. compromising on one's estimation of one's own art as far as its worth in financial terms is concerned

d. subjecting one's art to the buyer's interpretation of it

(*a*) Only a (*b*) only b and d

(c) b, c and d (*d*) only b

**16.** For an artist to sell his piece of art at a higher price range, he/she has to

(*a*) get endorsed by fellow artists and art critics.

(*b*) hold exhibitions or shows.

(c) gradually increase the collectibility of his/her art in the market place.

(*d*) all of the above.

**17.** The first piece of an artist that comes out in the market is seen as

(*a*) his masterpiece.

(*b*) the most collectible piece in his / her repertoire.

(c) a blueprint to discern the author's unique style and point of view.

(*d*) the inspiration for all his subsequent works.

**18.** From the point of view of the purist, the irony as far as pricing art is concerned is that:

a. a piece from his collection is eventually sold at the same price that he had estimated to be its real worth years earlier.

b. his art is subjected to the same market forces against which he strove his entire life.

c. "realities of the marketplace" is a concept that negates the very attributes that we associate with art- whim, fancy and imagination.

(*a*) only a (*b*) a and b

(c) only b (*d*) a, b and c

**For questions 19 and 20:** Each question consists of two capitalized words that have a certain relationship to each other, followed by 4 pairs of words. Choose the pair that is related to each other in the same way as the capitalized pair.

**19.** ENCUMBRANCE: BURDEN

(*a*) Mnemonic : Memory

(*b*) Blatant : Subtle

(c) Captious : Acrimonious

(*d*) Feral : Cultured

**20.** SUBSEQUENT : PREVIOUS

(*a*) Significant : Inconsequential

(*b*) Retrospect : Retrospective

(c) Visionary : Seer

(*d*) Caption : Legend

**21.** The synonym of the word PRECIPITATE in the context of the passage is

(*a*) Launch

(*b*) trigger

(c) provoke

(*d*) accelerate

**Passage for questions 22 to 27:**

Roger Rosenblatt's book 'Black Fiction', manages to alter the approach taken in many previous studies by making an attempt to apply literary rather than socio-political criteria to its subject. Rosenblatt points out that criticism of Black writing has very often served as a pretext for an expounding on Black history. The recent work of Addison Gayle's passes a judgment on the value of Black fiction by clear political standards, rating each work according to the ideas of Black identity, which it propounds.

Though fiction results from political circumstances, its author reacts not in ideological ways to those circumstances, and talking about novels and stories primarily as instruments of ideology circumvents much of the fictional enterprise. Affinities and connections are revealed in the works of Black fiction in Rosenblatt's literary analysis; these affinities and connections have been overlooked and ignored by solely political studies.

The writing of acceptable criticism of Black fiction, however, presumes giving satisfactory answers to quite a few questions. The most important of all, is there a sufficient reason, apart from the racial identity of the authors, for the grouping together of Black authors? Secondly, what is the distinction of Black fiction from other modem fiction with which it is largely contemporaneous? In the work Rosenblatt demonstrates that Black fiction is a distinct body of writing, which has an identifiable, coherent literary tradition. He highlights recurring concerns and designs, which are independent of chronology in Black fiction written over the past eighty years. These concerns and designs are thematic, and they come form the central fact of the predominant white culture, where the Black characters in the novel are situated irrespective of whether they attempt to conform to that culture or they rebel against it.

Rosenblatt's work does leave certain aesthetic questions open. His thematic analysis allows considerable objectivity; he even clearly states that he does not intend to judge the merit of the various works yet his reluctance seems misplaced, especially since an attempt to appraise might have led to interesting results. For example, certain novels have an appearance of structural diffusion. Is this a defeat, or are the authors working out of, or attempting to forge, a different kind of aesthetic? Apart from this, the style of certain Black novels, like Jean Toomer's Cane, verges on expressionism or surrealism; does this technique provide a counterpoint to the prevalent theme that portrays the fate against which Black heroes are pitted, a theme usually conveyed by more naturalistic modes of expressions?

Irrespective of such omissions, what Rosenblatt talks about in his work makes for an astute and worthwhile study. His book very effectively surveys a variety of novels, highlighting certain fascinating and little-known works like James Weldon Johnson's Autobiography of an Ex-Coloured Man. Black Fiction is tightly constructed, and levelheaded and penetrating criticism is exemplified in its forthright and lucid style.

**(AILET, 2011)**

**22.** The author of the passage raises an objection to criticism of Black fiction like that by Addison Gayle as it

(*a*) Highlights only the purely literary aspects of such works.

(*b*) Misconceive the ideological content of such fiction.

(*c*) Miscalculate the notions of Black identity presented in such fiction.

(*d*) Replaces political for literary criteria in evaluating such fiction.

**23.** The primary concern of the author in the above passage is

(*a*) Reviewing the validity of a work of criticism.

(*b*) Comparing various critical approaches to a subject.

(*c*) Talking of the limitations of a particular kind of criticism.

(*d*) Recapitulation of the major points in a work of criticism.

**24.** The author is of the opinion that Black Fiction would have been improved had Rosenblatt

(*a*) Undertaken a more careful evaluation of the ideological and historical aspects of Black Fiction

(*b*) Been more objective in his approach to novels and stories by Black authors

(*c*) Attempted a more detailed exploration of the recurring themes in Black fiction throughout its history

(*d*) Calculated the relative literary merit of the novels he analyzed thematically

**25.** Rosenblatt's discussion of Black Fiction is

(*a*) Pedantic and contentious

(*b*) Critical but admiring

(c) Ironic and Deprecating

(*d*) Argumentative but unfocused

**26.** According to the given passage the author would be LEAST likely to approve of which among the following?

(*a*) Analyzing the influence of political events on the personal ideology of Black writers

(*b*) Attempting a critical study which applies sociopolitical criteria to the autobiographies of Black authors

(*c*) A literary study of Black poetry that appraises the merits of poems according to the political acceptability of their themes

(*d*) Studying the growth of a distinct Black literary tradition within the context of Black history

**27.** From the following options, which does the author not make use of while discussing Black Fiction?

(*a*) Rhetorical questions

(*b*) Specific examples

(c) Comparison and contrast

(*d*) Definition of terms

**Passage for questions 28 to 32:**

In principle, a cohesive group - one whose members generally agree with one another and support one another's judgments – can do a much better job at decision making than it could if it were non-cohesive. When cohesiveness is low or lacking entirely, compliance out of fear of recrimination is likely to be strongest. To overcome this fear, participants in the group's deliberations need to be confident that they are members in good standing and that the others will continue to value their role in the group, whether or not they agree about a particular issue under discussion. As members of a group feel more accepted by the others, they acquire greater freedom to say what they really think, becoming less likely to use deceitful arguments or to play it safe by dancing around the issues with vapid or conventional comments. Typically, then, the more cohesive a group becomes, the less its members will deliberately censor what they say out of fear of being punished socially for antagonizing their fellow members.

But group cohesiveness can have pitfalls as well: while the members of a highly cohesive group can feel much freer to deviate from the majority, their desire for genuine concurrence on every important issue often inclines them not to use this freedom. In a highly cohesive group of decision makers, the danger is not that individuals will conceal objections they harbour regarding a proposal favoured by the majority, but that they will think the proposal is a good one without attempting to carry out a critical scrutiny that could reveal grounds for strong objections. Members may then decide that any misgivings they feel are not worth pursuing – that the benefit of any doubt should be given to the group consensus. In this way, they may fall victim to a syndrome known as "groupthink", which one psychologist concerned with collective decision making has defined as "a deterioration of mental efficiency, reality testing, and moral judgment that results from in-group pressures".

Based on analyses of major fiascos of international diplomacy and military decision making, researchers have identified groupthink behaviour as a recurring pattern that involves several factors: overestimation of the group's power and morality, manifested, for example, in an illusion of invulnerability, which creates excessive optimism; closed-mindedness to warnings of problems and to alternative viewpoints; and unwarranted pressures toward uniformity, including self-censorship with respect to doubts about the group's reasoning and a concomitant shared illusion of unanimity concerning group decisions. Cohesiveness of the decision-making group is an essential antecedent condition for this syndrome but not a sufficient one, so it is important to work toward identifying the additional factors that determine whether group cohesiveness will deteriorate into groupthink or allow for effective decision making.

**(AILET, 2012)**

**28.** Why does the author thinks that the cohesive group can do a much better job at decision making than it could if it were non-cohesive?

(*a*) The members of a highly cohesive group can feel much freer to deviate from the majority.

(*b*) Individuals will not conceal objections they harbour regarding a proposal favoured by the majority.

(*c*) Participants in the group's deliberations are confident that they are members in good standing and that the others will continue to value their role in the group, whether or not they agree about a particular issue under discussion.

(*d*) All of the above.

**29.** Which one of the following most accurately expresses the main point of the passage?

(*a*) Despite its value in encouraging frank discussions, high cohesion can lead to a debilitating type of group decision making called groupthink.

(*b*) Group members can guard against groupthink if they have a good understanding of the critical role played by cohesion.

(*c*) Groupthink is a dysfunctional collective decision-making pattern that can occur in diplomacy and military affairs.

(*d*) Low cohesion in groups is sometimes desirable when higher cohesion involves a risk of groupthink behaviour.

**30.** A group of closely associated colleagues has made a disastrous diplomatic decision after a series of meetings marked by disagreement over conflicting alternatives. It can be inferred from the passage that the author would be most likely to say that this scenario

(*a*) provides evidence of chronic indecision, thus indicating a weak level of cohesion in general.

(*b*) indicates that the group's cohesiveness was coupled with some other factor to produce a groupthink fiasco.

(*c*) provides no evidence that groupthink played a role in the group's decision.

(*d*) provides evidence that groupthink can develop even in some groups that do not demonstrate an "illusion of unanimity".

**31.** The passage mentions which one of the following as a component of groupthink?

(*a*) unjustified suspicions among group members regarding an adversary's intentions.

(*b*) strong belief that the group's decisions are right.

(*c*) group members working under unusually high stress, leading to illusions of invulnerability.

(*d*) the deliberate use of vapid, clichéd arguments.

**32.** It can be inferred from the passage that both the author of the passage and the researchers mentioned in the passage would be most likely to agree with which one of the following statements about groupthink?

(*a*) Groupthink occurs in all strongly cohesive groups, but its contribution to collective decision making is not fully understood.

(*b*) The casual factors that transform group cohesion into groupthink are unique to each case.

(*c*) The continued study of cohesiveness of groups is probably fruitless for determining what factors elicit groupthink.

(*d*) On balance, groupthink cannot be expected to have a beneficial effect in a group's decision making.

**Passage for questions 33 to 42:**

MY LOVE OF NATURE, goes right back to my childhood, to the times when I stayed on my grandparents' farm in Suffolk. My father was in the armed forces, so we were always moving and didn't have a home base for any length of time, but I loved going there. I think it was my grandmother who encouraged me more than anyone: she taught me the names of wild flowers and got me interested in looking at the countryside, so it seemed obvious to go on to do Zoology at University.

I didn't get my first camera until after I'd graduated, when I was due to go diving in Norway and needed a method of recording the sea creatures I would find there. My father didn't know anything about photography, but he bought me an Exacta, which was really quite a good camera for the time, and I went off to take my first pictures of sea anemones and starfish. I became keen very quickly, and learned how to develop and print; obviously I didn't have much money in those days, so I did more black and white photography than colour, but it was all still using the camera very much as a tool to record what I found both by diving and on the shore. I had no ambition at all to be a photographer then, or even for some years afterwards.

Unlike many of the wildlife photographers of the time, I trained as a scientist and therefore my way of expressing myself is very different. I've tried from the beginning to produce pictures which are always biologically correct. There are people who will alter things deliberately: you don't pick up sea creatures from the middle of the shore and take them down to attractive pools at the bottom of the shore without knowing you're doing it. In so doing you're actually falsifying the sort of seaweeds they live on and so on, which may seem unimportant, but it is actually changing the natural surroundings to make them prettier. Unfortunately, many of the people who select pictures are looking for attractive images and, at the end of the day, whether it's truthful or not doesn't really matter to them.

It's important to think about the animal first, and there are many occasions when I've not taken a picture because it would have been too disturbing. Nothing is so important that you have to get that shot; of course, there are cases when it would be very sad if you didn't, but it's not the end of the world. There can be a lot of ignorance in people's behavior towards wild animals and it's a problem, that more and more people are going to wild places: while some animals may get used to cars, they won't get used to people suddenly rushing up to them. The sheer pressure of people, coupled with the fact that there are increasingly fewer places where no-one else has photographed, means that over the years, life has become much more difficult for the professional wildlife photographer.

Nevertheless, wildlife photographs play a very important part in educating people about what is out there and what needs conserving. Although photography can be an enjoyable pastime, as it is to many people, it is also something that plays a very important part in educating young and old alike. Of the qualities it takes to make a good wildlife photographer, patience is perhaps the most obvious - you just have to be prepared to sit it out. I'm actually more patient now because I write more than ever before, and as long as I've got a bit of paper and a pencil, I don't feel I'm wasting my time. And because I photograph such a wide range of things, even if the main target doesn't appear I can probably find something else to concentrate on instead.

**(CLAT 2008)**

**33.** The writer decided to go to university and study Zoology because

(*a*) she wanted to improve her life in the countryside.

(*b*) she was persuaded to do so by her grandmother.

(*c*) she was keen on the natural world.

(*d*) she wanted to stop moving around all the time.

**34.** Why did she get her first camera?

(*a*) she needed to be able to look back at what she had seen.

(*b*) she wanted to find out if she enjoyed photography.

(*c*) her father thought it was a good idea for her to have one.

(*d*) she wanted to learn how to use one and develop her own prints.

**35.** She did more black and white photography than colour because

(*a*) she did not like colour photograph.

(*b*) she did not have a good camera.

(*c*) she wanted quality photograph.

(*d*) she didn't have much money in those days.

**36.** How is she different from some of the other wildlife photographers she meets?

(*a*) She tries to make her photographs as attractive as possible.

(*b*) She takes photographs which record accurate natural conditions.

(*c*) She likes to photograph plants as well as wildlife.

(*d*) She knows the best places to find wildlife.

**37.** What does 'them' refer to in the line "In so doing ... make 'them' prettier"?

(*a*) sea creatures (*b*) attractive pools

(c) seaweeds (*d*) natural surroundings

**38.** What the writer means by 'ignorance in people's behaviour' is

(*a*) altering things deliberately.

(*b*) people suddenly rushing up to animals.

(*c*) people taking photographs of wild animals.

(*d*) people not thinking about the animals in the first place.

**39.** The writer now finds it more difficult to photograph wild animals because

(*a*) there are fewer of them.

(*b*) they have become more nervous of people.

(*c*) it is harder to find suitable places.

(*d*) they have become frightened of cars.

**40.** Wildlife photography is important because it can make people realise that

(*a*) photography is an enjoyable hobby.

(*b*) we learn little about wildlife at school.

(*c*) it is worthwhile visiting the countryside.

(*d*) wildlife photographs educate people about wild animals.

**41.** Why is she more patient now?

(*a*) She does other things while waiting.

(*b*) She has got used to waiting.

(*c*) She can concentrate better than she used to.

(*d*) She knows the result will be worth it.

**42.** Which of the following describes the writer?

(*a*) proud (*b*) sensitive

(c) aggressive (*d*) disappointed

**Passage for questions 43 to 52:**

There is a fairly universal sentiment that the use of nuclear weapons is clearly contrary to morality and that its production probably so, does not go far enough. These activities are not only opposed to morality but also to law if the legal objection can be added to the moral, the argument against the use and the manufacture of these weapons will considerably be reinforced. Now the time is ripe to evaluate the responsibility of scientists who knowingly use their expertise for the construction of such weapons, which has **deleterious** effect on mankind.

To this must be added the fact that more than 50 percent of the skilled scientific manpower in the world is now engaged in the armaments industry. How appropriate it is that all this valuable skill should be devoted to the manufacture of weapons of death in a world of poverty is a question that must touch the scientific conscience.

A meeting of biologists on the Long-Term Worldwide Biological consequences of nuclear war added frightening dimension to those forecasts. Its report suggested that the long biological effects resulting from climatic changes may at least be as serious as the immediate ones. Sub-freezing temperatures, low light levels, and high doses of ionizing and ultraviolet radiation extending for many months after a large-scale nuclear war could destroy the biological support system of civilization, at least in the Northern Hemisphere. Productivity in natural and agricultural ecosystems could be severely restricted for a year or more. Post war survivors would face starvation as well as freezing conditions in the dark and be exposed to near lethal doses of radiation. If, as now seems possible, the Southern Hemisphere were affected also, global disruption of the biosphere could ensure. In any event, there would be severe consequences, even in the areas not affected directly, because of the inter-dependence of the world economy. In either case the extinction of a large fraction of the earth's animals, plants and microorganism seems possible. The population size of Homo sapiens conceivably could be reduced to prehistoric levels or below, and extinction of the human species itself cannot be excluded.

**(CLAT 2009)**

**43.** Choose the word, which is most opposite in meaning of the word, printed in bold as used in the passage Deleterious.

(*a*) Beneficial (*b*) Harmful

(c) Irreparable (*d*) Non-cognizable

**44.** The author's most important objective of writing the above passage seems to .....

(*a*) Highlight the use of nuclear weapons as an effective population control measures.

(*b*) Illustrate the devastating effects of use of nuclear weapons on mankind.

(*c*) Duly highlight the supremacy of the nations which possess nuclear weapons.

(*d*) Summarise the long biological effects of use of nuclear weapons.

**45.** The scientist engaged in manufacturing destructive weapons are......

(*a*) Very few in number

(*b*) Irresponsible and imcompetent

(*c*) More than half of the total number

(*d*) Engaged in the armaments industry against their desire

**46.** According to the passage, the argument on use and manufacture of nuclear weapons

(*a*) Does not stand the test of legality

(*b*) Possesses legal strength although it does not have moral standing

(*c*) Is acceptable only on moral grounds

(*d*) Becomes stronger if legal and moral considerations are combined

**47.** The author of the passage seems to be of the view that

(*a*) Utilization of scientific skills in manufacture of weapons is appropriate.

(*b*) Manufacture of weapons of death would help eradication of poverty.

(*c*) Spending money on manufacture of weapons may be justifiable subject to the availability of funds.

(*d*) Utilization of valuable knowledge for manufacture of lethal weapons is inhuman.

**48.** Which of the following is one of the consequences of nuclear war?

(*a*) Fertility of land will last for a year or so.

(*b*) Post-war survivors being very few will have abundant food.

(*c*) Lights would be cooler and more comfortable.

(*d*) Southern Hemisphere would remain quite safe in the Post-war period.

**49.** Which of the following best explains the word devoted, as used in the passage?

(*a*) Dedicated for a good cause

(*b*) Utilised for betterment

(c) Abused for destruction

(*d*) Underutilised

**50.** The biological consequences of nuclear war as given in the passage include all the following, except

(*a*) Fall in temperature below zero degree Celsius.

(*b*) Ultraviolet radiation

(*c*) High doses of ionizing

(*d*) Abundant food for smaller population.

**51.** It appears from the passage that the use of nuclear weapons is considered against morality by

(*a*) Only such of those nations who cannot afford to manufacture and sell weapons

(*b*) Almost all the nations of the world

(*c*) Only the superpowers who can afford to manufacture and sell weapons

(*d*) Most of the scientists devote their valuable skills to manufacture nuclear weapons.

**52.** Which of the following statements I, II, III, and IV is definitely true in the context of the passage?

I. There is every likelihood of survival of the human species as a consequence of nuclear war.

II. Nuclear war risks and harmful effects are highly exaggerated.

III. The post war survivors would be exposed to the benefits of non-lethal radiation.

IV. Living organisms in the areas which are not directly affected by nuclear was would also suffer.

(*a*) I (*b*) III

(c) II (*d*) IV

**Passage for questions 53 to 62:**

Antigone was one of the daughters of Oedipus, that tragic figure of male power who had been cursed by Gods for mistakenly killing his father and subsequently marrying his mother and assuming the throne of Thebes. After the death of Oedipus civil war broke out and a battle was waged in front of the seventh gate of Thebes- his two sons led opposing factions and at the height of the battle fought and killed each other. Oedipus' brother, Creon, uncle of Antigone, was now undisputed master of the city. Creon resolved to make an example of the brother who had fought against him, Polynices, by refusing the right of honourable burial. The penalty of death was promulgated against any who should defy this order.

Antigone was distraught. Polynices had been left unburied, unwept, a feast of flesh for keen eyed carrion birds. Antigone asks her sister Ismene, for it was a challenge to her royal blood. "Now it is time to show weather or not you are worthy of your royal blood. Is he not my brother and yours? Whether you like it or not? I shall never desert him-never!" But Ismene responds, "How could you dare- when Creon has expressly forbidden it? Antigone, we are women, it is not for us to fight against men". With a touch of bitterness, Antigone releases her sister from the obligation to help her, but argues she cannot shrug off the burden. "If I die for it what happiness! Live, if you will live, and defy the holiest of laws of heaven." **(CLAT 2010)**

**53.** What is the main theme of the story of Antigone?

(*a*) One must be truthful and honest

(*b*) There is a conflict between the laws of men and heavenly laws

(*c*) One must be true to one's kins

(*d*) War is an evil

**54.** Why did Antigone decide to defy the orders of Creon?

(*a*) She loved her brother

(*b*) She was to give an honorable burial to her brother

(*c*) She felt she was bound by her heavenly obligation

(*d*) To teach Creon a lesson

**55.** What, in your opinion, would have been the logical end of the story?

(*a*) Antigone might have agreed with her sister and refrained from giving a burial to Polynices

(*b*) Antigone might have been allowed by Creon to give a decent burial to her brother

(*c*) Antigone might have defied the order of Creon but forgiven by him

(*d*) Antigone might have been executed for defying the order of the king

**56.** What was the status of women in the contemporary society? They

(*a*) were liberated

(*b*) could have taken their own decisions

(*c*) considered themselves inferior and subordinate to men

(*d*) claimed equality with men

**57.** Why did a civil war break out in Thebes? The war broke out because

(*a*) of the curse of the Gods

(*b*) the brothers of Antigone were greedy

(*c*) there was a fight among sons of Oedipus for the inheritance of the kingdom

(*d*) there was a conflict between a son of Oedipus and Creon

**58.** A carrion bird is a bird

(*a*) of prey

(*b*) which eats human flesh

(*c*) which eats dead bodies

(*d*) which eats only grain

**59.** Why did Creon deny decent burial to Polynices? He did so because

(*a*) he did not love Polynices

(*b*) Polynices fought against Creon

(*c*) Polynices was disobedient to Creon

(*d*) Polynices did not show bravery

**60.** Why did Ismene not support Antigone? Ismene

(*a*) was weak and did not have the courage to defy orders of the powerful king

(*b*) did not consider it right to defy the king

(*c*) did not think it fit to defy her uncle especially after the death of her father

(*d*) did not believe that Polynices deserved better treatment

**61.** Why did the Gods curse Oedipus? Because Oedipus

(*a*) killed his father and married his mother

(*b*) killed his father

(*c*) married his mother

(*d*) committed an unknown sin

**62.** Does the story approve the principle of vicarious liability? If so how?

(*a*) No, it does not

(*b*) Yes, it does, because of the acts of Oedipus his children suffered

(*c*) Yes, it does, because his father was killed by Oedipus

(*d*) Yes, it does, because he married his mother

**Passage for questions 63 to 72:**

In 1954, a Bombay economist named A.D. Shroff began a Forum of Free Enterprise, whose ideas on economic development were somewhat at odds with those then influentially articulated by the Planning Commission of the Government of India. Shroff complained against the 'indifference, if not discouragement' with which the state treated entrepreneurs.

At the same time as Shroff, but independently of him, a journalist named Philip Spratt was writing a series of essays in favour of free enterprise. Spratt was a Cambridge communist who was sent by the party in 1920s to foment revolution in the subcontinent. Detected in the act, he spent many years in an Indian jail. The books he read in the prison, and his marriage to an Indian woman afterwards, inspired a steady move rightwards. By the 1950s, he was editing a pro-American weekly from Bangalore, called *MysIndia*. There he inveighed against the economic policies of the government of India. These, he said, treated the entrepreneur 'as a criminal who has dared to use his brains independently of the state to create wealth and give employment'. The state's chief planner, P.C. Mahalanobis, had surrounded himself with Western leftists and Soviet academicians, who reinforced his belief in 'rigid control by the government over all activities'. The result, said Spratt, would be 'the smothering of free enterprise, a famine of consumer goods, and the tying down of millions of workers to soul-deadening techniques.'

The voices of men like Spratt and Shroff were drowned in the chorus of popular support for a model of heavy industrialization funded and directed by the governments. The 1950s were certainly not propitious times for free marketers in India. But from time to time their ideas were revived. After the rupee was devalued in 1966, there were some moves towards freeing the trade regime, and hopes that the licensing system would also be liberalized. However, after Indira Gandhi split the Congress Party in 1969, her government took its 'left turn', nationalizing a fresh range of industries and returning to economic autarky.

**(CLAT 2011)**

**63.** Which of the following statements can most reasonably be inferred from the information available in the passage:

(*a*) P.C. Mahalanobis believed in empowering private entrepreneurs and promoting free market.

(*b*) Phillip Spratt preferred plans that would create economic conditions favourable for a forward march by the private enterprise.

(*c*) Restrictions on free markets enriched large Indian companies.

(*d*) Philip Spratt opposed the devaluation of rupee in 1966.

**64.** Which of the following statements is least likely to be inferred from the passage:

(*a*) Acceptance of A.D. Shroff's plans in the official circles smothered free enterprise in India.

(*b*) The views of the Forum of Free Enterprise ran against the conception of development then prevalent among the policy makers.

(*c*) A.D. Shroff believed that state should actively support the private sector.

(*d*) Philip Spratt had been educated in Cambridge.

**65.** Select the statement that best captures the central purpose of this passage:

(*a*) Highlight that even though there were advocates for free-market and private enterprise in the early years of independent India, they were crowded out by others who supported a dominant role for state over private enterprise.

(*b*) Explain the politics behind Indira Gandhi's decision to nationalise the banks.

(*c*) Demonstrate with the help of statistics how the preference of policy makers for Soviet-style economic policies prevented India's economic growth.

(*d*) Establish that devaluation of rupee in 1966 was vindicated by subsequent experience.

**66.** Philip Spratt came to India because he:

(*a*) Fell in love with an Indian women

(*b*) Wanted to protest against the economic policies of the Indian government.

(*c*) Was offered the editorship of *Mysindia*.

(*d*) Had been instructed to work towards the goal of inciting a revolution in India.

**67.** The author avers that A.D Shroff's ideas were somewhat at odds with the views of Planning Commission because:

(*a*) A.D. Shroff was in favour of rigid governmental control over all economic activities.

(*b*) Shroff had opposed government's decision to devalue Indian rupee.

(*c*) The hostility of the government to private entrepreneurs was complained against by A.D. Shroff.

(*d*) Shroff had been critical of the influence of Soviet academicians over India's economic policy.

**68.** The ideological shift of Philip Spratt to the right was caused by:

(*a*) The demise of the Soviet Union.

(*b*) The start of the weekly called *MysIndia*.

(*c*) The books that he encountered in the prison.

(*d*) The dissolution of his first marriage to his college friend.

**69.** Select the statement that could be most plausibly inferred from this passage:

(*a*) Philip Spratt and A.D. Shroff were members of the Forum for Free Enterprise.

(*b*) The first two Five Year Plans emphasised on the importance of private enterprise as the spearhead of economic growth.

(*c*) P.C. Mahalanobis had mooted the expulsion of foreign firms like Coca Cola and IBM from India.

(*d*) The hopes that the licensing regime would be liberalized after the devaluation of Indian rupee were belied in the aftermath of the split in the Congress Party.

**70.** The author alludes to nationalization of industries in 1969 in order to:

(*a*) Show the contradictions between AD Shroff's economic views and the official economic policies of the Government of India.

(*b*) Exemplify the shift of the Indira Gandhi led government to the 'left'

(*c*) Demonstrate the ideological changes in the worldview of Philip Spratt.

(*d*) Highlight the negative political repercussions of the decision to devalue the Indian currency.

**71.** "Neither Philip Spratt nor A.D. Shroff ______ able to convince Mahalanobis." Select the most appropriate phrase out of the four options for filling the blank space in the aforesaid sentence.

(*a*) Were (*b*) Are

(c) Was (*d*) Is.

**72.** The word 'inveighed' in this passage means:

(*a*) Praised (*b*) Recited

(c) Proclaimed (*d*) Remonstrated

**Passage for questions 73 to 82:**

In Manu Joseph's debut novel *Serious Men*, the protagonist, Ayyan Mani, is a <u>sly</u>, scheming Dalit-Buddhist who almost gets away with passing off his partially deaf son, Adi, as a prodigy, a genius who can recite the first 1,000 prime numbers. The garb of satire—where almost every character cuts a sorry figure—gives the author the licence to offer one of the most bleak and pessimistic portrayals of urban Dalits. Despite his savage portrayal of Dalit (and female) characters—or perhaps because of it?—*Serious Men* has won critical appreciation from a crosssection of readers and critics.

At a time when a formidable body of Dalit literature—writing by Dalits about Dalit lives—has created a distinct space for itself, how and why is it that a novel such as *Serious Men*, with its gleefully skewed portrayal of an angry Dalit man, manages to win such accolades? In American literature—and particularly in the case of African-American authors and characters—these issues of representation have been debated for decades. But in India, the sustained refusal to address issues related to caste in everyday life—and the continued and unquestioned predominance of a Brahminical stranglehold over cultural production—have led us to a place where non-Dalit portrayal of Dalits in literature, cinema and art remains the norm.

The journey of modern Dalit literature has been a difficult one. But even though it has not necessarily enjoyed the support of numbers, we must engage with what Dalits are writing—not simply for reasons of authenticity, or as a concession to identity politics, but simply because of the aesthetic value of this body of writing, and for the insights it offers into the human condition. In a society that is still largely unwilling to recognise Dalits as equal, rights-bearing human beings, in a society that is inherently indifferent to the everyday violence against Dalits, in a society unwilling to share social and cultural resources equitably with Dalits unless mandated by law (as seen in the anti-reservation discourse), Dalit literature has the potential to humanise non- Dalits and sensitise them to a world into which they have no insight. But before we can understand what Dalit literature is seeking to accomplish, we need first to come to terms with the stranglehold of non-Dalit representations of Dalits.

Rohinton Mistry's *A Fine Balance*, published 15 years ago, chronicles the travails of two Dalit characters—uncle Ishvar and nephew Omprakash—who migrate to Bombay and yet cannot escape brutality. While the present of the novel is set at the time of the Emergency, Ishvar's father Dukhi belongs to the era of the anti-colonial nationalist movement. During one of Dukhi's visits to the town, he chances upon a meeting of the Indian National Congress, where speakers spread the "Mahatma's message regarding the freedom struggle, the struggle for justice," and wiping out "the disease of untouchability, ravaging us for centuries, denying dignity to our fellow human beings."

Neither in the 1940s, where the novel's past is set, nor in the Emergency period of the 1970s— when the minds and bodies Ishvar and Omprakash, are savaged by the state—do we find any mention of a figure like BR Ambedkar or of Dalit movements. In his 'nationalist' understanding of modern Indian history, Mistry seems to have not veered too far from the road charted by predecessors like Mulk Raj Anand and Premchand. Sixty years after Premchand, Mistry's literary imagination seems stuck in the empathy-realism mode, trapping Dalits in abjection. Mistry happily continues the broad stereotype of the Dalit as a passive sufferer, without consciousness of caste politics. **(CLAT 2011)**

**73.** Which of the following is the closest description of the central argument of this passage:

(*a*) Manu Joseph's novel presents a scathing portrayal of Dalits.

(*b*) Contemporary American literature is very cautious on politically correct representation of minorities.

(*c*) The last two decades have witnessed the rise of a very vibrant Dalit literature.

(*d*) Portrayal of Dalits by non-Dalits merely as passive victims has been the dominant norm in Indian literature, cinema and art.

**74.** According to this passage, Premchand and Mulk Raj Anand:

(*a*) Presented a stereotyped version of Dalit characters in their writings.

(*b*) Excelled in writing satires on social inequality.

(*c*) Were politically opposed to the views of B.R. Ambedkar.

(*d*) Were closely involved with the leadership of the nationalist movement.

**75.** The writer refers to the 'anti-reservation discourse' in order to argue that:

(*a*) Dalit literature has had a very difficult journey since its origins.

(*b*) Manu Joseph is viscerally opposed to Dalits.

(*c*) Persons belonging to the upper castes are inherently indifferent to routine violence against Dalits.

(*d*) Indian society is not yet ready to equitably share, on its own, social, cultural and political space with Dalits.

**76.** Which of the following statements is least likely to be inferred from this passage:

(*a*) The author of *Serious Men* has used the literary device of satire to present an unflattering picture of women characters.

(*b*) Issues of representation of minorities have been debated extensively in American literature.

(*c*) The writer of this passage believes that engagement with Dalits is necessary only because such engagement affirms the importance of identity politics.

(*d*) The writer believes that Rohinton Mistry presented a stereotypical representation of Dalits character in his book.

**77.** According to the information available in the passage, the writer attributes the prevalence of representation of Dalits by non-Dalits in literature, art and media to:

(*a*) The nationalist understanding of Indian history.

(*b*) Marginalisation of B.R Ambedkar from nationalist movement.

(*c*) The anti-reservation discourse

(*d*) Brahminical control over cultural production.

**78.** Which of the following is not among the reasons suggested by the writer for engaging with Dalit writing:

(*a*) Dalit literature has the potential to sensitize non-Dalits about the experiences of the former.

(*b*) Dalit writing is more authentic than representation of Dalits by non-Dalits.

(*c*) Dalit literature does not have the support of numbers.

(*d*) The aesthetic value of Dalit writing.

**79.** Which of the following statement cannot be inferred from the passage:

(*a*) Upper-castes have dominated the instruments of cultural production in Indian society.

(*b*) Indian society is unwilling to recognise Dalits as equal, rights-bearing human beings.

(*c*) Dalit writers have carved out a space for writings on Dalit experience and world view.

(*d*) The judiciary in India, in its opposition to reservation, has betrayed its unwillingness to acknowledge Dalits as equal bearer of rights.

**80.** The writer of this passage is critical of Rohinton Mistry's *A Fine Balance* for the reason that:

(*a*) It is an example of a book on Dalit characters by a Non-Dalit.

(*b*) The book suggests that Dalits are nothing more than passive sufferers without any agency.

(*c*) The book ignores the everyday violence that Dalits have to confront with.

(*d*) It bares the passive literary style of the author, Rohinton Mistry.

**81.** Which of the following words would be the best substitute for the word 'sly' in this passage:

(*a*) Bright (*b*) wise

(c) devious (*d*) dim

**82.** "It is not as if Dalit movements ______ not active during the periods that form *A Fine Balance*'s backdrop." Select the most appropriate choice to fill in the blank in the above sentence:

(*a*) is (*b*) was

(c) were (*d*) are

**Passage for questions 83 to 92:**

In recent weeks, the writers William Dalrymple and Patrick French, among others, have come before a <u>fusillade</u> of criticism in India, much of it questioning not their facts, not their interpretations, but their foreignness.

"Who gets to write about India?" The Wall Street Journal asked on Wednesday in its own report on this Indian literary feuding. It is a complicated question, not least because to decide who gets to write about India, you would need to decide who gets to decide who gets to write about India. Rather than conjecturing some Committee for the Deciding of the Deciding of Who Gets to Write About India, it might be easier to let writers write what they please and readers read what they wish.

The accusations pouring forth from a section of the Indian commentariat are varied. Some criticism is of a genuine literary nature, fair game, customary, expected. But lately a good amount of the reproaching has been about identity.

In the case of Mr. Dalrymple, a Briton who lives in New Delhi, it is — in the critics' view — that his writing is an act of re-colonization. In the case of Mr. French, it is that he belongs to a group of foreign writers who use business-class lounges and see some merit in capitalism and therefore do not know the real India, which only the commentariat member in question does.

What is most interesting about these appraisals is that their essential nature makes reading the book superfluous, as one of my Indian reviewers openly admitted. (His review was not about the book but about his refusal to read the book.) The book is not necessary in these cases, for the argument is about who can write about India, not what has been written.

For critics of this persuasion, India surely seems a lonely land. A country with a millennial history of Hindus, Christians, Jews, Muslims and Buddhists living peaceably together; a country of hundreds of dialects in which so many Indians are linguistic foreigners to each other, and happily, tolerantly so; a country that welcomes foreign seekers (of yoga poses, of spiritual wisdom, of ancestral roots) with open arms; a country where, outside the elite world of South Delhi and South Bombay, I have not heard an Indian ask whether outsiders have a right to write, think or exist on their soil.

But it is not just this deep-in-the-bones pluralism that challenges the <u>who-gets-to-write-about- India contingent</u>. It is also that at the very heart of India's multifarious changes today is this glimmering idea: that Indians must be rewarded for what they do, not who they are. Identities you never chose — caste, gender, birth order — are becoming less important determinants of fate. Your deeds — how hard you work, what risks you take — are becoming more important.

It is this idea, which I have found pulsating throughout the Indian layers, that leaves a certain portion of the intelligentsia out of sync with the surrounding country.

As Mr. French has observed, there is a tendency in some of these writers to value social mobility only for themselves. When the new economy lifts up the huddled masses, then it becomes tawdry capitalism and rapacious imperialism and soulless globalization.

Fortunately for those without Indian passports, the nativists' vision of India is under demographic siege. The young and the relentless are India's future. They could not think more differently from these literatis.

They savour the freedom they are gaining to seek their own level in the society and to find their voice; and they tend to be delighted at the thought that some foreigners do the same in India and love their country as much as they do. **(CLAT 2011)**

**83.** Which of the following statements is least likely to be inferred from the passage:

(*a*) Younger generations of Indians are more tolerant of foreign scribes who write about their country.

(*b*) The writer believes that a section of Indian intelligentsia is very hostile to upward economic mobility.

(*c*) Mr. William Dalrymple has been accused of recolonising India through his writings.

(*d*) Most of the criticism that has been recently directed at Patrick French has emphasized mainly on the writer's underwhelming literary style.

**84.** Which of the following would be the best substitute for the word, 'fusillade' in the passage?

(*a*) Barrage (*b*) Breach

(c) Temper (*d*) Row

**85.** The writer uses the phrase, 'who-gets-to-write-about-India contingent' in this passage to refer to:

(*a*) Foreign writers who have written books on India.

(*b*) Critics who have attacked foreign writers writing on India for their mere foreignness.

(*c*) Elite residents of South Delhi and South Bombay.

(*d*) Cultural pluralists.

**86.** The writer believes that the most peculiar aspect of the criticisms that Patrick French and William Dalrymple have received is that:

(*a*) Most such condemnation has emerged from elite Indians.

(*b*) Such critics are hostile to upward immobility.

(*c*) These censures are not centered on the books of such writers or their literary styles but are targeted at their identity instead.

(*d*) These critics ignore the plural ethos of India.

**87.** Which of the following statements can be inferred from the passage:

(*a*) Ascriptive identities like caste, tribe, etc. are becoming more and more important with the passage of time.

(*b*) Patrick French believes that the new market friendly economic policies followed for the last decades have resulted in the rise of tawdry capitalism and rapacious imperialism.

(*c*) The writer is of the opinion that a section of the intelligentsia is divorced from the views of their compatriots.

(*d*) While India has historically been very hospitable to a variety of religions, it has not been equally open to linguistic foreigners.

**88.** According to the information available in the passage, the writer is of the opinion that:

(*a*) Writers like Patrick French do not know the real India.

(*b*) Most of the condemnation heaped on Dalrymple, French and himself has been on expected lines.

(*c*) India's reputation of pluralism is cosmetic at best, one that hides deep rooted hatred towards foreigners.

(*d*) The new generation of Indians have internalized the idea that people should be rewarded for what they do and not who they are.

**89.** The writer refers to the history of Hindus, Christians, Jews, Muslims and Buddhists living peaceably together in India for millions of years in order to:

(*a*) Show India's openness to foreigners who have visited Indian in the quest for yoga.

(*b*) Argue that India is a country of hundreds of dialects.

(*c*) Demonstrate the religiosity pervading in an average Indian.

(*d*) India's deep-in the bones pluralism.

**90.** The writer argues that the nature of criticism he, Dalrymple and French have received for their books renders reading their books superfluous because:

(*a*) Such criticism has been limited to a very small minority of Indians.

(*b*) These writers are popular among Indian youth, even among those who have not read their books.

(*c*) The literary styles of these writers are not the sole focus of such criticism.

(*d*) Such criticism is less about what has been written in their books than about who can write on India.

**91.** According to the passage, the question 'who gets to write about India' is complicated because:

(*a*) India has been historically open to and tolerant of foreign writers and artists.

(*b*) This issue can be satisfactorily resolved only if we can decide who gets to decide who gets to write about India.

(*c*) Ascriptive identities are becoming more and more important in a globalised world.

(*d*) This would result in a shift of attention from what has been written to who has written.

**92.** "But with many outsiders' India-related books recently hitting bookstores there, the sensitivity ______ flared into a bout of vigorous literary nativism, with equally vigorous counterpunches." Select the most appropriate choice to fill in the blank in the above sentence:

(*a*) Has (*b*) Have

(c) Was (*d*) did

**Passage for questions 93 to 102:**

If religion and community are associated with global violence in the minds of many people, then so are global poverty and inequality. There has, in fact, been an increasing tendency in recent years to justify policies of poverty removal on the ground that this is the surest way to prevent political strife and turmoil. Basing public policy – international as well as domestic – on such an understanding has some evident attractions. Given the public anxiety about wars and disorders in the rich countries in the world, the indirect justification of poverty removal – not for its own sake but for the sake of peace and quiet in the world – provides an argument that appeals to selfinterest for helping the needy. It presents an argument for allocating more resources on poverty removal because of its presumed political, rather than moral, relevance.

While the temptation to go in that direction is easy to understand, it is a perilous route to take even for a worthy cause. Part of the difficulty lies in the possibility that if wrong, economic reductionism would not only impair our understanding of the world, but would also tend to undermine the declared rationale of the public commitment to remove poverty. This is a particularly serious concern, since poverty and massive inequality are terrible enough in themselves, and deserve priority even if there were no connection whatsoever with violence. Just as virtue is its own reward, poverty is at least its own penalty. This is not to deny that poverty and inequality can – and do – have far reaching consequences with conflict and strife, but these connections have to be examined and investigated with appropriate care and empirical scrutiny, rather than being casually invoked with unreasoned rapidity in support of a 'good cause."

Destitution can, of course, produce provocation for defying established laws and rules. But it need not give people the initiative, courage, and actual ability to do anything very violent. Destitution can be accompanied not only by economic debility, but also by political helplessness. A starving wretch can be too frail and too dejected to fight and battle, and even to protest and holler. It is thus not surprising that often enough intense and widespread suffering and misery have been accompanied by unusual peace and silence.

Indeed, many famines have occurred without there being much political rebellion or civil strife or intergroup warfare. For example, the famine years in the 1840s in Ireland were among the most peaceful, and there was little attempt by the hungry masses to intervene even as ship after ship sailed down the river Shannon with rich food. Looking elsewhere, my own childhood memories in Calcutta during the Bengal famine of 1943 include the sight of starving people dying in front of sweetshops with various layers of luscious food displayed behind the glass windows, without a single glass being broken, or law or order being disrupted. **(CLAT 2011)**

**93.** Select the statement that can be most plausibly inferred from the aforesaid passage:

(*a*) A society plagued by recurrent famines can never witness political revolution.

(*b*) Religious discrimination inevitably leads to violence and strife.

(*c*) Destitution of the masses leads to peace and social stability.

(*d*) Famines and starvation do not necessarily result in political rebellion.

**94.** The author believes that it may not be advisable to emphasise on the connection between poverty and violence as:

(*a*) Emphasis on such connection appeals only to self-interest of persons.

(*b*) Linking poverty and violence undermines the moral character of anti-poverty measures.

(*c*) The absence of any essential connection between poverty and violence may then weaken the very rationale of anti-poverty policies.

(*d*) There is no necessary link between poverty and inequality.

**95.** Which of the following best captures the central argument of this passage:

(*a*) Religion is inextricably linked with violence

(*b*) Famines may not necessarily result in civil unrest.

(*c*) Global poverty and inequality are one of the fundamental causes of global violence and strife.

(*d*) Basing anti-poverty programmes on the need for avoidance of violence and strife is dotted with many pitfalls.

**96.** In the given passage, the word 'perilous' means:

(*a*) Scared (*b*) Costly

(c) Futile (*d*) Dangerous

**97.** The author refers to his own experience as a child during the Bengal famine of 1943 in order to:

(*a*) Illustrate how religiosity may instill passive acceptance of even the worst forms of starvation among people.

(*b*) Repudiate the argument that religious discrimination usually tends to inspire violent protests.

(*c*) Substantiate his assertion that it is not unusual to have the most intense suffering and misery coexist with complete peace.

(*d*) Demonstrate that people confronted with acute starvation are rendered too helpless to protest ever at all.

**98.** The word 'destitution' in this passage can be best substituted by:

(*a*) Dejection (*b*) Indigence

(c) Default (*d*) Dereliction

**99.** Which of the following statement is least likely to be inferred from the passage:

(*a*) History is replete with instance of famines that have occurred without there being much violent protest.

(*b*) Many writers and critics are increasingly advocating for stronger policies on poverty removal on the ground that this would help prevent political turmoil.

(*c*) The author believes that the links between poverty and violence must never be emphasized at all.

(*d*) Economic debility in turn inhibits political freedom.

**100.** The author asserts that basing anti-poverty measures on the avowed connections between poverty and violence has certain apparent benefits because:

(*a*) Poverty is similar to religious exploitation in terms of the potential violent consequences.

(*b*) It leads to allocation of more resources on anti-poverty policies.

(*c*) The widespread concern about war and violence provides a rationale for poverty removal that appeals to the 'self-interest' of persons.

(*d*) Otherwise, there would not have been the tendency to justify anti-poverty policies on the ground that they prevent political turmoil.

**101.** 'Economic reductionism' in this passage means;

(*a*) Neglecting the economic connection between poverty and violence

(*b*) Excessive accent on poverty and inequality

(*c*) Emphasizing on the linkage between violence, poverty and economic equality.

(*d*) The view that every conflict is caused by underlying economic tensions.

**102.** "A sense of encroachment, degradation and humiliation can be even easier __ mobilize for rebellion and revolt." Select the most appropriate word out of the four options for filling the blank space in the aforesaid sentence

(*a*) for (*b*) as

(c) into (*d*) to

**Passage for questions 103 to 112:**

The work which Gandhiji had taken up was not only regarding the achievement of political freedom but also the establishment of a new social order based on truth and non-violence, unity and peace, equality and universal brotherhood and maximum freedom for all. This unfinished part of his experiment was perhaps even more difficult to achieve than the achievement of political freedom. In the political struggle, the fight was against a foreign power and all one could do was either join it or wish it success and give it his/her moral support. In establishing a social order on this pattern, there was a strong possibility of a conflict arising between diverse groups and classes of our own people. Experience shows that man values his possessions even more than his life because in the former he sees the means for perpetuation and survival of his descendants even after his body is reduced to ashes. A new order cannot be established without radically changing the mind and attitude of men towards property and, at some stage or the other, the 'haves' have to yield place to the 'have-nots'. We have seen, in our time, attempts to achieve a kind of egalitarian society and the picture of it after it was achieved. But this was done, by and large, through the use of physical force.

In the ultimate analysis it is difficult, if not impossible, to say that the instinct to possess has been rooted out or that it will not reappear in an even worse form under a different guise. It may even be that, like a gas kept confined within containers under great pressure, or water held back by a big dam, once the barrier breaks, the reaction will one day sweep back with a violence equal in extent and intensity to what was used to establish and maintain the outward egalitarian form. This enforced egalitarianism contains, in its bosom, the seed of its own destruction.

The root cause of class conflict is possessiveness or the acquisitive instinct. So long as the ideal that is to be achieved is one of securing the maximum material satisfaction, possessiveness is neither suppressed nor eliminated but grows on what it feeds. Nor does it cease to be possessiveness, whether it is confined to only a few or is shared by many.

If egalitarianism is to endure, it has to be based not on the possession of the maximum material goods by a few or by all but on voluntary, enlightened renunciation of those goods which cannot be shared by others or can be enjoyed only at the expense of others. This calls for substitution of material values by purely spiritual ones. The paradise of material satisfaction, which is sometimes equated with progress these days, neither spells peace nor progress. Mahatma Gandhi has shown us how the acquisitive instinct inherent in man can be transmuted by the adoption of the ideal of trusteeship by those who 'have' for the benefit of all those who 'have not' so that, instead of leading to exploitation and conflict, it would become a means and incentive for the amelioration and progress of society respectively. **(CLAT 2012)**

**103.** According to the passage, egalitarianism will not survive if

(*a*) It is based on voluntary renunciation.

(*b*) It is achieved by resorting to physical force.

(*c*) Underprivileged people are not involved in its establishment.

(*d*) People's outlook towards it is not radically changed.

**104.** According to the passage, why does man value his possessions more than his life?

(*a*) He has inherent desire to share his possession with others.

(*b*) He is endowed with the possessive instinct.

(*c*) Only his possession helps him earn love and respect from his descendants.

(*d*) Through his possessions he can preserve his name even after his death.

**105.** According to the passage, which was the unfinished part of Gandhi's experiment?

(*a*) Educating people to avoid class conflict.

(*b*) Achieving total political freedom for the country.

(*c*) Establishment of an egalitarian society.

(*d*) Radically changing the mind and attitude of men towards truth and non-violence.

**106.** Which of the following statements is 'not true' in the context of the passage?

(*a*) True egalitarianism can be achieved by giving up one's possessions under compulsion.

(*b*) Man values his life more than his possessions.

(*c*) Possessive instinct is a natural desire of human beings.

(*d*) In the political struggle, the fight was against alien rule.

**107.** According to the passage, true egalitarianism will last only if

(*a*) It is thrust upon people.

(*b*) It is based on truth and non-violence.

(*c*) People inculcate spiritual values instead of material values.

(*d*) 'Haves' and 'have-nots' live together peacefully.

**108.** According to the passage, people ultimately overturn a social order ———

(*a*) which is based on coercion and oppression.

(*b*) which does not satisfy their basic needs.

(*c*) which is based upon conciliation and rapprochement.

(*d*) which is not congenital to the spiritual values of the people

**109.** According to the passage, the root cause of class conflict is

(*a*) The paradise of material satisfaction.

(*b*) Dominant inherent acquisitive instinct in man.

(*c*) Exploitation of the 'have-nots' by the 'haves'.

(*d*) A Social order where the unprivileged are not a part of the establishment.

**110.** Which of the following statements is 'not true' in the context of the passage?

(*a*) A new order can be established by radically changing the outlook of people towards it.

(*b*) Adoption of the ideal of trusteeship can minimize possessive instinct.

(*c*) Enforced egalitarianism can be the cause of its own destruction.

(*d*) Ideal of new order is to secure maximum material satisfaction

**111.** Which of the following conclusions can be deduced from the passage?

(*a*) A social order based on truth and non-violence alone can help the achievement of political freedom.

(*b*) After establishing the social order of Gandhiji's pattern, the possibility of a conflict between different classes of society will hardly exist.

(*c*) It is difficult to change the mind and attitude of men towards property.

(*d*) In an egalitarian society, material satisfaction can be enjoyed only at the expense of others.

**112.** According to the passage, what does "adoption of the ideal of trusteeship" mean?

(*a*) Equating peace and progress with material satisfaction.

(*b*) Adoption of the ideal by the 'haves' for the benefit of 'have-nots'.

(*c*) Voluntary enlightened remuneration of the possessive instinct by the privileged class.

(*d*) Substitution of spiritual values by material ones by those who live in the paradise of material satisfaction.

**Directions (Q. 113 - 118) :** The questions in this section is based on the passage. The questions are to be answered on the basis of what is **stated** or **implied** in the passage. For some of the questions, more than one of the choices could conceivably answer the question. However, you are to choose the **best** answer; that is, the response that most accurately and completely answers the question. **(AILET 2013)**

Although the legal systems of England and the United States are superficially similar, they differ profoundly in their approaches to and uses of legal reasons: substantive reasons are more common than formal reasons in the United States, whereas in England the reverse is true. This distinction reflects a difference in the visions of law that prevails in the two countries. In England, the law has traditionally been viewed as a system of rules; the United States favours a vision of law as an outward expression of community's sense of right and justice.

Substantive reasons, as applied to law, are based on moral, economic, political and other considerations. These reasons are found both "in the law" and "outside the law" so to speak. Substantive reasons inform the content of a large part of the law: constitutions, statutes, contracts, verdicts, and the like. Consider, for example, a statute providing that "no vehicles shall be taken into public parks." Suppose that no specific rationales or purposes were explicitly written into the statute, but that it was clear (from its legislative history) that the substantive purpose of the statute was to ensure quiet and safety in the park. Now suppose that a veterans' group mounts a World War II jeep (in running order but without a battery) as a war memorial on a concrete slab in the park, and charges are brought against its members. Most judges in the United States would find the defendants not guilty because what they did had no adverse effect on park's quiet and safety.

Formal reasons are different in that they frequently prevent substantive reasons from coming into play, even when substantive reasons are explicitly incorporated into the law at hand. For example, when a document fails to comply with stipulated requirements, the court may render the document legally ineffective. A Will requiring written witness may be declared null and void and, therefore, unenforceable for the formal reason that the requirement was not observed. Once the legal rule - that a Will is invalid for lack of proper witnessing - has been clearly established, and the legality of the rule is not in question, application of that rule precludes from consideration substantive arguments in favour of the Will's validity or enforcement.

Legal scholars in England and the United States have long bemused themselves with extreme examples of formal and substantive reasoning. On the one hand, formal reasoning in England has led to wooden interpretations of statutes and an unwillingness to develop the common law through judicial activism. On the other hand, freewheeling substantive reasoning in the United States has resulted in statutory interpretations so liberal that the texts of some statutes have ignored.

**113.** Which one of the following best describes the content of the passage as a whole?

(*a*) An analysis of similarities and differences between the legal systems of England and the United States

(*b*) A re-evaluation of two legal systems with the use of examples

(c) A contrast between the types of reasons embodied in the United States and English legal systems

(*d*) An explanation of how two distinct visions of the law shaped the development of legal reasoning.

**114.** It can be inferred from the passage that English judges would like to find the veterans' group discussed in the second paragraph guilty of violating the statute because

(*a*) not to do so would encourage others to act as the group did

(*b*) not to do so would be to violate the substantive reasons underlying the law

(*c*) the veterans failed to comply with the substantive purpose of the statute

(*d*) the veterans failed to comply with the stipulated requirements of the statute

**115.** From the discussion of Wills in the third paragraph it can be inferred that substantive arguments as to the validity of a Will might be considered under which one of the following circumstances?

(*a*) The legal rule that a Will be witnessed in writing does not stipulate the format of the V

(*b*) The legal rule requiring that a Will be witnessed stipulates that the Will must be witnessed in writing by two people

(*c*) The legal rule requiring that a Will be witnessed in writing stipulates that the witnessing must be done in the presence of a judge

(*d*) A judge rules that the law can be interpreted to allow for a verbal witness to a Will in a case involving a medical emergency

**116.** Which one of the following best describes the function of the last paragraph of the passage?

(*a*) It presents the consequences of extreme interpretations of the two types of legal reasons discussed by the author

(*b*) It shows how legal scholars can incorrectly use extreme examples to support their views

(*c*) It corrects inaccuracies in legal scholars' view of the nature of two types of legal systems

(*d*) It suggests how characterisations of the two types of legal reasons can become convoluted and inaccurate

**117.** The author of the passage suggests that in English law a substantive interpretation of a legal rule might be warranted under which one of the following circumstances?

(*a*) Social conditions have changed to the extent that to continue to enforce the rule would be to decide contrary to present-day social norms

(*b*) The composition of the legislature has changed to the extent that to enforce the rule would be contrary to the views of the majority in the present legislative assembly

(*c*) The legality of the rule is in question and its enforcement is open to judicial interpretation

(*d*) Individuals who have violated the legal rule argue that application of the rule would lead to unfair judicial interpretations

**118.** The author of the passage makes use of all of the following in presenting the discussion of the English and the United States legal systems except

(*a*) Comparison and contrast

(*b*) Generalisation

(c) Explication of terms

(*d*) A chronology of historical development

**Directions (Q. 119 – 128) :** *Read the given passage carefully and attempt the questions that follow and shade the appropriate answer in the space provided for it on the OMR answer sheet.* **(CLAT 2013)**

It is an old saying that knowledge is power. Education is an instrument which imparts knowledge and therefore, indirectly controls power. Therefore, ever since the dawn of our civilisation, persons in power have always tried to supervise or control education. It has been handmaid of the ruling class. During the Christian era, the ecclesiastics controlled the institution of education and diffused among the people the gospel of the Bible and religious teachings. These gospels and teachings were no other than a philosophy for the maintenance of the existing society. It taught the poor man to be meek and to earn his bread with the sweat of his brow, while the priests and the landlords lived in luxury and fought duels for the slightest offence. During the Renaissance, education passed more from the clutches of the priest into the hands of the prince. In other words, it became more secular. Under the control of the monarch, education began to devise and preach the infallibility of its masters, the monarch or king. It also invented and supported fantastic theories like "The Divine right Theory" and that the king can do no wrong, etc. With the advent of the industrial revolution, education took a different turn and had to please the new masters. It now no longer remained the privilege of the baron class, but was thrown open to the new rich merchant class of the society. The philosophy which was in vogue during this period was that of "Laissez Faire" restricting the function of the state to a mere keeping of laws and order while on the other hand, in practice the law of the jungle prevailed in the form of free competition and the survival of the fittest.

**119.** What does the theory "Divine Right of King" stipulate?

(*a*) The kings are God

(*b*) That the right of governing is conferred upon the kings by God

(*c*) They have the right to be worshipped like Gods by their subjects

(*d*) That the right of kings are divine and therefore sacred

**120.** Who controlled education during the Renaissance?

(*a*) The common people

(*b*) The prince

(*c*) The church and the priests

(*d*) None of these

**121.** What did the ruling class in the Christian era think of the poor man?

(*a*) That he is the beloved of God

(*b*) That he deserves all sympathy of the rich

(*c*) That he should be strong and lord over others

(*d*) That he is meant for serving the rich

**122.** Who controlled the institution of education during the Christian Era?

(*a*) The secular leaders of society

(*b*) The church and the priests

(*c*) The monarchs

(*d*) The common people

**123.** What does the word "infallibility" mean?

(*a*) That every man is open to error

(*b*) Sensitivity

(*c*) The virtue of not making mistake

(*d*) That some divine power is responsible for determining the fate of the man

**124.** What do you mean by the "sweat of his brow"?

(*a*) Very hard work

(*b*) The tiny droplets of sweat on the forehead

(*c*) The wrinkles visible on the forehead

(*d*) The sign of innocence

**125.** What does the policy of "Laissez Faire" stand for?

(*a*) Individual freedom in the economic field

(*b*) State control over law and order in society

(*c*) Joint control of the means of production by the state and private enterprise

(*d*) Decontrol over law and order by the ruling class

**126.** Which of the following describes the writer?

(*a*) Concerned (*b*) Unconcerned

(*c*) Aggressive (*d*) Frustrated

**127.** Choose the correct synonym out of the four choices given:

Gospels

(*a*) Chit chat

(*b*) A teaching or doctrine of a religious teacher

(*c*) Rumour

(*d*) Guidance

**128.** Choose the correct synonym out of the four choices given:

Vogue

(*a*) Uncertain

(*b*) Out-dated

(*c*) The prevailing fashion or style

(*d*) Journey

**Directions (Q. 129 – 135) :** The questions in this section are based on the passage. The questions are to be answered on the basis of what is **stated** or **implied** in the passage. For some of the questions, more than one of the choices could conceivably answer the question. However, you are to choose the **best** answer; that is, the response that most accurately and completely answers the questions.

Under very early common law, all felonies were punishable by death. The perpetrators of the felony were hanged whether or not a homicide had been committed during the felony. Later, however, some felonies were declared to be non-capital offences. The common law courts, in need of a deterrent to the use of deadly force in the course of these non-capital felonies, developed the "felony-murder" rule. The first formal statement of the rule stated: "Any killing by one in the commission of a felony is guilty of murder." The killing was a murder whether intentional or unintentional, accidental or mistaken. The usual requirement of malice was eliminated and the only criminal intent necessary was the intent to commit the particular underlying felony. All participants in the felony were guilty of murder-actual killer and non-killer confederates.

Proponents of the rule argued that it was justified because the felony demonstrated a lack of concern for human life by the commission of a violent and dangerous felony and that the crime was murder either because of a conclusive presumption of malice or simply by force of statutory definition.

Opponents of the rule describe it as a highly artificial concept and "an enigma wrapped in a riddle." They are quick to point out that the rule has been abandoned in England where it originated, abolished in India, severely restricted in Canada and a number of other commonwealth countries, is unknown in continental Europe, and abandoned in Michigan. In reality, the real strength of the opponents' criticism stems from the bizarre and of times unfair results achieved when the felony - murder rule is applied mechanically. Defendants have been convicted under the rule where the killing was purely accidental, or the killing took place after the felony during the later flight from the scene; or a third party killed another (police officer killed a citizen or vice versa; or a victim died of a heart attack 15 -20 minutes after the robbery was over; or the person killed was an accomplice in the felony).

Attacks on the rule have come from all directions with basically the same demand - re-evaluate and abandon the archaic legal fiction; restrict and limit vicarious criminal liability; prosecute killers for murder, not non-killers; increase punishment for the underlying felony as a real deterrent; and initiate legislative modifications. With the unstable history of the felony - murder rule, including its abandonment by many jurisdictions in this country, the felony - murder rule is dying a slow but certain death. **(AILET 2014)**

**129.** Which one of the following best states the central idea of the passage ?

(*a*) The felony - murder rule should be abolished.

(*b*) Some jurisdictions are about to abandon the felony — murder rule.

(*c*) The felony - murder rule can be unfair.

(*d*) Supreme Court of the United States.

**130.** The felony - murder rule was developed in order to

(*a*) deter felonies

(*b*) deter murders

(*c*) deter deadly force in felonies

(*d*) extend the definition of murder to any malicious act resulting in death

**131.** Arguments in favour of the felony - murder rule may include all of the following EXCEPT

(*a*) We can infer that anyone undertaking a dangerous felony demonstrates an indifference to human life.

(*b*) If the punishment for the use of deadly force whether intended or not is the same, criminals will be less likely to use deadly force.

(*c*) Because a life has been taken, the crime is murder by force of statutory definition.

(*d*) The victim of murder may be an accomplice of the felony.

**132.** According to the passage, opponents of the felony - murder rule have raised all of the following objections to the statute EXCEPT

(*a*) The felony - murder rule results in murder prosecutions of defendants who have not committed murder.

(*b*) The felony - murder rule assigns a criminal liability vicariously.

(*c*) The felony - murder rule is based upon a presumption of malice even if death is wholly accidental.

(*d*) The felony - murder rule deters the use of deadly force in non-capital felonies.

**133.** In which of the following situations would the defendant NOT be liable to the charge of murder under the felony — murder rule ?

(*a*) In escaping from an unsuccessful attempt to rob a bank, the defendant crashes his car, killing an innocent pedestrian in another city.

(*b*) A bank security officer, pursuing the defendant after a robbery, falls down a flight of stairs and suffers serious permanent brain and spinal cord injuries.

(*c*) The driver of the escape car, who has not entered the bank, crashes the car killing the armed gunman who committed the robbery.

(*d*) A bank teller, locked safely in the bank vault by the robber, has a stroke and dies.

**134.** According to the passage, the decline of support for the felony - murder rule is indicted by the abandoning of the rule in all of the following locations EXCEPT

(*a*) Continental Europe

(*b*) India

(*c*) England

(*d*) Canada

**135.** The author believes that the felony - murder rule is

(*a*) unconstitutional

(*b*) bizarre and unfair

(*c*) a serviceable rule unfairly attacked by the "intelligentsia"

(*d*) an unfair equating of intent to commit a felony and intent to commit murder

**Directions (Q. 136- 145) :** The questions in this section are based on a single passage. The questions are to be answered on the basis of what is stated or implied in the passage. Kindly note that more than one of the choices may conceivably answer some of the questions. However, you are to choose the most appropriate answer; that is, the response that most accurately and completely answers the question.

The spread of education in society is at the foundation of success in countries that are latecomers to development. In the quest for development, primary education is absolutely essential because it creates the base. But higher education is just as important, for it provides the ***cutting edge***. And universities are the life-blood of higher education. Islands of excellence in professional education, such as Indian Institutes of Technology (IITs) and Indian Institutes of Management (IIMs), are valuable complements but cannot be substitutes for universities which provide educational opportunities for people at large.

There can be no doubt that higher education has made a significant contribution to economic development, social progress and political democracy in independent India. It is a source of dynamism for the economy. It has created social opportunities for people. It has fostered the vibrant democracy in our polity. It has provided a beginning for the creation of a knowledge society. But it would be a mistake to focus on its strengths alone. It has weaknesses that are a cause for serious concern.

There is, in fact, a quiet crisis in higher education in India that runs deep. It is not yet ***discernible*** simply because there are pockets of excellence, an enormous reservoir of talented young people and an intense competition in the admissions process. And, in some important spheres, we continue to reap the benefits of what was sown in higher education 50 years ago by the founding fathers of the Republic. The reality is that we have miles to go. The proportion of our population, in the age group 18-24, that enters the world of higher education is around 7 per cent, which is only one-half the average for Asia. The opportunities for higher education, in terms of the number of places in universities, are simply not enough in relation to our needs. What is more, the quality of higher education in most of our universities requires substantial improvement.

It is clear that the system of higher education in India faces serious challenges. It needs a systematic overhaul, so that we can educate much larger numbers without diluting academic standards. This is imperative because the transformation of economy and society in the 21st century would depend, in significant part, on the spread and the quality of education among our people, particularly in the sphere of higher education. It is only an inclusive society that can provide the foundations for a knowledge society.

The challenges that confront higher education in India are clear. It needs a massive expansion of opportunities for higher education, to 1500 universities nationwide, that would enable India to attain a gross enrolment ratio of at least 15 per cent by 2015. It is just as important to raise the average quality of higher education in every sphere. At the same time, it is essential to create institutions that are exemplars of excellence at par with the best in the world. In the pursuit of these objectives, providing people with access to higher education in a socially inclusive manner is imperative. The realisation of these objectives, combined with access, would not only develop the skills and capabilities we need for the economy but would also help transform India into a knowledge economy and society.

**136.** The principal focus of the passage is: **(CLAT 2014)**

(*a*) Primary education

(*b*) Intermediate education

(*c*) Higher education

(*d*) Entire education system

**137.** The style of the passage can be best described as: **(CLAT 2014)**

(*a*) Academic (*b*) Critical and analytical

(*c*) Comparative (*d*) None of the above

**138.** What kind of society can provide the foundation for a knowledge society? **(CLAT 2014)**

(*a*) Elite society

(*b*) Contracted society

(*c*) Exclusive society

(*d*) Inclusive society

**139.** According to the passage, which one of the following is INCORRECT? **(CLAT 2014)**

(*a*) There are no quality institutes providing excellent professional education in India.

(*b*) Not many people go for higher education in India.

(*c*) Education is the basis of success.

(*d*) All the above options are correct.

**140.** According to the passage, the current state of affairs of higher education in India is: **(CLAT 2014)**

(*a*) Satisfactory

(*b*) Excellent, and there is no need of any expansion of opportunities for higher education

(*c*) Not good enough, and there is a need of expansion of opportunities for higher education, besides creating institutions and universities that are models of excellence

(*d*) Not explained in the passage

**141.** According to the passage, which of the following is NOT a challenge that confronts higher education in India? **(CLAT 2014)**

(*a*) Expanding opportunities for higher education

(*b*) Creating institutions and universities that are exemplars of excellence

(*c*) Substantial improvement in the quality of higher education in most of our universities

(*d*) Getting into World University Rankings

**142.** According to the passage, which of the following is CORRECT? **(CLAT 2014)**

(*a*) Primary education is very important

(*b*) Universities are the life-blood of higher education

(*c*) Transformation of economy and society in the 21st century would depend, in significant part, on the spread and the quality of education among our people, particularly in the sphere of higher education

(*d*) All the above propositions are correct

**143.** Should the entire university system in India be modelled on premier institutes, such as the IITs and the IIMs, providing professional education? **(CLAT 2014)**

(*a*) Yes

(*b*) For sure

(*c*) No

(*d*) The passage is silent on this question

**144.** What is the antonym of the expression 'cutting edge'? **(CLAT 2014)**

(*a*) Conventional (*b*) Avant-garde

(*c*) Advanced (*d*) Contemporary

**145.** What is the meaning of the word 'discernible'? **(CLAT 2014)**

(*a*) Unobtrusive

(*b*) Noticeable

(*c*) Unremarkable

(*d*) Inconspicuous

## Solutions

**1.** d. The answer is clearly option (*d*). The author begins by stating what Asimov believes in and mentions in the same breath that science itself was questioning whatever he supported in his time. This is roughly what the first paragraph does. The remaining part of the passage is an elucidation of this point. Option (*a*) and (*b*) are mere points mentioned in the passage, they do not form the main idea. Option (c) is neither stated nor implied in the passage. Hence, it cannot be the main point of the passage.

**2.** c In the last paragraph, the author reveals Asimov's beliefs as indicated through the foundation series. He also mentions several fields (like Physics, Biology and Maths) where the same beliefs were increasingly being proven wrong.

**3.** b The claim clearly illustates what the popular opinion was regarding Asimov's works. Refer to the lines, "Although the common claim ... have written a book in every category ..." It clearly shows that his works covered a broad range of areas.

**4.** d The author clearly indicates that the Seldon Plan, though naive it may sound, clearly reflects Isaac Asimov's attitude towards science. The last sentence of the second paragraph strongly points to this.

**5.** a 'The butterfly effect' is explained in the passage as a 'chaos theory' which 'showed that perfect prediction could take place only on the basis of perfect information, which was by nature impossible to obtain'. This idea is best captured in the example provided in Option (*a*). Option (c) and (*d*) are far from this principle. They talk about predictions being accurate which is opposite to the choas theory. Option (*b*) is incorrect because the perfect information angle is missing here. It talks about indeterminacy of the behaviour of subatomic particles, not imperfection of the data.

**6.** d The passage mainly talks about the viewpoint of philosophical anarchism which states that governments do not have a moral right to govern, but still people have non-legal moral duties to not harm other individuals. This point is best captured in option (*d*). Option (*a*) is incorrect as it is not the main point of the passage. The author has elaborated on how philosophical anarchism is not counter-intuitive. Option (*b*) and (c) are individually incorrect as they are only one of the claims of the commentators that the author has clarified.

**7.** a Refer to the line, *"It is also commonly supposed ... simply because it is the law."* Thus, the author has stated that following the laws is considered a moral obligation because of it being a law. Option (*a*) follows.

**8.** b In the last two paragraphs, the author is trying to clarify the ideas of philosophical anarchism. This implies that the author is in consonance with the ideas of the theory. This is highlighted in option (*b*). Option (*a*) is incorrect because of the word 'ardent' which makes the author biased towards the theory, which is clearly not the case. Options (c) and (*d*) are incorrect as the author is neither negative about the theory nor is he rejecting it.

**9.** a Options (*b*), (c) and (*d*) are incorrect as they are beyond the scope of information given in the passage. 'Counter-intuitive' is something that does not seem to be true when assessed using intuition or common sense. Only option (*a*) communicates the intention of the author correctly.

**10.** b The third paragraph highlights that people have a moral obligation to care for one another, which they might even discharge in their effort to support those in need. This is best expressed in the scenario given in option (*b*) where the executive quits her job (discharged her moral obligation to help others) learning of the harmful effects of the chemicals. Thus, option (*b*) is the correct choice.

**11.** c Refer to the line, *"Moreover, philosophical anarchists...to help those in need."* It is clear from this statement that people will support the laws and efforts of the government which are directed at helping those in need because of their inherent moral obligation to care for others. Thus, the author must agree to the statement given in option (*c*).

**12.** d Options (*a*), (*b*) and (c) are beyond the scope of the information of the question. Fourth paragraph clearly states that individuals should respect individual freedom. This makes option (*d*) the correct choice.

**13.** d The author in the last two paragraphs is trying to clarify the position of philosophical anarchism. Author is also trying to answer the critics on the issue by clarifying the doubts raised by the critics. Hence, option (*d*) is the correct answer.

**14.** d In the second paragraph, the author states, "That the artist can afford to be "purist" ..about what the art world or anyone else might think.." hence justifying the correctness of option (*d*).

**15.** d The author has mentioned in the passage that in order to sell one's work in the market, one has to price it for an amount that someone would be likely to pay for it. In other words, one cannot price it arbitrarily but must do so according to its market worth. Thus, statement b definitely follows. Statement a is the 'purist's vision' where the artist sees pricing his art as debasing it.

Statement c is incorrect as one need not compromise one one's estimation of one's own art always. Renowned artists often manage to get the price that they demand for their works. Statement d does not follow as pricing does not involve subjecting the art to buyer's interpretation. Thus, option (*d*), only b, is correct.

**16.** d For an artist to sell his piece of art at a higher price range, "the art world will have to recognize your art both critically and from the marketing standpoints, and you'll have to successfully produce, show, and see for many years" (paragraph 5).

**17.** d The author, in paragraph 5, states, "..drawing will hang framed and captioned as the first inspiration for all subsequent work." Option (*b*), though close, is incorrect since the first drawing according to the author, will be a "historically important document of your career" and hence would be a collectible piece in the artist's repertoire, maybe for a sentimental value, but nowhere does the author mention that this piece would also be the artist's most important piece. Similarly, options (*a*) and (*d*) are neither mentioned nor implied in the passage.

**18.** c In the last paragraph, the author states "Unless that artist leaves specific instructions..it (the art) will become subject to those market forces that the artist strived for a lifetime to avoid." So statement b is correct. Statement a on the other hand, is incorrect since the author claims that (only) when an artist becomes very successful and holds a retrospective exhibition and has his originally over-priced painting "a serious collector may well be willing to pay an extraordinary price to own this historically important document of your (the artist's) career". Thus statement a is incorrect as the price that the collector will be willing to pay may well be higher than what the artist thought. Statement c is out of scope of the passage. Moreover, 'purists' do not wish to sell their work so they would not take the 'realities of the market place' approach. Hence, the answer is statement b alone.

**19.** a Encumbrance is defined as a 'thing that impedes or is burdensome'. Hence, Encumbrance and Burden are synonyms. Out of the options given, the only that contains a pair that represents a similar relationship is option (*a*). Mnemonic is defined as 'of or relating to memory or mnemonics' and hence, Mnemonic represents a similar relationship with Memory like the one represented by the pair Encumbrance and Burden.

**20.** a Subsequent and previous are antonyms of one another. The only pair in the given options that represent a similar relationship is Significant and Inconsequential. Hence option (*a*) is correct.

**21.** b The word 'precipitate' is used in the passage in the line ".... the product of your two-minute moment precipitates a major transformational turning point in your career.'..Precipitate here is undoubtedly used in the context as something that 'triggers' a transformational change in the author/his art.

**22.** d Refer to the lines "The recent work of Addison Gayle's passes a judgment on the value of Black fiction by clear political standards, rating each work according to the ideas of Black identity, which it propounds." It is clear from these lines that rating by political standards (as done by Addison Gayle) is objectionable to the author.

**23.** a The author reviews the validity of a work of criticism. Roger Rosenblatt's book 'Black Fiction' is the book with respect to which criticism is being validated by the author. He raises an objection to the basis of criticism, states what is required before writing an acceptable criticism and discusses the strengths and weaknesses of the book 'Black Fiction'. Option (*b*) is incorrect because no critical approach is discussed in the passage. The author does not provide any data regarding the limitations of any kind of criticism. Recapitulation, which means a summary, of the major points in a work of criticism is not presented in the passage. Thus, option (*a*) is the correct choice.

**24.** d Refer to the lines "Rosenblatt's work does leave certain aesthetic questions open.especially since an attempt to appraise might have led to interesting results." Thus, option (*d*) is the correct answer.

**25.** b Refer to the last paragraph of the passage. "Irrespective of such omissions..Black Fiction is a tightly constructed, and levelheaded and penetrating criticism is exemplified in its forthright and lucid style." Thus, option (*b*) is the most suitable option.

**26.** c Refer to the lines "Roger Rosenbatt's book 'Black Fiction, manages expounding on Black History" and "The recent work of Addison Gayle's passes a judgment on the value of Black fiction by clear political standards, rating each work according to the ideas of Black identity, which it propounds." It is clear from these lines that rating by political standards (as done by Addison Gayle) is objectionable to the author. So he will be least likely to approve option (*c*).

**27.** d The passage does not provide definition of any of the terms mentioned in the passage (the words expressionism, surrealism demand a definition but definitions are not given). Thus, option (*d*) is the correct option.

**28.** d All of the reasons mentioned in options (*a*), (*b*) and (c) contribute to a cohesive group doing a better job at decision making than a non-cohesive group. It is mentioned in the passage that the members feel free to voice their opinion being part of a cohesive group. Refer to the lines, *"In a highly cohesive group...not that individuals will conceal objections..."* and *"...participants in the group's deliberations..."* Hence, option (*d*) is correct.

**29.** a The passage talks about group cohesiveness and its impact on decision making. The author begins by mentioning that cohesiveness in a group encourages people to be frank and open. In the second paragraph, he talks about the 'groupthink' syndrome that stems from the need to conform to group majority. Option (*a*), thus, is the right choice. Option (*b*) is incorrect because the passage does not go into how group members need to guard against groupthink. The passage is not about diplomacy and military affairs per se; rather they are just mentioned as examples. This negates option (c) as well. Option (*d*) is incorrect as the author does not conclude that low cohesion groups are better or worse than high cohesion groups.

**30.** b The scenario presented here is of a cohesive group where members initially put forth their conflicting ideas but due to lack of agreement, compromised on a disastrous diplomatic decision for the sake of arriving at a consensus. This is similar to the groupthink syndrome mentioned in the passage where a cohesive group gives in to the need to achieve group consensus. Option (*b*) is on the same lines and is the correct choice. Option (*a*) is incorrect as it is mentioned in the question that the group members are closely associated. Option (c) can be negated outright, since the scenario indeed is an evidence of groupthink. Option (*d*) is incorrect as the group did demonstrate an "illusion of unanimity" by coming to a 'diplomatic' decision that they were not convinced about.

**31.** b Groupthink, as given in the passage, is a syndrome wherein members stop attempting to carry out a critical scrutiny that could reveal grounds for objections. Rather, they give the benefit of doubt to the group consensus. Option (*b*) is correct. Groupthink's main component is the strong belief of the members that the group decision is right. Option (*a*) is incorrect; the passage doesn't talk about any suspicions between group members. Option (c) is incorrect as it is not stress that leads to illusions of invulnerability; rather they both are factors contributing to groupthink. Option (*d*) is characteristic of non-cohesive group, not groupthink.

**32.** a Option (*b*) is incorrect as the author states the researchers' findings that factors contributing to groupthink form a recurring pattern, meaning they are not unique to each case. Option (c) is incorrect, study of cohesiveness does contribute to determining the factors that elicit groupthink. The author does not make a conclusive statement about groupthink having or not having any beneficial effect on decision making. Hence, option (*d*) cannot be inferred. Option (*a*) is correct; the author mentions that highly cohesive groups experience this syndrome. Refer to the last line, "...it is important to work towards...whether group cohesiveness will deteriorate...or allow for effective decision making". It suggests that its contribution is still not fully understood.

**33.** c The answer might appear to one as option (*b*), but since her grandmother persuaded her to develop interest in the nature, and not to study zoology, the right answer is option (*c*).

**34.** a Refer to the line, "I didn't get my first camera until ... needed a method of recording the sea creatures ..." This clearly mentions that the author got her first camera to record what she had seen at the sea.

**35.** d Refer to the line, "I became keen very quickly ... didn't have much money...more black and white photography than color..." Thus, option (*d*) clearly follows from this line.

**36.** b The author talks about how some photographers pick up sea creatures from the shores to picture them in beautiful ponds. They do so to make their pictures attractive but in the process change the creature's natural surroundings drastically. The author finds herself different from other photographers in this respect. Thus, option (*b*) is the correct choice.

**37.** a The 'them' in the line "In so doing you're actually ... make *them* prettier" refers to sea creatures which are being captured by the photographers.

**38.** d Not thinking about the animals in the first place is what the author means by ignorance in people's behavior. This can be arrived at from the first few lines of the fourth paragraph.

**39.** b The author has stated in paragraph four that it has become difficult for the wildlife photographer to find and click wild animals. This is because of animals getting scared of people rushing towards them. Thus, option (*b*) is the correct choice.

**40.** d The passage clearly states that photography can "educate people about what is out there and what needs conserving". Thus, option (*d*) is an obvious choice.

**41.** a The last paragraph helps us to lead to this answer, as the author says that she is keeping herself busy through writing.

**42.** b The tone of the author is sensitive throughout the passage as she is concerned about the condition of the wild life.

**43.** a. Antonym for the word 'deleterious', which means 'harmful', is 'beneficial'.

**44.** b The most important objective of the author is to illustrate the devastating effects of the use of nuclear weapons on mankind. Option (*a*) and (c) are incorrect. The use of nuclear weapons is not highlighted as a population control measure neither has the author talked about the supremacy of the nations which possess nuclear weapons. Option (*b*) may seem correct but it is not. The author does talk about the long lasting biological effects of nuclear weapons but summarizing these effects is not his objective. He has done so to stress how harmful the use of nuclear weapons is to mankind which is the main objective of the author.

**45.** c The second paragraph states that more than fifty percent of the scientists are engaged in the manufacture of destructive weapons. The passage does not comment upon their number, their competence or whether they are engaged in the industry against their will. Thus, option (c) is the correct choice.

**46.** d The argument is that the use of nuclear weapons has a deleterious effect on mankind. The author states that this argument will become stronger if moral and legal considerations are combined. Thus, option (*d*) follows.

**47.** d The author has mentioned at several places that utilization of valuable skill for the manufacture of weapons of destruction,when it must be engaged in other constructive activities, is inhuman. Option (*a*) and (*b*) are complete opposites of this. The author doesn't bring in the availability of funds to justify the use of nuclear weapons. So, option (c) does not follow. Option (*d*) is correct since it brings out the author's view perfectly.

**48.** d There is no correct answer of this question. Only option (*d*) can be accepted as an answer.

**49.** c The author has used the word 'devoted' sarcastically to highlight how the valuable skill is being abused in making weapons of mass destruction. Thus, option (c) is the correct choice.

**50.** d Options (*a*), (*b*) and (c) are mentioned as the consequences of the nuclear weapon. Option (*d*) is not a consequence of nuclear weapon nor has it been mentioned in the passage.

**51.** b First line of the passage states, "There is a fairly ... far enough". This leads us to option (*b*).

**52.** d Statements I, II and III are all false according to the passage. The author talks about extinction of the human species, risks and harmful effects of nuclear war and post-war survivors being exposed to lethal radiations. Also, he talks about severe consequences in areas not affected directly. Thus, option (*d*) is correct.

**53.** c Antigone begs her sister Ismene to not desert their brother Polynices who lay dead and unburied, and thought of it as a challenge to her royal blood. She reminds Ismene of the "holiest law of heaven" which hints at one's responsibility towards one's kin.

**54.** c Antigone decides to defy the orders of Creon to fulfill her duty and prove that she is worthy of her royal blood. She believes that her sister must not "shrug off the burden" and "defy the holiest laws of heaven".

**55.** d Creon, the new king, "resolved to ...by refusing the right of honourable burial. The penalty of death was promulgated against any who should defy this order". This, coupled with Ismene's fear "how could you dare- when Creon has expressly forbidden it?" gives one enough reason to believe that Antigone might have been executed if she had attempted to stand up against Creon's orders and tried to give her brother an honourable burial.

**56.** c This is quite clear from Ismene's response to Antigone when the latter urges the former to defy Creon's orders and help her give their brother, Polynices, an honourable burial. ("Antigone, we are women, it is not for us to fight against men.")

**57.** d Option (*a*) is incorrect since the curse of the Gods was upon Oedipus and not his sons. Option (*b*) is incorrect since there was no mention of greed being the reason for the fight amongst the two brothers. Option (c) too, is incorrect since there is no mention of there being a conflict between Oedipus's sons over inheritance. Option (*d*) is correct since the passage says that "Creon resolved to make an example of the brother who had fought against him".

**58.** c A 'carrion' is a bird which eats dead animals' flesh.

**59.** b Refer to the line "Creon resolved to make an example of the brother who had fought against him, ...honourable burial."

**60.** a Refer to the lines, *"How could you dare...it is not for us to fight against men"*. Ismene was clearly afraid of the king because he had given orders of death penalty for anyone who would defy his orders. She did not have the courage to go against the king in order to help her sister. Thus, option (*a*) is the correct choice.

**61.** a This is clear from the beginning of the passage "..Oedipus, that tragic figure..who had been cursed by Gods for mistakenly killing his father and subsequently marrying his mother and assuming the throne of Thebes."

**62.** a Vicarious liability means the responsibility of the superior for the acts of their subordinate, or, in a broader sense, the responsibility of any third party that had the "right, ability or duty to control" the activities of a violator (Source: Wikipedia). In the passage, no one is responsible for other person's act and hence, option (*a*) is correct.

**63.** b Option (*a*) is incorrect as P.C. Mahalanobis believed in rigid control by the government over all activities. Option (c) is incorrect, as the effect of restrictions on large companies is not given in the passage. Option (*d*) is incorrect, as Spratt's views on the 'devaluation of the rupee' are not given. Option (*b*) can be inferred from the lines "...Philip Spratt was writing a series of essays in favor of free enterprise.".

**64.** a Option (*a*) cannot be inferred from the passage. Option (*b*) can be inferred from the first paragraph. Refer to lines "...Shroff began a forum.government, of India..". Option (c) can be inferred as he championed the cause of independent entrepreneur. Option (*d*) is indicated in the lines "Spratt was a Cambridge communist". Hence, the correct answer is option (*a*).

**65.** a Option (*a*) is correct as the author has tried to highlight the presence of advocates for free market by first mentioning Shroff and then Spratt. Option (*b*) is incorrect as the mention of Indira Gandhi and related politics is limited to only the last paragraph. Options (c) and (*d*) are beyond the scope of the passage.

**66.** d The correct answer is option (*d*). Refer to the line, "Spratt was a..revolution in the subcontinent."

**67.** c The correct answer is option (*c*). Refer to the first paragraph. Shroff complained that independent entrepreneurs were treated with indifference by the government.

**68.** c The correct answer is option (*c*). Refer to this line in second paragraph. "The books he read in the prison, and his marriage to an Indian woman afterwards, inspired a steady move rightwards."

**69.** d The correct answer is option (*d*). Refer to the last lines of the last paragraph - "After the rupee was devalued...and returning to economic autarky".

**70.** b Nationalization of industries in 1969 has been quoted by the author as a consequence of 'Indira Gandhi led politics'. Hence, correct answer is option (*b*).

**71.** c The correct answer is 'was'. In the given sentence, verb should agree with the closest available subject. Since A. D. Shroff is singular, hence, both 'is' and 'was' are correct. In light of the given passage, 'was' becomes more appropriate as we are referring to the past.

**72.** d 'Inveigh' means to criticize strongly or complain bitterly. The correct answer is 'remonstrate' which means to protest or complain about something/somebody.

**73.** d The passage talks about the strangeness in the non-Dalit representations of Dalits. He mentions two books, one by Manu Joseph and the other by Rohinton Mistry. Both these books are written by non- Dalits and both talk about Dalits without having any insight into the Dalit world. The non-Dalit portrayal of Dalits in literature, cinema and art has remained a norm in India but these portrayals fail to depict the truth about Dalit lives, their movements and figures like B.R. Ambedkar. Thus, option (*d*) is the correct choice.

**74.** a Refer to the lines, "Mistry seems to have not veered too far from the road charted by predecessors like Mulk Raj Anand and Premchand. Sixty years after Premchand, Mistry's literary imagination seems stuck in the empathy-realism mode, trapping Dalits in abjection." Hence, option (*a*) is the correct choice.

**75.** d Refer to this line in thrid paragraph, "In a society that is still largely unwilling to recognize Dalits as equal ....representation of Dalits." The correct answer is option (*d*).

**76.** c Refer to this line of third paragraph, ".we must engage with what Dalits are writing –not because for reasons of authenticity, or as a concession to identity politics, but simply because of the aesthetic value of this body of writing and for insights it offers into the human condition." Thus, option (c) cannot be inferred.

**77.** d Refer to last line of the second paragraph – "...and the continued and unquestioned predominance of a Brahminical stranglehold over cultural production have led us to a place where non-Dalit portrayal of Dalits in literature, cinema and art remains the norm." Hence, option (*d*) is correct.

**78.** c Option (c) has not been suggested in the passage; rest all three options are mentioned. Refer to the lines ".we must engage with what Dalits are writing –not because for reasons of authenticity, or as a concession to identity politics, but simply because of the aesthetic value of this body of writing and for insights it offers into the human condition." "Mistry seems to have not veered too far from the road charted by predecessors like Mulk Raj Anand and Premchand. Sixty years after Premchand, Mistry's literary imagination seems stuck in the empathy-realism mode, trapping Dalits in abjection. Mistry happily continues the broad stereotype of the Dalit as a passive sufferer, without consciousness of caste politics."

**79.** d Option (*d*) is neither mentioned nor implied in the passage and hence is the correct answer.

**80.** b The author has criticized Rohinton Mistry for presenting Dalits in the same stereotyped image that was created by Premchand and Mulk Raj Anand. Dalits have been perceived as passive sufferers. Refer to the lines "Mistry seems to have not veered too far from the road charted by predecessors like Mulk Raj Anand and Premchand. Sixty years after Premchand, Mistry's literary imagination seems stuck in the empathy-realism mode, trapping Dalits in abjection. Mistry happily continues the broad stereotype of the Dalit as a passive sufferer, without consciousness of caste politics." Hence, option (*b*) is the correct choice.

**81.** c 'Sly' means 'devious' in the passage. Option (c) is correct.

**82.** c As the subject is plural (Dalit movements) and the sentence is in past tense, the verb should be 'were' (plural verb).

**83.** d Refer to lines "The book is not necessary in these cases, for the argument is about who can write about India, not what has been written." "In recent weeks,.not their interpretations, but their foreignness." The author states that the criticism directed is mostly about the foreignness of authors rather than about their literary styles. Hence, the correct answer is option (*d*).

**84.** a 'Fusillade' refers to a spirited outburst of criticism; a number of shots fired simultaneously or in rapid succession. 'Barrage' refers to a rapid or overwhelming outpouring of many things at once. *"The teacher's rapid-fire barrage of homework assignments went by too fast for me to write them all down"*. Therefore, among the given options, barrage is the most suitable substitute for fusillade.

**85.** b Refer to paragraphs 1 and 6. Both talk about critics who have attacked foreign authors not for their literary styles but for their foreignness. Hence, the correct answer is option (*b*).

**86.** c Refer to lines "The book is not necessary in these cases, for the argument is about who can write about India, not what has been written." "In recent weeks,.not their interpretations, but their foreignness." The author states that the criticism directed is mostly about the foreignness of authors rather than about their literary styles. Option (c) is correct.

**87.** d Refer to paragraph 5 – "A country with a millennial history of Hindus, Christians, Jews...I have not heard an Indian ask whether outsiders have a right to write, think or exist on their soil." The correct answer is option (*d*).

**88.** d The author says that in today's India, outside of the elite intelligentsia, people think that a person should be awarded for what he does and not for who he is. Hence, the correct answer is option (*d*).

**89.** d The author has referred to the history of various religions living peaceably together in India in order to show its openness to unique cultural identities. Hence, the correct answer choice is option (*d*).

**90.** d According to the author, the criticism directed at these foreign authors has become more important than the book. This criticism is about the foreignness of these authors and not about the content of their books. Refer to the lines "What is more interesting about these appraisals...not what has been written." Hence, the correct answer is option (*d*).

**91.** b Refer to the second paragraph. The debate of 'who gets to write about India' has triggered another debate which is about who shall decide that 'who gets to write about India'. Hence, the correct answer choice is option (*b*).

**92.** a The correct answer is option (*a*). The subject 'sensitivity' is singular in number and the sentence is in present tense. Usage of present perfect tense is appropriate for the given blank. Therefore, 'has' is the apt verb.

**93.** d Refer to the penultimate and the last paragraphs. The author has given several examples to emphasize how poverty and starvation do not always result in revolt and how the link is not necessary. The correct answer is option (*d*).

**94.** b Refer to second paragraph. "Part of the difficulty lies in the possibility.the declared rationale of public commitment to remove poverty". Option (*c*) is incorrect as the passage does not definitely state that there is no connection between poverty and violence. The correct answer is option (*b*).

**95.** d The author stresses that policies of poverty removal should not be framed and justified on the premise that they are needed to avoid violence and strife as this notion has may shortcomings. Option (*d*) expresses the main idea of the passage effectively.

**96.** d 'Perilous' means involving potential loss or injury. Hence, 'dangerous' is the correct choice.

**97.** c The author states that it is not surprising that often enough intense and widespread suffering and misery have been accompanied by unusual peace and silence. He/She then gives the example of famines of Ireland and Calcutta to substantiate his/her assertion. Thus, option (c) is the correct choice. Option (*d*) is close but is narrow as it focuses only on people who are dying of starvation and fails to convey the broader idea of the author that deals with suffering and misery in general.

**98.** b 'Destitution' refers to the state of lack of sufficient money or material possessions. 'Indigence' is a state of extreme poverty. Therefore, option (*b*) is the correct choice.

**99.** c Option (*a*) can be inferred from the last paragraph. Option (*b*) can be inferred from the first paragraph, "There has, in fact been,.some evident attractions." Refer to the second paragraph, "This is not to deny that poverty and inequality can- and do-have far reaching consequences with conflict and strife, but these connections have to be examined and investigated with appropriate care and empirical scrutiny, rather than being casually invoked with unreasoned rapidity in support of a good cause." The author does not imply that links between poverty and violence must never be emphasized but advocates the need for prudence and empirical scrutiny before linking them. Thus, option (c) cannot be inferred. Option (*d*) can be inferred from the lines "Destitution can be accompanied not only by economic debility, but also by political helplessness."

**100.** c Refer to the lines "Basing public policy.rather than moral, relevance." Thus option (c) is correct.

**101.** c. Refer to the second paragraph of the passage. As per the reference to economic reductionism in the passage, option (c) states the meaning implied by the term effectively.

**102.** d As 'mobilize' is a verb, the preposition 'to' is appropriate. 'Into' is incorrect because it is used to show movement from exterior to interior position/location. It is used to show the state of movement; for example: I am going into the class. The phrase 'easier to mobilize' is grammatically correct.

**103.** d According to the passage, the new order of egalitarianism can be established only through radically changing the mind and attitude of people. Thus, it directly follows from the passage that egalitarianism won't survive if people's outlook towards it is not radically changed. So, option (*d*) is correct. Option (*a*) is what egalitarianism demands for its survival. It requires voluntary renunciation of material goods. Hence, option (*a*) is incorrect. Option (*b*) is incorrect since it speaks only in the context of India and is not the central reason for the death of egalitarianism.

**104.** d Option (*a*) is incomplete since it does not tell who these others are. Option (*b*) is merely stating the same thing as the question and doesn't answer it. Option (c) is close but love and respect from descendants are not talked about in the passage. Option (*d*) is given as the correct answer by CLAT but it is not. The reason that is mentioned in the passage for man valuing his possessions more than his life is that he wants perpetuation and survival of his descendants. Option (*d*) doesn't take into account preservation of his name through the 'descendants'. Hence, all options seem incorrect.

**105.** c Option (c) is the correct choice. Refer to the lines, *"the establishment of a new social order...this unfinished part of his experiment..."*. The 'social order' mentioned here refers to egalitarianism. Hence, establishment of an egalitarian society was the unfinished part of Gandhi's experiment. Option (*a*) is incorrect as nothing regarding educating people to avoid class conflict is mentioned in the passage. Option (*b*) is incorrect since he did achieve political freedom for the country and so it is not the unfinished part. Option (*d*) is a means to establish an egalitarian society. Hence, option (c) is the correct choice.

**106.** * The answer given by CLAT for this question is option (*b*). Option (*b*) certainly is correct i.e. not true in the context of the passage. Man values his possessions more than his life and not the other way round. However, even option (*a*) is correct. It says true egalitarianism can be achieved by giving up one's possessions under "compulsion". This is not true since the passage says there should be 'voluntary' renunciation of one's possessions. Hence, option (*a*) is not true in the context of the passage and is also a correct option. Options (c) and (*d*) are true; refer to the lines, "Mahatma Gandhi has shown us how the acquisitive instinct inherent in man..." and "In the political struggle, the fight was against a foreign power...".

**107.** c Refer to the lines, "If egalitarianism is to endure...This calls for substitution of material values by purely spiritual ones". Option (*a*) is completely incorrect; it should not be thrust upon the people. Option (*b*) is incorrect as it is incomplete. It should also be based on unity and peace, equality and universal brotherhood and so on. Option (*d*) is also incorrect. It is an outcome of a successful egalitarian society, not a way to make true egalitarianism last.

**108.** * Consider the second paragraph. It talks of a possibility of eventually breaking away from barriers that curtail the possessive instinct in an individual by force. Moreover, the line *"this enforced egalitarianism contains, in its bosom, the seed of its own destruction"* also hints at a social order based on oppression and coercion. However, it can't be said that people will overturn such a social order. The paragraph just talks of a possibility and that too in the context of possessiveness. Option (*b*) and (c) are incorrect since there is no mention of basic needs and conciliation and rapprochement in regard to a social order. Option (*d*) is incorrect as it talks of people overturning a social order not congenital to the spiritual values of people. This is nowhere mentioned in the passage. Hence, no option fits in perfectly here.

**109.** b It is directly mentioned in the third paragraph of the passage. Refer to the line, *"The root cause of class conflict is possessives or the acquisitive instinct"*. Hence, option (*b*) is the correct choice.

**110.** d Option (*a*) is true as the passage says, *"A new order cannot be established without radically changing the mind and attitude of men..."* Option (*b*) is true. Refer to the last couple of lines of the passage, *"...the acquisitive instinct inherent in man can be transmuted by the adoption of the ideal of trusteeship..."* Option (c) also follows directly from the passage, *"this enforced egalitarianism contains, in its bosom, the seed of its own destruction"*. Option (*d*) is false as the passage says the ideal of new order is to secure minimum material satisfaction and not maximum. Hence, option (*d*) is the correct answer.

**111.** * Option (*a*) cannot be deduced from the passage. The passage does not talk about how political freedom can be achieved and so we can't conclude that a social order based on truth and non-violence alone can help achieve it. Option (*b*) is given as the correct answer but in fact it is incorrect. Refer to the line, *"In establishing a new social order on this pattern, there was a* ***strong possibility*** *of a conflict"*. But the option says the opposite. It says such a possibility will 'hardly exist'. Thus, option (*b*) cannot be deduced from the passage and is incorrect. **Option (c) is the correct answer**. Property here refers to possessions. It is difficult to root out attachment to property because of an inherent acquisitive instinct in man. Option (*d*) is incorrect as in an egalitarian society, the 'haves' yield place to the 'have-nots' and do not enjoy material satisfaction at the expense of others.

**112.** b 'Adoption of the ideal of trusteeship' refers to sharing of wealth by the haves with the have-nots. This is given in option (*b*). Option (*a*) is incorrect as the passage says equating material satisfaction with progress neither spells peace nor progress. Option (c) is not the correct choice as the ideal of trusteeship doesn't mean voluntary remuneration of possessive instinct. Also, remuneration is incorrect with respect to the passage; the word should have been renunciation. Option (*d*) is incorrect. Material values should be substituted by spiritual values.

**113.** c The given passage talks about the legal systems of the United Stated and England and how different they are in their use of legal reasons. Therefore, option (c) is the correct answer. The passage doesn't talk of any similarities and differences between the legal systems of England and the United States, except that in their use of legal reasons. Hence, option (*a*) is incorrect. Option (*b*) is incorrect since the author uses examples not to re-evaluate the legal systems per se but to explain the use of substantive and formal reasons in their respective legal systems. Option (*d*) is incorrect as the passage doesn't talk of the development of legal reasoning in general but only as limited to England and the United States.

**114.** d In the first paragraph of the passage, the author tells us that formal reasons are more common in England than substantive reasons. Then the author goes on to describe what he means by formal reasons and as an example, says in the third paragraph that according to the laws that are followed in England, if a document fails to conform to the rules that have been specified, then the court has a right to make the document legally ineffective. So, it can be clearly inferred that the English judges would find the Veteran's group guilty because they have clearly violated the "stipulated requirements", which stated that no vehicles should be taken into public parks. Hence, option (*d*) is the correct answer.

**115.** d All of the first three options are circumstances under which the substantive arguments will not be considered as none of the options give valid reasons for the Will to be considered enforceable. Only option (*d*) is a circumstance when the Will may be considered valid without a written witness, since it is a case of a Judge allowing for a verbal witness during a medical emergency.

**116.** a The last paragraph of the passage describes what has happened as a result of following the extreme forms of legal reasoning (substantive reasons and formal reasons) in England and the United States. Therefore, option (*a*) is the correct answer.

**117.** c Option (c) is the correct answer. Refer to the line, "Once the legal rule.and the legality of the rule is not in question.". This clearly suggests that in case the legality of a rule is in question, substantive reasons might be warranted.

**118.** d The authors makes use of option (*a*) – comparison and contrast, when he talks about the different legal reasons that are used in England and the United States – formal reasons and substantive reasons respectively. He then goes on to use option (c) by describing these terms in separate paragraphs. The author also uses the process of generalization in the passage, especially in the second paragraph, when he gives the example of a statute and concludes the fact that most of the judges in the United States would find the defendants not guilty, based on a few facts and what is known about legal system in the United States. Option (*d*) – a chronology of the historical developments, is nowhere used in the passage and hence, it is the correct answer.

**119.** b The whole passage deals with governance and how the ruling class controls education to maintain it. Option (*a*) is unlikely to be the answer because it does not talk about rights while the phrase 'The Divine right Theory' contains the word. Option (*c*) and (*d*) are unlikely answers because they do not talk about governance. Therefore, option (*b*) turns out to be the best of all answer choices and is hence the correct answer.

**120.** b Refer to the following lines in the passage – "During the Renaissance, education passed.into the hands of the prince..Under the control of the monarch, education.".. From this, we can infer that the prince or the monarch ruled during the Renaissance. Hence, option (*b*) is correct.

**121.** d Refer to the following lines – "These gospels and teachings were no other than a philosophy for the maintenance of the existing society. It taught the poor man to be meek and to earn his bread with the sweat of his brow, while the priests and the landlords lived in luxury and fought duels for the slightest offence." From this, we can infer that the poor man was taught to serve the rich, who lived in luxury. Therefore, option (*b*) is correct. All other options are incorrect because the passage gives no evidence to support them.

**122.** b Refer to the following lines from the passage – "During the Christian era, the ecclesiastics controlled the institution of education and diffused among the people the gospel of the Bible and religious teachings." Ecclesiastics mean a priest or clergymen. Therefore, option (*b*) is the correct answer.

**123.** c 'Infallibility' means never wrong; never making mistakes. Therefore, option (*c*) is correct.

**124.** a The idiom 'sweat of one's brow' means by one's hard work. Therefore, option (*a*) is correct.

**125.** a The phrase 'Laissez Faire' means the policy of allowing private businesses to develop without government control. Therefore, option (*a*) is correct.

**126.** a Options (*c*) and (*d*) are clearly incorrect because nothing in the passage tells us that the author is aggressive or frustrated. Out of options (*a*) and (*b*), (*a*) is better of the two because the author appears concerned about the idea that education had always been a puppet that the ruling class could exploit to maintain their governance and rule. Phrases like "handmaid of the ruling class", "while the landlords.fought duels for the slightest offence" and "restricting the function of the state to a mere keeping of laws" somewhere suggests that the author is voicing his opinion about the matter. Moreover, 'unconcerned' shows 'lack of care because the topic is unimportant' and therefore, it has a slight negative connotation. So, option (*a*) appears to be the correct answer and not option (B); the answer is contentious nevertheless.

**127.** b 'Gospel' means a set of ideas that somebody believes in and tries to persuade others to accept. Therefore, option (*b*) is the correct answer. Option (*d*) is incorrect because it is vague and incomplete.

**128.** c 'Vogue' means a fashion for something. Therefore, option (*c*) is correct.

**129.** c The passage begins by stating what felony-murder rule is, what its proponents have to say in its favour but what is the real strength of the argument of its opponents is -the rule oft times is bizarre and unfair and so, owing to this, it is dying a slow but certain death. So, overall the passage states that the rule at times can be a faulty/unfair. Hence, option (*c*) is the correct answer. Option (*b*) is incorrect because although as per the passage it is true, it is not the passage's central theme. Although the answer key released with NLUD 2014 actual question paper says that the answer is option (*a*), option (*a*) is rather incorrect because the passage nowhere puts down his own opinion regarding the rule.

**130.** c Look at the fourth sentence of the second paragraph. It says that courts developed the "felony-murder" rule in order to deter the use of deadly forces. Hence, option (*c*) is the correct answer.

**131.** d Option (*a*) an be inferred by the first sentence of the third paragraph. It says that felony demonstrates a lack of concern for human life. It further says that crime is murder either because of a conclusive presumption of malice or by force of statutory definition. Option (*b*) can be inferred from the first paragraph of the passage, which states that the first formal statement of the rule said that any felony that involved killing was a murder and this rule was developed to deter people from using deadly force. This implies that option (*c*) can also be inferred. Option (*d*) is the answer as it is one of the objections raised by the opponents of the rule.

**132.** d Options (*a*) and (*c*) can be inferred from the third paragraph.It says that unfair results were achieved when rules were applied mechanically.

It further says that defendants have been convicted even when the killing was accidental. For example: if a person dies of heart attack 15-20 minutes after the robbery, the defendant is prosecuted. The last paragraph says that vicarious criminal liability should be restricted and limited. From this statement, option (*b*) can be inferred. Only option (*d*) cannot be from the opponents of felony - murder rule because it speaks in favour of felony - murder rule. Hence, option (*d*) is the answer.

**133.** b According to the passage, a defendant is charged of murder if death happens whether or not he intents to kill. In options (*a*), (*c*) and (*d*), the action of the defendant results in the death of innocent people. Therefore, the defendant is liable to charge of murder. Death does not occur in option (*b*) and hence, it is the answer.

**134.** d The passage states that "the rule has been abandoned in England where it originated, abolished in India, severely restricted in Canada and a number of other commonwealth countries, is unknown in continental Europe, and abandoned in Michigan". So, we can say that the felony - murder rule has not been abandoned in Canada but severely restricted there. Hence, option (*d*) is the correct answer. Option (*a*) is incorrect only in case the phrase 'is unknown in continental Europe' is understood to mean that the rule was abandoned so long back in time in continental Europe that it is unknown there. Otherwise, this question has two correct answers.

**135.** b Refer to the following sentence from the passage, "In reality the real strength of the opponent's criticism stems from the bizarre and of times unfair results achieved when the felony - murder rule is applied mechanically." From this, we can say that the author perceives that at times the rule is bizarre and unfair and hence, option (*b*) is the correct answer. Option (*d*) is incorrect because the author does not state that equating the intent to commit a felony and the intent to commit murder is unfair but that the rule overall is unfair at times.

**136.** c The passage talks about the role higher education plays in the development of the India, the quiet crisis in higher education in India and the challenges that impede the process of improvement and the spread of higher education in the country. Hence, option (*c*) is the correct answer.

**137.** b The passage analyzes and criticizes the existence of insufficient number of Universities to provide higher education in India and also states that the quality of education provided in most of them is not up to the mark. Hence, option (*b*) is the correct answer. Option (*a*) is incorrect because the theme/content of the passage is academic but the manner/style in which the passage is written cannot be called academic.

**138.** d Refer to the following sentence from the fourth paragraph, "It is only an inclusive society that can provide the foundations for a knowledge society." Hence, option (*d*) is the correct answer.

**139.** a Option (*a*) is incorrect because the first paragraph of the passage describes IITs and IIMs as "islands of excellence". Therefore, option (*a*) is the correct answer. Option (*b*) is true as evidenced from the following sentence of the second paragraph, "The proportion of our population.that enters the world of higher education is around 7 per cent, which is only one half the average of Asia." Option (*c*) is true as the passage talks about the importance of primary and higher education being essential for the growth of a country.

**140.** c The passage describes the sorry state of affairs concerning higher education in India and the need for improvement in this field. Hence, option (*c*) is the correct answer.

**141.** d Option (*d*) is false because it is not mentioned anywhere in the passage. Hence, it is the correct answer. All other options are true because the passage states the need of existence of excellent institutes, massive expansion of opportunities and substantial improvement in the quality of higher education.

**142.** d Options (*a*), (*b*) and (*c*) are all correct because the passage states that "primary education is absolutely essential because it is the base", "universities are the life-blood of higher education" and "transformation of economy and society in the 21st century would depend, in significant part, on the quality of education .particularly in the sphere of higher education". Hence, option (*d*) is the correct answer.

**143.** c Refer to the following sentence from the first paragraph, "Islands of excellence in professional education, such as Indian Institutes of Technology (IITs) and Indian Institutes of Management (IIMs), are valuable complements but cannot be substitutes for universities which provide educational opportunities for people at large." From this, we can infer that the passage states that not all universities should be modeled on these premier institutes. Hence, option (*c*) is the correct answer.

**144.** a 'Cutting Edge' means highly advanced; innovative or pioneering. So, 'conventional' is its apt antonym. Hence, option (*a*) is the correct answer.

**145.** b 'Discernible' means visible or noticeable. Hence, option (*b*) is the correct answer.

# REASONING

# 1

# VERBAL LOGIC

## CRITICAL REASONING

**Directions for questions 1 to 76:** The questions in this section are based on the reasoning contained in brief statements or passages. For some questions, more than one of the choices could conceivably answer the question. However, you are to choose the **best** answer, that is, the response that most accurately and completely answers the question. You should not make assumptions that are by commonsense standards implausible, superfluous or incompatible with the passage.

**1.** In France, children in pre-school programs spend a portion of each day engaged in a program of stretching and exercise. Pre-school programs in the United States, however, seldom devote time to a daily stretching and exercise program. In tests designed to measure cardiovascular fitness, children in the United States were out-performed by their French counterparts. It can therefore be determined that children attending pre-school programs in the United States can achieve cardiovascular fitness only by engaging in a daily school program of stretching and exercise.

Which one of the following is an assumption on which the argument depends?

(*a*) A daily program of stretching and exercise will allow all children to achieve cardiovascular fitness.

(*b*) Cardiovascular fitness is integral to one's overall health.

(*c*) It has been proven that children who participate in stretching and exercise programs in pre-school have better cardiovascular fitness than adults.

(*d*) Stretching and exercise are necessary components of French children's superior cardiovascular fitness programs. **(AILET, 2008)**

**2.** The level of blood sugar for many patients suffering from disease Q is slightly higher than the level of blood sugar in the general population. Nonetheless, most medical professionals believe that slightly increasing blood sugar levels is a successful means by which to treat disease Q.

This apparently contradictory argument can best be resolved by which one of the following statements?

(*a*) Blood sugar levels for patients who have been cured of disease Q are virtually identical to the level of blood sugar found in the general population.

(*b*) Many of the symptoms associated with severe cases of disease Q have been recognized in laboratory animals with experimentally induced high blood pressure, but none of the animals developed disease Q.

(*c*) The movement from inactive to advanced states of disease Q often occurs because the virus that causes Q flourishes during periods when blood sugar levels are slightly low.

(*d*) The blood sugar level in patients with disease Q fluctuates abnormally in response to changes in blood chemistry. **(AILET, 2008)**

**3.** Medical studies indicate that the metabolic rates of professional athletes are substantially greater than those of the average person. So, most likely, a person's speed and strength are primarily determined by that person's metabolic rate.

Which one of the following, if true, most strengthens the argument?

(*a*) Some professional athletes are either faster or stronger than the average person.

(*b*) Some professional athletes do not have higher metabolic rates than some people who are not professional athletes.

(*c*) The speed and strength of people who are not professional athletes are not primarily determined by choices of diet and exercise.

(*d*) Drugs that suppress metabolic rates have been shown to have the side-effect of diminishing the speed and strength of those who are not professional athletes. **(AILET, 2008)**

**4.** Since Oscar received extensive training in how to repair motorcycles, he is able to repair many of their most common mechanical problems. However, Oscar does not understand how internal combustion engines work. When Oscar was given Lucy's motorcycle to repair, he was able to fix the problem, despite the fact that he did not understand what was causing it.

From the above paragraph, which of the following can be properly inferred?

(*a*) The problem with Lucy's motorcycle involved its engine

(*b*) Not all mechanical problems can be repaired only by mechanics who understand how an internal combustion engine works

(*c*) At least some good mechanics are able to fix mechanical problems without an understanding of what is causing them

(*d*) Oscar's mechanical training in how to repair motorcycles was incomplete **(AILET, 2008)**

**5.** It cannot be true that the lack of success of third-party candidates in national elections is due to the difficulties such candidates encounter in securing space on national ballots. Everyone who identifies him or herself as a supporter of a third party has voted for a major-party candidate in at least one national election when a third-party candidate was listed on the ballot.

Which one of the following most accurately describes a reasoning flaw in the argument?

(*a*) The argument overlooks the possibility that the lack of success of third-party candidates in national elections may be due to the fact that their views on major issues prevent them from gaining broad support

(*b*) The argument takes for granted that the media coverage devoted to third-party candidates for national office is comparable to that devoted to major-party candidates for those same offices

(*c*) The argument treats as contradictory to some claim evidence that may instead provide support for that claim

(*d*) The argument draws its conclusion through the use of a set of facts, not all of which can be true **(AILET, 2008)**

**6. Consumer advocate:** Businesses are typically motivated primarily by the desire to make as great a profit as possible, and advertising helps business to achieve this goal. But it is clear that the motive of maximizing profits does not impel businesses to present accurate information in their advertisements. It follows that consumers should be skeptical of the claims made in advertisements.

Each of the following if true would strengthen the Consumer advocate's argument EXCEPT:

(*a*) Businesses know that they can usually maximize their profits by using inaccurate information in their advertisements.

(*b*) Businesses have often included inaccurate information in their advertisement.

(*c*) Many consumers have a cynical attitude toward advertising.

(*d*) Those who create advertisements are less concerned with the accuracy than with the creativity of advertisements. **(AILET, 2009)**

**7. Science columnist:** It is clear why humans have so many diseases in common with cats. Many human diseases are genetically based, and cats are genetically closer to humans than are any other mammals except nonhuman primates. Each of the genes identified so far in cats has an exact counterpart in humans.

Which one of the following if true, most weakens the science columnist's explanation for the claim that humans have so many diseases in common with cats?

(*a*) Cats have built up resistance to many of the disease they have in common with humans.

(*b*) Most diseases that humans have in common with cats have no genetic basis.

(*c*) Cats have more diseases in common with nonhuman primates than with humans.

(*d*) Many of the diseases human have in common with cats are mild and are rarely diagnosed.

**(AILET, 2009)**

**8. Psychologist:** It is well known that becoming angry often induces temporary incidents of high blood pressure. A recent study further showed, however, that people who are easily angered are significantly more likely to have permanently high blood pressure than are people who have more tranquil personalities. Coupled with the long established fact that those with permanently high blood pressure are especially likely to have heart disease, the recent findings indicate that heart disease can result from psychological factors.

Which one of the following would, if true, most **weaken** the psychologist's argument?

(*a*) Those who are easily angered are less likely to recover fully from episodes of heart disease than are other people.

(*b*) Medication designed to control high blood pressure can greatly affect the moods of those who use it.

(*c*) People with permanently high blood pressure who have tranquil personalities virtually never develop heart disease.

(*d*) The physiological factors that cause permanently high blood pressure generally make people quick to anger. **(AILET, 2009)**

**9.** A professor of business placed a case-study assignment for her class on her university's computer network. She later found out that instead of reading the assignment on the computer screen. 50 out of the 70 students printed it out on paper. Thus, it is not the case that books delivered via computer will make printed books obsolete.

Which one of the following, if true, most strengthens the argument?

(*a*) Several colleagues of the professor have found that, in their non-business courses, several of their students behave similarly in relation to assignments placed on the computer network.

(*b*) Studies consistently show that most computer users will print reading material that is more than a few pages in length rather than read it on the computer screen.

(*c*) Some people get impaired vision from long periods of reading printed matter on computer screens, even if they use high quality computer screens.

(*d*) Scanning technology is very poor, causing books delivered via computer to be full of errors unless editors carefully read the scanned versions.

**(AILET, 2009)**

**10.** Till Nineties, clearly the policy of the government was guided by the philosophy of socialism. Under its influence, the government tried to exercise control in every field. But today we hear about disinvestment and privatization. Hence, there is a clear shift from socialistic principles.

Which one of the following assertions, if true, contradicts the passage mentioned above?

(*a*) That government is the best government which governs least.

(*b*) Only enterprise in a free society contributes to the real progress.

(*c*) Not withstanding the alleged merits of laissez-faire implicit in the passage, lack of effective control by the state results in the exploitation of many by a few.

(*d*) The state is guilty of the dereliction of duty.

**(AILET, 2010)**

**11.** Geographical division of the Earth resulting in the so-called sovereign nations is artificial because it is man-made, just as division of society on the basis of religion, language, caste, etc., is artificial. While the so-called intellectuals raise hue and cry about the latter, they maintain divine silence about the former. Does it not amount to double standard ?

Which of the following statements, if true, is the essence of the passage mentioned above?

(*a*) Geographical division of the Earth is of divine origin.

(*b*) Only division of society on the basis of religion, language, etc., is man-made.

(*c*) The response to geographical and sociological divisions are very different.

(*d*) Patriotism is a barren concept.

**[Option C in the original paper was "The consequences of geographical and sociological divisions are very different". As none of the options are matching with the question, option (c) has been changed to fit the sprit of the question.] (AILET, 2010)**

**12.** It is argued that prosperity depends upon production which means more production more consumption. However, it is not the case. Consumption should be need based. Just as intake of food in excess of digestion is pointless so also consumption of natural resources beyond requirement is pointless.

Which of the following statements, if true, contradicts the spirit of the passage?

(*a*) Prosperity without consumption is ideal.

(*b*) Prosperity without consumption is shallow.

(*c*) Prosperity is possible when natural resources are not abused.

(*d*) To increase consumption we cannot have any alibi. **(AILET, 2010)**

**13.** It is true that agriculture is the backbone of a nation's economy. But it is fallacious to argue that only agriculture should receive overriding importance. Agriculture also depends upon other sectors like generation and distribution of power, irrigation, transportation, etc. If any one sector suffers, its fall-out is more than obvious.

Which of the following assertions, if true, is the summary of the given passage?

(*a*) Budget allocation for all fields must be equal.

(*b*) If adequate budget allocation in any one fiscal year for every sector is not possible, then each year one sector can be provided with adequate funds.

(*c*) Budget allocation for each sector should be need based, neither less nor more, i.e.it should be optimum.

(*d*) Reversion to ancient method of farming is the only way out. **(AILET, 2010)**

**14.** Education is one field which is totally non-remunerative. Still worse, it is a liability. But then the government is not a money-making institution. The bottom-line of prosperity is primary education. Hence the government should raise resources elsewhere only to pour it on primary education. But primary education cannot be provided without higher education. So higher education stands on par with primary education.

Which of the following statements, if true, contradicts the passage above?

(*a*) Money should produce money which means that that which does not generate money has no place.

(*b*) Education should raise its own resources.

(*c*) Education should be made as economical as possible.

(*d*) If the government cannot spread education, private enterprise should step in. **(AILET, 2010)**

**15.** Soaking dried beans overnight before cooking them reduces cooking time. However, cooking without pre-soaking yields plumper beans. Therefore, when a bean dish's quality is more important than the need to cook that dish quickly, beans should not be pre-soaked.

Which one of the following is an assumption required by the argument?

(*a*) Plumper beans enhance the quality of a dish.

(*b*) There are no dishes whose quality improves with faster cooking.

(*c*) A dish's appearance is as important as its taste.

(*d*) None of the other ingredients in the dish need to be pre-soaked. **(AILET, 2011)**

**16.** Everyone in Biba's neighbourhood is permitted to swim at Barton Pool at some time during each day that it is open. No children under the age of 6 are permitted to swim at Barton Pool between noon and 5 P.M. From 5 P.M. until closing, BartonPool is reserved for adults only.

If all the sentences above are true, then which one of the following must be true ?

(*a*) Few children under the age of 6 live in Biba's neighbourhood.

(*b*) If Biba's next door neighbour has a child under the age of 6, then Barton Pool is open before noon.

(*c*) If most children who swim in Barton Pool swim in the afternoon, then the pool is generally less crowded after 5 P.M.

(*d*) On days when Barton Pool is open, at least some children swim there in the afternoon.

**(AILET, 2011)**

**17.** Zack's Coffeehouse schedules free poetry readings almost every Wednesday. Zack's offers half-priced coffee all day on every day that a poetry reading is scheduled.

Which one of the following can be properly inferred from the information above?

(*a*) Wednesday is the most common day on which Zack's offers half-priced coffee all day.

(*b*) Most free poetry readings given at Zack's are scheduled for Wednesdays.

(*c*) Free poetry readings are scheduled on almost every day that Zack's offers half-priced coffee all day.

(*d*) Zack's offers half-priced coffee all day on most, if not all, Wednesdays. **(AILET, 2011)**

**18.** It is time that begging must be forbidden in all public places in India. Exploitation of charitable instincts in general, far from solving the problem of poverty, may infact aggravate it by inducing laziness.

Which of the following, if true, would support the above reasoning?

(*a*) Destitution is the result of unwillingness to work.

(*b*) Most beggars are really poor.

(*c*) All poor people do not beg.

(*d*) None of the above **(AILET, 2011)**

**19.** Yoga has become a very popular type of exercise, but it may not be for everyone. Before you sign yourself up for a yoga class, you need to examine what is it you want from your fitness routine. If you're looking for a high-energy, fast-paced aerobic workout, a yoga class might not be your best choice.

This paragraph best supports the statement that

(*a*) Yoga is more popular than high-impact aerobics.

(*b*) Before embarking on a new exercise regimen, you should think about your needs and desires.

(*c*) Yoga is changing the world of fitness in major ways.

(*d*) Most people think that yoga isn't a rigorous form of exercise. **(AILET, 2011)**

**20.** Before Robert Norman worked on 'Dip and Field Concept', his predecessor thought that the tendency of the magnetic needle to swing towards the poles was due to a point attractive. However, Norman showed with the help of experiment that nothing like point attractive exists. Instead, he argued that magnetic power lies is lodestone.

Which one of the following is the problem on which Norman and others worked?

(*a*) Existence of point attractive

(*b*) Magnetic power in lodestone

(*c*) Magnetic power in needle

(*d*) Swinging of magnetic needle **(AILET, 2011)**

**21.** In his study of conduction of heat, James Maxwell observed that quantities which are significant in such a study are 'temperature, flow of heat and conductivity'. Further, he noticed that the mathematical laws of the uniform motion of heat in homogenous media are identical in form with those of attractions varying inversely as the square of the distance. He thought source of heat, flow of heat and temperature correspond respectively to centre of attraction, accelerating effect of attraction and potential. On this ground, Maxwell observed that conduction of heat proceeds by an action between contiguous parts of a medium.

Which one of the following best explains Maxwell's method?

(*a*) Mathematical calculation

(*b*) Analogy

(*c*) Observation

(*d*) Experiment **(AILET, 2011)**

**22.** Henry Poincare argued that in space there are not only rectilinear triangles in which angles equal to two right angles, but also curvilinear triangles in which angles are less than two right angles. He, further, maintained that to name the first one straight is to subscribe to Euclidean geometry and to name the latter straight is tantamount to subscribing to non-Euclidean system.

Which one of the following accurately represents what is at stake?

(*a*) Acceptability of Euclidean system

(*b*) Acceptability of Non-Euclidean system

(*c*) Confusion in Geometry

(*d*) Choice of the definition of straight line **(AILET, 2011)**

**23.** For one academic year, all the students at a high school were observed. The aim was to test the hypothesis that studying more increased a student's chances of earning a higher grade. It turned out that the students who spent the most time studying did not earn grades as high as did many students who studied less. Nonetheless, the researchers concluded that the results of the observation supported the initial hypothesis.

Which one of the following, if true, most helps to explain why the researchers drew the conclusion described above?

(*a*) The students who spent the most time studying earned higher grades than did some students who studied for less time than the average.

(*b*) The students tended to get slightly lower grades as the academic year progressed.

(*c*) In each course, the more a student studied, the better his or her grade was in that course.

(*d*) The students who spent the least time studying tended to be students with no more than average involvement in extracurricular activities. **(AILET, 2012)**

**24. Educator:** It has been argued that our professional organization should take decision about important issues - such as raising dues and taking political stands - by a direct vote of all members rather than by having members vote for officers who in turn make the decisions. This would not; however, be the right way to decide these matters, for the vote of any given individual is much more likely to determine organizational policy by influencing the election of an officer than by influencing the result of a direct vote on a single issue.

Which one of the following principles would, if valid, most help to justify the educator's reasoning?

(*a*) No procedure for making organizational decisions should allow one individual's vote to weigh more than that of another.

(*b*) Outcomes of organizational elections should be evaluated according to their benefit to the organization as a whole, not according to the fairness of the methods by which they are produced.

(*c*) Important issues facing organizations should be decided by people who can devote their full time to mastering the information relevant to the issues.

(*d*) An organization's procedures for making organizational decisions should maximize the power of each member of the organization to influence the decisions made. **(AILET, 2012)**

**25. Mayor:** Local anti-tobacco activists are calling for expanded antismoking education programs paid for by revenue from heavily increased taxes on cigarettes sold in the city. Although the effectiveness of such education programs is debatable, there is strong evidence that the taxes themselves would produce the sought-after reduction in smoking. Surveys show that cigarette sales drop substantially in cities that impose stiff tax increases on cigarettes.

Which one of the following, if true, most undermines the reasoning in the argument above?

(*a*) A city-imposed tax on cigarette will substantially reduce the amount of smoking in the city if the tax is burdensome to the average cigarette consumer.

(*b*) Consumers are more likely to continue buying a product if its price increases due to higher taxes than if its price increases for some other reason.

(*c*) Usually, cigarette sales will increase substantially in the areas surrounding a city after that city imposes stiff taxes on cigarettes.

(*d*) People who are well informed about the effects of long-term tobacco use are significantly less likely to smoke than are people who are not informed. **(AILET, 2012)**

**26. Gotera:** Infants lack the motor ability required to voluntarily produce particular sounds, but produce various babbling sounds randomly. Most children are several years old before they can voluntarily produce most of the vowel and consonant sounds of their language. We can conclude that speech acquisition is entirely a motor control process rather than a process that is abstract or mental.

Which one of the following is an assumption required by Gotera's argument?

(*a*) Speech acquisition is a function only of one's ability to produce the sounds of spoken language.

(*b*) During the entire initial babbling stage, infants cannot intentionally move their tongues while they are babbling.

(*c*) The initial babbling stage is completed during infancy.

(*d*) The initial babbling stage is the first stage of the speech acquisition process. **(AILET, 2012)**

**27.** Reducing stress lessens a person's sensitivity to pain. This is the conclusion reached by researchers who played extended audiotapes to patients before they underwent surgery and afterward while they were recovering. One tape consisted of conversation; the other consisted of music. Those who listened only to the latter tape required less anaesthesia during surgery and fewer painkillers afterward than those who listened only to the former tape.

Which one of the following is an assumption on which the researchers' reasoning depends?

(*a*) All of the patients in the study listened to the same tape before surgery as they listened to after surgery.

(*b*) Anticipating surgery is no less stressful than recovering from surgery.

(*c*) Listening to music reduces stress.

(*d*) The psychological effects of music are not changed by anaesthesia or painkillers. **(AILET, 2012)**

**28.** Political turmoil in a country is mainly caused by widespread violence and flawed economic policies of successive governments. If at all this has to be crushed, it can be achieved only by a dictatorial government which rules with iron hand. Therefore, the need of the hour is to elect a government which imposes fresh set of stringent legislations.

The alternatives suggested (not necessarily all), if true, considerably weaken the argument. However, one of them is most forceful. Identify the same.

(*a*) It is not the imposition of new legislations which is required, but effective adherence to the existing legislations.

(*b*) That government is the best government which governs least.

(*c*) It is possible to overcome any evil by educating people.

(*d*) Only dialogue in a free society can eradicate political turmoil. **(CLAT 2008)**

**29. Under the same fact situation as above,** the alternatives suggested (not necessarily all), if true, significantly strengthen the argument. However, one of them is most forceful. Identify the same.

(*a*) Espionage activities by enemy nations, which contribute to political turmoil, can be prevented only if the government is very strong.

(*b*) The philosophy behind any economic policy, 'push from bottom, press from top' is to be followed to mitigate violence, and it is not observed.

(*c*) Political turmoil is due to corrupt establishment.

(*d*) Man is, by nature, a beast. **(CLAT 2008)**

**30.** Exploitation of poor by rich can be stemmed only if the state exercises complete control over agriculture and industrial production. But state control is beset by two evils; corruption and delay. The net result is that if man tries to escape from one evil, then he is trapped by another. Suffering, hence, is inescapable.

The argument presented above seems to imply the following conclusions. Identify the one which is least dubious. Apply common sense.

(*a*) If agriculture and industrial production can be abolished, we can free ourselves from all forms of evil.

(*b*) To avoid evil austere life shall be encouraged.

(*c*) The gap between poor and rich can be bridged by heavily taxing the rich and passing on the largesse to the poor.

(*d*) Man is, by nature, dishonest. **(CLAT 2008)**

**31.** That the human soul is immaterial is an undisputed fact. Significantly, what is not matter is not spatial and consequently, it is not vulnerable to motion. Evidently, no motion no dissolution. What escapes from dissolution is also free from corruptibility. Therefore, the human soul is immortal.

In this argument, one premise is missing. Complete the argument by choosing from the following:

(*a*) Nothing is free from dissolution

(*b*) What is incorruptible is immortal

(*c*) There is no motion

(*d*) Matter does not exist **(CLAT 2008)**

**32. Under the same fact situation as above,** which one of the following, if true, affects seriously the argument presented above?

(*a*) Matter is not bound by space

(*b*) Matter is indestructible

(*c*) Whatever exists is not necessarily affected by motion.

(*d*) What is not matter also is vulnerable to motion.

**(CLAT 2008)**

**33.** Protagonists of human rights vehemently oppose capital punishment. Their opposition stems mainly from three reasons. Firstly, man cannot terminate what he cannot generate. Secondly, the function of punishment is to reform the culprit. Thirdly, a culprit should be given an opportunity to repent. Admittedly, death penalty fails on all three counts. However, the defenders argue that a person is punished because he has to pay for his deeds. Reformation or repentance, according to them, is peripheral. Hence, death penalty is admissible.

Which one of the following is the focus of this debate?

(*a*) Man's rights and privileges

(*b*) Nature and purpose of punishment

(*c*) Prevention of crime

(*d*) Mercy and revenge **(CLAT 2008)**

**34.** Since Venus rotates slowly, Fred Whipple thought that like Mercury, Venus keeps one face always towards the Sun. If so, he said that the dark side would be very cold. However, he knew with the help of earlier study carried out by Petit and Nicholson that it was not the case. So, he concluded that the planet must rotate fairly often to keep the darker side warmer.

Which of the following is the original premise?

(*a*) Slow rotation of Venus

(*b*) Temperature of Venus.

(*c*) Frequent rotation of Venus

(*d*) Equality of the rate of rotation and revolution.

**(CLAT 2008)**

**35.** Before formulating the laws of motion, Galileo distinguished between mathematical study and empirical study. He, first, theoretically derived the relation between distances and times for uniformly accelerating motion by letting the ball roll a quarter, then half, then two-thirds and so on of the length of the groove and then measured the times on each occasion, which he repeated hundred times. He calculated, based on this study, that the distance travelled equalled the square of the time on all occasions.

Which one of the following characterizes Galileo's method?

(*a*) Speculation (*b*) Theoretical analysis

(*c*) Generalization (*d*) Statistical analysis

**(CLAT 2008)**

**36.** Read carefully a brief summary of one of the investigations of Sherlock Holmes: "While investigating the murders of Stangerson and Enoch Drebber he got into conversation with fellow detectives which runs as follows: "The last link...... My case is complete.... Could you lay your hands upon those pills". After he got those pills, Holmes cut one of them, dissolved it in water and placed it in front of the terrier. Contrary to his expectations, the animal survived. Though disappointed a bit, he thought for a while and then cut the other pill, dissolved it, added milk and placed before the animal. The moment it licked, the animal died. Those were the pills present at the scenes of crime.

Which one of the following aptly describes the method which this passage indicates?

(*a*) Imagination (*b*) Experiment

(*c*) Observation (*d*) Thought experiment

**(CLAT 2008)**

**37.** There has been much speculation concerning the origin of lunar craters. One hypothesis is that they are the results of the impact of heavy meteors on the surface of the moon while still soft. The most probable explanation is that they were produced by the gases liberated from the rocky matter. While solidification was taking place these gases and water vapors steadily escaped through viscous surface, raising giant bubbles. The reader can easily visualize the process that took place by watching frying of pancakes and noticing the formation of bubbles and craters on their surface.

Which one of the following actually helps us to determine the origin of lunar craters?

(*a*) Analogy

(*b*) Study of foreign body

(*c*) Course and effect relation

(*d*) Speculation **(CLAT 2008)**

38. "Perhaps the earliest work of Archimedes that we have is that on 'Plane Equilibrium'. In this, some fundamental principles of mechanics are set forth as rigorous geometric propositions. The work opens with famous postulate 'Equal weights at equal distances are in equilibrium; equal weights at unequal distances are not in equilibrium, but incline toward the weight at the greater distance".

According to this passage, which factor or factors determine equilibrium?

(*a*) weight

(*b*) distance

(*c*) weight & distance

(*d*) equality of weights & distances **(CLAT 2008)**

39. **According to the above passage,** which one of the following values can be assigned to the statement inequal weights at equal distances are in disequilibrium?

(*a*) true (*b*) false

(*c*) highly probable (*d*) highly improbable

**(CLAT 2008)**

40. **According to the above passage,** which one of the following values can be assigned to the statement 'inequal weights at inequal distances are in disequilibrium'?

(*a*) true (*b*) false

(*c*) uncertain (*d*) unverifiable

**(CLAT 2008)**

41. 'Gregor Mendel in examining tea-plants found two sharply marked races, the tall and the short. He experimentally fertilized flowers of tall plants with pollen of short. The off spring were tall plants. He next let the flowers of this first generation be fertilized with their own pollen. In the following generation, shortness reappeared. Tallness and shortness were distributed not at random but in a definite, constant, and simple ratio: three dominant talls to one recessive short'.

Which one of the following aptly describes the distribution of dominant and recessive characteristics?

(*a*) systematic (*b*) equal interval

(*c*) unpredictable (*d*) irregular interval

**(CLAT 2008)**

42. It is said that in his strongly worded reaction to quantum Physics, Einstein remarks 'God does not play dice' to which Bohr, another great physicist, reacted saying 'Do not tell God what to do'. Bohr, earlier had argued that we can never know what the properties of an isolated quantum system, though we can know the properties of macrocosmic objects.

Which one of the following is the focus of their debate?

(*a*) the behaviour of God

(*b*) probabilistic interpretation of the behaviour of quantum object

(*c*) limits of human knowledge

(*d*) irrelevance of microcosmic object

**(CLAT 2008)**

43. An efficient and diesel-independent public transport system is essential to the economic development of nation. Suppose that the government adopts a policy to that effect, then there is another favorable result. The pollution of environment is reduced to a greater extent. But, then it has two-pronged backlash. The sale and consequently the production of two and four wheelers reduce to the minimum which in turn render a large number of people jobless. Cash flow to the treasury also is adversely affected. Such a step, therefore, is self-defeating unless the government evolves a counter-strategy to nullify the adverse effects.

Which one of the following accurately projects the opinion of an imaginary speaker or author, as the case may be, of this passage?

(*a*) Abandon the idea of efficient and diesel-independent public transport system.

(*b*) Ensure sustained cash flow and create better job opportunities by inventing an alternate or more than one alternate.

(*c*) Public transport system shall be given up.

(*d*) Maintain production and sale at the same level by offering incentives. **(CLAT 2008)**

44. A moot question to be considered is whether democratic form of government is a boon or bane, no matter what Lincoln might or might not have said. Rather his most (in?) famous adage, 'by the people, for the people and of the people' misses the most pertinent question; which attitude works behind when a person declares that he is a (or the right?) candidate to serve the people, and does not hesitate to contest and fight tooth and nail the election, an euphemism for battle with or without bullets. Admittedly, the covert attitude is different from overt attitude. Hardly any one contests the election unwillingly. A contestant is not persuaded by any one, but driven by his own passions and dubious motives. Contrast this picture with Socrates' version; no honest man willingly takes up the job of ruler. If at all he accepts, he does so for fear of being ruled by one made up of inferior mettle. It is beyond even the wildest imagination, to expect an honest person to contest the election.

Assuming that every statement is true, identify from among the given alternatives the one which strictly follows from the passage.

(*a*) No assessment or appraisal of democracy is possible.

(*b*) Lincoln and Socrates are talking differently.

(*c*) Actually, Socrates scores over Lincoln on this issue.

(*d*) Rulers can be honest. **(CLAT 2008)**

**45.** According to the above passage, which one of the following correctly differentiates Lincoln's and Socrates' analyses?

(*a*) the nature of democracy

(*b*) merits and demerits of politicians

(*c*) qualities of election

(*d*) difference in mind set of respective men **(CLAT 2008)**

**46.** Many environmentalists either adopt double standard or do not know what they are talking about. A protagonist of environment, for obvious reasons, ought not to bat for any type of progress because progress without meddling with nature is a myth. But none can live without scientific and technological advance which has singularly made progress possible. Furthermore, environment includes not just forest wealth and hills, but animal wealth also. An honest environmentalist is obliged to address the following questions. First, should man in the interest of hygiene, kill any living being be it an insect purported to be harmful or stray dogs? After all, this world does not belong to man alone.

Which one of the following runs counter to the spirit of the passage?

(*a*) In the interest of health and cleanliness, our surroundings must be from disease-spreading bacteria

(*b*) Non-violence as a moral principle extends to all living creatures

(*c*) Vegetarian food is ideal to all men

(*d*) Man should protect his environment because he has to live **(CLAT 2008)**

**47.** Does our society need reservation in jobs? Before we defend reservation, we must consider some issues. Why do we need reservation? Obviously, reservation is required to lift the downtrodden and thereby achieve equality. How do you achieve this? Every individual, without exception, has a right to receive quality education. It is more so in the case of downtrodden people. Only a good-natured meritorious teacher can impart quality education. Suppose that a person who is neither good natured nor meritorious becomes a teacher thanks to reservation system. Then generations of students suffer.

Suppose that there is some merit in this argument. Then which of the following aptly describes the fall-out of this argument?

(*a*) Reservation is individual - centric, but not group - centric

(*b*) Reservation, in at least one field, is self-defeating

(*c*) The argument is biased

(*d*) Education is not required to uplift the downtrodden **(CLAT 2008)**

**48.** Under the same fact situation as above, which one of the following helps you to circumvent the situation?

(*a*) Replace education with money and make poor rich.

(*b*) To achieve equality encourage inter-caste marriage.

(*c*) Only downtrodden people should form the government.

(*d*) Identify good natured and meritorious people within downtrodden group to make them teachers. **(CLAT 2008)**

**49.** 'China has a higher literacy rate than India. This is due to the greater efficiency of the Communist system. Efficiency is sorely lacking in India's democratic system. Therefore, democracy is the biggest obstacle to India's achieving 100% literacy.'

Which of the following, *if true*, would directly undermine the above argument?

(*a*) Inefficiency is equally a problem in democracies and Communist countries.

(*b*) Communist systems do not respect human rights.

(*c*) Freedom is more important than literacy.

(*d*) China is slowly making the transition to democracy. **(CLAT 2011)**

**50.** 'In 399 BC, a jury in Athens condemned Socrates to death for impiety and corrupting the morals of the youth. Socrates' friends offered to help him escape, but Socrates refused. Socrates argued that the fact that he had lived in Athens for so many years meant that he had committed himself to obeying its laws. It would therefore be wrong for him to break those very laws he was implicitly committed to obeying.'

Which one of the following claims constitutes the most plausible challenge to Socrates' argument?

(*a*) Long residence only commits someone to obeying just laws and Socrates was convicted under an unjust law.

(*b*) Long residence by itself does not imply a commitment to obeying laws since one never made any explicit commitment.

(*c*) Obedience to the law is not always required.

(*d*) There is no point in escaping from prison since one will anyway be captured again. **(CLAT 2011)**

**51.** 'Soft drinks have been shown by scientists to be bad for the teeth. Therefore, the government would be justified in banning all soft drinks from the Indian market.'

Assuming that the factual claim in the above argument is true, what else needs to be assumed for the conclusion to follow?

(*a*) The government is justified in banning anything that is bad for dental health.

(*b*) Soft drinks are also bad for gastric health.

(*c*) Dental hygiene is a matter of great concern.

(*d*) No further assumptions are necessary.

**(CLAT 2011)**

**52.** 'In order to be eligible for election to the Lok Sabha, a person must be at least 25 years of age. Moreover, one must not be bankrupt. Therefore, Jatinder Singh, over 50 years of age and without any criminal convictions, cannot be the Speaker of the Lok Sabha since he has just filed for bankruptcy.'

Which of the following must be assumed for the conclusion to follow logically?

(*a*) Anyone over 50 years of ago is eligible to be Speaker of the Lok Sabha as long as he or she has no criminal convictions.

(*b*) People without criminal convictions cannot be elected to the Lok Sabha even if they are not bankrupt.

(*c*) Only those eligible for election to the Lok Sabha are eligible to be the Speaker of the Lok Sabha.

(*d*) There is no minimum age requirement for the Speaker of the Lok Sabha. **(CLAT 2011)**

**53**** 'As a century draws to a close, people start behaving much like people coming to the end of a long life. People approaching death often start reflecting on the events of their lives. Similarly, people alive in 1999 ______,

Which of the following most logically completes the paragraph above?

(*a*) ... started reflecting on the events of the twentieth century.

(*b*) ... started to reflect on the events of their lives.

(*c*) ... started to fear death.

(*d*) ... started to wonder what the year 2000 would bring. **(CLAT 2011)**

**54.** 'The Roman poet and philosopher Lucretius proposed the following thought experiment. If the universe has a boundary, we can throw a spear at this boundary. If the spear flies through, then it is not a boundary. If the spear bounces back, there must be something beyond this boundary that is itself in space, which means it is not a boundary at all. Either way, it turns out that the universe has no boundary.'

How best can the form of Lucretius' argument for the infinity of space be described?

(*a*) Lucretius shows that positing finite space leads to a contradiction.

(*b*) Lucretius shows that finite space is inconsistent with physics.

(*c*) Lucretius shows that finite space is inconsistent with mathematics.

(*d*) Lucretius shows that finite space is inconceivable.

**(CLAT 2011)**

**55.** 'Utilitarians believe that the right action is that which produces the most happiness.'

Which of the following claims is *incompatible* with the utilitarian view?

(*a*) The right thing to do is to make the consequences of our actions as good as possible.

(*b*) The right thing to do is to do our duty, whatever the consequences.

(*c*) The right thing to do is to act on a rule which, if followed widely, produces the most happiness.

(*d*) The right thing to do is to act from motivations which produce the most happiness.

**(CLAT 2011)**

**56.** 'Senthil goes to Ambala for the first time in his life. On the way from the railway station to his hotel, he sees twelve people, all of them male. He concludes that there are no women in Ambala. As a matter of fact, there are many thousands of women in Ambala.'

Which of the following best describes Senthil's error?

(*a*) Senthil was misled by irrelevant details.

(*b*) Senthil generalised on the basis of insufficient evidence.

(*c*) Senthil was biased against women.

(*d*) Senthil was bad at counting. **(CLAT 2011)**

**57.** 'It took many centuries before the countries of Europe could resolve their internal problems of violence and corruption to become the stable nation-states they are. Therefore, it will take many centuries for India to achieve internal stability.'

Assuming that the factual claims in the argument above are true, what must be assumed in order for the conclusion to follow?

(*a*) Countries everywhere must follow the same paths towards stability.

(*b*) India is gradually progressing towards internal stability.

(*c*) Indian can learn how to achieve stability by studying Europe's example.

(*d*) India has no hope of achieving stability in the near future. **(CLAT 2011)**

**Passage for questions 58-60**

'Instead of being concerned with what actually happens in practice ... [economics] is increasingly preoccupied with developing pseudo-mathematical formulas. These provide models of behaviour which never quite fit what actually happens, in a way which resembles the physical sciences gone wrong: instead of equations describing reality, economics produces equations describing ideal conditions and theoretical clarity of a type which never occurs in practice'.

**58.** Which of the following best summarises the argument of this paragraph?

(*a*) Economics ought to be more like the physical sciences.

(*b*) Theoretical clarity is undesirable in economics.

(*c*) The physical sciences are wrong to emphasise mathematic formulae.

(*d*) The mathematical equations used by economists do not accurately describe the real world. **(CLAT 2011)**

**59.** Which of the following claims is *not* implied in the paragraph above?

(*a*) Economists should stop using mathematical models.

(*b*) Equations describing ideal conditions should not be mistaken for equations describing reality.

(*c*) Theoretical clarity should not come at the expense of accuracy.

(*d*) Models of human behaviour should be true to the complexity of human nature. **(CLAT 2011)**

**60.** Which of the following, *if true*, would most *weaken* the argument of the passage above?

(*a*) The physical sciences are themselves reducing their reliance on mathematical formulae.

(*b*) The real world in fact closely approximates ideal theoretical conditions.

(*c*) We do not at present have the mathematical expertise to model the full complexity of the world economy.

(*d*) Academic economists need to be more sensitive to human nature. **(CLAT 2011)**

**Passage for questions 61-62**

'Religions, like camel caravans, seem to avoid mountain passes. Buddhism spread quickly south from Buddha's birth-place in southern Nepal across the flat Gangetic plain to Sri Lanka. But it took a millennium to reach China ... The religious belt stretched eventually to Mongolia and Japan, but in Afghanistan Buddhism filled only a narrow belt that left pagans among the valleys to the east and west in Kailash and Ghor'.

**61.** Which of the following best summarises the subject of this paragraph?

(*a*) The Afghan people were hostile to Buddhism.

(*b*) Geography has considerable impact on the spread of religions.

(*c*) Buddhism does not flourish in mountainous regions.

(*d*) Religion has a considerable impact on geography. **(CLAT 2011)**

**62.** Which of the following, if true, would most *weaken* the conclusion to the above argument?

(*a*) Christianity took several centuries to cross the Atlantic Ocean to America.

(*b*) The Hindukush mountains made no difference to the speed with which Islam spread.

(*c*) Buddhism is strongest in mountainous regions.

(*d*) Jainism is less popular in cold climates. **(CLAT 2011)**

**Passage for questions 63-64**

'Friendship was indeed a value for the villagers, more for men than for women. Two good friends were said to be 'like brothers' (literally, 'like elder brother-younger brother', *annatammandirahage*). I heard this expression several times and I could not help recalling the statement of an elderly English colleague who had told me that he and his brother were very close and had written to each other every week. He had added, 'We are very good friends.' That is, friendship connoted intimacy in England while in Rampura (as in rural India everywhere), brotherhood conveyed intimacy'.

**63.** Which of the following best summarises the conclusion of the argument of this paragraph?

(*a*) Friendship has greater value for men than for women.

(*b*) People in England have different attitudes to brotherhood and friendship than people in rural India.

(*c*) Brotherhood has greater value in rural India than in England.

(*d*) Friendship has greater value in England than in India. **(CLAT 2011)**

**64.** Which of the following, if true, would directly *contradict* the conclusion of the above argument?

(*a*) People are less likely to have large families in England.

(*b*) People in England are no longer close to their family members.

(*c*) People in England do not think that friendship connotes intimacy.

(*d*) People in rural India think that sisters cannot be intimate. **(CLAT 2011)**

**Passage for questions 65-66**

'A language is most easily learnt when it is in tune with the social context. To teach an Indian child in English at the primary stage ... strengthens distinctions of class and status and warps the mind. Failure to resort to regional languages in literacy campaigns also hampers their success'.

**65.** Which of the following best summarises the argument of the passage above?

(*a*) Learning English warps the mind.

(*b*) Language policy should be devised with an eye to social context.

(*c*) Literacy campaigns in India have failed.

(*d*) English should be taught at the secondary school level. **(CLAT 2011)**

**66.** Which of the following claims, if true, would *weaken* the argument in the passage above?

(*a*) Literacy campaigns are more successful when conducted in English.

(*b*) Learning English at an early age has been found to weaken class distinctions.

(*c*) Children who learn English at the primary-school stage have been found to show greater intellectual ability than those who learn English only at the secondary level.

(*d*) All of the above. **(CLAT 2011)**

**Passage for questions 67-69**

'The tribes should develop their own culture and make their contribution to the cultural richness of the country. It is unnecessary to cause them to change their customs, habits or diversions so far as to make themselves indistinguishable from other classes. To do so would be to rob rural and pastoral life of its colour and stimulating diversity'.

**67.** Which of the following conclusions is *not* implied by the passage above?

(*a*) It is good for India's tribal people to develop their culture.

(*b*) Tribal customs should not be allowed to change in any respect.

(*c*) Forcing tribal people to change their customs reduces the diversity of rural life.

(*d*) Tribal culture is part of the cultural richness of India. **(CLAT 2011)**

**68.** Which of the following claims runs directly counter to the spirit of the passage above?

(*a*) Tribal people should be able to decide what elements of the modern world to adopt.

(*b*) The government should make modern science and medicine available to tribal people.

(*c*) Tribal people should not be subjected to any coercion to conform to non-tribal cultural norms as long as they do not violate the law.

(*d*) The tribals should assimilate as far as possible into non-tribal culture as a condition of full citizenship. **(CLAT 2011)**

**69.** Which of the following is *not* an assumption required by the above argument?

(*a*) Colour and diversity are desirable things.

(*b*) Tribal people are capable of contributing to India's cultural diversity.

(*c*) Changing tribal customs is a necessary condition of making modern medicine available to tribal people.

(*d*) Rural life is presently full of colour and diversity. **(CLAT 2011)**

**Passage for questions 70-71**

'India is the only country in the world where, in the States which are governed by the Communist party, human rights are fully respected — and that is only because the Bill of Rights is firmly entrenched in our national Constitution. We can proudly say that our Constitution gave us a flying start and equipped us adequately to meet the challenges of the future.'

**70.** Which of the following conclusions is *not* implied by the passage above?

(*a*) Communist states often do not respect human rights.

(*b*) Communist states never respect human rights.

(*c*) The entrenchment of the Bill of Rights is what ensures that even Communist-governed states respect human rights.

(*d*) The Indian Constitution prepared India for the challenges of independence. **(CLAT 2011)**

**71.** Which of the following, if true, would *weaken* the above argument?

(*a*) Communist governments are motivated to respect human rights out of Communist principles, not Constitutional ones.

(*b*) The Constitution of India is itself sympathetic to Communist principles.

(*c*) Human rights need to be enforceable to have any meaning.

(*d*) Countries without a strong culture of human rights are prone to oppressing minorities.

**(CLAT 2011)**

**Passage for questions 72-73**

'Poverty is ... more restrictive and limiting than anything else. If poverty and low standards continue then democracy, for all its fine institutions and ideals, ceases to be a liberating force. It must therefore aim continuously at the eradication of poverty and its companion unemployment. In other words, political democracy is not enough. It must develop into economic democracy also'.

**72.** Which of the following is *not* implied by the above passage?

(*a*) Democracy has ceased to be a liberating force.

(*b*) Democracies should aim to eliminate poverty.

(*c*) Poverty and unemployment go hand in hand.

(*d*) Political democracy should develop into economic democracy. **(CLAT 2011)**

**73.** Which of the following views, if true, would *weaken* the argument of the above passage?

(*a*) Political democracy is inseparable from economic democracy.

(*b*) Poverty does not in fact restrict freedom.

(*c*) Democracy flourishes most in poor societies.

(*d*) Economic democracy is a necessary condition for the elimination of unemployment.

**(CLAT 2011)**

**74.** Yoga has become a very popular exercise, but it may not be for everyone. If you are interested in high energy and fast workouts, yoga may not be the best choice. Therefore, evaluate your fitness requirement before joining yoga classes.

This paragraph best supports the statement that:

(*a*) Yoga is more popular than high energy exercise

(*b*) Yoga is changing the concept of fitness in various ways

(*c*) Before opting for Yoga, assess your fitness requirements

(*d*) Yoga is a holistic fitness regime **(CLAT 2012)**

**75.** Statistics allows us to understand the reality. It indicates developmental directions. Statistics is good for exposing reality, but it can also be manipulated to perpetuate untruth and misunderstanding. Data has power to mislead people.

This paragraph best supports the statement that:

(*a*) Words are more truthful than numbers

(*b*) Study of statistics is more important than any other discipline

(*c*) Numbers never lie

(*d*) Numbers can be used to mislead people.

**(CLAT 2012)**

**76.** Technology has developed out of stone tools which were used in ancient times. At first, development of new technology was slow, but after neo-liberal economic policy was adopted there has been a tremendous growth in technology sector.

This paragraph best supports the statement that:

(*a*) Stone tools were not really technology

(*b*) Stone tools were in use in Ancient India

(*c*) Today new technologies are developing at a fast pace

(*d*) New technology has nothing in common with the stone tools **(CLAT 2012)**

**Directions for questions 77 to 114:** Answer the following questions carefully.

**77.** From among the alternatives, identify the statement which states the same fact as the statement 'The dual nature of light is an enigma'.

(*a*) The nature of light is an enigma.

(*b*) Light has some enigmatic properties.

(*c*) Two differing arguments regarding the nature of light are obviously wrong.

(*d*) It is surprising and puzzling that according to one study, light is made up of one type of constituents and according to another, light is made up another type of constituents.

**(AILET, 2010)**

**78.** Identify the statement which can be neither proved nor disproved.

(*a*) I have head-ache.

(*b*) Yesterday, New York recorded 20°C at 12 noon.

(*c*) The gang war that broke out last week was due to business rivalry.

(*d*) History of Kannada literature states that Nripatunga is the earliest poet.

**(AILET, 2010)**

**79.** Identify the statement which cannot be doubted.

(*a*) Sense experience provides true knowledge.

(*b*) It is reasonable to accept science and most unreasonable to believe any religion.

(*c*) I am alive.

(*d*) Whenever there is unrest in society, the police will be alert. **(AILET, 2010)**

**80.** If it is true that 'good governance ensures law and order', then identify the statement which has to be accepted along with the given statement.

(*a*) A healthy society is governed by maximum number of laws.

(*b*) A strong government uses force to enforce law.

(*c*) An able government very effectively uses the law to promote peace and prosperity.

(*d*) Law is indispensable for the society.

**(AILET, 2010)**

**81.** Identify the statement which cannot be accepted.

(*a*) Mahabharatha is an ancient epic.

(*b*) Many Indian languages have their origin in Sanskrit.

(*c*) According to the heliocentric theory, the Earth is the centre of the solar system.

(*d*) Indian Constitution has been amended many times. **(AILET, 2010)**

**82.** If it is true that 'religious fundamentalism is dangerous to society', which one of the following statements is also true?

(*a*) Religion without reason is dangerous to the society.

(*b*) Belief in religions is dangerous to the society.

(*c*) Religious pluralism is dangerous to the society.

(*d*) Disrespect for other religions is dangerous to the society. **(AILET, 2010)**

**83.** Identify the argument which has to be accepted when the premiss is accepted as true.

(*a*) A and B are subsets of C.

Therefore A and B must have at least one common element.

(*b*) Every man desires happiness.

Therefore happiness is desirable.

(*c*) God is not perceivable.

Therefore God does not exist.

(*d*) Nothing comes out of nothing.

Therefore something must have existed always.

**(AILET, 2010)**

**84.** Identify the argument which cannot be accepted.

(*a*) All Indians are Asians.

All Asians are dark-coloured.

Therefore All dark coloured are Indians.

(*b*) Amar is a friend of Basava.

Therefore Basava is a friend of Amar.

(*c*) All positive integers less than 100 have only 2 digits.

Therefore all positive integers with 2 digits are less than 100.

(*d*) All spinsters are unmarried women.

Therefore all unmarried women are spinsters.

**(AILET, 2010)**

**85.** 4 statements are given below. Group two of them in such a way that one is logically impossible and the other is empirically (factually) possible.

1. A plane equilateral triangle can also be a plane right angled triangle. (A)
2. Velocity of light in vacuum is constant. (B)
3. Consumption of fuel at this rate results in reversal to bullock-cart age. (C)
4. A tall man is a man. (D)

(*a*) A,B (*b*) B,D

(*c*) C,D (*d*) A,C **(AILET, 2010)**

**86.** 4 statements are given. Group two of them in such a way that one is logically possible and the other is empirically (factually) highly improbable.

1. No theories of science can explain the origin of the Universe satisfactorily. (A)
2. Solar energy is inexhaustible. (B)
3. Liberalisation and rise in consumerism are directly related. (C)
4. God exists. (D)

(*a*) A,B (*b*) A,C

(*c*) B,D (*d*) A,D **(AILET, 2010)**

**87.** Four statements are given below. One of them can be demonstrated with the help of reason, while another requires sense experience to ascertain the truth, Identify them.

1. Ravana killed Rama. (*a*)
2. Area of circle is given by the formula $pr^2$ (*b*)
3. Methane is poisonous (*c*)
4. The absolute is pure consciousness (*d*)

**(AILET, 2010)**

**88.** All faculties of understanding, which a human being enjoys, are necessarily limited in terms of performance. If so, which of the following alternatives is justified by the preceding statement ?

(*a*) Human knowledge is necessarily imperfect.

(*b*) Perfection one's own knowledge is a distinct possibility, but man does not know how to employ his faculties.

(*c*) When progress in knowledge is linear, one day or the other the ultimate truth will be discovered.

(*d*) Human knowledge is not necessarily perfect.

**(AILET, 2010)**

**89.** 'The Universe has necessarily a beginning and an end' and 'the Universe has boundary' together imply

(*a*) The universe is finite in space and time.

(*b*) The universe is infinite in space and time.

(*c*) The universe is infinite in space but not in time.

(*d*) The universe is finite in space but not in time.

**(AILET, 2010)**

**90.** Which of the following alternatives comes very close to the statement, 'Man is necessarily an evil by nature'?

(*a*) As a matter of fact, man is an evil by nature.

(*b*) Man is not an evil by nature, but circumstances tend to make him so.

(*c*) Man cannot be an evil by nature.

(*d*) Actually, man is not an evil. **(AILET, 2010)**

**91.** Which of the following alternatives is farthest from the statement, 'Sound waves cannot travel in vacuum'?

(*a*) Sound waves require some medium to travel.

(*b*) Sound waves may travel in vacuum very slowly.

(*c*) Sound waves can travel only in vacuum.

(*d*) Sound waves may not travel in vacuum.

**(AILET, 2010)**

**92.** Which of the following alternatives contradict the statement 'deterministic laws of physics are characteristically Newtonian'.

(*a*) Indeterminism and physics cannot go together.

(*b*) Indeterminism is inherent in Newtonian system.

(*c*) Determinism in physics is a flaw.

(*d*) Determinism in physics is only apparent.

**(AILET, 2010)**

**93.** Identify the alternative which best explains the relation between the arguments mentioned below:

**Arguments:**

1. It is highly probable that every student of law at University level would have done a course on principles of ethics and Rama being a student of law, in all probability, would have done a course on principles of ethics.
2. At University level, every faculty aims at super speciality for which emphasis is laid upon structuring the curricula in such a way that every faculty is treated as a closed system so that no inter-disciplinary study is acceptable. Principles of ethics being essentially an integral part of philosophy, most probably is out of any course on law.

(*a*) Two arguments are mutually independent.

(*b*) Two arguments are mutually supportive.

(*c*) Two arguments are supplementary.

(*d*) They are incompatible. **(AILET, 2010)**

**94.** 'Greater than' is said to be transitive (relation) since A is greater than B and B is greater than C imply A is greater than C. Similarly 'friend of' is said to be symmetric since if A is a friend of B, then B is a friend of A. If so, what kind of relation is 'analogous'?

(*a*) Transitive

(*b*) Symmetric

(*c*) Identical

(*d*) Transitive and symmetric **(AILET, 2010)**

**95.** Since an object is identical with itself, 'being identical' is called a reflexive relation and if a relation is transitive, symmetric and reflexive, then such a relation is called 'equivalence'. If so, what kind of relation is 'different'?

(*a*) Equivalence (*b*) Inequivalence

(*c*) Asymmetric (*d*) Transitive

**(AILET, 2010)**

**[Option D in the original paper was "Non-Transitive". As both options (B) and (D) are matching with the question, option (D) has been changed to "Transitive" to fit the question.]**

**96.** Which of the following having the same form contradicts the statement 'guilty should be punished'?

(*a*) Guilty will not be punished

(*b*) Guilty may not be punished

(*c*) Guilty are not punished

(*d*) Guilty should not be punished **(AILET, 2010)**

**97.** If it is true that 'no innocent persons should be punished' and' Socrates is innocent', which of the following is the correct conclusion?

(*a*) Socrates is not punished

(*b*) Socrates may not be punished

(*c*) Socrates should not be punished

(*d*) Socrates will not be punished **(AILET, 2010)**

**98.** Identify the alternative which gives true picture of the relation between the arguments listed below:

1. A healthy society is characterised by overall development of every section. As in the case of human body no organ is less prominent, so also in a society no section is less important. If any human organ is sick, then the human being is sick. Similarly, if any section of society is sick, then the society is sick.
2. It is fallacious to think that priority to production of agricultural products alone promotes the prosperity of farmers, Prosperity has too many discussions. Transportation, communication, network, sound economic policy, to mention a few are equally important to the economic wellbeing of farmers. Hence they also deserve consideration.

(*a*) These two are irrelevant

(*b*) They are interdependent

(*c*) They are analogous

(*d*) They are compatible **(AILET, 2010)**

**99.** From among the given alternatives, identify the missing premise.

1st Premise: If a plane triangle is possible, then perfect straight line is possible

2nd Premise: If perfect straight line is possible, then Euclid is right

3rd Premise :

4th Premise: But Riemann is right.

**Conclusion:** Therefore a plane triangle is not possible.

(*a*) If Riemann is right, then Euclid is right

(*b*) If Riemann is wrong, then Euclid is right

(*c*) If Euclid is right, then Riemann is wrong

(*d*) If Riemann is right, then Euclid is not wrong

**(AILET, 2010)**

**100.** If it is true that neither Rama is a brother of Krishna, nor is he a lecturer, then which of the following statements is true?

(*a*) Rama is not a brother of Krishna, but he is a lecturer.

(*b*) Rama is a brother of Krishna, but he is not a lecturer.

(*c*) Rama is a brother of Krishna and he is a lecturer.

(*d*) Rama is not a brother of Krishna and he is not a lecturer. **(AILET, 2011)**

**101.** "Make hay while the sunshine." is logically similar to

(*a*) Sleep when you are tired.

(*b*) Take the bull by horn.

(*c*) Losing hope is along everything.

(*d*) None of the above **(AILET, 2011)**

**102.** The Constitution has given the right of free speech. People speak freely in order to enjoy this right. Which of the following has the same logic?

(*a*) Smuggling is illegal. People indulge in smuggling because they want to violate laws.

(*b*) People have the right to live, but they die, since they do not want to exercise that right.

(*c*) Wealth gives power to enjoy material things. People enjoy these things by spending their wealth.

(*d*) All of the above **(AILET, 2011)**

**103.** Literature is the mirror in which the society can see itself. The above statement implies that

(*a*) no ugly society can produce good literature.

(*b*) writers are essentially like newspaper correspondents, reporting faithfully what they are observing,

(*c*) literature enables the people to comprehend the dimensions which they are unaware of.

(*d*) None of the above **(AILET, 2011)**

**104.** Child labour is only a reflection of the malaise in the society.

Which of the following, supports the above statement?

(*a*) Child labour is not abhorred by the public.

(*b*) The Government is not serious about eliminating child labour.

(*c*) Exploitation of the poor, weak and unorganized is not uncommon.

(*d*) All of the above **(AILET, 2011)**

**105.** If it is true that 'good governance ensures law and order', then identify the statement which has to be accepted along with the given statement.

(*a*) A healthy society is governed by maximum number of laws.

(*b*) A strong government uses force to enforce law.

(*c*) Law is indispensible for the society.

(*d*) All of the above **(AILET, 2011)**

**106.** If it is true that 'very rarely do we come across committed film directors', which one of the following is false beyond doubt?

(*a*) We can never come across committed film directors.

(*b*) No film director is committed.

(*c*) All film directors are committed, but we can never meet them.

(*d*) None of the above **(AILET, 2011)**

**107.** Consider a set of premises like this: If science and religion clash, then critical thinking and dogma will clash. Dogma is not acceptable and hence religion. But critical thinking shakes the foundation of morality.

Identify the conclusion which follows from the premises.

(*a*) If science is not accepted, then the foundations of morality are not shaken.

(*b*) If foundations of morality are shaken, then science is acceptable.

(*c*) If science is accepted, then foundations of morality are shaken.

(*d*) Though science is accepted, it cannot shake the foundation of morality. **(AILET, 2011)**

**108.** If Ramesh likes oranges more than grapes, strawberries more than apples, and apples more than oranges, then which one of the following is not true?

(*a*) He likes grapes more than strawberries.

(*b*) He likes strawberries more than grapes.

(*c*) He likes apples more than grapes.

(*d*) He likes strawberries more than apples.

**(AILET, 2011)**

**109.** "Justice should not only be done, but seen to have been done". The statement intends to convey the message that

(*a*) Court proceedings must be open to public.

(*b*) Public participation in judicial decision making is essential for timely justice.

(*c*) Court proceedings must be fair and judgments should be based on legal reasoning.

(*d*) All court cases must be publicized and reported to the public in their own language.

**(AILET, 2011)**

**110.** Which one of the following, if true, can be empirically tested?

(*a*) Violence is engineered by power-hungry politicians.

(*b*) Only poor are driven to violence.

(*c*) Faith in God alone can contain violence.

(*d*) Instinct to preserve one's own self is at the root of violence. **(AILET, 2011)**

**111.** Which one of the following, whether true or false, is irrelevant to the issue?

(*a*) Also, violence is due to the fact there is a tendency in man to enjoy when somebody suffers.

(*b*) Violence is commonplace in the world because men hardly learn philosophy.

(*c*) Violence is the overt manifestation of covert desire to be adventurous.

(*d*) Violence is the result of man's tendency to assert himself. **(AILET, 2011)**

**112.** Which one of the following makes the argument self-contradictory?

(*a*) The soul has finite existence.

(*b*) Whatever is corruptible is soluble.

(*c*) What is spatial is material.

(*d*) Motion is not a reality. **(AILET, 2011)**

**113.** "Some philosophers believe that a concept which cannot be verified can still be valid because of its inner logic which ennobles it."

In the light of the above statement, decide the status of the statement given below.

**Statement:** "Every person has certain inherent and inalienable rights which must be protected by Rule of Law."

(*a*) True

(*b*) False

(*c*) Difficult to determine

(*d*) Both True and False **(CLAT 2011)**

**114.** An argument is given below, on the basis of that argument; find out the parallel argument from the given list of subsequent arguments

**Argument:** Himalayan Sparrows are disappearing. This bird is an Indian bird; therefore, Indian birds are disappearing.

**Subsequent Arguments:**

(*a*) Industrialists pay most of the taxes. 'Z' is a wealthy man therefore 'Z' must pay most taxes

(*b*) A pineapple is a fruit, a mango is a fruit therefore pineapple is a mango

(*c*) Snow tigers are an endangered species; all endangered species must be protected; therefore snow-tiger must be protected

(*d*) John is his father's favorite son, and John knows this must be true because his father told him this; and no father would lie to his favorite son

**(CLAT 2012)**

**115.** Information that is published is part of the public record. But information that a reporter collects, and sources that he contacts, must be protected in order for our free press to function free of fear.

The above argument is most severely weakened by which one of the following statements ?

(*a*) Public information is usually reliable

(*b*) Undocumented evidence may be used to convict an innocent person

(*c*) Members of the press act ethically in most cases

(*d*) The sources that a reporter contacts are usually willing to divulge their identity **(AILET, 2013)**

**116.** Psychological novels are superior to novels of adventure. Immature readers prefer novels of adventure to novels with less action and greater psychological depth. The immature reader, who prefers James Bond's exploits to the subtleties of Henry James, can be identified easily by his choice of inferior reading matter.

A criticism of the logic of this argument would be likely to find fault with the author's

(*a*) Presupposing the conclusions he wishes to prove

(*b*) Failure to define "adventure" clearly

(*c*) Failure to cite possible exceptions to this rule

(*d*) Hasty generalisation on the basis of a limited specific case **(AILET, 2013)**

**117.** Many very effective prescription drugs are available to patients on a "one time only" basis. Suspicious of drug abuse, physicians will not renew a prescription for a medicine that has worked effectively for a patient. This practice denies a patient her right to health.

Which one of the following is a basic assumption made by the author ?

(*a*) A new type of medicine is likely to be more expensive

(*b*) Physicians are not concerned with a patient's health

(*c*) Most physicians prescribe inadequate amounts of medicine

(*d*) Patients are liable to suffer the same ailment repeatedly **(AILET, 2013)**

**118.** Vijay claimed that the large dent in the fender of the company-owned vehicle he had borrowed was caused by the careless act of another motorist, who backed into the car when it was parked in a public garage. Yet Vijay's own car has several dents in its fenders, all of which he acknowledges as having caused by his own careless driving. Therefore, Vijay's contention that the dent in the formerly undented company-owned vehicle was caused by the careless act of another person is not true.

The reasoning in this argument is vulnerable because it

(*a*) Fails to recognise that Vijay could be lying about the dents in his own vehicle

(*b*) Fails to recognise that the motorist who backed into him simply did not see him

(*c*) Fails to acknowledge that many such accidents occur in parking garages

(*d*) Presumes, without justification, that because Vijay has caused similar dents to his own car, he caused the dent in the company car

**(AILET, 2013)**

**119.** It takes a good telescope to see the moons of Neptune. I can't see the moons of Neptune with my telescope. Therefore, I do not have a good telescope.

Which one of the following most closely parallels the logic of this statement ?

(*a*) It takes two to tango. You are doing the tango. Therefore, you have a partner

(*b*) If you have a surfboard, you can surf. You do not have a surfboard. Therefore, you cannot surf

(*c*) You can write a letter to your friend with a pencil. You do not have a pencil. Therefore, you cannot write the letter

(*d*) If you know the area of a circle, you can find its circumference. You cannot figure out the circumference. Therefore, you do not know the area **(AILET, 2013)**

**120. Rahul :** One would have to be blind to the reality of moral obligation to deny that people who believe a course of action to be morally obligatory for them have both the right and the duty to pursue that action, and that no one else has any right to stop them from doing so.

Richa : But imagine an artist who feels morally obliged to do whatever she can to prevent works of art from being destroyed confronting a morally committed anti-pornography demonstrator engaged in destroying artworks he deems pornographic. According to your principle that artist has, simultaneously, both the right and duty to stop the destruction and no right whatsoever to stop it.

Which of the following, if substituted for the scenario invoked by Richa, would preserve the force of her argument? **(AILET 2014)**

(*a*) a medical researcher who feels a moral obligation not to claim sole credit for work that was performed in part by someone else confronting another researcher who feels no such moral obligation.

(*b*) a manufacturer who feels a moral obligation to recall potentially dangerous products confronting a consumer advocate who feels morally obliged to expose product defects.

(*c*) an architect who feels a moral obligation to design only energy-efficient buildings confronting, as a potential client, a corporation that believes its primary moral obligation is to maximise shareholder profits.

(*d*) a health inspector who feels morally obliged to enforce restrictions on the number of cats a householder may keep confronting a householder who, feeling morally obliged to keep every stray that comes along, has over twice that number of cats.

**121.** Between 1951 and 1963, it was illegal in the country of Geronia to manufacture, sell, or transport any alcoholic beverages. Despite this prohibition, however, the death rate from diseases related to excessive alcohol consumption was higher during the first five years of the period than it was during the five years prior to 1951, Therefore, the attempt to prevent alcohol use merely made people want and use alcohol more than they would have if it had not been forbidden.

Each of the following, if true, weakens the argument EXCEPT: **(AILET 2014)**

(*a*) Many who died of alcohol-related diseases between 1951 and 1963 consumed illegally imported alcoholic beverages produced by the same methods as those used within Geronia.

(*b*) Death from an alcohol-related disease generally does not occur until five to ten years after the onset of excessive alcohol consumption.

(c) The death rate resulting from alcohol-related diseases increased just as sharply during the ten years before and ten years after the prohibition of alcohol as it did during the years of prohibition.

(d) Between 1951 and 1963, among the people with pre-existing alcohol-related diseases, the percentage who obtained life-saving medical attention declined because of a social stigma attached to excessive alcohol consumption.

**122.** Unless they are used as strictly temporary measures, rent-control ordinances (municipal regulations placing limits on rent increase) have several negative effects for renters. One of these is that the controls will bring about a shortage of rental units. This disadvantage for renters occurs over the long run, but the advantage - smaller rent increases - occurs immediately. In many municipalities, especially in all those where tenants of rent-control units have a secure hold on political power and can get rent-control ordinances enacted or repealed, it is invariably the desire for short-term gain that guides those tenants in the exercise of that power.

If the statements above are true, which one of the following can be properly inferred from them? **(AILET 2014)**

(a) It is impossible for landlords to raise rents when rent controls are in effect.

(b) In many municipalities, rent-control ordinances are repealed as soon as shortages of rental units arise.

(c) In many municipalities there is now, or eventually will be, a shortage of rental units.

(d) in the long term, a shortage of rental units will raise rents substantially.

**123.** A government's proposed 8 percent cut in all subsidies to art groups will be difficult for those groups to absorb. As can be seen, however, from their response to last year's cut, it will not put them out of existence. Last year there was also an 8 percent cut, and though private fund-raising was very difficult for the art groups in the current recessionary economy, they did survive.

The reasoning in the argument is flawed because the argument **(AILET 2014)**

(a) Relies without warrant on the probability that the economy will improve.

(b) Overlooks the possibility that the cumulative effect of the cuts will be more than the arts group can withstand.

(c) Equates the mere survival of the arts groups with their flourishing.

(d) Does not raise the issue of whether there should be any government subsidies to arts groups at all.

**124.** Health insurance insulates patients from the expense of medical care, giving doctors almost complete discretion in deciding the course of most medical treatments. Moreover, with doctors being paid for each procedure performed, they have an incentive to over-treat patients. It is thus clear that medical procedures administered by doctors are frequently prescribed only because these procedures lead to financial rewards.

The argument uses which one of the following questionable techniques? **(AILET 2014)**

(a) Assigning responsibility for a certain result to someone whose involvement in the events leading to that result was purely coincidental.

(b) Inferring the performance of certain actions on no basis other than the existence of both incentive and opportunity for performing those actions.

(c) Presenting as capricious and idiosyncratic decisions that are based on the rigorous application of well-defined principles.

(d) Depicting choices as having been made arbitrarily by dismissing without argument reasons that have been given for these choices.

## Solutions

**1.** d The para in the question says how children in France do stretching and exercise on a daily basis, while their American counterparts do not do so. French students also outperform their American counterparts in tests that measure cardiovascular fitness. The author therefore concludes that the American students can achieve cardiovascular fitness only if they take up stretching and exercises. What the author has assumed here is that stretching and exercise is the only (or necessary) cause of cardiovascular fitness and no other factor plays a role in developing cardiovascular fitness. The answer is clearly option (d).

**2.** c The apparent contradiction in the argument is that patients suffering from disease Q report a slightly high level of blood sugar. But this abnormal condition of high blood sugar is considered a means to treat the very same disease of which it is a symptom. This contradiction/paradox is best explained in option (c) where it is explained that high blood sugar can stop the flourishing of the virus and as a consequence one may even benefit from high level of blood sugar.

**3.** d The argument is something like this— the metabolic rates of professional athletes are found to be substantially higher than that of ordinary people. So, author concludes that a person's speed and strength are primarily determined by his metabolic rate. This argument is best augmented in option (*d*) by providing evidence that drugs, when they supresss one's metabolic rate, also cause one's speed and strength to diminish.

**4.** b. In the question, Oscar was able to repair the motorcycle despite not knowing what was causing the problem. It is also known that he has received extensive training, can repair most mechanical problems and also does not understand how internal combustion engines work. We can clearly infer from here that there are some mechanical problems which do not require the understanding of internal combustion engines for solving them. The answer is clearly option (*b*). Option (*c*) is also a very close contender but this requires us to call Oscar a good mechanic and it is a far-fetched thing to do so.

**5.** c The claim is that third party candidates fail to succeed in the elections because they encounter difficulties in securing space on national ballots. 'Securing space on national ballots' means proper recognition as a party on the national level. The evidence provided in the argument ends up supporting the claim. Though option (*c*) is correct, it needs to be slightly reframed. The option should be rephrased as "The evidence provided in the argument instead of refuting / contradicting the claim, ends up supporting it."

**6.** c The argument states that businesses maximize their profits through advertisements which generally carry inaccurate information. Thus, the consumers should be wary of such advertisements. Only option (*c*) does not strengthen this argument since it states that consumers have a cynical attitude towards advertisements. This statement does not affect the argument at all and hence is the correct choice. Option (*a*), (*b*) and (*d*) all add to the consumer advocate's argument by substantiating his reasoning. Option (*a*) talks about businesses knowing that inaccurate information will help them make money. Option (*b*) restates the premise that businesses often include inaccurate information. Option (*d*) talks of advertisement makers also contributing to inaccurate information in the advertisements.

**7.** b The science columnist concludes that humans and cats have many similar diseases because of the similarity in their genetic makeup. He states that since many diseases in humans are genetic and humans and cats have similar genes, thus they also have common diseases. This is weakened by option (*b*) because it states that the diseases that humans and cats have in common are not genetic in nature. Thus, it negates the science columnist's reasoning of humans and cats having similar diseases because of their genetic similarity.

**8.** b The author of the passage links anger to permanent High B.P to heart diseases. He assumes a causal relationship between anger and High B.P. Option (*b*) makes this assumption incorrect as those with permanent high blood pressure will have to take medication for the same and this medication will make them quick to anger (mood swings). Hence, in light of option (*b*), being quick to anger is an effect of permanent high B.P and not the other way round. This means that both psychological factors and heart diseases are a result of permanent high blood pressure.

**9.** a The professor arrived at the conclusion that computers have not made books obsolete because of a majority of her students printing the material instead of reading it on the computer screen. This argument is strengthened by option (*a*) because it echoes the same sentiments as of the professor. It has been found by several colleagues of the same professor that their students also behave similarly. The rest of the options give different reasons for the conclusion which limits the scope of the professor's assertion. Thus, they cannot strengthen the argument.

**10.** d Here speaker equates exercising control with socialist influence. Disinvestments and privatization show less of control. Speaker reasons out that it is a shift from socialistic principles. However, if we show that the same phenomenon (less of control) comes due to laxity of the government, as in option (*d*), we can contradict the speaker's argument.

**11.** c Speaker observes two different responses from the intellectuals for two different events of similar nature. And he terms it as double standard. Option (*c*) shows the two different responses. It appears to him that "The response to geographical and sociological divisions are very different".

**12.** b Author argues that consumption should be need based and hence, prosperity should not depend on consumption. Option (*b*) says without consumption prosperity is shallow i.e. consumption is important to prosperity. Hence, option (*b*) contradicts the spirit of the passage.

**13.** c Speaker moots that even though agriculture is the backbone of a nation's economy, other sectors are no less important. Therefore, budget allocation should be need based.

**14.** a Speaker suggests to spend money on a field which is non-remunerative. Option (*a*) contradicts the same as it suggests that money should be spent on a field which generates money i.e, on a remunerative field.

**15.** a The argument says that beans are plumper when they are prepared without pre-soaking. So when the quality is more important then pre-soaking should be avoided. The assumption here is that plumper beans are of better quality. Thus, option (*a*) is correct.

**16.** b The argument says that children under six are not allowed from 12 to 5 P.M. and also after 5 P.M. to closing time. This means that they can go to the pool only before noon. Since everyone in the neighborhood is permitted to swim at the pool, if the neighborhood has a child under six, then the pool must be open for him/her before noon. Hence, option (*b*) is the correct choice.

**17.** d Option (*d*) is the most plausible inference. The argument says 'almost every Wednesday' so the best inference would be 'most if not all Wednesdays'. Options (*a*) is incorrect because the question does not say that half priced coffee is offered on only every Wednesday. Apart from it being done on almost every Wednesday, it may also be done on every Friday. In that case, the most common day will be Friday. Thus, option (*a*) cannot be inferred. Option (*b*) has the same error. Option (*c*) reverses the reasoning. There may be some days when half priced coffee is offered and free poetry readings are not scheduled. Half priced coffee may be given even without the poetry schedule because the question does not say that half priced coffee is offered only on those days when poetry is scheduled. Thus, (*c*) reverses the reasoning and becomes incorrect.

**18.** a The argument says that exploitation of charitable instincts of alms givers may aggravate poverty by inducing laziness in beggars. Option (*a*), which states that destitution (poverty) is a result of unwillingness to work (laziness), supports this reasoning. This statement means that beggars became poor and had to beg because they were lazy and unwilling to work. Now, if they are given alms, it will fulfill their needs and they may continue to be lazy.

19. b The argument states that one needs to choose one's exercise regime (yoga or aerobics) on the basis of one's requirements and expectations. Option (*b*) is best supported by the argument. Option (*d*) is close but can be negated easily because the argument says that yoga is not the best choice for those looking for a fast paced workout. It may not be the best but it may still be rigorous. Moreover, we cannot say that this is the opinion of most of the people. Thus, option (*d*) is negated as well.

**20.** d The argument is based on the reason for the tendency of a magnetic needle to swing towards the poles. Robert Norman and his predecessor offer different reasonings for this tendency. So, option (*d*) effectively expresses the problem they are working on.

**21.** b Analogy is the process of comparing one thing with another that has some similar features. In the given question, James Maxwell noticed that mathematical laws of uniform motion of heat are analogous to the laws of attraction and are inversely proportional to square of the distance. He thought that the source of heat is analogous to the center of attraction, flow of heat is analogous to the accelerating effect of attraction and temperature is analogous to potential. Thus, option (*b*) is correct.

**22.** d The issue here is the criterion to define a straight line. If 180 degree angle is used as the criterion to decide straight, then Euclidean geometry is followed. But, if less than 180 degree is also considered straight then we are referring to Non-Euclidean geometry. So, the choice of definition of a straight line is the issue at stake.

**23.** c The hypothesis states that the more a student studies, the higher are his grades. The observation is that the students who spent most time studying did not get grades as high as did many students who studied less. The hypothesis compares the performance of a student who studies say 4 hours a day with the same student if he/she were to study 6 hours a day. However, the observation compares the performance of one student with another. Option (*c*) helps in explaining why the observation does not undermine the hypothesis. It says when a student studies more, his performance improves relative to his own past performance. Option (*a*) is incorrect since it is a comparison across students, whereas the conclusion is about a particular student under different conditions. Option (*b*) is irrelevant since it does not provide any reason for researchers sticking to their conclusion. Option (*d*) is irrelevant too as we are not concerned as to what the students do when they are not studying.

**24.** d The argument of the educator is that it is known that the vote of an individual is much more likely to determine organizational policy by influencing the election of an officer by influencing the result of a direct vote. He concludes to say that it is better to take decisions through the election of an officer than direct vote. Option (*a*) is incorrect; the issue is not about one person's vote weighing more than any other. Option (*b*) can be ruled out on the same lines. The argument is how to take decisions, not how to evaluate the outcomes of these decisions. Option (*c*) supports the conclusion but does not provide a link between the premise and the conclusion. Option (*d*) is correct. If the main aim of the procedures of the organization is to maximize the influence of each individual on the decisions made and we know that an individual has greater influence in election of an officer then the decisions must be made through election of an officer.

**25.** b The argument states that higher taxes would produce reduction in smoking. Option (*a*) may strengthen the argument. It says that under some conditions a tax would have the desired effect. Option (*b*) is the best wrong answer. It makes it sound like people will continue to buy tobacco regardless. However, just because they're more likely to continue buying tobacco does not mean that there was not a reduction in the amount of tobacco consumed. Option (*c*) weakens the argument by showing that the tax would not reduce the amount of tobacco consumed; just shift the purchase to the neighboring town. Option (*d*) is irrelevant. Just because people are more likely to quit when they're well educated about the hazards of smoking does not mean that they wouldn't quit because of a tax imposed on tobacco. Option (*c*) is the correct choice, though NLU-D has given option (*b*) as the correct answer.

**26.** a The conclusion or the main point of the argument is that speech acquisition is *entirely* a motor control process rather than a process that is abstract or mental. In other words — the point at which we learn to talk is entirely based on when we learn how to physically control our mouths, and nothing else. If option (*a*) wasn't true, it would mean that there are other elements that impact speech acquisition. Option (*a*) is an answer that must be true in order for the argument to be true, and it is therefore correct. Option (*b*) doesn't have to be true — we don't need to know anything about the entire babbling stage (this is not discussed directly), and "intentionally move their tongues," though related to ability to create sounds of languages, is not the same thing, and therefore this is not directly relevant. Option (*c*) is not relevant to the argument and can be eliminated. Option (*d*) doesn't have to be true for the author to make his point.

**27.** c The argument is that those who listened to music instead of conversation required fewer painkillers and thus it can be concluded that reducing stress lessens the pain sensitivity. Option (*a*) is incorrect as it contradicts the argument. It says all the patients in the study listen to same tapes before and after a surgery. The argument, however, says that there were two types of tape that were used in the study. Option (*b*) is incorrect as we are not comparing which of the two, surgery or recovery, is more stressful. Similarly, option (*d*) is irrelevant as whatever be the psychological effects of music, the conclusion would still hold true.

**28.** b The argument bases itself on the premise that political turmoil is caused by violence and the government policies. It concludes that a dictatorial government which rules strictly and imposes stringent regulations can crush political turmoil. Option (*a*) does not weaken the argument much because it is not clear from the passage that existing legislations would be effective in curbing political turmoil. Option (*c*) talks about educating people which may weaken the argument somewhat but still does not address whether a strict government would be required or not. Option (*d*) also talks about the effectiveness of dialogue and that too in a certain type of society i.e.'free' society. Only option (*b*), if true, would directly weaken the need for a strict government which rules dictatorially.

**29.** b Only option (*b*), which mentions the economic policy of 'press from top', broadly strengthens the case for a dictatorial government which imposes strict rules from above. Option (*a*) talks about only one factor (espionage activities by enemy nations) that affects political turmoil and does not strengthen the conclusion that much. Option (*c*) which talks about 'corrupt establishment' also does not directly strengthen the case for a touch government. Option (*d*) makes a far-fetched statement not related to the issue at all.

**30.** b Only if an austere life is encouraged can one expect people to stop indulging in greed. In such a case one can expect both the state to be free of corruption and the rich to stop exploiting the poor. This is the least dubious of all conclusions that can emerge out of the para. Option (*a*) which talks about abolishing production is unrealistic. Option (*c*) does not address the issue of corruption at the state level. Also it does not address the impact that heavy taxation may have on the rich. Furthermore the passage does not mention taxation clearly as the only means of control the state has over industrial and agricultural production. Option (*d*) also makes a very broad statement about human dishonesty not clearly supported by the passage.

**31.** b This option establishes the link between incorruptibility and immortality and thus completes the argument.

**32.** d If what is not matter is also vulnerable to motion then the human soul will be subject to dissolution. This would seriously affect the argument.

**33.** b The debate talks about the merits and demerits of capital punishment as a form of punishment. Those who oppose it talk of man's rights and privileges. The defenders talk of punishing the criminal. However, these are reason that both the parties use to put forth their opinion regarding capital punishment. Hence, option (*a*) and (*c*) themselves are not the focus of the debate. Option (*d*) is irrelevant. Option (*b*) is the correct choice.

**34.** a The original premise was the 'Slow Rotation of Venus', which was changed by the scientist on the basis of his later conclusions. Since this is the only fact given in the passage and the rest are all assumptions and observations, option (*a*) is the apt answer.

**35.** b The passage clearly says 'He first theoretically derived the relation between distances and time.'. Therefore theoretical analysis characterised Galileo's method.

**36.** b The correct answer is option (*b*). The method used by Holmes is clearly one of 'Experiment'. This is not mere observation, because he experimented by dissolving the pills in water and then in milk.

**37.** a An analogy is drawn with the frying of pancakes in order to determine the formation of lunar craters.

**38.** d The passage says 'Equal weights at equal distances are in equilibrium.

**39.** c Since equilibrium is determined by both weight and distance and the passage clearly mentions that equal weights at unequal distances cause disequilibrium, it is highly probable that inequal weights at equal distances would be in disequilibrium. We cannot say it is 'true' because this case is not explicitly mentioned in the passage.

**40.** a Since the passage explicitly states that equal weights at inequal distances are in disequilibrium, then the statement 'inequal weights at inequal distances' can be considered to be true.

**41.** a 'Three dominant talls to one recessive short' indicates that the distribution of dominant and recessive characteristics is systematic.

**42.** b Einstein's remark with reference to playing dice (a game of probability) refers to his reservations about a probabilistic interpretation of the behaviour of quantum objects while Bohr expresses an opposing point of view suggesting that this could be possible.

**43.** b Since the issue with an environment friendly public transport system is the impact on cash flow to the treasury and better job opportunities, then developing alternatives that would reduce the adverse impact on these would be the opinion of the author of this passage.

**44.** a The opening sentence of the paragraph raises the question about the effectiveness of democratic government. It goes on to question Lincoln's view on the same by mentioning how he fails to clarify the real attitude that leads a candidate to seek election. The paragraph also quotes the view of Socrates that no honest man willingly seeks the position of a ruler. Therefore option (*a*) which more or less restates the question at the opening of the para follows strictly from the passage. The passage does not give enough information to verify any of the other options completely.

**45.** d According to Lincoln, no contestant to a democratic election takes part in it unwillingly. Rather he is driven by his own passions and motives. Socrates has a contrasting view on this and suggests that no honest man seeks democratic election willingly and does so only when he fears that he may otherwise serve under an inferior man. Thus option (*d*) which talks about difference in the mindset of respective men who seek election is the right answer choice.

**46.** a The last part of the passage suggests that it may be wrong to kill any living being in the interest of hygiene. Option (*a*) which suggests that disease-spreading bacteria should be eradicated in the interest of health and cleanliness therefore runs counter to the spirit of the passage.

**47.** b According to the passage if reservation holds true for those opting for the teaching profession then this may see the appointment of substandard teachers who have gained their qualifications not on the basis of merit but on the basis of reservation. If such teachers fail to impart quality education then every student including those benefiting from the reservation system will fail to derive the benefit of quality education. Therefore, at least in the field of ensuring quality teachers reservation will be self-defeating.

**48.** d Only if those who are meritorious among the downtrodden groups are made teachers can we ensure that they will impart quality education. Only this will circumvent the situation outlined in the para.

**49.** a The higher literacy rate in China is attributed to greater efficiency of the Communist system and the lesser literacy in India is attributed to the lack of efficiency in the democratic system. Among the given options, option (*a*) disproves the efficiency aspect, in the respective systems, in improving the literacy rate. Hence, it undermines the argument.

**50.** c Option (*a*) is not correct as we do not know if he was convicted under an unjust law. Option (*b*) makes Socrates' commitment to obeying law due to long residence a general argument of obeying law. Moreover, absence of explicit commitment may not be a factor in deciding whether to accept a pronouncement of offence. Option (*d*) does not refute the basic argument of Socrates in any way. Option (*c*) provides reasons to believe that Socrates need not necessarily obey the law that has implicated him.

**51.** a The argument states that the government is justified in banning all soft drinks from the Indian market because they have been shown by scientists to be bad for the teeth. The necessary assumption here is that the government is justified in banning anything that is bad for the teeth. Option (*b*) is irrelevant as it does not help us in arriving at the conclusion in any way. The concernfor dental hygiene also does not necessarily justify the government's action since we do not know if banning anything of great concern is justified or not. Thus, option (*a*) is the correct choice.

**52.** c Older than 25 years and not being bankrupt are the two criteria for being eligible for election to Lok Sabha. Jatinder Singh fulfills the criterion related to age but does not fulfill the one related to bankruptcy. So he is not eligible for election to Lok Sabha. As the conclusion says that he cannot be elected as the Speaker of the Lok Sabha, this means that the author has assumed that one who is not eligible for election to the Lok Sabha is also not eligible for being the Speaker of Lok Sabha. Thus, option (*c*) is correct.

**53.** a The passage states that the behavior of people at the end of the century is similar to the behavior of people that are at the end of their lives. Just as those who are at the end of their lives start reflecting on the past events of their lives similarly, those who are alive in 1999 (i.e. those who are at the end of the century) will reflect on the events of the century (twentieth). Thus, option (*a*) is the logically correct choice.

**54.** a The question asked is regarding the form of Lucretius's argument, not about what is the take–away from his thought experiment. Option (*b*) and (*c*) are out of scope as there is no mention of the thought experiment's inconsistency with mathematics or physics. Option (*d*) is incorrect as it does not answer the question. It gives a conclusive statement regarding the possibility of finite space, i.e. it is inconceivable. Option (*a*) is correct as it states that Lucretius showed that believing the space to be finite leads to a contradiction. This is to say that his thought experiment wherein he posited the space to be finite leads to contradictory results. This is consistent with the given argument and hence is the correct choice.

**55.** b Utilitarians believe that the action that produces maximum happiness is the right action. Option (*b*) states that one should do one's duty without giving any consideration to the consequences (happiness or misery). Thus, option (*b*) is incompatible with the belief of Utilitarians.

**56.** b Senthil draws his conclusion about the entire Ambala city on the basis of a limited and insufficient data. He had only seen the route from railway station to the hotel and not the entire city.

**57.** a A conclusion about the time that will be taken by India to achieve internal stability has been drawn on the basis of the data related to Europe. This may not be true unless the process of attaining internal stability follows a general pattern. Therefore, option (*a*) provides the correct assumption. Option (*b*) weakens the claim. Option (*c*) is irrelevant as the argument talks about the time span and not about the process of achieving stability.

**58.** d The argument states that the models and theories of economics (that are based on mathematical formulae) are too idealistic and far from realily. Option (*d*) summarizes the argument effectively.

**59.** a The argument demands the mathematical models used by economists to be more realistic than idealistic. It does not ask to stop the use of mathematical models.

**60.** b Option (*b*) would contradict the argument. If the conditions in the real word are very much similar to the theoretical conditions used in the mathematical models, then the argument that these models fail to incorporate real conditions gets contradicted.

**61.** b The paragraph talks about the spread of religion (Buddhism) vis-à-vis the geography of that place/country. Option (*b*) summarizes the paragraph effectively.

**62.** b The statement "The Hindkush mountains made no difference to the spread of Islam" nullifies the argument that geography (particularly mountains) played a role in the spread of religion.

**63.** b The conclusion of the argument is mentioned in its last lines "That is, friendship connoted intimacy in England while in Rural India, brotherhood conveyed intimacy." Therefore, the attitude of people of England towards brotherhood and friendship is different from that of rural India.

**64.** c The argument concludes that "friendship connotes intimacy in England". Option (*c*) which states that 'people in England do not think that friendship connotes intimacy' contradicts the argument.

**65.** b The argument discusses the importance of social context in making learning a language easier and effective. Option (*b*) summarizes the argument effectively.

**66.** d All of the given statements present facts that contradict the given argument and thus weaken it.

**67.** b The argument talks about the goodness/richness of tribal culture and the lack of need to dilute the richness of these cultures. The conclusions implied in the argument are: 1. Following/developing their own culture is good for tribes as well as for the country. 2. Tribal cultures do contribute to the diversity of the Indian culture. 3. Forceful adoption of another culture by tribal people would reduce their cultural distinctness and diversity. Option (*b*) which states "Tribal customs should not be allowed to change in any respect" takes the argument too far and is not implied in the passage.

**68.** d The argument talks about the goodness/richness of tribal culture and the lack of need to dilute the richness of these cultures. Option (*d*) which states "The tribes should assimilate as far as possible into non-tribal culture as a condition of full citizenship" contradicts the spirit as well as the essence of the passage.

**69.** c The argument does not mention the conditions that demand the tribal people to be flexible and change some of their customs. Moreover, the idea of modern medicines is beyond the scope of the passage. Thus, option (*c*) is not an assumption implicit in the argument.

**70.** b The passage itself states that in India, the states governed by the Communist party respect human rights. Option (*b*) contradicts this by stating that communist states never respect human rights. Thus, option (*b*) is not a conclusion implicit in the passage.

**71.** a The argument states that the concept of human rights enshrined in the constitution of India is the reason behind the Communist party's respect for human rights (in India). Option (*a*) weakens the argument by stating that the communist governments are not motivated by the principles of the constitution (of India). Instead they are motivated by their own Communist principles.

**72.** a The argument discusses that democracy ceases to be a liberating force if the people are poor and unemployed. Option (*a*) states that 'democracy has ceased to be a liberating force'. Thus, option (*a*) fails to convey the meaning implied in the argument and is incorrect.

**73.** a The argument is that in the absence of economic democracy, political democracy loses its luster and significance. Option (*a*) states that political democracy is inseparable from economic democracy i.e. they always co-exist. Hence, it weakens the argument.

**74.** c The paragraphs points to the fact that though Yoga is becoming a very popular form of exercise, it would not suit all fitness enthusiasts. Refer to the line, *"Therefore, evaluate your fitness requirements before joining yoga classes"*. Hence, option (*c*) is correct.

**75.** d Refer to the lines, *"Statistics...can also be manipulated to perpetuate untruth..."* and *"Data has power to mislead people"*. Option (*d*) directly follows from these lines and thus, is the correct choice.

**76.** c Refer to the line, *"At first, development of new technology was slow...there has been a tremendous growth in technology sector"*. These lines suggest that today technologies are developing rapidly. Hence, option (*c*) is correct.

**77.** d Enigmatic means puzzling. Option (*d*) brings out that puzzling fact about dual nature of light. Only (*d*) has the elements of 'dual nature' and 'enigma'.

**78.** a 'I have head-ache' is speaker's perception. No one else can prove or disprove it.

**79.** c If a speaker says 'I'm alive', one cannot doubt his/her statement as no dead person would be able to say so.

**80.** c Law-and-order (adj) means strict laws and their enforcement. Only option (*c*) talks of the same.

**81.** c Heliocentric system is a cosmological model in which the Sun is assumed to lie at or near a central point (e.g., of the solar system or of the universe) while the Earth and other bodies revolve around it. Therefore, (*c*) is obviously wrong.

**82.** d The meaning of fundamentalism is 'a movement or attitude stressing strict and literal adherence to a set of basic principles'. Option (*d*) is closet to this definition of fundamentalism.

**83.** b

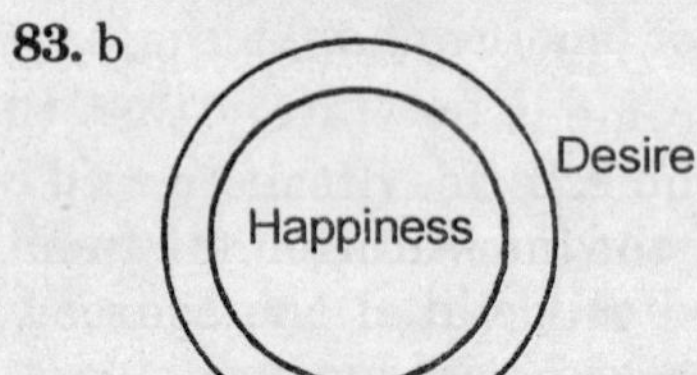


Only in option (*b*) the argument logically follows the given premise as happiness is a subset of desire.

**84.** * None of the options follow. Options (*a*) and (*d*) both seem correct as both the arguments are incorrect.

**85.** a Option (*b*) is factually correct and option (*a*) is logically impossible (it is impossible for an equilateral triangle to become right angle triangle)

**86.** a Option (*a*) is logically possible as we may not be able to explain the riddle of origin of the Universe even in the future. Option (*b*) is factually improbable.

**87.** * (a,b)

Area of circle can be arrived at with the help of reason. Whereas killing of someone can only be experienced by using the senses of vision. No option was given in the actual paper.

**88.** d When faculties of understanding become limited in their performance what suffers is perfection. However, it may not necessarily lead to imperfection. So option (*a*) is extreme. So is option (*b*). Option (*c*) is outside the scope. Only option (*d*) brings out the possibility of limited perfection in performance.

**89.** a First statement points at time and the second on space. Thus, universe is finite in space and time.

**90.** a Options (*b*), (*c*) & (*d*) negate the given statement. Option (*a*) states the given statement in a different way.

**91.** c Option (*a*) justifies the statement. Option (*b*), though goes against the statement, is somewhat uncertain. Option (*c*) says something completely opposite to the statement. Option (*d*), like option (*b*), is also somewhat uncertain. Thus, option (*c*) is the correct answer.

**92.** b If indeterminism is inherent in Newtonian System, then deterministic laws in Physics cannot be characteristically Newtonian. Thus, option (*b*) contradicts the given statement.

**93.** d 1 talks about a course in ethics in a Law University; 2, on the other hand, says the same course is most probably out of any course of law. Hence, the statements are incompatible with each other.

**94.** c* Though none of the options are completely correct, option (*c*) is the closest as 'analogous' is something that is comparable and alike in some respect to some other thing. Thus, identical comes the nearest to it.

**95.** b A 'different' relation may be symmetric as well as transitive. But it cannot be reflexive. So, it is inequivalence. Therefore, option (*b*) is the correct option.

**96.** d The words 'should be' in the given statement have some element of tentativeness in the suggestion. Only option (*d*) has such tentativeness in suggestion. Options (*a*) and (*c*) are assertive in nature. Option (*b*) is tentative but not a suggestion.

**97.** c Since Socrates is an element of the set 'innocent persons', whatever is true of the set must be true of Socrates. Thus, option (*c*) is correct.

**98.** c The speaker brings out the importance of each organ to the human body, each section of the society to the whole society and each element of the economy to the whole economy in the same vein. So they are analogous.

**99.** c 'But' in the fourth premise requires something in contrast with the statement. Only statement (*c*) brings out such a contrast.

**100.** d 'Rama is neither a brother of Krishna nor is he a lecturer' means that Rama is not a brother of Krishna and he is not a lecturer. Thus, option (*d*) is correct.

**101.** d 'Make hay while the sun shines' means to make the most of one's opportunities when one has the chance. None of the options is logically similar to it.

**102.** c 'The constitution has given the right of free speech. People speak freely in order to enjoy this right.' The argument with a similar logic is 'Wealth gives power to enjoy material things. People enjoy these things by spending their wealth.' Here, wealth is playing the same role as constitution. It empowers people. Constitution gives right of free speech and wealth gives power to enjoy. One exercises his right to free speech by speaking freely; one exercises the power to enjoy material things by spending money and buying them. Thus, these two arguments are analogous and have a similar pattern of reasoning.

**103.** d "Literature is the mirror in which the society can see itself." This statement implies that literature is a reflection of the society. The issues, ideologies, patterns, problems etc. of the society are reflected in the literature of that time. Literature enables people to get acquainted with the mass issues and ideologies. Option (*c*) does not correctly bring forward the meaning of the statement. It is a half-baked idea. Thus, option (*d*) would be a better answer.

**104.** a The statement that child labor is only a reflection of the malaise in the society means that the society is not in a good shape as depicted by the prevalence of child labor. This supports the statement that people do not abhor (hate) child labour (implied by its prevalence in the society).

**105.** c If the quality of governance is decided on the basis of law and order, it means that law must be indispensable (important) for society (that is why law and order has been used as a criterion). Other options are beyond the scope of the argument.

**106.** d All the options present possibilities which may be true. No option can be conclusively considered as a false inference.

**107.** c In the given argument, science and critical thinking are considered to be related. Similarly, religion is related to dogma. As dogma is not acceptable, therefore religion is not acceptable. The argument also says that critical thinking shakes the foundations of morality. Therefore, if science is accepted (which means critical thinking is accepted as they both are related), then the foundations of morality are shaken. Thus, option (*c*) is correct.

**108.** a Ramesh's liking for strawberries, apples, oranges and grapes can be expressed in the following order:

Strawberry > Apple > Orange > Grape

Thus, the statement that he likes grapes more than strawberries is false.

**109.** a The statement that "Justice should not only be done but also seen to have been done" means that people should know that justice is done; simply doing justice without making people aware of it is not enough. Option (*a*) is correct. The rest of the options are beyond the scope of the given statement.

**110.** b *Empirical* means based on experiments rather than theories. Faith and instinct are difficult to measure. So, options (*c*) and (*d*) are negated. Whether only poor people are driven to violence or not can be easily verified and tested. Thus, option (*b*) can be empirically tested. Engineer something (often disapproving) means to arrange for something to happen or take place, especially when this is done secretly in order to give yourself an advantage. This may be difficult to measure. Thus, option (*b*) is correct.

**111.** * The given question is incomplete.

**112.** * The given question is incomplete.

**113.** a The first statement means that according to some philosophers, a concept which can't be verified can still be considered valid because of the inner reasoning attached to it and which gives it a noble character.

The given statement is true in light of the above statement. It says that every person has 'certain inherent and inalienable rights' (i.e. concepts) which can't be verified i.e. ascertained whether they are justified or not, right or wrong. Because of the nature of such rights and the fact that they are inalienable to an individual, these rights are considered valid and given the status of protection by the Rule of Law.

**114.** c The argument is of the form A (Himalayan sparrows) is B (disappearing), A is C (Indian bird), and therefore B is C.

Option (*a*): It is completely out of sync with the given argument. It has four elements viz. industrialists, most taxes, Z and wealthy man. The given argument has only three elements and so both are not on the same line of reasoning.

Option (*b*): Here pineapple is a subset of fruit. Mango is also a subset of fruit. But they necessarily can't be the same sets. Hence, the reasoning is flawed and not on the same lines as in the argument.

Option (*c*): This option can be broken down as A (Snow tigers) is a subset of B (endangered species), B is a subset of C (protected) and so A is a subset of C. It follows the given argument exactly and hence is the correct answer.

Option (*d*): This option has both the premise (John is his father's favorite son) and conclusion (John is his father's favorite son) as the same. Therefore, this option does not follow the same line of reasoning.

**115.** b The given statement provides an argument on why undocumented evidence should be protected. Of all the given options, only option (*b*) gives a reason against the said argument, telling us how undocumented evidence can be dangerous and should thus, not remain undocumented. Therefore, the correct answer is option (*b*).

**116.** a The author does not prove his point, but instead fixates on the assumption that readers who prefer adventurous novels to psychological novels are inferior and while readers who have an opposite preference order are superior. He does not provide an explanation, and thus, option (*a*) is correct.

**117.** d If the patient suffers an ailment repeatedly for which he is not being given the drug more than one time, it could lead to problems, and thus denies the patient her right to health. This is the basic assumption made by the author. Hence, the correct answer is option (*d*).

**118.** d Even though Vijay has acknowledged causing dents on his own car due to his own recklessness, that does not necessarily mean he handled the office car with the same laxity. This makes the argument vulnerable and therefore, option (*d*) is the correct answer.

**119.** d The given statement has a negation in the second sentence, which is absent in option (*a*). Thus, it cannot be the answer. Option (*b*), though has the negation, follows the logic which is opposite to that given in the statement. Thus, option (*b*) is incorrect as well. Option (*c*) gives a condition where a pencil is not necessary and the required function can be fulfilled otherwise, unlike that in the given statement. Thus, option (*c*) is incorrect. Option (*d*) follows the logic presented by the given statement, and hence is the correct answer.

**120.** d The argument given by Richa shows a conflict of the moral obligations of two individuals. Option (*d*) is the correct answer because this is the only option that clearly shows two different moral obligations which contradict each other.

**121.** a The argument made by the author is that prohibition of alcohol increased the demand of alcohol. The increase in demand of alcohol has been concluded from the rise in deaths due to alcohol-related diseases during prohibition. Option (*b*) weakens this argument because it says that the rise in the diseases is due to the alcohol consumed before the prohibition. Option (*c*) also weakens the argument because it states that the rise in the death rate due to alcohol-related diseases has been constant in the period when it was prohibited and when it was not. Option (*d*) has also been ruled out because it attributes the rise in death rate to the decrease in availability of medical attention due to the social stigma attached to it. Option (*a*) is the correct answer as this does not affect/weaken the argument.

**122.** c According to the passage, a long-tern negative effect of enacting rent-control ordinances is that it will bring about a shortage of rental units. Hence, option (*c*) is the correct answer. Option (*a*) is incorrect because the passage states that there would be smaller rent increases when rent-control ordinances are in effect. Option (*b*) is incorrect because the passage talks about tenants of many municipalities having the power to enact or repeal ordinances but it does not state if these people would repeal ordinances passed 'as soon as' the negative effects of rent-control begin to surface. Option (*d*) is incorrect because it is difficult to say that the rents would increase 'substantially'.

**123.** b Option (*a*) talks of improvement of economy. This does not affect the argument as it does not assume a change in the state of economy. Option (*c*) defines 'survival' which again does not affect the argument. Option (*d*) questions the existence of government subsidies while the argument only talks about a cut and not elimination of subsidies. Moreover, this option will strengthen the argument. The correct answer is option (*b*) which states that just because the art groups have absorbed a decrease in subsidies, it is not necessary that they will be able to absorb another cut in their subsidies.

**124.** b According to the passage, doctors overtreat patients because they have an incentive for each procedure performed. Option (*a*) has been ruled out because the involvement of doctors is not coincidental. Option (*c*) is incorrect because the passage does not talk about any'well-defined principles' while option (*d*) is incorrect because no reasons have been given for the choices made. The correct answer is option (*b*) which talks of the opportunity as well as the incentive offered by it.

## STATEMENT-CONCLUSION

**Directions for questions 1 to 3:** In the following questions, a statement is followed by two conclusions. Taking the statement to be true, decide which of the given conclusions definitely follow from the given statement. Indicate your answer as (*a*) if only I follows, (*b*) if only II follows, (*c*) if neither I, nor II follows and (*d*) if both I and II follow.

**1. Statement:** The greatest advantage of democracy over all other forms of governments is not that the men who have gone to the top are exceptionally wise, but that since their power depends upon popular support, they know that they cannot retain their position if they are guilty of more than a modicum of injustice.

**Conclusions:**

**I.** In a democracy, persons in power cannot act arbitrarily.

**II.** Democratic countries cannot have excellent leaders. **(AILET, 2009)**

**2. Statement** : The Supreme Court gave a judgement that the maintenance of old age parents is the responsibility of the married girls, if they do not have brothers.

**Conclusions:**

**I.** Constitution is always interpreted to help oppressed people out.

**II.** Before the Supreme Court gave the verdict, a married girl must have denied to pay for the maintenance to her parents. **(AILET, 2012)**

**3. Statement :** Ideas given by our ancestors that were once discarded as uneconomical and unviable, turn out to be as functional and inevitable in present circumstances.

**Conclusions:**

**I.** In ancient period, ideas were considered either completely functional or totally infeasible.

**II.** Ideas cannot change from time to time.

**(AILET, 2012)**

**Directions (Q. 4 – 8):** *In each question below are given two statements numbered I and II.*

You have to take the two given statements as true even if they seem to be at variance with commonly known facts. Read all the conclusions and then decide which of the given conclusions logically follow from the given statements, disregarding commonly known facts. **(CLAT 2013)**

**4. I.** All vegetables have gravy.

**II.** All lunch has vegetable.

(*a*) All lunch has gravy.

(*b*) All gravy has lunch.

(*c*) Both (*a*) and (*b*).

(*d*) None of the above

**5. I.** Karan Johar is a good director.

**II.** Directors are intelligent.

(*a*) All intelligent are directors

(*b*) Karan Johar is intelligent.

(*c*) Both (*a*) and (*b*)

(*d*) None of the above

**6. I.** Some blues are green.

**II.** Pink is green

(*a*) Some blue is pink.

(*b*) Some green is pink.

(*c*) If either (*a*) or (*b*) follows.

(*d*) Some pinks are blues.

**7. I.** All boys are tall.

**II.** All Punjabi are tall.

(*a*) All boys are Punjabi.

(*b*) Some boys are Punjabi.

(*c*) Both of the above.

(*d*) None of the above.

**8. I.** All girls go to the college.

**II.** Rina does not go to the college.

(*a*) Rina is not a girl.

(*b*) Going to college is not essential to be a girl.

(*c*) Rina is a girl.

(*d*) None of the above.

**Directions (Q. 9 - 10) :** The question given below has a statement followed by two conclusions I and II. Consider the statement and the following conclusions. Decide which of the conclusions follow from the statement. Mark answer as: **(AILET 2014)**

(*a*) If conclusion I follows

(*b*) If conclusion II follows

(*c*) If both conclusions I and II follows

(*d*) If neither conclusion I follows nor 11 follows

**9. Statement :**

A degree in law is of the most wanted degrees by youth in India.

**Conclusions :**

I. A degree in law guarantees a good profession.

II. A degree in law is the first choice for youth in India.

**10. Statement :**

Any student who is caught red-handed using unfair means discredits his parents and teachers.

**Conclusions :**

I. Such students try to show that their teachers don't teach properly in the class.

II. Stringent actions must be taken against such students.

## Solutions

**1.** a The passage talks of top men depending upon popular support to exercise their power. This, in a way, means that their actions are closely watched by the public and so they cannot behave as they like. Thus, conclusion I definitely follows. Conclusion II is a far-fetched statement and thus, does not follow.

**2.** b Conclusion I does not follow from the statement. It cannot be generalized to say that the constitution is interpreted always to help oppressed people. Moreover, the statement is about Supreme Court and not about interpretation of the constitution. Conclusion II definitely follows. There has to be some observation on the part of The Supreme Court to give the judgement.

**3.** c Neither of the two conclusions follows. The statement says that the ideas that were given by our ancestors were then discarded for their unviability but presently they turn out to be functional and inevitable. Conclusion I does not follow since the statement does not talk about the classification of ideas. Conclusion II does not follow because the statement does not say that there are no new ideas in the present.

**4.** a

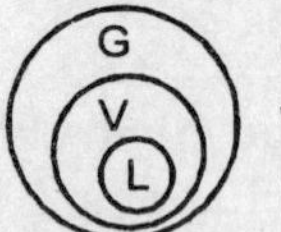


As we can see in the Venn diagram given above, option (A) follows and therefore, is the correct answer.

**5.** d

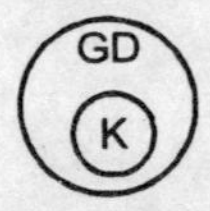

As we can see in the Venn diagram given above, option (D) follows and therefore, is the correct answer.

In case, they are taking 'good directors' and 'directors' as a single category, the following Venn diagram can be made. In that case option (B) would be the correct answer. However, the directions clearly state that the statements have to be true even if they seem to be at variance with commonly known facts. Thus, one cannot make such assumptions as mentioned above.

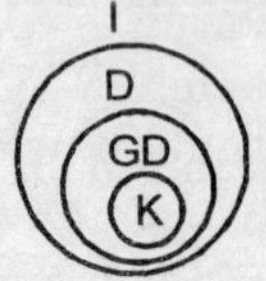


**6.** b

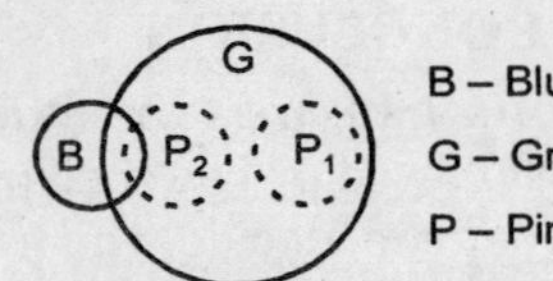


As we can see in the Venn diagram given above, option (B) follows and therefore, is the correct answer.

**7.** d

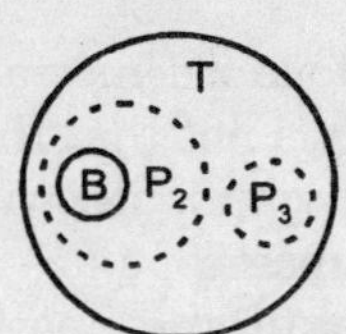


As we can see in the Venn diagram given above, option (D) follows and therefore, is the correct answer.

**8.** a

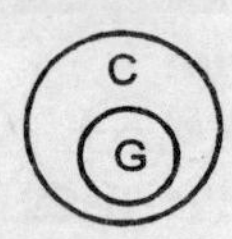


As we can see in the Venn diagram given above, option (A) follows and therefore, is the correct answer.

**9.** d Conclusion I does not follow because we cannot determine if a good profession is the reason behind the law degree being one of the most wanted degrees. Conclusion II also does not follow because the statement mentions 'one of the most'. Moreover, even if the law degree was the most wanted degree, conclusion II would not follow as each and every youth might not want that the majority of youth wants.

**10.** b The statement clearly shows that use of unfair means by students is undesirable. So, stringent actions must be taken against them to discourage this activity. This makes conclusion II valid. Conclusion I does not follow because we cannot judge the reason behind students using unfair means. So, the correct answer is option (*b*).

## STATEMENT-ASSUMPTION

**Direction for questions 1 to 21:** In each question below, a statement is followed by two assumptions numbered I and II. An assumption is something supposed or taken for granted. You have to consider the statement and the following assumptions and decide which of the assumptions is implicit in the statement. Mark answer:

(*a*) If only assumption I is implicit;

(*b*) If only assumption II is implicit;

(*c*) If neither I nor II is implicit; and

(*d*) If both I and II are implicit.

1. **Statement:** "Use 'M' Brand shoes. They are available in all sizes and last longer"- an advertisement in the newspaper 'A'.

**Assumption I:** Some people do not know about 'M' brand shoes.

**Assumption II:** People generally prefer shoes which last longer. **(AILET, 2012)**

2. **Statement:** Lack of stimulation in the first four or five years of life can have adverse consequences.

**Assumption I**: A great part of the development of observed intelligence occurs in the earliest years of life.

**Assumption II:** 50 per cent of the measurable intelligence at age 16 is predictable by the age of four. **(AILET, 2012)**

3. **Statement:** The patient's condition would improve after operation.

**Assumption I:** The patient can be operated upon in this condition.

**Assumption II:** The patient cannot be operated upon in this condition. **(CLAT 2009)**

4. **Statement:** Detergents should be used to clean cloths.

**Assumption I:** Detergent forms more lather.

**Assumption II:** Detergent helps to dislodge grease and dirt. **(CLAT 2009)**

5. **Statement:**. "As there is a great demand, every person seeking ticket of the programme will be given only five tickets".

**Assumption I:** The organizers are not keen on selling the tickets.

**Assumption II:** No one is interested in getting more than five tickets. **(CLAT 2009)**

6. **Statement:** Double your money in five months- An advertisement.

**Assumption I:** The assurance is not genuine.

**Assumption II:** People want their money to grow. **(CLAT 2009)**

7. **Statement:** Films have become indispensable for the entertainment of people.

**Assumption I:** Films are the only media of entertainment.

**Assumption II:** People enjoy films. **(CLAT 2009)**

8. **Statement:**. "To keep myself up-to-date, I always listen to 9.00 p.m. news on radio". – A candidate tells the interview board.

**Assumption I:** The candidate does not read newspaper.

**Assumption II:** Recent news are broadcast only on radio. **(CLAT 2009)**

9. **Statement:** Never before such a lucid book was available on the topic.

**Assumption I:** Some other books were available on this topic.

**Assumption II:** You can write lucid books on very few topics. **(CLAT 2009)**

10. **Statement:** In case of any difficulty about this case, you may contact our company's lawyer.

**Assumption I:** Each company has a lawyer of its own.

**Assumption II:** The company's lawyer is thoroughly briefed about this case. **(CLAT 2009)**

11. **Statement:** "Present day education is in shambles and the country is going to the dogs".

**Assumption I:** A good education system is essential for the well being of a nation.

**Assumption II:** A good education alone is sufficient for the well being of a nation. **(CLAT 2009)**

12. **Statement:** Children are influenced more by their teachers nowadays.

**Assumption I:** The children consider teachers as their models.

**Assumption II:** A large amount of children's time is spent in school. **(CLAT 2009)**

13. **Statement:** If Ram has finished reading the instructions, let him begin activities accordingly.

**Assumption I:** Ram has understood the instructions.

**Assumption II:** Ram would be able to act accordingly. **(CLAT 2010)**

14. **Statement:** Children below the age of seven should not be prosecuted for crimes.

**Assumption I:** Generally, children below seven cannot distinguish between right and wrong.

**Assumption II:** Children below the age of seven are generally mentally unsound. **(CLAT 2010)**

15. **Statement:** The employer has a right to reject the application of any candidate for employment without assigning any reason, while short listing candidates for interview.

**Assumption I:** The employer is impartial and believes in transparency in employment practices.

**Assumption II:** The employer wants to call only those candidates for interview, who in his opinion are eligible. **(CLAT 2010)**

16. **Statement:** The government has decided to reduce custom duty on computers.

**Assumption I:** The government wants to make computers accessible to larger number of people.

**Assumption II:** Prices in domestic market may go up in near future. **(CLAT 2010)**

**17. Statement:** You can win over new friends by your warm smile.

**Assumption I:** It is necessary to win over new friends.

**Assumption II:** It is always better to smile warmly to new persons. **(CLAT 2010)**

**18. Statement :** As poor people in India prefer and use jaggery rather than sugar, the government has decided to decontrol and scrap sugar distribution through Public Distribution System (PDS).

**Assumption I :** Jaggery is freely available at reasonable price to all poor people.

**Assumption II :** PDS has lost its utility.

**(AILET, 2013)**

**19. Statement :** Unless country 'X' achieves total literacy, it cannot achieve its mission of development.

**Assumption I :** It is possible to achieve total literacy in country 'X'.

**Assumption II :** No development is possible without a proper mission.

**(AILET, 2013)**

**20. Statement :** Many species of animals on our earth are still not studied scientifically and if we do not do this work urgently, many species will face extinction.

**Assumption I :** Earth may lose all types of life very shortly.

**Assumption II :** It is desirable and possible to study scientifically many animal species.

**(AILET, 2013)**

**21. Statement :** Herbs can safely be used for treating diseases of human animal species.

**Assumption I :** Herbs cannot be used for treating diseases of animals.

**Assumption II :** Herbs treatment is getting popular. **(AILET, 2013)**

## Solutions

**1.** d Both the assumptions are implicit. Had there been no one who would not know about 'M' brand shoes, there would be no point in giving such information. Assumption II is implicit. The statement says one should buy 'M' brand shoes because they are available in all sizes and last longer. It is clear that people would prefer shoes that last longer, and thus this is reason enough to convince them to buy these shoes. Option (*d*) is the correct choice.

**2.** c Neither of the assumptions is valid. The statement does not talk about the development of observed intelligence or measurable intelligence and such stuff. These are irrelevant to the statement and the statement lacks information to consider these assumptions valid.

**3.** a It has been suggested that the patient's condition will improve after the operation. This leads us to the assumption that the patient can be operated.

**4.** b The statement highlights that detergents should be used to clean the clothes. It implies that detergent will remove the stains of dirt and greese.

**5.** c It is clearly stated that there is a great demand of the tickets. This removes assumption I. As there is a restriction of five tickets we cannot assume that people are not willing to buy more than five tickets.

**6.** b The advertisement is created to attract people. So it can be assumed that people want their money to grow. But statement I is beyond the scope of information given in the question statement.

**7.** b The question states that films are indispensable for the entertainment of the people. So, II is definitely assumed. Assumption I is beyond the scope of information given in the question statement.

**8.** c The statement given does not tell us whether the candidate reads the newspaper. Nor does it tell that recent news are broadcast only on radio. Thus, both the assumptions are not implicit.

**9.** a The statement makes a comparison between the book in question with other books on the same topic. Thus, it assumes that other books were available on the topic. However, statement II is not implied in the statement.

**10.** b One cannot assume that all companies have a lawyer. The question statement highlights that the lawyer of the company can be called for further clarification. This implies that the lawyer is thoroughly briefed about the topic.

**11.** a Assumption I is implicit in the statement. Assumption II is not implicit as we cannot say that education alone is responsible for the nation.

**12.** a It is mentioned that children are influenced by their teacher. This implies that students consider their teachers role models. Duration of time spent is not related to the influence of teachers on the students.

**13.** a Assumption I follows as that is the condition for starting the activities. 'Reading the instructions' assumes that they are understood as well. Assumption II does not follow, as 'beginning the activity accordingly' may not mean 'would be able to act accordingly'. Therefore, (*a*) is the correct option.

**14.** a Assumption I follows as children do not generally know what is crime. Assumption II is tenuous. Therefore, (*a*) is the correct option.

**15.** c None of the Assumptions follow as right to reject entails an employer to reject for any reason. So 'impartiality or eligibility' cannot be assumed to be a factor. Therefore, (*c*) is the correct option.

**16.** c Governments' decision to reduce custom duty may lead to the outcome mentioned in I or II. But Government's decision may not have been based on these assumptions. Therefore, (*c*) is the correct option.

**17.** c Both the statements are far fetched. Therefore, (*c*) is the correct option.

**18.** d Government's decision to scrap sugar distribution through PDS assumes that jaggery is available to the poor at reasonable prices. If it were not true, the government's decision would have been illogical. Thus, assumption I is implicit in the given statement. Assumption II, if taken in the context of sugar distribution only, is also implicit in the given statement. This is so because the PDS, which earlier helped in distribution of goods to the poor, is no longer useful because the poor now have cheaper substitutes to those goods. Hence, option (*d*) is the correct answer.

**19.** a The statement talks of the mission of development which will only be possible when country 'X' achieves total literacy. Since a mission is a realistic possibility, therefore the condition of total literacy also has to be a realistic possibility. Therefore assumption I is implicit. We do not know if development is possible without a mission or not, so assumption II is not implicit. Option (*a*) is the correct answer.

**20.** b Though it is given in the statement that earth may lose many of its species, if it would lose all of its species cannot be commented on. Thus, assumption I is not implicit. Since there is talk of saving many species by studying them scientifically, therefore it is desirable and possible to study many animal species. Hence, assumption II is implicit. Option (*b*) is the correct answer.

**21.** b That herbs can be used to treat diseases of the humans does not, in any way, mean that animal diseases cannot be treated through the use of herbs. Hence, assumption I is not implicit. Since herbs have been found to have an important use, it can be concluded that its use as a treatment is getting popular. Option (*b*) is correct.

## ANALOGY

**Directions for questions 1 to 5:** In each question below, a pair of words is given. Select a pair from the given options which has a similar relationship as the given pair.

**1.** Frayed : Fabric

(*a*) Watered : Garden (*b*) Dilapidated : Building
(*c*) Frozen : Ice (*d*) Crumpled : Paper

**(AILET, 2008)**

**2.** Levitate : Magician

(*a*) Cook: Mother (*b*) Argue : Lawyer
(*c*) Float : Astronaut (*d*) Sky jump: Parachutists

**(AILET, 2008)**

**3.** Negotiable : cheque::

(*a*) Frozen : Asset
(*b*) Inventory : Merchandise
(*c*) Bank : Money
(*d*) Trade : Tariff **(AILET, 2009)**

**4.** Child : Fire

(*a*) Aged : Wisdom (*b*) Student : Examination
(*c*) Youth : Adolescence (*d*) Judge : Dishonour

**(AILET, 2012)**

**5.** Grain : Salt

(*a*) Shred : Wool (*b*) Cave : Stone
(*c*) Chip: Glass (*d*) Blades : Grass

**(AILET, 2012)**

**Direction for questions 6 to 32:** In each question below, word pairs are given which have a certain relation. Select a word to replace the question mark (?) so as to make a similar relational pair.

**6.** Hedger : Shrubbery :: ? : Stick

(*a*) snuffer (*b*) cougher
(*c*) Whittler (*d*) stickler **(AILET, 2009)**

**7.** Honour : Governor :: ? : Duke

(*a*) Excellency (*b*) Majesty
(*c*) Highness (*d*) Grace **(AILET, 2009)**

**8.** Carpet: Floor: : ? : Wall

(*a*) Wall paper (*b*) Wall hanging
(*c*) Scenery (*d*) Oil painting

**(AILET, 2011)**

**9.** Kaziranga: Rhino : : ? : Lion

(*a*) Corbett (*b*) Kanha
(*c*) Gir (*d*) Sunderbans

**(AILET, 2011)**

**10.** Legislation : Enactment :: Executive :?

(*a*) Minister (*b*) Officer
(*c*) Implementation (*d*) Leader **(CLAT 2009)**

**11.** UP : Uttranchal :: Bihar :?

(*a*) Jharkhand (*b*) Chhatisgarh
(*c*) Madhya Pradesh (*d*) Manipur **(CLAT 2009)**

**12.** Gold : Silver :: Cotton :?

(*a*) Yarn (*b*) Silk
(*c*) Fibre (*d*) Synthetic **(CLAT 2009)**

**13.** Botany : Flora ::Zoology :?

(*a*) Fauna (*b*) Biology
(*c*) Fossils (*d*) Pathology **(CLAT 2009)**

**14.** Cold wave : Winter :: Loo:?

(*a*) Humidity (*b*) Frostbite
(*c*) Summer (*d*) Storm **(CLAT 2009)**

**15.** King : Royal :: Saint :?

(*a*) Religious (*b*) Red
(*c*) Priesthood (*d*) Blue **(CLAT 2009)**

**16.** Sculptor : Statue :: Poet:?

(*a*) Painter (*b*) Singer
(*c*) Poem (*d*) Writer **(CLAT 2009)**

**17.** Laugh : Happy :: Cry :?

(*a*) Sad (*b*) Bickering
(*c*) Frown (*d*) Complain **(CLAT 2009)**

**18.** Black : Absence :: White :?

(*a*) Red (*b*) Presence
(*c*) Rainbow (*d*) Crystal **(CLAT 2009)**

**19.** Governor : President :: Chief-Minister :?

(*a*) Commissioner (*b*) Attorney General
(*c*) Justice (*d*) Prime-Minister **(CLAT 2009)**

**20.** Cat-Kitten; Goat-kid; Sheep-?

(*a*) colt (*b*) filly
(*c*) lamb (*d*) wool **(CLAT 2010)**

**21.** Cataract-eye; jaundice-liver; pyorrhea-?

(*a*) breath (*b*) tongue
(*c*) ears (*d*) teeth **(CLAT 2010)**

**22.** Blue-moon; blue-black; black-?

(*a*) sheep (*b*) goat
(*c*) sky (*d*) star **(CLAT 2010)**

**23.** Constituent Assembly : Constitution : : Parliament :?

(*a*) Statute (*b*) Legislative bills
(*c*) Speaker (*d*) Prime Minister **(CLAT 2010)**

**24.** Right : duty : : Power :?

(*a*) Wrong (*b*) Weak
(*c*) Powerless (*d*) Liability **(CLAT 2010)**

**25.** Elephant : Calf : : Tiger :?

(*a*) Pup (*b*) Tigress
(*c*) Cub (*d*) Baby Tiger **(CLAT 2010)**

**26.** Patient : Doctor : : Litigant :?

(*a*) Advisor (*b*) Help
(*c*) Legal aid (*d*) Lawyer **(CLAT 2010)**

**27.** Prosecutor : Accused : : plaintiff :?

(*a*) Appellant (*b*) Defendant
(*c*) Plaint (*d*) Suit **(CLAT 2010)**

**28.** Lok Sabha:Meera Kumar :: Rajya Sabha :?

(*a*) Hameed Ansari (*b*) Najma Heptullah
(*c*) Sushma Swaraj (*d*) Arun Jaitely **(CLAT 2010)**

**29.** President of India : 35 : : Member of Parliament (Rajya Sabha):?

(*a*) 18 (*b*) 21
(*c*) 25 (*d*) 30 **(CLAT 2010)**

**30.** India : Parliamentary System : : U.S.A. :?

(*a*) Democratic System (*b*) Presidential System
(*c*) Federal System (*d*) Republican system **(CLAT 2010)**

**31.** Executive : President : : Judiciary :?

(*a*) Supreme Court (*b*) Chief Justice
(*c*) Constitution (*d*) Government of India **(CLAT 2010)**

**32.** World War II : United Nations : : World War I :?

(*a*) Treaty of Versailles
(*b*) International Commission of Jurists
(*c*) League of Nations
(*d*) International court of Justice **(CLAT 2010)**

**Directions (Q. 33 – 37) :** *In each of the following questions, a related pair of words is followed by four pairs of words or phrases. Select the pair that best expresses a relationship similar to the one expressed in the question pair.* **(CLAT 2013)**

**33.** Action : Reaction

(*a*) Introvert : Extrovert
(*b*) Assail : Defend
(*c*) Diseased : Treatment
(*d*) Death : Rebirth

**34.** Sorrow : Misery

(*a*) Love : Obsession (*b*) Amity : Harmony
(*c*) Happiness : Joy (*d*) Enemy : Hatred

**35.** Drama : Audience

(*a*) Brawl : Vagabonds (*b*) Game : Spectators

(*c*) Art : Critic (*d*) Movie : Actors

**36.** Nuts : Bolts

(*a*) Nitty : Gritty (*b*) Bare : Feet

(*c*) Naked : Clothes (*d*) Hard : Soft

**37.** Book : Author

(*a*) Rain : Flood

(*b*) Light : Switch

(*c*) Symphony : Composer

(*d*) Song : Music

**Directions (Q. 38-41) :** *In the following set of analogies, one word is missing. Find it out from the given options.* **(AILET 2014)**

**38.** *Errata : ? : : Flaws : Jewels*

(*a*) Manuscripts (*b*) Books

(*c*) Literature (*d*) Prints

**39.** *inoculation : ?: : Exposure : Toughening*

(*a*) Immunity (*b*) Punctuality

(*c*) Vulnerability (*d*) Contagious

**40.** *Steel : Rails :: Alnico . ?*

(*a*) Aircraft (*b*) Machinery

(*c*) Silverware (*d*) Magnets

**41.** Conscience : Wrong : : Police : ?

(*a*) Thief (*b*) Law

(*c*) Discipline (*d*) Crime

**Directions (Q. 42-46):** *Two words, which have a certain relation, are paired. Select a correct option to substitute the question mark so as to make a similar relational pair with the word given after double colon (::).* **(CLAT 2014)**

**42.** Bow : Arrow :: Pistol : ?

(*a*) Gun (*b*) Shoot

(*c*) Rifle (*d*) Bullet

**43.** Eye : Wink :: Heart: ?

(*a*) Throb (*b*) Move

(*c*) Pump (*d*) Respirate

**44.** Ocean : Water :: Glacier : ?

(*a*) Cooling (*b*) Cave

(*c*) Ice (*d*) Mountain

**45.** *Prima facie* : On the first view :: *In pari delicto* : ?

(*a*) Both parties equally at fault

(*b*) While litigation is pending

(*c*) A remedy for all disease

(*d*) Beyond powers

**46.** Delusion : hallucination :: Chagrin : ?

(*a*) Illusion (*b*) Ordered

(*c*) Cogent (*d*) Annoyance

**Directions (Q. 47-49) :** *In each of the following questions, a related pair of words is followed by four pairs of words or phrases. Select the pair that best expresses a relationship similar to the one expressed in the question pair.* **(CLAT 2014)**

**47.** India : Tricolour

(*a*) China : Sickle and Hammer

(*b*) UK : Red Cross

(*c*) USA : Stars and Stripes

(*d*) None of the above

**48.** Statute : Law

(*a*) Proviso : Clause (*b*) Chapter : Exercise

(*c*) University : School (*d*) Section : Illustration

**49.** Buddhists : Pagoda

(*a*) Parsis : Temple (*b*) Christians : Cross

(*c*) Jains : Sun Temple (*d*) Jews : Synagogue

## Solutions

**1.** b 'Frayed' means to wear away. This is what happens to 'fabric' due to use over a period of time. The best answer is therefore 'dilapidated: building'. 'crumpled: paper' may seem close—nevertheless, when crumpled, paper is not exactly worn down.

**2.** d 'Levitate' is to float/fly up in the air and is a trick performed by magicians. In the same way, sky jump is a stunt performed by parachutists.

**3.** a Just as 'negotiable' is a quality of cheques, 'frozen' is a quality of 'asset'.

**4.** b Like a child is afraid of fire, a student is afraid of examination. Hence, option (*b*) is correct.

**5.** c The relation between 'a grain of salt' and 'a chip of glass' is that these are the smallest possible quantities by which the salt and glass can be described. Though 'a blade of grass' and 'a shred of wool' also make sense but these can be further broken down unlike 'a grain of salt' and 'a chip of glass'. Option (*b*) is irrelevant; it isn't analogous to grain:salt.

**6.** c A 'hedger' is a gardener who takes care of and trims the shrubbery. Similarly, a whittler carves decorative or functional objects by trimming and shaping a stick of wood.

**7.** d 'Honour' is used to address a 'Governor'. Likewise, 'grace' is used to address a 'duke'.

**8.** a Carpet covers the floor just as wall paper covers the wall.

**9.** c Kaziranga National Park is famous for rhinoceros. Similarly, Gir is famous for lions.

**10.** c Legislature is responsible for the enactment and executive is responsible for the implementation of laws.

**11.** a 'Uttaranchal' is carved out of UP. Similarly, Jharkhand is carved out of Bihar.

**12.** b Gold and silver are two different metals, similarly cotton and silk are two different fibres.

**13.** a Botany is a study of flora and zoology is a study of fauna.

**14.** c Cold wave is a phenomenon of winter and loo is a wind system of summer.

**15.** a King belongs to royalty similarly a saint belongs to a religion.

**16.** c Sculptor creates a statue and a poet composes a poem.

**17.** a Laughter is caused by happiness and someone cries because one is sad.

**18.** b Black and white are considered opposites. So, if black is to absence then white is to presence.

**19.** d What Governer is to the state, President is to the nation. Similarly, what Chief Minister is to the state, Prime Minister is to the nation.

**20.** c Lamb means young sheep.

**21.** d Pyorrhea is a disease of teeth.

**22.** a Blue-moon means something that happens in a long time. 'Blue-black' is a discoloration of the skin due to coagulation of blood. Blue sheep means unreliable or disreputable member in a family or society. Thus, all the given color phrases are idiomatic expressions.

**23.** a As a constituent assembly makes a constitution, similarly parliament formulates a statute, meaning a permanent rule made by a body or institution of the government.

**24.** d As a right brings along with it a duty, similarly power brings along liabilities.

**25.** c The young one of an elephant is called a calf, likewise, cub is the young one of tiger.

**26.** d As a patient approaches a doctor for help, similarly a litigant, which is a party involved in a law suit, approaches a lawyer.

**27.** b As a prosecutor is opposed to an accused; plaintiff, the complainant, is opposed to the defendant, the person being sued.

**28.** a The head of Lok Sabha is the Speaker, currently Ms. Meera Kumar. The chairperson of Rajya Sabha is the Vice-President of the country, currently Mr. Hameed Ansari.

**29.** d The minimum age for becoming the president of India is 35 years, similarly, the minimum age for becoming a member of Rajya Sabha is 30 years.

**30.** b India follows a parliamentary system while the US follows a presidential system.

**31.** b The real executive power lies with the President, similarly judiciary is headed by the Chief Justice.

**32.** c The United Nations was instituted after the World War II. League of Nations was instituted after World War I.

**33.** b The relationship between the key pair is of cause-effect. 'Action' is a cause and 'reaction', its effect. Similarly, 'assail', which means 'to attack violently', is a cause and 'defend' is its effect because one defends oneself only when one is attacked. Therefore, option (*b*) is correct. Option (*a*), like the key pair, is also a pair of antonyms but it is not the answer because option (*b*) also exhibits the cause-effect relationship that (*a*) does not. Other options are clearly incorrect because they do not exhibit that relationship.

**34.** a 'Misery' which means great suffering of the mind or body is a degree higher in intensity in comparison with 'sorrow'. Similarly, 'Obsession' is also a degree more intense than 'love'. Therefore, option (*a*) is correct. Option (*c*) and (*d*) are incorrect because there is no difference in terms of degree between the paired words in each pair. Option (*d*) is incorrect because one feels hatred for one's enemy.

**35.** b Just as audience are people that watch dramas, spectators are those that watch games. Therefore, option (*b*) is correct. Critics critique pieces of art, vagabonds (a person who has no home or job and who travels from place to place) have nothing to do with brawl (a noisy and violent fight involving a group of people, usually in a public place) and actors act in a movie.

**36.** a The idiom 'the nuts and bolts of something' means the basic practical details of a subject or an activity and 'nitty-gritty' also refers to the basic or most important details of an issue or a situation. All other options are unrelated and therefore, option (*a*) is the best of all the answer choices.

**37.** c Just as an author writes a book, a composer composes or writes symphonies, which is a long complicated piece of music for a large orchestra, in three or four main parts called movements. Therefore, option (*c*) is correct. Rains can cause flood, switch can be used to turn on lights and a song contains music.

**38.** b Errata is a list of errors in a printed work that are discovered after printing and are shown with its correction on a separate sheet. So, as flaws are related to jewels, errata will be related to books. Manuscript will not have errata and it is not a printed work. Literature is a subject and prints will also have flows and not errata. Hence, option (*b*) is the correct answer.

**39.** a Inoculate is to vaccinate i.e. to make a person immune against a disease. Similarly, exposure toughens a person or material. So, the correct answer is option (*a*).

**40.** d Just as steel is used to make rails, alnico is used to make magnets. Alnico is an acronym of a family of iron alloys. So, option (*d*) is the correct answer.

**41.** d A conscience stops you from doing anything wrong. Similarly, police stops you from committing a crime. Thus, option (*d*) is the correct answer.

**42.** d Just as an arrow is shot with a bow, a bullet is shot from a pistol.

**43.** a Just as an eye winks, the heart beats/throbs. Option (*c*) is incorrect because the beating of the heart is not called pumping of the heart; the heart pumps blood in the arteries.

**44.** c Just as an ocean comprises water, a glacier comprises ice.

**45.** a Just as 'prima facie' means 'on the first view', 'in pari delicto' means is a legal term used to indicate that two persons or entities are equally at fault.

**46.** d Just as 'delusion' and 'hallucination' are synonyms, which refer to the experience involving the apparent perception of something not present, 'chagrin' is a synonym of annoyance. 'Cogent' means conclusive.

**47.** c Just as the Indian flag contains tricolor, the USA flag contains stars and stripes.

**48.** a Just as 'statute' means law, 'proviso' means clause.

**49.** d Just as the Buddhist temple is called a 'pagoda', 'synagogue' is the place where the Jews meet for religious worship or instruction.

## PARAJUMBLES

**Directions for questions 1 to 5:** In each of the questions below, four sentences of a paragraph are jumbled. Arrange the four sentences in a logical sequence to make a coherent paragraph.

**1.** (i) The Supertag scanner could revolutionise the way people shop, virtually eradicating supermarket queues;

(ii) The face of retailing will change even more rapidly when the fibre optic networks being built by cable TV companies begin to be more widely used;

(iii) The scanner would have a double benefit for supermarkets - removing the bottleneck which causes frustration to most customers and reducing the number of checkout staff;

(iv) An electronic scanner which can read the entire contents of a supermarket trolley at a glance has just been developed.

The best sequence is:

(*a*) ii, i, iii, iv (*b*) iv, i, iii, ii
(*c*) iv, iii, ii, i (*d*) iii, i, iv, ii **(CLAT 2008)**

**2.** (i) Of course, modern postal services now are much more sophisticated and faster, relying as they do on motor vehicles and planes for delivery.

(ii) Indeed, the ancient Egyptians had a system for sending letters from about 2000 BC, as did the Zhou dynasty in China a thousand years later.

(iii) Letters, were, and are, sent by some form of postal service, the history of which goes back a long way.

(iv) For centuries, the only form of written correspondence was the letter.

**The best sequence is:**

(*a*) ii, i, iii, iv (*b*) iv, i, iii, ii
(*c*) iv, iii, ii, i (*d*) iii, i, iv, ii
**(CLAT 2008)**

**3.** (i) Converting money into several currencies in the course of one trip can also be quite expensive, given that banks and *bureaux de change* charge commission on the transaction.

(ii) Trying to work out the value of the various notes and coins can be quite a strain, particularly if you are visiting more than one country.

(iii) Travel can be very exciting, but it can also be rather complicated.

(iv) One of these complications is, undoubtedly, foreign currency.

**The best sequence is:**

(*a*) ii, i, iii, iv (*b*) iv, i, iii, ii
(*c*) iv, iii, ii, i (*d*) iii, iv, ii, i **(CLAT 2008)**

**4.** (i) She was right about three-curiosity, freckles, and doubt-but wrong about love.

(ii) "Four of the things I'd be better without: Love, curiosity, freckles, and doubt".

(iii) Love is indispensable in life.

(iv) So wrote Dorothy Parker, the American writer.

**The best sequence is:**

(*a*) ii, iv, i, iii
(*b*) ii, i, iii, iv
(*c*) ii, i, iv, iii
(*d*) iii, iv, i, ii **(CLAT 2008)**

5. (i) This clearly indicates that the brains of men and women are organised differently in the way they process speech.

(ii) Difference in the way men and women process language is of special interest to brain researchers.

(iii) However, women are more likely than men to suffer aphasia when the front part of the brain is damaged.

(iv) It has been known that aphasia - a kind of speech disorder - is more common in men than in women when the left side of the brain is damaged in an accident or after a stroke.

**The best sequence is:**

(*a*) ii, i, iv, iii (*b*) iv, i, iii, ii

(*c*) iv, iii, ii, i (*d*) ii, iv, iii, i **(CLAT 2008)**

**Direction (Q. 6 – 10):** *The sentences given in each question, when properly sequenced, form a coherent paragraph. Each sentenced is labelled with a letter. Choose the most logical order of sentences from among the given choices to construct a coherent paragraph. Shade the appropriate answer in the space provided for it in the OMR sheet.* **(CLAT 2013)**

6. A. People who start up their own business typically come from two extreme backgrounds: One is the business family background and the other is a steady professional family background.

B. Typically, people from different backgrounds face different kinds of basic problems.

C. The people from both the backgrounds find it very difficult to establish and manage an enterprise.

D. Starting up and managing a small business is no joke.

(*a*) D B C A (*b*) B A C D

(*c*) D A C B (*d*) C D A B

7. A. Venture capital is recommended as the ideal source of financing for a successfully small business.

B. Several companies including start ups have been funded by dedicated venture funds during this decade.

C. Despite this, an average Indian entrepreneur understands and appreciation of venture capital concept has been woefully inadequate.

D. In the Indian context, though venture capital has been a relatively late entrant, it has already made a reasonable impact.

(*a*) A B C D (*b*) A D B C

(*c*) A C B D (*d*) A D C B

8. A. Progress in diagnosis, in preventive medicine and in treatment, both medicinal and surgical,has been rapid and breathe taking.

B. Much in medicine which is not taken for granted was undreamt of even as recently as 20 years ago.

C. Presently small pox has been eradicated, poliomyelitis practically banished, tuberculosis has become curable and coronary artery disease surgically relievable.

D. The dramatic surge in the field of molecular biology and research by immunologists and geneticists has succeeded in controlling parasitic diseases like malaria and river blindness that affect millions of people round the world.

(*a*) B D C A (*b*) B A C D

(*c*) B C A D (*d*) B D A C

9. A. Instead, many deaths and injuries result from falling objects and the collapse of buildings, bridges and other structures.

B. Earthquakes almost never kill people directly.

C. Fire resulting from broken gas or power lines is another major danger during a quake.

D. Spills of hazardous chemicals are also a concern during an earthquake.

(*a*) C A B D (*b*) D A C B

(*c*) D C A B (*d*) B A C D

10. A. The Winchester or hard disk drives can store much more data than what can be stored on a floppy diskette.

B. Hard disks come sealed and they cannot be removed or changed like floppy diskettes.

C. Often floppy disk system is used in conjunction with the Winchester disk system.

D. This makes for an ideal system for secondary storage.

(*a*) C A B D (*b*) C B D A

(*c*) B A C D (*d*) A B C D

**Directions (Q. 11-15) :** *The sentences given in each question, when properly sequenced, form a coherent paragraph. Each sentence is labelled with a letter. Choose the most logical order of sentences from among the given choices to construct a coherent paragraph.*

11. (A) Payment for imports and exports is made through a system called foreign exchange. The value of the money of one country in relation to the money of other countries is agreed upon.

(B) The rates of exchange vary from time to time.

(C) For example, an American dollar or a British pound sterling is worth certain amounts in the money of other countries.

(D) Sometimes a US dollar is worth 60 rupees in India. **(CLAT 2014)**

(*a*) ABCD (*b*) BACD
(*c*) ACBD (*d*) CABD

**12.** (A) When a dictionary is being edited, a lexicographer collects all the alphabetically arranged citation slips for a particular word.

(B) The moment a new word is coined, it usually enters the spoken language.

(C) The dictionary takes note of it and makes a note of it on a citation slip.

(D) The word then passes from the realm of hearing to the realm of writing. **(CLAT 2014)**

(*a*) ABCD (*b*) ACBD
(*c*) BACD (*d*) BCAD

**13.** (A) The impression that corruption is a universal phenomenon persists and the people do not co-operate in checking this evil.

(B) So there is hardly anything that the government can do about it now.

(C) It is regrettable that there is a widespread corruption in the country at all levels.

(D) Recently several offenders were brought to book, but they were not given deterrent punishment. **(CLAT 2014)**

(*a*) CDAB (*b*) ADBC
(*c*) ADCB (*d*) CBAD

**14.** (A) In all social affairs convention prescribes more or less generally accepted rules of behaviour.

(B) Of course, there is nothing absolute about conventions.

(C) They vary from country to country, from age to age.

(D) Convention has a necessary part to play in the life of everyone. **(CLAT 2014)**

(*a*) ABCD (*b*) ADBC
(*c*) DACB (*d*) DABC

**15.** (A) In fact, only recently there have been serious studies to find out how many of us actually have nightmares.

(B) Now that is changing.

(C) The study of nightmares has been curiously neglected.

(D) While results so far are inconclusive, it seems fair to say that at least half the population has occasional nightmares. **(CLAT 2014)**

(*a*) CADB (*b*) ABDC
(*c*) ADCB (*d*) CBAD

## Solutions

**1.** b Sentence (iv) introduces the topic followed by (i), which talks about revolutionizing, followed by (iii) talking about the changes and benefits and then (ii) referring to the change expected in future.

**2.** c The paragraph talks of letters, with sentence (iv) introducing the topic, (iii) continuing the idea followed by (ii), and (i) being the last line talking of modern postal services.

**3.** d The paragraph is about the complications faced while travelling. (iii) introduces the topic, followed by (iv). And then (ii) and (i) elaborate the complications.

**4.** a The paragraph begins with the quote of the author, followed by her name in (iv), and then (i) and (iii) describing her quote.

**5.** d Sentence (ii) introduces the idea of the paragraph. Sentence (iv) talks about a speech disorder, (ii) describes it further and (i) concludes the paragraph.

**6.** c d is the opening sentence since it introduces the topic of the paragraph: starting and managing small business. a follows d since it discusses the backgrounds of those 'people who start up a business' mentioned in d. ac is a mandatory pair. 'Both the backgrounds' in c refers to the two backgrounds discussed in a, i.e., 'business family background' and 'steady professional family background'. b will follow c because c says that people from both the backgrounds will face difficulty and b adds that the difficulty faced by each will be different. Hence, the correct sequence is dacb, making option (*c*) the correct answer.

**7.** b A starts the paragraph by introducing the topic of discussion: venture capital. d follows a because where a talks about the success brought about by venture capital, d carries the idea forward by talking about its impact in the Indian context. bc is a mandatory pair because 'Despite this' in c refers to the information given in b. c says that an average Indian entrepreneur hardly appreciates venture capital, despite 'the latter being used by several companies', the information mentioned in b. Thus, the correct sequence is adbc, rendering option (*b*) the correct answer.

**8.** b bac is a mandatory sequence. b talks about the unparalleled progress made in the field of medicine and a tells us about the manner in which the progress was made - rapid and breath taking. c follows a by citing a few examples of the progress. This sequence is present only in option (*b*). Hence, option (*b*) is the correct answer.

**9.** d ba is a mandatory pair because b says that earthquakes usually do not kill people directly and a tells us how earthquakes kill indirectly. Both c and d cite concerns during earthquakes, they should therefore come together and follow a. Therefore, option (d) is the correct answer.

**10.** d cd is a mandatory pair. 'This' in d refers to the 'Winchester disk system' in c. a should precede b since a introduces the Winchester or hard disk drives and b gives more information about them. Hence, option (d) is the correct answer.

**11.** c The correct sequence is acbd. Statements (a) and (c) form a mandatory pair. Statement (a) discusses the system of rate of exchange i.e., there is a certain value of one currency with respect to that of another and statement (c) gives its example. Statements (b) and (d) form a mandatory pair because statement (b) states that the rate of exchange changes from time to time and statement (d) gives an example of it. Since only option (*c*) exhibits such a pairing, it is the correct answer.

**12.** d The correct answer is option (*d*) as the correct sequence is bcad. Statements (b) and (c) form a mandatory pair because the 'it' in (c) refers to the 'newly coined word' referred to in statement (b). Statement (c) should be followed by statement (a) because the former talks about noting down the newly coined word on a citation slip and the latter talks about arranging these citation slips when editing a dictionary. Statement (d) should come in the end because it concludes the idea (of passing of a word from the realm of hearing to that of writing) talked about in (b), (c) and (a).

**13.** a The correct sequence is cdab. Statement (c) should be followed by statement (d) because the former talks about the existence of corruption at all levels and the latter carries forward the idea by stating that such corrupt people have also been brought to the book. Statement (d) should be followed by statement (a) because (d) talks about offenders not being given deterrent punishment and (a) gives its reason. Statement (a) should be followed by statement (b) because (a) talks about people not checking corruption and (b) gives a consequence of it. Hence, option (*a*) is the correct answer.

**14.** d The correct sequence is dabc. Statement (d) is an apt beginning of the paragraph as it is a general statement that introduces the main idea - value of conventions in everyone's life. Statement (d) should be followed by statement (a) because (d) talks about conventions being necessary part of everyone's life and (a) carries the idea forward by telling what these conventions are. Statement (a) should be followed by statement (b) because (a) describes conventions as accepted rules (which may be considered absolute) and (b) immediately disclaims that these rules are not absolute but vary. Statement (b) should be followed by statement (c) because (c) further states how these conventions vary. Hence, option (*d*) is the correct answer.

**15.** d The correct sequence is cbad. Statements (c) and (b) form a mandatory pair because 'this' in (b) refers to 'study of nightmares being neglected' discussed in (c). Statement (b) should be followed by statement (a) because (b) talks about the fact that the study of nightmares is not neglected like before and (a) gives its example. Statements (a) and (d) form a mandatory pair because the 'results' in (d) refer to those of 'studies' referred to in (a). Hence, option (*d*) is the correct answer.

## PARAJUMBLES (6 SENTENCE TYPE)

**Directions (Q. 1-7) :** *In each question below, the first and the last phrase / sentence of the sentence / paragraph are given. Other phrases / sentences are given in jumbled form. Arrange the phrases / sentences to form a readable sentence / paragraph.*

**1.** 1. Some people seem to have a compulsive need to work continually, they may be called work-addicts.

M. However they never quite reach the top.

N. There are companies which expect everyone to be at work early and stay back late.

O. Because of their diligence they tend to get rapid promotion at first.

P. Work addicts generally end up in such organisations.

6. [in the original paper sentence 6 was missing]

The correct sequence should be:

(*a*) PNMO (*b*) MOPN
(*c*) OMNP (*d*) NPOM **(AILET, 2008)**

**2.** 1. If you feed a dog or tame a bear by hand

P. or until they succeed in getting it

Q. and tear and pull at it

R. they get their teeth into the meat

S. until they bite a piece off

6. all out of your hand.

The correct sequence should be:

(*a*) PSRQ (*b*) SQRP
(*c*) RPSQ (*d*) RQSP **(AILET, 2008)**

**3.** 1. St. Francis taught that

P. and that it was easier to be good

Q. if men would be happy

R. they must be good

S. and happy if one were poor

6. and did not trouble oneself about money

The correct sequence should be:

(*a*) PQRS (*b*) RPSQ

(*c*) QRPS (*d*) PSQR **(AILET, 2008)**

**4.** 1. When Mrs. Bates came down, the room was strangely empty, with a tension of expectancy.

P: Meantime her anger was turned pale with fear.

Q: She took up her sewing and stitched for some time without raising her head.

R: She rushed to the stair door and opened it, listening.

S: The clock struck eight and she rose suddenly, dropping her sewing on the chair.

6. Then she went out, locking the door behind her.

(*a*) S Q P R (*b*) Q P S R

(*c*) S R Q P (*d*) P R S Q

**(AILET, 2009)**

**5.** 1. Above all.

P: in the present age of light reading

Q: it is well if something heavier is cast now and then

R: of reading hastily and thoughtlessly

S: that is,

6. into the midst of the reading public.

(*a*) P Q R S (*b*) P S R Q

(*c*) P R QS (*d*) Q S R P

**(AILET, 2009)**

**6.** 1 : Two men held a struggling crazed dog down on a table.

P : Its mouth was smothered with saliva and a bite from its jaws might cause death.

Q : He put one end of the tube between his lips and lowered the other towards the foam covered jaws.

R : Beside them stood Louis Pasteur holding a narrow glass-tube in one hand.

S : As the animal writhed, he carefully sucked some of the saliva up the tube.

6 : The men watched him awe-struck.

The proper sequence should be

(*a*) P R Q S (*b*) P Q R S

(*c*) S R P Q (*d*) R P S Q

**(AILET, 2012)**

**7.** 1: There is only one monkey we can thoroughly recommend as an indoor pet

P : They quickly die from colds and coughs after the first winter fogs.

Q : It is the beautiful and intelligent Capuchin monkey.

R : The lively little Capuchins, however, may be left for years in an English house without the least danger to their health.

S : The Marmosets, it is true, are more beautiful than the Capuchins and just as pleasing, but they are too delicate for the English climate.

6: Finally, let me say that no other monkey has a better temper or more winning ways.

The proper sequence should be:

(*a*) P Q R S (*b*) Q R P S

(*c*) Q S P R (*d*) R P S Q **(AILET, 2012)**

**Directions (Q. 8-11) :** *In this section, each passage consists of five sentences. The first sentence is given in the beginning. The four sentences in each passage have been jumbled up. These are labeled P, Q, R and S. You are required to find out the proper sequence of the four sentences and mark accordingly on the Answer Sheet.* **(AILET 2014)**

**8.** $L_1$: It is significant that one of the most common objections to competition is that it is blind

P: This is important because in a system of free enterprise based on private property, chances are not equal and there is indeed a strong case for reducing that inequality of opportunity.

Q: Rather it is a choice between a system where it is the will of a few persons that decides which is to get what and one where it depends at least partly, on the ability and the enterprise of the people concerned.

R: Although competition and justice may have little else in common, it is as much a commendation of competition as of justice that it is no respector of persons.

S: The choice today is not between a system in which everybody will get what he deserves according to some universal standard and one where individual shares are determined by chance or goodwill.

$L_6$: The fact that opportunities open to the poor in a competitive society are much more restricted than those open to the rich, does not make it less true that in such a society the poor are more free than a person commanding much greater material comfort in a different type of society.

The proper sequence should be

(*a*) RSQP (*b*) SRQP

(*c*) PQRS (*d*) QPSR

**9.** $L_1$: The chain saw howled as I finished cutting through the branch.

P: The branch crashed to the ground, taking my spectacles with it.

Q: I almost dropped the saw as I shielded my face from the twigs that brushed by.

R: Howard retrieved my glasses and handed them up to me.

5: 1 pulled the saw away, and my husband tugged against the other end of the rope that I had tied just above the cut.

$L_6$: Are you okay? He asked.

The proper sequence should be

(*a*) QRPS (*b*) SQPR

(*c*) SRPQ (*d*) QSPR

**10.** $L_1$: All human beings are aware of the existence of a power greater than that of the mortals — the name given to such a power by individuals is an outcome of birth, education and choice.

P: Logically, therefore such a power should be remembered in good times also.

Q: Their other philanthropic contributions include the construction and maintenance of religious places such as temples or gurdwaras.

R: Industrial organizations also contribute to the veneration of this power by participating in activities such as religious ceremonies and festivities organized by the employees.

5: This power provides an anchor in times of adversity, difficulty and trouble..

$L_6$: The top management/ managers should participate in all such events, irrespective of their personal choices.

The proper sequence should be

(*a*) RPSQ (*b*) QRPS

(*c*) SPRQ (*d*) SQRP

**11.** $L_1$: A thorough knowledge of path or course to be followed is essential for achieving success.

P: Seniors must show the path clearly by laying down the precise expectations of the management in terms of job description, key result areas, and personal targets.

Q: They should also 'light the path' by personal examples.

R: Advice tendered or help offered must be objectively evaluated for its effectiveness in achieving the desired goals.

S: A display of arrogance and a false sense of 'self-worth', in order to belittle those who come to help, prove dysfunctional.

$L_6$: The individuality of each employee must be respected.

The proper sequence should be

(*a*) RSPQ (*b*) RPSQ

(*c*) QPSR (*d*) PQRS

## Solutions

**1.** d The paragraph begins by an introduction about work-addicts. N should follow it as we need to talk first about the perspective and ideology of the companies. 'Such organization' in P refers to the organization mentioned in N. Therefore, NP is a mandatory pair. O follows P as O mentions what happens when work-addicts start working in such organizations. M mentions the contrast. Thus, OM is a mandatory pair. Option (*d*) is the correct choice.

**2.** d The first sentence to follow 1 should be R, the 'they' in R refers to the animals described in 1. It also tells us the first thing that the animal is likely to do i.e., 'to get their teeth into the meat'. Q and S would follow this, telling what they would do after getting their teeth into the meat. Next should be P as it should directly precede 6.

**3.** c. Sentence 1 must be followed by Q since it tells about whom did St. Francis taught (men). Moreover, it begins with the conditional (if) that is appropriate after 1. Q begins the sequence in only one choice. Hence, option (*c*) is the correct choice.

**4.** b Q follows 1 because it tells what Mrs. Bates started doing after coming down. This is followed by P; 'meantime' refers to 'some time' for which she was sewing and stitching. SR is a mandatory pair which has a sequence of events ('rose suddenly' must be followed by 'rushed to the stair door'). Thus, option (*b*) is the correct choice.

**5.** b P must follow 1. This is followed by S and R which form a mandatory pair describing the 'present age of light reading'. Q has to precede 6 since 6 mentions where something heavier is cast (into the midst of the reading public).

**6.** b* RQ forms a mandatory pair as the 'he' in Q refers to 'Louis Pasteur' in R. Also, R introduces the glass-tube which has been mentioned later in Q and S. S follows Q as it explains what 'he' does with the tube. P cannot come anywhere but after the opening sentence. The 'its' in P refers to the 'dog' in 1. The RQ pair is in only one option i.e. option (*a*). Hence, option (*a*) should be correct, though the answer given by NLU-D is option (*b*).

**7.** c Q definitely follows 1 as it tells the name of the monkey talked about in the opening sentence. S follows Q as it compares the Capuchins with Marmosets that can also be candidates for the most recommended pet but for their delicacy. P explains what effect the English climate has on Marmosets and follows S. R comes after P as it explains how the Capuchins are better for the English climate. Thus, option (c) has the correct sequence.

**8.** a The correct sequence is RSQP. SQP is a mandatory sequence. S says that the choice is not between a system (in which everybody gets what he deserves) and individual share. Q follows it because it states what the choice is. P follows Q as P tells us why the choice given in Q is important. Hence, option (*a*) is the correct answer.

**9.** b The correct sequence is SQPR. The passage begins by saying that the writer finished cutting through the branch. S will follow L1 because the narrator pulls the saw away in S after cutting the branch in L1. Qshould follow S as the twigs brush the narrator's face in Q after her husband pulls the branch down in S.SQ should be followed by P because the branch falls in P after it is pulled in S and Q. P, R and L6 form a mandatory sequence because the narrator's spectacles fall down from the tree in P , which are picked by her husband Harwardin R, followed by Harward asking the narrator, his wife about her well-being.

**10.** c The correct sequence is SPRQ. L1 talks about a power that is greater than mortals and S follows it by saying that this power helps in times of need. RQL6 is a mandatory sequence because 'their' in Q refers to 'Industrial organizations' in R. L6 follows R because the 'events' in L6 refer to 'construction and maintenance of religious places' discussed in R. The sequence RQL6 should follow P since P talks about good times, which are discussed in R, Q and L6.

**11.** d The correct sequence is PQRS. P follows L1 because L1 states that a thorough knowledge of path is essential for success and P goes on to say that seniors must show this path. Q and P are mandatory pairs because 'they' in Q refer to 'seniors' in P. RS is a mandatory pair because R talks about the advise senior should give and S deals with what he should not.

## ASSERTION-REASON

**Directions for questions 1 to 15:** *Each question below consists of one Assertion (A) and one Reason (R). Examine them and select the correct answer using the code below.*

**Code:**

(*a*) Both A and R are individually true and R is the correct explanation of A.

(*b*) Both A and R are individually true but R is not the correct explanation of A.

(*c*) A is true but R is false.

(*d*) A is false but R is true.

**1. Assertion (A) :** A stranger to a contract has no right to enforce it against the parties to the contract.

**Reason (R):** Privity of contract between the parties is essential for enforcement of contract. **(AILET, 2009)**

**2. Assertion (A) :** A finder of a thing has title to it.

**Reason (R):** The finder's title to a thing is superior to that of the owner. **(AILET, 2009)**

**3. Assertion (A):** A minor is not competent to enter into any contract, even for necessaries.

**Reason (R):** For necessaries supplied to a minor, his estate can be made liable to reimburse. **(AILET, 2009)**

**4. Assertion (A):** A legal right is a legally protected interest.

**Reason (R):** An element of advantage is essential to constitute a right. **(AILET, 2009)**

**5. Assertion (A):** Customs to have the force of law must be immemorial.

**Reason (R):** Custom represents common consciousness of people. **(AILET, 2009)**

**6. Assertion (A):** Area along the Equator records the highest temperature throughout the year.

**Reason (R):** On the equator, days and nights are equal for the largest part of the year. **(CLAT 2009)**

**7. Assertion (A):** Commercial fisheries have not developed in tropics.

**Reason (R):** The demand for marine food from low income population is low in the tropics. **(CLAT 2009)**

**8. Assertion (A):** Lighting thunder and heavy rain accompany volcanic activity.

**Reason (R):** Volcanoes throw water vapour and charged particle in the atmosphere **(CLAT 2009)**

9. **Assertion (A):** Soils in some parts of Punjab, Haryana and Rajasthan are saline.

**Assertion (A):** Evaporation exceeds precipitation. **(CLAT 2009)**

10. **Assertion (A):** The monsoons arrive suddenly in India in June.

**Reason (R):** The monsoonal low pressure trough is well-developed over India. **(CLAT 2009)**

11. **Assertion (A):** India built dams and reservoirs to manage water resources

**Reason (R):** India had enough experience in canals. **(CLAT 2009)**

12. **Assertion (A):** The life expectancy in European countries is very high.

**Reason (R):** European countries have low mortality rate. **(CLAT 2009)**

13. **Assertion (A):** The nomadic herders slaughter their animals for meat.

**Reason (R):** Animals form the chief source of food and livelihood for nomadic herders. **(CLAT 2009)**

14. **Assertion (A):** Exploitation of equatorial rain forest of Amazon basin is not easy.

**Reason (R):** This region is very rich in several types of deadly animals and insects. **(CLAT 2009)**

15. **Assertion (A):** The Sea remains free from ice from British Columbia to Bering Sea.

**Reason (R):** Air moving off the comparatively warm waters of North Pacific Drift gives the coastal areas of British Columbia a warmer climate. **(CLAT 2009)**

**Directions (Q. 16 - 17) :** *Following items consist of two statements, one labeled as the 'Assertion (A)' and the other as 'Reason (R)' you are to examine these two statements carefully and select the answers to these items using the codes given below:* **(AILET 2014)**

**Codes :**

(*a*) Both A and R are individually true and R is the correct explanation of A.

(*b*) Both A and R are individually true but R is not the correct explanation of A.

(*c*) A is true but R is false.

(*d*) A is false but R is true.

16. **Assertion (A) :**

The phenomenon of nuclear fission generates great energy.

**Reason (R) :**

The process in which a nucleus is broken into two parts is called nuclear fission.

17. **Assertion (A) :**

The price of a stock is determined on the basis of demand and supply of the stock.

**Reason (R) :**

The value of the Sensex increases whenever there is a heavy demand for the stocks which form the Sensex.

## Solutions

**1.** a Both A and R are true and R is the correct explanation of A.

**2.** c The person who finds something would automatically have a title to it but it does not mean that his title is superior to that of the actual owner.

**3.** d A minor has all the right to enter into a contract for necessaries. R is true. This leads us to option (*d*).

**4.** c Yes, a legal right constitutes a legally protected interest. However, R is false. This leads us to option (*c*).

**5.** b Both the statements are independently true. This leads us to option (*b*).

**6.** a Both A and R are individually true and R is the correct explanation of option (*a*).

**7.** b Both A and R are individually true but R is not the correct explanation of A.

**8.** a Both A and R are individually true and R is the correct explanation of A.

**9.** a Both A and R are individually true and R is the correct explanation of A.

**10.** a Both A and R are individually true and R is the correct explanation of A.

**11.** b Both A and R are individually true but R is not the correct explanation of A.

**12.** b Both A and R are individually true but R is not the correct explanation of A.

**13.** a Both A and R are individually true and R is the correct explanation of A.

**14.** b Both A and R are individually true but R is not the correct explanation of A.

**15.** a Both A and R are individually true and R is the correct explanation of A.

**16.** b Both the statements are true but the reason behind the generation of energy is the binding of the nucleon. Hence, option (*b*) is the correct answer.

**17.** b Both the statements are true but (R) does not give the correct explanation of (A). So, the correct answer is option (*b*).

## STATEMENT-ARGUMENT

**Directions for questions 1 to 22**: *Each question below contains a Statement or a Question and two Arguments I and II. Assume the Statement or Question to be true and choose the correct answer according to the code given below.*

**Code:**

(*a*) If only argument I is strong.

(*b*) If only argument II is strong.

(*c*) If either argument I or II is strong.

(*d*) If neither argument I nor II is strong.

**1. Statement :** Should India adopt a Presidential system?

**Argument I:** Yes-Because our experience of Parliamentary democracy is disappointing

**Argument II:** No - Because it will concentrate power in the hands of a few people. **(AILET, 2009)**

**2. Statement :** Should the death sentence be abolished?

**Argument I:** Yes-The death sentence deprives the culprit of all chances of improving his behaviour.

**Argument II:** No - Capital punishment restrains criminal tendency. **(AILET, 2009)**

**3. Statement:** Should a total ban be put on trapping wild animals?

**Argument I:** Yes. Trappers are making a lot of money.

**Argument II:** No. Bans on hunting and trapping are not effective. **(CLAT 2009)**

**4. Statement:** Should school education be made free in India?

**Argument I:** Yes. This is the only way to improve the level of literacy.

**Argument II:** No. It would add to the already heavy burden on the exchequer. **(CLAT 2009)**

**5. Statement:** Should government jobs in rural areas have more incentives?

**Argument I:** Yes. Incentives are essential for attracting government servants there.

**Argument II:** No. Rural areas are already cheaper, healthier and less complex than big. So, why offer extra incentives! **(CLAT 2009)**

**6. Statement:** Should luxury hotels be banned in India?

**Argument I:** Yes. They are places from where international criminals operate.

**Argument II:** No. Affluent foreign tourists will have no place to stay. **(CLAT 2009)**

**7. Statement:** Should the political parties be banned?

**Argument I:** Yes. It is necessary to teach a lesson to the politicians.

**Argument II:** No. It will lead to an end of democracy. **(CLAT 2009)**

**8. Question:** Should there be complete ban on manufacture of fire crackers in India?

**Argument I:** No, This will render thousands of workers jobless.

**Argument II:** Yes, the fire cracker manufacturers use child labour. **(CLAT 2010)**

**9. Question:** Should private operators be allowed to operate passenger train service in India?

**Argument I:** No, private operators do not agree to operate on non profitable sectors.

**Argument II:** Yes, it will improve the quality of Indian Railway Service. **(CLAT 2010)**

**10. Question:** Should the system of reservation of posts for scheduled castes be introduced in private sector?

**Argument I:** Yes, this would give more opportunity of development to these groups.

**Argument II:** No, this would effect merit.

**(CLAT 2010)**

**11. Question:** Would the problem of old parents be solved if children are made legally responsible to take care of their parents in old age?

**Argument I:** Yes, such problems can be solved only through law.

**Argument II:** Yes, this will bring relief to old parents. **(CLAT 2010)**

**12. Question:** Should right to primary education be made a fundamental right?

**Argument I:** We should first complete other develop-mental projects, education of children can wait.

**Argument II:** Yes, without primary education for all there cannot be inclusive development.

**(CLAT 2010)**

**13. Statement:** Should the pay scale and conditions of service of government employees be made applicable to private sector employees?

**Argument I:** No, this will develop inertia, inefficiency and would adversely affect spirit of competition.

**Argument II:** Yes, this will enhance dedication to work and institutional loyalty. **(CLAT 2012)**

14. **Statement:** Should a strong institution of ombudsman be created in India?

**Argument I:** Yes, this will bring transparency and accountability in the administration.

**Argument II:** No, this will develop lack of initiative and flexibility in the administration. **(CLAT 2012)**

15. **Statement**: Should internal assessment in colleges and universities be abolished?

**Argument I:**Yes, this will eliminate the possibility of favoritism.

**Argument II:** No, teaching faculty will lose control over the students and this would adversely affect their academic growth. **(CLAT 2012)**

16. **Statement:** Should military training be made compulsory for all college and university students?

**Argument I:** Yes, this will develop in them a sense of punctuality and discipline.

**Argument II:** No, military training should be given only to those students who are physically fit. **(CLAT 2012)**

17. **Statement:** Should students' union in colleges and universities be abolished?

**Argument I:** Yes, it detracts students from academic and career development.

**Argument II:** No, all great leaders have been students' union leaders. **(CLAT 2012)**

18. **Statement:** Should the age of marriage be raised to 25 years for boys and 21 for girls?

**Argument I:** No, it is difficult to change a social practice in Indian conditions.

**Argument II:** Yes, by that age people develop a sense of responsibility and also complete their education. **(CLAT 2012)**

19. **Question:** Should Judicial Activism be discouraged?

**Argument I:** No, it would lead to executive dictatorship.

**Argument II:** Yes, Judiciary should stay in the constitutional limits. **(CLAT 2012)**

20. **Question:** Should the Judiciary be independent of Executive and Legislature?

**Argument I:** Yes, this is necessary to ensure impartiality in the administration of Justice.

**Argument II:** No, it will develop inertia in Executive and Legislature. **(CLAT 2012)**

21. **Question:** Should E-Governance be introduced at every level of public administration?

**Argument I:** Yes, it will reduce corruption.

**Argument II:** No, it will lead to unemployment. **(CLAT 2012)**

22. **Question:** Should there be a world Government?

**Argument I:** Yes, it will eliminate inter-state conflicts.

**Argument II**: No, Rich and Powerful countries will dominate it. **(CLAT 2012)**

## Solutions

**1.** b Only argument II is strong since it talks of a consequence which, if comes true, would greatly affect the nation. Argument I is not strong enough a reason to do away with the parliamentary democracy since disappointing past experience can be attributed to poor implementation of the same. It does not call for changing the system entirely. Thus, option (*b*) is the correct choice.

**2.** c. If we examine both the arguments, they are true independently depending on the individual situations. Hence, option (*c*) is correct.

**3.** d Argument I does not provide a strong reason for ban on trapping of wild animals. Just because trappers are earning a lot of money does not provide a reason for banning trapping of wild animals. Similarly, argument II is not strong because it is not a reason for not banning. It is merely a statement that tells that the bans are generally not effective.

**4.** c Both the arguments are strong. One highlights the need and second highlights the problem.

**5.** c Both the arguments are strong. Argument I gives the reason for offering more incentives. Argument II gives the reason for not increasing the incentives.

**6.** d Both the arguments are not strong. For curbing crimes, banning of hotels is not a solution since the international criminals can find another place to operate. Similarly, argument II is not true since banning luxury hotels does not mean that affluent tourists won't have any place to stay.

**7.** b Only argument II is strong. This highlights the problem of implementing the suggestion of the question statement. Argument I is not related to the question statement.

**8.** c Both are strong from two different perspectives. Therefore, (*c*) is the correct option.

**9.** b I is wrong as we do not know if Indian Railway is non profitable. Argument II is strong. Therefore, (*b*) is the correct option.

**10.** c Both are strong from two different perspectives. Therefore, (*c*) is the correct option.

**11.** d Even if only law can solve a problem then also it is not certain that the problem will be solved (use of necessary condition). Argument II is weak since it doesn't give any reason. It just states the benefit of solving the problem rather than answering the question. Therefore, (*d*) is the correct option.

**12.** b Only II is very strong as it justifies the necessity of such right. I doesn't give any substantial reason for not making it a fundamental right. Therefore, (*b*) is the correct option.

**13.** a The statement questions if there is a need for making pay scale and conditions of employees applicable to private sector employees. Argument I talks of inertia and inefficiency that may creep in to adversely affect the spirit of competition among the employees. It's a serious concern for any organization. Paying more and still having inefficient employees would be a bad situation. Hence, it is a strong argument. Argument II is not strong because there may be other methods that can enhance institutional loyalty. Moreover, paying more does not relate to greater dedication and loyalty. Option (*a*) is the correct choice here.

**14.** a Only argument I is strong in this case. Transparency and accountability are important parameters for the success of any administration. However, lack of flexibility and initiative is not a very big problem as compared to the benefits that it may have.

**15.** c Both arguments here are equally strong. Argument I talks about the possibility of favoritism which is a major issue. It may beat the entire purpose of assessing students; questions on its fairness can be raised. Argument II is strong because it is very important for the teaching faculty to have some control over the assessment of students. In the absence of internal assessment, students may not value their teachers because they would know that their marks would depend only on external assessment. Thus, option (*c*) is the correct answer.

**16.** a Only argument I is strong as it talks of punctuality and discipline, the two most important virtues of student life. Argument II is incorrect as it says military training should be given only to physically fit students. On the contrary, students who are physically unfit would require it the most. Thus, option (*a*) is correct.

**17.** a Argument I is strong since it talks about the distraction of students from academic pursuits. Students come to colleges primarily to study. Hence, any distraction in the same would kill the purpose of such an institution. Argument II is weak because all great leaders being from students' union leaders is not reason enough for keeping the unions. Option (*a*) is the correct choice.

**18.** b Here, only argument II is strong. It is fair to say that people are mature and responsible by this age and then they should get married. Inability of changing a social practice does not justify its existence. Hence, argument I is weak. Option (*b*) is correct.

**19.** d Both the arguments given in the question are weak. Judicial activism leading to executive dictatorship is an exaggeration of the situation. Similarly, 'Judiciary should stay in constitutional limits' is not reason enough. Why it should stay within constitutional limits or what effects it will have are not mentioned, making it a weak argument. Hence, correct option is (*d*).

**20.** a Argument I is strong since it is important to have impartiality in the judicial system which can be done by making it independent of executive and legislature. Argument II is a weak argument since it is an excuse and not a solid reason. Legislature and Executive may develop inertia even when they have judiciary under its purview. Thus, option (*a*) is correct.

**21.** c Both the given arguments are strong. The introduction of e-governance at every level of public administration may help weed out corruption. This is a very strong reason in support of e-governance. On the other hand, it may lead to unemployment which is a very serious problem. Hence, option (*c*) is correct.

**22.** b Only argument II is strong since there is all possibility that rich and powerful nations may dominate the world government, which beats the whole purpose of forming such a government. Argument I is weak because it talks of inter-state conflict. There is more to a world government than eliminating inter-state conflicts. There are other international organizations like the UN which aim to eliminate such conflicts. Hence, elimination of inter-state conflict is not a strong argument in favor of world government.

## SYLLOGISMS

**Directions for questions 1 to 24:** The following questions comprise of one or more statements. Answer the questions on the basis of the given statement(s). Accept the factual assumptions required by the question, even if you believe that the statement is false.

1. If it is true that 'men are seldom honest', which of the following statement conveys the same meaning?
   (*a*) At least one man is not honest.
   (*b*) Men are not honest.
   (*c*) At least on one occasion men are not honest.
   (*d*) Sometimes men are honest. **(AILET, 2010)**

2. If it is false that 'men always obey the law', which one of the following statements is doubtful ?
   (*a*) Sometimes men do not obey the law.
   (*b*) All men obey the law.
   (*c*) Men never obey the law.
   (*d*) Some men obey the law. **(AILET, 2010)**

**3.** If it is false that 'all men strive for the happiness of all', which one of the following statements is true beyond doubt ?

(*a*) All men seek their own happiness.

(*b*) There are men who do not desire for the happiness of all.

(*c*) No men strive for the happiness of all.

(*d*) There are men who do not strive for the happiness of all. **(AILET, 2010)**

**4.** If the statement "All men desire their own welfare always" is true, then which of the following statements must be false?

(*a*) There are men who desire their own welfare sometimes.

(*b*) Some men desire their own welfare always.

(*c*) There are men who always desire their and others' welfare.

(*d*) It is not the case that all men desire their own welfare always. **(AILET, 2010)**

**5.** From among the given alternatives, identify the conclusion of the following argument.

You cannot taste success in life unless you work hard.

You cannot be happy unless you taste success in life.

Therefore

(*a*) You can be happy unless you work hard.

(*b*) You cannot be happy unless you work hard.

(*c*) You cannot work hard unless you are happy.

(*d*) You can work hard unless you are happy.

**(AILET, 2010)**

**6.** If it is true that 'All men are honest' and 'All politicians are men', for which among the following is it impossible to follow from the given premises?

(*a*) Some politicians are not honest.

(*b*) All politicians are honest.

(*c*) One politician is honest.

(*d*) All honest persons are politicians. **(AILET, 2011)**

**7.** 'Where there is smoke, there is fire.' Which of the following statements, *if true*, would show that the above statement is false?

(*a*) There is sometimes smoke where there is no fire.

(*b*) There is sometimes fire where there is no smoke.

(*c*) There is no fire where there is no smoke.

(*d*) None of the above. **(CLAT 2011)**

**8.** 'Where there is poverty, there are always thieves.' Which of the following statements, *if true*, would show that the above statement is false?

(*a*) America is a rich country and there are thieves in America.

(*b*) Bhutan is a poor country and there are no thieves in Bhutan.

(*c*) Bangladesh is a poor country and there are many thieves in Bangladesh.

(*d*) Nepal is a rich country and there are no thieves in Nepal. **(CLAT 2011)**

**9.** Suleiman: All Communists are atheists. Sheeba: That is not true. Which of the following, *if true*, would make Sheeba's reply the most convincing?

(*a*) My uncle is an atheist but he is not a Communist.

(*b*) My uncle is a Communist but he is not an atheist.

(*c*) My uncle is a Communist and an atheist.

(*d*) My uncle is neither a Communist nor an atheist. **(CLAT 2011)**

**10. Statement 1:** All pingos are byronic.

**Statement 2:** Shalisto is byronic.

**Statement 3:** Therefore ________.

Fill in the blank.

(*a*) Shalisto is a pingo.

(*b*) Shalisto is not a pingo.

(*c*) Shalisto is not byronic.

(*d*) None of the above **(CLAT 2011)**

**11. Statement 1:** Some aeroplanes are balloons.

**Statement 2:** Some balloons are rockets.

Conclusions:

(A) Some aeroplanes are rockets.

(B) Some rockets are tables.

(C) All the rockets are balloons.

(D) All the balloons are aeroplanes.

Assuming that statements 1 and 2 are true, which conclusions follow:

(*a*) Only (B) and (D) (*b*) Only (A) and (C)

(*c*) Only (D) (*d*) None of the above.

**(CLAT 2011)**

**12. Statement 1:** All whales are fish.

**Statement 2:** Some fish are not amphibians.

**Statement 3:** All whales are amphibians.

**Statement 4:** Some amphibians are not fish.

Conclusions:

(A) Some fish are amphibians.

(B) Some amphibians are fish.

(C) Only whales are both fish and amphibians.

(D) All amphibians are fish.

Assuming only that Statements 1, 2, 3 and 4 are true, which of the above conclusions may be deduced?

(*a*) Only (A) and (B)

(*b*) Only (C)

(*c*) Only (D)

(*d*) None of the above **(CLAT 2011)**

**13. Statement 1:** All libraries are laboratories.

**Statement 2:** No laboratories are hostels.

**Conclusions:**

(A) All laboratories are libraries.

(B) Some hostels are libraries.

(C) Some libraries are hostels.

(D) No library is a hostel.

Assuming that statements 1 and 2 are true, which conclusions follow?

(*a*) Only (A) and (B) (*b*) Only (B) and (C)

(*c*) Only (C) and (D) (*d*) Only (D) **(CLAT 2011)**

**14. Statement 1:** Sugar is bad for people with diabetes.

**Statement 2:** Leela does not eat sugar.

Assuming that Statements 1 and 2 are true, which of the following statements follows?

(*a*) Leela has diabetes.

(*b*) Sugar is bad for Leela.

(*c*) People with diabetes do not eat sugar.

(*d*) None of the above. **(CLAT 2011)**

**15. Statement 1:** People who read fashion magazines do not like to read fiction. **Statement 2:** Tenzin does not read fashion magazines.

Assuming that Statements 1 and 2 are true, which of the following conclusions might be said to follow?

(*a*) Tenzin likes to read fiction.

(*b*) Tenzin may or may not like to read fiction.

(*c*) Tenzin does not like to read fiction.

(*d*) Tenzin does not like fashion magazines.

**(CLAT 2011)**

**16. Statement 1:** All girls are students.

**Statement 2:** All doctors are students.

Assuming that statement 1 and 2 are true, which of the above conclusions follow?

**Conclusions:**

I. All girls are students.

II. Some students are girls.

III. Some students are doctors.

IV. All doctors are girls.

(*a*) Only I follows.

(*b*) Only I and II follows.

(*c*) Only II and IV follow.

(*d*) Only I and II and III follows. **(CLAT 2012)**

**17. Statement 1:** All researchers are sociologists

**Statement 2:** Some researchers are professors.

Assuming that statement 1 and 2 are true, which of the above conclusions follow?

**Conclusions:**

I. All researchers are professors.

II. Some researchers are professors.

III. Some professors are sociologists.

IV. Some sociologists are researchers.

(*a*) Only III and II follow.

(*b*) Only II and IV follow.

(*c*) Only III follows.

(*d*) None follows. **(CLAT 2012)**

**18. Statement 1:** Some democracies are dictatorship.

**Statement 2:** No dictatorship is a monarchy.

Assuming that statement 1 and 2 are true, which of the above conclusions follow?

**Conclusions:**

I. No democracy is a monarchy.

II. No dictatorship is a democracy.

III. Some democracies are monarchy.

IV. Some dictatorships are democracies.

(*a*) None follows (*b*) Only IV follows.

(*c*) II and III follow. (*d*) I and IV follow.

**(CLAT 2012)**

**19. Statements:**

I. Cheese is bad for people with high-cholesterol.

II. Sumeet does not eat cheese.

Assuming that (i) and (ii) are true, which of the following statement follows?

(*a*) Sumeet has high-cholesterol.

(*b*) Cheese is bad for Sumeet.

(*c*) People with high-Cholesterol do not eat cheese.

(*d*) None of the above. **(CLAT 2012)**

**20. Statement:**

I. Democrats are secularists.

Which of the following statements, if true, would show that the above statement is false?

(*a*) My father is a secularist but he is not a democrat.

(*b*) My father is a democrat but he is not secularist.

(*c*) My father is a democrat and he is secularist.

(*d*) My father is neither a democrat nor a secularist. **(CLAT 2012)**

**21. Statement:**

"Where there is a cloud, there is a rain." Which of the following statements, if true, would show that the above statement is false?

(*a*) Sometimes there is cloud, but there is no rain.
(*b*) Sometimes there is rain, but there is no cloud.
(*c*) There is no rain where there is no cloud.
(*d*) None of the above. **(CLAT 2012)**

**22. Statements:**

I. No athletes are vegetarians.
II . All players are athletes.
III. Therefore ——————————

(*a*) no players are vegetarians.
(*b*) all players are vegetarian.
(*c*) some players are vegetarian.
(*d*) all vegetarians are players. **(CLAT 2012)**

**23. Statements :**

I. All persons who have done any creative work can be responsible critics.
II. Z has not done any creative work.
III. Therefore ——————————

(*a*) Z can be a responsible critic.
(*b*) Z cannot be a responsible critic.
(*c*) Z can become a responsible critic.
(*d*) Z cannot become a responsible critic. **(CLAT 2012)**

**24. Statement:**

I. One who has squared a circle is not a mathematician
II. Therefore ——————————

(*a*) No one who has squared a circle is a mathematician.
(*b*) All non-mathematicians have squared a circle.
(*c*) Some mathematicians have squared a circle.
(*d*) All mathematicians square a circle. **(CLAT 2012)**

**Directions for questions 25 to 28:** Each question given below, contains six statements followed by four sets of combination of three. Choose the set in which the statements are logically related.

**25. Statements:**

(i) X and Y are siblings.
(ii) X and Y do not quarrel.
(iii) Siblings are known to quarrel often.
(iv) X and Y quarrel often.
(v) All those who quarrel are siblings.
(vi) X and Y cannot be siblings.

(*a*) ii, iv,v (*b*) i, iv, vi
(*c*) i, iii, iv (*d*) i, ii, v **(CLAT 2012)**

**26. Statements:**

(i) All mangoes are fruits.
(ii) All mangoes are green.
(iii) All mangoes are oval shaped.
(iv) All fruits are sweet.
(v) All mangoes are sweet.
(vi) All fruits are expensive.

(*a*) i, ii, iii (*b*) i, iv, v
(*c*) ii, iii, iv (*d*) iv, v, vi **(CLAT 2012)**

**27. Statements:**

(i) All frogs are amphibians.
(ii) All amphibians are not frogs.
(iii) All amphibians are cold blooded.
(iv) All frogs lay eggs.
(v) All amphibians lay eggs.
(vi) Frogs are cold blooded.

(*a*) i, iii, vi (*b*) i, iv, v
(*c*) i, ii, v (*d*) ii, v, iv **(CLAT 2012)**

**28. Statements:**

(i) Some men are of short- height.
(ii) Short-heighted men are intelligent.
(iii) Sudhir is a man.
(iv) Sudhir is of short-height.
(v) Sudhir is intelligent.
(vi) All men are intelligent.

(*a*) i, ii, vi (*b*) iii, iv, ii
(*c*) ii, iv, v (*d*) ii, iv, vi **(CLAT 2012)**

**Directions (Q. 29-30) :** *Each question contains six statements followed by four sets of combinations of three. Choose the set in which the combinations are logically related.*

**29.** (1) Some buildings are not skyscrapers.
(2) Some skyscrapers are not buildings.
(3) No structure is a skyscraper.
(4) All skyscrapers are structures.
(5) Some skyscrapers are buildings.
(6) Some structures are not buildings. **(AILET 2014)**

(*a*) (1),(3),(5) (*b*) (2),(4),(6)
(*c*) (6),(4),(1) (*d*) (1),(3),(6)

**30.** (1) All bins are buckets.
(2) No bucket is a basket.
(3) No bin is a basket.
(4) Some baskets are buckets.
(5) Some bins are baskets.
(6) No basket is a bin. **(AILET 2014)**

(*a*) (2),(4),(5) (*b*) (1),(3),(2)
(*c*) (3),(4),(6) (*d*) (1),(2),(6)

**Directions (Q. 31-32) :** *Each question comprises two statements (numbered as I and II). You have to take the statements as true even if they seem to be at variance with commonly known facts. Read all the conclusions and then decide which of the given conclusions logically follow from the given statements, disregarding commonly known facts.* **(CLAT 2014)**

**31.** I. All contracts are agreements.

II. All agreements are accepted offers.

Which of the following derivations is correct?

(*a*) All accepted offers are contracts

(*b*) All agreements are contracts

(*c*) All contracts are accepted offers

(*d*) None of the above

**32.** I. Some beautiful women are actresses.

II. All actresses are good dancers.

Which of the following derivations is correct?

(*a*) Some beautiful women are good dancers

(*b*) All good dancers are actresses

(*c*) Both (*a*) and (*b*)

(*d*) None of the above

**Directions (Q. 33-35) :** *Two statements are given below followed by two conclusions (I and II). You have to consider the two statements to be true even if they seem to be at variance with commonly known facts. You have to decide which of the conclusions, if any, follow from the given statements.* **(CLAT 2014)**

**33. Statements:**

Some books are magazines.

Some magazines are novels.

**Conclusions:**

I. Some books are novels.

II. Some novels are magazines.

(*a*) Only (I) follows

(*b*) Only (II) follows

(*c*) Both (I) and (II) follow

(*d*) Neither (I) nor (II) follows

**34. Statements:**

All students like excursions.

Some students go for higher education.

**Conclusions:**

I. Students who go for higher education also like excursions.

II. Some students do not go for higher education, but like excursions.

(*a*) Only (I) follows

(*b*) Only (II) follows

(*c*) Both (I) and (II) follow

(*d*) Neither (I) nor (II) follows

**35. Statements:**

All good hockey players are in the Indian Hockey team.

'X' is not a good hockey player.

**Conclusions:**

I. 'X' is not in the Indian Hockey team.

II. 'X' wants to be in the Indian Hockey team.

(*a*) Only (I) follows

(*b*) Only (II) follows

(*c*) Both (I) and (II) follow

(*d*) Neither (I) nor (II) follows

**Directions (Q. 36-37) :** *Each question consists of, five statements (a-e) followed by options consisting of three statements put together in a specific order. Choose the option which indicates a valid argument; that is, where the third statement is a conclusion drawn from the preceding two statements.* **(CLAT 2014)**

**36.** a. Law graduates are in great demand.

b. Rajesh and Krishna are in great demand.

c. Rajesh is in great demand.

d. Krishna is in great demand.

e. Rajesh and Krishna are law graduates.

Choose the correct option:

(*a*) abe (*b*) ecd

(*c*) aeb (*d*) eba

**37.** a. All captains are great players.

b. Some captains are successful sports administrators.

c. Ritwik is a great player.

d. Ritwik is a captain and successful sports administrator.

e. Some successful sports administrators are great players.

Choose the correct option: **(CLAT 2014)**

(*a*) acd (*b*) abe

(*c*) dca (*d*) edc

## Solutions

**1.** c The given statement can be understood as 'men are rarely honest'. The emphasis here is not on the number of men but on number of occasions when they are honest or dishonest. This rules out option (*a*) and (*b*). Seldom implies rarely so we can conclusively say that men are dishonest on at least one occasion. This leads us to option (*c*). Also, option (*d*) cannot be definitely true since rarely can mean never too. In that case, option (*d*) would become false. Hence, only option (*c*) conveys the same meaning.

**2.** b If 'men always obey the law' is correct then 'all men obey law' (as in b) is also correct. But as the statement is false the statement 'all men obey law' (as in b) has to be wrong and hence, doubtful. The remaining three can be deduced in some limited scope; hence, cannot be doubtful completely.

**3.** d Only the statement in option (*d*) is exactly opposite to the given one. So, if the given one has to be false, option (*d*) must be correct.

**4.** d Statement in option (*d*) is directly opposite to the given statement.

**5.** b It is similar to 'only A leads to B and only B leads to C therefore, C occurs only if A occurs'. Option (*b*) is the correct answer.

**6.** a Politician is a subset of Men and Men is a subset of Honest. Thus, the conclusions that can be drawn are: 1. All politicians are honest. 2. At least one politician is honest.

All honest persons are politicians may or may not be true. Thus, option (*d*) is not a conclusion but a possibility. Options (*b*), (*c*) and (*d*) are negated. But some politicians are not honest is neither a conclusion nor a possibility. It does not follow from the given premises.

**7.** a

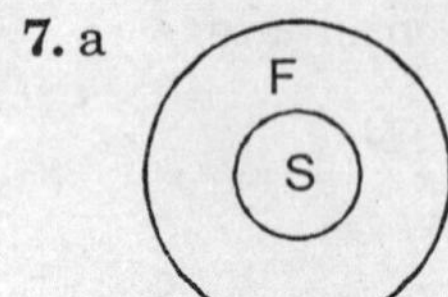


This argument is similar to 'if P then Q' type in which P is cause and Q is the effect. If this argument is true then whenever there is smoke there will be fire (smoke is cause and fire is the effect). Therefore, to make this argument false we have to show that at times smoke does not cause fire. Option (*a*) is correct.

**8.** b This argument is similar to 'if P then Q' type in which P is cause and Q is the effect. If this argument is true then whenever there is poverty there will be thieves ('poverty' is cause and 'thieves' is the effect). Therefore, to make this argument false we have to show that at times poverty does not leads to thieves. Option (*b*) shows that even if there is poverty in Bhutan there are no thieves.

**9.** b

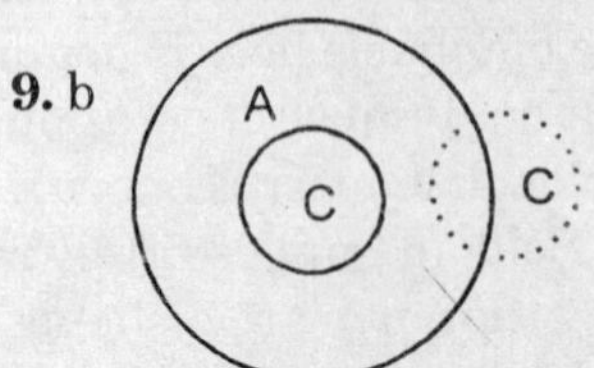


According to Suleiman, communists set must be a subset of atheist set (as shown in the figure). But if Sheeba contradicts this then at least a part of communists set must be outside the atheist set. Therefore option (*b*) is correct.

**10.** d

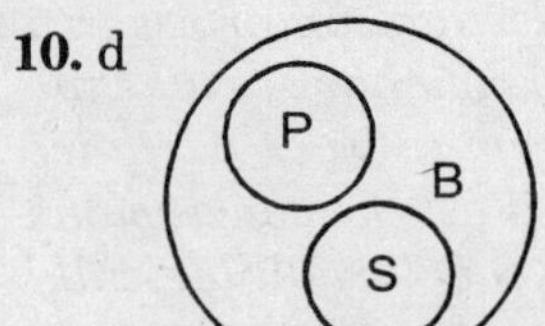


According to the figure drawn above, both pingos and Shalisto are subsets of Byronic but they do not necessarily intersect each other. Therefore, none of the options given in (*a*), (*b*) and (*c*) follow. Option (*d*) is correct.

**11.** d A, B, C or D do not follow. Therefore, option (*d*) is the correct choice.

**12.** a A and B can be concluded. Whales are both fish and amphibians is correct but only whales are both fish and amphibians is incorrect as data is not sufficient to conclude this. Thus, option (a) is the correct option.

**13.** d No laboratory is a hostel and library is a sub-set of laboratory. Therefore, no library is a hostel. Option (*d*) is the correct conclusion.

**14.** d Sugar is bad for people with diabetes. Leela does not eat sugar. From these statements, we cannot conclude whether Leela has diabetes or not. She may not be diabetic and still avoids taking sugar because she does not like sugar. So, option (*a*) and (*b*) do not follow. Option (*c*) cannot be concluded on the basis of the given statements. There is a chance that a person suffering from diabetes may still eat sugar because he is either unaware or less careful about his/her health. None of the above is the best choice.

**15.** b This argument is similar to 'if P then Q' type in which P is cause and Q is the effect. If this argument is true then whenever there is 'reading fashion magazine' there will be 'no reading fiction' ('reading fashion magazine' is cause and 'no reading fiction' is the effect). In this kind of argument, when the cause is not there we cannot say with certainity that the effect will also not be there. Therefore, option (*b*) is correct.

**16.** d Conclusion I: All girls are students.

This is same as statement I given in the question. So, conclusion I follows.

Conclusion II: Some students are girls.

It is given that all girls are students, so there will be some students who are girls. Thus, conclusion II follows.

Conclusion III: Some students are doctors.

It is given that all doctors are students, so there will be some students who are doctors. Thus, conclusion III also follows.

Conclusion IV: All doctors are girls.

Girls and doctors both are subsets of students. But we don't know how doctors and girls are related. They can be disjoined, intersecting or overlapping sets. Thus, conclusion IV doesn't follow.

Hence, option (*d*) is correct.

**17.** b*The answer given by CLAT is option (*b*). However, none of the options given have the correct combination. This is explained as follows. Conclusions II, III and IV follow. Conclusion II is same as statement II. Researchers are a subset of sociologists. Statement II says some researchers are professors. Combining these two, we can definitely say that there is atleast one professor who's a sociologist. Hence conclusion III also follows. Conclusion IV follows from statement I, since all researchers are sociologists, so there is at least one sociologist who's a researcher. Thus, the right answer should be II, III and IV which is given in none of the options.

**18.** b Conclusion I: No democracy is a monarchy.

Both the statements do not talk about the relation between democracy and monarchy. Democracy is an intersecting set with dictatorship while dictatorship and monarchy are disjoined sets. So monarchy and democracy can be anything, from disjoined and intersecting to overlapping. Hence, conclusion I does not follow.

Conclusion II: No dictatorship is a democracy.

It does not follow because we can conclude from statement one that at least one dictatorship is a democracy.

Conclusion III: Some democracies are monarchy.

It does not follow for the same reason as given for conclusion I.

Conclusion IV: Some dictatorships are democracies.

This conclusion follows because we can deduce from statement one that there is at least one dictatorship that is democracy.

Hence the correct answer is option (*b*).

**19.** c* CLAT has given the answer as option (*c*), but it does not follow from the question. It is incorrect as the given statements just say that cheese is bad for people with high cholesterol. It doesn't tell us whether people with high cholesterol eat it or not. It is possible that high cholesterol patients, despite knowing that it is bad for them, still eat it because they like it or are simple unaware of its ill effects and so eat it. Option (*a*) and (*b*) are incorrect as *'Sumit doesn't eat cheese'* may mean that probably he doesn't like it or doesn't eat it for some other reason, not necessarily that he has high cholesterol or it is bad for him respectively. Hence, Option (*d*) is the correct answer.

**20.** b The statement says that all democrats are secularists. Option (*b*) which says *'My father is a democrat but he is not a secularist'* makes the statement false because there is one democrat who is not a secularist. Thus, we can't say all democrats are secularists.

**21.** a The statement is *'if A then B'* type. It says that whenever there is a cloud (cause), there is rain (effect). Option (*a*) makes the statement false. It says that there are times when clouds (cause) are not followed by rain (effect). Option (*b*) is incorrect because it says that sometimes there is rain (effect) and no clouds (cause). It does not make the statement false since it is not mentioned that there is only one cause for rain i.e. clouds. It can rain because of some other reason too. Option (*c*) is incorrect as it doesn't affect it in any way.

**22.** a Athletes and vegetarians are disjoined sets. Players are a subset of athletes, so it can be concluded that no player is a vegetarian. Hence, option (*a*) is correct.

**23.** b*This statement is similar to *'if A then B'* type where A is the cause and (*b*) is the effect. It says all persons who have done any creative work (cause) can be responsible critics (effect). It doesn't mean that creative work (cause) is the **only** way to be a responsible critic (effect). This is so because the effect can have no or some other cause too. Hence, no conclusion about Z can be made given the two statements.

**24.** a Option (*a*) just rephrases the given statement; therefore it logically follows from it. The given statement is of the form *'A* (one who has squared a circle) *is not B* (mathematician)'. It can be logically concluded from here that *'No A* (no one who has squared a circle) *is B* (mathematician)'. Hence, option (*a*) is correct.

**25.** c X and Y are siblings and siblings are known to quarrel often. So, X and Y quarrel often can be logically deduced from the other two statements. Thus, statements i, iii and iv are logically related.

**26.** b Mangoes is a subset of fruits. 'Fruits' is a subset of sweet. Thus, 'mangoes' is a subset of sweet. This makes option (*b*) correct.

**27.** a Frogs is a subset of amphibians. 'Amphibians' is a subset of cold blooded. Thus, 'frogs' is a subset of cold blooded. So, statements in option (*a*) are logically related.

**28.** c Short-heighted men is a subset of intelligent. Sudhir is a subset of short-height. So, Sudhir falls in the set of intelligent. Hence, option (*c*) is correct.

**29.** b According to the venn diagram given below, option (*b*) is the correct answer.

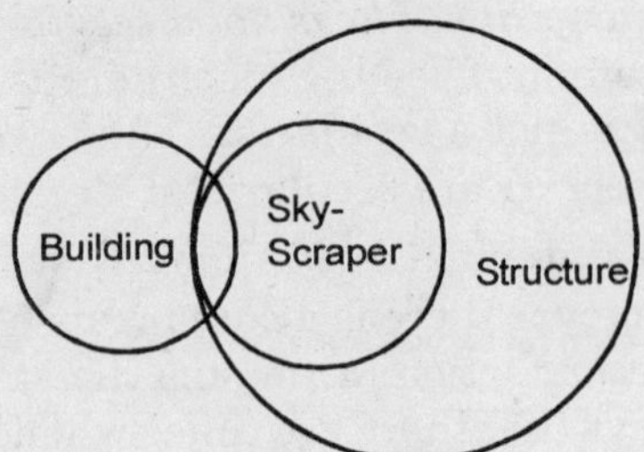


**30.** d According to the venn diagram given below, option (*d*) is the correct answer.

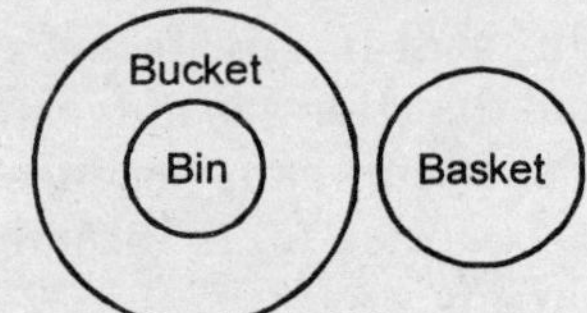


**31.** c

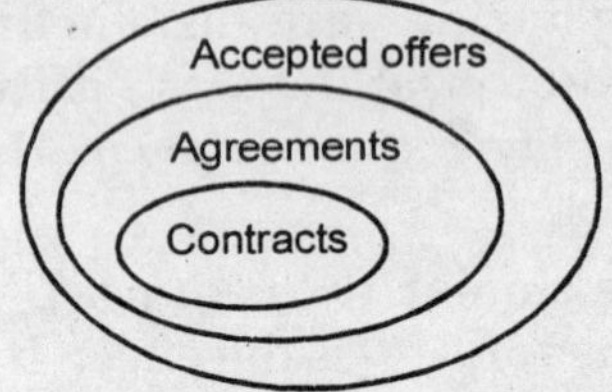


As we can see in the Venn diagram, option (*c*) follows and is therefore, the correct answer.

**32.** a

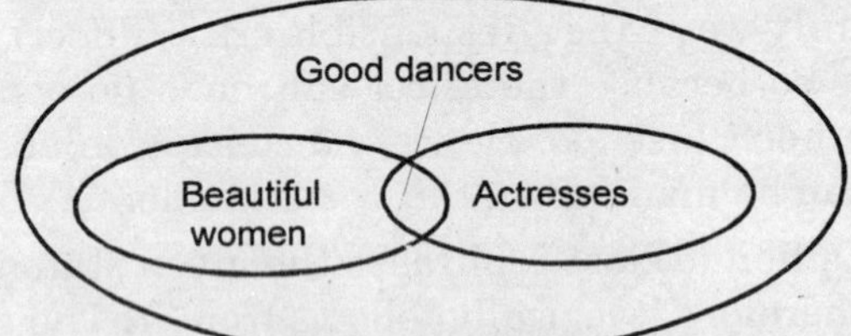


As we can see in the Venn diagram, only option (*a*) follows and is therefore, the correct answer.

**33.** b

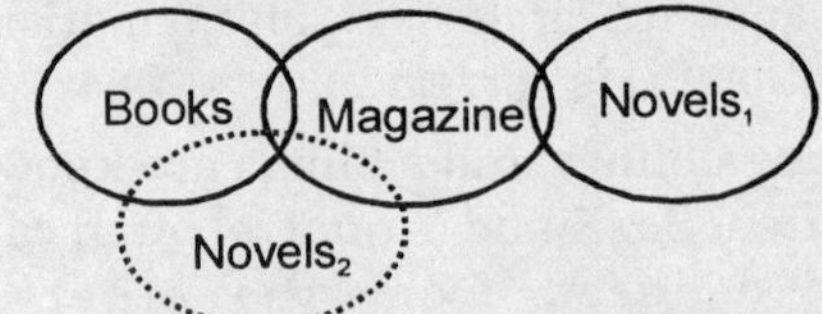


As we can see in the Venn diagram, only conclusion (II) follows and therefore, option (*b*) is the correct answer.

**34.** a

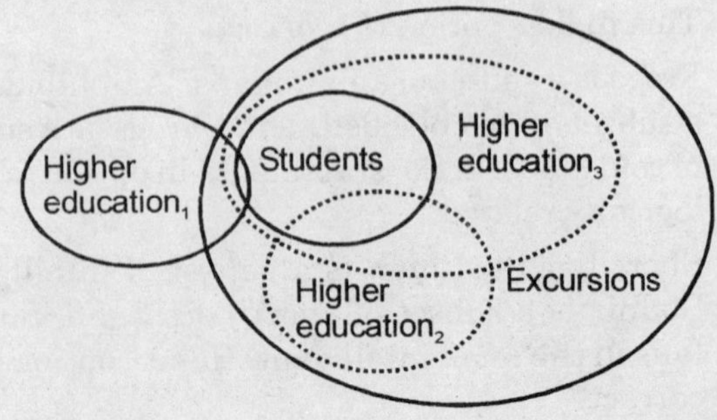


As we can see in the Venn diagram, only conclusion (I) follows and therefore, option (*a*) is the correct answer.

**35.** d

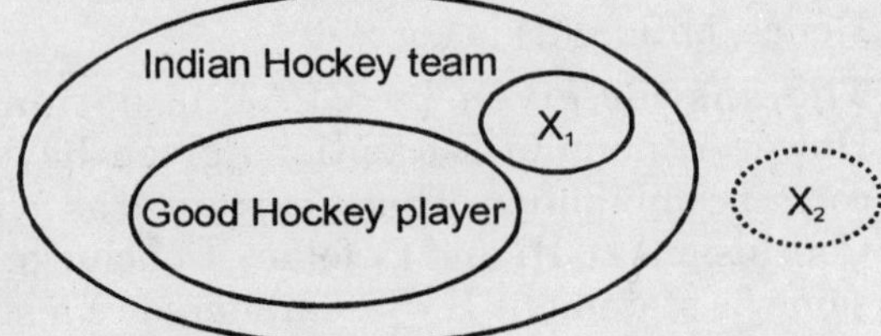


As we can see in the Venn diagram, neither of the conclusions follow and therefore, option (*d*) is the correct answer.

**36.** c

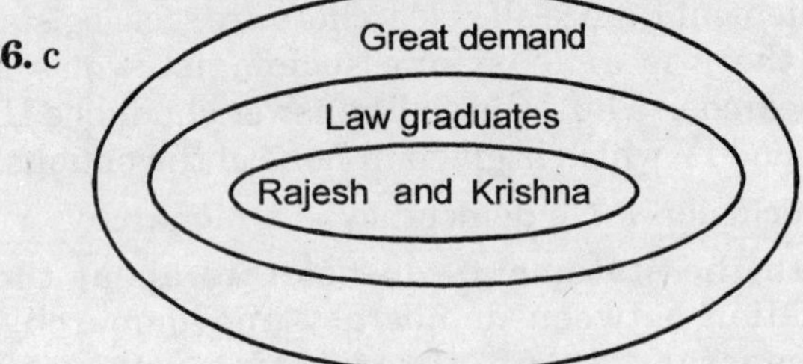


As can be seen in the Venn diagram given above, option (*c*) is the correct answer.

**37.** b

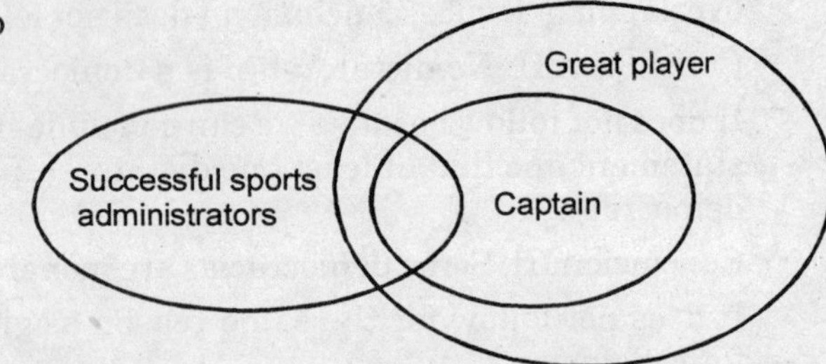


As can be seen in the Venn diagram given above, option (*b*) is the correct answer.

## SENTENCE JUMBLES

**Directions for questions 1 to 8:** The constituent phrases of a sentence are jumbled up. Select the most appropriate sequence to make the sentence meaningful.

**1.** (i) The Collector said that the Dams should receive

(ii) To ensure uninterrupted

(iii) Water up to a particular level

(iv) Supply of water for irrigation

**The best sequence is:**

(*a*) ii, i, iv, iii (*b*) i, iii, ii, iv

(*c*) iv, i, iii, ii (*d*) ii, iv, i, iii **(CLAT 2009)**

**2.** (i) He loved to distribute them among small kids.

(ii) He wore a long, loose shirt with many pockets.

(iii) And in doing so his eyes brightened.

(iv) The pockets of his shirt bulged with toffees and chocolates.

**The best sequence is:**

(*a*) ii, i, iii, iv (*b*) i, iv, ii, iii

(*c*) iv, i, iii, ii (*d*) ii, iv, i, iii **(CLAT 2009)**

**3.** (i) As we all know, a legislation

(ii) Needs the assent of the President

(iii) Passed by the Houses of Parliament

(iv) To become law.

**The best sequence is:**

(*a*) i, iii, ii, iv (*b*) i, iv, ii, iii

(*c*) iv, i, iii, ii (*d*) ii, iv, i, iii **(CLAT 2009)**

**4.** (i) The farmers grow food for the whole country.

(ii) And therefore it is our duty to improve their lot.

(iii) Yet these fellows are exploited by the rich.

(iv) Hence they are the most useful members of the society.

**The best sequence is:**

(*a*) ii, i, iv, iii (*b*) i, iv, ii, iii

(*c*) i, iv, iii, ii (*d*) ii, iv, i, iii **(CLAT 2009)**

**5.** (i) The ripples looked enchanting in the light of the Sun.

(ii) We went to the pond.

(iii) We flung stones to create ripples.

(iv) We stood knee-deep in the muddy water of the pond.

**The best sequence is:**

(*a*) ii, i, iv, iii (*b*) ii, iv, iii, i

(*c*) iv, i, iii, ii (*d*) iv, ii, i, iii **(CLAT 2009)**

**6.** (i) built on the site of a church destroyed

(ii) in the hilly area of the city is the famous Shandon Steeple

(iii) the bell tower of St. Anne's Church

(iv) when the city was besieged by the Duke of Marlborough

(*a*) ii, iii, i, iv (*b*) ii, i, iii, iv

(*c*) iv, iii, i, ii (*d*) iii, ii, i, iv **(CLAT 2010)**

**7.** (i) no law giving effect to the policy of the state towards securing all or any of the principles laid in part IV

(ii) notwithstanding anything contained in Article 13

(iii) and no law containing a declaration that it is for giving effect to such policy shall be called in question in any court on the ground that it does not give effect to such policy

(iv) shall be deemed to be void on the ground that it is inconsistent with or takes away or abridges any of the rights conferred by Article 14 or 19

(*a*) ii, i, iii, iv (*b*) iv, i, ii, iii

(*c*) ii, i, iv, iii (*d*) i, ii, iii, iv **(CLAT 2010)**

**8.** (i) neither House shall proceed further with the Bill,

(ii) if he does so, the houses shall meet accordingly

(iii) but the President may at any time after the date of his notification summon the Houses to meet in a joint sitting for the purpose specified in the notification and,

(iv) where the President has under clause (1) notified his intention of summoning the Houses to meet in a joint sitting,

(*a*) iv, i , iii, ii (*b*) iv, i, ii, iii

(*c*) iv, ii, iii, i (*d*) i, ii, iii, iv **(CLAT 2010)**

**Directions for questions 9 to 13:** Given below are the jumbled phrases of a sentence. The first and the last phrase of the jumbled sentence are given in correct order. Arrange the middle phrases in the correct sequence.

**9.** i. On one hand we are proud of being Indians,

ii. on the other hand we behave as if we were still at the dawn of our civilization

iii. murders of our own brothers and sisters is not the way to please Ram or Rahim

iv. the citizens of the land where Buddha and Gandhi taught

v. the principles of love and non-violence,

vi. nor does it fetch us any prosperity.

(*a*) ii, iii, iv, v (*b*) iii, iv, v, ii

(*c*) iv, v, iii, ii (*d*) iv, v, ii, iii **(CLAT 2012)**

**10.** i. On the basis of experiments with rats

ii. health experts here say that

iii. exercise more and consume vitamins,

iv. they will live up to 100 years or more

v. if humans eat less,

vi. and be vigorous in their eighties and nineties.

(*a*) ii, iii, v, iv (*b*) ii, v, iii, iv

(*c*) ii, v, iv, iii (*d*) v, ii, iii, iv **(CLAT 2012)**

**11.** i. The release of atomic energy is the greatest achievement which science has yet attained

ii. but the first invention to which their discoveries were applied was a bomb

iii. the atom was split by physicists whose minds were set on the search for knowledge

iv. it was more deadly than any other weapon invented so far

v. it is with dread that scientists regard the first use to which their greatest discovery was put

vi. however, they are gratified by the numerous applications of atomic energy for peaceful and constructive population.

(*a*) ii, iii, iv, v (*b*) v, iii, ii, iv
(*c*) iii, ii, iv, v (*d*) iv, v, iii, ii **(CLAT 2012)**

**12.** i. The problem of food is intimately connected with population

ii. wages will seldom rise in proportion to the rising prices

iii. the market is governed by demand and supply

iv. without enough food, such people lack health, strength of efficiency

v. if too many people demand goods to go round, prices will rise and poor classes will starve

vi. they fall an easy prey to all sorts of diseases.

(*a*) iii, v, ii, iv (*b*) ii, iii, iv, v
(*c*) iv, ii, v, iii (*d*) v, iii, iv, ii **(CLAT 2012)**

**13.** i. India's message has always been one of love and peace.

ii. our Buddha was the light of Asia

iii. it has been a source of light and wisdom to the rest of the world

iv. Ashoka, moved by the horrors of Kalinga War, adopted the message of non-violence

v. the greatest apostle of non-violence in recent years was Mahatma Gandhi

vi. he shook the foundation of the British rule in India through non-violence.

(*a*) ii, v, iii, iv (*b*) iv, ii, iii, v
(*c*) v, iv, iii, ii (*d*) iii, ii, iv, v **(CLAT 2012)**

## Solutions

**1.** b The correct sequence is given in option (*b*). (ii) starts the sentence which is followed by (iii) since it tells what the 'dams should receive'. The next part is (ii) followed by (iv) which completes the sentence. Starting the sentence with "to ensure ... the collector said..." is wrong. Thus, option (*d*) is incorrect. Option (*b*) is the correct choice.

**2.** d (ii) starts the sequence with the sentence talking about the 'person' and his 'shirt'. (iv) follows (ii) since it describes the pockets and what is contained in them. This is followed by (i), them referring to toffees and chocolates. (iv) ends the sequence by talking about the reaction of the man.

**3.** a (i) starts the topic, followed by (iii) which adds more to the description of the legislation. (ii) follows (iii) by providing the condition that the legislation needs fulfill to become a law as mentioned in (iv).

**4.** c (i) opens the paragraph by talking about what the farmers do for the country. This is followed by (iv) which concludes on (i)'s basis that they are the most useful members of the society. (iii) follows (iv) since it gives the other side of the story. (ii) comes last as it states that because of this exploitation it is our duty to protect them.

**5.** b The events mentioned are logically related in the sequence given in option (*b*). (ii), 'we went to the pond' starts the passage which is followed by (iv), 'stood knee-deep...' This is followed by (iii) which talks of throwing stones to create ripples. (i) comes after (iii) which describes the ripples.

**6.** a From the given jumbled sentences, (iv) logically follows (i) as (iv) shows when the church was destroyed. (ii) is a good introductory sentence. Looking at the options given, (*b*) and (*c*) get eliminated since in these two options, (iv) does not follow (i). Out of options (*a*) and (*d*), one can comprehend that the sequence in option (*a*) is logically correct.

**7.** c From the given jumbled sentences, one can see that (iv) logically follows (i) as it provides the verb to the subject mentioned in (i). This is because (i) is an incomplete sentence. Notice that sentence (iii) reads "and no law containing a declaration that it is for giving effect to such policy **shall be** called in question in any court on the ground that it does not give effect to such policy." and (i) and (iv) together form a complete sentence that is "no law giving effect to the policy of the state towards securing all or any of the principles laid in part IV **shall be** deemed to be void in the ground that it is inconsistent with or takes away or abridges any rights conferred by article 14 or 19". Since option (*c*) is the only option out of the ones given, that has (i) followed by (iv), option (*c*) is correct.

**8.** a From the given jumbled sentences, one can see that (ii) logically follows (iii) and that whatever may be the sequence, this pair would always come together. This is because (iii) talks about something that the President may (or may not) do and (ii), as an extension to (iii) reads that "if he does so", the action talked about in sentence (ii) shall take place, that is, 'if the President sends a notification summoning the Houses to meet in a joint sitting for the purpose specified in the notification, the Houses shall meet accordingly'. Now, only option (*a*) has this above mentioned pair in the required sequence. Therefore, option (*a*) is correct.

**9.** d (i) talks about Indians, which is described in (iv), hence (iv) follows (i). (v) completes (iv) because it tells what Buddha and Gandhi taught. (ii) follows (v) since it comes up with the other perspective of the sentence. (iii) follows (ii) and has to come before (vi) because the 'nor' in (vi) has to follow the 'not' in (iii). Hence, option (*d*) is the correct order.

**10.** b (i) tells us that there has to be an observation that follows it, since it has the words 'on the basis of experiments'. (ii) fits in here perfectly because we have health experts putting forth their results. (v) follows (ii), as it is the beginning of the condition for the conclusion that humans can live up to 100 years. (iii) adds to (v) with more conditions. (iv) gives the conclusion and falls in place before (vi). Option (*b*) has the correct order.

**11.** c (ii) and (iv) form a mandatory pair as the 'it' in (iv) refers to the bomb in (ii). This eliminates option (*a*) and (*d*). Similarly, (v) has to come before (vi) because the 'they' in (vi) refers to the 'scientists' in (v). Hence, option (*c*) is the correct choice.

**12.** a (iii) and (v) form a mandatory pair as the mechanism of demand and supply in (iii) is explained in (v). Such a combination is only there in option (*a*), hence it is the correct choice.

**13.** d (iii) follows the opening sentence and tells more about India. The 'it' in (iii) refers to India of (i). (ii) and (iv) fall together as both are examples of famous personalities who have had an impact on India and the world. (v) has to come before the last sentence as it talks about shaking the foundation of British rule in India which was done by Mahatma Gandhi. Hence, option (*d*) is correct.

## STATEMENT-REASON

**Directions for question 1:** Select the correct reason for the statement given below.

**1. Statement:** The Supreme Court of India is encouraging Public Interest Litigation

**Reasons:**

I. To increase the reach of justice to the disadvantaged sections of society.

II. To quicken the pace of Justice.

Identify the correct reason for the aforementioned statement.

(*a*) Both I and II are correct reasons of the statement.

(*b*) I is the correct reason of the statement.

(*c*) Both I and II are not correct reasons of the statement.

(*d*) II is the correct reason of the statement.

**(CLAT 2012)**

### Solution

**1.** b Only reason I is correct here. The Supreme Court of India is encouraging Public Interest Litigation so that people from different and disadvantaged sections of the society can benefit by filling PILs which are in their interest. PILs have nothing to do with quickening the pace of justice.

## CAUSE-EFFECT

**Directions for questions 1 to 5:** In each of the questions given below, two statements are given. There may or may not be cause and effect relationship between the two statements. Mark your answer using this code.

(*a*) Statement I is the cause and statement II is the effect.

(*b*) Statement II is the cause and statement I is the effect.

(*c*) Both the statements are independent causes.

(*d*) Both the statements are independent effects.

**1. Statement I:** School education has been made free for children of poor families.

**Statement II:** Literacy rate among the poor is steadily growing. **(CLAT 2010)**

**2. Statement I:** Hallmarking of gold jewellary has been made compulsory.

**Statement II:** Many persons do not prefer to buy Hallmarked jewellery. **(CLAT 2010)**

**3. Statement I:** Many vegetarians are suffering from stomach ailments.

**Statement II:** Many dead fish were found near the lake shore. **(CLAT 2010)**

**4. Statement I:** Ahmed is a healthy boy.

**Statement II:** His mother is very particular about the food he eats. **(CLAT 2010)**

**5. Statement I:** Rate of crime is very low in this city.

**Statement II:** The police is efficient in this city.

**(CLAT 2010)**

**Directions for questions 6 to 10 :** Given below is a pair of events I and II. You have to decide their nature of relationship. Assume that the given information is correct and final.

**6.** I. Prices of toys in the market have gone down.

II. Government has reduced import duty on toys.

(*a*) I is the main cause and II is the main effect

(*b*) I is effect but II is not the main cause

(*c*) II is the main cause and I is the main effect

(*d*) II is an effect but I is not the main cause.

**(CLAT 2012)**

**7.** I. Inflation rate in India has come down

II. Reserve Bank of India has increased interest rate.

(*a*) I is the main cause and II is the main effect

(*b*) I is effect but II is not the main cause

(*c*) II is the main cause and I is the main effect

(*d*) II is an effect but I is not the main cause

**(CLAT 2012)**

**8.** I. More and more students are opting for legal education

II. Bar Council of India has introduced Bar Examination

(*a*) I is the main cause and II is the main effect
(*b*) I is effect but II is not the main cause
(*c*) II is the main cause and I is the main effect
(*d*) II is an effect but I is not the main cause

**(CLAT 2012)**

**9.** I. Sea level is steadily rising
II. Global Warming is a serious problem which the world is facing
(*a*) I is the main cause and II is the main effect
(*b*) I is effect but II is not the main cause
(*c*) II is the main cause and I is the main effect
(*d*) II is an effect but I is not the main cause

**(CLAT 2012)**

**10.** I. Financial Institutions are largely unregulated
II. Today, world is passing through a serious phase of economic crisis
(*a*) I is the main cause and II is the main effect
(*b*) I is effect but II is not the main cause
(*c*) II is the main cause and I is the main effect
(*d*) II is an effect but I is not the main cause

**(CLAT 2012)**

### Solutions

**1.** a Because of the action in 1st statement the effect in the 2nd statement has taken place. Therefore, (*a*) is the correct option.

**2.** d Both the statements are unrelated i.e. are independent effects of some other cause.

**3.** d Both incidents in statements I & II could be (could not be) the result of same cause.. Therefore, (*d*) is the correct option.

**4.** b Ahmed is healthy because of his mother's care. Therefore, (*b*) is the correct option.

**5.** b Rate of crime is low in the city because of the efficiency of the police. Therefore, (*b*) is the correct option.

**6.** c Reduction of import duty II on toys has resulted in the decrease in their prices I. Thus II is the main cause and I is the main effect. Option (*c*) is the correct answer.

**7.** c Reserve Bank of India changes the interest rates to cater to the rise and fall of inflation rate in the country. Thus, decrease in inflation rate I is a result of increase in interest rates II by the government. Hence II is the main cause and I is the main effect. Option (*c*) is the correct choice.

**8.** d The introduction of Bar Examination by the Bar Council of India is an effect which can be caused by increasing number of students opting for legal education (cause) along with some other reasons. Thus, II is the main effect but I is not the main cause.

**9.** c The phenomenon of global warming is a serious problem (cause) and the rise in the sea level is a major effect of the same. So, II is the main cause and I is the main effect.

**10.** a Due to the unregulated nature of the financial institutions (cause), the economy is getting affected. As a result, the world is passing through an economic crisis (effect). Thus, I is the main cause and II is the main effect.

### STATEMENT-COURSE OF ACTION

**Directions for questions 1 to 5:** Each question below contains a Statement and two Courses of Action I and II. Assuming the statement to be true, decide which of the two suggested Courses of Action logically follows, using the Code given below.

**Code:**
(*a*) If only I follows.
(*b*) If only II follows.
(*c*) If either I or II follows.
(*d*) If neither I nor II follows.

**1. Statement:** One of the problems facing the food processing industry is the irregular supply of raw material. The producers of raw materials are not getting a reasonable price.

**Courses of Action :**

**I.** The government should regulate the supply of raw material to other industries also.

**II.** The government should announce an attractive package to ensure regular supply of raw material for food processing industry.

**(CLAT 2009)**

**2. Statement:** The Officer In-charge of a Company had a hunch that some money was missing from the safe.

**Courses of Action :**

**I.** He should get it recounted with the help of the staff and check it with the balance sheet.

**II.** He should inform the police. **(CLAT 2009)**

**3. Statement:** If the retired Professors of the same Institutes are also invited to deliberate on restructuring of the organisation, their contribution may be beneficial to the Institute.

**Course of Action:**

**I.** Management may seek opinion of the employees before calling retired Professors.

**II.** Management should involve experienced people for the systematic restructuring of the organisation. **(CLAT 2009)**

**4. Statement:** The sale of a particular product has gone down considerably causing great concern to the company.

**Course of Action:**

**I.** The company should make a proper study of rival products in the market.

**II.** The price of the product should be reduced and quality improved. **(CLAT 2009)**

**5. Statement:** Mr. X, an active member of the Union, often insults his superiors in the office with his rude behaviour.

**Course of Action:**

**I.** He should be transferred to some other department.

**II.** The matter should be referred to the Union.

**(CLAT 2009)**

**Directions (Q. 6 – 10):** *Each question contains one statement and two courses of action I and II. Assuming the statements to be true, decide which of the two courses of action most logically follows.* **(CLAT 2013)**

**Code:**

(*a*) If only I follows.

(*b*) If only II follows.

(*c*) If either I or II follows.

(*d*) If neither I nor II follows.

**6. Statement :** Indian children are very talented but are instead weak in science and mathematics.

**I.** Teaching and textbooks are not available in mother language.

**II.** Education based on experiments in both the subjects is lacking.

**7. Statement :** Despite of child labour laws, children can be seen working in hotels, shops, houses, very frequently.

**I.** The government should not make such laws which cannot be enforced.

**II.** A proper education system for the primary level particularly for lower caste community may eradicate this problem.

**8. Statement :** Kyoto protocol on environment is signed by almost every country of the world.

**I.** As a result air, water and soil pollution have come down.

**II.** Increasing production of automobiles, refrigerators and fertilisers do not affect our environment.

**9. Statement :** School dropout rate is very high in the rural areas as children support their parents in income earning activities.

**I.** Public awareness programme on primary education should be expanded immediately to educate parents.

**II.** Compensation is not a remedy.

**10. Statement :** Smoking is one of those human weaknesses which tend to test the will power of the smoker of the edge.

**I.** It is very difficult for the smoker to give up smoking even if they want to do so.

**II.** Human beings have other weaknesses as well

**Solutions**

**1.** b The question statement highlights the problem of the food processing industry. II is the course of action that will help solve the problem raised in the question statement. Course of action I is far-fetched.

**2.** a The officer is suspecting something but he is not sure. So, there is no need to call the police. He should first check the money. This makes I the desired course of action.

**3.** b The question statement is highlighting the importance of having experienced people in the team. Course of action II is an extension of the idea mention in the question statement. I is not a course of action.

**4.** a The sale of a product has gone down considerably so an enquiry into the rival product is a desirable course of action. II is not the desirable course of action.

**5.** b Since Mr. X is part of the union, his bad behaviour should be communicated to the union. But, transferring Mr. X will not solve the problem of bad behaviour.

**6.** d The solution to the problem at hand could have been suggestions that would have aided Indian students to improve in science and mathematics. However, I and II are impediments that are capable of further hindering the desired improvement. Therefore, option (D) is correct.

**7.** b I does not follows because it cannot be understood why the government can't forbid child labour by taking the requisite measures. Also, not making a law that must be made, only because you think it cannot be enforced is unjustified. Now, let's look at II. If proper education that enlightens the people towards the importance of education is imparted, there is a possibility that people start sending their children to school and the word 'may' in II talks about a possibility. Therefore, II is a valid course of action. Hence, option (B) is correct.

**8.** d I may or may not follow because the statement does not tell the details of Kyoto protocol. II also does not follow because it is unrelated to the statement. Hence, option (D) is correct.

**9.** a The problem at hand is high rate of school-dropouts. I follows because if parents are aware of the importance of education, they will try to educate their children instead of seeking their children's help to increase their income. II does not follow because it is unrelated to the statement. Hence, option (A) is correct.

**10.** c I follows because if the problem of smoking tests the will power of the smoker, it can be inferred that it is very difficult for a smoker to quit smoking even if he wills. II also follows because the statement refers to smoking as 'one of those human weaknesses'. So, option (C) is correct because both the statements follow.

## ASSERTION OF OPINION/FACT

**Directions for questions 1 to 3:** In the following questions, assume that a 'fact' expresses something that can be proved by clear and objective data. An opinion expresses a judgment, view, attitude, or conclusion that is not backed by data.

**1.** Which one of the following statements is best described as an assertion of opinion rather than an assertion of fact?

(*a*) Brazil, China and India are now among the largest emitters of greenhouse gases.

(*b*) Scientists agree that human activity is an important cause of climate change.

(*c*) The Indian government's policy on climate change is misguided.

(*d*) The Indian government's policy on climate change has changed significantly in the last five years. **(CLAT 2011)**

**2.** (A) The number of people migrating into Bengaluru has increased significantly in recent years.

(B) This is because Bengaluru provides more economic opportunities than the towns and villages from which these migrants come.

(C) This sudden influx of migrants has made the city less pleasant to live in.

(D) The success of the government's rural employment guarantee act might have the effect of stemming some rural-urban migration.'

Which one of the above statements is best described as an assertion of opinion rather than an assertion of fact?

(*a*) A (*b*) B

(*c*) C (*d*) D **(CLAT 2011)**

**3.** Which one of the following statements, if true, is best described as an assertion of opinion rather than an assertion of fact?

(*a*) Mumbai is larger than Pune.

(*b*) Mumbai is smaller than Pune.

(*c*) Mumbai is more cultured than Pune.

(*d*) Mumbai is more crowded than Pune.

**(CLAT 2011)**

### Solutions

**1.** c Option (*a*) can be verified therefore, it's a fact. Similarly, options (*b*) and (*d*) can also be verified. In Option (*c*), the issue of Indian policy being misguided is a subjective issue and cannot be verified. Hence, it's an opinion.

**2.** c What is more pleasant to live and what is less pleasant is a subjective issue and the answer about it may vary from subject to subject. It cannot be verified. Thus, it is not a fact but an opinion.

**3.** c Whether Mumbai is larger or smaller than Pune can be verified. So, option (*a*) and (*b*) are facts. Similarly, whether Mumbai is more crowded than Pune can be verified and is a fact. A place being more cultured than the other is a subjective issue and opinions on this may vary from subject to subject. Thus, option (*c*) is an opinion.

## ODD ONE OUT

**Directions for questions 1 to 8:** Of the four alternatives given in each of the following questions, find the one which is different from the rest.

**1.** (*a*) Cheese (*b*) Saffron
(*c*) Pepper (*d*) Lard **(AILET, 2009)**

**2.** (*a*) Hansom (*b*) Victoria
(*c*) Growler (*d*) Baroque **(AILET, 2009)**

**3.** (*a*) house (*b*) mortgage
(*c*) hypothecation (*d*) immovable property **(CAT 2010)**

**4.** (*a*) Law (*b*) Court
(*c*) Morality (*d*) Judge **(CAT 2010)**

**5.** (*a*) Freedom of speech (*b*) Right to equality
(*c*) Freedom of religion (*d*) Right to make contract **(CAT 2010)**

**6.** (*a*) Fast-Slow (*b*) Bright-Dark
(*c*) Day-Night (*d*) Valley-Depth **(CAT 2012)**

**7.** (*a*) Body-Hand (*b*) Foot-Ankle
(*c*) Eye-Ear (*d*) Wrist-Finger **(CAT 2012)**

**8.** (*a*) Snake-Frog (*b*) Goat-Hen
(*c*) Dog-Cat (*d*) Tiger-Deer **(CAT 2012)**

### Solutions

**1.** a Saffron, pepper and lard are all spices. Cheese is the odd one out.

**2.** c Hansom, Victoria and baroque are all horse-drawn carriages that were used in olden times in Europe. Growler is a person or thing that growls. Thus, it does not belong to the group.

**3.** a 'House' is the odd one out, rest three terms are technical financial terms.

**4.** c 'Morality' is a system of ideas of right and wrong conduct. Law, court and judge are all legal terms.

**5.** d The first three are fundamental rights, right to make a contract is not.

**6.** d Valley and depth are not antonyms while all other pairs of words are antonyms of each other. Thus, option (*d*) is the odd one out.

**7.** c All options except option (*c*) have the second part as an extension of the first, like hand being joined to the body, foot to the ankle and finger to the wrist. Eye and ear are separate and so option (*c*) is different from the others and thus, correct.

**8.** b The second animal in each option is a prey of the first. Goat doesn't eat hen. Option (*b*) is the correct choice.

## PARA-JUMBLES 5 SENTENCE TYPE

**Directions (Q. 1 - 3) :** In this section, each passage consists of five sentences. The first sentence is given in the beginning. The four sentences in each passage have been jumbled up. These are labeled P, Q, R and S. You are required to find out the proper sequence of the four sentences and mark accordingly on the Answer Sheet.

**1.** $S_1$ : A suicide bomber killed 18 people near a hospital of Baghdad, keeping violence on the boil after Iraq's landmark election and ahead of an important Shia religious ceremony.

P : The bomber drove his vehicle towards local government offices and a hospital in the town, but detonated it outside blast walls protecting buildings.

Q: Around 25 people were wounded in the attack, the second suicide car bombing in as many days.

R: "Looking at the partial result, it appears the Sistani list will have over 50% and Kurdish parties will come second," said a Sunni politician.

S : Meanwhile, the two electoral power houses representing Iraq's Shia and Kurdish communities are poised to clinch the country's two top jobs, with results from the landmark January 30 polls expected anytime.

The proper sequence should be

(*a*) SRPQ (*b*) SQPR

(*c*) PQSR (*d*) QPSR **(AILET, 2013)**

**2.** $S_1$ : It should be noted that Lenin, being the head of the government. held no official posts in the Party Central Committee, but presided over sessions of the Central Committee plenary meetings and also of the Political Bureau.

P : In performing his party duties, he was assisted by a secretary of the Central Committee, or the head of the Secretariat.

Q: Officially, such a post did not exist at the time, but in practice one of the secretaries was expected to

R: That being the case, Lenin not only heads the Council of People's commissars, but was also the de facto leader of the Party's Central Committee.

S: When Lenin's health deteriorated, the question arose of strengthening the secretariat and an authoritative leader has to be found who could supervise Perth's affairs in Lenin's absence.

The proper sequence should be

(*a*) PQRS (*b*) SRPQ

(*c*) SQPR (*d*) RPQS **(AILET, 2013)**

**3.** $S_1$: There is nothing in the world fascinating than watching a child grow and develop.

P: At first you think of it as just a matter of growing bigger.

Q: Then, as the infant begins to do things, you may think of it as "learning tricks".

R: In some ways, the development of each child retraces the whole history of the human race, physically and spiritually, step by step.

S: But, it's really more complicated and full of meaning than that.

The proper sequence should be

(*a*) PQSR (*b*) RPQS

(*c*) PQRS (*d*) RPSQ **(AILET, 2013)**

### Solutions

**1.** c P follows the opening sentence as it continues with the subject- the bomber, explaining his actions. Q further supports the facts presented in P. So, PQ forms a mandatory pair. "Looking at the partial result" in R refers to polls result mentioned in S. Hence, R follows S and SR forms another mandatory pair. Hence, option (*c*) is correct.

**2.** d Cleary R follows the opening statement, building further context on Lenin's leadership on different parties. P further talks about Lenin's performance; 'his' in P refers to Lenin. So, RP forms a mandatory pair. S follows Q as events in S are based on the facts mentioned in Q. Hence, option (*d*) is correct.

**3.** a Cleary P follows the opening statement, as 'it' in P refers to "watching a child grow" mentioned in the opening statement. Q builds the context further, by explaining infant's growth, referring to P, So, Q follows P. R provides support to the argument made in S. So, R follows S. Hence, option (*a*) is correct.

## WORD REARRANGEMENT

**Directions :** In questions **1** to **5,** a particular word is given. The word is followed by four words as given in the alternatives. One of these four words cannot be formed by using the letters given in the question.

1. ENTHUSIASTICALLY
(*a*) SATIATE
(*b*) HELMINTH
(*c*) SHALE
(*d*) TANTALUS **(AILET, 2013)**

2. CONCENTRATE
(*a*) CENTRE
(*b*) CONCERN
(*c*) REASON
(*d*) TREAT **(AILET, 2013)**

3. INTRANSIGENT
(*a*) STAIN
(*b*) GRATE
(*c*) TRACE
(*d*) RESIGN **(AILET, 2013)**

4. PERPETUATION
(*a*) REPUTE
(*b*) RETAIN
(*c*) PIPETTE
(*d*) PENANCE **(AILET, 2013)**

5. ESTRANGEMENT
(*a*) ENTANGLE
(*b*) RNTREAT
(*c*) GERMAN
(*d*) TANGEN **(AILET, 2013)**

### Solutions

**1.** b 'ENTHUSIASTICALLY' does not have an 'M' in it while 'HELMINTH' does. Thus, option (*b*) is the correct answer.

**2.** c 'CONCENTRATE' does not have an 'S' in it while 'REASON' does. Therefore, option (*c*) is the correct answer.

**3.** c 'INTRANSIGENT' does not have a 'C' in it while 'TRACE' does. Therefore, option (*c*) is the correct answer.

**4.** d 'PERPETUATION' does not have two 'N's' in it while 'PENANCE' does. Therefore, option (*d*) is the correct answer.

**5.** a 'ESTRANGEMENT' does not have an 'L' in it while 'ENTANGLE' does. Therefore, option (*a*) is the correct answer.

## ASSERTION OF OPINION/FACT/INFERENCE

**Directions (Q. 1-2) :** From the alternatives, choose the one which correctly classifies the four sentences as a

**F : Fact:** If it relates to known matter of direct observation, or an existing reality or something known to be true.

**J : Judgment :** If it is an opinion or estimate or anticipation of common sense or intention.

**I : Inference :** If it is a logical conclusion or deduction about something based on the knowledge of facts.

**1.** (1) If democracy is to survive, the people must develop a sense of consumerism.
(2) Consumerism has helped improve the quality of goods in certain countries.
(3) The protected environment in our country is helping the local manufacturers.
(4) The quality of goods suffers if the manufacturers take undue advantage of this. **(AILET 2014)**

(*a*) IJFJ (*b*) JFJI
(*c*) IJJF (*d*) 1FJJ

**2.** (1) Everyday social life is impossible without interpersonal relationships.
(2) The roots of many misunderstandings have been cited in poor relations among individuals.
(3) Assuming the above to be true, social life will be much better if people understand the importance of good interpersonal relations.
(4) A study reveals that interpersonal relations and hence life in general can be improved with a little effort on the part of individuals. **(AILET 2014)**

(*a*) FJIJ (*b*) JFIF
(*c*) FIFJ (*d*) IFFJ

### Solutions

**1.** b Statement (1) is a judgment as it is an opinion. So, the other options are ruled out and option (*b*) is the correct answer. Statement (2) is a fact as it can be checked using data while statement (3) is a judgment due to the subjective nature of 'protected environment'. Statement (4) is an inference based on the previous two statements.

**2.** b Statement (1) is an opinion of the author and hence, is a judgment. Statement (2) is expressed like an observation and hence, is a fact. Statement (3) is an inference based on the previous statements while statement (4) is again a fact that has been revealed by a study.

■■

# 2

# ANALYTICAL REASONING

## ANALYTICAL REASONING

**Directions for questions 1 to 4:** Some information is provided in the form of statements. On the basis of that information find the answer to the questions which follow.

Coach Balkishen is trying to put together a team of four players for a tennis tournament.

He has seven players available: males A, B and C and the females M, N, O and P. All players are of equal ability and there must be at least two males on the team. For a team of four, all players must be able to play with each other player.

Player B cannot play with player M

Player C cannot play with player P

Player M cannot play with player O **(AILET, 2008)**

**1.** If player O is selected and player B is rejected the team will consist of which foursome?

(*a*) A, C, M and O (*b*) A, C, N and O

(*c*) A, C, P and O (*d*) A, N, P and O

**2.** If player M is on the team, what other players must be on the team as well?

(*a*) A, B and N (*b*) A, C and N

(*c*) A, C and O (*d*) A, C and P

**3.** What statement is false?

(M) Player B and C are never selected together

(N) Player C and O are never selected together

(O) Player C and N are never selected together

(*a*) Only M (*b*) Only N

(*c*) Only O (*d*) All the three

**4.** Which statement must always be true?

(M) If M plays, A plays

(N) If O plays, B plays

(O) If M plays, O plays

(*a*) Only M (*b*) Only N

(*c*) Only O (*d*) Only M and O

**Directions for questions 5 to 9:** Answer the questions based on the following information.

Five adults A, B, C, D and E are sitting at Bharat Provision Store. In the group, there are one Manager, one Accountant, one Supplier of provisions. The Accountant, who has a child earns least money. A. who is married to C's sister, earns more than the Manager . D is an unmarried lady and does not do any work. There is one married couple in a group of which B is husband. E is the brother of C and is neither a Supplier nor an Accountatnt. No lady is a Supplier or Manager. C is neither a Supplier nor an 'Accountant'.

**(AILET, 2009)**

**5.** Who is Accountant?

(*a*) A (*b*) B

(*c*) C (*d*) D

**6.** Who is Supplier?

(*a*) A (*b*) B

(*c*) C (*d*) D

**7.** Who is the wife of B?

(*a*) A (*b*) B

(*c*) C (*d*) E

**8.** Who is earning the highest?

(*a*) A (*b*) B

(*c*) C (*d*) D

**9.** Who is the sister of C?

(*a*) A (*b*) B

(*c*) C (*d*) D

**Directions for questions 10 to 12:** Each group of questions in this section is based on a set of conditions. Choose the response that most accurately and completely answers each questions.

A panel reviews six contract bids - H, J, K, R, S, and T. No two bids have the same cost.

Exactly one of the bids is accepted. The following conditions must hold: **(AILET, 2009)**

1. The accepted bid is either K or R and is either the second or the third lowest in cost.
2. H is lower in cost than each of J and K.
3. If J is not the fourth lowest in cost, then J is higher in cost than each of S and T.
4. Either R or S is the fifth lowest in cost.

**10.** Which one of the following could be an accurate list of the bids in order from lowest to highest in cost?

(*a*) T, K, H, S, J, R (*b*) H, T, K, S, R, J

(*c*) H, S, T, K, R, J (*d*) H, K, S, J, R, T

**11.** Which one of the following bids CANNOT be the fourth lowest in cost?

(*a*) H (*b*) J

(*c*) K (*d*) R

**12.** Which one of the following bids CANNOT be the second lowest in cost?

(*a*) H (*b*) J

(*c*) K (*d*) R

**Directions for questions 13 and 14:** Answer the questions based on the following information.

Detectives investigating a city wide increase in burglaries questioned exactly seven suspects - S, T, V, W, X, Y and Z - each on a different one of seven consecutive days. Each suspect was questioned exactly once. Any suspect who confessed did so while being questioned.

The investigation conformed to the following:

1. T was questioned on day three.
2. The suspect questioned on day four did not confess.
3. S was questioned after W was questioned.
4. Both X and V were questioned after Z was questioned.
5. No suspects confessed after W was questioned.
6. Exactly two suspects confessed after T was questioned. **(AILET, 2009)**

**13.** Which one of the following could be true?

(*a*) X was questioned on day one.

(*b*) V was questioned on day two.

(*c*) Z was questioned on day four.

(*d*) W was questioned on day five.

**14.** If Z was the second suspect to confess, then each of the following statements could be true EXCEPT:

(*a*) T confessed. (*b*) T did not confess.

(*c*) V did not confess. (*d*) Y did not confess.

**Directions for questions 15 to 19:** Read the information and answer the following questions.

Six persons – P, Q, R, S, T and W work in an Organisation. Each of them likes different colours, viz., Black, White, Blue, Green, Red and Yellow and their salaries are also different. The person who earns maximum does not like Blue or White colour. The person who earns the least does not like Black or Red colour. R likes Yellow colour and his salary is the second maximum. P likes White colour and earns more than T but less than W. Q likes Black colour who earns less than P but more than T. S likes Blue colour and T likes Red colour. **(AILET, 2012)**

**15.** How many of them do earn more than Q?

(*a*) One (*b*) Two

(*c*) Three (*d*) Data inadequate

**16.** Who among them earns least?

(*a*) Q (*b*) P

(*c*) R (*d*) S

**17.** If they are arranged in the descending order according to their salaries, who will occupy the third position?

(*a*) P (*b*) R

(*c*) T (*d*) Data inadequate

**18.** W likes the colour

(*a*) White (*b*) Green

(*c*) Blue (*d*) Either White or Green

**19.** S likes which colour?

(*a*) White (*b*) Green

(*c*) Blue (*d*) Red

**Directions for questions 20 to 24:** Each group of questions is based on a set of conditions. Choose the response that most accurately and completely answers each question.

Mercotek carried out a study to compare the productivity of its night shift with that of its day shift. Every week the company's six crews – F, G, H, R, S and T – were ranked from first (most productive) to sixth (least productive). There were no ties. For any given week, either G and T were the two night-shift crews or else S and H were – the four other crews were the day-shift crews for that week. The following relationships held for every week of the study:

F is more productive than G

R is more productive than S

R is more productive than T

S is more productive than H

G is more productive than T **(AILET, 2012)**

**20.** Which of the following could be an accurate ranking of all the crews, in order from first to sixth, for a given week of the study?

(*a*) F, G, T, R, S, H

(*b*) F, R, G, T, H, S

(*c*) G, R, T, S, H, F

(*d*) R, F, G, S, H, T

**21.** If F is ranked third for a given week of the study, then which one of the following could also be true of that week?

(*a*) G ranks second (*b*) H ranks fourth

(*c*) R ranks second (*d*) S ranks fourth

**22.** Which one of the following CANNOT be the crew ranked fifth for any given week of the study?

(*a*) G (*b*) H

(*c*) R (*d*) S

**23.** For any given week of the study, the ranking of all the crews is completely determined if which one of the following is true?

(*a*) F ranks second that week

(*b*) G ranks fifth that week

(*c*) H ranks third that week

(*d*) R ranks third that week

**24.** If the night-shift crews rank fifth and sixth for a given week of the study, then which one of the following could also be true of that week?

(*a*) G ranks fourth (*b*) H ranks fifth

(*c*) R ranks third (*d*) S ranks fourth

**25.** A college received fifty applications for a certain course. In the qualifying examination, one-tenth of them secured marks in 90-95% range. Within remaining segment, three-fifths of them secured marks in 75-90% range. The rest secured below 75%. To get admission, the following restrictions hold good:

(i) No student who has scored below 75% can seek admission to Physics course.

(ii) No student is allowed to opt Physics without opting Mathematics.

(iii) No student is allowed to opt Physics and Astrophysics simultaneously.

(iv) To opt Mathematics or Astrophysics, a student should have scored at least 70% in the qualifying examination.

Which one of the following alternatives is possible?

(*a*) Ninety percent of the applicants are admitted to Physics course.

(*b*) Thirty-five percent of the applicants who are otherwise inelligible to join Physics course are admitted to Mathematics and Astrophysics course.

(*c*) Students of Physics course outnumber those of Mathematics.

(*d*) Whoever is eligible to study Mathematics is also eligible to study Physics. **(CLAT 2008)**

**Directions for questions 26 and 27:** Choose the appropriate option basis the given information.

**(CLAT 2008)**

**26.** A tourist can tour utmost four places out of A, B, C, D, E, F and G. Out of four, not more than two can come under holiday tour and at least two must come under business trip. The break up is as follows:

A, B C and D - Business tour; E, F and G - Holiday tour

The following restrictions hold good.

(*a*) If A is included, then both C and G are excluded.

(*b*) If neither E nor F is included, then B or G or both of them can be included.

(*c*) If G is included, then D cannot be included.

Which one of the following combinations is possible?

(*a*) A, C, E and F (*b*) B, G and E

(*c*) A, D and G (*d*) A, B and D

**27. Under the same fact situation as above,** suppose that the following restrictions hold good:

(*a*) A can be included provided C is included.

(*b*) E is included provided B or G is included but not both.

(*c*) C can be included provided at least D or F is excluded.

Which one of the following is a certainty?

(*a*) A, B, C, & E (*b*) A, C, D & F

(*c*) B, C, D & E (*d*) A, B, C & F

**28.** Four members have to be nominated to a Committee and there are six candidates: A, B, C, D, E and F. The following restrictions hold good:

(*a*) If A is nominated, then D does not find any place.

(*b*) If B is nominated, then either E or F has to be nominated, but not both.

(*c*) If C is nominated, then both D and E have to be nominated.

Which one of the following is an acceptable combination?

(*a*) A, B, C and E (*b*) A, B, C and D

(*c*) B, C, D and E (*d*) B, C, D and F

**(CLAT 2008)**

**29.** Six students A, B, C, D, E and F are sitting. A and B are from Mumbai, rest are from Delhi. D and F are tall but others are short. A, C, and D are girls, others are boys. Which is the tall girl from Delhi?

(*a*) F (*b*) D

(*c*) E (*d*) C **(CLAT 2010)**

**30.** Pramesh is heavier than Jairam but lighter than Gulab. Anand is heavier than Gulab. Mohan is lighter than Jairam. Who among them is the heaviest?

(*a*) Jairam (*b*) Anand

(*c*) Gulab (*d*) Pramesh **(CLAT 2010)**

**Directions for questions 31 to 33:** Read the following information carefully and then answer the questions.

Four friends W, X, Y and Z are students of Class $10^{th}$. W and X are good in Hindi but poor in English. W and Y are good in Science but poor in Mathematics. Y and Z are good in English but poor in Social Studies. Z and X are good in Mathematics as well as in Science.

**(CLAT 2012)**

**31.** Who amongst the following friends is not good in Mathematics but good in Hindi?

(*a*) W (*b*) Y

(*c*) X (*d*) Z

**32.** Which of the following pairs of friends are good, both in English and Science?

(*a*) W and Y (*b*) W and Z

(*c*) Y and Z (*d*) Z and X

**33.** Which of the following statements is definitely true?

(*a*) Y and Z are good in English as well as in Hindi

(*b*) All four friends are good in Science

(*c*) W is good in Social Studies, Hindi and Science

(*d*) Y is not good in Mathematics, Hindi and Social Studies

**Directions (Q. 34 - 39):** Each group of questions is based on a set of conditions. Choose the response that most accurately and completely answers each question.

At the snack cafe at a party, Ali, Bina, Champak and Diya are eating cookies. There are five kinds of cookies to choose from - chocolate chip cookies, oatmeal cookies, sugar cookies, peanut butter cookies and raisin cookies. Each of these four people eats at least two kinds of cookies. Their choices are governed by the following rules :

At most two of them eat oatmeal cookies

At least two of them eat sugar cookies

Ali does not eat any sugar cookies

Bina and Champak do not eat the same type of cookies

Bina eats chocolate chip cookies

Champak eats sugar cookies

No one eats both raisin cookies and sugar cookies

If someone eats raisin cookies, they also eat peanut butter cookies **(AILET, 2013)**

**34.** Which one of the following must be true ?

(*a*) Champak eats chocolate chip cookies

(*b*) Ali eats chocolate chip cookies

(*c*) Bina does not eat peanut butter cookies

(*d*) Diya does not eat raisin cookies

**35.** If Bina eats exactly three kinds of cookies, which one of the following must be true ?

(*a*) Champak eats exactly three kinds of cookies

(*b*) Diya eats only sugar cookies

(*c*) If Ali eats oatmeal cookies, Diya eats oatmeal cookies

(*d*) Champak eats oatmeal cookies

**36.** Which one of the following cannot be true ?

(*a*) No one eats raisin cookies

(*b*) Ali and Diya both eat oatmeal cookies

(*c*) All and Diya both eat chocolate chip cookies

(*d*) Bina and Champak eat the same number of kinds of cookies.

**37.** Which pair of cookie types could each be eaten by at least three different people ?

(*a*) Chocolate chip and oatmeal

(*b*) Oatmeal and peanut butter

(*c*) Chocolate chip and peanut butter

(*d*) Oatmeal and sugar

**38.** Which pair of cookie types contains a cookie type eaten by exactly two different people ?

(*a*) Chocolate chip and oatmeal

(*b*) Oatmeal and peanut butter

(*c*) Chocolate chip and peanut butter

(*d*) Sugar and raisin

**39.** Which cookie type could be eaten by none of the people ?

(*a*) Chocolate chip (*b*) Oatmeal

(*c*) Sugar (*d*) Raisin

**40.** Reaching a place of appointment on Friday, I found that I was two days earlier than the scheduled day. If I had reached on the following Wednesday, how many days late would I have been ?

(*a*) One day (*b*) Two days

(*c*) Three days (*d*) Four days

**(AILET, 2013)**

**41.** Kamala would like to complete all her home work before 10 p.m. in order to watch an important TV programme. She has 40 minutes assignment in each of her five subjects. What is the latest time at which she can start and still complete work in time for the programme ?

(*a*) 6.40 p.m. (*b*) 6.30 p.m.

(*c*) 7.10 p.m. (*d*) 7.20 p.m. **(AILET, 2013)**

**42.** What is the colour of the pole diagonally opposite to the Bronze coloured pole? **(CLAT 2013)**

(*a*) White (*b*) Silver

(*c*) Metallic (*d*) Golden

**43.** Which is the second tallest pole? **(CLAT 2013)**

(*a*) A (*b*) D

(*c*) B (*d*) Cannot be determined

**44.** Which is the colour of the tallest pole?

(*a*) Golden (*b*) Silver **(CLAT 2013)**

(*c*) Bronze (*d*) None of these

**Directions (Q. 45 – 46):** *Answer the questions on the basis of the information given below*:

The head of a newly formed Government desires to appoint five of the six elected ministers P, Q, R, S, T and U to portfolios of Foreign, Industry and Commerce, Agriculture, Rural Development and Human Resources. U does not want any portfolio if S gets one of the five. R wants either Foreign or Human Resources or no portfolio. Q says that if S gets Industry and Commerce or Rural Development then she must get the other one. T insists on a portfolio if P gets one. **(CLAT 2013)**

**45.** Which of the following is a valid assignment

(*a*) P- Foreign, Q- Industry and Commerce, R- Agriculture, S- Rural Development, T- Human Resources

(*b*) R- Foreign, S- Industry and Commerce, P- Agriculture, Q- Rural Development, T- Human Resources

(*c*) P- Foreign, Q- Industry and Commerce, T- Agriculture, S- Rural Development, U- Human Resources

(*d*) Q- Foreign, U- Industry and Commerce, T- Agriculture, R- Rural Development, P- Human Resources

**46.** If P gets Foreign and R gets Human Resources, then which is NOT a valid assignment of Agriculture and Rural Development

(*a*) S- Agriculture, Q- Rural Development

(*b*) U- Agriculture, Q- Rural Development

(*c*) Q- Agriculture, T- Rural Development

(*d*) Q- Agriculture, S- Rural Development

**Directions (Q. 47 – 51):** *Read the information given below to answer the questions.* **(CLAT 2013)**

*i.* Kareena's dieting schedule consists of having only one fruit on a given day of the week.

*ii.* Dietician has prescribed banana, papaya, pomegranate, apple and grape from Sunday to Friday, one day being a fasting day. Kareena cannot eat any fruit on Saturday.

*iii.* Pomegranate day is neither on the first day nor on the last day but earlier than the papaya day.

*iv.* Apple day is on the immediate next day of papaya day.

*v.* Banana day is on the immediate previous day of the fasting day.

*vi.* Apple day and grape day must have a gap of two days between them.

*vii.* Grape day is the day immediately following the fasting day.

**47.** Which of the following is the fasting day?

(*a*) Monday (*b*) Tuesday

(*c*) Wednesday (*d*) Thursday

**48.** Banana day and apple day have a gap of how many days between them?

(*a*) One (*b*) Two

(*c*) Three (*d*) Four

**49.** Which day is grape day?

(*a*) Monday (*b*) Tuesday

(*c*) Thursday (*d*) Sunday

**50.** Which day is pomegranate day?

(*a*) Sunday (*b*) Monday

(*c*) Tuesday (*d*) Wednesday

**51.** Which of the following is the correct statement?

(*a*) Apple day is after papaya day.

(*b*) Banana day is on Wednesday.

(*c*) Fasting day is on Tuesday.

(*d*) Papaya day is earlier than banana day.

**Directions (Q. 52–56):** *Read the information given below to answer the questions.* **(CLAT 2013)**

A, B, C, D, E, F, G and H want to have a dinner on a round table and they have worked out the following seating arrangements.

*i.* A will sit beside C

*ii.* H will sit beside A

*iii.* C will sit beside E

*iv.* F will sit beside H

*v.* E will sit beside G

*vi.* D will sit beside F

*vii.* G will sit beside B

*viii.* B will sit beside D

**52.** Which of the following is wrong?

(*a*) A will be to the immediate right of C

(*b*) D will be to the immediate left of B

(*c*) E will be to the immediate right of A

(*d*) F will be to the immediate left of D

**53.** Which of the following is correct?

(*a*) B will be to the immediate left of D

(*b*) H will be to the immediate right of A

(*c*) C will be to the immediate right of F

(*d*) B will be to the immediate left of H

**54.** A and F will become neighbours if:

(*a*) B agrees to change her sitting position

(*b*) C agrees to change her sitting position

(*c*) G agrees to change her sitting position

(*d*) H agrees to change her sitting position

**55.** During sitting:

(*a*) A will be directly facing C

(*b*) B will be directly facing C

(*c*) A will be directly facing B

(*d*) B will be directly facing D

**56.** H will be sitting between:

(*a*) C and B (*b*) A and F

(*c*) D and G (*d*) E and G

**Directions (Q. 57-62) :** Each group of questions is based on a set of conditions. Choose the response that most accurately and completely answers each question.

There are five flagpoles lined up next to each other in a straight row in front of a school. Each flagpole flies one flag (red, white, or blue) and one pennant (green, white, or blue). The following are conditions that affect the placement of flags and pennants on the poles:

On a given flagpole, the pennant and the flag cannot be the same colour.

Two adjacent flagpolescannot fly the same colour flags.

Two adjacent flagpoles cannot fly the same colour pennants.

No more than two of any colour flag or pennant may fly at one time.

**57.** If the 2nd and 5th pennants are blue, the 2nd and 5th flags are red, and the 3rd flag is white, then which one of the following must be true ?

(*a*) Two of the flags are white. **(AILET 2014)**

(*b*) Two of the pennants are white.

(*c*) The 4th pennant is green.

(*d*) If the 1st flag is white, then the 1st pennant is green.

**58.** If the 1st flag is red and the 2nd pennant is blue, then which one of the following is NOT necessarily true ? **(AILET 2014)**

(*a*) The second flag is white.

(*b*) If the 5th flag is red, then the 3rd flag is blue.

(*c*) If the 4th pennant is green, then the 1st pennant is white.

(*d*) If the 1st and 5th flags are the same colour, then the 3rd flag is blue.

**59.** If the 1st and 3rd flags are white and the 2nd and 4th pennants are blue, then which one of the following is false ? **(AILET 2014)**

(*a*) The 4th flag is red.

(*b*) The 1st pennant is green.

(*c*) The 3rd pennant is not red.

(*d*) The 5th pennant is green.

**60.** If the 1st and 4th flags are blue, and the 3rd pennant is white, then which one of the following must be true ? **(AILET 2014)**

(*a*) If the 1st pennant is green, then the 5th pennant is white.

(*b*) If the 5th pennant is white, then the 1st pennant is green.

(*c*) The 2nd flag is red.

(*d*) The 5th flag is red.

**61.** If the 2nd flag is red and the 3rd flag is white, and the 4th pennant is blue, then which one of the following must be true ? **(AILET 2014)**

(*a*) If the 5th flag is white, then the two of the pennants are blue.

(*b*) If the 1st flag is white, then the 2nd flag is white.

(*c*) If the 1st pennant is blue, then the 5th pennant is green.

(*d*) if the 1st pennant is green, then the 5th flag is not blue.

**62.** If the 1st flag and the 2nd pennant are the same colour, the 2nd flag and the 3rd pennant are the same colour, the 3rd flag and the 4th pennant are the same colour, and the 4th flag and the 5th pennant are the same colour, then which one of the following must be true ? **(AILET 2014)**

(*a*) The 1st pennant is white.

(*b*) The 2nd flag is not white.

(*c*) The 5th flag is red.

(*d*) The 3rd pennant is blue.

**63.** Nicky, who is Ronald's daughter, says to Irene, "Your mother Rita is the youngest sister of my father, who is the third child of Sylvester". How is Sylvester related to Irene ? **(AILET 2014)**

(*a*) Maternal uncle (*b*) Father

(*c*) Grandfather (*d*) Father-in-law

**64.** Pointing to a lady, a person says to his friend, "She is the grandmother of the elder brother of my father". How is the girl in the photograph related to the man? **(AILET 2014)**

(*a*) Niece (*b*) Sister

(*c*) Aunt (*d*) Sister-in-law

**65.** Pointing towards a boy, Aruna said to Pushpa, "The mother of his father is the wife of your grandfather (mother's father)". How is Pushpa related to that boy ? **(AILET 2014)**

(*a*) Sister (*b*) Niece

(*c*) Cousin (*d*) Wife

**66.** The front door of Kiran house is towards the south. From the backside of her house she walks 50 metres straight then turns towards the left and walks 100 metres and after that turns right and stops after walking 100 metres. Now Kiran is facing which direction ? **(AILET 2014)**

(*a*) East (*b*) South

(*c*) West (*d*) North

**67.** If Northwest becomes south and southwest becomes east and all the other directions change in the similar manner, then what will be the direction for north? **(AILET 2014)**

(*a*) Southeast (*b*) Northeast

(*c*) North (*d*) Southwest

**68.** A policeman goes 20 km east and then turning to the south he goes 30 km and then again turns to his left and goes 10 km. How far is he from his starting point? **(AILET 2014)**

(*a*) 30 km (*b*) 20 km
(*c*) 10 km (*d*) 40 km

**Directions (Q. 69-72) :** *In the following number series, find out the missing number:* **(AILET 2014)**

**69.** 31, 32, 36, 45, ?

(*a*) 55 (*b*) 56
(*c*) 62 (*d*) 61

**70.** 1, 3, 2, 5, 3, 7, 4, 9, 5, 11, 6, ?

(*a*) 10 (*b*) 11
(*c*) 13 (*d*) 9

**71.** 300, 296, 287, 271, ?, 210

(*a*) 246 (*b*) 250
(*c*) 244 (*d*) 261

**72.** 12, 15, 19, ?, 30, 37

(*a*) 25 (*b*) 21
(*c*) 23 (*d*) 24

**Directions (Q. 73-74) :** Each question is followed by two statements, I and II. Answer each question using the following instructions. **(AILET 2014)**

**Choose (a) :** *If the question can be answered by using statement I alone but not by using II alone.*

**Choose (*b*) :** *If the question can be answered by using Statement II alone but not by using I alone.*

***Choose* (*c*) :** *If the question can be answered by using either statement alone.*

**Choose (*d*) :** *If the question can be answered by using both the statements together but not by either statement.*

**73.** In a cricket match the 'man of the match' award is given to the player scoring the highest number of runs. In case of tie, the player (out of those locked in the tie) who has taken the higher number of catches is chosen. Even thereafter, if there is a tie, the player (out of those locked in the tie) who has dropped fewer catches is selected. Aakash, Biplab and Chirag who were contenders for the award dropped at least one catch each. Biplab dropped 2 catches more than Aakash did, scored 50, and took 2 catches. Chirag got two chances to catch and dropped both. Who was the 'man of the match'?

I. Chirag made 15 runs less than both Aakash and Biplab.

II. The catches dropped by Biplab are 1 more than the catches taken by Aakash.

**74.** Four friends, A,B,C and D got the top four ranks in a competitive examination, but A did not get the first, B did not get the second, C did not get the third, and D did not get the fourth rank. Who secured which rank ?

I. Neither A nor D were among the first 2.

II. Neither B nor C was third or fourth.

**Directions (Q. 75-77) :** *Read the following information carefully and answer the questions given below:*

Five friends Satish, Rajesh, Rehman, Rakesh, and Vineet, — each presents one paper to their class on Physics, Zoology, Botany, English, or Geology — one day a week, Monday through Friday.

(i) Vineet does not present English and does not give his presentation on Tuesday.

(ii) Rajesh makes the Geology presentation, and does not do it on Monday or Friday.

(iii) The Physics presentation is made on Thursday.

(iv) Rehman makes his presentation, which is not on English, on Wednesday.

(v) The Botany presentation is on Friday, and not by Rakesh.

(vi) Satish makes his presentation on Monday.

**75.** What day is the English presentation made?

(*a*) Friday (*b*) Monday **(CLAT 2014)**
(*c*) Tuesday (*d*) Wednesday

**76.** What presentation does Vineet do? **(CLAT 2014)**

(*a*) English (*b*) Geology
(*c*) Physics (*d*) Botany

**77.** What day does Rakesh make his presentation on?

(*a*) Monday (*b*) Tuesday **(CLAT 2014)**
(*c*) Wednesday (*d*) Thursday

**Directions (Q. 78-82) :** *Each question contains a statement on relationship and a question regarding relationship based on the statement. Choose the correct option.*

**78.** Pointing to a photograph, a man said, "I have no brother or sister but that man's father is my father's son". Whose photograph was that? **(CLAT 2014)**

(*a*) His father's (*b*) His own
(*c*) His son's (*d*) His nephew's

**79.** Ranjan introduces Abhay as the son of the only brother of his father's wife. How is Abhay related to Ranjan? **(CLAT 2014)**

(*a*) Son (*b*) Brother
(*c*) Cousin (*d*) Uncle

**80.** Pointing to a lady on the stage, Bhumika said, "She is the sister of the son of the wife of my husband. How is the lady related to Bhumika? **(CLAT 2014)**

(*a*) Cousin (*b*) Sister-in-law
(*c*) Sister (*d*) Daughter

**81.** Pinky, who is Victor's daughter, says to Lucy, "Your mother Rosy is the younger sister of my father, who is the third child of Joseph". How is Joseph related to Lucy? **(CLAT 2014)**

(*a*) Father-in-law (*b*) Father
(*c*) Maternal uncle (*d*) Grandfather

**82.** Pramod told Vinod, "Yesterday I defeated the only brother of the daughter of my grandmother". Whom did Pramod defeat? **(CLAT 2014)**

(*a*) Father (*b*) Son
(*c*) Father-in-law (*d*) Cousin

**Directions (Q. 83-87) :** *Read the information given below to answer the questions.*

(i) In a family of six persons, there are people from three generations. Each person has separate profession and also each one likes different colours. There are two couples in the family.
(ii) Charan is a CA and his wife neither is a doctor nor likes green colour.
(iii) Engineer likes red colour and his wife is a teacher.
(iv) Vanita is mother-in-law of Namita and she likes orange colour.
(v) Mohan is grandfather of Raman and Raman, who is a principal, likes black colour.
(vi) Sarita is granddaughter of Vanita and she likes blue colour. Sarita's mother likes white colour.

**83.** Who is an Engineer? **(CLAT 2014)**

(*a*) Sarita (*b*) Vanita
(*c*) Namita (*d*) Mohan

**84.** What is the profession of Namita? **(CLAT 2014)**

(*a*) Doctor (*b*) Engineer
(*c*) Teacher (*d*) Cannot be determined.

**85.** Which of the following is the correct pair of two couples? **(CLAT 2014)**

(*a*) Mohan — Vanita and Charan — Sarita
(*b*) Vanita — Mohan and Charan — Namita
(*c*) Charan — Namita and Raman — Sarita
(*d*) Cannot be determined

**86.** How many ladies are there in the family?

(*a*) Two (*b*) Three **(CLAT 2014)**
(*c*) Four (*d*) None of these

**87.** Which colour is liked by CA? **(CLAT 2014)**

(*a*) White (*b*) Blue
(*c*) Black (*d*) None of these

**Directions (Q. 88-92) :** *Read the information given below carefully and answer the questions.*

**88.** Two buses start from the opposite points of a main road, 150 kms apart. The first bus runs for 25 kms and takes a right turn and then runs for 15 kms. It then turns left and runs for another 25 kms and takes the direction back to reach the main road. In the meantime, due to a minor breakdown, the other bus has run only 35 kms along the main road. What would be the distance between the two buses at this point? **(CLAT 2014)**

(*a*) 65 kms (*b*) 75 kms
(*c*) 80 kms (*d*) 85 kms

**89.** 'G', 'H', 'I', 'J', 'K', 'L', 'M', 'N' are sitting around a round table in the same order for group discussion at equal distances. Their positions are clock wise. If 'M' sits in the north, then what will be the position of 'J'? **(CLAT 2014)**

(*a*) East (*b*) South-East
(*c*) South (*d*) South-West

**90.** Roshan, Vaibhav, Vinay and Sumit are playing cards. Roshan and Vaibhav are partners. Sumit faces towards North. If Roshan faces towards West, then who faces towards South? **(CLAT 2014)**

(*a*) Vinay (*b*) Vaibhav
(*c*) Sumit (*d*) Data is inadequate

**91.** Five boys are standing in a row facing East. Pavan is to the left of Tavan, Vipin, Chavan. Tavan, Vipin, Chavan are to the left of Nakul. Chavan is between Tavan and Vipin. If Vipin is fourth from the left, then how far is Tavan from the right? **(CLAT 2014)**

(*a*) First (*b*) Second
(*c*) Third (*d*) Fourth

**92.** One morning after sunrise, Suraj was standing facing a pole. The shadow of the pole fell exactly to his right. Which direction was Suraj facing?

(*a*) West (*b*) South **(CLAT 2014)**
(*c*) East (*d*) Data is inadequate

**Directions (Q. 93-94) :** *Read the information given below to answer the questions.*

Diana is three times older than Jackson; Edward is half the age of Stephen. Jackson is older than Edward. **(CLAT 2014)**

**93.** Which one of the following can be inferred?

(*a*) Jackson is older than Stephen
(*b*) Diana is older than Stephen
(*c*) Diana may be younger than Stephen
(*d*) None of the above

**94.** Which one of the following information will be sufficient to estimate Diana's age?

(*a*) Edward is 10 year old

(*b*) Both Jackson and Stephen are older than Edward by the same number of years

(*c*) Both A and B above

(*d*) None of the above

**Directions (Q. 95-99) :** *Study the sequence / pattern of letters or numbers carefully to work out the pattern on which it is based, and answer what the next item in the sequence must be. For example, the sequence A, C, E, G, ?' has odd numbered letters of alphabet; therefore, the next item must be T.* **(CLAT 2014)**

**95.** 0, 3, 8, 15, ?

(*a*) 24 (*b*) 26

(*c*) 35 (*d*) None

**96.** 8, 16, 28, 44, ?

(*a*) 60 (*b*) 64

(*c*) 62 (*d*) 66

**97.** 0, 6, 24, 60, 120, 210, ?

(*a*) 290 (*b*) 240

(*c*) 336 (*d*) 504

**98.** POQ, SRT, VUW, ?

(*a*) XYZ (*b*) XZY

(*c*) YZY (*d*) YXZ

**99.** A1, C3, F6, J10, O15, ?

(*a*) U21 (*b*) V21

(*c*) T20 (*d*) U20

## Solutions

**For questions 1 to 4**: Going by the information, combinations BM , CP and MO are not possible. So the possible combinations are ABCN, ABCO, ABNO, ABNP, ABOP, BCNO, ACMN ACNO, APMN, APNO

**1.** b If player O is selected and player B is rejected then Option (*a*) and (*c*) are straightaway discounted as these consist of combinations MO and CP respectively. Option (*d*) is not acceptable as it consists of only a single male. Only option (*b*) does not violate any restriction.

**2.** b explanation same as in Q 1

**3.** d All the three statements are false

**4.** a From the possible combinations it is clear whenever M plays, A plays but same is not true for other cases.

**For questions 5 to 9:** If we arrange all of the given information, then there are a total of 7 conditions.

From condition 2, we can say that A is not Manager. Using condition 1, 2, 4 and 5 we can say that B is the husband of C and she is the sister of E. Now, using condition 6, we can say that E is manager. Thus, we can conclude that A earns more than E, Manager. Using condition 1, we can conclude that B is accountant and A is supplier. The final arrangement would look like this:

| | Manager | Accountant | Supplier | |
|---|---|---|---|---|
| A | × | × | √ | Male |
| B | × | √ | × | Male |
| C | × | × | × | Female |
| D | × | × | × | Female (unmarried) |
| E | √ | × | × | Male |

**5.** b **6.** a **7.** c **8.** a **9.** d

**For questions 10 to 12:**

**10.** b Option (*a*) is not true as it violates condition 2. Option (*c*) is not true as it violates condition 1. Option (*d*) is not true as it violates condition 3. Thus, option (*b*) is correct as it satisfies all the condition.

**11.** a Based on the given conditions the following combinations are possible:

1. J R S K T H 2. J S R K T H
3. J R S T K H 4. J S K R T H
5. J R T K S H 6. J R T K H S
7. J S K T R H

Thus, H cannot be fourth lowest in cost.

**12.** b Based on the above given combinations, we can say that J cannot be the second lowest in cost.

**For questions 13 and 14:** Using the conditions we can infer that exactly two confess after T which leaves us with 5, 6 and 7. Also using the condition 5 and 6 we can say that W can not be placed before T. Now following combinations are possible.

| 1 | Z | Z | Y | Y | |
|---|---|---|---|---|---|
| 2 | X | V | Z | Z | |
| 3 | T | T | T | T | |
| 4 | V | X | X | V | ×C |
| 5 | Y | Y | V | X | C |
| 6 | W | W | W | W | C |
| 7 | S | S | S | S | ×C |

**13.** b **14.** d

**For questions 15 to 19:**

The given information can be tabulated as follows:

| Rank in earnings | 1 | 2 | 3 | 4 | 5 | 6 |
|---|---|---|---|---|---|---|
| Person | W | R | P | Q | T | S |
| Colour | Green | Yellow | White | Black | Red | Blue |

**15.** c W, R and P earn more than Q.

**16.** d S has the lowest earnings.

**17.** a In such a case, P will earn the third highest among them.

**18.** b Green

**19.** c Blue

**For questions 20 to 24:**

The given information about productivity is:

F > G, R > S, R > T , S > H, G > T.

Also, the night-shift crews are either G and T or S and H.

**20.** d Option (*a*) is incorrect as it reads T > R, which is not true.

Option (*b*) is incorrect as it reads H > S, which is not true.

Option (*c*) is incorrect as it reads G > F, which is not true.

Only option (*d*) follows all the rules.

**21.** b Clearly, we know that three crews, S, T and H are less productive than R.

So R is either ranked first or second.

Also, G is less productive than the third ranked crew F.

So G must be in the bottom 3 ranks.

If R is at the second place, the bottom three positions will have 4 contenders, which is not true.

∴ R is placed first.

Also, G and T are surely in the bottom three (since F > G > T).

Of the remaining, S > H.

Thus, S will be ranked second and H will be in bottom three.

**22.** c Clearly, we know that three crews, S, T and H are less productive than R.

So R cannot be ranked fifth in any week.

**23.** c If H is ranked third for any week, then the ranking of the crew is as follows:

| Rank | 1 | 2 | 3 | 4 | 5 | 6 |
|---|---|---|---|---|---|---|
| Crew | R | S | H | F | G | T |

**24.** c The fifth and sixth ranked crews can be either G and T or S and H.

So H can never be ranked fifth.

If S and H are ranked fifth and sixth, two arrangements (in desending order) are possible:

F G R T S H or R F G T S H

We find that G cannot be fourth and R can be ranked third.

**25.** b Going by the information, 10% of the students i.e. 5 students scored in the 90%-95% range. 3/5[th] of the remaining 45 students, i.e. 27 students scored in the range of 75% - 90%. The remaining 18 students scored below 75%. Option A is not possible because a maximum of 32 students who have scored 75% and above can opt for Physics. This is maximum of 64%. Option C is also not possible because at best 32 students can opt for Physics and each of them has to opt for Mathematics as per restrictions given. Even if no student who scores below 75% opts for Mathematics, the number of students taking Physics will still equal the number of students taking Mathematics. D is also not possible. To be eligible to study Physics, a student has to score above 75% while to study Mathematics, a student has to score above 70%. So there would be some students scoring between 70% and 75% who would be eligible to study Mathematics but not Physics. B is the only possible option. If 35% of those who scored below 75% scored between 75% and 70%, then they can opt for Mathematics and Astrophysics.

**26.** d Option (*a*) violates restriction A. Option (*b*) violates restriction B. Option (*c*) violates restriction C. Only option (*d*) does not violate any restriction.

**27.** a Option (*b*) and (*d*) are straightaway discounted. Option (*d*) includes C,D and F and violates restriction C. Option (*d*) includes B but does not include E. Therefore, it violates restriction B. Option (*c*) is not a certainty but a possibility because in option (*c*) while C is included. A is not included. This does not fulfill restriction A at all. Option (*a*) meets all the restrictions and is therefore a certainty.

**28.** c Option (*a*) is not acceptable because it includes C and E but not D. Therefore, it violates restriction C. Option (*b*) is not acceptable because it includes both A and D which violates restriction A. Option (*d*) is not acceptable because it includes C and D but not E which again violates restriction C. Only option (*c*) meets all the restrictions and is therefore an acceptable combination.

**29.** b

| Student | City | Height | Gender |
|---|---|---|---|
| A | Mumbai | Short | Girl |
| B | Mumbai | Short | Boy |
| C | Delhi | Short | Girl |
| D | Delhi | Tall | Girl |
| E | Delhi | Short | Boy |
| F | Delhi | Tall | Boy |

Hence, (*b*) is the correct option.

**30.** b Anand > Gulab > Pramesh > Jairam > Mohan
Thus, Anand is the heaviest.

**Solutions for questions 31 to 33:** According to the information given, the following can be concluded.

| Friends | Good | Bad |
|---|---|---|
| W | Hindi, Science | English, Mathematics |
| X | Hindi, Science, Mathematics | English |
| Y | English, Science | Social Studies Mathematics |
| Z | English, Mathematics, Science | Social Studies |

**31.** a W is not good in Mathematics but good in Hindi. Hence, Option (*a*) is correct.

**32.** c From the table above, it is seen that Y and Z both are good in English and Science.

**33.** b Only option (*b*) is true that all four friends are good in science.

**For questions 34 to 39:** After satisfy all the given condition, we will get the following table.

| Persons | Cookies | | | | |
|---|---|---|---|---|---|
| | Chocolate | Oatmeal | Sugar | Peanut | Raisin |
| Ali | | | × | | |
| Bina | √ | | × | | |
| Champak | × | | √ | | × |
| Diya | | | √ | | × |

**34.** d Diya does not eat raisin cookies.

**35.** d Only possible combination for Bina and Champak when Bina eats exactly 3 cookies is

| Persons | Cookies | | | | |
|---|---|---|---|---|---|
| | Chocolate | Oatmeal | Sugar | Peanut | Raisin |
| Bina | √ | × | × | √ | √ |
| Champak | × | √ | √ | × | × |

**Option (a) :** As Bina eats exactly three kinds of cookies, therefore Champak cannot eats exactly three kinds of cookies. (There are only five kinds of cookies and Bina and Champak do not eat the same type of cookies)

**Option (b) :** It is not trure because each of these four people eats at least two kinds of cookies.

**Option (c) :** If Ali eats oatmeal cookies, Diya cannot eat oatmeal cookies.

**36.** b If Ali and Diya both eat oatmeal cookies, then one of the Bina and Champak cannot eat at least two types of cookies.

**37.** c At most two people eat oatmeal cookies, therefore none of the options (*a*), (*b*) and (*d*) are true.

∴ Only chocolate chip and peanut butter cookies could be eaten by atleast three different people.

**38.** d As no one eats both raisin cookies and sugar cookies, therefore these two cookies is eaten by exactly two different people.

**39.** d One of the possible combination is

| Persons | Cookies | | | | |
|---|---|---|---|---|---|
| | Chocolate | Oatmeal | Sugar | Peanut | Raisin |
| Ali | √ | √ | × | | × |
| Bina | √ | √ | × | | × |
| Champak | × | | √ | √ | × |
| Diya | | | √ | √ | × |

∴ Raisin cookies could be eaten by none of the people.

**40.** c I reached on Friday 2 days earlier than scheduled day, so scheduled day was Sunday. If I had reached on the following Wednesday, then I would have been late by 3 days.

**41.** a Kamala takes 40 minutes for each assignment and she has to complete 5 assignments, so she will take $40 \times 5 = 200$ minutes to complete all 5 assignments.

Hence, she can start latest by 6.40 p.m.

**For questions 42 to 44** : *From the given information, the following table can be drawn,*

| A(White) | F(Black)(Shortest) | D(Golden) |
|---|---|---|
| | | |
| C (Bronze) | B(Metallic) | E(Silver)(Tallest) |

**42.** d

**43.** d

**44.** b

**45.** b Since R wants either Foreign or Human Resources or no portfolio, options A and D can be ruled out. U does not want any portfolio if S gets one of the five. But in option C, both U and S have got portfolios. Thus, option C can also be ruled out. Hence, the correct option is option B, as it doesn't violate any condition.

**46.** d Since Q says that if S gets Industry and Commerce or Rural Development then she must get the other one, option D is not a valid assignment.

**For questions 47 to 51:** *The following table shows the days and corresponding fruit prescribed for that day.*

| Sunday | Monday | Tuesday | Wednesday | Thursday | Friday |
|---|---|---|---|---|---|
| Banana | Fast | Grape | Pomegranate | Papaya | Apple |

**47.** a

**48.** d

**49.** b

**50.** d

**51.** a

**For questions 52 to 56 :** *The following diagram represents the possible sitting arrangements.*

**52.** c

**53.** * We can see that both options (*a*) and (*b*) are possible.

**54.** d

**55.** c

**56.** b

**57.** d Applying the condition given in the question, the colour of flag and pennant is given below.

| No. | Flag | Pennant |
|---|---|---|
| 1 | White | Green |
| 2 | Red | Blue |
| 3 | White | Green |
| 4 | Blue | white |
| 5 | Red | Blue |

**58.** c Goindthrought each option we find that option (*c*) is not necessarily true as the colour of the first pennant can be green also.

| No. | Flag | Pennant |
|---|---|---|
| 1 | Red | Green/white |
| 2 | | Blue |
| 3 | | White |
| 4 | | Green |
| 5 | | |

**59.** d Applying the condition given in the question, the colour of flag and pennant is given below.

| No. | Flag | Pennant |
|---|---|---|
| 1 | white | Green |
| 2 | Red | Blue |
| 3 | white | Green |
| 4 | Red | Blue |
| 5 | Blue | White |

**60.** b Applying the condition given in the question, the colour of flag and pennant is given below.

| No. | Flag | Pennant |
|---|---|---|
| 1 | Blue | |
| 2 | White | |
| 3 | Red | White |
| 4 | Blue | |
| 5 | | |

If the fifth pennant is white then first cannot be white or blue. Hence, it must be green.

**61.** a Applying the condition given in the question, the colour of flag and pennant is given below.

| No. | Flag | Pennant |
|---|---|---|
| 1 | Blue | White |
| 2 | Red | Blue |
| 3 | White | Green |
| 4 | Red | Blue |
| 5 | White | Green |

**62.** c As there are two colours which are common in flag and pennants (i.e. Blue and White). So, among the first four flag two will be blue and other two will be white. Hence the colour of the fifth flag must be red.

**63.** c the relation is shown below.

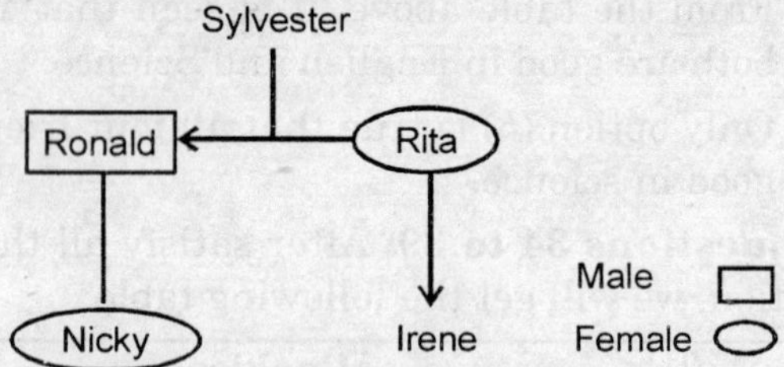


**64.** a Grandmother of elder brother of father is great grandmother. Which is not present in any option.

**65.** c As the paternal grandfather of the boy is the maternal grandfather of Pushpa. Hence, they are cousin.

**66.** d The movement of Kiran is shown below

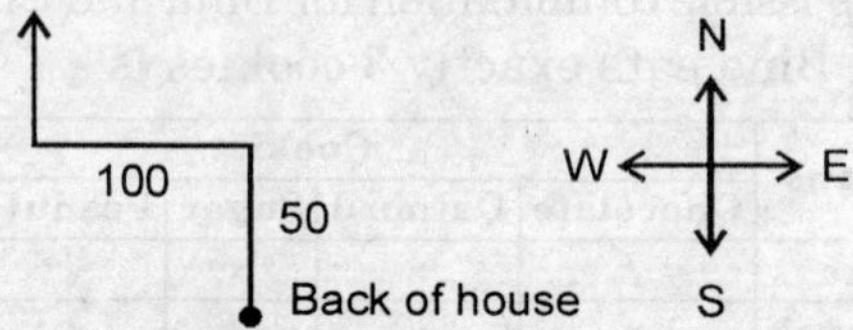


Hence, Kiran is now facing north.

**67.** d Each direction is rotaed by 135 degree in AWC. Hence north become southwest.

**68.** c

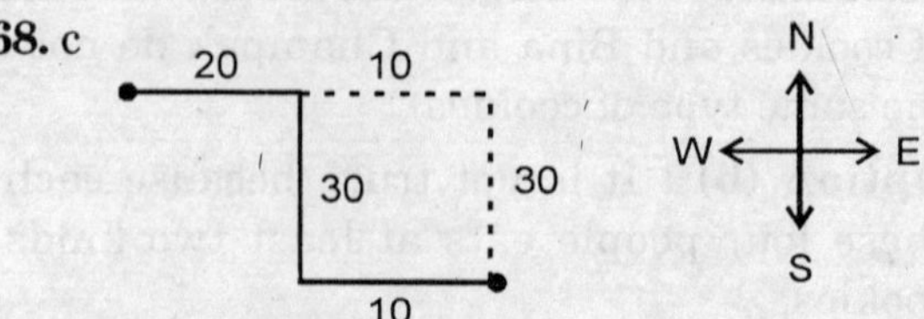


The required distance = $\sqrt{30^2 + 30^2} = 30\sqrt{2}$

Which is not present in any option.

**69.** d The series is following the given pattern:

$31 + 1^2 = 32$

$32 + 2^2 = 36$

$36 + 3^2 = 45$

$45 + 4^2 = 61$

**70.** c The given series is combination of two series

I. 1, 2, 3, 4, 5, 6

II. 3, 5, 7, 9, 11, 13

Hence, the m × t term is 13.

The series is following the given pattern.

**71.** a $300 - 2^2 = 296$

$296 - 3^2 = 287$

$287 - 4^2 = 271$

$271 - 5^2 = 246$

$246 - 6^2 = 210$

**72.** d $12 + 3 = 15$

$15 + 4 = 19$

$19 + 5 = 24$

$24 + 6 = 30$

$30 + 7 = 37.$

**73.** d Using both the statement together

| | Score | Catch taken | Catch drop |
|---|---|---|---|
| Akash | 50 | x+1 | x |
| Biplab | 50 | 2 | x+2 |
| Chirag | 35 | | |

as $x \geq 1$ hence, Akash was man of the match.

**74.** c Using statement I alone, rank of the four persons is as follow:

| Rank | Person |
|---|---|
| 1 | B |
| 2 | C |
| 3 | D |
| 4 | A |

Using statement II alone, rank of the four persons is as follow:

| Rank | Person |
|---|---|
| 1 | B |
| 2 | C |
| 3 | D |
| 4 | A |

Hence, either of the statement is sufficient.

**For 75 to 77**

The information given is summarized as follow:

| Day | Persons | Subjects |
|---|---|---|
| Monday | Satish | English |
| Tuesday | Rajesh | Geology |
| Wednesday | Rehman | Zoology |
| Thursday | Rakesh | Physics |
| Friday | Vineet | Botany |

**75.** b

**76.** d

**77.** d

**78.** c Since the man has no sister or brother, so the man's father's son is the man himself.

Hence, the person in the photograph is his son.

**79.** c The son of only bothers of father's wife in the son of maternal uncle.

Hence, they are cousin.

**80.** d The wife of Bhumika's husband is Bhumika herself and her son's sister is her daughter.

**81.** d The family relation is represented below.

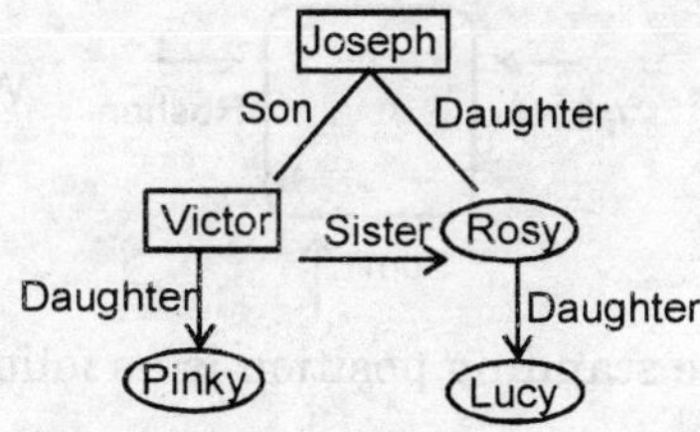


Hence, Josheph is the grandfather of Lucy.

**82.** a The daughter of Pramod's grandmother is his aunt and her only bother is father of Pramod.

**For 83 to 87.** *The information given is summarized as follow:*

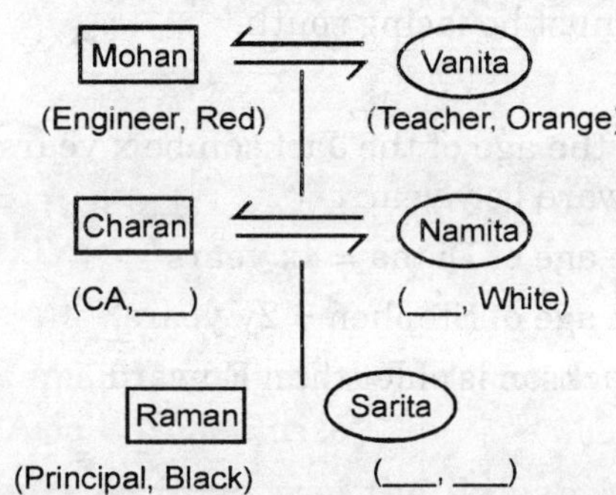


**83.** d

**84.** d

**85.** b

**86.** b

**87.** d

**88.** a The movement of the first bar $B_1$ and second bar $B_2$ is shown below

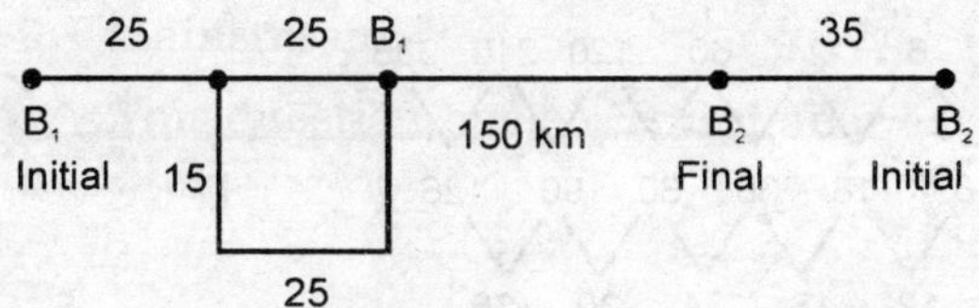


The required distance = 150 − (25 + 25 + 35)

= 65 km.

**89.** d Sitting arrangement is shown below

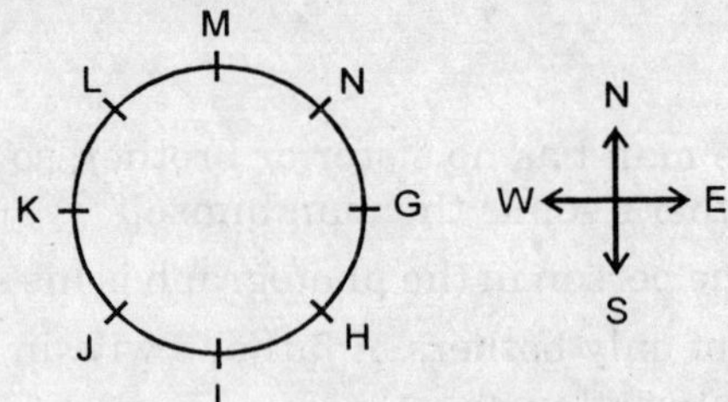


Hence, J is in South-West.

**90.** a The sitting positions the persons and the direction they are facing is shown below.

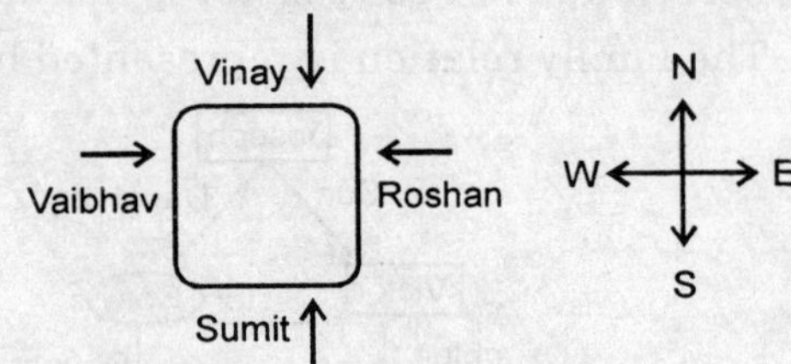


**91.** d The standing position is as follow.

Pavan Tavan Chavan Vipin Nakul

Hence, Tavan is fourth from the right.

**92.** b The shadow of the pole fell exactly to right of Suraj. Hence the sun is in the left of Suraj, so he must be facing south.

**For 93-94**

Let the age of the Jackson be x years and that Edward be y years.

The age of Diana = 4x years

The age of Stephen = 2y years.

$\because$ Jackson is older than Edward

$\therefore x > y$

**93.** B

**94.** c Both the statements are required to find the age of Diana.

**95.** a The pattern of the series is as follows:

$0 \xrightarrow{+3} 3 \xrightarrow{+5} 8 \xrightarrow{+7} 15 \xrightarrow{+9} 24.$

**96.** b The pattern of the series is as follows:

$8 \xrightarrow{+8} 16 \xrightarrow{+12} 28 \xrightarrow{+16} 44 \xrightarrow{+20} 64.$

**97.** c The pattern of the series is as follows:

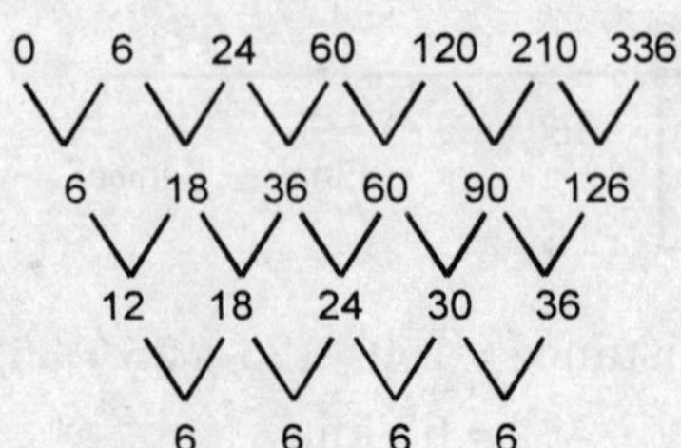


**98.** d The pattern of the series is as follows:

$P \xrightarrow{+3} S \xrightarrow{+3} V \xrightarrow{+3} Y$

$O \xrightarrow{+3} R \xrightarrow{+3} U \xrightarrow{+3} X$

$Q \xrightarrow{+3} T \xrightarrow{+3} W \xrightarrow{+3} Z$

**99.** a The pattern of the series is as follows:

$\underset{1}{A} \xrightarrow{+2} \underset{3}{C} \xrightarrow{+3} \underset{6}{F} \xrightarrow{+4} \underset{10}{Z} \xrightarrow{+5} \underset{15}{O} \xrightarrow{+6} \underset{21}{U}$

## BLOOD RELATIONS

**1.** K is L's wife's husband's brother. M is the sister of K. N is the sister of L. How is K related to M?

(*a*) Sister-in-law (*b*) Brother

(*c*) Daughter (*d*) Wife **(AILET, 2009)**

**2.** Atul is the son of Zamir. Alka is the daughter of Aman. Sheela is the Wife of Aman, Mohan is the son of Sheela. How is Alka related to Mohan?

(*a*) Sister (*b*) Uncle

(*c*) Son (*d*) Father **(AILET, 2009)**

**Directions for questions 3 and 4:** Read the following directions and answer the questions.

A is the father of C. But C is not his son. E is the daughter of C. F is the spouse of A. B is the brother of C. D is the son of B. G is the spouse of B. H is the father of G. **(AILET, 2012)**

**3.** Who is the son-in-law of H?

(*a*) C (*b*) A

(*c*) D (*d*) B

**4.** Who is the grand-daughter of A?

(*a*) H (*b*) D

(*c*) B (*d*) E

**5.** Pointing to a photograph, a lady tells Ram, "I am the only daughter of this lady and her son is your maternal uncle". How is the speaker related to Ram's father? **(CLAT 2009)**

(*a*) Sister-in-law (*b*) Wife

(*c*) Either (*a*) or (*b*) (*d*) Neither (*a*) nor (*b*)

**6.** Introducing a man, a woman said, "He is the only son of my mother." How is the woman related to the man?

(*a*) Mother (*b*) Aunt

(*c*) Sister (*d*) Niece **(CLAT 2009)**

**7.** Shyam said, " This girl is the wife of the grandson of my mother". Who is Shyam to the girl?

(*a*) Father

(*b*) Grandfather

(*c*) Husband

(*d*) Father-in-law **(CLAT 2009)**

**8.** Pointing to a man on the stage, Sunita said, "He is the brother of the daughter of the wife of my husband". How is the man on the stage related to Sunita?

(*a*) Son (*b*) Husband
(*c*) Cousin (*d*) Nephew **(CLAT 2009)**

**9.** Introducing a man to her husband, a woman said, "His brother's father is the only son of my grandfather". How is the woman related to this man?

(*a*) Mother (*b*) Aunt
(*c*) Sister (*d*) Daughter **(CLAT 2009)**

**10.** P is the brother of Q. R is the sister of Q. S is the Sister of R. How is Q related to S?

(*a*) brother
(*b*) sister
(*c*) brother or sister
(*d*) son **(CLAT 2010)**

**11.** Ravi is the brother of Amit's son. How is Amit related to Ravi? **(CLAT 2010)**

(*a*) Cousin (*b*) Father
(*c*) Son (*d*) Grandfather

**Directions (Q. 12–14):** *Read the following directions and answer the questions that follow.*

Sunita, Rahul and Suraj are children of Mrs. and Mr. Ahuja. Rani, Rohan and Shyam are children of Mrs. and Mr. Malik. Shyam and Sunita are married and Arjun and Sohan are their children. Gunjan and Romesh are children of Mrs. and Mr. Gandhi. Gunjan is married to Suraj and has three children named Rupali, Sonu and Ravi.

**12.** How is Rahul related ot Arjun ? **(AILET, 2013)**

(*a*) Brother-in-law (*b*) Cousin
(*c*) Uncle (*d*) Maternal uncle

**13.** Rani is Sohan's **(AILET, 2013)**

(*a*) Niece (*b*) Sister
(*c*) Aunt (*d*) Sister-in-law

**14.** Shyam and Suraj are related as **(AILET, 2013)**

(*a*) Brother-in-law (*b*) Cousin
(*c*) Brother (*d*) Nephew

**Directions (Q. 15 – 19) :** *Each question contains a statement on relationship and a question regarding relationship based on the statement. Select the correct option.* **(CLAT 2013)**

**15.** Moni is daughter of Sheela. Sheela is wife of my wife's brother. How Moni is related to my wife?

(*a*) Cousin (*b*) Niece
(*c*) Sister (*d*) Sister-in-law

**16.** Annu is daughter of my mother's brother Abahi. Pari is grand daughter of my mother. Pari should call Annu as

(*a*) Maternal Aunt (*b*) Sister
(*c*) Cousin (*d*) Niece

**17.** Markandey is Rajiv's mother's father. Markandey is three brother One of them has grandson Abahi. Rajan is son of Abahi. Rajan is related to Rajiv as

(*a*) Brother (*b*) Nephew
(*c*) Cousin (*d*) Uncle

**18.** Deepak said to Nitin, "That boy playing with the football is the younger of the two brothers of the daughter of my father's wife". How is the boy playing football related to Deepak?

(*a*) Son (*b*) Brother
(*c*) Cousin (*d*) Brother-in-law

**19.** Pointing to a woman in the photograph, Rajesh said, "The only daughter of her grandfather is my wife". How is Rajesh related to that woman?

(*a*) Uncle (*b*) Father
(*c*) Maternal Uncle (*d*) Brother

## Solutions

**1.** b All of the given information can be represented as-

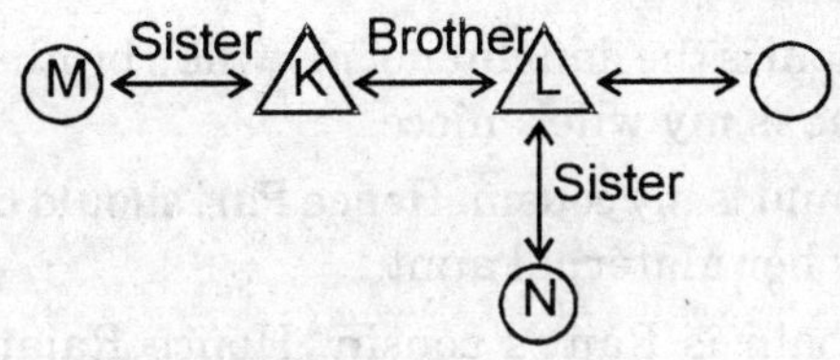


∴ K is brother of M.

**2.** a All of the given information can be represented as:

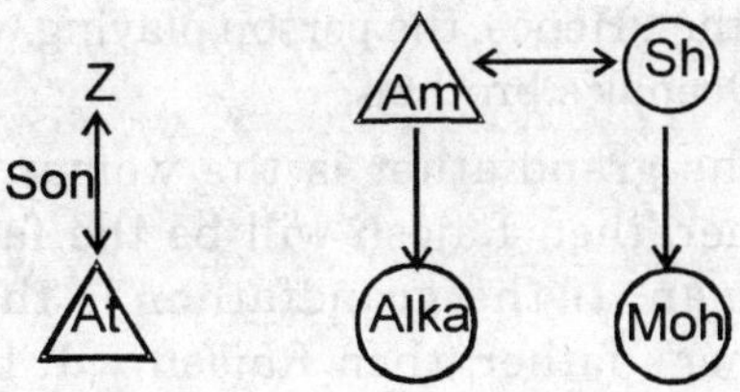


∴ Alka is the sister of Mohan.

**3.** d B is the brother of C

⇒ B is a male.

G is the spouse of B and H is the father of G.

⇒ B is the son-in-law of H.

**4.** d A is the father of C and E is the daughter of C.

⇒ E is the granddaughter of A.

**5.** b The lady in the photograph is the mother of the speaker and Ram's maternal grandmother. Thus, the speaker is the wife of Ram's father.

**6.** c The man is the only son of that woman who is that woman's mother. Thus, the woman is that man's sister.

**7.** d The grandson of Shyam's mother is Shyam's son and his son's wife is his daughter-in-law. Or Shyam is her father-in-law. This is the best possible answer as he could be her father-in-law's brother.

**8.** a Sunita's husband's wife is she herself. Now, the man is the brother of her daughter. It means that the man is Sunita's son.

**9.** c Man's brother's father is that man's father. Now, that woman's grandfather is also that Man's grandfather. This in turn implies that the man and the woman are siblings.

**10.** c P, Q, R and S are siblings. Since, the gender of Q is not clear, Q can be either brother or sister of S. Therefore, (c) is the correct option.

**11.** b Amit's son's brother is Amit's son. Therefore, Amit is the father of Ravi.

**For solutions: 12 to 14:**

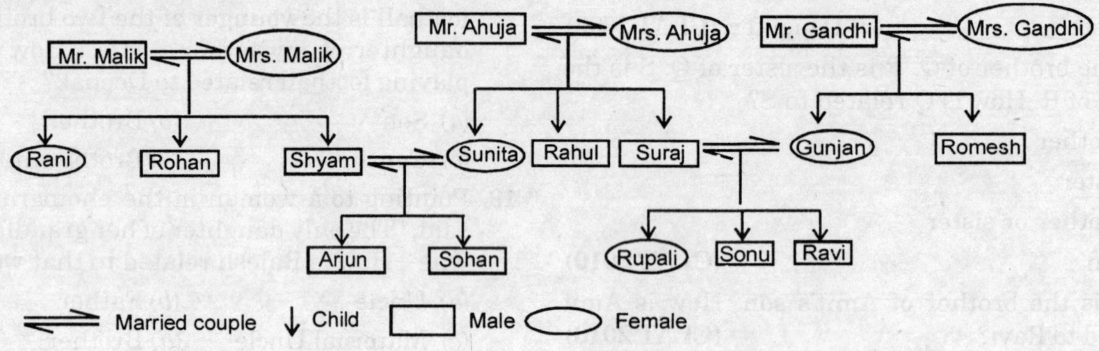


**12.** d

**13.** c

**14.** a

**15.** b Moni is the daughter of my wife's brother. Hence she is my wife's niece.

**16.** a Annu is my cousin. Hence Pari should call Annu as her Maternal aunt.

**17.** b Abahi is Rajiv's cousin. Hence Rajan will be Rajiv's nephew.

**18.** b Daughter of Deepak's father's wife will be his sister. The brother of her sister will be his brother. Hence, the person playing with football is Deepak's brother.

**19.** * If the grandfather is the woman's mother's father, then Rajesh will be the father of the woman. If the grandfather is the woman's father's father, then Rajesh will be woman's uncle. Hence, either of the options A or B is possible.

## DIRECTIONS

**1.** The door of my house is towards east direction. From the backside of my house I drove straight 100 metres, then turned towards right and drove for 100 metres, then turned towards left and drove for 50 metres and reached my destination. In what direction am I from the starting point?

(*a*) North-west (*b*) West
(*c*) North (*d*) East **(AILET, 2008)**

**2.** I go 100 metres towards North from my house, then I turn left and go 200 metres, then turning left I go 200 metres, then again turning left I go 100 metres. and then turning left again I go 100 metres. In which direction am I now from my house?

(*a*) West (*b*) East
(*c*) North (*d*) South **(AILET, 2009)**

**3.** Ram is facing North-West. He turns in clockwise direction by 90°, then 180° in the anti-clockwise direction and then another 90° in the same direction. Which direction is he facing now?

(*a*) South-West (*b*) West
(*c*) South (*d*) South-East

**(AILET, 2011)**

**4.** One morning after sunrise, Vikram and Shailesh were standing in a lawn with their backs towards each other. Vikram's shadow fell exactly towards left hand side. Which direction was Shailesh facing?

(*a*) East (*b*) West
(*c*) North (*d*) South **(AILET, 2011)**

**5.** A child crawls 20 feet towards North, turns right and crawls 30 feet, turns right again and crawls 35 feet. He turns left now and crawls 15 feet. He turns left again and crawls 15 feet. Finally he turns to his left to crawl another 15 feet. How far is he from his starting point and in which direction?

(*a*) 45 feet North-East (*b*) 30 feet East
(*c*) 30 feet West (*d*) 15 feet West

**(AILET, 2012)**

**6.** Ram is facing North-West. He turns in clockwise direction by 90°, then 180° in the anti-clockwise direction and then another 90° in the same direction. Which direction is he facing now?

(*a*) South-West (*b*) West **(AILET, 2012)**

(*c*) South (*d*) South-East

**7.** One morning after sunrise, Vikram and Shailesh were standing in a lawn with their backs towards each other. Vikram's shadow fell exactly towards left hand side.

Which direction was Shailesh facing?

(*a*) East (*b*) West

(*c*) North (*d*) South **(AILET, 2012)**

**8.** Y travels 15 kilometers due South, then 5 kilometers due West, then 18 kilometers due North, then 3 kilometers due South, then 5 kilometers due East. How far is he from the starting point? **(CLAT, 2012)**

(*a*) 6 kilometers (*b*) 3 kilometers

(*c*) 0 kilometers (*d*) 9 kilometers

**9.** Shyam travels 5 km towards East and turns left and moves 6 km further. He then turns right and moves 9 km. Finally, he turns once again to his right and moves 6 km. How far is he from the starting point ? **(AILET, 2013)**

(*a*) Brother-in-law (*b*) Cousin

(*c*) Uncle (*d*) Maternal uncle

## Solutions

**1.** a

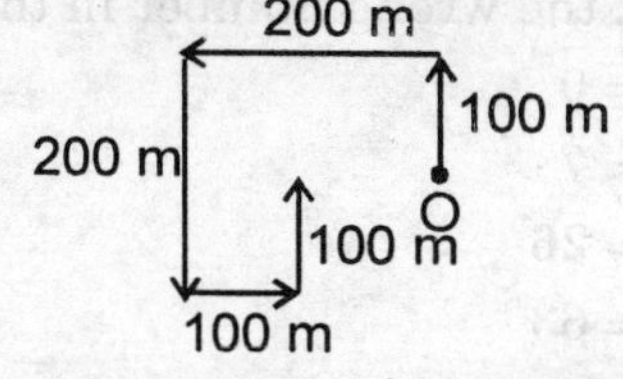


**2.** a I am in West direction with respect to my house.



**3.** d

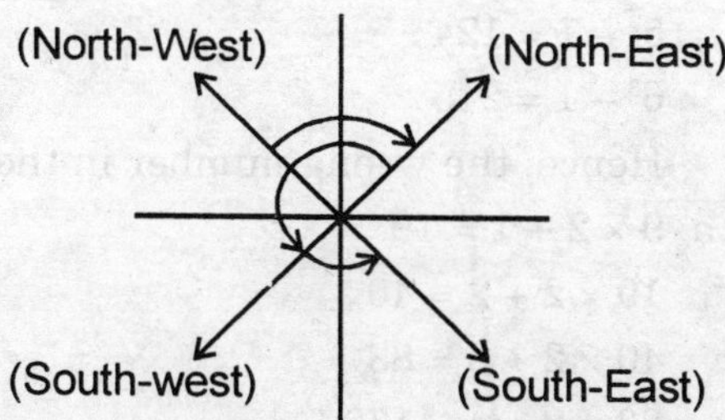


Therefore, Ram is facing South-East direction now.

**4.** d Sun rises in the East in morning.

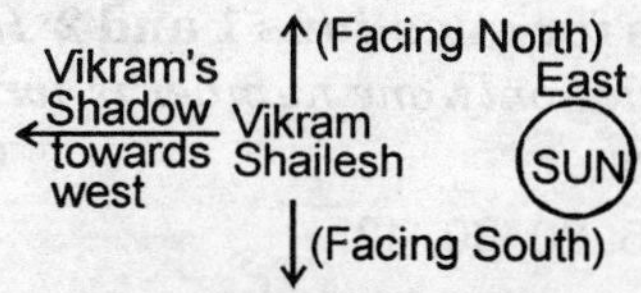


Therefore, Shailesh was facing South direction.

**5.** b



Clearly, the child is 30 feet to the East of the starting point.

**6.** d Initially Ram is facing North-West direction. After turning $90^0$ CW, he will be facing North-East direction. By turning $180^0$ ACW, he will be facing South-West direction. Finally, he turns 90° ACW which will make him face in the South-East direction.

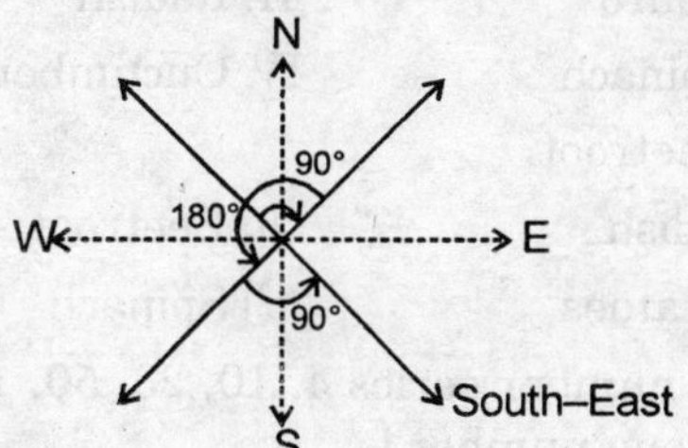


**7.** d If a man stands facing the North, at the time of sunrise his shadow will be towards his left. So Vikram was facing the North. Hence, Shailesh was facing the South.

**8.** c



As both the starting point and the finishing point of 'Y' is A, therefore, 'Y' is 0 km away from his starting point.

**Disclaimer:** We have considered the gender of the person according to their names (Indian context), otherwise the question cannot be solved.

**9.** c

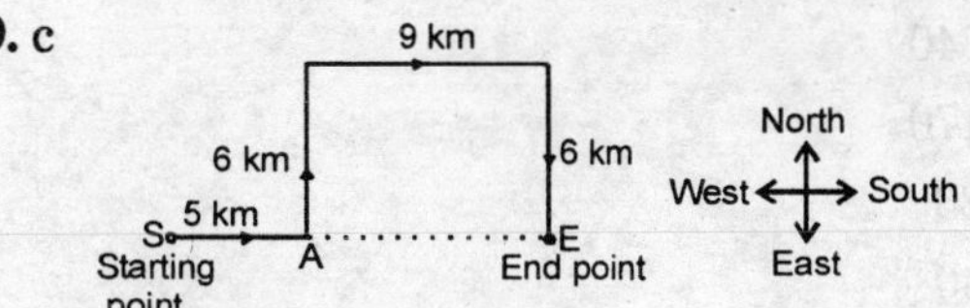


Required distance = SA + AE = 5 + 9 = 14 km.

## ODD ONE OUT

**Directions for questions 1 and 2:** *In the following number series only one number is **wrong**. Find out that number.* **(AILET, 2012)**

**1.** 1, 2, 6, 15, 20, 30, 42

(*a*) 30 (*b*) 15
(*c*) 6 (*d*) 1

**2.** 2, 5, 10, 17, 26, 37, 50, 64

(*a*) 50 (*b*) 17
(*c*) 26 (*d*) 64

**Directions for questions 3 and 4:** *Four of the given five options are alike in a certain way and form a group. Which is the one that does not belong to that group?* **(CLAT 2010)**

**3.** I. 217 II. 43
III. 214 IV. 157
V. 131

(*a*) I (*b*) V
(*c*) I (*d*) III

**4.** I. Gourd II. Radish
III. Spinach IV. Cucumber
V. Beetroot

(*a*) Radish (*b*) Beetroot
(*c*) Potatoes (*d*) Spinach

**5.** In the number series 4, 10, 23, 50, 104, 216, 439 the wrong number is

(*a*) 10 (*b*) 23
(*c*) 104 (*d*) 50 **(CLAT 2012)**

**Direction (Q. 6 – 9):** *In the following number series only one number is wrong.*

**(CLAT 2013)**

**6.** 21, 28, 33, 35, 37, 36

(*a*) 33 (*b*) 35
(*c*) 21 (*d*) 36

**7.** 5, 13, 29, 61, 120, 253

(*a*) 61 (*b*) 29
(*c*) 120 (*d*) 253

**8.** 0, 7, 28, 63, 124, 215

(*a*) 7 (*b*) 63
(*c*) 28 (*d*) 215

**9.** 9, 19, 40, 83, 170, 340, 340

(*a*) 340
(*b*) 170
(*c*) 83
(*d*) 40

## Solutions

**1.** b The series is of the form $n^2 + n$ (where n is a natural number).

1

$1^2 + 1 = 2$

$2^2 + 2 = 6$

$3^2 + 3 = 12$ **(15)**

$4^2 + 4 = 20$

$5^2 + 5 = 30$

$6^2 + 6 = 42$

So the incorrect number is 15.

**2.** d The pattern followed in the series is as follows:

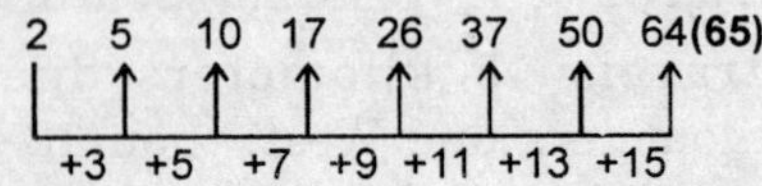


So the incorrect number is 64.

**3.** d Except 214, all other are odd numbers.

**4.** d Spinach is the only leafy vegetable of the group. Rest all roots.

**5.** c $10 = 4 \times 2 + 2$

$23 = 10 \times 2 + 3$

$50 = 23 \times 2 + 4$

(105) (104) $= 50 \times 2 + 5$

$216 = 105 \times 2 + 6$

$439 = 216 \times 2 + 7$

Hence, 104 is the wrong number in the series.

**6.** b 21 28 33 36 37 36
+7 +5 +3 +1 −1
−2 −2 −2 −2

Hence, the wrong number in the series is 35.

**7.** c 5 13 29 61 125 253
$2^3$ $2^4$ $2^5$ $2^6$ $2^7$

Hence, the wrong number in the series is 120.

**8.** c $1^3 - 1 = 0$

$2^3 - 1 = 7$

$3^3 - 1 =$ **26**

$4^3 - 1 = 63$

$5^3 - 1 = 124$

$6^3 - 1 = 215$

Hence, the wrong number in the series is 28.

**9.** a $9 \times 2 + 1 = 19$

$19 \times 2 + 2 = 40$

$40 \times 2 + 3 = 83$

$83 \times 2 + 4 = 170$

$170 \times 2 + 5 =$ **345**

Hence, the wrong number in the series is 340.

## SEQUENCE AND SERIES

**Directions for questions 1 to 4:** *In each of the following questions, a series of letters or numbers has been arranged in some sequence. Below each are given alternative responses. Find out the* ***correct*** *response.* **(AILET, 2008)**

**1.** 2, 6, 14, 11, 15, 23, 20, 24,___ , 29
(*a*) 31 (*b*) 29
(*c*) 28 (*d*) 32

**2.** 97, 86, 73,______, 45, 34
(*a*) 54 (*b*) 56
(*c*) 58 (*d*) 60

**3.** MOQ, SUM, YAC, ______
(*a*) FIL (*b*) DHJ
(*c*) EGI (*d*) XAD

**4.** KWZ, MOX, OIV, QET, _____
(*a*) SAQ (*b*) SUR
(*c*) RAP (*d*) SAR

**Directions for questions 5 and 6:** *Find out the missing term.* **(AILET, 2011)**

**5.** AOP, CQR, EST, GUV, ?
(*a*) IYZ (*b*) HWX
(*c*) IWX (*d*) JWX

**6.** 6, 11, 21, 36, 56, ?
(*a*) 66 (*b*) 76
(*c*) 81 (*d*) 86

**Directions for questions 7 to 10:** *Find out the missing alphabet / number.* **(AILET, 2012)**

**7.** D, H, L, R, ?
(*a*) T (*b*) X
(*c*) I (*d*) O

**8.** 3, 7, 15, 31, 63, ?
(*a*) 92 (*b*) 115
(*c*) 127 (*d*) 131

**9.** D, H, L, R, ?
(*a*) T (*b*) X
(*c*) I (*d*) O

**10.** 3, 7, 15, 31, 63, ?
(*a*) 92 (*b*) 115
(*c*) 127 (*d*) 131

**11.** Which number should fill the blank space to complete the series: 1, 2, 4, 5, 7, 8, 10, 11...
(*a*) 12 (*b*) 13
(*c*) 14 (*d*) 15 **(CLAT 2009)**

**12.** Find out the wrong number in the series: 3,8,15,24,34,48,63
(*a*) 24 (*b*) 34
(*c*) 15 (*d*) 63 **(CLAT 2009)**

**Directions for questions 13 and 14:** *Select appropriate numbers to fill in the blanks in the given series.* **(CLAT 2010)**

**13.** 3, 9, ......, 6561
(*a*) 18 (*b*) 27
(*c*) 81 (*d*) 61

**14.** 100, 50, 33.33, ......, 20
(*a*) 25 (*b*) 30
(*c*) 22 (*d*) 21

**Directions for questions 15 to 17:** *Select one of the given numbers to replace the question mark in the series.* **(CLAT 2010)**

**15.** 2, 3, 4, 6, 7, 8, 9, 11, 12, 13, 14, 15, 17, 18, 19, 20, 21, ?
(*a*) 22 (*b*) 23
(*c*) 24 (*d*) 25

**16.** 117, 104, 91, 78, ?
(*a*) 39 (*b*) 60
(*c*) 65 (*d*) 36

**17.** 88, 96, 104, ?
(*a*) 100 (*b*) 110
(*c*) 120 (*d*) 112

**Directions for questions 18 to 25:** *Study the sequence of letters, numbers or words carefully to work out the pattern on which it is based, and therefore what the next item in the sequence must be. For example, the sequence 'A, C, E, G, __', has odd-numbered letters of the alphabet; therefore, the next item must be 'I'. The meanings of the words are irrelevant.* **(CLAT 2011)**

**18.** A, B, D, G, K, P, ___ What is the last alphabet in this sequence?
(*a*) Z (*b*) Y
(*c*) V (*d*) X

**19.** B, C, E, G, K, M, Q, S, _ What is the next alphabet in this sequence?
(*a*) T (*b*) U
(*c*) V (*d*) W

**20.** Z, X, T, N, _ What is the next alphabet in this sequence?
(*a*) E (*b*) F
(*c*) G (*d*) H

**21.** 'Apple, Application, ______, Approval, Apricot, April' Which of the following best fits in the blank?
(*a*) Arrogant (*b*) April
(*c*) Appropriate (*d*) Apiary.

**22.** 'Sunday, Monday, Wednesday, Saturday, Wednesday, Monday, Sunday, ___________' Which of the following best fits in the blank?
(*a*) Sunday (*b*) Tuesday
(*c*) Saturday (*d*) Thursday

**23.** '387924, ________, 3724, 423, 32, 2'. Which is the missing number?

(*a*) 42978 (*b*) 42183
(*c*) 42983 (*d*) 42783

**24.** 'Gym, hymn, lynx, pygmy, rhythm' Which one of the following words does not belong to the above set?

(*a*) Myrrh (*b*) Mythic
(*c*) Flyby (*d*) Syzygy

**25.** Aadvark, Eerie, Iiwi, Oolong, ________ Which one of the following words follow the pattern of this series?

(*a*) Uvula (*b*) Uulium
(*c*) Uranium (*d*) Uranus

**Directions (Q. 26–30):** *Complete the series by choosing the correct option.* **(CLAT 2013)**

**26.** 0, 1, 1, 2, 3, 5, 8, 13, 21, ?

(*a*) 34 (*b*) 35
(*c*) 33 (*d*) 36

**27.** A -10, E -15, I -20, M -25,....

(*a*) Q-5 (*b*) Q-30
(*c*) P-30 (*d*) R-30

**28.** 17, 36, 74, 150, ? , 606

(*a*) 250 (*b*) 303
(*c*) 300 (*d*) 302

**29.** 2, 1, 4, 3, 6, 5, 8, ?

(*a*) 9 (*b*) 10
(*c*) 7 (*d*) 8

**30.** 1, 4, 27, 256, ?

(*a*) 625 (*b*) 3125
(*c*) 3025 (*d*) 1225

## Solutions

**1.** d 2, 6, 14, 11, 15, 23, 20, 24, ?, 29

The logic here is that:

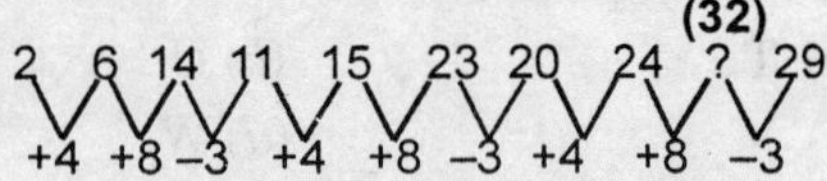


**2.** c There is no certain logic for this question. But assuming that the question is true, then among the best possible answer it should be 58.

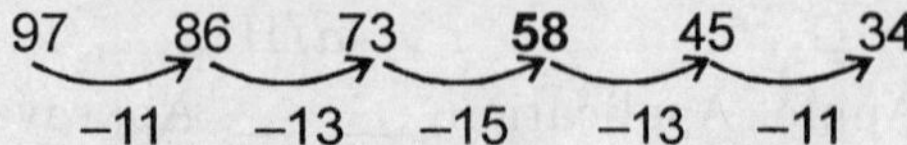


**3.** c* MOQ, SUM, YAC, ?

There is some error in the question at it should be 'W' in place of 'M' in second term.

The logic here is that:

M + 6 = S, S + 6 = Y, Y + 6 = E(5)

O + 6 = U, U + 6 = A, A + 6 = G(7)

Q + 6 = W, W + 6 = C, C + 6 = I(9)

Hence, best possible answer is option (*c*).

**4.** d* KWZ, MOX, OIV, QET, ?

The logic here is that-

K + 2 = M, M + 2 = O, O + 2 = Q, Q + 2 = S

W – 8 = O, O – 6 = I, I – 4 = E, E – 2 = C

Z – 2 = X, X – 2 = V, V – 2 = T, T – 2 = R

There is some error in the question. As no option is matching. But, we know that answer is between b and d. Then the best possible answer is option (*d*).

**5.** c The alphabetical position number of the three letters in each successive term increases by 2.

Hence, required term is IWX.

**6.** c The series is moving as:

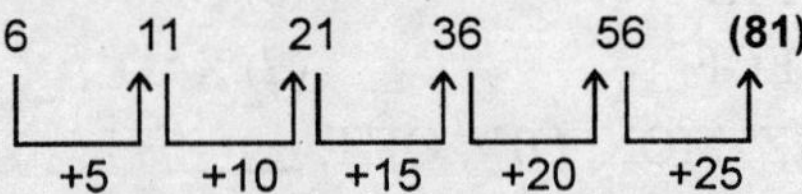


**7.** b The alphabetical position number of each successive term increases by 4, 4, 6, 6 and so on.

The required term is X(24).

**8.** c The series is moving as:

$3 = 2^2 - 1$

$7 = 2^3 - 1$

$15 = 2^4 - 1$

$31 = 2^5 - 1$

$63 = 2^6 - 1$

**(127) = $2^7 - 1$**

**9.** b D(4) + 4 → H(8)

H(8) + 4 → L(12)

L(12) + 6 → R(18)

So the next term will be R(18) + 6 → X(24).

**10.** c

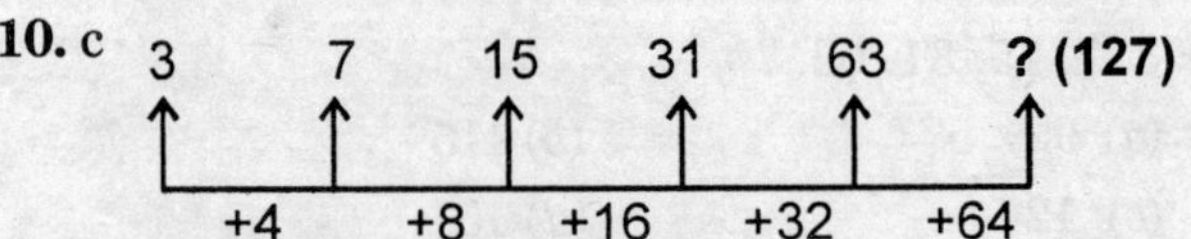


So the next term will be

63 + (2 × 32) = 63 + 64 = 127.

**11.** b The logic here is that two alternate series are given as (2, 5, 8, 11) and (1, 4, 7, 10,?).

Now, the term replacing (?) would be

10 + 3 = 13.

**12.** b The series is moving as ($n^2 - 1$), where n is a natural number starting from 2. Thus, 34 doesn't satisfy the given condition.

**13.** c The series is:

9 = 3 × 3

81 = 9 × 9

6561 = 81 × 81

Thus, the missing term is 81.

**14.** a The series is:

$$\frac{100}{1}, \frac{100}{2}, \frac{100}{3}, \frac{100}{4}, \frac{100}{5}$$

i.e., 100, 50, 33.33, 25, 20.

Thus, the missing term is 25.

**15.** a From the natural numbers written in ascending order, the numbers taken out are 1, 5, 10, 16, ... These numbers follow the following pattern:

1 5 10 16 **(23)**
differences: 4 5 6 7

Thus, the required term is 22.

or

(2, 3, 4), (6, 7, 8, 9), (11, 12, 13, 14, 15), (17, 18, 19, 20, 21, 22).

**16.** c The series is:

117 = 13 × 9

104 = 13 × 8

91 = 13 × 7

78 = 13 × 6

<u>65</u> = 13 × 5

Thus, the required term is 65.

**17.** d The series is:

88 = 8 × 11

96 = 8 × 12

104 = 8 × 13

<u>112</u> = 8 × 14

Thus, the required term is <u>112</u>.

**18.** c A(1) B(2) D(4) G(7) K(11) P(16) <u>V(22)</u>
+1 +2 +3 +4 +5 +6

**19.** d Position number of the letters B, C, E, G, K, M, Q, S are 2, 3, 5, 7, 11, 13, 17 and 19 respectively i.e. increasing prime numbers. Therefore, the position number of the next letter will be 23. Hence, the next letter will be W.

**20.** b Z(26) X(24) T(20) N(14) <u>F(6)</u>
– 2 – 4 – 6 – 8

**21.** c All the words in the given series are in the order of how they will appear in a dictionary. For example 'Apple' will come before 'Application' in a dictionary. Hence the word that fits the blank best will be 'Appropriate'.

**22.** a The difference between every two consecutive days in the given series is increasing by 1, 2, 3, 4, 5, 6 and 7. Hence, the next term will be Sunday.

**23.** d In each term, larger number is removed and the remaining numbers are rearranged in reverse order in the next step. Hence, missing term will be 42783.

**24.** b None of the words contains any vowel but Mythic does.

**25.** b In the given series, in each word first two letters are same. Hence, the next word will be Uulium.

**26.** a In the given series, each term is the sum of previous two terms. Hence the next term will be 34.

**27.** b The letters are increasing by 4 in alphabetical order and the corresponding numbers are increasing in AP with common difference of 5. Hence the next term will be Q-30.

**28.** d Each term is 2 more than the previous term multiplied by 2. Hence the missing term will be 302.

**29.** c The given sequence is a combination of two sequences 2, 4, 6, 8 and 1, 3, 5, 7.

**30.** b Each term is of the form of $n^n$. Hence the next term will be $5^5$ i.e. 3125.

## CLOCKS

**1.** A clock gains 5 minutes every hour. Then the angle traversed by the seconds hand in one minute will be

(*a*) 390° (*b*) 380°

(*c*) 360.5° (*d*) 360° **(AILET, 2010)**

### Solutions

**1.** a Gain in 60 min = 5 min

Gain in 1 min = $\frac{5}{60}$ min = $\frac{5}{60} \times 60$ sec. = 5 sec

∴ Angle traversed by second hand

$$= 360° + \frac{5}{60} \times 360° = 390°.$$

## CUBE BASED

**Directions for questions 1 and 2:** Some information is provided in the form of statements. On the basis of that information, find the answer to the questions which follow.

**A.** A cube has six sides each of a different colour

**B.** The red side is opposite black

**C.** The green side is between red and black

**D.** The blue side is adjacent to white

**E.** The brown side is adjacent to blue

**F.** The red side is face down. **(AILET, 2009)**

**1.** The side opposite to brown is

(*a*) Red (*b*) Black

(*c*) White (*d*) Green

**2.** The four colours adjacent to green are______

(*a*) Red, Black, Blue and White

(*b*) Red, Black, Brown and Blue

(*c*) Red, Black, Brown and White

(*d*) Black, Blue. White and Red

### Solutions

**For questions 1 and 2:**

All of the given information can be represented as

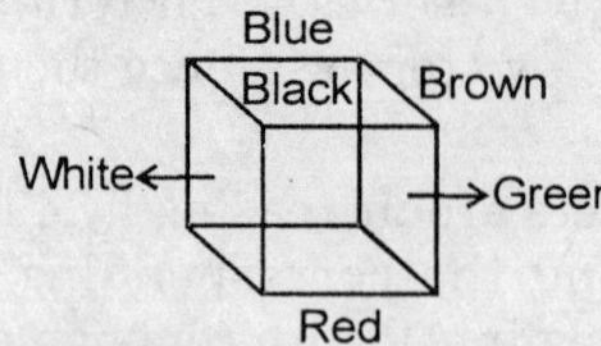


**1.** c The side opposite to 'Brown' is 'White'.

**2.** c Four colors adjacent to 'Green' are 'White', 'Black', 'Brown' and 'Red'.

## CALENDAR

**1.** India's Republic day in 1996 fell on Friday. Which week day it will be celebrated in the year 2000?

(*a*) Tuesday (*b*) Wednesday

(*c*) Thursday (*d*) Friday **(AILET, 2010)**

**2.** If day before yesterday was Tuesday, the day after tomorrow will be

(*a*) Monday (*b*) Wednesday

(*c*) Friday (*d*) Saturday

**(AILET, 2011)**

**3.** If day before yesterday was Tuesday, the day after tomorrow will be

(*a*) Monday (*b*) Wednesday

(*c*) Friday (*d*) Saturday

**(AILET, 2012)**

**4.** My brother is 562 days older to me, while my sister is 75 weeks older to him. If my sister was born on Tuesday, on what day was I born?

(*a*) Sunday (*b*) Monday

(*c*) Tuesday (*d*) Wednesday

**(AILET, 2012)**

**5.** X was born on March, 6, 1993. The same year Independence Day was celebrated on Friday. Find out the birth day of X.

(*a*) Thursday (*b*) Saturday

(*c*) Friday (*d*) Wednesday

**(AILET, 2013)**

### Solutions

**1.** b 26 Jan. 1996 is Friday

Number of odd days from:

27 Jan. 1996 to 26 Jan. 1997 = 2

27 Jan. 1997 to 26 Jan. 1998 = 1

27 Jan. 1998 to 26 Jan. 1998 = 1

27 Jan. 1999 to 26 Jan. 2000 = 1

Total number of odd days

$= 2 + 1 + 1 + 1 = 5$

Five days after Friday is Wednesday.

**2.** d Day before yesterday was Tuesday.

Yesterday was Wednesday.

Today is Thursday and tomorrow will be Friday.

So day after tomorrow will be Saturday.

**3.** d If day before yesterday was Tuesday, then today is Thursday.

$\Rightarrow$ The day after tomorrow will be Saturday.

**4.** a My sister was born $(562 + 75 \times 7) = 1087$ days before me and it was a Tuesday.

Number of odd days (i.e. remainder left when 1087 is divided by 7) is 2.

$\Rightarrow$ I was born on a Sunday.

**5.** a Independence Day was celebrated after [25 (March) + 30 (April) + 31 (May) + 30 (June) + 31 (July) + 15 (August)]

$= 162$ days $= 23 \times 7 + 1$

$= 23$ weeks $+ 1$ days

$\therefore$ Number of odd days = 1

Hence, X was born on Thursday.

## CODING-DECODING

**1.** It is possible to make a meaningful word with the third, the fourth, and the eleventh letters of word 'CONTROVERSIAL' write the first letter of that word.

(*a*) I (*b*) N

(*c*) S (*d*) T **(AILET, 2008)**

**2.** If (*a*) Chip din chunk means student attends class; (*b*) din sunk dink means Arjuna is student; (*c*) jump nink sink means schools are good; (*d*) dink mup chimp means teacher is good. Then what is the code for Arjuna?

(*a*) din (*b*) sunk

(*c*) dink (*d*) chunk **(AILET, 2008)**

**3.** If SIR is written as PSPIPR, then MAN can be written as

(*a*) PMANP (*b*) PMPAPN

(*c*) MANP (*d*) MPANP **(AILET, 2011)**

**4.** In a certain code language, 35796 is written as 44887. How is 46823 written in that code?

(*a*) 57914 (*b*) 55914

(*c*) 55934 (*d*) 55714 **(AILET, 2011)**

**5.** PLANING is coded in a certain language as UFFHSCSA. How will AUTHORITY be coded in the same language?

(*a*) FOYBTLNND

(*b*) FYOTBNNLT

(*c*) FBOYTLNTN

(*d*) FBOYTNLTN

**(AILET, 2012)**

**6.** In certain code ELECTION is written as GLGCVIQN, then VOTER will be coded as:

(*a*) XOVET (*b*) VOXET

(*c*) WPUFU (*d*) VQTGR **(AILET, 2012)**

**7.** In a code, every letter of the alphabet is replaced by some other letter. The code for the name Ram Kumar is

(*a*) Ten Ronet

(*b*) Len Finol

(*c*) Pen Sinet

(*d*) Elephant **(CLAT 2010)**

**8.** If CABLE is coded as ZCDAY, then STABLE will be coded as

(*a*) TPADAY (*b*) TPCDCY

(*c*) TPCDAY (*d*) TPCYAY **(CLAT 2010)**

**9.** If CHARTER is coded as UMOEPYE then PARTNER will be coded as **(CLAT 2011)**

(*a*) AONPCYE

(*b*) AEEPCYE

(*c*) AOEACYE

(*d*) AOEPCYE

**10.** In a certain code, TEAMWORK is written as NBFUJQNV and SOME is written as PTDL. How is PERSON written in that code ? **(AILET, 2013)**

(*a*) QDOOPT

(*b*) QDOMNR

(*c*) SFQMNR

(*d*) SFQOPT

**11.** In certain code, BASKET is written as 5$3%#1 and TRIED is written as 14*#2. How is SKIRT written in that code ?

(*a*) 3%*41 (*b*) 3*%41

(*c*) 3%#41 (*d*) 3#4%1 **(AILET, 2013)**

## Solutions

**1.** d Third letter = N, fourth letter = T and eleventh letter = I. Hence, the meaningful word is TIN.

**2.** b From statements (*a*) and (*b*), 'student' is coded as 'din'.

From statements (*b*) and (*d*), 'is' is coded as 'dink'. Hence, 'Arjuna' is coded as 'sunk'.

**3.** b P is added before each letter of SIR.

Therefore, MAN can be written as PMPAPN.

**4.** b The coding follows the pattern:

$3 + 1 = 4$

$5 - 1 = 4$

$7 + 1 = 8$

$9 - 1 = 8$

$6 + 1 = 7$

Therefore, code for 46823 in the same code language will be 55914.

**5.** a Consider PLANING as PLANNIG.

A(1) + 5 = F(6)

U(21) – 6 = O(15)

T(20) + 5 = Y(25)

H(8) – 6 = B(2)

O(15) + 5 = T(20)

R(18) – 6 = L(12)

I(9) + 5 = N(14)

T(20) – 6 = N(14)

Y(25) + 5 = D(4)

Hence, the code of PLANNING is FOYBTLNND.

**6.** a The letters in the odd number of places are increased by 2 positions while those at the even number of places remain same.

Hence, the code for VOTER is XOVET.

**7.** a From option (*a*), the code for Ram is Ten i.e., R = T, A = E and M = N. Therefore, the code for Kumar should be _ _ net. Option (*a*) satisfies this. Hence, the code for Ram Kumar is Ten Ronet.

**8.** c From CABLE, ABLE is coded as CDAY. Therefore, STABLE is coded as TPCDAY.

**9.** d From CHARTER, ARTER is coded as OEPYE. Therefore, PARTNER is coded as AOEPCYE.

**10.** c

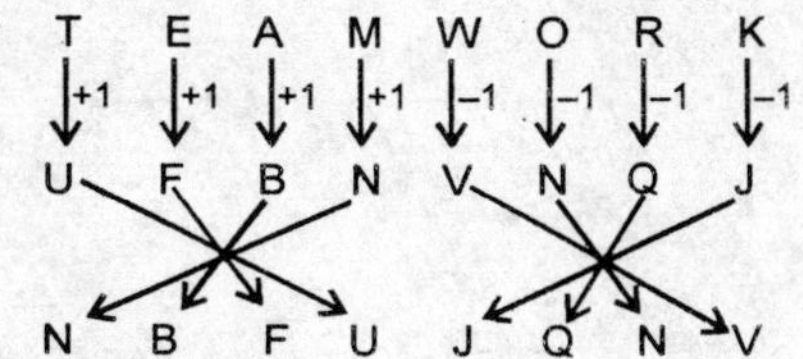


Hence, PERSON will be coded as SFQMNR in that code language.

**11.** a In this code language every letter is coded with a distinct symbol or integer as follow.

B – 5

A – $

S – 3

K – %

E – #

T – 1

R – 4

I – *

D – 2

Hence, SKIRT will be coded as 3%*41 in that code language.

## ANALOGY

**1.** Eagle : Swoops : : Duck : ?

(*a*) Swims (*b*) Flits

(*c*) Waddles (*d*) Floats **(AILET, 2013)**

**2.** APPLE : 50 : : ORANGE : ?

(*a*) 61 (*b*) 63

(*c*) 60 (*d*) 69 **(AILET, 2013)**

### Solutions

**1.** c Movement of Eagle is like swooping, similarly the movement of Duck is Waddle.

**2.** c Sum of position numbers of all the alphabets of the words

APPLE : 1+16 +16 + 12 + 5 = 50

Similarly, ORANGE :

15 + 18 + 1 + 14 + 7 + 5 = 60.

■■

# QUANTITATIVE APTITUDE

# 1

# NUMBER SYSTEM

1. Find the sum of all two-digit numbers that give a remainder of 3 when they are divided by 7.
   (*a*) 686 (*b*) 676
   (*c*) 666 (*d*) 656 **(AILET, 2008)**
2. Find the least number that when divided by 16, 18 and 20 leaves a remainder 4 in each case, but is completely divisible by 7.
   (*a*) 364 (*b*) 2254
   (*c*) 2884 (*d*) 3234 **(AILET, 2009)**
3. What is the location value of 7 in the figure 9872590?
   (*a*) 72590 (*b*) 7
   (*c*) 70000 (*d*) 7000 **(CLAT 2009)**
4. The square root of 289 is
   (*a*)13 (*b*) 17
   (*c*) 27 (*d*) 23 **(CLAT 2010)**
5. Find the factors of 330. **(CLAT 2010)**
   (*a*) $2 \times 4 \times 5 \times 11$ (*b*) $2 \times 3 \times 7 \times 13$
   (*c*) $2 \times 3 \times 5 \times 13$ (*d*) $2 \times 3 \times 5 \times 11$
6. Find the factors of 1122. **(CLAT 2010)**
   (*a*) $3 \times 9 \times 17 \times 2$ (*b*) $3 \times 11 \times 17 \times 2$
   (*c*) $9 \times 9 \times 17 \times 2$ (*d*) $3 \times 11 \times 17 \times 3$
7. Which of the following is not a prime number?
   (*a*) 23 (*b*) 29
   (*c*) 43 (*d*) 21 **(CLAT 2010)**
8. If the numbers from 1 to 24, which are divisible by 2 are arranged in descending order, which number will be at the 8th place from the bottom?
   (*a*) 10 (*b*) 12
   (*c*) 16 (*d*) 18 **(CLAT 2010)**
9. Square root of 400 is
   (*a*) 40 (*b*) 25
   (*c*) 20 (*d*) 100 **(CLAT 2010)**
10. What is the place (location) value of 5 in 3254710?
    (*a*) 10000 (*b*) 5
    (*c*) 54710 (*d*) 50000 **(CLAT 2010)**
11. $6 \times 3\ (3 - 1)$ is equal to
    (*a*) 53 (*b*) 36
    (*c*) 20 (*d*) 19 **(CLAT 2010)**
12. Which of the following is a prime number?
    (*a*) 19 (*b*) 20
    (*c*) 21 (*d*) 22 **(CLAT 2010)**
13. Difference between two numbers is 9 and difference between their squares is 981. Lowest of the two numbers is:
    (*a*) 40 (*b*) 50
    (*c*) 55 (*d*) 59 **(CLAT 2011)**
14. The least value of x for which the expression $x^2 + x + 17$ will not give a prime number, is
    (*a*) 7 (*b*) 11
    (*c*) 13 (*d*) 17 **(CLAT 2012)**
15. The difference between the number of numbers from 2 to 100 which are not divisible by any other number except 1 and itself and the numbers which are divisible by atleast one more number along with one and itself.
    (*a*) 25 (*b*) 50 **(AILET 2013)**
    (*c*) 49 (*d*) none of these
16. The average of three prime numbers lying between 47 and 74 is 191/3. The greatest possible sum between any two out of the 3 prime numbers is
    (*a*) 120 (*b*) 138
    (*c*) 132 (*d*) 136 **(AILET 2013)**
17. Three consecutive positive even numbers are such that thrice the first number exceeds double the third by 2, the third number is
    (*a*) 10 (*b*) 14
    (*c*) 16 (*d*) 12 **(AILET 2013)**
18. 2 / 3 is a rational number whereas $\sqrt{2}/\sqrt{3}$ is
    (*a*) Also a rational number **(CLAT 2013)**
    (*b*) An irrational number
    (*c*) Not a number
    (*d*) A natural periodic number
19. Greatest number which divides 926 and 2313, leaving 2 and 3 remainders, respectively, is
    (*a*) 52 (*b*) 54 **(CLAT 2013)**
    (*c*) 152 (*d*) 154
20. Two whole numbers whose sum is 64 can be in the ratio of ? **(AILET 2014)**
    (*a*) 7 : 2 (*b*) 7: 6
    (*c*) 3 : 1 (*d*) 8 : 7
21. P, Q and R are three consecutive odd numbers in ascending order. If the value of three times P is 3 less than two times R, find the value of R.
    (*a*) 5 (*b*) 7 **(AILET 2014)**
    (*c*) 9 (*d*) 11

**22.** The next number in the sequence is: 19, 29, 37, 43, ........... **(CLAT 2014)**

(*a*) 45 (*b*) 47
(*c*) 50 (*d*) 53

**23.** The Least Common Multiple (L.C.M.) of 0.12, 9.60 and 0.60 is: **(CLAT 2014)**

(*a*) 9.60 (*b*) 0.12
(*c*) 0.6 (*d*) None of these

**24.** Value of "A" in the expression,

$5+12\times10\div\frac{120}{240}=A\times10$, is: **(CLAT 2014)**

(*a*) 11 (*b*) 24.5,
(*c*) 34 (*d*) 6.5

### Solutions

**1.** c The two digit numbers that give remainder 3 when divided by 7 are 17, 24, 31, 38 .......... 94, which is an A.P. with

a = 17, d = 7 and l = 94.

Therefore, $Sn=\frac{12}{2}\{17+94\}=666$.

**2.** c LCM of (16, 18, 20) = 720

Required number = 720 + 4 = 724

Series of such a number would be of the form

n × 720 + 4,

where n is a natural number.

Among the given options, 2884 satisfies the condition 2884 = 4 × 720 + 4 and is divisible by 7 too.

**3.** c Place value of 7 = 7 × $10^4$ = 70000.

**4.** b $\sqrt{289}=\sqrt{17\times17}=17$.

**5.** d 330 = 2 × 3 × 5 × 11.

**6.** b 1122 = 2 × 3 × 11 × 17.

**7.** d 21 is divisible by 3 and 7. However, all the other numbers are divisible by 1 and the number itself. Therefore, 21 is not a prime number.

**8.** c All the even numbers from 1 to 24 are divisible by 2, i.e., 24, 22, 20, 18, 16, 14, 12, 10, 8, 6, 4 and 2.

∴ 16 will be at the $8^{th}$ place from the bottom.

**9.** c $\sqrt{400}=\sqrt{20\times20}=20$.

**10.** a 3254710 = 3000000 + 200000 + 50000 + 4000 + 700 + 10 + 0

∴ Place value of 5 is 50,000.

**11.** b 6 × 3(3 – 1) = 6 × 3(2) = 6 × 6 = 36.

**12.** a From the given options:

20 is divisible by 2 and 5,

21 is divisible by 3 and 7,

22 is divisible by 2 and 11,

19 is divisible by only 1 and itself.

Thus, 19 is a prime number.

**13.** b Let x and y be two numbers, where x > y.

$x - y = 9$ ...(i)

$x^2 - y^2 = 981$

⇒ $(x - y)(x + y) = 981$

⇒ $x + y = 109$ ...(ii)

Solving (i) and (ii), we get

x = 59 and y = 50

Hence, lowest of the two numbers is 50.

**14.** d By putting x = 17, we get the least value of x i.e. 17 × 19 = 323, a non-prime number.

**15.** c The numbers which are not divisible by any other number except 1 are prime numbers and there are 25 prime numbers from 2 to100. Therefore, the numbers from 2 – 100 which are not prime (i.e. composite) = 99 – 25 = 74

Hence, the difference = 74 – 25 = 49.

**16.** b Three prime numbers lying between 47 and 74, whose average is $\frac{191}{3}$ are (53, 67, 71) and (59, 61, 71).

Hence, the required sum = 67 + 71 = 138.

**17.** b Let the third number be x, then the first number is (x – 4) and the second number is (x – 2).

Now, 3 × (x – 4) = 2 + 2x

⇒ x = 14.

**18.** b A rational number is of the form $\frac{p}{q}$, where *p* and *q* are integers and $q \neq 0$.

Hence $\frac{\sqrt{2}}{\sqrt{3}}$ is an irrational number.

**19.** * (Correct answer not present in the given options)

Required number will be the HCF of (926 – 2) and (2313 – 3), i.e. 924 and 2310.

The HCF of 924 and 2310 is 462.

Hence, the required number is 462.

**20.** c If Ratio of two number is x : y, then sum of the number must be divisible by x + y.

Among the given option only option (*c*) is satisfying.

**21.** c Let P = x

∴ Q = x +2 and R = x + 4

According to question,

3 x = 2(x + 4) – 3 ⇒ x = 5

∴ R = 5 + 4 = 9.

**22.** b Each term of the sequence is as follows:

$19 \xrightarrow{+10} 29 \xrightarrow{+8} 37 \xrightarrow{+6} 43 \xrightarrow{+4} 47$

**23.** a L.C.M. of 0.12, 9.60 and 0.60

$= \text{LCM of } \frac{3}{25}, \frac{48}{5} \text{ and } \frac{3}{5}$

$= \frac{\text{LCM (3, 48 and 3)}}{\text{HCF of (25, 5 and 5)}} = \frac{48}{5} = 9.6.$

**24.** b $5+12\times10\div\frac{120}{240}=A\times10$

$\Rightarrow 5+120\times2=A\times10$

$\Rightarrow A = 24.5.$

# 2

# ARITHMETIC

## AVERAGE

**1.** The average age of three boys is 15 years. If their ages are in the ratio 3 : 5 : 7, the age of the youngest boy is
(*a*) 21 years (*b*) 18 years
(*c*) 15 years (*d*) 9 years **(AILET, 2009)**

**2.** The average height of 10 students in a class is 105 cms. If 20 more students with an average height of 120 cms join them, what will be the average height be?
(*a*) 105 cms (*b*) 110 cms
(*c*) 112 cms (*d*) 115 cms **(AILET, 2010)**

**3.** Before 3 years, the average age of a five-member family was 17 years. A baby having been born and the average of family is now 17 years. The present age of the baby is:
(*a*) 3 years (*b*) 2 years
(*c*) 1 year (*d*) none of these
**(AILET, 2012)**

**4.** The average age of A, B and C is 25 years. The ratio of their ages is 3 : 5 : 7. Find the age of A
(*a*) 21 years (*b*) 18 years **(AILET, 2012)**
(*c*) 15 years (*d*) Data Inadequate

**5.** Of the three numbers, the first is one third of the second and twice the third. The average of these numbers is 27. The largest of these numbers is
(*a*) 18 (*b*) 36
(*c*) 54 (*d*) 108 **(CLAT 2008)**

**6.** The average monthly income of a person in a certain family of 5 members is ₹ 1000. What will be monthly average income of one person in the same family if the income of one person increased by ₹ 12,000 per year?
(*a*) ₹ 1200 (*b*) ₹ 1600
(*c*) ₹ 2000 (*d*) ₹ 3400 **(CLAT 2009)**

**7.** The average age of 29 boys of a class is equal to 14 years. When the age of the class teacher is included the average becomes 15 years. Find the age of the class teacher.
(*a*) 44 years (*b*) 40 years
(*c*) 52 years (*d*) 66 years **(CLAT 2009)**

**8.** 10 sheep and 5 pigs were brought for ₹ 6,000. If the average price of a sheep is ₹ 450, find the average price of a pig.
(*a*) ₹ 380 (*b*) ₹ 410
(*c*) ₹ 340 (*d*) ₹ 300 **(CLAT 2009)**

**9.** Average age of ten persons learning yoga is 32 years. When the age of their instructor is added, the average age becomes 34 years. The age of their instructor is
(*a*) 54 (*b*) 52
(*c*) 46 (*d*) 56 **(CLAT 2010)**

**10.** Ms. Jhulan Goswami scores 102 runs in the 18th innings of her career and thus increases her average by 5. After the 18th inning, her average is:
(*a*) 17 (*b*) 21
(*c*) 26 (*d*) 28 **(CLAT 2011)**

**11.** In a school for midday meal food is sufficient for 250 students for 33 days, if each student is given 125 gm meals. 80 more students joined the school. If same amount of meal is given to each student, then the food will last for **(CLAT 2013)**
(*a*) 20 days (*b*) 40 days
(*c*) 30 days (*d*) 25 days

**12.** Table shows the daily expenditure on food of 25 households in a locality: **(CLAT 2013)**

| ₹ | **Households** |
|---|---|
| 100 – 150 | 4 |
| 150 – 200 | 5 |
| 200 – 250 | 12 |
| 250 – 300 | 2 |
| 300 – 350 | 2 |

The mean daily expenditure on food is
(*a*) ₹ 111 (*b*) ₹ 161
(*c*) ₹ 211 (*d*) ₹ 261

**13.** The average marks of a student in ten papers are 80. If the highest and the lowest score are not considered the average is 81. If his highest score is 92, what is the lowest score ? **(AILET 2014)**
(*a*) 55 (*b*) 60
(*c*) 62 (*d*) 61

**14.** There are 30 boys and 40 girls in a class. If the average age of boys is 10 yr and average age of girls is 8 yr, then the average age of the whole class is: **(CLAT 2014)**
(*a*) 8 yr (*b*) 8.86 yr
(*c*) 8.2 yr (*d*) 9 yr

## Solutions

**1.** d Total age of three boys = $3 \times 15 = 45$ years

Age of youngest boy

$$= \frac{3}{3+5+7} \times 45 = \frac{3}{15} \times 45 = 9 \text{ years.}$$

**2.** d Average height of 10 students = 105 cm

Total height of 10 students = $105 \times 10 = 1050$ cm

Average height of 20 new students = 120 cm

Total height of 20 new students

$= 120 \times 20 = 2400$ cm

Total height of the class = $1050 + 2400 = 3450$ cm

Average height of the class $= \frac{3450}{30} = 115$ cm.

**3.** b Three years before, sum of the ages of all five members in the family = $17 \times 5 = 85$ years

At present, their sum of ages

$= 85 + 3 \times 5 = 100$ years.

But, since a baby was born, the present sum of the age of six-member family = $17 \times 6 = 102$ years.

$\therefore$ Present age of the baby = $102 - 100 = 2$ years.

**4.** c Let the ages of A, B and C be 3x, 5x and 7x years respectively.

$\therefore \quad 3x + 5x + 7x = 25 \times 3$

$\Rightarrow \quad 15x = 75$

$\Rightarrow \quad x = 5$

Hence, age of A is $(3 \times 5) = 15$ years.

**5.** c Let the three numbers be a, b and c.

Now, $a = \frac{b}{3}$ and $a = 2c$.

Also, $\frac{a+b+c}{3} = 27$

$\Rightarrow \quad a + b + c = 81$

$\therefore \quad a + 3a + \frac{a}{2} = 81$

$\Rightarrow \quad a = 18, b = 54, c = 9$

$\therefore$ Largest of the three numbers is 54.

**6.** a Total monthly income of 5 members in the family

$= 5 \times 1000 =$ ₹ 5,000

Total yearly income of 5 members in the family

$= 5000 \times 12 =$ ₹ 60,000

Total yearly income of 5 members in the family after increment

$= 60,000 + 12,000 =$ ₹ 72,000

Increased average yearly income of 5 members

$= \frac{72000}{12} =$ ₹ 6,000

Increased average monthly income of 5 members

$= \frac{6000}{5} =$ ₹ 1,200.

**7.** a Total age of 29 boys in the class

$= 29 \times 14 = 406$ years

Total age of 29 boys and the class teacher

$= 30 \times 15 = 450$ years

Age of the class teacher = $450 - 406 = 44$ years

**8.** d Total price of 10 sheeps = $10 \times 450 =$ ₹ 4500

Total price of 5 pigs = ₹ 6000 – ₹ 4500 = ₹ 1500

Average price of a pig = ₹ $\frac{1500}{5}$ = ₹ 300.

**9.** a Average age of 10 persons = 32 years

Total age of 10 persons = $32 \times 10 = 320$ years

Average age of 10 persons and instructor

= 34 years

Total age of 10 persons and instructor

$= 34 \times 11 = 374$ years

$\therefore$ Age of the instructor = $374 - 320 = 54$ years.

**10.** a Let x be the average score of Ms. Jhulan Goswami after 17[th] innings. Then,

$$\frac{17 \times x + 102}{18} = x + 5$$

$\Rightarrow \quad x = 12$

Hence, after 18[th] innings, her average score

$= 12 + 5 = 17$.

**11.** d Total amount of food available

$= (250 \times 33 \times 125)$ gm = 1031250 gm.

Total number of students in the school after new students joined = $250 + 80 = 330$.

Required number of days $= \left[\frac{1031250}{330 \times 125}\right] = 25$.

**12.** c The daily mean expenditure on food

$$= \frac{(125\times4+175\times5+225\times12+275\times2+325\times2)}{4+5+12+2+2}$$

= ₹ 211

**13.** b Let the lowest score be x.

$\therefore 80 \times 10 = 81 \times 8 + 92 + x \Rightarrow x = 60$

**14.** b The average age of the whole class

$$= \frac{30\times10+40\times8}{30+40} = 8.86 \text{ years.}$$

## RATIO AND PROPORTION

**1.** In Ramnagar Colony, the ratio of school going children to non-school going children is 5 : 4. If in the next year, the number of non-school going children is increased by 20% making it 35,400. what is the new ratio of school going children to non-school going children?

(*a*) 4 : 5 (*b*) 3 : 2 **(NLDU 2009)**

(*c*) 25 : 24 (*d*) None of these

**2.** ₹ 324 is divided among three friends Sonu, Monu and Hari in the ratio 5: 6 : 7. What is Monu's share of money?

(*a*) 68 (*b*) 108
(*c*) 60 (*d*) 120 **(NLDU 2011)**

**3.** A purse contains some coins consisting of rupees, fifty paise coins and twenty five paise coins. If coins be in the ratio of 2 : 3 : 10 and their total value is ₹72, the number of twenty-five paise coins will be:

(*a*) 100 (*b*) 140
(*c*) 120 (*d*) 80 **(NLDU 2012)**

**4.** Raju earns twice as much in March as in each of the other months of the year. What part of his annual earnings he earns in that month?

(*a*) 1/5 (*b*) 5/7
(*c*) 2/13 (*d*) 1/10 **(CLAT 2008)**

**5.** The monthly salary of A, B and C are in the ratio 2 : 3 : 5. If C's monthly salary is ₹ 1,200 more than that of A, find B's annual salary.

(*a*) ₹ 2000 (*b*) ₹ 1000
(*c*) ₹ 1500 (*d*) ₹ 1200 **(CLAT 2009)**

**6.** In a town there are 94500 people. 2/9 of them are foreigners, 6400 are immigrants and the rest are natives. How many are natives?

(*a*) 67100 (*b*) 27400
(*c*) 77600 (*d*) 88100 **(CLAT 2009)**

**7.** Total salary of three persons A, B and C is ₹ 1,44,000. They spend 80%, 85% and 75% respectively. If their savings are in the ratio 8 : 9 : 20, find C's salary.

(*a*) 48000 (*b*) 64000
(*c*) 40000 (*d*) 32000 **(CLAT 2009)**

**8.** The ratio of two numbers is 4 : 5. But, if each number is increased by 20, the ratio becomes 6 : 7. The sum of such numbers is:

(*a*) 90 (*b*) 95
(*c*) 100 (*d*) 60 **(CLAT 2011)**

**9.** During the academic session 2009-10, in Banaras Hindu University, Varanasi, the number of students studying Arts, Law and Commerce was in the ratio of 5 : 6 : 7. If during the academic session 2010-11 the number of students studying Arts, Law and Commerce increased by 20%, 30% and 40% respectively, what will be new ratio?

(*a*) 26 : 42 : 63 (*b*) 36 : 44 : 73
(*c*) 26 : 39 : 49 (*d*) 30 : 39 : 49
**(CLAT 2011)**

**10.** A sum was divided among P, Q & R. R got double than P who got double than Q. If the difference between the shares of Q and R is ₹3675.00, then the sum in rupees is

(*a*) 4900 (*b*) 8575
(*c*) 11025 (*d*) 7350 **(CLAT 2012)**

**11.** If the ratio of the areas of two squares is 25 : 36, then the ratio of their perimeters is

(*a*) 5 : 6 (*b*) 25 : 36
(*c*) 6 : 5 (*d*) 36 : 25 **(CLAT 2012)**

**12.** The denominator of a fraction is greater than its numerator by 11. If 8 is added to both its numerator and denominator, then it becomes $\frac{3}{4}$. The fraction is

(*a*) $\frac{25}{26}$ (*b*) $\frac{35}{26}$
(*c*) $\frac{26}{35}$ (*d*) $\frac{25}{36}$ **(CLAT 2012)**

**13.** A and B started a business with a total capital of ₹ 30,000. At the end of the year, they shared the profit in the ratio of their investments. If their capitals were interchanged, then A would have received 175% more than what he actually received. Find out the capital of B. **(AILET 2014)**

(*a*) ₹ 20,000 (*b*) ₹ 22,000
(*c*) ₹ 21,000 (*d*) ₹ 23,000

**14.** The ratio in which Aman and Bimal have contributed to the capital of a company is 3 : 4. Bimal has invested his capital for only 3 months and has received half as much profit as Aman, at the end of the year. Find out for how much time has Aman invested his capital in the company.

(*a*) 8 months (*b*) 14 months
(*c*) 15 months (*d*) 1 year **(AILET 2014)**

**15.** An employer reduces the number of employees in the ratio 8:5 and increases their wages in the ratio 7:9. Therefore, the overall wages bill is:

(*a*) Increased in the ratio 45:56 **(CLAT 2014)**
(*b*) Decreased in the ratio 56:45
(*c*) Increased in the ratio 13:17
(*d*) Decreased in the ratio 72:35

**16.** A starts a business with ₹5000 and B joins the business 5 months later with an investment of ₹ 6000. After a year, they earn a profit of ₹ 34000. Find the shares of A and B in the profit amount depending on their individual investment. **(CLAT 2014)**

(*a*) ₹20000, ₹14000 (*b*) ₹16000, ₹16000
(*c*) ₹14000, ₹20000 (*d*) None of these

## Solutions

**1.** c Let the number of school going children and non-school going children be 5x and 4x respectively.

New number of non-school going children
$= 4x \times 1.2$

Hence, new ratio $= \frac{5x}{4x \times 1.2} = \frac{25}{24}$ or 25 : 24.

**2.** b Share of Monu $= \frac{6}{18} \times 324 =$ ₹ 108.

**3.** c Let the number of 1 rupee, fifty paise and twenty five paise coins be 2x, 3x and 10x respectively.

$\therefore \quad 2x \times 1 + 3x \times \frac{1}{2} + 10x \times \frac{1}{4} = 72$

$\Rightarrow \quad 2x + \frac{3x}{2} + \frac{5x}{2} = 72$

$\Rightarrow \quad 6x = 72$

$\Rightarrow \quad x = 12$

Hence, the number of twenty five paise coins

$= 10 \times 12 = 120.$

**4.** c Let Raju earns ₹ x in each of the other eleven months.

Then, Raju's earning in March = ₹ 2x

Raju's annual earning = ₹ (11x + 2x) = ₹ 13x

$\therefore \quad$ Required fraction $= \frac{2x}{13x} = \frac{2}{13}$

**5.** d Let the monthly salary of A, B and C be ₹ 2x, ₹ 3x and ₹ 5x respectively.

Difference between the monthly salary of C and A

= 5x – 2x = ₹ 3x

According to the question,

$3x = 1200$

$\Rightarrow \quad x = 400$

B's monthly salary = 3x = 3 × 400 = ₹ 1200

**It seems that B's monthly salary is asked instead of his/her annual salary. None of the options are close to B's annual salary. So we have kept it to B's monthly salary.**

**6.** a Number of foreigners = $94500 \times \left(\frac{2}{9}\right) = 21000$

Number of immigrants = 6400

Number of natives = 94500 – (21000 + 6400)

= 94500 – 27400 = 67100

**7.** b All of the given information can be tabulated as:

| | **A** | **B** | **C** |
|---|---|---|---|
| **Income** | A | B | C |
| **Expenditure** | 0.80A | 0.85B | 0.75C |
| **Saving** | 0.20A | 0.15B | 0.25C |

Their savings are in the ratio of 8 : 9 : 20.

$\therefore$ For 0.20 A = 8, A = 40

For 0.15B = 9, B = 60

For 0.25C = 20, C = 80

Now, A + B + C = 144000

$\Rightarrow \quad 40x + 60x + 80x = 144000$

$\Rightarrow \quad 180x = 144000$

$\Rightarrow \quad x = 800$

Thus, C's salary = 80 × 800 = ₹ 64,000.

**8.** a Let 4x and 5x be two numbers. Then,

$\frac{4x + 20}{5x + 20} = \frac{6}{7}$

$\Rightarrow \quad x = 10$

Therefore, numbers are 40 and 50.

Hence, sum of two numbers = 40 + 50 = 90.

**9.** d Let 5x, 6x and 7x be the number of students studying in Arts, law and commerce respectively.

After increment, new ratio

$= 5x \times 1.2 : 6x \times 1.3 : 7x \times 1.4$

$= 30 : 39 : 49.$

**10.** b Let Q's share be ₹x.

Then, P's share = ₹2x and R's share = ₹4x

According to the question, we get

$4x - x = 3675$

$\Rightarrow \quad 3x = 3675$

$\Rightarrow \quad x = 1225$

Hence, the total sum = 2x + x + 4x = 7x

= 7 × 1225 = ₹8,575.

**11.** a Ratio of the areas of two squares = 25 : 36

$\therefore$ Ratio of the lengths of their sides

$= \sqrt{25} : \sqrt{36} = 5 : 6$

$\Rightarrow$ Ratio of their perimeters = 5 : 6.

**12.** d Let the numerator be x.

Therefore, denominator = x + 11

and the original fraction = $\frac{x}{x+11}$

New fraction $= \frac{x+8}{x+11+8} = \frac{x+8}{x+19}$

According to the question, $\frac{x+8}{x+19} = \frac{3}{4}$

$\Rightarrow \quad x = 25$

Hence, the original fraction is $\frac{25}{36}$.

**13.** b When their capitals were interchanged, then A would have received175% more than what he actually received it means in actual B received 175% more than A.

Ratio of their investment of A to B

= 1 : 2.75 = 4 : 11.

$\therefore \quad$ Capital of B $= \frac{11}{4+11} \times 30000 = 22000.$

**14.** a Let Aman invested his capital for x months.

$\therefore \frac{4 \times 3}{3 \times x} = \frac{1}{2} \Rightarrow x = 8.$

**15.** b The required ratio = 8 . 7 : 5 . 9 = 56 :45.

**16.** a The ratio of investment of A to B = 5000 . 12 : 6000 . 7 = 10 : 7.

## PERCENTAGE AND FRACTION

**1.** The petrol prices shot up by 7% as a result of the hike in the price of crudes. The price of petrol before the hike was ₹ 28 per litre. Vawal travels 2400 kilometers every month and his car gives a mileage of 18 kilometers to a litre. Find the increase in the expenditure that Vawal has to incur due to the increase in the price of petrol (to the nearest rupee)?

(*a*) ₹ 270 (*b*) ₹ 262

(*c*) ₹ 276 (*d*) ₹ 272 **(NLDU 2008)**

**2.** Two cubes of bronze have their total weight equivalent to 60 kg. The first piece contains 10 kg of pure zinc and the second piece contains 8 kg of pure zinc. What is the percentage of zinc in the first piece of bronze if the second piece contains 15 percent more zinc than the first?

(*a*) 15% (*b*) 25%

(*c*) 55% (*d*) 24% **(NLDU 2008)**

**3.** A's salary is first increased by 25% and then decreased by 20%. The result is the same as B's salary increased by 20% and then reduced by 25%. Find the ratio of B's salary to that of A's.

(*a*) 4 : 3 (*b*) 11 : 10

(*c*) 10 : 9 (*d*) 12 : 11 **(NLDU 2009)**

**4.** Which one of the following is same as 30% of 40% of 560? **(NLDU 2010)**

(*a*) 60% of 40% of 280 (*b*) 15% of 80% of 280

(*c*) 30% of 40% of 280 (*d*) 15% of 80% of 140

**5.** The number of the members of a club is increased by 10% every year. If the initial number of the members is 500, then what will be the number at the beginning of the third year?

(*a*) 610 (*b*) 615

(*c*) 620 (*d*) 605 **(NLDU 2011)**

**6.** A company declares a dividend of 12% on ₹ 100 shares. A housewife buys such shares and gets 15% on her investment. At what price she bought the shares?

(*a*) ₹ 80 (*b*) ₹ 85

(*c*) ₹ 125 (*d*) ₹ 76 **(NLDU 2011)**

**7.** The price of an article is cut by 10%. To restore it to the original value, the new price must be increased by

(*a*) 10% (*b*) $9\frac{1}{11}\%$

(*c*) 11% (*d*) $11\frac{1}{9}\%$ **(NLDU 2011)**

**8.** The value of a car depreciates every year at the rate of 10% on its value at the beginning of the year. If the present value of the car is ₹ 52,488, its worth four years ago was

(*a*) ₹ 68,232 (*b*) ₹ 68,234

(*c*) ₹ 69,862 (*d*) ₹ 80,000 **(NLDU 2011)**

**9.** In an examination, a student who secured 25% of the maximum marks fails by 60 marks but another candidate who secures 45% of the maximum marks gets 10 marks more than required passing marks. The maximum number of marks is:

(*a*) 450 (*b*) 350 **(NLDU 2012)**

(*c*) 525 (*d*) None of these

**10.** The length of a square is increased by 15% and breadth decreased by 15%. The area of the rectangle so formed is

(*a*) neither increases nor decreases

(*b*) decreases by 2.25%

(*c*) increases by 2.25%

(*d*) decreases by 22.5% **(CLAT 2008)**

**11.** Change 1/8 into percentage

(*a*) 12.5% (*b*) 15%

(*c*) 8% (*d*) 25% **(CLAT 2009)**

**12.** 12.5% of 80 is equal to

(*a*) 8 (*b*) 20

(*c*) 10 (*d*) 40 **(CLAT 2009)**

**13.** The smallest of the fractions given below

(*a*) 9/10 (*b*) 11/12

(*c*) 23/28 (*d*) 32/33 **(CLAT 2009)**

**14.** Three friends shared the cost of a television. If Amit, Bharat and Dinesh each paid ₹ 3000 and ₹ 1800 respectively, then Dinesh paid what percent of the total cost?

(*a*) 10% (*b*) 20%

(*c*) 30% (*d*) 40% **(CLAT 2009)**

**15.** Ram's income is 20% less than Shyam's. How much is Shyam's income more than Ram's in percentage terms?

(*a*) 20% (*b*) 30%

(*c*) 25% (*d*) 15% **(CLAT 2009)**

**16.** The population of a town is 155625. For every 1000 males, there are 1075 females. If 40% of the males and 24% of the females are literate, find the literacy percentage in the town.

(*a*) 33.7% (*b*) 32.7%

(*c*) 31.7% (*d*) 30.7% **(CLAT 2009)**

**17.** Find 12% of 5000.

(*a*) 620 (*b*) 600

(*c*) 680 (*d*) 720 **(CLAT 2010)**

**18.** Which of the following fractions has the highest value?

3/5, 4/3, 2/5, 1/2

(*a*) 3/5 (*b*) 4/3

(*c*) 2/5 (*d*) 1/2 **(CLAT 2010)**

**19.** Jogen's taxable income for 2010-11 is ₹ 5,00,000. The tax rates are (i) nil for first 1,50,000, (ii) 10% for 150,001—3,00,000, and (iii) 20% for the remaining. His Tax liability is:

(*a*) ₹ 45,000 (*b*) ₹ 50,000

(*c*) ₹ 55,000 (*d*) ₹ 60,000 **(CLAT 2011)**

**20.** If the length and height of a brick increases by 10% each respectively, and the breadth reduces by 20%, what is the percentage change in the volume of the brick?

(*a*) 2.8 (*b*) 3.0

(*c*) 3.2 (*d*) 3.6 **(CLAT 2011)**

**21.** If 0.06% of a number is 84, then 30% of that number is

(*a*) 25.2 (*b*) 420

(*c*) 42000 (*d*) 2520 **(CLAT 2012)**

**22.** In a factory, the production of scooters rose to 48400 from 40000 in 2 years. The rate of growth per annum is

(*a*) 20% (*b*) 10%

(*c*) 30% (*d*) 8% **(CLAT 2012)**

**23.** Out of the total income, X spends 20% on house rent and 70% of the remaining amount on household expenditure. If X saves ₹ 1800, the total income is

(*a*) ₹ 8000 (*b*) ₹ 9500

(*c*) ₹ 7500 (*d*) ₹ 8500 **(CLAT 2012)**

**24.** Divya purchased 6 mangoes, 10 oranges and 5 apples for a certain amount. With 40% less amount Anu could purchase 3 mangoes, 5 oranges and 4 apples. What percentage of the total amount did Divya spend on apples ?

(*a*) 25% (*b*) 33.333% **(AILET 2013)**

(*c*) 40% (*d*) can't be determined

**25.** A single discount equivalent to a discount series 15% and 5% is **(CLAT 2013)**

(*a*) 32% (*b*) 20%

(*c*) 10% (*d*) 8.5%

**26.** The population of a city is 250 thousand. It is increasing at the rate of 2% every year. The growth in the population after 2 years is **(CLAT 2013)**

(*a*) 2500 (*b*) 10000

(*c*) 252000 (*d*) 10100

**27.** Mohan credits 15% of his salary into his bank and spends 30% of the remaining amount on household articles. If cash on hand is ₹ 2,3801-, what is his salary ? **(AILET 2014)**

(*a*) ₹ 5,000 (*b*) ₹ 4,500

(*c*) ₹ 4,000 (*d*) ₹ 3,500

**28.** 72% of students in a class took Physics and 44% took Mathematics. If each student took Physics or Mathematics and 40 took both, the total number of students in the class would be

(*a*) 200 (*b*) 240 **(AILET 2014)**

(*c*) 250 (*d*) 320

**29.** If 80% of A = 20% of B and B = 5x% of A, then the value of x is: **(CLAT 2014)**

(*a*) 75 (*b*) 80

(*c*) 90 (*d*) 85

## Solutions

**1.** b Price of petrol before the hike = ₹28 per liter

Price of petrol after the hike = ₹ (1.07 × 28) per liter = ₹29.96 per liter.

For traveling 2400 kms, total quantity of petrol consumed

$$= \frac{2400}{18} = 133.33 \text{ liters}$$

Increase in expenditure = ₹(29.96 – 28) × 133.33

= ₹261.32 = ₹262

**2.** b Consider first and second piece of bronze be x kg and (60 – x) kg respectively.

According to the given condition:

$$\frac{8}{60-x} - \frac{10}{x} = \frac{15}{100}$$

$$\frac{8x - 600 + 10x}{x(60-x)} = \frac{3}{20}$$

3x^2 + 180 x – 12000 = 0

x = 40

therefore % age of zinc in in the first piece of bronze

$$= \frac{10}{40} \times 100 = 25\%$$

**3.** c Let A's salary be ₹A and B's salary be ₹B

Final salary of A = A × 1.25 × 0.8

Final salary of B = B × 1.20 × 0.75

∵ Result is same.

⇒ A × 1.25 × 0.80 = B × 1.20 × 0.75

$$\Rightarrow \frac{B}{A} = \frac{1.25 \times 0.80}{1.20 \times 0.75} = \frac{10}{9} \text{ or } 10:9$$

**4.** a 30% of 40% of 560 $= \frac{30}{100} \times \frac{40}{100} \times 560$

$$= \frac{12}{100} \times 560 = 67.2$$

Also, 60% of 40% of 280

$$= \frac{60}{100} \times \frac{40}{100} \times 280$$

$$= \frac{24}{100} \times 280 = 67.2.$$

**5.** d Initial number of members = 500

Number of members at beginning of 3rd year

$$= 500 \times \left(1 + \frac{10}{100}\right)^2 = 605.$$

**6.** a Present value of share = ₹100

Dividend on ₹ 100 shares = ₹12

Let the value of share at the time of purchase be ₹ x. Then,

$$\frac{15}{100} \times x = 12 \text{ or } x = 80$$

The shares were bought at price of ₹ 80.

**7.** d Let the price of the article be ₹100.

New price = 0.9 × 100 = ₹90

Hence, required percentage increase

$$= \frac{10}{90} \times 100 = 11\frac{1}{9}\%.$$

**8.** d Let the value of car 4 years ago be ₹x

According to question,

$$x\left(1-\frac{10}{100}\right)^4 = 52,488 \text{ or } x = 80,000$$

Hence, required answer = ₹ 80,000.

**9.** b Let the maximum number of marks be x.

$$\therefore \quad \frac{45}{100}x - \frac{25}{100}x = 70$$

$$\Rightarrow \quad \frac{20}{100}x = 70$$

$$\Rightarrow \quad x = 70 \times 5 = 350$$

Hence, the maximum number of marks is 350.

**10.** b Let the original length of the rectangle be x and original breadth be y.

∴ Original area = xy

Now, new length = 1.15x

New breadth = 0.85y

∴ New area = 0.9775xy

Percentage change

$$= \frac{0.9775xy - xy}{xy} \times 100 = -2.25\%,$$

where negative sign shows a decrease in the area of rectangle so formed.

**Short cut:**

Using successive percentage change method:

$$= -15 + 15 - \frac{15 \times 15}{100} = -2.25\%$$

**11.** a Required percentage $= \frac{1}{8} \times 100 = 12.5\%$.

**12.** c As we know that 12.5% is equivalent to $\left(\frac{1}{8}\right)$ of a certain quantity.

Thus, required value $= \left(\frac{1}{8}\right) \times 80 = 10$

**13.** c Option (*a*) $= \frac{9}{10} = 0.9$; Option (*b*) $= \frac{11}{12} = 0.9167$

Option (*c*) $= \frac{23}{28} = 0.82$; Option (*d*) $= \frac{32}{33} = 0.96$

Thus, $\frac{23}{28}$ is the smallest among the given fractions.

**14.** * **There is some error in the question as no information is given regarding the amount paid by any one of them.**

**15.** c Let us assume Shyam's income be ₹ 100.

Thus, Ram's income = 100 – 20 = ₹ 80

Difference in their income = ₹ 100 – ₹ 80 = ₹ 20

Required percentage $= \left(\frac{20}{80}\right) \times 100 = 25\%$.

**16.** c Ratio between male to female

= 1000 : 1075 = 40 : 43

Number of males in the town

$$= 155625 \times \left(\frac{40}{83}\right) = 75000$$

Number of females in the town

$$= 155625 - 75000 = 80625$$

Number of literate, in town

$$= 75000 \times 0.4 + 80625 \times 0.24$$

$$= 30000 + 19350 = 49350$$

Required percentage $= \frac{49350}{155625} \times 100 = 31.7\%$

**17.** b 12% of 5000 $= \frac{12}{100} \times 5000 = 12 \times 50 = 600$.

**18.** b $\frac{3}{5} = 0.6$, $\frac{4}{3} = 1.33$, $\frac{2}{5} = 0.4$ and $\frac{1}{2} = 0.5$

Also, it is clear from the options that the numerator is greater than the denominator only in case of $\frac{4}{3}$. Thus, $\frac{4}{3}$ has the highest value.

**19.** c (i) Tax for first ₹1,50,000 = 0

(ii) Tax for ₹1,50,001 to ₹3,00,000

$$= (3,00,000 - 1,50,000) \times \frac{10}{100} = ₹\ 1,500$$

(iii) Tax for ₹ 3,00,001 to ₹5,00,000

$$= (5,00,00 - 3,00,000) \times \frac{20}{100} = ₹\ 40,000$$

Total tax liability of Jogen

= 0 + ₹ 15,000 + ₹40,000 = ₹55,000.

**20.** c Let l, b and h be length, breath and height of the brick respectively.

Original volume of the brick = lbh

Volume after change in dimensions

= 1.1l × 1.1h × 0.8b = 0.968 lbh

∴ Required percentage change in volume

$$= \frac{lbh - 0.968lbh}{lbh} \times 100 = 3.2\%.$$

**21.** c Let the number be x.

According to the question, we get

0.06% of x = 84

⇒ x = 140000

∴ 30% of x = 30% of 140000

$$= \frac{30}{100} \times 140000 = 42000.$$

**22.** b Let the rate of growth per annum be r%.

According to the question, we get

$$48400 = 40000\left(1+\frac{r}{100}\right)^2$$

$$\Rightarrow \left(\frac{22}{20}\right)^2 = \left(1+\frac{r}{100}\right)^2$$

$\Rightarrow$ r = 10%.

**23.** c Let the total income be ₹x.

Amount spent on house rent = ₹0.2x

Remaining amount = (x – 0.2x) = ₹0.8 x.

Amount spent on household expenditure

= 0.7 × 0.8x = ₹0.56x

His savings = ₹1,800.

**24.** b Let the price of 1 Mango, 1 Orange and 1 Apple be M, O and A respectively. If ₹ x be the total amount with Divya, then

6M + 10O + 5A = x ...(i)

3M + 5O + 4A = 0.6x ...(ii)

Multiply (ii) by 2 and then subtract (i) from it, we get

$$A = \frac{0.2x}{3}$$

Hence, percentage of total amount spend an apples

$$= \frac{5A}{x} \times 100 = 33.33\%.$$

**25.** * (Correct answer not present in the given options)

Let the amount on which discount is being offered be ₹ 100

SP after the first discount of 15%

= ₹ (100 – 15) = ₹ 85

SP after second discount of 5 %

$$= ₹\left(85 - \frac{5}{100}\times 85\right) = ₹\ 80.75$$

Hence net discount percentage

$$= \frac{100-80.75}{100}\times 100 = 19.25\%$$

**26.** d Population of the city after two years

$$= 250000\times\left(1+\frac{2}{100}\right)^2 = 260100.$$

Hence the required growth

= 260100 – 250000 = 10100.

**27.** c Let the salary of Mohan be ₹x.

$\therefore x\times(1-0.15)\times(1-0.3) = 2380 \Rightarrow x = 4000.$

**28.** c The percentage of students who took both the subjects = (72 + 44) – 100 = 16.

the total number of students in the class $\frac{60}{0.16} = 375.$

**29.** b A . 0.80 = B . 0.20 $\Rightarrow \frac{B}{A} = 4 \Rightarrow 5x\% = 4 \Rightarrow x = 80$

## PROFIT, LOSS AND DISCOUNT

**1.** The cost of setting up the type of a magazine is ₹ 1000. the cost of running the printing machine is ₹ 120 per 100 copies, the cost of paper, ink and so on is 60 paise per copy. The magazines are sold at ₹ 2.75 each. 900 copies are printed, but only 784 copies are sold. What is the sum to be obtained from advertisements to give a profit of 10% on the cost?

(*a*) ₹ 730 (*b*) ₹ 720

(*c*) ₹ 726 (*d*) ₹ 736 **(AILET, 2008)**

**2.** A man sells 5 articles for ₹15 and makes a profit of 20%. Find his gain or loss percent if he sells 8 such articles for ₹8.40. **(AILET, 2009)**

(*a*) 2.22% profit (*b*) 2.22% loss

(*c*) 8% loss (*d*) 8%profit

**3.** A shopkeeper mixes two varieties of Tea, one costing ₹40/kg and another ₹50/kg in the ratio 3 : 2. If he sells the mixed variety of Tea at ₹48/kg, his gain or loss percent is

(*a*) 48.4% gain (*b*) 48.4% loss

(*c*) 10% gain (*d*) 10% loss **(AILET, 2011)**

**4.** A publisher sells books to retailer at marked price which is 20% above his outlay. If on cash payment, he allows a discount of 10% on the marked price. The publisher thus gains:

(*a*) 12% (*b*) 10%

(*c*) 8% (*d*) 14% **(AILET, 2012)**

**5.** Sanjay sold his watch for ₹ 1140 and thereby loses 5%. In order to gain 5% he has to sell the watch for

(*a*) ₹ 1254 (*b*) ₹ 1260

(*c*) ₹ 1197 (*d*) ₹ 1311 **(CLAT 2008)**

**6.** A dishonest shopkeeper uses a weight of 800 gm for a kg and professes to sell his good at cost price. His profit is

(*a*) 20% (*b*) 21%

(*c*) 24% (*d*) 25% **(CLAT 2009)**

**7.** By selling 11 oranges for a rupee, a man loses 10%. How many oranges for a rupee should he sell to gain 10%?

(*a*) 9 (*b*) 10

(*c*) 8 (*d*) 5 **(CLAT 2009)**

**8.** A customised jewellery was sold at ₹1000 with 90% discount on the 'making charges'. If the payment made for making charges was ₹100, what is the *approximate* rate of discount on the product?

(*a*) 35 (*b*) 45

(*c*) 47 (*d*) 90 **(CLAT 2011)**

**9.** Francis has 18 eggs, out of which 12 eggs were sold at 10% loss than the cost price. At what mark up price should he sell the remaining eggs to cover his losses?

(*a*) 5% (*b*) 10%

(*c*) 15% (*d*) 20% **(CLAT 2008)**

**10.** P sells a table to Q at a profit of 10% and Q sells it to R at a profit of 12%. If R pays ₹246.40 for it, then how much had P paid for it?
(*a*) 200.00 (*b*) 300.00
(*c*) 248.00 (*d*) 346.00 **(CLAT 2012)**

**11.** A dealer buys an article for ₹ 380.00. What price should he mark so that after allowing a discount of 5% he still makes a profit of 25% on the article?
(*a*) ₹500 (*b*) ₹475
(*c*) ₹95 (*d*) ₹465 **(CLAT 2012)**

**12.** Devendra, a computer accessories vendor gave a discount of 20% on a pen-drive and his profit reduced from ₹ 200 to ₹ 100. What is Devendra's cost price ?
(*a*) ₹ 300 (*b*) ₹ 200 **(AILET 2013)**
(*c*) ₹ 400 (*d*) None of these

**13.** By selling a cycle for ₹ 2345, a student loses 19%. His cost price is nearly **(CLAT 2013)**
(*a*) ₹ 4000 (*b*) ₹ 5000
(*c*) ₹ 3000 (*d*) ₹ 3500

**14.** If selling price of 10 articles is equal to cost price of 11 articles, then gain is **(CLAT 2013)**
(*a*) 8% (*b*) 9%
(*c*) 8.5% (*d*) 10%

**15.** A dealer marked his goods 20% above the cost price and allows a discount of 10%. Then the gain percent is:
(*a*) 2% (*b*) 4% **(CLAT 2014)**
(*c*) 6% (*d*) 8%

## Solutions

**1.** c Total Cost Price = ₹ (1000 + 120 × 9 + 0.60 × 900) = ₹2620

Total Selling Price = ₹ (784 × 2.75) = ₹ 2156

For having 10% profit, the selling price should be ₹ (1.1 × 2620) = ₹ 2882

Sum to be obtained from the advertisements = ₹ (2882 – 2156) = ₹726

**2.** c CP of 5 articles = $\frac{15}{1.2}$ = ₹12.5

∴ CP of 1 article = $\frac{12.5}{5}$ = ₹ 2.5

∴ CP of 8 such articles = 8 × 2.5 = ₹20

∴ SP of 8 such articles = ₹18.40

∴ Loss = ₹20 – ₹18.40 = ₹1.60

Hence, loss percentage = $\frac{1.60}{20} \times 100 = 8\%$.

**3.** c Using alligations,

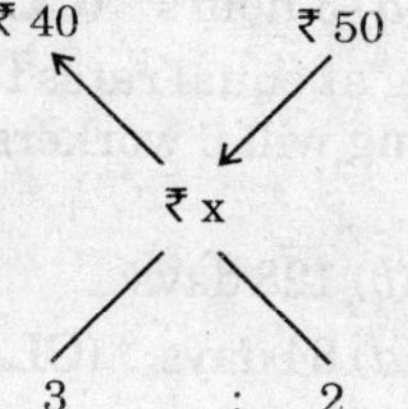


$$\frac{50 - x}{x - 40} = \frac{3}{2} \text{ or } x = 44$$

Hence, required profit percentage

$$= \frac{4}{44} \times 100 = 9.09\%$$

**4.** c Let the marked price be ₹x.

Then, cost price is $\frac{1}{1.2}x = ₹\ \frac{5}{6}x$

And the selling price is $\frac{90}{100}x = ₹\ \frac{9}{10}x$

∴ Profit percentage = $\frac{\text{S.P.} - \text{C.P}}{\text{C.P}} \times 100$

$$= \frac{\frac{9}{10}x - \frac{5}{6}x}{\frac{5}{6}x} \times 100 = 8\%.$$

**Alternate solution:**

$$20 - 10 - \frac{20 + 10}{100} = 8\%$$

**5.** b Let the new S.P. be x.

Then, 1st S.P. = $\frac{\text{C.P.} \times (100 - \text{loss}\%)}{100}$

$\Rightarrow \frac{1140 \times 100}{(100 - 5\%)} = \text{C.P.}$

2nd S.P. = $\frac{\text{C.P.} \times (100 + \text{Gain}\%)}{100}$

$\Rightarrow x = \frac{1140 \times (105)}{95}$

⇒ New S.P. = ₹ 1260.

**6.** d It should be noted that he uses 800 gm weight for 1000 gm.

Difference in weight = 1000 – 800 = 200 gm

Profit percentage = $\frac{200}{800} \times 100 = 25\%$

**7.** a SP of 11 oranges = Re. 1

SP of an orange = Re. $\frac{1}{11}$

CP of an orange (Using the concept of multiplying index)

$$\text{MF} = \frac{\text{SP}}{\text{CP}}$$

$$\text{CP} = \frac{\left(\frac{1}{11}\right)}{0.9} = \text{Re. } \frac{10}{99}$$

SP of an orange if sold on profit (Using the concept of multiplying index)

$$\text{SP} = 1.1 \times \frac{10}{99} = \text{Re. } \frac{1}{9}$$

Number of oranges sold for a rupee = 1/(1/9) = 9

**8.** c Since 10% of making charges is ₹100, total making charges = ₹1,000.

Marked Price = 1000 + 900 = ₹1,900

Discount offered in percentage

$$= \frac{900 \times 100}{19} \times 100 \approx 47\%.$$

**9.** d Let x (in ₹) be the price of one egg.

Then, price of 12 eggs = ₹12x

Selling price of 12 eggs =₹12x × 0.9 = ₹10.8x

Price to be recovered by selling 6 eggs

= 1.2x + 6x = ₹7.2x

∴ Percentage mark-up

$$= \frac{7.2x - 6x}{6x} \times 100\% = 20\%.$$

**10.** a Let P paid ₹x for the table.

Then, 1.1 × 1.12x = 246.40

⇒ x = 200.

**11.** a Let the marked price of the article be ₹x.

Therefore, discount = ₹0.05x

S.P. = x – 0.05x = ₹0.95x

$$\Rightarrow \quad 0.95x = \frac{(100 + 25) \times 380}{100}$$

$$\Rightarrow \quad x = \frac{125 \times 380}{95}$$

⇒ x = 500

Hence, marked price of the article is ₹500.

**12.** a Let ₹ c be Devendra's cost price, then

(c + 200) × 0.2 = 200 – 100

⇒ c = 300.

**13.** * (Correct answer not present in the given options)

Let the CP be ₹ x.

Loss = ₹ (x – 2345)

$$\text{Loss percent} = \frac{x - 2345}{x} \times 100 = 19$$

⇒ x = 2895.

Hence the CP was ₹ 2895.

**14.** d Let the cost price of 1 article be ₹ 1.

Cost price of 10 articles = ₹ 10.

Selling price of 10 articles

= Cost price of 11 articles = ₹ 11.

$$\text{Profit} = \frac{(11 - 10)}{10} \times 100 = 10\%.$$

**15.** d Let the CP of the goods be Rs. 100.

$SP = 100 \times 1.2 \times 0.9 = 108$

Percentage profit = 8.

## TIME AND WORK

**1.** The Bubna dam has four inlets. Through the first three inlets, the dam can be filled in 12 minutes; through the second, the third and the fourth inlet, it can be filled in 15 minutes; and through the first and the first inlet, in 20 minutes. How much time will it take all the four inlets to fill up the dam?

(*a*) 8 min (*b*) 10 min
(*c*) 12 min (*d*) None of these

**(AILET, 2008)**

**2.** Ajit can do as much work in 2 days as Baljit can do in 3 days and Baljit can do as much in 4 days as Diljit in 5 days. A piece of work takes 20 days if all work together. How long would Baljit take to do all the work by himself?

(*a*) 82 days (*b*) 44 days
(*c*) 66 days (*d*) 50 days **(AILET, 2009)**

**3.** 10 men can finish the construction of a hut in 8 days. How many men are needed to finish the same in half a day?

(*a*) 80 (*b*) 100
(*c*) 120 (*d*) 160 **(AILET, 2010)**

**4.** 16 men can do a piece of work in 16 days. 4 days after they started the work, 8 more men joined them. How many days will they now take to complete the remaining work?

(*a*) 10 days (*b*) 6 days
(*c*) 8 days (*d*) 12 days **(AILET, 2011)**

**5.** A group of workers accepted to do a piece of work in 25 days. If 6 of them did not turn up for the work and the remaining workers did the work in 40 days, then the original number of workers was

(*a*) 22 (*b*) 18
(*c*) 20 (*d*) 16 **(AILET, 2012)**

**6.** Two taps 'A' and 'B' can fill a water reservoir in 8 and 6 hours respectively. A third tap 'C' can empty the tank completely in 24 hours. How long would it take to fill the empty tank when all the taps are open?

(*a*) 4 hours (*b*) 5 hours
(*c*) 6 hours (*d*) 3 hours **(AILET, 2012)**

**7.** A tank can be filled up by two pipes A and B in 2 hours and 3 hours respectively. A third pipe C can empty the full tank in 6 hours. If all the taps can be turned on at the same time, the tank will be full in

(*a*) 1 hour (*b*) 40 minutes
(*c*) 1 1/2 hours (*d*) 3 hours **(CLAT 2008)**

**8.** It takes 8 people working at equal rates to finish a work in 96 days. How long will 6 workers take for the same work?

(*a*) 92 days (*b*) 128 days
(*c*) 111 days (*d*) 84 days **(CLAT 2009)**

**9.** Four gardeners with four grass mowers mow 400 square meters of ground in four hours. How long would it take for eight gardeners with eight grass mowers to mow 800 square meters of ground?

(*a*) 8 hours (*b*) 6 hours

(*c*) 12 hours (*d*) 4 hours **(CLAT 2010)**

**10.** 120 men had food provision for 200 days. After 5 days, 30 men died of an epidemic. The food will last for further

(*a*) 280 days (*b*) 260 days

(*c*) 290 days (*d*) 252 days **(CLAT 2012)**

**11.** A contractor Abhay Singh employed some men to do a piece of work which can be done by 16 men in 14 days. At the end of 5 days, 7 of the men stopped working and 3 days later half of the remainder stopped working; the rest finished the work in 5 days. What is the number of men originally employed ?

(*a*) 25 (*b*) 27

(*c*) 29 (*d*) 33 **(AILET 2013)**

**12.** There is leak in the bottom of a tank. This leak can empty a full tank in 8 hours. When the tank is full, a tap is opened into the tank which admits 6 litres per hour and the tank is now emptied in 12 hours. What is the capacity of the tank ?

(*a*) 28.8 litres (*b*) 36 litres **(AILET 2013)**

(*c*) 144 litres (*d*) 145 litres

**13.** Pipe A can fill a tank in 10 hours and pipe B can fill the same tank in 12 hour. Both the pipes are opened to fill the tank and after 3 hours pipe A is closed. Pipe B will fill the remaining part of the tank in **(CLAT 2013)**

(*a*) 5 hours (*b*) 4 hours

(*c*) 5 hours 24 minutes (*d*) 3 hours

**14.** In a call centre, 6 employees working for 10 hours complete a certain task. They started working at 11:00 am. This continued till 5:00 pm and after that, for each hour one more employee is added till the work gets completed. At what time will they complete the work ? **(AILET 2014)**

(*a*) 7:10 pm (*b*) 8:00 pm

(*c*) 7:35 pm (*d*) 6:35 pm

**15.** 'A' can do a piece of work in 20 days and 'B' can do the same work in 15 days. How long will they take to finish the work, if both work together?

(*a*) $13\frac{1}{2}$ days (*b*) 10 days **(CLAT 2014)**

(*c*) $8\frac{4}{7}$ days (*d*) $17\frac{1}{2}$ days

## Solutions

**1.** b Consider the 4 inlet pipes be A, B, C and D

According to given condition :

$$\frac{1}{A}+\frac{1}{B}+\frac{1}{C}=\frac{1}{12} \quad (1)$$

$$\frac{1}{B}+\frac{1}{C}+\frac{1}{D}=\frac{1}{15} \quad (2)$$

$$\frac{1}{A}+\frac{1}{D}=\frac{1}{20} \quad (3)$$

adding the above equations :

$$2\left(\frac{1}{A}+\frac{1}{B}+\frac{1}{C}+\frac{1}{D}\right)=\frac{1}{12}+\frac{1}{15}+\frac{1}{20}$$

therefore , $\frac{1}{A}+\frac{1}{B}+\frac{1}{C}+\frac{1}{D}=\frac{1}{10}$

ie. The four inlets can fill the dam in 10 min.

**2.** c Ratio of time taken by Ajit, Baljit and Daljit

$= 8 : 12 : 15 = 8x : 12x : 15x$

According to the given condition,

$\Rightarrow \frac{1}{8x}+\frac{1}{12x}+\frac{1}{15x}=\frac{1}{20}$

$\Rightarrow \frac{15+10+8}{120x}=\frac{1}{20}$

$\Rightarrow \frac{33}{120x}=\frac{1}{20}$

$\Rightarrow x=\frac{11}{2}$

Hence, time taken by Baljit alone to complete the work

$=12\times\frac{11}{2}=66$ days.

**3.** d $M_1 \times D_1 = M_2 \times D_2$

$\Rightarrow 10 \times 8 = M_2 \times \frac{1}{2}$

$\Rightarrow M_2 = 160.$

**4.** c Number of men days required = $16 \times 16 = 256$

Number of men days completed in 4 days

$= 16 \times 4 = 64$

Number of men on work after 4 days

$= 16 + 8 = 24$

From this instant onwards work will be completed in

$\frac{256-64}{24}=8$ days.

**5.** d Let the original number of workers who could complete the work in 25 days be x.

So one worker would have completed the work in 25x days.

Also, the number of workers who completed the work in 40 days = x – 6

$\therefore$ One worker completed the work in 40(x – 6) days.

As the number of days required by one worker to complete the work is constant, therefore,

$25x = 40(x - 6).$

On solving the above equation, we get x = 16.

Hence, original number of workers was 16.

**6.** a Part of the tank filled in one hour by 'A' = $\frac{1}{8}$

Part of the tank filled in one hour by 'B' = $\frac{1}{6}$

Part of the tank emptied in one hour by 'C' = $\frac{1}{24}$.

$\therefore$ Part of the tank filled in one hour by the three pipes together

$= \frac{1}{8}+\frac{1}{6}-\frac{1}{24}=\frac{1}{4}$

$\therefore$ The entire tank will be filled by the three pipes together in 4 hours.

**Alternate solution**

Capacity of the tank = LCM(8, 6, 24) = 24 units

Number of units filled by tap A in one hour = 3

Number of units filled by tap B in one hour = 4

Number of units emptied by tap C in one hour = 1

Number of units filled by all three taps in one hour

= 3 + 4 – 1 = 6

Hence, the tank will be filled in $\frac{24}{6} = 4$ hours.

**7.** c Net part filled in 1 hour = $\frac{1}{2}+\frac{1}{3}-\frac{1}{6}=\frac{4}{6}$

$\therefore$ The tank will be full in $\frac{6}{4}$ hours, i.e. $1\frac{1}{2}$ hours.

**8.** b Let us assume that 6 workers will take 'n' days. Then,

$8 \times 96 = 6 \times n$

$n = 8 \times \left(\frac{96}{6}\right) = 8 \times 16 = 128$ days

**9.** d In both the cases, one gardener is using one grass mower.

We know, $\frac{(M_1 \times H_1)}{W_1} = \frac{(M_2 \times H_2)}{W_2}$

$\therefore \quad \frac{(4\times 4)}{400} = \frac{(8\times H_2)}{800}$

$\Rightarrow \quad H_2 = 4$ hours.

**10.** b Originally, the food would have lasted for 200 days.

Number of men who died after 5 days = 30

$\therefore$ Number of men left = 90

Let the food that would have been consumed by 120 men in 195 days was consumed by 90 men in x days.

$\therefore \quad 120 \times 195 = 90 \times x$

$\Rightarrow \quad x = 260$ days.

**11.** a Let the number of men originally employed be x, then

$\Rightarrow \quad 16\times 14 = x\times 5 + (x-7)\times 3 + \frac{(x-7)}{2}\times 5$

$\Rightarrow \quad x = 25.$

**12.** c Let x litres per hour be the rate at which water comes out from the leak, then

$x \times 8 = (x - 6) \times 12$

$\Rightarrow \quad x = 18$

Hence, capacity of the tank = 18 × 8 = 144 litres.

**13.** c Part of the tank filled by pipe A and pipe B together in 3 hours = $\left(\frac{1}{10}+\frac{1}{12}\right)\times 3 = \frac{33}{60}$.

Remaining part of the tank to be filled = $\frac{27}{60}$

Time taken by B to fill the remaining part of the tank = $\frac{\left(\frac{27}{60}\right)}{\left(\frac{1}{12}\right)} = \frac{27}{5}$ hours

i.e. 5 hours and 24 minutes.

**14.** b Let the total work to be done is 60 units.

Unit of work done 11 am to 5 pm = 6 × 6 = 36.

Remaining work = 24 units.

From 5 pm onwards the unit of work done in every consecutive hours will be 7, 8, 9 and so on.

Hence, in three hours after 5pm (at 8 pm) the remaining work will get completed i.e. 7 + 8 + 9 = 24 units.

**15.** c The part of work done by A and B together in one day $= \frac{1}{20}+\frac{1}{15}=\frac{7}{60}$

The required number of day $= \frac{60}{7} = 8\frac{4}{7}$.

## SIMPLE INTEREST AND COMPOUND INTEREST

**1.** A sum is divided between A and B in the ratio of 1 : 2. A purchased a car from his part, which depreciates per annum and B deposited his amount in a bank, which pays him 20% interest per annum compounded annually. By what percentage will the total sum of money increase after two years due to this investment pattern (approximately).

(*a*) 20% (*b*) 26.66%
(*c*) 30% (*d*) 25% **(AILET, 2008)**

**2.** What is the simple interest for 9 years on a sum of ₹800 if the rate of interest for the first 4 years is 8% per annum and for the last 4 years is 6% per annum?

(*a*) 400 (*b*) 392 **(AILET, 2009)**
(*c*) 352 (*d*) Cannot be determined

**3.** Kirti took loan of ₹800 at the rate of 11% per year for 7 months. After seven months she has to pay

(*a*) ₹851 (*b*) ₹852
(*c*) ₹950 (*d*) ₹951 **(AILET, 2011)**

**4.** A certain sum of money was deposited in a bank and it became two-fold in 10 years. What is the rate of simple interest?

(*a*) 8% (*b*) 10%
(*c*) 12% (*d*) 13% **(AILET, 2012)**

**5.** If ₹80 amounts to ₹140 in 4 years, what will ₹ 96 amount to in 10 years at the same rate of interest per annum?

(*a*) ₹276 (*b*) ₹306
(*c*) ₹386 (*d*) ₹300 **(AILET, 2012)**

**6.** Ram borrows ₹520 from Govind at a simple interest of 13% per annum. What amount of money (in ₹) should Ram pay to Govind after six months to be absolved of the debt?

(*a*) 552.80 (*b*) 553.80
(*c*) 453.80 (*d*) 353.80 **(CLAT 2010)**

**7.** The difference between the simple interest and the compound interest (compounded annually) on ₹2000 for 2 yr at 8% per annum will be:

(*a*) ₹10 (*b*) ₹20
(*c*) ₹13 (*d*) ₹25 **(CLAT 2014)**

### Solutions

**1.** a Let the total amount be ₹ 300

Amount with A and B is ₹100 and ₹200 respectively.

Value of the car bought by A after 2 years

$$= 100\left(1-\left(\frac{1}{7}\right)\right)^2 = ₹\,73.469$$

Value of the money deposited by B after 2 years

$= 200\ (1 + 0.2)^2 = ₹\ 288$

Total worth of money with A and B after 2 years

= ₹ 73.469 + ₹ 288 = ₹ 361.469

Percentage increase (approximate)

= ((361.469 – 300)/300) x 100 = 20%

**2.** d The answer to the question is "cannot be determined". As no information is given regarding one of the years.

**3.** a $\text{S.I.} = P \times T \times \frac{R}{100}$

Amount to be paid after 7 months

$$= 800 + 800 \times \frac{7}{12} \times \frac{11}{100} \approx ₹851.$$

**4.** b Let the principal be ₹P and the rate of interest per annum be r%.

As the amount became two-folded in 10 years, it implies that the simple interest for 10 years is equal to the principal, ₹P.

Hence, $P = \frac{P \times r \times 10}{100} \Rightarrow r = 10\%$.

**5.** a Let the simple rate of interest per annum be r%.

$$\therefore \quad (140 - 80) = \frac{80 \times r \times 4}{100}$$

$$\Rightarrow \quad r = \frac{100 \times 60}{80 \times 4} = \frac{75}{4}$$

Again, for 10 years,

$$\text{S.I.} = \frac{96 \times \frac{75}{4} \times 10}{100} = ₹180$$

Hence, amount after 10 years

= S.I. + ₹96 = ₹276.

**6.** b $\text{S.I.} = \frac{P \times r \times t}{100}$, where P is principal, r is rate of interest and t is time.

$$\text{S.I.} = 520 \times \frac{1}{2} \times \frac{13}{100} = ₹\,33.80$$

Total amount to be paid

= ₹ 520 + ₹ 33.80 = ₹ 553.80.

**7.** c The required difference

$$= P\left(\frac{r}{100}\right)^2 = 2000 \times \left(\frac{8}{100}\right)^2 = 12.8 \approx 13.$$

## TIME, SPEED AND DISTANCE

**1.** An ant moved for several seconds and covered 3 mm in the first second and 4 mm more in each successive second than in its predecessor. If the ant had covered 1 mm in first second and 8 m more in each successive second, then the difference between the path it would cover during the same time and the actual path would be more than 6 mm but less than 30 mm. Find the time for which the ant moved (in seconds).

(*a*) 5 s (*b*) 4 s **(AILET, 2008)**
(*c*) 6 s (*d*) None of these

**2.** A train travels with a speed of 20 m/s in the first 10 minutes, goes 8.5 kms in the next 10 minutes, 11 kms in the next 10 minutes, 8.5 kms in the next 10 and 6 kms in the next 10 minutes. What is the average speed of the train in kilometer per hour for the journey described? **(AILET, 2008)**

(*a*) 42 kmph (*b*) 35.8 kmph
(*c*) 55.2 kmph (*d*) 46 kmph

**3.** Amar and Akbar left Bhubaneshwar simultaneously and travelled towards Cuttack. Amar's speed was 15 km/h and that of Akbar was 12km/h. Half an hour later, Anthony left Bhubaneshwar and travelled in the same direction. Some time later, he overtook Akbar and 90 minutes further on he overtook Amar. Find Anthony's speed.

(*a*) 18 kmph (*b*) 24 kmph
(*c*) 12 kmph (*d*) 16 kmph

**(AILET, 2009)**

**4.** An express train travels at an average speed of 120 km per hour, stopping for 4 minutes after every 80 kms. How long will it take the train to reach a destination 960 km away? **(AILET, 2010)**

(*a*) 8 hrs 40 mts (*b*) 8 hrs 44 mts
(*c*) 8 hrs 48 mts (*d*) 8 hrs 56 mts

**5.** A student rides a bicycle at 8 km/hr and reaches the school 2.5 minutes late. The next day he increases the speed to 10 km/hr and reaches school 5 minutes early. How far is the school from his house?

(*a*) 4 kms (*b*) 8 kms
(*c*) 5 kms (*d*) 10 kms **(AILET, 2011)**

**6.** A train 100 meters long running at 54 km/hr takes 20 seconds to pass a bridge. The length of the bridge is

(*a*) 50 mt (*b*) 150 mt

(*c*) 200 mt (*d*) 620 mt **(CLAT 2008)**

**7.** A person takes 3 hours to walk a certain distance and riding back. He could walk both ways in 5 hours. How long could it take to ride both ways.

(*a*) 1.5 hr (*b*) 1 hr

(*c*) 0.5 hr (*d*) 2 hrs **(CLAT 2009)**

**8.** A man walks from his house to the Railway Station to catch a train, which is running as per schedule. If he walks at 6 km/hr, He misses the train by 9 minutes. However, if he walks at 7 km/hr, he reaches the station 6 minutes before the departure of train. The distance between his home and the Railway Station is:

(*a*) 20 km (*b*) 15 km

(*c*) 10.5 km (*d*) 12.5 km **(CLAT 2011)**

**9.** A train 300 meters long is running at a speed of 25 meters per second, it will cross a bridge 200 meters long in **(CLAT 2012)**

(*a*) 5 seconds (*b*) 10 seconds

(*c*) 20 seconds (*d*) 25 seconds

**10.** Ram is travelling by car at the rate of 40 kmph. After 80 km he rests for 20 minutes. How long will he take to cover a distance of 240 kms ?

(*a*) 6 hrs 40 min (*b*) 6 hrs 11 min

(*c*) 5 hrs 11 min (*d*) 7 hrs 15 min

**(AILET 2013)**

**11.** A and B walk from X to Y, a distance of 27 km at 5 km/hr and 7 km/hr, respectively. B reaches Y and immediately turns back meeting A at Z. What is the distance from X to Z ?

(*a*) 25 km (*b*) 22.5 km

(*c*) 24 km (*d*) 20 km **(AILET 2013)**

**12.** A person covers a certain distance by car at a speed of 30 km/h and comes back at a speed of 40 km/h. The average speed during the travel is:

(*a*) 34.3 km/h (*b*) 35 km/h **(CLAT 2014)**

(*c*) 37.5 km/h (*d*) 32.8 km/h

**13.** A man can row 5 km/h in still water. If the speed of the current is 1 km/h, it takes 3 h more in upstream than in the downstream for the same distance. The distance is: **(CLAT 2014)**

(*a*) 36 km (*b*) 24 km

(*c*) 20 km (*d*) 32 km

## Solutions

**1.** c Let the ant move for 't' seconds

Required Difference

$= (0.5t(2 + (t - 1)8)) - (0.5t(6 + (t - 1)4))$

$= 4t^2 - 3t - (2t^2 + t) = 2t^2 - 4t$

Also, $6 < 2t^2 - 4t < 30$

So, from the options the value of 't' should be 4s.

**2.** c Distance travelled with speed 20 m/s in the first 10 min. = 12 km

Total distance travelled

$= (12 + 8.5 + 11 + 8.5 + 6) = 46$ km

Total Time = (10 + 10 + 10 + 10 + 10) = 50 min

Therefore Average speed

$$= \frac{46 \,.\, 60}{50} = 55.2 \text{ km/h}$$

**3.** a Let the speed of Anthony be S km/hr and t be the time taken to over took Akbar.

$$\Rightarrow \quad \frac{6}{S-12} = t \quad \text{...(i)}$$

$$\text{and} \quad \frac{7.5}{S-15} = t + \frac{3}{2} \quad \text{...(ii)}$$

On solving equation (i) and (ii), we get

S = 10 or 18 (but Anthony's speed must be greater than that of Amar)

Hence, S = 18 km/hr.

**4.** b Time taken to cover 80 km

$$= \frac{80}{120} \text{hr.} = \frac{2}{3} \times 60 \text{ min} = 40 \text{ min}$$

Stoppage time after 80 km = 4 min

∴ Effective time to cover 80 km

= 40 + 4 = 44 min

As, 960 = 80 × 12

∴ Time taken to cover 960 km

= (44 × 11 + 40) min = 484 + 40 min

= 524 min = 8 hr. 44 min.

(Since, there will be no stoppage after covering the last 80 km)

**5.** c Let the school begins at 't' minutes after the boy leaves his home.

According to question,

$$8 \times \left(\frac{t + 2.5}{60}\right) = 10 \times \left(\frac{t - 5}{60}\right)$$

$\Rightarrow$ 2t = 70 or t = 35

Hence, required distance

$$= 8 \times \left(\frac{t + 2.5}{60}\right) = 10 \times \left(\frac{t - 5}{60}\right) = 5 \text{ km.}$$

**6.** c Time taken by the train to pass a bridge = 20 sec

Let the length of the bridge be 'x' m.

$$\therefore \quad \frac{100 + x}{20} = 15$$

$\Rightarrow$ 100 + x = 300

$\Rightarrow$ x = 200 m

**7.** b Let the time taken in walking and riding the distance be W hrs and R hrs respectively.

$$W + R = 3 \quad \text{...(i)}$$

$$W + W = 5 \quad \text{...(ii)}$$

Using the above two equations, we get

W = 2.5 hrs and R = 0.5 hrs

Thus, time taken to ride both ways

$$= 2 \times 0.5 = 1 \text{ hr.}$$

**8.** c Let D be the distance between man's house and railway station. Then,

$$\frac{D}{6} - \frac{D}{7} = \frac{9+6}{60} = \frac{15}{60} = \frac{1}{4}$$

$\Rightarrow$ D = 10.5 km.

**9.** c Time taken by the train to cross the bridge

$$= \frac{\text{Length of the train + length of the bridge}}{\text{Speed of the train}}$$

$$= \frac{300 + 200}{25} = 20 \text{ seconds.}$$

**10.** a Ram after travelling 80 km (in $\frac{80}{40} = 2$ hours), rests for 20 minutes, therefore in the journey of 240 kms, he will rest twice after travelling 80 kms and 160 kms.

$\therefore$ Total duration of journey

$$= (2 \times 3) \text{ hrs} + (20 \times 2) \text{ min}$$

$$= 6 \text{ hrs } 40 \text{ min.}$$

**11.** b Let the x km be the distance from X to Z, then distance travelled by B before they meet

$$= 27 + (27 - x).$$

$$\therefore \frac{27 + (27 - x)}{7} = \frac{x}{5}$$

$\Rightarrow$ $x = 22.5$.

**12.** a The average speed (in km/h)

$$= \frac{2 \times 30 \times 40}{30 + 40} \approx 34.3$$

**13.** a Let the distance be $x$ km.

$$\therefore \frac{x}{(5-1)} - \frac{x}{(5+1)} = 3 \Rightarrow x = 36.$$

## MIXTURE AND SOLUTIONS

**1.** Two solutions of 90% and 97% purity are mixed resulting in 21 litres of mixture of 94% purity. How much is the quantity of the first solution in the resulting mixture?

(a) 15 liters (b) 12 litres
(c) 9 litres (d) 6 litres **(AILET, 2008)**

**2.** A mixture of 40 litres of milk and water contains 10% of water. How much water is to be added to the mixture so that the water may be 20% in the new mixture. **(CLAT 2008)**

(a) 5 Litres (b) 4 Litres
(c) 6.5 Litres (d) 7.5 Litres

**3.** The ratio of milk and water in 60 Litres of adulterated milk is 2 : 1. If the ratio of milk and water is to be 1 : 2, then the amount of water to be added further is

(a) 20 Litres (b) 30 Litres
(c) 40 Litres (d) 60 Litres **(CLAT 2008)**

**4.** A mixture of 40 L of alcohol and water contains 10% water. How much water should be added to this mixture, so that the new mixture contains 20% water? **(CLAT 2014)**

(a) 9L (b) 5L
(c) 7L (d) 6L

### Solutions

**1.** c By aligation : The ratio in which two solutions are mixed

$$= \frac{97 - 94}{94 - 90} = \frac{3}{4}$$

ie . 3 : 4

Therefore quantity of the first solution in the 21 liters of resulting mixture

$$= 3 \times \frac{21}{7} = 9 \text{ liters}$$

**2.** a Mixture of 40 litres of milk and water contains 10% of water.

$\Rightarrow$ Milk = 36 litres and water = 4 litres

Now let quantity of water to be added be x litres.

New mixture contains 20% of water

$$\therefore \frac{4 + x}{40 + x} \times 100 = 20$$

$$\Rightarrow 20 + 5x = 40 + x$$

$$\Rightarrow x = 5 \text{ litres.}$$

**3.** d Quantity of milk $= \left(60 \times \frac{2}{3}\right)$ litres = 40 litres

Quantity of water = (60 – 40) = 20 litres

New ratio = 1 : 2

Let the quantity of water to be added be x litres.

Then, milk : water $= \frac{40}{(20 + x)}$

$$\therefore \frac{40}{20 + x} = \frac{1}{2}$$

$$\Rightarrow 20 + x = 80$$

$$\Rightarrow x = 60$$

Quantity of water to be further added = 60 litres.

**4.** b Le the amount of water to be added be $x$ L.

$$\therefore \frac{0.1 \times 40 + x}{40 + x} = \frac{20}{100} \Rightarrow x = 5.$$

3

# GEOMETRY AND MENSURATION

## GEOMETRY

1. A flag pole 18 m high casts a shadow 9.6 m long. What is the distance of the top of the pole from the far end of the shadow? **(CLAT 2011)**
   (a) 20 metres (b) 20.04 metres
   (c) 20.4 metres (d) 24 metres

2. Ranjeetha walks around the circular park in 15 minutes. If she walks at the rate of 5 km/hr, how much distance would she have to travel, at the minimum, to reach the centre of the park from any point on its perimeter? **(CLAT 2011)**
   (a) 100 metre (b) 200 metre
   (c) 250 metre (d) 300 metre

3. An angle in a semi circle is **(CLAT 2013)**
   (a) $\pi$ (b) $\frac{\pi}{4}$
   (c) $\frac{\pi}{2}$ (d) $2\pi$

4. If a point $(x, y)$ in a OXY plane is equidistant from (–1, 1) and (4, 3) then **(CLAT 2013)**
   (a) $10x + 4y = 23$ (b) $6x + 4y = 23$
   (c) $-x + y = 7$ (d) $4x + 3y = 0$

5. Angles of a quadrilateral are in the ratio 3 : 4 : 5 : 8. The smallest angle is **(CLAT 2013)**
   (a) 54° (b) 72°
   (c) 36° (d) 18°

### Solutions

**1.** c Let AB be the pole and C be the far end of the shadow.

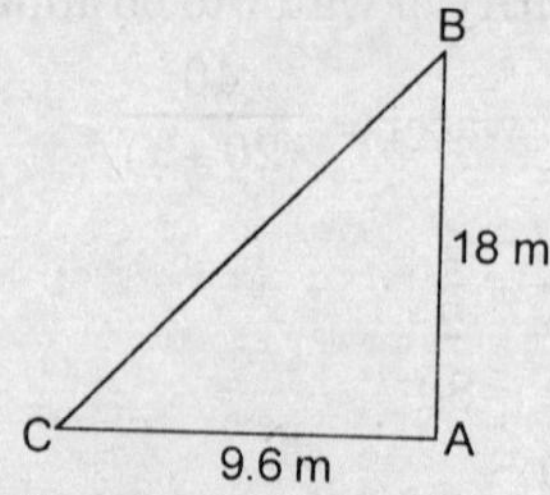


Using Pythagoras' Theorem,

$BC^2 = (18)^2 + (9.6)^2$

$\Rightarrow$ BC = 20.4 meters.

**2.** b Let 'r' be the radius of the park. Then,

$2\pi r = \frac{15}{60} \times 5 \quad \Rightarrow \quad 2 \times \frac{22}{7} \times r = \frac{5}{4}$

$\Rightarrow$ r ≈ 0.200 km or 200 meters.

**3.** c The angle in a semici rcle is $\frac{\pi}{2}$.

**4.** a Point (x, y) in a OXY plane is equidistant from (–1, 1) and (4, 3).

$\Rightarrow \quad (x+1)^2 + (y-1)^2 = (x-4)^2 + (y-3)^2$

$\Rightarrow \quad 10x + 4y = 23.$

**5.** a Let the angles of the quadrilateral be 3x, 4x, 5x and 8x.

Sum of all angles of a quadrilateral = 360°.

$\Rightarrow \quad 3x + 4x + 5x + 8x = 360°$

$\Rightarrow \quad x = 180°$

Hence the smallest angle = 3x = 54°.

## MENSURATION

1. A right circular cone and a right cylinder have the same radius and the same volume. The ratio of the height of the cone to that of the cylinder is
   (a) 5 : 3 (b) 5 : 2
   (c) 1 : 3 (d) 3 : 1 **(AILET, 2010)**

2. A cylindrical tennis ball container can contain maximum three balls stacked on one another. The top and bottom balls also touch the lid and the base of the container respectively. If the volume of a tennis ball is 240 cm³, then what is the volume of the container?
   (a) 1080 cm³ (b) 840 cm³
   (c) 1440 cm³ (d) 720 cm³ **(CLAT 2011)**

3. If the volume of a sphere is divided by its surface area, we obtain 27 cm. The radius of the sphere is
   (a) 9 cm (b) 81 cm **(CLAT 2012)**
   (c) 27 cm (d) 24 cm

4. Diagonals of a rhombus are 1 meter and 1.5 meter in lengths. The area of the rhombus is
   (a) 0.75 m² (b) 1.5 m **(CLAT 2013)**
   (c) 1.5 m² (d) 0.375 m²

5. A rod of 2 cm diameter and 30 cm length is converted into a wire of 3 meter length of uniform thickness. The diameter of the wire is **(CLAT 2013)**
   (a) $\frac{2}{10}$ cm (b) $\frac{2}{\sqrt{10}}$ cm
   (c) $\frac{1}{\sqrt{10}}$ cm (d) $\frac{1}{10}$ cm

**6.** Two straight poles of unequal length stand upright on a ground. The length of the shorter pole is 10 meter. A pole joins the top of the two vertical poles. The distance between the two tops is 5 meter. The distance between the poles along the ground is 4 meter. The area thus formed by the three poles with the ground is **(CLAT 2013)**

(*a*) 52 meter$^2$ (*b*) 46 meter$^2$

(*c*) 20 meter$^2$ (*d*) 50 meter$^2$

**7.** A ground $100 \times 80$ m$^2$ has two cross roads in its middle. The road parallel to the length is 5 meter wide and the other road is 4 meter wide, both roads are perpendicular to each other. The cost of laying the bricks at the rate of ₹ 10 per m$^2$, on the roads, will be **(CLAT 2013)**

(*a*) ₹ 7000 (*b*) ₹ 8000

(*c*) ₹ 9000 (*d*) ₹ 10000

**8.** A square field has its area equal to 324 m$^2$. The perimeter of the field is: **(CLAT 2014)**

(*a*) 36 m (*b*) 72 m

(*c*) 18 m (*d*) 6561 m

**9.** A closed metal box measure 30 cm x 20 cm x 10 cm. Thickness of the metal is 1 cm. The volume of the metal required to make the box is: **(CLAT 2014)**

(*a*) 1041 cm$^3$ (*b*) 6000 cm$^3$

(*c*) 4536 cm$^3$ (*d*) 1968 cm$^3$

## Solutions

**1.** d Let the height of the cylinder be $h_1$

And the height of the cone be $h_2$

$\therefore \quad \frac{1}{3}\pi r^2 h_2 = \pi r^2 h_1$

$\Rightarrow \quad \frac{h_2}{h_1} = \frac{3}{1}$ i.e. 3 : 1.

**2.** a

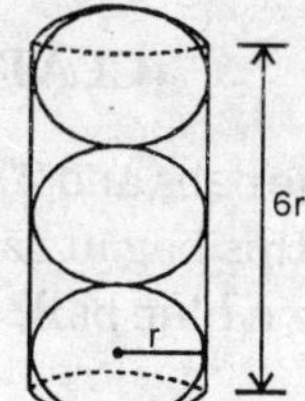


Let 'r' be the radius of balls, so radius and height of the cylinder will be r and 6r.

$\therefore$ Volume of a tennis ball $= \frac{4}{3}\pi r^3 = 240$

$\Rightarrow \quad \pi r^3 = 180$

Volume of the container $= \pi r^2 \times h = \pi r^2(6r)$

$= 6\pi r^3 = 6 \times 180$

$= 1080$ cm$^3$.

**3.** b Let the radius of the sphere be r cm.

Then, volume of the sphere $= \frac{4}{3}\pi r^3$

and surface area of the sphere $= 4\pi r^2$

According to the question, we get

$$\frac{\frac{4}{3}\pi r^3}{4\pi r^2} = 27$$

$\Rightarrow \quad r = 81.$

**4.** a Required area $= \frac{1}{2} \times 1 \times 1.5 = 0.75\text{m}^2$.

**5.** b The volume will be the same in both the cases.

$\Rightarrow \quad \pi \times (1)^2 \times 30 = \pi \times (r)^2 \times 300$

$\Rightarrow \quad r = \frac{1}{\sqrt{10}}$ cm

Hence, the required diameter $= \frac{2}{\sqrt{10}}$ cm.

**6.** b

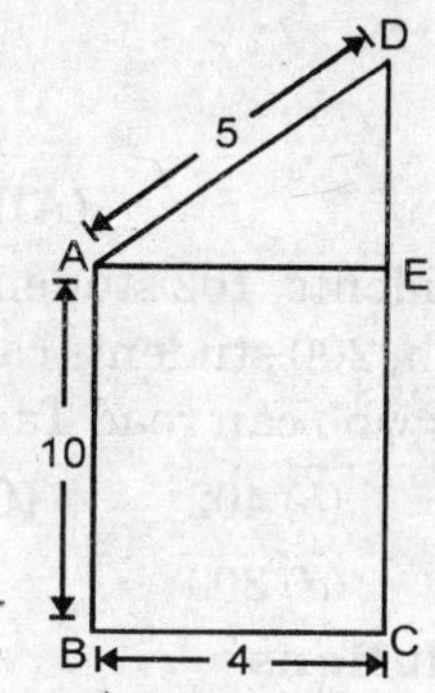


Let AB and DC be the two poles standing on the ground and AD be the pole touching the top of both the poles.

DE $= \sqrt{(5)^2 - (4)^2} = 3$m.

Required area = Area of the trapezium ABCED

$= \frac{1}{2} \times (10 + 13) \times 4 = 46\,\text{m}^2$.

**7.** b Total area of the road

$(100 \times 5 + 80 \times 4) - 5 \times 4 = 800\,\text{m}^2$

Required cost = 800 × 10 = ₹ 8000.

**8.** b The side of the field $= \sqrt{324} = 18$m

Perimeter = 4 . 18 = 72m.

**9.** d The volume of metal = outer volume – inner volume

= 30 . 20 . 10 – (30 – 2) . (20 –2) . (10 – 2)

= 1968 cm$^3$.

# 4

# MODERN MATHS

## PERMUTATION AND COMBINATION

**1.** The number of natural numbers of two or more than two digits in which digits from left to right are in increasing order is

(*a*) 127

(*b*) 128

(*c*) 502

(*d*) 501 **(AILET, 2008)**

**2.** Five boys and three girls are sitting in a row of eight seats. In how many ways can they be seated so that not all girls sit side by side?

(*a*) 36,000

(*b*) 45,000

(*c*) 24,000

(*d*) None of these **(AILET, 2009)**

**3.** In a school of 500 students, 102 students can read Hindi and Tamil both, 200 students can read only Hindi. The students who can read Tamil are

(*a*) 98 (*b*) 402 **(CLAT 2013)**

(*c*) 302 (*d*) 300

### Solutions

**1.** c Total number of two digit numbers

$$= 8 + 7 + 6 + .... + \frac{8 \times 9}{2} = 36$$

Total number of three digit numbers

$$= 28 + 21 + 15 + 10 + 6 + 3 + 1 = 84$$

Total number of four digit numbers

$$= 56 + 35 + 20 + 10 + 4 + 1 = 126$$

Total number of five digit numbers

$$= 70 + 35 + 15 + 5 + 1 = 126$$

Total number of six digit numbers

$$= 56 + 21 + 6 + 1 = 84$$

Total number of seven digit numbers

$$= 28 + 7 + 1 = 36$$

Total number of eight digit numbers

$$= 8 + 1 = 9$$

Total number of nine digit numbers = 1

Hence, total required numbers = 502.

**2.** a Required number of ways

= All of them are arranged

– when 3 girls are arranged together

$= 8! - 6! \times 3! = 36000.$

**3.** * As we do not know that each of the students can read at least one of the two given languages, the correct answer can not be determined.

## PROBABILITY

**1.** A bag contains 5 red, 4 green and 3 black balls. If three balls are drawn out of it at random, find the probability of drawing exactly 2 red balls.

(*a*) 7/22 (*b*) 10/33

(*c*) 7/12 (*d*) 7/11 **(AILET, 2009)**

**2.** A box contains 90 discs which are numbered from 1 to 90. If one disc is drawn at random from the box, the probability that it bears a perfect square number is:

(*a*) $\frac{1}{10}$ (b) $\frac{1}{11}$

(*c*) $\frac{1}{90}$ (*d*) $\frac{1}{9}$ **(CLAT 2011)**

**3.** Two coins are tossed simultaneously. The probability of getting at the most one head is:

(*a*) $\frac{1}{4}$ (*b*) $\frac{1}{2}$

(*c*) $\frac{3}{4}$ (*d*) 1 **(CLAT 2011)**

**4.** A bag contains 19 red balls, 37 blue balls and 27 green balls. If a ball is picked up from this bag at random, what is the probability of picking a blue ball?

(*a*) $\frac{19}{83}$ (*b*) $\frac{37}{87}$

(*c*) $\frac{34}{81}$ (*d*) None of the above

**(CLAT 2011)**

**5.** A box contains 24 marbles, some are green and others are blue. If a marble is drawn at random from the jar, the probability that it is green is 2/3. The number of blue balls in the jar is

(*a*) 13 (*b*) 12

(*c*) 16 (*d*) 8 **(CLAT 2013)**

**6.** An unknown man is found murdered. The corpse has one gold plated tooth, right ear is pierced and a healed fracture of left hand thumb. A man with these characteristics is reported missing. What are the chances (probability) of the corpse being the missing man? (Given the occurrence of the gold-plated teeth in the area, 1 in 5000, left hand thumb fractures 1 in 20000 and of right ear pierces 1 in 100). **(CLAT 2014)**

(*a*) 1 in 1000 (*b*) 1 in 1000,000

(*c*) 1 in 1000,000,000 (*d*) 1 in 10,000,000,000

## Solutions

**1.** a Required probability $= \frac{{}^5c_2 \times {}^7c_1}{{}^{12}c_3} = \frac{7}{22}$.

**2.** a Perfect square numbers from 1 to 90 are 1, 4, 9, 16, 25, 36, 49, 64 and 81.

$\therefore$ Required probability $= \frac{9}{90} = \frac{1}{10}$.

**3.** c Total number of cases are: {HT, HH, TH, TT}

$\therefore$ Required probability $= \frac{3}{4}$.

**4.** d Total number of balls = 19 (Red) + 37 (Blue) + 27 (Green) = 83

$\therefore$ Required probability $= \frac{37}{83}$.

**5.** d Let the number of green marbles in the jar be x.

If a marble is drawn at random from the jar, the probability that it is green $= \frac{x}{24}$

$\Rightarrow \frac{x}{24} = \frac{2}{3}$

$\therefore$ x = 16.

Hence the number of blue balls in the jar

= 24 – 16 = 8.

**6.** d The required probability

$= \frac{1}{5000} \times \frac{1}{20000} \times \frac{1}{100} = \frac{1}{10000000000}$.

■■

# 5

# ALGEBRA

1. If $\frac{x}{y} = \frac{4}{5}$, then the value of $\left(\frac{4}{7} + \frac{2y - x}{2y + x}\right)$ is

(a) $\frac{3}{7}$ (b) 2

(c) 1 (d) $\frac{8}{7}$ **(AILET, 2010)**

2. Anil is half his father's age now. Fifteen years ago, he was one-third of his father's age. How old will Anil be after five years?

(a) 45 years (b) 40 years

(c) 35 years (d) 30 years

**(AILET, 2010)**

3. In a family, the father took one-fourth of the cake and he had three times more than the others had. The total number of family members is

(a) 3 (b) 7

(c) 10 (d) 12 **(AILET, 2010)**

4. A father is now three times as old as his son. Five years back, he was four times as old as his son. The age of the son is

(a) 12 (b) 15

(c) 18 (d) 20 **(AILET, 2011)**

5. A bus for Delhi leaves every thirty minutes from a bus stand. An enquiry clerk told a passenger that the bus had already left ten minutes ago and the next bus will leave at 9.35 a.m. At what time did the enquiry clerk give this information to the passenger?

(a) 9.10 a.m. (b) 8.55 a.m.

(c) 9.08 a.m. (d) 9.15 a.m.

**(AILET, 2011)**

6. In an examination, every candidate took either Physics or Mathematics or both. 84% of the candidates took Physics and candidates who took Mathematics were half of those who took Physics. The total number of candidates being 1000, how many took both Physics and Mathematics?

(a) 200 (b) 240

(c) 250 (d) 260 **(AILET, 2011)**

7. A is older by 4 years to B at one stage. After 16 years of this stage, A will be thrice his present age and B will be five times his present age. How old would A and B be two years before the initially indicated stage?

(a) 8 and 4 (b) 10 and 6

(c) 6 and 2 (d) 12 and 8 **(AILET, 2012)**

8. In a tour, I spent every day as many ten rupee (notes) as the number of days I had been away from the home. My total expenditure was ₹18,300. How long did I stay away from the home?

(a) 1 month (b) 2 months

(c) 3 months (d) 4 months

**(AILET, 2012)**

9. Sameer is as much younger to Mohan as he is older to Arun. If the sum of the ages of Mohan and Arun is 48, the age of Sameer is

(a) 20 years (b) 24 years

(c) 30 years (d) cannot be determined

**(CLAT 2008)**

10. A piece of cloth costs ₹ 70. If the piece is 4 metre longer and each metre costs ₹ 2 less, the cost remains unchanged. The length of the piece is

(a) 8 m (b) 9 m

(c) 10 m (d) 12 m **(CLAT 2008)**

11. Ram weighs 25 kg more than Shyam. Their combined weight is 325 kg. How much does Shyam weigh?

(a) 150 kg (b) 200 kg

(c) 125 kg (d) 160 kg **(CLAT 2009)**

12. Akbar will turn 50 when his son Jehangir turns 18. What will be Akbar's age when it will be exactly 5 times that of Jehangir?

(a) 36 (b) 40

(c) 44 (d) 48 **(CLAT 2011)**

13. Arun can climb a Coconut tree by 1.5 feet by each lift; however he slips 0.5 feet every time he makes the next lift. How many individual lifts will he have to make to reach the top of the Coconut tree of 18.5 feet?

(a) 20 (b) 19

(c) 18 (d) 17 **(CLAT 2011)**

**14.** In a staff room of 25 teachers, 13 drink black coffee, 7 drink milk coffee, 9 drink both tea and either type of coffee, and everyone drinks either of the beverages. How many teachers drink only tea?

(*a*) Insufficient information

(*b*) 5

(*c*) 6

(*d*) 9 **(CLAT 2011)**

**15.** The 10th term of the series: 5, 8, 11, 14, ... is:

(*a*) 32 (*b*) 35

(*c*) 38 (*d*) 185 **(CLAT 2011)**

**16.** If $\left(\frac{9}{7}\right)^3 \times \left(\frac{49}{81}\right)^{2x-6} = \left(\frac{7}{9}\right)^9$, then the value of *x* is:

(*a*) 12 (*b*) 9

(*c*) 8 (*d*) 6 **(CLAT 2011)**

**17.** The value of $\frac{1}{x^2}+\frac{1}{y^2}$, where $x = 2+\sqrt{3}$ and $y = 2-\sqrt{3}$, is

(*a*) 12 (*b*) 16

(*c*) 14 (*d*) 10 **(CLAT 2012)**

**18.** One-third of one fourth of a number is 12. Then the number is

(*a*) 96 (*b*) 144

(*c*) 108 (*d*) 36 **(CLAT 2012)**

**19.** The price of 2 trousers and 4 shirts is ₹1,600. With the same amount one can buy 1 trouser and 6 shirts. If one wants to buy 12 shirts, he has to pay

(*a*) ₹2400 (*b*) ₹4800

(*c*) ₹1200 (*d*) ₹3700 **(CLAT 2012)**

**20.** If $x = \left(\frac{3}{2}\right)^2\left(\frac{2}{3}\right)^{-4}$, the value of $x^{-2}$ is

(*a*) $\left(\frac{2}{3}\right)^{12}$ (*b*) $\left(\frac{3}{2}\right)^{12}$

(*c*) $\left(\frac{6}{5}\right)^{-12}$ (*d*) $\left(\frac{5}{6}\right)^{-12}$ **(CLAT 2012)**

**21.** If $x+\frac{1}{x} = 3$, then $x^2+\frac{1}{x^2}$ will be

(*a*) 9 (*b*) 10

(*c*) 27 (*d*) 7 **(CLAT 2012)**

**22.** When $16x^4 + 12x^3 - 10x^2 + 8x + 20$ is divided by $4x - 3$, the quotient and the remainder are, respectively

(*a*) $4x^3 + 6x^2 + 2x$ and $\frac{61}{2}$

(*b*) $4x^3 + 6x^2 + \frac{7}{2}$ and $\frac{51}{2}$

(*c*) $6x^2 + 2x + \frac{2}{7}$ and $\frac{61}{2}$

(*d*) $4x^3 + 6x^2 + 2x + \frac{7}{2}$ and $\frac{61}{2}$ **(CLAT 2012)**

**23.** The sum of two numbers is 2490. If 6.5% of one number is equal to 8.5% of the other, the numbers are

(*a*) 1411 and 1079 (*b*) 1412 and 1080

(*c*) 1141 and 1709 (*d*) 1214 and 1800

**(CLAT 2012)**

**24.** Military camp is having the provisions for 300 people consuming 600 grams daily for 75 days. They are joined by 60 more men and daily ration was reduced by 100 grams. How long will the provisions last approximately ?

(*a*) 61 days (*b*) 67 days

(*c*) 75 days (*d*) 88 days **(AILET 2013)**

**25.** The value of *k* for which *kx*+ 3*y*− *k* + 3 = 0 and 12*x* + *ky* = *k*, have infinite solutions, is

(*a*) 0 (*b*) – 6 **(CLAT 2013)**

(*c*) 6 (*d*) 1

**26.** Sum of first 15 multiples of 8 is **(CLAT 2013)**

(*a*) 960 (*b*) 660

(*c*) 1200 (*d*) 1060

**27.** Ten years ago, Sunil was half of Sudip's age. If the age of both at present is in the ratio of 3 : 4, what will be the total of their present age? **(AILET 2014)**

(*a*) 20 years (*b*) 30 years

(*c*) 35 years (*d*) 45 years

**28.** Amar is twice as fast as Rohit and Rohit is thrice as fast as Chanda is. The journey covered by Chanda in 42 minutes will be covered by Amar in **(AILET 2014)**

(*a*) 14 min 25 sec (*b*) 7 min

(*c*) 28 min 37 sec (*d*) 54 min 35 sec

**29.** A person spends $\frac{1}{3}$ part of his income on food, $\frac{1}{4}$ part on house rent and remaining ₹630 on other items. The house rent is: **(CLAT 2014)**

(*a*) ₹504 (*b*) ₹1512

(*c*) ₹378 (*d*) None of these

**30.** Father is 3 years older than the mother and the mother's age is now twice the daughter's age. If the daughter is 20 years old now, then the father's age when the daughter was born is:

(*a*) 20 yr. (*b*) 40 yr. **(CLAT 2014)**

(*c*) 43 yr. (*d*) 23 yr.

**31.** A farmer has some hens and some goats. If the total number of animal heads is 80 and the total number of animal feet is 200, what is the total number of goats? **(CLAT 2014)**

(*a*) 40 (*b*) 60

(*c*) 20 (*d*) Cannot be determined

**32.** A man went to the Reserve Bank of India with ₹2000. He asked the cashier to give him ₹10 and ₹20 notes only in return. The man got 150 notes in all. How many notes of ₹10 did he receive?

(*a*)100 (*b*) 150 **(CLAT 2014)**

(*c*) 50 (*d*) 70

## Solutions

**1.** c On dividing both numerator and denominator in $\frac{2y-x}{2y+x}$ by 'y', we get:

$$\frac{4}{7}+\frac{\left(2-\frac{x}{y}\right)}{\left(2+\frac{x}{y}\right)}=\frac{4}{7}+\frac{\left(2-\frac{4}{5}\right)}{\left(2+\frac{4}{5}\right)}$$

$$=\frac{4}{7}+\frac{\frac{6}{5}}{\frac{14}{5}}=\frac{4}{7}+\frac{6}{14}=\frac{4}{7}+\frac{3}{7}=1.$$

**2.** c Let present age of the father be 2x years.

∴ Anil's age = x years

∴ $3 \times (x-15) = 2x - 15$

⇒ $3x - 45 = 2x - 15$

⇒ $x = 30$ years

Anil's age after five years = 30 + 5 = 35 years.

**3.** c Let the number of members be n.

And the quantity of cake = 4x kg

Share of the father = x kg

Share of each of the other member

$$= \frac{3x}{(n-1)} \text{ kg}$$

∴ $x = 3 \times \frac{3x}{(n-1)}$

⇒ $n = 10$

Total number of members = 10.

**4.** b Let the present age (in years) of son and father be x and 3x respectively. Then,

$4(x-5) = 3x - 5$ or $x = 15$

∴ The age of son is 15 years.

**5.** d As the next bus is at 9:35 a.m., the last bus must have left at 9:05 a.m.

Therefore, the enquiry clerk gave this information at 9:15 a.m.

**6.** d The given information can be shown with help of Venn diagram.

(84%) Physics Mathematics (42%)

x y z

$x + y = 0.84 \times 1000 = 840$ ...(i)

$y + z = 0.42 \times 1000 = 420$ ...(ii)

$x + y + z = 1000$ ...(iii)

Adding equations (i) and (ii), then subtracting equation (iii) from it, we get y = 260.

**7.** c Let the age of A be 'a' years at one stage.

Then the age of B will be (a – 4) years at this stage.

After 16 years, $a + 16 = 3a$

⇒ $2a = 16$

⇒ $a = 8$

∴ At initial stage, age of A = 8 years; B = 4 years

Two years before this stage, ages of A and B were 6 years and 2 years respectively.

**8.** b Let the total number of days of my tour away from home be 'n'.

My expenditure, on day 1 = 10 × 1,

on day 2 = 10 × 2,

on day 3 = 10 × 3 and so on.

Therefore, on day n = 10 × n

⇒ $10 \times 1 + 10 \times 2 + 10 \times 3 + ... + 10 \times n = 18300$

⇒ $10[1 + 2 + 3 + ... + n] = 18300$

⇒ $1 + 2 + 3 + ... + n = 1830$

⇒ $\frac{n(n+1)}{2} = 1830$

⇒ $n(n + 1) = 3660 = 60 \times 61$

⇒ $n = 60$

Hence, my tour lasted for a total of 2 months.

**9.** b According to the given condition, we have

Mohan's age - Sameer's age

= Sameer's age – Arun's age

∴ Mohan's age + Arun's age = 2 Sameer's age

Also, Mohan's age +Arun's age = 48

⇒ 2 Sameer's age = 48

∴ Sameer's age = 24 years.

**10.** c Let the length of the piece be 'x' m.

Then, cost of 1 m of piece = ₹ $\frac{70}{x}$

∴ $(x+4)\left(\frac{70}{x}-2\right) = 70$

$\Rightarrow \quad (x + 4)(70 - 2x) = 70x$

$\Rightarrow \quad 70x - 2x^2 + 280 - 8x = 70x$

$\Rightarrow \quad 2x^2 + 8x - 280 = 0$

$\Rightarrow \quad (x + 14)(x - 10) = 0$

$\Rightarrow \quad x = 10$ m

**11.** a Let Shyam's weight be x kg.
Therefore, Ram's weight = (x + 25) kg
According to the question,

$x + x + 25 = 325$

$\Rightarrow \quad x = 150$

$\therefore$ Shyam's weight = 150 kg.

**12.** b Let 'x' years ago, Akbar's age was exactly 5 times that of Jahangir.
Then, 50 – x = 5 (18 – x)

$\Rightarrow \quad 4x = 40$

$\Rightarrow \quad x = 10$

Hence, required Akbar's age = 50 – 10 = 40 years.

**13.** c Net effect of each lift (prior considering height of next lift) = 1.5 – 0.5 = 1 feet

$\therefore$ Required number of lifts = 17 + 1 = 18.

**14.** a On the basis of the given information, we cannot find out the number of teachers who drink only black coffee and milk coffee and all the three beverages. So we cannot find the number of teachers who drink only tea.

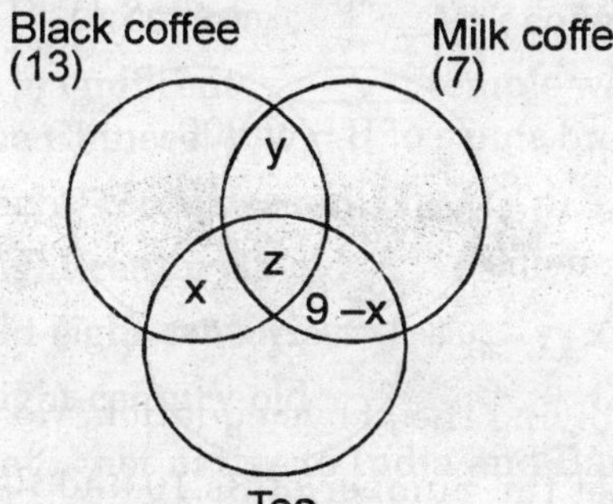


**15.** a The given series is an A.P. whose first term is 5 and common difference is 3.

$\therefore \quad T_{10} = 5 + 9 \times 3 \qquad [\because T_n = a + (n - 1)d]$

$= 32$

**16.** d Given expression can be rewritten as,

$$\left(\frac{7}{9}\right)^{-3} \times \left(\frac{7}{9}\right)^{2(2x-6)} = \left(\frac{7}{9}\right)^{9}$$

$$\Rightarrow \quad \left(\frac{7}{9}\right)^{4x-12-3} = \left(\frac{7}{9}\right)^{9}$$

$\therefore \quad 4x - 15 = 9$

$\Rightarrow \quad x = 6.$

**17.** c Given, $x = 2 + \sqrt{3},\ y = 2 - \sqrt{3}$

$$\frac{1}{x^2} + \frac{1}{y^2} = \frac{1}{\left(2+\sqrt{3}\right)^2} + \frac{1}{\left(2-\sqrt{3}\right)^2}$$

$$= \frac{\left(2-\sqrt{3}\right)^2 + \left(2+\sqrt{3}\right)^2}{\left(2+\sqrt{3}\right)^2\left(2-\sqrt{3}\right)^2}$$

$$= \frac{4+3+4+3}{\left\{(2)^2 - \left(\sqrt{3}\right)^2\right\}^2} = 14.$$

**18.** b Let the number be x.
According to the question, we get

$\frac{1}{3} \times \frac{1}{4} \times x = 12$

$\Rightarrow \quad x = 144$

**19.** a Let the price of a trouser and a shirt be ₹x and ₹y respectively.
According to the question, we get

$2x + 4y = 1600$

$\Rightarrow \quad x + 2y = 800 \qquad$ ...(i)

And, $\quad x + 6y = 1600 \qquad$ ...(ii)

On solving (i) and (ii), we get

$y = 200$

Hence, for 12 shirts, one has to pay
₹(200 × 12) = ₹2400.

**20.** a $x = \left(\frac{3}{2}\right)^2 \left(\frac{2}{3}\right)^{-4}$

$$\Rightarrow \quad x = \left(\frac{3}{2}\right)^2 \left(\frac{3}{2}\right)^4$$

$$\Rightarrow \quad x = \left(\frac{3}{2}\right)^6$$

$$\Rightarrow \quad x^2 = \left(\frac{3}{2}\right)^{12}$$

$$\Rightarrow \quad x^{-2} = \left(\frac{2}{3}\right)^{12}$$

**21.** d Given, $x + \frac{1}{x} = 3$.
On squaring both the sides, we get

$$x^2 + \frac{1}{x^2} + 2 = 9$$

$$\Rightarrow \quad x^2 + \frac{1}{x^2} = 7.$$

**22.** d

$$\begin{array}{r} 4x^3+6x^2+2x+\frac{7}{2} \\ 4x-3\overline{)16x^4+12x^3-10x^2+8x+20} \\ 16x^4-12x^3 \\ (-)\quad(+) \\ \hline 24x^3-10x^2+8x+20 \\ 24x^3-18x^2 \\ (-)\quad(+) \\ \hline 8x^2+8x+20 \\ 8x^2-6x \\ (-)\quad(+) \\ \hline 14x+20 \\ 14x-\frac{21}{2} \\ (-)\quad(+) \\ \hline \frac{61}{2} \end{array}$$

Therefore, the quotient is $4x^3+6x^2+2x+\frac{7}{2}$ and the remainder is $\frac{61}{2}$.

**23.** a Let the first number be x.

Therefore, the second number is 2490 – x.

According to the question, we get

8.5% of x = 6.5% of (2490 – x)

$\Rightarrow$ 8.5x = 6.5(2490 – x)

$\Rightarrow$ $8.5x = 6.5\times2490 - 6.5x$

$\Rightarrow$ $15x = 16185$

$\Rightarrow$ $x = 1079$

Therefore, the two numbers are 1079 and 1411.

**24.** c Let the provisions when 60 more men join last for x days, then

$300 \times 600 \times 75 = 360 \times (600 - 100) \times x$

$\Rightarrow$ x = 75.

**25.** c For the given equations to have infinite number of solutions, $\frac{k}{12}=\frac{3}{k}=\frac{k-3}{k}$

Hence, k = 6.

**26.** a Sum of first 15 multiples of 8

$= 8\times1+8\times2+8\times3+\ldots+8\times14+8\times15$

$= 8\times(1+2+3+\ldots+14+15) = 8 \times 120 = 960.$

**27.** c Let the present age of Sunil and Sudip is 3x and 4x years respectively.

$\therefore \frac{3x-10}{4x-10}=\frac{1}{2}\Rightarrow x=5$

**28.** b Amar = 2 × Rohit and Rohit = 3 × Chanda

Amar = 6 × Chanda

Time taken by Amar = $\frac{42}{6}=7\text{min.}$

**29.** c Let the total income be Rs.x.

$\therefore x-\left(\frac{x}{3}+\frac{x}{4}\right)=630\Rightarrow x=1512$

House rent $=\frac{1512}{4}=378.$

**30.** d Father's present age = 2 . 20 + 3 = 43 years.

The father's age when the daughter was born

= 43 – 20 = 23 years.

Share of A = $\frac{10}{17}\times34000=20000$

And share of B = 14000.

**31.** a let the total number of goats be x and that of hens be y.

$\therefore x+y=80$ and $4x+2y=200$

Solving the above equation, we get x = 20.

**32.** a Let the number of Rs.10 and Rs.20 be x and y respectively.

$\therefore x+y=150$ and $10x+20y=2000$

Solving the above equation, we get x = 100.

# LEGAL APTITUDE

# 1

# TORTS

1. .........are words, which appear innocent, but have a latent defamatory meaning

(*a*) Libel (*b*) Slander

(*c*) Innuendo (*d*) None of the above

**(AILET, 2008)**

2. Unliquidated damages mean

(*a*) Damage to something solid.

(*b*) Damage caused by a firm which has gone in liquidation.

(*c*) Damage to a firm in the hands of receivers.

(*d*) Damage to be assessed by a Court as these are not pre-determined. **(AILET, 2008)**

3. Assault and nuisance are

(*a*) Wrong under Criminal law.

(*b*) Wrong under tort.

(*c*) Wrong under neither.

(*d*) Wrong under both. **(AILET, 2008)**

4. **PRINCIPLE:** An occupier is not normally liable to a trespasser except in respect of willful act intended to cause him harm or done with reckless disregard.

**FACTS:** Tony, a richman, had kept a ferocious dog to guard his house. He strictly instructed all his servants not to go near the dog. Further a special attender was hired to take care of the dog. Visitors were warned by a prominent warning sign board about this dog.

One day, a 13 year old boy playing in the neighborhood, running after his ball got into the house. The dog attacked him and killed him. Tony was sued for damages.

(*a*) Tony was not liable because the boy was trespasser.

(*b*) Tony is not liable because a 13 year old boy ought to have known about the presence of the ferocious dog.

(*c*) Tony is liable of the negligence of his servant to keep watch on such a ferocious dog during the day time.

(*d*) Both (*a*) and (*b*) **(AILET, 2008)**

5. **PRINCIPLE:** A master will be liable for the wrongful acts of his servants in the course of employment.

**FACTS:** Maria was an old widow who opened an account with the Indian Overseas Bank, whereby she should deposit ₹ 5/- everyday in the bank. Stephen was her neighbour who used to collect the amount and deposit them in the bank. Stephen would get a small commission from the bank for the money deposited. One day it was discovered that Stephen, who had not deposited the money for more than three months, had vanished with the amount. Maria filed a suit against the Bank.

(*a*) Bank would not be liable because Stephen was not a employee of the bank.

(*b*) Bank would not be liable because Stephen was paid commission by the bank for doing its work.

(*c*) Bank would be liable because Stephen was paid commission by the bank for doing its work.

(*d*) None of the above **(AILET, 2008)**

6. **PRINCIPLE:** The occupier of a premises owes a duty of care to all his invitees and visitors.

**FACTS:** Devi, who was the owner of a big home with a compound wall, constructed an underground tank to store water. This was covered by jute bags since the work was incomplete. The postman who came inside to deliver registered letter, fell into this tank and hurt himself. There was also a box on the outside of the compound wall, where all the mail could be deposited. The injured man filed a suit against Devi claiming compensation.

(*a*) Devi is not liable, because she did not invite the postman to her house.

(*b*) Devi is not liable, because the postman could have delivered the letter in the box on the outside of the compound wall.

(*c*) Devi is not liable because the postman was required to take care of himself.

(*d*) Devi is liable because the postman came into the premises in the course of his duty.

**(AILET, 2008)**

**7. PRINCIPLE:** Even if the sovereign functions of the State are discharged negligently the State is not vicariously liable in tort.

**FACTS:** A' was a trader in gold. There he was arrested by Police and was detained in the police lock up after search. The gold with him along with sundry other things were seized. Later he was discharged. His possessions seized by the police were returned, except the gold. He moved against the State in tort. In the words of Supreme Court, "There can be no escape from the conclusion that the Police Officers were negligent in dealing with the property after it was seized." One of the Constables was a Muslim. He fled with gold to Pakistan.

(*a*) 'A' succeeded because the servants of the State were negligent and thus caused injury.

(*b*) 'A' failed because the Constable who seized the gold had fled to Pakistan and the gold was not with the State at all.

(*c*) 'A' failed because the acts of search and seizure by the Police Office were part of the sovereign function of the State.

(*d*) There was some other relief given to 'A'

**(AILET, 2008)**

**8.** X, duly posts a letter of acceptance to Y. But the letter is lost in transit by the negligence of the Post Office

(*a*) There is no contract concluded because the acceptance has not reached the proposer.

(*b*) There is no contract concluded because the proposer had not received the letter.

(*c*) The contract is concluded because the acceptance is complete from the date of despatch not with standing any delay or miscarriage in its arrival from causes not within the acceptor's control.

(*d*) None of these **(AILET, 2009)**

**9.** Libel is addressed to the eye: slander to the ear: State which of the following statement are slander

(*a*) slanderous words are uttered by the characters on the dramatic stage.

(*b*) slanderous words are uttered by the characters on the cinema screen.

(*c*) abuses recorded in the gramophone disc.

(*d*) both (*b*) and (*c*) **(AILET, 2009)**

**10.** What is the legal meaning of the word 'Battery'?

(*a*) Cells as used in torch, tape recorder etc.

(*b*) Battering a person to death.

(*c*) Actual or intended striking of another person.

(*d*) Assault resulting in, at least, 6 months hospitalisation. **(AILET, 2009)**

**Directions:** Given below is a statement of principle followed by a fact. Apply the principle to the facts given below and select the most appropriate answer.

**11. PRINCIPLE:** The occupier of a premises owes a duty of care to all his invitees and visitors.

**FACTS:** Laloo was running a dairy from his house. People used a part of his farm as a short cut to get to a nearby railway station. Laloo who did not approve of this, put up a notice that "Trespassers will be prosecuted". However, since a number of these people were also his customers he tolerated them. One day a person who was using this short cut was attacked by a bull belonging to the farm. The injured person filed a suit against him.

**DECISION:**

(*a*) Laloo is liable for having kept a bull on his farm.

(*b*) Laloo is not liable in view of the clear notice against trespassers.

(*c*) Laloo is liable because in fact he allowed the people to use his premises.

(*d*) Laloo is not liable to the people other than his customers. **(AILET, 2009)**

**12. PRINCIPLE:** A libel is a publication of a false and defamatory statement tending to injure the reputation of another person without lawful justification or excuse. A slander is a false and defamatory statement by spoken words or gestures tending to injure the reputation of another.

A wrote a letter to B calling him a cheat. B' s clerk C opened the letter, as he normally did (a fact which was known to A) and placed it on B's table. B alleges that A has committed libel.

(*a*) B will succeed since A has published a defamatory statement against A.

(*b*) B will not succeed because it was not written in a newspaper.

(*c*) B will not succeed because everyone knew that A was a cheat.

(*d*) B will not succeed since A did not follow up the letter with a speech. **(AILET, 2010)**

**13. PRINCIPLE:** A Master is liable for the acts of his Servant as long as he can control the working of his servant.

A owned a taxi agency. She had hired B to drive one of her cars. On January 1, 2010, C called up A's taxi agency and asked for a car to drop him from his house to his place of work. On the way, because of the driver's negligence, the car hit a road divider and C was injured. He sued A for damages.

(*a*) A is not liable because A was not driving the car.

(*b*) A is not liable because A was not in the car.

(*c*) A is liable because B was employed be her and was in her control.

(*d*) A is not liable because B was driving as per C's instructions. **(AILET, 2010)**

**14. PRINCIPLE:** A, Master is liable to third persons for every such wrong of his servant, as committed in the course of service. For acts committed beyond the scope of employment, the master is liable only if he has expressly authorised the act. **(Common for Q. No. 14, 15 and 16)**

A owned a bus and he had hired B to drive it and C to be the conductor. One day, when B had stepped out of the: bus to have a cup of coffee, C decided to turn the bus around so that it was ready for its next trip. While doing so, C ran over D's leg, causing major injuries to him. D sued A for damages.

(*a*) D will succeed since C was employed by A.

(*b*) D will not succeed since A had not authorised C to drive the bus.

(*c*) D will not succeed since the bus was not on an official trip.

(*d*) D will succeed since turning the bus was in the course of employment. **(AILET, 2010)**

**15.** A owned a truck and he had hired B to drive it. On one of its trips, C flagged the truck down and asked to be dropped to a nearby city. B agreed to do so for a small amount of money. The truck met with an accident *en route*, in which C was badly injured. C sued A for damages.

(*a*) A will be liable since B did the act in the course of his employment.

(*b*) A will be iiable since he had not instructed B not to pick up passengers.

(*c*) A will not be liable since taking passengers in a truck had no connection with his business.

(*d*) A will not be liable because B was an experienced driver. **(AILET, 2010)**

**16.** A handed over ₹ 5,000 to her neighbour B, who was an employee of a bank, and asked him to deposit the money in her account. Instead of doing so, B spent the money. A sues the bank for damages.

(*a*) The bank will be liable since B was its employee.

(*b*) The bank will not be liable since B was not authorised to collect money from A.

(*c*) The bank will not be liable since A gave money to B in his capacity as a neighbour and not as an employee of the bank.

(*d*) The bank will not be liable since this is a criminal act. **(AILET, 2010)**

**17. PRINCIPLE:** A person is liable for any damage which is the direct consequence of his/ her unlawful act, as long as the consequence could have been foreseen by a reasonable person.

During a scuffle, A knocked B unconscious and then placed B at the foot of a hill at night, when the temperature was around one degree centigrade. B suffered from hypothermia and had to be hospitalised for a week. B sues A.

(*a*) B will be liable for the act, since the consequence was a direct and foreseeable consequence of his act.

(*b*) B will not be liable because he had no intention of causing hypothermia.

(*c*) B will not be liable because he did not know that A would suffer from hypothermia.

(*d*) B will be liable since A was hospitalised.

**(AILET, 2010)**

**18. PRINCIPLE:** Trespass to land is the wrongful and unwarranted entry upon the land of another.

A purchased a ticket to watch a movie in a theatre. After the show got over, A refused to leave the theatre. The owner of the theatre sues A for trespass

(*a*) He will not succeed since A had purchased a ticket.

(*b*) He will not succeed since A has a right to remain wherever he wants to after the show gets over.

(*c*) He will succeed since A's authorisation to remain in the theatre ends with the show.

(*d*) He will not succeed since A did not have the intention to trespass. **(AILET, 2010)**

**19. PRINCIPLE:** Negligence is the breach of a duty caused by an omission to do something which a reasonable person would do or an act which a prudent and reasonable person would not do. An action for negligence proceeds upon the principle that the person has an obligation or duty on the part of the defendant, which he/she breaches, leading to damage.

A, a surgeon operated on B. Subsequent to the operation, B complained of pain in his abdomen. On examination, it was discovered that A had left a mop in B' s stomach while operating.

(*a*) A will be liable for negligence, since there is a breach of the duty of care.

(*b*) A will not be liable for negligence since it was an accident.

(*c*) A will not be liable for negligence since no real damage was done.

(*d*) A will not be liable for negligence since it is not a reasonable act. **(AILET, 2010)**

20. **PRINCIPLE:** A master shall be responsible for the wrongful acts of his servants in the course of his employment.

**FACTS:** The Syndicate Bank was running a small savings scheme under which its authorised agents would go round and collect small savings from several people on daily basis. These agents would get commission, on the deposits so collected. Ananth was one such agent, collecting deposits from factory workers engaged on daily wages. Though he regularly carried on his business for sometime, slowly he started appropriating deposits for his personal use and one day he just disappeared. One Fatima, who had been handing over her savings to him found that nearly for a month before his disappearance, he was not depositing her savings at all. The Bank, when approached, took the stand that Ananth was not its regular and paid employee and therefore, it was not responsible for his misconduct. She files a suit against the Bank

(*a*) The Bank is not liable, since Ananth was not its salaried employee.

(*b*) The Bank is liable, since Ananth was projected as its employee.

(*c*) The Bank is not liable, since it did not know about misappropriation by Ananth.

(*d*) None of the above **(AILET, 2011)**

21. **PRINCIPLE:** Interfering with another's goods in such a way as to deny the latter's title to the goods amounts to conversion and it is a civil wrong.

**FACTS:** Ram went to the bicycle stand to park his bicycle and he found the stand fully occupied. Ram removed a few bicycles in order to rearrange the stand and make some space for his bicycle. He parked his bicycle properly and put back all the bicycles except the one belonging to Shyam. It was rather negligent on the part of Ram and he was in fact in a hurry to get into his office. Somebody came on the way and took away Shyam's cycle. The watchman of the stand did not take care of it assuming that the cycle was not parked inside the stand. Shyam filed a suit against Ram for conversion

(*a*) Shyam would succeed because Ram's act led to the stealing of his bicycle.

(*b*) Shyam would not succeed, because Ram did not take away the bicycle himself.

(*c*) Ram would not be held responsible for the negligence of the watchman.

(*d*) None of the above **(AILET, 2011)**

22. **PRINCIPLE:** Nobody shall make use of his property in such a way as to cause damage to others. Any such use constitutes private nuisance, a wrongful act under Law of Torts.

**FACTS:** Vasan was owing a house, adjacent to a cluster of houses, owned by Varadan. Varadan was leasing out these houses whereas Vasan was living in his house. When Vasan was transferred to another place, he leased out his house to a person suffering from AIDS. Fearing the spread of AIDS, the tenants moved out of Varadan's houses. Varadan requested Vasan to evict AIDS patient and he offered to fix a suitable tenant for Vasan's house, if the AIDS patient is evicted. But Vasan refused by arguing that AIDS would not spread as feared by V aradan's tenants. Varadan filed a suit against Vasan.

(*a*) Varadan will win, because Vasan knowingly caused him fmancial damage.

(*b*) Varadan will not win, because Vasan could lease his house to whomever he wanted.

(*c*) Varadan will not win, because Vasan should not be held responsible for public mis-perception.

(*d*) None of the above **(AILET, 2011)**

23. **PRINCIPLE:** One has to compensate another for the injury caused due to his wrongful act. The liability to compensate is reduced to the extent the latter has contributed to the injury through his own negligence. This is the underlying principle of contributory negligence.

**FACTS:** Veerappa owns a farm at a distance of half a furlong from the railway track. He stored in his land the stacks of dried up straw after the cultivation as is normal in farming. One day when the train was passing through the track, the driver was negligently operating the locomotive by allowing it to emit large quantities of spark. The high wind, normal in open fields, carried the sparks to the stacks stored by Veerappa and the stacks caught fire thereby causing extensive damage. Veerappa filed a suit against the Railways claiming damages. The Railways while acknowledging liability alleged contributory negligence on the part of Veerappa.

(*a*) Veerappa was not liable since his use of land was lawful.

(*b*) Veerappa's farm being at a reasonable distance from the railway track, he cannot be held responsible for the high winds.

(*c*) Veerappa should have anticipated the possibility and hence he is liable for contributory negligence.

(*d*) None of the above **(AILET, 2011)**

**24. PRINCIPLE:** A person is entitled to protect his property by using lawful means.

**FACTS:** Ramlal is growing valuable vegetables and fruits in his farm and he has fenced the farm to prevent the cattle from entering into it. In addition he has kept a ferocious dog to chase away intruding urchins and cattles. Some children were playing in a nearby playground and the ball slipped into the farm. A boy running after the ball came near the fence and shouted for the ball. But when there was no response, he managed to creep into the farm to get the ball. The dog which was surreptitiously waiting attacked the boy and badly mauled him. The boy's parents filed a suit against Ramlal.

(*a*) Ramlal is not liable, since the fence and the dog are lawful means of protecting the property.

(*b*) Ramlal is not liable for the boy trespassing and getting badly injured in that process.

(*c*) Ramlal is liable, since an ordinary barking dog would have sufficed for the purpose.

(*d*) None of the above **(AILET, 2011)**

**25. PRINCIPLE:** A person who commits an unlawful act towards another which can be imputed to him, must repair the damage which the other person suffers as a consequence thereof.

**FACTS:** Mr. Rajender Singh was riding his scooter on the right side of the road which is illegal as per the Traffic Rules. Mr. Rajesh Chawla was driving his car in the opposite direction. The two vehicles collided and resulted in loss of ₹ *50,000/-* to Mr. Rajender Singh. This includes his medical expenses and damage to the scooter. In this accident there is no fault on the part of Mr. Rajesh Chawla.

(*a*) Mr. Rajendra Singh will not get any amount as damages.

(*b*) Mr. Rajendra Singh will get full compensation.

(*c*) Mr. Rajendra Singh will get part of compensation.

(*d*) None of the above **(AILET, 2011)**

**26. PRINCIPLE:** Whoever does any act so rashly or negligently as to endanger human life or the personal safety of others is said to have committed an offence.

**FACTS:** Mr. Mangeskar owns a Yamaha motorcycle which has very good pick up and speed. He is studying in the IV semester of Mechanical Engineering degree course. One day it was getting late for the college as he woke up late in the morning. He got ready and was rushing to the college so that he would not miss the class. He was riding the motor cycle at a speed of 140 km per hour in Bangalore city which was crowded. He was very good in riding the motorcycle. People who were using the road got annoyed scared with the way Mr. Mangeskar was riding the motorcycle.

(*a*) Mr. Mangeskar has committed an act of rash and negligent driving.

(*b*) Mr. Mangeskar is very good in driving, so there is no need for others to be panicky about his driving.

(*c*) Mr. Mangeskar is very studious student and he does not want to miss any class in the College.

(*d*) None of the above **(AILET, 2011)**

**27. PRINCIPLE:** The standard to determine whether a person has been guilty of negligence is the standard of care which, in the given circumstances, a reasonable man could have foreseen.

**FACTS:** The Agricultural University constructed 200 houses for its employees in its premises. Two huge bore wells were sunk and motors were installed. They did not cover the pump rooms properly. A child, 6 years old, from one of the quarters was playing near the pumphouse. On hearing the noise of the pump, she was curious to see the motor. She touched the motor that was not covered properly and three of her fingers were cut.

(*a*) The parents of the child cannot sue the University on any grounds.

(*b*) Inspite of the child's act, her parents can successfully sue the University for damages.

(*c*) The University can be made liable only to the extent of the cost of treatment as the child also contributed to the incident.

(*d*) None of the above **(AILET, 2011)**

**28. PRINCIPLE:** A person is liable for all the injurious consequences of his careless act.

**FACTS:** Ram, a snake charmer, was exhibiting his talents to a group of people. One of the snakes escaped and bit a child who had to be hospitalised for two days for treatment.

(*a*) Ram is liable to compensate the child's family for his careless act.

(*b*) Ram is not liable to anything as such things keep happening.

(*c*) Ram is not in a position to compensate as he is poor.

(*d*) None of the above **(AILET, 2011)**

**29. PRINCIPLE:** A citizen is expected to take reasonable duty of care while driving on the road and not to cause injuries to any person. (Common for **Q.29, 30 and 31**)

**FACTS:** X, the owner of a car, asked his friend Y to drive the car to his office. As the car was near his (X' s) office, it hit a pedestrian P on account of Y' s negligent driving and injured him seriously. P sued X for damages. Which one of the following is correct?

(*a*) X is not liable as it was the negligence of Y.

(*b*) The liability was solely of Y as X was not accompanying him.

(*c*) As Y was driving under X's care and authority, X is liable.

(*d*) X is not liable under the principle of inevitable accident. **(AILET, 2011)**

**30.** The standard of care generally used in cases of negligence is the

(*a*) skill and care of a professional person.

(*b*) care taken by an intelligent and prudent man.

(*c*) foresight of a prudent man.

(*d*) skill and foresight of an ordinary person of prudence and competence. **(AILET, 2011)**

**31.** Two persons are said to be joint tort-feasors when

(*a*) a person on account of his negligence gives opportunity to another for committing a tort.

(*b*) two or more persons are simultaneously involved in committing a wrong.

(*c*) a tort is committed by two or more persons or any one of them when they are engaged in furtherance of a concerted purpose.

(*d*) two persons together cornmit a tort.

**(AILET, 2011)**

**32. PRINCIPLE:** A man would be responsible for all direct consequences of his act, in so far as he could reasonably foresee them as arising from his act.

**FACTS:** A ship carrying petroleum was moving on the high sea. On a short halt in a port, the master of the ship engaged some stevedores to load some metallic planks onto the ship. While loading the planks, a plank slipped from the hands of stevedore and the spark, emitted thereby, ignited petroleum vapour and caused considerable damage to the goods. The owner of the goods filed a suit against the master of the ship.

**DECISION:**

(*a*) The master of the ship is not liable, because he was not responsible for the act of stevedore.

(*b*) The master of the ship is liable, because he is responsible for the acts of stevedores since he engaged them.

(*c*) The master is liable, because he should have foreseen the consequences of the stevedore's act.

(*d*) None of the above answer is correct.

**(AILET, 2012)**

**33. PRINCIPLES**

1. If A is asked to do something by B, B is responsible for the act, not A.
2. If A, while acting for B commits a wrong, A is responsible for the wrong, not B.
3. If A is authorised to do something for B, but in the name of A without disclosing B's presence, both A and B may be held liable.

**FACTS:** Somu contracted with Amar whereunder Amar would buy a pumpset to be used in Somu's farm. Such a pumpset was in short supply in the market. Gulab, a dealer, had such a pumpset and he refused to sell it to Amar. Amar threatened Gulab of serious consequences if he fails to part with the pumpset. Gulab filed a complaint against Amar.

**PROPOSED DECISION**

(*a*) Amar alone is liable for the wrong though he acted for Somu.

(*b*) Amar is not liable for the wrong, though he is bound by the contract with Somu.

(*c*) Somu is bound by the contract and liable for the wrong.

(*d*) Both Somu and Amar are liable for the wrong.

**SUGGESTED REASONS**

(i) Amar committed the wrong while acting for the benefit of Somu.

(ii) Amar cannot do while acting for Somu something which he cannot do while acting for himself.

(iii) Both Amar and Somu are liable since they are bound by the contract.

(iv) Somu has to be responsible for the act of Amar committed for Somu's benefit.

**YOUR DECISION WITH THE REASON**

(*a*) (*a*) (i) (*b*) (*a*) (ii)

(*c*) (*c*) (iii) (*d*) (*d*) (iv) **(CLAT 2008)**

**34. PRINCIPLES**

1. An employer shall be liable for the wrongs committed by his employees in the course of employment.
2. Third parties must exercise reasonable care to find out whether a person is actually acting in the course of employment.

**FACTS:** Nandan was appointed by Syndicate Bank to collect small savings from its customers spread over in different places on daily basis. Nagamma, a housemaid, was one of such customers making use of Nandan's service. Syndicate Bank after a couple of years terminated Nandan's service. Nagamma, unaware of this fact, was handing over her savings to Nandan who misappropriated her. Nagamma realised this nearly after three months, when she went to the Bank to withdraw money. She filed a complaint against the Bank.

**POSSIBLE DECISION**

(*a*) Syndicate Bank shall be liable to compensate Nagamma.

(*b*) Syndicate Bank shall not be liable to compensate Nagamma.

(*c*) Nagamma has to blame herself for her negligence.

**POSSIBLE REASONS**

(i) Nandan was not acting in the course of employment after the termination of his service.

(ii) A person cannot blame others for his own negligence.

(iii) Nagamma was entitled to be informed by the Bank about Nandan.

(iv) The Bank is entitled to expect its customers to know actual position.

**YOUR DECISION WITH THE REASON**

(*a*) (*b*) (i) (*b*) (*c*) (ii)

(*c*) (*a*) (iii) (*d*) (*b*) (iv) **(CLAT 2008)**

**35. PRINCIPLES**

1. A master shall be liable for the fraudulent acts of his servants committed in the course of employment.
2. Whether an act is committed in the course of employment has to be judged in the context of case.
3. Both master and third parties must exercise reasonable care in this regard.

**FACTS:** Rama Bai was an uneducated widow and she opened a S.B. account with Syndicate Bank with the help of her nephew by name Keshav who was at that time working as a clerk in the Bank. Keshav used to deposit the money of Rama Bhai from time to time and get the entries done in the passbook. After a year or so, Keshav was dismissed from the service by the Bank. Being unaware of this fact, Rama Bai continued to hand over her savings to him and Keshav misappropriated them. Rama Bai realised this only when Keshav disappeared from the scene one day and she sought compensation from the Bank.

**POSSIBLE DECISIONS**

(*a*) Syndicate Bank shall be liable to compensate Rama Bai.

(*b*) Syndicate Bank shall not be liable to compensate Rama Bai.

(*c*) Rama Bai cannot blame others for her negligence.

**POSSIBLE REASONS**

(i) Keshav was not an employee of the Bank when the fraud was committed.

(ii) The Bank was not aware of the special arrangement between Rama Bai and Keshav.

(iii) It is the Bank's duty to take care of vulnerable customers.

(iv) Rama Bai should have checked about Keshav in her own interest.

**Your decision with the reason**

(*a*) (*a*) (iii) (*b*) (*c*) (iv)

(*c*) (*b*) (ii) (*d*) (*b*) (i) **(CLAT 2008)**

**36. PRINCIPLES**

1. A person is liable for negligence, if he fails to take care of his neighbour's interest.
2. A neighbour is anyone whose interests should have been foreseeable by a reasonable man while carrying on his activities.

**FACTS:** A cricket match was going on in a closed door stadium. A cricket fan who could not get into the stadium was watching the game by climbing up a nearby tree and sitting there. The cricket ball in the course of the game went out of the stadium and hit this person and injured him. He filed a suit against the organizers.

**POSSIBLE DECISIONS**

(*a*) The organizers are liable to compensate the injured person.

(*b*) The organizers are not liable to compensate the injured person.

(*c*) The injured person should have avoided the place where he might be hit by the cricket ball.

**POSSIBLE REASONS**

(i) The organizers are responsible for the people inside the stadium.

(ii) The organizers could not have foreseen somebody watching the game by climbing up a tree.

(iii) A person crazy about something must pay the price for that.

(iv) The organizers shall be liable to everybody likely to watch the game.

**YOUR DECISION WITH THE REASON**

(*a*) (*a*) (iv)

(*b*) (*a*) (iii)

(*c*) (*b*) (iii)

(*d*) (*c*) (i) **(CLAT 2008)**

**37. PRINCIPLES**

1. When a person unlawfully interferes in the chattel of another person by which the latter is deprived of its use, the former commits the tort of conversion.
2. Nobody shall enrich himself at other's expense.

**FACTS:** A patient suffering from stomach ailment approached a teaching hospital. He was diagnosed as suffering from appendicitis and his appendix was removed. He became alright. The hospital however found some unique cells in the appendix and using the cell lines thereof, it developed drugs of enormous commercial value. When the erstwhile patient came to know about it, he claimed a share in the profit made by the hospital.

**POSSIBLE DECISIONS**

(*a*) The hospital need not share its profits with the patient.

(*b*) The hospital may share its profits on ex gratia basis.

(*c*) The hospital shall share its profits with the patient.

**POSSIBLE REASONS**

(i) The patient, far from being deprived of the use of his appendix, actually benefitted by its removal.

(ii) The hospital instead of throwing away the appendix conducted further research on it on its own and the development of drug was the result of its own effort.

(iii) The hospital could not have achieved its success without that appendix belonging to the patient.

(iv) Everybody must care for and share with others.

**YOUR DECISION WITH THE REASON**

(*a*) (*a*) (i) (*b*) (*a*) (ii)

(*c*) (*c*) (iii) (*d*) (*c*) (iv) **(CLAT 2008)**

**38.** When the master is held liable for the wrongful of his servant, the liability is called

(*a*) Strict liability

(*b*) Vicarious liability

(*c*) Tortous liability

(*d*) Absolute liability **(CLAT 2009)**

**39.** The act of unlawfully entering into another's property constitutes

(*a*) Trespass

(*b*) Restraint

(*c*) Appropriation

(*d*) Encroachment **(CLAT 2009)**

**40.** 'No-fault liability' means

(*a*) liability for damage caused through negligence.

(*b*) liability for damage caused through fault.

(*c*) absolute liability even without any negligence or fault.

(*d*) freedom from liability. **(CLAT 2010)**

**[For questions 41 to 45]**

**RULES**

A. A person is an employee of another if the mode and the manner in which he or she carries out his work is subject to control and supervision of the latter.

B. An employer is required to provide compensation to his or her employees for any injury caused by an accident arising in the course of employment. The words 'in the course of the employment' mean in the course of the work which the employee is contracted to do and which is incidental to it.

**FACTS:** Messrs. ZafarAbidi and Co. (Company) manufactures bidis with the help of persons known as 'pattadars'. The pattadars are supplied tobacco leaves by the Company and are required to roll them into bidis and bring the bidis back to the Company. The pattadars are free to roll the bidis either in the factory or anywhere else they prefer. They are not bound to attend the factory for any fixed hours of work or for any fixed number of days. Neither are they required to roll up any fixed number of bidis. The Company verifies whether the bidis adhere to the specified instructions or not and pays the pattadars on the basis of the number of bidis that are found to be of right quality. Aashish Mathew is one of the pattadars of the Company. He was hit by a car just outside the precinct of the factory while he was heading to have lunch in a nearby food-stall. Aashish Mathew has applied for compensation from the Company.

**41.** Which of the following statements can most plausibly be inferred from the application of the rules to the given facts:

(*a*) Aashish Mathew is an employee of the Company because the latter exercises control over the manner in which Aashish Mathew carries out his work.

(*b*) Aashish Mathew is not an employee but an independent contractor as he does not have a fixed salary.

(*c*) Aashish Mathew is an employee because the Company exercises control over the final quality of the bidis.

(*d*) Verification of the quality of bidis amounts to control over the product and not control over the mode and method of work and therefore, Aashish Mathew is not an employee of the Company. **(CLAT 2011)**

**42.** In case the pattadars were compulsorily required to work in the factory for a minimum number of hours every day, then it would be correct to state that:

(*a*) The injury was not caused by an accident in the course of employment.

(*b*) Aashish Mathew would not be an employee as the Company would have still not exercised control over the manner of work.

(*c*) The injury suffered by Aashish Mathew could not be held to be one caused by an accident.

(*d*) Stipulations on place and hours of work relate to manner and mode of work and therefore, Aashish Mathew would be held to be an employee of the Company. **(CLAT 2011)**

**43.** According to the facts and the rules specified, which of the following propositions is correct:

(*a*) The Company is not liable to pay compensation as the injury to Aashish Mathew was not caused by an accident arising in the course of employment.

(*b*) The Company is liable to pay the compensation.

(*c*) Since the injury did not arise in the course of employment, the Company would not be liable to pay the compensation even though Aashish Mathew is an employee of the company.

(*d*) The Company is liable to pay the compensation as Aashish Mathew is a contracted pattadar with the company. **(CLAT 2011)**

**44.** Select the statement that could be said to be most direct inference from specified facts:

(*a*) The injury to Aashish Mathew did not arise in the course of employment as he was not rolling bidis at the time when he was hit by the car.

(*b*) Since the Ashish Mathew is a contracted pattadar with the Company, it shall be presumed that the injury was caused by an accident in the course of employment.

(*c*) Since there was no relationship of employment between Aashish Mathew and the Company, the injury suffered by Aashish Mathew could not be held to be one arising in 'the course of employment' notwithstanding the fact that the concerned injury was caused while he was involved in an activity incidental to his duties.

(*d*) As the concerned injury was caused to Aashish Mathew while he was involved in an activity incidental to his duties, the injury did arise in the course of employment. **(CLAT 2011)**

**45.** If the pattadars were compulsorily required to work in the factory for a minimum number of hours every day, then the Company would have been liable to pay compensation to Aashish Mathew if the latter:

(*a*) Had been assaulted and grievously hurt by his neighbour inside the factory precincts over a property dispute.

(*b*) Had slipped and fractured his arm while trying to commute on a city bus from his home to the factory.

(*c*) Had been injured while commuting on a bus provided by the Company and which he was required by his contract to use every day.

(*d*) Had been caught in the middle of a cross-fire between police and a gang of robbers while travelling to work on a city bus. **(CLAT 2011)**

**[For questions 46-50]**

**Rule A**: An owner of land has the right to use the land in any manner he or she desires. The owner of land also owns the space above and the depths below it.

**Rule B:** Rights above the land extend only to the point they are essential to any use or enjoyment of land.

**Rule C:** An owner cannot claim infringement of her property right if the space above his or her land is put to reasonable use by someone else at a height at which the owner would have no reasonable use of it and it does not affect the reasonable enjoyment of his or her land.

**Ramesh's case:** Ramesh owns an acre of land on the outskirts of Sullurpeta, Andhra Pradesh. The Government of India launches its satellites into space frequently from Sriharikota, near Sullurpeta. The Government of India does not deny that once the satellite launch has traveled the distance of almost 7000 kilometres it passes over Ramesh's property. Ramesh files a case claiming that the Government of India has violated his property rights by routing its satellite over his property, albeit 7000 kilometres directly above it.

**46.** Applying **only** Rule A to Ramesh's case, as a judge you would decide:

(*a*) In favour of the Government of India because the transgression was at a height at which Ramesh could not possibly have any use for.

(*b*) That ownership of land does not mean that the owner's right extends infinitely into space above the land.

(*c*) In favour of Ramesh because he has the right to infinite space above the land he owns.

(*d*) In favour of the Government of India because it would lead to the absurd result that Ramesh and most other property owners would have a claim against airline companies and other countries of the world whose satellites orbit the earth. **(CLAT 2011)**

**Shazia's case:** Shazia owns a single storeyed house in Ahmedabad which has been in her family for more than 75 years. The foundation of the house cannot support another floor and Shazia has no intention of demolishing her family home to construct a bigger building. Javed and Sandeep are business partners and own three storey house on either side of Shazia's house. Javed and Sandeep are also Ahmedabad's main distributors for a major soft drinks company. They have erected a huge hoarding advertising their products, with the ends supported on their roofs but the hoarding also passes over Shazia's house at 70 feet and casts a permanent shadow on her terrace. Shazia decides to hoist a huge Indian flag, going up to 75 feet, on her roof. She files a case, asking the court to order Javed and Sandeep to remove the hoarding for all these reasons.

**47.** Applying **only** Rule B to Shazia's case, you would decide in favour of:

(*a*) Javed and Sandeep because Shazia can easily hoist a flag below 70 feet.

(*b*) Shazia because she has the right to put her land to any use and the court cannot go into her intentions for hoisting a flag at 75 feet.

(*c*) Shazia because she has the absolute right to the space above her land.

(*d*) Javed and Sandeep because hoisting a flag 75 feet above one's roof is not essential to the use and enjoyment of the land. **(CLAT 2011)**

**48.** Applying **only** Rules A **and** B to Shazia's case, you would decide:

(*a*) In favour of Shazia only under Rule A.

(*b*) In favour of Shazia under Rule A as well as B.

(*c*) Against Shazia under Rule B.

(*d*) Against Shazia under Rule A as well as B.

**(CLAT 2011)**

**49.** Applying **only** Rule B **and** C to Ramesh's case, you would decide:

(*a*) In favour of Ramesh only under Rule B.

(*b*) In favour of Ramesh under Rule B as well as C.

(*c*) Against Ramesh under Rule C.

(*d*) Against Ramesh under Rule B as well as C.

**(CLAT 2011)**

**50.** Applying Rule C to Shazia's case, you would decide:

(*a*) In her favour because hoisting a 75 feet high flag is reasonable.

(*b*) Against her because hoisting a 75 feet high flag is not reasonable.

(*c*) Against her because the hoarding is a reasonable use of the space above her land.

(*d*) In her favour because the permanent shadow cast by the hoarding affects the reasonable enjoyment of her land. **(CLAT 2011)**

**51. PRINCIPLE:** *Injuria Sine Damnum* i.e. Injury (violation of legal right) without damage

**FACTS:** X, who was the returning officer at a polling booth in Amethi, wrongly refused to register a duly tendered vote of Y in the recent UP elections, even though Y was an eligible voter. The candidate in whose favour Y wanted to vote, was declared elected. Give the appropriate answer-

(*a*) Y can sue X on the ground that he was denied the right to cast vote, which is a fundamental right.

(*b*) Y can sue X on the ground that he was denied the right to cast vote, which is a legal right.

(*c*) Y cannot sue X because there is no injury or damage caused to Y.

(*d*) Y cannot sue X because the candidate in whose favor he wanted to vote was declared elected. **(CLAT 2012)**

**52. PRINCIPLE:** Any direct physical interference with goods in somebody's possession without lawful justification is called trespass of goods.

**FACTS:** Z purchased a car from a person who had no title to it and sent it to a garage for repair. X believing wrongly that the car was his, removed it from the garage.

(*a*) X can be held responsible for trespass of goods.

(*b*) X cannot be held responsible for trespass of goods as he was under a wrong belief.

(*c*) X has not committed any wrong.

(*d*) None of the above. **(CLAT 2012)**

**Instructions for question 53:** Given question consists of two statements, one labeled as 'Assertion' (A) and other as 'Reason' (R). You are to examine these two statements carefully and select the correct answer.

**53. Assertion (A):** In the Event of violation of any legal right (tort) the aggrieved party is entitled to recover unliquidated damages.

**Reason (R):** The object of awarding damages to the aggrieved party is to put him in the same position in which he would have been if the wrong would not have been committed. Damages are therefore, assessed on that basis.

(*a*) Both A and R are individually true and R is the correct explanation of A.

(*b*) Both A and R are individually true but R is not the correct explanation of A

(*c*) A is true but R is false

(*d*) A is false but R is true **(CLAT 2012)**

**54.** The Railway authorities allowed a train to be over crowded. In consequence, a legitimate passenger Mr. X got his pocket picked. Choose the appropriate answer:

(*a*) Mr. X can sue the Railway authorities for the loss suffered.

(*b*) Mr. X cannot sue because he had given his consent to travel in a over-crowded train.

(*c*) Mr. X cannot sue railway authorities because there was no infringement of his legal right and mere fact that the loss was caused does not give rise to a cause of action.

(*d*) None of these **(CLAT 2012)**

**55.** Ms. Usha wants to file a suit against Bhagyalaxmi Theatre praying for a permanent injunction (stay order) restraining the theatre from running the film named "Jai Santoshi Maa". Her contention is that the film hurt her religious feelings and sentiments as Goddess Saraswati, Laxmi and Parvati were depicted as jealous and were ridiculed.

(*a*) She cannot file a suit because injury to religious feelings is not a legally recognized right.

(*b*) She cannot file a suit because the Theatre has a fundamental right to speech and expression.

(*c*) She can file a suit as injury to religious feelings has been legally recognized as a right (*injuria sine damnum*)

(*d*) It is a case of complete judicial discretion. **(CLAT 2012)**

**56.** X went to Y's house and forgot his bag which contained 1 kg sweets. Y's children consumed the sweets. Decide the liability of Y.

(*a*) Y is bound to pay the price of sweets to X

(*b*) Y is not bound to pay anything

(*c*) Y is bound to pay half the price of sweets.

(*d*) Y would not have to pay anything because X loves Y's children. **(CLAT 2012)**

**Directions (Q. 57 - 65) :** Given below is a statement of legal principle followed by a factual situation. Apply the principle to the facts given below and select the most appropriate answer.

**57. LEGAL PRINCIPLE:** If a person brings anything dangerous on his land which may prove harmful if escapes, then that person must keep it at his peril. If a man fails to do so then he must be made responsible to all natural consequences of its

**FACTUAL SITUATION :** A grows poisonous trees on his own land and lets the projection of the branches of his trees on the B's land. B's cattle die because of nibbling the poisonous leaves.

**DECISION :**

(*a*) A is not liable to B because B must have taken due care to control his cattle.

(*b*) A is not liable to B because trees are still on A's land and there is no escape of dangerous thing.

(*c*) A is liable to B because projection of branches with poisonous leaves amounts to escape.

(*d*) A is not liable to B because he is not acting negligently. **(AILET 2013)**

**58. LEGAL PRINCIPLE :** Master/Principal is vicariously liable for the tort committed by an servant/agent, in the performance of his duties as an servant/agent.

**FACTUAL SITUATION :** A gave some cash and cheques to his friend B, who was an employee of the State Bank of India, to deposit the same in that Bank in the account of A. B misappropriated the amount. If A sues the Bank for damages, then the Bank is

**DECISION :**

(*a*) Liable to pay because it was the employer of B.

(*b*) Liable to pay because the employee did it during business hours and while working as an employee.

(*c*) Not liable because he turned out to be the friend of the plaintiff's husband Not liable because while committing the fraud, he was not acting as the agent or employee of the Bank. **(AILET 2013)**

**59. LEGAL PRINCIPLE :** Master / Principal is vicariously liable for the tort committed by an servant / agent, in the performance of his duties as an servant / agent.

**FACTUAL SITUATION :** The plaintiff a bullion merchant was arrested by the police on a charge of purchasing stolen goods. Some of the gold and silver ornaments were seized from the plaintiff and were kept in the police station custody. The duty constable appropriated the gold ornaments and escaped to a foreign country. The plaintiff after being acquitted brought an action against the State for the compensation. In this case, compensation is

**DECISION :**

(*a*) Payable as there is misappropriation by the servants of the State.

(*b*) Payable due to the fact that police constable has escaped to a foreign country.

(*c*) Payable by the police constable himself and not by the State.

(*d*) Not payable as the act was committed in discharge of sovereign function. **(AILET 2013)**

**60. LEGAL PRINCIPLES :**

(1) Joint tort-feasers means joint wrong doers. People can be joint tort-feasors in case of common action, in fact or in law.

(2) Joint tort-feasers are jointly and severally liable.

**FACTUAL SITUATION :** Two dogs belonging to two different owner acting in concert attacked a flock of sheep and injured several sheeps. In an action for damages brought against the owners of the dogs, if one of them puts a defence claiming that he was liable for one half only of the damage, then which one of the following statements is legally sustainable in the above case ?

**DECISION :**

(*a*) Neither of the owners is liable for damages done by his dog.

(*b*) Each owner was responsible for one half of the damage.

(*c*) The owners themselves are not joint tort-feasers.

(*d*) None of the above **(AILET 2013)**

**61. LEGAL PRINCIPLES :**

(1) Negligence is the omission to do something which a reasonable man, guided upon those considerations which ordinarily regulate the conduct of human affairs, would do or doing something which a prudent or reasonable man would not do.

(2) Defendant's duty of care depends on the reasonable foreseeability of injury which may be caused to the plaintiff on breach of duty.

**FACTUAL SITUATION :** The defendants employees of the Municipal Corporation opened a manhole in the street and in the evening left the manhole open and covered it by a canvass shelter, unattended and surrounded by warning lamps. The plaintiff, an eight years old boy, took one of the lamps into the shelter and was playing with it there, when he stumbled over it and fell into the manhole. A violent explosion followed and the plaintiff suffered burn injuries. The defendants are:

**DECISION :**

(*a*) Not liable because the injury to plaintiff is not foreseeable.

(*b*) Liable because they should have completed the work before they left.

(*c*) Not liable because they acted reasonably.

(*d*) Liable because they acted unreasonably.

**(AILET 2013)**

**62. LEGAL PRINCIPLES :**

(1) Master / Principal is vicariously liable for the tort committed by an servant / agent, in the performance of his duties as an servant / agent.

(2) Negligence is the omission to do something which a reasonable man, guided upon those considerations which ordinarily regulate the conduct of human affairs, would do or doing something which a prudent or reasonable man would not do.

**FACTUAL SITUATION :** A patient is brought to a hospital maintained by B. The patient is to be operated upon. As a result of faulty oxygen supply, the patient dies on the operation theatre table, then

**DECISION :**

(*a*) B would not be liable because the surgeon was negligent.

(*b*) B would be liable because there is master and servant relationship between B and the surgeon.

(*c*) B would not be liable because there is no_ master and servant relationship between B and the surgeon.

(*d*) B would not be vicariously liable because surgery is a highly skilled work on which B would have no control. **(AILET 2013)**

**63. LEGAL PRINCIPLE:** Defamation means publication of a false and derogatory statement about another person without lawful justification.

**FACTUAL SITUATION:** A writes a defamatory letter to B containing defamatory remarks in reference of B in Urdu language. A is aware that B does not know Urdu. B goes to C who knows Urdu and the letter is read over by C to him. B sues A for defamation.

**DECISION :**

(*a*) A is liable.

(*b*) A is not liable because he addresses the letter to B and not to C.

(*c*) A is not liable because there is no publication of defamatory statement.

(*d*) A is not liable because he is unaware that the letter can be read over by someone else to B.

**(AILET 2013)**

**64. LEGAL PRINCIPLES:** A private nuisance may consist of :

(1) Any interference with a person's use or enjoyment of land.

(2) The act of wrongfully causing or allowing the escape of deletesthings into another person's land e.g. water, smoke, smell, etc.

**FACTUAL SITUATION:** D erected a brick grinding machine adjoining the premises of P, a medical practitioner. The dust from the machine polluted the atmosphere and caused inconvenience to P and his patients. Here

**DECISION:**

(*a*) P cannot stop D because D is carrying on lawful business.

(*b*) D has fundamental right to carry on any kind of business.

(*c*) P can claim compensation because D's activity amounts **to nuisance** for P.

(*d*) D can claim compensation from P because P is trying to **maliciously prosecute** D.

**(AILET 2013)**

**65. LEGAL PRINCIPLES:** In a suit for malicious prosecution, the plaintiff must prove the following essentials:

(1) That he was prosecuted by the defendant.

(2) That the proceeding complained was terminated in favour of the present plaintiff.

(3) That the prosecution was instituted against him without any just or reasonable cause.

(4) That the prosecution was instituted with a malicious intention, that is, not with the mere intention of getting the law into effect, but with an intention, which was wrongful in fact.

(5) That he suffered damage to his reputation or to the safety of person, or to security of his property.

**FACTUAL SITUATION:** A recovered a large sum of money from Railway Co. for personal injuries. Subsequently, Railway Co. came to know that injuries were not real and were created by doctor B. Railway Co. prosecuted B for playing fraud on the company, but B was acquitted. B sued Railway Co. for malicious prosecution. In the light of these facts which of the following statements is true ?

**DECISION:**

(*a*) Railway Co. is guilty of malicious prosecution because it acted without reasonable cause.

(*b*) Railway Co. is not guilty of malicious prosecution because the Co. took reasonable care in determining the facts and honestly believed them to be true.

(*c*) Railway Co. is liable because it acted negligently.

(*d*) None of the above **(AILET 2013)**

**66. Principle:** *res ipsa loquitur* i.e. the thing speaks for itself. **(CLAT 2013)**

Facts: Seema got herself operated for the removal of her uterus in the defendant's hospital, as there was diagnosed to be a cyst in one of her ovaries. Due the negligence of the surgeon, who performed the operation, abdominal pack was left in her abdomen. The same was removed by a second surgery.

(*a*) Surgeon cannot be held responsible because it is merely a human error.

(*b*) Surgeon can be held responsible but Seema will have to prove in the court of law that the surgeon was grossly negligent.

(*c*) Surgeon will be responsible and Seema need not to prove surgeon's negligence because presence of abdominal pack in her abdomen is sufficient proof therefor.

(*d*) None of the above

**67. Principle:** Whoever by words either spoken or intended to be read, or by signs or by visible representations, makes or publishes any imputation concerning any person intending to harm, or knowing or having reason to believe that such imputation will harm, the reputation of such person, is said to defame that person. **(CLAT 2013)**

**Facts:** In a community there is a custom of stealing shoes of bridegroom during the marriage ceremony. The shoes of the bridegroom were stolen by Y. 'A' announced that Z has stolen the shoes. Everyone present in the marriage party started staring at Z with great surprise. Z felt very ashamed.

(*a*) A defamed Z

(*b*) A did not defame Z

(*c*) A defamed Z for Z felt very ashamed

(*d*) A defamed the whole marriage party

**68. Principle:** An employer is liable for the negligence of his employee. But an employer is not liable for the negligence of his employee if the victim of such negligence is one of his other employees. **(CLAT 2013)**

**Facts:** 'A' and 'B' were working in a factory as unskilled labourers. A was carrying a basket of stones on his head. B was sitting on the ground. When A crossed B, all of a sudden a stone fell down from the basket and hit B on his head. B died immediately.

(*a*) The owner of the factory will be liable

(*b*) A and the owner of the factory shall be jointly liable

(*c*) The owner of the factory will not be liable

(*d*) None of the above

**69. Principle:** Damages are the money recompense, as far as money can do, for the violation of a right. **(CLAT 2013)**

**Facts:** A, an Indian citizen, having a right to vote, was not allowed to cast his vote on the polling booth, by the returning officer. Name of A was mentioned in the voter's list. A has also reported at the polling booth in time. However, the candidate in whose favour A would have cast his vote won the election. A filed a suit claiming damages.

(*a*) A will be entitled to damages

(*b*) A will not be entitled to damages

(*c*) A will be entitled to only nominal damages

(*d*) A will be entitled to exemplary damages

**70. Principle:** When a person voluntarily agrees to suffer some harm, he is not allowed to complain for that. **(CLAT 2013)**

Facts: 'A' was one of the spectators at a formula one car race, being held at Gurgaon, on a track owned by one 'M' company. During the race, there was a collision between two racing cars, one of which was thrown away amidst spectators, thereby causing an injury to 'A'. 'A' claims damages for the injuries caused to him.

(*a*) M company will be liable for damages because the injury was caused during the race organized by it

(*b*) M company will not be liable for damages because A had come to see the race on his own will.

(*c*) M company will not be liable for damages because the collision between the cars was beyond its control

(*d*) M company will be liable because it has earned huge revenue by way of sale of tickets for the event

**71. Principle:** An unlawful interference with a person's use or enjoyment of land, or some right over, or in connection with it, is a nuisance in law of tort. **(CLAT 2013)**

**Facts:** During the scarcity of onions, long queues were made outside the defendant's shop who having a license to sell fruits and vegetables used to sell only 1 Kg. of onion per ration card. The queues extended on to the highway and also caused some obstruction to the neighbouring shops. The neighboring shopkeepers filed a suit for nuisance against the defendant. Which one of the following decisions will be correct in this suit?

(*a*) The defendant is liable for nuisance

(*b*) The defendant is not liable for nuisance

(*c*) The defendant is liable under the principle of strict liability

(*d*) The plaintiff's suit should be decreed in favour of the neighbouring shopkeeper

**Directions (Q. 72 - 79) :** Given below is a statement of legal principle followed by a factual situation. Apply the principle to the facts given below and select the most appropriate answer. **(AILET 2014)**

**72. LEGAL PRINCIPLE :** The occupier of a premise owes a duty of care to all his invitees and visitor.

**FACTUAL SITUATION :** Radhika's brother, Akash, had come to visit at her place. After seeing her wealth, Akash decided to commit theft that night. While he was trying to escape that night he got electrocuted by the wires which were fixed on the boundary walls. Akash plans to sue Radhika. Will his claim succeed?

**DECISION :**

(*a*) Yes, because in Indian tradition, guests are like Gods.

(*b*) No, because one has to be himself cautious about his safety.

(*c*) Yes, because it is the occupiers' duty to take care of its visitors.

(*d*) No, because he himself is guilty of theft. He is no longer an invitee or visitor.

**73. LEGAL PRINCIPLES :**

1. An unlawful intrusion which interferes with one's person or property constitutes trespass.
2. An easement is the right to use another person's land for a stated purpose and has been in use for quite some time. It can involve a general or specific portion of the property.

**FACTUAL SITUATION :** Vijay wanted to construct a shed on his window to stop the water from leaking to his house. The shed was constructed but it protruded in Namit's house. Vijay claims it is his easementary right. Will Vijay's claim succeed?

**DECISION :**

(*a*) Yes, because he has a reason to do the same.

(*b*) Yes, because right of easement exists.

(*c*) No, because there exists no right of easement.

(*d*) No, because this is encroachment on Namit's property.

**74. LEGAL PRINCIPLE :** A person is responsible for that which he could have reasonably foreseen or prevented.

**FACTUAL SITUATION :** A chemist sold a hair conditioner to Jyoti. The conditioner was locally manufactured and the contents, harmful chemicals, were listed on the bottle. The chemist, however, represented to Jyoti that the chemicals used were harmless and beneficial for the hair. On using it, Jyoti's hair was badly damaged and she had to get hair treatment done for the same. Jyoti filed a complaint against the chemist. Will the chemist be liable?

**DECISION :**

(*a*) Yes, as he should have informed Jyoti that the ingredients are not known.

(*b*) Liable because he was aware of the side effects of the ingredients.

(*c*) Not liable because it was the buyer's duty to be aware about the product she is buying.

(*d*) Not liable as it is a natural tendency of shopkeepers to extol the virtues of the product they are selling.

**75. LEGAL PRINCIPLE :** Defamation means publication of a statement injuring the reputation of a person without lawful justification. Such statement must reflect on a person's reputation and tends to lower him in the estimation of right thinking members of the society generally or tends to make them shun or avoid him.

**FACTUAL SITUATION :** Madam Tussauds Ltd. decided to keep a waxwork exhibition, and placed an effigy of Babloo Prasad with a gun, in a room adjoining the "Chamber of Horrors". Mr. Babloo Prasad had been tried for murder in India and released on a verdict of "not proven guilty" and a representation of the scene of the alleged murder was displayed in the Chamber of Horrors. Is it amount to defamation?

**DECISION :**

(*a*) No Defamation as Babloo was an accused.

(*b*) Defamation as his guilt was not proved and he was released by the court.

(*c*) No defamation as there was not proper publication.

(*d*) None of the above.

**76. LEGAL PRINCIPLES :**

1. No fault liability means liability of a person even without any negligent act on his part and even if he has taken due care and caution.
2. If a person brings and keeps any dangerous thing on his land, then he is liable for any damage caused if the thing escapes.
3. No one can be penalized for an Act of God which is unforeseeable and unpredictable.

**FACTUAL SITUATION :** B owned and managed a company supplying electricity to the nearby locality. On a particular windy and stormy day, one of the wires snapped and was hanging down. A, a cyclist who was driving in the night, saw the wire from a distance. There was a nearby street light with low visibility. He came in contact with the wire and was electrocuted immediately. His heirs sued A on ground of strict liability. Decide.

**DECISION :**

(*a*) A is not liable because B must have stayed indoor on a windy day.

(*b*) A is not liable because B's negligence caused him injury.

(*c*) A is liable because supplying electricity is an inherently dangerous use of land and he should have been careful.

(*d*) A is not liable because sudden storm and winds without A's negligence was an Act of God.

**77. LEGAL PRINCIPLE :** The master/principal is liable for all acts done by his duly appointed servant/agent for all acts done by him lawfully in the course of his employment.

**FACTUAL SITUATION :** A had an agency which used to lend carpenters to people on need basis. A deputed B to do some repair work in C's shed. While so doing, B lit up a cigarette and threw it as soon as he saw someone coming there. The cigarette remaining lit caused a fire and the shed was reduced to ashes. C sued A and B. Decide.

**DECISION :**

(*a*) A is liable as B was his servant.

(*b*) A is liable as he should have chosen responsible people.

(*c*) A is not liable as B's act was not an authorised act.

(*d*) A is not liable but B is liable.

**78. LEGAL PRINCIPLE :** Where the parents of a minor child due to their negligence allow the child an opportunity to commit a tort, the parents are liable.

**FACTUAL SITUATION :** The father supplied an airgun to his son who was about to turn 18 next month. After some complaints of mischief, the father took the gun away and placed it in a corner of their storeroom which was used by the family to store surplus and other unnecessary stuff. The son took it out of the store and shot A. A sued his father. Is the father liable?

**DECISION :**

(*a*) No he took all necessary steps to prevent the son from using the gun.

(*b*) Yes, he was the one who gave the gun and allowed him to use it by giving an opportunity.

(*c*) No, the son was almost 17 years and 11 months of age; hence, he could think about his well being and interest.

(*d*) Yes, the father was negligent in disposing off the gun.

**79. LEGAL PRINCIPLES :**

1. Medical professionals are not immune from liability in tort on ground of negligence.
2. Services rendered to a patient by a doctor (except when given free of charge) by way of consultation, diagnosis and treatment fall in the definition of "service" under the Consumer Protection Act. In case of negligence, the doctors are liable in tort as well as under the Consumer Protection Act.

**FACTUAL SITUATION :** A was the only child of his parents. Once he had high fever and his parents called a doctor at home. This doctor used to work at a respectable hospital in Delhi. The doctor administered certain medicines and asked the nurse to stay with him for the night and administer to him a chloroquine injection. This injection was generally not suitable for young children. The nurse, without prior test, followed instructions of the doctor and gave the injection. As a result of an allergic reaction, the child died. The parents sued the nurse and the doctor.

**DECISION :**

(*a*) Doctor was rendering a "service"; hence liable to pay compensation.

(*b*) Doctor was not liable as he came to their home to give personal treatment and was not in the Hospital.

(*c*) This is not a service; hence not liable.

(*d*) Only the nurse is liable.

**Directions (Q. 80 - 90) :** *This section consists of ten (10) questions.*

Each question consists of legal propositions/principles (hereinafter referred to as 'principle') and facts. These principles have to be applied to the given facts to arrive at the most reasonable conclusion. Such principles may or may not be true in the real sense, yet you have to conclusively assume them to be true for the purposes of this section. In other words, in answering the following questions, you must not rely on any principles except the principles that are given herein below for every question. Further, you must not assume any facts other than those stated in the question. The objective of this section is to test your interest towards study of law, research aptitude and problem solving ability even if the 'most reasonable conclusion' arrived at may be unacceptable for, any other reason. It is not the object of this section to test your knowledge of law. **(CLAT 2014)**

**80. Principle:** Vicarious liability is the liability of the Master or Principal for the tort committed by his servant or agent, provided the tort is committed in the course of employment. The Master or Principal is not liable for private wrongs of the servant/ agent.

**Facts:** 'X' hands over some cash money at his house to 'Y', who is his (X's) neighbour and is also, cashier in a bank, to be deposited in A's account in the bank. Instead of depositing the money, 'Y' misappropriates it.

Which of the following statements depicts correct legal position in this given situation?

(*a*) The bank would not be liable because 'Y' did not do any wrong in the course of his employment

(*b*) The bank would be vicariously liable because 'Y' was the employee of the bank

(*c*) The bank would not be liable because 'Y' did not do any wrong

(*d*) The bank would be liable because 'Y' acted as bank's agent

**81. Principle:** A person has no legal remedy for an injury caused by an act to which he has consented.

**Facts:** 'R', a cricket enthusiast, purchases a ticket to watch a T20 match organised by the Indian Premier League (IPL). During the match, a ball struck for six hits 'R' on his body and injures him. He sues IPL for compensation for the medical expenses.

Which of the following derivations is CORRECT?

(*a*) 'R' should be compensated as he purchased the ticket to get entertainment and not to get injured

(*b*) 'R' would fail in his action, as he voluntarily exposed himself to the risk

(*c*) IPL would be liable as it did not ensure that the spectators were protected from the risk of such injuries

(*d*) None of the above

**82. Principle:** Ignorance of law excuses no one.

**Facts:** 'X' fails to file his income tax returns for a considerable number of years. The Income Tax department serves upon him a 'show-cause notice' as to why proceedings should not be initiated against him for the recovery of the income tax due from him with interest and penalty.

Which of the following derivations is CORRECT?

(*a*) 'X' may defend himself by taking the plea that his legal advisor had not advised him to file the return

(*b*) 'X' would have to pay the due, as ignorance of law and failure to comply with law is no legal ground of defence

(*c*) 'X' may defend himself successfully by taking the plea that he was unaware of any such law being in force

(*d*) None of the above

**83. Principle:** Damage without the violation of a legal right is not actionable in a court of law. If the interference with the rights of another person is not unlawful or unauthorised, but a necessary consequence of the exercise of defendant's own lawful rights, no action should lie.

**Facts:** There was an established school ('ES') in a particular locality. Subsequently, a new school ('NS') was set up in the same locality, which charged lower fees, on account of which people started patronising the new school. Because of the competition, 'ES' had to reduce its fees. 'ES' filed a case against 'NS' saying that 'NS' had caused it ('ES') financial loss and, thus, claimed compensation.

Which of the following derivations is CORRECT?

(*a*) Since no legal right of 'ES' had been violated, therefore, as such, no compensation could be granted

(*b*) Since damage is caused to 'ES', therefore, it should be awarded compensation

(*c*) 'ES' should be awarded compensation, as opening of school in competition is not good

(*d*) No compensation could be granted, as reduction in fees is good for the public

**84. Principle:** Whenever there is an invasion of a legal right, the person in whom the right is vested, is entitled to bring an action though he has suffered no actual loss or harm, and may recover damages (compensation).

**Facts:** 'A' was a qualified voter for the Lok Sabha election. However, a returning officer wrongfully refused to take A's vote. In spite of such wrongful refusal, the candidate, for whom 'A' wanted to vote, won the election. But, 'A' brought an action for damages:

Which of the following derivations is CORRECT?

(*a*) Since no legal right of 'A' had been violated, therefore, as such, no compensation could be granted

(*b*) Since legal right of 'A' had been violated, therefore, compensation should be granted

(*c*) No compensation could be granted, as 'A' had suffered no loss as his candidate won the election

(*c*) Since no fundamental right of 'A' had been violated, therefore, as such, no compensation could be granted

**85. Principle:** In a civil action for defamation, truth of the defamatory matter is an absolute defence. However, the burden of proving truth is on the defendant; and he is liable if he does not successfully discharge this burden.

**Facts:** 'D', who was the editor of a local weekly, published a series of articles mentioning that 'P', who was a government servant, issued false certificates, accepted bribe, adopted corrupt and illegal means to mint money and was a 'mischief monger'. 'P' brought a civil action against 'D', who could not prove the facts published by him.

Under the circumstances, which of the following derivations is CORRECT?

(*a*) 'D would be liable, since he could not prove the facts published by him

(*b*) 'D' would not be liable, as such an action could curtail the right of expression and speech of press

(*c*) 'D' would not be liable, as media could publish anything

(*d*) None of the above

**86. Principle:** Negligence is a breach of duty or a .failure of one party to exercise the standard of care required by law, resulting in damage to the party to whom the duty was owed. A plaintiff can take civil action against the respondent, if the respondent's negligence causes the plaintiff injury or loss of property.

**Facts:** 'D' went to a cafe and ordered and paid for a tin/can of soft drink. The tin was opaque, and, therefore, the contents could not be seen from outside. She ('D') consumed some of the contents and then lifted the tin to pour the remainder of the content into a tumbler. The remains of a snail in decomposed state dropped out of the tin into the tumbler. 'D' later complained of a stomach pain and her doctor diagnosed her as having gastroenteritis and being in a state of severe shock. She sued the manufacturer of the drink for negligence.

Applying the afore-stated principle, which of the following derivations is CORRECT as regards liability of the manufacturer in the given situation?

(*a*) The manufacturer is liable for negligence, as it owed a duty (to consumers) to take reasonable care to ensure that its products are safe for consumption

(*b*) The manufacturer is not liable for negligence, as there is no direct contract between 'D' and the manufacturer. No duty is owed by the manufacturer towards a particular consumer ('D')

(*c*) The manufacturer is not liable for negligence because it would otherwise become very difficult for the manufacturers to do business

(*d*) The manufacturer could be made liable under criminal law, but not for tort of negligence

**87. Principle:** Master is liable for the wrongful acts committed by his servant; provided the acts are committed during the course of employment. However, the master is not liable if the wrongful act committed by his servant has no connection, whatsoever, with the servant's contract of employment.

**Facts:** 'D' is a driver employed by 'M', who is the owner of a company. During the lunch time, 'D' goes to a closeby tea shop to have a cup of tea. There he ('D') picks up fight with the tea shop owner ('T'), which resulted in some damage to his shop. 'T' wants to sue 'M' for claiming compensation for the damage caused by the fight.

Which of the following derivations is CORRECT?

(*a*) 'M' will be liable because 'D' is his servant

(*b*) Both 'M' and 'D' will be liable

(*c*) 'M' will not be liable because the wrongful act (picking up fight) was not committed in the course of D's employment

(*d*) 'M' will be liable albeit the wrongful act (picking up fight) was not committed in the course of D's employment

**88. Principle:** Trespass to land means direct interference with the possession of land without lawful justification. Trespass could be committed either by a person himself entering the land of another person or doing the same through some tangible object(s).

**Facts:** 'A' throws some stones upon his neighbour's (B's) premises.

Which of the following derivations is CORRECT?

(*a*) 'A' has committed trespass

(*b*) 'A' has not committed trespass, as he has not entered B's premises

(*c*) 'A' has committed nuisance

(*d*) None of the above

**89. Principle:** Nuisance is an unlawful interference with a person's use or enjoyment of land or some right over or in connection with it. If the interference is 'direct', the wrong is trespass; whereas, if the interference is 'consequential, it amounts to nuisance.

**Facts:** 'A' plants a tree on his land. However, he allows its branches to project over the land of 'B'.

Which of the following derivations is CORRECT?

(*a*) 'A' has committed trespass

(B 'A' has committed nuisance

(*c*) 'A' has not committed nuisance

(*d*) None of the above

## Solutions

**1.** c An innuendo is an insinuation or intimation about a person or thing, especially of a disparaging or a derogatory nature. It can also be a remark or question, typically disparaging (also called insinuation), that works obliquely by allusion. In the latter sense, the intention is often to insult or accuse someone in such a way that one's words, taken literally, are innocent.

**2.** d Unliquidated damages means the damages or compensation which are not pre-fixed. It is determined by the court considering the loss actually suffered by the party.

**3.** d Whoever makes any gesture, or any preparation intending or knowing it to be likely that such gesture or preparation will cause any person present to apprehend that he who makes that gesture or preparation is about to use criminal force to that person, is said to commit as assault. Nuisance means that which causes offence, annoyance, trouble or injury. A nuisance can be either public (also "common") or private.Both these offences are recognized in criminal law as well as law of torts.

**4.** d There is nothing to show that Tony had intended to cause any harm, or had acted with reckless disregard. Option (*b*) is not exactly fitting into the principle, but you have to take the best from among what is available.

**5.** a Undoubtedly, the Bank is liable because the Bank had authorized its agent Stephen to collect money. Even though on commission basis, Stephen was acting on behalf of and for the Bank when he collected the amount from Maria. The rule of 'course of employment' is clearly made out in this case.

**6.** d Devi is liable because postman was acting in course of his since the letter was a registered post under a duty to handover the letter to Devi.

**7.** c The principle absolves all the liability of the State even if the act was done in a negligent manner. Therefore, applying the principle over facts, even if the Police Officers were negligent in their act they shall not be held liable.

**8.** c Section 4 of the Indian Contract Act 1872 states that the communication of an acceptance is complete, as against the proposer, when it is put in a course of transmission to him so as to be out of the power of the acceptor and; as against the acceptor, when it comes to the knowledge of the proposer.

**9.** c Gramophone disc once played shall address to ear, hence it will constitute slander.

**10.** c Battery is the tort of intentionally and voluntarily bringing about an unconsented harmful or offensive contact with a person or to something closely associated with them. Unlike assault, battery involves an actual contact.

**11.** d Laloo can not be held liable as he had taken the due care by putting up a caution board. Law does not prohibit tolerance towards customers or visitors, it only mandates duty of care which was duly complied by Laloo.

**12.** a The moment when the clerk reads the letter it is considered to be published and the libel is complete.

**13.** c B being a servant, was acting under the control and direction of A and B and was doing the work assigned by A' only. Hence A shall be held liable.

**14.** b In the facts A only authorized the conductor for cleaning the bus or for issuing ticket and never authorized him to drive the bus. Conductor's act here is beyond the scope of employment which was not authorized by the master.

**15.** c The act of B' by stopping the truck and giving the lift is an unauthorized act which A' never expressly authorized. Hence A will not be liable.

**16.** b Bank will not be held liable because 'B' even though was an employee of the Bank, he acted beyond the scope of his employment and did an act which was not authorized by the Bank.

**17.** a A' will be liable as the direct consequence or effect of putting someone on the foothills at that time when the temperature is one degree would be hypothermia. So it could be said that it was reasonably foreseeable and the person is therefore liable.

**18.** c By virtue of the movie ticket, A was authorized to enter the theatre till the time movie show gets over. Once this time lapses, the presence of A in the theatre will be considered unauthorized and shall amount to trespass.

**19.** a Since surgeon has breached the duty and the moment he does that negligence is complete.

**20.** b Undoubtedly, the Bank is liable because the Bank had authorized its agent Ananth to collect money. Though on commission basis, Ananth was acting on behalf of the Bank when he collected the amount from Fatima. The rule of 'course of employment' is clearly made out in this case.

**21.** a Shyam would succeed because denial of title (depriving Shyam of his bicycle) was actually caused by Ram. Ram displaced the cycle from its place leaving open the possibility of it being stolen.

**22.** c Vasan can not be held liable for nuisance merely on the ground that firstly: he has leased out his house to a person who is suffering from AIDS and secondly that the tenants of Varadan's house are apprehensive that AIDS will spread in the locality. The correct option further clarifies that Vasan should no be held responsible for 'public misperception'.

**23.** b Veerappa's farm was at a distance of half a furlong which is a reasonable distance hence cannot held liable. The principle of law is Reasonability outweighs the liability.

**24.** a According to the principle Ramlal is not liable as Ramlal is entitled to protect his property by using lawful means. Ramlal has protected his farm in a very reasonable and legal manner as neither the fencing nor keeping a dog is illegal in order to protect one's farm.

**25.** a Mr. Rajender will not get any compensation as he violated the traffic rules by riding the scooter on the right side of the road. He was himself at fault hence is not entitled to any compensation.

**26.** a The fact that Mangeshkar was driving at 140 km/hr in Bangalore which is crowded and secondly his act scared the people using the road makes the act rash and negligent.

**27.** b The university is under an obligation to take reasonable care to prevent injury which a reasonable person would foresee. The injury caused to the child in the given case is foreseeable and not remote. Thus the university would be held liable for negligence.

**28.** a The snake charmer is liable as because of his carelessness the child was injured. The snake charmer is under a duty to see that the snakes do not escape.

**29.** a According to the principle citizens is expected to take reasonable duty of care, the fact that Y injured P proves that Y did not observe reasonable care on his behalf. X cannot be made liable for the same.

**30.** d Standard of care is based on the foresight of an ordinary prudent person. Law takes into account what a reasonable and prudent man foresee and not what the parties to the suit thinks on their own.

**31.** c Tort-feasors are the persons who commit the 'tort' jointly or together.

**32.** c The master of the ship was knowing that he was carrying highly inflammable substance and therefore he should have been more careful. Even if the planks slipped from the hands of stevedores the accident which occurred was reasonably foreseeable hence master should be held liable.

**33.** a It is clear from the facts that Amar has committed a wrong while acting on behalf of Somu. This directly falls within the purview of principle 2, hence only Amar will be liable.

The facts do not state as to whether or not Amar had disclosed before Gulab that he is acting under the authorisation of Somu, hence principle 3 is not attracted in this case.

**34.** c Upon reading the facts, it is clear that principle 2 applies in this case. Nagamma must exercise reasonable care to find out whether a person is actually acting in the course of employment.

**35.** c It is clear from the facts that the arrangement between Rama Bai and Keshav was private in nature, based upon the mutual understanding between two relatives. The Course of employment has to be decided in view of facts and circumstances. It is important to note that Keshav was already out of the service when the cause of action took place. The transaction between Rama Bai and Keshav had no involvement with that of the Syndicate bank.

**36.** c From the facts it is clear that the cricket fan volunteered to watch the match from a place where the cricket organisers failed to foresee any danger of injury being caused to the spectators. Hence by applying principle 1 and 2 it is evident that the organisers of the cricket match are not at fault and therefore not liable to compensate the cricket fan for any injury caused to him by the cricket ball.

**37.** a From the facts it is clear that as soon as the appendix is operated out of the patient it becomes the property of the hospital. Thereafter, the research work that fetched the commercially viable drug was conducted solely under the initiative of the hospital and no one else. Thus, the patient has no right to claim share from the profit earned by the hospital from the use of the removed appendix.

**38.** b Vicarious liability

(*a*) Strict liability- A rule which makes a person legally responsible for the damage and loss caused by his or her acts and omissions regardless of culpability (including fault in criminal law terms, typically the presence of mens rea).

(*c*) Tortous liability- Obligation of one party to a victim as a result of a civil wrong or injury.

(*d*) Absolute liability – commonly used to describe offences in which it is not open to an accused to avoid criminal liability on the ground that he acted under a reasonable mistake of fact which, if the facts had been as the accused believed them to be, would have made his act innocent.

**39.** a Tresspass to property is the unauthorised invasion to the property of another. If someone enters onto another's land without his permission the person entering shall be liable for tresspass. In tresspass possession of the property is sufficient, ownership is not essentially required.

**40.** c Absolute liability even without any negligence or fault.

The principle of "No fault liability" is encapsulated under Section 140 of the Motor Vehicles Act 1988 which provides for liability of the owner of the Motor Vehicles to pay compensation in certain cases, on the principle of no fault. This means that the claimant need not prove negligence on the part of the motorist. Liability is automatic.

**41.** d Application of Principle A leads us to infer that Ashish Mathew is not an employee of the company. Now out of option (*b*) and (*d*), the latter is more appropriate due to better reasoning.

**42.** d Rule A talks about "mode and manner of carrying out the work". Clearly by regulating the work hours Ashish becomes an employee of the company.

**43.** a The concept of "during the course of employment" is not applicable to the present facts in the absence of any employer employee relationship. Therefore the company is not liable for any compensation and 'a' is the most appropriate answer.

**44.** c There was no direct relationship between Ashish and the company and therefore the concept of "during the course of employment" is not applicable to the present facts even though the act in question by Ashish while he got injured was incidental to his duties.

**45.** c Out of all the situations mentioned in the options, option c best explains "during the course of employment" as he was required to travel in the bus as per his contract.

**46.** c Rule A provides no classification and gives the owner an infinite right over the space above and beneath his property.

**47.** d Hoisting a flag of 75 ft is not essential to the enjoyment of rights of a person to his property. Please note that out of option (*a*) and (*d*), the latter is chosen because of the reasoning that relates to the principle.

**48.** a Since the right provided to an owner under Rule A is without any limitation, Shazia shall succeed under Rule A only.

**49.** d Ramesh had no reasonable use of property at such a height and the satellite passing over his property at such a great height does not interfere with his right to use or enjoyment of property.

**50.** d In her favour because, Rule C talks about the fact that reasonable enjoyment of the land shall not be affected. The permanent shadow casted by the hoarding affects the reasonable use and enjoyment of Shazia's property.

**51.** b 'Injuria Sine Damno' means violation of legal rights without causing any damage i.e. there is injury though there is no damage. Even in the absence of any damage, if there is violation of legal right, the plaintiff can claim damage.

**52.** a X can be held responsible since he had no lawful justification for removing the car from the garage.

**53.** a Damages are assessed on the basis of actual loss suffered by the party and is meant to reinstate the party in a position, had the loss would not have occured to him.

**54.** c The fact that Mr.X got his pocket picked because of overcrowding is a remote consequence and hence to that extent railway authorities can not be sued.

**55.** a No person can obtain a permanent injunction restraining the theatre from running the film just on the ground that his personal religious feelings and sentiments are being hurt.

**56.** b Law does not take account of trifle and trivial acts. If Y's children consumed 1 kg. of sweets, no offence is made out on part of Mr.Y hence he can not be held liable in law.

**57.** c A is liable because growing of poisonous trees is a dangerous thing and its projection into B's land amounts to escape. And hence, B should be made liable for the consequences i.e. death of B's cattle, due to the escape of the poisonous leaves.

**58.** d The Bank does not have any liability because the cash and the cheques handed over to B by A was made in the capacity of a friend. B was not working as an employee of the Bank while taking them. Therefore, the Bank cannot be made liable under the Master-servant/ Principle-Agent relationship.

**59.** a The State here is liable to pay the compensation because the constable was discharging his duties under the sovereign functions of the Government and hence comes under the ambit of Master-Servant relationship making the Govt liable to pay for the misappropriated goods.

**60.** b The dogs of both the owners acted in concert and injured the sheep. As there is a common action, the owners of both the dogs are jointly and severally liable and if one of them claims liability for one half of the damage then the other is also liable to pay for the other half.

**61.** d The Defendant employees of Municipal Corporation did not take requisite precaution and left the manhole unattended and covered it merely with a canvass shelter. There was a reasonable foresight that someone might stumble over and fall into the manhole. Hence, the Defendants acted unreasonably in not covering the manhole and are thus liable.

**62.** b The hospital in the present case is maintained by B. The fault was on the part of the Hospital in providing with the faulty oxygen. The surgeon was acting only as an agent of the Hospital in conducting the operation. Therefore, B would be liable.

**63.** a A is liable because he wrote a defamatory letter which was read by C as B did not know Urdu. Reading by a third party amounts to publication of those defamatory remarks and therefore A is guilty of Defamation.

**64.** c P can claim compensation from D. It is so because the dust from the brick grinding machine was causing pollution in the atmosphere causing inconvenience for P and his patients. It will amount to wrongful escape of deleterious thing into another's land interfering with his use. Therefore, it is nuisance and D is liable to compensate.

**65.** b There is no malicious prosecution in the present matter. Malice or dishonest intention is an essential requirement for malicious prosecution. Here, the Railway Co. did not have any wrong intention but based their act on the honest belief that the injuries were created by Doctor B. Hence, the Railway Co. is not guilty of malicious prosecution.

**66.** c The principle given is not self-explanatory and requires legal knowledge to be applied. But going by the understanding of the principleOption "C" would be the correct answer as leaving the abdominal pack inside cannot be justified in any way by a surgeon.

**67.** b A has not defamed Z because there was no intention to harm his reputation and moreover, it was done as a marriage ritual.

**68.** c The death of the employee was caused due to the negligence of the other employee making the employer devoid of the liability as stated in the principle.

**69.** a A will be entitled to damages as his right to vote has been violated. It does not matter if the candidate he wanted to vote for has won the election anyways. Hence, (A) is the correct option.

**70.** b M company will not be liable for damages because A had voluntarily came to see the race and was aware of the fact that there are chances of accidents happening in such races.

**71.** a Although the shopkeeper has not committed any wrongful act but indirectly his act was the cause of unlawful interference with other's use and enjoyment of land. Hence, the shopkeeper will be liable for nuisance.

**72.** d Though the occupier of a premise is under an obligation to take care of his invitees and visitors but he does not owe the same duty towards thieves. Therefore Radhika is not liable

**73.** c Vijay does not have easement rights over the property of Namit. Therefore his shed protruding on Namit's property is an act of trespass.

**74.** b The chemist is liable because he could have foreseen that the chemicals would harm Jyoti and still he lied about them

**75.** b There is a clear case of defamation as there is a clear intention of depicting Babloo Prasad as a murderer even after he has been proven not guilty by the courts of law in India.

**76.** b Though the wire snapped because of storms and winds but the wind and storm cannot be taken as an act of god which was unforeseeable and unpredictable. It is clear that B is liable.

**77.** a As per the facts of the case, B was under the course of employment when he went to work in C's shed and threw a lit cigarette leading to the fire. Therefore A being his employer is liable for his acts.

**78.** d It was the duty of the father to dispose of the air gun in a such a manner that his son cannot use it again. The facts state that the gun was merely taken away and kept at a place where it was easily accessible to the minor. The father is therefore liable.

**79.** d The act of the doctor in providing consultation and diagnosis clearly falls in the definition of service. He is therefore liable to pay compensation.

**80.** a X gave money to Y in his house not only because he was a cashier, but because he was his neighbor and X trusted him. Y as an employee was not told by the bank to collect money from X at his house. Therefore the Bank is not vicariously liable for the act of Y as it was committed outside the course of employment.

**81.** b The very Act of purchasing ticket match signifies 'X' consenting to the injury as it is common knowledge that in a cricket match, the ball, hit by batsmen does falls into spectator area occasionally.

**82.** b X does not have any remedy and will have to pay all his dues as he cannot take ignorance of law as a defence.

**83.** a It can be established that damage was being caused to ES as they had to reduce their school fee but at the same time it can also be established that there was no violation of legal rights of ES.

**84.** b There was no damage caused to A as the candidate he wanted to vote for won. But his legal right to vote was violated; therefore he has to be compensated.

**85.** a D would be liable as he published defamatory material against P and had no evidence to prove whatever he published was true.

**86.** a It was failure on the part of manufacturer to exercise the standard of care required by law, resulting in damage to D who was the consumer and was getting directly affected.

**87.** c The act of going for tea to a shop and picking up a fight is in no way connected to D's employment.

**88.** a 'A' was directly interfering with 'B's premises with the help of tangible object (stone).

**89.** b Had A directly planted a tree on B's land, it would have had amounted to trespass. However A planted a tree on his own land and consequently the branches started projecting on B's land which would amount to nuisance.

# 2

# LAW OF CONTRACTS

**1.** The law forbids the number of partner is partnership. According to law, the maximum number of people who can form a partnership firm is

(*a*)10 (*b*) 20

(*c*) 30 (*d*) No limit

**(AILET, 2008)**

**2. PRINCIPLE:** When a contract has been broken, the party who suffers by such breach is entitled to receive, from the party who has broken the contract, compensation for any loss or damage caused to him thereby, which naturally arose in the usual course of things from such breach, or which the parties knew, when they made the contract to be likely to result from the breach of it. Such compensation is not given for any remote or indirect loss or damage sustained by reason of the breach.

Decide, whether and to what extent B is entitled to damages in the following situation.

**FACTS:** A contracts with B to sell him 1,000 tons of iron at ₹100/- per tone. B tells A that he needs the iron for export purposes, and that he would be selling the iron at ₹ 200/- per tonne. A breaks the contract. When the question comes about damages, A says he will pay only ₹ 5,000/- as damages because the some variety of iron was available in the market at ₹ 105/- per tonne. B however contends that he should be given ₹ 1,00,000/- because that was the profit which he would have made had A fulfilled the contract. B had actually bought the iron at ₹ 110/- and had exported it. B is

(*a*) not entitled to damages.

(*b*) entitled to ₹ 10,000 as damages.

(*c*) entitled to ₹ 5.000 as damages.

(*d*) entitled to ₹ 1,00,000 as damages.

**(AILET, 2008)**

**3. PRINCIPLE:** Contract is an agreement freely entered into between the parties.

**FACTS:** Tapan was a dealer in mustard oil. The Government of India by an order issued under the Essential Commodities Act, fixed the price of mustard oil, and also the quantity which a person can buy from the dealer. Tapan carried on his business under this order for a while, but he refused to pay sales tax on his sale transactions on the ground that these were not the contracts freely entered into by him.

(*a*) Tapan would succeed because the price and quantity were not negotiated by him.

(*b*) Tapan would not succeed because free consent between the parties was there despite the restriction on price and quantity.

(*c*) He would succeed because the Government under the new order forced him to enter into contracts.

(*d*) Both (*a*) and (*c*) **(AILET, 2008)**

**4. PRINCIPLE:** Vishal, a famous artist was requested by Arun, an industrialist to draw the portrait of his deceased wife and paid ₹ 20,000/- in advance and agreed to pay when the work was completed, sum of ₹ 2 lakhs. When the portrait was half drawn, Vishal died due to heart attack. His son also a fine artist completed his father's work and demanded the money from Arun. Arun refused to pay and to accept the portrait drawn by Vishal's son and also demanded the advance to be returned.

(*a*) Arun cannot demand the advance amount from the son of Vishal, because in normal cases the son is not responsible for the father's contractual obligation.

(*b*) Son of Vishal cannot demand the rest of amount from Arun because Arun has not assigned him the work.

(*c*) Arun can demand the rest of the amount.

(*d*) Both (*a*) and (*b*) **(AILET, 2008)**

**5.** Ramesh asks his servant to sell his cycle to him at a price less than that of market price. This contract can be avoided by the servant on the ground of

(*a*) fraud

(*b*) mistake

(*c*) undue influence

(*d*) coercion **(AILET, 2009)**

**6.** In book depot, a catalogue of books enlisting the price of each book and specifying the place where the particular book is available is

(*a*) an invitation to offer.

(*b*) an offer.

(*c*) an invitation to visit the book shop.

(*d*) just a promise to make available the particular book at a particular place at the listed price.

**(AILET, 2009)**

**7.** Mark the **incorrect** answer

The main purpose of the Law of Contract is:

(*a*) The satisfaction of human desires in the highest practicable degree.

(*b*) Where there are conflicting human interests and desires by establishing a judicial and administrative system that acts with reasonable degree of uniformity.

(*c*) To do something in accordance with the norm of prescribed law.

(*d*) All of the above **(AILET, 2009)**

**8.** Frustration of contract implies

(*a*) Commercial hardship.

(*b*) Physical impossibility due to disappearance of the subject matter of the contract or the object has failed to materialise.

(*c*) Both (*a*) & (*b*)

(*d*) Neither (*a*) nor (*b*) **(AILET, 2009)**

**9.** According to law, the maximum number of people who can form a partnership firm is

(*a*) 10 (*b*) 20

(*c*) 30 (*d*) No limit

**(AILET, 2009)**

**Directions:** The following two (2) items consist of two statements, one labelled the **'Assertion A'** and the other labelled the **'Reason R'**. You are to examine these two statements carefully and decide if the Assertion A and the Reason R are individually true and if so whether the Reason is a correct explanation of the Assertion. Select your answers to these items using the codes given below and mark your answer-sheet accordingly.

**Code:**

(A) Both A and R are true and R is the correct explanation of A.

(B) Both A and R are true but R is not a correct explanation of A.

(C) A is true but R is false.

(D) A is false but R is true.

**10. Assertion (A) :** A stranger to a contract has no right to enforce it against the parties to the contract.

**Reason (R) :** Privacy of contract between the parties is essential for enforcement of contract.

**(AILET, 2009)**

**11. Assertion (A) :** A minor is not competent to enter into any contract, even for necessaries.

**Reason (R) :** For necessaries supplied to a minor, his estate can be made liable to reimburse.

**(AILET, 2009)**

**12. PRINCIPLE:** A contract requires a proposal and an acceptance of the proposal. It is necessary to make a binding contract, not only that the proposal be accepted, but also that the acceptance is notified to the proposer. **(Common for Q. No. 12, 13 and 14)**

A sent a letter to B stating that he was willing to sell to B, 10 bags of rice at ₹ 20/- each. B made telephone call to A to inform him, that he had accepted the offer. Just as he was stating his acceptance, a very noisy aircraft flew over B' s house. A was not able to hear the acceptance.

(*a*) There is no contract since the acceptance has not been notified to A.

(*b*) There is no contract since the reply also has to be in writing.

(*c*) This is a valid contract since B conveyed his acceptance to A. It does not matter if A heard it or not.

(*d*) None of the above **(AILET, 2010)**

**13.** A sent a letter to B stating that he was willing to sell to B, 10 bags of rice at ₹ 20/- each. B wrote a letter to A accepting the offer and posted it,

(*a*) The contract is entered into the moment B posts the letter.

(*b*) The contract is entered into only after A receives and reads the letter.

(*c*) The contract is entered into only after A receives the letter, reads it and then gets back to B.

(*d*) The contract is entered into the moment A makes the offer. **(AILET, 2010)**

**14.** A sent a letter to B stating that he was willing to sell to B, 10 bags of rice at ₹ 20/- each. B sent an e-mail to the address mentioned in the letter-head, accepting the offer.

(*a*) The contract is entered into the moment the mail reaches A' s server.

(*b*) The contract is entered into only after A sees the e-mail.

(*c*) The contract is entered into when A sent the letter.

(*d*) The contract is entered into the moment B receives an automated delivery receipt.

**(AILET, 2010)**

**15. PRINCIPLE:** An agreement becomes a contract when it is entered into between two or more people with each other's free consent. Two or more people are said to consent when they agree to the same thing in the same sense. Consent is said to be free when it is not caused by coercion, undue influence, fraud, misrepresentation or mistake.

A went to a doctor to get himself treated. The doctor asked him to sign a "consent form" and said that unless he signs it, he will not examine him. A signed the form waiving his right to sue the doctor.

(*a*) This is a valid contract since A understood and consented to the terms.

(*b*) This is not a valid contract since A had not other option, but to sign.

(*c*) This is a valid contract since it is a doctor-patient relationship .

(*d*) None of the above **(AILET, 2010)**

**16. PRINCIPLE:** Where both parties to an agreement are under a mistake as to matter of fact essential to the agreement, the agreement is void.

A had a piece of land. He believed that the value of the land was ₹ 1,000 per square foot. B knew that the value of the land was infact ₹ 1,500 per square foot. However, he did not inform A and purchased the land at ₹ 1,000.

(*a*) The contract is valid since A should have been more careful.

(*b*) The contract is valid since B paid for the land.

(*c*) The contract is void since A was mistaken about the cost of the land.

(*d*) The contract is valid since the land has already been purchased. **(AILET, 2010)**

**17. PRINCIPLE:** The object of an agreement is lawful unless it is forbidden by law; is of such a nature that, if permitted, it would defeat the provisions of any law; is fraudulent; involves or implies injury to the person or property of another person; the court regards it as immoral; it is opposed to public policy. **(Common for Q. No. 17, 18, 19 and 20)**

A and B entered into a contract, whereby A agreed to get married to B, if her parents paid A ₹ 1,00,000 before the wedding. B' s parents failed to pay the promised amount. A sues B and her parents.

(*a*) A will succeed because all the requirements of a contract are met.

(*b*) A will succeed since the payment of the amount was the condition precedent for the wedding.

(*c*) A will not succeed since the contract is void, its object being against the law.

(*d*) A will not succeed since B was not a party to the contract. **(AILET, 2010)**

**18.** A was arrested by the police for committing an offence and was subsequently granted bail by the Court. One of the conditions imposed by the Court for granting bail was that A arrange for a surety for ₹ 50,000. A approached B to be a surety. B agreed, but insisted that they enter into a contract whereby A would deposit ₹ 50,000 into B's account, which would be returned to A by B after the case was over.

(*a*) The contract would be void since its effect is to defeat the provisions of the Cr. P.C.

(*b*) The contract would be void because A cannot enter into a contract when a criminal case is going on against him.

(*c*) The contract would be void because the Court is not a party to it.

(*d*) The contract would be valid. **(AILET, 2010)**

**19.** A and B, a Hindu couple were married to each other. Owing to differences between them, they decided to get divorced. They entered into a contract laying down the conditions that both parties had to adhere with. One of the terms of the contract was that their children would not be entitled to claim the ancestral property of A, the husband.

(*a*) The contract will be void since the children are not a party to the contract.

(*b*) The contract will be void since its terms since it is opposed to the personal laws of the parties.

(*c*) The contract will be valid.

(*d*) The contract will be void since a woman cannot enter into a contract with her husband.

**(AILET, 2010)**

**20.** The BCCI decided to hold an auction to sell IPL teams. 12 bidders registered for the auction. Unknown to the BCCI, these 12 bidders had entered Into a contract that they would not bid more than a certain amount.

(*a*) The contract will be void because BCCI is not a party to it.

(*b*) The contract will be void since the object of the contract is to cause a loss to the BCCI.

(*c*) The contract will be void since the maximum number of parties to a contract as per Indian law is 10.

(*d*) The contract will be valid. **(AILET, 2010)**

**21. PRINCIPLE:** Every agreement by which anyone is restrained from exercising a lawful profession, trade or business of any kind, to that extent is void.

A company entered into a contract with Coca Cola Ltd. to bottle soft drinks produced by Coca Cola. One of the terms of the contract was that the company would not bottle soft drinks for any other competitor of Coca Cola during the pendency of the contract.

(*a*) The contract is void since it restrains the lawful right of the company to engage in business.

(*b*) The contract is void because there is no consider ration being paid.

(*c*) The contract is valid.

(*d*) The contract is valid since the competitor is not a party to the contract. **(AILET, 2010)**

**22. PRINCIPLE:** An agreement is void to the extent that it restricts absolutely, a party from enforcing his contractual rights by usual rights by usual proceedings in any ordinary court.

A and B entered into a transaction in Delhi for sale of goods based in Delhi. The contract stated that in case of a dispute, only civil courts in Chennai would have jurisdiction. Neither A, nor B resided or carried on business in Chennai.

(*a*) The contract is valid since it is still an Indian court that has jurisdiction.

(*b*) The contract is void since it ousts the jurisdiction of the competent court.

(*c*) The contract is void since the consent of the court is required before entering into such a contract.

(*d*) The contract is valid since Chennai courts have expertise with respect to contractual matters. **(AILET, 2010)**

**23. PRINCIPLE:** An Agreement, the meaning of which is not certain, or capable of being made certain, is void.

A and B, who were brothers, entered into an agreement which stated that A would sell his entire share of the ancestral property to B. The agreement did not mention the specific details (like survey number) of the property.

(*a*) The contract will be void since it is vague.

(*b*) The contract will be void because it is not possible to ascertain the property which is being referred to.

(*c*) The contract will be void since it is illegal.

(*d*) The contract is valid since there is clarity about the property sought to be sold. **(AILET, 2010)**

**24. PRINCIPLE:** When the parties to an agreement agree on the same thing in the same sense, there arises legally binding obligations between them.

**FACTS:** Zaverilal's antique shop was a well-known shop of the locality. Taradevi, a socialite of the locality, went to the shop and she was attracted by an earthern jar on display. Zaverilal explained to her that the jar belonged to Hoysala period; and despite its earthern composition, it was very strong and almost unbreakable. Taradevi replied to him that she was so captivated by the jar that it was immaterial to her as to which period it belonged. She bought the jar and came home. She placed the jar in a prominent place in her drawing room. One of her friends, an art critique, who happened to visit her, told her that the jar was not at all an Antique, but Taradevi did not bother about it. One day, it accidentally fell down and broke into pieces. Taradevi took up the matter with Zaverilal that his both statements were wrong and therefore, he should pay damages to her.

(*a*) Zaverilal must compensate her, since his both the statements concerning jar were wrong.

(*b*) Zaverilal need not to compensate, since, Taradevi was not concerned with its antique value at all.

(*c*) Zaverilal must compensate, because he carelessly made the statements.

(*d*) None of the above **(AILET, 2011)**

**25. PRINCIPLE:** Damages are payable for breach of contract and the purpose of damages is to compensate for the loss suffered and not to improve position more than what it would have been if the contract had been duly performed.

**FACTS:** A wanted to buy a house and he contracted with a surveyor S to inspect a particular house and value it for him. S surveyed the house and valued it for ₹ 10 lakhs. S, however, failed to notice the defective plumbing system in the house and had he taken note of it, the house would have been worth only ₹ 8 lakhs. A followed S' s advice and bought the house for ₹ 8 lakhs and thereafter spent ₹ 4 lakhs for repairing the plumbing system. He filed a suit against S claiming ₹ 4 lakhs as damages.

(*a*) A should get ₹ 4 lakhs, because that was the amount that he had to spend finally to make the house worth living.

(*b*) A should get ₹ 2 lakhs, since he paid additional ₹ 2 lakhs on account of S 's negligence.

(*c*) A should get ₹ 4 lakhs, since that loss was attributable to S's negligence.

(*d*) None of the above **(AILET, 2011)**

26. **PRINCIPLE:** When there is breach of contract, the resulting damages will have to be paid by the party breaching the contract to the aggrieved party. However, the parties are free to agree as to damages payable in advance in case there is breach of contract.

**FACTS:** Mr. Ramesh entered into a contract with Mr. Ramakrishna for selling his green Alto Car for ₹ 3 lakhs. Mr. Ramakrishna was to pay ₹ 3 lakhs on or before 25th April 2005 and take possession of the car. The party failing to honour the contract has to pay ₹ 40,000/- as damages to the other party.

Mr. Ramakrishna has not performed his part of the contract. Mr. Ramesh is claiming ₹40,000/-.

(*a*) Mr. Ramesh can sell the car in the second hand market and if he suffers any loss, then only he can claim that amount from Mr. Ramakrishna.

(*b*) Mr. Ramakrishna is liable to pay the agreed damages.

(*c*) Mr. Ramesh has to prove that he has suffered ₹ 40,000/- as damages to get it.

(*d*) None of the above **(AILET, 2011)**

27. **PRINCIPLE:** Contractual liability is completely irrelevant to the existence of liability in tort (civil wrong).

**FACTS:** X purchased a bottle of ginger-beer from a retailer. As she consumed more than 3/4 of the contents of the bottle, she found a decomposed remains of a snail in the bottle. After seeing the remains of a snail, she fell sick on the thought of what she consumed. She sued the manufacturer of the beer for negligence, though there is no contractual duty on the part of the manufacturer.

(*a*) X cannot sue the manufacturer for negligence in the absence of a contract.

(*b*) X cannot sue the retailer.

(*c*) X can sue the manufacturer as he had a duty to take care to see that bottles did not contain any other substance than the beer and hence liable to have broken that duty.

(*d*) None of the above **(AILET, 2011)**

28. **PRINCIPLE:** A contingent contract is a contract to do or not to do something, if some event, collateral to such contract, does or does not happen.

**FACTS:** A agrees to pay B a sum of ₹ 1 lakh if B marries C within a period of six months. B marries C during the seventh month as the marriage hall was available only during that month. B claims ₹ 1 lakh from A.

(*a*) B can successfully claim ₹ 1 lakh from A.

(*b*) B cannot claim ₹ 1 lakh from A as B married C after the duration set in the contract.

(*c*) B can claim ₹ 1 lakh as well as special damages from A for having married C.

(*d*) None of the above **(AILET, 2011)**

29. **PRINCIPLE:** A contract without consideration is void. When at the desire of one party the other party does something, the consideration is said to flow from the latter to the former.

**FACTS:** A's house was on fire and a child was trapped inside the house. Everyone was shouting for help. A brave onlooker, hearing the shrieks of child, went inside the house and brought him out. The father of the child promised to pay the rescuer ₹10,000. Subsequently, he backtracked his promise. The rescuer sued the promise for the breach.

(*a*) The father of the child must pay for the service rendered by the rescuer.

(*b*) The rescuer is not entitled to the payment, since he acted on his own.

(*c*) Commercial considerations cannot be applied to humanitarian instincts.

(*d*) None of the above **(AILET, 2011)**

**Directions (Q. 30- 34):** Given below is a statement of principle followed by a factual situation. Apply the principle to the facts given below and select the most appropriate answer.

30. **PRINCIPLE:** In case of a breach of contract, compensation can be awarded for the personal inconvenience suffered by a party by reason of the breach, which naturally arose in the usual course of things from such breach, or which the parties knew, when they made the contract to be likely to result from the breach of it.

**FACTS:** Sunita and Sushmita bought bus tickets for a journey from Adyar to Mandaveli. The bus was to go to St. Thomas Mount via Mandaveli. However, the driver mistakenly took a wrong direction and the two girls were dropped at a distance of 2½ miles from Mandaveli on the highway. With no other transportation in sight nor a place to stay, the two had to walk 2½ miles at midnight.

Later they filed a case against the bus company and claimed ₹ 5000 as damages for inconvenience caused in having to walk and ₹ 6500 for Sushmita having fallen ill by catching cold during the night.

**DECISION:**

(*a*) Both the amounts are liable to be paid because Sunita and Sushmita suffered loss for no fault of theirs.

(*b*) The bus company is liable to pay both the amounts claimed because the loss was suffered on account of the fault of the bus company and the inconvenience suffered and illness arose was in the normal course of things from breach of contract.

(*c*) The compensation for inconvenience suffered by being forced to walk at night is liable to be paid by the bus company. However, no compensation for Sushmita's illness because this was not expected on account of breach of contract.

(*d*) The bus company is not liable to pay any amount, because it was the driver's fault.

**(AILET, 2012)**

**31.** All contracts are agreements. All agreements are accepted offers.

Which of the following derivation is correct?

(*a*) All accepted offers are contracts.

(*b*) All agreements are contracts.

(*c*) All contracts are accepted offers.

(*d*) None of the above. **(CLAT 2008)**

**32.** No minor can enter into a contract of work. Working in a shop can be done only by a contract.

Which of the following derivation is correct?

(*a*) A minor cannot work in a shop.

(*b*) A shop cannot contract with a minor.

(*c*) There cannot be a contract to which minor is a party.

(*d*) None of the above. **(CLAT 2008)**

**33.** A contract contravening public policy is void. There cannot be a general definition of public policy.

Which of the following is correct derivation from the above?

(*a*) There cannot be a general definition of contract.

(*b*) Since public policy is uncertain, contract is also uncertain.

(*c*) The impact of public policy on contract is to be judged in individual cases.

(*d*) None of the above **(CLAT 2008)**

**34.** X, a shopkeeper, leaves a sealed 5 kilogram bag of a branded wheat flour at the door of Y with a note "you will like this quality wheat flour and pay Rupees 100 for this bag" without being asked to do so. Y on coming back, collects the bag from his door, opens the seal of the bag, and uses a quarter of kilogram for making chapattis (unleavened bread). But next day returns the bag. Is he bound to pay for the bag? He is

(*a*) not bound to pay as he did not ask the shopkeeper to deliver the bag.

(*b*) bound to pay as he has opened the bag.

(*c*) bound to pay only for the quantity used.

(*d*) neither bound to pay nor return the bag.

**(CLAT 2010)**

**<u>(For questions 35 to 39)</u>**

**Rules:** A. A minor is a person who is below the age of eighteen. However, where a guardian administers the minor's property the age of majority is twenty-one. B. A minor is not permitted by law to enter into a contract. Hence, where a minor enters into a contract with a major person, the contract is not enforceable. This effectively means that neither the minor nor the other party can make any claim on the basis of the contract. C. In a contract with a minor, if the other party hands over any money or confers any other benefit on the minor, the same shall not be recoverable from the minor unless the other party was deceived by the minor to hand over money or any other benefit. The other party will have to show that the minor misrepresented her age, he was ignorant about the age of the minor and that he handed over the benefit on the basis of such representation.

**Facts** Ajay convinces Bandita, a girl aged 18 that she should sell her land to him. Bandita's mother Chaaru is her guardian. Nonetheless Bandita, without the permission of Chaaru, sells the land to Ajay for a total sum of rupees fifty lakh, paid in full and final settlement of the price. Chaaru challenges this transaction claiming that Bandita is a minor and hence the possession of the land shall not be given to Ajay. Thus Ajay is in a difficult situation and has no idea how to recover his money from Bandita.

**35.** Chaaru is justified in challenging the sale transaction because:

(*a*) Bandita is of unsound mind and is not in a position to make rational decisions.

(*b*) Though Bandita is eighteen year old, she will be treated as a minor, as Chaaru is her guardian.

(*c*) Though Bandita is eighteen year old, she cannot sell the land without the permission of her mother.

(*d*) Though Bandita is eighteen year old she should not be treated like a person who has attained the age of majority. **(CLAT 2011)**

**36.** Ajay can be allowed to recover the money only if he can show that:

(*a*) He was deceived by Bandita who misrepresented her age.

(*b*) He honestly believed that Bandita was empowered under the law to sell the land.

(*c*) He was an honest person who had paid the full price of the land to Bandita.

(*d*) Both (*a*) and (*b*). **(CLAT 2011)**

**37.** In order to defend the sale, Bandita will need to show that

(*a*) Bandita has attained the age of majority.

(*b*) Bandita is mature enough to make rational decisions regarding her own affairs.

(*c*) The sale transaction was beneficial to her interest and will enhance her financial status.

(*d*) None of the above. **(CLAT 2011)**

**38.** Which of the following is correct?

(*a*) Ajay should be allowed to recover the money because even though there is no contract, Bandita and Chaaru should not be allowed to unjustly benefit from Ajay's money.

(*b*) Ajay should be allowed the possession of the land because Chaaru can always decide to approve the transaction between Ajay and Bandita.

(*c*) Ajay should not be allowed to recover because he induced Bandita, a minor, to sell the land.

(*d*) None of the above. **(CLAT 2011)**

**39.** Which of the following is correct?

(*a*) If Ajay is allowed to recover the money, that will defeat the law framed for protecting the minors against fraudulent persons.

(*b*) If Ajay is not allowed to recover that will cause him injustice as he has not paid off the entire sale price.

(*c*) If Ajay is allowed to recover, Chaaru will benefit from both the money and the land.

(*d*) None of the above. **(CLAT 2011)**

**(For questions 40 and 43)**

**Rules**

A. The act of using threats to force another person to enter into a contract is called coercion.

B. The act of using influence on another and taking undue advantage of that person is called undue influence.

C. In order to prove coercion, the existence of the use of threat, in any form and manner, is necessary. If coercion is proved, the person who has been so threatened can refuse to abide by the contract.

D. In order to prove undue-influence, there has to be a pre-existing relationship between the parties to a contract. The relationship has to be of such a nature that one is in a position to influence the other. If it is proven that there has been undue influence, the party who has been so influenced need not enforce the contract or perform his obligations under the contract.

**FACTS:** Aadil and Baalu are best friends. Aadil is the son of multi millionaire business person, Chulbul who owns Maakhan Pharmaceuticals. Baalu is the son of a bank employee, Dhanraj. One day, Aadil is abducted from his office by Baalu. Chulbul receives a phone call from Dhanraj telling him that if he does not make Baalu the CEO of Maakhan Pharmaceuticals, Aadil will be killed. Chulbul reluctantly agrees to make the Baalu the CEO. Subsequently Chulbul and Baalu sign an employment contract. However as soon as Aadil is released and safely returns home, Chulbul tells Baalu that he shall not enforce the employment contract. Baalu and Dhanraj are not sure as to what is to be done next ?

**40.** As per the rules and the given facts, who coerces whom:

(*a*) Aadil coerces Baalu.

(*b*) Baalu coerces Chulbul.

(*c*) Dhanraj coerces Chulbul

(*d*) None of the above. **(CLAT 2011)**

**41.** In the above fact situation:

(*a*) There is undue influence exercised by Dhanraj on Baalu.

(*b*) There is undue influence exercised by Aadil on Chulbul.

(*c*) There is no undue influence.

(*d*) None of the above. **(CLAT 2011)**

**42.** Chulbul is:

(*a*) Justified in refusing to enforce the employment contract as Chulbul was coerced by Dhanraj.

(*b*) Justified in refusing to enforce the employment contract as Baalu was complicit in the coercive act.

(*c*) Not justified in refusing to enforce the employment contract as Baalu was an innocent person and has not coerced Chulbul.

(*d*) Both (*a*) and (*b*). **(CLAT 2011)**

**43.** Baalu will succeed in getting the employment contract enforced if he can show that

(*a*) He is the best friend of Aadil.

(*b*) It was his father, and not he, who used coercion against Chulbul.

(*c*) Chulbul has promised his father to employ him.

(*d*) None of the above. **(CLAT 2011)**

**44. PRINCIPLE:** When one person signifies to another his willingness to do or abstain from doing anything, with a view to obtaining the assent of that person to such an act or abstinence, he is said to have made a proposal.

**FACT:** "Ramanuj telegraphed to Shyam Sunder, writing: *"Will you sell me your Rolls Royce CAR? Telegram the lowest cash price."* Shyam Sunder also replied by telegram: *"Lowest price for CAR is ₹20 lakh."* Ramanuj immediately sent his consent through telegram stating: *"I agree to buy the CAR for ₹20 lakh asked by you."* Shyam Sunder refused to sell the car.

(*a*) He cannot refuse to sell the CAR because the contract has already been made.

(*b*) He can refuse to sell the CAR because it was only invitation to offer and not the real offer.

(*c*) It was not a valid offer because willingness to enter into a contract was absent.

(*d*) None of these **(CLAT 2012)**

**45. PRINCIPLE:** Every person, who is of the age of majority, is competent to contract according to the law to which he is subject.

**FACTS:** A minor mortgaged his house in favour of Thakur Das, a money lender, to secure a loan of ₹ 20000. A part of this, i.e. ₹ 10500 was actually advanced to him. While considering the proposed advance, the attorney who was acting for the money lender, received information that the plaintiff was still a minor. Subsequently the minor commenced an action stating that he was underage when he executed the mortgage and the same should, therefore, be cancelled. He prayed for setting aside the mortgage. The mortgagee money lender prayed for the refund of ₹ 10500 from the minor.

(*a*) As a minor's contract is void, any money advanced to a minor can be recovered.

(*b*) A minor's contract is void ab initio, any money advanced to a minor cannot be recovered.

(*c*) A minor's contract is voidable; any money advanced to a minor can be recovered.

(*d*) Advanced money can be recovered because minor has given wrong information about his age. **(CLAT 2012)**

**46. PRINCIPLE**: A person is said to be of sound mind for the purpose of making a contract if, at the time when he makes it, he is capable of understanding it and of forming a rational judgment as to its effect upon his interests.

**FACTS:** Mr. X who is usually of sound state of mind, but occasionally of unsound state of mind, enters into a contract with Mr. Y when he was of unsound state of mind. Mr. Y having come to know about this fact afterwards, wants to file a suit against Mr. X

(*a*) Mr. X cannot enter into contract because he is of unsound state of mind when he entered into contract.

(*b*) Mr. X can enter into contract but the burden is on the other party to prove that he was of unsound state of mind at the time of contract.

(*c*) Mr. X can enter into contract but the burden is on Mr. X to prove that he was of sound state of mind at the time of contract.

(*d*) None of these **(CLAT 2012)**

**47. PRINCIPLE:** Proposal (communication) + Acceptance (communication) + Consideration = Contract. The communication of a proposal is complete when it comes to the knowledge of the person to whom it is made.

**FACTS:** X's nephew absconded from home. He sent his servant in search of the boy. After the servant had left, X by handbills offered to pay ₹ 501 to anybody finding his nephew. The servant came to know of this offer only after he had already traced the missing child. He, therefore, brought an action to recover the reward.

(*a*) His action would fail because he was not aware of the offer.

(*b*) His action would not fail because it was a general offer.

(*c*) The fact that he was not aware of the offer does not make any difference and hence it was a valid contract. It is a mere formality.

(*d*) None of the above **(CLAT 2012)**

**48. PRINCIPLE:** Agreements, the meaning of which is not certain, or not capable of being made certain, are void.

**FACTS:** A horse was bought for a certain price coupled with a promise to give ₹500 more if the horse is proved lucky.

(*a*) This is a valid agreement.

(*b*) This agreement is void for uncertainty because it is very difficult to determine what luck, bad or good, the horse has brought to the buyer.

(*c*) The agreement is partially valid and partially void.

(*d*) None of the above. **(CLAT 2012)**

**49. PRINCIPLE:** Mere silence as to the facts likely to affect the willingness of a person to enter into a contract is not a fraud, unless the circumstances of the case are such that, on close examination it is found to be the duty of the person keeping silent to speak, or unless his silence is, in itself, equivalent to speech.

**FACTS:** X sells by auction to Y, a horse which X knows to be of unsound state of mind. X says nothing to Y about the horse's unsound state of mind. Give the correct answer-

(*a*) X can be held liable for fraud.

(*b*) X can be held liable for misrepresentation

(*c*) X cannot be held liable, because he did not say anything positive about the mental state of the horse.

(*d*) X cannot be held liable because it is the buyer who must be aware of the things. **(CLAT 2012)**

**Instructions (50):** Given question consists of two statements, one labeled as 'Assertion' (A) and other as 'Reason' (R). You are to examine these two statements carefully and select the correct answers.

**50. Assertion (A):** A void contract is not necessarily illegal

**Reason (R):** Every illegal contract is void.

(*a*) Both A and R are individually true and R is the correct explanation of A.

(*b*) Both A and R are individually true but R is not the correct explanation of A.

(*c*) A is true but R is false.

(*d*) A is false but R is true. **(CLAT 2012)**

**51.** P, Q and R made a joint promise to give S a sum of ₹3000. S recovered the whole amount from P. Q was declared insolvent and cannot give anything. Which statement out of the following is correct?

(*a*) P cannot get anything from R.

(*b*) P can recover ₹1000 from R.

(*c*) P can recover ₹1500 from R

(*d*) P can recover ₹2000 from R. **(CLAT 2012)**

**Directions (Q. 52 - 53) :** Given below is a statement of legal principle followed by a factual situation. Apply the principle to the facts given below and select the most appropriate answer.

**52. LEGAL PRINCIPLE:** When at the desire of the promisor, the promisee has done or abstained from doing, or does or abstains from doing, or promises to do or abstain something, such an act or abstinence or promise is called consideration for the promise.

**FACTUAL SITUATION:** A daughter promises to give maintenance to her uncle in consideration of her mother making a gift of certain properties to her. The daughter pleads lack of consideration when the uncle seeks to enforce the contract. She says that the uncle is a stranger to the consideration and so he cannot enforce the contract. The daughter:

**DECISION:**

(*a*) will succeed because uncle being a stranger to the consideration cannot enforce it.

(*b*) will not succeed because uncle is a near relative and in such cases consideration is not necessary.

(*c*) cannot succeed because consideration might move from any person.

(*d*) none of the above **(AILET 2013)**

**53. LEGAL PRINCIPLES:**

(1) Parties to contract should be capable of entering in to contract, only then they can lay the foundation of a valid contract.

(2) Every person is competent to contract who is of the age of majority.

**FACTUAL SITUATION:** A minor agreed with B to become a tenant of his house and to pay ₹ 1,000/- for the furniture therein. He paid ₹ 800/- in cash and gave a promissory note for the balance. A occupied the premises and used the furniture for some months and then brought an action for refund of consideration, in this case

**DECISION:**

(*a*) A is liable to pay ₹ 1,000.

(*b*) A is liable to pay remaining ₹ 200.

(*c*) A is liable to refund of ₹ 800.

(*d*) Neither B is liable to refund ₹ 800 nor A is under obligation to pay ₹ 200. **(AILET 2013)**

**54.** A post dated cheque bears ______ date.

(*a*) past (*b*) no

(*c*) future (*d*) present **(AILET 2013)**

This section consists of fourteen (14) questions. Each question consists of legal propositions/ principles (hereinafter referred to as 'principle') and facts. These principles have to be applied to the given facts to arrive at the most reasonable conclusion. Such principles may or may not be true in the real sense, yet you have to conclusively assume them to be true for the purposes of this section. In other words, in answering the following questions, you must not rely on any principles except the principles that are given herein below for every question. Further you must not assume any facts other than those stated in the question. The objective of this section is to test your interest towards study of law, research aptitude and problem solving ability even if the "most reasonable conclusion" arrived at may be unacceptable for any other reason. It is not the objective of this section to test your knowledge of law. **(CLAT 2013)**

**55. Principle:** When an offer is accepted by a person to whom it is made, it becomes a promise. But this promise will become legally binding only when the acceptance of the offer is unconditional.

**Facts :** Ram makes an offer to sell his house to Shyam for ₹ 50 lacs. Shyam accepts this offer but wants to pay the price of the house in five quarterly instalments. Ram does not agree to it. Thereafter Shyam agrees to pay the price of the house in the way as originally desired by Ram. But Ram does not reply to it. Can Shyam compel Ram to sell his house to him?

(*a*) Shyam can compel Ram to sell his house because Shyam ultimately agrees to pay the price as originally desired by Ram

(*b*) Shyam can compel Ram to sell his house because Shyam in the first instance substantially complied with the desire of Ram

(*c*) Shyam can compel Ram to sell his house because Ram's offer does not exclude the payment of price in instalments

(*d*) Shyam can not compel Ram to sell his house because Shyam imposes a new condition about payment of price of the house while accepting the offer which is not ultimately accepted by Ram.

**56. Principle:** Generally an agreement without consideration is not valid. Therefore, in order to make a valid agreement, some consideration which may have some value in the eyes of law, is essentially required. **(CLAT 2013)**

**Facts:** William has an old car of which he makes seldom use. He voluntarily enters into an agreement with Smith to sell this car for rupees ten thousand. Thereafter one Anson approaches William and offers to buy that car for rupees one lac as the car was one which Anson has been searching for long. Now William wants to cancel his agreement with Smith and refuses to deliver the car to him saying that consideration (price) for the car promised by Smith is negligible and, therefore, agreement with him can not be said to be valid one.

(*a*) William can cancel his agreement with Smith as the consideration involved in that is really inadequate.

(*b*) William can not cancel his agreement with Smith as the sale of car for rupees ten thousand was voluntary and this price has some value in the eyes of law.

(*c*) William can cancel his agreement with Smith as he was ignorant about the value / price of the car for which it could be sold.

(*d*) William can cancel his agreement with Smith as he is entitled to get full market value/price of his car.

**57. Principle:** A Contract can not be enforced by or against a person who is not a party to it. However, where some benefit is conferred on third party by the contract itself, there third party can be allowed to enforce that contract to get such benefit. **(CLAT 2013)**

**Facts:** Dinesh is liable to pay ₹ 50000/- to Suresh. In order to discharge this liability Dinesh enters into a contract with Ramesh by which Dinesh sells his car to Ramesh for ₹ 1 lac. Ramesh takes the delivery of the car and promises/ assures to pay its price at the earliest. Dinesh separately informs Suresh about this contract for his satisfaction. Ramesh fails to pay the car's price. Suresh wants to join Dinesh in filing suit against Ramesh for the recovery of price of the car. Whether Suresh is entitled to do so?

(*a*) Suresh is entitled to do so because the contract was made for his benefit.

(*b*) Suresh is entitled to do so because Dinesh is liable to him and discharge of this liability depends upon the payment of the price of the car by Ramesh.

(*c*) Suresh is not entitled to do so because liability of Dinesh does not depand upon any assurance of Ramesh

(*d*) Suresh is not entitled to do because he is not a party to the contract between Dinesh and Ramesh.

**58. Principle:** If a contract is made by post between two persons living in two different cities, then the contract is said to be complete as soon as the letter of acceptance is properly posted, and the place of completion of the contract is that city where acceptance is posted. It is worth mentioning here that in every contract there is always an offer from one party and the acceptance of the offer from the other party. **(CLAT 2013)**

**Facts:** Sani, a resident of Patna, gives an offer by post to sell his house for ₹ 25 lacs to Hani, a resident of Allahabad. This offer letter is posted on 1st January 2013 from Patna and reaches

Allahabad on 7th January 2013. Hani accepts this offer and posts the letter of acceptance on 8th January 2013 from Allahabad which reaches Patna on 16th January 2013. But Sani presuming that Hani is not interested in accepting his offer, sells his house to Gani at same price on 15th of January, 2013. Hani files a suit against Sani for the breach of contract in the competent court of Allahabad. Whether Hani will succeed?

(*a*) Hani can not succeed as Sani can not be compelled by law to wait for the answer from Hani for an indefinite period of time.

(*b*) Hani can not succeed as he could use some other effective and speedy mode for communicating his acceptance in minimum possible time

(*c*) Hani can succeed as he properly posted the letter of acceptance and the delay was beyond his control

(*d*) Hani can succeed as contract became complete in the eyes of law on the date of posting the letter of acceptance

**59. Principle:** If the object of an agreement is or becomes unlawful or immoral or opposed to public policy in the eyes of law, then the courts will not enforce such agreements. Law generally prohibits Child labour. **(CLAT 2013)**

**Facts:** P enters into an agreement with T by which P has to let his house to T for two years and T has to pay ₹ 20000.00 per month to P as rent. T starts a child care centre in that house. But after some time in order to earn some money for the maintenance of the centre, T starts sending the children of the centre on the rotation basis to work for four hour a day in some nearby chemical and hazardous factories. When P comes to know about this new development, he asks T either to stop the children from working in factories or to leave his house immediately. T neither agrees to leave the house nor to stop the children from working in the factories. P files a suit in the court of law for appropriate relief/ action

(*a*) P can not succeed as the agreement was for the two years and it can not be terminated before the expiry of that period

(*b*) P can not succeed as the object at the time of making of the agreement was not clear

(*c*) P will succeed as the object of the agreement has become unlawful.

(*d*) P will not succeed if T agrees to share the wages of the children with P

**60. Principle:** An agreement to do an act impossible in itself cannot be enforced by a court of law. **(CLAT 2013)**

**Facts:** Ramesh agrees with his girl friend Shilpa to pluck stars from the sky through his extraordinary will power, and bring them down on earth for her within a week. After the expiry of one week, Shilpa filed a suit for damages against Ramesh for the breach of contract as Ramesh failed to perform his promise.

(*a*) Shilpa can succeed in getting damages as Ramesh has deceived her.

(*b*) Ramesh cannot be held liable as he honestly believes that his love for Shilpa is true and, therefore, he will succeed in his endeavour.

(*c*) The court cannot entertain such suits as the act promised under the agreement is impossible in itself.

(*d*) Ramesh can be held liable for making an absurd promise.

**61. Principle:** An agreement may be oral or written. However, if a law specifically requires that an agreement must be in writing then the agreement must be in writing. A law specifically requires that the agreements relating to transfer of the copyright in novel between an author of a novel and the producer of a motion picture must be in writing. **(CLAT 2013)**

**Facts:** The author of a novel, *Love at Lost Sight*, had several rounds of discussion with a producer of motion picture regarding making of a motion picture based on *Love at Lost Sight*. During the last discussion, they decided to make a motion picture on *Love at Lost Sight*. The producer made a motion picture on *Love at Lost Sight* after making a payment of ₹ 10, 00,000/- (Ten Lac Only) in cash to the author who happily accepted this amount as full and final payment. Later on, on the advice of his lawyer, the author brought a case in a court of law against the producer on the ground that there is no written agreement between the producer and him.

(*a*) The author is likely to succeed in the case as the agreement is not in accordance with the law

(*b*) The author cannot succeed in the case as he has given his consent to the agreement

(*c*) The author is not likely to succeed in the case because he has already accepted the amount of ₹ 10,00,000/- as full an final payment

(*d*) The author can succeed in the case as the consideration is not adequate

**62. Principle:** A person is said to be of sound mind for the purpose of making a contract if, at the time when he makes it, he is capable of understanding it and of forming a rational judgment as to its effect upon his interest. **(CLAT 2013)**

**Facts:** X who is usually of sound mind, but occasionally of unsound mind enters into a contract with Y when he (X) is of unsound mind. Y came to know about this fact afterwards and now wants to file a suit against X.

(*a*) X cannot enter into contract because he is of unsound mind when he entered into contract.

(*b*) X can enter into contract but the burden is on the other party to prove that he was of unsound mind at the time of contract.

(*c*) X can enter into contract but the burden is on X to prove that he was of sound mind at the time of contract.

(*d*) None of these.

**63. Principle:** When at the desire of one person, any other person has done or abstained from doing something, such act or abstinence or promise is called a consideration for the promise. Only a promise coupled with consideration is enforceable by law. **(CLAT 2013)**

**Facts:** X, the uncle of Y, made a promise to pay him an amount of ₹ 10,000/- as reward if Y quits smoking and drinking within one year. X also deposited the above mentioned amount in a bank and informed Y that the said amount will be paid to him if he quits smoking and drinking within one year. Within a period of six months of making the promise X died. After the expiry of one year of making the promise by X, Y made a request to the legal heirs of X demanding the promised money. The legal heirs of X declined the request of Y.

(*a*) The promise of X to Y is enforceable by law because Y has quitted smoking and drinking

(*b*) The promise of X to Y is not enforceable by law because Y has benefitted by quitting smoking and drinking

(*c*) The promise of X to Y is enforceable by law because the amount of ₹ 10, 000/- has been deposited in a bank

(*d*) The promise of X to Y is enforceable by law because X has died within a period of six months of making the promise

**64. Principle:** Mere silence as to facts likely to affect the decision of a person to enter into a contract does not amount to fraud, unless his silence is in itself equivalent to speech. **(CLAT 2013)**

**Facts:** A sells to B a horse which A knows to be of unsound mind. B says to A that if A does not say anything about the state of mind of horse, then B shall presume that the horse is of sound mind. A says nothing to B about the mental condition of horse.

(*a*) A has committed fraud

(*b*) A has committed misrepresentation

(*c*) There cannot be a fraud because A says nothing about the mental condition of the horse

(*d*) There can not be a fraud because B did not ask A whether the horse is of sound mind

**65. Principle:** When a party to a contract has refused to perform, or disabled himself from performing, his promise in its entirety, the other party may put an end to the contract. **(CLAT 2013)**

**Facts:** A engaged B on April 12 to enter his service on June 1, but on May 11, A wrote to B that his services would not be needed. On May 22, B joined C for employment.

(*a*) B must wait till June 1

(*b*) B must have joined C on May 11

(*c*) B is not bound to wait till June 1

(*d*) A must pay damages to B

**66. Principle:** A condition precedent must be complied with before the happening of the event to which such a condition is attached. Fulfillment of such a condition after the happening of the event is no fulfillment of condition. **(CLAT 2013)**

**Facts:** A transfers ₹ 5000 to B on condition that he shall marry with the consent of C, D and E. As C, D and E had to go abroad for some business purposes and as the date of marriage was already fixed, therefore, B marries without the consent of C, D and E, but obtains their consent after the marriage when C, D and E return to their country.

(*a*) B has fulfilled the condition

(*b*) B has not fulfilled the condition

(*c*) B was free to marry any one without the consent of any body

(*d*) B must divorce his wife as he married her without fulfilling the condition

**67. Principle:** In an agreement, a condition subsequent must be complied with, to claim the benefit of that agreement. **(CLAT 2013)**

**Facts:** A agrees to transfer a farm to B, provided that, if B does not go to England within three years after the date of the agreement, his interest in the farm shall cease. B does not go to England within the term prescribed.

(*a*) B's interest in the farm continues

(*b*) B's interest in the farm does not continue

(*c*) B has a fundamental right to go to England or not to go to England and hence the condition was illegal

(*d*) The agreement between A and B was void

**68. Principle:** Every agreement in restraint of the marriage of any person, other than a minor, is void. **(CLAT 2013)**

**Facts:** Qadir Khan died in a road accident. Two co-widows, Sultana and Marjina enter into an agreement that if any of them will remarry, would forfeit her right to her share in the deceased husband's property.

(*a*) The agreement is void because it was restraint of marriage

(*b*) The agreement is not void because no restraint was imposed upon either of two widows for remarriage.

(*c*) The restraint was partial so agreement is valid

(*d*) None of the above

**Directions (Q. 69 - 77) :** Given below is a statement of legal principle followed by a factual situation. Apply the principle to the facts given below and select the most appropriate answer. **(AILET 2014)**

**69. LEGAL PRINCIPLE :** Every partner is liable, jointly with all the other partners and also severally, for all acts of the firm done while he is a partner.

**FACTUAL SITUATION :** A and B started a partnership firm for providing vehicle repairing services. C approached the firm for getting his car repaired and noticed that only B was present in the office. C informed the problem, and B started repairing the car. While B was repairing, he filled petrol instead of oil in the engine. As a consequence, a small blast occurred and damaged the car. Now, C sued both A and B for the damage so caused. Decide.

**DECISION :**

(*a*) Both liable since B was authorised to carry out the work of the firm.

(*b*) A is not liable since A has not authorised B to do something which was not for the benefit of the firm.

(*c*) A is not liable since it was B's fault and for that only B can be held liable.

(*d*) A is liable since it was negligence on his part that he was not resent in the office when C came.

**70. LEGAL PRINCIPLE :** Every agreement, by which any party is restricted absolutely from enforcing his rights in respect of any contract, by the usual legal proceedings in the ordinary tribunals, is void to that extent.

**FACTUAL SITUATION :** Feroz and Pinto entered into an agreement for rendering certain services. As per the prevailing law, the agreement may be enforced either at Jaipur or Udaipur. The agreement itself, however, specifies that upon breach, the parties can only approach courts at Jaipur. Feroz breaches the contract and Pinto, being a resident of Udaipur, would like to sue him in Udaipur. He challenged the validity of the clause.

**DECISION :**

(*a*) Pinto will succeed as Feroz had made him suffer and the law must take his convenience into account and allow him to sue in Udaipur.

(*b*) Pinto will succeed as the contract does not allow him to institute any legal proceedings in any court or tribunal in Udaipur.

(*c*) Pinto will fail as the contract does not restrain him from instituting legal proceedings in Jaipur.

(*d*) Pinto will fail as he was of sound mind while entering into contract and having accepted it, he cannot now deny his obligation.

**71. LEGAL PRINCIPLES :** A contract is an agreement enforceable by law.

**FACTUAL SITUATION :** Amita invited Bina to her house for dinner. Bina accepted the invitation but later did not go. On Bina's failure to attend, Amita filed a suit against Bina for the price of non-consumed food. Will the law enforce this agreement?

**DECISION :**

(*a*) No, it is a social agreement.

(*b*) Yes, Amita can recover amount for non-consumed food.

(*c*) No, as Bina did not accept the invitation in writing.

(*d*) No, because the law does not take account of trivial things.

**72. LEGAL PRINCIPLES :**

1. Once a person accepts another's offer, and signifies such acceptance to the former, a contract comes into existence between them.
2. Uncertain agreements are void agreements.
3. Rejected offers can be accepted only if renewed.

**FACTUAL SITUATION :** Bakshi wanted to purchase a particular land. He sent a letter to his cousin, Dutt, offering him ₹ 4 lakhs for it. Dutt replied that he would not sell it below 5 lakhs. Bakshi communicated his willingness to pay this amount. Dutt did not sell the land to Bakshi. Bakshi sued him for breach of contract.

**DECISION :**

(*a*) Dutt is liable because once he communicates an offer to Bakshi and Bakshi accepts it, a contract comes into existence.

(*b*) Dutt is liable as he has misled Bakshi by his actions.

(*c*) Dutt is not liable because he has rejected the offer by giving a counter offer which is also not specific.

(*d*) Dutt is not liable as there is no legally enforceable contract.

**73. LEGAL PRINCIPLE :** An agreement is void if the court regards it as opposed to the public policy.

**FACTUAL SITUATION :** Sunita, while her husband Shankar was alive, promised to marry Neel in the event of Shankar's death. Subsequently, Shankar died, but Sunita refused to marry Neel. Neel sues Sunita for damages for breach of promise.

**DECISION :**

(*a*) Sunita is liable as she is to bound to marry Neel.

(*b*) She is liable to compensate Neel for breach of promise.

(*c*) Neel can marry someone else.

(*d*) She is not liable as the contract is opposed to public policy and so void.

**74. LEGAL PRINCIPLE :** An agreement is void if its object is unlawful.

**FACTUAL SITUATION :** Sunil had a rich uncle who owned prime property in Chennai and had lot of money in the bank. Being the only heir, Sunil was sure that he would inherit the property. One day, the uncle called him to his room and announced that he planned to marry again. This angered Sunil and he plans to murder his uncle so he hired Anuj, a murderer and entered into a contract with him to kill his uncle. Sunil agreed to pay As. 10 lakhs to Anuj and even paid 5 lakhs as advance. The following night Anuj entered the uncle's house intending to kill him. On reaching there, he realised that Sunil's uncle was already dead so he left without doing anything. Next day, after post mortem report, it transpired that Sunil's uncle had died due to heart attack. Now, Sunil wants to recover the advance from Anuj. Will he succeed?

**DECISION :**

(*a*) Yes

(*b*) No

(*c*) Anuj is liable to return the amount as the act was done by him.

(*d*) None of the above.

**75. LEGAL PRINCIPLES :**

1. Consideration must be of value in the eyes of law.
2. Consideration is not real if it is illusory.

**FACTUAL SITUATION :** Arjun received summons to appear at a trial as a witness on behalf of Bitu, the accused. Bitu promised to pay him a sum of ₹ 1,000 for his trouble. On default by Bitu, Arjun filed a suit to recover the said sum. Will he succeed?

**DECISION :**

(*a*) No, as the consideration is of no value in the eyes of law.

(*b*) Yes, as the contract is supported by consideration.

(*c*) No, as there is no consideration for the promise.

(*d*) Yes, as he appeared before court only after Bitu agreed to pay him the amount of ₹ 1,000.

**76. LEGAL PRINCIPLE :** A minor is not competent to contract.

**FACTUAL SITUATION :** Deep, a 9th standard student realizes that he being a minor, he is not permitted by law to execute a contract, appoints Mandeep as his agent to conclude purchase of a land to gift it to his mother on her birthday. Mandeep accordingly prepares the papers for the transaction but at the last minute the seller who had agreed to sell it now refuses to sell it contending that he does not wish to sell the land to a minor. Deep seeks to enforce the contract against the seller.

**DECISION :**

(*a*) Deep can enforce the contract - since Mandeep is his agent, Deep is deemed to have personally entered into a contract.

(*b*) Deep cannot enforce the contract - only Mandeep can, since seller has entered into the contract with Mandeep.

(*c*) Deep cannot enforce the contract since he is a minor.

(*d*) Deep can neither appoint an agent nor enforce the contract since he is a minor.

**77. LEGAL PRINCIPLES :**

1. Acceptance must be given only by the person to whom the offer is made.
2. Communication of acceptance to a person who did not make the offer does not bind the offeror.

**FACTUAL SITUATION :** Pal sold his business to Sam without disclosing it to his customers. Mani, an old customer sent an order for goods to Pal by name. Sam, the new owner, executed the order. Mani refuses to accept the goods from Sam as he intended to deal only with Pal. In a suit by Sam against Mani:

**DECISION :**

(*a*) Sam cannot recover as Mani never intended to deal with him.

(*b*) Can recover the price as he had supplied goods only against the order made by Mani.

(*c*) Sam cannot recover as it was only an invitation to offer by Mani on which no acceptance can be given by Sam.

(*d*) Sam can recover as the price of the goods as an offer once accepted results in a contract.

**Directions (Q. 78 to 87) :** *This section consists of ten (10) questions.*

Each question consists of legal propositions/principles (hereinafter referred to as 'principle') and facts. These principles have to be applied to the given facts to arrive at the most reasonable conclusion. Such principles may or may not be true in the real sense, yet you have to conclusively assume them to be true for the purposes of this section. In other words, in answering the following questions, you must not rely on any principles except the principles that are given herein below for every question. Further, you must not assume any facts other than those stated in the question. The objective of this section is to test your interest towards study of law, research aptitude and problem solving ability even if the 'most reasonable conclusion' arrived at may be unacceptable for, any other reason. It is not the object of this section to test your knowledge of law. **(CLAT 2014)**

**78. Principle:** When one person signifies to another his willingness to do or to abstain from doing anything, with a view to obtaining the assent of that other to such act or abstinence, he is said to make a proposal. The expression of willingness/ desire results in a valid proposal only when it is made/addressed to some person(s).

**Facts:** 'X' makes the following statement in an uninhabited hall: 'I wish to sell my mobile phone for '1,000.'

Which of the following derivations is CORRECT?

(*a*) 'X' made a statement that resulted in a promise

(*b*) 'X' made a statement that resulted in a proposal

(*c*) 'X' made a statement that did not result in any proposal

(*d*) 'X' made a statement that resulted in an agreement

**79. Principle:** A proposal (offer) should be made with an intention that after its valid acceptance, a legally binding promise or agreement will be created. The test for the determination of such intention is not subjective, rather it is objective. The intention of the parties is to be ascertained from the terms of the agreement and the surrounding circumstances under which such an agreement is entered into. As a general rule, in the case of arrangements regulating social relations, it follows as a matter of course that the parties do not intend legal consequences to follow. On the contrary, as a general rule, in the case of arrangements regulating business affairs, it follows as a matter of course that the parties intend legal consequences to follow. However, the above rules are just presumptive in nature, and hence, can be rebutted.

**Facts:** One morning while having breakfast, 'X', the father, says to 'Y' (X's son), in a casual manner, 'I shall buy a motorbike for you if you get through the CLAT.'

Which of the following derivations is CORRECT?

(*a*) 'X' made a statement that resulted in an enforceable promise

(*b*) 'X' made a statement that resulted in a valid proposal

(*c*) 'X' made a statement that resulted in an enforceable agreement

(*d*) 'X' made a statement that did not result in any enforceable agreement

**80. Principle:** Acceptance (of offer) must be communicated by the offeree to the offeror so as to give rise to a binding obligation. The expression 'by the offeree to the offeror' includes communication between their authorised agents.

**Facts:** 'X' made an offer to buy Y's property for a stipulated price. 'Y' accepted it and communicated his acceptance to 'Z', a stranger.

Which of the following derivations is CORRECT?

(*a*) Y's acceptance resulted in an agreement

(*b*) Y's acceptance did not result in any agreement

(*c*) Y's acceptance resulted in a contract

(*d*) Y's acceptance resulted in a promise

**81. Principle:** Acceptance should be made while the offer is still subsisting. The offeror is free to retract his offer at any time before his offer gets accepted by the offeree. Once the offer is withdrawn or is lapsed, it is not open to be accepted so as to give rise to a contract. Similarly, if a time is prescribed within which the offer is to be accepted, then, the offer must be accepted within the prescribed time. And, if no time is prescribed, then, the acceptance must be made within a reasonable time. 'What is a reasonable time', is a question of fact which is to be determined by taking into account all the relevant facts and surrounding circumstances.

**Facts:** 'X' makes an offer to 'Y' to sell his equipment for ₹ 1,000.00. No time is specified for the acceptance. 'Y' sends his reply two years after receiving the offer.

Which of the following derivations is CORRECT?

(*a*) There arises a contract between 'X' and 'Y' to sell/buy the equipment in question for ₹ 1,000.00

(*b*) There does not arise any contract between 'X' and 'Y' to sell/buy the equipment in question for ₹ 1,000.00

(*c*) 'X' is bound by his offer, and hence, cannot reject the acceptance made by 'Y'

(*d*) There arises a promise by 'Y' to buy the equipment

**82. Principle:** Minor's agreement is void from the very beginning. It can never be validated. It cannot be enforced in the court of law.

**Facts:** 'A', a boy of 16 years of age, agrees to buy a camera from 'B', who is a girl of 21 years of age.

Which of the following derivations is CORRECT?

(*a*) There arises a contract between 'A' and 'B' to sell/buy the camera in question

(*b*) There arises an enforceable agreement between 'A' and 'B' to sell/buy the camera in question

(*c*) There does not arise any contract between 'A' and 'B' to sell/buy the camera in question

(*d*) There arises a voidable contract between 'A' and 'B', to sell/buy the camera in question

**83. Principle:** A contract which is duly supported by real and lawful consideration is valid notwithstanding the fact that the consideration is inadequate. The quantum of consideration is for the parties to decide at the time of making a contract, and not for the courts (to decide) when the contract is sought to be enforced. An agreement to which the consent of the promisor is freely given is not void merely because the consideration is inadequate; but the inadequacy of the consideration may be taken into account by the Court in determining the question whether the consent of the promisor was freely given.

**Facts:** 'A' agrees to sell his mobile phone worth ₹20,000/- for ₹100/- only to 'B'. A's consent is freely given.

Which of the following derivations is CORRECT?

(*a*) There is a contract between 'A' and 'B'

(*b*) There is no contract between 'A' and 'B' because consideration is not adequate

(*c*) There is no contract between 'A' and 'B' because a mobile phone worth ₹20,000/- cannot be sold for just ₹100/-

(*d*) None of the above.

**84. Principle:** The consideration or object of an agreement is unlawful if it is forbidden by law. Every agreement of which the object or consideration is unlawful is void.

**Facts:** 'X', promises to pay 'Y' ₹50,000, if he ('Y') commits a crime. 'X' further promises to indemnify him ('Y') against any liability arising thereof. 'Y' agrees to act as per X's promise.

Which of the following derivations is CORRECT?

(*a*) There is a contract between 'X' and 'Y'

(*b*) There is an agreement between 'X' and 'Y' which can be enforced by the court of law

(*c*) There is an agreement between 'X', and 'Y' which cannot be enforced by the court of law

(*d*) There is a voidable contract between 'X' and 'Y'

**85. Principle:** The consideration or object of an agreement is unlawful if the Court regards it as opposed to public policy. Every agreement of which the object or consideration is unlawful is void.

**Facts:** 'X' promises to obtain for 'Y' an employment in the public service; and 'Y' promises to pay ₹ 5,00,000/- to 'X'.

Which of the following derivations is CORRECT?

(*a*) There is a contract between 'X' and 'Y'

(*b*) There is a voidable contract between 'X' and 'Y'

(*c*) There is an agreement between 'X' and 'Y' which can be enforced by the court of law

(*d*) There is an agreement between 'X', and 'Y' which cannot be enforced by the court of law

**86. Principle:** Two or more persons are said to consent if they agree upon the same thing in the same sense. Consent is said to be free when it is not caused by coercion, or undue influence, or fraud, or misrepresentation, or mistake. When consent to an agreement is caused by coercion, undue influence, fraud or misrepresentation, the agreement is a contract voidable (rescindable or terminable) at the option of the party whose consent was so caused. However, when consent to an agreement is caused by mistake as to a matter of fact essential to the agreement, the agreement is void.

**Facts:** 'X' threatens to gun down 'Y', if he ('Y') does not sell his property worth ₹20,00,000/- for ₹1,00,000/- only. As a consequence, 'Y' agrees to sell it as demanded by A'.

Which of the following derivations is CORRECT?

(*a*) There is a contract between 'X' and 'Y'

(*b*) There is an agreement between 'X' and 'Y' which can be enforced by the court of law

(*c*) There is an agreement between 'X', and 'Y' which cannot be enforced by the court of law

(*d*) There is a contract between 'X' and 'Y' which voidable at the option of 'Y'

**87. Principle:** Agreements in restraint of marriage are void.

**Facts:** 'X' enters into an agreement with 'Y' where under he agrees not to marry anybody else other than a person whose name starts with the letter 'A', and promises to pay ₹1,00,000/- to 'Y' if he ('X') breaks this agreement.

Which of the following derivations is CORRECT?

(*a*) There is a contract between 'X' and 'Y'

(*b*) There is an agreement between 'X' and 'Y' which can be enforced by the court of law

(*c*) There is an agreement between 'X', and 'Y' which cannot be enforced by the court of law

(*d*) There is a voidable contract between 'X' and 'Y'

## Solutions

**1.** b The minimum number of partners must be two, while the maximum number can be 10 in case of banking business and 20 in all other types of business.

**2.** c In normal course of business, the same iron was available in the market at ₹ 105 per ton. B, however, bought it for ₹ 110 per ton and suffered a loss of ₹ 10,000, being the amount more than what he would have paid under the contract. As per the principle, the loses which naturally arose in the usual course of things would be the loss which was incurred by B over and above the market rate at which that iron was available in the market at the time when the contract was breached. Thus, the difference between the loss incurred and the market rate is the rightful amount which can be claimed by B, i.e., 10,000 - 5,000 = 5,000.

**3.** b It is also essential to remember in this regard that the duty to abide by legal obligations does not affect free consent in any way whatsoever.

**4.** c Even though Vishal's son finished the portrait, Arun is under no obligation to accept it. Vishal was given the contract because of his own artistic skills which cannot be transferred or inherited by his son. Without performing his part of the contract Vishal died. When his son completed the portrait himself, he ratified the contract and also all the obligations thereunder. As a result, Vishal's son must repay the advance paid by Arun.

**5.** c A contract is said to be induced by "undue influence" where the relations subsisting between the parties are such that one of the parties is in a position to dominate the will of the other and uses that position to obtain an unfair advantage over the other. Ramesh being the master in this case there exists all possibility that undue influence may be exercised on his part.

**6.** a When someone displays an article indicating its price, law of contract considers it to be an invitation to offer and not offer. In simple terms, the person invites others to offer which he may or may not accept.

**7.** a Law of Contract primarily aims to avoid commercial hardships and losses which occur to the parties in business transactions. It is never concerned towards fulfillment of human desires and wishes.

**8.** b A contract to do an act which, after the contract is made, becomes impossible, or, by reason of some event which the promisor could not prevent, unlawful, becomes void when the act becomes impossible or unlawful.

**9.** b The minimum number of partners must be two, while the maximum number can be 10 in case of banking business and 20 in all other types of business.

**10.** 'Privacy of contract' means a contract can't confer rights of obligation to any person except the parties to it.

**11.** A minor is an individual under the age of 18 years.

**12.** a In the present fact the contract is not complete as the acceptance to the contract never reached to the offeror. Acceptance was not communicated to the offeror.

**13.** b B only posted the letter but the contract would be complete when A receives the letter and reads it. The agreement shall transform into a contract once the letter of acceptance is received by A and not before that.

**14.** b Communication of acceptance is an essential element of contract. A contract shall be entered into only after A reads the email otherwise it will remain incomplete.

**15.** a No force or compulsion was used and the consent given for examination was free consent. So it is a valid contract.

**16.** c Both the parties were under mistake of the actual price of the property and therefore the agreement was never complete and it was a void agreement.

**17.** c Object or purpose of the contract is against the public policy and morals. As getting married in return of the money is not correct morally and also it is a crime in the law. So the contract is not valid contract.

**18.** a The purpose of the agreement in the facts was to defeat provision of Criminal procedure code which wants a third person to take the surety of the accused on individual and independent basis. So it has defeated the provision of the requisite law.

**19.** b Correct answer should be (*b*) and not (*c*). In present facts by entering into the contract couple disentitled there children from the ancestral property and right over ancestral property cannot be taken away or limited. So contract entered to do the same is not a valid contract.

**20.** b The bidders by entering into the contract wanted to cause loss to the BCCI which is against the principle of bidding and against the public policy so the contract entered is void.

**21.** a Contract is void as contract is restricting company in there lawful trade.

**22.** a Contract is valid as it does not absolutely restrict the party to approach to any court; rather it just restricts the party to go to the other court. So restriction was not absolute and this is a valid contract.

**23.** b The certainty to the contract is not present. Since the property an important part of the contract has not been described briefly. Also the certainty to the property is missing in the contract so it is not a valid contract. Entire ancestral property is a very general term, for a valid transfer, law requires that it must be specifically mentioned.

**24.** d Zaverilal should compensate as he said that the article was strong and almost unbreakable. The fact that the article broke will hold Zaverilal liable. None of the options given explore this possibility. Hence it's none of the above.

**25.** a The principle states that the purpose of damages is to compensate the injured person and not to improve his position, the amount has spent 4 lakhs thus he should get back the amount he has spent.

**26.** b Ramakrishna is liable to pay ₹40,000/- as agreed in the contract. Second half of the principle is applicable in this case as it was already agreed between the parties at the time of contract that whoever will commit breach, will pay the amount.

**27.** c The manufacturers of a commodity are under a duty of care for the products it sells to its consumers. The fact that the bottle of beer contained a snail makes the manufacturer liable. Whether there was a contractual obligation or not is irrelevant here.

**28.** b The collateral factor in this contract was that B should have married C within a period of 6 months. Since B married in 7th month, A is under no obligation to pay ₹1 Lakh.

**29.** b The rescuer is not entitled for the payment as the rescuer had no idea of the promise when he acted to save the child.

**30.** c Illness caused to Sushmita was not a natural thing or which naturally arose in the usual course of things, hence the liability of the Bus company will only be to the extent of inconvenience caused by walking only.

**31.** c Contracts are agreements which are enforceable by law. It is essential for all agreements to have a valid acceptance to the offer made in the agreement. Therefore it is clear, in order to a contract come into existence, it is necessary that an offer made in the agreement is accepted. However, keep in mind, All Contracts are Agreements but all Agreements are not Contracts.

**32.** a Applying the principle of syllogism it is clear from the facts that a minor cannot work in a shop.

One of the essential element for a valid contract is competency of parties. Under section 11 of the Indian Contract Act, 1872 it is stated that any person may become a party to the contract except for who is a minor or of unsound mind or forbidden by law.

**33.** c It is a well settled rule to the effect that contract will not be enforced if it is in violation of law. In any society, governmental entities enact laws and make policies. Public policy can be generally defined as a system of laws, regulatory measures, courses of action, and funding priorities concerning a given topic promulgated by a governmental entity or its representatives. Thus a subject matter of a contract which is opposed to the public policy cannot be validated.

**34.** a Not bound to pay as he did not ask the shopkeeper to deliver the bag.

The action of leaving the flour bag at the doorstep of Y was uncalled for. Besides, the message that X leaves with the bag does not constitute any offer but is a mere statement. Usage of flour by Y does not amount to any acceptance or a counter offer. Y is not bound to pay anything to X. This could be compared with sample sachets that are given with a newspaper/magazine copy. Mere usage of those samples by the consumer does not bind him to pay to the provider, irrespective of any message that is given with the sample.

**35.** b The principle clearly states that in case of a guardian the age of majority becomes 21. And being a minor if she enters into a contract with Ajay, the same is not enforceable as per the principle. Chaaru can justifiably challenge the sale transaction.

**36.** a The only exception wherein money can be recovered from a minor is if the other party was deceived. The principle makes no reference to honest belief. Hence, a is the correct answer.

**37.** a The sale would be valid and enforceable only if Bandita is a major.

**38.** c It is the only appropriate option as knowing the Bandita is 18 years and the property is being looked after by her mother Ajay had induced rather than convincing Bandita to sell the land.

**39.** a It will surely defeat the purpose of law if Ajay is allowed to recover, as the protection is rendered to minor persons considering they may not be able to make a rational decision. Therefore any transaction entered into with a minor is not enforceable. If Ajay is allowed to recover then the purpose of law to offer protection to minors would be of no value and effect.

**40.** c Refer Rule C. Dhanaraj calls Chulbul and threatens him.

**41.** c The case here is one of coercion and not of undue influence. Undue influence is exercised in cases where one person has a position of authority over the other and manipulates such to unduly influence the other person. This is a case of coercion.

**42.** a Chulbul was coerced by Dhanraj entering into the employment contract and hence he is justified in refusing the enforcement. Out of option (*a*) and (*b*) the reasoning provided in (*a*) is more logical and relatable to the principle.

**43.** b Baalu had not coerced Chulbul in the given case and if this is proved, he would be entitled to get the job.

**44.** b When Shyam replied that lowest price for car is 20 lakhs that was an invitation to offer and Ramanuj had to make another offer to which Shyam could have given an acceptance or refusal.

**45.** b Section 11 of Indian Contract Acts provides the definition of "who are competent to contract". In the case of *Mohri Bibi v. Dharmadas Ghose* it was held that any agreement with a minor is void ab initio.

**46.** c Burden of proof lies on the person who first asserts the fact, and not on the one who denies that fact to be true. The responsibility of the defendant to prove a fact to be true would start only when the authenticity of the fact is proved by the plaintiff.

**47.** a The servant did not know about the offer when he traced the missing child. Hence, his action would fail.

**48.** b Here the word luck has not been defined in the agreement. Hence it is void of uncertainty.

**49.** c X cannot be held liable because he did not say anything about the mental state of the horse.

**50.** b All illegal contract are void, but not all void contracts are illegal.

**51.** c The promise had been made jointly by P, Q and R. Since Q has been declared insolvent he is out of the picture and P can claim ₹ 1500 from R.

**52.** c Though the correct answer marked in the question is '(c)', but the question is ambiguous.

**53.** d In the present matter, A is a minor and hence does not have the capacity to contract. Therefore, the contract entered by him with B is not a valid contract. And since it is not a valid contract A is not liable to pay anything to B. Therefore, (*d*) is the right answer.

**54.** c In banking, postdated refers to cheques which have been written by the drawer for a date in the future.

**55.** d As per the principle, a promise is legally binding only when acceptance is unconditional. Shyam's acceptance was accompanied by another condition which amounts to counter offer. Hence, Shyam cannot compel Ram to sell his house.

**56.** b Although Smith's offer is negligible when it is compared with Anson's offer, however It does have a substantial value in the eyes of law and hence is a valid consideration.

**57.** * The facts seem to be insufficient because it is not clear whether Suresh was the third party to the contract or not. He was merely being assured by Dinesh that his profit from the contract would be used to repay his debt. However, if we assume Suresh to be the third party, then option "D" would be the most appropriate.

**58.** d As per the principle, acceptance is complete when the letter of acceptance is properly posted and in the present scenario, this was done before Sani sold his house to Gani. Hence option D would be the correct answer.

**59.** * The facts are insufficient to state the object of the agreement entered between P and T. If we consider the object to be the benefit of children through a child care centre, then we can narrow down on option "C" as the answer.

**60.** c The agreement is based on an act which is impossible in nature, and as per the principle any such impossible act cannot be enforced by the court of law. Hence, "C" is the correct answer.

**61.** a Since the law specifically provides for the agreement relating to transfer of the copyright in novel between author of a novel and the producer need to be in writing, author will succeed.

**62.** * The principle and facts are insufficient to conclusively reach an answer. The principle only states who is a person of unsound mind but is silent upon the repercussions of the agreement entered into by a person of unsound mind. So, Legal knowledge had to be applied in this case. Option "A" and "D" are equally possible answer

**63.** * The principle and facts are insufficient to reach at a conclusive answer. The facts are silent on the aspect whether Y had quit smoking and drinking. Going with the assumption that he had quit smoking and drinking, we can mark option "A" as the answer.

**64.** a B specifically asked A to state the mental condition of the horse. A stayed silent but his silence amounted to speech indicating that the mental state of the horse is sound. Thus, it would amount to fraud.

**65.** c When A wrote to B on 11th May that his services will not be needed, he had refused to perform his part of the contract giving B the liberty to end the contract and go ahead with other options.

**66.** b Condition precedent means that the condition should be carried out before the happening of the event. In this case, B married without the consent of C,D and E. Obtaining their consent after the marriage is not fulfilling the condition precedent.

**67.** b To claim the benefit of the agreement, the condition subsequent i.e. the condition that follows the agreement, needs to be fulfilled which in the present case has not been. B did not go to England and hence, his interest in the farm does not continue.

**68.** b The agreement between Sultana and Marjina is valid as it only provides that in case of remarriage, forfeiture of right over husband's property would happen which cannot be considered as a restrain on marriage.

**69.** a Both are liable as the principle clearly mentions that partners are jointly and severally liable for the wrongs committed.

**70.** c The contract has only restrained the parties from starting proceedings in Udaipur. Pinto is free to begin proceedings in Jaipur. Thus this is not a total restriction against approaching a tribunal for proceedings and therefore the clause is not void.

**71.** a Inviting someone for Dinner is just a social obligation and not a legally enforceable contract.

**72.** c Dutt is not liable because he did not accept the offer given by Bakshi but gave a counter offer which was not specific. Therefore there is no contract in the present case.

**73.** d the fact that the initial agreement between Sunita and Neel was against public policy (law does not allow a woman or man to marry during the subsistence of a current marriage) makes the agreement void.

**74.** b The object of the agreement in this case was to kill Sunil's Uncle. Thus the object being unlawful, the contract between Sunil and Anuj is void.

**75.** c Every person is supposed to appear before a court of law when summoned. Any consideration to do an act which a person is bound to do by law is no consideration.

**76.** d The principle clearly states that a minor is not competent to contract. Therefore Deep can neither enter into an agreement of agency with Mandeep nor a general contract with any buyer.

**77.** a It is clear from the facts that Mani wanted to deal only with Pal as he had sent in his order to Pal only. Therefore Sam cannot accept the offer when it was not made to him in the first place. Therefore Sam cannot recover in the suit.

**78.** a,c

A person has to signify his willingness to do or to abstain from doing anything to another person according to the principle. In the present scenario, there is no other person present and therefore there is no proposal.

**79.** d As per the principle, in the case of arrangements regulating social relations, it follows as a matter of course that the parties do not intend legal consequences to follow. The present case is a general agreement regulating a social relation (father son relation.)

**80.** b Communication of acceptance to 'z', a complete stranger does not give rise to any legally binding obligation.

**81.** b Two years cannot be determined as a reasonable period of time taking into account that the equipment worth was Rs. 1000, which would vary due to various factors such as inflation etc. in two years of time.

**82.** c The agreement becomes void from the very beginning as 'A' is a minor.

**83.** a The consideration is real and it does not matter is it is adequate or not.

**84.** c The agreement is void as the object is unlawful and hence, cannot result into a contract.

**85.** d The agreement is void as the object is unlawful and hence, cannot result into a contract.

**86.** d Since consent of 'Y' was obtained through coercion, the contracts becomes voidable at the option of 'Y'.

**87.** c This is an Agreement in restraint of marriage and hence is void (cannot be enforced in a court of law).

■■

# 3

# CRIMINAL LAW

1. 'A' by cutting the moorings of a boat in which a man and a women were sitting, caused in them a fear for life. He is liable for
   (*a*) Criminal use of force.
   (*b*) Assault.
   (*c*) Mischief.
   (*d*) None of these. **(AILET, 2008)**
2. In Criminal law, intention is an essential constituent of an offence. In law of 'Torts
   (*a*) Intention is relevant.
   (*b*) Intention is irrelevant.
   (*c*) Intention is relevant only in some torts.
   (*d*) None of these. **(AILET, 2008)**
3. You send your servant with a typewriter to be delivered to your friend. The servant takes the typewriter home and uses it over a period of time. You discovered this a fortnight later and report him for
   (*a*) Cheating (*b*) Embezzlement
   (*c*) Fraud (*d*) Forgery
   **(AILET, 2008)**

**DIRECTIONS:** Answer the question, which follow from application of the under-mentioned legal principle:

4. **PRINCIPLE:** Nothing is an offence which is done in the exercise of right of private defence. This right also extends to lawfully causing the death of the assailant, if the offence which occasions the exercise of the right of private defence, be –
   (i) an assault which reasonably causes the apprehension of death or grievous hurt (very serious hurt).
   (ii) an assault which causes reasonable apprehension of rape.
   (iii)an assault which causes reasonable apprehension of kidnapping This right is available for protecting one's own body, as well as the body of any other, provided the assault is not self invited.

   Decide whether the right of private defence is available in the following situations.

   **FACTS:** A was holding the birthday party of his daughter. Some of his friends decided to present her with a car. To create an element of surprise, they decided to kidnap her for few minutes while the party was in full swing and then get her back in the new car. They put the plan into action. While they were kidnapping, A got alarmed and asked the guards to open fire. The guards killed all the five friends. A is
   (*a*) not protected.
   (*b*) protected because he did not kill, the guards did.
   (*c*) not protected because A's own body was not involved.
   (*d*) protected because to any ordinary person there would have appeared a reasonable apprehension of kidnapping. **(AILET, 2008)**
5. Sometimes an accused seeks pardon from the court and offers to give evidence against all others involved in a crime. He is called..........
   (*a*) witness (*b*) clone
   (*c*) approver (*d*) accomplice
   **(AILET, 2009)**
6. Culpable homicide means causing death
   (*a*) With the intention of causing death.
   (*b*) With the intension of causing such bodily injury as is likely to cause death.
   (*c*) With the knowledge that by such act death is likely to be caused.
   (*d*) All the above **(AILET, 2009)**
7. X takes away a girl out of the custody of her lawful guardians. Which of the following statements is a complete defence if X is charged under section 361 of the Indian Penal Code for kidnapping on the ground that the girl was below the age of eighteen years when taken away?
   (*a*) The girl was a student in a college and could understand what was right or wrong for her.
   (*b*) The girl was maltreated by the guardians and X promised her a better life.
   (*c*) The girl looked more than 18 years of age and the accused had satisfied himself that she was more than 18 years of age.
   (*d*) None of these **(AILET, 2009)**

**8. PRINCIPLE:** An assault is an attempt to do a corporeal hurt to another, coupled with an apparent present ability and intention to do that act. A battery is the intentional and direct application of any physical force to the person of another.

A was sitting on a chair reading a book. His friend, B decided to play a practical joke on him. Accordingly, he pulled the chair from under him, as a result of which A landed on the floor.

(*a*) B's act amounts to a battery.

(*b*) B's act amounts to an assault.

(*c*) B' s act amounts to an assault till the time A lands on the floor.

(*d*) B' s act amounts to neither because there was no intention. **(AILET, 2010)**

**9. PRINCIPLE:** False imprisonment is a total restraint of the liberty of a person, for how so ever short period of time, without lawful excuse. **(Common for Q. No. 9 and 10)**

A was driving down a road heading to her house. As she reached close to her house, she found that a few people led by B, protesting against an unfair law had blocked the road. There was no alternate road to her house and hence she was stuck there for around 5 minutes.

(*a*) B and his group are liable for having falsely imprisoned A.

(*b*) B and his group are not liable for falsely imprisoning A, since they were exercising their right to protest.

(*c*) B and his group are not liable for falsely imprisoning A, since they did not totally restrain the liberty of A.

(*d*) B and his group are not liable for falsely imprisoning A, since 5 minutes is too short a time. **(AILET, 2010)**

**10.** A was suspected of having committed the murder of B. C, a policeman who was investigating into B' s murder, saw A in a market. He went up to him, caught hold of his hand and prevented him from going anywhere.

(*a*) C is liable for having falsely imprisoned A, since to arrest a person, a policeman requires permission from a Magistrate.

(*b*) C is not liable for having falsely imprisoned A, since for the offence of murder, a policeman need not take the permission of a Magistrate to arrest.

(*c*) C is not liable for having falsely imprisoned A since the restraint was not total.

(*d*) C is not liable for having falsely imprisoned A since he did not take him to a prison. **(AILET, 2010)**

**11. PRINCIPLE:** When a criminal act is done by one person in furtherance of the common intention of himself and some other persons, each of such person is liable for the act in the same manner as if it were done by each one of them.

A, B and C decided to commit burglary. They broke into a locked house. However, before they had finished their work, a domestic servant appeared from the out-house and started shouting. A, B and C left the house and started running away. They were pursued by a small crowd. A, on being caught by X, one of the persons pursuing them, stabbed him and ran away. By the time B and C had disappeared. X died on account of the stab wounds. Later, the police arrested all the three. They were charged for attempted burglary and murder of X.

(*a*) Along with A (the person who stabbed X) B and C are also guilty of murder because A stabbed X in furtherance of common intention.

(*b*) Along with A, B and C are also guilty of murder because A, at the time of stabbing X, was acting on behalf of B and C and he wanted to save not only himself but B and C as well.

(*c*) A alone is guilty of murder because though there was common intention to commit the offence of burglary, there was no common intention to commit the offence of murder.

(*d*) None of the above **(AILET, 2010)**

**12. PRINCIPLE:**

Whoever intending to take dishonestly (with an intention to cause wrongful loss to another or wrongful gain to himself) any moveable property without that person's consent moves that property in order to such taking, is said to commit theft.

**(Common for Q. No. 12 and 13)**

A had lent his watch to B for a month. Two days after he had done so, he walked into B' s office to find the watch on B' s table. He decided to take the watch back. A was prosecuted for theft.

(*a*) A is not guilty of the offence since he owned the watch.

(*b*) A is not guilty of the offence since he was not doing the act dishonestly.

(*c*) A is guilty of the offence since he caused wrongful loss to B.

(*d*) A is not guilty of the offence since he had lent the watch to B only for a short period of time.

**13.** A handed over his watch to B for safekeeping. B sells the watch to C, which he was not authorised to do. B is prosecuted for theft.

(*a*) B is guilty of theft because he gained from the act.

(*b*) B is not guilty of theft because he was in possession of the watch.

(*c*) B is not guilty of theft because A had given him the watch.

(*d*) B is guilty of theft because caused wrongful loss to A. **(AILET, 2010)**

**14. PRINCIPLE:** Whoever intentionally puts any person in fear of any injury to that person, or to any other, and thereby dishonestly induces that person so put in fear to deliver to any person any property, commits extortion.

A entered B' s house, caught hold of B' s daughter C and threatened to stab her if B did not give him ₹ 10,000 immediately. B did so. A is prosecuted for extortion.

(*a*) A has committed theft, not extortion.

(*b*) A has committed extortion.

(*c*) A has committed both theft and extortion.

(*d*) A has not committed any offence.

**(AILET, 2010)**

**15. PRINCIPLE:** Theft is robbery if in order to committing of the theft, or in committing the theft, or in carrying away or attempting to carry away property obtained by theft, the offender, for that end, voluntarily causes or attempts to cause to any person death or hurt or fear of instant death or instant hurt. **(Common for Q. No. 15 and 16)**

A entered B's house to take away her TV. When he was carrying the TV out of the house, he encountered B near the door. He left the TV behind and ran away.

(*a*) A has committed theft.

(*b*) A has committed robbery.

(*c*) A has committed both theft and robbery.

(*d*) A has neither committed theft nor robbery.

**(AILET, 2010)**

**16.** A entered B' s house and was taking away her wallet and leaving the house, when he encountered B. He dropped the wallet, but shot her while escaping

(*a*) A has committed robbery.

(*b*) A has committed theft, but not robbery.

(*c*) A has neither committed theft, nor robbery.

(*d*) A has committed both- theft and robbery.

**(AILET, 2010)**

**17. PRINCIPLE:** Whoever with the intent to cause, or knowing that he is likely to cause wrongful loss or damage to the public or to any person, causes the destruction of property, or any such change in any property or in the situation thereof as destroys or diminishes its value or utility, of affects it injuriously, commits mischief. **(Common Q. No. 17 and 18)**

A went to B' s house for dinner. He saw that B had a statue made of ice, which was kept in a freezer, A removed the statue from the freezer for a few minutes, which led to the hand of the statue changing shape.

(*a*) A has not committed mischief, since he did not have the intention to change the shape of the hand of the statue.

(*b*) A has committed mischief because he should have known that his act was likely to damage the statue.

(*c*) A has not committed mischief because the statue did not get destroyed.

(*d*) A did not commit mischief because the value of the statue has not diminished.

**(AILET, 2010)**

**18.** A lent his laptop to B. When in possession of the laptop, B inserted a pen drive into the laptop. When he did a virus scan, he realised that the pen drive was infected. Since he urgently required a file that was on the laptop, he nevertheless opened the files on the pen drive, in the process infecting the laptop .

(*a*) A has committed mischief because he has affected the laptop injuriously.

(*b*) A has not committed mischief because he did not intend to do so.

(*c*) A has not committed mischief because the laptop continued working.

(*d*) A has not committed mischief because the laptop was in his possession. **(AILET, 2010)**

**19. PRINCIPLE:** Whoever enters into or upon property in the possession of another with the intent to commit an offence or to intimidate, insult or annoy any person in possession of such property or having lawfully entered into or upon such property, unlawfully remains there with an intent to intimidate, insult or annoy any such person, or with the intent to commit an offence commits criminal trespass.

A went to Delhi Law College to participate in a competition. After participating in the competition, A hid inside the campus so that he could steal a few books from the library,

(a) A has committed theft.

(b) A has committed criminal trespass.

(c) A has not committed criminal trespass, because he entered with permission.

(d) A has not committed any offence.

**(AILET, 2010)**

**20. PRINCIPLE:** Every person has a right of self defence, if his life is under imminent threat.

**FACTS:** Mr. Prashanth threatens Mr. Krishna that he will kill Mr. Krishna. After saying so, Mr. Prashanth goes to his house saying that he would get his axe

(a) Mr. Krishna will have to run away.

(b) Mr. Krishna will have to go to the Police Station and file a complaint.

(c) Mr. Krishna cannot exercise the right of self defence.

(d) None of the above **(AILET, 2011)**

**21. PRINCIPLE:** When two or more persons agree to do an illegal act, it is criminal conspiracy punishable with imprisonment.

**FACTS:** Mr. Bharath is a student of B.E. in Computer Science. He loves his computer very much. He considers his computer as his close friend and companion. On 1.4.2006, while interacting with his computer, he hacked into the Bank account of Mr. Javed and was successful in withdrawing money from Mr. Javed's bank account. He did it to please his girl friend.

(a) Mr. Bharath has committed an offence.

(b) Mr. Bharath has committed a cyber crime.

(c) Mr. Bharath has not committed the offence of criminal conspiracy.

(d) None of the above **(AILET, 2011)**

**22. PRINCIPLE:** The law permits citizens to use force only for protection when necessary against imminent attack. (Common for **Q. 22, 23 & 24**)

**FACTS:** P with the intention of committing theft entered the house of Q. Q, on seeing him entering, struck him with a lathi and P fell down unconscious. Thereafter, Q gave him another blow of lathi on his head which caused his death. On being prosecuted for murder, Q took the plea of private defense. Which of the following argument is valid?

(a) Since Q was acting in the exercise of right of private defense of his property, he had taken a valid defence.

(b) Since in the defence of one's property one cannot cause death of the intruder, Q has no defense.

(c) Q has used excessive force as once P fell unconscious; there was no need for the second blow.Hence, Q' s plea of right of private defence will not succeed.

(d) If P committed house breaking in the night, Q has the right to cause death in defense of his property, and thus Q's plea should prevail.

**(AILET, 2011)**

**23.** To whom, among the following, is the right of private defence is available?

1. Only to the defender being a preventive right.
2. An aggressor, while facing action on the part of the defender which is excessive.

Select the correct answer using the code given below:

(a) 1 only (c) 2 only

(b) Both 1 and 2 (d) Neither 1 nor 2

**(AILET, 2011)**

**24.** X's farm house in outskirts of Delhi was attacked by a gang of armed robbers. X without informing the police, at first warned the robbers by firing in the air. As they were fleeing from the farm, he fired and killed one of them. At the trial -

I. X can avail the right of private defence as he was defending his life and property.

II. X cannot avail the right as he failed to inform the police.

III. X cannot avail the right as he caused more harm than was necessary to ward off the danger.

IV. X can avail of the right as at first he only fires in the air.

(a) I and IV (b) II only

(c) II and III (d) IV only **(AILET, 2011)**

**25. PRINCIPLE:** Conspiracy is a combination between two or more persons formed for the purpose of doing either an unlawful act or a lawful act by unlawful means.

**FACTS:** X and Y conspire to poison Z. X in pursuance of the conspiracy procures the poison and delivers it to Y in order that he may administer it to Z. Y in pursuance of the conspiracy administers the poison in the presence of X and thereby causes Z's death. What offence, if any has been committed by X and Y, respectively? (Common **for Q. 25, 26 & 27**) (*a*) Y has committed the offence of murder and X was an abettor.

(*b*) Both X and Y have committed the offence of criminal conspiracy.

(*c*) X has committed the offence of murder and Y was an abettor.

(*d*) Both X and Y have committed the offence of murder. **(AILET, 2011)**

**26.** Suppose X & Y were apprehended by A before administering poison to Z . What is the offence committed by X & Y ?

(*a*) X & Y are not guilty of conspiracy as they did not cause death of Z.

(*b*) Liability of X comes to an end and Y is only liable.

(*c*) As no offence is committed and none of them are responsible.

(*d*) X & Y are to be punished as it is immaterial whether illegal act is ultimate object of the agreement or merely incidental to that object. **(AILET, 2011)**

**27.** The gist of the offence of criminal conspiracy is

(*a*) agreement is necessary between two or more persons to do or cause to be done an illegal act.

(*b*) a legal act by illegal means followed by an overt act to be done or cause to be done according to agreement.

(*c*) both (*a*) and (*b*)

(*d*) None of the above **(AILET, 2011)**

**28. PRINCIPLE:** Contributory negligence in an accident is a defence to a charge in criminal law.

**FACTS:** X, the deceased was negligently crossing the busy road at Connaught place in Delhi while Y's car hit him resulting in death of X. What is the liability of Y?

(*a*) Y is liable for death of X.

(*b*) Y is partly liable as X contributed to his own death.

(*c*) Y is absolved from liability based on the principle of contributory negligence.

(*d*) None of the above **(AILET, 2011)**

**29. PRINCIPLE:** A contract procured by coercion is bad under Indian Contract Act. Coercion is defined as committing or threatening to commit any act forbidden by Indian Penal Code. Attempt to commit suicide is an offence under India Penal Code.

**FACTS:** A wanted his wife B to part with some property given to her by her father. B resisted fearing that her husband would squander it away. A threatened her that if she does not sign the deed transferring the property to him (i.e., A), he would commit suicide. B signed the deed. Subsequently, she challenged the deed on the ground that the deed was bad under law.

(*a*) The deed is valid under the law.

(*b*) The transfer of property is complete once the deed 'is entered between the owner of the property and the buyer.

(*c*) The deed is not valid as it was signed under the threat of suicide by her husband which amounts to coercion and vitiates the contract.

(*d*) Husband has a right over the property of the wife that was voluntarily transferred to the buyer. **(AILET, 2011)**

**30. PRINCIPLES:**

(1) If a person commits an act by which death is caused to another person and the act is done with the intention of causing death, that person is liable for murder.

(2) A person has a right of self defence to the extent of causing death to another provided he apprehends death by the act of the latter.

**FACTS:** Shiva went to a hardware shop owned by Anup. Bargaining on some item led to altercation between the two and Shiva picked up a sharp object and hit at Anup. When Anup started bleeding, his wife Mridula intervened and she was also hit by Shiva and she became unconscious. Finding himself totally cornered, Anup delivered a severe blow to Shiva with a sharp object. Shiva died instantly.

**<u>Possible decisions</u>**

(a) Anup murdered Shiva.

(b) Anup killed Shiva with the intention of killing to save himself and his wife.

(c) Anup killed Shiva without any intention to do so just to save himself and his wife.

**<u>Probable reasons for the decision</u>**

(i) If a person kills another instantly on the spot, the intention to kill is obvious.

(ii) Anup used force apprehending death of himself and his wife.

(iii) Anup used disproportionate force.

(iv) There was nothing to show that Shiva wanted to kill Anup or his wife.

**<u>Your decision with the reason</u>**

(*a*) (*a*) (i) (*b*) (*a*) (iii)

(*c*) (*c*) (ii) (*d*) (*b*) (i) **(CLAT 2008)**

**31.** When a person is prosecuted for committing a criminal offence, the burden of proof is on

(*a*) Accused

(*b*) Prosecution

(*c*) Police

(*d*) Complainant **(CLAT 2009)**

**32.** Offence which can be compromised between the parties is known as

(*a*) Conjugal right

(*b*) Cognizable offence

(*c*) Compoundable offence

(*d*) Complainant **(CLAT 2009)**

**33.** Which of the following is not true about a criminal proceeding?

(*a*) the court may ask to pay a fine.

(*b*) the court may order the transfer of the ownership of the property.

(*c*) there is prosecution.

(*d*) the court may discharge an accused.

**(CLAT 2010)**

**34.** X, the servant of Y, takes a hundred rupee note from Y's pocket and hides it under the carpet in the house of Y. X tells Z another servant of Y, about the currency note and both agree to share the money when the currency note is taken by X from the hiding place. Before X could recover the note, it was found by Y. Decide if an offence was committed and if so who committed the offence?

(*a*) No offence was committed.

(*b*) Only X committed the offence.

(*c*) Both X and Z committed the offence.

(*d*) Only Z committed the offence. **(CLAT 2010)**

**(For questions 35 to 39)**

**Rules:**

A. Whoever intending to take any moveable property out of the possession of any person without that person's consent, moves that property out of his or her possession, is said to commit theft.

B. A person who, without lawful excuse, damages any property belonging to another intending to damage any such property shall be guilty of causing criminal damage.

C. Damage means any impairment of the value of a property.

**Facts:** Veena, an old lady of 78 years, used to live with her granddaughter Indira. Veena was ill and therefore bed-ridden for several months. In those months, she could not tolerate any noise and it became quite difficult to clean her room. After she died, Indira hired a cleaner, Lucky, to clean the room and throw away any rubbish that may be there.

There was a pile of old newspapers which Veena had stacked in a corner of her room. Lucky asked Indira if he should clear away the pile of old newspapers, to which she said yes. Lucky took the pile to a municipality rubbish dump. While Lucky was sorting and throwing away the newspapers, he was very surprised to find a beautiful painting in between two sheets of paper. He thought that Indira probably wouldn't want this old painting back, especially because it was torn in several places and the colour was fading. He took the painting home, mounted it on a wooden frame and hung it on the wall of his bedroom. Unknown to him, the painting was an old masterpiece, and worth twenty thousand rupees. Before mounting the painting, Lucky pasted it on a plain sheet of paper so that it does not tear any more. By doing so, he made its professional restoration very difficult and thereby reduced its value by half.

Lucky's neighbour Kamala discovered that the painting belonged to Indira. With the motive of returning the painting to Indira, Kamala climbed through an open window into Lucky's room when he was away one afternoon and removed the painting from his house.

**35.** Has Lucky committed theft?

(*a*) Yes, Lucky has committed theft of the newspapers and the painting.

(*b*) No, Lucky has not committed theft because he had Veena's consent.

(*c*) Yes, Lucky has committed theft of the painting, but not of the newspapers.

(*d*) No, Lucky has not committed theft because he has not moved the painting out of Veena's possession. **(CLAT 2011)**

**36.** Is Lucky guilty of criminal damage?

(*a*) No, Lucky is not guilty of criminal damage as he did not intentionally impair the value of the painting.

(*b*) Yes, Lucky is guilty of criminal damage as he intentionally stuck the paper on to the painting.

(*c*) No, Lucky is not guilty of criminal damage as he does not have the painting in his possession anymore.

(*d*) No, Lucky is not guilty of criminal damage as he has not destroyed the painting.

**(CLAT 2011)**

**37.** If Lucky had discovered the painting before leaving Indira's house rather than at the rubbish dump, would he have been guilty of theft in this case?

(*a*) Yes, he would be guilty of theft of the newspapers and the paintings.

(*b*) No, he would not be guilty of theft.

(*c*) Yes, he would be guilty of theft of the painting.

(*d*) None of the above. **(CLAT 2011)**

**38.** Is Kamala guilty of theft?

(*a*) No, Kamala is not guilty of theft since the person she took the painting from (Lucky) was not its lawful owner.

(*b*) No, Kamala is not guilty of theft since she took the painting only with the motive of returning it to Indira.

(*c*) Yes, Kamala is guilty of theft as she took the painting out of Lucky's possession without his consent.

(*d*) None of the above

**39.** Which of the following propositions could be inferred from the facts and the rules specified,

(*a*) Kamala is guilty of criminal damage as the person she took the painting from (Lucky) was not its lawful owner.

(*b*) Kamala is guilty of criminal damage as she took the painting without Lucky's consent.

(*c*) Kamala is not guilty of criminal damage as the painting has not been completely destroyed.

(*d*) None of the above. **(CLAT 2011)**

**40. PRINCIPLE:** Nothing is an offence merely by reason of its being done with the knowledge that it is likely to cause harm, if it be done without any criminal intention to cause harm, and in good faith for the purpose of preventing or avoiding other harm to a person or property.

**FACTS:** Mr. Sharman, the Captain of a steam vessel, suddenly and without any fault or negligence on his part, finds himself in such a position that, before he can stop his vessel, he must inevitably run down a boat B, with twenty or thirty passengers on board, unless he changes the course of his vessel, and that, by changing his course, he must incur the risk of running down a boat C with only two passengers on board and which he may possibly clear.

(*a*) Sharman has committed no offence because this was done out of necessity.

(*b*) Sharman can be held responsible for the act of criminal negligence.

(*c*) Sharman can be held responsible for culpable homicide.

(*d*) This is a clear case of accident so Sharman cannot be held responsible. **(CLAT 2012)**

**41. PRINCIPLE:** Willful rash driving is an offense.

**FACTS:** Mr. Tiwari was driving his car after drinking alcohol. Police books him for willful negligent driving. Is the act of the police lawful?

(*a*) No, because Mr. Tiwari was not driving rashly; he was drunk while driving.

(*b*) No, this is not a negligent act.

(*c*) Yes, because Mr. Tiwari was driving rashly.

(*d*) Yes, because the police has the power to arrest a person driving rashly. **(CLAT 2012)**

**42. PRINCIPLE:** Whoever, intending to take dishonestly any movable property out of the possession of any person without that person's consent, moves that property with an intention to take it, is said to commit theft.

**FACTS:** Y cuts down a tree on Z's ground, with the intention of dishonestly taking it out of Z's possession without Z's consent. Y could not take away the tree.

(*a*) Y can be prosecuted for theft.

(*b*) Y cannot be prosecuted for theft.

(*c*) Y can be prosecuted for attempt to theft.

(*d*) Y has neither committed theft nor attempted to commit theft. **(CLAT 2012)**

**43. PRINCIPLE:** Nothing is an offence which is done by a person who, at the time of doing it, by reason of unsound state of mind, is incapable of knowing the nature of the act, or something that he is doing is either wrong or contrary to law.

**FACT:** X takes his son Y who is three years old, for bathing to the well. He throws his son inside the well so that the son can have a good bath. After 10 minutes he also jumps into the well to take bath and get his son out of the well. Both were rescued by the villagers but his son was found dead.

(*a*) X has committed culpable homicide amounting to murder.

(*b*) X has committed murder.

(*c*) X has done no offence as he can plead the defense of unsound state of mind.

(*d*) X's family should be held responsible for allowing him to take the child to the well.

**(CLAT 2012)**

**Instructions (44 to 49 ):** Each of the next three questions consists of two statements, one labeled as 'Assertion' (A) and other as 'Reason' (R). You are to examine these two statements carefully and select the correct answers.

**44. Assertion (A):** X, because of unsound state of mind and not knowing the nature of the act, attacks Y, who in self defense and in order to ward off the attack, hits him thereby injuring him. Y has not committed an offence.

**Reason (R):** Y had a right of private defense against X under Section 98 of the Indian Penal Code.

(*a*) Both A and R are individually true and R is the correct explanation of A.

(*b*) Both A and R are individually true but R is not the correct explanation of A.

(*c*) A is true but R is false.

(*d*) A is false but R is true. **(CLAT 2012)**

**45. Assertion (A):** X and Y independently entertained the idea to kill Z. Accordingly, each of them separately inflicted wounds on Z who died as a consequence. X and Y are liable for murder under 341 IPC.

**Reason (R):** When a criminal act is done by several persons in furtherance of common intention of all, each of such persons is liable as if the whole act was done by him alone.

(*a*) Both A and R are individually true and R is the correct explanation of A.

(*b*) Both A and R are individually true but R is not the correct explanation of A.

(*c*) A is true but R is false.

(*d*) A is false but R is true. **(CLAT 2012)**

**46. Assertion (A):** The essence of joint liability under section 149 of the IPC is that the criminal act must have been done with a view to fulfill the common object of an unlawful assembly.

**Reason (R):** Any sudden and provocative act done by a member of an unlawful assembly would render the other members of that assembly liable.

(*a*) Both A and R are individually true and R is the correct explanation of A.

(*b*) Both A and R are individually true but R is not the correct explanation of A.

(*c*) A is true but R is false.

(*d*) A is false but R is true. **(CLAT 2012)**

**47.** Z is carried off by a tiger. X fires at the tiger, knowing that the shot might kill Z, but with no intention to kill Z, and in good faith trying to save Z. X's shot, however, gives Z a mortal wound. Choose the correct option –

(*a*) X has committed an offence of a grievous nature.

(*b*) X has no moral duty to save Z therefore he can be held liable.

(*c*) X has not committed any offence, as the act was in good faith and for the benefit of Z.

(*d*) None of the above **(CLAT 2012)**

**48.** Y makes an attempt to steal some jewels by breaking open a box and finds, after opening the box, that there is no jewel in it. Choose the appropriate answer.

(*a*) Y is not guilty of attempt to theft because the box was empty.

(*b*) Y is guilty of attempt to commit theft.

(*c*) Y is guilty of trespass.

(*d*) Y is not guilty of any offence. **(CLAT 2012)**

**49.** A lady wanted to get a railway ticket but finding a crowd near the ticket window at the station, asked Raju, who was near the window, to get a ticket for her and handed him money for the same. Raju took the money and instead of getting the ticket, ran away with it. What offence has been committed by Raju?

(*a*) No offence

(*b*) Criminal breach of trust

(*c*) Criminal misappropriation

(*d*) Theft **(CLAT 2012)**

**Directions (Q. 50 - 53) :** Given below is a statement of legal principle followed by a factual situation. Apply the principle to the facts given below and select the most appropriate answer.

**50. LEGAL PRINCIPLE:** False imprisonment is the confinement of a person without just cause or excuse. There must be a total restraint of the person and the onus of proving reasonable cause is on the defendant.

**FACTUAL SITUATION:** A entered in B's park where there was an artificial lake for the boating. A paid ₹ 100 for entering the park and has to pay **₹ 100 at** the time of exit. A waited for 30 minutes but no boat was available. A came **out,** however, denied to pay ₹ 100 for exit, B did not allow A to leave the park unless he paid ₹ 100 for exit. A sued B for false imprisonment.

**DECISION:**

(*a*) B is guilty of false imprisonment.

(*b*) B is not guilty of false imprisonment.

(*c*) A can lawfully refuse to pay ₹ 100 when no boat was available.

(*d*) A can ask for even ₹ 100 given for entering the park as B's services are deficient in the park and can sue B for false imprisonment.

**(AILET 2013)**

**51. LEGAL PRINCIPLE:** Attempt is an act done with an intent to commit crime, and forming part of the series of acts which would constitute actual commission of the crime, if not interrupted.

**FACTUAL SITUATION:** A intending to murder B by poison, purchases poison and mixes the same with a glass of water. He gave to the bearer to serve B. The bearer while approaching B, loses the balance and the glass drops out of his tray.

**DECISION:**

(*a*) A has not committed any offence.

(*b*) A has committed the offence of murder.

(*c*) A has committed the offence of attempt to murder.

(*d*) A has not committed an offence of attempt to murder because nothing happened to B.

**(AILET 2013)**

**52. LEGAL PRINCIPLES:**

(1) The concept of joint liability comes under Section 34 of IPC which states that "when a criminal act is done by several persons, in furtherance of the common intention of all, each of such persons is liable for that act in the same manner as if it were done by him alone."

(2) A person abets an offence, who abets either the commission of an offence, or the commission of an act which would be an offence, if committed by a person capable by law of committing an offence with the same intention or knowledge as that of the abettor.

(3) A criminal conspiracy takes place when two or more people get together and plan to commit a crime and then take some action toward carrying out that plan. The action taken does not have to be a crime itself to further the conspiracy.

**FACTUAL SITUATION:** X and Y conspire to poison Z. X in pursuance of the conspiracy procures the poison and delivers it to Y in order that he may administer it to Z. Y in pursuance of the conspiracy, administer the poison in the presence of X and thereby causes Z's death. What offences X and Y have committed ?

**DECISION:**

(*a*) Y has committed the offence of murder and X was an abettor.

(*b*) Both X and Y has committed the offence of criminal conspiracy.

(*c*) X has not committed any offence.

(*d*) Both X and Y has committed the offence of murder. **(AILET 2013)**

**53. LEGAL PRINCIPLES:**

(1) Whoever, intending to take dishonestly any movable property out of the possession of any person without that person' s consent, moves that property in order to such taking, is said to commit theft.

(2) Whoever dishonestly misappropriates or converts to his own use any movable property, shall be punished with imprisonment of either description for a term which may extend to two years, or with fine, or with both.

**FACTUAL SITUATION:** A takes umbrella belonging to Z out of Z's possession in good faith, believing at the time when he took it, that the property belongs to himself. His wife points out after some days that the umbrella does not belong to them but to Z. After coming to know that, A dishonestly keeps the umbrella.

**DECISION:**

(*a*) A is guilty of criminal misappropriation.

(*b*) A is guilty of criminal breach of trust.

(*c*) A is guilty of theft.

(*d*) Both A and his wife are guilty of criminal misappropriation. **(AILET 2013)**

**54.** In India, the reckoning date for the determination of the age of the juvenile is the

(*a*) date of offence.

(*b*) date of trial.

(*c*) date of judgment.

(*d*) date of arrest. **(AILET 2013)**

**55.** An offence of breaking a divine idol

(*a*) Blasphemy (*b*) Salus populi

(*c*) Crime (*d*) Sacrilege

**(AILET 2013)**

**Directions (Q. 56-67) :** This section consists of twelve (12) questions. Each question consists of legal propositions/ principles (hereinafter referred to as 'principle') and facts. These principles have to be applied to the given facts to arrive at the most reasonable conclusion. Such principles may or may not be true in the real sense, yet you have to conclusively assume them to be true for the purposes of this section. In other words, in answering the following questions, you must not rely on any principles except the principles that are given hereinbelow for every question. Further you must not assume any facts other than those stated in the question.The objective of this section is to test your interest towards study of law, research aptitude and problem solving ability even if the "most reasonable conclusion" arrived at may be unacceptable for any other reason. It is not the objective of this section to test your knowledge of law.

**56. Principle:** Whosoever commits any act forbidden by the Indian Penal code with a view to obtain the consent of any person to enter into an agreement, he cannot get the agreement enforced by law but the person whose consent has been so obtained may get the agreement enforced by law. The Indian Penal code defines various offences and prescribes punishments therefor. **(CLAT 2013)**

**Facts:** A obtains the consent of B to enter into an agreement by an act amounting to criminal intimidation under the Indian Penal Code. A brings a case against B for performance of agreement.

(*a*) A will succeed in the case

(*b*) A may succeed in the case

(*c*) B will succeed in the case

(*d*) B will not succeed in the case

**57. Principle:** Whoever takes away anything from the land of any person without that person's consent is said to commit theft. A thing so long as it is attached to the earth is not the subject of theft; but it becomes capable of being the subject of theft as soon as it is severed from the earth. **(CLAT 2013)**

**Facts:** Y cuts down a tree standing on the land of X with the intention of dishonestly taking the tree out of X's possession without the consent of X. But Y is yet to take away the tree out of X's possession.

(*a*) Y has committed theft as soon as he came to the land of X

(*b*) Y has committed theft as soon as the tree has been completely cut down by him

(*c*) Y has committed theft as soon as he has started cutting down the tree

(*d*) Y has not committed theft because he is yet to take away the tree out of X possession

**58. Principle:** Whoever takes away with him any minor person less than sixteen years of age if a male, or less than eighteen years of age if a female out of the keeping of parents of such minor person without the consent of such parent, is said to kidnap such minor person. **(CLAT 2013)**

**Facts:** A female born on January 01, 1995 got admitted to an undergraduate program of a reputed University on July 01, 2012. She became friendly with one of the boys, born on June 01, 1994, of her class. The boy and the girl decided to marry. The parents of the boy agreed but the family of the girl did not agree. On December 15, 2012 the girl made a call from her Blackberry to the boy. The girl told the boy to come in his car at a particular place and time. The boy reached the stipulated place before the stipulated time. He waited there for about half an hour. The girl reached the stipulated place. She opened the door of the car and sat beside the boy who was on the driving seat. Without exchanging any pleasantries, the boy drove the car to an unknown place. The father of the girl lodged an FIR in the nearest police station on January 20, 2013.

(*a*) The boy has committed the offence of kidnapping

(*b*) The boy has not committed the offence of kidnapping

(*c*) The boy has not committed the offence of kidnapping for there is a delay in filing the FIR

(*d*) The boy has not committed the offence of kidnapping because the girl was his classmate

**59. Principle:** Whoever voluntarily has carnal intercourse against the order of nature with any man, woman or animal shall be punished. **(CLAT 2013)**

**Facts:** Two adult men were found engaged in carnal intercourse by the police. The police arrested the men and produced them before the Court.

(*a*) Court will punish the police officer who arrested the men

(*b*) Court will not punish the men for they were adults

(*c*) Court will punish the men

(*d*) Court may be requested to declare the law unconstitutional.

**60. Principle:** Wherever the causing of a certain effect, or an attempt to cause that effect, by an act or by an omission, is an offence, it is to be understood that the causing of that effect partly by an act and partly by an omission is the same offence. **(CLAT 2013)**

**Facts:** A intentionally omitted to give food to his father. He also used to beat his father. Consequently A's father died.

(*a*) A did not commit any offence

(*b*) A committed only the offence of omitting to give food to his father

(*c*) A committed only the offence of beating of his father

(*d*) A committed the offence of killing of his father

61. **Principle:** Nothing is an offence which is done by a child under seven years of age. **(CLAT 2013)**

**Facts:** A, a child born on January 01, 2005 killed another child 'B' on December 30, 2011.

(*a*) A has committed no offence.

(*b*) A has committed the offence as it is heinous crime

(*c*) Killing of one child by another child is not an offence

(*d*) A has not committed the offence for on the date of killing of B, A was a minor

62. **Principle:** A pact, other than a pact to commit suicide, to suffer any harm is not an offence, provided the age of the person who has given his consent to suffer harm is above eighteen year **Facts:** A enters into a pact with B, a boy of less than 18 years of age, to fence with each other for amusement. They agreed to suffer any harm which, in the course of such fencing, may be caused without foul play. **(CLAT 2013)**

(*a*) A, while playing fairly, hurts B, A commits no offence

(*b*) A, while playing only unfairly, hurts B, A commits an offence

(*c*) A, while playing fairly, hurts B, A commits an offence

(*d*) A, while playing unfairly, hurts B, A commits no offence

63. **Principle:** When an act, which would otherwise be an offence, is not that offence by reason of the youth, the want of maturity of understanding, the unsoundness of mind or the intoxication of the person doing that act, every person has the same right of private defence against that act which he would have if the act were that offence. Nothing is an offence which is done in the exercise of the right of private defence. **(CLAT 2013)**

**Facts:** A, under the influence of madness, tempts to kill B. B in order to save his life causes grievous hurt to A.

(*a*) A has committed an offence

(*b*) A has not committed an offence

(*c*) B has committed an offence

(*d*) B has not committed any offence

64. **Principle:** Whoever by words, either spoken or written brings or attempts to bring into hatred or contempt, or excites or attempts to excite disaffection towards the Government established by law in India shall be punished. However, comments expressing disapprobation of the administrative or other action of the Government without exciting or attempting to excite hatred, contempt or disaffection, do not constitute an offence. **(CLAT 2013)**

**Facts:** A renowned professor of economics wrote a critical comment on the economic policies of the Government of India in a National Daily. This piece of writing generated academic debate not only in the print media but also on television and internet. A student of law asked the fellow Indians on a social networking website to assemble at a particular place for peaceful and silent demonstration against the said economic policies on a stipulated date and time. The crowed assembled at that venue and started shouting anti-government slogans. Police arrested the professor.

(*a*) The professor has committed the offence

(*b*) The professor has not committed any offence

(*c*) The student of law has committed the offence

(*d*) The crowed has committed an offence

65. **Principle:** Whoever attempts to commit an offence punishable by the Indian Penal Code and in such attempt does any act towards the commission of the offence, shall be punished. Stealing is an offence punishable by the Indian Penal Code. **(CLAT 2013)**

**Facts:** A makes an attempt to steal some jewels by breaking open a box, and after so opening the box, finds that there is no jewel in it.

(*a*) A has committed no offence

(*b*) A has committed the offence of stealing

(*c*) A has attempted to commit the offence of stealing

(*d*) None of the above

66. **Principle:** Whoever desires any Court to give judgment about any legal right or liability which depends on the existence of those facts which he asserts, must prove that those facts exist. **(CLAT 2013)**

**Facts:** A asserts that B, C and D have committed an offence of criminal conspiracy and therefore A desires a Court to give judgment that B, C and D shall be punished for that crime which A says B, C and D have committed.

(*a*) A must prove that B, C, and D have committed the crime

(*b*) B, C, and D must prove that they have not committed the crime

(*c*) A must prove that B, C, and D were present at the place of crime

(*d*) Police must prove that B, C, and D have committed the crime

67. **Principle:** Nothing is an offence merely by reason of its being done with the knowledge that it is likely to cause harm, if it be done without any criminal intention to cause harm, and in good faith for the purpose of preventing or avoiding other harm to a person or property. **(CLAT 2013)**

**Facts:** Mr. Sharman, the Italian captain of a steam vessel, suddenly and without any fault or negligence on his part, finds himself near the Kochi coast in such a position that before he can stop his vessel, he must inevitably run down a boat B with twenty or thirty passengers on board, unless he changes the course of his vessel, and that by changing his course, he must incur risk of running down a boat C with only two passengers on board, which he may possibly clear.

Whether Sharman has committed an offence?

(*a*) Sharman has committed no offence because this was done out of necessity

(*b*) Sharman can be held responsible for the act of criminal negligence

(*c*) Sharman can be held responsible for culpable homicide

(*d*) This is a clear case of accident so Sharman cannot be held responsible

**Directions (Q. 68 - 75) :** Given below is a statement of legal principle followed by a factual situation. Apply the principle to the facts given below and select the most appropriate answer. **(AILET 2014)**

**68. LEGAL PRINCIPLES :**

1. An act done by the consent of a person above 18 years is not an offence; provide the offender did not intend to cause death or grievous hurt.
2. Mere pecuniary benefit is not a 'thing done for a person's benefit'.

**FACTUAL SITUATION :** A, poor man, is in dire need of money to pay off his money lenders. A approaches Z, a doctor, to operate on him to remove one of his kidneys so that he can donate it to needy people and earn money. The doctor explains to him the risks and thereafter proceeds to remove his kidney. In the process, some complications develop and A develops an abdominal tumour. Is Z guilty?

**DECISION :**

(*a*) Yes, donating kidney for money is illegal and amounts to trafficking of organs.

(*b*) Yes, removing kidney for money is not an act protected by this exception.

(*c*) No, Z performed the operation with A's consent and fully explained him the risks involved.

(*d*) No, Z's act was done for A's benefit so that he can pay off the money lenders.

**69. LEGAL PRINCIPLES :**

1. An act done, even if without the consent of a person is not an offence, provided the offender did not intend to cause death, and the act was done for the person's benefit, in good faith.
2. Mere pecuniary benefit is not a 'thing done for a person's benefit'.

**FACTUAL SITUATION :** A is in a house which is on fire, with Z, a child. People below hold out a blanket. A drops the child from the house top, knowing it to be likely that the fall may kill the child but intending to save him from the fire. Unfortunately, the child is killed. Is A guilty?

**DECISION :**

(*a*) Yes, A had knowledge of his dangerous act. His act was not justified.

(*b*) Yes, A should have tried a less dangerous alternative.

(*c*) No, his act was done in good faith to save the child.

(*d*) No, he had the best of intentions and this was the only alternative.

**70. LEGAL PRINCIPLE :** Nothing is an offence which is done by any person who is, or who by reason of mistake of fact, in good faith, believes himself to be bound by law to do it.

**FACTUAL SITUATION :** A, soldier, fires on a mob by the order of his superior officer, in conformity with the commands of the law. B is killed due to such firing. Is A guilty of murder?

**DECISION :**

(*a*) Yes, he should have taken care to avoid any innocent person from being killed.

(*b*) No, he is bound by law to do it.

(*c*) Yes, as he has killed a person.

(*d*) The superior officer is guilty.

**71. LEGAL PRINCIPLE :** Whoever intending to take dishonestly any movable property out of the possession of any person without that person's consent, moves that property in order to such taking, is said to commit theft.

**FACTUAL SITUATION :** A, in good faith, believing property belonging to B to be A's own property, sells the property to C. Has A committed theft?

**DECISION :**

(*a*) No, because he did not have a dishonest intention.

(*b*) No, he did not move the property.

(*c*) No, he did not move the property that was in B's possession.

(*d*) Yes, the constituent elements of theft are satisfied in this case.

**72. LEGAL PRINCIPLES :**

1. Preparation to commit an offence is not an offence.
2. After one has finished preparation to commit an offence, any act done towards committing the offence with the intention to commit it, is an attempt to commit the offence which is by itself an offence.

**FACTUAL SITUATION :** Manish wanted to kill Nandini and had therefore gone to the market to buy explosives to plant in her house. Manish kept those explosives in his godown as he planned to plant them early next morning. But as the explosives were stolen in the night he could not plant them in Nandini's house. However, Nandini came to know about Manish's plan and therefore wants to file a complaint against him. Will she succeed?

**DECISION :**

(*a*) Yes, because he has done something more than mere preparation.

(*b*) No, because Nandini did not die.

(*c*) Yes, because there existed a mala fide intention.

(*d*) No, because mere preparation is no offence.

**73. LEGAL PRINCIPLE :** Whoever intentionally uses force to any person, without that person's consent, in order to committing of any offence, or intending by the use of such force to cause, or knowing it likely to cause injury, fear, or annoyance to the person to whom the force is used, is said to use criminal force to that other.

**FACTUAL SITUATION :** Akash was burning some crackers in his house when his dog got scared and got unruly which scared his brother Mohsin. Can this be called criminal force?

**DECISION :**

(*a*) Yes, because he did it intentionally.

(*b*) No, because law doesn't account for trivial things.

(*c*) Yes, because it led to annoyance of Mohsin.

(*d*) No, because there was no mala fide intention.

**74. LEGAL PRINCIPLE :** No person shall be convicted of any offence except for violation of a law in force at the time of commission of the act charged as an offence, nor subjected to a penalty greater than which might have been inflicted under the law in force at the time of commission of the offence.

**FACTUAL SITUATION :** A boy of 16 years was convicted of house trespass and theft. He was sentenced to imprisonment for 6 months and fine was also imposed. After the judgement, the Probation of Offenders Act came into force. It provided that a person below 21 years may not ordinarily be sentenced to imprisonment. Now the boy claims the benefit of this Act. Should he get it?

**DECISION :**

(*a*) No

(*b*) The rule of beneficial interpretation required that the benefit of ex post facto law can be applied to reduce his sentence.

(*c*) A boy below 18 years is a minor and so should not be punished.

(*d*) None of the above.

**75. LEGAL PRINCIPLE :** To be held guilty of an offence, one should have done the act that causes the intended result.

**FACTUAL SITUATION :** A, with the intention to murder B stabs him repeatedly with a knife. B is taken to the hospital and is found to be out of danger. Thereafter, due to the doctor's negligence, B's wounds are infected and he requires surgical interventions. During the time of operation to remove his infected leg, B died on account of administration of general anaesthesia.

**DECISION :**

(*a*) A is guilty of murder.

(*b*) A is not guilty of murder though he may be guilty of attempt to murder.

(*c*) A is not guilty of murder but he may be guilty of causing hurt.

(*d*) The doctor is liable as he was negligent.

**Directions (Q. 76 - 90) :** *This section consists of fifteen (15) questions.*

Each question consists of legal propositions/principles (hereinafter referred to as 'principle') and facts. These principles have to be applied to the given facts to arrive at the most reasonable conclusion. Such principles may or may not be true in the real sense, yet you have to conclusively assume them to be true for the purposes of this section. In other words, in answering the following questions, you must not rely on any principles except the principles that are given herein below for every question. Further, you must not assume any facts other than those stated in the question. The objective of this section is to test your interest towards study of law, research aptitude and problem solving ability even if the 'most reasonable conclusion' arrived at may be unacceptable for, any other reason. It is not the object of this section to test your knowledge of law. **(CLAT 2014)**

**76. Principle:** Nothing is an offence which is done by a person who is bound by law to do it.

**Facts:** 'A', a police officer, without warrant, apprehends, who has committed murder.

(*a*) 'A' is guilty of the offence of wrongful confinement

(*b*) 'A' is not guilty of the offence of wrongful confinement

(*c*) 'A' may be guilty of the offence of wrongful restraint

(*d*) 'A' cannot apprehend 'Z' without a warrant issued by a court of law

**77. Principle:** When a criminal act is done by several persons in furtherance of the common intention of all, each of such persons is liable for that act in the same manner as if it were done by him alone.

**Facts:** Roshan along with two of his friends, Tushar and Tarang proceeded to the house of Darshan in order to avenge an insult made by the brother of Darshan. They opened fire on the members of Darshan' s family. It was found that the shots of Roshan did not hit anyone, but the shots of Tushar and Tarang succeeded in killing Darshan.

(*a*) Roshan was not liable for the offence of murder of Darshan, as Roshan's shots did not hit Darshan

(*b*) Only Tushar and Tarang were liable for the offence of murder of Darshan, as their shots hit Darshan

(*c*) Roshan along with Tushar and Tarang was liable for the offence of murder of Darshan

(*d*) Roshan was liable to a lesser extent comparing to his friends for the offence of murder of Darshan, as Roshan' s shots did not hit Darshan

**78. Principle:** No communication made in good faith is an offence by reason of any harm to the person to whom it is made, if it is made for the benefit of that person.

**Facts:** 'A', a surgeon, in good faith, communicates to a patient his opinion that he cannot live. The patient dies in consequence of the shock.

(*a*) 'A' has committed the offence of causing death of his patient

(*b*) 'A' has not committed the offence of causing death of his patient

(*c*) 'A' has only partially committed the offence of causing death of his patient

(*d*) None of the above

**79. Principle:** Whoever, being legally bound to furnish information on any subject to any public servant, as such, furnishes, as true, information on the subject which he knows or has reason to believe to be false, has committed a punishable offence of furnishing false information.

**Facts:** Sawant, a landholder, knowing of the commission of a murder within the limits of his estate, willfully misinforms the Magistrate of the district that the death has occurred by accident in consequence of the bite of a snake.

(*a*) Sawant is not guilty of the offence of furnishing false information to the Magistrate

(*b*) Sawant is guilty of the offence of furnishing false information to the Magistrate

(*c*) Sawant is not legally bound to furnish true information to the Magistrate

(*d*) Sawant has the discretion to furnish true information to the Magistrate, as the murder was committed within the limits of his estate

**80. Principle:** Whoever unlawfully or negligently does any act which is, and which he knows or has reason to believe to be, likely to spread the infection of any disease dangerous to life, shall be guilty of a negligent act likely to spread infection of disease dangerous to life.

**Facts:** 'K', a person, knowing that he is suffering from Cholera, travels by a train without informing the railway officers of his condition.

(*a*) 'K' has committed an unlawful and negligent act, which is likely to spread the infection of Cholera disease dangerous to the life of fellow-passengers

(*b*) Railway officers are guilty of an unlawful and negligent act, as 'K' who is suffering from Cholera disease has travelled by the train

(*c*) 'K' has not committed an unlawful and negligent act, which is likely to spread the infection of Cholera disease dangerous to the life of fellow-passengers

(*d*) Both 'K' and Railway officers are guilty of an unlawful and negligent act, which is likely to spread the infection of Cholera disease dangerous to the life of fellow passengers

**81. Principle:** Whoever drives any vehicle, or rides, on any public way in a manner so rash or negligent as to endanger human life, or to be likely to cause hurt or injury to any other person, has committed an offence, which shall be punished in accordance with the law.

**Facts:** 'X', a truck driver, driving his vehicle rashly and negligently at a high speed climbed the footpath and hit 'Y', a pedestrian, from behind causing his death.

(*a*) 'X' is not guilty of rash and negligent driving

(*b*) 'Y' should have taken sufficient care on the footpath

(*c*) 'X' is guilty of rash and negligent driving

(*d*) 'X' is only in part guilty of rash and negligent driving

**82. Principle:** Whoever causes death by doing an act with the intention of causing death, or with the intention of causing such bodily injury as is likely to cause death, or with the knowledge that he is likely by such act to cause death, commits the offence of culpable homicide.

**Facts:** 'A' knows 'Z' to be behind a bush. 'B' does not know it. 'A', intending to cause, or knowing it to be likely to cause Z's death, induces 'B' to fire at the bush. 'B' fires and kills 'Z'.

(*a*) 'B' has committed the offence of culpable homicide

(*b*) 'A' has committed the offence of culpable homicide

(*c*) Both 'A' and 'B' have committed the offence of culpable homicide

(*d*) None of them has committed the offence of culpable homicide

**83. Principle:** Whoever, intending to take dishonestly any movable property out of the possession of any person without that person's consent, moves that property in order to such taking, is said to commit theft.

**Facts:** 'Z', going on a journey, entrusts his plate to the possession of 'A', the keeper of a warehouse, till 'Z' shall return. Then, 'A' carries the plate to a goldsmith and sells it.

(*a*) 'A' has committed theft

(*b*) 'A' has not committed theft

(*c*) 'A' lawfully sold the plate to the goldsmith

(*d*) None of the above is true

**84. Principle:** Whoever makes any false document or part of a document with intent to cause damage or injury, to the public or to any person, or to support any claim or title, or to cause any person to part with property, or to enter into any express or implied contract, or with intent to commit fraud or that fraud may be committed, commits forgery.

**Facts:** 'A' without Z's authority, affixes Z's seal to a document purporting to be a conveyance of an estate from 'Z' to 'A', with the intention of selling the estate to 'B' and thereby of obtaining from 'B' the purchase-money.

(*a*) 'B' has committed forgery

(*b*) 'Z' has committed forgery

(*c*) 'A' has committed forgery

(*d*) 'A' and 'B' have committed forgery

**85. Principle:** Whoever intentionally uses force to any person, without that person's consent, in order to the committing of any offence, or intending by the use of such force to cause, or knowing it to be likely that by the use of such force he will cause injury, fear or annoyance to the person to whom the force is used, is said to use criminal force to that other.

**Facts:** 'Z' is riding in a palanquin. 'A', intending to rob 'Z', seizes the pole and stops the palanquin. Here 'A' has caused cessation of motion to 'Z', and 'A' has done this by his own bodily power.

(*a*) 'A' has used criminal force to 'Z'

(*b*) 'A' has no intention to use criminal force to 'Z'

(*c*) 'A' has used force with the consent of 'Z'

(*d*) None of the above is correct

**86. Principle:** Every person shall be liable to punishment under the Indian Penal Code and not otherwise for every act or omission contrary to the provisions of the Code of which he shall be guilty within the territory of India. In other words, the exercise of criminal jurisdiction depends upon the locality of the offence committed, and not upon the nationality or locality of the offender.

**Facts:** 'X', a Pakistani citizen, while staying at Karachi, made false representations to 'Y', the complainant, at Bombay through letters, telephone calls and telegrams and induced the complainant to part with money amounting to over rupees five lakh to the agents of 'X' at Bombay, so that rice could be shipped from Karachi to India as per agreement. But the rice was never supplied to the complainant.

(*a*) The offence of cheating under section 420 of the Code was committed by 'X' within India, even though he was not physically present at the time and place of the crime

(*b*) The offence of cheating as per section 420 of the Code was not committed by 'X' within India, as he was not physically present at the time and place of the crime

(*c*) Only the agents of 'X' had committed the offence of cheating under section 420 of the Code within India, as they were physically present at the time and place of the crime

(*d*) 'Y' was also liable for the offence of cheating under section 420 of the Code within India, as he was physically present at the time and place of the crime

**87. Principle:** When two or more persons agree to do, or cause to be done, (1) an illegal act, or (2) an act which is not illegal by illegal means, through such an agreement such persons are said to have been engaged in a criminal conspiracy to commit an offence. It is said that no consummation of the crime need be achieved or even attempted.

**Facts:** 'X', 'Y' and 'Z' plan to kill 'D'. They agree that only one among them, that is 'Z', will execute the plan. In pursuance of it 'Z' buys a gun and loads it.

(*a*) Only 'Z' can be charged with criminal conspiracy to kill 'D'

(*b*) All of them, i.e., 'X', 'Y' and 'Z', can be charged with criminal conspiracy to kill 'D'

(*c*) 'X' and 'Y' cannot be charged with criminal conspiracy to kill 'D'

(*d*) None of them can be charged with criminal conspiracy to kill 'D'

**88. Principle:** 'Wrongful gain' is gain by unlawful means of property to which the person gaining is not legally entitled. 'Wrongful loss' is the loss by unlawful means of property to which the person losing it is legally entitled.

**Facts:** 'X' takes away Y's watch out of Y's possession, without Y's consent and with the intention of keeping it.

(*a*) 'X' causes 'wrongful gain' to 'Y'

(*b*) 'Y' causes 'wrongful gain' to 'X'

(*c*) 'X' causes 'wrongful loss' to 'Y'

(*d*) 'Y' causes 'wrongful loss' to 'X'

**89. Principle:** Nothing is an offence by reason that it causes, or that it is intended to cause, or that it is known to be likely to cause, any harm, if that harm is so slight that no person of ordinary sense and temper would complain of such harm.

**Facts:** 'X' takes a plain sheet of paper from Y's drawer without Y's consent to write a letter to his friend.

(*a*) 'X' has committed an offence in the above context

(*b*) 'X' has committed no offence in the above context

(*c*) 'Y' can sue 'X' for an offence in the above context

(*d*) None of the above is correct in the above context

**90. Principle:** When an act which would otherwise be a certain offence, is not that offence, by reason of the youth, the want of maturity of understanding, the unsoundness of mind or the intoxication of the person doing that act, or by reason of any misconception on the part of that person, every person has the same right of private defence against that act which he would have if the act were that offence.

**Facts:** 'X', under the influence of madness, attempts to kill 'Y'.

(*a*) 'Y' has the right of private defence against 'X'

(*b*) 'Y' does not have the right of private defence against 'X'

(*c*) 'Y' has the right of private defence against 'X', only if 'X' is not under the influence of madness

(*d*) 'X' has the right of private defence against 'Y'

## Solutions

**1.** a Criminal Force has been defined under Section 350 of IPC as whoever intentionally uses force to any person, without that person's consent, in order to the committing of any offence, or intending by the use of such force to cause, or knowing it to be likely that by the use of such force he will cause injury, fear or annoyance to the person to whom the force is used, is said to use criminal force to that other.

**2.** c There are certain Torts where element of 'intention' is relevant while committing the act. For eg: assault, battery, false imprisonment, trespass etc.

**3.** b The act is dishonest embezzlement of the property as the servant has put the typewriter to his own use which was entrusted to him for a specified purpose. In Indian Penal Code, it is an offence and is recognized as criminal Breach of Trust.

**4.** d A clearly in the present case was under reasonable apprehension of kidnapping. He exercised private defense for his daughter on seeing an act which to an ordinary person would considered (as facts of the case are silent about A's knowledge of surprise) kidnapping in progress.

**5.** c The term approver is neither defined nor used in the Criminal Procedure Code, but is usually applied to a person, supposed to be directly or indirectly concerned in an offence and to whom a pardon is granted by the court with a view to securing his testimony/statement against other persons guilty of the offence.

**6.** d Section 299 of IPC defines Culpable Homicide as who ever causes death by doing an act with the intention of causing death, or with the intention of causing such bodily injury as is likely to cause death, or with the knowledge that he is likely by such act to cause death, commits the offence of culpable homicide.

**7.** d As per Section 361 of IPC, whoever takes or entices any minor under 1[sixteen] years of age if a male, or under [eighteen] years of age if a female, or any person of unsound mind, out of the keeping of the lawful guardian of such minor or person of unsound mind, without the consent of such guardian, is said to kidnap such minor or person from lawful guardianship hence none of the given options would be taken as a defence of kidnapping.

**8.** d The correct option is (*d*) as in the abovementioned facts B' never had the intention to hurt his friend and he was only playing a joke and he never used the required force which would make him liable for the offence of Battery or Assault.

**9.** c A's movement was not completely stopped or restrained as required by the principle. He had the option to return.

**10.** b There is a lawful excuse with the policeman who was trying to catch suspected criminal.

**11.** c The common intention formed by A,B and C was to commit burglary and not murder. It was in course of running away that A was caught and he stabbed X which was never conspired or preconceived amongst A, B and C.

**12.** b The intention at the time when A took back the watch was not dishonest. He neither caused wrongful loss to B nor wrongful gain to himself. So he is not liable for theft.

**13.** b Since B has the entrusted possession of the property therefore this is a case of breach of trust rather than theft. Theft is done when something is taken out of possession without that person's consent, but breach of trust is done when someone gives the property in trust and other misuse or misappropriates the property against trust created.

**14.** b By direct application of principle it is clear that threat and fear were used for getting the money so there is extortion.

**15.** a A has committed theft only and not robbery as he moved the property without using force.

**16.** a 'A' is the correct answer because A shot at B while escaping after taking away the wallet i.e. it was an attempt to cause to any person death or hurt. Hence, A has committed robbery.

**17.** b In present set of facts A is liable as he knew that his act is likely to cause wrongful loss and damage to the property and therefore it is mischief.

**18.** a A is the correct option as he possessed the knowledge that his action is likely to cause destruction of the property and therefore he is guilty of mischief.

**19.** b Answer is very clear as intention of A is to remain in the campus unlawfully in order to commit the offence of theft.

**20.** c Krishna cannot exercise the right to self defense as there is no imminent threat to his life. In this case, it is just an intimidation and not an imminent threat. Imminent threat arises where there is no intermittent act except the act which may result in harm to the person.

**21.** c The principle clearly states that when two or more persons in the facts only Bharat is the person who has committed the act, thus its not criminal conspiracy. In legal context, a computer does not fall in the category of a person.

**22.** c The first blow is for self defense, but when the thief is unconscious after the first blow, there is no eminent threat to Q's life or property, thus the second blow is unreasonable. The right of self defence seized to exist once the thief fell unconscious.

**23.** a Private defence is only available only against the defender. There is no self-defence against self defence. Right of private defence is preventive in nature and can never be aggressively used. It has to be exercised with utmost care and caution.

**24.** c Here right of 'private defence' cannot be claimed as the robbers were fleeing and there was no imminent danger to the property. However as none of the options cover this scenario singularly, option c is the best choice.

**25.** b As both X and Y conspired to poison Z, thus both are liable. As per the given facts, answer (*d*) is also correct but as the principle is about determining and identifying the criminal conspiracy, option B is the appropriate answer.

**26.** d Though murder has not taken place, but both X and Y did conspire, making both of them liable for criminal conspiracy. As there is no option which covers this directly, option d is the best choice.

**27.** c Criminal Conspiracy has been defined under Section 120-A of IPC which states that When two or more persons agree to do, or cause to be done,— an illegal act, or an act which is not illegal by illegal means, such an agreement is designated a criminal conspiracy.

**28.** b As the principle of Contributory Negligence is given, and the facts clearly states that due to the negligent act of X, X died. Y would be only partly liable to the extent of his negligent act.

**29.** c The agreement is not valid as it was signed under threat of suicide which amounts to coercion as per the principle.

**30.** c Even death of a person would not be an offence if it is proved it was for self-defence.

**31.** b Prosecution

**32.** c Compoundable offence

**33.** b The court may order the transfer of the ownership of the property.

**34.** b Only X committed the offence of theft.

**35.** c Lucky had only taken the pile of newspapers with the consent of Indira, but not the painting. Moreover he did not return the painting to Indira after discovering it and this establishes the theft.

**36.** a The rule of criminal damage talks about the intention of the person in question. Here Lucky had only pasted the painting in order to prevent it from tearing any further. Therefore in the absence of any intention of reducing the value of the property, Lucky has not committed any criminal damage.

**37.** c Lucky would still be guilty of theft as long as he did not have Indiras consent on it. Indira had only asked him to take away the pile of newspapers. Removing anything apart from that from the possession of Indira would amount to theft.

**38.** c Kamala is liable for theft as the rule talks about having the intention to take property from the possession of another without his consent. The person in question need not necessarily be an owner. All other requirements of Rule A is established and hence it makes Kamala liable for theft as per the principle.

**39.** d No act done by Kamala amounts to reducing the value of the property in question. Hence there was no criminal damage. Options a and b are thus ruled out. The facts do not make any reference to damage of property after it is in Kamala's possession. Therefore, (*d*) becomes the only appropriate answer.

**40.** a Sharman acted on necessity in order to avoid a bigger harm and acted in good faith without any criminal intention, hence, he has committed no offence.

**41.** a In the present case the police can book Mr. Tiwari for drunken driving but not for willful negligent driving.

**42.** a Y moved the property (severed it from the ground) with the dishonest intention of taking it. Therefore, Y can be prosecuted for theft.

**43.** * The options are incorrect. The correct answer should be "X has committed culpable homicide NOT amounting to murder". Besides, there is nothing in the facts to show that X has committed the act in unsound state of mind.

**44.** a Undue influence renders on contract voidable at the option of party so influenced.

**45.** d Coersion renders on contract voidable at the option of party so coerced.

**46.** c Every individual shall be treated equally by the state. (In equal circumstances).

**47.** c X had not committed any offence and had no intention to kill Z and in good faith he was trying to save Z.

**48.** b Y is guilty of attempt to commit theft because Y with a dishonest intention acted in order to steal the jewels.

**49.** b Raju will be held guilty of Criminal breach of trust as he misappropriated by running away with the money which was entrusted upon him by the lady.

**50.** b There is no false imprisonment in this case as there was a just cause with B to stop A from leaving the park. B was justified in asking ₹100 to be paid at the time of exit. Hence, B is not guilty of false imprisonment.

**51.** c A has committed the offence of attempt to murder. A had the intention to commit crime and formed a series of acts by purchasing poison and giving the same to the bearer to be served to B in a drink. The act was interrupted as the glass dropped and hence, the actual commission of offence got limited to attempt. Hence, A is guilty of the offence of attempt to murder.

**52.** d Though the correct answer marked in the question is '(*d*)', but the question is ambiguous.

**53.** a A is guilty of Criminal Misappropriation. When he took the umbrella out of the possession of Z, he took it in good faith believing it to be his own. Therefore, the act will not amount to theft because theft needs taking property dishonestly out of the possession. But later, after knowing that it did not belong to him, converted it for his own use, hence, misappropriating the same.

**54.** a The Supreme Court in various cases has held that the age at the date of the commission of the offence will be the reckoning date for determination of the age of the juvenile.

**55.** d Sacrilege is the violation or injurious treatment of a sacred object or person.

**56.** c Since A had used criminal intimidation to obtain B's consent, B will succeed and A will not be able to enforce the agreement.

**57.** d Since taking away from the land or possession is an important part of theft and has not yet been executed, option D would be correct.

**58.** a Consent has no part in kidnapping as per the principle. The boy took away the minor girl out of the keeping of her parents. He would be liable for kidnapping.

**59.** * Facts provided are insufficient to reach a conclusive answer. However, taking assumption that the men were voluntarily having carnal intercourse against the order of nature, we can mark "C" as the correct option.

**60.** d The omission of A of not giving food to his father and his act of beating his father together resulted in his father's death.

**61.** a A is not seven years of age on December 30, 2011 and hence, as per the principle, not qualified to commit an offence. Therefore, A is the correct answer.

**62.** c Since B was a minor, he could not have entered in a pact to suffer harm, Hence A has committed an offence.

**63.** d Although A is not committing an offence because of his madness, B has the right to defend himself as per the principle, hence option D is correct.

**64.** b The professor has not committed any offence as he wrote a comment in a National Daily which generated an academic debate and no sort of disaffection towards the government. Hence, the professor has not committed any offence.

**65.** * The principle given in this question is incomplete as the definition of 'stealing' is not provided. But if we go by the general understanding of the offence of stealing, then "C" would be the most appropriate answer. It would be an attempt to steal because A opened the box in which the jewel s used to be kept but he did not steal as there was no jewel in the box. By opening of the box, it is clear that he made an attempt to steal the jewel. Hence, he has committed the offence of attempt to stealing.

**66.** a Since A is asserting the facts in the given situation, hence, A must prove that B, C and D have committed the crime.

**67.** * The facts are insufficient in the given question. We do not know the final course of action taken by Mr. Sharman at the end. Assuming that he ran down the boat with only two passengers aboard, "A" would be the most appropriate answer. The act of killing two passengers on boat C would result from the necessity of saving more lives which is exactly what the principle provides.

**68.** b The facts clearly illustrate that selling kidney, even though done on a person's own consent, is not a "thing done for a person's own benefit" as per the principles given. Therefore Z is guilty

**69.** c A acted in good faith with to save the life of the child. He anyways did not have any other option. Therefore he is not guilty

**70.** b As given in the principle the soldier is bound by duty to obey his senior as per law. Therefore he is not guilty.

**71.** a A did not have the dishonest intention to move B' property. He under good faith believed that the property of his own. He is therefore not guilty of theft.

**72.** d The act of keeping explosives in the garage can only amount to preparation for the crime. Manish has not done any act after that to achieve his objective of killing Nandini. There is no offence by Manish.

**73.** d Akash never had the intention to use criminal force against his brother. He further never knew that his act of bursting a cracker was likely to get his brother scared. There is no offence by Akash

**74.** a the principle herein talks about giving the same amount of punishment and penalty to a person as is applicable at the time of commission of the offence. Therefore the boy should not be allowed the benefit of the Probation of offenders act. (AILET official answer key gives option 'B' as answer)

**75.** b A is not guilty of murder because the death of B was not result of his stabbing B but the negligence of Hospital doctors. He can at best be charged with the offence of attempt to murder.

**76.** b Apprehending someone who has committed murder is not unlawful by a police officer even without a warrant.

**77.** c The act of killing Darshan was done togather in furtherance of a common intention and hence all of them would be liable.

**78.** b A was communicating his diagnosis to his patient in good faith which cannot amount to any offence.

**79.** b Sawant knowingly and willfully furnished false information to the magistrate of the murder happening on his property and hence is liable.

**80.** a K knows that his act of travelling while having cholera is likely to spread the infection of a disease dangerous to life and he still does it. Therefore, K is guilty.

**81.** c X's action of rash and negligent driving caused a pedestrian's death and hence he is guilty.

**82.** b A knew Z was behind the bush. He intentionally and knowingly made B to fire at the bush and hence A is guilty of culpable homicide.

**83.** b Z voluntarily gave the plate to A and it was not taken out of Z's possession without his consent. Therefore A has not committed theft.

**84.** c A used Z's seal in order to sell the estate to B. A has committed forgery.

**85.** a A stopped Z's ride by use of force in order to rob him. A is guilty of using criminal force on Z.

**86.** a It does not matter whether X was physically present in India or not. The very fact the offence of cheating was committed in Bombay (India) makes him liable for cheating.

**87.** b All of them are guilty since they conspired to commit the crime even though no crime was committed or even attempted.

**88.** c Since X took the Watch away from Y without his consent, X is causing wrongful loss to Y.

**89.** b No person in his ordinary senses would have complaint of taking a plain sheet of paper from his drawer.

**90.** a Since X was insane his actions would not amount to an offence, still Y would get a chance to defend himself according to principle.

■■

# 4

# CONSTITUTIONAL LAW AND LEGAL FRAMEWORK

1. The Supreme Court of India enjoys:
   (*a*) Only original jurisdiction.
   (*b*) Only appellate jurisdiction.
   (*c*) Only advisory jurisdiction.
   (*d*) All the above types of jurisdictions.
   **(AILET, 2008)**

2. A money bill can be introduced in Parliament by:
   (*a*) The Finance Minister alone.
   (*b*) Any minister.
   (*c*) Any member of Parliament.
   (*d*) Any member of the ruling party.
   **(AILET, 2008)**

3. Members of Rajaya Sabha are not associated with
   1. Public Accounts Committee.
   2. Estimates Committee.
   3. Committee on Public Undertakings.
   (*a*) 1 and 2 (*b*) 3
   (*c*) 2 (*d*) 1 and 3 **(AILET, 2008)**

4. According to the Constitution, amendments cannot be proposed in either House to
   (*a*) The Annual Financial Statement.
   (*b*) Appropriation Bill.
   (*c*) Demand for Grants.
   (*d*) All of the above **(AILET, 2008)**

5. Which article of our Constitution provides that the State shall make effective provision for securing right to work?
   (*a*) Article 41 (*b*) Article 39
   (*c*) Article 21 (*d*) Article 45
   **(AILET, 2008)**

6. Who of the following does not constitute an exception for 'equality before law' (Article 14)?
   (*a*) The Foreign Diplomats.
   (*b*) The Prime Minister.
   (*c*) The Governor.
   (*d*) The President. **(AILET, 2008)**

7. The Constitution of India Describes India as:
   (*a*) A Quasi-Federal Country.
   (*b*) Union of States.
   (*c*) A federation of States and Union territories.
   (*d*) None of the above. **(AILET, 2008)**

8. Which one of the following Fundamental Rights has been the subject of maximum litigation and controversies?
   (*a*) Right to Property.
   (*b*) Right to Equality.
   (*c*) Right to Freedom of Religion.
   (*d*) Right to Freedom. **(AILET, 2008)**

9. The Fundamental Duties of the Indian Citizens:
   (*a*) Formed a part of the original Constitution.
   (*b*) Were added by the Forty-Second Amendment.
   (*c*) Were added by the Forty-Fourth Amendment.
   (*d*) Were defined by the Parliament through a law enacted during the emergency. **(AILET, 2008)**

10. What is contained in the Eleventh Schedule to the Constitution of India?
   (*a*) Forms of oath of affirmation.
   (*b*) Provisions regarding disqualification on grounds of defection.
   (*c*) Items in respect of which Panchayats shall have powers and authority to function as institutions of Self-Government.
   (*d*) Items on which Municipalities shall have powers and authority to function as institutions of Self-Government. **(AILET, 2008)**

11. The strength of the Council of Ministers:
   (*a*) has been fixed by the Constitution.
   (*b*) has been fixed by the Parliament under Representation of People's Act, 1950.
   (*c*) is determined by the Prime Minister keeping in view the requirement of the time.
   (*d*) is determined by the President.
   **(AILET, 2008)**

**12.** The advisory Powers of the Supreme Court of India imply that:

(*a*) it renders advice to the Government of India on all constitutional matters.

(*b*) it renders advice to the Prime Minister on legal matters.

(*c*) it renders advice to the President on question of law or fact which is of public importance.

(*d*) it has power to render advice to all the above persons. **(AILET, 2008)**

**13.** The provision under which the Supreme Court can grant 'special leave' to appeal against decisions of lower courts and tribunals is contained in:

(*a*) Section 10 of Supreme Court Rules.

(*b*) Article 136 of Indian Constitution.

(*c*) Article 226 of Indian Constitution.

(*d*) Article 139 of Indian Constitution.

**(AILET, 2008)**

**14.** The display of articles in a show room indicating their prices amounts to

(*a*) offer

(*b*) counter offer

(*c*) invitation to an offer

(*d*) mere advertisement **(AILET, 2008)**

**15.** Which one of the following conditions regarding acquisition of citizenship by naturalisation has been **wrongly** listed?

(*a*) He belongs to a country where citizens of India are permitted to acquire citizenship by naturalisation.

(*b*) He has been residing in India or serving the Government of India for at least 10 years preceding the date of application.

(*c*) He possesses workable knowledge of an Indian language.

(*d*) He has consistently supported the Indian cause at various national and international forums. **(AILET, 2009)**

**16.** Which one of the following statements is **correct**?

(*a*) The Right to Private Property was incorporated in the Constitution by the Forty-Second Amendment.

(*b*) The Right to Private Property granted by the original Constitution but it has since been removed from the list of Fundamental Rights.

(*c*) The Right to Private Property was never a Fundamental Right under the Indian Constitution.

(*d*) The Right to Private Property which was granted by the original Constitution has been made more sacrosanct by the Forty-Forth Amendment. **(AILET, 2009)**

**17.** Which one of the following Directive Principles is non Gandhian?

(*a*) Promotion of cottage industries in rural areas.

(*b*) Prohibition of the use of intoxicants except for medicinal purposes.

(*c*) Prevention of slaughter of cow, calves and other milch cattle.

(*d*) Provision o free and compulsory education for all the children up to the age of fourteen years.

**(AILET, 2009)**

**18.** Which one of the following steps cannot be taken by the President during the Financial Emergency?

(*a*) He can direct the Union and State Governments to observe such canons of financial propriety as he deems desirable.

(*b*) He can suspend the Fundamental Rights of the Indian citizens.

(*c*) He can order reduction of salaries and allowances of all civil servants.

(*d*) He can order the reduction of the salaries of the Supreme Court and High Court judges.

**(AILET, 2009)**

**19.** How many members are required to support the introduction of a No-Confidence Motion in the Lok Sabha?

(*a*) Two-thirds of the membership of the House.

(*b*) 50 members.

(*c*) 80 members.

(*d*) 60 members. **(AILET, 2009)**

**20.** The decision of a High Court is

(*a*) binding on other High Courts

(*b*) not binding on other High Courts

(*c*) occasionally binding on other High Courts

(*d*) of no value for other High Courts

**(AILET, 2009)**

**21.** With the approval of the Parliament the National Emergency can continue for

(*a*) a maximum period of three years.

(*b*) a maximum period of one year.

(*c*) an indefinite period.

(*d*) a maximum period of six months. **(AILET, 2009)**

**22.** The 39th Amendment laid that election of any person to Lok Sabha holding the office of Prime Minister cannot be challenged before a Court of Law, but only before an authority established by Parliament. This was declared unconstitutional by the Supreme Court in

(*a*) Keshvananda Bharti Case.

(*b*) Menaka Gandhi Case.

(*c*) Indira Gandhi v. Raj Narain Case.

(*d*) None of these **(AILET, 2009)**

**23.** Once appointed, judges of Supreme Court serve till they attain the age of

(*a*) 62 years.

(*b*) 63 years.

(*c*) 64 years.

(*d*) 65 years. **(AILET, 2009)**

**24.** Gangaram is a wood-cutter. He earns his livelihood by cutting forest trees in Nainital, Uttranchal. The State of Uttranchal makes a law prohibiting the cutting of forest trees. Is Gangaram's Constitutional right infringed?

(*a*) Yes. Because he may not like to do any other job to earn his bread and butter.

(*b*) No. Because the Government is sovereign and can make any law.

(*c*) Yes. Because he has a fundamental right to life and livelihood under Article 21 of the Constitution and the Government cannot snatch away his bread and butter by making such a law.

(*d*) No. Because the Government has power to make a law for prohibiting the cutting of forest trees under Article 48A of the Constitution.

**(AILET, 2009)**

**25. PRINCIPLE:** Right to carry on any occupation, trade or business is a Fundamental Right under the Indian Constitution. The State is under an obligation under the Directive Principles of State Policy to organize agriculture and animal husbandry on scientific lines, and towards that goal, take steps to prohibit cow slaughter.

**FACTS:** The State of X passed a legislation totally prohibiting cow slaughter. A, a butcher, trading in meat of all animals including cows, challenged this legislation as violating the fundamental right to carry on his business.

(*a*) The State of X cannot make a law taking away any fundamental right. Such law is null and void.

(*b*) The State can prohibit cow slaughter to organize animal husbandry in scientific lines.

(*c*) The right to carry on any occupation, trade or business is subject to reasonable restrictions.

Banning cow-slaughter is such a restriction to better animal husbandry production and it is within the power of State.

(*d*) None of the above. **(AILET, 2011)**

**26. PRINCIPLE:** The Constitution guarantees freedom of religion and expects the citizen to respect national anthem as a fundamental duty.

**FACTS:** According to the religions tenets of a particular sect, singing the praise of any entity other than God is forbidden. The child, belonging to that sect, refuses to sing national anthem in the course of school assembly, in which every child must compulsorily participate. When the disciplinary action was instituted against the child, the parents challenged the school's order of singing the national anthem.

(*a*) The School can take disciplinary action against the child as it is the fundamental duty to respect national anthem.

(*b*) The fundamental right to freedom of religion cannot be abridged by a fundamental duty imposed by the State.

(*c*) The girl is free to follow the religion of her choice and follow its rules. It cannot be said to be disrespect on the part of the girl if she refuse to sing national anthem.

(*d*) None of the above **(AILET, 2011)**

**27. PRINCIPLE:** All citizens shall have the right to freedom of speech and expression.

**FACTS:** X, a famous writer and Novelist criticized another novelist, B stating that: "the novel of B is foolish, he is a weakman, his Novel is indecent, his mind is impure, he is not of a good character, he should write decent and good Novels" Can X be sued for defamation?

(*a*) He is not liable because he has just expressed his personal views.

(*b*) He is liable to be sued for defamation if his statement, was not true or said in *mala fide* intention.

(*c*) He cannot be liable because he has fundamental right to freedom of speech and expression.

(*d*) He cannot be sued, because both are writer and novelists and both can criticize each other. **(AILET, 2011)**

**28.** What is minimum duration of stay essential before a person can apply for citizenship of India?

(*a*) Five years.

(*b*) Seven years.

(*c*) Nine years.

(*d*) Twelve years. **(AILET, 2012)**

**29.** The Ordinances issued by the Governor are subject to the approval by

(*a*) State legislature.

(*b*) President.

(*c*) Central Government.

(*d*) Parliament. **(AILET, 2012)**

**30.** Scheduled Castes and Scheduled Tribes

(*a*) have been specified by the Presidential Orders issued in consultation with the Governors of the respective States.

(*b*) have been specified in the Constitution by the Constitution makers in the form of a Schedule.

(*c*) have to be specified and notified by the Parliament after detailed discussions about the backward nature of these people.

(*d*) are the Castes and Tribes notified by the State Government after detailed discussion as to their socio-economic conditions. **(AILET, 2012)**

**31.** Free legal aid for an accused is a

(*a*) Fundamental right.

(*b*) Fundamental duty of the State.

(*c*) Directive Principles of State Policy.

(*d*) Discretion of the State. **(AILET, 2012)**

**32.** The concept of Secular State is that the State will not make any discrimination on the ground of religion, caste or community against any person professing any particular form of religious faith. The Secularism is embodied in

(*a*) Preamble of Constitution.

(*b*) Directive Principles of State Policy.

(*c*) Fundamental Rights.

(*d*) Judicial Interpretation of Fundamental Rights. **(AILET, 2012)**

**33.** The Constitution of India does not mention the post of

(*a*) The Deputy Speaker of the Lok Sabha.

(*b*) The Deputy Speaker of the State Legislative Assembly.

(*c*) The Deputy Chairman of the Rajya Sabha.

(*d*) The Deputy Prime Minister. **(AILET, 2012)**

**34.** A Judge of the Supreme Court of India or High Court of any State can be removed by the President of India only

(*a*) when the Principles of Natural Justice are followed and the alleged misconduct is proved in an impartial enquiry.

(*b*) if he is satisfied through the report made by the Chief Justice of India that the misconduct of the judge has been proved.

(*c*) when an address is made by both the Houses of Parliament in the same session asking for his/her removal on the grounds of proven misbehaviour and incapacity.

(*d*) when the President and the Prime Minister are satisfied that he or she has committed a misconduct and the same has been proved before a competent authority. **(AILET, 2012)**

**35.** The Constitution of India is the result of considerable imitation and adaptation rather than originality because

(*a*) makers of Indian Constitution drew much from the American Constitution, Canadian Constitution and British made Government of India Act, 1935.

(*b*) makers of Indian Constitution drew much from Swiss Constitution, German Constitution and Government of India Act of 1919.

(*c*) makers of Indian Constitution drew much from Constitution of Singapore, Constitution of Sri Lanka and Government of India Act of 1919.

(*d*) makers of Indian Constitution drew from Constitution of South Africa, Constitution of Netherlands and Government of India Act of 1919. **(AILET, 2012)**

**36.** A seat of a M.P. can be declared vacant if he absents himself from the House for a continuous period of

(*a*) six months.

(*b*) two months.

(*c*) three months.

(*d*) one year. **(AILET, 2012)**

**37.** What is true with Members of Parliament's immunity from arrest?

(*a*) In civil cases while the Legislature is in Session, for 40 days before and after and in criminal cases no arrest during Parliament Session.

(*b*) In civil cases, while Legislature is in Session and for 40 days before and after and in criminal cases arrest can be made at any time.

(*c*) In civil cases while the Legislature is in Session, for 20 days before and after and in criminal cases no arrest during Parliament Session.

(*d*) In civil cases, while Legislature is in Session and for 20 days before and after and in criminal cases arrest can be made at any time. **(AILET, 2012)**

**38.** Dealing with the chapter of citizenship under the Constitution, the Supreme Court has held that Sonia Gandhi, the President of Congress (I) is not an Italian citizen, but is an Indian citizen because she is governed by

(*a*) Article 10, Constitution of India.

(*b*) Article 11, Constitution of India.

(*c*) The Citizenship Act, 1955.

(*d*) Article 5, Constitution of India.

**(AILET, 2012)**

**39.** What is true with appointment of Attorney General for India?

(*a*) He can be appointed by President of India and is qualified to be appointed a Judge of Supreme Court.

(*b*) He can be appointed by President of India and is qualified to be appointed a Judge of High Court.

(*c*) He can be appointed by a Special Commission and is qualified to be appointed as Law Minister.

(*d*) He can be appointed by Chief Justice of India and is qualified to be appointed as a Judge of Supreme Court. **(AILET, 2012)**

**40.** The right to constitutional remedies in India is available to

(*a*) only the citizen of India.

(*b*) all persons in case of infringement of any fundamental right.

(*c*) any person for enforcing any rights conferred on them.

(*d*) an aggrieved individual alone. **(AILET, 2012)**

**41.** While a proclamation of emergency is in operation, the State Government

(*a*) cannot legislate.

(*b*) can legislate only on subjects in the Concurrent List.

(*c*) can legislate on the subjects in the State List.

(*d*) is suspended. **(AILET, 2012)**

**Directions** Given below is a statement of legal principle followed by a facts . Apply the principle to the facts given below and select the most appropriate answer.

**42. FACTS:** In order to ensure that people live in an amicable atmosphere the Government of India decided to abolish courts and constituted Dispute Settlement Boards. Further to achieve this objective, the law stipulated that lawyers should not be allowed to espouse the claims of parties, and instead their claims be espoused by social workers.

**PRINCIPLES:**

I. Any law made by the Parliament that infringes the fundamental rights of the citizens is invalid and unenforceable.

II. Freedom to carry on trade or profession of one's own choice is a fundamental right.

III. The Parliament is competent to impose reasonable restrictions on the exercise of this right.

IV. If the restrictions, on fundamental rights imposed by the Parliament, totally removes or nullifies any fundamental right then it will be construed as an unreasonable restriction.

**DECISION:**

(*a*) The law made by the Parliament is valid as it does not infringe any fundamental right.

(*b*) The law made by the Parliament is valid as even though there is restriction of fundamental right, such a restriction is reasonable.

(*c*) The law made by the Parliament is invalid as it constitutes an infringement of fundamental rights and the restriction imposed is not reasonable.

(*d*) None of the above answer is correct.

**(AILET, 2012)**

**43. PRINCIPLES**: All minorities, whether based on religion or language shall have the rights to establish and administer educational institution of their choice.

**FACTS**: Md. Yusuf wants to establish an educational institution to help the poor person of his community and to educate the children of the community. Yusuf being a very rich man has no problem regarding finance for institution. Therefore he applies to state government to grant him permission to establish and administer the institution. State government rejects his plea on ground that said institution will create communal tension in the proposed area. Yusuf has following remedies:

(*a*) He should file a civil suit in District Court.

(*b*) He should file a special leave petition before Supreme Court.

(*c*) He has no remedy under the law.

(*d*) He could file a writ petition either before the High Court or the Supreme Court.

**(AILET, 2012)**

**44.** The right of a party to initiate an action and be heard before a Court of law is called

(*a*) Right in rem. (*b*) Right in personam.

(*c*) Fundamental right. (*d*) Locus standi.

**(CLAT 2009)**

**45.** Indian Parliament is based on the principle of Bicameralism

(*a*) Universal Adult Franchise

(*b*) Dyarchy

(*c*) Federalism

(*d*) None of these **(CLAT 2009)**

**46.** Supreme Court held that Preamble as a basic feature of Constitution cannot be amended in the case of

(*a*) Golknath V. State of Punjab.

(*b*) Maneka Gandhi V. Union of India.

(*c*) S. R. Bommai V. Union of India.

(*d*) Kesavananda Bharti V. State of Kerala.

**(CLAT 2009)**

**47.** The offence of inciting disaffection, hatred or contempt against Government is

(*a*) Perjury. (*b*) Forgery.

(*c*) Sedition. (*d*) Revolt. **(CLAT 2009)**

**48.** No one can be convicted twice for the same offence. This doctrine is called

(*a*) Burden of proof.

(*b*) Double conviction.

(*c*) Double jeopardy.

(*d*) Corpus delicti. **(CLAT 2009)**

**49.** Who have constitutional right to audience in all India Courts?

(*a*) President.

(*b*) Chief Justice of India.

(*c*) Attorney General.

(*d*) Solicitor General. **(CLAT 2009)**

**50.** Which of the following is not included in the Preamble to the Constitution?

(*a*) Morality. (*b*) Justice.

(*c*) Sovereign. (*d*) Socialist. **(CLAT 2009)**

**51.** 'Court of Record' is a Court which?

(*a*) Maintains records.

(*b*) Preserves all its records.

(*c*) Can Punish for its contempt.

(*d*) Is competent to issue writs. **(CLAT 2009)**

**52.** A judge of the Supreme Court can be removed from office only on grounds of

(*a*) gross inefficiency.

(*b*) delivering wrong judgments.

(*c*) senility.

(*d*) proven misbehaviour or incapacity.

**(CLAT 2009)**

**53.** Fiduciary relationship means a relationship based on

(*a*) trust.

(*b*) money.

(*c*) senility.

(*d*) blood relation. **(CLAT 2009)**

**54.** The concept of judicial review has been borrowed from the Constitution of

(*a*) U.S.S.R.

(*b*) U.K.

(*c*) U.S.A.

(*d*) Switzerland. **(CLAT 2009)**

**55.** Which of the following is not a fundamental right in India?

(*a*) Right to form association.

(*b*) Freedom of religion.

(*c*) Right to property.

(*d*) Right to move throughout the territory of India.

**(CLAT 2010)**

**56.** The President of India is elected by an electoral college consisting of

(*a*) all the members of both the Houses of Parliament and all the members of all the Legislative Assemblies.

(*b*) all the elective members of both the Houses of Parliament and all the members of all the Legislative Assemblies.

(*c*) all the members of both the Houses of Parliament and all the elected members of all the Legislative Assemblies.

(*d*) all the elected members of both the Houses of Parliament and all the elected members of all the Legislative Assemblies. **(CLAT 2010)**

**57.** Which of the following is not a fundamental right?

(*a*) Freedom of speech.

(*b*) Right to life.

(*c*) Right to equality.

(*d*) Right to work. **(CLAT 2010)**

**(For questions 58 to 62)**

**Rules**

A. The fundamental right to freedom of association includes the right to form an association as well as not join an association.

B. The fundamental right to freedom of association also includes the freedom to decide with whom to associate.

C. The fundamental right to freedom of association does not extend to the right to realise the objectives of forming the association.

D. Fundamental rights are applicable only to laws made by or administrative actions of the State and do not apply to actions of private persons.

E. Any law in contravention of fundamental rights is unconstitutional and therefore cannot bind any person.

**Facts** Gajodhar Pharmaceuticals, a private company, offered an employment contract of two years to Syed Monirul Alam. One of the clauses in the employment contract provided that Syed Monirul Alam must join Gajodhar Mazdoor Sangh (GMS), one of the trade unions active in Gajodhar Pharmaceuticals.

**58.** Decide which of the following propositions can be most reasonably inferred through the application of the stated legal rules to the facts of this case:

(*a*) The employment contract offered to Monirul Alam to join GMS is legal as it does not restrict his freedom not to join any association.

(*b*) The condition requiring Monirul Alam to join GMS cannot bind him as it impinges on his freedom not to join any association.

(*c*) Syed Monirul Alam cannot claim a fundamental right to freedom of association against Gajodhar Pharmaceuticals and therefore, the contract would bind him even though his freedom of association is restricted.

(*d*) The employment contract infringes Syed Monirul Alam's freedom to decide with whom to associate and therefore is legally not enforceable. **(CLAT 2011)**

**59.** If Parliament enacts a law which requires every employee to join the largest trade union in their workplace mandating Syed Monirul Alam to join GMS, then:

(*a*) such a law would merely govern private action to which fundamental rights do not apply.

(*b*) such a law would not curtail any individual's right to freedom of association.

(*c*) neither the employment contract, nor the law of the parliament would be enforceable as they would curtail the freedom of association.

(*d*) the law of parliament would violate an individual's freedom not to join any association and therefore be unconstitutional.

**(CLAT 2011)**

**60.** If Parliament enacts a law that requires a trade union to open its membership to all the employees, then

(*a*) such a law would not infringe any fundamental right to freedom of association.

(*b*) the law of the parliament would curtail an individual's right not to join any association.

(*c*) such a law would curtail the union members' right to decide with whom they would like to associate.

(*d*) such a law would render the employment contract offered by Gajodhar Pharmaceuticals to Syed Monirul Alam unenforceable.

**(CLAT 2011)**

**61.** If Gajodhar Pharmaceuticals enters into an agreement with GMS wherein the former agrees to hire only the existing members of GMS as employees, then:

(*a*) the agreement would be illegal as it would curtail the union members' right to decide with whom they would like to associate.

(*b*) such an agreement would infringe the union's right to decide with whom to associate and therefore is legally not enforceable.

(*c*) the agreement would not be enforceable as it would infringe upon the employer's right not to join an association.

(*d*) the constitutionality of this agreement cannot be contested on grounds of contravention of fundamental rights as such rights are not applicable to private persons. **(CLAT 2011)**

**62.** If Parliament enacts a legislation prohibiting strikes by trade unions of employees engaged in pharmaceutical industry, then:

(*a*) the legislation would not violate the right to freedom of association.

(*b*) the legislation would curtail the right of trade unions to strike, and therefore violate freedom of association.

(*c*) since strike is only one of the objectives with which a trade union is formed, right to strike is not protected by the right to freedom of association.

(*d*) none of the above **(CLAT 2011)**

**(For questions 63 to 67)**

**Rules**

**A:** The State shall not discriminate, either directly or indirectly, on the grounds of sex, race, religion, caste, creed, sexual orientation, marital status, disability, pregnancy, place of birth, gender orientation or any other status.

**B:** Direct discrimination occurs when for a reason related to one or more prohibited grounds a person or group of persons is treated less favourably than another person or another group of persons in a comparable situation.

**C:** Indirect discrimination occurs when a provision, criterion or practice which is neutral on the face of it would have the effect of putting persons having a status or a characteristic associated with one or more prohibited grounds at a particular disadvantage compared with other persons.

**D:** Discrimination shall be justified when such discrimination is absolutely necessary in order to promote the well-being of disadvantaged groups, such as women, dalits, religious minorities, sexual minorities or disabled persons.

**Facts:** On 2nd October 2010, the Governor of the state of Bihar ordered the release of all women prisoners who were serving sentence of less than one year imprisonment to mark the occasion of Mahatma Gandhi's birthday.

**63.** Which of the following is correct with respect to the Governor's order?

(*a*) It discriminates directly on the ground of sex.

(*b*) It discriminates indirectly on the ground of sex.

(*c*) It does not discriminate on the ground of sex.

(*d*) It discriminates directly as well as indirectly on the ground of sex. **(CLAT 2011)**

**64.** Is the governor's order justified under Rule D?

(*a*) Yes, because it is for the well-being of women prisoners.

(*b*) No, because it is not absolutely necessary for the well-being of women prisoners.

(*c*) No, because it does not promote the well-being of women prisoners or the society.

(*d*) None of the above **(CLAT 2011)**

**65.** Assume that the Governor also made a second order requiring the release of all persons under the age of 25 and over the age of 65 who were serving a sentence of less than one year's imprisonment. Under the Rules, this order is:

(*a*) directly discriminatory.

(*b*) indirectly discriminatory.

(*c*) not discriminatory.

(*d*) discriminatory, but justifiable. **(CLAT 2011)**

**66.** Assume further that the government made a third order, releasing all graduate prisoners who are serving a sentence of less than one year's imprisonment. Which of the following statistics would have to be true for this order to be indirectly discriminatory?

(*a*) Only 13% of the prison population in Bihar have a graduation degree.

(*b*) Of the graduate prisoners, 89% belong to upper castes.

(*c*) Only 25% women in Bihar get a graduation degree.

(*d*) All of the above. **(CLAT 2011)**

**Rule E:**

'A discriminatory act shall be justified if its effect is to promote the well-being of disadvantaged groups, such as women, dalits, religious minorities, sexual minorities or disabled persons.'

**67.** Would the first Order of release of all women prisoners be justified under Rule E?

(*a*) Yes, because it promotes the well-being of women.

(*b*) No, because it does not promote the well-being of women prisoners

(*c*) No, because it does not promote the well-being of all disadvantaged groups equally.

(*d*) None of the above. **(CLAT 2011)**

**(For questions 68 to 71)**

**Rule A:**

When a State undertakes any measure, the effects of the measure must be the same for all those who are affected by it.

**Facts:** 100 mountaineers embarked on an extremely risky climbing expedition in Leh. Weather conditions worsened five days into the expedition and the mountaineers are trapped under heavy snow. The government received information of this tragedy only two weeks after the unfortunate incident and has only 24 hours in which to send rescue helicopters. Weather stations across the world confirm that this particular region of Leh will experience blizzards of unprecedented intensity for almost two weeks after this 24 hour window rendering any helicopter activity in the region impossible and certain death for anyone left behind. The government has only five rescue helicopters with a maximum capacity of 50 people (excluding pilots and requisite soldiers) and these helicopters can fly only once in 24 hours to such altitudes.

As the Air Force gets ready to send the helicopters, an emergency hearing is convened in the Supreme Court to challenge this measure as this would leave 50 people to die.

**68.** If you were the judge required to apply Rule A, you would decide that:

(*a*) As many lives must be saved as possible.

(*b*) If everyone cannot be rescued, then everyone must be left behind.

(*c*) A measure cannot be upheld at the cost of 50 lives.

(*d*) It must be left to those who are trapped to decide if they want half amongst them to be saved and leave the rest to die. **(CLAT 2011)**

**Rule B:**

When a State undertakes any measure, everyone affected must have an equal chance to benefit from it.

**69.** As the government prepares to send in rescue helicopters, which option would be acceptable only under Rule B and not Rule A:

(*a*) A lottery to choose the 50 survivors excluding those diagnosed with terminal illnesses from participating in the lottery.

(*b*) A lottery to decide the 50 survivors with single parents of children below five years of age automatically qualifying to be rescued.

(*c*) The 50 youngest people should be rescued.

(*d*) None of the above. **(CLAT 2011)**

**70.** Choosing 50 survivors exclusively by a lottery would be:

(*a*) permissible under Rules A and B.

(*b*) impermissible under Rule A and B.

(*c*) permissible only under Rule B.

(*d*) permissible only under Rule A. **(CLAT 2011)**

**71.** If the government decides that it will either save everyone or save none, it would be:

(*a*) permissible under Rules A and B.

(*b*) impermissible under Rules A and B.

(*c*) permissible only under Rule A.

(*d*) permissible only under Rule B. **(CLAT 2011)**

**72. PRINCIPLE:** Only Parliament or State Legislatures have the authority to enact laws on their own. No law made by the State can take away a person's fundamental right.

**FACTS:** Parliament enacted a law, which according to a group of lawyers is violating the fundamental rights of traders. A group of lawyers files a writ petition challenging the Constitutional validity of the statute seeking relief to quash the statute and further direct Parliament to enact a new law.

(*a*) No writ would lie against Parliament, as the court has no authority to direct Parliament to enact or re-enact a law.

(*b*) The court can quash existing law if it violates fundamental rights and can direct Parliament to make a new law.

(*c*) The court can quash the existing law if it violates fundamental rights but cannot direct Parliament to make a new law.

(*d*) None of these **(CLAT 2012)**

**73. PRINCIPLE:**

(1) The state shall not deny to any person equality before the law and equal protection of the laws within the territory of India.

(2) The State shall not discriminate against any citizen on grounds only of religion, race, caste, sex and place of birth or any of them.

**FACTS:** The Government of Rajasthan, passed an order providing for reservations for the Scheduled Castes/ Scheduled Tribes and Socially and Educationally Backward Classes (including Muslims), and Women, in all institutions of higher education, including private educational institutions, both aided as well as unaided, in the following manner: Scheduled Caste- 15%; Scheduled Tribe- 7.5%, Socially and Educationally Backward Classes (including Muslims) - 27%

I. The reservation policy of the government is violative of the principle of equality envisaged in the Constitution

II. The reservation policy is unconstitutional because it is based on 'caste' which is a prohibited marker

III. Reservation does not violate equality clause as it entails "like should be treated like and unlike should be treated differently."

IV. Reservation does not violate equality clause as the Constitution itself enables the State to make special provision for the advancement of socially and educationally backward classes of citizens or for the Scheduled Castes and Scheduled Tribes.

(*a*) I is correct.

(*b*) I and II are both correct answers.

(*c*) III is correct answer.

(*d*) III and IV both are correct answers.

**(CLAT 2012)**

**Instructions (74 to 80) :** Each of the next nine questions consists of two statements, one labeled as 'Assertion' (A) and other as 'Reason' (R). You are to examine these two statements carefully and select the correct answers.

**74. Assertion (A):** The Indian Constitution was adopted on 26th November, 1949.

**Reason (R):** Law Day is celebrated in India on 26th November every year.

(*a*) Both A and R are individually true and R is the correct explanation of A.

(*b*) Both A and R are individually true but R is not the correct explanation of A.

(*c*) A is true but R is false.

(*d*) A is false but R is true. **(CLAT 2012)**

**75. Assertion (A):** The state shall not make any law, which takes away or abridges the rights conferred by Part III (Fundamental Rights) and any law made in contravention of this clause shall, to the extent of the contravention, be void.

**Reason (R):** The fundamental rights are the rights reserved by the people and for this reason they are eternal and sacrosanct.

(*a*) Both A and R are individually true and R is the correct explanation of A.

(*b*) Both A and R are individually true but R is not the correct explanation of A.

(*c*) A is true but R is false.

(*d*) A is false but R is true. **(CLAT 2012)**

**76. Assertion (A):** Directive Principles of State Policy contained in Part IV shall not be enforceable by any court, but the principles therein laid down are nevertheless fundamental in the governance of the country and it shall be the duty of the State to apply these principles in making laws.

**Reason (R):** Directive Principles of State Policy and Fundamental Rights are both complementary to each other but in case of any controversy fundamental rights will prevail.

(*a*) Both A and R are individually true and R is the correct explanation of A.

(*b*) Both A and R are individually true but R is not the correct explanation of A.

(*c*) A is true but R is false.

(*d*) A is false but R is true. **(CLAT 2012)**

**77. Assertion (A):** All minorities, whether based on religion or language, shall have the right to establish and administer educational institutions of their choice.

**Reason (R):** Institutions established by the minorities are not entitled to governmental aid and government is not under an obligation to give aid.

(*a*) Both A and R are individually true and R is the correct explanation of A.

(*b*) Both A and R are individually true but R is not the correct explanation of A.

(*c*) A is true but R is false.

(*d*) A is false but R is true. **(CLAT 2012)**

**78. Assertion (A):** The right to move the Supreme Court under Article 32 of the Constitution by appropriate proceedings for the enforcement of the fundamental rights is guaranteed as a fundamental right.

**Reason (R):** Supreme Court of India has been appointed as the guardian of the Constitution.

(*a*) Both A and R are individually true and R is the correct explanation of A.

(*b*) Both A and R are individually true but R is not the correct explanation of A.

(*c*) A is true but R is false.

(*d*) A is false but R is true. **(CLAT 2012)**

**79. Assertion (A):** If the budget presented to the Rajya Sabha in not passed in the stipulated period, the budget proposals are not affected.

**Reason (R):** The Lok Sabha is more powerful, in financial matters, than the Rajya Sabha.

(*a*) Both A and R are individually true and R is the correct explanation of A.

(*b*) Both A and R are individually true but R is not the correct explanation of A.

(*c*) A is true but R is false.

(*d*) A is false but R is true. **(CLAT 2012)**

**80. Assertion (A):** Freedom of Speech is the most important civil liberty of people in a democratic polity.

**Reason (R):** State can regulate free speech in the interest of public order.

(*a*) Both A and R are individually true and R is the correct explanation of A.

(*b*) Both A and R are individually true but R is not the correct explanation of A.

(*c*) A is true but R is false.

(*d*) A is false but R is true. **(CLAT 2012)**

**81.** The following are enshrined in the Preamble of the Constitution of India **(CLAT 2012)**

I. Equality of status and of opportunity.

II. Liberty of thought, expression, belief, faith and worship.

III. Justice-social, economic and political.

IV. Fraternity assuring the dignity of the individual.

V. Unity and Integrity of the nation.

Which of the following is the correct order in which they appear in the preamble?

(*a*) V-I-II-IV-III (*b*) III-II-I-IV-V

(*c*) III-I-II-V-IV (*d*) I-II-IV-III-V

**82.** Which one of the following statements is correct?

Right to free and compulsory education for all children of the age of 6 to 14 years is:

(*a*) a fundamental right enforceable in law.

(*b*) a fundamental duty.

(*c*) a directive principle of state policy.

(*d*) a fundamental right which, however, can be enforced only if the state makes an enabling legislation. **(CLAT 2012)**

**83.** Affirmative action connotes:

I. Measures taken by the state to help the socially disadvantaged groups. **(CLAT 2012)**

II. Positive discrimination.

III. Strict quotas for the socially and educationally backward class in school/college admissions and jobs.

Which of the above mentioned is true?

(*a*) I and II only. (*b*) II only.

(*c*) I,II and III. (*d*) II and III only.

**84.** Identify the correct statement:

(*a*) Federalism implies a system of government which embodies a division of powers between a central and a number of regional authorities.

(*b*) Federalism implies a system of government which embodies a division of powers between Legislature, Executive and Judiciary.

(*c*) Federalism implies a system of Government which embodies Parliamentary supremacy.

(*d*) None of these. **(CLAT 2012)**

**85.** Which one of the following is not correct?

(*a*) Freedom of speech and expression includes freedom of press. **(CLAT 2012)**

(*b*) Right to life and personal liberty includes right to carry on any trade and profession

(*c*) Right to equality includes the principles of natural justice

(*d*) Freedom of conscience includes the wearing and carrying of kirpans by the Sikhs

**86.** The Right to Equality is guaranteed by-

(*a*) Article 14 to 18. (*b*) Article 14.

(*c*) Article 14 and 15. (*d*) Article 14, 15 and 16. **(CLAT 2012)**

**87.** Mr. Samay was severely hurt while working in his factory and fell unconscious. He was rushed to a hospital by his fellow workers. In the hospital (at emergency/casualty ward) the doctors opined that he should be operated immediately. While conducting preliminary examinations, he was found to be HIV positive. The doctors are in a dilemma regarding what should they do first-

(*a*) Doctors should operate first. **(CLAT 2012)**

(*b*) Doctors should inform his family members.

(*c*) Doctors should inform his employers.

(*d*) Doctors should not inform anyone because it would violate patient's right of privacy.

**88.** Match the schedule I and II and choose the appropriate answer-

| **Schedule I** | **Schedule II** |
|---|---|
| i. Republic | 1. Head of the state is elected by the people. |
| ii. Secular | 2. State does not recognize any religion as religion of the state. |
| iii. Democracy | 3. The government which gets authority from the will of the people. |

| | i | ii | iii |
|---|---|---|---|
| (*a*) | 1 | 2 | 3 |
| (*b*) | 1 | 3 | 2 |
| (*c*) | 2 | 3 | 1 |
| (*d*) | 3 | 2 | 1 |

**(CLAT 2012)**

**89.** Which of the following rights is not available to the citizens of India under Article 21 of the Constitution? **(AILET 2013)**

(*a*) Right to Privacy.

(*b*) Right to Die.

(*c*) Right to Health and Medical Assistance.

(*d*) Right to Get Pollution free Water and Air.

**90.** When a judge makes certain remarks in the course of his judgement, which are said "by the way" and do not have direct bearing on the facts at hand, such remarks are called **(AILET 2013)**

(*a*) Ratio Decidendi. (*b*) Obiter Dictum.

(*c*) Observations. (*d*) Comments ordinaralis.

**91.** Who is the Chairperson of the 20th Law Commission of India?

(*a*) Justice Altmas Kabir.

(*b*) Justice P.V. Reddy.

(*c*) Justice A. R. Lakshmanan.

(*d*) Justice D. K. Jain. **(AILET 2013)**

**92.** _________ of the Constitution of India lays down that Union of India and the States are juristic person and can sue and be sued. **(AILET 2013)**

(*a*) Article 225. (*b*) Article 268.

(*c*) Article 300. (*d*) Article 348.

**93.** High Courts has been constituted in all these States in January, 2013 except **(AILET 2013)**

(*a*) Assam. (*b*) Meghalaya.

(*c*) Manipur. (*d*) Tripura.

**Directions (Q. 94-96) :** This section consists of three (3) questions. Each question consists of legal propositions/ principles (hereinafter referred to as 'principle') and facts. These principles have to be applied to the given facts to arrive at the most reasonable conclusion. Such principles may or may not be true in the real sense, yet you have to conclusively assume them to be true for the purposes of this section. In other words, in answering the following questions, you must not rely on any principles except the principles that are given herein below for every question. Further you must not assume any facts other than those stated in the question.The objective of this section is to test your interest towards study of law, research aptitude and problem solving ability even if the "most reasonable conclusion" arrived at may be unacceptable for any other reason. It is not the objective of this section to test your knowledge of law.

**94. Principle:** All citizens shall have the Fundamental Right to carry on any occupation, trade or business. But reasonable restrictions on the exercise of such rights can be imposed by law in the interest of the general public. **(CLAT 2013)**

**Facts:** A large number of persons had been carrying on the business of dyeing and printing in Rajkot area for the last 25 years providing employment to about 30000 families. From these business places untreated dirty water was being discharged on the roads thereby causing damage to the public health. A notice, therefore, was given to close this business till necessary measures to protect public health as provided under the environmental statutes were taken by those business men.

(*a*) Notice can not be justified as it will cause loss of employment to 30000 families.

(*b*) Notice can not be justified as it amounts to violation of the fundamental right of the persons who have been carrying on the business for the last 25 years.

(*c*) The notice can not be justified on the ground of damage to public health as the persons in that area have been voluntarily residing for long and have become used to that environment.

(*d*) The notice can be justified as the right to business is not absolute and reasonable restriction can be imposed by law in the interest of the public.

**95. Principle:** A contract between the father and his son is a contract of utmost good faith. In such a type of contract law presumes that at the time of entering into the contract the father was in a position to dominate the will of his son. Where one of the parties was in position to dominate the will of the other party, the contract is enforceable only at the option of the party whose will was so dominated. **(CLAT 2013)**

**Facts:** Ram had advanced a sum of ₹ 10,000/- to his minor son Shyam. When Shyam became major, his father Ram misused his parental position and entered into an agreement with Shyam and obtained a bond from him for a sum of ₹ 30,000 in respect of the advance. Whether this agreement is enforceable?

(*a*) The agreement is enforceable against Shyam only for ₹ 10,000/-, the actual amount of money advanced to him

(*b*) The agreement is enforceable against Shyam for ₹ 30,000/- because he has signed the bond

(*c*) The agreement is enforceable against Shyam because he was major at the time of agreement.

(*d*) The agreement is not enforceable against Shyam because Ram has misused his position as father to obtain an unfair advantage.

**96. Principle:** Only the Parliament or the State Legislatures have the authority to enact laws on their own. No law made by State can take away a person's fundamental right. **(CLAT 2013)**

**Facts:** Parliament enacted a law, which according to a group of lawyers is violating the fundamental rights of traders. The group of lawyers filed a writ petition against the Parliament for enacting such law and requests the court to quash the law and to direct the Parliament to make a new law.

(*a*) No writ would lie against the Parliament, as the Court has no authority to direct the Parliament to enact or re-enact a law.

(*b*) The Court can quash the existing law if it violates fundamental right and can direct to make a new law.

(*c*) The Court can quash the existing law if it violates fundamental right but cannot direct the Parliament to make a new law.

(*d*) None of these

**Directions (Q. 97) :** Given below is a statement of legal principle followed by a factual situation. Apply the principle to the facts given below and select the most appropriate answer. **(AILET 2014)**

**97. LEGAL PRINCIPLE :** No one can be punished for the same offence twice.

**FACTUAL SITUATION :** Aditya is accused of harassing his colleague Nimisha. She complains to her superior and a departmental inquiry is initiated against Aditya. Aditya tries to intimidate Nimisha and continues harassing her following which she complains to the police. The departmental inquiry finds him guilty and terminates his services. Later, he is found guilty by a court and is jailed for 2 years. He claims that he has been punished twice.

**DECISION :**

(*a*) He has been punished twice for the same offence.

(*b*) He has not been punished twice for the same offence.

(*c*) He has been punished for different offences.

(*d*) None of the above

**Directions (Q. 98 - 99) :** *This section consists of two (2) questions.*

Each question consists of legal propositions/principles (hereinafter referred to as 'principle') and facts. These principles have to be applied to the given facts to arrive at the most reasonable conclusion. Such principles may or may not be true in the real sense, yet you have to conclusively assume them to be true for the purposes of this section. In other words, in answering the following questions, you must not rely on any principles except the principles that are given herein below for every question. Further, you must not assume any facts other than those stated in the question. The objective of this section is to test your interest towards study of law, research aptitude and problem solving ability even if the 'most reasonable conclusion' arrived at may be unacceptable for, any other reason. It is not the object of this section to test your knowledge of law. **(CLAT 2014)**

**98. Principle:** The Constitution of India guarantees the 'right to life', which means 'right - to live with human dignity'. The right to life under the Constitution, however, does not include the right to die.

**Facts:** 'M', who is 90, lives all alone as he has no family or children or grandchildren. He suffers from physical and mental distress, as there is no one to look after him. He has little means to foot his medical expenses. Under these circumstances, he approaches the court with a prayer that he should be granted the right to die with dignity because he does not want to be a burden on the society. Further, as it is his life, he has a right to put an end to it.

Which of the following derivations is CORRECT?

(*a*) The prayer can be granted, as suicide is not an offense in India

(*b*) The prayer can be granted, as the right to life under the Constitution includes the right to die

(*c*) The prayer can be granted, as a person cannot be forced to enjoy right to life to his detriment, disadvantage and disliking

(*d*) The prayer cannot be granted, as the right to life under the Constitution does not include the right to die

**99. Principle:** One of the principles of natural justice is *Nemo judgx in causa sua,* which means that no one should be a judge in his own cause. In other words, no person can judge a case in which he has an interest.

**Facts:** 'X', a member of the selection board for a government service, was also a candidate for selection for the same service. 'X' did not take part in the deliberations of the board when his name was considered and approved.

(*a*) Selection of 'X' is against the principle of natural justice.

(*b*) Selection of 'X' is not against the principle of natural justice.

(*c*) Non-selection of 'X' will be against the principles of natural justice.

(*d*) Non-participation of 'X' in the board deliberations will render his selection valid.

## Solutions

**1.** d The Constitution of India confers three types of jurisdictions on Supreme Court of India, these are;

1. Original Jurisdiction under Article 131 of the Constitution.
2. Appellate Jurisdiction under Article 132, 133 and 136 of the Constitution.
3. Advisory Jurisdiction under Article 143 of the Constitution.

**2.** b A Money Bill is introduced by a Minister who is also a Member of Lok Sabha. The question that whether a bill is ordinary bill or a money bill is decided by the Speaker of Lok Sabha.

**3.** c Members of Rajya Sabha are associated with Public Accounts Committee and Committee on Public Undertakings with 7 Members (from Rajya Sabha). It is infact Estimates Committee which does not constitute any member from Rajya Sabha. Estimates Committee has 30 Members, all from Lok Sabha. Correct answer is (*c*).

**4.** d It is a peculiar provision in parliamentary business that amendment to Annual Financial Statement (Budget), Appropriation Bill, Demand for Grants can not be proposed in either house of the Parliament.

**5.** a Article 41 states that the State shall, within the limits of its economic capacity and development, make effective provision for securing the right to work, to education and to public assistance in cases of unemployment, old age, sickness and disablement, and in other cases of undeserved want.

**6.** b Correct answer should be B (not A as mentioned). The principle of equality under India Constitution recognizes the following exceptions:

1. Foreign Sovereigns and Diplomats enjoy immunity from jurisdiction of the courts therefore they are at the most expelled from the country for any offence committed instead of any punishment.
2. Article 361 of the Constitution of India protects the President and Governor during the tenure of their Office from the jurisdiction of the courts.

**7.** b Article-1 of the Constitution of India declares that India, that is Bharat shall be the Union of States.

**8.** b Right to equality, being the most important fundamental right has been subjected to largest interpretation by the Court and therefore this issue has been under litigation for the maximum number of times.

**9.** b The Forty-second Amendment of the Constitution of India, enacted in 1976, attempted to reduce the power of the Indian Supreme Court and High Courts to pronounce upon the constitutional validity of laws. It also declared India to be a socialist and secular republic and as securing fraternity assuring the unity "and integrity" of the Nation, by adding these words to the Preamble of the Constitution of India. It laid down the Fundamental Duties of Indian citizens to the nation. This amendment brought about the most widespread changes to the Constitution until then and is often called a "mini-Constitution".

**10.** c There are total 12 Schedules in the Constitution of India. Schedules are the lists in the Constitution that categorize and tabulate bureaucratic activity and policy of the government.

**11.** a By virtue of Constitution(Ninety First Amendment) Act of 2003, Clause(1-A) was inserted in Article 75 of the Constitution which declares that the total number of Ministers including the Prime Minister, in the Council of Ministers shall not exceed 15% of the total number of House of People.

**12.** d .If at any time it appears to the President that a question of law or fact has arisen, or is likely to arise, which is of such a nature and of such public importance that it is expedient to obtain the opinion of the Supreme Court upon it, he may refer the question to that Court for consideration and the Court may, after such hearing as it thinks fit, report to the President its opinion thereon. Further, the President may, refer a dispute of the kind mentioned to the Supreme Court for opinion and the Supreme Court shall, after such hearing as it thinks fit, report to the President its opinion thereon.

**13.** b As per Article 136 of the Constitution, the Supreme Court may in its discretion grant special leave to appeal from any judgment, decree, determination, sentence or order in any cause or matter passed or made by any court or tribunal in the territory of India.

**14.** c When someone displays an article indicating its price, law of contract considers it to be an invitation to offer and not offer. In simple terms, the person invites others to offer which he may or may not accept.

**15.** d Supporting Indian cause at various national and international level is not a criteria for acquiring citizenship either in Citizenship Act 1955 of under Part II of the Constitution of India.

**16.** b The Constitution originally provided for the right to property under Articles 19 and 31. Article 19 guaranteed to all citizens the right to acquire, hold and dispose of property. The Forty-Forth Amendment of 1978 deleted the right to property from the list of fundamental rights. A new provision, Article 300-A, was added to the constitution which rendered it merely a constitutional right and not a fundamental right.

**17.** d The Right of Children to Free and Compulsory Education Act or Right to Education Act (RTE), which was passed by the Indian parliament on 4 August 2009, describes the modalities of the provision of free and compulsory education for children between 6 and 14 in India under Article 21A of the Indian Constitution. India became one of 135 countries to make education a fundamental right of every child when the act came into force on 1 April 2010.

**18.** b In case of a financial emergency under Article 360, the President can reduce the salaries of all government officials, including judges of the Supreme Court and High Courts. All money bills passed by the State legislatures are submitted to the President for his approval. He can direct the state to observe certain principles (economy measures) relating to financial matters. He can not suspend the fundamental rights of the citizens.

**19.** b Motions of no confidence against the government can only be introduced and passed in the Lok Sabha. If passed by a majority vote, the Prime Minister and the Council of Ministers resign collectively. The Rajya Sabha has no power over such a motion and hence, no real power over the executive. Thus, both the executive and the legislature in India have checks and balances over each other.

**20.** b The decision of a High Court is not binding on other High Courts. A judgment passed by the High Court of one state has only persuasive value for other states.

**21.** c Once approved by the Parliament, the emergency remains in force for a period of six months from the date of proclamation. In case it is to be extended beyond six months, another prior resolution has to be passed by the Parliament. In this way, such emergency continues indefinitely.

**22.** c Smt. Indira Nehru Gandhi vs Shri Raj Narain. Decided on 7 November, 1975.

**23.** d Correct answer is D and not A. The Supreme Court of India comprises of the Chief Justice and 30 other Judges appointed by the President of India. Supreme Court Judges retire upon attaining the age of 65 years.

**24.** c Cutting wood being the sole source of livelihood for Gangaram, the government's action is not justified. His wood cutting can be regulated in a reasonable manner but it can not be absolutely restrained.

**25.** b State of X has not absolutely prohibited the right to carry on trade or business rather it has taken an obligatory step under DPSP by merely prohibiting the cow slaughter.

**26.** c Right to Religion is a Fundamental Right, the mere fact of not singing the national anthem in the morning does not amount to disrespect .Moreover it is stated in the principle that the Constitution expects a citizen to respect national anthem as a fundamental duty. No mandatory compliance of such is mentioned.

**27.** b True that freedom of speech & expression has been conferred upon citizens but this right is not absolute in nature. Right to freedom of expression does not authorize another person to defame any person.

**28.** a The question is ambiguous since there are numerous criteria stipulated in Citizenship Act 1955 and under Part II of the Constitution of India to acquire citizenship. Besides the criteria of minimum duration of stay to acquire citizenship there are other criteria which are simultaneously required to be fulfilled. Amongst the given options, (A) is closest answer to the question.

**29.** a An Ordinance promulgated shall have the same force and effect as an Act of Legislature of the State assented to by the Governor, but every such Ordinance shall be laid before the Legislative Assembly of the State, or where there is a Legislative Council in the State, before both the houses, and shall cease to operate at the expiration of six weeks from the reassembly of the Legislature.

**30.** a Scheduled Castes and Scheduled Tribes are specified by the Presidential Orders issued in consultation with the Governors of the respective States and in case of Union Territories, their respective Lieutenant Governors.

**31.** c The State shall secure that the operation of the legal system promotes justice, on a basis of equal opportunity, and shall, in particular, provide free legal aid, by suitable legislation or schemes or in any other way, to ensure that opportunities for securing justice are not denied to any citizen by reason of economic or other disabilities.

**32.** a The words 'Socialist' and 'Secular' were added to the preamble of the Constitution in the year 1976. The term 'Secular' means that the State shall not have any religion of its own.

**33.** d Constitution of India does not mention the post of Deputy Prime Minister. This post has been recognised in India for practical convenience otherwise there is no constitutional mandate that along with Prime Minister there shall be a Deputy Prime Minister.

**34.** c Article 217(1){b} and 124(4) of the Constitution of India provides in detail, the legislative procedure through which a Judge of a High Court or Supreme Court (as the case may be) shall be removed. The Constitution of India reflects only 2 grounds of removal i.e. proven misbehaviour and incapacity.

**35.** a The founding fathers of our Constitution had before them the accumulated experience from the working of all the known constitutions of the world and were aware of the difficulties faced in the working of those constitutions. Hence, besides incorporating some provisions from the other constitutions, a number of provisions were included to avoid some of the difficulties experienced in the working of these constitutions. This is an important reason for making our Constitution the lengthiest and the most comprehensive of all the written constitutions of the world. It is pertinent here to mention that in the process of drafting the Constitution, the most profound influence was exercised by The Government of India Act -1935.

**36.** b Clause (4) of Article 101 of the Constitution of India mandates that if for a period of sixty days a member of either House of Parliament is without permission of the House absent from all meetings thereof, the House may declare his seat vacant: Provided that in computing the said period of sixty days no account shall be taken of any period during which the House is prorogued or is adjourned for more than four consecutive days.

**37.** b There are certain privileges provided to the Members of Parliament which have been incorporated under Article 105 and 194 of the Constitution of India.

**38.** c The case is named as : Hari Shankar Jain Vs. Sonia Gandhi, decided on 12th September 2001 in favour of Mrs. Sonia Gandhi.

**39.** a As per Article-76 Clause (1) of the Constitution of India the President shall appoint a person who is qualified to be appointed a Judge of the Supreme Court to be Attorney General for India.

**40.** c Article 32 confers the power on Supreme Court of India and Article 226 confers the power upon High Courts in India to ensure the protection of rights to any person.

**41.** c In case of National Emergency, the State Government can legislate on the subjects mentioned in the state list.

**42.** c Lawyers have a right to livelihood which was completely restricted by the government and principle (iv) clearly states that any restriction on fundamental right imposed by Parliament which totally removes or nullifies any fundamental right will be construed as unreasonable.

**43.** d If the right to establish and administer educational institution of one's choice has been conferred upon a person, it can not be denied by State Government merely on the basis of unjustified prediction on part of state government that such institution will create communal tension in the proposed area. The State Government can not restrict a Fundamental Right merely on a presumption of communal tension.

**44.** d Locus standi

(*a*) Right 'in rem'- property rights enforceable against the entire world.

(*b*) Right 'in Personem' - personal right attached to a specific person, such as contract rights, a tort award against a defendant, or a license.

(*c*) Fundamental Rights- basic human freedoms which every Indian citizen has the right to enjoy for a proper and harmonious development of personality.

**45.** a Bicameralism

The Legislative body of India having two houses: House of the people (Lok Sabha) and Council of states (Rajya sabha).

(*b*) Universal adult franchise- All citizens with age above 18 have the right to vote.

(*c*) Dyarchy- A form of government controlled by two rulers

(*d*) Federalism- A form of government wherein union of states under a central government is distinct from the individual governments of the separate states.

**46.** d Keshavananda Bharti V. State of Kerala

(*a*) Golaknath V. State of Punjab- Supreme Court held that Parliament could not curtail any of the Fundamental Rights in the Constitution.

**47.** c Sedition includes all acts which create hatred or contemp for, or dissatisfaction towards the government established by law.

**48.** c Double Jeopardy

(*a*) Burden of proof- A duty placed upon a civil or criminal defendant to prove or disprove a disputed fact

(*b*) Double conviction- a convict found guilty of an offence after transportation.

(*d*) Corpus Delicti- Term which refers to the principle that a crime must have been proven to have occurred before a person can be convicted of committing that crime

**49.** c Attorney General

The Attorney General of India is appointed by the President of India under Article 76 of the Constitution of India. It is the duty of the Attorney General for India to give advice to the Government of India upon such legal matters and to perform such other duties of legal character as may be referred or assigned to him by the President. In the performance of his duties, he has the right of audience in all Courts in India as well as the right to take part in the proceedings of Parliament without the right to vote. In discharge of his functions, the Attorney General is assisted by a Solicitor General and four Additional Solicitors General.

**50.** a The word 'morality' doesn't find its mentioned in the preamble of the Constitution of India.

**51.** c A Court of Record is the court which has been conferred the power to punish and impose fine for its contempt.

**52.** d Proven misbehaviour or incapacity

According to article 124(4) of the Indian constitution: A member of higher judiciary which is the chief justice of India and the state high courts can be removed from the service through the process of impeachment on the ground of proven misbehaviour. In India, there is no other process by a judge can be removed from the office before his or her term comes to an end.

As per the judge's inquiry act 1986, the impeachment of judges can be done on grounds of "proven Misbehaviour" and "incapacity", if the judge of India is to be Impeached than the recommendation have to be made by the Chief Justice of India to the president of India. The motion is passed by the two-third majority members present and voting must be done separately in the each house of the parliament. If the motion is passed than the formal announcement is done by the President of India.

**53.** a Trust

Fiduciary relationship is a relationship where one person places complete confidence in another in regard to a particular transaction or one's general affairs or business. The relationship is not necessarily formally or legally established as in a declaration of trust, but can be one of moral or personal responsibility, due to the superior knowledge and training of the fiduciary as compared to the one whose affairs the fiduciary is handling. Ex: Lawyer- Client, Doctor-Patient, Teacher-Student relationships.

**54.** c U.S.A

Judicial Review is a constitutional doctrine that gives to a court system the power to annul legislative or executive acts which the judges declare to be unconstitutional. The Constitution of USA does not expressly provide that the federal judiciary has the power of judicial review. However, after the Marbury Vs. Madison case judicial review was exercised by the American judiciary under Article III of the constitution of America.

**55.** c Right to property

The Forty-Forth Amendment of 1978 deleted the right to property from the list of fundamental rights. A new provision, Article 300-A, was added to the constitution which provided that "no person shall be deprived of his property save by authority of law". Thus, the right to property is no longer a fundamental right, though it is still a constitutional right.

**56.** d All the elected members of both the Houses of Parliament and all the elected members of all the Legislative Assemblies.

The President is elected, from a group of nominees, by the elected members of the Parliament of India (Lok Sabha and Rajya Sabha) as well as of the state legislatures (Vidhan Sabhas) for a term of 5 years. Whenever the office becomes vacant, the new President is chosen by an electoral college consisting of the elected members of both houses of Parliament, the elected members of the State Legislative Assemblies (Vidhan Sabha) and the elected members of the legislative assemblies of the Union Territories of Delhi and Pondicherry.

**57.** d Right to work
The Indian constitution refers to the right to work under the "directive principles of state policy". Article 39 urges the State to ensure that "the citizens, men and women equally, have the right to an adequate means to livelihood", and that "there is equal pay for equal work for both men and women. Further, Article 41 stresses that "the state, shall within the limits of its economic capacity and development, make effective provision for securing right to work..."

**58.** c Refer to Rule D. Fundamental Rights can only be enforced against the State and the administrative actions of the state. Gajodhar Pharmaceuticals being a private limited company, no fundamental rights can be enforced against it.

**59.** d Applying Rule D and B to the facts, we can derive that, one Fundamental Rights can be enforced by Syed since this is a law made by the State, two, the law in question curtails Syed's freedom to decide whom to associate with. Therefore option d is the most relevant choice.

**60.** a Neither of the rules are applicable to the given facts nor does the law in question forces any individual to join any association. Therefore a is an appropriate answer.

**61.** d Applying Rule D to the question. Refer explanation to 156.

**62.** c The right to freedom of association does not extend to realizing the objectives of forming such an association. Strikes are only an objective in the given case and therefore would not amount to any violation of the fundamental rights as mentioned in the rules.

**63.** a Direct application of Rule A qualifies the act of the State as discrimination. Rule D, the exception to Rule A is not applicable as the discrimination in question in not justified on any of the grounds mentioned in the Rule. Now, out of Rule B and C, the former is applicable and therefore this amounts to a direct discrimination being made on the grounds of sex alone.

**64.** b The point to consider is whether the action taken by the Governor is 'absolutely necessary' the given case. It cannot be found to be such and though it promotes the well being of the women it is not 'absolutely necessary'.

**65.** a The discrimination based on age would fall under 'any other status' under Rule A. It does not get protected under Rule D. Therefore this is a case of direct discrimination.

**66.** d There is no mention of percentage of graduate population in Bihar in the question itself. No answer can be possibly arrived at. Hence the given option D should be taken as 'None of the above' instead of All of the above.

**67.** a Note the absence of phrase "absolutely necessary" in Rule E as against Rule D above. The order can now be justified as is promotes the well-being of women, who were being held in prison, and had a punishment period of less than one year.

**68.** b Since the question demands applicability of Rule A, option b would hold good. A measure,. the outcome of which is certain and would amount to violation of Rule A, should not be put to enforced.

**69.** d The qualifications in the lottery mentioned in each other option is very arbitrary and just not ensure equal chance as is required under Rule B. Therefore, option is the only appropriate choice.

**70.** c Rule B talks about equal chance. Hence, a lottery for all without any further qualification can be upheld under Rule A.

**71.** c Here the measure is sending helicopters and if that is not provided for everyone equally, Rule A would be defeated.

**72.** c As per the Constitutional structure, Court is the custodian of Fundamental Rights. The principle clearly states that only Parliament or State Legislature can enact laws. Courts can only interfere if there is violation of Fundamental Right. It is an interpreter of the Constitution of India and not a law making body.

**73.** d Art 14 is a general provision which ensures equality but simultaneously Art. 15 have been interpreted by the Courts as an exception to Article 14. Art. 15 talks of positive discrimination wherein unequals are to be treated differently.

**74.** b Supreme Court Bar Association declared 26 January, Law day in the year 1979.

**75.** a The eternal nature of Fundamentals Rights ensure states law's conformity with its law making power.

**76.** a The state shall frame its policy in lines with Directive Principles of State Policy (DPSP) keeping inview the scheme of Fundamental Rights envisaged under part III of the Constitution of India.

**77.** c The government shall (through financial aids) promote religious and minority institutions. As mandated under Constitution of India.

78. * The Supreme Court of India is a final interpreter of the Constitution of India.

79. d Since the member of Lok Shabha are elected by the people of India the appropriation of public money (viz. money bill) is entrusted upon them.

80. a The state can impose 'reasonable restrictions' upon the freedom of speech.

81. b The preamble state as following: "WE, THE PEOPLE OF INDIA, having solemnly resolved to constitute India into a SOVEREIGN SOCIALIST SECULAR DEMOCRATIC REPUBLIC and to secure to all its citizens: JUSTICE, social, economic and political; LIBERTY of thought, expression, belief, faith and worship; EQUALITY of status and of opportunity; and to promote among them all FRATERNITY assuring the dignity of the individual and the unity and integrity of the Nation".

82. d Art. 21A. The State shall provide free and compulsory education to all children of the age of six to fourteen years in such manner as the State may, by law, determine. (Eighty -sixth Amendment Act, 2002)

83. c Affirmative actions are basically the measures taken by the State which are aimed to ensure equality of status and opportunity in the society. These are also called, positive actions of the state.

84. a A principle of government that defines the relationship between the central government at the national level and its constituent units at the regional, state, or local levels.

85. b Article 19 states Protection of certain rights regarding freedom of speech, etc.—(1) All citizens shall have the right - (*s*) to practice any profession, or to carry on any occupation, trade or business; Article 21 talks about Right to Protection of life and personal liberty

86. * The answer should be A. Right to equality is enshrined under Part III of the Constitution which runs from Article 14-18. Hence the correct answer should be A and not (*d*).

87. a The emergent situation in this case is that Mr. Samay is severely hurt and hence should be operated first.

88. a Republic means head of the State is elected by the people. Secular means that the State does not recognize any religion as the religion of the State. Democracy is a form of government where will of the people prevails, i.e. they are free to elect their representative.

89. b The true meaning of the word 'life' in Article 21 means life with human dignity. Any aspect of life which makes life dignified may be include in it but not that which extinguishes it. The 'Right to Die' if any, is inherently inconsistent with the "Right to Life".

90. b In English, "obiter dicta" translates to "things said by the way". In other words, obiter dicta are the judicial ponderings said in a case that are not directly relevant to the outcome of the case but that have the potential to inform or guide future decision-making.

91. d Law Commission of India is an executive body established by an order of the Government of India. Its major function is to work for legal reform. Its membership primarily comprises legal experts, who are entrusted a mandate by the Government. The Commission is established for a fixed tenure and works as an advisory body to the Ministry of Law and Justice.

92. c Article 300 of the Constitution of India lays down that Union of India and the States are juristic person and can sue and be sued.

93. a High Courts have been constituted in all these States in January, 2013 except in **Assam.**

94. d As per the principle, reasonable restrictions can be imposed on fundamental rights by law in the interest of general public. And the restrictions imposed by authorities fall in that category.

95. d The father has misused his position as a father to obtain a bond of ₹ 30,000 from his son Shyam. And as per the principle, such an agreement is not enforceable.

96. * From the given facts and principle, it is not clear whether the court can direct the Parliament to make a new law. Hence, "B" and "C", both remain debatable options. The court cannot enact laws according to principle, however the court can very well quash a law if it violates fundamental rights.

97. b Departmental inquiry was not a proceeding for the offence of harassment but an in house method by the company to punish bad employees. Therefore Aditya has been punished only once.

98. d It has been clearly provided in the principle that right to life does not include right to die and hence it cannot be granted.

99. a Even after not taking part in the selection process, Selection of A would be invalid.

■■

# 5

# MISCELLANEOUS

1. The Indian Territory which fell under the states on the eve of Independence was:
   (a) Only 20 Percent. (b) Over 80 percent.
   (c) 54 percent. (d) 46 percent.
   **(AILET, 2008)**
2. The most powerful legislature in the world is the:
   (a) Indian Parliament. (b) U.S. Congress.
   (c) Swiss Legislature. (d) British Parliament.
   **(AILET, 2008)**
3. In the U.S.A., residuary powers or reserve of powers are:
   (a) Left to the federal government.
   (b) Left to the States.
   (c) Not defined properly.
   (d) Given to local government. **(AILET, 2008)**
4. Match the following:
   A. Nagpur session (1920).
   B. Madras session.
   C. Calcutta session (1928).
   D. Lahore session (1929).
   E. Karachi session (1930).
   (i) Poorna Swaraj.
   (ii) Changes in the Constitution of Congress.
   (iii) Resolution of Fundamental Rights and National Economics Policy.
   (iv) Return of Gandhiji to active politics after 6 years.
   (v) Independence resolution passed for the first time.

|  | A | B | C | D | E |
|---|---|---|---|---|---|
| (a) | iii | i | ii | v | iv |
| (b) | i | ii | iv | v | iii |
| (c) | ii | v | iv | i | iii |
| (d) | i | iii | ii | v | iv |

**(AILET, 2008)**

5. An idol of Lord Krishna in a temple is
   (a) A natural person.
   (b) A legal person.
   (c) Not a person in the eyes of law become only the priest of the temple will be a person.
   (d) Not a person because no personality can be conferred on God. **(AILET, 2008)**
6. When a court sends some one in judicial custody, what does it mean by judicial custody
   (a) Sent to jail.
   (b) Sent to police look up.
   (c) Sent to home under judicial protection.
   (d) None of these. **(AILET, 2008)**
7. The term of office of a judge of the International Court of Justice is
   (a) 10 years. (b) 9 years.
   (c) 7 years. (d) 5 years. **(AILET, 2008)**
8. The democratic device, used in constitutional states, by which important political questions, particularly question relating tot he states of a region, may be referred to the people of the region for their final decision, is called
   (a) Plebiscite. (b) Referendum.
   (c) Recall Vote. (d) Quorum.
   **(AILET, 2008)**
9. Ancient treatise on law?
   (a) Vedas. (b) Upanishads.
   (c) Smritis. (d) Shrutis. **(AILET, 2008)**
10. Muslim religious foundations
    (a) Ulema. (b) Jihad.
    (c) Quzat. (d) Wakfs. **(AILET, 2008)**
11. The maximum litigation in Courts is caused by
    (a) businessmen. (b) middle class.
    (c) government. (d) criminals.
    **(AILET, 2008)**
12. The first-regular adjudicatory mobile court in the country has been inaugurated at Punbanna village in:
    (a) Haryana. (b) Bihar.
    (c) Andhra Pradesh. (d) Punjab. **(AILET, 2008)**
13. Dissolution of Muslim Marriage Act, 1939 provides grounds of dissolution of Muslim marriage to
    (a) Spouses.
    (b) Only males.
    (c) Only females.
    (d) Muslim parents and parents-in-law.
    **(AILET, 2008)**

**14.** A married man commits adultery if he has sexual intercourse with a/an

(*a*) unmarried women.

(*b*) married woman.

(*c*) any woman except his wife.

(*d*) unmarried woman without her consent.

**(AILET, 2008)**

**15.** A husband is obliged to maintain his divorced wife

(*a*) For ever.

(*b*) For 20 years.

(*c*) Till the children grow up.

(*d*) Till she gets remarried. **(AILET, 2008)**

**16.** Match the following:

(I) Default A. Failure to do something required by law.

(II) Delict B. A wrongful act.

(III) Derelict C. A thing thrown away by its owner.

(IV) Dictum D. A judge's observation.

(*a*) I-A, II- C, III-D, IV-B (*b*) I-D,II-C,III-B,IV-A

(*c*) I-C, II-D, III-A, IV-B (*d*) I-A,II-B,III-C,IV-D

**(AILET, 2008)**

**17.** India and Britain have signed an 'Extradition treaty'. Extradition means

(*a*) Exports with double taxation.

(*b*) Order of Indian Courts will apply to Indians living in the UK.

(*c*) Indian and the U.K. will deport criminals on reciprocal basis to each other.

(*d*) None of above. **(AILET, 2008)**

**18.** Genocide occurred in all but one case

(*a*) Bosnia.

(*b*) Nazi Germany.

(*c*) Rwanda.

(*d*) Gulf War. **(AILET, 2008)**

**19.** High sea is

(*a*) Sea lying more than 5 km beyond the coast of a country.

(*b*) Sea lying beyond a distance of 3 miles from the coast of any country.

(*c*) Sea beyond 200 km of a cost of any country.

(*d*) Both (*a*) & (*b*). **(AILET, 2008)**

**20.** Which Inn of Court called Gandhiji to the Bar?

(*a*) Inner Temple.

(*b*) Middle Temple.

(*c*) Lincoln's Inn.

(*d*) Gray's Inn. **(AILET, 2008)**

**DIRECTIONS:** Answer the questions (Q. 21-23), which follow from application of the under-mentioned principle:

**21. PRINCIPLE:** Ignorance of law is not an excuse in India with the practice that every person in India should be acquainted with the law of the land.

**FACTS**: Mr. Jackson, a foreigner, came to Delhi in the winter season. He saw the people in Delhi set fire on road side during night and get their body warm. One night he came out of his hotel and asked two labourers to cut down a dry tree in Pandara Road and when they agreed he paid them ₹ 150/- Indian currency for cutting down the tree. They cut and made the long into small pieces and the foreigner along with the tree cutters set fire and got their body warm. After some time, the Police Patrol car watched it and arrested the foreigner and two labourers on the spot. The foreigner pleaded that the tree was dry and he did not know the cutting of tree from road side is a offence in India.

(*a*) The foreigner shall not be responsible for the offence because he himself has not cut the tree but got it cut through the Indian people.

(*b*) The foreigner shall be punished because in India cutting of tree from road side is an offence.

(*c*) The pretence that he does not know such act is an offence is not an excuse for a foreigner also.

(*d*) Both (*b*) and (*c*) **(AILET, 2008)**

**22.** A death sentence by a lower court

(*a*) Must be confirmed by High Court.

(*b*) Must be confirmed by Supreme Court.

(*c*) Is operational if no appeal is made to higher courts.

(*d*) Must be confirmed by the President.

**(AILET, 2009)**

**23.** The Supreme Court in its judgment held that non-payment of minimum wages is a type of forced labour:

(*a*) Asiad workers case.

(*b*) Minerva Mills case.

(*c*) Lokhandwala Mills case.

(*d*) T. Krishnamachari case. **(AILET, 2009)**

**24.** Choose the **correct** statement

Doctrine of double jeopardy means

(*a*) a person should not be punished more than once for the same offence.

(*b*) a person should be punished more than once for the same offence.

(*c*) a man may be put twice in peril for the same offence.

(*d*) a man may commit the same offence twice but will get punishment once only. **(AILET, 2009)**

**25.** "What cannot be done directly cannot be done indirectly". This statement epitomises the doctrine of

(*a*) pith and substance.

(*b*) implied powers.

(*c*) ancillary powers.

(*d*) colourable legislation. **(AILET, 2009)**

**26.** The Janata Party Government of Morarjee Desai constituted.........to find out the truth about the excesses committed by the Indira Gandhi Government during emergency (1975-77)

(*a*) Shahbano Commission.

(*b*) Jagmohan Commission.

(*c*) Shah Commission.

(*d*) Nayyar Commission. **(AILET, 2009)**

**27.** Public holidays are declared under

(*a*) Negotiable Instruments Act, 1881.

(*b*) Contract Act, 1872.

(*c*) Public Employees Act, 1967.

(*d*) None of the above. **(AILET, 2009)**

**28.** A Hindu wife can marry immediately after divorce. A Muslim wife

(*a*) can also marry immediately.

(*b*) has to wait till period of Iddat (seclusion) is over.

(*c*) has to wait for one year.

(*d*) None of the above. **(AILET, 2009)**

**29.** Under the Motor Vehicles Act, 1988, the minimum compensation to be awarded in case of death (vide 1994 amendment) is

(*a*) ₹ 25,000. (*b*) ₹ 30,000.

(*c*) ₹ 40,000. (*d*) ₹ 50,000. **(AILET, 2009)**

**30.** Match the following:

| | |
|---|---|
| A. Malfeasance | I. One who falsely pretends to be sick. |
| B. Malingerer | II. Minor offences. |
| C. Misdemeanor | III. Improper performance of legal duty. |
| D. Misfeasance | IV. Doing an unlawful act. |

(*a*) I-A II-B III-C IV-D

(*b*) I-B II-C III-D IV-A

(*c*) I-C II-D III-A IV-B

(*d*) I-D II-A III-B IV-C **(AILET, 2009)**

**Directions for 31 to 33:** The following three (3) items consist of two Statements, one labelled the **'Assertion A'** and the other labelled the **'Reason R'**. You are to examine these two Statements carefully and decide if the Assertion A and the Reason R are individually true and if so whether the Reason is a correct explanation of the Assertion. Select your answers to these items using the codes given below and mark your answer-sheet accordingly.

**Code:**

(*a*) Both A and R are true and R is the correct explanation of A.

(*b*) Both A and R are true but R is not a correct explanation of A.

(*c*) A is true but R is false.

(*d*) A is false but R is true.

**31. Assertion (A) :** A finder of a thing has title to it.

**Reason (R) :** The finder's title to a thing is superior to that of the owner. **(AILET, 2009)**

**32. Assertion (A) :** A legal right is a legally protected interest.

**Reason (R) :** An element of advantage is essential to constitute a right. **(AILET, 2009)**

**33. Assertion (A) :** Customs to have the force of law must be immemorial.

**Reason (R) :** Custom represents common consciousness of people. **(AILET, 2009)**

**34. PRINCIPLE:** The owner of a land is entitled to the column of air space above the surface *ad infinitum*. But, the right is restricted to such height as is necessary for the ordinary use and employment of his land, and the structure on it.

A had constructed a single-storeyed house on a corner site. He had no intention of building an additional floor. B his neighbour, who ran an internet parlour got a hoarding made, which protruded over A's house at a height of around 6 feet above the terrace. A sues B for trespass.

(*a*) A will succeed since B's act amounts to trespass.

(*b*) A will not succeed since he was anyway not planning to build an additional storey.

(*c*) A will not succeed since the hoarding is not obstructing him.

(*d*) A will not succeed since B has a right to erect a hoarding. **(AILET, 2010)**

**35. PRINCIPLE:** A second suit will not be heard on the same facts between the same parties.

**(Common for 35 and 36)**

Nakshatra files a suit against Chandra for getting possession of a house on the ground: that the property passed on to her through the will executed by Surya before his death. The suit gets dismissed as Nakshatra fails to produce the will. Nakshatra files another suit against Chandra to get the same house from the latter, on the ground that she was entitled to the house as being the nearest heir of Sljfya.

(*a*) Nakshatra will succeed as she is the nearest heir of Surya.

(*b*) Nakshatra will not succeed as the facts in both the cases are the same.

(*c*) Nakshatra will succeed as the facts in the two cases deal with different situations.

(*d*) Nakshtra will succeed as the grounds in the second case were not taken in the' first one owing to the mistake of her advocate.

**(AILET, 2010)**

**36.** Mr. Sampath went to a party alone in his wife Sunanda's car. He usually used his wife's car after office hours and his wife never objected to it. At the party, he got drunk. Instead of taking the risk of driving the car, he requested his friend Mr. Vivek to drive him back home in Sunanda's car. Mr. Vivek was quite sober since he had moderately consumed alcohol. On the way, Vivek knocked down a boy and injured his leg. Subsequently, on behalf of the boy a claim for compensation was brought against Mrs. Sunanda since the car belonged to her and it was registered in her name. The insurance company refuses to pay compensation because the police report says that the person driving the car at the time of accident had consumed alcohol.

(*a*) Sunanda is liable to pay compensation, although she did not authorize Mr. Vivek to drive the car which caused the accident, yet it was registered in her name.

(*b*) Sunanda is not liable to pay compensation because it is the liability of Mr. Sampath who had permission to drive the car and on the basis of this permission, he requested Mr. Vivek who was driving the car at the time of the accident.

(*c*) Mr. Vivek is liable to compensate the boy fully because he was negligent in driving the car.

(*d*) Sunanda, Sampath and Vivek are all jointly liable to compensate the boy. **(AILET, 2010)**

**37. PRINCIPLE:** A right of action cannot arise out of an illegal activity.

**FACTS:** A and B were thieves engaged in stealing cars and other vehicles. Once they stole a car; and while driving off, they had to cross a city. They engaged a driver to drive them through the city, since they did not know the route inside. The indicator lamp of the car was not working and the thieves had not realised this and therefore, had not told about it to the driver. While driving, through the city, the car was hit by another vehicle because of the faulty indicator. In the accident, the driver was injured and he filed a suit against A and B.

(*a*) The driver would lose, because he was driving a stolen car.

(*b*) The driver would win, because he was not a party to the stealing.

(*c*) The driver would win, because he did not know anything about the stealing.

(*d*) None of the above. **(AILET, 2011)**

**38. PRINCIPLE:** Law does not take notice of trifles.

**FACTS:** A proposes to his neighbour B that they both should go together for a morning walk. B agrees to the proposal and it is decided that both of them would meet at a particular point at 6 AM from where they would set off for the morning walk. Inspite of the agreement, B does not turn up. A waits for him at 6 AM every day for a continuous period of seven days. Thereafter he files a suit against B claiming damages for the agony and mental torture suffered by him. Decide.

(*a*) B is guilty of breach of contract and is liable to pay damages.

(*b*) There is no intention to enter into legal relations.

(*c*) The matter is too small and the court will refuse to go into it.

(*d*) None of the above. **(AILET, 2011)**

**39. PRINCIPLE:** Limitation bars the remedy, not the right.

**FACTS:** After the expiry of the period of limitation of three years, debtor Rohan makes a part payment of debt to creditor Sohan. Sohan then files a suit against Rohan for recovery of the debt after two years from the date of part payment. Decide.

(*a*) The part payment extends the period of limitation.

(*b*) The suit is time barred as part payment is made after the expiry of period of limitation.

(*c*) Fresh period of limitation begins from the date of part payment.

(*d*) None of the above. **(AILET, 2011)**

**40. PRINCIPLE:** Ignorance of law is no excuse.

**FACTS:** A fails to file his income tax returns for ten years. The Income tax department issues to him notice to show cause why proceedings should not be initiated against him for the recovery of the income tax due from him with interest and penalty. Advise.

(*a*) He may take the plea that his advocate had advised him not to file the return as his income was not taxable.

(*b*) He may request the department to waive the interest and penalty.

(*c*) A must pay the tax due as ignorance of law cannot be ground of defence.

(*d*) None of the above. **(AILET, 2011)**

**41.** The National Development Council consists of

(*a*) Members of Planning Commission.

(*b*) Cabinet Ministers and State Chief Ministers.

(*c*) Representatives of Union Territories.

(*d*) All of the above. **(AILET, 2012)**

**42.** Who allocates portfolios among the Ministers?

(*a*) Prime Minister.

(*b*) President.

(*c*) President on the recommendation of the Prime Minister.

(*d*) Chairperson of Ruling Political Party. **(AILET, 2012)**

**43.** Which Indian language is given the status of 'Classical language' by the Central Government?

(*a*) Sanskrit (*b*) Telugu

(*c*) Tamil (*d*) Pali **(AILET, 2012)**

**44.** Each member of the Security Council has one vote. Decisions on procedural matters are to be taken by .............. permanent members. Here veto does not apply. On all other matters, there must be nine affirmative votes including those of five permanent members.

(*a*) 6 (*b*) 7

(*c*) 8 (*d*) 5 **(AILET, 2012)**

**45.** The first venture of Mahatma Gandhi in all India Politics was

(*a*) Non-cooperation Movement.

(*b*) Dandi March.

(*c*) Champaran Movement.

(*d*) Rowlatt Satyagrah. **(AILET, 2012)**

**46.** The "Right to Information" (RTI) is a

(*a*) Constitutional Right.

(*b*) Statutory Right.

(*c*) Fundamental Right.

(*d*) Contractual Right. **(AILET, 2012)**

**47.** Which of the following committees has recommended measures for banning and controlling ragging in educational establishments in India?

(*a*) The Raghavan Committee.

(*b*) Jasraj Committee.

(*c*) Narsimhan Committee.

(*d*) Soli Sorabjee Committee. **(AILET, 2012)**

**48.** For transfer of accused person from a foreign State to India for any offence within India or relating to India is done

(*a*) by previous repatriation agreement between India and concerned foreign country.

(*b*) by instant repatriation agreement between India and concerned foreign country.

(*c*) at the desire of ambassador representing India in concerned foreign country.

(*d*) at the desire of the ambassador who represents concerned foreign country in India. **(AILET, 2012)**

**49.** Whether a Bill is a Money Bill or not is certified by the ________ and his decision is conclusive.

(*a*) President

(*b*) Chairman of Rajya Sabha

(*c*) Speaker of Lok Sabha

(*d*) Chairman of Public Accounts Committee **(AILET, 2012)**

**50.** ________ seats are reserved in all Panchayats at all levels for women

(*a*) One-fourth (*b*) One-third

(*c*) One-half (*d*) Two-third **(AILET, 2012)**

**51.** The maximum duration of the zero hour in Lok Sabha can be

(*a*) one hour (*b*) unspecified

(*c*) 30 minutes (*d*) two hours **(AILET, 2012)**

**52.** The earliest Codified Laws (Civil and Criminal) that defined and demarcated for first time in India during 335-345 A.D. was followed in the

(*a*) Huna reign. (*b*) Sakka reign.

(*c*) Mughal reign. (*d*) Gupta reign. **(AILET, 2012)**

**53.** Which of the following statements is/are not correct about the Objectives Resolution?

I. It was moved by Jawaharlal Nehru in the Constituent Assembly.

II. It called for just right for minorities.

III. It formed the basis for the chapter on Fundamental Rights.

IV. It called for the establishment of a socialist and secular polity.

(*a*) I and II

(*b*) I, II and III

(*c*) III and IV

(*d*) Only III **(AILET, 2012)**

**54.** Money bills can be introduced in the State Legislature with the prior consent of the

(*a*) President.

(*b*) Governor.

(*c*) Speaker.

(*d*) Chief Minister. **(AILET, 2012)**

**55.** A political party is recognised by the Election Commission only if

I. it has been engaged in political activity for a continuous period of five years.

II. has returned at least one member of the Lok Sabha for every 25 members of that House or any fraction of that number elected from that State.

III. has polled not less than six per cent of the total number of valid votes polled by all contesting candidates at the general elections.

IV. has contested elections in four or more states in three consecutive general elections.

(*a*) I and II (*b*) I, III and IV
(*c*) I, II and III (*d*) I, II, III and IV

**(AILET, 2012)**

**56.** Electioneering has to stop in a constituency

(*a*) one day before the election.
(*b*) 48 hours before election starts.
(*c*) 36 hours before a poll commences.
(*d*) 48 hours before the closing hour of polling.

**(AILET, 2012)**

**57. PRINCIPLE:** A right to action cannot arise out of an illegal activity.

**FACTS:** A and B were thieves engaged in stealing cars and other vehicles. Once they stole a car; and while driving off, they had to cross a city. They engaged a driver to drive them through the city, since they did not know the route inside. The indicator lamp of the car was not working and the thieves had not realised this, and therefore, had not told about it to the driver. While driving, through the city, the car was hit by another vehicle because of the faulty indicator. In the accident, the driver was injured and he filed a suit against A and B.

**DECISION:**

(*a*) The driver would lose, because he was driving a stolen car.
(*b*) The driver would win, because he was not a party to the stealing of car.
(*c*) The driver would win because he did not know anything about the stealing.
(*d*) None of the above answer is correct.

**(AILET, 2012)**

**58. PRINCIPLES:**

(1) On the death of husband, the widow shall inherit the property of her deceased husband along with children equally.

(2) A widow can not claim the property of the deceased if on the date when the question of succession opens, she has remarried.

(3) A female acquiring property in any way has the absolute title to the property.

Apply the above three principles and decide the case of the following fact situation:

**FACTS:** When Sudhir died, he had 1/3rd share of the family property, which the three brothers Rudhir, Sudhir and Yasu inherited from their father, B.

Sudhir died on September 23rd 2006 without having any issue. The widow of Sudhir, Ms. Win remarried on January 1, 2007.

Rudhir and Yasu refused 'Win' the share from Sudhir's portion when Win claimed the entire property belonging to Sudhir on January 30, 2007.

Select your decision from the possible decisions given in list I and the appropriate reason from the indicated reasons given in list II given below:

**List I - Decisions**

A. Widow cannot inherit the property of Sudhir.
B. Widow can inherit the property of Sudhir.

**List II - Reasons**

(i) Widow does not belong to the family.
(ii) Widow was remarried.
(iii) Her claim was on the date of Sudhir's death.
(iv) Her claim was submitted after she was remarried.

**Your decision and reason**

**Shade the right decision with reason from the following**

(*a*) (A) (i) (*b*) (A) (ii)
(*c*) (B) (iii) (*d*) (B) (iv) **(CLAT 2008)**

**59. PRINCIPLES:**

(1) Consumable goods which are not fit for consumption are not marketable.

(2) A consumer shall not suffer on account of unmarketable goods.

(3) A seller is liable for knowingly selling unmarketable goods.

(4) A manufacturer shall be liable for the quality of his products.

**FACTS:** Ram bought a Coca Cola bottle from Shama's shop. Back at home, the server opened the bottle and poured the drink into the glasses of Ram and his friend Tom. As Tom started drinking, he felt irritation in his throat. Immediately, Ram and Tom took the sample to test and found Nitric acid in the content. Ram filed a suit against Shama, Coca Cola company and the bottler, Kishen and Co.

**Suggested Decisions**

A. Ram cannot get compensation.
B. Tom can get compensation.
C. Both Ram and Tom can get compensation.

**Suggested Reasons**

(i) Shama did not know the contents of sealed bottle.

(ii) Ram did not actually suffer though he bought the bottle.

(iii) Tom did not buy the bottle.

(iv) Coca Cola company is responsible since it supplied the concentrate.

(v) Kishen & Co, is responsible since it added water, sugar, etc., and sealed the bottle.

(vi) Shama is responsible for selling the defective product.

**Your decision with the reason**

(*a*) (A) (ii) (*b*) (B) (vi)
(*c*) (C) (v) (*d*) (C) (iv) **(CLAT 2008)**

**60. PRINCIPLES:**

1. The owner of a land has absolute interest on the property including the contents over and under the property.
2. Water flowing below your land is not yours though you can use it.
3. Any construction on your land belongs to you.
4. All mineral resources below the land belongs to the State.

**FACTS:** There is a subterranean water flow under Suresh's land surface. Suresh constructed a huge reservoir and drew all subterranean water to the reservoir. As a result, the wells of all adjacent property owners have gone dry. They demanded that either Suresh must demolish the reservoir or share the reservoir water with them.

**Proposed Decision**

(A) Suresh need not demolish the reservoir.

(B) Suresh has to demolish the reservoir.

(C) Suresh has to share the water with his neighbours.

(D) The Government can take over the reservoir.

**Possible reasons**

(i) Water cannot be captured by one person for his personal use.

(ii) The Government must ensure equitable distribution of water.

(iii) Whatever is under Suresh's land may be used by him.

(iv) Suresh has to respect the rights of others regarding water.

**Your decision with the reason**

(*a*) (A) (iii) (*b*) (B) (i)
(*c*) (C) (iv) (*d*) (D) (ii) **(CLAT 2008)**

**61. PRINCIPLES:**

1. Copying including attempt to copy in examinations is a serious offence.
2. One shall not take any unauthorised materials into the examination hall.

**FACTS:** Rohini, an examinee in PUC., was thoroughly checked while entering into the examination hall. She did not have anything other than authorised materials such as pen, instrument box, etc., with her. As she was writing her paper, an invigilator found close to her feet a bunch of chits. The invigilator on scrutiny found that the chits contained answers to the paper being written by Rohini. Rohini's answers tallied with the answers in the chits. A charge of copying was levelled against Rohini..

**Probable Decisions**

A. Rohini shall be punished for copying.

B. Rohini cannot be punished for copying.

**Probable Reasons**

(i) Something lying near the feet does not mean that the person is in possession of that thing.

(ii) The fact that she was checked thoroughly while getting into the hall must be conclusive.

(iii) Similarities between her answers and the answers in the chit indicate that she used those chits.

(iv) After using those chits, she must have failed to dispose of them properly.

**Your decision with the reason**

(*a*) (A) (iii) (*b*) (A) (iv)
(*c*) (B) (iii) (*d*) (B) (i) **(CLAT 2008)**

**62.** All motor vehicles are required to have third party insurance. Any vehicle not using mechanical device is not a motor vehicle.

Which of the following is correct derivation from the above?

(*a*) All Third Party Insurances relate to motor vehicles.

(*b*) Vehicles not using mechanical device need not have Third Party Insurance.

(*c*) All vehicles must have Third Party Insurance.

(*d*) None of the above. **(CLAT 2008)**

**63.** International Law is the law between sovereign states. A sovereign is the supreme authority not bound by legal constraints.

Which of the following is correct derivation from the above?

(*a*) International law is not law binding on the sovereign states.

(*b*) International Law is only a positive morality.

(*c*) International law is in the nature of pact between sovereign states.

(*d*) None of the above. **(CLAT 2008)**

**64.** Which is the oldest Code of Law in India?
(*a*) Naradasmriti. (*b*) Manusmriti.
(*c*) Vedasmriti. (*d*) Prasarsmriti.
**(CLAT 2009)**

**65.** Private international law is also called....
(*a*) Civil Law (*b*) local laws
(*c*) conflict of laws (*d*) common law
**(CLAT 2009)**

**66.** A nominal sum given as a token for striking a sale is called
(*a*) Earnest money. (*b*) advance.
(*c*) interest. (*d*) solatium. **(CLAT 2009)**

**67.** Joint heirs to a property are called
(*a*) co-heirs. (*b*) coparceners.
(*c*) successors. (*d*) joint owners.
**(CLAT 2009)**

**68.** The Supreme Court held that evidence can be recorded by video-conferencing in the case...
(*a*) State of Maharashtra V. Prafull B.Desai.
(*b*) Paramjit Kaur V. State of Punjab.
(*c*) Pappu Yadav V. State of Bihar.
(*d*) Bachan Singh V. State of Punjab. **(CLAT 2009)**

**69.** Which Parliamentary Committee in India system of democracy is shared by a member of Opposition Party?
(*a*) Estimates Committee.
(*b*) Joint Parliamentary Committee.
(*c*) Public Accounts Committee.
(*d*) Finance Committee. **(CLAT 2009)**

**70.** In the year 2002 the Competition Act was enacted replacing
(*a*) Trade Marks Act. (*b*) Copy Right Act.
(*c*) Contract Act. (*d*) MRTP Act.
**(CLAT 2009)**

**71.** A right to recover time barred debt is
(*a*) universal right. (*b*) perfect right.
(*c*) imperfect right. (*d*) Fundamental Right.
**(CLAT 2009)**

**72.** The law relating to prisoners of war has been codified by
(*a*) Geneva Convention. (*b*) Vienna Convention.
(*c*) Paris Convention. (*d*) None of the above.
**(CLAT 2009)**

**73.** Public holidays are declared under
(*a*) Criminal Procedure Code.
(*b*) Civil Procedure Code.
(*c*) Constitution of India.
(*d*) Negotiable Instruments Act. **(CLAT 2009)**

**74.** Husband and wife have a right to each others company. The right is called
(*a*) Conjugal right. (*b*) Human right.
(*c*) Civil right. (*d*) Fundamental right.
**(CLAT 2009)**

**75.** A person 'dying intestate' means he
(*a*) Died without legal heirs.
(*b*) Died without making a will.
(*c*) Died without any property.
(*d*) Died without a son. **(CLAT 2009)**

**76.** If a witness makes a statement in Court, Knowing it to be false, he commits the offence of
(*a*) forgery. (*b*) falsehood.
(*c*) perjury. (*d*) breach of trust.
**(CLAT 2009)**

**77.** A child born after father's death is
(*a*) posthumous. (*b*) heir.
(*c*) intestate. (*d*) bastard. **(CLAT 2009)**

**78.** A formal instrument by which one person empowers another to represent him is known as
(*a*) affidavit. (*b*) power of attorney.
(*c*) will. (*d*) declaration.
**(CLAT 2009)**

**79.** The temporary release of a prisoner is called
(*a*) parole. (*b*) amnesty.
(*c*) discharge. (*d*) pardon. **(CLAT 2009)**

**80.** India became the member of United Nations in the Year
(*a*) 1956 (*b*) 1945
(*c*) 1946 (*d*) 1950 **(CLAT 2009)**

**81.** A party to the suit is called
(*a*) Accused. (*b*) Plaintiff.
(*c*) Litigant. (*d*) Complainant.
**(CLAT 2009)**

**82.** Who heads the four member committee appointed to study the Centre-State relations especially the changes took place since Sarkaria Commission
(*a*) Justice M.M.Punchi. (*b*) Justice Nanavati.
(*c*) Justice Barucha. (*d*) Justice Kuldip Singh.
**(CLAT 2009)**

**83.** A participant in commission of crime is popularly known as
(*a*) respondent. (*b*) under-trial.
(*c*) defendant. (*d*) accomplice.
**(CLAT 2009)**

**84.** Which of the following is not payable to Central Government?
(*a*) Land revenue. (*b*) Customs duty.
(*c*) Income tax. (*d*) Wealth tax.
**(CLAT 2009)**

**85.** Where is the National Judicial Academy located?
(*a*) Kolkata (*b*) Bhopal
(*c*) Delhi (*d*) Mumbai **(CLAT 2009)**

**86.** Every duty enforceable by law is called
(*a*) accountability. (*b*) obligation.
(*c*) burden. (*d*) incidence. **(CLAT 2009)**

**87.** The killing of a new born child by its parents is
(*a*) malfeasance. (*b*) infanticide.
(*c*) abortion. (*d*) foeticide. **(CLAT 2009)**

**88.** Offence of breaking a divine idol is
(*a*) Salus populi.
(*b*) Infanticide.
(*c*) Sacrilege.
(*d*) Blasphemy. **(CLAT 2009)**

**89.** A person who goes under-ground or evades the jurisdiction of the Court is known as
(*a*) offender. (*b*) under-ground.
(*c*) absentee. (*d*) absconder. **(CLAT 2009)**

**90.** What is a caveat?
(*a*) A warning. (*b*) An injunction.
(*c*) Writ. (*d*) Certiorari. **(CLAT 2009)**

**91.** Muslim religious foundations are known as
(*a*) Deen. (*b*) Wakfs.
(*c*) Ulema. (*d*) Zakat. **(CLAT 2009)**

**92.** Beyond what distance from the coast, is the sea known as "High Sea"?
(*a*) 20 miles (*b*) 300 miles
(*c*) 200 kms. (*d*) 12 miles **(CLAT 2009)**

**93.** An 'encumbrance' in legal parlance is a
(*a*) liability on property. (*b*) grant of property.
(*c*) gift of property. (*d*) restriction on property. **(CLAT 2010)**

**94.** A husband and wife have a right to each other's company. This right is called
(*a*) matrimonial right. (*b*) consortium right.
(*c*) marital right. (*d*) conjugal right. **(CLAT 2010)**

**95.** Release of prisoner before completion of his sentence is called
(*a*) release. (*b*) parole.
(*c*) acquittal. (*d*) lease. **(CLAT 2010)**

**96.** Result of successful prosecution is
(*a*) acquittal.
(*b*) discharge.
(*c*) conviction.
(*d*) charge sheeting. **(CLAT 2010)**

**97.** The manager of waqf is known as
(*a*) Sajjadanashin. (*b*) Khadim.
(*c*) Mutawalli. (*d*) Mujawar. **(CLAT 2010)**

**98.** "Ipso facto" means
(*a*) in place of. (*b*) by reason of that fact.
(*c*) by the same source. (*d*) by the way. **(CLAT 2010)**

**99.** 'Requisition' means
(*a*) permanent transfer of the title of the property.
(*b*) supervision of property.
(*c*) taking control of property temporarily.
(*d*) taking possession permanently. **(CLAT 2010)**

**100.** 'Corroborative evidence' means
(*a*) main evidence in a case.
(*b*) evidence which supports other evidence.
(*c*) evidence that proves the guilt of an accused person.
(*d*) evidence of a person who supports the accused. **(CLAT 2010)**

**101.** Ex-parte decision means a decision given
(*a*) after hearing both the parties.
(*b*) without proper procedure.
(*c*) after observing proper procedure.
(*d*) without hearing the opponent. **(CLAT 2010)**

**102.** Which of the following constitutions is a unitary constitution
(*a*) U.S. (*b*) British.
(*c*) Indian. (*d*) Australian. **(CLAT 2010)**

**103.** Which of the following marriages is approved by Islamic law? Between a Muslim
(*a*) male and a Christian female.
(*b*) female and a Hindu male.
(*c*) female and a Christian male.
(*d*) female and a Jew male. **(CLAT 2010)**

**104.** Which of the following constitutions when framed did not provide for judicial review?
(*a*) Indian.
(*b*) Pakistani.
(*c*) U.S.
(*d*) Australian. **(CLAT 2010)**

**105.** Ratio decidendi means
(*a*) a judicial decision.
(*b*) part of the judgment which possesses authority.
(*c*) any observation made by the court which goes beyond the requirement of the case.
(*d*) an observation made by a judge. **(CLAT 2010)**

**106.** 'Dyarchy' under the government of India Act 1919 meant

(*a*) division of powers between the central and provincial government.

(*b*) separation of judiciary from executive.

(*c*) division of executive departments under elected ministers and the members of the governor's executive council.

(*d*) separation between legislature and executive. **(CLAT 2010)**

**107.** Fringe benefit tax is a tax

(*a*) paid by an employer in respect of the fringe benefits provided or deemed to have been provided by an employer to his employee.

(*b*) paid by an employer for the benefits which he enjoys.

(*c*) paid by a person for the benefits which he gets from his employer.

(*d*) paid by a member of scheduled castes and scheduled tribes for benefits they receive from the government. **(CLAT 2010)**

**108.** In Ram V/S Shayam, Ram cannot be a

(*a*) plaintiff. (*b*) appellants.

(*c*) defendant. (*d*) prosecutor. **(CLAT 2010)**

**109.** Cr.P.C. stands for

(*a*) Criminal proceedings code.

(*b*) Criminal proceedings court.

(*c*) Crime prevention code.

(*d*) Criminal Procedure code. **(CLAT 2010)**

**110.** Medical Science used for investigating crimes is known as

(*a*) Criminal Medicine.

(*b*) Epistemological Science.

(*c*) Forensic science.

(*d*) Ontological Science. **(CLAT 2010)**

**111.** Apuisne judge of a High Court is

(*a*) a judge other than a Chief Justice.

(*b*) the Chief Justice.

(*c*) a temporary judge.

(*d*) a retired judge. **(CLAT 2010)**

**112.** Intra vires means

(*a*) within the powers.

(*b*) outside the powers.

(*c*) within the scope of fundamental rights.

(*d*) regular. **(CLAT 2010)**

**113.** Moots, in law schools, are

(*a*) exercises of law teaching.

(*b*) legal problems in the form of imaginary cases, argued by two opposing students before a bench pretending to be a real court.

(*c*) imaginary class room where a student acts as a teacher.

(*d*) a debate on a legal problem. **(CLAT 2010)**

**114.** Scheduled Tribe status is

(*a*) restricted to Hindus.

(*b*) religiously neutral.

(*c*) restricted to Hindus and Christians.

(*d*) restricted to Hindus and Muslims. **(CLAT 2010)**

**115.** Which of the following has not been a woman judge of the Supreme Court of India, till 2009?

(*a*) Justice Gyan Sudha Mishra.

(*b*) Justice Sujata Manohar.

(*c*) Justice Ruma Pal.

(*d*) Justice Fathima Beevi. **(CLAT 2010)**

**116.** What is the meaning of chattel?

(*a*) Any property. (*b*) Immovable property.

(*c*) Movable property. (*d*) Cattle.

**(CLAT 2010)**

**117.** In a civil suit, the person who files suit and the person against whom the suit is filed are called

(*a*) accused, prosecutor.

(*b*) accuser, defendant.

(*c*) appellant, respondent.

(*d*) plaintiff, defendant. **(CLAT 2010)**

**118.** In a criminal case, an accused person, who in consideration of his non- prosecution offers to give evidence against other accused, is called

(*a*) accomplice. (*b*) hostile witness.

(*c*) approver. (*d*) hostile accomplice.

**(CLAT 2010)**

**119.** International Labour Organization has its headquarters at

(*a*) The Hague. (*b*) Geneva.

(*c*) New York. (*d*) London. **(CLAT 2010)**

**120.** The Child Marriage Restraint Act 2006 is applicable to

(*a*) only Hindus.

(*b*) all Indians except Muslims as the minimum age of marriage among Muslim girls is puberty (beginning of menstruation) in Muslim personal law.

(*c*) all irrespective of religion.

(*d*) all except Muslim, Christians and Jews.

**(CLAT 2010)**

**121.** Within the jurisdiction of which High Court does Lakshdweep fall
(*a*) Bombay High Court. (*b*) Kerala High Court.
(*c*) Madras High Court. (*d*) Delhi High Court.
**(CLAT 2010)**

**122.** Which of the following is not the function of the International Court of Justice? It
(*a*) gives advisory opinion at the request of general Assembly.
(*b*) gives advisory opinion at the request of Security Council.
(*c*) interprets treaties when considering legal disputes brought before it by nations.
(*d*) decides international crimes. **(CLAT 2010)**

**123.** Bank nationalization case relates to the nationalization of
(*a*) some banks by the government of India after economic liberalisation in 1991.
(*b*) some banks under a law during the Prime Ministership of Mrs. Indira Gandhi.
(*c*) all the private Indian Banks during the Prime Ministership of Narasimha Rao.
(*d*) all the private Indian Banks during the Prime Ministership of Mrs. Indira Gandhi
**(CLAT 2010)**

**124.** Which of the following is not included within the meaning of intellectual property
(*a*) Patents.
(*b*) Copyrights.
(*c*) Trade mark.
(*d*) Property of an intellectual. **(CLAT 2010)**

**125.** The main aim of the competition Act 2002 is to protect the interests of
(*a*) the multinational corporation.
(*b*) the Indian companies.
(*c*) the consumers.
(*d*) the market. **(CLAT 2010)**

**126.** Which of the following judges had never been the chairman of the Law Commission of India?
(*a*) Justice R.C. Lahoti.
(*b*) Justice A.R. Lakshamanan.
(*c*) Justice Jeevan Reddy.
(*d*) Justice Jagannadha Rao. **(CLAT 2010)**

**127.** Who among the following was the first chief Information Commissioner of India?
(*a*) Wajahat Habibullah.
(*b*) Irrfan Habib.
(*c*) Tahir Mahmood.
(*d*) Najma Heptullah. **(CLAT 2010)**

**128.** R.T.I. stands for
(*a*) Revenue transactions in India.
(*b*) Research and Technology Institute.
(*c*) Rural and Transparency infrastructure.
(*d*) Right to information. **(CLAT 2010)**

**129.** Fiduciary relationship is relationship based on
(*a*) contract. (*b*) trust.
(*c*) blood relationship. (*d*) money. **(CLAT 2010)**

**130.** Human rights day is observed on
(*a*) 14th February.
(*b*) 26th November.
(*c*) 2nd October.
(*d*) 10th December. **(CLAT 2010)**

**(For questions 131 to 133)**

**Rule:** Whoever finds an unattended object can keep it unless the true owner claims that object. This does not affect the property owner's right to the ownership of the property on which the object is found. The right to ownership of a property does not include the right to ownership of unattended objects on that property.

**Facts**: Elizabeth is the CEO of a global management services company in Chennai and is on her way to Ranchi to deliver the convocation address at India's leading business school on the outskirts of Ranchi. Flying business class on Dolphin Airlines, she is entitled to use the lounge owned by the airline in Chennai Airport while waiting for her flight. She finds a diamond ear-ring on the floor of the lounge and gives it to the staff of Dolphin Airlines expressly stating that in the event of nobody claiming the ear-ring within six months, she would claim it back. The airline sells the ear-ring after eight months and Elizabeth files a case to recover the value of the ear-ring from the airline when she is informed about its sale.

**131.** As a judge you would order that:
(*a*) Elizabeth is not entitled to compensation because the ear-ring was found on the property of the airline and therefore, the airline is entitled to sell it.
(*b*) The airline must compensate Elizabeth because owning the lounge does not give the airline the right over all things that might be found on it.
(*c*) The airline must compensate Elizabeth because while accepting the ear-ring from Elizabeth they had agreed to return it if nobody claimed it within six months.
(*d*) Elizabeth is not entitled to compensation because she did not claim the ear-ring after the expiry of six months and the airline waited for a couple more months before selling it.
**(CLAT 2011)**

132. Assume now that Elizabeth was only an economy class passenger and was not entitled to use the airline's lounge. However, she manages to gain entry and finds the ear-ring in the lounge. The rest of the above facts remain the same. Will her illegal entry into the Lounge affect Elizabeth's right to keep the ear-ring (or be compensated for its value)?

(*a*) Yes, the airline claims that Elizabeth's entry into the lounge was illegal and therefore she has no right over anything she found there

(*b*) No, because Elizabeth's class of travel has no bearing on the outcome in this case

(*c*) Cannot be determined as we need to know how Elizabeth was able to access the airline's lounge.

(*d*) None of the above. **(CLAT 2011)**

133. To the original fact scenario, the following fact is added: In the lounge there are numerous signboards which proclaim 'Any unattended item will be confiscated by Dolphin Airlines'. In this case, you would:

(*a*) Order the airline to pay compensation to Elizabeth because the board in the lounge cannot grant property rights over unattended objects to the airline.

(*b*) Deny Elizabeth compensation because the signboard makes it evident that the airline, as owner of the lounge, is exercising all rights over all unattended items in the lounge and the ear-ring is one such item.

(*c*) Deny Elizabeth compensation because she knew any unattended item belonged to the airline.

(*d*) Order the airline to pay compensation to Elizabeth because the property rights of the airline are relevant only if the item is unattended. The moment Elizabeth found the earring, it belonged to her. **(CLAT 2011)**

**[For questions 134-137]**

**Rules:**

A. When land is sold, all 'fixtures' on the land are also deemed to have been sold.

B. If a moveable thing is attached to the land or any building on the land, then it becomes a 'fixture'.

**FACTS:** Khaleeda wants to sell a plot of land she owns in Baghmara, Meghalaya and the sale value decided for the plot includes the fully-furnished palatial six-bedroom house that she has built on it five years ago. She sells it to Gurpreet for sixty lakh rupees. After completing the sale, she removes the expensive Iranian carpet which used to cover the entire wooden floor of one of the bedrooms. The room had very little light and Khaleeda used this light-coloured radiant carpet to negate some of the darkness in the room. Gurpreet, after moving in, realises this and files a case to recover the carpet from Khaleeda.

134. As a judge you would decide in favour of:

(*a*) Gurpreet because when the price was agreed upon, Khaleeda did not inform her about removing the carpet.

(*b*) Gurpreet because the carpet was integral to the floor of the bedroom and therefore attached to the building that was sold.

(*c*) Khaleeda because a fully-furnished house does not entail the buyer to everything in the house.

(*d*) Khaleeda because by virtue of being a carpet it was never permanently fixed to the floor of the building. Assume that in the above fact scenario, Khaleeda no longer wants the carpet. She removes the elaborately carved door to the house after the sale has been concluded and claims that Gurpreet has no claim to the door. The door in question was part of Khaleeda's ancestral home in Nagercoil, Tamil Nadu for more than 150 years before she had it fitted as the entrance to her Baghmara house. **(CLAT 2011)**

135. As a judge you would decide in favour of:

(*a*) Khaleeda because while the rest of the building belongs to Khaleeda exclusively, the door is ancestral property and therefore the decision to sell it cannot be Khaleeda's alone.

(*b*) Gurpreet because the door is an integral part of the building as it is attached to it.

(*c*) Khaleeda because the door can be removed from the building and is therefore not attached to it.

(*d*) Gurpreet because the contract is explicitly for the whole house and since the door is part of house, it cannot be removed subsequent to the sale. **(CLAT 2011)**

136. Amongst the following options, the most relevant consideration while deciding a case on the basis of the above two principles would be:

(*a*) Whether the moveable thing was included in the sale agreement.

(*b*) Whether the moveable thing was merely placed on the land or building.

(*c*) Whether the moveable thing had become an inseparable part of the land or building.

(*d*) Whether the moveable thing could be removed. **(CLAT 2011)**

**137. Rule C:** If a moveable thing is placed on land with the intention that it should become an integral part of the land or any structure on the land it becomes a fixture. Applying Rules A and C, to the fact situations in questions 192 and 193, as a judge you would decide in favour of:

(*a*) Khaleeda in both situations.

(*b*) Gurpreet only in 192.

(*c*) Khaleeda only in 193.

(*d*) Gurpeet in both situations. **(CLAT 2011)**

**138. PRINCIPLE:** Ignorance of Fact is excused but ignorance of law is no excuse.

**FACT:** X was a passenger from Zurich to Manila in a Swiss Plane. When the plane landed at the Airport of Bombay on 28 Nov. 1962 it was found on searching that X carried 34 kg of Gold Bars on his person and that he had not declared it in the 'Manifest for Transit'. On 26th Nov. 1962 the Government of India had issued a notification modifying its earlier exemption, making it mandatory now that the gold must be declared in the "Manifest" of the aircraft.

(*a*) X cannot be prosecuted because he had actually no knowledge about the new notification issued two days ago.

(*b*) X cannot be prosecuted because ignorance of fact is excusable.

(*c*) X can be prosecuted because ignorance of law is not excusable.

(*d*) X's liability would depend on the discretion of the court. **(CLAT 2012)**

**139. Assertion (A)**: During inflation, there is increase in money supply and rise in price level.

**Reason (R):** The rise in prices is due to shortage in supply of essential consumer goods.

(*a*) Both A and R are individually true and R is the correct explanation of A.

(*b*) Both A and R are individually true but R is not the correct explanation of A.

(*c*) A is true but R is false.

(*d*) A is false but R is true. **(CLAT 2012)**

**140. Assertion (A):** A person claims compensation for his non-gratuitous act.

**Reason (R):** A person who enjoys benefit from lawful, non-gratuitous act of another must compensate him even though there is no contract.

(*a*) Both A and R are individually true and R is the correct explanation of A.

(*b*) Both A and R are individually true but R is not the correct explanation of A.

(*c*) A is true but R is false.

(*d*) A is false but R is true. **(CLAT 2012)**

**141. Assertion (A):** Austin's concept of law is known as imperative theory.

**Reason (R):** Austin emphasized on the commanding character of law.

(*a*) Both A and R are individually true and R is the correct explanation of A.

(*b*) Both A and R are individually true but R is not the correct explanation of A.

(*c*) A is true but R is false.

(*d*) A is false but R is true. **(CLAT 2012)**

**142.** Consider the following statements:

I. In a recent Supreme Court verdict pronounced by Justice Markandeya Katju and Justice Gyan Sudha Mishra, the court upheld the constitutionality of the Haj subsidy.

II. Muslims are not the only beneficiaries of the secular state's generosity. Hindus have also received substantial financial support from the Government.

With reference to the statements mentioned above, which of the following is correct?

(*a*) I only. (*b*) II only.

(*c*) Both I and II. (*d*) Neither I nor II.

**(CLAT 2012)**

**143.** X, a married woman, agreed to live in adultery with B and also agreed to serve him as his housekeeper. In return, B agreed to pay X ₹ 500 per month for living in adultery and ₹ 500 per month for housekeeping. The agreement is

(*a*) valid.

(*b*) void.

(*c*) void as to the first object but valid with respect to the second object.

(*d*) unlawful as being opposed to public policy.

**(CLAT 2012)**

**144.** Ramu applied for the post of Director in an organization. The governing body of the organization passed a resolution appointing him to the post. After the meeting, one of the members of the governing body informed him privately of the resolution. Subsequently, the resolution was rescinded. Ramu claims damages. Which one of the following is the correct legal proposition in the case?

(*a*) Ramu cannot claim damages as he had not resigned from his existing post in anticipation of getting the appointment letter.

(*b*) Ramu cannot claim damages as there was no formal communication.

(*c*) Ramu can claim damages as governing body cannot rescind the resolution once passed.

(*d*) Ramu can claim damages as there was private communication. **(CLAT 2012)**

**145.** Match schedule one and two and choose the appropriate answer-

| **Schedule I** | **Schedule II** |
|---|---|
| i. Concurrent list | 1. Constitution of Japan |
| ii. Rule of Law | 2. Constitution of Ireland |
| iii. Directive Principle of State Policy | 3. British Constitution |
| iv. Procedure established by law | 4. Constitution of Australia |

| | i | ii | iii | iv |
|---|---|---|---|---|
| (*a*) | 1 | 2 | 3 | 4 |
| (*b*) | 2 | 4 | 3 | 1 |
| (*c*) | 1 | 3 | 4 | 2 |
| (*d*) | 4 | 3 | 2 | 1 |

**(CLAT 2012)**

**146.** In which of the following cases can a Constitutional amendment be passed just by a simple majority in Parliament?

(*a*) Election matters.

(*b*) Change in the name and boundaries of states.

(*c*) Powers of the President.

(*d*) None of the above. **(CLAT 2012)**

**147.** "Begar" means

(*a*) voluntary work without payment.

(*b*) involuntary work without payment.

(*c*) involuntary work with payment.

(*d*) voluntary work with payment. **(AILET 2013)**

**148.** The "Eco-mark" is given by the Ministry of Environment and Forest to the consumer products which

(*a*) are degradable.

(*b*) are environment friendly.

(*c*) conform to the standards of ISI.

(*d*) are electricity saver. **(AILET 2013)**

**149.** The EIA is abbreviated form of

(*a*) Environment Impact Assessment.

(*b*) Environment Implementation Arrangement.

(*c*) Environment Impact Apparatus.

(*d*) Environmental Institute of Awareness.

**(AILET 2013)**

**150.** ______ was the leader of "Chipko Movement".

(*a*) Medha Patkar (*b*) Subhash Gheising

(*c*) Balasaheb Doeras (*d*) Sunderlal Bahuguna

**(AILET 2013)**

**151.** When two persons descend from a common ancestor but by different wives, they are said to be related to each other by **(AILET 2013)**

(*a*) Sapinda relationship. (*b*) Half blood.

(*c*) Full blood. (*d*) None of the above.

**152.** "*Pacta sunt Servanda*" means that

(*a*) the states are not bound to respect the agreements entered into by them

(*b*) the agreements entered into by the States will be respected and followed by them in good faith

(*c*) the states are under no obligation to follow the agreements in good faith

(*d*) though the states are bound to recognise an agreement entered into by them but cannot be compelled to follow it **(AILET 2013)**

**153.** What is Plea Bargaining ?

(*a*) A conference between opposing lawyers and judge to determine the time a case should take place.

(*b*) A procedure by which an accused pleads guilty in exchange for a lesser punishment.

(*c*) A conference between opposing lawyers to settle the claim.

(*d*) A conference between the victim and the accused to settle the claim. **(AILET 2013)**

**154.** The act by members of a trade union, persuading others not to work is called as **(AILET 2013)**

(*a*) non-cooperation. (*b*) picketing.

(*c*) sit-in-strike. (*d*) strike.

**155.** In India, cyber terrorism is an offence punishable under

(*a*) information Technology Act.

(*b*) POTA.

(*c*) TADA.

(*d*) Indian Penal Code. **(AILET 2013)**

**156.** In Extradition Treaty, extradition means

(*a*) Order of Indian Court will apply to Indian living elsewhere than India.

(*b*) Export without double taxation.

(*c*) Two countries will deport criminal on reciprocal basis to each other.

(*d*) None of the above. **(AILET 2013)**

**157.** According to the Doctrine of_____, every generation is obliged to preserve its natural and cultural heritage for the enjoyment of the future generations.

(*a*) Sustainable development

(*b*) Polluter pay principle

(*c*) Precautionary principle

(*d*) Inter-generational equity **(AILET 2013)**

**158.** Which of the following is not recommended by the Justice Verma Committee ? **(AILET 2013)**

(*a*) Minimum sentence for a rapist should be enhanced from 7 years to 10 years.

(*b*) The age of juvenile should not be lowered from 18 to 16 years.

(*c*) Life imprisonment must always mean jail for "the entire natural life of the convict".

(*d*) Death sentence for "rarest of rare cases" of rape.

**Directions (Q. 159-173) :** This section consists of fifteen (15) questions. Each question consists of legal propositions/ principles (hereinafter referred to as 'principle') and facts. These principles have to be applied to the given facts to arrive at the most reasonable conclusion. Such principles may or may not be true in the real sense, yet you have to conclusively assume them to be true for the purposes of this section. In other words, in answering the following questions, you must not rely on any principles except the principles that are given herein below for every question. Further you must not assume any facts other than those stated in the question.The objective of this section is to test your interest towards study of law, research aptitude and problem solving ability even if the "most reasonable conclusion" arrived at may be unacceptable for any other reason. It is not the objective of this section to test your knowledge of law.

**159. Principle:** In order to be illegible to appear in the semester examination, a student is required to attend, under all circumstances, at least 70% of the total classes held in that semester as per University rules. **(CLAT 2013)**

**Facts:** Anand, an economically poor but a very brilliant student of LL.B. final semester, while going to his University bycycle received some leg injuries in road accident. Consequently Anand could not attend his classes for one week as he was advised rest by his doctor for that period. Due to this absence from the University, Anand failed to have 70% attendance essential to appear in the examination and, therefore, he was debarred from appearing in the examination by the University authorities. Anand challenges this decision in the court of law

(*a*) Anand will succeed in the court of law as the accident was beyond his control

(*b*) Anand will definitely get favour of the court on humanitarian ground as he comes from a economically poor family and may not afford to take readmission

(*c*) Anand will not succeed as he could very easily fulfill eligibility criteria for appearing in the examination by being reasonably regular in the class throughout the semester.

(*d*) Anand will succeed as requirement of 70% attendance may be declared arbitrary and, therefore, unreasonable by the court of law.

**160. Principle:** A seller of goods cannot transfer better rights than he himself possesses in the goods sold to the buyer. **(CLAT 2013)**

**Facts:** Komal leaves his watch by mistake on a seat in the park. Sonal finds that watch and immediately sells the same for good price to Monal who without inquiring whether Sonal is its owner or not. Komal later on claims that watch from Monal. Decide whether Komal can succeed?

(*a*) Komal cannot succeed as Monal has paid good price of the watch.

(*b*) Komal cannot succeed as Monal is unaware of the fact that Sonal is not its owner.

(*c*) Komal can not succeed as it was his carelessness and nothing else which enabled Sonal to sell the watch to Monal.

(*d*) Komal can not succeed as Sonal is merely finder of the watch and, therefore, cannot transfer ownership rights thereon to Monal.

**161. Principle:** He, who goes to the court of law to seek justice, must come with clean hands.

**Facts:** P enters into a contract with S under which S has to construct a house for P and has to complete the same within one year from the date of the contract. This contract includes two very important terms. According to first term if there is price hike of the materials to be used in the construction, then the escalation charges at a particular rate shall be payable by P to S. According to second term if the construction of the house is not completed within the period prescribed for it, then S will have to pay penalty at a particular rate to P. Before the completion of the construction work the workers of S go on strike and strike continues up to three months even after the expiry of one year. After that period workers return and the construction work again starts. During the last three months period of strike there was a considerable rise in the price of the building material. S claimed escalation cost from P. P did not agree to it. S filed a suit in the court of law either to order the payment of the price of the building material on the basis of escalated price or to allow him to stop the work without incurring any penal liability towards P. **(CLAT 2013)**

(*a*) S will succeed as strike by his workers was unexpected and beyond his control.

(*b*) S can succeed as there is an escalation clause in the contract

(*c*) S can not succeed as he has failed to complete the construction work in time and strike can not be treated as a valid excuse for delay in work.

(*d*) S can succeed if he pays penalty to P for delay.

**162. Principle:** whosoever by his act or omission causes environmental pollution shall be held liable for any loss caused by such pollution. It shall be no defence in such cases that all due diligence or reasonable care was taken while carrying out the act or omission in question. **(CLAT 2013)**

**Facts:** Hari is carrying on a chemical and fertilizer industry near a bank of a river. In order to prevent and control any kind of harm to the environment, suitable waste treatment and disposal plants were installed in the factory. Due to some sudden mechanical/ technical problem, these plants ceased to work properly and, therefore, caused environmental pollution, which ultimately caused substantial harm to the environment and to the people living around the factory. Victims of such pollution file a suit for suitable remedy.

(*a*) Victims can not succeed as necessary precautions to prevent any harm were taken by Hari.

(*b*) Victims can not succeed as the mechanical/ technical problem was sudden and, therefore, beyond the control of Hari.

(*c*) Victims can succeed as it is the duty of Hari to see that no harm is caused to the environment/ people due to his activity under any circumstances.

(*d*) Victims could succeed if treatment/ disposal plant were not installed in the factory.

**163. Principle:** If a person transfers movable or immovable property with its full ownership and without any consideration to some other person, then it is called a gift. **(CLAT 2013)**

**Facts:** S, who has no child of his own, makes a gift of his house worth ₹ 25 lacs to his nephew R. After completing all the legal formalities required for a valid gift, S says to R that in case of need R will provide that house to S for use without any questions. R does not react to it. After one year of this gift, S really needs that house and request R to make the house available to him, but R refuses to do so.

(*a*) R cannot refuse as he got the house without paying any consideration for that.

(*b*) R cannot refuse as S is without children.

(*c*) R can refuse as he has become full owner of the house.

(*d*) R can refuse as he himself may be in need of that house.

**164. Principle:** 'Work' means literary work, artistic work, dramatic work, musical work, cinematographic film and sound recording but does not include acting in a cinematographic film. **(CLAT 2013)**

Only the works, as enumerated above, can be protected under copyright law.

**Facts:** A very famous actor acted in a cinematographic film. The actor was also the producer and director of cinematographic film.

(*a*) The acting of the actor can be protected under copyright law

(*b*) The acting of the actor can be protected under copyright law only as an artistic work

(*c*) The acting of the actor cannot be protected under copyright law

(*d*) The acting of the actor cannot be protected under copyright law as a cinematographic film

**165. Principle:** In case where the government is a party, the government shall be the first owner of thecopyright in the work unless there is an agreement to the contrary. **(CLAT 2013)**

**Facts:** The Government of the State of X entered into an agreement with a retired Professor of Botany. The Professor agreed to write a text book on Botany. The Government agreed to pay a sum of ₹ Ten Lacs to the Professor for this work.

(*a*) The Government of the State of X shall be first owner of copyright in the text book

(*b*) The Professor shall be first owner of copyright in the text book

(*c*) Both the Government of the State of X and the Professor shall be the joint owners of copyright in the text book

(*d*) The Professor shall be first owner of copyright in the text book only if he refuses to accept the amount of ₹ Ten Lacs from the Government

**166. Principle:** Licence is an agreement whereby the owner of the copyright agrees to grant an interest in the copyright to the licencee. Assignment is an agreement whereby the owner of the copyright transfers all the property rights to the assignee. Property right is a bundle of rights consisting of right to possess, right to use, right to alienate, and the right to exclude other **(CLAT 2013)**

**Facts:** A, an owner of copyright in a cinematographic film enters into an agreement with B, a film distributer. B agrees to distribute the film only in Mumbai. A also enters into many such agreements with other distributers for distribution of his film in other cities.

(*a*) The agreement between A and B is more in the nature of assignment than in the nature of licence

(*b*) The agreement between A and B is more in the nature of licence than in the nature of assignment

(*c*) The agreement between A and B is both in the nature of assignment and licence

(*d*) The agreement between A and B is neither in the nature of assignment nor in the nature of licence

**167. Principle:** *Qui facit per alium facit per se*, i.e. he who does things through others does it himself. **(CLAT 2013)**

**Facts:** Nisha, the owner of a car, asked her friend Saurabh to take her car and drive the same to her office. As the car was near her office, it hit a pedestrian Srikant on account of Saurabh's negligent driving and injured him seriously. Now Srikant files a suit for damages against Nisha.

(*a*) Nisha is not liable as it was the negligence of Saurabh.

(*b*) Saurabh is solely liable as Nisha was not driving the car.

(*c*) Nisha is liable as Saurabh was driving under her authority and for her purpose.

(*d*) Saurabh will be exempted from liability under the principle of inevitable accident.

**168. Principle:** Words describing quality of things cannot be registered as trade mark. However, such words may be registered as trade mark if they acquire a secondary meaning. Words acquire secondary meaning when people start associating the descriptive words with a person specific. **(CLAT 2013)**

**Facts:** A hatchery located in Raipur is owned by 'X'. X has been using the slogan "new laid eggs sold here" since 1970 to describe the quality of eggs sold in his hatchery. Over a period of time because of continuous use of this slogan, people started associating this slogan with X. X filed an application for registration of the words "new laid eggs" as trade mark in the year 1970.

(*a*) The words will be registered as trade mark

(*b*) The words will not be registered as trade mark

(*c*) The words may be registered as trade mark

(*d*) The words may not be registered as trade mark

**169. Principle:** Where two or more persons have made a complaint for the grant of compulsory licence to the Copyright Board, the licence shall be granted to that complainant only who, in the opinion of the Copyright Board, would best serve the interests of the general public. **(CLAT 2013)**

**Facts:** Four persons made a complaint for the grant of compulsory licence to the Copyright Board.

(*a*) Licence shall be granted to only one complainant

(*b*) Licence may be granted to two complainants

(*c*) Licence may be granted to three complainants

(*d*) Licence must be granted to all the four complainants

**170. Principle:** Any police officer, not below the rank of a sub-inspector, may, if he is satisfied that an offence in respect of the infringement of copyright in any work has been, is being, or is likely to be, committed, seize without warrant, all copies of the work, and all plates used for the purpose of making infringing copies of the work, wherever found, and all copies and plates so seized shall, as soon as practicable, be produced before a Magistrate. **(CLAT 2013)**

**Facts:** A Superintendent of Police (SP) conducted a raid on a shop and found pirated copies of books. The SP formed an opinion that infringement of copyright is taking place. He arrested the shop owner without warrant in the light of above mentioned propositions.

(*a*) The arrest of the shop owner was within the power of the SP

(*b*) The arrest of the shop owner was not within the power of the SP

(*c*) The shop owner can never be arrested

(*d*) SP was not competent to know whether infringement of copyright has taken place

**171. Principle:** An interest which is created on a transfer of property and depends upon the fulfillment of a condition will fail if the fulfillment of the condition is impossible or is forbidden by law or is of such a nature that, if permitted, it would defeat the provisions of any law or is fraudulent or involves or implies injury to the person or property of another or the court regards it as immoral or opposed to public policy. **(CLAT 2013)**

**Facts:** A gives ₹ Ten Lacs to B on condition that B shall marry A's daughter C. On the date on which A gave ₹ Ten Lacs to B, C was dead.

(*a*) B's interest in ₹ Ten Lacs fails because of impossibility

(*b*) B's interest in ₹ Ten Lacs fails because of immorality

(*c*) B's interest in ₹ Ten Lacs fails because of prohibition by law

(*d*) B's interest in ₹ Ten Lacs does not fail

**172. Principle:** Existence of all the alleged facts is relevant whether they occurred at the same time and place or at different times and places.

**Facts:** A, a permanent resident in a foreign country who never visited India, is accused of waging war against the Government of India by taking part in an armed insurrection in which property is destroyed, troops are attacked and prisons are broken open. **(CLAT 2013)**

(*a*) The existence of all the above mentioned alleged facts is relevant

(*b*) Only the alleged fact that A is accused of waging war against the Government of India is relevant

(*c*) The fact that A was a permanent resident in a foreign country who never visited India is not relevant

(*d*) Only the alleged fact of taking part by A in armed resurrection is relevant

**173. Principle:** The fact that any person was born during the continuance of a valid marriage between his mother and any man, or within two hundred and eighty days after its dissolution, the mother remaining unmarried, shall be conclusive proof that he is the legitimate son of that man, unless it can be shown that the parties to the marriage had no access to each other at any time when he could have been begotten. **(CLAT 2013)**

**Facts:** X and Y married on January 15, 1995. Y, the wife of X, never left her parental home and never went to her husband's home. A boy was born to Y on July 15, 1995. For the Court:

(*a*) There shall be a conclusive proof that the boy is the legitimate son of X

(*b*) There shall be no conclusive proof that the boy is the legitimate son of X

(*c*) There shall be a conclusive proof that the boy is the illegitimate son of X

(*d*) There shall be no evidence at all.

**Directions (Q. 174) :** Given below is a statement of legal principle followed by a factual situation. Apply the principle to the facts given below and select the most appropriate answer. **(AILET 2014)**

**174. LEGAL PRINCIPLE :** A person shall not be guilty of contempt of court on the ground that he has published any matter which interferes with or obstructs or tends to obstruct the course of justice in connection with any civil or criminal proceeding pending at the time of the publication, if at that time he had no reasonable grounds for believing that the proceeding was pending.

**FACTUAL SITUATION :** X delivered a lecture at the local Rotary Club in favour of an accused who is prosecuted for assaulting a police officer. He said that the accused is a victim of prevailing corruption in the judiciary and he knows that the accused is going to be punished by the court for being honest. Is X guilty of contempt of court?

**DECISION :**

(*a*) No, not guilty of contempt of court.

(*b*) Yes, guilty of contempt of court.

(*c*) Yes, X has dishonoured judiciary.

(*d*) No, X is an honest man.

**175.** Who was among the following honoured with Arjun Award in Chess for the year 2013? **(CLAT 2014)**

(*a*) Kavita Chahal

(*b*) Parimarjan Negi

(*c*) Ronjan Sodhi

(*d*) Abhijeet Gupta

**Directions (Q. 176 - 188) :** *This section consists of thirteen (13) questions.*

Each question consists of legal propositions/principles (hereinafter referred to as 'principle') and facts. These principles have to be applied to the given facts to arrive at the most reasonable conclusion. Such principles may or may not be true in the real sense, yet you have to conclusively assume them to be true for the purposes of this section. In other words, in answering the following questions, you must not rely on any principles except the principles that are given herein below for every question. Further, you must not assume any facts other than those stated in the question. The objective of this section is to test your interest towards study of law, research aptitude and problem solving ability even if the 'most reasonable conclusion' arrived at may be unacceptable for, any other reason. It is not the object of this section to test your knowledge of law. **(CLAT 2014)**

**176. Principle:** A gift comprising both existing and future property is void as to the latter.

**Facts:** 'X' has a house which is owned by him. He contracted to purchase a plot of land adjacent to the said house, but the sale (of the plot of land) in his favour is yet to be completed. He makes a gift of both the properties (house and land) to 'Y'.

Under the afore-mentioned circumstances, which of the following derivations is CORRECT?

(*a*) Gift of both the properties is valid

(*b*) Gift of both the properties is void

(*c*) Gift of house is void, but the gift of the plot of land is valid

(*d*) Gift of house is valid, but the gift of the plot of land is void

**177. Principle:** Caveat emptor, i.e. 'let the buyer beware' stands for the practical skill and judgment of the buyer in his choice of goods for purchase. It is the business of the buyer to judge for himself that what he buys has its use and worth for him. Once bought, and if the buy is not up to his expectations, then he alone is to blame and no one else.

**Facts:** For the purpose of making uniform for the employees, 'A' bought dark blue coloured cloth from 'B', but did not disclose to the seller (B') the specific purpose of the said purchase. When uniforms were prepared and used by the employees, the cloth was found unfit. However, the cloth was fit ' for a variety of other purposes (such as, making caps, boots and carriage lining, etc).

Applying the afore-stated principle, which of the following derivations is CORRECT as regards remedy available to 'A' in the given situation?

(*a*) 'A' (the buyer) would succeed in getting some remedy from 'B' (the seller)

(*b*) 'A' (the buyer) would not succeed in getting any remedy from 'B' (the seller)

(*c*) 'A' (the buyer) would succeed in getting refund from 'B' (the seller)

(*d*) 'A' (the buyer) would succeed in getting a different variety of cloth from 'B' (the seller), but not the refund

**178. Principle:** The transferor of goods cannot pass a better title than what he himself possesses.

**Facts:** 'X' sells a stolen bike to 'Y' buys it in good faith.

As regards the title to bike, which of the following derivations is CORRECT? **(CLAT 2014)**

(*a*) The real owner cannot get back the bike from 'Y'

(*b*) 'Y' will get no title, as transferor's (X's) title was defective

(*c*) 'Y' will get good title, as he is a *bona fide* buyer

(*d*) 'Y' will get good title, as has not committed any wrong (stolen the bike)

**179. Principle:** Interference with another's goods in such a way as to deny the latter's title to the goods amounts to conversion, and thus it is a civil wrong. It is an act intentionally done inconsistent with the owner's right, though the doer may not know of, or intend to challenge, the property or possession of the true owner.

**Facts:** 'R' went to a cycle-stand to park his bicycle. Seeing the stand fully occupied, he removed a few bicycles in order to rearrange a portion of the stand and make some space for his bicycle. He parked his bicycle properly, and put back all the bicycles except the one belonging to 'S'. In fact, 'R' was in a hurry, and therefore, he could not put back S's bicycle. Somebody came on the way and took away S's bicycle. The watchman of the stand did not take care of it assuming that the bicycle was not parked inside the stand. 'S' filed a suit against 'R' for conversion.

Which of the following derivations is CORRECT?

(*a*) 'R' could not be held liable for the negligence of the watchman

(*b*) 'S' would succeed because R's act led to the stealing of his bicycle

(*c*) 'S' would not succeed because 'R' did not take away the bicycle himself

(*d*) 'S' would not succeed because R's intention was not bad

**180. Principle:** One of the essential conditions for a marriage between any two persons to be solemnized under the Special Marriage Act, '1954 is that at the time of the marriage the male has completed the age of twenty-one years and the female the age of eighteen years. If the said condition is not fulfilled such a marriage is null and void.

**Facts:** 'A', a male aged twenty-two years, proposes to many 'B', a female aged sixteen years, at Delhi in the month of June 2014 under the Special Marriage Act, 1954. **(CLAT 2014)**

(*a*) Marriage between 'A' and 'B' can be legally solemnized under the Special Marriage Act, 1954

(*b*) Marriage between 'A' and 'B' cannot be legally solemnized under the Special Marriage Act, 1954

(*c*) Marriage between 'A' and 'B' can remain valid for A under the Special Marriage Act, 1954

(*d*) None of the above is correct

**181. Principle:** Under the Hindu Marriage Act, 1955 either the husband or the wife can move a petition for a decree of divorce on the ground of desertion. The term 'desertion' means desertion of the petitioner by the other party to the marriage for a continuous period of not less than two years immediately preceding the presentation of the petition, without reasonable cause and without the consent or against the wish of such party and includes the willful neglect of the petitioner by the other party to the marriage, and its grammatical variations and cognate expressions shall be construed accordingly. It is also said that desertion is withdrawal not from a place but from a state of things.

**Facts:** Rohan, a technocrat, went to US in January 2011 for pursuing his higher studies for a period of three years. In fact, Rohan went to US with the consent of his wife Basanti, who stayed at her parents' home, and with a promise of his return to India upon the completion of his studies. From US he has quite often been in touch with his wife. Subsequently, Rohan has got a job there in US and he wishes to take his wife. She refuses to go to US and, in the meanwhile, she files a petition for a decree of divorce on the ground of desertion by her husband.

(*a*) Rohan's three year stay in US in the above context can amount to a ground of desertion for divorce.

(*b*) Rohan's three year stay in US in the above context cannot amount to a ground of desertion for divorce.

(*c*) Rohan's continued stay after three years can amount to a ground of desertion for divorce.

(*d*) Basanti's refusal can amount to a ground of desertion for divorce.

**182. Principle:** Under the Hindu Adoptions and Maintenance Act, 1956, no person shall be capable of being taken in adoption unless he or she is a Hindu, he or she not already been adopted, he or she has not been married, unless there is a custom or usage applicable to the parties which permits persons who are married being taken in adoption, and he or she has not completed the age of fifteen years, unless there is a custom or usage applicable to the parties which permits persons who have completed the age of fifteen years being take in adoption.

**Facts:** Vijay being natural father had given Tarun, a boy aged 10 years, in adoption to Manoj in March 2010 in accordance with the Hindu Adoptions and Maintenance Act, 1956. In May 2012 Manoj gave Tarun in adoption to Sanjay. Subsequently in December 2013, Sanjay gave Tarun in adoption to Vijay.

(*a*) Adoption of Tarun by Sanjay is valid

(*b*) Adoption of Tarun by Vijay is valid

(*c*) Adoption of Tarun by Manoj is valid

(*d*) None of the above adoptions is valid

**183. Principle:** Under copyright law copyright subsists in original literary works also. A literary work need not be of literary quality. Even so prosaic a work as an index of railway stations or a railway guide or a list of stock exchange quotations qualifies as a literary work if sufficient work has been expended in compiling it to give it a new and original character.

**Facts:** Michael works hard enough, walking down the streets, taking down the names of people who live at houses and makes a street directory as a result of that labour.

(*a*) Michael's exercise in making a street directory is sufficient to justify in making claim to copyright in that work which is ultimately produced

(*b*) Michael's exercise in making a street directory is not enough to justify in making claim to copyright in that work

(*c*) A street directory cannot be enough to be considered as a literary work

(*d*) None of the above statements is correct

**184. Principle:** Where a person fraudulently or erroneously represents that he is authorized to transfer certain immovable property and professes to transfer such property for consideration, such transfer shall, at the option of the transferee, operate on any interest which the transferor may acquire in such property at any time during which the contract of transfer subsists.

**Facts:** 'A', a Hindu who has separated from his father 'B', sells to 'C' three fields, X, Y and Z, representing that 'A' is authorized to transfer the same. Of these fields Z does not belong to 'A', it having been retained by 'B' on the partition; but on B's dying 'A' as successor obtains Z, and at that time 'C' had not cancelled the contract of sale.

(*a*) 'A' can sell Z to a third party

(*b*) 'A' is not required to deliver Z to 'C'

(*c*) 'A' is required to deliver Z to 'C'

(*d*) None of the above statements is correct

**185. Principle:** Under the Transfer of Property Act, 1882 a property must be transferred by one living person to another living person. The Act deals only with transfer of property between living persons.

**Facts:** 'X' wants to transfer his property to the presiding deity in a temple situated within the estate of 'A'.

(*a*) Transfer of property by 'X' will be valid

(*b*) Transfer of property by 'X' will be invalid

(*c*) Transfer of property by 'X' to the presiding deity will become a valid transfer to 'A'

(*d*) None of the above is correct

**186. Principle:** Where there is transfer of ownership of one thing for the ownership of some other thing it is called exchange; while transfer of ownership for consideration of money is called sale, whereas, without consideration it becomes gift.

**Facts:** 'A' transfers his house worth ₹50 Lakhs to 'B' for a shopping building worth the same amount, as consideration, from 'B'. **(CLAT 2014)**

(*a*) The transaction is a gift

(*b*) The transaction is a sale

(*c*) The transaction is an exchange

(*d*) The transaction is a mortgage

**187. Principle:** Strike is a collective stoppage of work by workmen undertaken in order to bring pressure upon those who depend on the sale or use of the products of work; whereas, lock-out is a weapon in the hands of the employer, similar to that of strike in the armoury of workmen, used for compelling persons employed by him to accept his terms or conditions of or affecting employment. While in closure there is permanent closing down of a place of employment or part thereof, in lay-off an employer, who is willing to employ, fails or refuses or is unable to provide employment for reasons beyond his control.

**Facts:** Workmen of a textile factory went on strike as per law, demanding the payment of bonus. Employer of the factory refused to pay any extra allowances, including bonus, and besides he closed down the factory till the strike was stopped.

(a) Act of closing down the factory by the employer amounted to strike

(b) Act of closing down the factory by the employer amounted to lay-off

(c) Act of closing down the factory by the employer amounted to lock-out

(d) Act of closing down the factory by the employer amounted to closure

**188. Principle:** Trade dispute means any dispute between employers and workmen or between workmen and workmen, or between employers and employers which is connected with the employment or non-employment, or the terms of employment or the conditions of labour, of any person. Disputes connected with the non-employment must be understood to include a dispute connected with a dismissal, discharge, removal or retrenchment of a workman.

**Facts:** 'X', an employee in a sugar factory, raised a dispute against 'Y', the employer, through trade union regarding certain matters connected with his suspension from the employment.

(a) Matters connected with suspension can amount to a trade dispute

(b) Matters connected with suspension cannot amount to a trade dispute

(c) Only after dismissal, matters connected with suspension can amount to a trade dispute

(d) None of the above is correct.

**189.** The main objectives of the Judicial Standards Accountability Bill 2010 is

1. Is a legislation which aims to increase accountability of the higher judiciary in India
2. It seeks to devise a new "complaint procedure" under which any person may be able to file a complaint in writing against any judge of a superior court
3. The issue of Judicial Standards must be seen in the context of Article 124(4) of the Constitution
4. The Bill seeks to provide a straight jacketed definition of misbehaviour in Clause 2(k)

Select the correct code: **(AILET 2014)**

(a) 1 and 2 (b) 1, 2 and 3

(c) only 4 (d) 3 and 4

**190.** On April 2013, the Supreme Court held that the modification of a well known cancer fighting drug is not a patentable new invention against which pharmaceutical firm? **(AILET 2014)**

(a) GlaxoSmithkline (b) Novartis

(c) Ranbaxy (d) Cipla

**191.** Criminal Law (Amendment) Act, 2013 does not provide that: **(AILET 2014)**

(a) A rape convict can be sentenced to a term not less than 20 years

(b) Death sentence to repeat offenders

(c) Stalking and voyeurism are bailable offences

(d) Acid attack convicts can get a 10 year jail term

**192.** In India, Uniform Civil Code is applicable in the State of: **(AILET 2014)**

(a) Goa (b) Nagaland

(c) Jammu & Kashmir (d) Maharashtra

**193.** NOTA is introduced in the voting machine as one among the options based on **(AILET 2014)**

(a) Representation of Peoples Act, 1950

(b) Representation of Peoples Act, 1951

(c) Decision of the Supreme Court of India

(d) Direction of the Election Commission

**194.** How many duties are provided under Part - IV A of the Constitution? **(AILET 2014)**

(a) 10 (b) 11

(c) 12 (d) 08

**195.** The Inter State Council has been constituted based on the recommendation of **(AILET 2014)**

(a) Second Administrative Reforms Commission

(b) National Commission to Review the Working of the Constitution

(c) Sarkaria Commission

(d) Punchhi Commission

**196.** Which of the following is not a constitutional body ? **(AILET 2014)**

(a) Finance Commission

(b) State Public Service Commissions

(c) Election Commission

(d) Planning Commission

## Solutions

**1.** c 54% of the Indian territory was constituted to form the Union of States in the year 1947.

**2.** a Indian Parliament is the most powerful legislature with an elaborate set of powers to legislate which extends from regular legislative business to the amendment procedures. The power has been conferred by the Constitution of India.

**3.** a USA being a federal polity, its residuary powers are vested in the Federal government.

**4.** c Nagpur Session 1920: Changes were made in the Constitution of the Congress, in Madras Session: Independence Resolution was passed for the first time, in Calcutta Session of 1928: Gandhiji returned to active politics, in Lahore

Session (1928): slogan of Poorna Swaraj was raised and in Karachi Session of 1930:Resolution of Fundamental Rights and National Economic Policy was made.

**5.** b For determining rights and liabilities in a law suit, the idols of God are considered to be a legal person.

**6.** a Where during the continuance of proceedings, the court finds it necessary to keep the person in custody, it may order to send the accused to judicial custody which in simple terms means that the accused shall be in jail till further orders of the court.

**7.** b As per Article 13 of the Statute of ICJ, the Judges of the Court shall be elected for 9 years and may also be re-elected. There are total 15 Judges in ICJ.

**8.** a A plebiscite or a vote on a ballot question is a direct vote in which an entire electorate is asked to either accept or reject a particular proposal, usually a piece of legislation which has been passed into law by the local legislative body and signed by the pertinent executive official(s). This may result in the adoption of a new constitution, a constitutional amendment, a law, the recall of an elected official or simply a specific government policy. It is a form of direct democracy.

**9.** a Correct answer/option is (*a*) and not (*c*). Vedas are considered to be the oldest treatise amongst the ancient texts on Hindu religion. Smritis were recorded later.

**10.** a None of the given options absolutely qualifies itself to be Muslim religious foundation. Question is ambiguous.

**11.** c Since the government has been entrusted by law to meet the ends of social justice and good governance of the society at large, in this process enforcement through courts becomes an indispensable option.

**12.** d First regular adjudicatory mobile court was inaugurated in Punbanna village of Punjab.

**13.** a Under Dissolution of Muslim Marriage Act, 1939, grounds of dissolution is available to both husband and wife.

**14.** c Adultery under Section 497 of Indian Penal Code has been defines as, whoever has sexual intercourse with a person who is and whom he knows to be the wife of another man, without the consent of that man, is guilty of the offence of adultery. In such case the wife shall not be punishable as an abettor.

**15.** d Once the divorced wife gets remarried, the obligation of her ex-husband to maintain her seizes.

**16.** d Default means failure to do something required by law; Delict means a wrongful act; Derelict means a thing which is thrown away or disowned by its owner and Dictum is the observation of a Judge in a law suit.

**17.** c India has signed repatriation treaty or extradition treaty with various other nations which makes it possible to secure the presence of accused in India wherein he can be tried as per the Indian criminal justice system.

**18.** d In wake of Gulf War 1991 Saddam Hussein and his government inhumanely crushed rebellions by Shia Muslims and by Kurds in the north of the country at a massive scale.

**19.** c High sea is the open ocean, esp. that not within any country's jurisdiction. As per maritime law, the extent of high sea commences beyond 200 Nautical Miles. Amongst the given options, none of them seems to be correct. Firstly because, as per maritime law, the extent of territorial waters is always measured in Nautical Miles (NM) but the given options are either in miles or in kilometres. The correct answer 'would' have been C if, instead of 200 Kms, it would have been mentioned as 200 Nautical Miles.

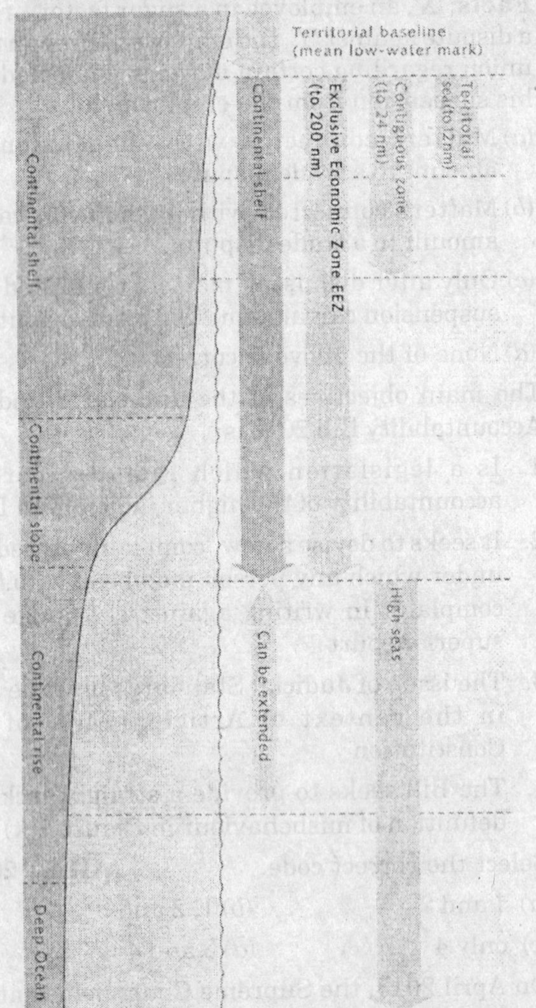


**20.** a Gandhiji was called to Bar by Inner Temple in London.

**21.** d The principle in law is 'ignorantia legis non excusat' i.e. ignorance of law is no excuse and the same applies to the given facts.

**22.** a Criminal Procedure Code mandates that if a death sentence is passed by a Court of Session (Sessions Judge), it must essentially be confirmed by the concerned High Court.

**23.** a Peoples Union for Democratic Rights V. Union of India: [AIR 1982 SC 1473] Also known as the Asiad Workers case. The Supreme Court held that non payment of minimum wages is a type of forced labour.

**24.** a A partial protection against double jeopardy is a Fundamental Right guaranteed under Article 20 (2) of the Constitution of India. This states that ""No person shall be prosecuted and punished for the same offence more than once". This provision enshrines the concept of *autrefois convict*, that no one convicted of an offence can be tried or punished a second time.

**25.** d The doctrine of colourability is the idea that when the legislature wants to do something that it cannot do within the constraints of the constitution, it colours the law with a substitute purpose which will still allow it to accomplish its original goal.

**26.** c Shah Commission was a commission of inquiry appointed by Government of India in 1977 to inquire into all the excesses committed in the Indian Emergency (1975 - 77). It was headed by Justice J.C. Shah, a former chief Justice of India.

**27.** a Section 25 of Negotiable Instrument Act 1881, the expression" public holiday" includes Sundays and any other day declared by the Central Government, by notification in the Official Gazette, to be a public holiday.

**28.** b In Islam, iddah or iddat is the period of waiting which a woman must observe after the death of her spouse or after a divorce, during which she may not marry another man.

**29.** d Under Section 140 of Motor Vehicle Act, the minimum compensation to be awarded in death cases id ₹50,000/.

**30.** b Malfeasance means committing an unlawful act; Malingerer means one who falsely pretends to be sick; Misdemeanor constitutes minor offences and Misfeasance means improper performance of duty.

**31.** c A finder of a thing doesn't becomes its owner.

**32.** c A right's definition doesn't include of element of advantage.

**33.** b Although the custom represents common conscience but this feature of custom has no bearing of it being 'force of law'.

**34.** c Since the height of 6 feet is not sufficient air space in consideration of the problem. Therefore A will not succeed because the hoarding being at a height of 6ft.was not causing obstruction in the ordinary use of A's house.

**35.** b The ultimate object in both the cases is to obtain possession through the order of the court. In both the cases, facts and cause of action are same and suit cannot be initiated again on the same fact.

**36.** a In absence of any relevant Principle, (*a*) is the most appropriate answer as it was Sunanda's car.

**37.** b Here the illegal activity is the act of stealing. The driver was oblivious of this fact and his 'right to action' for getting injured ensues as a result of his legal act of driving. Driver was acting in complete bonafide belief.

**38.** c The principle states that the court should not take notice of trifles, the fact speaks about a matter which is a trifle and of a trivial nature for the Court to entertain the same.

**39.** c Apply the principle over facts. The Limitation Act can only bar the filing of suit but it can not bar the right of Sohan to recover his debt. After the limitation period ends Rohan makes a part payment; this brings forth the commencement of a fresh period of limitation. As the cause of action starts from the date of part payment, recovery of debt would be allowed.

**40.** c Since A failed to pay the income tax, he can not take the plea that he was not aware about his legal duty to pay the tax. Law presumes that every citizen should be aware about the existing law in force.

**41.** d The National Development Council (NDC) or the Rashtriya Vikas Parishad is the apex body for decision making and deliberations on development matters in India, presided over by the Prime Minister. It was set up on August 6, 1952 to strengthen and mobilize the effort and resources of the nation in support of the Plan, to promote common economic policies in all vital spheres, and to ensure the balanced and rapid development of all parts of the country. The Council comprises the Prime Minister, the Union Cabinet Ministers, Chief Ministers of all States or their substitutes, representatives of the union territories and the members of the Commissions. It is an extra-constitutional and non-statutory body. Its status is advisory to planning commission but not binding.

**42.** c The President, as soon as practicable after taking office, by writing signed by him, allocate among the members of the Cabinet (including himself if he so desires) the portfolios of Ministers of Finance, Minister of Foreign Affairs, Minister of Communications and Transportation, Minister of Resources and Development, Minister of Social Welfare, Minister of Public Works and such other portfolios as may be necessary or desirable for giving to a member of the Cabinet the primary responsibility for any Department or function of government. The President has the primary responsibility for any Department or function of government in respect of which no allocation of a portfolio is for the time being in force.

**43.** c The question is ambiguous. In 2004, the Government of India declared that languages that met certain requirements could be accorded the status of a "Classical Language in India". Languages thus far declared to be Classical are Tamil (in 2004), Sanskrit (in 2005), Kannada and Telugu (in 2008).

**44.** d Each Security Council member has one vote. Decisions on procedural matters are made by an affirmative vote of at least nine of the 15 members. Decisions on substantive matters require nine votes, including the concurring votes of all five permanent members. This is the rule of "great power unanimity", often referred to as the "Veto" power.

**45.** d In Champaran, a district in state of Bihar, tens of thousands of landless serfs, indentured laborers and poor farmers were forced to grow indigo and other cash crops instead of the food crops which was necessary for their survival. Now in the throes of a devastating famine, the British levied an oppressive tax which they insisted on increasing in rate. Without food and without money, the situation was growing progressively unlivable and the peasants in Champaran revolted against indigo plant cultivation in 1914 (at Pipra) and 1916 (Turkaulia) and Raj Kumar Shukla took Mahatma Gandhi to Champaran and the Champaran Satyagraha began. Gandhi arrived in Champaran with a team of eminent lawyers.

**46.** b RTI is a statutory right. As the name suggests, a statutory right is one which is conferred by a statute i.e. a legislative enactment. Consumer Protection Act is another example of statutory right as it confers certain rights to consumers.

**47.** a In 1997, the state of Tamil Nadu first passed laws related to ragging Subsequently, a major boost to anti-ragging efforts was given by a landmark judgement of the Supreme Court of India in May 2001,in response to a Public Interest Litigation filed by the Vishwa Jagriti Mission. The Ministry of Human Resources Development (MHRD), following a directive by the Supreme court, appointed a seven member panel headed by ex-CBI director Dr. R. K. Raghavan to recommend anti-ragging measures. The Supreme Court of India based on the recommendations dated May 16, 2007 makes it obligatory for academic institutions to file official First Information Reports with the police in any instance of a complaint of ragging. This would ensure that all cases would be formally investigated under criminal justice system, and not by the academic institutions own ad-hoc bodies.

**48.** a India has signed repatriation treaty or extradition treaty with various other nations which makes it possible to secure the presence of accused in India wherein he can be tried as per the Indian criminal procedure code.

**49.** c If there arises any question over the validity of the Money Bill, the decision of the Speaker of Lok Sabha is final. The Speaker duly certifies the Bill as Money Bill because this Bill passes through special procedures (Article 109 of the Constitution of India.)

**50.** c The correct answer should be (c) instead of 'B'. The proposal for enhancing reservation for women in Panchayats from the present 33 per cent to 50 per cent has been approved with the provision being applicable to all seats filled through direct election, office of chairpersons and of offices reserved for SC/ST. The provision of reserving half the seats for women in Panchayats applies to the total number of seats filled by direct election.

**51.** b The time immediately following the Question Hour and laying of papers and before any listed business is taken up in the House has come to be popularly known as 'zero hour'. As it starts around 12 noon, this period is euphemistically termed as 'zero hour'. For raising matters during the so-called zero hour in Lok Sabha, members give notice before 10 a.m. everyday to the Speaker stating clearly the subject which they consider to be important and wish to raise in the House. The maximum duration of the zero hour is unspecified.

**52.** d The earliest codified laws (civil and criminal) that defined and demarcated for the first time in India during 335-345 AD was followed during Gupta reign.

**53.** c Jawahar Lal Nehru introduced "Objective Resolution" in the Constituent Assembly in the on December-13, 1946. This resolution as accepted by the Constituent Assembly forms the basis of Indian political system. It also guided the constitution drafting process.

**54.** b Money Bill can be introduced in the State Legislature only with the prior recommendation of the Governor.

**55.** c Following is the criteria followed by Election Commission of India to recognize a political party in a State, (A) that such party – has been engaged in political activity for a continuous period of five years; and has, at the last general election in that State to the House of the People, or, to the Legislative Assembly of the State, returned - either

(i) at least one member to the House of the People for every twenty-five members of that House or any fraction of that number from that State; or

(ii) at least one member to the Legislative Assembly of that State for every thirty members of that Assembly or any fraction of that number;

(B) that the total number of valid votes polled by all the contesting candidates set up by such party at the last general election in the State to the House of the People, or as the case may be, to the Legislative Assembly of the State, is not less than six per cent of the total number of valid votes polled by all the contesting candidates at such general election in the State.

**56.** d As per the Model Code of Conduct For Guidance of Political Parties & Candidates, issued by Election Commission of India, electioneering has to be stopped in a constituency 48 hrs. before the closing hour of polling.

**57.** b The driver of the car was acting in the bona fide belief, he was not knowing that the car is stolen and therefore he can still exercise his right to sue.

**58.** b If a widow is remarried when the 'question of succession' is opened then she cannot claim property.

**59.** d The principle 2 talks about consumers, which includes both Ram and Tom. Now by applying principle 4 to the facts of the case it is clear that it is the manufacturer "Coca-Cola Company" who is responsible for the quality of the products, which contained nitric acid. The seller, being unaware of the quality of the product will definitely not be liable for selling unmarketable goods.

**60.** c Crucial here is Principle 2- that although you can use the water flowing below your land, you cannot have ownership over it. This means that you cannot deprive others of their right to the water even if it is flowing under the land owned by you. The question of demolishing the tank does not arise due to 2 reasons: one, because of principle 3, any construction on your land belongs to you, and second, the neighbours had given him an option to share the water instead of being forced to demolish it.

**61.** d Here, you have to read the facts very, very carefully, and then apply plain and simple logic, and nothing else! The facts tell you that she was thoroughly checked before being allowed to enter the examination hall, so the search must have been conclusive, and this satisfies reason (ii). However, reason (i) is the most appropriate, because it tells you what can be reasonably and correctly presumed, and what cannot.

**62.** b A simple rule of syllogism is to deduce reasoning from a major premise and connect it to a minor premise. Here, the major premise is the first sentence of the problem which talks of an obligation for all motor vehicle to have a third party insurance. The Second sentence by way of merely defining what qualifies as motor vehicle becomes the minor premise in the problem. Now, by way of connecting the minor premise to that of the major premise it is clear that vehicles without mechanical devices are not motor vehicles and thus, vehicles which are not motor vehicles falls out of the purview of "All Motor vehicles" (as given in the first sentence). Hence it is deduced that vehicles which are not motor vehicles need not have Third Party Insurance.

**63.** a The answer should be (*a*), because it has the most direct link with the principle.

**64.** b Manusmriti

Manismriti (translated "Laws of Manu") is regarded as the foundational work of Hindu law and ancient Indian society, compiled and written in c.200 CE in India. It is attributed to the legendary first man and lawgiver, Manu. It is also known as Mânava-Dharmaúâstra.

**65.** c Conflict of laws

The term Conflict of law describes the body of law of each country or state that is designed to resolve problems arising from the differences between legal system of different countries.

(*a*) Civil law- seeks to resolve non-criminal disputes such as disagreements over the meaning of contracts, property ownership, divorce, child custody, and damages for personal and property damage.

(*b*) Local laws- laws passed by a legislative body and intended to apply only to one part of the area under its jurisdiction.

(*d*) Common law- laws developed by judges through decisions of courts.

**66.** a Earnest money.

When a-buyer makes an offer to buy residential real estate, he/she generally signs a contract and pays a sum acceptable to the seller by way of earnest money.

(*b*) Advance- is the part of a contractually due sum that is paid or received in advance for goods or services, while the balance included in the invoice will only follow the delivery.

(*c*) Interest- amount paid by a borrower of assets to the owner as a form of compensation for the use of the assets. It is most commonly the price paid for the use of borrowed money, or money earned by deposited funds.

(*d*) Solatium- is a form of compensation for emotional rather than physical or financial harm.

**67.** a Co-heirs

(*b*) Coparceners- two or more people inherit a title equally between them.

(*c*) Successors- a person who succeeds another in an office, position, or the like.

(*d*) Joint owners- two parties owning property together.

**68.** a State of Maharashtra v. Prafull B. Desai

**69.** c Public Accounts Committee: The Public Accounts Committee (PAC) is a committee of selected members of Parliament, constituted by the Parliament of India, for the auditing of the expenditure of the Government of India. The PAC is formed every year with a strength of not more than 22 members of which 15 are from Lok Sabha, the lower house of the Parliament, and 7 from Rajya Sabha, the upper house of the Parliament.

**70.** d MRTP Act

The Monopolies and Restrictive Trade Practices Act, 1969 was promulgated with the aim to prevent concentration of economic power to the common detriment, provide control for control of monopolies and probation of monopolistic, restrictive and unfair trade practices, and protect consumer interest. It has been replaced by Competition Act, 2002.

**71.** c Imperfect right

Imperfect right is a right recognized by law, but could not be enforceable due to its form or some other defects

(*a*) Universal right- One which is correspondent to legal duty which is common to all purposes, conditions, or situations:

(*b*) Perfect right- one which is correspondent to legal duty, and not only recognized by law but also enforced by law.

(*d*) Fundamental rights- is defined as basic human freedoms which every citizen has the right to enjoy.

**72.** a Geneva Convention.

The Geneva Conventions are rules that apply in times of armed conflict and seek to protect people who are not or are no longer taking part in hostilities. These include the sick and wounded of armed forces on the field, wounded shipwrecked members of armed forces at sea, prisoners of war and civilians. This convention comprises of four treaties, and three additional protocols that establish the standards of international law for the humanitarian treatment of the victims of war. The singular term Geneva Convention denotes the agreements of 1949, negotiated in the aftermath of the Second World War (1939–45), which updated the terms of the first three treaties (1864, 1906, 1929), and added a fourth treaty.

**73.** d Negotiable Instruments Act

Negotiable Instruments Act, 1881 defines "Public Holiday" in the explanation of its Section 25.

**74.** a Conjugal right.

**75.** b Died without making a will.

**76.** c Perjury.

**77.** a Posthumous.

**78.** b Power of Attorney.

(*a*) Affidavit-A written statement confirmed by oath or affirmation, for use as evidence in court.

(*c*) Will- A document in which a person specifies the method to be applied in the management and distribution of his estate after his death.

(*d*) Declaration- a paper subscribed by a grantee of property, acknowledging that he holds it in trust for the purposes and upon the terms set forth.

**79.** a Parole

The conditional release of a person convicted of a crime prior to the expiration of that person's term of imprisonment, subject to both the supervision of the correctional authorities during the remainder of the term and a resumption of the imprisonment upon violation of the conditions imposed.

(*b*) Amnesty- An official pardon for people who have been convicted of political offences.

(*c*) Discharge- a release, as of a person held under legal restraint.

(*d*) Pardon- The action of an executive official of the government that mitigates or sets aside the punishment for a crime.

**80.** b 1945

India was a founding member of United Nations in October 1945, despite it being a British colony. India, Canada, the Union of South Africa, New Zealand and Australia were all British colonies but were given independent seats in the UN General Assembly.

**81.** c Litigant

A party to a lawsuit; "plaintiffs and defendants are both litigants".

(*a*) Accused- a person charged with a crime.

(*b*) Plaintiff- A person who brings a case against another in a court of law.

(*d*) Complainant- Synonymous to Plaintiff

**82.** a Justice M. M. Punchi

The commission was constituted on April 28, 2007 to take a fresh look at the relative roles and responsibilities of the various levels of government and their inter-relations. The terms of reference of the Justice Punchhi Commission are comprehensive and are a step forward from the Justice Sarkaria Commission set up in 1983.

Justice Punchi was the 28th Chief Justice of India from January 18, 1998 until his retirement on October 9, 1998.

(*b*) Justice Nanavati- The Justice G..T. Nanavati commission was established by the Indian Government in 2000 to investigate the 1984 anti-sikh riots.

(*c*) Justice Bharucha- Justice Sam Piroj Bharucha was the 30th Chief Justice of India, serving from November 2001 until his retirement in 2002. Justice Bharucha is responsible for many significant legal decisions. He was part of the five judge constitutional panel which unanimously ruled on the 2001 dismissal of J. Jayalalitha as Chief Minister of Tamil Nadu. It was the first and only such dismissal of a chief minister in India's history.

(*d*) Justice Kuldip Singh- Acted as the Chair person of the Delimitation Commission set up on 12th July, 2002. This commission is established by Government of India under the provisions of the Delimitation Commission Act. The main task of the commission is to redraw the boundaries of the various assembly and Lok Sabha constituencies based on a recent census.

**83.** d Accomplice.

**84.** a Land Revenue.

**85.** b Bhopal.

National Judicial Academy is a government funded training institute established on August 17, 1993 under the Societies Registration Act, 1860. This institution focuses on training judicial officers working in the Supreme Court and High Courts during their services.

**86.** b Obligation.

**87.** b Infanticide.

**88.** c Sacrilege.

**89.** d Absconder.

**90.** a Warning.

(*b*) An injunction- A court order by which an individual is required to perform, or is restrained from performing, a particular act

(*c*) Writ- An order issued by a court requiring that something be done or giving authority to do a specified act.

(*d*) Certiorari- A type of writ wherein a higher court issues an order to review the decision and proceedings in a lower court and determine whether there were any irregularities.

**91.** b Wakfs

Wakf Board is a statuary body constituted under the Wakf Act to administer, control and manage the Wakf properties comprising of any moveable or immoveable property which is pious , religious, or charitable. Charity is the dominant feature of a Wakf. The creator of a Wakf is called Wakif. The income of the Wakf Property is utilized for charity, assistance to the poor and needy, maintenance of the Mosque, Dargah, Graveyards, Khankah, educational institution, hospitals. A Wakf is managed by the mutawalli or a managing committee or directly by the Wakf Board.

**92.** — High sea is the open ocean, esp. that not within any country's jurisdiction. As per maritime law, the extent of high sea commences beyond 200 Nautical Miles from the coastline. Amongst the given options, none of them seems to be correct. Firstly because, as per maritime law, the extent of territorial waters is always measured in Nautical Miles (NM) but the given options are either in miles or in kilometres. The correct answer 'would' have been C if, instead of 200 Kms, it would have been mentioned as 200 Nautical Miles

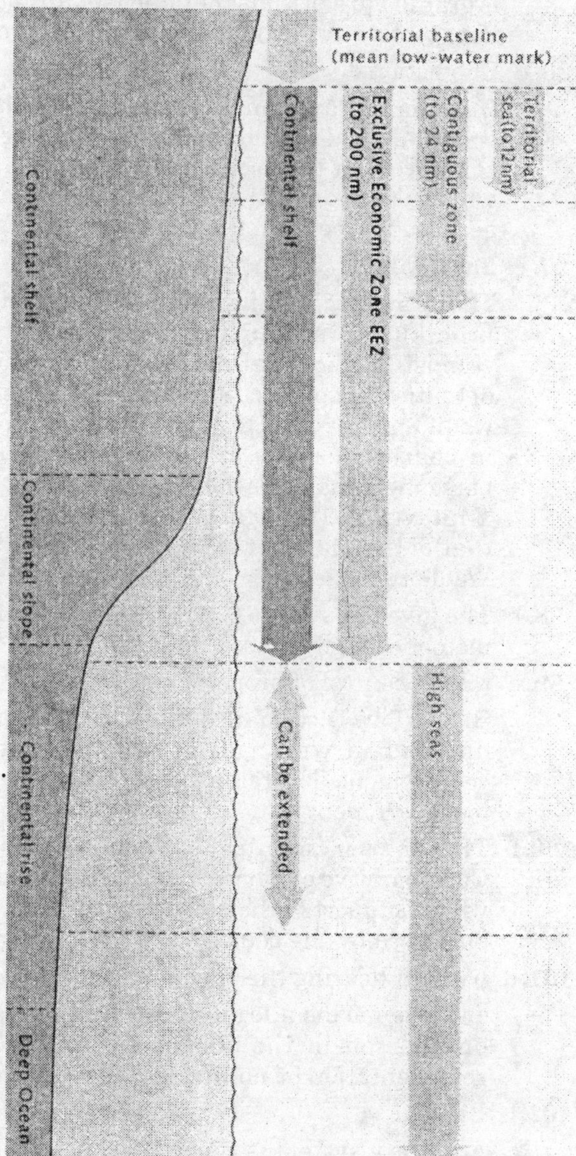

**93.** a liability on property

An encumbrance means a legal liability on property. It constitutes a burden on the title which diminishes the value of the land. It may be a mortgage or a deed of trust or a lien of an easement. An encumbrance, thus, must be a charge on the property. It must run with the property.

**94.** d Conjugal Right

Conjugal means belonging to marriage. Conjugal Rights include fellowship of husband and wife, and the right of each to the company, society, co-operation, affection and aid of the other.

**95.** b Parole.

Parole is a legal sanction that lets a prisoner leave the prison for a short duration, on the condition that s/he behaves appropriately after release and reports back to the prison on termination of the parole period. While parole is granted to a prisoner detained for any offence irrespective of the duration of imprisonment.

**96.** c Conviction.

In criminal law, conviction is the result of a criminal trial which ends in a judgment or sentence that the accused is guilty as charged whereas an acquittal formally certifies the accused is free from the charge of an offense.

**97.** c Mutawalli

The term waqf literally means "confinement and prohibition" or causing a thing to stop or standstill. The legal meaning of Waqf is the detention of specific thing in the ownership of waqif and the devoting of its profit or products in charity of poors or other good objects. A person,who manages the Waqf property is called "Mutawalli". The legal position of Mutawalli is that of the Manager or Superintendent of the Waqf properties.

**98.** b The given answer is C but it should be B. Ipso facto means, by reason of that fact.

**99.** c taking control of property temporarily

Blacks Law Dictionary defines Requisition as a demand in writing, or formal request or requirement. The taking or seizure of property by government.

**100.** b The answer should be (*b*) instead of (C). Corroborative evidence means those evidences which supports other evidence already taken on record by the court.

**101.** d without hearing the opponent

*ex parte* means a legal proceeding brought by one person in the absence of and without representation or notification of other parties.

**102.** b British.

A unitary system is governed constitutionally as one single unit, with one constitutionally created legislature. The UK is an example of a unitary system.

**103.** a male and a Christian female.

The Quran explicitly allows Muslim men to marry chaste women of the People of the Book, a term which includes Jews and Christians.

**104.** c Under the United States Constitution, the power of *judicial review* i.e subjecting the actions of the legislature and the executive to the scrutiny of the Judiciary, is not explicit and has been inferred from the structure, provisions, and history of the Constitution. After the Marbury v/s. Madison case judicial review was exercised by the American judiciary under Article III of the constitution of America.

**105.** b The part of the judgment which possesses authority is called Ratio Decidendi. It is the rationale for a decision passed by the Court and as a general rule, binding on courts of lower and later jurisdiction unlike obiter dicta which is a remark or an observation make by the Judge which does not necessarily form part of the Court's decision.

**106.** a Division of powers between the central and provincial government.

The Act, passed during British India, provided a dual form of government (a "dyarchy") for the major provinces. In each such province, control of some areas of government were given to the Provincial Council. All other areas of government remained under the control of the Viceroy.

**107.** a Paid by an employer in respect of the fringe benefits provided or deemed to have been provided.

Employees get many benefits at the cost of the employers. Where the benefits are usually enjoyed collectively by the employees and cannot be attributed to individual employees, they shall be taxed in the hands of the employer, and this tax is called Fringe Benefit Tax. An employer is liable for fringe benefit tax even if they do not have any income which is chargeable to the income tax. The fringe benefit tax was abolished in the 2009.

**108.** d Ram can never be a prosecutor because in criminal cases prosecution is always brought on behalf of the state.

**109.** d The Code of Criminal Procedure is the main legislation on procedure for administration of substantive criminal law in India.

**110.** c Forensic science.

Forensic Science is the application of a broad spectrum of sciences to answer questions of interest to a legal system. This may be in relation to a crime or a civil action.

**111.** a A judge other than a Chief Justice

The word Puisne means junior and is used to distinguish High Court judges from senior judges sitting at the Court of Appeal. The term is only used in relation to judges of a superior court, *e.g.*, the Supreme Court or the High Court of a jurisdiction. The equivalent term in the United States is Associate Justice.

**112.** a Within the powers

*It is a latin term which implies "within the powers" as opposed to Ultra vires* which means "beyond the powers" If an act requires legal authority and it is done with such authority, it is characterised in law as *intra vires* If it is done without such authority, it is *ultra vires*.

**113.** b Legal problems in the form of imaginary cases, argued by two opposing students before a bench pretending to be a real court. A moot court is an extracurricular activity at law schools in which participants take part in hypothetical court proceedings, which usually involves drafting briefs (or memorials) and participating in oral argument.

**114.** b Religiously neutral.

The Scheduled Castes (SCs), also known as the Dalit, and the Scheduled Tribes (STs) are two groupings of historically disadvantaged people that are given express recognition in the Constitution of India are not based on any religion.

**115.** a Justice Gyan Sudha Mishra.

The first woman to be appointed to the Supreme Court was Justice Fatima Beevi in 1987. She was later followed by Justices Sujata Manohar(1994), Ruma Pal (2000) and Gyan Sudha Mishra(2010).

**116.** c Movable property.

An article of personal property; any species of property not amounting to a freehold or fee in land. All property which is not real estate is said to be chattel.

**117.** d Plaintiff, defendant.

Plaintiff is the term used for the party who initiates a law suit. Defendant is the party who has been formally charged or accused by the plaintiff. The party who appeals a court's decision is called the Appellant. Accused is the person who is charged with a crime. A person who initiates legal proceedings against someone is called a prosecutor.

**118.** c Approver.

The term "approver" is usually applied to a person, supposed to be directly or indirectly concerned in or privy to an offence to whom a pardon is granted under Section 306 of the Code with a view to securing his testimony against other persons guilty of the offence.

**119.** b Geneva

The International Labour Organization (ILO) is an agency of the United Nations that deals with labour issues pertaining to international labour standards and decent work for all. Its headquarters are in Geneva, Switzerland.

**120.** c All irrespective of religion.

The Act applies to the citizens per se and its applicability is not restricted to any religion.

**121.** b Kerala High Court.

The state of Kerala was formed by the States Reorganisation Act, 1956. which also created the Kerala High Court. The Act also extended the jurisdiction of the Kerala High Court to Lakshadweep.

**122.** d Decides international crimes.

ICJ is the primary judicial organ of the United Nations. Its main functions are to settle legal disputes submitted to it by states and to provide advisory opinions on legal questions submitted to it by duly authorized international organs, agencies, and the UN General Assembly.

**123.** b Banks were nationalised under a law during the Prime Ministership of Mrs. Indira Gandhi. *R.C.Cooper Vs. Union of India (1970) (the Bank Nationalisation Case).*

**124.** d Property of an intellectual.

Rest options are a form of intellectual property which is given protection under various laws.

**125.** a The multinational corporation.

The Competition Act, 2002 was introduced, inter alia, to repeal MRTP Act and prevent activities that have an adverse effect on competition in India.

**126.** a Justice R.C. Lahoti.

Law Commission of India is an executive body established by an order of the Government of India. Its major function is to work for legal reform. Justice B. P. Jeevan Reddy was the Chairman of the Commission from 2000-01 followed by Justice M. Jagannadha Rao who served as the Chairman of the Commission until 2007 after which Justice A. R. Lakshmanan took over.

**127.** a Wajahat Habibullah was the first chief Information Commissioner of India.

**128.** d R.T.I. stands for Right To Information

**129.** b Trust.

A fiduciary is someone who has undertaken to act for and on behalf of another in a particular matter in circumstances which give rise to a relationship of trust and confidence. Such relationships could be termed as fiduciary relationships.

**130.** d 10th December.

The date was chosen to honor the United Nations General Assembly's adoption and proclamation, on 10 December 1948, of the Universal Declaration of Human Rights (UDHR), the first global enunciation of human rights and one of the first major achievements of the new United Nations.

**131.** b Applying the first part of the rule, Elizabeth is entitled to keep the ear ring unless the true owner claims it. In the absence of any claim, airport cannot presume ownership of the ear ring just because it was found on its property (applying third part of the principle). Therefore, selling of the ear ring by the airport is wrong and Elizabeth should be compensated for the same. Now, out of option (*b*) and (*c*) , both of which talk about compensating Elizabeth, the reasoning of the former is more appropriate as it relates with the principle given in the question.

**132.** b Elizabeths travelling in a particular class is not relatable. The first part of the principle talks about "finding of an unattended object" and this without any qualifications or limitations.

**133.** d The right to confiscation can be exercised on any object that is unattended and is found by the Airlines Staff. However, when Elizabeth finds the ear ring, as per the principle, she has the right to keep it till the true owner claims it back. Therefore, applying the same explanation as in 161, in the absence of any claim by the true owner, the air line is liable to compensate Elizabeth for selling the ear ring further.

**134.** d Only fixtures are deemed to be sold with the land. But as per Rule B, the carpet was never attached to the land, and therefore was not a fixture. Khaleeda had the right to remove the carpet after sale.

**135.** b Door was a fixture and was attached to the house and therefore cannot be removed as per Rule A. Out of options (*b*) and (*d*), the former is more appropriate as it relates to the principle.

**136.** b For the fixture to be deemed to be sold with the land, it is relevant to know if it amounts to fixture or not. Applying Rule B, the test would be to see if the moveable thing was merely placed on the building and were fixed to it or not.

**137.** d Applying the new rule, carpet also become a fixture and thus could not have been removed. Hence the case would be in favour of Gurpreet in both the situations.

**138.** c X can be prosecuted because he was ignorant about the new notification that was passed and the law says that ignorance of law is non-excusable.

**139.** a Price is set by market forces of demand and supply.

**140.** a Regardless of a contract, a non-gratuitous act must be compensated.

**141.** a Imperative theory advocates "Law is a command of the sovereign".

**142.** c Rafique Bhikan V/S Union of India

**143.** d An agreement with an unlawful object is against public policy and hence, unlawful.

**144.** b One of the members in his private capacity informed Ramu about the decision of the body. Hence, Ramu cannot claim damages

**145.** d Concurrent List = Australia

Rule of Law = Britian

Directive Principles of State Policy = Ireland.

Procedure established by Law = Japan

**146.** b The answer given in CLAT key sheet is D but it should be B. A Bill regarding admission or establishment of a new State, formation of new States and alteration of areas, boundaries or names of the existing ones (Article 2,3 and 4) requires to be passed by simple majority.

**147.** b Begar was a system of forced labour in India wherein the labour did involuntary work without payment . But now it is prohibited under Article 23 of the Constitution of India.

**148.** b Ecomarkor Eco mark is a certification mark issued by the Bureau of Indian Standards (the national standards organization of India) to products conforming to a set of standards aimed at the least impact on the ecosystem.

**149.** a An environmental impact assessment (EIA) is an assessment of the possible positive or negative impacts that a proposed project may have on the environment, consisting of the environmental, social and economic aspects.

**150.** d The Chipko movement or Chipko Andolan is a movement that practiced the Gandhian methods of satyagraha and non-violent resistance, through the act of hugging trees to protect them from being felled. Sunderlal Bahuguna, took a 5,000-kilometre trans-Himalaya foot march in 1981–83, spreading the Chipko message to a far greater area.

**151.** b Two persons are said to be related by 'half blood' where the male parent/ancestor is the same, but the female parent/ancestor, through whom each makes a claim, is different.

**152.** b Pactasuntservanda is a latin term which means agreements must be kept. It is the principle in international law which says that international treaties should be upheld by all the signatories. The rule of pactasuntservanda is based upon the principle of good faith.

**153.** b Plea-Bargaining can be defined as Pre-Trial procedure whereby a bargain or deal is struck between the accused of an offence and the prosecution with the active participation of the trial judge. In India, the system of plea bargaining is in its experiment stage.

**154.** b Standing or parading near a business or government office usually with signs of protest or claims in labor disputes or public policy controversies (peace marches to pro- or anti-abortion advocates). Picketing is constitutionally guaranteed as free speech, but in some cases it may be limited by court order to prevent physical combat, blocking of entrances or threats to the public safety.

**155.** a Cyber terrorism is the use of Internet based attacks in terrorist activities, including acts of deliberate, large-scale disruption of computer networks, especially of personal computers attached to the Internet, by the means of tools such as computer viruses. The Information Technology Act The aims to provide for the legal framework so that legal sanctity is accorded to all electronic records and other activities carried out by electronic means.

**156.** c Extradition comes into play when a person charged with a crime under state statutes flees the state. Extradition between nations is usually based on a treaty between the country where the accused is currently located and the country seeking to place him or her on trial for an alleged crime.

**157.** d **Intergenerational Equity**: The present generation does not destroy or deplete resources or significantly alter anything; rather it saves resources for future generations and preserves the same level of quality in all aspects of the environment.

**Sustainable Development**: Right to wholesome environment is a fundamental right protected under Article 21 of the Constitution of India. But Development comes through industrialization, which in turn the main factor behind the degradation of environment. Hence, we follow the doctrine called 'Sustainable Development', i.e. there must be balance between development and ecology.

**158.** d Justice Verma Committee was constituted to recommend amendments to the Criminal Law so as to provide for quicker trial and enhanced punishment for criminals accused of committing sexual assault against women. The Committee submitted its report on January 23, 2013.

**159.** c A margin of 30% has been provided to students for miscellaneous contingencies (as was the case here). As per the university rules no student is allowed to appear in exams under any condition without attending minimum 70% of classes. Hence, Anand's challenge will fail.

**160.** * All the options state that Komal cannot succeed. But, if we read option "D" as "Komal can succeed..". then it would be closest to the principle because Komal was the owner of the watch. Since Sonal did not had the ownership of the watch and mere possession, she could not have transferred ownership to anyone including Monal.

**161.** c S never went to court with clean hands.Had he fulfilled his part of the agreement and then asked for relief, he would have had succeeded but strike cannot be granted as a valid excuse.

**162.** c It does not matter whether Hari had taken proper precautions or not in the present scenario. Damage was due to an act (Carrying on a chemical and fertilizer industry) of Hari and damages need to be paid.

**163.** * There is no nexus between the Principle and facts because the principle is silent upon the legal implications after making a gift. However, if we have to go ahead with the options given, option "C" would be considered the best out of the lot.

**164.** c It has been made clear in the principle that acting in a cinematographic film will not be considered as 'work', it cannot be protected under copyright law.

**165.** a Since government is party to this agreement, they are the first owner of the copyright in the work, as there was no agreement to the contrary by the professor.

**166.** b Only a certain kind of restricted rights have been granted to B, that of distribution that to in Mumbai only. Hence the agreement is in the nature of license.

**167.** * Although this question involves application of Legal Knowledge contrary to the instructions given, still "C" would be the most appropriate answer

**168.** * There is insufficiency in the principle and facts provided. The principle only state what can be registered as a trademark but is silent on the legal technicality of registration. Hence, there is no conclusive answer which can be arrived at.

**169.** a The principle states that where more than one person have made a complaint for the grant of compulsory license, it shall be granted to that complainant 'only' who would best serve the interests of general public. The principle shows that the license will be granted to only one complainant.

**170.** b The principle mentions that any police officer not below the rank of sub-inspector shall be competent to 'seize' without warrant in case any copyright infringement is found. In the facts given, the Superintendent of Police (SP) made an 'arrest' which as per the principle is not within his power.

**171.** a When A gave Rs 10 lacs to B, C was already dead making the condition impossible to be carried out.

**172.** a All the alleged facts are relevant in this case. There is no fact which does not hold importance with respect to the fact scenario.

**173.** * The facts are insufficient in the given question. Based on various assumptions, options A, B and C, all three can be possible correct choices.

**174.** b X is guilty of contempt of court because his comment was made in connection with a criminal proceeding which he knew was pending in a court of law. More over, he has made categorical remarks on the judiciary and questioned the veracity of the judicial process.

**175.** d The Arjuna Awards were instituted in 1961 by the government of India to recognize outstanding achievement in National sports. The award carries a cash prize of Rs. 500,000, a bronze statuette of Arjuna and a scroll.

**176.** d The principal clearly states that gift of uture property would be void. Since the sale of adjacent land has not been completed, it would be considered a future property with respect to 'X' gifting it away.

**177.** b 'A' should have been cautious and had tested out whether the cloth he is purchasing is fit for his purpose i.e. for making uniforms or not. Since he has not done that, therefore he cannot succeed in getting a remedy against the Seller.

**178.** b Since 'X' himself had obtained the bike illegally, he cannot sell the bike as an owner and therefore 'Y' has no title.

**179.** b The Action of R(taking out S's bike and not putting it back again) led to S's bike getting stolen away and hence amounts to conversion.

**180.** b since B (16) is not of legal age (18), she is not eligible to marry under the special marriage Act.

**181.** b Rohit went to US with a reason and with the consent of his wife. This cannot amount to desertion.

**182.** c As per the principle a person once given in adoption cannot be given in adoption again. Hence first adoption i.e. adoption of Tarun by Manoj is valid.

**183.** a Sufficient work has been expended Michael in making the street directory and hence it can be copyrighted.

**184.** c Since Z (property) was transferred to A after B's death, such transfer shall, at the option of the transferee($c$), operate on any interest which the transferor($a$) may acquire in such property at any time during which the contract of transfer subsists.

**185.** b Since the deity is not a living person, X cannot transfer his property as this would be invalid according to the principle.

**186.** c There is no money involved and transfer of one property is being done in lieu of other. According to the principle this transaction is exchange.

**187.** c Closing down of the factory by the employer till the strike ends would amount to lock-out.

**188.** a Suspension is a dispute between workmen and employer which is connected with employment and non-employment of the workmen. Hence it can be brought under the purview of trade disputes.

**189.** d Judicial Standards Accountability Bill, 2010 aims to bring in standards for judicial accountability. It does not give a definition of misbehavior.

**190.** b It was held in the case of Novartis v. Union of India that the modification of well known cancer fighting drug is not patentable.

**191.** c Under the Criminal Law (Amendment) Act, 2013 stalking and voyeurism are non bailable offences.

**192.** a Uniform Civil Code is applicable in the state of Goa.

**193.** c NOTA or none of the above was introduced in the voting machine as result of a Decision of the Supreme Court

**194.** b Part IV-A of the constitution contains 11 duties

**195.** c The inter state council has been constituted on the recommendation of the Sarkaria Commission.

**196.** d Planning Commission is not a constitutional body. It was created by an executive order of the Government of India.

■■

# GENERAL KNOWLEDGE

# 1

# CONSTITUTION AND POLITY

**1.** The Supreme Court of India enjoys:

(*a*) Only original jurisdiction.

(*b*) Only appellate jurisdiction.

(*c*) Only advisory jurisdiction.

(*d*) All the above types of jurisdictions.

**(NLUD 2008)**

**2.** A money bill can be introduced in Parliament by:

(*a*) The Finance Minister alone.

(*b*) Any minister.

(*c*) Any member of Parliament.

(*d*) Any member of the ruling party.

**(NLUD 2008)**

**3.** In the U.S.A., residuary powers or reserve of powers are:

(*a*) Left to the federal government.

(*b*) Left to the States.

(*c*) Not defined properly.

(*d*) Given to local government. **(NLUD 2008)**

**4.** Members of Rajya Sabha are not associated with

1. Public Accounts Committee.

2. Estimates Committee.

3. Committee on Public Undertakings.

(*a*) 1 and 2 (*b*) 3

(*c*) 2 (*d*) 1 and 3 **(NLUD 2008)**

**5.** According to the Constitution, amendments cannot be proposed in either House to

(*a*) The Annual Financial Statement.

(*b*) Appropriation Bill.

(*c*) Demand for Grants.

(*d*) All of the above. **(NLUD 2008)**

**6.** Which article of our Constitution provides that the State shall make effective position for securing right to work?

(*a*) Article 41.

(*b*) Article 39.

(*c*) Article 21.

(*d*) Article 45. **(NLUD 2008)**

**7.** Who of the following does not constitute an exception for 'equality before law' (Article 14)?

(*a*) The Foreign Diplomats.

(*b*) The Prime Minister.

(*c*) The Governor.

(*d*) The President. **(NLUD 2008)**

**8.** The Constitution of India Describes India as:

(*a*) A Quasi-Federal Country.

(*b*) Union of States.

(*c*) A federation of States and Union territories.

(*d*) None of the above. **(NLUD 2008)**

**9.** Which one of the following Fundamental Rights has been the subject of maximum litigation and controversies?

(*a*) Right to Property.

(*b*) Right to Equality.

(*c*) Right to Freedom of Religion.

(*d*) Right to Freedom.

**(NLUD 2008)**

**10.** The Fundamental Duties of the Indian Citizens:

(*a*) Formed a part of the original Constitution

(*b*) Were added by the Forty-Second Amendment

(*c*) Were added by the Forty-Fourth Amendment

(*d*) Were defined by the Parliament through a law enacted during the emergency

**(NLUD 2008)**

**11.** What is contained in the Eleventh Schedule to the Constitution of India?

(*a*) Forms of oath of affirmation.

(*b*) Provisions regarding disqualification on grounds of defection.

(*c*) Items in respect of which Panchayats shall have powers and authority to function as institutions of Self-Government.

(*d*) Items on which Municipalities shall have powers and authority to function as institutions of Self-Government.

**(NLUD 2008)**

**12.** The strength of the Council of Ministers:

(*a*) Has been fixed by the Constitution.

(*b*) Has been fixed by the Parliament under Representation of People's Act, 1950.

(*c*) Is determined by the Prime Minister keeping in view the requirement of the time.

(*d*) Is determined by the President. **(NLUD 2008)**

**13.** The advisory Powers of the Supreme Court of India imply that:

(*a*) it renders advice to the Government of India on all constitutional matters.

(*b*) it renders advice to the Prime Minister on legal matters.

(*c*) it renders advice to the President on question of law or fact which is of public importance.

(*d*) it has power to render advice to all the above persons. **(NLUD 2008)**

**14.** The provision under which the Supreme Court can grant 'special leave' to appeal against decisions of lower courts and tribunals is contained in:

(*a*) Section 10 of Supreme Court Rules.

(*b*) Article 136 of Indian Constitution.

(*c*) Article 226 of Indian Constitution.

(*d*) Article 139 of Indian Constitution.

**(NLUD 2008)**

**15.** There were .......... Articles and ........... Schedules in the draft of the Constitution of India.

(*a*) 315, eight

(*b*) 319, nine

(*c*) 327, ten

(*d*) 317, nine **(NLU-D 2009)**

**16.** Almost all political parties participated and contributed their share in the formation of Indian Constitution. Which one of the following party was not associated with the Constituent Assembly?

(*a*) Communist Party of India.

(*b*) Indian National Congress.

(*c*) Hindu Mahasabha.

(*d*) Scheduled Castes Freedom. **(NLU-D 2009)**

**17.** The expenditure from the Consolidated Fund of India for which the approval of Parliament is not necessary according to the Constitution of India, is called

(*a*) Charged Expenditure.

(*b*) Extra Expenditure.

(*c*) Special Provision Fund.

(*d*) None of these. **(NLU-D 2009)**

**18.** How many official languages are mentioned in Schedule VIII to the Constitution of India

(*a*) 18 (*b*) 22

(*c*) 14 (*d*) 28 **(NLU-D 2010 )**

**19.** The first President of the Constituent Assembly of India established in 1946 was

(*a*) Rajendra Prasad. (*b*) Sachidananda Sinha.

(*c*) Rajagopalachari. (*d*) B.R. Ambedkar.

**(NLU-D 2010 )**

**20.** The Constitution of India was adopted on

(*a*) 26 November 1949. (*b*) 26 January 1950.

(*c*) 26 November 1947. (*d*) 26 January 1949.

**(NLU-D 2010 )**

**21.** If the Anglo-Indian Community is not adequately represented in the election, the President can nominate to Lok Sabha from that community

(*a*) not more than 5. (*b*) not more than 2.

(*c*) not more than 1. (*d*) none.

**(NLU-D 2010)**

**22.** The right to vote in India is a

(*a*) Constitutional right.

(*b*) Legal right.

(*c*) Fundamental right.

(*d*) None. **(NLU-D 2010)**

**23.** The state having the maximum number of seats in Rajya Sabha is

(*a*) Maharastra. (*b*) Uttar Pradesh.

(*c*) Tamil Nadu. (*d*) Andhra Pradesh.

**(NLU-D 2011)**

**24.** Rajya Sabha members are elected for a period of

(*a*) 5 years. (*b*) 4 years.

(*c*) 2 years. (*d*) 6 years.

**(NLU-D 2011)**

**25.** The maximum number of nominated members to Lok Sabha is

(*a*) One.

(*b*) Two.

(*c*) Three.

(*d*) No one can be nominated. **(NLU-D 2011)**

**26.** The constitutional advisor to the Constituent Assembly was

(*a*) Rajendra Prasad.

(*b*) B. N. Rau.

(*c*) B. R. Ambedkar.

(*d*) Kamat. **(NLU-D 2011)**

**27.** Name the Finance Minister who presented the highest number of Budgets in the Parliament so far:
(*a*) P. Chidambaram.
(*b*) Morarji Desai.
(*c*) Manmohan Singh.
(*d*) T.T. Krishnamachari. **(CLAT 2008)**

**28.** Which of the following is considered as bulwark of personal freedom?
(*a*) Mandamus.
(*b*) Habeus Corpus.
(*c*) Certiorari.
(*d*) Quo Warranto. **(CLAT 2008)**

**29.** Article 1 of Indian Constitution defines India as
(*a*) Federal State.
(*b*) Unitary State.
(*c*) Union of State.
(*d*) Quasi-Federal State. **(CLAT 2008)**

**30.** Which is the highest body that approves Five Year Plans in India ?
(*a*) Parliament.
(*b*) Planning Commission.
(*c*) National Development Council.
(*d*) Council of Ministers. **(CLAT 2008)**

**31.** Plea bargaining is
(*a*) permissible in India.
(*b*) illegal in India.
(*c*) mandatory in India.
(*d*) allowed subject to the permission of the court. **(CLAT 2008)**

**32.** The person appointed by two parties to settle a dispute is known as:
(*a*) Judge. (*b*) Arbitrator.
(*c*) Solicitor. (*d*) Conciliator. **(CLAT 2008)**

**33.** Right to travel is a fundamental right under
(*a*) Article 19 of the Constitution.
(*b*) Article 21 of the Constitution.
(*c*) Article 14 of the Constitution.
(*d*) None of the above. **(CLAT 2008)**

**34.** Legal aid for an accused is
(*a*) fundamental right.
(*b*) legal right.
(*c*) Directive Principles of State Policy.
(*d*) Discretion of State. **(CLAT 2008)**

**35.** The members of Constituent Assembly who framed the Constitution were:
(*a*) directly elected by the people.
(*b*) indirectly elected.
(*c*) nominated.
(*d*) appointed by political parties. **(CLAT 2008)**

**36.** Ambedkar acted in Constituent Assembly as:
(*a*) President of the Assembly.
(*b*) Chairman of the Drafting Committee.
(*c*) the leading spokesman of weaker sections.
(*d*) a strong defender of fundamental rights. **(CLAT 2008)**

**37.** In India, international treaties are ratified by
(*a*) Parliament. (*b*) President.
(*c*) Prime Minister. (*d*) The Union Cabinet. **(CLAT 2008)**

**38.** It is a constitutional requirement that the Parliament shall meet at least
(*a*) twice in a year. (*b*) thrice in a year.
(*c*) once in a year. (*d*) none of the above. **(CLAT 2008)**

**39.** Governor of a State can be removed by
(*a*) impeachment by State Legislature.
(*b*) the President.
(*c*) by the State Cabinet.
(*d*) the Union Government at the request of the Chief Minister. **(CLAT 2008)**

**40.** Sovereignty under the Constitution belongs to
(*a*) The Parliament.
(*b*) The People.
(*c*) The Supreme Court.
(*d*) The President along with Parliament. **(CLAT 2008)**

**41.** The Supreme Court upheld Mandal Commission Report in
(*a*) *Bommai v. Union of India.*
(*b*) *Indra Sawhney v. Union of India.*
(*c*) *Unnikrishan v. Union of India.*
(*d*) *Maneka Gandhi v. Union of India.* **(CLAT 2008)**

**42.** Under our Constitution, right to property is
(*a*) fundamental right.
(*b*) basic structure of the Constitution.
(*c*) Constitutional right.
(*d*) a mere legal right. **(CLAT 2008)**

**43.** Right to education emanates from:

(*a*) right to culture and education under Articles 29 and 30

(*b*) right to equality under Article 14

(*c*) freedom of speech & expression under Article 19

(*d*) right to life and personal liberty under Article 21 **(CLAT 2008)**

**44.** The Monopolies and Restrictive Trade Practices Act was repealed by:

(*a*) Competition Act

(*b*) Consumer Protection Act

(*c*) Foreign Trade (Development and Regulation) Act

(*d*) Liberalization Policy of the Government **(CLAT 2008)**

**45.** Lok Adalats have been created under:

(*a*) Legal Services Authority Act

(*b*) Arbitration and Conciliation Act

(*c*) Administration of Justice Act

(*d*) None of the above **(CLAT 2008)**

**46.** The Third World leader who has been defying the U.S.A:

(*a*) Fidel Castro (*b*) Hugo Chavez

(*c*) Robert Mughabe (*d*) Hu Jintao **(CLAT 2008)**

**47.** Indo-Pak summit between Parvez Musharraf and Atal Bihari Bajpayee was held in 2001 at

(*a*) Delhi (*b*) Shimla

(*c*) Agra (*d*) Mumbai **(CLAT 2010)**

**48.** Who was the founder editor of"Kesari"?

(*a*) Lala Lajpat Rai

(*b*) Bal Gangadhar Tilak

(*c*) Gopal Krishna Gokhle

(*d*) Dadabhai Naoroji **(CLAT 2010)**

**49.** Identify the main principle on which the Parliamentary system operates?

(*a*) Responsibility of executive to legislature

(*b*) Supremacy of democracy

(*c*) Rule of law

(*d*) Supremacy of the constitution **(CLAT 2010)**

**50.** Which of the following is the national song of India?

(*a*) Vande Mataram...

(*b*) Jana gana mana adhinayak...

(*c*) Ye mera chaman, ye mera chaman...

(*d*) Sarejahari se achchha... **(CLAT 2010)**

**51.** Who is chairing the Joint Parliamentary Committee (JPC) on the 2G Spectrum allocation issue?

(*a*) Murli Manohar Joshi

(*b*) A Raja

(*c*) M. Thambi Durai

(*d*) P.C. Chacko **(CLAT 2011)**

**52.** Justice P.C. Phukan Commission of Inquiry was constituted to enquire into which of the following incidents?

(*a*) Clashes between Nagas and Lepchas in Nagaland on 14th August 2008

(*b*) Clashes between Bodos and Muslims in Northern Assam's Udalguri district on August 14th 2008

(*c*) Clashes between Assamese and Bengalis in Guwahati on August 14th 2008

(*d*) None of the above **(CLAT 2011)**

**53.** Under whose premiership was the Women's Reservations Bill (to secure quotas for women in Parliament and state legislative assemblies) first introduced in Parliament?

(*a*) Rajiv Gandhi

(*b*) HD Deve Gowda

(*c*) Atal Bihari Vajpayee

(*d*) Manmohan Singh **(CLAT 2011)**

**54.** Which of the following report brought out the 2G spectrum scam?

(*a*) CBI report

(*b*) WikiLeaks

(*c*) CAG report

(*d*) None of the above **(CLAT 2011)**

**55.** Which one of the following was not awarded a portion of the contested land by the judgment of the Allahabad High Court in 2010 pertaining to the Ayodhya dispute?

(*a*) Nirmohi Akhada

(*b*) Sunni Central Board of Waqfs

(*c*) Rashtriya Swayamsevak Sangh

(*d*) Bhagwan Sri Ram Lala Virajman **(CLAT 2011)**

**56.** The Right of Children to Full and Compulsory Education Act 2009 requires private schools to ensure that ___ percent of their students come from weaker sections and disadvantaged groups?

(*a*) 2 (*b*) 15

(*c*) 25 (*d*) 40 **(CLAT 2011)**

**57.** Srikrishna Committee, which recently submitted its report, was constituted for which of the following issues?

(*a*) Mumbai bomb blast case

(*b*) Malegaon blast case

(*c*) Telengana issue

(*d*) 2G Spectrum corruption issue **(CLAT 2011)**

**58.** Who presides over the joint sitting of both houses of Parliament?

(*a*) Speaker of Lok Sabha

(*b*) President

(*c*) Chairman of Rajya Sabha

(*d*) Prime Minister **(CLAT 2012)**

**59.** Supreme Court recently declared 'Salva Judum' unconstitutional. What is 'Salva Judam'?

(*a*) A terrorist outfit

(*b*) An armed civilian group formed to combat Maoists

(*c*) A money-chain business

(*d*) Custom of killing a girl for inter-caste marriage in the name of honour **(CLAT 2012)**

**60.** Which of the following is/are listed among the Directive Principles in Part IV of the Constitution of India ?

I. Equal pay for equal work

II. Uniform Civil Code

III. Small family norm

IV. Education through mother tongue at primary level

(*a*) I, II and Ill (*b*) l and II

(*c*) II and III (*d*) I, II and IV

**(AILET 2013)**

**61.** Who decides whether a Member of Parliament is subject to any disqualification?

(*a*) President

(*b*) Speaker

(*c*) Election Commissioner

(*d*) None of the above **(AILET 2013)**

**62.** Regarding No-Confidence Motion

(*a*) it is expressed against an individual minister or council of ministers

(*b*) no grounds have to be set out for the motion

(*c*) not less than 100 members have to support it for the Speaker to grant leave for its introduction

(*d*) it is always brought against the Prime Minister

**(AILET 2013)**

**63.** Who is responsible for the registration of voters in India?

(*a*) Government

(*b*) Voters

(*c*) Political parties

(*d*) Election Commission **(AILET 2013)**

**64.** The Constitution (One Hundred Seventeenth Amendment) Bill, 2012 makes provisions regarding **(CLAT 2013)**

(*a*) Reservation in matters of promotions for Scheduled Castes and Scheduled Tribes

(*b*) Reservation in matters of appointments for Scheduled Castes and Scheduled Tribes

(*c*) Reservation in matters of appointments and promotions for Scheduled Castes and Scheduled Tribes

(*d*) None of the above

**65.** The number of High Courts in India is

(*a*) 18 (*b*) 24 **(CLAT 2013)**

(*c*) 21 (*d*) 28

**66.** The chairman of Fundamental Rights Sub-Committee of the Constituent Assembly was **(CLAT 2013)**

(*a*) Rajendra Prasad (*b*) B.R. Ambedkar

(*c*) Jawaharlal Nehru (*d*) J.B. Kripalani

**67.** The Environment Protection Act was passed by the Parliament of India in the year

(*a*) 1976 (*b*) 1986 **(CLAT 2013)**

(*c*) 1996 (*d*) 2006

**68.** How many High Courts are there in India as on January 2014? **(AILET 2014)**

(*a*) 18 (*b*) 21

(*c*) 28 (*d*) 24

**69.** The Parliament of India voted to remove

(*a*) Justice V. Ramaswami **(AILET 2014)**

(*b*) Justice P. Dinakaran

(*c*) Justice Soumitra Sen

(*d*) None

**70.** The maximum penalty that can be imposed by CIC / SIC under the Right to Information Act, 2005 is **(AILET 2014)**

(*a*) ₹ 5,000 (*b*) ₹ 25,000

(*c*) ₹250 (*d*) 10,000

**71.** How many members can be nominated to the Rajya Sabha by the President ? **(AILET 2014)**

(*a*) 10 (*b*) 20

(*c*) 12 (*d*) 16

**72.** Who among the following was the first Law Minister of India ? **(AILET 2014)**

(*a*) Jawaharlal Nehru

(*b*) Maulana Abul Kalam Azad

(*b*) Dr. B.R. Ambedkar

(*d*) T. Krishnamachari

**73.** Which of the following statements is INCORRECT about Fundamental Duties under the Constitution of India? It shall be the duty of every citizen of India — **(CLAT 2014)**

(*a*) To uphold and protect the sovereignty, unity and integrity of India.

(*b*) To strive towards excellence in all spheres of individual and collective activity so that the nation constantly rises to higher levels of endeavour and achievement.

(*c*) Who is a parent or guardian to provide opportunities for education to his child or, as the case may be, ward between the age of six and fourteen years.

(*d*) To vote in public elections.

**74.** Who was not a Chief Justice of India?

(*a*) Justice M Patanjali Sastri **(CLAT 2014)**

(*b*) Justice KN Wanchoo

(*c*) Justice HR Khanna

(*d*) Justice MN Venkatachaliah

**75.** Who was the first Attorney-General for India? **(CLAT 2014)**

(*a*) CK Daphtary

(*b*) MC Setalvad

(*c*) Niren De

(*d*) LN Sinha

**76.** Which one of the following is NOT correctly matched? **(CLAT 2014)**

United Nations Specialized Agency Headquarters

(*a*) International Civil Aviation Organization Montreal

(*b*) World Trade Organization Geneva

(*c*) United Nations Industrial Development Organization Brussels

(*d*) International Fund for Agricultural Development Rome

**77.** Which one of following offices is held during the pleasure of the President of India? **(CLAT 2014)**

(*a*) Vice-President

(*b*) Governor of a State

(*c*) Chief Justice of India

(*d*) Comptroller and Auditor General of India

**78.** Which one of following is the highest peacetime gallantry award of India? **(CLAT 2014)**

(*a*) Param Vir Chakra (*b*) Ashok Chakra

(*c*) Maha Vir Chakra (*d*) Kirti Chakra

## Solutions

**1.** d The Supreme Court has three types of jurisdiction -:

1. **Original Jurisdiction:** (Article 131): This refers to the power to entertain those disputes which can be initiated at Apex court at first Instance.
2. **Appellate Jurisdiction:** (Article 132-133) This refers to power to entertain those civil and constitutional disputes which any High Court has given 'certificate of appeal' to the Apex Court.
3. **Advisory Jurisdiction:**(Article 143)

   This refers to the power to render an opinion by Supreme Court of India on any question of public importance on being asked by The President of India.

**2.** b Any minister can introduce money bill in the parliament but no Money Bill can be introduced except on the recommendation of the President. It can be introduced in Lok Sabha only, not in Rajya Sabha. Article 110 of Indian Constitution defines money bill. It should be remembered that only speaker of the Lok Sabha certifies whether a bill is money bill or not.

**3.** a In the U.S.A. residuary powers or reserve of powers are vested with states as they have one list i.e. Federal List so all the other subjects fall under the ambit of state legislations.

**4.** c Estimates Committee does not have any members from Rajya Sabha. It is a convention which has been model on the lines with Westminster Model.

**5.** d As per our constitution, amendments regarding the Annual Financial Statement, Appropriation Bill and Demand for Grants cannot be proposed in either House.

**6.** a Article 41of our Constitution provides that the State shall make effective position for securing right to work.

**7.** a The Foreign Diplomats does not constitute an exception for 'equality before law' mentioned under article 14 of the Constitution of India.

**8.** b The Constitution of India Describes India as a union of states. (Article 1 of the Constitution of India).

**9.** b Right to Equality is a fundamental right, which has been the subject of maximum litigation and controversies.

**10.** b The Fundamental Duties of the Indian Citizens were added by the Forty-Second Amendment in they year 1976 which obliged them morally to perform mentioned duties therein.

**11.** c Eleventh Schedule to the Constitution of India contain Items in respect of which Panchayats shall have powers and authority to function as institutions of Self-Government.

**12.** a The strength of the Council of Ministers has been fixed by the constitution. Article 164 of the Constitution of India. The Constitution (91st Amendment) Act, 2003, which limits the size of all ministries in India, comes into force on July 7, 2004. This Act stipulates that the strength of a council of ministers should not exceed 15 percent of the total number of members in the Lok Sabha (in case of the central government) or the relevant state assembly. An exception has been made only for smaller states such as Sikkim, Mizoram and Goa where the strength of the assembly is 40 or less. There, the state government can have a maximum of 12 ministers.

**13.** c The advisory Powers of the Supreme Court of India (mentioned under *Article* 143 of the Constitution.) imply that it renders advice to the President on question of law or fact, which is of public importance.

**14.** b Under article 136 of Indian Constitution, the Supreme Court can grant 'special leave' to appeal against decisions of lower courts and tribunals.

**15.** a There are currently 448. Articles and 12 Schedules in the Constitution of India.

**16.** c Hindu Mahasabha did not participated and contributed it's share in the formation of Indian Constitution.

**17.** a The expenditure from the Consolidated Fund of India for which the approval of Parliament is not necessary, according to the Constitution of India, is called charged Expenditure. (Article 112 of the Constitution of India.)

**18.** b In Schedule VIII to the Constitution of India 22 official languages have been listed. Recently there is a motion in the parliament for inclusion of one more language "bhojpuri" into that list.

**19.** b Sachidananda Sinha was the first President of the Constituent Assembly of India which was established in the year 1946.

**20.** a The Constitution of India was adopted on 26 November 1949.

**21.** b If the Anglo-Indian Community is not adequately represented in the election, the President can nominate not more than 2 members to Lok Sabha from that community.

**22.** a The right to vote in India is a constitutional right. Article 326 of the Constitution of India provides the mandates adult suffrage, which means that every person who is a citizen of India and who is not less than 18 years of age can vote.

**23.** b Uttar Pradesh largest state in India in terms of territory and also has maximum number of seats in Rajya Sabha.

**24.** d The member of Rajya Sabha are elected for the period of 6 year. Rajya Sabha is a permanent House and is not subject to dissolution. However, one-third Members of Rajya Sabha retire after every second year

**25.** b Two members of the Anglo-Indian Community are nominated by the President in the lock Sabha.

**26.** b B. N. Rau was the constitutional advisor to the Constituent Assembly.

**27.** b Former Prime Minister Morarji Desai. Morarji Desai presented the maximum number of times. He held the finance portfolio from 1959-64, 1967-70 and between 1977 and 1979. He is seconded by Current President of India Mr. Pranab Mukherjee who has presented it seven times.

**28.** b Article 32 of the Constitution of India empowers Supreme Court of India to issue five kinds of Writs for enforcement of fundamental rights viz. Prohibition, Habeas Corpus, Certiorari, Mandamus, Quo Warranto.

**29.** c Article 1 of Indian Constitution defines India as an 'Union of States'.

**30.** c National Development Council (NDC) was setup in 1951 with a view to bringing about a coordination of plans between the Central Ministers and the State Governments. The Prime Minister of India heads it.

**31.** d Plea Bargaining was dealt by the 144th report of Law Commission of India and was included through amendment in 2005 which came force in 2006.

**32.** b Arbitrator is the term used to describe the person appointed by two parties to settle a dispute.

**33.** b In Menka Gandhi case, it was held that right to travel outside India is included under Article 21 of the Constitution of India.

**34.** a The right to legal aid is recognized under article 21 of the Constitution of India. (Hussainara Khantoon Case).

**35.** b The members of Constituent Assembly who framed the Constitution were indirectly elected.

**36.** b B. R. Ambedkar was the Chairman of the Drafting Committee in the Constituent Assembly.

**37.** a Parliament is the Sovereign body of India. The Legislative powers solely vest in the legislature unless it falls under exceptions mentioned in Indian Constitution.

**38.** a It is a constitutional requirement that the Parliament shall meet at least thrice in a year.

**39.** b The Governor of a State can be removed by The President of India.

**40.** b The Sovereignty under the Constitution belongs to the people.

**41.** b The Supreme Court upheld Mandal Commission Report in Indra Sawhney v/s. Union of India.

**42.** c The Indian Constitution does not recognize property right as a fundamental right. In the year 1977, the 44th amendment eliminated the right to acquire, hold and dispose of property as a fundamental right. However, in another part of the Constitution, Article 300 (A) was inserted to affirm that no person shall be deprived of his property save by authority of law.

**43.** d Right of Children to Free and Compulsory Education Act, 2009 has been notified recently. The apex court upheld the constitutional validity of the Act and directed all schools, including privately run schools, irrespective of the board they are affiliated to, to admit from this academic year (2012-13) at least 25% students from socially and economically backward families. These students will be guaranteed free education from class I till they reach the age of 14.

**44.** a The Competition Act has been enacted in the year 2002. The Competition Commission's chairperson is presently Mr. Ashok Chawla.

**45.** a Legal Aid scheme was first introduced by Justice P.N. Bhagwati. Legal Services Authority Act 1987 was introduced keeping in mind Article 39A of the Constitution of India which provides that "State shall secure that the operation of the legal system promotes justice on a basis of equal opportunity, and shall in particular, provide free legal aid, by suitable legislation or schemes or in any other way, to ensure that opportunities for securing justice are not denied to any citizen by reason of economic or other disability.

**46.** a Fidel Castro defied the United States of America.

**47.** c Indo-Pak 2001 summit was held in Agra.

**48.** b Kesari is a newspaper founded in 1881 by LokmanyaBalGangadharTilak, a prominent leader of the Indian Independence movement. Bal GangadharTilak used to run his two newspapers, the Kesari, in Marathi and Maratha in English from Kesari Wada. The Wada still has the offices of Kesari, and mementos of Tilak, including his writing desk original letters and documents, and the first India national flag unfurled by Madame Cama.

**49.** a Responsibility of executive to legislature is the principle on which parliamentary democracy operates.

**50.** a Vande Mataram ("I bow to thee, Mother") is a poem from the famed novel Anandamath which was written by Bankim Chandra Chattopadhyay in 1882. It was written in Bengali and Sanskrit. In 1950 (after India's independence), the song's first two verses were given the official status of the "national song" of the Republic of India, distinct from the national anthem of India, Jana GanaMana.

**51.** d P.C. Chacko chaired the Joint Parliamentary Committee (JPC) on the 2G Spectrum allocation issue.

**52.** b Justice P.C. Phukan Commission of Inquiry was constituted to enquire into Clashes between Bodos and Muslims in Northern Assam's Udalguri district on August 14th 2008

**53.** b Under HD Deve Gowda 's premiership the Women's Reservations Bill (to secure quotas for women in Parliament and state legislative assemblies) was first introduced in Parliament.

**54.** d 2-G Spectrum scam was brought from the Central Vigilance Commission (CVC) action on the illegalities in the spectrum allocation.

**55.** c Rashtriya Swayamsevak Sangh was not awarded a portion of the contested land by the judgment of the Allahabad High Court in the year 2010 pertaining to the Ayodhya dispute.

**56.** c The Right of Children to Full and Compulsory Education Act 2009 requires private schools to ensure that 25 percent of their students come from weaker sections and disadvantaged groups. Supreme Court has recently upholded constitutionality of the aforementioned act when a writ petition was filed challenging its' constitutionality in the case *Society for Unaided Private Schools of Rajasthan Vs. Union of India*.

**57.** c Srikrishna Committee submitted its report in the year 2011 on Telengana issue.

**58.** a The Speaker of Lok Sabha presides over the joint parliament session.

**59.** b SalwaJudum (meaning "Peace March" or "Purification Hunt" in Gondi language) refers to a militia in Chhattisgarh, India, which is aimed at countering the Maoist(Naxalite) violence in the region. The militia consisting of local tribal youth receives support and training from the Chhattisgarh state government. On July 5, 2011, the Supreme Court of India declared the militia as illegal and unconstitutional. The court directed the Chhattisgarh government to recover all the firearms given along with the ammunition and accessories. It also ordered the government to investigate all instances of alleged criminal activities of SalwaJudum. The use of SalwaJudum by the government for anti naxal operations was criticized for its violations of human rights, use of child soldiers and poorly trained uneducated youth for counter-insurgency roles.

**60.** b Equal pay for equal work and uniform civil code are listed among Directive Principles in part 4 of the Indian constitution.

**61.** b Speaker of Lok Sabha is authorised under para 8 of the Tenth Schedule to disqualify any member of parliament.

**62.** b Regarding no confidence motion no grounds have been set out for the motion.

**63.** d Election Commission of India is responsible for the registration of voters in India.

**64.** a Reservation in matters of promotions for Scheduled Castes and Scheduled Tribes

**65.** b 24

**66.** d J B Kripalani

**67.** b 1986

**68.** d There are 24 High Courts at the state and union territory level of India which, together with the Supreme Court of India at the national level, comprise the country's judicial system. Each High Court has jurisdiction over a state, a union territory or a group of states and union territories.

**69.** a V. Ramaswami was the Justice of the Supreme Court of India and the first judge against whom impeachment proceedings were initiated in independent India. The only other judge to face impeachment proceedings is Justice "Soumitra Sen" of Calcutta High Court, proceedings against whom were initiated in Rajya Sabha on 17 August 2011.

**70.** b The maximum penalty that can be imposed by CIC/SIC under the Right to Information Act, 2005 is ₹ 25,000.

**71.** c The Rajya Sabha or Council of States is the upper house of the Parliament of India. Membership is limited to 250 members, 12 of whom are nominated by the President of India for their contributions to art, literature, science, and social services.

**72.** c Dr. B.R. Ambedkar was the first Law Minister of Independent India.

**73.** d The right to vote is the fundamental right that has been the source of the most significant Supreme Court litigation. Rights and Duties are inseparable. So as we have Fundamental Rights that we can enjoy there are also some Fundamental Duties that we must follow & do. It is very true that the original constitution didn't contain fundamental duties. The 42nd Constitutional Amendment, 1976, has added it to the constitution.

**74.** c Justice HR Khanna was never a Chief Justice of India.

**75.** b The Attorney General for India is the Indian government's chief legal advisor, and its primary lawyer in the Supreme Court of India. He is appointed by the President of India and holds office during the pleasure of the President. M C Stelvad was the first Attorney-General of India (1950-1963).

**76.** c The United Nations Industrial Development Organization (UNIDO), French/Spanish/Portuguese acronym ONUDI, is a specialized agency in the United Nations system, headquartered in Vienna, Austria.

**77.** b In a public interest litigation it was argued that "a Governor, as the Head of the State, holds a high constitutional office which carries with it important constitutional functions and duties; that the fact that the Governor is appointed by the President and that he holds office during the pleasure of the President does not make the Governor an employee or a servant or agent of the Union Government; and that his independent constitutional office is not subordinate or subservient to the Union Government and he is not accountable to them for the manner in which he carries out his functions and duties as Governor". Thus was submitted "a Governor should ordinarily be permitted to continue in office for the full term of five years; and though he holds office during the pleasure of the President, he could be removed before the expiry of the term of five years, only in rare and exceptional circumstances, by observing the following constitutional norms and requirements."

**78.** b The Ashok Chakra is an Indian military decoration awarded for valor, courageous action or self-sacrifice away from the battlefield. It is the peace time equivalent of the Param Vir Chakra, and is awarded for the "most conspicuous bravery or some daring or pre-eminent valour or self-sacrifice" other than in the face of the enemy. The decoration may be awarded either to military or civilian personnel and may be awarded posthumously.

■■

# 2

# CURRENT AFFAIRS

1. Which country has recently adopted its new National Anthem?
   (a) Israel (b) Bangladesh
   (c) Indonesia (d) Nepal **(NLUD 2008)**

2. Which among the following films has got the 'Swarna Kamal Award' for Best Feature Film in 53rd National Film Awards?
   (a) Parineeta (b) Sringarm
   (c) Iqbal (d) Kaalpurush
   **(NLUD 2008)**

3. The 2009 Nobel Peace Prize was awarded to
   (a) Al Gore (b) Jane Adams
   (c) Mohammed Yunus (d) Barak Hussein Obama
   **(NLUD 2010)**

4. The present Prime Minister of Bangladesh is
   (a) Sheik Hasina. (b) Khaleda Zia
   (c) Ziaur Rahman (d) None **(NLUD 2010)**

5. The President of South Africa at present is
   (a) Nelson Mandela (b) Jacob Zuma
   (c) Thabo Mbeki (d) Kgalema Motlanthe
   **(NLUD 2010)**

6. The former President who committed suicide in May 2009 was
   (a) Kim Jong II of North Korea
   (b) Maumoon Abdul Gayoom of Maldives
   (c) Meghavati Sukarnoputri of Indonesia
   (d) Roh Moo-Hyun of South Korea **(NLUD 2010)**

7. The present Chief Election Commissioner of India is
   (a) T.N. Seshan (b) Navin Chawla
   (c) N.S. Gopalaswami (d) V.S. Sampath
   **(NLUD 2010)**

8. 76 CRPF jawans were killed recently by the Maoist in an ambush near
   (a) Dantewada in Chattisgarh
   (b) Konarkhurd in Bihar
   (c) Gadhchiroli in Maharashtra
   (d) Karimnagar in Andhra Pradesh
   **(NLUD 2010)**

9. The former Chief Election Commissioner to be appointed as a Union Minister is
   (a) Sukumar Sen (b) T. Swaminathan
   (c) R.K. Trivedi (d) M.S. Gill **(NLUD 2010)**

10. The present Committee on Centre-State Relations in India is headed by
    (a) Justice Punnchi (b) Justice Ahmedi
    (c) Justice Anand (d) Justice Ruma Pal
    **(NLUD 2010)**

11. The recently constituted Telangana Committee by the Central Government is headed by
    (a) Justice P.V. Reddy
    (b) Justice Sri Krishna
    (c) Justice Venkatachala
    (d) Justice Banerjee **(NLUD 2010)**

12. At the Beijing Olympics, highest number of medals were won by
    (a) China (b) USA
    (c) Russia (d) Germany
    **(NLUD 2010)**

13. Maximum number of gold medals won by an individual at Olympics in any event is
    (a) 3 (b) 5
    (c) 7 (d) 8 **(NLUD 2010)**

14. The present UN' Secretary General Ban Ki Moon is from
    (a) South Korea (b) North Korea
    (c) China (d) Mongolia
    **(NLUD 2010)**

15. The Minority Affairs Minister of Pakistan who was assassinated in March 2011
    (a) Salman Taseer (b) Nawaaz Paintal
    (c) Shahbaz Batti (d) None
    **(NLUD 2011)**

16. The present Central Chief Information Commissioner is
    (a) Wajhat Habibullah (b) Satyananda Mishra
    (c) M. L. Sharma (d) Sushma Singh
    **(NLUD 2011)**

**17.** The present Chief Election Commissioner of India is

(*a*) S. Y. Quraishi (*b*) H. S. Brahma
(*c*) V. S. Sampath (*d*) Navin Chawla

**(NLUD 2011)**

**18.** India's Foreign Exchange Reserve has become the _____ largest in the world.

(*a*) Eighth (*b*) Twelfth
(*c*) Fourth (*d*) Eleventh

**(NLUD 2011)**

**19.** The first ever woman Secretary-General of SAARC, Ms. Fathimath Dhiyana Saeed is from

(*a*) Pakistan (*b*) Bangladesh
(*c*) India (*d*) Maldives

**(NLUD 2011)**

**20.** The country that recently joined the South Asian Association for Regional Co-operation was

(*a*) Myanmar (*b*) Iran
(*c*) Iraq (*d*) Afghanistan

**(NLUD 2011)**

**21.** The 123 Agreement was entered into between

(*a*) Canada and India (*b*) France and India
(*c*) USA and India (*d*) China and India

**(NLUD 2011)**

**22.** The Supreme Court recently declared the appointment *non-est* of

(*a*) Navin Chawla (*b*) S. C. Mishra
(*c*) P. J. Thomas (*d*) Both (*b*) and (*c*)

**(NLUD 2011)**

**23.** The special reservation of 4% in favour of Muslims was struck down as unconstitutional by

(*a*) High Court of Madras
(*b*) High Court of Andhra Pradesh
(*c*) High Court of Delhi
(*d*) High Court of Kerala **(NLUD 2011)**

**24.** The Year Book of Industrial Statistics 2010 released by the UN Industrial Development Organization ranks India among

(*a*) Top 12 countries (*b*) Top 15 countries
(*c*) Top 4 countries (*d*) Top 10 countries

**(NLUD 2011)**

**25.** The European Union member states decided to temporarily withdraw the preferential tariff benefits from August 2010 on the ground that there are significant shortcomings in the implementation of three UN Human Rights Conventions in

(*a*) Sri Lanka (*b*) India
(*c*) Pakistan (*d*) Nepal **(NLUD 2011)**

**26.** The Eleventh South Asian Games was held in

(*a*) Kathmandu, Nepal (*b*) Hyderabad, India
(*c*) Dhaka, Bangladesh (*d*) Colombo, Sri Lanka

**(NLUD 2011)**

**27.** Dr. Jean Mayer Award for Global Citizenship by the Tufts University, USA, was awarded in 2010 to

(*a*) Justice Verma (*c*) Narayana Murthy
(*b*) M. C. Mehta (*d*) Sanjoy Hazarika

**(NLUD 2011)**

**28.** Kyoto Protocol which was replaced by Cancun in December 2010 relates to

(*a*) Climate (*b*) Water
(*c*) Air (*d*) Soil **(NLUD 2011)**

**29.** What is the venue for the 20th Commonwealth Games in 2014?

(*a*) Glasgow (*b*) Beijing
(*c*) London (*d*) Italy **(NLUD 2012)**

**30.** Who among the following leaders topped 2011 Forbes List of "World's Most Powerful Person"?

(*a*) Mr. Barak Obama
(*b*) Ms. Pratibha Patil
(*c*) Mr. Manmohan Singh
(*d*) Mr. Hu Jintao **(NLUD 2012)**

**31.** According to the Srikrishna Committee, which is the most workable option out of the six option suggested by the Committee to resolve the Telengana issue?

(*a*) Second (*b*) Fourth
(*c*) Sixth (*d*) First **(NLUD 2012)**

**32.** Who is convicted to death in the Beant Singh assassination case on March 31, 2012?

(*a*) Kehar Singh
(*b*) Balwant Singh Rajoana
(*c*) Karnail Singh
(*d*) Dilawar Singh Babbar **(NLUD 2012)**

**33.** Which news corporation was recently alleged to have been using illicit hacking into voicemail messages of prominent people to find stories?

(*a*) News of the World (NoW)
(*b*) BBC
(*c*) CNN
(*d*) AajTak **(NLUD 2012)**

**34.** Ms. Aung San Suu Kyi, Myanmar's democracy icon, has been released from _____ of home arrest.

(*a*) 16 years (*b*) 15 years
(*c*) 10 years (*d*) 20 years **(NLUD 2012)**

**35.** The country that set the record as the one with the longest time without government, in April 2011?

(*a*) Burundi (*b*) Belgium
(*c*) Turkey (*d*) Taiwan **(NLUD 2012)**

**36.** The Supreme Court of India upheld the decision to implement the quota for other backward classes (OBCs) in higher educational institutions. The court, however, excluded the "creamy layer" from being a beneficiary. The reason is:

(*a*) Creamy layer is not an OBC; it is a forward caste
(*b*) Creamy layer is politically powerful
(*c*) It can complete with others on equal footing
(*d*) The inclusion of creamy layer would be unjust **(CLAT 2008)**

**37.** Name the latest State which declared independence in 2008

(*a*) Serbia (*b*) Kosovo
(*c*) Kurdistan (*d*) Tibet **(CLAT 2008)**

**38.** The CEO of Microsoft Corporation is

(*a*) Bill Gates
(*b*) Warren Buffett
(*c*) Steve Ballmer
(*d*) John Wallace **(CLAT 2008)**

**39.** The current impasse in Doha Round of Negotiations is centered around:

(*a*) access to cheaper drugs
(*b*) access to markets of developed countries
(*c*) agricultural subsidies provided by developed countries
(*d*) removal of non-tariff barriers **(CLAT 2008)**

**40.** The Managing Director of Delhi Metropolitan Railway Corporation

(*a*) Chairman of Indian Railway Board
(*b*) Lt. Governor of Delhi
(*c*) C. Sreedharan
(*d*) Sheela Dikshit **(CLAT 2008)**

**41.** Bali Road map adopted in December 2007 provides for

(*a*) fixation of greenhose gas emission limits
(*b*) launching of an adaptation fund
(*c*) amendment to UN Framework Convention on Climate Change
(*d*) special and differential treatment for developing countries **(CLAT 2008)**

**42.** Indian who won Raman Magasaysay award in 2007:

(*a*) Arun Roy (*b*) P. Sainath
(*c*) Medha Patkar (*d*) Ruth Manorama **(CLAT 2008)**

**43.** The person who won Jawaharlal Nehru award in 2007:

(*a*) Lula de Silva (*b*) Hugo Chavez
(*c*) Aung Saan Suu Ki (*d*) Fidel Castro **(CLAT 2008)**

**44.** The space shuttle which successfully carried Sunita Williams to space:

(*a*) Challenger (*b*) Atlantis
(*c*) Discovery (*d*) Columbus **(CLAT 2008)**

**45.** Name the winner of 2007 Nobel Prize for Literature

(*a*) Dorris Lessing (*b*) V.S. Naipaul
(*c*) Doras Lessing (*d*) Salman Raushdie **(CLAT 2008)**

**46.** Recent Nepal elections are globally significant because

(*a*) Communists came to power through ballot box for the first time in the world
(*b*) Monarchy was defeated by democratic forces
(*c*) a militant movement joined the mainstream
(*d*) secularism triumphed over theocracy **(CLAT 2008)**

**47.** From which river would the National River Project be started?

(*a*) Yamuna (*b*) Gomti
(*c*) Ganga (*d*) Krishna **(CLAT 2009)**

**48.** Kandhamal, the worst affected town by sectarian violence in September-October 2008 is situated in

(*a*) Orissa (*b*) Gujarat
(*c*) Andhra Pradesh (*d*) Karnataka **(CLAT 2009)**

**49.** Which organization is headed by Indian Environmentalists R.K. Pachauri, a Nobel Laureate?

(*a*) International Environment Panel
(*b*) International Panel on Climate Change
(*c*) International Pollution Control Panel
(*d*) International Panel on Global Warming **(CLAT 2009)**

**50.** Government has launched E – Passport Scheme and first E – Passport was issued to

(*a*) Mr. Arjun Singh
(*b*) Mrs. Sonia Gandhi
(*c*) Dr. Man Mohan Singh
(*d*) Mrs. Pratibha Patil **(CLAT 2009)**

**51.** Which State has launched the "Aarogya Sri" a health Insurance Scheme for families below poverty line?
(*a*) Andhra Pradesh (*b*) Uttar Pradesh
(*c*) Maharasthra (*d*) Kerala **(CLAT 2009)**

**52.** Who emerged the fastest woman of the world at Beijing Olympics?
(*a*) Sheron Sumpson (*b*) Kerron Stewart
(*c*) Ann Fraster (*d*) Elina Basiena
**(CLAT 2009)**

**53.** In which State "Kanya Vidyadhan Yojna' is operational?
(*a*) Andhra Pradesh (*b*) Uttar Pradesh
(*c*) Rajasthan (*d*) Haryana **(CLAT 2009)**

**54.** Dr. A.P.J. Abdul Kalam has been appointed as Chancellor of
(*a*) IIM Mumbai
(*b*) IIT Kanpur
(*c*) IIM Ahmedabad
(*d*) IIST Thiruvananthapuram **(CLAT 2009)**

**55.** The youngest recipient of Padma Shri so far is
(*a*) Sachin Tendulkar
(*b*) Shobana Chandrakumar
(*c*) Sania Mirza
(*d*) Billy Arjan Singh **(CLAT 2009)**

**56.** Who is the Central Chief Information Commissioner of India?
(*a*) Prof. Ansari
(*b*) Mrs. Padma Subramanian
(*c*) Mr. Wajahat Habibullah
(*d*) Dr. O.P. Kejariwal **(CLAT 2009)**

**57.** Which country recently produced the world's first cloned rabbit using a biological process that takes cells from a fetus?
(*a*) U.K. (*b*) China
(*c*) U.S.A. (*d*) Germany **(CLAT 2009)**

**58.** Indian Judge in the UN Law of the Sea Tribunal is
(*a*) Dr. P.S. Rao
(*b*) Dr. P.C. Rao
(*c*) Mr. Justice Jagannath Rao
(*d*) Mr. Justice Rajendra Babu **(CLAT 2009)**

**59.** Who among the following Indians became Citigroup's Investment Banking head?
(*a*) L. N. Mittal (*b*) A.K. Subramaniyam
(*c*) Vineet Seth (*d*) Vikram Pandit
**(CLAT 2009)**

**60.** Out standing Parliamentarian Award (2006) was presented in 2007 to
(*a*) P. Chidambram (*b*) Sarad Pawar
(*c*) Mani Shankar Aiyar (*d*) Sushma Swaraj
**(CLAT 2009)**

**61.** The Railway Budget for 2007-2008 has declared the year 2007 as the year of
(*a*) Cleanliness
(*b*) Passenger Comfort
(*c*) Staff Welfare
(*d*) Computerization of Reservations **(CLAT 2009)**

**62.** The president of Maldives is
(*a*) Maumoom Abdul Gayoom
(*b*) Mohammad Ashraf
(*c*) Mahmood Alam
(*d*) Mohammed Nasheed **(CLAT 2010)**

**63.** Arabinda Rajkhowa is a member of
(*a*) B.J.P. (*b*) Assam Gana Parishad
(*c*) Maoist Centre (*d*) Ulfa **(CLAT 2010)**

**64.** Before the Indian team left for Conference on Climate Change at Copenhagen, Jairam Ramesh announced that India would work for voluntary reduction of
(*a*) 40 to 45 percent
(*b*) 20 to 25 percent
(*c*) 30 to 35 percent
(*d*) 10 to 15 percent in energy intensity in 2020 compared to 2005 **(CLAT 2010)**

**65.** Who is the foreign minister of European Union?
(*a*) Baroness Ashlon (*b*) Massimo D' Alema
(*c*) David Miliband (*d*) Carl Bildt
**(CLAT 2010)**

**66.** Why was Arundhati Roy investigated for sedition?
(*a*) For committing contempt of court
(*b*) For saying that Kashmir is not an integral part of India
(*c*) For sympathising with the Maoists
(*d*) For condemning nuclear tests conducted by India **(CLAT 2011)**

**67.** Damon Galgut's 'In a Strange Room' was recently in news for:
(*a*) Man Booker Prize shortlist
(*b*) Winning the Pulitzer Prize
(*c*) Winning the Orange Prize for fiction
(*d*) None of the above **(CLAT 2011)**

**68.** Who was recently in the news when the Supreme Court of India rejected her plea for Euthanasia, but paved the way for legalization of passive euthanasia?
(*a*) Aruna Shanbaug
(*b*) Aruna Roy
(*c*) Mary Roy
(*d*) Medha Patkar **(CLAT 2011)**

**69.** Nagoya Protocol, signed by India on 30th October, 2010 is:

(*a*) an international treaty of bilateral investment between India and Japan

(*b*) an international treaty to ensure that local produce are exploited only under license and for the common good of the mankind

(*c*) an international treaty to ensure that the benefits of natural resources and their commercial derivatives are shared with local communities

(*d*) None of the above. **(CLAT 2011)**

**70.** Julian Assange, the founder of WikiLeaks, was arrested in which of the following nations?

(*a*) U.K (*b*) Sweden

(*c*) U.S.A (*d*) Denmark **(CLAT 2011)**

**71.** Which of the following are the five countries that have decided to bid for 2017 World Athletics Championships?

(*a*) Qatar, USA, China, Sri Lanka and Brazil

(*b*) Germany, Britain, Hungary, Qatar and Spain

(*c*) Germany, Qatar, India, Spain and China

(*d*) Germany, Britain, China, Qatar and Spain **(CLAT 2011)**

**72.** The recent Tunisian revolution is known as:

(*a*) Orange Revolution (*b*) Jasmine Revolution

(*c*) Purple Revolution (*d*) Crescent Revolution **(CLAT 2011)**

**73.** Who replaced Lalit Modi as the IPL Chairman and Commissioner from this year's edition of the IPL?

(*a*) Chirayu Amin (*b*) Rajiv Shukla

(*c*) Ratnakar Shetty (*d*) Shashank Manohar **(CLAT 2011)**

**74.** Which one of the following films was officially selected to compete in the *Un Certain Regard* (A Certain Glance) category at the 2010 Cannes Film Festival?

(*a*) Udaan (*b*) My Name is Khan

(*c*) Wednesday (*d*) Dhobi Ghat **(CLAT 2011)**

**75.** In which case did the Nagpur Bench of the Bombay High Court on July 14, 2010 commute the death sentence of six accused to rigorous life imprisonment?

(*a*) Khairlanji case (*b*) Bhopal Gas Leak case

(*c*) Bhagalpur case (*d*) Nithari Case **(CLAT 2011)**

**76.** The Shunglu panel was constituted for which of the following issues?

(*a*) Investigate the 2G Spectrum Scam

(*b*) Suggest Civil Service Reforms

(*c*) Probe the Commonwealth Games Scam

(*d*) Suggest reforms on centre-state relationship **(CLAT 2011)**

**77.** Who was appointed as the Chairman of the National Innovation Council in August 2010?

(*a*) Shashi Tharoor

(*b*) Chetan Bhagat

(*c*) Arindam Chaudhury

(*d*) Sam Pitroda **(CLAT 2011)**

**78.** Name the Kenya-born political lobbyist who runs a firm called Vaishnavi Corporate Communications, and has recently been in news?

(*a*) Barkha Dutt (*b*) Vir Sanghhvi

(*c*) Vina Ramani (*d*) Nira Radia **(CLAT 2011)**

**79.** Thein Sein is the newly-appointed President of which of the following nations?

(*a*) Indonesia (*b*) Malaysia

(*c*) Myanmar (*d*) Thailand **(CLAT 2011)**

**80.** On 25th January 2011, BJP leaders Sushma Swaraj and Arun Jaitley were prevented from entering Srinagar and unfurl the national flag. What was that *Rath Yatra* called?

(*a*) Swabhimaan Yatra (*b*) Ekta Yatra

(*c*) Mukti Yatra (*d*) Swaraj Yatra **(CLAT 2011)**

**81.** Saina Nehwal recently defeated Ji Hyun Sung of South Korea to win which of the following titles?

(*a*) Swiss Open Grand Prix Gold Badminton

(*b*) Commonwealth Games

(*c*) Singapore Open

(*d*) Hong Kong Open **(CLAT 2011)**

**82.** '*Moner Manush*', the film to win the 'Golden Peacock' at the 41st International Film Festival of India was based on the life of which legendary 19th century folk singer and spiritual leader?

(*a*) Kabir (*b*) Surjya Sen

(*c*) Kabir Suman (*d*) Lalan Fakir **(CLAT 2011)**

**83.** In February 2011, Gopa Sabharwal was appointed as the first Vice Chancellor of which University of international stature?

(*a*) Jawaharlal Nehru University

(*b*) Azim Premji University

(*c*) Visva-Bharati University

(*d*) Nalanda International University **(CLAT 2011)**

**84.** With which of the following do you associate the name P.J Thomas?

(*a*) Central Vigilance Commission

(*b*) Lokpal

(*c*) Anti corruption Ombudsman

(*d*) Banking Ombudsman **(CLAT 2011)**

**85.** The 17th Commonwealth Law Conference was held in which city?
(*a*) Delhi (*b*) Bangalore
(*c*) Kolkata (*d*) Hyderabad
**(CLAT 2011)**

**86.** Sania Mirza claimed silver in the tennis mixed doubles category in the Asian Games in Guanzhou in November 2010. Who was her Partner?
(*a*) Mahesh Bhupathi (*b*) Somdev Devvarman
(*c*) Leander Paes (*d*) Vishnu Vardhan
**(CLAT 2011)**

**87.** China objected to the Dalai Lama's recent visit to Tawang in Arunachal Pradesh. What was he visiting in Tawang?
(*a*) A Buddhist monastery
(*b*) A memorial to Tibetans massacred by the Chinese army
(*c*) The residence of Panchen Lama
(*d*) None of the above **(CLAT 2011)**

**88.** Which prominent Barrister-politician, who was closely linked with the emergency proclamation of 1975, breathed his last in Kolkata on 6th November 2010?
(*a*) Jyoti Basu.
(*b*) Siddhartha Shankar Ray.
(*c*) Hiren Mukherjee.
(*d*) Indrajit Gupta **(CLAT 2011)**

**89.** Mohammad Asif, Mohammad Amir and Salman Butt (Cricket players of Pakistan) have been banned for being found guilty of spot fixing. To which of the following institutions have they appealed?
(*a*) Pakistan Cricket Board
(*b*) Anti-Corruption Tribunal of the Asian Cricket Council
(*c*) Court of Arbitration for Sport
(*d*) Anti-Corruption Tribunal of the International Cricket Council. **(CLAT 2011)**

**90.** Indian driver Karun Chandok was recently in the news for which of the following?
(*a*) Being selected as a reserve driver by Team Force India for the 2011 Formula One season.
(*b*) Being selected as a reserve driver by Team Lotus for the 2011 Formula One season.
(*c*) Being selected as a reserve driver by Team Ferrari for the 2011 Formula One season.
(*d*) None of the above. **(CLAT 2011)**

**91.** The United Nations Framework Convention on Climate Change meeting of 2010 December was held in which of the following places?
(*a*) Colorado. (*b*) Canberra.
(*c*) Cancun. (*d*) None of the above.
**(CLAT 2011)**

**92.** The II Africa-India Summit was held in May 2011 in
(*a*) New Delhi (*b*) Lagos
(*c*) Nairobi (*d*) Addis Ababa
**(CLAT 2012)**

**93.** Who was awarded the Nobel Prize for literature in 2011?
(*a*) Paul Lauterbur (*b*) Bill Clinton
(*c*) Tomas Transtromer (*d*) Shirin Ebadi
**(CLAT 2012)**

**94.** Who was awarded the UNESCO King Sejong Literacy Prize in 2011?
(*a*) Nelson Mandela
(*b*) National Literacy Service, Burundi
(*c*) Medha Patkar
(*d*) National Literacy Mission, India **(CLAT 2012)**

**95.** Identify the Indian Tennis player who has turned Hollywood filmmaker?
(*a*) Vijay Amritraj (*b*) Mahesh Bhupathi
(*c*) Leander Paes (*d*) Ashok Amritraj
**(CLAT 2012)**

**96.** Where will the next Olympic Games be held in 2012?
(*a*) Tokyo (*b*) Berlin
(*c*) London (*d*) Toronto **(CLAT 2012)**

**97.** Which of the following teams has won the Santosh Trophy Football Championship in 2011?
(*a*) Punjab (*b*) West Bengal
(*c*) Goa (*d*) Railways **(CLAT 2012)**

**98.** India became a member of UNO in
(*a*) 1945 (*b*) 1947
(*c*) 1950 (*d*) 1952 **(CLAT 2012)**

**99.** In which city was Osama Bin Laden killed in May 2011?
(*a*) Islamabad (*b*) Abbottabad
(*c*) Faisalabad (*d*) Peshawar **(CLAT 2012)**

**100.** The IV summit of BRICS was held in New Delhi on
(*a*) 11th January 2012 (*b*) 1st April 2012
(*c*) 29th March 2012 (*d*) 28th February 2012
**(CLAT 2012)**

**101.** An indigenous nuclear submarine still under construction has been named as
(*a*) Chakra (*b*) Sudarshan
(*c*) Arihant (*d*) Ghaatak **(CLAT 2012)**

**102.** Government of India has launched a publicity campaign for census 2011 in association with which of the following UN organization?
(*a*) United Nations Development Programme (UNDP)
(*b*) World Health Organization (WHO)
(*c*) United Nations Children's Fund (UNICEF)
(*d*) United Nations Population Fund (UNPF)
**(CLAT 2012)**

**103.** Name the actor who has been honoured with the Dadasaheb Phalke Award in 2012.
(*a*) Naseerudin Shah
(*b*) Kamal Hasan
(*c*) Soumitra Chatterjee
(*d*) Amol Paleker **(CLAT 2012)**

**104.** In which city was the Arab Summit held in the last week of March 2012?
(*a*) Bagdad (*b*) Cairo
(*c*) Beirut (*d*) Riyadh **(CLAT 2012)**

**105.** The two Supreme Court Judges who delivered the famous 2-G judgment in February 2012 were
(*a*) Justice G.S. Singhvi and Justice Gyan Sudha Mishra
(*b*) Justice G.S. Singhvi and Justice A.K. Ganguly
(*c*) Justice S.H. Kapadia and Justice A.K. Ganguly
(*d*) Justice Chandramauli Kumar Prasad and Justice H.L. Gokhale **(CLAT 2012)**

**106.** Which countries co-hosted the One-day cricket World Cup in 2011?
(*a*) India, Bangladesh and Sri Lanka
(*b*) India, Bangladesh and Pakistan
(*c*) India, Sri Lanka and Pakistan
(*d*) India, Sri Lanka, Bangladesh and Pakistan **(CLAT 2012)**

**107.** Priyanka Chopra has been named National Ambassador of
(*a*) WHO
(*b*) UNICEF
(*c*) UNESCO
(*d*) International Red Cross Society **(CLAT 2012)**

**108.** Who is leading in the Republican primaries to contest the American Presidential election scheduled in November 2012?
(*a*) Sara Palin (*b*) Newt Gingrich
(*c*) Rick Santorum (*d*) Mitt Romney **(CLAT 2012)**

**109.** The U. N. Climate Change Conference 2011 was held in
(*a*) New Delhi (*b*) Doha
(*c*) Durban (*d*) Geneva **(CLAT 2012)**

**110.** Who is, presently, the Director of the National Judicial Academy ?
(*a*) Prof. N.R. Madhava Menon
(*b*) Dr. Balram K. Gupta
(*c*) Prof. M.P. Singh
(*d*) Prof. K.N.Chandrasekharan Pillai **(AILET 2013)**

**111.** Name the Indian woman weight-lifter who in January 2013 won Maiden National Title in National Weightlifting Championship, 2013.
(*a*) Binitha Devi (*b*) Amanpreet Kaur
(*b*) Manpreet Kaur (*d*) Karnam Malleswari **(AILET 2013)**

**112.** Which of the following Indian company got the top rank among Indian companies in Top 500 companies list of Fortune India ?
(*a*) Indian Oil Corporation
(*b*) ONGC
(*c*) RIL
(*d*) SAIL **(AILET 2013)**

**113.** The Report of Transparency International India released in December, 2012 places India at ______ rank among 176 nations of the basis of Corruption Percentage Index.
(*a*) 93rd (*b*) 94th
(*c*) 95th (*d*) 96th **(AILET 2013)**

**114.** Who is crowned as Pond's Femina Ms. India, 2013?
(*a*) Zoya Afroz
(*b*) Sobhita Dhulipala
(*c*) Navneet Kaur Dhillon
(*d*) Anukriti Gusain **(AILET 2013)**

**115.** Which Hindi film was awarded 60th National Film Award, 2013 for Best Feature Film
(*a*) Paan Singh Tomar
(*b*) Barfi
(*c*) Gangs of Wasseypur
(*d*) Vicky Donor **(AILET 2013)**

**116.** Who is elected as the 266th Pope of the Roman Catholic Church at Rome In March, 2013?
(*a*) John Paul I (*b*) John Paul II
(*c*) Benedict XVI (*d*) Francis **(AILET 2013)**

**117.** Which country joined WTO in August 2012 ?
(*a*) Russia (*b*) Belgium
(*c*) Turkey (*d*) Taiwan **(AILET 2013)**

**118.** India in 2008 successfully put CHANDRAYAAN-1 into its initial orbit by **(CLAT 2013)**
(*a*) PSLV- C12 (*b*) PSLV- C11
(*c*) PSLV-14 (*d*) GSLV-D3

**119.** Kapilvastu Relics (fragments of Lord Buddha's bone), for the second time in 114 years, recently travelled from India to **(CLAT 2013)**
(*a*) China (*b*) Sri Lanka
(*c*) Myanmar (*d*) Japan

**120.** Who was crowned the Miss World 2012 on August 18, 2012? **(CLAT 2013)**

(*a*) Ms. Jessica Kahawaty
(*b*) Ms. Wenxia Yu
(*c*) Ms. Vanya Mishra
(*d*) Ms. Sophie Moulds

**121.** The present Pope chosen in March 2013 hails from which country? **(CLAT 2013)**

(*a*) Brazil (*b*) Mexico
(*c*) Argentina (*d*) Panama

**122.** In which place, on Feb 21, 2013, two powerful explosive devices planted on bicycles had exploded in Andhra Pradesh? **(CLAT 2013)**

(*a*) Dilrubnagar (*b*) Dilsukhnagar
(*c*) Dilkushnagar (*d*) Dilshaknagar

**123.** On which date Maha Kumbh Mela started in Prayag this year? **(CLAT 2013)**

(*a*) 14-1-2013 (*b*) 1-1-2013
(*c*) 26-1-2013 (*d*) 4-1-2013

**124.** Hugo Chavez who died on March 5, 2013 after losing his battle with cancer, was the President of which country? **(CLAT 2013)**

(*a*) Argentina (*b*) Cuba
(*c*) Brazil (*d*) Venezuela

**125.** Carlos Slim, who tops the list of world's wealthiest people, for the fourth year in a row, belongs to which country? **(CLAT 2013)**

(*a*) USA (*b*) England
(*c*) Mexico (*d*) Germany

**126.** Which is the richest temple in India?

(*a*) Balaji Temple of Tirupathi **(CLAT 2013)**
(*b*) Padmanabha Swamy Temple of Thiruvananthapuram
(*c*) Shirdi Sai Baba Temple
(*d*) Jagannatha Temple of Puri

**127.** In the month of March, 2013 the Supreme Court of India issued a notice that the ambassador of the following country shall not leave India without the permission of the Supreme Court **(CLAT 2013)**

(*a*) Germany (*b*) Maldives
(*c*) Italy (*d*) Nepal

**128.** Where was 16th NAM Summit held? **(CLAT 2013)**

(*a*) Tehran (*b*) Mehran
(*c*) Turban (*d*) Bagdad

**129.** The Aircraft Carrier inducted in to the Indian Navy recently is **(AILET 2014)**

(*a*) INS Virat (*b*) INS Vikrant
(*c*) INS Vikramaditya (*d*) None

**130.** Which of the following countries impeached its Chief Justice recently ? **(AILET 2014)**

(*a*) Bangladesh (*b*) Pakistan
(*c*) Sri Lanka (*d*) Maldives

**131.** With which of the following country India signed an Extradition treaty that came into force during October 2013 ? **(AILET 2014)**

(*a*) Afghanistan (*b*) Kenya
(*c*) China (*d*) Bangladesh

**132.** The present Chief Election Commissioner of India is **(AILET 2014)**

(*a*) Dr. Nasim Zaidi (*b*) V. S. Sampath
(*c*) H. S. Brahma (*d*) None

**133.** According to the recent World population data of 2013, the second most populous city in the world is

(*a*) New Delhi (*b*) Tokyo **(AILET 2014)**
(*c*) Mexico (*d*) Beijing

**134.** Indira Gandhi Prize for Peace, Disarmament and Development for the year 2013 has been conferred on: **(AILET 2014)**

(*a*) Ms. Angela Merkel (*b*) Mr. Nelson Mandela
(*c*) Mr. Uhuru Kenyatta (*d*) Mr. Hamid Karzai

**135.** Which of the following was declared by the United Nations General Assembly as "International Year for Water Co-operation" ? **(AILET 2014)**

(*a*) 2011 (*b*) 2012
(*c*) 2013 (*d*) 2014

**136.** Which one of the following is included in the World List of Biosphere Reserves by UNESCO? **(AILET 2014)**

(*a*) Kinnaur Region (*b*) Spiti Valley
(*c*) Nallamalai Hills (*d*) Sunderbans

**137.** Which one of the following countries is not a UN member country? **(AILET 2014)**

(*a*) Greece (*b*) Taiwan
(*c*) Portugal (*d*) Australia

**138.** What is known as Jasmine Revolution ? **(AILET 2014)**

(*a*) Czech uprising (*b*) Sudan uprising
(*c*) Arab Spring (*d*) Libyan uprising

**139.** Which one of the following statements about NATO is not correct ? **(AILET 2014)**

(*a*) NATO has 28 independent member states
(*b*) The US is an ex-officio member of NATO
(*c*) NATO is a collective defence organisation in Europe
(*d*) Turkey is a member of NATO

**140.** V.R. Krishna lyer was ______ before he became a Judge. **(AILET 2014)**

(*a*) A minister (*b*) An ambassador

(*c*) A Governor (*d*) A bureaucrat

**141.** Who is the founder of facebook? **(AILET 2014)**

(*a*) Jimmy Wales (*b*) Larry Page

(*c*) Mark Zuckerberg (*d*) Brian Acton

**142.** Shashi Kant Sharma was appointed in 2013 as the **(AILET 2014)**

(*a*) Attorney General of India

(*b*) Comptroller and Auditor General of India

(*c*) Commissioner of Linguistic Minorities

(*d*) Chairman of the National Commission for SCs & STs

**143.** Which of the following Judges of the Supreme Court of India is famously known as the 'Green Judge'?

(*a*) Justice VR Krishna lyyar **(CLAT 2014)**

(*b*) Justice PN Bhagwati

(*c*) Justice Kuldip Singh

(*d*) Justice BN Kirpal

**144.** Law Day is observed on: **(CLAT 2014)**

(*a*) 26th January (*b*) 26th May

(*c*) 15th August (*d*) 26th November

**145.** In which year, Defence Research & Development Organisation (DRDO) was formed by the amalgamation of the Technical Development Establishment (TDE) of the Indian Army and the Directorate of Technical Development & Production (DTDP) with the Defence Science Organisation (DSO): **(CLAT 2014)**

(*a*) 1955 (*b*) 1958

(*c*) 1959 (*d*) 1963

**146.** Match List I with List II and select the correct answer using the codes given below the lists:

| | List I (Person) | | List II (Position) |
|---|---|---|---|
| (a) | Nagendra Singh | (1) | Chief Election Commissioner of India |
| (b) | SH Kapadia | (2) | President of the International Court of Justice |
| (c) | NR Madhava Menon | (3) | Former Chief Justice of India |
| (d) | VS Sampath | (4) | Legal educator and Founder-Director of National Law School of India University |

**Codes:** **(CLAT 2014)**

(*a*) a-2; b-3; c-l; d-4 (*b*) a-4; b-3; c-2; d-1

(*c*) a-1; b-2; c-4; d-3 (*d*) a-2; b-3; c-4; d-1

**147.** Who is the winner of the coveted Dadasaheb Phalke Award for the year 2013? **(CLAT 2014)**

(*a*) Javed Akhtar (*b*) Gulzar

(*c*) AR Rahman (*d*) Indeevar

**148.** Who among the following has been recently appointed as brand ambassador for Central Reserve Police Force (CRPF): **(CLAT 2014)**

(*a*) Aamir Khan

(*b*) Mahendra Singh Dhoni

(*c*) MC Mary Kom

(*d*) Sania Mirza

**149.** Till date (2014), how many people have been awarded the Bharat Ratna Award?

(*a*) 40 (*b*) 41 **(CLAT 2014)**

(*c*) 42 (*d*) 43

**150.** Which country Malala Yousafzai belongs to? **(CLAT 2014)**

(A Pakistan (*b*) Afghanistan

(*c*) The USA (*d*) England

**151.** Who recently became the first woman chief of the State Bank of India? **(CLAT 2014)**

(*a*) Arundhati Bhattacharya

(*b*) Shubhalakshmi Panse

(*c*) Vijaylakshmi Iyer

(*d*) Chanda Kochhar

**152.** Who is the Chairman of the 14th Finance Commission? **(CLAT 2014)**

(*a*) Dr M Govinda Rao (*b*) Dr Vijay Kelkar

(*c*) Dr YV Reddy (*d*) Dr Raghuram Rajan

**153.** The Chairperson of the Seventh Pay Commission is: **(CLAT 2014)**

(*a*) Justice BN Srikrishna

(*b*) Justice DK Jain

(*c*) Justice AP Shah

(*d*) Justice AK Mathur

**154.** Who was appointed as the 23rd Governor of the Reserve Bank of India? **(CLAT 2014)**

(*a*) KC Chakrabarty (*b*) Urijit Patel

(*c*) Raghuram Rajan (*d*) D Subbarao

**155.** Who was the first winner of the prestigious Jnanpith Award? **(CLAT 2014)**

(*a*) Tarasankar Bandyopadhyay

(*b*) Kuppali Venkatappagowda Puttappa

(*c*) G Sankara Kurup

(*d*) Umashankar Joshi

**156.** Who was sworn in as the Prime Minister of Italy on 22nd February 2014? **(CLAT 2014)**

(*a*) Oleksandr Turchynov

(*b*) Matteo Renzi

(*c*) Enrico Letta

(*d*) Giorgio Napolitano

**157.** Which year was designated by the United Nations as International Women's Year? **(CLAT 2014)**

(*a*) 1974 (*b*) 1975
(*c*) 1976 (*d*) 1977

**158.** General Election is being held in India from 7 April to 12 May 2014 to constitute: **(CLAT 2014)**

(*a*) 14th Lok Sabha (*b*) 15th Lok Sabha
(*c*) 16th Lok Sabha (*d*) 17th Lok Sabha

**159.** Mention the name of the current Chief Justice of India: **(CLAT 2014)**

(*a*) Justice Altamas Kabir
(*b*) Justice P Sathasivam
(*c*) Justice R M Lodha
(*d*) Justice H L Dattu

**160.** The 9th Ministerial Conference of the WTO, held during 3 December-6 December 2013, was concluded at: **(CLAT 2014)**

(*a*) Geneva, Switzerland
(*b*) Kaula Lumpur, Malaysia
(*c*) Warsaw, Poland
(*c*) Bali, Indonesia

**161.** Nobel Prize in Literature for the year 2013 was awarded to: **(CLAT 2014)**

(*a*) Mo Yan
(*b*) James E Rothman
(*c*) Lars Peter Hansen
(*d*) Alice Munro

**162.** Which one of the following satellites was successfully launched by the ISRO's Polar Satellite Launch Vehicle (PSLV-C24) on 4th April 2014? **(CLAT 2014)**

(*a*) IRNSS-1B (*b*) GSAT-14
(*c*) INSAT-3D (*d*) SARAL

**Solutions**

**1.** d Nepal in the year 2008 adopted a new National Anthem.

**2.** d Kaalpurush.

**3.** d Incumbent President of the United States, Mr. Barrak Obama was awarded Nobel Peace Prize in 2009. He is the also holds the first rank in the list of world s most powerful Leaders by Forbes.

**4.** a Sheik Hasina is the current president of the Bangladesh.

**5.** b The Incumbent President of South Africa is Jacob Zuma.

**6.** d Roh Moo-Hyun who was Ex- President of South Korea committed suicide.

**7.** b Mr. V. S. Sampath is the incumbent Chief election Commissioner of India.

**8.** a In the year 2010, 76 CRPF jawans were killed by the Maoist in an ambush near Dantewada in Chattisgarh.

**9.** d M.S. Gill was appointed in 2010 as a Union Minister.

**10.** a Justice Punnchi headed the committee on Centre-State Relations in India.

**11.** b Justice Sri Krishna headed Telangana Committee.

**12.** a China in 2010 Beijing Olympics won highest number of medals.

**13.** d Till now maximum number of gold medals won by an individual at Olympics in any event stands at 8 medals.

**14.** a The present UN' Secretary General Ban Ki Moon is from South Korea.

**15.** c Shahbaz Batti who was then Minority Affairs Minister of Pakistan was assassinated in March 2011.

**16.** b Satyanand Mishra is the incumbent Chief Information Commissioner of India.

**17.** a V. S. Sampath is the incumbent chief Chief Election Commissioner of India.

**18.** c India's Foreign Exchange Reserve has become the fourth largest in the world in year 2011.

**19.** d Mr. Ahmed Saleem from Maldives is the current Secretary General of SAARC. Ms. Fathimath Dhiyana Saeed from same country was the first ever woman president of SAARC.

**20.** d Afghanistan joined SAARC in year 2011.

**21.** c 123 Agreement is between Indian and USA dealing with Nuclear power Plants including only Civil Nuclear power plants excluding defence one.

**22.** c A claim of *non est factum*(Latin for "it is not [my] deed") means that the signature on the contract was signed by mistake, without knowledge of its meaning, but was not done so negligently. If an appointment is illegal, it is *non est or non existent* in the eye of the law, which renders the appointment to be a nullity. The Supreme Court in 2011 declared the appointment *non-est* of P. J. Thomas. The High Power Committee which recommended the name of P.J. Thomas did not did not consider charge sheet relating to a corruption case pending against him.

**23.** b High Court of Andhra Pradesh struck down the special reservation of 4% in favour of Muslims in 2011.

**24.** d The Year Book of Industrial Statistics 2010 released by the UN Industrial Development Organization ranked India among top 4 countries.

**25.** a The European Union member states decided to temporarily withdraw the preferential tariff benefits from August 2010 on the ground that there are significant shortcomings in the implementation of three UN Human Rights Conventions in Shri Lanka. Recently also, United Nations Warned Shi Lanka for the Human Rights violations reported by many international NGOs.

**26.** c The 2013 South Asian Games, officially the XII South Asian Games, is an upcoming major multi-sport event, scheduled to take place in Delhi, India in February, 2013.

**27.** d Dr. Jean Mayer was a World-renowned nutritionist. An Award under his name viz. 'Dr. Jean Mayer Global Citizenship Award' was established in the year 1993. In the present year this award is conferred to Susannah Sirkin. She is a deputy director of the organisation Physicians for Human Rights (PHS).

**28.** * Cancun Summit occurred in Mexico in 2010 with an aim to continue efforts towards an international deal on cutting carbon emissions. COP16 was the official name of the Cancún summit, which is the 16th Conference of the Parties (COP) under the United Nations Framework Convention on Climate Change (UNFCCC).

**29.** a Glasgow city, which is in Scotland, UK. the venue of common wealth games in 2014.

**30.** a The President of USA. Barrak Obama retained as a top leader in Forbes list of "World's Most Powerful Persons". From India Sonia Gandhi is on 11 the rank in the list and Incumbent prime minister of India Mr. Man Mohan Singh is on 17th Rank.

**31.** c The sixth option presented by Srikrishna Committee was the most workable option i.e."Keeping the State united by simultaneously providing certain definite Constitutional/ Statutory measures for socio-economic development and political empowerment of Telangana region through creation of a statutorily empowered Telangana Regional Council".

**32.** b Balwant Singh Rajoana recently has been convicted in the Beant Singh assassination case on March 31, 2012. Beant Singh was the Ex-Chief Minister of state of Punjab.

**33.** a News of the World (NOW) has been recently alleged using illicit hacking into voicemail messages of prominent people to find stories.

**34.** b Ms. Aung San Suu Kyi who has recently accepted the prestigious Nobel prize conferred to her in the year 1993. She was released after 15 years of house arrest.

**35.** b Belgium set the record as the one with the longest time without government, in April 2011. Herman Van Rompuy was re-elected head of the states recently.

**36.** c Creamy Layer is excluded on the basis of the Mandal commission's recommendations. 'Creamy layer' is interpreted by the court as 'socially-advanced Persons and hence were excluded from the other eligible castes for availing reservation Benefits.

**37.** b Kosovo declared itself as Independent in the year 2008.

**38.** c Setve Balmer 's personal wealth in the present year has been estimated at $15.7 billion, ranking number 19 on the Forbes 400.

**39.** c The Impasse in the year 2008 in Doha Round of Negotiations was centered around agricultural subsidies provided by developed countries.

**40.** c E. Sreedharan is the Managing Director of Delhi Metropolitan Railway Corporation.

**41.** a Bali Road map adopted in December 2007 provided for fixation of greenhose gas emission limits.

**42.** b Raman Magsaysay award is also considered as "Asia 's Nobel Prize"

**43.** a Lula de Silva won the Raman Magasaysay award in 2007.

**44.** c Sunita Williams has again ventured into another space mission and this time she is accompanied with Russian cosmonaut Yury Malenchenko and Japan's Akihito Hoshide.

**45.** a Dorris Lessing won Nobel Prize for Literature in the year 2007.

**46.** c In 2008 Nepal elections were globally significant because a militant movement joined the mainstream.

**47.** * This question has no correct answer.

Note: The National River Linking Project (NRLP) is designed to ease water shortages in western and southern India while mitigating the impacts of recurrent floods in the eastern parts of the Ganga basin. The NRLP, if and when implemented, will be one of the biggest interbasin water transfer projects in the world.

**48.** a Kandhamal is a district of the state of Orissa, India. The district headquarters of the district is Phulbani.

**49.** b The Intergovernmental Panel on Climate Change (IPCC) is a scientific intergovernmental body, set up at the request of member governments.It was first established in 1988 by two United Nations organizations, the World Meteorological Organization (WMO) and the United Nations Environment Programme (UNEP). Its mission is to provide comprehensive scientific assessments of current scientific, technical and socio-economic information worldwide about the risk of climate change caused by human activity, its potential environmental and socio-economic consequences, and possible options for adapting to these consequences or mitigating the effects. It is chaired by Rajendra K. Pachauri.

**50.** d In Malaysia, the word 'bhumiputra' refers to Buddhists.

**51.** a State of Andra Pradesh launch a health insurance scheme 'Aarogya Sri' for the below poverty line families.

**52.** c Parvez was the name of Emperor Shahjahan before he became Emperor.

**53.** b In Uttar Pradesh 'Kanya Vidyandhan Yojna' is operational.

**54.** d Bharat Ratna Dr. Avul Pakir Jainulabdeen Abdul Kalam born October 15, 1931, Tamil Nadu, India, usually referred to as Dr. A. P. J. Abdul Kalam, who was the eleventh President of India, serving from 2002 to 2007 has been appointed as the Chancellor of IIST Trivandrum.

**55.** c Sania Mirza is the youngest recipient of Padma Shri so far. Padma Shri (also Padmashree) is the fourth highest civilian award in the Republic of India, after the Bharat Ratna, the Padma Vibhushan and the Padma Bhushan. It is awarded by the Government of India.

**56.** c Sumatra is the largest island in the world (if Australia is not considered an island).

**57.** b The University of Bombay established in the year 1857.

**58.** b The International Tribunal for the Law of the Sea (ITLOS) based in Hamburg, Germany is an intergovernmental organization created by the mandate of the Third United Nations Conference on the Law of the Sea. It was established by the United Nations Convention on the Law of the Sea, signed at Montego Bay, Jamaica, on December 10, 1982. The Convention entered into forçe on November 16, 1994. Mr. P. Chandrasekhara Rao is the Indian judge in the tribunal that has a set of 21 serving judges from a variety of states parties.

**59.** d Vikram Shankar Pandit (born 14 January 1957) is an Indian-born American banker.He is the chief executive of Citigroup, a position he has held since December 2007.

**60.** c The Outstanding Parliamentarian Award is an award given by the Indian Parliamentary Group to an outstanding sitting Member of the Indian Parliament. It was instituted in 1995 by Shivraj Patil who was then the Speaker, Lok Sabha from 1991-96. In 2007, the award was conferred upon Mr. Mani Shankar Aiyar.

**61.** a Indian Railways has declared the Year 2007 as 'Cleanliness Year' as part of which special campaigns to ensure cleanliness in station complexes, passenger trains, railway lines, waiting rooms etc. will be undertaken.

**62.** d Mohmmad Naseed is the incumbent President of Maldives.

**63.** d Arvinda Rajkhwa is a member of United Liberation Front of Assam (ULFA).

**64.** b 20 to 25% is the limit which was announced by Jairam Ramesh that India would work for voluntary reduction before Indian team left for Kopen Hagen Conference.

**65.** d Carl Bildt is the Foreign Minister of European Union.

**66.** b Arundhati Roy investigated in the year 2011 for sedition for saying that Kashmir is not an integral part of India. Section 124 of Indian Penal Code 1860 makes such a kind of act punishable.

**67.** a For Man Booker Prize Damon Galgut's 'In a Strange Room" was short-listed in the year 2011.

**68.** a

**69.** c Nagoya Protocol, signed by India on 30th October, 2010 is an international treaty to ensure that the benefits of natural resources and their commercial derivatives are shared with local communities.

**70.** a Julian Assange, the founder of WikiLeaks, was arrested in United Kingdom in the year 2011.

**71.** b Germany, Britain, Hungary, Qatar and Spain are the countries who have decided to bid for 2017 World Athletics Championships.

**72.** b Jasmine revolution or the Tunisian revolution which occurred in the year 2011 in which in which President Zine El Abidine Ben Ali was forced out of the presidency by popular protests, Currently, Moncef Marzouki holds the presidency in Tunisia.

**73.** a Rajiv Shukla is the incumbent chief of *Indian Premier League* (*IPL*).

**74.** a The movie 'Uddan' is directed by Mr. Vikramaditya Motwane.

**75.** a The Kherlanji massacre refers to the 2006 lynching-style murders of a Dalit family by members of the politically dominant Kunbi "OBC ". The killings took place in a small village in India named Khairlanji, located in the Bhandara district of the state of Maharashtra.

**76.** a The Shunglu panel was constituted to probe the Commonwealth Games Scam.

**77.** d Sam Pitroda

**78.** d Nira Radia is currently investigated by Serious Fraud Investigation Office of Ministry of Corporate Affairs for 2-G spectrum scam.

**79.** c *Thein Sein* is the president of Burma (Mayanmar).

**80.** d Swaraj Yatra

**81.** a Swiss Open Grand Prix Gold Badminton

**82.** d Moner Manush is a Bengali feature film based on the life and philosophy of Fakir Lalan Shah, a noted spiritual leader, poet and folk singer of Bengal in the 19th century. The film is directed by Goutam Ghose.

**83.** d Gopa Sabharwal was appointed as the first Vice Chancellor ofNalanda International University in the year 2011.

**84.** a PJ Thomas headed Central Vigilance Commission

**85.** d In Hyderabad 70th Common Wealth Law Conference was held.

**86.** d Vishnu Vardhan belong to the sports of tennis.

**87.** a The Shunglu panel was constituted to investigate the 2G spectum scam.

**88.** b Siddartha Shankar Rai who died in year 2011 was a politician.

**89.** c Courts of Arbitration for sports has headquarter in Swizerland (Lausanni)

**90.** c Karun Chandok is a Formula One driver.

**91.** c The United Nations Framework Convention on Climate Change meeting of 2010 December was held in Cancun.

**92.** d The 2$^{nd}$Africa-India Summit was held at Addis Ababa, with India and 15 African Countries participating. The leaders discussed significant aspects of the India-Africa partnership with the objective of enhancing and widening its ambit for mutual benefit.

Africa and India agree to continue their cooperation in the areas enumerated below:

1. Economic Cooperation
2. Political Cooperation
3. Cooperation in Science, Technology, Research and Development
4. Cooperation in Social Development and Capacity Building
5. Cooperation in Health, Culture and Sports
6. Cooperation in Tourism
7. Cooperation in Infrastructure, Energy and Environment
8. Cooperation in the area of Media and Communications

**93.** c The Swedish Academy has awarded the 2011 Nobel prize for literature to one of its own: the Swedish poet Tomas Tranströmer.

Tranströmer becomes the eighth European to win the world's premier literary award in the past 10 years, following the German novelist HertaMüller in 2009, the French writer JMG le Clézio in 2008 and the British novelist Doris Lessing in 2007.

**94.** b 2011 Winners of UNESCO King Sejong Literacy Prize was ***National Literacy Service - Burundi***. The UNESCO King Sejong Literacy Prize was created in 1989 through the generosity of the Government of the Republic of Korea and rewards the activities of governments or governmental agencies and non-governmental organizations (NGOs) displaying merit and achieving particularly effective results in contributing to the fight for literacy. It gives special consideration to the creation, development and dissemination of mother-tongue languages in developing countries.The Prize consist of a sum of US$20,000, a silver medal and a certificate.

**95.** d Ashok Amritraj is an Indian American film producer, former tour professional tennis player, and chairman of Hyde Park Entertainment. Amritraj has produced over 100 films, including Hollywood films such as Antitrust, Walking Tall, and Bringing Down the House, which starred Steve Martin and Queen Latifah and Tamil film Jeans. Among his upcoming movies are projects based on Lee Falk's comic strip characters Mandrake the Magician and The Phantom.

**96.** c The 2012 Summer Olympic Games, officially the Games of the XXX Olympiad, also known informally as London 2012, began in London, United Kingdom on 27 July and will continue until 12 August 2012.

**97.** b West Bengal won the Santosh Trophy Football Championship in 2011. Santosh Trophy is an annual Indian football tournament which is contested by states and government institutions. The first winners were Bengal, who also lead the all-time winners list with 31 titles till date.

**98.** a India was a founding member in October 1945, despite being a British colony. India, Canada, the Union of South Africa, New Zealand and Australia were all British colonies but were given independent seats in the UN General Assembly.

**99.** b Osama bin Laden was killed in Abbottabad, Pakistan on May 2, 2011, shortly after 1:00am local time by a United States special forces military unit. The operation, code-named Operation Neptune Spear, was ordered by United States President BarackObama and carried out in a U.S. Central Intelligence Agency (CIA) operation by a team of United States Navy SEALs from the United States.

**100.** c The 2012 BRICS summit was the fourth annual BRICS summit, an international relations conference attended by the heads of state or heads of government of the five member states Brazil, Russia, India, China and South Africa. The summit was held at at TajMahal Hotel in New Delhi, India on 29 March 2012 and began at 10:00 Indian Standard Time. This is the first time that India has hosted a BRICS summit. The theme of the summit was "BRICS Partnership for Global Stability, Security and Prosperity.

**101.** c The Arihant class submarines are nuclear-powered ballistic missile submarines under development by the Indian Navy. The lead vessel of the class, INS Arihant, is expected to complete its harbour acceptance trials in February 2012. Four vessels of the class are under development and expected to be in commission by 2015. The Arihant class vessels are India's first indigenously designed and built nuclear submarine. They were developed under the US$2.9 billion Advanced Technology Vessel (ATV) project to design and build nuclear-powered submarines.

**102.** c Amir Khan is the brand ambesddor of UNICEF.

**103.** c Legendary Bengali actor Soumitra Chatterjee was conferred with the prestigious Dadasaheb Phalke Award by Vice-President HamidAnsari at the 59th National Awards for 2011 at Vigyan Bhawanon 3rd May 2012 for his outstanding contribution to the growth of Indian cinema.

Dadasaheb Phalke Award is India's highest award in cinema given annually by the Government of India for lifetime contribution to Indian cinema.The Award is given to a prominent personality from the Indian film industry, noted and respected for significant contributions to Indian cinema. A committee consisting eminent personalities from the Indian film industry is appointed to evaluate the award. Introduced in 1969, the birth centenary year of DadasahebPhalke, considered as the father of Indian cinema, award is given to recognise the contribution of film personalities towards the development of Indian Cinema and for distinguished contribution to the medium, its growth and promotion.

**104.** a The 23rd Arab League Summit was the third one held in Baghdad and the first one since 1990, before the start of the Gulf War. The decision to grant the host rights to Iraq was made at the previous summit in Syria. Among the subjects discussed were the Iraqi debts to its neighbors and the uprising in Syria. The summit marked the first time since the Invasion of Kuwait that an acting Emir (Sabah Al-Ahmad Al-Jaber Al-Sabah) paid a visit to Iraq.

**105.** b The divisioanl bench of Justice G.S. Singhvi and Justice Gyan Sudha Mishra delivered the 2-G judgment.

**106.** a The 2011 ICC Cricket World Cup was the tenth Cricket World Cup. It was played in India, Sri Lanka, and (for the first time) Bangladesh. Pakistan was also scheduled to be a co-host, but after the 2009 attack on the Sri Lanka national cricket team in Lahore, the International Cricket Council (ICC) cancelled that, and the headquarters of the organising committee, originally in Lahore, was transferred to Mumbai. Pakistan was to have held 14 matches, including one semi-final. Eight of the games (including the semi-final) were awarded to India, four to Sri Lanka, and two to Bangladesh.

**107.** b The United Nations Children's Fund (UNICEF) has chosen Bollywood actress and former Miss World Priyanka Chopra as one of their brand ambassadors.

In a statement, Karin Hulshof, the UNICEF representative to India said that the signing ceremony will take place on August 10 in New Delhi, after which the actress will be seen supporting UNICEF in the promotion of child and adolescent rights.

**108.** d The 2012 Republican primaries are the selection processes by which the Republican Party selects delegates to attend the 2012 Republican National Convention from August 27–30. The series of primaries, caucuses, and state conventions culminates in the national convention where the delegates vote on and select a candidate. A simple majority (1,144) of the total delegate votes (2,286) is required to become the party's nominee. On May 29, according to projected counts, Mitt Romney crossed the threshold of 1,144 delegates to become the party's presumptive nominee.

**109.** c The 2011 United Nations Climate Change Conference was held in Durban, South Africa, from 28 November to 11 December 2011 to establish a new treaty to limit carbon emissions. The conference agreed to a legally binding deal comprising all countries, which will be prepared by 2015, and to take effect in 2020.There was also progress regarding the creation of a Green Climate Fund (GCF) for which a management framework was adopted. The fund is to distribute US$100 billion per year to help poor countries adapt to climate impacts.

While the president of the conference, Maite Nkoana-Mashabane, declared it a success, scientists and environmental groups warned that the deal was not sufficient to avoid global warming beyond 2 °C as more urgent action is needed.

**110.** b Dr Balram Gupta was appointed as the Director, National Judicial Academy, Bhopal in March 2013. His appointment to the coveted post of the prestigious institution of the country has been made by the Chief Justice of India, as the National Judicial Academy comes under the Supreme Court of India.

**111.** c Manpreet Kaur, of All India Police claimed the women's +75kg gold medal in the final day of the National weightlifting championship at SRM University campus, Uttar Pradesh on 10 January 2013. Manpreet Kaur lifted 189 kg to secure maiden National title.

**112.** a Indian Oil Corporation (IOC) is the biggest company in terms of revenue, followed by Reliance Industries, according to the Fortune 500 list of Indian companies for 2012.

**113.** b Transparency International's Corruption Perception Index (CPI) placed India at 94th rank out of 176 nations this year in report for Transparency International India released in December ,2012.

**114.** c Navneet Kaur Dhillon was crowned as Pond's Miss India 2013 .

**115.** a Tigmanshu Dhulia's *Paan Singh Tomar* , about an athlete-turned-dacoit, won the best film award at 60th National Award for best feature film.

**116.** d Cardinal Jorge Mario Bergoglio of Argentina known as Pope Francis I, the 266 Pope of the Roman Catholic Church.

**117.** a Russia joined the WTO in August 2012 after negotiations, which spanned 18 years.

**118.** b PSLV C 11

**119.** b Sri Lanka

**120.** b Ms Wenxia Yu

**121.** c Argentina

**122.** b Dilsukhnagar

**123.** a 14-1-2013

**124.** d Venezuela

**125.** c Mexico

**126.** b Padmanabha Swamy Temple of Thiruvananthapuram

**127.** c Italy

**128.** a Tehran

**129.** c Aircraft carrier INS Vikramaditya inducted into Indian Navy recently.

**130.** c Sri Lanka impeached its Chief Justice recently.

**131.** d The extradition treaty between Bangladesh and India came into effect with the handing over of the instruments of ratification of the much-awaited pact. The two countries will now be able to exchange convicts or under trials as and when required.

**132.** b Veeravalli Sundaram Sampath is the current Chief Election Commissioner (CEC) of the Election Commission of India.

**133.** a As per World Population Data 2013, Delhi and its extended suburbs is the second most populous urban sprawl in the world after Tokyo.

**134.** a Ms. Angela Merkel, the Chancellor of Germany. The Indira Gandhi Peace Prize or the Indira Gandhi Prize for Peace, Disarmament and Development is the prestigious award accorded annually by India to individuals or organizations in recognition of creative efforts toward promoting international peace, development and a new international economic order; ensuring that scientific discoveries are used for the larger good of humanity, and enlarging the scope of freedom.

**135.** c 2013 has been declared as the "International Year for Water Conservation"

**136.** d The Sundarbans mangrove forest, one of the largestsuch forests in the world (140,000 ha), lies on the delta of the Ganges, Brahmaputra and Meghna rivers on the Bay of Bengal. It is adjacent to the border of India's Sundarbans World Heritage site inscribed in 1987. The site is intersected by a complex network of tidal waterways, mudflats and small islands of salt-tolerant mangrove forests, and presents an excellent example of ongoing ecological processes. The area is known for its wide range of fauna, including 260 bird species, the Bengal tiger and other threatened species such as the estuarine crocodile and the Indian python.

**137.** b Taiwan is not a UN member country.

**138.** c Arab Spring is known as Jasmine revolution.

**139.** b The U.S. is not an ex-officio member of NATO but was a part of founding members alongwith 12 other member countries. The founding countries are Belgium, Canada, Denmark, France, Iceland, Italy, Luxembourg, the Netherlands, Norway, Portugal, the United Kingdom, and the United States. In 1952, Greece and Turkey became members of the Alliance.

**140.** a Before becoming the Judge of Supreme Court of India V.R. Krishna was the minister of law, power, prisons, irrigation and social welfare in the Government of Kerala, he was instrumental in bringing about many significant changes in these sectors. In 1973, he was sworn in as a Judge of the Supreme Court of India; as of 2011, he is the last Supreme Court judge to have previously served as a politician. He was conferred with Padma Vibhushan in the year 1999.

**141.** c Mark Elliot Zuckerberg (born May 14, 1984) is an American computer programmer, Internet entrepreneur, and philanthropist. He is best known as one of five co-founders of the social networking website Facebook.

**142.** b Shashi Kant Sharma is the Comptroller and Auditor General of India. He succeeded Vinod Rai as the supreme auditor of the Constitutional body on 22 May 2013.

**143.** c Justice Kuldip Singh is known as the 'Green Judge' as he has created fear among the polluting industries and anti-environment lobbies, including, bureaucracy has petitioned the apex court for justice.

**144.** d National Law Day in India is celebrated on 26 November. It marks the anniversary of the drafting of the constitution by the constituent assembly in 1949.

**145.** b The DRDO was formed in 1958 following the merger of the Technical Development Establishment (TDE) of the Indian Army, the Directorate of Technical Development & Production (DTDP) and the Defense Science Organisation (DSO).

**146.** d a-2, b-3, c-4, d-1.

Nagendra Singh was an Indian lawyer and administrator who served as President of the International Court of Justice from 1985 to 1988. Sarosh Homi Kapadia was the thirty-eighth Chief Justice of India. N. R. Madhava Menon is a legal educator from India. He was instrumental in setting up the National Law School of India University (NLSIU) in Bangalore, and was its founder-director. He was the founder and vice-chancellor of West Bengal National University of Juridical Sciences

(NUJS) in Calcutta, run on the NLSIU model. He was the founder Director of the National Judicial Academy, Bhopal, and an institute for training judges. Madhava Menon has worked for nearly five decades to improve Indian legal education. He is Scholar-in-Residence of Faculty of Law; A.M.U. Veeravalli Sundaram Sampath is the current chief election commissioner (CEC) of the Election Commission of India.

**147.** b Veteran poet and film lyricist Gulzar has been chosen for the coveted Dadasaheb Phalke Award for 2013 announced by the ministry of information and broadcasting. The multi-faceted Gulzar, whose real name is Sampooran Singh Kalra, is a lyricist, director, screenwriter, producer and poet. He is the 45th winner of the Dadasaheb Phalke Award.

**148.** c India's largest paramilitary force CRPF has appointed five-time world boxing champion and Olympic bronze medallist Mary Kom as its brand ambassador.

**149.** d The award can be considered to be conferred only if the recipient's name is published in The Gazette of India-a public journal and an authorised legal document of the Government of India, and a recipients' register maintained under the direction of the President. Till date (2014) 43 individuals have been bestowed the award including 11 posthumous declarations.

**150.** a Malala Yousafzai is a Pakistani school pupil and education activist from the town of Mingora in the Swat District of Pakistan's northwestern Khyber Pakhtunkhwa province. She is known for her activism for rights to education and for women, especially in the Swat Valley, where the Taliban had at times banned girls from attending school.

**151.** a Arundhati Bhattacharya has taken over, as the new chairperson of the State Bank of India (SBI). She is the first woman to be appointed to the top job.

**152.** c The Fourteenth Finance Commission has been set up under the Chairmanship of Dr. Y.V.Reddy [Former Governor Reserve Bank of India].

**153.** d Justice A.K. Mathur is the Chairperson of the Seventh Pay Commission.

**154.** c Dr. Raghuram Rajan assumed charge as the 23rd Governor of the Reserve Bank of India.

**155.** c G. Sankara Kurup, better known as Mahakavi G (The Great Poet G), was the first winner of the Jnanpith Award, India's highest literary award.

**156.** b Matteo Renzi, 39, has been sworn in as Italy's youngest prime minister ever.

**157.** b International Women's Year (IWY) was the name given to 1975 by the United Nations. Since that year March 8 has been celebrated as International Women's Day, and the United Nations Decade for Women, from 1976-1985, was also established.

**158.** c The general elections for 2014 is taking place in 9 phases and encounters to be the longest election poll in the country's history from 7th April to 12th May, 2014 to constitute 16th Lok Sabha in India. The voting is carried out in all 543 parliamentary constituencies of India for electing members of parliament in Lok Sabha.

**159.** c Justice Rajendra Mal Lodha, the senior most judge of the Supreme Court, was on Sunday sworn in as the 41st Chief Justice of India by President Pranab Mukherjee.

**160.** d The ninth Ministerial Conference of the WTO, held during 3 December - 6 December 2013, was concluded at Bali, Indonesia.

**161.** d The Nobel Prize in Literature 2013 was awarded to Alice Munro "master of the contemporary short story".

**162.** a ISRO's Polar Satellite Launch Vehicle, PSLV-C24, successfully launched IRNSS-1B, the second satellite in the Indian Regional Navigation Satellite System (IRNSS), on April 04, 2014 from Satish Dhawan Space Centre SHAR, Sriharikota.

■■

# 3

# EVERYDAY SCIENCE

1. The Hindustan-Tibet road connects
   (a) Kalimpong with Lhasa
   (b) Shimla with Gangtok
   (c) Leh and Lhasa
   (d) Gangtok with Gyangyse (NLUD 2008)

2. The Aswan Dam is constructed at a point where
   (a) there are several waterfalls
   (b) there are several cataracts
   (c) there are several pigeon towers to facilitate the collection of droppings needed to keep the land productive
   (d) the old traditional basic irrigation facility exists (NLUD 2008)

3. The difference in time per degree longitude between any two places on globe is
   (a) 4 minutes (b) 5 minutes
   (c) 15 minutes (d) 30 minutes (NLUD 2008)

4. The best anti-knock compound used in petrol to increase mileage is
   (a) Ethyl-magnesium chloride
   (b) Sodium ethoxide
   (c) Zinc ethyl
   (d) Tetraethyl lead (NLUD 2008)

5. Rainbow is produced when sunlight falls on drops of rain. Which of the following physical phenomena are responsible for this?
   I. Dispersion II. Refraction
   III. Internal Reflection
   (a) II and III only (b) I and II only
   (c) I, II and III (d) I and III only (NLUD 2008)

6. Which of the following bombs, when dropped on a city, will kill only the inhabitants?
   (a) Atom Bomb (b) Hydrogen Bomb
   (c) Chemical Bomb (d) Neutron Bomb (NLUD 2008)

7. Which of the following will you use to remove rust stains on cloth?
   (a) Alcohol (b) Oxalic acid solution
   (c) Kerosene oil (d) Lime (NLUD 2008)

8. "Mach Number" is a term associated with the speed of
   (a) ships (b) cars
   (c) aeroplanes (d) light (NLUD 2008)

9. If an object is placed midway between two parallel plane mirrors facing each other, then the number of images that will appear in mirrors is
   (a) Four
   (b) Infinite
   (c) Two
   (d) Zero because the images will cancel each other (NLUD 2008)

10. The spherical shape of rain drops is due to
   (a) Atmospheric friction of air
   (b) Gravity of spherical earth
   (c) Surface tension of rain water
   (d) Viscosity of rain water (NLUD 2008)

11. What is the colour of pure diamond?
   (a) Light green (b) Light yellow
   (c) Light blue (d) Light pink (NLUD 2008)

12. Geiger counter is an instrument
   (a) determine is the heart beat rate
   (b) two detect radioactive radiation
   (c) to measure intensity of visible light
   (d) to count the baggage of an airport (NLUD 2008)

13. The film of oil and soapy water owe their brilliant colours to a combination of light reflection and
   (a) Refraction (b) Polarisation
   (c) Diffraction (d) Interference (NLUD 2008)

14. When a ship enters a sea from a river, its portion under water will
   (a) increase
   (b) decrease
   (c) show no change
   (d) increase or decrease alternatively (NLUD 2008)

**15.** For digestion of food, hydrochloric acid is secreted into stomach at a p*H* value of
(*a*) 2 (*b*) 4
(*c*) 6 (*d*) 18 **(NLUD 2008)**

**16.** Which of the following diseases is genetically linked?
(*a*) Epilepsy (*b*) Diabetes
(*c*) Colour blindness (*d*) Leucoderma
**(NLUD 2008)**

**17.** An eye defect in which one cannot distinguish between vertical and horizontal lines is called
(*a*) Myopia (*b*) Astigmatism
(*c*) Trachoma (*d*) Glaucoma
**(NLUD 2008)**

**18.** The gland which is attached to the digestive system but does not have any role to play in digesting food is
(*a*) Salivary gland (*b*) Liver
(*c*) Spleen (*d*) Pancreas
**(NLUD 2008)**

**19.** A reptile with a four-chambered heart is
(*a*) Snake (*b*) Lizard
(*c*) Crocodile (*d*) Turtle **(NLUD 2008)**

**20.** At a particular speed, a bus starts vibrating violently due to the phenomenon of
(*a*) Pitch (*b*) Resonance
(*c*) Rumbling (*d*) None of the above
**(NLUD 2009)**

**21.** When a bullet is fired upward vertically, it gains in
(*a*) speed (*b*) acceleration
(*c*) kinetic energy (*d*) potential energy
**(NLUD 2009)**

**22.** A motorcycle passing by disturbs radio and TV reception. The disturbance is caused because
(*a*) Intense sound waves shake the delicate electronic components of the receiver
(*b*) Metallic parts of the vehicle deflect the radio waves
(*c*) The sparking in the spark-plug of the vehicle generates electromagnetic radiation
(*d*) Modern motorcycle contains an electronic ignition system which emits ratio waves
**(NLUD 2009)**

**23.** Match the following scientists with their contributions

| | |
|---|---|
| (*a*) Weismann | I. Theory of Mutation |
| (*b*) Darwin | II. Principle of Independent Assortment |
| (*c*) Mendal | III. Theory of Evolution |
| (*d*) Hugo-de-varis | IV. Continuity of Germplasm |

(*a*) I - (*a*) II - (*b*) III - (*c*) IV - (*d*)
(*b*) I - (*b*) II - (*c*) III - (*d*) IV - (*a*)
(*c*) I - (*d*) II - (*c*) III - (*a*) IV - (*b*)
(*d*) I - (*d*) II - (*c*) III - (*b*) IV - (*a*) **(NLUD 2009)**

**24.** A Public Works Department was set up in India by
(*a*) Lord Dalhousie
(*b*) Lord Ripon
(*c*) Lord Warren Hastings
(*d*) Lord William Bentinck **(NLUD 2009)**

**25.** A cyclone is a system of wind in which the wind blows spirally
(*a*) towards the centre of low pressure
(*b*) towards central region of high pressure
(*c*) towards a region of low pressure
(*d*) outwards from a central region of high pressure
**(NLUD 2009)**

**26.** Contour bunding is used
(*a*) to stop the winds in sandy deserts
(*b*) to irrigate desert areas
(*c*) to prevent erosion in hilly areas
(*d*) None of the above **(NLUD 2009)**

**27.** The orbit of the earth is an ellipse and not a circle. The distance between earth and sun thus varies. On January 3, earth is closest to the sun (Perihelion). Similarly, earth is said to be at Aphelion, when it is farthest from the sun on
(*a*) March, 23 (*b*) July, 4
(*c*) December, 23 (*d*) April, 21
**(NLUD 2009)**

**28.** You are standing in a lift. The force on the floor of the lift due to your weight will
(*a*) become zero when the lift moves up with an acceleration of 9.8 m/s$^2$
(*b*) become zero when the lift moves down with an acceleration of 9.8 m/s$^2$
(*c*) become zero when the lift moves with an acceleration of 9.8 m/s$^2$ in any direction
(*d*) remain unchanged whatever be the value of acceleration of the lift **(NLUD 2012)**

**29.** What happens to the level of mercury in a barometer tube when it is taken down a coal mine? It
(*a*) falls
(*b*) remain unaltered
(*c*) rises
(*d*) rises and then falls **(NLUD 2012)**

**30.** A popping sound is heard in the ear when yawning or swallowing. This is caused by
(*a*) air in the cochlea
(*b*) the opening of the Eustachian tubes
(*c*) air entering the perilymph
(*d*) the moving of the jaws **(NLUD 2012)**

**31.** The body's thermostat is in the
(*a*) pineal (*b*) hypothalamus
(*c*) thyroid (*d*) pituitary
**(NLUD 2012)**

**32.** Which of the following theories has no connection with the origin of the earth?
(*a*) Nebular hypothesis of Laplace
(*b*) Tidal hypothesis of Jeans and Jeffreys
(*c*) Binary star theory of Lyttleton
(*d*) Convection current theory of Holmes
**(NLUD 2012)**

**33.** The blood enters the aorta from
(*a*) left ventricle (*b*) left auricle
(*c*) right ventricle (*d*) right auricle
**(NLUD 2012)**

**34.** Desert plants would be characterised by
(*a*) vivipary (*b*) aerenchyma
(*c*) aerial roots (*d*) sunken stomata
**(NLUD 2012)**

**35.** Why is sprouted gram considered more nutritious?
(*a*) seeds are storehouses of energy
(*b*) germinating seeds produce enzymes which are a rich source of protein
(*c*) seeds have plenty of amino acids and glucose
(*d*) sprouted gram is not more nutritious; it is just an old wives' tale that it is **(NLUD 2012)**

**36.** The edible portion of which of the following vegetables is not a stem?
(*a*) Potato (*b*) Sweet potato
(*c*) Ginger (*d*) Corn of Colocasia
**(NLUD 2012)**

**37.** A nautical mile is equal to
(*a*) 1825 metres (*b*) 2000 metres
(*c*) 1575 metres (*d*) 2050 metres
**(CLAT 2008)**

**38.** Enriched uranium, used in a nuclear reactor, is
(*a*) uranium freed of all impurities
(*b*) uranium treated with radiation
(*c*) uranium mixed with isotopes
(*d*) uranium alloy with aluminum **(CLAT 2008)**

**39.** Bio-fuels have become controversial because,
(*a*) they increase environmental pollution
(*b*) they slow down industrialization
(*c*) they reduce food cultivation
(*d*) they lead to degeneration of soil **(CLAT 2008)**

**40.** Why is Ozone Layer important?
(*a*) It absorbs greenhouse gases
(*b*) It protects Earth from ultraviolet radiation
(*c*) It maintains Earth's temperature
(*d*) It is a buffer against extra-terrestrial hazards
**(CLAT 2008)**

**41.** Genetically modified seeds have become controversial mainly because of
(*a*) adverse impact on human health
(*b*) adverse impact on flora around
(*c*) adverse impact on ozone layer
(*d*) emission of greenhouse gases **(CLAT 2008)**

**42.** What is the full form of the scanning technique CAT?
(*a*) Complete Anatomical Trepanning
(*b*) Computerized Automatic Therapy
(*c*) Computerized Axial Tomography
(*d*) Complete Axial Transmission **(CLAT 2009)**

**43.** Blue revolution refers to
(*a*) forest Development
(*b*) fishing
(*c*) poultry Farming
(*d*) horticulture **(CLAT 2009)**

**44.** Which one of the following Vitamins is responsible for blood clotting? **(CLAT 2009)**
(*a*) Vitamin A (*b*) Vitamin E
(*c*) Vitamin C (*d*) Vitamin K

**45.** The Ozone Layer thins down as a result of a chain chemical reaction that separates from the layer
(*a*) Oxygen (*b*) Chlorine **(CLAT 2009)**
(*c*) Nitrogen (*d*) Hydrogen

**46.** Galvanometer is an instrument to measure
(*a*) relative density of liquids
(*b*) electric currents
(*c*) pressure of gases
(*d*) distances **(CLAT 2010)**

**47.** The breakthrough in the ideas of Darwin on the evolution of species came after his visit to a cluster of islands and where he saw that each island supported its own form of finch. Name the islands?
(*a*) Ice land (*b*) Greenland
(*c*) Galapagos (*d*) Christian Islands
**(CLAT 2010)**

**48.** Which of the following trees has medicinal value?
(*a*) Pine (*b*) Teak
(*c*) Oak (*d*) Neem **(CLAT 2010)**

**49.** Which is the largest gland in human body?
(*a*) Pancreas (*b*) Liver
(*c*) Thyroid (*d*) Pituitary **(CLAT 2012)**

**50.** The largest living flightless bird is
(*a*) Emu (*b*) Kiwi
(*c*) Ostrich (*d*) Penguin **(CLAT 2012)**

**51.** Which of the following oceans has the shape of the English letter 'S'?
(*a*) Atlantic (*b*) Pacific
(*c*) Indian (*d*) Arctic **(CLAT 2012)**

**52.** Leukemia is a disease related to
(*a*) Kidney (*b*) Throat
(*c*) Blood (*d*) Eyes **(CLAT 2012)**

**53.** Light year is a unit of
(*a*) Distance (*b*) Time **(CLAT 2012)**
(*c*) Sound (*d*) Light intensity

**54.** Which one of the following is the most effective carrier of communications ? **(AILET 2013)**
(*a*) Cables (*b*) Radio waves
(*c*) Microwaves (*d*) Optical fibres

**55.** Which one of the following compounds is used as a sedative ? **(AILET 2013)**
(*a*) Potassium Bromide (*b*) Calcium Chloride
(*c*) Ethyl Alcohol (*d*) Phosphorus Trichloride

**56.** In a fire siren, a jet of air is directed against a series of evenly spaced holes in a rotating disc. As the disc speeds up, the tone
(*a*) maintains constant pitch
(*b*) drops in pitch
(*c*) increases in wavelength
(*d*) increases in frequency **(AILET 2013)**

**57.** After death, the
I. arteries are usually empty of blood
II. blood in arteries clots
III. veins are empty of blood
IV. veins are full of clots
(*a*) I and II (*b*) I only
(*c*) I and IV (*d*) III only **(AILET 2013)**

**58.** A victim of a road accident is unconscious. Put in correct order the steps in First- Aid.
I. Treating for cardiac arrest
II. Treating for asphyxia
III. Treating for shock
IV. Arrest Haemorrhage
V. Cleanse and cover wounds
(*a*) I, II, III, IV, V (*b*) II, I, IV, Ill, V
(*c*) II, III, I, IV, V (*d*) V, I, Ill, IV
**(AILET 2013)**

**59.** A feature 'Bluetooth' now common in mobile phones, gets its name from a **(CLAT 2013)**
(*a*) Chinese 10th Century King
(*b*) UK Software Company
(*c*) Greek Goddess
(*d*) Danish 10th Century King

**60.** Light Year is the unit of **(CLAT 2013)**
(*a*) Time (*b*) Distance
(*c*) Light (*d*) None of these

**61.** The leaning tower of Pisa does not fall because
(*a*) It is tapered at the top **(CLAT 2013)**
(*b*) It covers a large base area
(*c*) Its C.G. is inside the tower
(*d*) The vertical line passing through the C.G. of the tower falls within its base

**62.** Potential Energy is described by the expression: **(CLAT 2013)**
(*a*) PE = mgh (*b*) PE = ngh
(*c*) PE = oph (*d*) PE = pph

**63.** The latest country to launch a satellite during January 2013 from its soil and join the club of space-faring nations is **(AILET 2014)**
(*a*) South Korea (*b*) North Korea
(*c*) Ukraine (*d*) Iran

**64.** On January 1, 2013, internet has completed **(AILET 2014)**
(*a*) 26 years (*b*) 30 years
(*c*) 32 years (*d*) 28 years

**65.** Cloves, used as a spice, are derived from which of the following plant parts ?**(AILET 2014)**
(*a*) Seeds (*b*) Fruits
(*c*) Flower buds (*d*) Young leave

**66.** What does airbag, used for safety of car driver, contain ? **(AILET 2014)**
(*a*) Sodium bicarbonate (*b*) Sodium azide
(*c*) Sodium nitrite (*d*) Sodium peroxide

**67.** Which colour of heat radiation represents the highest temperature ? **(AILET 2014)**
(*a*) Blood red (*b*) Dark cherry
(*c*) Salmon (*d*) White

**68.** Mist is a result of which one of the following ? **(AILET 2014)**
(*a*) Condensation (*b*) Evaporation
(*c*) Sublimation (*d*) Saturation

**69.** Solvents are the substances used to dissolve other substances. Consider the following substances: (1) Water (2) Ether (3) Toluene (4) Chloroform (5) Ethanol **(CLAT 2014)**

Which of the above can be used as solvents?

(*a*) 1 and 2 (*b*) 2 and 3

(*c*) 3, 4 and 5 (*d*) All of these

**70.** Viruses are parasitic, having DNA/RNA; but, they can be crystallised and lack respiration. Therefore, they are treated as: **(CLAT 2014)**

(*a*) Living beings

(*b*) Non-living beings

(*c*) Both living and non-living beings

(*d*) None of the above

**71.** The change in the colour of stars is linked to: **(CLAT 2014)**

(*a*) Variation in their surface temperature

(*b*) Variation in their distance from the earth

(*c*) Fluctuations in their composition and size

(*d*) Irregular absorption or scattering in earth's atmosphere

**72.** Which one of the following gases is lighter than air? **(CLAT 2014)**

(*a*) Carbon dioxide (*b*) Chlorine

(*c*) Oxygen (*d*) Hydrogen

**73.** Name the scientist who is known as the father of modern genetics: **(CLAT 2014)**

(*a*) Jean-Baptiste Lamarck

(*b*) Hugo de Vries

(*c*) Gregor Johann Mendel

(*d*) Charles Darwin

**74.** Mention the correct abbreviation for ATM:

(*a*) Automated Teller Machine **(CLAT 2014)**

(*b*) Any Time Money

(*c*) All Time Money

(*d*) Auto-limited Teller Machine

## Solutions

**1.** b The Hindustan-Tibet road connects Shimla with Gangtok. The Hindustan-Tibet road, which passes through Himachal Pradesh, is a 300-mile (480km) highway which runs through Shimla, once the summer capital of India, and crosses the Indo-Tibetan border near Shipki Pass.

**2.** d The Aswan Damis an embankment dam situated across the Nile River in Aswan, Egypt.

**3.** a Chandrasekher limit is the limit beyond which stars suffer internal collapse.

**4.** d Tetraethyl lead is the compound which is used in petrol to increase mileage.

**5.** c Rainbow is produced because of the combine phenomena of dispersion, refraction and internal reflexation.

**6.** c Chemical bomb will kill only the inhabitant in use in the city.

**7.** b Oxalic acid solution is used to remove rust stains on cloth.

**8.** c "Mach Number" is a term associated with the speed of Aeroplanes.

**9.** b If an object is placed midway between two parallel plane mirrors facing each other, then the number of images that will appear in mirrors will be Infinite.

**10.** c It is due to Surface tension of rainwater that gives raindrop a spherical shape.

**11.** * A pure diamond is colorless.

**12.** b Geiger counter is an instrument to detect radioactive radiation.

**13.** d The film of oil and soapy water owe their brilliant colours to a combination of light reflection and Refraction.

**14.** b When a ship enters a sea from a river, its portion under water will decrease.

**15.** a For digestion of food, hydrochloric acid is secreted into stomach at a pH value of 2.

**16.** c Color blindness is a disease, which is genetically linked.

**17.** b Astigmatism is the disease in which one cannot distinguish between vertical and horizontal lines.

**18.** c Spleen is the gland, which is attached to the digestive system but does not have any role to play in digesting food.

**19.** c Crocodile is a reptile with a four-chambered heart.

**20.** b Due to the phenomena of resonance at a particular speed, if attained by a bus its starts vibrating violent.

**21.** d A built fired in the sky gains potential energy.

**22.** d

**23.** d The principle of independent assortment is given by Mendal.

**24.** a Sir Charles Wood's Dispatch for the first time in India setup a Public Works Department.

**25.** a A cyclone is a system of wind in which the wind blows spirally towards the centre of low pressure.

**26.** c Contour bunding is used to prevent soil erosion in hilly areas.

**27.** c Aphelion happens on December 23rd.

**28.** b The cardinal principles of physics dictate that during free fall because of force of gravity, which happens at the rate of 9.8 m/ s2, any physical body falling will not experience weight.

**29.** c The density of air rises if we go below sea level that's why the level of mercury rises in a barometer tube when it is taken down a coal mine.

**30.** b Eustachian tubes forms the part of middle ear. It was discovered by the sixteenth-century anatomist Bartolomeo Eustachi.

**31.** b Hypothalamus is the part of the brain that connects nervous system to endocrine system. Hypothalamus is responsible for certain activities concerning metabolism and automatic nervous system.

**32.** d Thermal Convection Current Theory propounded by Arthur Holmes contributes to the understanding of evolution of various landforms on earth due to thermal convection currents it does not deal with origin of earth. The theory describes the origin of for mountain building, continental drift, volcanism and formation of ocean trenches etc.

**33.** a The "Aorta" is the largest artery in the body, originating from the left ventricle of the heart and extending down to the abdomen,

**34.** d Sunken Stomata are found in predominantly in desert plants where moisture may be unavailable or in short supply for at least part of the year The aforementioned adaptation helps survival of such plants in the regions having low supply of moisture or none by reducing water loss.

**35.** b Enzymes are proteins that are involved in digestion and every chemical reaction in our body. According to food enzyme researcher, Dr. Edward Howell, "Without enzymes, no activity at all would take place. Neither vitamins, minerals, or hormones can do any work — without enzymes."

**36.** b Sweet potato is the root of the plant.

**37.** a A nautical mile is equal to 1825 metres.

**38.** a Enriching uranium increases the proportion of uranium atoms that can be "split" by fission to release energy (usually in the form of heat) that can be used to produce electricity.

**39.** c Bio fuels began to be in controversy because it was found out that they reduce food cultivation.

**40.** b Ozone Layer protects Earth from ultraviolet radiation.

**41.** b Genetically modified seeds are controversial because they have adverse impact on flora around.

**42.** c X-ray computed tomography, also computed tomography (CT scan) or computed axial tomography (CAT scan), is a medical imaging procedure that utilizes computer-processed X-rays to produce tomographic images or 'slices' of specific areas of the body. These cross-sectional images are used for diagnostic and therapeutic purposes in various medical disciplines

**43.** b Blue Revolution is the water equivalent of the green revolution and primarily refers to the management of water resources that can steer humanity to achieve drinking water and crop irrigation security.

**44.** d Vitamin K is necessary for normal blood clotting and synthesis of proteins found in plasma, bone, and kidneys and is found in spinach, lettuce, kale, cabbage, cauliflower, wheat bran, organ meats, cereals, some fruits, meats, dairy products, eggs.

**45.** a Ozone the layer of gas that forms a protective covering in the Earth's upper atmosphere is formed when oxygen molecules absorb ultraviolet photons and undergo a chemical reaction known as photo dissociation or photolysis, where a single molecule of oxygen breaks down to two oxygen atoms. The Ozone Layer thins down as a result of a chain chemical reaction that separates from the Oxygen layer.

**46.** b A galvanometer is a type of ammeter: an instrument for detecting and measuring electric current.

**47.** c The breakthrough in the ideas of Darwin on the evolution of species came after his visit to Galapagos, which is a cluster of islands. Wherein, he saw that each island supported its own form of finch.

**48.** d Products made from Neem trees have been used in India for over two millennia for their medicinal properties: Neem products are believed to be anthelmintic, antifungal, antidiabetic, antibacterial and antiviral. Neem products are also used in selectively controlling pests in plants. It is considered a major component in Ayurvedic and Unani medicine and is particularly prescribed for skin disease.

**49.** b The liver is the largest gland and the largest internal organ in the human body. A gland is defined as any group of cells that manufactures and releases substances for use somewhere else in the body. The liver not only makes and secretes substances, but it has over 5,000 functions that have been identified, including immune protection, waste removal, metabolism and energy storage.

**50.** c Ostrich is the largest living flightless bird. There are about forty species of flightless birds in existence today, the best known being the Ostrich, Emu, Cassowary, Rhea, Kiwi, and Penguin.

**51.** a The Atlantic Ocean shaped like the letter S is the second-largest of the world's oceanic divisions. With a total area of about 106,400,000 square kilometres (41,100,000 sq mi), it covers approximately 20% of the Earth's surface and about 26% of its water surface area. The first part of its name refers to Atlas of Greek mythology, making the Atlantic the "Sea of Atlas".

**52.** c Leukemia (from the Greek leukos "white", and haima "blood") is a type of cancer of the blood or bone marrow characterized by an abnormal increase of immature white blood cells called "blasts". Leukemia is a broad term covering a spectrum of diseases. In turn, it is part of the even broader group of diseases affecting the blood, bone marrow, and lymphoid system, which are all known as hematological neoplasms.

**53.** a Light-year is a unit of length equal to just under 10 trillion kilometres (or about 6 trillion miles). As defined by the International Astronomical Union (IAU), a light-year is the distance that light travels in a vacuum in one Julian year.

1 light-year
= 9460730472580800 metres (exactly)
= 5878625 million miles
= 63241.1 astronomical units
= 0.306601 parsecs

**54.** c Microwaves are most effective carrier whereas optical fibres are widely used in long distance propagation of waves in communications.

**55.** a Potassium bromide is a salt, widely used as an anti convulsant and a sedative .

**56.** d The pitch of a tone depends upon its frequency ,the tone with the higher pitch have the higher frequency.

**57.** c After death arteries empty out bloods and it starts settling down and the veins are full of blood clots.

**58.** b Priorities of Casualty Treatment
- Asphyxia
- Cardiac Arrest
- Severe Haemorrhage (Bleeding)
- Shock
- Cleaning and covering of wounds

**59.** d Danish 10th Century King

**60.** b Distance

**61.** d The vertical line passing through the C.G. of the tower falls within the base

**62.** a mgh

**63.** a South Korea is the latest country to launch a satellite during January 2013 from its soil and join the club of space-firing nations..

**64.** b On January 1, 2013, internet has completed 30 years.

**65.** c Cloves is nothing but the dried flower buds of the plant named Syzygium aromaticum.

**66.** b Inside the airbag is a gas generator containing a mixture of $NaN_3$, $KNO_3$, and $SiO_2$. Therefore the correct answer is sodium azide($NaN_3$).

**67.** d White color represents high intensity and hence high heat of radiation.

**68.** a Mist is formed by condensation. Although mist and fog look like smoke, they are actually tiny drops of water floating in the air. In fact, they are clouds that have formed at ground level.

**69.** d All of these. Water, Ether, Ethanol, Toluene, Chloroform and Ethanol are all used to dissolve other substances.

**70.** c It has been argued extensively whether viruses are living organisms. Most virologists consider them non-living, as they do not meet all the criteria of the generally accepted definition of life. They are similar to obligate intracellular parasites as they lack the means for self-reproduction outside a host cell, but unlike parasites, viruses are generally not considered to be true living organisms. A primary reason is that viruses do not possess a cell membrane or metabolize on their own - characteristics of all living organisms. Since they can be crystallized for years together, they remain inactive and dormant without the host, this is a trait similar to that of non-living.. Therefore, viruses can be considered both living and non-living.

**71.** a The color of a star is linked to its temperature and its temperature is linked to what processes are taking place in and on the surface of the star. Stars evolve during their lives, going through different phases of elements burning. Say a star has finished burning its hydrogen and goes to the helium burning phase, this will change the temperature (hence the color) of the star.

**72.** d Hydrogen, being the lightest existing gas (14 times less dense than air), seems to be the most appropriate gas for lifting.

**73.** c Gregor Mendel is currently known as the father of modern genetics. This lesson goes through a brief history of his life, workings as a scientist, and his findings.

**74.** a Automated teller machine is an electronic telecommunications device that enables the customers of a financial institution to perform financial transactions without the need for a human cashier, clerk or bank teller.

■■

# 4

# GEOGRAPHY

1. The Indian Territory which fell under the states on the eve of Independence was:
(a) only 20 Percent (b) over 80 percent
(c) 54 percent (d) 46 percent
**(NLUD 2008)**

2. High sea is
(a) the sea lying more than 5 km beyond the coast of a country
(b) the sea lying beyond a distance of 3 miles from the coast of any country
(c) the sea beyond 200 km of a cost of any country
(d) both (a) & (b) **(NLUD 2008)**

3. Which of the following is/ are included in the UNESCO's natural heritage site in India?
(1) Keoladeo
(2) Kaziranga National Park
(3) Manag Tiger Project
(4) Nanda Devi Biosphere Reserve
(a) 1 and 2 (b) 2 and 3
(c) 3 and 4 (d) All **(NLUD 2008)**

4. The metal that is most abundant in the earth is
(a) Silicon (b) Iron
(c) Aluminium (d) Nickel **(NLUD 2009)**

5. Which of the following is not a closed sea?
(a) Caspian sea (b) Aral sea
(c) Black sea (d) Red sea **(NLUD 2009)**

6. If Greenwich Mean Time is ahead by 12 hours, the place may be (10 = 4 minutes)
(a) 1800 West (b) 1800 East
(c) 900 West (d) None of the above
**(NLUD 2009)**

7. The largest country in terms of territory is
(a) Russia (b) Canada
(c) USA (d) China **(NLUD 2010)**

8. Which of the following mountains has oldest rocks in India?
(a) Aravallis (b) Himalayas
(c) Siwaliks (d) None **(NLUD 2011)**

9. Aurorae are a result of the interaction of earth's magnetosphere with
(a) the solar wind (b) the ozone layer
(c) radio waves (d) none of the above
**(NLUD 2012)**

10. Unlike the fluid core of the earth, the core of the moon is
(a) plasma (b) volatile gas
(c) viscous liquid (d) solid **(NLUD 2012)**

11. Which of the following theories has no connection with the origin of the earth?
(a) Nebular hypothesis of Laplace
(b) Tidal hypothesis of Jeans and Jeffreys
(c) Binary star theory of Lyttleton
(d) Convection current theory of Holmes
**(NLUD 2012)**

12. The contentious Baglihar dam is built on the river
(a) Indus (b) Jheelum
(c) Chenab (d) Satlez **(CLAT2008)**

13. The phenomenon called "Equinox" is due to the
(a) rotation of the Earth on its own axis
(b) revolution of the Earth on its inclined axis
(c) oblate-spheroid shape of the Earth
(d) gravitational pull of the planet **(CLAT2008)**

14. How many minutes for each degree of longitude does the local time of any place vary from the Greenwich time ?
(a) Four minutes (b) Two minutes
(c) Eight minutes (d) Ten minutes
**(CLAT2008)**

15. Which of the following is the largest peninsula in the world ?
(a) Indian Peninsula (b) Arabian Peninsula
(c) Malay Peninsula (d) Chinese Peninsula
**(CLAT2008)**

16. The Great Barrier Reef refers to
(a) Coral formation (b) Tidal waves
(c) Hill range (d) Man-made walls
**(CLAT2008)**

**17.** Which of the following is concerned with land forms ?

(*a*) Geology (*b*) Geomorphology
(*c*) Ecology (*d*) Geography

**(CLAT2008)**

**18.** The World's largest river is

(*a*) Brahmaputra (*b*) Amazon
(*c*) Nile (*d*) Mississippi

**(CLAT2008)**

**19.** Tsunami is caused by

(*a*) plate tectonics
(*b*) underwater ridges
(*c*) underwater volcanic activity
(*d*) pressure from Earth's core **(CLAT2008)**

**20.** Suez Canal connects

(*a*) Mediterranean Sea and Red Sea
(*b*) Mediterranean Sea and Black Sea
(*c*) Baltic Sea and Red Sea
(*d*) Baltic Sea and Black Sea **(CLAT2009)**

**21.** Savannath grasslands are found in

(*a*) North America (*b*) Africa
(*c*) Australia (*d*) East Asia **(CLAT2009)**

**22.** Periyar Wild-Life sanctuary is situated in the state of

(*a*) Tamilnadu (*b*) Karnataka
(*c*) Kerala (*d*) Andhra-Pradesh

**(CLAT 2010)**

**23.** Harare is the capital of

(*a*) Zambia (*b*) Zaire Republic
(*c*) Zimbabwe (*d*) Yemen **(CLAT 2010)**

**24.** Which is the largest island in the world (if Australia is not considered an island)?

(*a*) Iceland (*b*) Borneo
(*c*) Sumatra (*d*) Greenland

**(CLAT 2010)**

**25.** Which of the following is not a union territory?

(*a*) Tripura (*b*) Daman and Diu
(*c*) Lakshadweep (*d*) Puducherry

**(CLAT 2010)**

**26.** Baglihar dam has been a matter of dispute between which nations?

(*a*) Bangladesh and Myanmar
(*b*) Myanmar and China
(*c*) India and China
(*d*) India and Pakistan **(CLAT 2011)**

**27.** The famous Akshardham temple is situated in the city of

(*a*) Jamnagar (*b*) Gandhinagar
(*c*) Jammu (*d*) Madurai **(CLAT2012)**

**28.** Which strait separates Europe from Africa

(*a*) Mallaica (*b*) Gibralter
(C) Berring (*d*) Palk **(CLAT2012)**

**29.** Which is the longest shipping canal in the world?

(*a*) Panama Canal
(*b*) Suez Canal
(*c*) White Sea-Baltic Canal
(*d*) Kiel Canal **(CLAT2012)**

**30.** The longest highway in India runs from

(*a*) Kolkata to Jammu
(*b*) Shillong to Amritsar
(*c*) Ambala to Nagercoil
(*d*) Varanasi to Kanyakumari **(CLAT2012)**

**31.** The longest irrigation canal in India is called

(*a*) Upper Bari Doab Canal
(*b*) Indira Gandhi Canal
(*c*) Sirhind Canal
(*d*) Yamuna Canal **(CLAT2012)**

**32.** The sun reaches its maximum angular distance from the equator at the

(*a*) zenith
(*b*) solstice
(*c*) equinox
(*d*) noon time **(AILET 2013)**

**33.** The difference in the duration of day and night increases as one move from

(*a*) West to East
(*b*) East and West of the prime meridian
(*c*) Poles to equator
(*d*) Equator to poles **(AILET 2013)**

**34.** When can one record the lowest temperature of air ?

(*a*) Just before sunrise (*b*) At midnight
(*c*) At 3 a.m. (*d*) At sunrise

**(AILET 2013)**

**35.** What is the difference between a geyser and a hot spring ?

(*a*) Water is ejected explosively in a geyser
(*b*) Water from a geyser may be cold
(*c*) Geysers are formed on volcanic mountains
(*d*) Geysers are more common in cold countries

**(AILET 2013)**

**36.** The Headquarter of European Union is situated in **(CLAT 2013)**

(*a*) England (*b*) Germany

(*c*) France (*d*) Belgium

**37.** Dr. Norman Borlaugh is famous as father of the Green Revolution in 1960s. His initial goal was to create varieties of wheat adapted to the climate of **(CLAT 2013)**

(*a*) Mexico (*b*) India

(*c*) USA (*d*) China

**38.** Which pair of states does not touch each other

(*a*) Meghalaya, Manipur **(CLAT 2013)**

(*b*) Chhattisgarh, U.P.

(*c*) Rajasthan, Punjab

(*d*) J.K., H.P.

**39.** Baglihar dam, is constructed on river

(*a*) Ravi (*b*) Chenab **(CLAT 2013)**

(*c*) Indus (*d*) Sutlej

**40.** The first person to set foot on the moon on July 20, 1969 and who died on Aug. 25, 2012 was **(CLAT 2013)**

(*a*) Nevil Armstrong (*b*) Neil Armstrong

(*c*) Gagan Narang (*d*) Michael Phelps

**41.** The earlier name of which city was New Amsterdam? **(CLAT 2013)**

(*a*) Chicago (*b*) California

(*c*) Washington D.C. (*d*) New York City

**42.** Where did Kuchipudi, an eminent dance form, originate? **(CLAT 2013)**

(*a*) Kerala (*b*) Andhra Pradesh

(*c*) Uttar Pradesh (*d*) Tamil Nadu

**43.** Who founded the Red Cross? **(CLAT 2013)**

(*a*) Henry Dunant (*b*) Alexander

(*c*) James Cook (*d*) Bismark

**44.** How many states are there in the European Union ? **(AILET 2014)**

(*a*) 28 (*b*) 24

(*c*) 36 (*d*) 22

**45.** Which of the following divides India into Northern and Southern parts ? **(AILET 2014)**

(*a*) Equator (*b*) Tropic of Cancer

(*c*) Tropic of Capricorn (*d*) Arctic Circle

**46.** With which one of the following countries, India shares maximum length of the border ? **(AILET 2014)**

(*a*) Bangladesh (*b*) Pakistan

(*c*) China (*d*) Nepal

**47.** Which of the following planets has the maximum number of natural satellites? **(CLAT 2014)**

(*a*) Earth (*b*) Mars

(*c*) Jupiter (*d*) Saturn

**48.** Which one of the following does NOT remain to be a planet now? **(CLAT 2014)**

(*a*) Neptune (*b*) Uranus

(*c*) Pluto (*d*) Venus

## Solutions

**1.** c Over 54 percent of the Indian Territory fell under the states on the eve of Independence.

**2.** a High sea is that part of the sea which lays more than 5 km beyond the coast of a country

**3.** d Recently, Western Ghats from India has been included into UNESCO's World natural heritage site.

**4.** a Silicon is the most abundant metal in the earth.

**5.** d Red Sea is not a closed sea.

**6.** b If the GMT is a head by 12 hours the place may be 1800 east.

**7.** a Russia is the largest country in terms of territory. India is the 7$^{th}$ Largest in the List.

**8.** * The literal meaning of the term "Arravali" is "Line of Peaks" . It a range of mountains in western India and eastern Pakistan running approximately 800 km from northwest to southwest across Indian states of Rajasthan, Haryana, and Gujarat and Pakistani provinces of Punjab and Sindh.

**9.** a Aurora is the physical phenomenon associated with the display of natural light he sky particularly in the high latitude (Arctic and Antarctic) regions, caused by the collision of energetic charged particles with atoms in the high altitude atmosphere.

**10.** d The Core of the Moon consists of volatile Gas. Recently China declared that it will launch an unmanned lunar rover Chang'e-3 on moon in the year 2013.

**11.** d Thermal Convection Current Theory propounded by Arthur Holmes contributes to the understanding of evolution of various landforms on earth due to thermal convection currents it does not deal with origin of earth. The theory describes the origin of for mountain building, continental drift, volcanism and formation of ocean trenches etc.

**12.** c Chenab River is located in State of Jammu and Kashmir.

**13.** b An equinox occurs twice a year (around 20 March and 22 September), when the tilt of the Earth's axis is inclined neither away from nor towards the Sun, the center of the Sun being in the same plane as the Earth's equator.

**14.** a Greenwich Mean Time is an absolute time reference and does n't change with seasons. It was established in 1884 at the International Meridian Conference, when it was decided to place the Prime Meridian at Greenwich, England.

**15.** b Arabian Peninsula is the largest peninsula in the world.

**16.** a The Great Barrier Reef is the World 's Largest Coral Reef System. The reef is located in the Coral Sea, off the coast of Queensland in northeast Australia. It is the world's biggest single structure made by living organisms.

**17.** b Geomorphology (Geo= earth, morph=form, Logos=study) is the scientific study of landforms and the processes that shape them. It aims to understand why landscapes look the way they do, to understand landform history and dynamics.

**18.** b Nile is the world's largest river.

**19.** c Tsunami is caused by underwater volcanic activity.

**20.** a The Suez Canal, also known by the nickname "The Highway to India", is an artificial sea-level waterway in Egypt, connecting the Mediterranean Sea and the Red Sea. Opened in November 1869 after 10 years of construction work, it allows transportation by water between Europe and Asia without navigation around Africa.

**21.** b A savanna, or savannah, is a grassland ecosystem characterized by the trees being sufficiently small or widely spaced so that the canopy does not close. The open canopy allows sufficient light to reach the ground to support an unbroken herbaceous layer consisting primarily of grasses. Among the given options largest amount of Savannah is in Africa, therefore, Africa is the most likely correct response.

**22.** c Periyar Wildlife Sanctuary is a protected area in the districts of Idukki and Pathanamthitta in Kerala, South India. It is notable as an elephant reserve and a tiger reserve. The protected area covers an area of 925 km2 (357 sq mi). 350 km2 (140 sq mi) of the core zone was declared as the Periyar National Park in 1982.

**23.** c Harare (known as Salisbury before 1982) is the largest city and capital of Zimbabwe. It has an estimated population of 1,606,000 (2009), with 2,800,000 in its metropolitan area (2006). Administratively, Harare is an independent city equivalent to a province. It is Zimbabwe's largest city and its administrative, commercial, and communications centre. The city is a trade centre for tobacco, maize, cotton, and citrus fruits. Manufactures include textiles, steel, and chemicals, and gold is mined in the area.

**24.** d Traditionally, landmasses completely or mostly surrounded by water are classified as continents (when they are large enough) or islands. According to this classification, mainland Australia (7.6 million km$^2$) is the smallest continent and Greenland (2.1 million km$^2$) is the largest island.

**25.** a Tripura is a state in Northeast India, and one of the Seven Sister States. The third-smallest state of India, it occupies an area of 4,051 sq mi (10,490 sq.km). Tripura is surrounded by Bangladesh on the north, south, and west. The Indian states of Assam and Mizoram lie to its east. The state capital is Agartala. A landlocked state, Tripura's geography is characterized by several north-south hill ranges with intervening valleys, and plain in the western part of the state.

**26.** d Baglihar dam is on the river Chenab in the state of Jammu and Kashmir it has been the matter of controversy between India and Pakistan as Pakistan claimed that design parameters of Baglihar project violated the Indus Water Treaty.

**27.** b Akshardham (inGandhinagar) is one of the largest temples in the Indian state of Gujarat. The temple complex combines art, architecture, education, exhibitions and research at one place. The temple came to international attention when two heavily armed terrorists attacked it in September 2002.It was inaugurated on November 2, 1992, during the centenary celebrations of Yogiji Maharaj.

**28.** b The Strait of Gibraltar is a narrow strait that connects the Atlantic Ocean to the Mediterranean Sea and separates Gibraltar and Spain in Europe from Morocco in Africa. The name comes from the Rock of Gibraltar, which in turn originates from the Arabic Jebel Tariq (meaning "Tariq's mountain") .Europe and Africa are separated by 7.7 nautical miles (14.3 km; 8.9 mi) of ocean at the strait's narrowest point. The Strait's depth ranges between 300 and 900 metres (160 and 490 fathoms; 980 and 3,000 ft)

**29.** c The White Sea – Baltic Sea Canal opened on 2 August 1933, is the longest ship canal in the world. It connects the White Sea with Lake Onega, which is further connected to the Baltic Sea.

**30.** d National Highway 44, commonly referred to as NH 44(old NH 7), is the longest Highway in India that runs through the states of Uttar Pradesh, Madhya Pradesh, Maharashtra, Andhra Pradesh, Karnataka, and Tamil Nadu.

**31.** b Indira Gandhi Canal is the longest canal in India.It starts from the Harike Barrage at Sultanpur, a few kilometers below the confluence of the Sutlej and Beas rivers in Punjab state.

**32.** b Solstice, happens at the two instants when the Sun is at its greatest angular distance from the celestial equator. During the course of a year, the apparent motion of the Sun as seen from Earth moves from south to north and back to south again. When the Sun changes direction from north to south or vice verse, it seems to stands still momentarily. This point of time is known as the solstice.

**33.** d As one moves from the equator towards pole the difference in length between daylight and darkness becomes greater, and so therefore does the difference in length between day and night hours.

**34.** a The lowest temperature of air is recorded just before the sun is about to come out i.e just before sunrise.

**35.** a Hot springs are bubbling of water that comes from under ground ,a geyser happens when underground water turns to steam and rushes through out the surface.

**36.** d Belgium

**37.** a Mexico

**38.** a Meghalaya, Manipur

**39.** b Chenab

**40.** b Neil Armstrong

**41.** d New York City

**42.** b Andhra Pradesh

**43.** a Henry Dunant

**44.** a The European Union (EU) is a politico-economic union of 28 member states that are primarily located in Europe. The EU operates through a system of supranational independent institutions and intergovernmental negotiated decisions by the member states.

**45.** b Tropic of Cancer divides India into Northern and Southern parts.

**46.** a India shares maximum length of the border with Bangladesh.

**47.** c The planet with the most moons in the Solar System is Jupiter, with a total of 63 confirmed moons (as of 2009). Eight of Jupiter's moons are regular satellites, with 4 large, spherical moons, and 4 smaller moons that orbit closer to Jupiter. Jupiter has an additional 55 tiny irregular satellites.

**48.** c To qualify as a planet in orbit around our Sun, a chunk of rock must have been made round by its own gravity; have cleared its neighbourhood of other debris; and not be a satellite of another planetary body. Mercury, Venus, Earth, Mars, Jupiter, Saturn, Uranus and Neptune all fulfil these criteria. But Pluto is just one of many bits of icy debris in orbit at the edge of our Solar System, known as trans-neptunian objects. Pluto's membership of the trans-neptunians disqualifies it from being a fully-fledged planet because it has not 'cleared its orbit'.

■■

# 5

# HISTORY

**1.** Match the following:

A. Nagpur session (1920)
B. Madras session
C. Calcutta session (1928)
D. Lahore session (1929)
E. Karachi session (1930)

(i) Poorna Swaraj
(ii) Changes in the Constitution of Congress
(iii) Resolution of Fundamental Rights and National Economics Policy
(iv) Return of Gandhiji to active politics after 6 years
(v) Independence resolution passed for the first time

| | A | B | C | D | E |
|---|---|---|---|---|---|
| (*a*) | iii | i | ii | v | iv |
| (*b*) | i | ii | iv | v | iii |
| (*c*) | ii | v | iv | i | iii |
| (*d*) | i | iii | ii | v | iv |

**(NLUD 2008)**

**2.** Genocide occurred in all but one case
(*a*) Bosnia (*b*) Nazi Germany
(*c*) Rwanda (*d*) Gulf War **(NLUD 2008)**

**3.** Which Inn of Court called Gandhiji to the Bar?
(*a*) Inner Temple (*b*) Middle Temple
(*c*) Lincoln's Inn (*d*) Gray's Inn **(NLUD 2008)**

**4.** The island of Bombay was acquired by the East India Company from
(*a*) Netherlands (*b*) France
(*c*) Portugal (*d*) Spain **(NLUD 2008)**

**5.** The outstanding achievement of Todar Mal was in the field of
(*a*) Military Conquests
(*b*) Revenue Administration
(*c*) Religious Reforms
(*d*) Art and Architecture **(NLUD 2008)**

**6.** The deity most praised in Rigveda is
(*a*) Indra (*b*) Agni
(*c*) Mitra (*d*) Varuna **(NLUD 2008)**

**7.** The Peacock throne of Shahjahan was taken away by
(*a*) Changez Khan (*b*) Timur
(*c*) Nadir Shah (*d*) Ahmad Shah Abdali **(NLUD 2008)**

**8.** Shivaji's Council of Ministers was called
(*a*) Nava Patnas (*b*) Ashta Pradhans
(*c*) Ashta Diggajas (*d*) Mantri Parishad **(NLUD 2008)**

**9.** Charak was the court physician of
(*a*) Asoka
(*b*) Kanishka
(*c*) Chandragupta Maurya
(*d*) Samudragupta **(NLUD 2008)**

**10.** Who was the first Sultan of Delhi to introduce the practice of 'Sijda'?
(*a*) Balban (*b*) Muhammad Tughlaq
(*c*) Alauddin Khilji (*d*) Firoz Tughlaq **(NLUD 2009)**

**11.** Which of the following is rightly regarded as a milestone in the field of education in India?
(*a*) Sir Charles Wood's Despatch
(*b*) Stanley's Despatch
(*c*) Hunter Commission Report
(*d*) University Commission **(NLUD 2009)**

**12.** The Calcutta session of the Indian National Congress held in September 1920, passed a resolution which led to the
(*a*) Non-Cooperation Movement
(*b*) Civil Disobedience Movement
(*c*) Home Rule Movement
(*d*) Quit India Movement **(NLUD 2009)**

**13.** One of the following statements was not among the Simon Commission's recommendations
(*a*) dyarchy to be abolished in the provinces
(*b*) reconstitution of the Central Legislature
(*c*) establishment of the Provincial Public Service Commission for all Provinces
(*d*) Indian Council is not needed to advice the Secretary of State for India. **(NLUD 2009)**

**14.** Which of the following are the principal features of Government of India Act, 1919

1. Introduction of dyarchy in the executive government of the provinces
2. Introduction of separate communal electorate for Muslims
3. Devolution of legislative authority by the Centre to the Provinces
4. Expansion and reconstitution of Central and Provincial Legislature

**Codes:**

(*a*) 1, 2 and 3 (*b*) 1, 2 and 4
(*c*) 2, 3 and 4 (*d*) 1, 3 and 4 **(NLUD 2009)**

**15.** The Indian National Congress asserted in ............ that India would not accept any constitution made by anyone other then people of India and without outside interference.

(*a*) 1942 (*b*) 1936
(*c*) 1927 (*d*) 1935 **(NLUD 2009)**

**16.** Proclamation of Emergency on the ground of internal disturbance was for the first time made in

(*a*) 1971 (*b*) 1972
(*c*) 1974 (*d*) 1975 **(NLUD 2009)**

**17.** The first sitting Head of the State to be charged with 'War crimes and crimes against humanity' by the International Criminal Court is

(*a*) President Manuel Zelaya of Honduras
(*b*) President Omar al-Bashir of Sudan
(*c*) President Siad Bane of Somalia
(*d*) President Martin Torrijos of Panama **(NLUD 2010)**

**18.** India's Imperial Capital was officially shifted from Calcutta to Delhi in

(*a*) 1912 (*b*) 1935
(*c*) 1947 (*d*) 1872 **(NLUD 2010)**

**19.** In India, women were allowed to contest election and to public offices for the first time in

(*a*) 1909 (*b*) 1919
(*c*) 1935 (*d*) 1926 **(NLUD 2010)**

**20.** The person who promoted the establishment of the International Committee of the Red Cross was

(*a*) Charles Dickens
(*b*) Henry Dunant
(*c*) Henry Ford
(*d*) Robert Frost **(NLUD 2010)**

**21.** Which of the following states got separated from India in 1937 ?

(*a*) Pakistan (*b*) Sikkim
(*c*) Sri Lanka (*d*) Burma **(NLUD 2010)**

**22.** Which of the following statements are correct with regard to the Indus Valley civilisation?

I. The people of this civilisation were the earliest to make use of cotton.
II. They did not cremate their dead.
III. A grid system was followed in city planning.
IV. Stone was the chief building material.

(*a*) I and II
(*b*) II and III
(*c*) III and IV
(*d*) I and III **(NLUD 2012)**

**23.** The famous queen Chand Bibi who fought gallantly against Akbar belonged to

(*a*) Berar
(*b*) Ahmadnagar
(*c*) Bijapur
(*d*) Golconda **(NLUD 2012)**

**24.** Who among the following Indian rulers established embassies in foreign countries on modern lines?

(*a*) Haider Ali
(*b*) Mir Qasim
(*c*) Shah Alam II
(*d*) Tipu Sultan **(NLUD 2012)**

**25.** Which one of the following may be called a 'political' cause of the 1857 Revolt?

(*a*) The subsidiary alliance system of Wellesley
(*b*) The Religious Disabilities Act of 1856
(*c*) Low pay and poor prospects of the sepoys
(*d*) Dalhousie's annexation policy **(NLUD 2012)**

**26.** The first time that Mahatma Gandhi tried out his method of *satyagraha* was

(*a*) in South Africa against racist policies
(*b*) against indigo planters in Champaran
(*c*) in the Kheda no-rent campaign
(*d*) at Bardoli **(NLUD 2012)**

**27.** The Royal Indian Navy ratings revolted in February 1946 to protest against

(*a*) the treatment meted out to them
(*b*) the punishment meted out to the INA officials
(*c*) the firing on some ratings of the *HMIS Talwar*
(*d*) the Government's suppression of Congress activities **(NLUD 2012)**

**28.** The Preamble enshrines certain ideals that were first spelt out in
(*a*) the speech by Jawaharlal Nehru on the banks of Ravi when he called for *Purna Swaraj*
(*b*) the Nehru Report
(*c*) a resolution adopted at Karachi session of the Indian National Congress
(*d*) the Objectives Resolution adopted by the Constituent Assembly **(NLUD 2012)**

**29.** Vande Mataram is composed by
(*a*) Rabindranath Tagore
(*b*) Sharatchandra Chatterji
(*c*) Bankimchandra Chatterjee
(*d*) Surendranath Banerji **(CLAT 2008)**

**30.** The monk who spread Buddhism in Tibet and Far-East:
(*a*) Ananda (*b*) Nagarjuna
(*c*) Padmasambava (*d*) Mahendra
**(CLAT 2008)**

**31.** By signing which pact with Gandhiji did Ambedkar give up his demand for separate electorates:
(*a*) Poona Pact (*b*) Aligarh Pact
(*c*) Deccan Pact (*d*) Delhi Pact
**(CLAT 2008)**

**32.** The Chipko movement is associated with
(*a*) preventing the felling of trees
(*b*) afforestation
(*c*) transparency in public life
(*d*) sustainable development **(CLAT 2008)**

**33.** The first Great Indian Empire was
(*a*) Magadhan Empire (*b*) Kuru Empire
(*c*) Pandava Empire (*d*) Gandhara Empire
**(CLAT 2008)**

**34.** The first President of Indian National Congress
(*a*) A.O. Hume (*b*) W.C. Banerji
(*c*) Dadabhai Nauroji (*d*) Phirozeshah Mehta
**(CLAT 2008)**

**35.** The King who gave permission to establish East India Company in India
(*a*) Jahangir (*b*) Aurangzeb
(*c*) Shahjahan (*d*) Shershah
**(CLAT 2008)**

**36.** The person who conceptualized the idea of Pakistan
(*a*) M.A. Jinnah (*b*) Hakim Azmal Khan
(*c*) Mohammad Iqbal (*d*) Liaqusat Ali Khan
**(CLAT 2008)**

**37.** Khilafat movement was organized
(*a*) for getting Muslim Homeland
(*b*) as a protest against British suppression of Turks
(*c*) to preserve Turkish Empire with Khilafat as temporal head
(*d*) as a protest against communal politics
**(CLAT 2008)**

**38.** The pattern of Centre-State relations in India can be traced back to
(*a*) The U.S. Constitution
(*b*) The Government of India Act, 1935
(*c*) Motilal Nehru Committee Report
(*d*) Ambedkar's vision **(CLAT 2008)**

**39.** First woman Prime-Minister in the World was from
(*a*) Sri Lanka (*b*) Bhutan
(*c*) India (*d*) Nepal **(CLAT 2009)**

**40.** Who destroyed the Somnath temple in Gujarat?
(*a*) Mohammed Ghouri
(*b*) Mahmud Ghaznavi
(*c*) Changhez Khan
(*d*) Taimur Lang **(CLAT 2010)**

**41.** In Cape Trafalgar, the famous battle of Trafalgar was fought in 1805. Where is Cape Trafalgar situated?
(*a*) Italy (*b*) Greece
(*c*) Spain (*d*) Portugal
**(CLAT 2010)**

**42.** Lumbini is the place where the Buddha
(*a*) attained nirvana
(*b*) attained enlightenment
(*c*) was born
(*d*) was married **(CLAT 2010)**

**43.** Who wrote 'Mudra Rakshasa'?
(*a*) Vishakhadatta (*b*) Bana Bhatta
(*c*) Kaliclasa (*d*) Jaya Dev **(CLAT 2010)**

**44.** The venue of Asian Games in 1970 was
(*a*) Beijing (*b*) Jakarta
(*c*) Bangkok (*d*) New Dethi
**(CLAT 2010)**

**45.** 1929 is known for
(*a*) visit of Simon Commission to India
(*b*) congress resolution for complete independence of India
(*c*) coming of Indian National Congress under the leadership of Mahatma Gandhi
(*d*) burma was made a part of India **(CLAT 2010)**

**46.** I.N.S. Airavat is India's
(*a*) amphibious ship (*b*) submarine
(*c*) destroyer (*d*) frigate **(CLAT 2010)**

**47.** In which year Bastille fell on 14th of July?
(*a*) 1879 (*b*) 1789
(*c*) 1787 (*d*) none of them
**(CLAT 2010)**

**48.** Which of the following was not the base of L.T.T.E. before being captured by Srilankan Forces?
(*a*) Elephant Pass (*b*) Kilinochchi
(*c*) Mullaithivu (*d*) Murid ke
**(CLAT 2010)**

**49.** Which political party does Raj Babbar belong to?
(*a*) Samajwadi
(*b*) Bharatiya Janata Party
(*c*) Congress
(*d*) Bahujan Samaj Party **(CLAT 2010)**

**50.** Mahatma Gandhi never became a Nobel Laureate, but he was nominated five times. In which of the following years he was not nominated?
(*a*) 1937 (*b*) 1939
(*c*) 1948 (*d*) 1940 **(CLAT 2010)**

**51.** When was the University of Bombay established?
(*a*) 1861 (*b*) 1857
(*c*) 1909 (*d*) 1890 **(CLAT 2010)**

**52.** In May 2009, in the final of Sultan Azlan Shah Championship Indian men's Hockey team defeated
(*a*) Pakistan (*b*) Argentina
(*c*) New Zealand (*d*) Malaysia
**(CLAT 2010)**

**53.** With whose permission did the English set up their first factory at Surat?
(*a*) Akbar (*b*) Shahjahan
(*c*) Jahangir (*d*) Aurangzeb
**(CLAT 2010)**

**54.** The group of nations known as G-8 started as 0-7. Which among the following was not one of them?
(*a*) Canada (*b*) Italy
(*c*) Russia (*d*) Japan **(CLAT 2010)**

**55.** Emperor Akbar the Great, died in the year
(*a*) 1505 (*b*) 1605
(*c*) 1606 (*d*) 1590 **(CLAT 2010)**

**56.** What was the name of Emperor Shahjahan before he became Emperor?
(*a*) Kusrau (*b*) Khurram
(*c*) Parvez (*d*) Shaheryar
**(CLAT 2010)**

**57.** Prophet Mohammed was born in
(*a*) 570 A.D. (*b*) 720 A.D.
(*c*) 620 A.D. (*d*) 510 A.D. **(CLAT 2010)**

**58.** When was the First World Wan declared?
(*a*) 1914 (*b*) 1915
(*c*) 1918 (*d*) 1913 **(CLAT 2010)**

**59.** Which *Gharana* of Classical singing did Late Pandit Bhimsen Joshi belong to?
(*a*) Dhrupad (*b*) Maihar
(*c*) Kirana (*d*) Etawah **(CLAT 2011)**

**60.** 14$^{th}$ March 2011 was the 80$^{th}$ Anniversary of the first Indian sound Film (talkie). Which Movie was it?
(*a*) Jahan Ara (*b*) Alam Ara
(*c*) Noorjehan (*d*) None of the above
**(CLAT 2011)**

**61.** Whose teaching inspired the French Revolution?
(*a*) Rousseau (*b*) Locke
(*c*) Hegel (*d*) Wagner **(CLAT 2012)**

**62.** Taiwan was earlier known as
(*a*) Fuchow (*b*) Marshall Island
(*c*) Formosa (*d*) Macau **(CLAT 2012)**

**63.** Le Corbusier, the architect of Chandigarh was a national of
(*a*) Britain (*b*) Portugal
(*c*) France (*d*) Netherlands
**(CLAT 2012)**

**64.** The first ever formula one race in India was held in
(*a*) Greater Noida (*b*) New Delhi
(*c*) Faridabad (*d*) Pune **(CLAT 2012)**

**65.** Sher Shah is well-known for his administrative skill, especially his
(*a*) Market control steps
(*b*) Land revenue system
(*c*) Mansabdari system
(*d*) Law and order' **(AILET 2013)**

**66.** A monument resembling Taj Mahal was created by Aurangzeb in
(*a*) Ahmedabad (*b*) Aurangabad
(*c*) Hoshangabad (*d*) Daulatabad
**(AILET 2013)**

**67.** The maximum work in popularising female education in the nineteenth century was done by

(*a*) Ishwar Chandra Vidyasagar

(*b*) J.E.D. Bethune

(*c*) D.K. Karve

(*d*) Raja Ram Mohan Roy **(AILET 2013)**

**68.** The most learned ruler of the Delhi Sultanate who was well versed in various branches of learning including Astronomy, Mathematics and Medicine was

(*a*) Iltutmish

(*b*) Alauddin Khalji

(*c*) Muhammad Bin Tughlaq

(*d*) Sikandar Lodhi **(AILET 2013)**

**69.** Permanent Settlement was introduced to

(*a*) help the ryots

(*b*) earn a fixed and regular revenue

(*c*) help the landlords

(*d*) improve the prospects of agriculture

**(AILET 2013)**

**70.** Navjivan Trust was instituted with the objectives of propagating peaceful means of attaining third Swaraj, by **(CLAT 2013)**

(*a*) Mohan Das Karam Chand Gandhi

(*b*) Lala Lajpat Rai

(*c*) Bal Gangadhar Tilak

(*d*) Dr. Ambedkar

**71.** The grant of Diwani of Bengal, Bihar and Orissa is associated with **(CLAT 2013)**

(*a*) Nawab Shuja-ud-Daula

(*b*) Nawab Asif-ud-Daula

(*c*) Shah Alam I

(*d*) Shah Alam II

**72.** The last British Emperor of India was

**(CLAT 2013)**

(*a*) King George I (*b*) King George III

(*c*) King George V (*d*) King George VI

**73.** Palaeolithic period is also known as

**(CLAT 2013)**

(*a*) Mesolithic Age (*b*) Late Stone Age

(*c*) Old Stone Age (*d*) Neolithic Age

**74.** Capital of India was transferred from Calcutta to Delhi in the year **(CLAT 2013)**

(*a*) 1901 (*b*) 1911

(*c*) 1921 (*d*) 1922

**75.** The first Shaka king in India was **(CLAT 2013)**

(*a*) Rudradaman (*b*) Menadar

(*c*) Maues (*d*) Damanrudra

**76.** Lord Buddha's image is sometimes shown with the hand gesture, called 'Bhumisparsha Mudra'. It signifies: **(CLAT 2014)**

(*a*) Buddha's calling of the Earth to watch over Mara and to prevent Mara from disturbing his meditation.

(*b*) Buddha's calling of the Earth to witness his purity and chastity despite the temptations of Mara.

(*c*) The gesture of debate or discussion/argument.

(*d*) Both (*a*) and (*b*) are correct.

**77.** Which one of the following scripts of ancient India was mostly written from right to left?

(*a*) Nandnagari (*b*) Brahmi **(CLAT 2014)**

(*c*) Kharoshti (*d*) Sharada

**78.** During the time of which Mughal Emperor did the East India Company establish its first factory in India? **(CLAT 2014)**

(*a*) Akbar (*b*) Jahangir

(*c*) Shahjahan (*d*) Aurangzeb

**79.** Who, among the following, first translated the Bhagwat Gita into English? **(CLAT 2014)**

(*a*) Charles Wilkins

(*b*) Alexander Cunningham

(*c*) William Jones

(*d*) James Prinsep

**80.** Match List I with List II and select the correct answer using the codes given below the lists:

| | List I (Author) | | List II (Work) |
|---|---|---|---|
| (a) | Devaki Nandan Khatri | (1) | Chandrakanta |
| (b) | Premchand | (2) | Durgeshnandini |
| (c) | Bankim Chandra Chattopadhyay | (3) | Nil Daman |
| | | (4) | Seva Sadan |

**Codes:** **(CLAT 2014)**

(*a*) a-4; b-3; c-1 (*b*) a-1; b-4; c-3

(*c*) a-2; b-1; c-3 (*d*) a-1; b-4; c-2

**81.** Under the leadership of Mahatma Gandhi, the Civil Disobedience Movement, launched in 1930, started from? **(CLAT 2014)**

(*a*) Sabarmati

(*b*) Dandi

(*c*) Sevagram

(*d*) Champaran

**82.** Match List I with List II and select the correct answer using the codes given below the lists:

| | List I (Events) | | List II (Results) |
|---|---|---|---|
| (a) | Dandi March | (1) | Communal electorate |
| (b) | Chauri Chaura | (2) | Illegal manufacture of salt |
| (c) | Simon Commission | (3) | Country-wise agitation |
| (d) | Morley Minto Reforms | (4) | Withdrawal of a movement |

**Codes:** **(CLAT 2014)**

(*a*) a-1; b-2; c-3; d-4 (*b*) a-4; b-3; c- 2; d-1

(*c*) a-2; b-4; c-3; d-1 (*d*) a-1; b-4; c-3; d-2

**83.** Find out the correct chronological sequence of the following persons' visit to India at one time or another: (1) Fa-Hien (2) I-Tsing (Yijing) (3) Megasthanese (4) Hiuen-Tsang. **(CLAT 2014)**

(*a*) 1, 3, 2, 4 (*b*) 1, 3, 4, 2

(*c*) 3, 1, 4, 2 (*d*) 3, 1, 2, 4

**84.** Which was the first newspaper to be published in India? **(CLAT 2014)**

(*a*) Bombay Samachar (*b*) The Hindu

(*c*) Bengal Chronicle (*d*) Bengal Gazette

**85.** Match List I with List II and choose the correct answer: **(CLAT 2014)**

| **List I** | **List II** |
|---|---|
| (a) Visakhadatta | (1) Surgery |
| (b) Varahamihira | (2) Drama |
| (c) Sushruta | (3) Astronomy |
| (d) Brahmagupta | (4) Mathematics |

**Codes:**

| | (a) | (b) | (c) | (d) |
|---|---|---|---|---|
| (*a*) | 1 | 3 | 4 | 2 |
| (*b*) | 2 | 1 | 3 | 4 |
| (*c*) | 2 | 3 | 1 | 4 |
| (*d*) | 3 | 4 | 1 | 2 |

## Solutions

**1.** c Nagpur session (1920) related to changes in the Constitution of Congress. Madras session (1929) is related to Independence resolution passed for the first time. Calcutta session (1928) is related to Return of Gandhiji to active politics after 6 years. Lahore session (1929) is related to Poorna Swaraj. Karachi session (1930) is related to Resolution of Fundamental Rights and National Economics Policy.

**2.** d Genocide didn't occurred in Gulf War.

**3.** a The Inner Temple called Gandhiji to Bar.

**4.** c The island of Bombay was acquired by the East India Company from the Portugal.

**5.** b Todarmal was the Diwan-I- Ashraf or the revenue or Finance Minister in Akbar's Darbar of the Mughal empire (one of the 'Navratnas' of Akbar's court). Akbar introduced fresh reforms in the land-revenue system with his assistance.

**6.** a Indra is the chief gods described in Rigveda under Hindu Mythology.

**7.** c Nadir Shah took the Peacock throne of Shahjahan.

**8.** b The council of eight ministers of Chhtrapati Shivaji were known as "Ashta Pradhans".

**9.** b Charak was the court physician of Kanishka. Charak wrote the Charaksamhita in the second century A.D

**10.** a Balban was the first Sultan of Delhi to introduce the practice of 'Sijda.

**11.** c The Hunter Commission published its detailed report in 1884 with its main focus was to explain the failure of Charles Wood's Education Dispatch of 1854 and to recommend reform. The principal objective of Wood's Dispatch was to spread government and mission education to the broader population in India.

**12.** a Non-Cooperation Movement was started pursuant to the resolution of Calcutta assembly in September 1920.

**13.** d Simon Commission's recommendations did not mentioned that Indian Council is not needed to advice the Secretary of State for India.

**14.** d Introduction of separate communal electorate for Muslims was not one of the features of the principal features of Government of India Act, 1919.

**15.** b The Indian National Congress asserted in the year 1936 that India would not accept any constitution made by anyone other then people of India and without outside interference.

**16.** d Proclamation of Emergency on the ground of internal disturbance was for the first time made in year 1975. In 1975, Fakhruddin Ali Ahmed (then The President of India) was advised by Prime Minister Indra Gandhi to declare such a sate of emergency under Article 352, which empowers such state to declare on ground of internal disturbance.

**17.** b President Omar al-Bashir of Sudan was the first head of state to be charged with 'War crimes and crimes against humanity' by the International Criminal Court.

**18.** a In 1912, the imperial capital was officially shifted from Calcutta to Delhi to mark the entry of the Governor-general of India into the new Capital.

**19.** b In 1919, Women were allowed first time in India to contest election and to hold public offices.

**20.** b Heneri Dunant promoted the establishment of the International Committee of the Red Cross.

**21.** d Burma got separated from India in the year 1937.

**22.** d Indus Valley Civilization also known as Harrapan Civilization was a Bronze age civilization located in south Asia.

**23.** b Chand Bibi was a Indian Muslim Warrior Muslim defended Ahmednagar against the Mughal forces of Emperor Akbar.

**24.** d Tipu Sultan (also known as Tiger of Mysore) was son of Hyder Ali.

**25.** d The 1857 revolt began in the town of Meerut. Sir Sayed Ahmed Khan wrote critiques in 1859 by title of "The Causes of the Indian Mutiny" in 1859.

**26.** a Mahatma Gandhi's book is entitled "My Experiments with Truth".

**27.** a The Royal Indian Navy mutiny (also called the Bombay Mutiny) refers to the strike by the total strike followed by the mutiny by the Indian sailors of the Royal Indian Navy.

**28.** d The extant Preamble in our constitution embodying our cherished ideals (Liberty, equality and Justice etc.) were first introduced through 'the Objectives resolution' which was moved in the Constituent Assembly on December 13, 1946 by Pt. Jawaharlal Nehru.

**29.** c Bankimchandra Chatterjee composed Vande Mataram.

**30.** c Padmasambava was the monk who spread Buddhism in Tibet and Far-East regions.

**31.** a By signing Poona Pact in the year 1932 with Gandhiji, Ambedkar gave up his demand for separate electorates.

**32.** a Chipko Movement followed gandhian priciples of non-violent resistance. The modern Chipko movement started in the early 1970s in the Garhwal Himalayas of Uttarakhand, Then in Uttar Pradesh with growing awareness towards rapid deforestation.

**33.** a Magadhan Empire was the first Great Indian Empire.

**34.** b W.C. Banerji was the first President of Indian National Congress.

**35.** a Jahangir gave permission to establish East India Company in India.

**36.** c Mohammad Iqbal conceptualized the idea of Pakistan.

**37.** c The Khilafat movement (1919–1924) was a pan-Islamic, political protest campaign launched by Muslims in British India to influence the British government and to protect the Ottoman Empire during the aftermath of World War.

**38.** c The Nehru Report (1928) was a memorandum containing a proposed new dominion constitution for India.

**39.** a Sirimavo Bandaranaike (April 17, 1916 – October 10, 2000) was a ***Sri Lankan*** politician and the modern world's first female head of government. She served as Prime Minister of Ceylon and Sri Lanka three times, 1960–65, 1970–77 and 1994–2000, and was a long-time leader of the Sri Lanka Freedom Party.

**40.** b In 1024 CE, the Somnath Temple located in the Prabhas Kshetra near Veraval in Saurashtra, on the western coast of Gujarat was destroyed by Mahmud of Ghazni.

**41.** c Cape Trafalgar (Spanish: Cabo Trafalgar) is a headland in the Province of Cádiz in the south-west of Spain. It lies on the shore of the Atlantic Ocean, northwest of the Strait of Gibraltar at 36°10'58"N, 6°2'2"W. The International Hydrographic Organization defines the Western limit of the strait as a line that joins Cape Trafalgar to the North to Cape Spartel to the South.

**42.** c Lumbinî is a Buddhist pilgrimage site in the Rupandehi district of Nepal. It is the place where Queen Mayadevi gave birth to Siddhartha Gautama, who as the Buddha Gautama founded the Buddhist tradition. The Buddha lived between roughly 563 and 483 BCE. Lumbini is one of four magnets for pilgrimage that sprang up in places pivotal to the life of the Buddha, the others being at Kushinagar, Bodh Gaya and Sarnath.

**43.** a The Mudrarakshasa ("The Signet of the Minister") is a historical play in Sanskrit by Vishakhadatta that narrates the ascent of the king Chandragupta Maurya to power in Northern India. It is dated variously from the late 4th century[1] to the 8th century.

**44.** c The 6th Asian Games were held from December 9, 1970 to December 20, 1970 in Bangkok, Thailand.

**45.** b The year 1929 is known for congress resolution for complete independence of India.

**46.** a INS Airavat (L24) is the third Shardul class amphibious warfare vessel of the Indian Navy and was built by Garden Reach Shipbuilders & Engineers in Kolkata at Yard 3016

**47.** b

**48.** d Muridke was not the base of L.T.T.E. before being caputured b Srilankan Forces.

**49.** c Raj Babbar belongs to Congress Party.

**50.** d Gandhi was nominated in 1937, 1938, 1939, 1947 and, finally, a few days before he was murdered in January 1948. The omission has been publicly regretted by later members of the Nobel Committee; when the Dalai Lama was awarded the Peace Prize in 1989, the chairman of the committee said that this was "in part a tribute to the memory of Mahatma Gandhi".

**51.** b The University of Mumbai (informally known as Mumbai University or MU) is a public state university located in Mumbai, Maharashtra, India. It was known as the University of Bombay until 1996 when the city of Bombay was renamed as Mumbai. University of Mumbai was established in 1857 consequent upon "Wood's Education Dispatch", and is one amongst the first three Universities in India.

**52.** d In 2009, Sultan Azlan Shah Chaimponship (Hockey) Indian team defeated Malaysian team.

**53.** c Jahangir (the mughal emperor) gave permission to Hawkins (ambassador of King James) to set up a factory at Surat 1612.

**54.** c The Group of Eight (G8) is a forum for the governments of eight of the world's largest economies. (It excludes, however, two of the actual eight largest economies by nominal GDP: China, 2nd, and Brazil, 6th). The forum originated with a 1975 summit hosted by France that brought together representatives of six governments: France, Germany, Italy, Japan, the United Kingdom, and the United States, thus leading to the name Group of Six or G6. The summit became known as the Group of Seven or G7 the following year with the addition of Canada. In 1997, Russia was added to group which then became known as the G8.

**55.** b Jalal-ud-Din Muhammad Akbar, also known as Shahanshah Akbar-e-Azam or Akbar the Great (14 October 1542 – 27 October 1605), was the third Mughal Emperor. He was of Timurid descent; the son of Emperor Humayun, and the grandson of the Mughal Emperor Zaheeruddin Muhammad Babur, the ruler who founded the Mughal dynasty in India. At the end of his reign in 1605 the Mughalempire covered most of northern and central India. He is most appreciated for having a liberal outlook on all faiths and beliefs and during his era, culture and art reached a zenith as compared to his predecessors.

**56.** b Shah Jahan was born as Prince Shihab-ud-din Muhammad Khurram, in 1592 in Lahore, Pakistan as the third and favourite son of the emperor Jahangir from his Rajput wife Gossaini. The name Khurram-Persian for 'joyful'-was given by his grandfather Akbar. His early years saw him receive a cultured, broad education and he distinguished himself in the martial arts and as a military commander while leading his father's armies in numerous campaigns against Mewar (1615), the Deccan Sultanates (1617 and 1621), Kangra Fort (1618).

**57.** a Muhammad (c. 570 – c. 8 June 632 was a leader from Mecca who unified Arabia into a single religious polity under Islam. He is believed by Muslims and Baháís to be a messenger and prophet of God, and by most Muslims as the last prophet sent by God for mankind. Muhammad is generally considered to be the founder of Islam, although this is a view not shared by Muslims. Muslims consider him to be the restorer of an uncorrupted original monotheistic faith of Adam, Noah, Abraham, Moses, Jesus and other prophets.

**58.** a World War I (WWI) was a global war centred in Europe that began on 28 July 1914 and lasted until 11 November 1918. It was predominantly called the World War or the Great War from its occurrence until the start of World War II in 1939, and the First World War or World War I thereafter. It involved all the world's great powers, which were assembled in two opposing alliances: the Allies (based on the Triple Entente of the United Kingdom, France and Russia) and the Central Powers (centred around the Triple Alliance of Germany, Austria-Hungary and Italy)

**59.** c Late Pandit Bhimsen Joshi belonged to Kirana *Gharana* of Classical singing.

**60.** d Alam Ara is the film directed by Ardeshir Irani. It was the first sound film.

**61.** * Jaean-Jacques Rousseau's ( 1712 – 1778) teachings and philosophy influenced the French Revolution as well as the overall development of modern political, sociological and educational thought. He is a Genevan philosopher, writer, and composer of 18$^{th}$century Romanticism of French expression. This Solitary Walker exemplified the late 18th-century movement known as the Age of Sensibility, featuring an increasing focus on subjectivity and introspection that has characterized the modern age. His Discourse on the Origin of Inequality and his On the Social Contract are cornerstones in modern political and social thought.

**62.** c Taiwan, officially the Republic of China, is a state in East Asia. Originally based in mainland China, the Republic of China now governs the island of Taiwan (formerly known as **Formosa**), which makes up over 99% of its current territory, as well as Penghu, Kinmen, Matsu, and other minor islands. Neighboring states include the People's Republic of China to the west, Japan to the east and northeast, and the Philippines to the south. Taipei is the capital city and economic and cultural centre of the country, while New Taipei is the most populous city.

**63.** c Charles-Édouard Jeanneret, better known as Le Corbusier ( October 6, 1887 – August 27, 1965), was an architect, designer, urbanist and writer, famous for being one of the pioneers of what is now called modern architecture. He was born in Switzerland and became a French citizen in 1930. His career spanned five decades, with his buildings constructed throughout Europe, India and America.

**64.** a The Indian Grand Prix (sometimes referred to as the Grand Prix of India) is a race in the calendar of the FIA Formula One World Championship. It is currently held at the Buddh International Circuit in Greater Noida, Uttar Pradesh, India. The first event took place on 30 October 2011 as the 17th race of the 2011 Formula One season, The new race track was officially homologated on 1 September by Charlie Whiting, and the inaugural race was won by Germany's Sebastian Vettel.

**65.** b Sher Shah was a very able administrator and is remembered for his rule and the land reforms he introduced. He divided his empire into provinces known as Sarkars, these were further sub-divided into Parganas and these were again divided into smaller units. He is believed to be the first one to introduce "Rupaiya" and "paisa' in place of "Tanka". He is also credited with the introduction of custom duty, which is followed even today.

**66.** b Bibi Ka Maqbara is a maqbara located in Aurangabad,Maharastra. It was commissioned by the sixth Mughal Emperor Aurangzeb in the late 17th century in the memory of his first wife, Dilras Banu Begam (posthumously known as Rabia-ud-Daurani). It bears a striking resemblance to the famous Taj Mahal, the mausoleum of his mother, Mumtaz Mahal.

**67.** a Vidyasagar in Calcutta and many other reformers in Bombay set up schools for girls. Vidhyasagar was associated with other reformers, who founded schools for girls. He devoted himself for female education and widow remarriage acts.

**68.** c Muhammad bin Tughluq,the ruler of the Tughluq dynasty who was well versed in Astronomy, Mathematics and Medicine.

**69.** b Permanent settlement was an agreement between the East India Company and Bengali landlords to fix revenues to be raised from land and which can be gained out regularly.

**70.** a Mohan Das Karam Chand Gandhi

**71.** d Shah Alam II

**72.** d King George VI

**73.** c Old Stone Age

**74.** b 1911

**75.** c Maues

**76.** d One of the most common and popular mudras, which are found, depicted in Buddha statues is the Bhumisparshamudra, translated as the earth touching gesture. Buddha statues with this mudra are commonly known as the "earth-witness" Buddha and these iconographic representations are one of the most popular Buddhas you can find anywhere in the world.

**77.** c The Ashokan inscriptions were I two scripts. Kharoshti in the north-western version and Brahmani in the rest. This script is known to write from right to left. Brahmi, written from left to right is ascribed to Brahma who, in iconic terms, is shown to hold a sheaf of palmleaves in his right hand.

**78.** b In 1615 Sir Thomas Roe was instructed by King James I to visit the Mughal Emperor Jahangir, who ruled over 70% of the Indian subcontinent. The meeting was a success and a commercial treaty was made which gave the British East India Company exclusive rights to trade to and from India and England. Emperor Jahangir sent a letter to the King through Sir Thomas Roe.

**79.** a Sir Charles Wilkins was an English typographer and Orientalist, notable as the first translator of Bhagavad Gita into English in 1785 in London, England.

**80.** d a-1, b-4, c-2

Chandrakanta is a popular Hindi novel by Devaki Nandan Khatri. It is considered to be the first work of prose in the modern Hindi language. Durgeshnandini is a Bengali historical romance novel written by Indian writer Bankim Chandra Chattopadhyay in 1865. Premchand wrote over three hundred short stories and fourteen novels, many essays and letters, plays and translations. "seva Sadan", the novel was originally written in Urdu under the title Bazaar-e-Husn, but was first published in Hindi from Calcutta, under the title Seva Sadan ("The House of Service"), in 1919.

**81.** b Under the leadership of Gandhiji, the Civil Disobedience Movement was launched in AD 1930. It began with the Dandi March. On 12 March 1930, Gandiji with some of his followers left the Sabarmati Ashram at Ahmedabad and made their way towards Dandi, a village on the west coast of India. After travelling for twenty-five days and covering a distance of three hundred and eighty-five kms, the group reached Dandi on 6 April 1930. Here, Gandhiji protested against the Salt Law (salt was a monopoly of the government and no one was allowed to make salt) by making salt himself and throwing up a challenge to the British government. The Dandi March signified the start of the Civil Disobedience Movement.

**82.** c a-2, b-4, c-3, d-1

a. Dandi March-Illegal manufacture of salt

b. Chauri-Chaura - Withdrawal of movement

c. Simon Commission -Country-wise agitation

d. Morley Minto Reforms - Communal Electorate.

**83.** c The chronological sequence of the persons who visited India at one time or another is:

Megasthanese -> Fa-Hien -> Hiuen-Tsang -> I-Tsing (Yijing)

**84.** d Bengal Gazette (founded in 1779) was the first newspaper of India published in Calcutta, the editor of which was James Augustus Hickey who was a pioneer in bringing the start of journalistic activities in the country.

**85.** c a-2, b-3, c-1, d-4

a. Vishakhadatta-Drama

b. Varahamihira-Astronomy

c. Sushruta-Surgery

d. Brahmagupta-Mathematics

■■

# 6

# ECONOMICS

1. What is Phishing?
   (a) A Government Plan
   (b) A stem cell
   (c) Fradulent way of acquiring PIN and bank passwords using e-mail
   (d) None of these **(NLUD 2008)**

2. The Theory of Economics Drain from India to England was propounded by
   (a) R. C. Dutt (b) B. G. Tilak
   (c) Dadabhai Naoroji (d) L. K. Jha **(NLUD 2009)**

3. What is the meaning of 'Gilt edged market'?
   (a) Market in Government securities
   (b) Market in smuggled goods
   (c) Market of auctioned goods
   (d) None of the above **(NLUD 2009)**

4. "Reduction in rate of taxation leads to more than proportionate increase in tax yield". This law is known as
   (a) Giffins Effect (b) Laffer Effect
   (c) Gresham's Law (d) None of the above **(NLUD 2009)**

5. The VDIS-Voluntary Disclosure of Income Scheme was the brainchild of
   (a) P. Chidambaram
   (b) Ram Jethmalani
   (c) Atal Behari Vajpayee
   (d) Sonia Gandhi **(NLUD 2009)**

6. A company is said to be 'Sick' when the accumulated loss at the end of any financial year leads to erosion of ...... percent of its net wealth.
   (a) 100% (b) 75%
   (c) 50% (d) 25% **(NLUD 2009)**

7. Wealth tax on agricultural property is levied by
   (a) Central Government
   (b) State Government
   (c) Both Central and State Governments
   (d) Non of the above **(NLUD 2009)**

8. What is the sequence in which the Indian economy has undergone the process of convertibility?
   I. Rupee floated on trade account
   II. Part convertibility under a dual exchange rate system
   III. Introduction of exim scrips
   IV. Rupee made convertible on current account
   (a) I, II, III, IV (b) II, I, III, IV
   (c) III, II, I, IV (d) IV, I, II, III **(NLUD 2012)**

9. Which of the following currency exchange rate mechanisms has been adopted by India?
   (a) Free Float
   (b) Managed Float
   (c) Floating with a Band
   (d) Fixed-but-Adjustable **(NLUD 2012)**

10. The national income estimates of India are prepared by
    (a) Ministry of Finance
    (b) National Sample Survey
    (c) Central Statistical Organisation
    (d) Indian Statistical Institute **(NLUD 2012)**

11. A very rapid growth in prices in which money loses its value to the point where even barter may be preferable is known as
    (a) inflation (b) hyper-inflation
    (c) deflation (d) disinflation **(NLUD 2012)**

12. Hegde fund is a fund
    (a) used for absorbing inflation
    (b) used for cushioning health risks
    (c) applied to minimize the risk of financial market transactions
    (d) applied for absorbing the risk in commodity trading **(CLAT 2008)**

13. What does strong Rupee as against the dollar mean to India?
    (a) There is a Balance of Payments surplus
    (b) Indian economy is globally respected
    (b) It is a sign of economic buoyancy
    (d) Income from exports is falling **(CLAT 2008)**

**14.** Indo-U.S. nuclear deal was opposed in Parliament mainly because

(*a*) all Indian nuclear reactors would fall under American supervision

(*b*) Nuclear energy sector will be dominated by American corporations

(*c*) Nuclear relations between India and the U.S.A will be governed by the Hyde Act

(*d*) The USA will dictate Indian policies

**(CLAT 2008)**

**15.** The country which stands for Gross National Happiness in contradistinction to Gross National Product

(*a*) Sweden (*b*) Switzerland

(*c*) Bhutan (*d*) Finland **(CLAT 2008)**

**16.** Capital account convertibility signifies

(*a*) guaranteeing the right to investment to foreigners

(*b*) ensuring the right of buyers to make international payments

(*c*) ensuring free international movement of capital

(*d*) ensuring the right of an individual to invest in foreign capital markets **(CLAT 2008)**

**17.** The purpose of Kyoto Protocol is

(*a*) to promote tourism

(*b*) to contribute sustainable development

(*c*) to promote renewable sources of energy

(*d*) to put a limit on greenhouse gas emissions by states **(CLAT 2008)**

**18.** What do carbon credits signify?

(*a*) Credits given in the course of carbon products sales

(*b*) Entitlements to emit certain quantity of green house gases

(*c*) Permissible amount of Carbon dioxide in the atmosphere

(*d*) The extent of carbon required to ensure sustainable development **(CLAT 2008)**

**19.** The practice of selling goods in a foreign country at a price below their domestic selling price is called

(*a*) discrimination

(*b*) dumping

(*c*) double pricing

(*d*) predatory pricing **(CLAT 2008)**

**20.** Which is the highest body that approves Five Year Plans in India ?

(*a*) Parliament

(*b*) Planning Commission

(*b*) National Development Council

(*d*) Council of Ministers **(CLAT 2008)**

**21.** The economist who for the first time scientifically determined national income in India:

(*a*) Dr. D.R. Gadgil

(*b*) Dr. V.K.R.V. Rao

(*c*) Dr. Manmohan Singh

(*d*) Dr. Y.V. Alagh **(CLAT 2008)**

**22.** The person responsible for economic model for Indian Planning:

(*a*) Jawaharlal Nehru (*b*) P.C. Mahalanobis

(*c*) Tarlok Singh (*d*) V.T. Krishnamachari

**(CLAT 2008)**

**23.** Social Forestry aims at

(*a*) Ensuring fuel and forest produces to weaker sections

(*b*) Medicinal and fruit plantation

(*c*) Large scale afforestation

(*d*) Scientific forestry **(CLAT 2008)**

**24.** TRIPs, forming part of the World Trade Organization is intended

(*a*) to provide for stronger patent protection

(*b*) to promote transnational corporate interests

(*c*) to harmonize IPR regime internationally

(*d*) to replace World Intellectual Property Organization **(CLAT 2008)**

**25.** Carbon dating method is used to determine the age of

(*a*) rocks (*b*) fossils

(*c*) trees (*d*) ancient monuments

**(CLAT 2008)**

**26.** The scientist responsible for developing atomic energy in India

(*a*) C.V. Raman (*b*) H.J. Bhabha

(*c*) H.K. Sethna (*d*) Vikram Surabhai

**(CLAT 2008)**

**27.** Affirmative action in Indian context signifies:

(*a*) providing security to weaker sections

(*b*) welfare measures to alleviate the sufferings of poor people

(*c*) providing positive opportunities to deprived sections

(*d*) giving incentives to start industries

**(CLAT 2008)**

28. Special Economic zones are
(*a*) the places where industries can operate without any control
(*b*) the places wherein any person can start any industry
(*c*) the places where industries get certain tax advantages
(*d*) the places wherein the national labour laws do not apply **(CLAT 2008)**

29. Evergreening of patents means
(*a*) granting patents in perpetuity
(*b*) granting patents for 100 years
(*c*) granting protection to incremental inventions having no substantial significance
(*d*) patenting of green technology **(CLAT 2008)**

30. India earns maximum foreign exchange from the export of
(*a*) Garments
(*b*) Jute
(*c*) Gems and Jewelleries
(*d*) Light engineering goods **(CLAT 2008)**

31. The author of the management principle - In a hierarchy, every employee tends to rise to his level of incompetence
(*a*) Prof. Ducker (*b*) Prof. J. Peter
(*c*) Prof. C.H. Prahlad (*d*) Prof. Schmitthoff
**(CLAT 2008)**

32. The World Trade Organization was earlier known as
(*a*) UNCTAD (*b*) GATT
(*c*) UNIDO (*d*) UNCITRAL
**(CLAT 2008)**

33. Capital market means
(*a*) Mutual Funds (*b*) Money Market
(*c*) Securities Market (*d*) Banking Business
**(CLAT 2009)**

34. "The Audacity of Hope" is a book written by
(*a*) Bill Clinton (*b*) Barack Obama
(*c*) Gorge Bush (*d*) Bill Gates **(CLAT 2009)**

35. 'WPI' is used as an acronym for
(*a*) World Price Index
•(*b*) World Price Indicators
(*c*) Wholesale Price Index
(*d*) Wholesale Price Indicators **(CLAT 2009)**

36. If the tax rate increases with the higher level of income, it shall be called
(*a*) Progressive Tax (*b*) Proportional Tax
(*c*) Lump sum Tax (*d*) Regressive Tax
**(CLAT 2009)**

37. The territorial waters of India extend up to?
(*a*) 12 Nautical Miles (*b*) 6 Km
(*c*) 10 Nautical Miles (*d*) 15 Nautical Miles
**(CLAT 2009)**

38. What is the meaning of 'Gilt Edged Market'?
(*a*) Market in Government securities
(*b*) Market of smuggled goods
(*c*) Market of auctioned goods
(*d*) Market of Gold products **(CLAT 2009)**

39. Excess of money supply as compared to supply of goods results in
(*a*) depression (*b*) deflation
(*c*) trade deficit (*d*) inflation **(CLAT 2012)**

40. To which country does India export the largest quantity of iron ore?
(*a*) USA (*b*) Japan
(*c*) Egypt (*d*) Germany **(CLAT 2012)**

41. The XI Five Year Plan envisaged the highest growth in the sector of
(*a*) industry (*b*) agriculture
(*c*) services (*d*) manufacturing
**(CLAT 2012)**

42. Mahatma Gandhi National Rural Employment Guarantee Act (MGNREGA) completed how many years of operation in 2011?
(*a*) 3 years (*b*) 4 years
(*c*) 5 years (*d*) 6 years **(CLAT 2012)**

43. As per the Indian Union Budget of 2012-13, the income-tax exemption limit for persons below 65 years of age is
(*a*) ₹ 175000 (*b*) ₹ 200000
(*c*) ₹ 250000 (*d*) ₹ 190000 **(CLAT 2012)**

44. The term fiscal deficit means
(*a*) total receipts minus expenditure
(*b*) total receipts minus interest payments on external debt
(*c*) revenue receipts minus expenditure
(*d*) revenue receipts minus defence expenditure
**(AILET 2013)**

45. The functions of the Reserve Bank of India are
I. issuing all notes and coins
II. distributing all notes and coins
III. formulating monetary policy
IV. acting as agent of government in respect of India's membership of the IMF
(*a*) I, II and III (*b*) II and III
(*c*) II, III and IV (*d*) I, II, III and IV
**(AILET 2013)**

**46.** What do you understand by Bear Raid ?

(*a*) An attempt to bring down the price of strong short selling

(*b*) Simultaneous buying of shares and debentures in view of getting more values in near future

(*c*) Higher rate of price paid for particular government share or debentures

(*d*) Any of the above **(AILET 2013)**

**47.** The foreign exchange reserves of India include

(*a*) Gold (*b*) SDRs

(*c*) Foreign currencies (*d*) All of these

**(AILET 2013)**

**48.** Among the remedies of inflation, we cannot include

(*a*) better capacity utilisation

(*b*) lowering bank rate

(*c*) reducing budgetary deficit

(*d*) an efficient public distribution system

**(AILET 2013)**

**49.** In 2012-13, India's target is to restrict the fiscal deficit to $x$ % of the GDP, where $x$ is

(*a*) 10 (*b*) 8.3 **(CLAT 2013)**

(*c*) 15 (*d*) 5.1

**50.** POSCO steel project to come up but being strongly protested by the people is located in

**(CLAT 2013)**

(*a*) Chhattisgarh (*b*) Jharkhand

(*c*) Odisha (*d*) Andhra Pradesh

**51.** Bharat Ratna and Padma Awards in our country were instituted in the year **(CLAT 2013)**

(*a*) 1952 (*b*) 1954

(*c*) 1962 (*d*) 1964

**52.** Duration of which Five Year Plan was 2007-2012

(*a*) X (*b*) XII **(CLAT 2013)**

(*c*) IX (*d*) XI

**53.** As per census 2011, which State has the lowest sex ratio (877:1000) ? **(CLAT 2013)**

(*a*) Punjab (*b*) Haryana

(*c*) Uttar Pradesh (*d*) Bihar

**54.** The phrase 'Bitcoins' refers to **(AILET 2014)**

(*a*) Cryptocurrency introduced by the United States

(*b*) Cryptocurrency introduced by France

(*c*) Cryptocurrency introduced by the World Bank

(*d*) None

**55.** The main component of India's import items from China is **(AILET 2014)**

(*a*) Rice

(*b*) Iron ore

(*c*) Pharmaceuticals

(*d*) Telecom equipments and Machinery

**56.** The Reserve Bank of India was established in the year: **(CLAT 2014)**

(*a*) 1858 (*b*) 1935

(*c*) 1947 (*d*) 1950

**57.** In India, the interest rate on savings accounts in all the nationalised commercial banks is fixed by? **(CLAT 2014)**

(*a*) Union Ministry of Finance

(*b*) Union Finance Commission

(*c*) Indian Banks' Association

(*d*) None of the above

**58.** The First Five Year Plan of India was based on:

(*a*) John W Miller Model **(CLAT 2014)**

(*b*) PC Mahalanobis Model

(*c*) Gadgil Yojana

(*d*) Herrod-Domar Model

**59.** Which one of the following measures is NOT likely to aid in improving India's balance of payment position? **(CLAT 2014)**

(*a*) Promotion of import substitution policy

(*b*) Devaluation of rupee

(*c*) Imposition of higher tariff on imports

(*d*) Levying the higher duty on exports

**60.** Economic growth rate projected by the IMF for India in the fiscal year 2014-15 is: **(CLAT 2014)**

(*a*) 5.4 percent (*b*) 5.5 percent

(*c*) 5.6 percent (*d*) 5.7 percent

## Solutions

**1.** c Phishing refers to the act of fraudulent way of acquiring PIN and bank passwords using e-mail.

**2.** * Dadabhai Naoroji propounded the theory of economic drain. He also authored a book by name of Poverty and un-Britrish rule in India.

**3.** a Gilt Edged Market is the market of government securities. These securities are No risk securities.

**4.** b Laffer Effect states "Reduction in rate of taxation leads to more than proportionate increase in tax yield". The aforementioned is the long-term affect described by the theory and short-term affect "arithmetic affect" leads to shortage of government revenue.

**5.** a VDIS-Voluntary Disclosure of Income Scheme was brainchild of P.Chidambaram.

**6.** a A company is said to be 'Sick' when the accumulated loss at the end of any financial year leads to erosion of 50 % percent of its net wealth during the immediately preceding ***four*** financial years.

**7.** b Wealth tax on agricultural property is levied by state government because it is the subject of state list under the seventh schedule of constitution of India.

**8.** c Capital Account Convertibility (CAC) or a floating exchange rate means the freedom to convert local financial assets into foreign financial assets and vice versa at market determined rates of exchange. This means that capital account convertibility allows anyone to freely move from local currency into foreign currency and back. In India there exists full Current Account Convertibility i.e. Indian Currency rupee is convertible to any other currency. The capital account convertibility is sought to be achieved by RBI in the future if suitable macro-economic conditions such as fiscal consolidation is achieved.

**9.** b Manage floating or dirty floating refers to the regime of financial practice where the central bank of a country as on required basis only attempt to influence their countries exchange rate and in normal circumstances allow the market forces (i.e. demand and supply) to determine the exchange rate of their domestic currency. India follows dirty floating system.

**10.** c Central Statistical Organization was setup in year 1951. It is responsible for coordination of statistical activities in India including but not limited to evolving and maintaining statistical Standards.

**11.** b Inflation is measured through Wholesale Price Index (WPI) in India. There are two types of Inflation Demand Pull and Cost Pull Inflation. Hyperinflation occurs due to continuing supply of money, which results into the real value of domestic currency not being reflected by the prices of the commodities.

**12.** c A "Hedge fund" term is used to describe a very generic form of funds, which can undertake a wider range of investment and trading activities. The primary aim of hedge funds is to minimize the risk of financial transaction.

**13.** a A balance of payment surplus is the desirable positive state of account in a nation's balance of payments in which payments made by the country are less than payments received by the country. This is also termed a favorable balance of payments. It's considered favorable because more currency is flowing into the country than is flowing out.

**14.** c The Hyde act of the United States had a extraterritorial jurisdiction so as to effect the sovereignty of India in matters of nuclear relations with United States. Parliament is only recognized by the constitution of India as the sovereign not any foreign or domestic institution.

**15.** c The term "Gross National Happiness" was coined in 1972 by Bhutan's fourth Dragon King, Jigme Singye Wangchuck is intended to comprehend not only economic aspect of growth but psychological and social progress in an attempt to be more holistic.

**16.** c Capital Account Convertibility (CAC) also known as Capital Asset Liberation is a feature of a nation's financial regime that centers on the ability to conduct transactions of local financial assets into foreign financial assets freely and at country determined exchange rates. Reserve Bank of India coined the term. The Tarapore Committee has given its report on CAC.

**17.** d Kyoto protocol is the United Nations Framework Convention on Climate Change (UFCCC) aimed at reducing Global Warming. The Protocol was initially adopted on 11 December 1997 in Kyoto, Japan, and entered into force on 16 February 2005.

**18.** b Carbon Credits which is an prominent concept of environmental economics are allotted under the Kyoto Protocol and are tradable certificates representing the right to emit one tonne of carbon dioxide or the mass of another greenhouse gas with a carbon dioxide equivalent ($tCO_2e$) equivalent to one tonne of carbon dioxide

**19.** b Dumping is an economic offence and is prohibited by World Trade Organization 's Anti-Dumping treaties.

**20.** c National Development Council (NDC) was setup in 1951 with a view to bringing about a coordination of plans between the Central Ministers and the State Governments. The Prime Minister of India heads it.

**21.** b V. K. R. V. Rao (Vijayendra Kasturi Ranga Varadaraja Rao) was a prominent Indian economist, politician, professor and educator. The prize instituted on his name i.e. VKRV Prize is given for the development in the field of social science research in India.

**22.** b Prasanta Chandra Mahalanobis founded Indian Statistician Institute.

**23.** a The Term 'Social Forestry' first used in 1976 by The National Commission on Agriculture, Government of India. It was then that India embarked upon a social forestry project with the aim of taking the pressure off currently existing forests by planting trees on all unused and fallow land.

**24.** c TRIPS stand for Trade Related aspects of Intellectual Property Rights. In the year 2005 India brought The Patents (Amendment) Act 2005 to make it compatible with TRIPS.

**25.** b Carbon dating method is used to determine the age of Fossils

**26.** b Homi Jehangir Bhabha, is also known as father of Indian nuclear program.

**27.** b Affirmative Action refers to the governmental policies, which includes factors like "race, color, religion, gender, sexual orientation, or national origin". In India reservation system represents affirmative action.

**28.** c Special Economic Zones in India were setup with the aim of promotion of exports. The Special Economic Zone Act 2005 regulates functioning of such zones in India.

**29.** c Evergreening is the strategy used by the pharmaceutical companies to reap the benefits of patent beyond the normal span allotted by the law of 20 years. These patent term extension strategies entail using the intricacies of patent prosecution procedures. The Indian Patents Act is rather rigid as to the time lines for priority, patent term and patentable subject matters. Hence, 'Evergreening' in India is not a serious concern.

**30.** c The maximum amount of foreign exchange is earned by India through export of jams and Jewelleries.

**31.** b J. Peters is the author of the management principle viz. In a hierarchy, every employee tends to rise to his level of incompetence.

**32.** b The Uruguay Round, which was the 8th round of Multilateral trade negotiations (MTN) conducted within the framework of the General Agreement on Tariffs and Trade (GATT), spanning from 1986-1994 and embracing 123 countries as "contracting parties". The Round transformed the GATT into the World Trade Organization.

**33.** c A capital market is a market for ***securities*** (debt or equity), where business enterprises (companies) and governments can raise long-term funds. It is defined as a market in which money is provided for periods longer than a year, as the raising of short-term funds takes place on other markets (e.g., the money market). The capital market includes the stock market (equity securities) and the bond market (debt). Money markets and capital markets are parts of financial markets.

**34.** b "The Audacity of Hope: Thoughts on Reclaiming the American Dream" is the second book written by then-Senator Barack Obama. In the book, Obama expounds on many of the subjects that became part of his 2008 campaign for the presidency

**35.** c The Wholesale Price Index or WPI is "the price of a representative basket of wholesale goods. Some countries use the changes in this index to measure inflation in their economies, in particular India – The Indian WPI figure was earlier released weekly on every Thursday and influenced stock and fixed price markets. The Indian WPI is now updated on a monthly basis. The Wholesale Price Index focuses on the price of goods traded between corporations, rather than goods bought by consumers, which is measured by the Consumer Price Index. The purpose of the WPI is to monitor price movements that reflect supply and demand in industry, manufacturing and construction. This helps in analyzing both macroeconomic and microeconomic conditions.

**36.** a A progressive tax is a tax by which the tax rate increases as the taxable base amount increases. "Progressive" describes a distribution effect on income or expenditure, referring to the way the rate progresses from low to high, where the average tax rate is less than the marginal tax rate. It can be applied to individual taxes or to a tax system as a whole; a year, multi-year, or lifetime. Progressive taxes attempt to reduce the tax incidence of people with a lower ability-to-pay, as they shift the incidence increasingly to those with a higher ability-to-pay.

**37.** a The territorial waters of India extend up to 12 nautical miles.

**38.** a Gilt edged market deals in securities issued by central, state and autonomous govt authoritie such as municipalities, city corporations, state electricity boards etc and development financial institutions such as IDBI,I FCI, NABARD etc.

Since government issues these classes of securities, they all are considered to be quite safe and liquid for investment. Hence the term "gilt -edged securities"

**39.** d Excess of money supply as compared to supply of goods results in Inflation.

**40.** b India exports the largest quantity of iron ore to Japan. In May 2012, it has been decided that India will export two million tonne of iron ore to Japan annually for the next three years and initiate the process for the Japanese government's equity participation in Delhi Mumbai Industrial Corridor Development Corporation to the extent of 26%

**41.** c The XIth Five Year Plan envisaged the highest growth in the sector of Services.

**42.** c The Mahatma Gandhi National Rural Employment Guarantee Act (MGNREGA) is an Indian job guarantee scheme, enacted by legislation on August 25, 2005. The scheme provides a legal guarantee for one hundred days of employment in every financial year to adult members of any rural household willing to do public work-related unskilled manual work at the statutory minimum wage of 120 (US$2.17) per day in 2009 prices. The Central government outlay for scheme is 40,000 crore (US$7.24 billion) in FY 2010–11.

**43.** b As per the Indian Union Budget of 2012-13, the income-tax exemption limit for persons below 65 years of age is Rs.2,00,000.

**44.** c When a government's total expenditures exceed the revenue that it generates (excluding money from borrowings). Deficit differs from debt, which is an accumulation of yearly deficits.

**45.** c The broad objectives of the Reserve Bank are:

(*a*) Regulating & distributing of currency in India.

(*b*) Keeping the foreign exchange reserves of the country;

(*c*) Establishing the monetary stability in the country; and

(*d*) Developing the financial structure of the country on sound lines consistent with the national socio-economic objectives and policies.

**46.** a A bear raid is a type of stock market strategy, where a trader (or group of traders) attempts to force down the price of stock to cover a short position.

**47.** d Foreign-exchange reserves should only include foreign currency deposits and bonds, also adds Gold Reserves, Special drawing rights (SDRs), and International monetary funds (IMF) reserve positions.

**48.** b Among remedies of inflation we do not include lowering down of bank rates.

**49.** d 5.1 %

**50.** c Odisha

**51.** b 1954

**52.** d XI

**53.** b Haryana

**54.** d Bitcoin is a digital currency (also called crypto-currency) that is not backed by any country's central bank or government. Bitcoins can be traded for goods or services with vendors who accept Bitcoins as payment. In short, a digital currency in which transactions can be performed without the need for a central bank.

**55.** d The main component of India's import items from China is Telecom equipments and Machinery.

**56.** b The Reserve Bank of India was established on April 1, 1935 in accordance with the provisions of the Reserve Bank of India Act, 1934. Though originally privately owned, since nationalisation in 1949, the Reserve Bank is fully owned by the Government of India.

**57.** d In most countries, interest rates on savings bank accounts are set by commercial banks based on market conditions. In India, RBI fixes the interest rate on savings accounts in all the nationalized commercial banks.

**58.** d First Plan (1951 - 56), was based on Harrod-Domar Model. Community Development Program launched in 1952.It was focused on agriculture, price stability, power and transport. It was a successful plan primarily because of good harvests in the last two years of the plan.

**59.** d Levying the higher duty on exports does not aid in improving India's balance of Payment.

**60.** a The economic growth rate projected by the IMF for India in the fiscal year 2014-15 is 5.4 percent.

■■

# 7

# MISC. (QUOTES, DAYS, BOOKS TITLES, SPORTS, BASIC LEGAL CONCEPTS)

**1.** .........are words, which appear innocent, but have a latent defamatory meaning

(*a*) Libel (*b*) Slander **(NLUD 2008)**

(*c*) Innuendo (*d*) None of the above

**2.** The most powerful legislature in the world is the:

(*a*) Indian Parliament (*b*) U.S. Congress

(*c*) Swiss Legislature (*d*) British Parliament **(NLUD 2008)**

**3.** Unliquidated damages mean

(*a*) Damage to something solid

(*b*) Damage caused by a firm which has gone in liquidation

(*c*) Damage to a firm in the hands of receivers

(*d*) Damage to be assessed by a Court as these are not pre-determined **(NLUD 2008)**

**4.** Assault and nuisance are

(*a*) wrong under Criminal law

(*b*) wrong under tort

(*c*) wrong under neither

(*d*) wrong under both **(NLUD 2008)**

**5.** The display of articles in a show room indicating their prices amounts to **(NLUD 2008)**

(*a*) offer (*b*) counter offer

(*c*) invitation to an offer (*d*) mere advertisement

**6.** An idol of Lord Krishna in a temple is

(*a*) a natural person

(*b*) a legal person

(*c*) not a person in the eye of law become only the priest of the temple will be a person

(*d*) not a person because no personality can be conferred on God **(NLUD 2008)**

**7.** When a court sends some one in judicial custody, what does it mean by judicial custody

(*a*) sent to jail

(*b*) sent to police look up

(*c*) sent to home under judicial protection

(*d*) none of these **(NLUD 2008)**

**8.** The term of office of a judge of the International Court of Justice is

(*a*) 10 years (*b*) 9 years

(*c*) 7 years (*d*) 5 years **(NLUD 2008)**

**9.** The democratic device, used in constitutional states, by which important political questions, particularly question relating tot he states of a region, may be referred to the people of the region for their final decision, is called **(NLUD 2008)**

(*a*) Plebiscite (*b*) Referendum

(*c*) Recall Vote (*d*) Quorum

**10.** Ancient treatise on law?

(*a*) Vedas (*b*) Upanishads

(*c*) Smritis (*d*) Shrutis **(NLUD 2008)**

**11.** Muslim religious foundations

(*a*) Ulema (*b*) Jihad

(*c*) Zakat (*d*) Wakfs **(NLUD 2008)**

**12.** The maximum litigation in Courts is caused by

(*a*) businessmen (*b*) middle class

(*c*) government (*d*) criminals **(NLUD 2008)**

**13.** The first-regular adjudicatory mobile court in the country has been inaugurated at Punbanna village in:

(*a*) Haryana (*b*) Bihar

(*c*) Andhra Pradesh (*d*) Punjab **(NLUD 2008)**

**14.** Dissolution of Muslim Marriage Act, 1939 provides grounds of dissolution of Muslim marriage to **(NLUD 2008)**

(*a*) spouses

(*b*) only males

(*c*) only females

(*d*) muslim parents and parents-in-law

**15.** A married man commits adultery if he has sexual intercourse with a/an **(NLUD 2008)**

(*a*) unmarried women

(*b*) married woman

(*c*) any woman except his wife

(*d*) unmarried woman without her consent

**16.** A husband is obliged to maintain his divorced wife

(*a*) for ever

(*b*) for 20 years

(*c*) till the children grow up

(*d*) till she gets remarried **(NLUD 2008)**

**17.** Match the following:

| | | | |
|---|---|---|---|
| (A) | Failure to do something required by law | (I) | Default |
| (B) | A wrongful act | (II) | Delict |
| (C) | A thing thrown away by its owner | (III) | Derelict |
| (D) | A judge's observation | (IV) | Dictum |

| | A | B | C | D |
|---|---|---|---|---|
| (*a*) | I | IV | II | III |
| (*b*) | IV | III | II | I |
| (*c*) | III | IV | I | II |
| (*d*) | I | II | III | IV |

**(NLUD 2008)**

**18.** India and Britain have signed an 'Extradition treaty'. Extradition means

(*a*) Exports with double taxation

(*b*) Order of Indian Courts will apply to Indians living in the UK

(*c*) Indian and the U.K. will deport criminals on reciprocal basis to each other

(*d*) None of above **(NLUD 2008)**

**19.** The limit beyond which stars suffer internal collapse is called

(*a*) Chandrasekher limit

(*b*) Eddington limit

(*c*) Hoyle limit

(*d*) Fowler limit **(NLUD 2008)**

**20.** Ahmedabad-based Pioma Industries is best known for which brand?

(*a*) Maggi (*b*) Kissan

(*c*) Brooke-Bond (*d*) Rasna **(NLUD 2008)**

**21.** Australian cricketer Brett Lee models for which watch company?

(*a*) Timex (*b*) HMT

(*c*) Titan (*d*) All of these

**(NLUD 2008)**

**22.** Which game will be played for the first time in Asian Games, 2010?

(*a*) Kabaddi (*b*) Twenty20 Cricket

(*c*) Squash (*d*) Kho-Kho

**(NLUD 2008)**

**23.** Who is the Managing Director of the Delhi Metro Railway Corporation?

(*a*) B.L. Joshi, Lt. Governor of Delhi

(*b*) Sam Pitroda

(*c*) Chairman of the Indian Railway Board

(*d*) Shri. E. Sreedharan **(NLUD 2008)**

**24.** Gunnar Myradal has dealt with the problem of Asian countries in her book ASIAN DRAMA 'regarding

(*a*) poverty

(*b*) modern industries

(*c*) military dictatorship

(*d*) neo-colonialism **(NLUD 2009)**

**25.** Who among the following has not won an Oscar?

(*a*) A.R. Rahman (*b*) Satyajit Ray

(*c*) Bhanu Athaiya (*d*) Dev Patel

**(NLUD 2010)**

**26.** The National Dairy Research Insdtute in Haryana cloned a buffalo calf and named it as

(*a*) Gowri (*b*) Tusna

(*c*) Garima (*d*) Shakthi **(NLUD 2010)**

**27.** The former Chief Justice of India who did not become the Chairperson of the National Human Rights Commission is

(*a*) Justice S. Rajendra Babu

(*b*) Justice M. N. Venkatachalaiah

(*c*) Justice Lahoti

(*d*) Justice Verma **(NLUD 2010)**

**28.** The first Women's University was established in Pune during

(*a*) 1909 (*b*) 1928

(*c*) 1915 (*d*) 1968 **(NLUD 2010)**

**29.** The Committee on Reforming Criminal Justice System in India was headed by

(*a*) Justice K.T. Thomas

(*b*) Justice Krishna Iyer

(*c*) Justice V.S. Malimath

(*d*) Justice Mohan **(NLUD 2010)**

**30.** The film that won 14 Oscar nominations was

(*a*) Gandhi (*b*) Slumdog Millionaire

(*c*) Benhur (*d*) All about Eve

**(NLUD 2010)**

**31.** The first Indian to get a medal at the World Boxing Championship was

(*a*) Jayadev Bisht (*b*) Suvanjoy Singh

(*c*) Vijender Singh (*d*) Rajkumar Sangwan

**(NLUD 2010)**

**32.** The maximum fine that the Central or State Information Commission can impose on Public Information Officer for not furnishing the information within the stipulate time is

(*a*) Rs. 10,000/- (*b*) Rs. 15,000/-
(*c*) Rs. 25,000/- (*d*) Rs. 30,000/-

**(NLUD 2010)**

**33.** The first African to become the Secretary General of United Nations was

(*a*) Kofi Annan
(*b*) Dag Hammarskjold
(*c*) Boutros Boutros Ghali
(*d*) U Thant **(NLUD 2010)**

**34.** Who said that Swaraj is my birth right?

(*a*) M.K. Gandhi
(*b*) Balagangadhar Tilak
(*c*) Jawaharlal Nehru
(*d*) Mohammed Ali Jinnah **(NLUD 2010)**

**35.** The first woman Prime Minister was

(*a*) Indira Gandhi (*b*) Srimavo Bandaranaike
(*c*) Golda Meir (*d*) Elizabeth Domitien

**(NLUD 2010)**

**36.** The phrase 'cloud computing' means

(*a*) Delivery of hosted services over the internet
(*b*) Study of clouds to predict rains and thunderstorms
(*c*) Study of conditions of clouds for 'cloud seeding'
(*d*) Use of different software for financial accounting **(NLUD 2010)**

**37.** The world's largest nuclear power station is

(*a*) Chernobyl (*b*) Kashiwazki-Kariwa
(*c*) Fukushima-Daiichi (*d*) Kalpakkam

**(NLUD 2011)**

**38.** The First International Women's Day was celebrated on

(*a*) 17.3.1911 (*b*) 8.3.1911
(*c*) 18.3.1911 (*d*) 9.3.1911 **(NLUD 2011)**

**39.** The nature and extent of nuclear accident in power plants is indicated as International Nuclear and Radiological Event (INRE) and quantified in terms of the highest as

(*a*) Level 10 Accident (*b*) Level 12 Accident
(*c*) Level 7 Accident (*d*) Level 6 Accident

**(NLUD 2011)**

**40.** The country that gets highest percentage of electricity from nuclear power stations is

(*a*) U. S. A. (*b*) Japan
(*c*) China (*d*) France **(NLUD 2011)**

**41.** Which of the following Chief Justices of India also became the Vice President of India?

(*a*) Patanjali Sastri (*b*) Hidayatullah
(*c*) Sikri (*d*) None **(NLUD 2011)**

**42.** Air-conditioning was invented by

(*a*) Carrier (*b*) Voltas
(*c*) A. Volta (*d*) Sinclair **(NLUD 2011)**

**43.** Motor Cycle was invented by

(*a*) Davidson
(*b*) G. Daimler
(*c*) Benz
(*d*) MacMillan **(NLUD 2011)**

**44.** Which of the following has the largest territory?

(*a*) U.S.A (*b*) Brazil
(*c*) Canada (*d*) China **(NLUD 2011)**

**45.** According to the survey conducted in India during 2001-2003, the highest percentage of deaths were due to

(*a*) Cancer (*b*) Heart diseases
(*c*) Asthma (*d*) HIV-AIDS

**(NLUD 2011)**

**46.** The largest state in India in terms of territory is

(*a*) Uttar Pradesh (*b*) Madhya Pradesh
(*c*) Maharastra (*d*) Rajasthan

**(NLUD 2011)**

**47.** The first judge who was sought to be impeached under the Constitution was

(*a*) Justice V.Ramaswami
(*b*) Justice Dinakaran
(*c*) Justice Sen
(*d*) None **(NLUD 2011)**

**48.** Census takes place in India

(*a*) every 20 years (*c*) every 10 years
(*b*) every 15 years (*d*) every 5 years

**(NLUD 2011)**

**49.** INTERPOL, a 147-nation Police Commission, has its Headquarters at

(*a*) Paris (*b*) Lyons
(*c*) London (*d*) Frankfurt **(NLUD 2011)**

**50.** Red Cross is an international society for relief of suffering in the time of war or disaster which has headquarters at Geneva was founded in 1863 on the advocacy of

(*a*) Herbert Spencer
(*b*) J.H. Dunant
(*c*) W.H. Morgan
(*d*) C.A. Barnord **(NLUD 2011)**

**51.** The Maastrich Treaty is for
(*a*) Nuclear weapons free world
(*b*) Chemical weapons free world
(*c*) Biological weapons free world
(*d*) Common European Union **(NLUD 2011)**

**52.** Who among the following was the Chairman of Sixth Pay Commission?
(*a*) Justice Rathnaval Pandian
(*b*) Justice Venkatachalliah
(*c*) Justice A.K. Majumdar
(*d*) Justice B.N. Srikrishna **(NLUD 2011)**

**53.** The 'Year of Great Divide' refers to
(*a*) rapid growth rate in population after 1921
(*b*) the declining sex ratio after 1921
(*c*) the slow down in death rate after 1921
(*d*) all of the above **(NLUD 2012)**

**54.** India is divided into how many PIN code zones?
(*a*) Six (*b*) Seven
(*c*) Eight (*d*) Nine **(NLUD 2012)**

**55.** More than 50 Sikh shrines in India are named after?
(*a*) Flowers (*b*) Trees
(*c*) Birds (*d*) Animals **(NLUD 2012)**

**56.** It has been the practice to have ——————as the Managing Director of the IMF.
(*a*) an American (*b*) a European
(*c*) an Australian (*d*) an Arab **(NLUD 2012)**

**57.** Who is the Chairman of 13th Finance Commission constituted in 2007?
(*a*) Vijay Kelkar (*b*) C. Rangrajan
(*c*) Ashok Lahiri (*d*) K.C.Pant
**(CLAT 2008)**

**58.** The Indian industrialist who bought Tippu Sultan's sword in an auction in London was
(*a*) Vijay Mallya (*b*) Anil Ambani
(*c*) Amar Singh (*d*) Lakshmi Mittal
**(CLAT 2008)**

**59.** Which country has its richest man as the head of the Government?
(*a*) The USA (*b*) Italy
(*c*) Saudi Arabia (*d*) Russia **(CLAT 2008)**

**60.** Who is the person known as the Father of Modern Indian Retail Trade?
(*a*) Mukhesh Ambani
(*b*) Kishore Bijani
(*c*) Aditya Birla
(*d*) Anil Ambani **(CLAT 2008)**

**61.** The largest software service company in Asia is
(*a*) WIPRO
(*b*) INFOSYS
(*c*) Tata Consultancy Services
(*d*) Satyam Computers **(CLAT 2008)**

**62.** Taikonaut means
(*a*) a character in comic strips
(*b*) a character in Russian opera
(*c*) astronaut in China
(*d*) a delicious Japanese dish **(CLAT 2008)**

**63.** The highest paid head of the government in the world at present is in
(*a*) The USA (*b*) Russian Federation
(*c*) Singapore (*d*) Japan **(CLAT 2008)**

**64.** The Director-General of the World Trade Organization is
(*a*) Renalto Ruggiero (*b*) Pascal Lamy
(*c*) Arthur Dunkell (*d*) Oliver Long
**(CLAT 2008)**

**65.** The country known as the Land of Midnight Sun
(*a*) Sweden (*b*) Norway
(*c*) Finland (*d*) Denmark **(CLAT 2008)**

**66.** 18 carat gold signifies
(*a*) 18 parts of gold and 82 parts of other metal
(*b*) 18 parts of gold and 6 parts of other metal
(*c*) 82 parts of gold and 18 parts of other metal
(*d*) None of the above **(CLAT 2008)**

**67.** Salwa Judum practised in certain places in India refers to **(CLAT 2008)**
(*a*) witchcraft
(*b*) arming civilians to fight militants
(*c*) training civilians in the use of fire arms
(*d*) training civilians to be home guards

**68.** The leader who led the country in atoning for the past wrongs: **(CLAT 2008)**
(*a*) John Howard (*b*) Desmond Tutu
(*c*) Kevin Rudd (*d*) Jimmy Carter

**69.** Gandhiji expounded his economic ideas in
(*a*) Hind Swaraj
(*b*) My Experiments with Truth
(*c*) Unto the Last
(*d*) Economics of Permanence **(CLAT 2008)**

**70.** Sunita Williams, renowned astronaut of Indian origin, spent a record of _____ days in space
(*a*) 195 (*b*) 185
(*c*) 200 (*d*) 160 **(CLAT 2008)**

**71.** The second biggest greenhouse gas emitter (after the USA) in the world is:

(*a*) Russia (*b*) Germany
(*c*) China (*d*) Japan **(CLAT 2008)**

**72.** The "wailing wall" is associated with

(*a*) Christians (*b*) Bahais
(*c*) Jews (*d*) Shias **(CLAT 2008)**

**73.** An Education Minister who got Bharata Ratna in India

(*a*) G.B. Pant (*b*) M.C. Chagla
(*c*) Abul Kalam Azad (*d*) Humayun Kabir **(CLAT 2008)**

**74.** Why is Ozone Layer important?

(*a*) It absorbs greenhouse gases
(*b*) It protects Earth from ultraviolet radiation
(*c*) It maintains Earth's temperature
(*d*) It is a buffer against extra-terrestrial hazards **(CLAT 2008)**

**75.** Who was the first recipient of Jnanapith award?

(*a*) Amrita Pritam (*b*) Dinkar
(*c*) D.V. Gundappa (*d*) G. Shankara Kurup **(CLAT 2008)**

**76.** The Chairman of Sixth Pay Commission

(*a*) Justice B.N. Srikrishna
(*b*) Justice Ratnavel Pandian
(*c*) Justice Jagannatha Shetty
(*d*) Justice A.K. Majumdar **(CLAT 2008)**

**77.** International Court of Justice is:

(*a*) an independent international institution
(*b*) a principal organ of the U.N.O.
(*c*) a subsidiary organ of the U.N.O.
(*d*) an European Institution **(CLAT 2008)**

**78.** The Liberhan Commission which received repeated extensions has been inquiring into:

(*a*) Godhra riots
(*b*) Mumbai riot
(*c*) demolition of Babri Masjid
(*d*) killing of Sikhs in Delhi **(CLAT 2008)**

**79.** Only Judge against whom a motion of impeachment was introduced into Parliament

(*a*) Justice Subba Rao (*b*) Justice Ramaswami
(*c*) Justice Mahajan (*d*) Justice Viraswami **(CLAT 2008)**

**80.** The Mallimath Committee Report deals with:

(*a*) judicial delays in India
(*b*) criminal justice administration
(*c*) stock market reforms
(*d*) review of Constitutional system **(CLAT 2008)**

**81.** The first Woman Chief Justice of High Court in India

(*a*) Leila Mukherji (*b*) Leila Seth
(*c*) Fatima Bibi (*d*) Ruma Pal **(CLAT 2008)**

**82.** Who is the Director of "Chak De India"?

(*a*) Shimit Amiro (*b*) Yash Chopra
(*c*) Shahrukh Khan (*d*) Ram Gopal Verma **(CLAT 2009)**

**83.** Who got the world Food Prize?

(*a*) Kofi Annan (*b*) Man Mohan Singh
(*c*) Hillary Clinton (*d*) Bhumibol Adulyadej **(CLAT 2009)**

**84.** ISO 9000 is a

(*a*) Quality Standard Mark
(*b*) Space Project
(*c*) Trade Technique
(*d*) Loan Security **(CLAT 2009)**

**85.** What is 'AGMARK'?

(*a*) Name of Brand
(*b*) A Marketing Research Organisation
(*c*) Eggs supplied by Government-run cooperative
(*d*) Agriculture marketing for agro products **(CLAT 2009)**

**86.** "Saras" is the name of

(*a*) an Aircraft (*b*) a Tank
(*c*) a Missile (*d*) a Submarine **(CLAT 2009)**

**87.** Who was felicitated with 'Nishan-e-Pakistan'?

(*a*) Shatrughan Sinha
(*b*) Maulana Azad
(*c*) Dilip Kumar
(*d*) Khan Abdul Gaffar Khan **(CLAT 2009)**

**88.** World "No Tobacco Day" is observed on

(*a*) January 10 (*b*) June 1
(*c*) May 31 (*d*) March 5 **(CLAT 2009)**

**89.** The Hindu outfit 'Hindraf' has been banned in

(*a*) Pakistan (*b*) Thailand
(*c*) Malaysia (*d*) Bangladesh **(CLAT 2009)**

**90.** In May 2007 Air Sahara acquired by Jet Airways is being operated as a separate airline under the name of

(*a*) Jet Lite (*b*) Jet Sahara
(*c*) Air Jet Line (*d*) Jet Sahara Lite **(CLAT 2009)**

**91.** The first nuclear reactor of India is named

(*a*) Rohini (*b*) Vaishali

(*c*) Apsara (*d*) Kamini **(CLAT 2009)**

**92.** 'Samjhouta Express' runs between the Railway Stations of

(*a*) New Delhi - Wagah (*b*) New Delhi - Lahore

(*c*) Amritsar - Lahore (*d*) New Delhi – Islamabad

**(CLAT 2009)**

**93.** Who is the Director of the film "Elizabeth : The Golden Age Cast"?

(*a*) Rama Nand Sagar (*b*) Ram Gopal Verma

(*c*) Karan Johar (*d*) Shekhar Kapur

**(CLAT 2009)**

**94.** Joint SAARC University of eight SAARC Nations has been established in **(CLAT 2009)**

(*a*) Colombo (*b*) Dhaka

(*c*) Kathmandu (*d*) New Delhi

**95.** The Green Revolution in India has been identified with

(*a*) Dr. Man Mohan Singh

(*b*) Dr. Montek Singh Ahluwalia

(*c*) Mr. Rajendra Singh 'waterman'

(*d*) Dr. M.S. Swaminathan **(CLAT 2009)**

**96.** World's longest sea bridge has taken shape in to 2007 in

(*a*) China (*b*) Japan

(*c*) Singapore (*d*) U.S.A. **(CLAT 2009)**

**97.** In the world of Hindi Cinema, who was affectionately called as 'Dada Moni'?

(*a*) Balraj Sahni (*b*) Prithviraj Kapoor

(*c*) Ashok Kumar (*d*) Utpal Dutt

**(CLAT 2009)**

**98.** Great tennis player Bjorn Borg belongs to which country?

(*a*) Italy (*b*) Latvia

(*c*) U.S.A. (*d*) Sweden **(CLAT 2010)**

**99.** Which country was known as sick man of Europe?

(*a*) Greece (*b*) Latvia

(*c*) Turkey (*d*) Austria **(CLAT 2010)**

**100.** in Malaysia, the word 'bhumiputra' refers to

(*a*) Malays (*b*) Chinese

(*c*) Indians (*d*) Buddhists

**(CLAT 2010)**

**101.** What was the real name of Munshi Premchand?

(*a*) Nabab Rai

(*b*) Dhanpat Rai

(*c*) Ram Chandra Srivastava

(*d*) Han Shankar **(CLAT 2010)**

**102.** Who is the author of 'Old Man and the Sea'?

(*a*) John Ruskin (*b*) Raja Rao

(*c*) Gunter Grass (*d*) Ernest Hemingway

**(CLAT 2010)**

**103.** 'The Naïve and the Sentimental Novelist' is a 2010 publication of Harvard University Press of which of the following authors? **(CLAT 2011)**

(*a*) Orhan Pamuk (*b*) J.M Coetzie

(*c*) Partha Chatterjee (*d*) Ben Okri

**104.** Rani Kumudini Devi, whose birth centenary is being celebrated in 2011, was the:

(*a*) First woman barrister of India

(*b*) First woman Mayor of Hyderabad

(*c*) First woman photographer in India

(*d*) First woman doctor of India **(CLAT 2011)**

**105.** The Supreme Court in 2010 upheld an order of the Bombay High Court to lift a four-yearold ban imposed by the Maharashtra government on publication and circulation of a controversial book, authored by American scholar James Laine. Identify the book from the following.

(*a*) Chatrpati Shivaji

(*b*) Shivaji – The Warrior King

(*c*) Shivaji - The Hindu King in Muslim India

(*d*) None of the above. **(CLAT 2011)**

**106.** Irom Sharmila has been fasting for the last 10 years to protest against which of the following issues?

(*a*) Rape cases against Indian Army in Manipur

(*b*) Emergency in Manipur

(*c*) Prevention of Terrorism Act 2005

(*d*) Application of the Armed Forces (Special Powers) Act 1958 in Manipur **(CLAT 2011)**

**107.** Who is the author of the book "TINDERBOX - The Past and Future of Pakistan"?

(*a*) Husain Haqqani

(*b*) Yasmeen Niaz Mohiuddin

(*c*) Ishrat Husain

(*d*) M.J. Akbar **(CLAT 2011)**

**108.** The first woman Secretary General of SAARC is from which country?

(*a*) Maldives (*b*) Bhutan

(*c*) Sri Lanka (*d*) India **(CLAT 2011)**

**109.** Which Irish player scored the fastest Century in the history of World Cup Cricket?

(*a*) Niall O' Brien (*b*) Kevin O' Brien

(*c*) A. Cusack (*d*) Ed Joyce **(CLAT 2011)**

**110.** With which Hindutva association are Sadhvi Pragya Singh Thakur and Swami Aseemanand allegedly associated?

(*a*) Vishwa Hindu Parishad
(*b*) Shri Ram Sena
(*c*) Abhinav Bharat
(*d*) Arya Samaj **(CLAT 2011)**

**111.** Gustavo Santaolall who composed the music to the song "Stranger Lives" in the movie "Dhobi Ghat", is from which of the following nations?

(*a*) Chile (*b*) Peru
(*c*) Argentina (*d*) Mexico **(CLAT 2011)**

**112.** Which one of the following tribes lives in the Niyamgiri Hills, which is at the heart of the controversy surrounding Vedanta Resources' mining operations? **(CLAT 2011)**

(*a*) Manna Dhora (*b*) Dongria Kondh
(*c*) Pardhan (*d*) Mal Pahariya

**113.** Who is the author of the book 'Great Soul: Mahatma Gandhi and his Struggle with India', criticised for its content? **(CLAT 2011)**

(*a*) Nirad C. Chaudhury (*b*) Joseph Lelyveld
(*c*) Khushwant Singh (*d*) Hermann Kallenbach

**114.** Which internationally renowned musician collaborated with Rahul Sharma to release a music album titled '*Namaste India*'? **(CLAT 2011)**

(*a*) Richard Clayderman (*b*) Kenny G
(*c*) Yanni (*d*) Ricky Martin

**115.** "War on Terrorism or American Strategy for Global Dominance" is authored by which of the following authors? **(CLAT 2011)**

(*a*) Noam Chomsky (*b*) Demetrios Caraley
(*c*) Lea Brilmayer (*d*) Manzoor Alam

**116.** Which of the following pairings is incorrect?

(*a*) Muammar Gaddafi – Syria.
(*b*) Fidel Castro – Cuba.
(*c*) Pol Pot – Cambodia.
(*d*) Hosni Mubarak – Egypt. **(CLAT 2011)**

**117.** Who said that, 'Man is a social animal'?

(*a*) Socrates (*b*) Aristotle
(*c*) Kahn (*d*) Plato **(CLAT 2012)**

**118.** World Computer Literacy day is celebrated on

(*a*) November 14 (*b*) November 3
(*c*) December 2 (*d*) July 5 **(CLAT 2012)**

**119.** Who out of the following was the recipient of Dhyan Chand Award in 2011?

(*a*) Satish Pillai (*b*) Hukam Singh
(*c*) Shabbir Ali (*d*) Mukh Bain Singh
**(CLAT 2012)**

**120.** Name the annual fair of Rajasthan that is famous for its camel trading event. **(CLAT 2012)**

(*a*) Maru Mela (*b*) Pushkar Mela
(*c*) Suraj Kund Mela (*d*) Sonepur Mela

**121.** December 10 is observed as **(CLAT 2012)**

(*a*) World Health Day (*b*) U. N. Day
(*c*) Red Cross Day (*d*) Human Rights Day

**122.** The book titled 'The Google Story' has been authored by **(CLAT 2012)**

(*a*) David A. Vice (*b*) Shobha Dey
(*c*) Fredrick Forsyth (*d*) Vikram Seth

**123.** Christian Lagarde heads the

(*a*) World Bank
(*b*) UNICEF
(*c*) International Monetary Fund
(*d*) WHO **(CLAT 2012)**

**124.** The seat of International Criminal Court is at

(*a*) The Hague (*b*) Geneva
(*c*) Washington (*d*) Tokyo **(CLAT 2012)**

**125.** First Indian to ski to North Pole is

(*a*) Arun Nayyar
(*b*) Ajeet Bajaj
(*c*) Sq. Ldr. Sanjay Thapar
(*d*) Neal Paramjeet **(CLAT 2012)**

**126.** First woman Director General of Police in India was

(*a*) Kanchan Choudhary
(*b*) Kavitha Choudhary
(*c*) Kiran Bedi
(*d*) Aswathy Tonge **(CLAT 2012)**

**127.** The 9th Postal Zone of India covers

(*a*) Andhra Pradesh
(*b*) Army Post Office
(*c*) Goa
(*d*) Andaman and Nicobar Islands **(AILET 2013)**

**128.** Which one of the following international organisations does India disapprove of?

(*a*) ASEAN (*b*) NATO
(*c*) FAO (*d*) OPEC **(AILET 2013)**

**129.** Which space agency released surprising pictures of the remains of huge river which ran across Mars at some point of time on January 17, 2013 ?

(*a*) NASA
(*b*) European Space Agency
(*c*) Australian Space Agency
(*d*) ISRO **(AILET 2013)**

**130.** Which of the following are included in the definition of Sexual Harassment under the new Sexual Harassment of Women at Workplace (Prevention Prohibition and Redressal) Bill?

(*a*) Physical contact and advances

(*b*) Demand or request for sexual favours

(*d*) Making sexually coloured remarks

(*d*) All of the above **(AILET 2013)**

**131.** Vishwanathan Anand retained the World Chess Championship in 2012 by defeating Boris Gelfand. Mr. Gelfand belongs to **(CLAT 2013)**

(*a*) Israel (*b*) Russia

(*c*) Poland (*d*) USA

**132.** World Cup Football 2014 and Olympics 2016 will be held in **(CLAT 2013)**

(*a*) USA (*b*) Brazil

(*c*) Russia (*d*) South Africa

**133.** Vishwaroopam is a 2013 Tamil spy thriller film written, directed and co-produced by ______ who also enacts the lead role. **(CLAT 2013)**

(*a*) Prakash Raj (*b*) Rajni Kant

(*c*) Kamal Haasan (*d*) Chiranjeevi

**134.** Vijay Kumar, who clinched a silver medal in London Olympics in 2012 is associated with **(CLAT 2013)**

(*a*) Boxing (*b*) Shooting

(*c*) Weight Lifting (*d*) Wrestling

**135.** Sushil Kumar who won a silver medal in London Olympics in 2012 is associated with

(*a*) Shooting (*b*) Boxing **(CLAT 2013)**

(*c*) Wrestling (*d*) Weight lifting

**136.** How many medals did India win in London Olympics 2012? **(CLAT 2013)**

(*a*) 3 (*b*) 4

(*c*) 5 (*d*) 6

**137.** On which date International Women's Day is celebrated? **(CLAT 2013)**

(*a*) 18th March (*b*) 8th March

(*c*) 28th March (*d*) 18th Feb

**138.** In the name P. Chidambaram, the present Union Finance Minister, what does 'P' stands for? **(CLAT 2013)**

(*a*) Palghat (*b*) Pallakudi

(*c*) Palaniappan (*d*) Perumal

**139.** "Paradise Regained" was written by **(CLAT 2013)**

(*a*) John Milton (*b*) Michel Angelo

(*c*) John Keats (*d*) Lord Byron

**140.** World Literacy Day is celebrated on **(CLAT 2013)**

(*a*) 5th September (*b*) 6th September

(*c*) 8th September (*d*) None of these

**141.** South African Paralympics icon Oscar Pistorius has been accused of killing **(CLAT 2013)**

(*a*) Julia Kamp (*b*) Reeva Steenkamp

(*c*) Pistorius Kamp (*d*) Shakeera Kamp

**142.** International Year of Biodiversity is/was/will be

(*a*) 2010 (*b*) 2011 **(CLAT 2013)**

(*c*) 2012 (*d*) 2014

**143.** Who won the Women's Singles at the Malaysian Gran Prix Badminton Championship in 2013 ? **(AILET 2014)**

(*a*) Saina Nehwal (*b*) Juan Gu

(*c*) P. V. Sindhu (*d*) Ratchanok Intanon

**144.** Who is the oldest woman tennis player to be ranked No. 1 in the world ? **(AILET 2014)**

(*a*) Venus Williams

(*b*) Chris Evert

(*c*) Martina Navratilova

(*d*) Serena Williams

**145.** Who has won the Golden Shoe Award in Soccer three times ? **(AILET 2014)**

(*a*) Diego Maradona (*b*) Christiano Ronaldo

(*c*) Lionel Messi (*d*) Pele

**146.** Who was conferred the Col. C. K. Nayudu Life Achievement Award in Cricket during 2012 ? **(AILET 2014)**

(*a*) Sunil Gavaskar (*b*) Sachin Tendulkar

(*c*) Dhoni (*d*) Kapildev

**147.** The highest award for sporting excellence in India is **(AILET 2014)**

(*a*) Arjuna Award (*b*) Dronacharya Award

(*c*) Bharat Ratna (*d*) Khel Ratna

## Solutions

**1.** c Innuendos are words, which appear innocent, but have a latent defamatory meaning.

**2.** a The British Parliament is the most powerful legislature in the world.

**3.** d Unliquidated damages means damage to be assessed by a Court as these are not pre-determined

**4.** d Assault and nuisance are wrong under both tort and criminal law.

**5.** c The dispaly of the goods by the seller is an 'invitation to offer'.

**6.** b An ideal of Shri Krishna is a legal person and treated having juristic personality.

**7.** a When a court sends some one in judicial custody, it means he is sent to jail.

**8.** b The term of office of a judge of the International Court of Justice is 9 years.

**9.** a The democratic device, used in constitutional states, by which important political questions, particularly question relating tot he states of a region, may be referred to the people of the region for their final decision, is called 'Plebiscite'.

**10.** c Shrutis are ancient treatise on law.

**11.** d Wakfs are the Muslim religious foundations.

**12.** c Government cause maximum litigation in Courts.

**13.** d The first-regular adjudicatory mobile court in the country has been inaugurated at Punbanna village in Punjab.

**14.** a Dissolution of Muslim Marriage Act, 1939 provides grounds of dissolution of Muslim marriage to Spouses.

**15.** c A married man commits adultery if he has sexual intercourse with any woman except his wife.

**16.** d A husband is obliged to maintain his divorced wife till she gets remarried.

**17.** d (i) Default = Failure to do something required by law

(ii) Delict = A wrongful act

(iii) Derelict =A thing thrown away by its owner

(iv) Dictum = A judge's observation.

**18.** c India and Britain have signed an 'Extradition treaty'. Extradition means Indian and the U.K. will deport criminals on reciprocal basis to each other.

**19.** a Tetraethyl lead is the best anti-knock compound used in petrol to increase mileage.

**20.** d Rasna is the Ahmedabad-based Pioma Industries. Recently, the rasna girl Taruni Sachdeva died in a plan crash in Nepal.

**21.** a Brett Lee acted as a model for Timex.

**22.** b T-20 has been included in Asian Games since the year 2010.

**23.** d Shri. E. Sridharan is the incumbent Managing Director of Delhi Metro Railway Corporation.

**24.** a Gunnar Myradal has dealt with the problem of poverty in Asian countries in her book ASIAN DRAMA.

**25.** d Dev Patel the protagonist in the world famous Indian movie Slumdog Millionaire has not won the Oscar.

**26.** c Garima is the name of the cloned buffalo calf created by The National Dairy Research Insdtute in Haryana.

**27.** d Ex- Chief Justice of India Hon'ble Justice Lahoti did not became the chairperson of National Human Right Commission.

**28.** c In the year 1915 Shreemati Nathibai Damodar Thackersey (SNDT) the first Women's university in India was established.

**29.** c Justice V.S. Malimath headed committee on reforming Criminal Justice System.

**30.** b Slumdog Millionaire got 14 Oscar nominations.

**31.** c Vijender Singh was the first Indian to get a medal at the World Boxing Championship.

**32.** c Rs. 25,000 is the maximum amount of fine that can be imposed by the Central or State Information Commission on Public Information Officer for not furnishing the information.

**33.** c Boutros Boutros Ghali was the first African to become the Secretary General of United Nations not Kofi Annan.

**34.** b Balagangadhar Tilak gave the slogan "Swaraj is my birth right".

**35.** b Srimavo Bandaranaike was the first woman Prime Minister.

**36.** a Cloud Computing is a Internet based computing model. Cloud Computing has No sole Inventor.

**37.** a Kashiwazaki-kariwa Japan is the world's largest nuclear power Station. Kallpakam is a small town in Tamil Naidu and is famous for its nuclear power plants affiliated research installations.

**38.** d The first International Day for women was celebrated on 19th March 1911. After that it is celebrated every year at March 8. New Zealand is the first country in the world to give women the right to vote.

**39.** c Chernobyl nuclear accident occurred on 26 April 1986 at the Chernobyl Nuclear power Plant in the Ukraine (then part of the Soviet Union) It is the only one classified as a level 7 event on the International Nuclear Event Scale which is the highest.

**40.** d France gets highest percentage of electricity from nuclear power stations i.e. (78.8%).

**41.** b Justice M. Hidayatullah also became acting vice-president while serving the post of Chief Justice of India.

**42.** a Air-conditioning was invented Carrier.

**43.** b Motor Cycle was invented by G. Daimler.

**44.** c Canada has the largest territory among U.S.A, Brazil and China.

**45.** d According to the survey conducted in India during 2001-2003, the highest percentage of deaths were due to HIV/ AIDS.

**46.** d Uttar Pradesh largest state in India in terms of territory.

**47.** a Justice V.Ramaswami was the only Supreme Court who was sought to be impeached under the Constitution.

**48.** b Census takes place in India every 10 years. The Latest Census was took in the year 2011.

**49.** b In Lyons Frans INTERPOL, a 147-nation Police Commission has its Headquarters.

**50.** b J.H. Dunant founded Red Cross in 1863 which has its' Headquarter in Geneva.

**51.** d The European Union came into existence through the 'Maastricht Treaty' in the year 1992 and it (treaty) also let to the creation of the single European currency, the Euro. Recently the economics comprising the European Union commonly known as PIGGS (Portugal, Italy, Greece and Spain) were in International News because of relentless deepening of economic crisis.

**52.** * Justice B.N. Srikrishna was the Chairman of Sixth Pay Commission.

**53.** a The year of 1921 is referred, as year of great divide is as it marked the massive growth rate of population revealed by the census.

**54.** d A Pin Code consists of 6 digits. First Digit represents the Zone. First and Second Digits combined indicate the Postal Circle or States (except for North-Eastern India as its a Postal Circle). Third Digit indicates the Sorting Unit/ District of the respective postal circle. Last three digits indicate the delivery Post Office.

**55.** b More than 50 Sikh Shrines in India are named after trees.

**56.** b The Current President of IMF is Christine Lagarde from France. She is also the first woman president if IMF.

**57.** a Vijay Kelkar was the Chairman of $13^{the}$ Finance Commission constituted in the year 2007.

**58.** a Vijay Mallaya the Indian business tycoon has recently been in spotlight because of grave financial issues surrounded his company kingfisher airlines.

**59.** c Saudi Arabia 's king "Abdullah (Abdullah bin Abdulaziz al Saud) " is the monarch of Saudi Arabia.

**60.** b Kishore Biyani is the CEO of future group and managing director of Pantaloon Retail.

**61.** c Tata Consultancy Services has retained its position at the top and in terms of revenue in the present year has widened the revenue gap with its business rival Infosys.

**62.** c The term "Taikonaut" is used for an astronaut of Chinese Ethnicity. Similarly the term "Cosmonaut" is for an astronaut of Russian descent.

**63.** c Singapore's government is one of the "cleanest" in the world largely because its top ministers are paid exorbitant salaries (in excess of $1-million) annually.

**64.** b Pascal Lamy is the Current Director-General of the World Trade Organization.

**65.** b Norway is known as the Land of Midnight Sun

**66.** b 18 carat gold signifies 18 parts of gold and 6 parts of other metal

**67.** b Salwa Judam (meaning Purification Hunt) refers to the militant movement in state of chhattisgarh India which is aimed at countering the naxalite violence in that region.

**68.** c Kevin Rudd led the country in atoning for the past wrongs.

**69.** b In My Experiments with Truth, Gandhiji expounded his economic ideas.

**70.** a Sunita William made a record for spending of 195 days in 2008.

**71.** c China in the year 2008 was the second biggest greenhouse gas emitter (after the USA) in the world.

**72.** c The "wailing wall" is associated with Jews.

**73.** c The Ex-President Abul Kalam Azad who was also Education Minister got Bharat Ratna also.

**74.** b Ozone Layer protects Earth from ultraviolet radiation.

**75.** d Jnapath Award is given for Literature It is presented by the trust Bharatiya Jnanpith.

**76.** a Justice B.N.Srikrishna was the Chairman of Sixth Pay Commission.

**77.** b International Court of Justice is situated at The Hague in the Netherlands. Justice Dalveer Bhandari from India has been appointed to ICJ recently.

**78.** c The Liberhan Commission which received repeated extensions has been inquiring into demolition of Babri Masjid.

**79.** b Justice Ramaswami is the only judge against whom a motion of impeachment was introduced into Parliament

**80.** a Malimath Committee suggested reforms on Criminal Justice System.

**81.** b Leila Seth was the first Woman Chief Justice of High Court in India.

**82.** a Chak De! India is a 2007 Indian woman's sports film about field hockey in India. Directed by Shimit Amin and produced by Yash Raj Films, the film stars Shahrukh Khan as Kabir Khan, the former captain of the Indian hockey team.

**83.** * This question has no correct answer.
Note : The 2009 World Food Prize was awarded to Dr. Gebisa Ejeta of Ethiopia, whose sorghum hybrids resistant to drought and the devastating Striga weed have dramatically increased the production and availability of one of the world's five principal grains, enhancing the food supply of hundreds of millions of people in sub-Saharan Africa.

**84.** a The ISO 9000 family of standards is related to quality management systems and designed to help organizations ensure that they meet the needs of customers and other stakeholders while meeting statutory and regulatory requirements related to the product. The standards are published by ISO, the International Organization for Standardization, and available through National standards bodies.

**85.** d AGMARK is a certification mark employed on agricultural products in India, assuring that they conform to a set of standards approved by the Directorate of Marketing and Inspection, an agency of the Government of India. The AGMARK is legally enforced in India by the Agricultural Produce (Grading and Marking) Act of 1937 ( amended in 1986). The present AGMARK standards cover quality guidelines for 205 different commodities spanning a variety of Pulses, Cereals, Essential Oils, Vegetable Oils, Fruits & Vegetables, and semi-processed products like Vermicelli.

**86.** a The NAL Saras (Sanskrit: Crane) is the first Indian multi-purpose civilian aircraft in the Light Transport Aircraft category designed by the National Aerospace Laboratories (NAL). The first Saras (PT1) completed its maiden flight at the HAL airport in Bangalore on 29 May 2004.

**87.** c Dilip Kumar has been Awarded Nishan-E-Pakistan, the highest civilian award conferred by government of Pakistan, for his effort to bridge gap between India and Pakistan.

**88.** c World No Tobacco Day (WNTD) is observed around the world every year on May 31. It is meant to encourage a 24-hour period of abstinence from all forms of tobacco consumption across the globe. The day is further intended to draw global attention to the widespread prevalence of tobacco use and to negative health effects, which currently lead to 5.4 million deaths worldwide annually. The member states of the World Health Organization (WHO) created World No Tobacco Day in 1987.

**89.** c HINDRAF or Hindu Rights Action Force with its slogan of People's Power began as a coalition of 30 Hindu non-governmental organisations committed to the preservation of Hindu community rights and heritage in a multiracial Malaysia. . HINDRAF has made a major impact to the political landscape of Malaysia in staging the 2007 HINDRAF rally. After several warnings by the Malaysian government HINDRAF was officially banned on October 15, 2008.

**90.** a 'Jet lite' airlines of today is an offspring of Jet Airways and Sahara.

**91.** c India's First Nuclear Reactor was Apsara. It was also the first nuclear reactor in Asia. Apsara went critical at Bhabha Atomic Research Centre (BARC), Trombay on August 4, 1956. It heralded the arrival of India's nuclear energy programme. Dr. Homi Bhabha himself conceptualised the design of the reactor and the reactor was built entirely by Indian engineers in a record time of about 15 months.

**92.** b The Samjhauta Express commonly called the Friendship Express, is a twice-weekly train – Tuesdays and Fridays – that runs between Delhi and Attari in India and Lahore in Pakistan. The word samjhauta means "Understanding", "accord" and "compromise" in both Hindi and Urdu.

**93.** d

**94.** d The South Asian University is an International University sponsored by the eight Member States of the South Asian Association for Regional Cooperation (SAARC). The eight countries are: Afghanistan, Bangladesh, Bhutan, India, Maldives, Nepal, Pakistan and Sri Lanka. South Asian University started admitting students in 2010, as a temporary campus at Akbar Bhawan, India. Its permanent campus will be at Maidan Garhi in South Delhi, India, next to Indira Gandhi National Open University (IGNOU).

**95.** d Maankombu Sambasivan Swaminathan (born 7 August 1925) is an Indian geneticist and international administrator, renowned for his leading role in India's "Green Revolution," a program under which high-yield varieties of wheat and rice seedlings were planted in the fields of poor farmers.

**96.** a The world's largest sea bridge that has taken shape in 2007 is in China. The 26-mileJiaozhou Bay crossing connecting the port city of Qingdao, south-east of Beijing, to the industrial district of Huangdao is currently the longest sea bridge in the world.

**97.** c Ashok Kumar (13 October 1911 – 10 December 2001) also fondly called Dadamoni in Bengali, was an Indian film actor. Born in Bhagalpur, Bengal Presidency he attained iconic status in Indian cinema. The Government of India honoured him with the Dadasaheb Phalke Award and the Padma Bhushan in 1998 for his contributions to Indian cinema.

**98.** d Björn Rune Borg ( born 6 June 1956) is a former world no. 1 tennis player from Sweden. Between 1974 and 1981 he won 11 Grand Slam singles titles. He won five consecutive Wimbledon singles titles (a record equalled by Roger Federer) and six French Open singles titles (a record broken by Rafael Nadal). He is considered by many to be one of the greatest tennis players of all time.

**99.** c "Sick man of Europe" is a nickname that has been used to describe a European country experiencing a time of economic difficulty and/ or impoverishment. The term was first used in the mid-19th century to describe the Ottoman Empire (Modern Turkey) but has since been applied at one time or another to nearly every other mid-to-large-sized country in Europe.

**100.** a Bumiputera or Bumiputra is a Malaysian term to describe Malay race and the indigenous peoples of Southeast Asia, and particularly in Malaysia. The term comes from the Sanskrit word bhumiputra, which can be translated literally as "prince of land" (bhumi= earth or land, putra=prince).

In the 1970s, the Malaysian government implemented policies which The Economist called "racially discriminatory" designed to favour bumiputras (including affirmative action in public education) to create opportunities, and to defuse inter-ethnic tensions following the extended violence against Chinese Malaysians in the 13 May Incident in 1969. These policies have succeeded in creating a significant urban Malay middle class. They have been less effective in eradicating poverty among rural communities. Some analysts have noted a backlash of resentment from excluded groups, in particular the sizeable Chinese and Indian Malaysian minorities.

**101.** b Premchand who was born as Dhanpat Rai was an Indian writer famous for his modern Hindi-Urdu literature. He is one of the most celebrated writers of the Indian subcontinent, and is regarded as one of the foremost Hindi-Urdu writers of the early twentieth century.

**102.** d The Old Man and the Sea is a novel written by the American author Ernest Hemingway in 1951 in Cuba, and published in 1952. It was awarded the Pulitzer Prize for Fiction in 1953 and was cited by the Nobel Committee as contributing to the awarding of the Nobel Prize in Literature to Hemingway in 1954.

**103.** a The Naïve and the Sentimental Novelist' has been written by Orhan Pamuk.

**104.** b Rani Kumudini Devi was the first woman barrister of India.

**105.** c James Laine authored the book Shivaji - The Hindu King in Muslim India.

**106.** d Irom Sharmila has been fasting for the last 10 years to protest against Application of the Armed Forces (Special Powers) Act 1958 in Manipur.

**107.** d TINDERBOX - The Past and Future of Pakistan is the name of the book written by M.J. Akbar who is a leading journalist and editorial director of popular magazine 'India Today'.

**108.** a Fathimath Dhiyana Saeed, from Maldives is the first woman Secretary General of SAARC.

**109.** b Kevin O' Brien from his country Ireland scored the fastest Century in the history of World Cup Cricket.

**110.** a Pradeep Kumar is the Incumbent chief Commissioner of Central Vigilance Commission.

**111.** c Gustavo Santaolall who composed the music to the song 'Stranger Lives' in the movie 'Dhobi Ghat' is from Argentina.

**112.** b Dongria Kondh is the tribe living in the Niyamgiri Hills, which is at the heart of the controversy surrounding Vedanta Resources' mining operations.

**113.** b Joseph Lelyveld is the author of the book 'Great Soul: Mahatma Gandhi and his Struggle with India', which was criticized for its content.

**114.** b Kenny G, collaboration with Rahul Sharma in the music album 'Namste India'

**115.** d "War on Terrorism or American Strategy for Global Dominance" is written by Manzoor Alam.

**116.** a Munammar Gaddafi is from Libya.

**117.** b Aristotle (384 BC – 322 BC) the famous Greek philosopher and polymath is the person to whom the given quote is attributed. He is a student of Plato and teacher of Alexander the Great and his writings cover many subjects, including physics, metaphysics, poetry, theater, music, logic, rhetoric, linguistics, politics, government, ethics, biology, and zoology. Together with Plato and Socrates (Plato's teacher), Aristotle is one of the most important founding figures in Western philosophy. Aristotle's writings were the first to create a comprehensive system of Western philosophy, encompassing morality, aesthetics, logic, science, politics, and metaphysics.

**118.** c December 2nd is World Computer Literacy Day. The aim of World computer literacy day at is to educate and spread awareness among the masses about the benefits of using computers.

**119.** c DhyanChand Award is India's highest award for lifetime achievement in sports and games, given by the Government of India.The award is named after the legendary Indian hockey player DhyanChand. The award was initiated in 2002 and carries a cash prize of INR 5 lakh, a statuette,ceremonial dress and a scroll of honour.

In August 2011, the following 3 sports personalities were awarded the DhyanChand Award : ***Shabbir Ali*** (Football), SushilKohli (Swimming), and Rajkumar (Wrestling).

**120.** b The Pushkar Fair, or Pushkar ka Mela, is the annual five-day camel and livestock fair, held in the town of Pushkar in the state of Rajasthan, India. It is one of the world's largest camel fairs, and apart from buying and selling of livestock it has become an important tourist attraction and its highlights have become competitions such as the "matkaphod", "longest moustache", and "bridal competition".

**121.** d Human Rights Day is celebrated annually across the world on 10 December.

The date was chosen to honor the United Nations General Assembly's adoption and proclamation, on 10 December 1948, of the Universal Declaration of Human Rights (UDHR), the first global enunciation of human rights and one of the first major achievements of the new United Nations. The formal establishment of Human Rights Day occurred at the 317th Plenary Meeting of the General Assembly on 4 December 1950, when the General Assembly declared resolution 423(V), inviting all member states and any other interested organizations to celebrate the day as they saw fit.

**122.** a David A. Vise, formerly a Pulitzer Prize-winning reporter for The Washington Post, authored the book titled ' The Google Story ' which chronicles the birth and rise of Google as a search engine giant.

**123.** c Christine Lagarde is a French lawyer and Union for a Popular Movement politician who has been the Managing Director (MD) of the International Monetary Fund (IMF) since 5 July 2011. Previously, she held various ministerial posts in the French government: she was Minister of Economic Affairs, Finances and Industry and before that Minister of Agriculture and Fishing and Minister of Trade in the government of Dominique de Villepin. Lagarde was the first woman ever to become Minister of Economic Affairs of a G8 economy, and is the first woman to ever head the IMF.

On 28 June 2011, she was named as the next MD of the IMF for a five-year term, starting on 5 July 2011, replacing Dominique Strauss-Kahn. Her appointment is the 11th consecutive appointment of a European to head the IMF. In 2011, Lagarde was ranked the 9th most powerful woman in the world by Forbes magazine.

**124.** a The International Criminal Court (commonly referred to as the ICC) is a permanent tribunal to prosecute individuals for genocide, crimes against humanity, war crimes, and the crime of aggression (although it cannot, until at least 2017, exercise jurisdiction over the crime of aggression).

It came into being on 1 July 2002—the date its founding treaty, the Rome Statute of the International Criminal Court, entered into force and it can only prosecute crimes committed on or after that date. The Court's official seat is in The Hague, Netherlands, but its proceedings may take place anywhere.

**125.** b Ajeet Bajaj (born 1965) is the first Indian to ski to the North Pole and the South Pole within a year and has undertaken travel in 17 countries spanning six continents. In July 2008 he kayaked along the coast of Greenland as part of an Indo-American team. The expedition's aim was to create awareness about the effect of global warming on glaciers.

**126.** a Kanchan Chaudhary Bhattacharya,an IPS officer of the 1973 batchis the first woman Director General of Police of any state. Popular Hindi teleserial 'Udaan' was based on her life. She retired as the DGP of Uttarakhand state in the year 2007.

**127.** b The 9 th Postal zone of India covers Army Post office (APO) and Field Post office (FPO).

**128.** b India does not approves North Atlantic Treaty Organisation (NATO) .

**129.** b The European Space Agency released surprising pictures of the remains of huge river which ran across the Red Planet, Mars at some point of time, on 17 January 2013.

**130.** d All of these are included in the definition of sexual harassment under the new sexual harassment of woman at workplace.

**131.** a Israel

**132.** b Brazil

**133.** c Kamal Hasan

**134.** b Shooting

**135.** c Wrestling

**136.** d 6

**137.** b 8th March

**138.** c Palaniappan

**139.** a John Milton

**140.** c 8th September

**141.** b Reeva Steenkamp

**142.** a 2010

**143.** c She won Malaysian open title 2013, beating her opponent from Singapore Juan Gu. This is Sindhu's maiden Grand Prix Gold title.

**144.** d According to the Women's Tennis Association (WTA), Serena Williams is the oldest female player to earn the top ranking.

**145.** c Lionel Messi and Cristiano Ronaldo are currently the only players to have won the European Golden Shoe three times, with Messi being the only one to have thrice been the stand-alone winner.

**146.** a Sunil Gavaskar was conferred the Col. C.K. Nayudu Life Achievement Award in Cricket during 2012.

**147.** d Rajiv Gandhi Khel Ratna - India's highest honour given for achievement in sports. Arjuna Award - recognizes outstanding achievement in National sports. Dronacharya award- an award presented by the government of India for excellence in sports coaching. Bharat Ratna is the highest civilian award of the Republic of India and not the sports award.

■■

# Chapter-Wise
# Solved Papers

# CLAT-2015
# CHAPTER-WISE

## ENGLISH

### VOCABULARY

**Directions (Qs. 1–5) :** *For the word a contextual sentence is given. Pick the word from the alternatives given that is most inappropriate in the given context.*

**1. SPECIOUS :** A specious argument is not simply a false one but one that has the ring of truth.

(*a*) Deceitful (*b*) Fallacious
(*c*) Credible (*d*) Deceptive

**2. OBVIATE :** The new mass transit system may obviate the need for the use of personal cars.

(*a*) Prevent (*b*) Forestall
(*c*) Preclude (*d*) Bolster

**3. DISUSE :** Some words fall into disuse as technology makes objects obsolete.

(*a*) Prevalent (*b*) Discarded
(*c*) Obliterated (*d*) Unfashionable

**4. PARSIMONIOUS:** The evidence was constructed from every parsimonious scraps of information.

(*a*) Prevalent (*b*) Penurious
(*c*) Thrifty (*d*) Altruistic

**5. FACETIOUS:** When I suggested that war is a method of controlling population, my father remarked that I was being facetious.

(*a*) Jovian (*b*) Jovial
(*c*) Jocular (*d*) Joking

**Directions (Qs. 6–8) :** *In the question, a related pair of words or phrases is followed by a pair of words or phrases. Select the pair that best expresses a relationship similar to the one expressed in the original pair.*

**6.** Dulcet : Raucous

(*a*) Sweet : Song
(*b*) Crazy : Insane
(*c*) Palliative : Exacerbating
(*d*) Theory : Practical

**7.** Malapropism : Words

(*a*) Anachronism : Time (*b*) Ellipsis : Sentence
(*c*) Jinjanthropism : Apes (*d*) Catechism : Religion

**8.** Peel : Peal

(*a*) Coat: Rind (*b*) Laugh : Bell
(*c*) Rain : Reign (*d*) Brain : Cranium

**Direction (Qs. 9–11) :** *Choose the option closest in meaning to the Capitalized word.*

**9. GRANDIOSE**

(*a*) imposing (*b*) unpretentious
(*c*) boring (*d*) lanky

**10. SPRY**

(*a*) doubtful (*b*) nimble
(*c*) prognosticate (*d*) leave

**11. FUDGE**

(*a*) to sweeten (*b*) smear
(*c*) irritate (*d*) falsify

### ANSWERS

| | | | | |
|---|---|---|---|---|
| **1.** (c) | **2.** (d) | **3.** (a) | **4.** (d) | **5.** (a) |
| **6.** (c) | **7.** (a) | **8.** (c) | **9.** (a) | **10.** (b) |
| **11.** (d) | | | | |

### EXPLANATIONS

1. *Specious* means superficially plausible, but actually wrong. Apart from option (c), the other options are synonyms of *specious*. *Credible* is an antonym.
2. Options other than (d) are synonymous words. All the words refer to preventing or stalling something. *Bolster* means to support or strengthen. It can also mean a long, thick pillow that is placed under other pillows for support.
3. *Obsolete* means something which is out of vogue or archaic. Hence, options (b), (c) and (d) are synonyms. Option (a) is the odd one out.
4. *Parsimonious* refers to someone who is unwilling to spend money. Options (a), (b) and (c) are synonyms. Option (d) is *altruistic* which means showing a disinterested and selfless concern for the well-being of others or being unselfish.
5. *Facetious* means treating serious issues with deliberately inappropriate humour; flippant. *Jovian* relates to Jove or Jupiter. Hence, option (a) is inappropriate.
6. (Incorrect)

   The CLAT answer key is option (b). However, we believe that option (c) is the correct answer. *Dulcet* refers to a sweet and soothing sound while *raucous* means a loud noise. Hence, *dulcet* and *raucous* are antonyms. Similarly, *palliative* refers to relieving or soothing of pain whereas, *exacerbate* refers to worsening of something. *Palliative* and *Exacerbate* can be considered as antonyms. Option (d) also refers to antonyms and hence, can be the correct answer but it has to be kept in mind that *Theory* is noun while *Practical* is adjective. Option (b) refers to synonyms.

7. *Malapropism* refers to the mistaken use of a word in place of a similar-sounding one, often with an amusing effect. Hence, *Malapropism* is closely associated with words. Similarly, *Anachronism* refers to a thing belonging or appropriate to a period other than that in which it exists, especially a thing that is conspicuously old-fashioned. Hence, *Anachronism* is closely associated with time. The relation is the same as *Malapropism* and *words*.
8. This is an example of homophone. Both the words have the same pronunciation but have different meaning and spellings.
9. *Grandiose* (adj.) refers to something *magnanimous* or *huge*. *Imposing* is another synonym of *Grandiose*.
10. *Spry* (adj.) refers to someone who is active, agile or lively. *Nimble* is another synonym of *spry*.
11. *Fudge* (n. and vb.) refers to tampering with something. It can also mean evading something. *Falsify* is a good synonym of *fudge*.

## GRAMMAR

**Direction (Qs. 1–3) :** *In the question, there are five sentences. Each sentence has pairs of words/phrases that are italicized and highlighted. From the italicized and highlighted word(s)/phrase(s), select the most appropriate word(s)/phrase(s) to form correct sentences. Then, from the options given, choose the best one.*

1. The **further [A]/farther [B]** he pushed himself, the more disillusioned he grew.

   For the crowd it was more of a **historical [A]/historic [B]** event, for their leader it was just another day.

   The old has a healthy **distrust [A]/mistrust [B]** for all new technology.

   The film is based on a **worthy [A]/true [B]** story.

   She coughed **discreetly [A]/discretely [B]** to announce her presence.

   (*a*) BABAB
   (*b*) ABBBA
   (*c*) BAABA
   (*d*) BBAAB

2. **Regrettably [A]/ Regretfully [B]** I have to decline your invitation.

   The critics **censored [A]/censured [B]** the new movie because of its social unacceptability.

   He was **besides [A]/beside [B]** himself with range when I told him what I had done.

   Anita had a beautiful **broach [A]/brooch [B]** on the lapel of her jacket.

   He has the same capacity as an adult to **consent [A]/assent [B]** to surgical treatment.

   (*a*) BABBA (*b*) BBAAB
   (*c*) ABBBA (*d*) BABAB

3. The prisoner's **interment [A]/internment [B]** came to an end with his early release

   She managed to bite back the **ironic [A]/caustic [B]** retort on the tip of her tongue.

   Jeans that **flair [A]/flare [B]** at the bottom are in fashion these days.

   They heard the bells **peeling [A]/pealing [B]** far and wide.

   The students **baited [A]/bated [B]** the instructor with irrelevant questions.

   (*a*) BBABB (*b*) ABBBB
   (*c*) BABBA (*d*) BBBBA

**Direction (Qs. 4-6) :** *Identify the incorrect sentence/ sentences.*

4. A. I want to do an MBA before going into business.
   B. Priti's husband has been on active service for three months.
   C. The horse suddenly broke into a buckle.
   D. I need to file an insurance claim.

   (*a*) B and A (*b*) C only
   (*c*) B and C (*d*) B, C and D

5. A. I must run fast to catch up with him
   B. The newly released took is enjoying a popular run.
   C. The doctor is on a hospital round.
   D. You can't run over him like that.

   (*a*) A and C (*b*) D only
   (*c*) A, C and D (*d*) A only

6. A. The letter was posted to the address.
   B. Your stand is beyond all reasons.
   C. How do you deal with friend who doesn't listen to a reason?
   D. My wife runs profitable business in this suburb.

   (*a*) A only (*b*) D only
   (*c*) B and C (*d*) C and D

**Direction (Qs. 7–12) :** *Fill up the blanks, numbered [1] [2] [3] [4] [5] and [6] in the passage given below with the most appropriate word from the options given for each blank.*

"Between the year 1946 and the year 1995, I did not file any income tax returns." With that [1] statement, Soubhik embarked on an account of his encounter with the Income Tax Department. "I originally owed Rs. 20,000 in unpaid taxes. With [2] and [3], the 20,000 became

60,000. The Income Tax Department then went into action, and I learned first-hand just how much power the Tax Department wields. Royalties and trust funds can be [4]; automobiles may be [5], and auctioned off. Nothing belongs to the [6] until the case is settled."

**7.** Fill up the blank [1]

(*a*) devious (*b*) blunt

(*c*) tactful (*d*) pretentious

**8.** Fill up the blank [2]

(*a*) interest (*b*) taxes

(*c*) principal (*d*) returns

**9.** Fill up the blank [3]

(*a*) sanctions (*b*) refunds

(*c*) fees (*d*) fines

**10.** Fill up the blank [4]

(*a*) closed (*b*) detached

(*c*) attached (*d*) impounded

**11.** Fill up the blank [5]

(*a*) smashed (*b*) seized

(*c*) dismantled (*d*) frozen

**12.** Fill up the blank [6]

(*a*) purchaser (*b*) victim

(*c*) investor (*d*) offender

**Directions (Qs. 13–15) :** *In the following sentence, a part of the sentence is underlined. Beneath each sentence, four different ways of paraphrasing the underlined part are indicated. Choose the best alternative among the four options.*

**13.** The management can still hire freely but cannot scold freely.

(*a*) cannot scold at will

(*b*) cannot give umbrage

(*c*) cannot take decision to scold

(*d*) cannot scold willfully

**14.** This government has given subsidies to the Navratnas but there is no telling whether the subsequent one will do.

(*a*) whether the subsequent government will do so

(*b*) if the government to follow will accept the policy

(*c*) if the government to follow will adhere to the policy

(*d*) no telling whether the subsequent one will do so

**15.** The Romanians may be restive under Soviet direction but they are tied to Moscow by ideological and military links.

(*a*) they are close to Moscow from ideological and military perspective

(*b*) they are preparing for a greater revolution

(*c*) secretly they rather enjoy the prestige of being protected by the mighty Soviets

(*d*) there is nothing they can do about it

## ANSWERS

| | | | | |
|---|---|---|---|---|
| **1.** (b) | **2.** (a) | **3.** (d) | **4.** (b) | **5.** (b) |
| **6.** (d) | **7.** (b) | **8.** (a) | **9.** (d) | **10.** (c) |
| **11.** (b) | **12.** (d) | **13.** (a) | **14.** (a) | **15.** (a) |

## EXPLANATIONS

**1.** The correct sequence is ABBBA. *Farther* refers to a physical distance whereas *further* refers to something over a great expanse of time and space. *Historic* refers to something which is famous or important in history while history refers to something concerning history. In the context of the sentence it will be *historic. Mistrust* refers to suspicion and then, a film can only be based on a *true* story. *Discreet* means to be careful while *discrete* refers to something separate or distinct.

**2.** (Incorrect) The CLAT answer key is option (a). However, we believe that the correct answer should be BBBBA (option not given). Critics cannot *censor* but *censure*. "Censure" means disapproval of something. Furthermore, in the 3rd option, *range* is incorrect. The word should be *rage*.

**3.** *Interment* refers to burial of a corpse while *internment* refers to imprisonment. *Caustic* refers to something *acerbic. Flare* refers to a gradual widening of shape, especially towards the hem of a garment. *Pealing* refers to the sound of bells. *Bait* means to taunt or annoy someone.

**4.** *Buckle* refers to a flat, typically rectangular frame with a hinged pin, used for joining the ends of a belt or strap. *Break into a buckle* does not have any meaning.

**5.** *Run over* means to *overflow* or *exceed.* It can also mean a pedestrian being hit by a car. In the context of the sentence *run over* is wrong. Hence, statement D is incorrect.

**6.** In statements C and D, there should be the indefinite article 'a' before *friend* and *profitable* respectively.

**7.** The statement made by the author is obviously very *blunt. Blunt* in the context of the sentence means a straightforward or direct statement.

**8.** A principal amount accrues interest. Hence, *interest* is the answer.

**9.** Apart from *fines*, the other options are incorrect in the context of the sentence.

**10.** Properties are often *attached* when taxes are not paid. Hence, *attached* is the right answer.

**11.** *Seized* is the most appropriate word in the context of the sentence. Automobiles can be *seized* if taxes are not paid.

**12.** *Offender* is the right word because a tax payer who has not paid taxes regularly has committed an offence in the eyes of the law.

**13.** Option (a) is grammatically correct. The sentence wants to say that the management cannot scold as and when they wish. *Umbrage* in option (b) means *annoyance.*Typing Error: In the question 'but' should not have been underlined.

**14.** Option (a) is grammatically correct. The other options are grammatically incorrect. Typing Error: In the question 'no telling' should not have been underlined.

**15.** The sentence wants to say that Romanians are close to Moscow in terms of ideological and military aspects. Hence, option (a) is the answer.

## READING COMPREHENSION

**Directions (Qs. 1–2) :** *Four alternative summaries are given the text. Choose the option that best captures the essence of the text.*

**1.** Some decisions will be fairly obvious-"no-brainers". Your bank account is low, but you have a two-week vacation coming up and you want to get away to some place warm to relax with your family. Will you accept your in-laws, offer of free use of their Florida beachfront condo? Sure. You like your employer and feel ready to move forward in your career. Will you step in for your boss for three weeks while she attends a professional development course? Of course.

A. Some decisions are obvious under certain circumstances. You may, for example, readily accept a relative's offer of free holiday accommodation. Or step in for your boss when she is away.

B. Some decisions are no-brainers. You need not think when making them. Examples are condo offers from in-laws and job offers from bosses when your bank account is low or boss is away.

C. Easy decisions are called "no-brainers" because they do not require any cerebral activity. Examples such as accepting free holiday accommodation abound in our lives.

D. Accepting an offer from in-laws when you are short on funds and want a holiday is a no-brainer. Another no-brainer is taking the boss's job when she is away.

(*a*) A (*b*) B
(*c*) C (*d*) D

**2.** Physically, inertia is a feeling that you just can't move; mentally, it is a sluggish mind. Even if you try to be sensitive, if your mind is sluggish, you just don't feel anything intensely. You may even see a tragedy enacted in front of your eyes and not be able to respond meaningfully. You may see one person exploiting another, one group persecuting another, and not be able to get angry. Your energy is frozen. You are not deliberately refusing to act; you just don't have the capacity.

A. Inertia makes your body and mind sluggish. They become insensitive to tragedies, exploitation, and persecution because it freezes your energy and decapacitates it.

B. When you have inertia you don't act although you see one person exploiting another or one group persecuting another. You don't get angry because you are incapable.

C. Inertia is of two types - physical and mental. Physical inertia restricts bodily movements. Mental inertia prevents response to events enacted in front of your eyes.

D. Physical inertia stops your body from moving; mental inertia freezes your energy and stops your mind from responding meaningfully to events, even tragedies, in front of you.

(*a*) A (*b*) B
(*c*) C (*d*) D

**Directions (Qs. 3–4) :** *Answer the question based on the following information. Indicate which of the statements given with that particular question consistent with the description of unreasonable man in the passage below.*

Unreasonableness is a tendency to do socially permissible things at the wrong time. The unreasonable man is the sort of person who comes to confide in you when you are busy. He serenades his beloved when she is ill. He asks a man who has just lost money by paying a bill for a friend to pay a bill for him. He invites a friend to go for a ride just after the friend has finished a long car trip. He is eager to offer services which are not wanted, but which cannot be politely refused. If he is present at an arbitration, he stirs up dissension between the two parties, who were really anxious to agree. Such is the unreasonable man.

**3.** The unreasonable man tends to

(*a*) entertain women

(*b*) be a successful arbitrator when dissenting parties are anxious to agree

(*c*) be helpful when solicited

(*d*) tell a long story to people who have heard it many times before

**4.** The unreasonable man tends to

(*a*) bring a higher bidder to a salesman who has just closed a deal

(*b*) disclose confidential information to others

(*c*) sing the praise of the bride when he goes to a wedding

(*d*) sleep late and rise early

**Directions (Qs. 5–14) :** *In view of the passage given below. Choose the best option for question.*

When talks come to how India has done for itself in 50 years of Independence, the world has nothing but praise for our success in remaining a democracy. On other fronts, the applause is less loud. In absolute terms, India has not done too badly, of course, life expectancy has increased. So has literacy. Industry, which was barely a fledging, has grown tremendously. And as far as agriculture is concerned, India has been transformed from a country perpetually on the edge of starvation into a success story held up for others to emulate. But these are competitive times when change is rapid, and to walk slowly when the rest of the world is running is almost as bad as standing still on walking backwards.

Compared with large chunks of what was then the developing world South Korea, Singapore, Malaysia, Thailand, Indonesia, China and what was till lately a separate Hong Kong-India has fared abysmally. It began with a far better infrastructure than most of these countries had. It suffered hardly or not at all during the Second World War. It had advantages like an English speaking elite, quality scientific manpower (including a Nobel laureate and others who could be ranked among the world's best) and excellent business acumen. Yet, today, when countries are ranked according to their global competitiveness, it is tiny Singapore that figures at the top. Hong Kong is an export powerhouse. So is Taiwan. If a symbol were needed of how far we have fallen back, note that while Korean Cielos are sold in India, no one is South Korea is rushing to buy an Indian car. The reasons list themselves. Topmost is economic isolationism.

The government discouraged imports and encouraged self-sufficiency. Whatever the aim was, the result was the creation of a totally inefficient industry that failed to keep pace with global trends and, therefore, became absolutely uncompetitive. Only when the trade gates were opened a little did this become apparent. The years since then have been spent in merely trying to catch up. That the government actually sheltered its industrialists from foreign competition is a little strange. For in all other respects, it operated under the conviction that businessmen were little more than crooks how were to be prevented from entering the most important areas of the economy, how were to be hamstrung in as many ways as possible, how were to be tolerated in the same way as an inexcisable wart. The high expropriatory rates taxation, the licensing laws, the reservation of whole swathes of industry for the public sector, and the granting of monopolies to the public sector firms were the principle manifestations of this attitude. The government forgot that before wealth could be distributed, it had to be created.

The government forgot that it itself could not create, but only squander wealth. Some of the manifestations of the old attitude have changed. Tax rates have fallen. Licensing has been all but abolished. And the gates of global trade have been opened wide. But most of these changes were first by circumstances partly by the foreign exchange bankruptcy of 1991 and the recognition that the government could no longer muster the funds of support the public sector, leave alone expand it. Whether the attitude of the government itself, or that of more than handful of ministers, has changed, is open to question. In many other ways, however, the government has not changed one with. Business still has to negotiate a welter of negotiations. Transparency is still a longer way off. And there is no exit policy. In defending the existing policy, politicians betray an inability to see beyond their noses. A no-exit policy for labour is equivalent to a no-entry policy for new business. If one industry is not allowed to retrench labour, other industries will think a hundred times before employing new labour. In other ways too, the government hurts industries.

Public sector monopolies like the department of telecommunications and Videsh Sanchar Nigam Ltd. make it possible for Indian business to operate only at a cost several times that of their counterparts abroad. The infrastructure is in a shambles partly because it is unable to formulate a sufficiently remunerative policy for private business, and partly because it does not have the stomach to change market rates for services. After a burst of activity in the early nineties, the government is dragging its feet. At the rate it is going, it will be another fifty years before the government realises that a pro-business policy is the best pro-people policy. By then of course, the world would have moved even farther ahead.

**5.** The writer's attitude towards the Government is...

(*a*) critical (*b*) ironical

(*c*) sarcastic (*d*) derisive

**6.** The writer is surprised at the Government's attitude towards its industrialists because.......

(*a*) the government did not need to protect its industrialists.

(*b*) the issue of competition was non-existent.

(*c*) the government looked upon its industrialists as crooks.

(*d*) the attitude was a conundrum.

**7.** The Government was compelled to open the economy due to....

(*a*) pressure from international market.

(*b*) pressure from domestic market.

(*c*) foreign change bankruptcy and paucity of funds with the government.

(*d*) All of the above.

**8.** The writer ends the passage on a note of.....

(*a*) cautious optimism (*b*) pessimism

(*c*) optimism (*d*) pragmatism

**9.** According to the writer India should have performed better than the other Asian nations because.......

(*a*) it had adequate infrastructure

(*b*) it had better infrastructure

(*c*) it had better politicians who could take the required decisions.

(*d*) All of the above.

10. India was in better condition than the other Asian nations because....
(*a*) it did not face the ravages of the Second World War
(*b*) it had an English speaking populace and good business sense.
(*c*) it had enough wealth through its exports.
(*d*) Both (a) and (b) above

11. The major reason for India's poor performance is........
(*a*) economic isolationism
(*b*) economic mismanagement
(*c*) inefficient industry
(*d*) All of these

12. One of the factors of the government's projectionist policy was......
(*a*) encouragement of imports
(*b*) discouragement of imports
(*c*) encouragement of exports
(*d*) discouragement of exports

13. The example of the Korean Cielo has been presented to highlight......
(*a*) India's lack of stature in the international market.
(*b*) India's poor performance in the international market.
(*c*) India's lack of credibility in the international market
(*d*) India's disrepute in the international market.

14. According to the writer.....
(*a*) India's politicians are myopic in their vision of the country's requirements.
(*b*) India's politicians are busy lining their pockets.
(*c*) India's politicians are not conversant with the needs of the present scenario.
(*d*) All of the above.

## ANSWERS

| | | | | |
|---|---|---|---|---|
| **1.** (a) | **2.** (d) | **3.** (d) | **4.** (a) | **5.** (a) |
| **6.** (c) | **7.** (c) | **8.** (b) | **9.** (b) | **10.** (d) |
| **11.** (a) | **12.** (d) | **13.** (b) | **14.** (a) | |

## EXPLANATIONS

1. The title is the most appropriate because it covers all the aspects of the passage. It includes the in-law's offer as well as the professional aspect.

2. The title covers the two types of inertia and their effect on a human being. No aspect in the passage is left excluded in the title.

3. After reading the passage, option (d) seems to be the most likely answer because an unreasonable man will try to do things which are inappropriate in a particular moment.

4. After reading the passage, we know that an unreasonable man will do things which are inappropriate in the context of a particular time. Hence, option (a) seems to be the most likely answer.

5. The author's attitude is certainly critical. S/he furnishes examples and elaborate explains his point to examine and analyse India's economic policies.

6. Refer to the sixth sentence of the third paragraph. The author clearly mentions that the government believed that businessmen were crooks and adopted unholy practices.

7. Refer to the sixth sentence of the second last paragraph. The explains why the government changed its economic policies. Furthermore, there is a typographical error in option (c). The word *change* should have been *exchange*.

8. The author ends the passage with a note of pessimism. The ending of the passage reflects the frustration of the author.

9. Refer to the second sentence in the second paragraph. The author mentions that India had a better infrastructure compared to the other South Asian countries. India did not suffer significantly during the Second World War.

10. Both statements A and B are correct. Refer to the third sentence in the second paragraph where the author mentions that India suffered hardly during World War II. Furthermore, refer to the following sentence where the author mentions that India had a population who could speak English and had business skills or acumen.

11. Refer to the third paragraph where the author mentions that India isolationism in the global economic arena was to be blamed for India's poor performance.

12. (Incorrect)

The CLAT answer key is option (a). We believe that the correct answer choice should be option (b). Refer to the first sentence of the third paragraph. Secondly, there is a typing error. *Projectionist* should have been *protectionist*.

13. The author cites the example of the car Cielo to highlight the popularity of the car in the Indian market. Furthermore, the comment also shows that India has been a poor performer in the international market. Refer to the second last sentence of the second paragraph.

14. Refer to the fourth last sentence in the second last paragraph. "To see beyond their noses" means shortsightedness or myopic character.

# REASONING

## VERBAL LOGIC

**Direction (Qs. 1–3) :** *From the alternatives given below.*

Choose the best option that correctly classifies the four sentences as a :

**F : Fact :** If it relates to a known matter of direct observation, or an existing reality or something known to be true.

**J : Judgment :** If it is an opinion or estimate or anticipation of common sense or intention.

**I : Inference :** if it is a logical conclusion or deduction about something based on the knowledge of facts.

**1.** A. Everyday social life is impossible without interpersonal relationships.

B. The root of many misunderstandings has been cited in poor relations among individuals.

C. Assuming the above to be true, social life will be much better if people understand the importance of good interpersonal relations.

D. A study reveals that interpersonal relations and hence life in general can be improved with a little effort on the part of individuals.

(a) FJIJ (b) JFIF
(c) FIFJ (d) IFFJ

**2.** A. The Cabinet minister definitely took the wrong step in giving the government contract.

B. Under the circumstances, he had many other alternatives.

C. The Prime Minister is embarrassed due to the minister's decision.

D. If he has put the government in jeopardy, the minister must resign.

(a) JFFI (b) IFJI
(c) FFJI (d) IFIJ

**3.** A. If democracy is to survive, the people must develop a sense of consumerism.

B. Consumerism has helped improve the quality of goods in certain countries.

C. The protected environment in our country is helping the local manufacturers.

D. The quality of goods suffers if the manufacturers take undue advantage of this.

(a) IJFJ
(b) JFJI
(c) IJJF
(d) IFJJ

**Direction (Qs. 4–6) :** *Question consists of five statements followed by options consisting of three statements put together in a specific order. Choose the best option which indicates a valid argument, that is, where the third statement is a conclusion drawn from the preceding two statements.*

**4.** A. Traffic congestion increases carbon monoxide in the environment.

B. Increase in carbon monoxide is hazardous to wealth.

C. Traffic congestion is hazardous to health.

D. Some traffic congestion does not cause increase carbon monoxide.

E. Some traffic congestion is not hazardous to health

(a) CBA (b) BDE
(c) CDE (d) BAC

**5.** A. MBAs are in great demand.

B. Samrat and Akshita are in great demand.

C. Samrat is in great demand.

D. Akshita is in great demand.

E. Samrat and Akshita are MBAs

(a) ABE (b) ECD
(c) AEB (d) EBA

**6.** A. All software companies employ knowledge workers.

B. Infotech employees are knowledge workers.

C. Infotech is a software company.

D. Some software companies employ knowledge workers.

E. Infotech employs only knowledge workers.

(a) ABC (b) ACB
(c) CDB (d) ACE

**Direction (Qs. 7–9) :** *The question contains two statements numbered I and II.*

You have to decide whether the information provided in the statements are sufficient to answer the question. Read both the statements and give your answer as:

Answer (1) If the information in the statement I alone are sufficient to answer the questions.

Answer (2) If the information in the statement II alone are sufficient to answer the questions.

Answer (3) If the information either in the statement I alone or in statement II alone are sufficient to answer the questions.

Answer (4) If the information even in both statement I and II together are not sufficient to answer the questions.

7. Can a democratic system operate without an effective opposition?
   I. The opposition is indispensable.
   II. A good politician always learns more from his opponents than from his fervent supporters.
   (a) Answer (1) (b) Answer (2)
   (c) Answer (3) (d) Answer (4)
8. Do habits make men's life rigid?
   I. It is out of habit that people envy others.
   II. Men become slave of habits.
   (a) Answer (1) (b) Answer (2)
   (c) Answer (3) (d) Answer (4)
9. Does intelligence predict the child's ability to learn?
   I. Intelligence is unaffected by bad teaching or dull home environment.
   II. Children from poor home backgrounds do not do well in their school-work.
   (a) Answer (1) (b) Answer (2)
   (c) Answer (3) (d) Answer (4)

**Direction (Qs. 10–11) :** *The question contains two statements and two conclusions numbered I and II.*

You have to take the two given statements to be true even if they seem to be at variance from commonly known facts and decide which of the given conclusion (s) logically follow(s) from the two given statements.

Answer (1) If only conclusion I follows.

Answer (2) If only conclusion II follows.

Answer (3) If neither I nor II follows.

Answer (4) If both I and II follows.

10. **Statements:**
    I. Some players are singers.
    II. All singers are tall.
    **Conclusions:**
    I. Some players are tall.
    II. All players are tall.
    (a) Answer (1) (b) Answer (2)
    (c) Answer (3) (d) Answer (4)
11. **Statements:**
    I. Some vegetables are fruits.
    II. No fruit is black.
    **Conclusions:**
    I. Some fruits are vegetables.
    II. No vegetable is black.
    (a) Answer (1) (b) Answer (2)
    (c) Answer (3) (d) Answer (4)

## ANSWERS

| | | | | |
|---|---|---|---|---|
| **1.** (b) | **2.** (*) | **3.** (b) | **4.** (*) | **5.** (c) |
| **6.** (*) | **7.** (a) | **8.** (b) | **9.** (d) | **10.** (a) |
| **11.** (a) | | | | |

## EXPLANATIONS

1. Statements B and D are certainly facts. Statement C begins with "assuming" which means the sentence is an inference.
2. (Incorrect)
   The CLAT answer key is option (a). However, statement B is a *judgment* and not a *fact* as suggested by the answer. Hence, option (a) is incorrect. The correct answer choice is not given.
3. Statements A and C are certainly judgments because they reflect the opinion of the author. Statement B is clearly a fact while statement D is an inference because it is based on certain premises.
4. (Incorrect)
   The CLAT answer key is option (a). However, we believe that option (d) is the correct answer because option (d) represents the correct sequence of inference. There is a printing error in statement (b). *Wealth* should have been *health.*
5. The correct sequence is AEB. Since MBAs are in great demand (a) and we know that Samrat and Akshita are MBAs (E), we can infer that Samrat and Akshita will be in great demand as well.
6. (Incorrect)
   The CLAT answer key is option (b). However, we believe the answer choice is wrong. Statement B states: Infotech employees are knowledge workers which means all Infotech employees are knowledge workers. However, statement A and C combined imply that Infotech employs knowledge workers. It does not necessarily mean that All Infotech employees are knowledge workers.
7. (Incorrect)
   The CLAT answer key is option (c). Statement II in this question is unnecessary. The answer can be inferred from Statement I itself. Hence the correct choice is option (a).
8. When a person becomes a slave to a certain habit, s/he finds it difficult to try anything else. Hence, his/her life becomes rigid. The first statement doesn't answer the question. Envying others and becoming out of habit are two different things.
9. "Bad teaching" or "dull home environment" does not include the ability to learn. Hence, statement I is insufficient. Furthermore, statement II is off the mark because possessing intelligence and performing well in school are two completely different things.
10. It is clear from the Venn diagram that all players are not tall. Hence, only conclusion I follows.
11. From the Venn diagram, it is evident that no fruit is black and some fruits are vegetables. However, the second conclusion cannot be inferred. Hence, option (a) is correct.

## ANALYTICAL REASONING

**Direction (Qs. 1–8) :** *W, X, Y, and Z are four friends, who do not mind exchanging items. X has two chessboards each costing Rs. 500, and a record player. Z originally had a cycle and a walkman. Each cricket bat costs Rs. 700. Both W and Z got a cricket bat from Y. X gave his record player costing Rs. 2000 to Y. Z get a camera costing Rs. 1500 from W. The cycle of Z costs Rs. 1000 and the walkman is for Rs. 700. Y had three cricket bats at the beginning and W had two cameras the total cost of which is Rs. 5000. X gave one of his chessboards to Z and took Z's cycle. Z gave his walkman to W.*

**1.** Total cost of materials Z had at the beginning was :

(a) Rs. 1500 (b) Rs. 1700

(c) RS. 1000 (d) RS. 2000

**2.** At the beginning who had the costliest items :

(a) W (b) X

(c) Y (d) Z

**3.** Who did not have a cricket bat after the exchange of items was over?

(A) W (B) X

(C) Y (D) Z

**4.** Who became the gainer by highest amount through exchange?

(A) W (B) X

(C) Y (D) Z

**5.** The person incurring the highest amount of financial loss through exchange lost an amount of:

(a) Rs. 600 (b) Rs. 1000

(c) None (d) Rs. 500

**6.** The amount of price of all the things remaining with the four persons lie between:

(a) Rs. 800 - Rs. 900

(b) Rs.10000 -12000

(c) Rs. 9000-RS.10000

(d) Rs.10000-Rs. 11000

**7.** Even after exchanges, an item of highest value remained in possession of:

(a) W (b) X

(c) Y (d) Z

**8.** Among the things exchanged, which one faced the highest exchange value in percentage term.

(a) Cricket Bat

(b) Record Player

(c) Camera

(d) Cycle

**Direction (Qs. 9–13) :** *Read the following information and choose the best option.*

Recently, the answers of a test held nationwide were leaked to a group of unscrupulous people. The investigative agency has arrested the mastermind and nine other people A, B, C, D, E, F, G, H and I in this matter. Interrogating them, the following facts have been obtained regarding their operation. Initially, the mastermind obtains the correct answer-key. All the others create their answer-key from one or two people who already possess the same. These people are called his/her "sources". If the person has two sources, then he/she compares the answer-keys obtained for both sources. If the key to a question from both sources is identical, it is copied, otherwise it is left blank. If the person has only one source, he/she copies the source's answer into his/her copy. Finally, each person compulsorily replaces one of the answers (not a blank one) with a wrong answer in his/her answer key.

The paper contained 200 questions; so the investigative agency has ruled out the possibility of two or more of them introducing wrong answers to the same question. The investigative agency has a copy of the correct answer key and has tabulated the following data. This data represents question numbers.

| Name | Wrong Answer(s) | Blank Answerfs) |
|---|---|---|
| A | 46 | --- |
| B | 96 | 46,90,25 |
| C | 27,56 | 17,46,90 |
| D | 17 | --- |
| E | 46,90 | --- |
| F | 14,46 | 92,90 |
| G | 25 | --- |
| H | 46,92 | --- |
| I | 27 | 17,26,90 |

**9.** Which one of the following must have two sources?

(a) A

(b) B

(c) C

(d) D

**10.** How many people (excluding the mastermind) needed to make answer keys before C could make his answer key?

(a) 2

(b) 3

(c) 4

(d) 5

**11.** Both G and H were sources to .... Options :

(a) F (b) B

(c) A (d) None of the above

**12.** Which of the following statement is true?

(a) introduced the wrong answer to question 27

(b) E introduced the wrong answer to question 46

(c) F introduced the wrong answer to question 14

(d) H introduced the wrong answer to question 46

**13.** Which of the following two groups of people has identical sources?

I. A, D and G

II. E and H

(a) Only (I) (b) Only (II)

(c) Neither (I) nor (II) (d) Both (I) and (II)

**Direction (Qs. 14–18) :** *In the following question, a group of numerals is given followed by four groups of symbol/letter combinations lettered (a), (b), (c) and (d). Numerals are to be coded as per the codes and conditions.*

You have to find out which of the combinations (a), (b), (c) and (d) is correct and indicate your answer accordingly.

| Numerals: | 3 | 5 | 7 | 4 | 2 | 6 | 8 | 1 | 0 | 9 |
|---|---|---|---|---|---|---|---|---|---|---|
| Letter/symbol code: | * | B | E | A | @ | F | K | % | R | M |

Following conditions apply:

1. If the first digit as well as the last digit is odd, both are to be coded as 'X'.
2. If the first digit as well as the last digit is even, both are to be coded as '$'.
3. If the last digit is 'O', it is to be coded as #.

**14.** Find out the combination for : 487692

(a) $KEFM@ (b) AKEFM@

(c) AKFEM@ (d) $KEFM$

**15.** Find out the combination for : 713540

(a) X%*BA#

(b) E%*BA#

(c) E%*BAR

(d) None of the above

**16.** Find out the combination for : 765082

(a) EFB#K@

(b) XFBRK@

(c) EFBRK@

(d) None of the above

**17.** Find out the combination for : 364819

(a) *FAK%X (b) XFAK&M

(c) *FAK%M (d) None of the above

**18.** Find out the combination for : 546839

(a) XAFK*X (b) XAFK*M

(c) BAFK*X (d) None of the above

**Direction (Qs. 19–20) :** *Read the following information carefully to choose best option for the question:*

A. 'L % M' means that M is brother of L.

B. 'L × M' means that L is mother of M.

C. 'L ÷ M' means that L is the sister of M.

D. 'L = M' means that M is father of L.

**19.** Which of the following means "I is the nephew of Q?"

1. Q % J = I
2. Q ÷ M × B % I
3. C ÷ I = B % Q

(a) Only 3 (b) Only 1

(c) Only 2 (d) None of the above

**20.** If 'A $ B' means that A is the father of B, 'A * B' means that A is the mother of B, 'A @ E' means that A is the wife of B, then which of the following means that M is the grand-mother of N?

(a) M * R $ T @ N (b) M * R @ T @ N

(c) M * T $ N @ R (d) M * T $ N @ R

**Direction (Qs. 21–23) :** *In the following question some capital alphabets are written in a row, below them their coding has been given. In the question, a particular word has been coded in a particular manner using codes as given below the capital letters.*

You have to understand the pattern of coding and have to answer the question asked subsequently.

| A | B | C | D | E | F | G | H | I | J | K | L | M | N | O | P | Q | R | S | T | U | V | W | X | Y | Z |
|---|---|---|---|---|---|---|---|---|---|---|---|---|---|---|---|---|---|---|---|---|---|---|---|---|---|
| U | a | 2 | v | b | w | 3 | t | 4 | x | s | y | 5 | z | 6 | c | d | 8 | 7 | e | r | h | 9 | l | p | q |

**21.** If DASH is 2a84, then SMASH is?

(a) 7 5 U 7 t (b) e y a 8 4

(c) 8 z q e 3 (d) 8 z q e 4

**22.** If FASHION is z64t7w, then POSITION is?

(a) z 6 4 e 4 7 6 c

(b) z 6 4 e 4 7 c 6

(c) c 6 7 4 e 4 6 z

(d) c 6 7 4 e 4 z 6

**23.** If LONDON is 5c62z5, then EUROPE is?

(a) w h 7c d w (b) w h 7 z 6 v
(c) b r 7 6 c b (d) w h 7 6 c b

**24.** Amit first goes in South direction, then he turns towards left and travel for some distance. After that he turns right and moves certain distance. At last he turns left and travels again for some distance. Now, in which direction is he moving?

(a) South (b) West
(c) East (d) None of the above

**25.** There are six houses in a row. Mr. Aalekh has Mr. Mishra and Mr. Iliyas as neighbours. Mr. Mritynjay has Mr. Sandeep and Mr. Nayak as neighbours. Mr. Sandeep's house is not next to Mr. Mishra or Mr. Iliyas and Mr. Nayak does not live next to Mr. Iliyas. Who are Mr. Mishra's next door neighbours?

(a) Mr. Aalekh and Mr. Mishra
(b) Mr. Aalekh and Mr. Iliyas
(c) Mr. Nayak and Mr. Aalekh
(d) None of the above

**26.** From the word 'LAPAROSCOPY', how many independent meaningful English words can be made without changing the order of the letters and using each letter only once?

(a) 1 (b) 2
(c) 3 (d) 4

**27.** If Monday falls on 1st of October, which day will fall three days after the 20th in that month?

(a) Monday (b) Tuesday
(c) Saturday (d) Wednesday

**28.** In the word GRAPHOLOGIST, if 1st and 7th letters, 2nd and 9th letters, 3rd and 11th letters, 4th and 8th letters and 5th and 12th letters are mutually interchanged then which letter will be 6th letter from the left of 10th letter from the left side?

(a) S
(b) T
(c) G
(d) None of the above

**29.** The son of M is the father of N and grandfather (Mother's father) of R. S is the daughter of N and sister of B. On the basis of this information, how is M related to B?

(a) Grandfather
(b) Grandmother
(c) Grandmother's mother
(d) None of the above

## ANSWERS

| | | | | |
|---|---|---|---|---|
| **1.** (b) | **2.** (a) | **3.** (b) | **4.** (d) | **5.** (c) |
| **6.** (b) | **7.** (a) | **8.** (*) | **9.** (b) | **10.** (c) |
| **11.** (d) | **12.** (c) | **13.** (d) | **14.** (d) | **15.** (b) |
| **16.** (c) | **17.** (d) | **18.** (a) | **19.** (c) | **20.** (*) |
| **21.** (c) | **22.** (a) | **23.** (b) | **24.** (c) | **25.** (c) |
| **26.** (*) | **27.** (b) | **28.** (d) | **29.** (d) | |

## EXPLANATIONS

**For questions 1 to 8:**

X had items: 2 chessboard cost of each is Rs.500 & 1 record player of cost Rs. 2000

so X had in beginning items of total cost of Rs. = 3000

after transaction he had only 1 cycle of cost Rs. = 1000 & 1 chessboard of his own loss in transaction = 1500

Y had items: 3 cricket bat each of Rs.700

So Y had in beginning items of total cost of Rs = 2100

after transaction he had only 1 record player of cost Rs = 2000 & 1 bat of his own profit in transaction = 600

Z had items: 1 cycle cost of Rs.1000 & 1 walkman of cost Rs.700

So Z had in beginning items of total cost of Rs. = 1700

after transaction he had only 1 bat of cost Rs. = 700 & 1 chessboard of cost = 500 and 1 camera = 1500

total = 2700

**W had items: 2 camera cost and profit = 1000** of one is Rs. 1500 & other one of cost Rs.3500

so X had in beginning items of total cost of Rs. = 5000

after transaction he had only 1batof cost Rs. = 700 & 1 camera of his own of cast Rs. = 3500 & a walkman of Rs. 700 loss in transaction = 100.

1. Rs.1700
2. W has the costiest items.
3. X does not have cricket bat after exchange.
4. Z gained the highest.
5. The maximum less is Rs.1500.
6. (Incorrect)

   The total amount is Rs.11,800, so the correct answer should be option (b). While the official answer key is option (d).
8. (Incorrect)

   Walkman faced the highest exchange value, which is not in the option.

**For questions 9 to 13:** The last row of table should be

| I | 27 | 17, 46, 90 |
|---|---|---|

and according to this the solution as follow.

If a person copies from one source, he must have the same blank answers as the source and exactly one wrong answer more than the source (as the copier has introduced one wrong answer on his own). If the person copies from two sources, the distinct wrong answers from the two sources would be left blank by the copier and the same wrong answers in the two sources would be copied as it is.

**9.** A and D have only one source since they have only one wrong answer each.

C may have copied from only one source i.e. I and hence, only B has two sources.

**10.** I did it before C since 27 is the wrong choice for I. Similarly, A, D and E made keys before C. Hence, 4 people made their keys before C.

**11.** Both G and H can't be sources to any of F, B or I and hence, (d) is the correct option.

**12.** F introduced wrong answer to question 14, because nobody else has done question 14 wrong.

**13.** A, D and G have one distinct wrong answer and no blank answers. So they must have the same source. E and H also have a common wrong answer and no blanks.

Hence, both the groups had identical sources.

**14.** The first as well as the last digit is even. Hence the correct code is $KEFM$.

**15.** The last digit is 0. Hence, the correct code is E%*BA#

**16.** The correct code is EFBRK@

**17.** The first as well as the last digit is odd. Hence the correct code is XFAK%X

**18.** The first as well as the last digit is odd. Hence the correct code is XAFK*X

**19.** (Incorrect)

Applying condition 2 the relation represented below

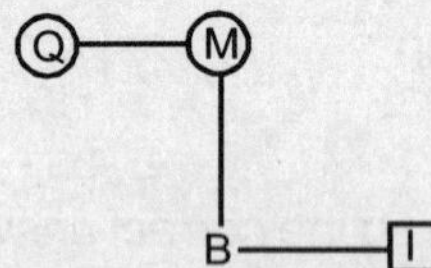


Which represent I is nephew of Q. The official answer key is option (d) which is wrong.

**20.** (Incorrect)

Option (c) and (d) are same. Any can be correct answer.

**21.** Letters at the odd places have been moved one place back, and letters at the even places have been moved one place ahead regarding the position of codes given in the table

**22.** Wrong Question, The correct question should be FASHION is z64t7Uw, then POSITION is. Assuming this, the correct answer is option (a).

**23.** Letters have been moved one place right regarding the position of codes given in the table

**24.** The movement is as follows

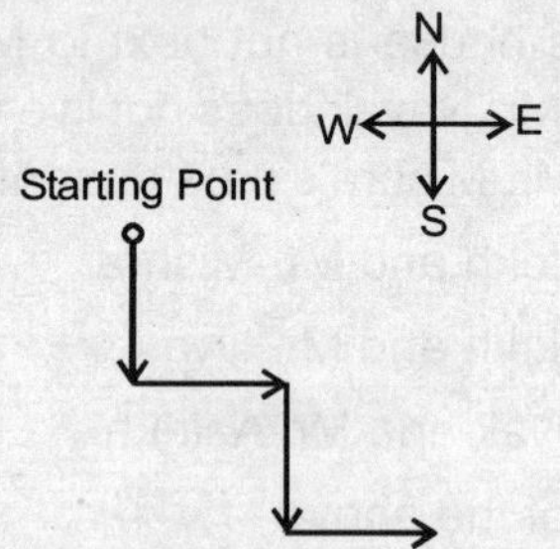


**25.** The arrangement of the houses is as follows:

| Sandeep | Mrintuyay | Nayak | Mishra | Aalekh | Iliyas |
|---|---|---|---|---|---|

[It may be in reverse order also but answer will be same in the both the cases].

**26.** (Incorrect)

The CLAT answer key is option (b). However, option (b) is incorrect because we can make at least 3 words from *Laparoscopy* / *Lap, Par* and *Coy.*

**27.** Number of odd days is 22 i. e. 1. Hence the required day is Tuesday

**28.** The order of letter after interchanging is as follows:

L G S [O] T O G P R I A H

**29.** The family diagram is represented below:

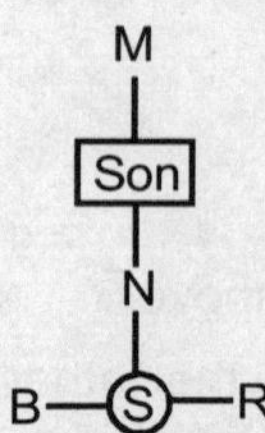


M is great grandmother/father of B.

# QUANTITATIVE APTITUDE

## NUMBER SYSTEM

(c) 6 (d) 7

1. What is the value of (x) in the following equation? $x^{0.4}/16 = 32/x^{2.6}$
2. The simplified value of $[(0.111)^3 + (0.222)^3 - (0.333)^3 + (0.333)^2 \times (0.222)]^3$ is:

   (a) 0.999 (b) 0.111

   (c) 0 (d) 8.888
3. When 2½ is added to a number and the sum is multiplied by 4½ and then 3 is added to the product and then the sum is divided by $1^{1/5}$, the quotient becomes 25. What is that number?

   (a) 2½ (b) 3 ½

   (c) 4 ½ (d) 5 ½
4. If $x = (16^3 + 17^3 + 18^3 + 19^3)$, then x divided by 70 leaves a remainder of ....

   (a) 0 (b) 1

   (c) 69 (d) 35
5. The sum of all the natural numbers from 200 to 600 (both inclusive) which are neither divisible by 8 nor by 12 is:

   (a) 1, 23, 968 (b) 1, 33, 068

   (c) 1, 33, 268 (d) 1, 87, 332
6. What are the last two digits of $7^{2008}$?

   (a) 01 (b) 21

   (c) 61 (d) 71

## ANSWERS

**1.** (a) **2.** (c) **3.** (b) **4.** (a) **5.** (c) **6.** (a)

## EXPLANATIONS

**1.** $\frac{x^{0.4}}{16} = \frac{32}{x^{2.6}} \Rightarrow x^3 = 512 \Rightarrow x = 8$

**2.** $[(0.111)^3 + (0.222)^3 - (0.333)^3 + (0.333)^2 + (0.222)]^3$

$= [(0.111)^3 + (0.222)^3 + (-0.333)^3 - 3(0.111)(0.222)(0.333)]^3 = 0$

[If $a + b + c = 0$, then $a^3 + b^3 + c^3 - 3abc = 0$]

**3.** Let the number be x.

$$\therefore \quad \frac{\left(x+\frac{5}{2}\right)\times\frac{9}{2}+3}{\frac{6}{5}} = 5$$

$$\Rightarrow \quad \left(x+\frac{5}{2}\right)\times\frac{9}{2}+3 = 30$$

$$\Rightarrow \quad x = \frac{7}{2}$$

**4.** $x = 16^3 + 17^3 + 18^3 + 19^3$ is an even number

Therefore, 2 divides x.

$\Rightarrow$ a + b always divides $a^3 + b^3$.

Therefore, $16^3 + 19^3$ is divisible by 35.

$18^3 + 17^3$ is divisible by 35.

Thus, x is divisible by 70.

Hence, option (a) is the correct choice.

**5.** The sum of the number divisible by either 8 or 12 = (the sum of number divisible by 8) + = (the sum of number divisible by 12) – = (the sum of number divisible by both)

$(200 + 208 + \ldots\ldots.. 600) + (204 + 216 + \ldots\ldots + 600) - (216 + 240 + \ldots\ldots.+ 60)$

$= \frac{51}{2}(200+600) + \frac{34}{2}(204+600) - \frac{17}{2}(216+600)$

$= 27132$

Sum of all the number $= \frac{401}{2}[200+600] = 160400$

Hence, the sum of the number which are divisible by 8 nor by 12 = 160400 – 27132 = 133268.

**6.** $7^{2008} = (7^4)^{502} = (2401)^{502} = (2400 + 1)^{502}$

$= k \times 100 + 1$

$\therefore$ The last 2 digits = 01.

## ARITHMETIC

1. Two trains, one from Howrah to Patna and other from Patna to Howrah, start simultaneously. After they meet, the trains reach their destinations after 9 hours and 16 hours respectively. The ratio of their speed is...

   (a) 2:03 (b) 4:03

   (c) 6:07 (d) 9:06
2. A watch which gains uniformly is 2 minutes slow at noon on Monday and is 4 minute 48 second fast at 2 p.m. on the following Monday. When was it correct?

   (a) 2 p.m. on Tuesday (b) 2 p.m. on Wednesday

   (c) 3 p.m. on Thursday (d) 1 p.m. on Friday
3. A speaks truth in 75% cases and B in 80% of the cases. In what percentage of cases are they likely to contradict each other, narrating the same incident?

   (a) 5% (b) 15%

   (c) 35% (d) 45%

## ANSWERS

**1.** (b) **2.** (b) **3.** (c)

## EXPLANATIONS

1. As we know $\frac{v_1}{v_2} = \sqrt{\frac{t_2}{t_1}} = \sqrt{\frac{16}{9}} = 4:3.$
2. The total time gain in 24 × 7 + 2 hrs = 6 minutes 48 seconds (i.e. 6.8 minutes)

   To show the correct time it will have to gain 2 minutes

   2 minutes gain can obtain in $\frac{24\times2+2}{6.8}\times2 = 50\text{hrs}$

   Hence it will sow the correct time at 2 pm on Wednesday.
3. The required percentage = 0.75 × 0.2 + 0.8 × 0.25 = 35.

## MODERN MATHS

**Direction (Qs. 1–5) :** *Answer the questions based on the information given in the following table. A, B, C, D, E denote companies and 2006, 2007, 2008, 2009 & 2010 denote years.*

Number of Units Manufactured (M) and Number of Units Sold (S) (in hundreds) by five different companies over the years.

| | A | | B | | C | | D | | E | |
|---|---|---|---|---|---|---|---|---|---|---|
| | M | S | M | S | M | S | M | S | M | S |
| 2006 | 2.8 | 1.3 | 3.3 | 2.2 | 2.6 | 1.7 | 3.0 | 2.2 | 1.9 | 1.4 |
| 2007 | 3.2 | 2.0 | 2.4 | 1.6 | 2.2 | 1.5 | 2.5 | 1.9 | 2.0 | 1.7 |
| 2008 | 1.9 | 0.9 | 2.9 | 1.6 | 2.1 | 1.0 | 2.3 | 1.5 | 1.6 | 1.1 |
| 2009 | 1.0 | 0.4 | 2.4 | 1.3 | 2.8 | 1.4 | 2.1 | 1.2 | 3.2 | 2.5 |
| 2010 | 2.5 | 1.5 | 2.3 | 1.2 | 2.6 | 2.1 | 1.8 | 1.1 | 3.1 | 2.6 |

1. What is the total number of units manufactured by Company C over all the years together?

   (a) 1420 (b) 1030

   (c) 1230 (d) 1320
2. What is the approximate percent increase in the number of units sold by Company E in the year 2007 from the previous year?

   (a) 17 (b) 36

   (c) 27 (d) 21
3. The number of units sold by Company D in the year 2006 is what percent of the number of units manufactured by it in that year? (rounded off to two digits after decimal)

   (a) 52.63 (b) 61.57

   (c) 85.15 (d) 73.33
4. What is the respective ratio of total number of units manufactured by Company A and B together in the year 2009 to those sold by them in the same year?

   (a) 2 : 01 (b) 3 : 02

   (c) 5 : 02 (d) None of the Above
5. What is the average number of units sold by Company D over all the years together?

   (a) 166 (b) 158

   (c) 136 (d) 147
6. A man has 9 friends: 4 boys and 5 girls. In how many ways can he invite them, if there have to be exactly 3 girls in the invitees?

   (a) 320 (b) 160

   (c) 80 (d) 200
7. A group of 630 children is arranged in rows for a group photograph session. Each row contains three fewer children than the row in front of it. What number of rows is not possible?

   (a) 3 (b) 4

   (c) 5 (d) 6
8. A die is rolled twice. What is the probability that the sum of the numbers on the two faces is 5?

   (a) 3/13 (b) 4/13

   (c) 6/13 (d) 1/9

## ANSWERS

| | | | | |
|---|---|---|---|---|
| 1. (c) | 2. (d) | 3. (d) | 4. (a) | 5. (b) |
| 6. (b) | 7. (d) | 8. (d) | | |

## EXPLANATIONS

1. Total number of units manufactured by company C overall the years together

   = (2.6 + 2.2 + 2.1 + 2.8 + 2.6) × 100

   = 12.3 × 100 = 1230
2. Required increase percentage

   $= \frac{(1.7-1.4)}{1.4}\times100$

   $= \frac{0.3}{1.4}\times100 = 21.42\% = 21\%$ (Approx.)
3. Required percentage $= \frac{2.2}{3}\times100 = 73.33\%$
4. Total number of units manufactured by company A and B together in the year 2009

   = (1 + 2.4) × 100 = 3.4 × 100 = 340

   Total number of units sold by company A and B together in the year 2009

   =(0.4 + 1.3) × 100 = 1.7 × 100 = 170

   Hence, required ratio = 340 : 170 = 2 : 1
5. Required average number of units

$$= \frac{(2.2+1.9+1.5+1.2+1.1)\times 100}{5}$$

$$= \frac{7.9\times 100}{5} = \frac{790}{5} = 158$$

**6.** Out of the 5 girls, 3 girls can be invited in $^5C_3$ ways. Nothing is mentioned about the number of boys that he has to invite. He can invite one, two, three, four or even no boys. Each boy can be invited or not. He can invite them in $2^4$ ways. Thus, the total number of ways is $^5C_3 \times (2)^4 = 10 \times 16 = 160$.

**7.** Let the no. of students in front row be x.

So, the no. of students in next rows be x – 3, x – 6, x – 9,.... so on

If n i.e. no. of rows be 3, then

$x + (x - 3) + (x - 6) = 630$

$\Rightarrow \quad 3x = 639$

$\Rightarrow \quad x = 213$

So possible.

Similarly, for n = 4,

$x + (x - 3) + (x - 6) + (x - 9) = 630$

$\Rightarrow \quad 4x - 18 = 630$

$\Rightarrow \quad x = \frac{648}{4} = 162$

$\therefore$ x = 4 to possible.

If n = 5,

$(4x - 18) + (x - 12) = 630$

$\Rightarrow \quad 5x - 30 = 630$

$\Rightarrow \quad x = 120$

Again n = 5 is possible.

If n = 6,

$(5x - 30) + (x - 15) = 630$

$\Rightarrow \quad 6x - 45 = 630$

$\Rightarrow \quad 6x = 675$

$\Rightarrow x \neq$ Integer

Hence, $n \neq 6$.

**8.** Number of possible outcomes = 36

Favorable outcomes = (1, 4), (4,1), (2, 3) and (3, 2)

The required probability $= \frac{1}{9}$

## ALGEBRA

**1.** In a tournament, there are n teams $T_1$; $T_2$,.......$T_n$, with n > 5. Each team consists of k players, k > 3. The following pairs of teams have one player in common $T_1$ and $T_2$, $T_2$ and $T_3$, ....., $T_{n-1}$ and $T_n$ and $T_n$ and $T_1$. No other pair of teams has any player in common. How many players are participating in the tournament, considering all the n teams together?

(a) k(n – 1) (b) n(k – 2)
(c) k(n – 2) (d) n(k – 1)

**2.** If $n^2$ = 12345678987654321, what is n?

(a) 12344321 (b) 1235789
(c) 111111111 (d) 11111111

**3.** Along a road lie an odd number of stones placed at intervals of 10m. These stones have to be assembled around the middle stone. A person can carry only one stone at a time. A man carried out the job starting with the stone in the middle, carrying stones in succession, thereby covering a distance of 4.8 km. Then, the number of stones is:

(a) 35 (b) 15
(c) 31 (d) 29

## ANSWERS

**1.** (d) **2.** (c) **3.** (c)

## EXPLANATIONS

**1.** In each team, $T_j$ there are two players, one it shares with $T_{j-1}$ and other with $T_{j-1}$. Other (k – 2)players team $T_j$ shares with no other team. So, total players which play for only one team = (k – 2)n.

One player is common in $T_1$ and $T_2$, one in $T_2$ and $T_3$ and so on.

Number of such players = number of pairs = n

So, total players = (k – 2)n + n = n(k – 1)

**2.** $111111111^2 = 12345678987654321$.

**3.** Let the number of stones be 'n'.

As the person covers 4.8 km, he covers 2.4 km on one side and 2.4 km on other side.

So total distance covered by him = 20 + 40 + 60 +.......

$\therefore \quad 2400 = \frac{n}{2}\left[2\times 20+(n-1)20\right] = 10n(n+1)$

(Here n is the number of stones)

After solving, we get n = 15

$\therefore$ Total number of stones = 15 + 15 + 1 = 31

# LEGAL APTITUDE

## TORTS

**Direction (Qs. 1–10) :** *The question consist of two statements, one labelled as PRINCIPLE and other as FACT. You are to examine the principle and apply it to the given facts carefully and select the best option.*

1. **PRINCIPLE :** Whoever, intending to take dishonestly any movable property out of the possession of any person without that person's consent moves that property, such taking is said to commit theft.

   **FACT :** RAMU cuts down a tree on RINKU'S ground, with the intention of dishonestly taking the tree out of RINKU'S possession without RINKU'S consent. A could not take the tree away.

   (a) RAMU can be prosecuted for theft
   (b) RAMU cannot be prosecuted for theft
   (c) RAMU can be prosecuted for attempt to theft
   (d) RAMU has neither committed theft nor attempt to commit theft

2. **PRINCIPLE :** injuria sine damnum i.e. injury without damage.

   **FACT :** SONU, who was a returning officer at a polling booth, wrongly refused to register a duly tendered vote of MONU, though he was a qualified voter. The candidate, whom MONU sought to vote, was declared elected.

   (a) MONU can sue SONU on the ground that he was denied to cast vote, which is a fundamental right.
   (b) MONU can sue SONU on the ground that he was denied to cast vote, which is a legal right.
   (c) MONU cannot sue SONU because there is no injury or damage cause to MONU.
   (d) MONU cannot sue SONU because to whom he sought to vote was declared elected.

3. **PRINCIPLE :** When one person signifies to another his willingness to do or to abstain from doing anything, with a view to obtaining the assent of that other to such act or abstinence, he is said to make a proposal.

   **FACT :** "Ramanuj telegrammed to the Shyamsunder, writing: "will you sell me your Rolls Royce CAR? Telegram the lowest cash price." Shyamsunder replied, too by telegram: 'Lowest price for CAR is Rs. 20 lacs.' Ramanuj immediately sends his consent through telegram stating: 'I agree to buy the CAR for Rs. 20 laks asked by you.' Now Shyamsunder refused to sell the CAR.

   (a) He cannot refuse to sell the CAR because the contract has already been made.
   (b) He can refuse to sell the CAR because it was only invitation to offer and not the real offer.
   (c) It was not a valid offer because willingness to enter into a contract was absent.
   (d) None of the above.

4. **PRINCIPLE :** A master is liable for the acts committed by his servant in the course of employment.

   **FACT :** Sanjay is a driver working in Brookebond and Co. One day, the Manager asked him to drop a customer at the airport and get back at the earliest. On his way back from the airport, he happened to see his fiance Ruhina waiting for a bus to go home. He offered to drop her at home, which happened to be close to his office. She got into the car and soon thereafter; the car somersaulted due to the negligence of Sanjay. Ruhina was thrown out of the car and suffered multiple injuries. She seeks compensation from Brookebond and Co.

   (a) Brookebond and Co., shall be liable, because Sanjay was in the course of employment at the time of accident
   (b) Brookebond and Co., shall not be liable, Sanjay was not in the course of employment when he took Ruhina inside the car.
   (c) Ruhina got into the car at her own risk, and therefore, she cannot sue anybody.
   (d) None of the above.

5. **PRINCIPLE:** ignorantia juris non excusat and ingnorantia facit excusat

   **FACT:** George was a passenger from Zurich to Manila in a Swiss Plane. When the plane landed at the airport at Bombay on 28th Nov. 1962 it was found on search that George carried 34 kgs of gold bars in person and that he had not declared it in the 'Manifest for transit'. On 26th Nov. 1962 Government of India issued a notification and modified its earlier exemption and now it is necessary that, the gold must be declared in the "Manifest" of the aircraft.

   (a) George cannot be prosecuted because he had actually no knowledge about the new notification issued only two days ago.
   (b) George cannot be prosecuted because it is mistake of fact which is excusable.
   (c) George's will be prosecuted because mistake of law is not excusable.
   (d) George liability would depend on the discretion of the court

6. **PRINCIPLE :** Everybody is under a legal obligation to take reasonable care to avoid an act or omission which he can foresee would injure his neighbor. The neighbor for this purpose, is any person whom he should have in his mind as likely to be affected by his act.

**FACT :** Krishnan, while driving a car at high speed in a crowded road, knocked down a cyclist. The cyclist died on the spot with a lot of blood spilling around, Lakshmi, a pregnant woman passing by, suffered from a nervous shock, leading to abortion. Lakshmi filed a suit against Krishnan claiming damages.

(a) Krishna will be liable, because he owed a duty of reasonable care to everybody on the road including Lakshmi

(b) Krishna will not be liable, because he could not have foreseen Lakshmi suffering from nervous shock as a result of his act.

(c) Krishna will be liable to Lakshmi because he failed to drive carefully

(d) None of the above

7. **PRINCIPLE:** Preparation is not an offence except the preparation of some special offences.

**FACT:** Ramesh keeps poisoned halua in his house, wishing to kill Binoy whom he invited to a party and to whom he wishes to give it. Unknown to Ramesh, his only son takes the halua and dies. In this case

(a) Ramesh is liable for the murder.

(b) He is not liable for murder since it is a preparation alone.

(c) He is liable for culpable homicide

(d) None of the above

8. **PRINCIPLE:** Any direct physical interference with the goods in somebody's possession without lawful justification is called trespass to goods.

**FACT:** A purchased a car from a person who had no title to it and had sent it to a garage for repair. X, believing, wrongly, that the car was his, removed it from the garage.

(a) X can be held responsible for trespass to goods.

(b) X cannot be held responsible for trespass to good as he was under a wrong belief.

(c) X has not committed any wrong.

(d) None of the above.

9. **PRINCIPLE:** "Nobody shall unlawfully interfere with a person's use or enjoyment of land, or some right over, or in connection with it. The use or enjoyment, envisaged herein, should be normal and reasonable taking into account surrounding situation."

**FACT:** Jeevan and Pavan were neighbours in a residential locality. Pavan started a typing class in a part of his house and his typing sound disturbed Jeevan who could not put up with any kind of continuous noise. He filed a suit against Pavan.

(a) Pavan is liable, because he should not have started typing class in his house

(b) Pavan is liable, because as a neighbour, he should have realised Jeevan's delicate nature

(c) Pavan is not liable, because typing sound did not disturb anyone else other than Jeevan

(d) None of the above.

10. **PRINCIPLE:** Doctrine of Double Jeopardy: No person shall be prosecuted and punished for the same offence twice.

**FACT:** Maqbool brought some gold into India without making any declaration to Custom department on the airport. The custom authorities confiscated the gold under the Sea Customs Act. Maqbool was later charged for having committed an offence under Foreign Exchange Regulation Act.

(a) He cannot be prosecuted because it would amount to double jeopardy.

(b) He can be prosecuted because confiscation of good by custom authorities does not amount to prosecution by the Court.

(c) Maqbool ought to have known that he can be stopped by the custom authorities.

(d) None of the above.

## ANSWERS

| | | | | |
|---|---|---|---|---|
| **1.** (a) | **2.** (b) | **3.** (b) | **4.** (a) | **5.** (c) |
| **6.** (b) | **7.** (b) | **8.** (a) | **9.** (d) | **10.** (b) |

## EXPLANATIONS

1. The principle clearly stresses on the intention to take property out, and since Ramu cut the tree with the intention of taking it away, he can be prosecuted for theft.

2. This question requires legal knowledge since the meaning of injury and damage has not been clearly explained. However, this fact situation is also one of the first examples of injuria sine damnum that's given while teaching. It is clear that even though there was no actual harm from Monu's inability to cast his vote, his right to vote nonetheless got violated (causing him legal injury) and he can sue.

3. First telegram had asked 2 questions, one regarding the willingness to sell and the other regarding the lowest price. In reply, only lowest price was quoted and this quoting of price was not an offer. Third telegram 'I agree to buy' was an offer and not an acceptance of the offer. Since this offer has not been accepted, there is no binding contract.

Quoting the price is always an invitation to offer, and not an offer which means that the Parties are at the stage of negotiation only. The principle doesn't elaborate on the distinction between offer and invitation to offer, so it presumes legal knowledge.

4. Clearly, getting back from the airport was part of the task the Manager had assigned to Sanjay. Anything that happened during the course of that time was the Master's responsibility to compensate for. So Brookebond is liable.

5. This question presumes legal knowledge in a reasoning question. The maxims translate to 'ignorance of law is not an excuse' and 'ignorance of fact can be.'

   The fact situation clearly tells us that the law was in force before George carried that gold. He was at fault for not declaring it in the Manifest for transit.

6. This question pertains to remoteness of damage, and the question here is whether or not Krishnan could reasonably have foreseen that a pregnant woman would experience nervous shock on seeing the blood on the road and have an abortion. He could reasonably have foreseen the cyclist's death, but not the remote consequence of someone else facing problems with that death.

7. Preparation means to arrange necessary measures for the commission of the intended criminal acts. Intention alone or intention followed by preparation is not enough to constitute the crime. Preparation has not been made punishable except in few cases because a person might change his mind last minute and not commit the act even after having made all necessary preparations.

   However, the answer may also be (d) since the principle doesn't specify what special offenses are, and whether the attempt to kill someone qualifies as a special offense, we don't really know if preparation would be an offense in this case or not.

8. Removing someone's car, however innocently, amounts to direct physical interference. Since the principle says nothing about the intention of the person doing it, X can be held responsible.

9. The principle deals with the reasonableness of the interference, which none of the options deals with. Pavan may be liable for nuisance only if it is proved that any reasonable person will be disturbed by the typing sound. But options A, B and C do not provide proper explanation. Hence, the answer would be (d).

10. The principle states that prosecution and punishment are both needed. Confiscation doesn't amount to prosecution or punishment. Maqbool will be liable because confiscation of gold by the custom authorities does not amount to prosecution. Judicial proceedings alone can be said to constitute prosecution and can lead to punishment.

## LAW OF CONTRACTS

**Direction (Qs. 1–5) :** *The question consist of two statements, one labelled as PRINCIPLE and other as FACT. You are to examine the principle and apply it to the given facts carefully and select the best option.*

1. **PRINCIPLE :** A person is said to be of sound mind for the purpose of making a contract if, at the time when he makes it, he is capable of understanding it and of forming a rational judgment as to its effect upon his interests.

   **FACT:** Mr. X who is usually of sound mind, but occasionally of unsound mind enters into a contract with Mr. Y when he is of unsound mind. Y came to know about this fact afterwards and now wants to file a suit against Mr. X.

   (A) Mr. X cannot enter into contract because he is of unsound mind when he entered into contract.

   (B) Mr. X can enter into contract but the burden is on the other party to prove that he was of unsound mind at the time of contract.

   (C) Mr. X can enter into a contract but the burden is on Mr. X to prove that he was of unsound mind at the time of contract.

   (D) None of the above.

2. **PRINCIPLE:** Nuisance as a tort (civil wrong) means an unlawful interference with a person's use or enjoyment of land, or some right over, or in connection with it.

   **FACT:** During the scarcity of onions, long queues were made outside the defendant's shop who having a license to sell fruits and vegetables used to sell only 1 Kg. of onion per ration card. The queues extended on to the highway and also caused some obstruction to the neighboring shops. The neighboring shopkeepers brought an action for nuisance against the defendant.

   (a) The defendant is liable for nuisance

   (b) The defendant was not liable for nuisance

   (c) The defendant was liable under the principle of strict liability

   (d) The plaintiffs suit should be decreed in his favour

3. **PRINCIPLE:** Nothing is an offence which is done by a person who, at the time of doing it, by reason of unsoundness of mind, is incapable of knowing the nature of the act, or that he is doing what is either wrong or contrary to law.

   **FACT:** A takes his son B who is three years old, for a bath to the well. He throws his son inside the well so that he could have a good bath. After 10 minutes he also jumped in the well to take a bath and take his son out of the well. Both were rescued by the villagers but his son was found dead.

(a) A has committed culpable homicide not amounting to murder
(b) A has committed murder
(c) A has done no offence as he can plead the defence of unsoundness of mind
(d) A's family should be responsible for this incident to let him to take child to the well

4. **PRINCIPLE :** Agreements, the meaning of which is not certain, or capable of being made certain, are void.

**FACT :** A horse was bought for a certain price coupled with a promise to give Rs. 500 more if the horse proved lucky.

(a) This is a valid agreement.
(b) This agreement is void for uncertainty because it is very difficult to determine what luck, bad or good, the horse had brought to the buyer.
(c) The agreement is partially valid and partially void.
(d) None of the above.

5. **PRINCIPLE:** Mere silence as to facts likely to affect the willingness of a person to enter into a contract is not fraud, unless the circumstances of the case are such that, regard being had to them, it is the duty of the person keeping silence to speak, or unless his silence is, in itself, equivalent to speech.

**FACT:** A sells, by auction, to B, a horse which A knows to be unsound. A says nothing to B about the horse's unsoundness.

(a) A can be held liable for fraud
(b) A can be held liable for misrepresentation
(c) A cannot be held liable, because he did not say anything positive about the soundness of horse.
(d) A cannot be held liable because it is the buyer who must be aware of the things.

## ANSWERS

**1.** (a) **2.** (a) **3.** (c) **4.** (b) **5.** (c)

## EXPLANATIONS

1. The official answer key says (c) but the correct answer should be A.

The focus of the principle is on the competence to contract and not on the burden of proof. The principle clearly states that the person should be of sound mind at the time of entering into the contract, and says nothing about burden of proof. Using that, the answer should be A since Mr. X was not of a sound state of mind at the time of entering into the contract.

2. The principle defines nuisance as unlawful interference with someone's enjoyment of their land, and the long queues due to the defendant's actions definitely interfered with the other shopkeepers' right to enjoy their property.

3. A's actions of throwing his son inside the well and then jumping in himself show that he was incapable of understanding the consequences of what he was doing.

4. This agreement is not capable of being made certain as it is difficult to determine what luck, good or bad, the horse had brought to the buyer. Hence, the agreement which is uncertain or incapable of being made certain, is void.

5. As per the principle, A would have a duty to speak only in situations where the circumstances are such that his silence could amount to speech. Since no discussion regarding the soundness of the horse was initiated at the auction either by A or by B, A had no obligation to speak up.

## CRIMINAL LAW

**Direction (Qs. 1–3) :** *Read the definition and elements of the attempt, apply them on the given fact situations and answer the question:*

**Definition of Attempt :** Lord Blackburn has said that "there is no doubt that there is difference between a preparation antecedent to an attempt and the actual attempt, but if the actual transaction has commenced which would have ended in the crime if not interrupted, there is clearly an attempt to commit the crime."

1. Fault element: Intention or knowledge requisite for committing an offence; and
2. Conduct Element: does any act towards its commission and has crossed the stage of preparation. This act is so closely connected with, and proximate to the commission that it fails in object because of facts not known to him or because of circumstances beyond his control.

1. 'RANI' ran to a well stating that she would jump into it, and she started running towards the well but she was caught before she could reach it.

(a) She is not guilty of attempt to commit suicide because she might have changed her mind before jumping into the well.
(b) She is guilty of attempt to commit suicide
(c) Right to life includes rights right to die hence a person should not be held responsible for attempt to commit suicide.
(d) None of the above.

2. 'SINY' with an intention to pick-pocket puts his hand into MINU's pocket. MINU had a loaded pistol in his pocket. The thief touches the pistol and trigger goes on, whereby MINU is shot dead.

(a) SINY will be liable only for attempting to pick-pocket and not for killing because she cannot be treated differently from all other pick-pockets who steal under exactly similar circumstances and same intention, with no risk of causing death and with no greater care to avoid it.

(b) SINY will be liable for attempting to murder

(c) SINY will be liable for culpable homicide not amounting to murder as his intention was definitely not to kill.

(d) None of the above

3. 'JAM' denied food to his wife JANE for several days by keeping her confined in a room with an intention to accelerate her death. JANE ultimately managed to escape.

(a) JAM is guilty for attempt to murder his wife.

(b) JAM is not guilty for attempt to murder his wife and he was only doing preparation.

(c) JAM is not guilty for attempt to murder his wife as she always had option to escape.

(d) None of the above.

## ANSWERS

1. (a) 2. (a) 3. (a)

## EXPLANATIONS

1. The principle establishes the threshold for an act being considered attempt, and says that it's only when if not for an external event, the person would definitely have gone ahead with the deed, would their actions be considered attempt.

Here, Rani could've changed her mind before jumping into the well at any point between the starting point and her actually jumping, so her action of starting to run doesn't qualify as attempt.

2. The reasoning given in the option is self-explanatory. SINY cannot be held liable for something he never intended to do.

3. Here, JAM's actions match the threshold for attempt. Had it not been for JANE managing to escape by herself, JAM had done enough to ensure that she ended up dead.

## CONSTITUTIONAL LAW AND LEGAL FRAMEWORK

**Direction (Qs. 1–10) :** *The question consist of two statements, one labelled as Assertion (A) and other as Reason (R). You are to examine the two statements carefully and select the best option.*

1. **Assertion (A):** Custom per se is law, independent of prior recognition by the sovereign or the judge.

**Reason (R) :** Custom is source of law but by itself is not law.

(a) Both A and R are individually true and R is correct explanation to A

(b) Both A and R are individually true but R is not correct explanation of A

(c) A is true but R is false.

(d) A is false but R is true.

2. **Assertion (A) :** Idol is a person who can hold property.

**Reason (R) :** Only human being can be called person not the lifeless things.

(a) Both A and R are individually true and R is correct explanation to A

(b) Both A and R are individually true but R is not correct explanation of A

(c) A is true but R is false.

(d) A is false but R is true.

3. **Assertion (A) :** Laws are means of achieving an end namely social control.

**Reason (R) :** The ultimate end of law is to secure greatest happiness to greatest number.

(a) Both A and R are individually true and R is correct explanation to A

(b) Both A and R are individually true but R is not correct explanation of A

(c) A is true but R is false.

(d) A is false but R is true.

4. **Assertion (A) :** Every person should have the freedom of speech and expression.

**Reason (R) :** If a person is stopped from speaking then mankind will lose the truth.

(a) Both A and R are individually true and R is correct explanation to A

(b) Both A and R are individually true but R is not correct explanation of A

(c) A is true but R is false.

(d) A is false but R is true.

5. **Assertion (A) :** Attempt to commit an offence though does not result in any harm, should also be punished.

**Reason (R) :** A person who tries to cause a prohibited harm and fails, is, in terms of moral culpability, not materially different from the person who tries and succeeds.

(a) Both A and R are individually true and R is correct explanation to A

(b) Both A and R are individually true but R is not correct explanation of A

(c) A is true but R is false.

(d) A is false but R is true.

6. **Assertion (A) :** In India, every state has a High Court in its territory.

**Reason (R) :** The Constitution of India provides for a High Court in each state.

(a) Both A and R are individually true and R is correct explanation to A

(b) Both A and R are individually true but R is not correct explanation of A

(c) A is true but R is false.

(d) A is false but R is true.

7. **Assertion (A) :** The Council of Ministers at the centre is collectively responsible both to the Lok Sabha and Rajya Sabha.

**Reason (R) :** The members of both Lok Sabha and Rajya Sabha are eligible to be ministers of the Union Government.

(a) Both A and R are individually true and R is correct explanation to A

(b) Both A and R are individually true but R is not correct explanation of A

(c) A is true but R is false.

(d) A is false but R is true.

8. **Assertion (A) :** The reservation of thirty-three percent of seats for women in Parliament and State Legislature does not require Constitutional Amendment.

**Reason (R) :** Political parties contesting elections can allocate thirty-three per cent of seats they contest to women candidates without any Constitutional Amendment.

(a) Both A and R are individually true and R is correct explanation to A

(b) Both A and R are individually true but R is not correct explanation of A

(c) A is true but R is false.

(d) A is false but R is true.

9. **Assertion (A) :** We, the people of India, having solemnly resolved to constitute India into a Democratic Republic.

**Reason (R) :** A republic will ensure we have a head of state that is democratically elected and accountable to voters. As a result the head of state will be a more effective constitutional safeguard.

(a) Both A and R are individually true and R is correct explanation to A

(b) Both A and R are individually true but R is not correct explanation of A

(c) A is true but R is false.

(d) A is false but R is true.

10. **Assertion (A) :** Republic Day is celebrated on 26th January every year in the country.

**Reason (R) :** The Constitution of India came into force on 26th January 1950.

(a) Both A and R are individually true and R is correct explanation to A

(b) Both A and R are individually true but R is not correct explanation of A

(c) A is true but R is false.

(d) A is false but R is true.

**Direction :** *Fill in the blanks: Choose the pair of words which complete the sentence to make logical sense.*

11. The NDA led Government notified the ................ ..and the National Judicial Appointments Commission Act, thus ending the over two-decade-old .................of appointing judges of Supreme Court and high courts. Under the new law, a six-member panel headed by.................... will select judges of the apex court and state high courts.

(a) 99th Constitutional (Amendment) Act 2015, collegium system, the Chief Justice of India

(b) 121st Constitutional (Amendment) Act 2015, collegium system, the Union Law Minister

(c) 121st Constitutional (Amendment) Act 2015, collegium system, the Prime Minister

(d) 99th Constitutional (Amendment) Act 2015, cabinet system, the Prime Minister

12. **Choose the best option for the following statement:**

No one can be compelled to sing the National Anthem since:

1. It will be violative of the right to freedom of speech and expression.
2. It will be violative of the right to freedom of conscience and practice & propagation of religion.

3. There is no legal provision obliging anyone to sing the National Anthem.
(a) 1 and 2 are correct
(b) 2 and 3 are correct
(c) 1, 2 and 3 are correct
(d) None is correct

**13.** Union Government recently approved 33 per cent Reservation for Women in:
(a) Horizontally and each category (OBC, SC, ST, and others) in direct recruitment in all non-gazetted Police Posts in all Union Territories including Delhi.
(b) Horizontally and each category (OBC, SC, ST, and others) in direct recruitment in all gazetted Police Posts in all Union Territories including Delhi.
(c) Horizontally and each category (OBC, SC, ST, and others) in direct recruitment in all gazetted and non-gazetted Police Posts in all Union Territories including Delhi.
(d) Horizontally and each category (OBC, SC, ST, and others) in direct recruitment in all gazetted and non-gazetted Posts in all Union Territories including Delhi.

**14.** In a recent case a Supreme Court bench comprising of Justice Dipak Misra and Justice Prafulla C Pant held that the amount of maintenance to be awarded under Section 125 of CrPC cannot be restricted for the iddat period (three months) only as the inherent and fundamental principle behind Section 125. Also, it said that an order under Section 125 CrPC can be passed if a person, despite having sufficient means, neglects or refuses to maintain the wife.
(a) Shamima Farooqui v. Shahid Khan
(b) Mohd. Ahmad Khan v. Shah Bano Begum
(c) Hamida Bano v. Abdul Rasheed
(d) Abdul Kadir v. Salima

**15. Select the correct statements on Social Justice Bench constituted on social issue**
1. Constituted by Supreme Court on 3 December 2014
2. Started operation on 12 December 2014
3. The brainchild of Chief Justice of India H L Dattu
4. Two-judge bench to be headed by Justice Madan B Lokur
5. The other member is Justice U U Lalit
(a) 1, 2 & 5 are correct (b) 1, 2 & 3 are correct
(c) 1, 3 & 4 are correct (d) All are correct

**16.** Select the correct statements about 14th Finance Commission which submitted its report to President
1. It covers the period between 1 April 2015 and 31 March 2020.
2. The Commission headed by former RBI Governor Y V Reddy.
3. Provides for devolution of tax receipts from the Centre to the States.
4. Article 280 of Constitution provides for appointment of Finance Commission.
5. 1st and 13th Finance Commission was headed by K C Neogy & Dr Vijay Kelkar respectively.
Options :
(a) 1, 3 & 5 are correct (b) 1, 2 & 3 are correct
(c) 1, 3 & 4 are correct (d) All are correct

**17.** Who administers oath of office to the Governor of a State?
(a) President of India
(b) Chief Justice of High Court of the respective state
(c) Chief Justice of India
(d) Speaker of State Assembly

**18.** Governor of a State can make Laws during recess of State Legislative Assembly through..............
(a) Act (b) Bills
(c) Notification (d) Ordinance

## ANSWERS

| | | | | |
|---|---|---|---|---|
| **1.** (d) | **2.** (c) | **3.** (b) | **4.** (b) | **5.** (a) |
| **6.** (*) | **7.** (d) | **8.** (d) | **9.** (a) | **10.** (a) |
| **11.** (a) | **12.** (c) | **13.** (a) | **14.** (a) | **15.** (d) |
| **16.** (d) | **17.** (b) | **18.** (d) | | |

## EXPLANATIONS

**1.** Custom derives its force from the fact that it has been the standard practice for a while, and recognized as such by the community. Custom can be recognized by the Sovereign or the Court only later in time but the question of any prior recognition does not arise in the case of custom. So A is false.

Custom can be codified into law by an act of the Parliament making it a source of law, but it isn't law by itself. So R is true.

**2.** There are two types of person namely, Natural person and Juristic person. Juristic persons are created by law. Idol is a Juristic person, capable of holding the property. A is factually true, but R isn't because 'person' can refer to lifeless things like corporations, religious and charitable institutions.

**3.** Social control refers to the act of establishing rules that must be followed by the members of a society, and law is how that control is achieved. It signifies the role of law in maintaining peace and harmony in the society. So A is true.

As per Utilitarian philosophy, yes, the ultimate aim of law should be to attain the greatest happiness for the greatest number of people. So R is also true, but R isn't the correct explanation for A because laws don't exist for Utilitarian purposes alone.

**4.** The official answer key says (a) but the correct option should be (b).

A and R are factually true, but the purpose of having freedom of speech and expression is grounded in the individual's right to speak their mind in a democracy as every person is equal in the eyes of law and should have the freedom of speech and expression. It has also been provided for in our fundamental rights guaranteed by the Constitution of India in consonance with the guiding principle. It doesn't have to do with mankind's quest for truth.

**5.** Both A and R are factually true, and R is the reasoning behind making attempt punishable. If not for external circumstances, the person would've ended up committing the crime, so it doesn't make him very different from the person who succeeds.

**6.** Correct option not provided

The official answer key provides (d) as the correct answer, but according to us the correct answer should be - Both A and R are false.

A is false because several High Courts serve more than one state or union territory. For instance, the High Court of Punjab and Haryana looks after Punjab, Haryana and Chandigarh. While there are 29 States, there are only 24 High Courts in India.

R is false because Article 214 of the Constitution of India states that "There shall be a High Court for each State" and not "in each State".

**7.** A is false because the Council of Ministers is accountable only to the Lok Sabha. Theoretically, there is nothing to bar a Rajya Sabha member from becoming a Union Minister, it is not the usual practice. Interestingly, Indira Gandhi wasn't a member of either house when she became the Minister for Information and Broadcasting in 1964, and got elected to the Rajya Sabha only later.

**8.** A is false because 33% reservation across the legislatures requires Constitutional Amendment, whereas R is true because allocation of seats by the political party is an internal matter for the party.

**9.** A is factually true, as it's been quoted verbatim from the Preamble. As per the Preamble, India is a democratic republic and R is the intent of the Preamble.

R is a sound explanation for having a democratically elected Head of State, and explains the rationale for calling the country a Democratic Republic.

**10.** Both are factually true, and 26th January is celebrated as the Republic Day because the Constitution came into force that day.

**11.** Also called the National Judicial Appointments Commission Bill, it was passed by the Lok Sabha on 14th August 2014.

**12.** The Constitution of India doesn't make it obligatory for anyone to sing the National Anthem as it would violate the right to freedom of speech and expression and also, the right to freedom of conscience and practice and propagation of religion.

**13.** The Union Cabinet approved 33 per cent reservation for women in police forces of all Union Territories, including the Delhi Police, through direct recruitment in non-gazetted posts. The move aims at increasing representation of women in police and to make the force gender sensitive. This reservation for women will be applicable "horizontally and in each category (SC/ST/OBC and others) through direct recruitment in non-gazetted posts - from constables to sub-inspectors." The reservation will be available to women against all such vacancies existing on the date of issue of order and vacancies arising thereafter.

**15.** The Supreme Court of India has set up a Social Justice Bench, which comprises of two judges devoted to the delivery of speedy justice in a range of social issues related to the downtrodden and socially marginalised groups. It's a brainchild of Chief Justice of India H.L. Dattu and the Bench is headed by Justice Madan B. Lokur and also has Justice U.U. Lalit. The purpose behind constituting the new Bench was to streamline cases highlighting social issues before one court and thus facilitate the Supreme Court's monitoring and review of the government's action in such cases. The social justice bench has been set up to ensure three-dimensional justice, as provided for in the Preamble. This Bench would function from 12th December 2014 and in order to ensure that these matters are monitored on regular basis, will continue to sit on every working Friday at 2.00 p.m.

**16.** The purpose of the 14th finance commission was to give recommendations on specified aspects of Centre-State fiscal relations during 2015-20.

17. As per article 159, the Chief Justice of the concerned High Court administers oath to the Governor.

18. Article 123 of the Indian Constitution empowers the President to promulgate ordinances during the recess of the Parliament. The ordinances are temporary laws having the effect of an act. It is considered one of the important legislative powers of the President, however it is subject to limitations. An ordinance is valid for six months from the date of the start of the next session.

## MISCELLANEOUS

**Direction (Qs. 1–3) :** *Fill in the blanks: Choose the pair of words which complete the sentence to make logical sense.*

1. The ................Legislative Assembly on 31st March 2015 passed a controversial Anti-Terrorism Law. Earlier, the passed bill was rejected two times by the then ................ in 2004 and 2008.
   (a) Bihar, Presidents
   (b) Madhya Pradesh, Governors
   (c) Gujarat, Presidents
   (d) Maharashtra, Governors

2. The Union Government on the recommendation of the ............under the chairmanship of ................ has decided to decriminalise Section..............of the Indian Penal Code.
   (a) 20th Law Commission, Justice A.P. Shah & 309
   (b) 20th Law Commission, Justice M.P. Shah & 307
   (c) Supreme Court, Justice H.L. Dattu & Section 309
   (d) Planning Commission, Law Minister, section 309

3. A bench headed by ............... quashed allocation of 214 ......... ...as ...................
   (a) Justice H L Dattu, coal blocks, illegal and arbitrary
   (b) Justice R. M. Lodha, coal blocks, illegal and arbitrary
   (c) Justice T. S. Thakur, licenses, illegal and arbitrary
   (d) None of the above.

4. Five years' experience is a must to be able to practice as an advocate in the Supreme Court of India. This rule was prescribed by the .........
   (a) Bar Council of India
   (b) Supreme Court of India
   (c) High Court of Delhi
   (d) Ministry of Law and Justice, Government of India

5. As per Indian Protocol, who among the followings ranks highest in the order of precedence?
   (a) Deputy Prime Minister
   (b) Former President
   (c) Governor of a State within his State
   (d) Speaker of Lok Sabha

6. Consider the following statements and choose the best option:
   1. The Chairman of the National Legal Services Authority (NALSA) is the Chief Justice of India.
   2. Chief Justice Mr. Justice H. L Dattu is the present Chairman of NALSA.
   3. The Chairman of the National Legal Services Authority (NALSA) is the senior most judge (after CJI) of the Supreme Court of India.
   4. Hon'ble Mr. Justice T. S. Thakur is the present Chairman of NALSA.

   (a) 1 and 2 are correct
   (b) 2 and 3 are correct
   (c) 3 and 4 are correct
   (d) None is correct

7. India and Britain recently signed an "extradition treaty". Extradition means -
   (a) Exports without double taxation
   (b) Order of Indian courts will apply to Indians living in the U.K.
   (d) India and the U.K. will deport criminals on reciprocal basis to each other
   (d) None of the above

8. What is a 'moot'?
   (a) A basic point of law
   (b) A basic fact of case
   (c) Mock court for practice by students in general
   (d) Another name for magistrate's court

9. The temporary release of a convicted prisoner from jail for a fixed period is called -
   (a) Bail (b) Parole
   (c) Acquittal (d) Discharge

10. The Railway authorities allowed a train to be over-crowded. In consequence, a legitimate passenger, Mr. X got his pocket picked. Choose appropriate answer -
    (a) Mr. X can sue the railway authorities for the loss suffered.
    (b) Mr. X cannot sue because he had given his consent to travel in a over-crowded train.
    (c) Mr. X cannot sue the railway authorities because there was no infringement of legal right and mere fact that the loss was caused does not give rise to a cause of action.
    (d) None of the above

**11. Choose the best option for the following statement:**

The distinction between fraud and misrepresentation:

1. Fraud is more or less intentional wrong, whereas misrepresentation may be quite innocent.
2. In addition to rendering the contract voidable, is a cause of action in tort for damages. Simple misrepresentation is not a tort but a person who rightfully rescinds a contract is entitled to compensation for any damages which he has sustained through the non-fulfilment of the contract.
3. A person complaining of misrepresentation can be met with the defence that he had "the means of discovering the truth with ordinary diligence". But excepting fraud by silence in other cases of fraud it is no defence that "the plaintiff had the means of discovering the truth by ordinary diligence".
4. None of the above.

(a) 1 is correct.
(b) 1 & 2 are correct.
(c) 1, 2 & 3 are correct.
(d) Only 4 is correct.

**12.** Who called Indian Constitution as Quasi-Federal?
(a) Austin
(b) K. C. Wheare
(c) H. M. Servai
(d) Jennings

**13.** President of India exercises his powers..........
(a) Either directly or through officers subordinate to him
(b) Through ministers
(c) Through Prime Minister
(d) Through Cabinet

**14.** Vote on accounts is meant for..........
(a) Vote on the report of CAG
(b) To meet un for seen expenditure
(c) Appropriating funds pending passing of budget
(d) Budget

## ANSWERS

| | | | | |
|---|---|---|---|---|
| **1.** (c) | **2.** (a) | **3.** (b) | **4.** (a) | **5.** (c) |
| **6.** (c) | **7.** (c) | **8.** (c) | **9.** (b) | **10.** (c) |
| **11.** (c) | **12.** (b) | **13.** (a) | **14.** (c) | |

## EXPLANATIONS

**1.** Brought in by former Chief Minister Narendra Modi and known as The Gujarat Control of Terrorism and Organized Crime Bill, 2015, it empowers police to tap telephonic conversations and submit them as evidence in court. It also makes confessions before police officers admissible in court, and has therefore been the cause of much controversy. The new Bill is a re-worked version of the Gujarat Control of Organised Crime Bill (GUJCOC), 2003, which was earlier rejected twice by the President due to some of its contentious provisions.

**2.** 20th Law Commission headed by Justice (retd.) A P Shah in its 210$^{th}$ Report on Humanization and Decriminalization of Attempt to Suicide had recommended that Section 309 of IPC needed to be effaced from the statute book because the provision is inhuman, irrespective of whether it is constitutional or unconstitutional. 18 States and four Union Territories have backed the government's decision. S. 309 of the IPC deals with attempt to commit suicide. It was understood as a cruel and irrational provision, since it only caused additional trauma to someone who would already be dealing with the consequences of not being able to commit suicide. It also has implications for the right to die and the euthanasia debate.

**3.** The Supreme Court of India scrapped 214 coal blocks out of 218 coal blocks. The four coal blocks spared in the judgment were those of Reliance Power, NTPC and SAIL.

**4.** Under the new Certificate of Practice and Renewal Rules, 2014, the Bar Council of India has stated that an advocate cannot start his/her practice in the Supreme Court unless they have at least five year practice experience in the lower and High Court of India.

**5.** The Governor within his state is the supreme executive head.

**6.** The NALSA was established to provide free and competent legal services to the weaker sections of the society, so that their economic disabilities don't prevent them from getting justice. Hon'ble Mr. Justice H. L. Dattu, the Chief Justice of India is the Patron-in-Chief and Hon'ble Mr. Justice Tirath Singh Thakur, Judge, Supreme Court of India is the Executive Chairman of the Authority.

**7.** The purpose of extradition is to ensure that criminals are prosecuted under the more appropriate jurisdiction. Such treaties ease the rendition of criminals from one country to another.

8. It is a mock court at which students argue imaginary cases for practice. There are international as well as domestic moots.
9. Parole is usually given after proven good behavior within the prison, before the expiry of the sentence. In India, the grant of Parole is largely governed by the rules made under the Prison Act, 1894 and Prisoner Act, 1900. Each of the States has its own parole rules. There are two types of parole- custody and regular. The custody parole is granted in emergency circumstances like death in the family, serious illness or marriage in the family. It is limited to a time span of six hours during which the prisoner is escorted to the place of visit and return there from. The grant of parole is subject to verification of the circumstances from the concerned police station and is granted by the Superintendent of Jail. Regular Parole is allowed for a maximum period of one month, except in special circumstances, to convicts who have served at least one year in prison. It is granted on certain grounds such as: Serious Illness of a family member, accident or death of a family member, marriage of a member of the family, delivery of child by wife of the convict, maintain family or social ties, serious damage to life or property of the family of convict by natural calamities, pursue filing of a Special Leave Petition etc. Certain categories of convicts are not eligible for being released on parole like prisoners involved in offences against the State, or threats to national security, non-citizens of India etc. People convicted of murder and rape of children or multiple murders etc. are also exempted except at the discretion of the granting authority.
10. This question doesn't have a principle, so one would have to rely on legal knowledge alone. The principle of damnum sine injuria would apply as there's damage but no legal injury. Over-crowding is a common enough occurrence on trains, and there cannot be a remedy against it. Authorities are not legally bound to ensure the convenience of every passenger.
11. All three are correct
    (i) Fraud is committed with a dishonest intention whereas representation is when you believe something to be actually true.
    (ii) Misrepresentation renders the contract voidable i.e. it gives an option to the innocent party to avoid the contract but under torts, one can claim damages if the contract is rescinded rightfully or if one has suffered damages because of non-fulfillment of the contract.
    (iii) One cannot complain of mis-representation if had the means of discovering the truth with ordinary diligence and even in cases where fraud has been committed by maintaining silence.
12. A quasi-federal state combines the features of a federal government and those of a unitary government. India is not a true federation. It combines the features of a federal government and the features of a unitary government which can also be called the non-federal features. Because of this, India is regarded as a semi-federal state. Prof. K. C. Wheare describes it as "a quasi-federal state". The Supreme Court of India also describes it as "a federal structure with a strong bias towards the Centre".
13. As per Article 53, Presidential executive powers can be exercised either directly or through officers subordinate to him.
14. The vote on accounts deals only with the expenditure in a government's budget. The government gives an estimate of the funds it needs to meet the expenditure it incurs during the first 3-4 months of a financial year.

    The Indian Constitution says that all revenues received by the Union government and the loans raised by it are to be put into the Consolidated Fund of India. This does not include anything that is put into a Contingency Fund. Since Parliament is not able to vote the entire budget before the commencement of the new financial year, it is necessary to keep enough money at the disposal of government to allow it to run the administration of the country. When the government needs to withdraw any money from the Consolidated Fund of India to cover its expenditure (especially during the time when elections are underway and a caretaker government is in place), it has to seek approval from the Parliament. A special provision is, therefore, made for a vote-on-account by which the government obtains the vote of Parliament for a sum sufficient to incur expenditure on various items for a part of the year. This sanction of Parliament for withdrawal of money from the Consolidated Fund of India to meet the government's expenses is generally known as a vote-on-account.

# GENERAL KNOWLEDGE

## CONSTITUTION AND POLITY

1. Which of the following Acts formally introduced the principle of elections for the first time?
   (a) The Indian Councils Act, 1909
   (b) Government of India Act, 1919
   (c) The Government of India Act, 1935
   (d) India's Independence Act, 1947

## ANSWER

1. (a)

## EXPLANATION

1. The Indian Councils Act 1909 effectively allowed the election of Indians to the various legislative councils in India for the first time. Previously some Indians had been appointed to legislative councils. The majorities of the councils remained British government appointments. Moreover the electorate was limited to specific classes of Indian nationals.

## CURRENT AFFAIRS

1. In February 2015, which Indian Cricket legend has been inducted into the ICC Hall of Fame?
   (a) Rahul Dravid
   (b) Anil Kumble
   (c) Sachin Tendulkar
   (d) Mohammad Azharuddin
2. IRCTC has recently launched a new service called 'RuPay prepaidcards' which will enable passengers to book their tickets, do shopping and pay service bills online. This service was launched in collaboration with which bank?
   (a) Union Bank of India
   (b) State Bank of India
   (c) ICICI Bank
   (d) Bharatiya Mahila Bank
3. Name India's Beyond Visual Range (BVR) Air-to-Air missile which was successfully test fired on 19 March 2015 from a Sukhoi-30 fighter aircraft?
   (a) Astra (b) K-100
   (c) Mitra (d) Tejas
4. The ISRO has developed a "Flood Hazard Atlas" by mapping flood prone and vulnerable areas in which state?
   (a) Kerala
   (b) Maharashtra
   (c) Assam
   (d) Tripura
5. Which South East Asian country has recently banned surrogacy service to end its flourishing rent-a-womb industry?
   (a) Singapore (b) Laos
   (c) Thailand (d) Vietnam
6. The name of new Andhra Pradesh Capital is likely to be ..........
   (a) Amaravathi (b) Badrachala
   (c) Krishna Nagar (d) Varshavathi
7. The Ufa city, where annual BRICS summit-2015 is scheduled to be held is in which country?
   (a) China (b) Russia
   (c) South Africa (d) Brazil
8. Prime Minister Modi has launched the "Give It Up" campaign for voluntarily giving up ..........
   (a) Use of tobacco products
   (b) LPG Subsidy
   (c) Use of incandescent bulbs
   (d) Use of plastics
9. The recently announced Paramparagat Krishi Vikas Yojana aims to boost __?
   (a) Organic Farming (b) Drip Irrigation
   (c) Horticulture crops (d) Vegetable production
10. The winner of 2015 Malaysian Grand Prix is __?
    (a) Sebastian Vettel (b) Kimi Raikkonen
    (c) Lewis Hamilton (d) Jenson Button
11. Name the golfer who won the Indian Open title on 22 February 2015.
    (a) SSP Chowrasia (b) Anirban Lahiri
    (c) Siddikur Rahman (d) Daniel Chopra
12. Which space agency has successfully launched the world's first all electric satellites in March, 2015?
    (a) Russia Federal Space Agency
    (b) China National Space Administration
    (c) SpaceX
    (d) European Space Agency
13. Bhalchandra Nemade who has been selected for the 50th Jnanpith Award for 2014, on 6 February 2015, is a famous writer in which language?
    (a) Marathi (b) Oriya
    (c) Malayalam (d) Urdu
14. Recently, which country became the first member country to the UN Framework Convention on Climate Change (UNFCCC) to submit its action plan on Intended Nationally Determined Contribution (INDC)?
    (a) India (b) Switzerland
    (c) Australia (d) Singapore

15. Which city has become India's first fully WiFi-enabled metro city on 5 February 2015?
(a) Mumbai (b) Kolkata
(c) Chennai (d) Delhi

16. Indian Space Research Organisation was recently conferred 'Space Pioneer Award' by the National Space Society (NSS) of which country over the historic feat on successfully sending an orbit to Martian atmosphere in its very first attempt?
(a) France (b) European Union
(c) China (d) USA

17. Recently in which country did Indian Prime Minister Narendra Modi inaugurate the first of the eight Coastal Surveillance Radar Systems (CSRS) being set up by India?
(a) Mauritius (b) Maldives
(c) Sri Lanka (d) Seychelles

18. Name the Indian industrialist on whose 175th birth anniversary, Union government launched the commemorative stamp on 6th January 2015?
(a) G D Birla
(b) T V Sundaram Iyengar
(c) Kasturbhai Lalbhai
(d) Jamsetji Nusserwanji Tata

19. Which state is to host the 36th National Games in 2016?
(a) Karnataka (b) Goa
(c) Tamil Nadu (d) Telangana

20. Project Varsha, India's new naval base under construction is near which of the following cities?
(a) Kochi (b) Karwar
(c) Visakhapatnam (d) Chennai

21. Young Indian shuttler K. Srikanth on 15 March 2015 won which of the following major badminton championship?
(a) China Grand Prix Gold
(b) Australian Grand Prix Gold
(c) Swiss Grand Prix Gold
(d) Indonesian Grand Prix Gold

22. What is the name given to the dedicated TV channel for farmers that was announced in the Union Budget for 2014-15 and Rs. 100 crore was set aside for its establishment?
(a) Kisan (b) Farmers Show
(c) Krishi Channel (d) None of the above

23. President Pranab Mukherjee on 6th January 2015 signed the ordinance to amend Citizenship Act, 1955. Which of the statements in this regard is/are right?
I. The ordinance exempts Person of Indian Origin (PIO) from appearing before the local police station on every visit
II. It replaced the clause that says foreigners marrying Indians must continuously stay in the country for a period of six months before they get an Indian citizenship
(a) I Only (b) II Only
(c) Both I and II (d) Neither I nor II

24. Name the renowned Indian ecologist who has been chosen for the prestigious 2015 Tyler Prize for Environmental Achievement on 23 March 2015?
(a) MS Swaminathan
(b) Kasthuri Rangan
(c) Jayaram Ramesh
(d) Madhav Gadgil

## ANSWERS

| | | | | |
|---|---|---|---|---|
| 1. (b) | 2. (a) | 3. (a) | 4. (c) | 5. (c) |
| 6. (a) | 7. (b) | 8. (b) | 9. (a) | 10. (a) |
| 11. (b) | 12. (c) | 13. (a) | 14. (b) | 15. (b) |
| 16. (d) | 17. (d) | 18. (d) | 19. (b) | 20. (c) |
| 21. (c) | 22. (a) | 23. (a) | 24. (d) | |

## EXPLANATIONS

1. Anil Kumble, the former India captain and Betty Wilson, one of the greatest women's cricketers of all-time, were inducted into the ICC Cricket Hall of Fame during the ICC Cricket World Cup 2015.

2. On 24 March 2015 IRCTC in collaboration with Union Bank of India (UBI) launched IRCTC RuPay Debit Card exclusively for booking train tickets on railway portal. RuPay card is India's first payment gateway system launched by National Payments Corporation of India (NPCI).

3. India's Beyond Visual Range (BVR) air-to-air missile ASTRA was successfully test fired by the Indian Air Force off the coast of Odisha near the Integrated Test Range, Balasore. The missile has been indigenously designed and developed by the Defence Research and Development Organisation (DRDO). In test flight an ASTRA missile carrying telemetry equipment in place of the warhead was fired from a Sukhoi-30 aircraft against a Lakshya (Pilotless Target Aircraft) target. The target was successfully engaged and it was captured by Telemetry and Electro-optical tracking stations.

4. The Indian Space Research Organization has developed a Flood Hazard Atlas by mapping flood prone and vulnerable areas in Assam.

5. Thailand's military-dominated parliament passed a law criminalising and banning foreigners from seeking surrogacy services in the South-East Asian country. The law prohibits non-Thai couples and same-sex couples accessing surrogacy services, ending a booming "rent-a-womb" industry that made Thailand a top destination for fertility tourism.
6. Amaravathi is the new capital of Andhra Pradesh.
7. Ufa is the capital city of the Republic of Bashkortostan, Russia, and the industrial, economic, scientific and cultural center of the republic.
8. Prime Minister of India has launched the Give it Up campaign for voluntarily giving up LPG subsidy. Through this campaign he appealed to well-to-do sections of Indian society to voluntarily give up LPG subsidy, so that the benefit of the same could be shared more widely with poor sections of the society.
9. Paramparagat Krishi Vikas Yojana (Traditional Farming Improvement Programme) has been launched by Government of India to support and promote organic farming and thereby improving soil health.
10. Sebastian Vettel won 2015 Malaysian Grand prix.
11. Indian golfer Anirban Lahiri's purple patch continued as he clinched the Hero Indian Open.
12. A SpaceX rocket blasted off from Cape Canaveral Air Force Station to put the world's first all-electric communications satellites into orbit.
13. Bhalchandra Vanaji Nemade is a Marathi writer from Maharashtra, India. Famous for his books "Hindu" & "Kosala". Also he is known for his novel "Hindu jagnyachi samrudhha adgal". He is winner for 2014 Jnanpith Award.
14. Switzerland is the First country to officially submit INDC.
15. Kolkata, West Bengal's capital city, has become India's first fully WiFi-enabled metro city. Reliance JIO is reportedly providing the services.
16. Space Pioneer award for the year 2015 was presented to Indian Space Research Organisation (ISRO) in the Science and Engineering category during the 34th Annual International Space Development Conference held at Toronto in Canada.
17. Prime Minister Narendra Modi unveiled CSRS radar in Seychelles.
18. In order to honour Tata Group founder Jamsetji Nusserwanji Tata by releasing commemorative coins to mark his 175th birth anniversary. The coins, a first for an industrialist, are being minted on the instructions of the Prime Minister's Office with an eye to enthuse Indian businesses for Modi's 'Make in India' campaign.
19. Goa will organise the 36th National Games 2016.
20. NS Varsha is a new naval base being developed under Project Varsha for the Indian Navy. This base will be the home of the navy's new fleet of nuclear submarines and ships. It was planned to be located within a radius of approximately 200 kilometres from Visakhapatnam, the headquarters of the navy's Eastern Naval Command.
21. K Srikanth won Swiss Grand Prix Gold.
22. Finance minister Arun Jaitley, in his Union Budget 2014, announced a new 24-hour TV channel Kisan for farmers that will be dedicated to the agriculture sector, with an outlay of Rs.100 crore for providing real-time information to farmers.
23. Only option (a) A is correct.
24. Madhav Gadgill was chosen for Tyler prize 2015.

## EVERYDAY SCIENCE

1. Lysosomes, which are known as suicide bags, are produced by which organelle?
   (a) Mitochondria (b) Golgi body
   (c) Ribosome (d) Peroxisome
2. The protein CA-125 (Cancer Antigen-125) is used as biomarker for detection of which type of cancer?
   (a) Ovarian cancer
   (b) Bone cancer
   (c) Lung cancer
   (d) Oral cancer

## ANSWERS

1. (b) 2. (a)

## EXPLANATIONS

1. Lysosomes are called suicide sacks. They are produced by the Golgi body. They consist of a single membrane surrounding powerful digestive enzymes. It acts as the "garbage disposal" of the cell by breaking down cell components that are no longer needed as well as molecules or even bacteria that are ingested by the cell.
2. CA-125 is a protein that is found more in ovarian cancer cells than in other cells. This blood test is often used to monitor women who have been diagnosed with ovarian cancer. The test is useful if CA-125 level was high when the cancer was first diagnosed.

## GEOGRAPHY

1. Which of the following is incorrect option?
   (a) Within the Arctic and Antarctic Circles there is at least one day in the year during which the sun does not set and at least one day on which it never rises.
   (b) At the North Pole there is darkness for half the year.
   (c) At the summer solstice, the sun shines vertically over the Tropic of Capricorn.
   (d) The sun shines vertically over the Equator twice in the year.

## ANSWER

**1.** (c)

## EXPLANATION

1. A solstice happens when the sun's zenith is at its furthest point from the equator. In June solstice it reaches its northernmost point and the Earth's North Pole tilts directly towards the sun, at about 23.5 degrees. It's also known as the northern solstice because it occurs when the sun is directly over the Tropic of Cancer in the Northern Hemisphere.

## HISTORY

1. Who among the following 18th century Indian rulers has been called 'Plato of his tribe'?
   (a) Sawai Jai Singh
   (b) Badam Singh
   (c) SurajMal
   (d) Guru Gobind Singh
2. What is the correct sequence of the following movements in chronological order?
   1. Civil Disobedience Movement
   2. Khilafat Movement
   3. Home Rule Movement
   4. Quit India Movement

   (a) 1, 2, 3, 4
   (b) 4, 3, 2, 1
   (c) 3, 2, 1,4
   (d) 2, 4, 1, 3

## ANSWERS

**1.** (c) **2.** (c)

## EXPLANATIONS

1. Maharaja Suraj Mal or Sujan Singh was ruler of Bharatpur in Rajasthan, India. Historians has described him as "the Plato of the Jat people" and by a modern writer as the "Jat Odysseus".
2. Option (c) is the correct choice.

## ECONOMICS

1. Which of the following is the oldest share market in India?
   (a) Bombay (b) Madras
   (c) Calcutta (d) Delhi
2. Which committee was constituted by RBI to review governance of boards of banks in India?
   (a) P J Nayak Committee
   (b) H R Khan Committee
   (c) Harsh Vardhan Committee
   (d) K Subramanian Committee
3. Which is the single policy rate to unambiguously signal the stance of monetary policy as recently recommended by RBI?
   (a) PLR (b) Repo
   (c) Bank (d) CLR
4. Which of the following is a Direct Tax?
   (a) Excise duty (b) Sales tax
   (c) Income tax (d) None of the above
5. How much Foreign Direct Investment (FDI) in country's defence sector was proposed in the Union Budget 2014-15 presented on 10 July 2014?
   (a) 51% (b) 49%
   (c) 29% (d) 10%

## ANSWERS

**1.** (a) **2.** (a) **3.** (b) **4.** (c) **5.** (b)

## EXPLANATIONS

1. The Bombay Stock Exchange, popularly known as BSE, is the oldest one in Asia. BSE was established in 1875 as The Native Share and Stock Brokers Association.
2. The Reserve Bank of India has constituted an expert committee to review the governance of bank boards in India. Chaired by P.J. Nayak, former Chairman and CEO of Axis Bank, the committee members include S. Raman, whole-time member, SEBI; Shubhalakshmi Panse, Chairperson and Managing Director, Allahabad Bank; Pratip Kar, former Executive Director, SEBI, and Joydeep Sengupta, Director, McKinsey & Company.
3. Repo is the single policy rate to unambiguously signal the stance of monetary policy as recommended by RBI.
4. Income Tax is a direct tax while the rest are indirect taxes.

5. As part of military modernisation drive, The government today allocated Rs 2.29 lakh crore for the Defence Ministry in the Budget, marking an increase of around 12.5 per cent from the last fiscal as it raised the FDI limit in the defence sector up to 49 per cent from 26 per cent now.

## MISCELLANEOUS (QUOTES, DAYS, BOOKS TITLES, SPORTS, BASIC LEGAL CONCEPTS)

1. Attukal Pongal festival, which is figured in Guinness Book of World Records is celebrated in ..........
(*a*) Tamil Nadu (*b*) Kerala
(*c*) Telangana (*d*) Goa

2. Garuda Shakti III is the military exercise between India and which country?
(*a*) Nepal (*b*) Russia
(*c*) Indonesia (*d*) China

3. Match List-I with List-II and select the best option using the code given below the lists:

| **List-I** *(Organization/Centers)* | **List-II** *(Locations)* |
|---|---|
| A. High Altitude Warfare School | 1. Chennai |
| B. Indian Air force Training Center | 2. Gulmarg |
| C. National Defense College | 3. New Delhi |
| D. Institute of National Integration | 4. Pune |

| | A | B | C | D |
|---|---|---|---|---|
| (a) | 2 | 1 | 3 | 4 |
| (b) | 1 | 2 | 3 | 4 |
| (c) | 1 | 2 | 4 | 3 |
| (d) | 2 | 1 | 4 | 3 |

4. The "Ease of Doing Business Index" is prepared and published by ...........
(a) World Trade Organisation
(b) World Bank Group
(c) United Nations
(d) European Union

5. Which one of the following Railway Zones and the corresponding Headquarter pairs is not correctly matched?
(a) North Eastern Railway : Gorakhpur
(b) South Eastern Railway : Bhubaneswar
(c) Eastern Railway : Kolkata
(d) South East Central Railway : Bilaspur

6. Which among the following is the world's largest e-commerce company?
(a) Amazon (b) eBay
(c) Alibaba (d) Flipkart

7. Which one of the following is essentially a solo dance nowadays performed in group as well?
(a) Kuchipudi (b) Kathak
(c) Manipuri (d) Mohiniattam

8. Who among the following was the author of Rajtarangini, commonly regarded as the first genuine history of India written by an Indian?
(a) Banbhatta (b) Ravikirti
(c) Pushpananda (d) Kalhana

9. A Snickometer is associated with which sports?
(a) Tennis (b) Cricket
(c) Hockey (d) Football

10. Who among the following is India's first chief of Cyber Security?
(a) B. J. Srinath
(b) Gulshan Rai
(c) A. S.Kamble
(d) Amardeep S. Chawla

11. Which one of the following is the online grievances monitoring portals launched by union government for Indians living abroad?
(a) Madad (b) Sankalp
(c) Mythri (d) Rakshan

12. Greece and Turkey are working to resolve their dispute over sovereignty and related rights in the area of which sea?
(a) Black Sea
(b) Sea of Marmara
(c) Aegean Sea
(d) Mediterranean Sea

13. Which one of the following pairs is not correctly matched?
(a) Kunal Bahl & Rohit Bansal- Snapdeal
(b) Sachin Bansal & Binny Bansal- Red Bus
(c) Deepinder goyal & Pankaj Chaddah - Zomato
(d) Bhavish Aggarwal & Ankit Bhati - Ola Cab

14. The "Friends for Life" - an elephant conservation project has been launched by World Wide Fund for Nature India and ...........
(a) Aditya Birla Group (b) Muthoot Group
(c) Manapuram Group (d) Reliance Ltd

**15.** The National Industrial Corridor (NIC) that was proposed to be established in the Union Budget of 2014-15, will have its headquarters at which city?

(a) Pune

(b) Bhubaneswar

(c) Bangalore

(d) Hyderabad

## ANSWERS

| | | | | |
|---|---|---|---|---|
| **1.** (b) | **2.** (c) | **3.** (a) | **4.** (b) | **5.** (b) |
| **6.** (c) | **7.** (d) | **8.** (d) | **9.** (b) | **10.** (b) |
| **11.** (a) | **12.** (c) | **13.** (b) | **14.** (b) | **15.** (a) |

## EXPLANATIONS

**1.** Attukal Pongala is an extremely popular, essentially women's festival celebrated in ancient Bhagavathy temple (Mudippura) at Attukal in Thiruvananthapuram district of Kerala.

**2.** Exercise 'GARUDA SHAKTI-III' is the third one in the ongoing series of joint exercises between armies of India and Indonesia.

**3.** Option (a) is the correct answer.

**4.** The ease of doing business index is an index created by the World Bank Group. Higher rankings (a low numerical value) indicate better, usually simpler, regulations for businesses and stronger protections of property rights.

**5.** The South Eastern Railway (SER) is one of the seventeen railway zones in India. It is headquartered at Garden Reach, Kolkata, West Bengal, India.

**6.** Alibaba is world's largest e-commerce company.

**7.** Kuchipudi was never a solo affair and required a number of performers. Kuchipudi was performed in the open air by performers who were given a vigorous training in abhinaya, music, dancing and singing. Kathak is traditionally a solo dance form. Mohiniattam, essentially a solo dance, is nowadays being performed in groups as well. The repertoire of Mohiniattam closely follows that of Bharatanatyam. There are a number of forms in Manipuri. These are the Ras Lila, the Pung Cholom, Nupa Cholom, Thoibi and a host of others.The Ras Lila is the most important dance form in the Manipuri style. The theme revolves around the love of Krishna and the milkmaids (gopinis).

**8.** Rajtarangini is a metrical historical chronicle of north-western Indian subcontinent, particularly the kings of Kashmir, written in Sanskrit by Kashmiri Brahman Kalhana in 12th century.

**9.** Snickometer is associated with cricket.

**10.** The Narendra Modi government has created a cyber-security chief's position under the Prime Minister's Office and has appointed Gulshan Rai.

**11.** Union foreign ministry has launched "Madad" an online grievances monitoring portal for Indians living abroad. The portal will help the Indians living abroad to approach the government easily for any help. Madad is a combined effort of MEA and MOIA to enhance collaboration and contact with Indians abroad.

**12.** The evolution of the Law of the Sea, which gives countries new spaces of sovereignty and areas of jurisdiction without specifying their delimitation, is the source of the dispute between Greece and Turkey in the Aegean Sea.

**13.** Sachin Bansal & Binny Bansal are founders of Flipkart.

**14.** The Muthoot Group, as a part of its CSR initiative Muthoot Haathi Mera Saathi, in partnership with World Wide Fund for Nature- India (WWF-India) has launched "Friends for Life" an elephant conservation project that is dedicated towards effective management of human-elephant conflict (HEC) and protecting the habitats of Asian elephants across six states in India.

**15.** The National Industrial Corridor (NIC) is proposed to be established in Pune (Maharashtra).

■■

# AILET-2015 CHAPTER-WISE

## ENGLISH

### VOCABULARY

**Directions (Q. 1 - 5) :** For each of the following words below, a context is provided. From the alternatives given, pick the word or phrase that is closest in meaning in the given context.

1. **Alphanumeric :** The inclusion of alphanumeric features in cellular phones has made sending SMSs very convenient.
(a) using only alphabets
(b) using digital codes
(c) using OSCOLA
(d) using both letters and numerals

2. **Oligarchy :** Mrigank argued that all political parties, including those which profess democratic values become the instruments of their leaders who eventually become a self-interested and self-satisfied oligarchy.
(a) rule of a mob or crowd
(b) small group of people having control of state
(c) an iron-rule of democrats
(d) a socialist rule of activists

3. **Perestroika :** In the 1980's, the "state socialist' tradiiion became totally discredited as Gorbachev's programme of perestroika revealed the fundamental failures of the planned economies of the Communist bloc.
(a) closing off all entries (b) manifesto of failure
(c) opening up (d) nagging policies

4. **Bequeath :** In consequences, they bequeathed to their followers no clear vision of the economics of socialism, that is state ownership and planning the means of production, distribution and exchange, and others had to advocate market socialism, the state regulation of capital rather than state ownership of planning.
(a) hand down or pass on
(b) a powerful will of the people
(c) a method of governing
(d) to gjve in promise

5. **Redundancy :** Communication is a subtle, complex and continuously fluctuating process, affected by a multitude of factors both external and internal, and two such elements are noise and redundancy.
(a) that part of message that is predictable or conventional
(b) that word or phrase which is surprising
(c) that meaning of a word which is sparingly used
(d) that message which has no clear meaning

**Directions (Q. 6 - 9) :** In the following questions, choose the word which is odd one out.

6. (a) bedlam (b) anarchy
(c) anatomise (d) insurrection

7. (a) miscreant (b) defendant
(c) accused (d) plaintiff

8. (a) assault (b) extortion
(c) sub-poena (d) battery

9. (a) barrister (b) attorney
(c) juror (d) advocare

**Direction (Q. 10 - 14) :** Choose the exact meaning of the idioms/phrases.

10. Alpha and Omega
(a) related to science
(b) the beginning and the end
(c) A to Z
(d) none of these

11. Ante-diluvium
(a) old time (b) up-to-date
(c) time period (d) against dualism

12. To play truant
(a) to make a narrow escape
(b) to run away from work without permission
(c) to be clever
(d) none of these

13. To see red
(a) to find fault with (b) to be very angry
(c) to criticise others (d) to victimise someone

14. To flog a dead horse
(a) to do a thing in vain
(b) to act in a foolish way
(c) to criticize strongly
(d) try to revive interest in a subject that is out of date

**Direction (Q. 15 - 24) :** Fill in the blanks with the most appropriate word:

**15.** When you are living with your ——— values and principles, you can be straight forward, honest and ———

(a) inherited, distinct
(b) core, upfront
(c) innate, durable
(d) cultural, perceptive

**16.** The quality of ——— between individuals and the organisation for which they work can be ——— to the benefit of both parties.

(a) life, conceptualised (b) interactions, improved
(c) service, evaluated (d) work, better

**17.** Genetic engineering in humans should be used to ——— diseases, not to ——— genetic uniformity.

(a) treat, foster (b) eradicate, cater
(c) cure, generate (d) avoid, promote

**18.** Stating that the ATM operations are ——— losses, the nation's largest bank, the State Bank plans to ——— the management of some of its ATMs.

(a) generating, resource
(b) generating, close
(c) incurring, outsource
(d) reporting, tighten

**19.** Most journalistic writing could do with ——— of paragraphs to make the prose more ———

(a) suppression, legible
(b) removal, argumentative
(c) simplification, abstruse
(d) deletion, succinct

**20.** Angered by bureaucrat's ——— comments, the reporter insisted for a more ——— response.

(a) redundant, repetitive
(b) tactless, immediate
(c) circumlocutions, direct
(d) sarcastic, beneficial

**21.** One of the most productive researches ——— in contemporary neurosciences is devoted to ——— maps of human consciousness.

(a) trajectories, reconnoitring
(b) designs, enunciating
(c) paradigms, elucidating
(d) declensions, obfuscating

**22.** But ——— are now regularly written not just for tools but well-established practices, organisations and institutions not all of which seem to be ——— away

(a) reports, withering
(b) stories, trading
(c) books, dying
(d) obituaries, fading

**23.** In this context, the ——— of the British Labour Movement is particularly ———

(a) affair, weird
(b) activity, moving
(c) experience, significant
(d) atmosphere, gloomy

**24.** Indian intellectuals may boast if they are so inclined of being ——— to the most elitist among the intellectual ——— of the world

(a) subordinate, traditions
(b) heirs, cliques
(c) ancestors, societies
(d) heir, traditions

## ANSWERS

| | | | | |
|---|---|---|---|---|
| **1.** (d) | **2.** (b) | **3.** (c) | **4.** (a) | **5.** (a) |
| **6.** (c) | **7.** (d) | **8.** (c) | **9.** (c) | **10.** (b) |
| **11.** (a) | **12.** (b) | **13.** (b) | **14.** (d) | **15.** (d) |
| **16.** (b) | **17.** (a) | **18.** (c) | **19.** (d) | **20.** (c) |
| **21.** (c) | **22.** (d) | **23.** (c) | **24.** (d) | |

## EXPLANATIONS

**1.** An 'Alphanumeric' code refers to both letters and numerals.

**2.** An 'oligarchy' refers to a small group of people having control of a country or organisation.

**3.** 'Perestroika' (used in erstwhile USSR) refers to the policy or practice of restructuring or reforming the economic and political system. First proposed by Leonid Brezhnev in 1979 and actively promoted by Mikhail Gorbachev, perestroika originally referred to increased automation and labour efficiency, but later, came to entail greater awareness of economic markets and the ending of central planning. Hence, 'opening up' can be considered to be a definition of 'Perestroika.'

**4.** 'Bequeth' refers to the action of leaving property to a person or other beneficiary by a will. Hence, the word is very similar to 'hand down' or 'pass on.'

**5.** In the context of the sentence, option (a) is the correct answer. 'Redundancy' refers to something that is superfluous and unnecessary. So, any part of message that is predictable or conventional can be considered unnecessary or redundant.

6. 'Bedlam', 'Anarchy' and 'Insurrection' refer to a period of chaos or a violent uprising against a government or an authority. Anatomise means to 'examine or analyse something in detail'. The word can also mean 'to dissect a body'.

7. 'Miscreant' refers to a person who has done an unlawful activity. 'Defendant' refers to an individual or an institution accused in a court of law. 'Accused' relates to a person who has been charged with something. Hence, all the three words refer to someone who is on the receiving side of law. Plaintiff is a person who brings a case against another in a court of law. Hence, plaintiff is a person who brings a charge and is not on the receiving side of the law. Therefore, option (d) is the correct answer.

   ****However, option (a) can also be the answer. 'Accused', 'Defendant' and 'Plaintiff' refer to persons who have a close association with a court of law. However, 'miscreant' is a person who commits a crime. He is not associated with a court of law unless caught.

8. A subpoena is a writ ordering a person to attend a court. On the other hand, extortion is the practice of obtaining something, especially money, through force or threats. Assault is to make a physical attack on someone. Battery refers to a fortified emplacement for heavy guns. Hence, extortion, assault and battery relate to threat and attack while subpoena is a writ ? a legal term.

9. Juror is a member of a jury while the other options refer to the position of a lawyer.

10. 'Alpha and Omega' refer to the beginning and the end (used by Christians as a title for Jesus).

11. 'Ante-diluvium' refers to the period before the biblical flood, e.g., 'antediluvian man'. It can also refer to a very old time period.

12. 'To play truant' refers to the act of remaining absent from work without an approval. It can also mean to run away from work without permission.

13. 'To see red' is to become very angry.

14. 'To flog a dead horse' is to revive interest in a topic which is out of vogue or date. It can also refer to a futile endeavor.

15. Let's fill in the second blank space first. 'Durable' in option (c) does not make any sense because a person cannot be durable. A person cannot be 'upfront'. Hence, option (b) is out. The qualities mentioned by the narrator are straight forward and honest. Taking cue from these qualities, the only possible option 'perceptive.'

16. 'Quality of *interactions*' can '*improve*' work. The other options cannot be true.

17. Genetic engineering in humans is certainly a mode of treatment. 'Foster' means to 'encourage the development of something.' The other options are inappropriate in the contaxt of the sentence.

18. Losses can only be 'incurred.' Furthermore, it is a common practice to outsource the management of a department in order to counter the losses. Hence, option (c) is the answer.

19. 'Succinct' refers to something briefly and clearly stated. 'Deletion' of paragraphs can make the prose more 'succinct.' Hence, option (d) is the answer.

20. 'Circumlocutious' means explaining something in a roundabout and unnecessary wordy manner. 'Direct' can be considered to the opposite of 'circumlocutious.' Both the words when used together in the sentence makes sense.

21. 'Paradigm' means 'pattern'. Research pattern in contemporary neurosciences is devoted to explaining the maps of human consciousness. 'Elucidate' means 'to explain.' 'Reconnoitring' refers to military observation. 'Enunciate' means 'to pronounce clearly. 'Obfuscate' means to make something unintelligible. None of the other options other than 'elucidate' is making any sense in the context of the sentence.

22. You don't write reports or stories or books for tools, but 'obituaries' ? yes, as tools do get obsolete. Also 'practices' do not wither or trade or die away, but they do fade away with time.

23. Option (a) with 'wird' as an option can be removed and similarly, option (d) with 'gloomy.' They are both using words that are not first-priority as they are somewhat informal. Out of the other choices, 'activity' in option (b) is not qualified as 'moving' (emotional). Option (c) fits in the best and is the best answer.

24. Option (a) can be easily eliminated since 'being subordinate' and 'boasting' of it do not go together. Option (c) is incorrect because 'intellectuals' (individuals) being ancestors to societies (collectively) is incorrect. Also present Indian intellectuals cannot possibly be ancestors either. Option (b) is incorrect because 'intellectual cliques' is odd especially since 'cliques' is used in a somewhat negative sense. Option (d) is correct.

## GRAMMAR

**Directions (Q. 1 - 5) :** In this section, each passage consists of four/five sentences. The sentences in each passage have been jumbled up. These are labelled P, Q, R, S and T. You are required to find out the proper sequence of the sentences and mark accordingly on the Answer Sheet.

1. **P :** You couldn't have asked for a nicer, more respectable-looking fellow than Jack, the day he arrived in town for grandpa's funeral.

   **Q :** He'd just arrived that morning, got the word that the old Judge was gone' he said.

   **R :** He rode into the yard on his motorbike - the one he'd sold last summer, which wasn't a patch on the big red one he'd bought later.

   **S :** He was glad he was in time for the services. He sat with Paresh all through the funeral; he even cried - or if it wasn't crying, it was a darned good show.

   The proper sequence should be

   (a) QRPS (b) QRSP
   (c) SPQR (d) PRQS

2. **P :** Anything to do with his parents had always been vague to Manish.

   **Q :** He had been too young to remember them; he only knew the story of the fatal weekend at the Airondack camel and the overturned canoe.

   **R :** Then, as the years swept by and the tragedy faded into time, they began taking him there; and the lake again became a quite lake in the foothills' a camping place where the three of them had a good time.

   **S :** Grandpa had still owned the camp a long while afterwards he and Grandma hadn't gone there.

   The proper sequence should be

   (a) PQRS (b) QRSP
   (c) PQSR (d) QPSR

3. **P :** The role of Western values in contemporary Indian society is a subject on which I have pondered for years.

   **Q :** Moreover, various stakeholders of our company - employees, investors, customers and vendors - come from across the globe.

   **R :** An organisation is representative of society, and some of the lessons that I have learnt from the West regarding values are, I think, applicable to us as a nation. Here are some of them:

   **S :** I come from a company that is built on strong values.

   **T :** In dealing with them over the years, I have come to appreciate several aspects of the West's value system.

   The proper sequence should be

   (a) PQSTR (b) PSQTR
   (c) SQTRP (d) SQRPT

4. **P :** "To play great music," he said, "you must keep your eyes on a distant star."

   **Q :** Eleven years old, I was taking a violin lesson with Georges Enesco, my teacher, in his Paris studio.

   **R :** At the time, I took this to mean, simply, "Give your very best to every piece."

   **S :** A deep-chested, powerful man with a rugged, gentle face, Enesco looked at me across the violin he held under his chin, and shook his bow.

   The proper sequence should be

   (a) QPRS (b) QSPR
   (c) SPRQ (d) SPQR

5. **P :** On the one hand, I want very much for someone else to clean our house, as neither I nor my husband, Ed, has shown any aptitude for it.

   **Q :** No one but me, for instance, should have to clean up the dental floss heaped up like spaghetti near the wastebasket where I toss it each night, never catching on that floss is not something that can be thrown with a high degree ot accuracy.

   **R :** On the other hand, I'd feel guilt in flicting such distasteful drudgery on another human being.

   **S :** Have always wanted and not wanted a cleaning person.

   The proper sequence should be

   (a) SPRQ (b) RQPS
   (c) RPQS (d) PQSR

## ANSWERS

**1.** (d) **2.** (c) **3.** (b) **4.** (b) **5.** (a)

## EXPLANATIONS

1. Statement P introduces the topic. It says that Jack arrived in town for grandpa's funeral. Statement R says, "he rode into the yard on his motorbike ..." The 'he' in statement R refers to Jack in statement P. Hence, R follows P. Statement Q follows next since it refers to the demise of the old judge who is the grandfather of Jack. Statement S comes last since the statement refers to his presence during the funeral service.

2. Statement P introduces the topic. Statement Q follows statement P. The 'he' in statement P actually refers to Manish. Statement S is followed by statement R because statement R speaks of the camp which was visited by Manish and his grandparents.

3. Statement P introduces the topic. Statement S talks about the narrator's background which logically follows statement P. Statement Q is a continuation of statement S. The transition word 'Moreover' hints towards that. Statement T talks about the Western world's value system and statement R further talks about the values of the Western world. Hence, statement R comes last.
4. Statement Q introduces the topic. Statement S describes the violin teacher Georges Enesco. Statement P is an advice by Georges Enesco and Statement R is the reaction of the narrator to this advice.
5. Statement S introduces the topic and reflects the requirement of a person who can clean. Statement P follows statement S. Statement P portrays the requirement of the narrator while Statement R reflects the narrator's guilt when she asks someone to clean the house. Hence, statements P and R are a pair. Statement Q comes last because it sums up the paragraph.

## READING COMPREHENSION

**Directions (Q. 1 - 6) :** The questions in this section are based on the passage. The questions are to be answered on the basis of what is **stated** or **implied** in the passage. For some of the questions, more than one of the choices could conceivabiy answer the question. However, you are to choose the best answer; that is, the response that most accurately and completely answers the questions.

The Constitution ofthe United States protects both property rights and freedom of speech. At times these rights conflict. Resolution then requires a determination as to the type of property involved. If the property is private and not open to the general public, the owner may absolutely deny the exercise of the right of free speech thereon. On the other hand, if public land is at issue, the First Amendment protections of expression are applicable. However, the exercise of free speech thereon is not absolute. Rather it is necessary to determine the appropriateness of the forum. This requires that consideration be given to a number of factors including: character and normal use of the property, the extent to which it is open to the public, and the number and types of persons who frequent it. If the forum is clearly public or clearly private, the resolution of the greater of rights is relatively straight forward.

In the area of quasi-public property, balancing these rights has produced a dilemma. This is the situation when a private owner permits the general public to use his property. When persons seek to use the land for passing out handbills or picketing, how is a conflict between property rights and freedom of expression resolved?

The precept that a private property owner surrenders his rights in proportion to the extent to which he opens up his property to the public is not new. In 1675, Lord Chief Justice Hale wrote that when private property is "affected with a public interest, it ceases to be private.' Throughout the development of Anglo-American law, the individual has never possessed absolute dominion over property. Land becomes clothed with a public interest when the owner devotes his property to a use in which the public has an interest in support of this position the chairman of the board of the Wilde Lake Shopping Centre in Columbia, Maryland said :

The only real purpose and justification of any of these centres is to serve the people in the area-not the merchants, not the developers, not the architects. The success or tailure of a regional shopping centre will be measured by what it does for the people it seeks to serve.

These doctrines should be applied when accommodation must be made between a shopping centre owner's private property rights and the public's right to free expression. It is hoped that when the Court is asked to balance these conflicting rights it will keep in mind what Justice Black said in 1945: "When we balance the constitutional rights of owners of property against those of the people to enjoy (First Amendment) freedom(s) ..... we remain mindful of the fact that the latter occupy a preferred position."

1. In which one of the following cases would the owner of the property probably be most free to restrict the freedom of speech ?
   (a) an amusement park attended by five million people each year owned by a multinational company.
   (b) a small grocery shopping mall owned by a husband and wife
   (c) an enclosed shopping mall owned by a single woman
   (d) an eight-unit residential apartment building owned by a large real estate company
2. A conflict between property rights and freedom of speech might arise in all of the following situations, EXCEPT
   (a) protestors carrying signs outside a cinema in an enclosed shopping mall
   (b) a disgruntled employee passing out leaflets in front of a hairdresser's salon
   (c) a religious order soliciting funds and converts in the swimming pool area ot a condominium
   (d) a candidate for mayor handing out flyers in front of his opponent's headquarters

3. According to the passage, an owner's freedom to deny freedom of speech on his property is determined by all of the following EXCEPT
   (a) whether or not the land is open to the public
   (b) the nature of and the usual use of the property
   (c) the type of persons who frequents the land
   (d) the nature of character of the owner
4. We can infer from the passage that the author believes that shopping malls in America
   (a) should be in the service of the people who frequent them
   (b) have a right to prohibit distribution of advertising handbills
   (c) have a right to control any distributed materials
   (d) should permit any charitable solicitations
5. According to the passage, the idea that a property owner's rights decline as the property is more used by the general public
   (a) is peculiar to recent Supreme Court decisions
   (b) is attested by a three-hundred-year-old opinion
   (c) conflicts with the idea that property affected with a public interest ceases to be private
   (d) is now universally accepted in Great Britain and in Canada
6. All other things being equal, the courts must
   (a) favour First Amendment rights over property rights
   (b) favour property rights over First Amendment rights
   (c) treat property rights and First Amendment rights equally
   (d) protect property rights of the owners

## ANSWERS

**1.** (d) **2.** (c) **3.** (d) **4.** (a) **5.** (b)
**6.** (a)

## EXPLANATIONS

1. In the first paragraph, the author says that if a property is private and not open to the general public, the owner can restrict the freedom of speech. Options (a), (b) and (c) talk about public places which are open to the general public.
2. 'Quasi-public' property refers to seemingly public property. Options (a), (b) and (d) refer to quasi-public places. Option (c) is not a quasi-public property. Hence, conflict should not arise in the situation mentioned in option (c). Refer to the second paragraph.
3. In the fourth sentence of the first paragraph, the author mentions that if the property is private and not open to the general public, the owner may absolutely deny the exercise of the right of free speech thereon. Hence, it can be assumed that the nature of the character of the owner determines whether the owner will deny the freedom of speech or not.
4. In the second last paragraph, the author mentions that the main purpose of the shopping malls is to serve the people in the area and not the merchants, developers or the architects. Therefore, it can be inferred that the author believes shopping malls in America should be in the service of the people who frequent them.
5. In the third paragraph, the author mentions that in 1675, Lord Chief Justice Hale wrote about private property ceasing to be private when it is affected with a public interest.
6. Refer to the last paragraph of the passage. The author quotes Justice Black who said in 1945 that the courts must favour First Amendment rights over property rights if the two come into conflict.

# REASONING

## VERBAL LOGIC

1. At birth we have no self-image. We cannot distinguish anything from the confusion of light and sound around us. From this beginning of no-dimension, we gradually begin to differentiate our body from our environment and develp a sense of identity, with the realisation that we are a separate and independent human being. We then begin to develop a conscience, the sense of right and wrong. Further, we develop social consciousness, where we become aware that we live with other people. Finally, we develop a sense of values, which is our overall estimation of our worth in the world.

   Which one of the following would be the best completion of this passage?
   (a) The sum total of all these developments we call the self-image or the self-concept.
   (b) This estimation of worth is only relative to our value system.
   (c) Therefore, our social consciousness is dependent on our sense of values.
   (d) The sum total of living with other people and developing a sense of values makes us a total person.

**2.** Violence against racial and religious minority groups increased sharply throughout the country last year, despite a slight decline in state wide figures. Compiling incidents from police departments and private watchdog groups, the County Human Relations Committee reported almost 500 hate crimes in the year, up from only 200 last year. It was the first increase since the committee began to report a yearly figure six years ago. The lower state wide figures are probably in error due to underreporting in other countries; underreporting is the major problem that state surveyors face each year.

All of the following, if true, would support the conclusion or the explanation of the discrepancy in the state and country figures EXCEPT:

(a) The number of hate crimes and those resulting in fatalities has increased in neighbouring states.

(b) Anti-immigration sentiment was fanned this year by an anti-immigration ballot referendum.

(c) Many law-abiding members of minority groups are fearful or distrustful of the police.

(d) All of the countries in the state have active private watchdog groups that carefully monitor hate crimes.

**3.** In the last three years, the numbers of arrests for burglary and robbery in Sandy Beach has declined by more than 30 percent. At the same time, the city has reduced the size of its police force by 25 percent.

Which one of the following helps to resolve an apparant discrepancy in the information above?

(a) Neighbourhood Watch programs have always been active in Sand Beach.

(b) The number of reported burglaries and robberies in Sandy Beach has increased in the last three years.

(c) Compared to other cities in the state, Sandy Beach has one of the lowest crime rates.

(d) Many of the residents of Sandy Beach have installed expensive security systems in their homes.

**4.** To be admitted to Bigshot University, you must have a 3.5 grade-point average (GPA) and a score of 800 on the admission test, a 3.0 GPA and a score of 1,000 on the admission test, or a 2.5 GPA and a score of 1,200 on the admission test. A sliding scale exists for the other scores and GPAs.

Which one of the following is inconsistent with the above?

(a) Jagan was admitted with a 2.7 GPA and a score of 1,100 on the admission test.

(b) No student with a score less than 800 on the admission test and a 3.4 GPA will be admitted.

(c) More applicants had a GPA of 3.5 than had a GPA of 2.5.

(d) Some of the students with a score of less than 1,200 on the admissions test and a GPA of less than 2.5 were admitted.

**5.** Only 75 years ago, the best fishing in the world was the Grand Banks of the North Atlantic. But now overfishig and man's pollution have decimated the area. There will be no fishing industry in the Americas in a few years. The waters off Newfoundland now yield less than the catch of five years ago, and less than one quarter of the total of ten years ago. The cod has almost disappeared. The numbers of fisherman in Newfoundland and New England have declined, and their yearly earnings are now at an all-time low. Yet radar has made fishing methods more efficient than ever.

Which one of the following identifies most clearly a faulty assumption in the reasoning of this passage?

(a) The argument fails to consider that the decline in the catch may be due to factors other than pollution.

(b) The argument assumes that the waters off Newfound land are representative of all the American oceans.

(c) The pollution of the sea may have been caused by natural as well as human forces.

(d) The argument does not allow for the possibility that the catch may increase in size in the next five years.

**6.** A number of lawsuits have been brought against popular singing groups charging that suicidal themes in their songs have led to teenage suicides. So far, the courts have found that the lyrics are protected under the Constitution. But what if this should change and a court decides that suicidal themes in popular songs are dangerous? In fact, the songs that have been charged so far are anti-suicide; they present sardonically the self-destructive behaviour of drinking, drugs, and escape by death. They describe a pitiful state of mind, but they do not endorse it.

Blaming suicide on the arts is nothing new. In the late eighteenth centrury, Goethe's popular novel *The Sorrows of Young Werther* was said to be the cause of a rash of suicides in imitation of the novel's hero. If we begin to hold suicide in books or music responsible for suicides in real life, the operas of Verdi and Puccini will have to go, and *Romeo and Juliet* and *Julius Caesar* will disappear from the high school reading lists.

Which one of the following is an assumption necessary to the author s argument?

(a) A lyric presenting suicide in a favourable light should not have Constitutional protection.

(b) Literature or music cannot directly influence human behaviour

(c) Freedom of speech is most threatened by our personal freedom

(d) The audience, not the performer, is responsible for the audience's actions.

**7.** Archaeologists have come to the support of Arctic anthropologists. A small minority of anthropologists assert that stone Age tribes of the Arctic domesticated wolves and trained them to haul sleds. Excavations have recently found evidence to support this claim. Archaeologists have found wolf bones near the site of a Stone Age village. They have also found walrus bones that might have been used on primitive sleds. The small minority of anthropologists believe that their theories have been proved.

Which one of the foliowing is true of the evidence cited in the paragraph above ?

(a) It conclusively contradicts the anthropologists' conclusions.

(b) It neither supports nor refutes the anthropologist' conclusions positivety.

(c) It conclusively supports only a part of the anthropologists' conclusions.

(d) It supports the anthropologists' conclusions authoritatively.

**Direction (Q. 8 - 11):** Each question contains four arguments of three sentences each. Choose the set in which the third statement is a logical conclusion of the first two.

**8.** (1) Some bikes are mopeds. All mopeds are scooters. Some bikes are scooters.

(2) All children are hairs. No hairs are red. No children are red.

(3) No pencil is pen. Some pens are markers. Some pencils are markers.

(4) Every man has a wife. All wives are devoted. No devoted has a husband.

(a) (1), (2), and (3) (b) (1) and (2)

(c) (3) and (2) (d) (1), (2), (3) and (4)

**9.** (1) No moon is not red. All stars are moon. All stars are red.

(2) All doors are open. No open is outdoors. All door are not outdoors.

(3) No Japanese can fire. All Chinese are books. Japanese and Chinese can fight.

(4) No A is B. No B is C. No A is C.

(a) (1) only (b) (2) only

(c) (1) and (2) only (d) (4) only

**10.** (1) All envelopes are rectangles. All rectangles are rectangular. All envelopes are rectangular.

(2) Some things are smart. Some smart things are tiny. Some things are tiny.

(3) Learneds are well read. Well read know. Learneds know.

(4) Dieting is good for health. Healthy foods are rare. Dieting is rare.

(a) (4) only (b) (3) only

(c) Both (1) and (3) (d) All of these

**11.** (1) Shahrukh is an actor. Some actors are pretty. Shahrukh is pretty.

(2) Some executives are soldiers. All soldiers are patriotic.

(3) All cricketers are patriotic. Some executives are soldiers. Some executives are patriotic.

(4) All actors are pretty. Shahrukh is not an actor. Shahrukh is not pretty.

(a) (4) only (b) (2) only

(c) (1) only (d) (2) and (3)

**Direction (Q. 12 - 14) :** Each question has a main statement, followed by four statements labelled. I, II, III and IV. Choose the ordered pair of statement, where the first statement implies the second, and the two statements are logically consistent with the main statement.

**12.** Whenever Vijay reads late into the night, his grandfather reprimands him.

I. His grandfather does not reprimand Vijay.

II. Vijay reads late into the night.

III. Vijay reads early in the morning.

IV. Vijay's grandfather reprimands him in the morning

(a) III,IV (b) II,IV

(c) I, II (d) none of the above

**13.** Either Amir is angry, or he shows mock anger.

I. Amir shows mock anger.

II. Amir is angry.

III. Amir does not show mock anger.

IV. Amir is not angry.

(a) III, II only (b) IV, I only

(c) I, II only (d) III, II and IV, I

**14.** Every player will become a champ.

I. Rajesh is a player.

II. Rajesh will become champ.

III. Rajesh is not a player.

IV. Rajesh will not become a champ.

(a) I, IV (b) IV, I

(c) III, IV (d) IV, III

**Direction (Q. 15 - 18) :** The question given below has a statement followed by two courses of action numbered I and II. You have to assume everything in the statement to be true. Then decide which of the two suggested course of action logically follows for pursuing.

Mark answer as :

(a) If only I follows

(b) If only II follows

(c) II both I and II follows

(d) It neither I follows nor II follows

**15. Statement:**

The number of people who die on the roads every year is so alarming that the numbers every year are also close to the numbers which can be attributed to the major diseases of the world.

**Course of Action :**

I. There should be an active campaign for sensitising people towards road safety norms.

II. There should be an increased emphasis on enforcing speed limits, road safety rules and traffic management on roads across the world.

**16. Statement:**

An unacceptable number of children die during the first year of their lives. The high incidence of infant death is a major cause for concern for the health ministry.

**Course of Action :**

I. All government hospitals should be privatized to improve health care facilities.

II. Government should commit higher levels of their budget to health services.

**17. Statement:**

The cream of India's Cricket team is likely to retire in the next three years leaving a vacuum which the Indian Cricket team is going to struggle to overcome.

**Course of Action :**

I. The BCCI should start to induct youngsters into the team and start to give them exposure to pressure situations.

II. There should be a rotation policy adopted for senior players in order to prolong their careers and keep them injury free.

**18. Statement:**

The lack of employment and income during economic depression leads to an increase in the crime rates.

**Course of Action :**

I. The government should provide an unemployment compensation as done in advanced countries.

II. The government should encourage greater economic activity and increase the number of industries in order to reduce crime rates.

## ANSWERS

| | | | | |
|---|---|---|---|---|
| **1.** (a) | **2.** (d) | **3.** (b) | **4.** (d) | **5.** (b) |
| **6.** (d) | **7.** (b) | **8.** (b) | **9.** (c) | **10.** (c) |
| **11.** (b) | **12.** (d) | **13.** (d) | **14.** (d) | **15.** (c) |
| **16.** (b) | **17.** (c) | **18.** (c) | | |

## EXPLANATIONS

**1.** Option (a) sums up the entire essence of the passage. The passage deals with the different stages of emotional and psychological development. Option (a) offers the perfect conclusion to the discussion. "These developments" in option (a) indicate that certain developments in the passage are being referred to. The "developments" are mentioned in the passage. Option (b) introduces additional information. However, it does not conclude the passage. Option (c) cannot be inferred. Similarly, option (d) does not offer the perfect ending to the discussion.

**2.** Option (d) does not support the above premise. If there were active watchdog groups, hate crimes would certainly have been lesser and there wouldn't have been any discrepancy in the figures. Options (a), (b) and (c) offer an explanation. If the crime rate in neighboring states has increased, there would be a discrepancy between the state and county figures. Therefore, option (a) can be rejected. Similarly, if there was an anti-immigration sentiment going on, discrepancy between the figures of state and county would be evident. Hence, option (b) can be ruled out. If people do not trust law enforcement agencies, reports of crimes would be lesser and this can lead to a disparity in crime figures between states and counties.

**3.** If it is assumed that burglaries and robberies in Sandy Beach have increased in the last three years, the information can explain the apparent discrepancy in the data provided in the statement. Options (a), (c) and (d) do not mention any timeframe. Thus, it is impossible to infer whether the cited measures have been instrumental in curbing the crime figures.

**4.** Option (d) cannot be calculated. We do not know what score and GPA are being referred to. Less than 1200 and less than 2.5 can mean any number below the cited figures. Hence, the information given is insufficient and therefore, inconsistent with the provided data. The data do not provide any benchmark or cut-off mark. Furthermore, the data given in option (d) is contradicting the trend mentioned in the paragraph. A student with a score of less than 1200 should have a GPA of more than 2.5 to be admitted. The other options offer specific data which can be calculated and are in line with the given trend.

5. Option (b) is a wrong assumption. It is incorrect to infer that Newfoundland reflects the entire scenario in and around America. The passage does not discuss any factor other than over fishing and pollution. Hence, option (a) cannot be the answer. Option (c) is categorically stated in the second sentence while option (d) is a possibility even if we take into account the declining number of fishes.

6. Option (d) if assumed, is necessary for the author's argument. The author believes that literature or art cannot influence human behavior. Had it been the case, *Romeo and Juliet* and other works would have been banned. Option (a) if assumed negates the argument. Option (a) is exactly opposite of what the author says. Option (b) cannot be inferred because the author does not talk about human behavior being influenced by literature or music per se. Instead, he states that literature or music cannot be held responsible if a person commits suicide. Option (c) appears to be too generic, wide in scope and out of context.

7. Option (b) is the answer because a few anthropologists believe that their findings have been proved. It means other anthropologists have different views about the findings. Thus, it is not very clear at the moment whether the findings positively support or refute the anthropologists' conclusions. Option (a) cannot be true because the evidence is not contradicting the anthropologists' conclusions. Rather, the evidence has encouraged a small section of anthropologists to believe that their theories have been proved. Option (c) cannot be the answer because some anthropologists believe that their conclusions have been entirely proved by the archaeologists' findings. Option (d) cannot be true because the last sentence mentions that only a small minority of anthropologists believe that their theories have been substantiated. Hence, there is an iota of doubt in the findings.

8. Refer to the venn diagrams given below:

(1)

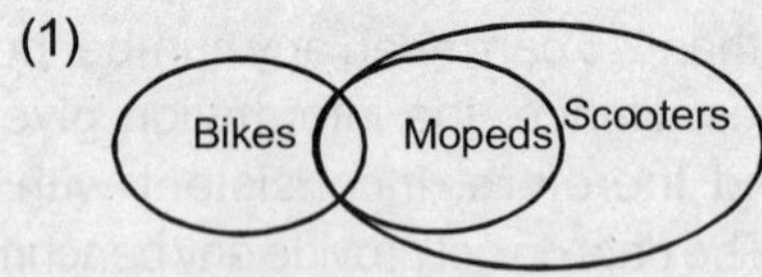


(2)

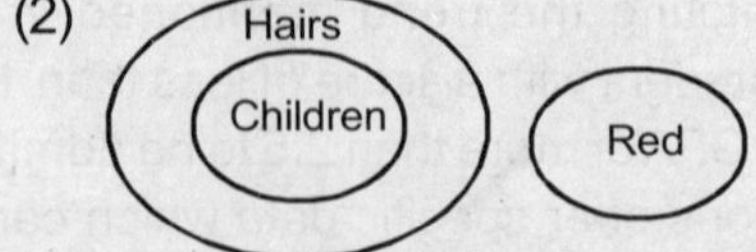


9. Refer to the venn diagrams given below:

(1)

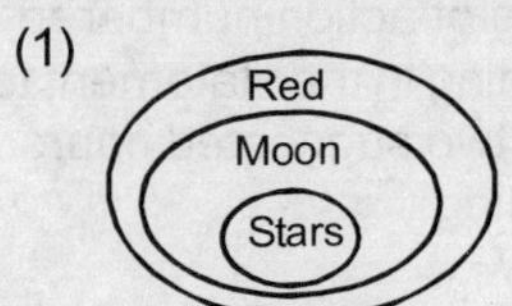


(2)

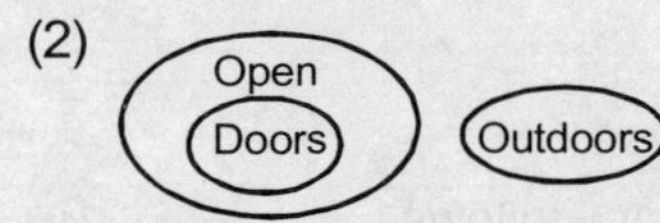


10. Refer to the venn diagrams given below:

(1)

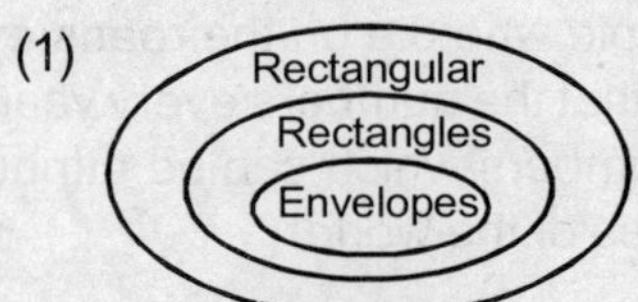


(3)

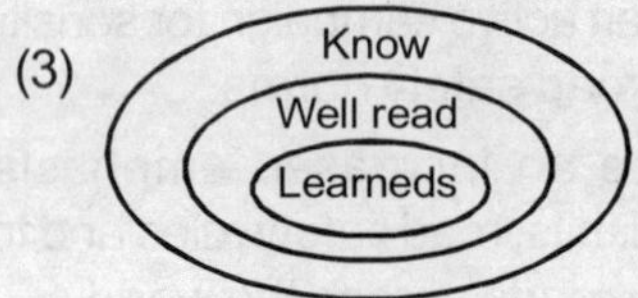


11. Refer to the venn diagram given below:

(2)

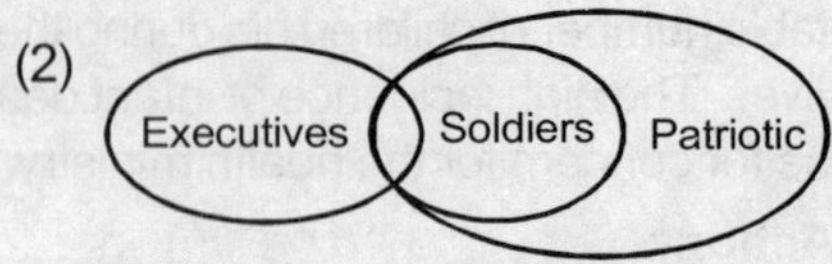


12. The given statement is like an 'if..then' clause. Options (a) and (b) are negated because the statement does not talk about the grandfather reprimanding Vijay 'in the morning'. If the effect does not happen, we can be sure that the cause did not exist. So, option (c) can also be ruled out. So, the correct answer is option (d).

13. The given statement means that Amir is in only one of the two situations at a time: angry and show mock anger. If Amir is angry, he is not showing mock anger and if Amir is not angry, he is showing mock anger. So, the correct answer is option (d).

14. This statement is like an 'if..then' clause. If the cause happens, the effect will happen but if the effect happens, we cannot be sure of the cause. Similarly, we cannot be sure that if the cause does not happen, the effect will also not happen. So, options (a), (b) and (c) are ruled out. . If the effect does not happen, we can be sure that the cause did not exist. So, the correct answer is option (d).

15. Both statements I and II address the issue of road safety and can certainly bring fatalities related to road accidents. Hence, option (c) is the correct answer.

16. Statement I is incorrect because we cannot infer that government hospitals lack infrastructure. Hence, statement I can be rejected. However, statement II is a possible course of action and government intervention in the form of allotting more funds for the betterment of health services can be a way to address the issue.

17. Both the courses of action are valid. BCCI can certainly play a pivotal role in the development of new talent in cricket. Furthermore, a rotation policy is a very good idea to help the senior players stay in shape, remain free from injuries and play for a longer time. This in turn, will avert a possible vacuum in the Indian cricket team.

18. Both statements I and II are valid courses of action. If the government provides a compensation package for the unemployed people, it will help them deal with lack of income. This in turn, will lead to a decline in the crime rate. Similarly, statement II is valid because a greater economic activitythat combines with growth of industry will help in generating employment and income which can again lead to a reduction in the crime graph.

## ANALYTICAL REASONING

**Direction (Q. 1 - 6) :** Each group of questions is based on a set of conditions. Choose the response that most accurately and completely answers each question.

A science student has exactly four flasks-1, 2, 3 and 4-originally containing a red, a blue, a green and an orange chemical, respectively. An experiment consists of mixing exactly two of these chemicals together by completely emptying the contents of one of the flasks into another of the flasks. The following conditions apply;

The product of an experiment cannot be used in further experiments.

Mixing the contents of 1 and 2 produces a red chemical.

Mixing the contents of 2 and 3 produces an orange chemical.

Mixing the contents of 3 with the contents of either 1 or 4 produces a blue chemical.

Mixing the contents of 4 with the contents of either 1 or 2 produces a green chemical.

1. If the student performs exactly one experiment, which one of the following could be the colours of the chemicals in resulting three non-empty flasks ?
   (a) blue, blue, green
   (b) blue, orange, orange
   (c) blue, orange, red
   (d) green, green, red

2. If the student performs exactly two experiments, which one of the following could be the colours of the chemicals in the resulting two non-emptv flasks ?
   (a) blue, blue (b) blue, orange
   (c) blue, red (d) green, red

3. If the student performs exactly one experiment and none of the resulting three non-empty flasks contains a red chemical, which one of the following could be the colours of the chemicals in the three flasks ?
   (a) blue, blue, green
   (b) blue, green, green
   (c) blue, green , orange
   (d) blue, orange, orange

4. If the student performs exactly one experiment and exactly one of the resulting three non-empty flasks contains a blue chemical, which one of the following must be the colours of the chemicals in other two flasks ?
   (a) both green (b) both orange
   (c) both red (d) one green and one red

5. If the students will perform exactly two experiments and after the first experiment exactly one of the resulting three non-empty flasks contains an orange chemical, then in the second experiment the student could mix together the contents of flasks
   (a) 1 and 2 (b) 1 and 3
   (c) 2 and 3 (d) 3 and 4

6. If the student performs exactly one experiment and none of the resulting three none-empty flasks contains an orange chemical, then the student must have mixed the
   (a) flask 1 with flask 2
   (b) flask 2 with flask 4
   (c) flask 2 with one of the other flasks
   (d) flask 4 with one of the other flasks

**Direction (Q, 7 - 9):** Read the following information carefully and answer the questions given below.

In a joint family of seven persons L, M, N, O, P, Q and R, two are married couple. 'R' is a housewife and her husband is a lawyer. 'N' is the wife of 'M', 'L' is an engineer and is the grand-daughter of 'R' and 'O' is the father-in-law of 'N', a doctor, and father of 'P', a professor. 'Q' is L's brother and M's son.

7. How is P related to M ?
   (a) Son (b) Brother
   (c) Daughter (d) Uncle

**8.** How is Q related to O ?

(a) Grandfather (b) Uncle
(c) Grandson (d) brother

**9.** Who is M's father ?

(a) O (b) R
(c) N (d) P

**Direction (Q. 10 - 12) :** Read the following information carefully and answer the questions given below.

The city K is 30 km to the southeast of Z while Y is 50 km to the northwest of K. Also, H is 38 km to the southeast of Y. L lies in the direct route between Y and K and its distance from H is 14 km. G also lies on this route and is exactly midway between L and Y.

**10.** A car starting from K at 9 a.m. and running at a constant speed towards Y reaches H at 9.24 a.m. and then reaches G at

(a) 9.18 a.m. (b) 10.16 a.m.
(c) 10.36 a.m. (d) 10.42 a.m.

**11.** If M is 1 km to the southeast of L, then it is exactly midway between

(a) H and L (b) Y and K
(c) H and Z (d) None of these

**12.** The distance from G to H is

(a) 26 km (b) 24 km
(c) 12 km (d) 16 km

**Direction (Q. 13 - 17):** Read the questions below very carefully and choose the correct answer.

On an island 'Neverland' the inhabitants always answer any question with two sentences - one of which is always true and the other always false.

Perhaps due to this peculiar habit, there's been a high rate of suicides on the island. As a doctor, you have to identify potentially suicidal people and counsel them. You know that all people who are suicidal feel that the life is futile. On questioning three inhabitants, these are the answers you get:

Anuj : Himanshu is suicidal. I am not suicidal.
Himanshu : I do not want to die. Akshay does not want to die.
Akshay : Life is futile. I am suicidal.

**13.** Who among the three is suicidal ?

(a) Akshay
(b) Himanshu
(c) Himanshu and Akshay
(d) None of these

**14.** Which one of them is lying about another person's tendencies ?

(a) Akshay (b) Himanshu
(c) Anuj and Himanshu (d) Anuj

Going around the village, you come across three people. One of them is a dentist, one is a barrister and one is a professor. You want to know who is who.

Peter : I am not a professor. Shina is not a professor.
Matt : Peter is not a barrister. Shina is a professor.
Shina : Peter is not a dentist. I am not a professor.

**15.** Which of the following is true ?

(a) Shina is the professor
(b) Peter is the dentist
(c) Matt is the barrister
(d) None of the above

Further, you come across three women, one of whom is an excellent singer. You start questioning them, when you notice that Minaxi is wearing a flower in her hair.

Madhuri : I am not the singer. The singer wears a flower in her hair.
Minaxi : I am the singer. The singer is amongst us.
Jaya : Madhuri is the singer. Minaxi is not the singer.

**16.** Who is the singer ?

(a) Madhuri
(b) Minaxi
(c) Jaya
(d) Cannot be ascertained

You want to expand your horizons and decide to go to the village of "Where is Who" which is deep inside the island. You come the border of "Kya Kya" and see a road sign. One leads to left and the other right. Threre are no other roads. You ask the inhabitants.

Maroof : I do not speak to the strangers. I am new to these parts.
Nafish : Take road to the right. I am married to Ayesha.
Ayesha : I am not Nafish's wife. Maroof is not new to these parts.

**17.** Which one of the following is true ?

(a) The road to the right leads to "Where is Who"?
(b) The road to the left leads to "Where is Who"?
(c) Nafish is married to Ayesha
(d) None of the above

## ANSWERS

| | | | | |
|---|---|---|---|---|
| **1.** (d) | **2.** (c) | **3.** (b) | **4.** (a) | **5.** (d) |
| **6.** (d) | **7.** (b)* | **8.** (c) | **9.** (a) | **10.** (b) |
| **11.** (b) | **12.** (a) | **13.** (d) | **14.** (*) | **15.** (a) |
| **16.** (c) | **17.** (a) | | | |

## EXPLANATIONS

**For questions 1 to 6:** The initial colours of the chemicals is as follows

| Flask | Colour |
|---|---|
| 1 | Red |
| 2 | Blue |
| 3 | Green |
| 4 | Orange |

The final results of various experiments are shown below:

| Experiment No | Experiments | Final colour | Colors in rest of two flask |
|---|---|---|---|
| 1 | Mixing 1 and 2 | Red | Green, Orange |
| 2 | Mixing 2 and 3 | Orange | Red, Orange |
| 3 | Mixing 3 and 1 | Blue, | Blue, Orange |
| 4 | Mixing 3 and 4 | Blue | Blue, Red |
| 5 | Mixing 4 and 1 | Green | Blue, Green |
| 6 | Mixing 4 and 2 | Green | Red, Green |

1. From the above table we can say that option (d) is correct.
2. If a student preforms two experiments then it can be (i) Experiment number 1 and 4, (ii) Experiment number 2 and 5 and (iii) Experiment number 3 and 6. Among given options (c) is correct.
3. According to condition experiment number 3 or 4 are possible.

**For questions 7 to 9:** Family relation is shown below:

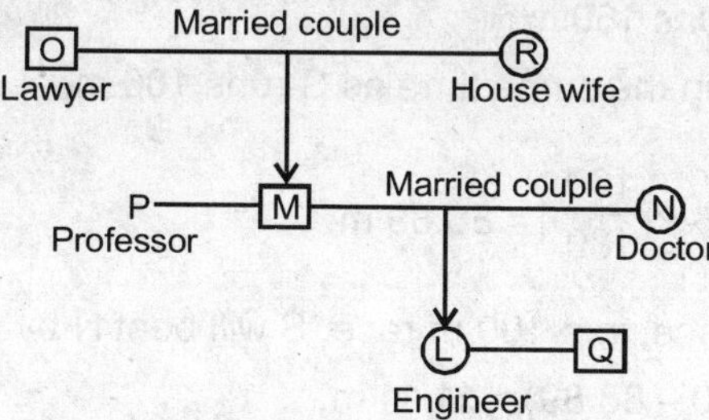


7. P is either brother or sister of M.
8. Q is grandson of O.
9. O is the father of M.

**For questions 10 to 12:** The position of cities is shown below:

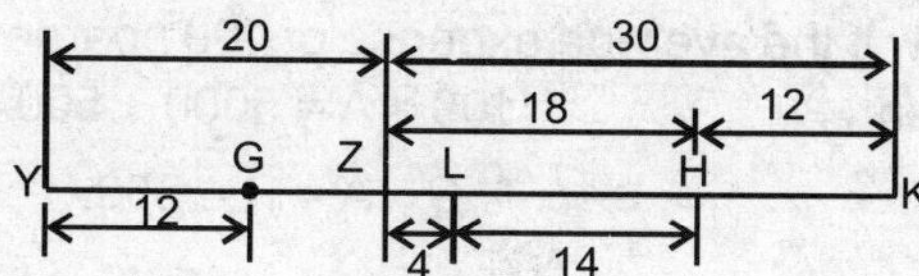


10. The speed of the car $= \frac{12}{24} = 0.5$ km/min.

    The time taken to reach G from K $= \frac{38}{0.5} = 76$ min

    Hence, the required time is 10:16 a.m.
11. If m is 1 km to the south-east of L, then it is exactly midway between Y and K.
12. The distance from G to H is 26 km.
13. The correct answer is option (d) because Anuj and Himanshu are suicidal. The official answer key is (a) which is wrong.
14. No one is lying about other person tendencies. Which is not given in the any option.
15. According to Peter's statement either Peter or Shina is professor. If Peter is professor, then both statement of Shina will be true, which is not possible. Therefore, Shina is the professor.
16. Start with Minaxi's statement: If the first statement is true, then the second becomes also true, which is not possible (because one is true and one is false). The first statement of Minaxi is false it means she is not the singer. Now come to Jaya statement, her second statement is true so the first must be false, hence Madhuri is also not the singer. Therefore, Jaya is the singer
17. Start with Maroof statement: The first statement must be false, (because he is talking to strange and saying that he does not speak to the stranger), so his second statement is true it means Maroof is new to these part.. Now come to Ayesha's statements: The second statement of Ayesha is false, so first must be true, it means she is not the wife Nafish. Now come to Nafish statement, his second statement is false so the first must be true. Hence, the road to the left leads to "Where is Who".

# QUANTITATIVE APTITUDE

## ARITHMETIC

1. A piece of string is 40 centimetres long. It is cut into three pieces. The longest piece is 3 times as long as the middle-sized and the shortest piece is 23 centimetres shorter than the longest piece. Find length of the shortest piece (in cm).

   (a) 27cm (b) 5 cm

   (c) 4 cm (d) 9 cm
2. Fresh grapes contain 90% water by weight while dried grapes contain 20% water by weight. What is the weight of dry grapes available from 20 kg of fresh grapes ?

   (a) 2 kg (b) 2.4 kg

   (c) 2.5 kg (d) 2.6 kg

3. A group of men decided to do a job in 8 days. But since 10 men dropped out every day, the job got completed at the end of the 12[th] day. How many men were there at the beginning ?
(a) 165 (b) 175
(c) 80 (d) none of these

4. In a race of 200 m run, A beats S by 20 m and N by 40 m. If S and N are running a race of 100 m with exactly same speed as before, then by how many metres will S beat N ?
(a) 11.11 m (b) 10 m
(c) 12 m (d) 25 m

5. Total expenses of a boarding house are partly fixed and partly varying linearly with the number of boarders. The average expense per boarder is Rs. 700 when there are 25 boarders and Rs. 600 when there are 50 boarders. What is the average expense per boarder when there are 100 boarders ?
(a) Rs. 550 (b) Rs. 580
(c) Rs. 540 (d) Rs. 570

6. Three maths classes: X, Y and Z take an algebra test. The average score of class X is 83. The average score of class Y is 76. The average score of class Z is 85. The average score of class X and Y is 79 and average score of class Y and Z is 81. What is the average score of classes X, Y and Z ?
(a) 81.5 (b) 80.5
(c) 83 (d) 78

7. You can collect rubies and emeralds as many as you can. Each ruby is worth Rs. 4 crore and each emerald is worth of Rs. 5 crore. Each ruby weighs 0.3 kg and each emerald weighs 0.4 kg. Your bag can carry at the most 12 kg. What you should collect to get the maximum wealth?
(a) 20 rubies and 15 emeralds
(b) 40 rubies
(c) 28 rubies and 9 emeralds
(d) none of these

8. A man has 9 friends: 4 boys and 5 girls. In how many ways can he invite them, if there have to be exactly 3 girls in the invitee's list ?
(a) 320 (b) 160
(c) 80 (d) 200

## ANSWERS

**1.** (c) **2.** (c) **3.** (a)* **4.** (a) **5.** (a)
**6.** (a) **7.** (b) **8.** (b)

## EXPLANATIONS

1. Let the largest piece $= 3x$

Middle $= x$

Shortest $= 3x - 23$

$\therefore \quad 3x + x + (3x - 23) = 40$

$\Rightarrow \quad x = 9$

$\therefore$ the shortest piece $= 3(9) - 23$

$= 4$

2. 20 kg fresh grapes will contain $(0.9 \times 20) = 18$ kg water and 2 kg mass. If the dry grape has to contain 2 kg mass, it should constitute 80% of that. Hence, if 80% of dry grapes corresponds to 2 kg, its total weight will be $\left(\frac{2}{0.8}\right) = 2.5$ kg.

3. If x men were there on day one, there would be $(x - 110)$men on the 12th day.

Hence, on an average, there were $(x - 55)$ men.

The job takes $\frac{3}{2}$ times the normal time.

Hence, the average number of people $= \frac{2}{3}$.

$\Rightarrow \quad x - 55 = \frac{2}{3}x$

Hence, $\quad x = 165$

The official answer key is (d), which is wrong.

4. In the same time as A runs 200 m in the race, S runs 180 m and N runs 160 m.

In other words, in the same time as S runs 180 m, N runs 160 m.

So in the same time as S runs 100 m, N will run

$\left(100 \times \frac{160}{180}\right) = 88.89$ m.

Hence, in a 100 m race, S will beat N by $(100 - 88.89) = 11.11$ m.

5. Let x be the fixed cost and y the variable cost. Then,

$17500 = x + 25y \quad \ldots(i)$

$30000 = x + 50y \quad \ldots(ii)$

Solving the equation (i) and (ii), we get

$x = 5000, y = 500$

Now if the average expense of 100 boarders be 'A'.

Then, $\quad 100 \times A = 5000 + 500 \times 100$

$\Rightarrow \quad A = $ Rs. 550.

6. Let the number of students in classes X, Y and Z be a, b and c respectively. Then,

total of X = 83a; total of Y = 76b; total of Z = 85c

Also $\frac{83a+76b}{a+b} = 79 \Rightarrow 4a = 3b;$

and $\frac{76b+85c}{b+c} = 81 \Rightarrow 4c = 5b$

Hence, $b = \frac{4}{3}a,\ c = \frac{5}{4}b = \frac{5}{4} \times \frac{4}{3}a = \frac{5}{3}a$

Average of X, Y and Z

$$= \frac{83a + 76b + 85c}{a+b+c}$$

$$= \frac{83a + 76 \times \frac{4}{3}a + 85 \times \frac{5}{3}a}{a + \frac{4}{3}a + \frac{5}{3}a}$$

$$= \frac{978}{12} = 81.5$$

7. To maximise the value of the wealth, we must carry more of the one whose value per kilogram is more. Value per kilogram of ruby

$$= \left(\frac{4}{0.3}\right)$$

= Rs 13.33 crore, and value per rupee of each emerald

$$= \left(\frac{5}{0.4}\right) = \text{Rs. } 12.5 \text{ crore.}$$

It is obvious that we should carry entire 12 kg of ruby. This would amount to $\left(\frac{12}{0.3}\right) = 40$ rubies.

8. Out of the 5 girls, 3 girls can be invited in $^5C_3$ ways. Nothing is mentioned about the number of boys that he has to invite. He can invite one, two, three, four or even no boys. Each boy can be invited or not. He can invite them in $2^4$ ways. Thus, the total number of ways is

$^5C_3 \times (2)^4 = 10 \times 16 = 160.$

# GENERAL KNOWLEDGE

## CONSTITUTION AND POLITY

1. Election Commission (EC) has announced to launch Electoral Roll Authentication Mission (ERAM) and Purification Drive. What is the aim of the mission ?
(a) To enlist all the eligible voters in voters list
(b) To create awareness about the voting right
(c) To weed out bogus voters from the voters list
(d) (a) and (c)

## ANSWER

1. (c)

## EXPLANATION

1. Election Commission (EC) on has announced to launch Electoral Roll Authentication Mission (ERAM) and Purification Drive in order to weed out bogus voters from the voters list.

## CURRENT AFFAIRS

1. Which State has become first to fix minimum educational qualification for panchayat polls ?
(a) Kerala (b) Gujarat
(c) Rajasthan (d) Karnataka

2. Which country was chosen to chair Partnership in Population and Development (PPD) for the year 2015 ?
(a) India (b) China
(c) SriLanka (d) Ghana

3. Recently, the Prime Minister has launched the "Give it Up" campaign for voluntarily giving up
(a) use of tobacco products
(b) use of plastic
(c) LPG subsidy
(d) black money

4. Who bagged the best actress award at the 62nd National Film Awards ?
(a) Priyanka Chopra (b) Vidya Balan
(c) Kangana Ranaut (d) Rani Mukherji

5. Simona Halep, who has won the Indian Wells Open Tennis Women's Singles Title 2015, hails from which country ?
(a) Belgium (b) Romania
(c) Switzerland (d) Sweden

6. The winner of prestigious Dadasaheb Phalke Award 2014 is
(a) Mohan Lal (b) Shashi Kapoor
(c) Mani Ratnam (d) Girish Karnad

7. Recently, the Union Government has appointed Amitabh Bachchan as the brand ambassador for its campaign against which disease ?
(a) Swine Flu
(b) Tuberculosis
(c) Hepatitis B
(d) Diabetes

**8.** Which Country has launched the "Let Girls Learn" initiative aimed at educating 62 million girls around the World ?

(a) United States
(b) New Zealand
(c) India
(d) Australia

**9.** Which among the following parties declared victory in the 2015 Israel Legislative Election ?

(a) Zionist Union (b) Likud
(c) Yesh Atid (d) Joint List

**10.** What is the name of the innovative Council proposed in the Railway Budget -2015 to promote innovation ?

(a) Navachar (b) Rail Tech
(c) Kayakalp (d) Sankalp

**11.** India's rank in the recently released World Press Freedom Index (WPFI) 2015 is

(a) 120 (b) 135
(c) 136 (d) 140

**12.** Recently, UNICEF and which football legend has launched protection fund named "7" to protect the World's most vulnerable youngsters ?

(a) David Beckham (b) Lionel Messi
(c) Christiano Ronaldo (d) Zinedine Zidane

**13.** According to the latest data, which among the following States has attracted maximum Foreign Direct Investment (FDI) in the country ?

(a) Gujarat (b) Tamil Nadu
(c) Maharashtra (d) Karnataka

**14.** Which one of the following countries will hold the presidency of the BRICS New Development Bank for the first six years ?

(a) India (b) China
(c) South Africa (d) Russia

**15.** Which among the following States has won the 10th National Award for Excellence work in Mahatma Gandhi National Rural Employment Guarantee Act ?

(a) Karnataka (b) West Bengal
(c) Haryana (d) Madhya Pradesh

**16.** Who is the newly appointed Chairman of the empowered Committee of State Finance Ministers on Goods & Services Tax (GST) ?

(a) J. K. George
(b) K. M. Mani
(c) Amit Mitra
(d) Saurabh Patel

**17.** What is the code name of the military operation in Yemen against Shia Houthi Group ?

(a) Operation Destruction Storm
(b) Operation Decisive Storm
(c) Operation Desert Storm
(d) Operation Black Star

**18.** Who was sworn in as the President of Sri Lanka in January 2015 ?

(a) Mahinda Deshapriya
(b) Mahinda Rajapaksa
(c) Gotabhaya Rajapaksa
(d) Mithripala Sirisena

**19.** Who won the title Miss India 2015 ?

(a) Aafreen Rachel (b) Vartika singh
(c) Koyal Fana (d) Aditi Arya

**20.** ________, the 'founding father' and 'architect' of modern Singapore passed away on 23 March 2015.

(a) Mr. Lee Kuan Yew
(b) Mr. Lee Hsien Loong
(c) Mr. Lim Hng Kiang
(d) Mr. Lee Li Lian

**21.** What is the name of the party of the Australian Prime Minister Tony Abbott that saw a confidence vote on spilling the top leadership in February 2015 ?

(a) Liberal Party
(b) Australian Greens
(c) Labour Party
(d) Palmer United Party

## ANSWERS

| | | | | |
|---|---|---|---|---|
| **1.** (c) | **2.** (b) | **3.** (c) | **4.** (c) | **5.** (b) |
| **6.** (b) | **7.** (c) | **8.** (a) | **9.** (b) | **10.** (c) |
| **11.** (c) | **12.** (a) | **13.** (c) | **14.** (a) | **15.** (d) |
| **16.** (b) | **17.** (b) | **18.** (d) | **19.** (d) | **20.** (a) |
| **21.** (a) | | | | |

## EXPLANATIONS

**1.** Rajasthan became the first State in the country to fix a minimum educational qualification for contesting elections to the Panchayati Raj Institutions. The State Assembly passed Rajasthan Panchayati Raj (amendment) Bill, 2015, which makes Class VIII pass mandatory for the post of sarpanch except in tribal reserved areas, where the minimum qualification is Class V and Class X for Zila Parishad or Panchayat Samiti elections.

2. China was selected to head the Partnership in Population and Development (PPD), an inter-governmental body promoting South-to-South collaboration in the fields of reproductive health, population and development.
3. Prime Minister of India has launched the Give it Up campaign for voluntarily giving up LPG subsidy. Through this campaign he appealed to well-to-do sections of Indian society to voluntarily give up LPG subsidy, so that the benefit of the same could be shared more widely with poor sections of the society.
4. Bollywood actress Kangana Ranaut has bagged the National award for Best Actress for her performance in Vikas Bahl's 'Queen', which was announced on March 24, 2015.
5. Simona Halep is from Romania.
6. Shashi Kapoor got the prestigious Dada Saheb Phalke award for contribution to Indian Cinema for the year 2014.
7. The government has roped in Amitabh Bachchan as brand ambassador for its campaign against hepatitis B, a critical public health problem facing India.
8. President Barack Obama and first lady Michelle Obama put their weight behind Let Girls Learn, an initiative to help girls around the world attend secondary school and complete their education.
9. The incumbent Prime Minister, Benjamin Netanyahu's Likud party has won the Israel election with Likud party picking up the highest number of votes.
10. Kaya kalp the innovative Council proposed in the Railway Budget 2015 to promote innovation.
11. India has improved its ranking from 140 to 136 in the World Press Freedom Index (WPFI) 2015, released by Reporters Without Borders (RWB).
12. Football legend David Beckham and UNICEF has launched new protection fund '7' to protect the world's most vulnerable youngsters. The fund, named after Beckham's lucky number on his England and Manchester United shirts. The fund will focus on children at risk of violence, abuse or disease.
13. According to the latest data Maharashtra has attracted maximum Foreign Direct Investment (FDI) in the country.
14. The BRICS bank, aimed at funding infrastructure projects in developing nations, will be based in Shanghai, China, and India will preside over its operations for the first six years, followed by five-year terms for Brazil and then Russia, leaders of the five-country group announced at the 6th BRICS - Brazil, Russia, India, China and South Africa - summit.
15. Madhya Pradesh won the 10th National Award for excellent work in Mahatma Gandhi National Rural Employment Guarantee Act, 2005 (MGNREGA) in February 2015.
16. Kerala Finance Minister K M Mani is appointed as the Chairman of the Empowered Committee of State Finance Ministers on Goods and Services Tax (GST).
17. Decisive Storm, is the international war against Houthi militias in Yemen, is currently under way. The international alliance led by Saudi Arabia is currently fighting against the Houthi militants in Yemen.
18. President Maithripala Sirisena was elected as the new President of Sri Lanka in the presidential election held on January 8, 2015.
19. Aditi Arya was crowned fbb Femina Miss India World 2015.
20. First Prime Minister (PM) of Singapore Lee Kuan Yew passed away on 23 March 2015. He was 91. Mr. Lee is described as the 'founding father' and 'architect' of modern Singapore. He is also considered as pioneer for transforming the island country from a small port city into a wealthy global hub after its independence from United Kingdom and separation from Malaysia.
21. Anthony John "Tony" Abbott is the 28th and current Prime Minister of Australia. He has held this position since 2013, and been Leader of the Liberal Party since 2009. Abbott is the Member of Parliament representing the Sydney-based Division of Warringah.

## EVERYDAY SCIENCE

1. Which is the only regenerative organ in human body ?
   (a) Brain (b) Liver
   (c) Pancreas (d) Lungs
2. Lysosomes, which are known as suicidal bags, are produced by which organelle ?
   (a) Mitochondria
   (b) Golgi body
   (c) Ribosome
   (d) Peroxisome

## ANSWERS

1. (b) 2. (b)

## EXPLANATIONS

1. The liver is the only human internal organ capable of natural regeneration of lost tissue; as little as 25% of a liver can regenerate into a whole liver.

2. Lysosomes are called suicide sacks. They are produced by the Golgi body. They consist of a single membrane surrounding powerful digestive enzymes. It acts as the "garbage disposal" of the cell by breaking down cell components that are no longer needed as well as molecules or even bacteria that are ingested by the cell.

## GEOGRAPHY

1. Which part of the World is referred to as the Fertile Crescent ?
   (a) Latin Americas
   (b) South East Asia
   (c) Middle East
   (d) Scandinavia

## ANSWER

**1.** (c)

## EXPLANATION

1. Fertile Crescent is an arc-shaped important event which covers large parts of Middle East. The country in which it falls is Israel, Lebanon, Jordan, Syria and Iraq.

## ECONOMICS

1. Which of the following measures the value of a currency against a basket of other currencies ?
   (a) Real Exchange Rate
   (b) Effective Exchange Rate
   (c) Real Effect Exchange Rate
   (d) Nominal Exchange Rate
2. Which of the following banks launched 'Pocket', India's first digital bank on mobile phones ?
   (a) Axis Bank (b) ICICI Bank
   (c) HDFC Bank (d) SBI

## ANSWERS

**1.** (c) **2.** (b)

## EXPLANATIONS

1. Real Effect Exchange Rate (REER) is the weighted average of a country's currency relative to an index or basket of other major currencies adjusted for the effects of inflation.
2. ICICI Bank, India's largest private sector bank, launched 'Pockets', India's first digital bank for the youth.

## MISCELLANEOUS (QUOTES, DAYS, BOOKS TITLES, SPORTS, BASIC LEGAL CONCEPTS)

1. Which is the only Central University in India which has Prime Minister as its Chancellor ?
   (a) Banaras Hindu University
   (b) Indira Gandhi National Open University
   (c) Rajiv Gandhi University
   (d) Visva Bharti University
2. Who among the following is often called the "Greenest Chief Minister of India" ?
   (a) Pawan Kumar Chamling
   (b) Anandiben Patel
   (c) Prakash Singh Badal
   (d) Nabam Tuki
3. Who is the new Chief Election Commissioner?
   (a) H.S. Brahma
   (b) Vinod Zutshi
   (c) Nasim Zaidi
   (d) R. Balakrishnan
4. A minor planet is named after which one of the following Indian Legends ?
   (a) Viswanathan Anand
   (b) Sachin Tendulkar
   (c) A. B. Rahman
   (d) Milkha Singh

## ANSWERS

**1.** (d) **2.** (a) **3.** (c) **4.** (a)

## EXPLANATIONS

1. "The President in his capacity as the Visitor of Visa Bharati (Acharya) has appointed Prime Minister Narendra Modi as the Chancellor of Viswa Bharati for a term of three years.
2. Pawan Kumar Chamling is often called the "Greenest Chief Minister of India".
3. Election Commissioner Nasim Zaidi became the new Chief Election Commissioner (CEC) of India in April, 2015.
4. Minor planet was named after India's chess legend and first grandmaster Vishwanathan Anand by the Minor Planet Center. His name was given to the minor planet which was previously identified as planet 4538. Now the planet will be called as 4538 Vishyanand and is located somewhere between the Mars and Jupiter.

# LEGAL APTITUDE

## TORTS

**Directions (Q. 1 - 9) :** Given below is a statement of legal principle followed by a factual situation. Apply the principle to the facts given below and select the most appropriate answer.

1. **LEGAL PRINCIPLE :** A statement is defamatory in nature if it is injurious to a person's reputation and if the statement has been published.

   **FACTUAL SITUATION :** Rudra had been dating a girl named Kiara for three weeks. But he had introduced himself to heras Ricky Thakur (who is one of Rudra's friends) and he continued to be Ricky for the rest of their relationship. But ultimately the relationship ended badly and Kiara being upset and angry at Rudra started a website named 'ricky-thakur-is-a-jerk.com'. She created this website so as to warn other girls about 'Ricky Thakur'. The real Ricky Thakur files a suit for defamation. Decide.

   **DECISION :**

   (a) Kiara shall be held liable for defamation as she published a statement which was injurious to Ricky's reputation.

   (b) Rudra shall be held liable as he had led Kiara into thinking that he was Ricky Thakur and moreover, it was his fault in the first place that made Kiara create this website.

   (c) Kiara cannot be held liable as she had actually been referring to Rudra and not the real Ricky Thakur.

   (d) Kiara cannot be held liable as her act was done in good faith as she intended to warn other girls.

2. **LEGAL PRINCIPLE :** Whoever stores a substance which could cause damage on escape shall be absolutely liable (i.e. liable even when he has exercised necessary care) for any damage caused by the escape of the substance.

   **FACTUAL SITUATION:** Union Carbide India Limited (UCIL) manufactured methyl isocyanate, an extremely toxic gas. Due to a storm, the gas that was being stored in sealed containers got released. Before much could happen, the local municipal authorities managed to contain the disaster. The authorities filed a suit against UCIL for the costs that were incurred in decontamination. However, later it was realized that the clean-up by the authorities could have been done without spending as much resources and the damage was not that significant. UCIL argued that it would pay only part of the amount demanded by the authorities, which could have dealt with the contamination.

   **DECISION :**

   (a) UCIL is liable only to the extent of contamination caused. It does not need to pay the authorities the entire amount demanded by them.

   (b) The authorities are entitled to the whole sum, as UCIL shall be held liable for all the repercussions of their act even if they had exercised due care.

   (c) UCIL can plead that the escape of the gas had been caused by a storm and not due to its own negligence. It was an inevitable accident.

   (d) The municipal authorities should have analyzed the damage first before jumping into action. It was due to their own negligence because of which they had to shell out more than required.

3. **LEGAL PRINCIPLE :** Everybody is under a legal obligation to take reasonable care to avoid act or omission which he can foresee would injure his neighbour, the neighbour for this purpose is any person whom he should have in his mind as likely to be affected by his act.

   **FACTUAL SITUATION :** Krish, while driving a car at a high speed in a crowded road, knocked down a cyclist. The cyclist died on the spot with a lot of blood spilling around, Lekha, a pregnant woman passing by, suffered from a nervous shock, leading to abortion. Lekha filed a suit against Krishnan claiming damages.

   **DECISION :**

   (a) Krish will be liable, because he owed a duty of reasonable care to everybody on the road including Lekha.

   (b) Krish will not be liable, because he could not have foreseen Lekha suffering from nervous shock as a result of his act.

   (c) Krish will be liable to Lekha because he failed to drive carefully.

   (d) None of the above.

4. **LEGAL PRINCIPLE :** The occupier of a premise owes a duty of care to all his invitees and visitors.

   **FACTUAL SITUATION :** Lalit was running a dairy from his house. People used a part of his farm as shortcut to get to a nearby railway station. Lalit who did not approve of this, put up a notice that "Trespassers will be prosecuted". However since a number of these people were also his customers he tolerated them. One day a person who was using this short cut was attacked by a bull belonging to the farm. The injured person filed a suit against him.

DECISION :

(a) Lalit is not liable in view of the clear notice against trespassers.

(b) Lalit is liable for having kept a bull on his farm.

(c) Lalit is not liable to the people other than his customers.

(d) Lalit is liable because in fact he allowed the people to use his premises.

5. **LEGAL PBINCIPLE :** A master shall be liable for the acts of his servants done in the course of employment.

**FACTUAL SITUATION :** PUL, a public sector undertaking, is operating a number of bus services for its employees in Pune. These buses are quite distinct in their appearance and carry the board "for PUL employees only". M, a villager from neighbouring state, was waiting for a regular bus in one of the bus stops in Pune. A bus belonging to PUL happened to stop nearby and number of people got into the bus. M, without realizing that it was PUL bus, got into the bus and soon-thereafter, the bus met with an accident due to driver's negligence. M, along with several others, was injured in the accident. M seeks to file a suit against PUL claiming damages.

**DECISION :**

(a) M will succeed, because he got into the bus without realizing that it was PUL bus.

(b) M will not succeed, because it was for him to find out whether it was a public transport.

(c) M will succeed, because the driver was anyhow duty-bound to drive carefully.

(d) PUL is not liable as the bus met with an accident due to drive's negligence.

6. **LEGAL PRINCIPLE :** Any direct physical interference with goods in somebody's possession without lawful justification is called trespass of goods.

**FACTUAL SITUATION :** Z purchased a car from a person who had no title to it and sent it to a garage for repair. X believing wrongly that the car was his, removed it from the garage. Has X committed any offence?

**DECISION :**

(a) X cannot be held responsible for trespass of goods as he was under a wrong belief.

(b) X can be held responsible for trespass of goods.

(c) Z has no right over the car as he purchased it from a person who has no title over it.

(d) None of the above.

7. **LEGAL PRINCIPLE :** The master principal is liable for all acts done by his duly appointed servant/agent for all acts done by him lawfully in the course of his employment.

**FACTUAL SITUATION :** A, B, C and D carried on a business in partnership. While making a deal with another company, B bribed the clerk there. Is the partnership firm vicariously liable ?

**DECISION :**

(a) No, as bribing is not in course of employment of the partners.

(b) Yes, as partners are agent of the firm.

(c) Yes, as B can be said to have implied authority for the same.

(d) No, as this act was not authorised by the others.

8. **LEGAL PRINCIPLE :** Nobody shall unlawfully interfere with a person's use or enjoyment of land, or some right over, or in connection with it. The use or enjoyment, envisaged herein, should be normal and reasonable taking into account surrounding situation.

**FACTUAL SITUATION :** Jogi and Prakash were neighbours in a residential locality. Prakash started a typing class in a part of his house and his typing sound disturbed Jogi who could not put up with any kind of continuous noise. He filed a suit against Prakash.

**DECISION :**

(a) Prakash is liable, because he should not have started typing class in his house.

(b) Prakash is liable, because as a neighbour, he should have realised Jogi's delicate nature.

(c) Prakash is not liable, because typing sound did not disturb anyone else other than Jogi

(d) None of the above.

9. **LEGAL PRINCIPLES :** Necessity knows no law, and any person facing danger may do all that is necessary to avert the same till he can take recourse to public authorities.

**FACTUAL SITUATION :** Akshay, a law abiding citizen decided to remove the weed of corruption from India society. One day, confronted with a bribing official, Akshay decided to teach him a lesson and punched him on his face. Akshay

(a) Can plead defence of necessity as he was being bribed which is a crime.

(b) Cannot plead defence of necessity as there was no necessity to act in the manner he acted.

(c) Can plead defence of necessity as aware and vigilant citizenry forms the basis of a good democracy.

(d) Can plead defence of necessity as there was no time to take recourse to public authorities.

## ANSWERS

**1.** (a) **2.** (b) **3.** (b) **4.** (d) **5.** (c)
**6.** (b) **7.** (a) **8.** (d) **9.** (b)

## EXPLANATIONS

1. On a straightforward application of the principle, we find that regardless of Kiara's intent, the real Ricky did get defamed because the website was injurious to his reputation and put in the public domain. Kiara will be liable because intention is irrelevant in defamation. Mere publication of injurious statement about a particular person is sufficient to cause the offence. Further, the principle is limited and does not deal with any exceptions. Thus, we cannot presume any exceptions or defenses unless specifically mentioned in the question.
2. UCIL would be liable for all the damages as mandated by the principle. Here, escape of dangerous substance has occurred and authorities bore the expenses for decontaminating the substance to avert any further loss of lives and property. It would not matter what precautions they took, UCIL would be responsible for any damage caused as a result of the gas.
3. As per the official answer key, option A is the correct answer. According to us, the correct answer should be option B. This question also featured in the CLAT 2015 paper.

   Krish will not be liable because he cannot foresee that a pregnant lady will suffer a nervous shock by witnessing a road accident that had resulted in the death of a person. Krish was under an obligation to take care only of those people he could reasonably have foreseen as being affected by his act. He could reasonably have foreseen the harm he could cause to the cyclist, but not to Lekha since the damage to her was too remote.
4. Since Lalit tolerated the passers-by, they can be considered visitors and therefore Lalit has a duty to watch out for them. Lalit will be liable despite the fact that he had put up a board "Trespassers will be prosecuted" because he did not strictly prohibit the entry of outsiders on his premises and continued to allow people to use the same.
5. PUL will be liable for damages towards all the persons travelling in the bus irrespective of the fact that they are employee or not. The principle says master would be liable for the act of servant done in the course of employment. Hence, the driver has caused the accident due to his negligent driving and he will be considered in course of employment because he was driving the bus to pick up the employees of the company. Further, since driving the bus carefully was within the purview of the driver's duties, the master will be liable for whatever happens during the course of the discharge of that duty. PUL is, therefore, liable.
6. This question also featured in the CLAT 2015 paper. Removing a car from the garage amounts to direct physical interference with goods, regardless of the innocence of X's intention. Hence it would amount to trespass as per the principle.
7. The principle states that the partners would be liable for something that one of them does lawfully in the course of employment. Bribery isn't lawful, and thus they stand absolved of liability.
8. This question also featured in the CLAT 2015 paper. Options A, B and C do not match the criteria as mandated by the principle. The principle specifies normal and reasonable use, which isn't evaluated by any of the options, hence D.
9. Akshay was not facing any danger of an imminent nature such as to justify usage of all necessary means to avert it before taking recourse to public authorities.

## LAW OF CONTRACTS

**Directions (Q. 1 - 4) :** Given below is a statement of legal principle followed by a factual situation. Apply the principle to the facts given below and select the most appropriate answer.

1. **LEGAL PRINCIPLE :** A partner is liable for the debts incurred by the other partners in the course of Partnership.

   **FACTUAL SITUATION :** Satwik and Prateek enter into a partnership to produce a film, wherein Satwik also directs the movie. The movie bombed at the box office. Consequently, they run into financial difficulties and the partnership ends. Prateek goes to Abbas to borrow some money, which Abbas understands is for-repaying the debts from the partnership. Prateek takes the money and absconds to Malibu. Abbas sues Satwik for the amount. Decide

   **DECISION :**

   (a) Satwik is liable to return the money as it was his partner, Prateek, who directed the movie.

   (b) Abbas has been negligent in not properly enquiring the purpose for which Prateek borrowed the money. Satwik is not liable to pay him back according to the principle of contributory negligence

(c) Satwik is not liable as prateek absconded with the money instead of using it to payoff the debts in the partnership.

(d) Satwik is not liable as by the time Prateek borrowed money from Abbas, the partnership was no more in existence

2. **LEGAL PRINCIPLE :** When one person signifies to another his willingness to do or abstain from doing anything, with a view to obtaining the assent of that person to such an act or abstinence, he is said to have made a proposal.

**FACTUAL SITUATION :** Ram sends a telegram to Sohan, writing : "Will you sell me your Rolls Royce car? Telegram the lowest cash price." Sohan also replied by telegram: "Lowest price for car is Rs. 20 lakh." Ram immediately sent his consent through telegram stating "I agree to buy the cat for Rs. 20 lakh asked by you.", Sohan refused to sell the car

(a) He cannot refuse to sell the car because the contract has already been made.

(b) He can refuse to sell the car because it was only invitation to offer and not the real offer.

(c) It was not a valid offer because willingness to enter into a contract was absent.

(d) It was not a valid contract as offer and acceptance is conveyed through telegram.

3. **LEGAL PRINCIPLE :** A person is said to be of sound mind for the purpose of making a contract if, at the time when he makes it, he is capable of understanding it and of forming a rational judgement as to its effect upon his interests.

**FACTUAL SITUATION :** Mr. X who is usually of sound state of mind, but occasionally of unsound state of mind, enters into a contract with Mr. Y when he was of unsound state of mind. Mr. Y having come to know about this fact afterwards, wants to file a suit against Mr. X.

**DECISION :**

(a) Mr. X cannot enter into contract because he is of unsound state of mind when he entered into contract.

(b) Mr. X can enter into contract but the burden is on the other party to prove that he was of unsound state of mind at the time of contract.

(c) Mr. X can enter into contract but the burden is on Mr. X to prove that he was of sound state of mind at the time of contract.

(d) Contract with a person of unsound mind is void.

4. **LEGAL PRINCIPLE :** A contract which is impossible to perform becomes void.

**FACTUAL SITUATION :** Surender agreed to deliver a specific quality of rice to Sonakshi identified by both of them. Before delivery, the rice was burnt by short circuit. Is Surender discharged from the performance of the contract?

**DECISION :**

(a) Surender is discharged from performance as the subject matter of the contract is destroyed.

(b) Surender is discharged from performance as the subject matter has been specifically identified.

(c) Surender is not discharged from performance as he can procure rice from other sources.

(d) None of the above.

## ANSWERS

**1.** (d) **2.** (b) **3.** (a) **4.** (b)

## EXPLANATIONS

1. Satwik will not be liable because Prateek took the money from Abbas only after termination of the partnership which is clearly mentioned in the facts.The partnership ended right after the movie bombed, and since at the time of borrowing the money from Abbas, the partnership was no longer in existence, Satwik cannot be sued for the amount.

2. This question also featured in the CLAT 2015 paper. Here, Sohan can refuse to sell the car because he quoted the lowest price of the car asked by Ram. Quoting the price is always an invitation to offer, and not an offer which means that the Parties are at the stage of negotiation only. It was now down to Ram to send an offer saying that he'd like to buy the car for 20 lakhs, and it would then have been down to Sohan to accept or reject it.

3. As per the official answer key, option C is the correct answer. According to us, the correct answer should be option A. This question also featured in the CLAT 2015 paper.

   The focus of the principle is on the competence to contract and not on the burden of proof. The principle clearly states that the person should be of sound mind at the time of entering into the contract, and says nothing about burden of proof. Using that, the answer should be A since Mr. X was not of a sound state of mind at the time of entering into the contract.

4. The contract was for a specific quality of rice as identified by both the contracting parties and that had gotten destroyed, Surender stands discharged.

## CRIMINAL LAW

**Directions (Q. 1 - 9) :** Given below is a statement of legal principle followed by a factual situation. Apply the principle to the facts given below and select the most appropriate answer.

1. **LEGAL PRINCIPLE :** Ignorance of Fact is excused but ignorance of law is not an excuse to criminal liability.

   **FACTUAL SITUATION :** X was a passenger from Zurich to Manila in a Swiss Plane. When the plane landed at the Airport of Bombay on 22 November 2014 it was found on searching the X carried 34 kg of Gold Bars on his person and that he had not declared it in the 'Manifest for Transit'. On 24 Novemeber 2014, the Government of India has issued a notification modifying its earlier exemption, making it mandatory now that the gold must be declared in the "Manifest" of the aircraft.

   **DECISION :**

   (a) X cannot be prosecuted because he had actually no knowledge about the new notification issued two days ago

   (b) X cannot be prosecuted because ignorance of fact is excusable

   (c) X can be prosecuted because ignorance of law is not excusable

   (d) X's liability would depend on the discretion of the court.

2. **LEGAL PRINCIPLES :** Whoever dishonestly takes away any property from the possession of another, with an intention of such taking away, without his permission is liable for theft.

   **FACTUAL SITUATION :** Raja, a famous gangster, moves into an apartment in Kankurgachi, Calcutta. There, he discovers that the previous owner of the apartment had left behind a pair of beautiful ivory handled combs. Mesmerized by their beauty and confused as to whom he should be returning them to, he decides to retain them and starts using them. The previous owner of the combs gets to know; this and registers an FIR for theft against Raja. Is Raja liable ?

   **DECISION :**

   (a) Raja is liable for theft as he failed to return the property even when he knew it was someone else's property.

   (b) Raja is not liable as he is not taken it away from anyone else's possession and there was no dishonest intention.

   (c) Raja is liable as you don't expect anything better from a gangster.

   (d) Raja is not liable as he was confused as to whom he should be returning the property to.

3. **LEGAL PRINCIPLE :** Whoever dishonestly misappropriates or converts to his own use any movable property is guilty of criminal misappropriation of property.

   **FACTUAL SITUATION :** A finds a government promissory note belonging to Z, bearing a blank endorsement. A knowing that the note belongs to Z, pledges it with a banker as security for a loan, intending to restore it to Z at a future time. Has A committed criminal misappropriation ?

   **DECISION :**

   (a) Yes since he deprived Z from using his property and used it for his own use.

   (b) No, since he intended to return the property to Z in the future.

   (c) No, it is theft and not criminal misappropriation.

   (d) Yes since he deprived Z from using his property.

4. **LEGAL PRINCIPLES :**

   1. Whoever causes death by doing an act with the intention of causing death or with the intention of causing such bodily injury as is likely to cause death or with the knowledge that he is likely by such act to cause death commits the offence of culpable homicide.
   2. Mens rea and actus reus must concur to result in a crime which is punishable by the law.

   **FACTUAL SITUATION :** A and B went for shooting. A knows Z to be behind a bush. B does not know it. A induces B to fire at the bush. B fires and kills Z. Has an offence been committed ?

   **DECISION :**

   (a) A had mens rea but no actus reus. B had actus reus but no mens rea. No one is guilty.

   (b) A induced B to fire at the bush with the knowledge that Z is there. A is guilty c.culpable homicide but B is not guilty of any offence.

   (c) Both A and B are guilty.

   (d) None of the above.

5. **LEGAL PRINCIPLES :**

   1. The crime of kidnapping involves taking someone away from the custody of their lawful guardian.

   3. The crime abduction involves inducing or forcing somebody to go away from some place against their will.

   **FACTUAL SITUATION :** A steals B's slave. Is it a crime ?

**DECISION :**

I. Kidnapping II. Abduction III. Neither

**REASON :**

(A) Slavery is illegal.

(B) A has taken him away from B's lawful custody.

(C) A has forced somebody to go with him against his will.

**DECISION :**

(a) I (B) (b) II (C)

(c) III (A) (d) I (A)

6. **LEGAL PRINCIPLE :** Whoever delivers to another person as genuine any counterfeit currency which he knows to be counterfeit, but which that other person is not aware of at the time when he received it, is guilty of counterfeiting currency.

**FACTUAL SITUATION :** While returning home one day, Roshni realizes that the local shopkeeper has given her a fake note ot Rs. 1,000. Disappointed, she goes to the same shop and buys cosmetics worth Rs. 600. She then passes the same fake note to the shopkeeper. The shopkeeper while inspecting the note finds out that it is fake. Is Roshni guilty ?

**DECISION :**

(a) No, as she was merely attempting to return the note to the same shopkeeper who gave her the note.

(b) No, she is not guilty of any offence as neither did she manufacture the note nor did she circulate it with a view to deceive the public.

(c) Yes, as she attempted to pass on a note which she knew was counterfeit.

(d) No, the shopkeeper is guilty as he was the one who circulated the counterfeit note to Roshni.

7. **LEGAL PRINCIPLES :**

1. To constitute a punishable criminal offence, guilty intention must accompany an illegal act.
2. Criminal mischief means causing damage to public property intentionally or with the knowledge that harm may occur.

**FACTUAL SITUATION :** Neel being a Shahrukh Khan fan went for the premier of Happy New Year. As usual, he carried his pen-knife, a gift from his dead mother. At the security check, impatient of waiting in the queue, Neel slunk past the guards and the metal detector when no one was watching. Later, he was apprehended in the hall and charged for mischief and possession of a weapon when it was expressly forbidden.

**DECISION :**

(a) Neel is not criminally liable since he had no intention to commit mischief.

(b) Liable for possession of the weapon since it was expressly forbidden and mere possession was enough; although he might not be liable for mischief as he did not do anything.

(c) Neel is not liable since the pen knife has an emotional value and rather the guards should be punished for the security breach.

(d) Liable for both possession of weapon and criminal mischief since he slunk past the guards which shows his intention to commit the crime.

8. **LEGAL PRINCIPLE :**

1. Everyone has a right to defend their life and property against criminal harm provided it is not possible to approach public authorities and more harm than is necessary has been caused to avert the danger.
2. Nothing is an offence which is done in the exercise of the right of private defence.

**FACTUAL SITUATION :** The accused found the deceased engaged in sexual intercourse with his 15 years old daughter. The accused assaulted the deceased on the head with a spade which resulted in his death. Accused claimed private defence and the prosecution claimed that the sexual intercourse was with the consent of the daughter. Here,

**DECISION :**

(a) Accused is entitled to the right of private defence since the girl was only 15 years old.

(b) Accused exceeded the right of private defence.

(c) Accused is not entitled to private defence as the intercourse was consensual.

(d) Accused is not entitled to private defence as the right of private defence is available for defending one's life and property only.

9. **LEGAL PRINCIPLES :**

1. Preparation to commit an offence is not an offence.
2. After one has finished preparation to commit an offence, any act done towards committing the offence with the intention to commit it, is an attempt to commit the offence which is by itself an offence.

**FACTUAL SITUATION :** A wanted to kill B and had therefore gone to the market to buy explosives to plant in his house. After A has planted the bomb, he felt guilty and went back to remove the bomb but while he was doing so, B saw him and called the police. Can A be held liable ?

**DECISION :**

(a) Yes, because he has done something more than mere preparation.

(b) No, because B did not die.

(c) Yes, because there existed a mala fide intention.
(d) No, because he had removed before anything could happen.

## ANSWERS

| | | | | |
|---|---|---|---|---|
| 1. (c) | 2. (b) | 3. (a) | 4. (b) | 5. (c) |
| 6. (c) | 7. (b) | 8. (a) | 9. (a) | |

## EXPLANATIONS

1. This question also featured in the CLAT 2015 paper.

   Since ignorance of law cannot be an excuse, it is presumed that X knew of the law regarding declaration of gold. There appears to be a typographical mistake in the facts. X was arrested on 22nd November and changes in the law were notified on 24th November as stated in the facts while option (A) says "...he had actually no knowledge about the new notification issued two days ago". Assuming 20th November as the date of notification of law, the answer will be C.
2. The ivory combs were not dishonestly taken from the possession of their previous owner; they had been lying around the house. Raja will not be liable for theft because he did not take any property from the possession of the owner or without his consent as he found the article upon entering the apartment.
3. What makes his intention dishonest is that he knew that the promissory note belonged to Z and decided to use it for his own purposes despite the knowledge.
4. A had the knowledge that firing into the bush could cause severe harm or death to Z, so he is guilty of culpable homicide. B had neither knowledge nor intention, so he wouldn't be liable for any offence.
5. It would be neither kidnapping nor abduction, since slavery per se is illegal. We don't know anything as to the willingness of the slave, and he was definitely not under his owner's lawful guardianship.
6. Regardless of the fact that she was cheated first, Roshni's act of passing on a counterfeit note with the knowledge that it was counterfeit is punishable.
7. Neel may be liable for possession of illegal arms but not for mischief because he has not destroyed any public property.
8. Here, Accused can take the right of private defense as consent of the 15 year old girl for sexual intercourse with deceased is immaterial.
9. Preparation would've stopped at buying the explosives, but actually planting them in B's house amounts to an attempt since barring any external interference, B would've died because of the explosives. So he can be held guilty for attempt.

## CONSTITUTIONAL LAW AND LEGAL FRAMEWORK

**Directions (Q. 1 - 2) :** Given below is a statement of legal principle followed by a factual situation. Apply the principle to the facts given below and select the most appropriate answer.

1. **LEGAL PRINCIPLE :** Only Parliament or State Legislatures have the authority to enact laws on their own. No law made by the State can take away a person's fundamental right.

   **FACTUAL SITUATION :** Parliament enacted a law, which according to a group of lawyers is violating the fundamental rights of traders. A group of lawyers files a writ petition challenging the Constitutional validity of the statute seeking-relief to quash the statute and further direct Parliament to enact a new law.

   **DECISION :**

   (a) The court can quash the existing law if it violates fundamental rights but cannot direct Parliament to make a new law.
   (b) The court can quash existing law if it violates fundamental rights and can direct Parliament to make a new law.
   (c) No writ would lie against Parliament, as the court has no authority to direct Parliament to enact or re-enact a law.
   (d) The court cannot quash the law as reasonable restrictions can be put on the fundamental rights.
2. **LEGAL PRINCIPLES :** The state shall make special laws for the upliftment of citizens of the country, and these laws can be made for the benefit of any specific caste, class or sex of people living in the society.

   **FACTUAL SITUATION :** The state of Hindu Pradesh comes out with a law, which provided for reservation to Muslims in all government and government aided institutions. This law is challenged in the High Court of Hindu Pradesh, as being arbitrary and contrary to the established laws. Can the challenge be successful ?

   **DECISION :**

   (a) Yes, since people from other religions would also start making such demand's which would jeopardize the unity and integrity of the country.
   (b) No, since the state has the right to make special laws for the upliftment of the citizens of the country.
   (c) Yes, since the state has not been mandated to make reservation, based on a person's religion.
   (d) No, since the Government cannot neglect the minorities.

3. The Supreme Court of India constituted _____ Bench in December 2014.
   (a) Constitution (b) Arbitration
   (c) Social Justice (d) Fast-Track
4. Who is the author of the book "Indian Parliamentary Diplomacy - Speaker's Perspective" ?
   (a) Sumitra Mahajan (b) Somnath Chaterjee
   (c) Meira Kumar (b) Manohar Joshi
5. Which of the following recently became 123rd State party to the International Criminal Court?
   (a) Israel (b) Palestine
   (c) Jordan (d) Bangladesh
6. Which body has launched the "Group of Friends Against Terrorism" ?
   (a) United Nations (b) European Union
   (c) ASEAN (d) SAARC
7. Which one of the following Committee was constituted to review environmental law in the country ?
   (a) Subramanian Committee
   (b) Kasturi Ranjan Committee
   (c) Madhav Nair Committee
   (d) Ullas Karanth Committee
8. Which South-East Asian country has recently banned surrogacy services to end its flourishing rent-a-womb industry?
   (a) Singapore (b) India
   (c) Thailand (d) Vietnam
9. The Third National Lok Adalat which disposed of 56000 cases in a single day was held under the chairmanship of
   (a) Justice H. L. Dattu
   (b) Justice T. S. Thakur
   (c) Justice Jagdish Singh Khehar
   (d) Justice Anil R Dave
10. In which of the following cases, the Supreme Court, recently, held that demand for dowry can be made at any time and not necessarily before marriage ?
   (a) State of uttarakhand v. Bhim Singh & Anr
   (b) State of Bihar v. Arnesh Kumar & Anr
   (c) State ot Rajasthan v. Prem Kumar
   (d) State of Punjab v. Kans Raj & Ors
11. National Green Tribunal ruled _____ old diesel vehicles cannot ply on Delhi roads.
   (a) 15 years (b) 10 years
   (c) 20 years (d) 5 years
12. Supreme Court struck down which Section of the Information Technology Act 2000, in Shreya Singhal v. U. O. I, as unconstitutional ?
   (a) 66 B (b) 66 A
   (c) 66 C (d) 66

## ANSWERS

| | | | | |
|---|---|---|---|---|
| 1. (a) | 2. (c) | 3. (c) | 4. (c) | 5. (b) |
| 6. (a) | 7. (a) | 8. (c) | 9. (b) | 10. (a) |
| 11. (b) | 12. (b) | | | |

## EXPLANATIONS

1. The court is perfectly within its rights to strike down a law if it violates fundamental rights as per article 13 of the Constitution; but the task of making new laws is that of the legislature alone.
2. The principle specifies that reservations can be made on grounds of caste, class or sex but doesn't mention religion. According to the principle, the reservations are invalid.
3. This question also featured in the CLAT 2015 paper. The Supreme Court of India has set up a Social Justice Bench, which comprises of two judges devoted to the delivery of speedy justice in a range of social issues related to the downtrodden and socially marginalised groups. It's a brainchild of Chief Justice of India H.L. Dattu and the Bench is headed by Justice Madan B. Lokur and also has Justice U.U. Lalit. The purpose behind constituting the new Bench was to streamline cases highlighting social issues before one court and thus facilitate the Supreme Court's monitoring and review of the government's action in such cases.The social justice bench has been set up to ensure three-dimensional justice, as provided for in the Preamble. This Bench would function from 12th December 2014 and in order to ensure that these matters are monitored on regular basis, will continue to sit on every working Friday at 2.00 p.m.
4. Former Lok Sabha speaker Meira Kumar is the author of "Indian Parliamentary Diplomacy – Speaker's Perspective" and this book was released at a function in Rashtrapati Bhavan on March 19th, 2015. The President of India, Pranab Mukherjee received the 1st copy of the book from Sumitra Mahajan, Speaker, Lok Sabha who formally released it. The book features an account of the parliamentary diplomacy and its role in furthering foreign policy and strengthening international relations. It is also a collection of select speeches and reports by Kumar during her stint as Lok Sabha speaker and as leader of Indian parliamentary delegations at several international fora.

5. Palestine became the 123rd member of the International Criminal Court. 123 countries are States Parties to the Rome Statute of the International Criminal Court. Out of them 34 are African States, 19 are Asia-Pacific States, 18 are from Eastern Europe, 27 are from Latin American and Caribbean States, and 25 are from Western European and other States.

6. Group of Friends Against Terrorism is a United Nations initiative launched to combat terrorism. The group was launched at the initiative of Morocco, and it was presided over by Morocco's Permanent Representative to the UN Ambassador Omar Hitale. Created at the initiative of Morocco, the group consists of thirty countries. Group of Friends Against Terrorism will aim, among others; to create synergies between all initiatives implemented within the UN, promoting international cooperation in combating terrorism, share and exchange good practices in the fight against this scourge that threatens international peace and security. India and Pakistan, as well as the five permanent members of the Security Council are among the 30 nations who have joined hands. In addition to China, France, Russia, UK and the US, the group has representation from the five continents and is composed of African countries (Morocco, Ethiopia, Egypt, Chad, Kenya, Senegal and South Africa),Western Europe (Spain, Germany, Norway and Turkey), from Eastern Europe (Czech Republic and Bulgaria), Asia (India, Indonesia, Jordan, Pakistan, Saudi Arabia and United Arab Emirates), Latin America (Argentina, Brazil and Colombia) and Oceania (New Zealand and Australia)

7. T S R Subramanian Committee was constituted to review environmental laws in India. The committee has submitted its recommendations to the government recently. The report has been criticized for failing to make the environmental regulation more participatory and democratic.

8. Thailand has passed a law that bans foreigners from seeking surrogacy services to end the "rent-a-womb" industry that made the South-east Asian country a top destination for fertility tourism. Several surrogacy scandals were reported in Thailand last year, including allegations that an Australian couple had abandoned their Down's Syndrome baby with his Thai birth mother taking only his healthy twin sister back to Australia with them. Another case involved a Japanese man who fathered at least 16 babies using Thai surrogates in what local Thai media called the "baby factory". The law makes commercial surrogacy a crime and aims to stop Thai women's wombs from becoming the world's womb. This law bans foreign couples from coming to Thailand to seek commercial surrogacy services and stipulates that surrogate mothers must be Thai and over 25. The important part is if the couple seeking surrogacy services is Thai or the couple is mixed-race, they can find a Thai woman to be their surrogate provided she is over 25 and the violation of the law carries a "severe prison sentence".

9. The third National Lok Adalat was organised on 14 February 2015 throughout India involving the Supreme Court, High Courts, Districts Courts and taluka-level courts, except in Assam and Uttar Pradesh. It was organised under the patronage of Chief Justice of India (CJI) H L Dattu and the chairmanship of Supreme Court Judge Justice T S Thakur. Nearly 56,000 cases were disposed of by the third National Lok Adalat in a single day. It also saw disbursal of Rs 265 crore as claims towards final settlement in bank recovery and cheques bounce cases. Third Lok Adalat was organised by the National Legal Service Authority (NALSA) to dispose cases related to bank recovery, cheque bounce cases, particularly under Section 138 of the Negotiable Instruments Act, 1881. Several banks, financial institutions and others had participated in it. First National Lok Adalat was held in November 2013 and had settled a record 71.50 lakh cases pending in various courts. The second National Lok Adalat was held in December 2014 and had disposed of over 1.25 crore cases.

10. In State of *Uttarkhand* v. *Bhim Singh & Anr.*, it was held that the demand of dowry can be made at any time, even post marriage.

11. The NGT has been established for speedy disposal of cases relating to environmental protection and conservation of forests and other natural resources. The National Green Tribunal (NGT) banned all diesel vehicles over 10 years old and all petrol vehicles over 15 years old from plying on Delhi roads.

12. The Shreya Singhal case has been hailed as a welcome development in the Indian free speech jurisprudence. It was the outcome of a petition following the misuse of Section 66 A by political parties for suppressing valid expression of dissent on social media. It also has implications for intermediary liability. The Supreme Court declared Section 66A of Information Technology Act as unconstitutional and struck it down. This section had been widely misused by police in various states to arrest innocent persons for posting critical comments

about social and political issues and political leaders on social networking sites. The court said such a law hit at the root of liberty and freedom of expression, two cardinal pillars of democracy.

## MISCELLANEOUS

**Direction :** Given below is a statement of legal principle followed by a factual situation. Apply the principle to the facts given below and select the most appropriate answer.

**1. LEGAL PRINCIPLES :**

1. Bigamy is not permitted under Hindu law.
2. A Hindu of sound mind can adopt a child of the gender they don't already have a child of.
3. Only the child's father, mother or guardian has the capacity to give the child up in adoption, under Hindu law.

**FACTUAL SITUATION :** Ramesh comes from a family where from the past two generations; all male members have had two wives. He also wants to continue this tradition and thus he married Suman first and then Tania. Ramesh has a son, Gunjan,with Suman. However, with Tania, he is childless. He thus wishes to adopt some children. Rajat is the child of Ramesh's brother. However, Rajat's parents decide to go off to Dubai for 5 years and they leave their son under the care of Ramesh's sister. Ramesh and Tania ask for Rajat in adoption from his sister who agrees and Rajat is adopted. Later, Ramesh and Suman want to adopt a daughter as well and they do adopt a girl-Sara-from an orphanage. However, at the time of signing the adoption deed, Ramesh was dead drunk. Ramesh and his entire family member are Buddhists. Keeping in mind the given principles and facts, solve the questions. Is Rajat's adoption a valid adoption ?

**DECISION :**

(a) No, because Ramesh already has a son.

(b) No, because Ramesh's sister has no authority to give Rajat up in adoplron.

(c) Yes, it is a valid adoption because Ramesh has no child with Tania ano Ramesh's sister is Rajat's guardian for 5 years at least.

(d) Both (a) and (b)

## ANSWER

1. (d)

## EXPLANATION

1. Since Ramesh already has a son, he cannot adopt another. Ramesh's sister, not being the legal guardian of Rajat, could not have consented to give Rajat up for adoption.

■■

# CLAT-2016 CHAPTER-WISE

## ENGLISH

### VOCABULARY

**Direction for questions 1-5 :** Choose the correct spellings in questions given below:

**1.** Choose the correct spellings
(*a*) sacribegous
(*b*) sacrilegious
(*c*) sacrilegiuos
(*d*) saereligious

**2.** Choose the correct spellings
(*a*) barrister (*b*) barisster
(*c*) berister (*d*) berrister

**3.** Choose the correct spellings
(*a*) deceive (*b*) decieve
(*c*) diecieve (*d*) deceeve

**4.** Choose the correct spellings
(*a*) colaborate (*b*) collaborrate
(*c*) collaborat (*d*) collaborate

**5.** Choose the correct spellings
(*a*) integrity
(*b*) integerity
(*c*) integerety
(*d*) intigerity

**Direction for Questions 6-9:** Choose the correct option for each of the following questions:

**6.** "Faux pas" means:
(*a*) false
(*b*) expected to happen
(*c*) fake identity
(*d*) social blunder

**7.** "To bury the hatchet" means:
(*a*) to plant grass in the field
(*b*) to end a feud with an enemy
(*c*) to hide some treasure
(*d*) to cremate carcass of an animal

**8.** "Ab initio" means:
(*a*) from the beginning
(*b*) in connection with the future
(*c*) in continuation with
(*d*) in defence of a comment

**9.** "Amicus curiae" means:
(*a*) One among the parties to the dispute
(*b*) One among the expert witnesses in a case
(*c*) One of the judges of the court
(*d*) A friend of the court

**Direction for Questions 10-11:** Complete the proverb, in the following questions:

**10.** When ______ is bliss, it is ______ to be wise.
(*a*) knowledge, better
(*b*) bachelorhood, single
(*c*) ignorance, folly
(*d*) romance, boring

**11.** ______ waters run ______.
(*a*) Stagnant, leisurely (*b*) Still, deep
(*c*) Muddy, slow (*d*) Hot, fast

### ANSWERS

| | | | | |
|---|---|---|---|---|
| **1.**(*b*) | **2.**(*a*) | **3.**(*a*) | **4.**(*d*) | **5.**(*a*) |
| **6.**(*d*) | **7.**(*b*) | **8.**(*a*) | **9.**(*d*) | **10.**(*c*) |
| **11.**(*b*) | | | | |

### EXPLANATIONS

**1.** The correct spelling of the word is 'sacrilegious'. Hence, option (b) is the correct answer.

**2.** The correct spelling of the word is 'barrister'. Hence, option (a) is the correct answer.

**3.** The correct spelling of the word is 'deceive'. Hence, option (a) is the correct answer.

**4.** The correct spelling of the word is 'collaborate'. Hence, option (d) is the correct answer.

**5.** The correct spelling of the word is 'integrity'. Hence, option (a) is the correct answer.

**6.** 'Faux pas' means social blunder. Hence, option (d) is the correct answer.

**7.** 'Burry the hatchet' means to end a feud with an enemy. Hence, option (b) is the correct answer.

**8.** 'Ab initio' is a Latin phrase which means from the beginning.

**9.** The literal translation of 'amicus curiae' is friend of the court. Hence, option (d) is the correct answer.

**10.** 'When ignorance is bless it is folly to be wise' is an idiom which means if knowing something makes you unhappy, it would be betternot to knowit. Hence, option (c) is the correct answer.

**11.** 'Still waters run deep' is a proverb which means a quiet or placid manner may conceal a passionate nature. Hence, option (b) is the correct answer.

## GRAMMAR

**Direction for Questions 1-10:** Fill in the blanks by choosing the most appropriate option:

**1.** I like reading journals __________ novels.
(*a*) the less than (*b*) most than
(*c*) the best (*d*) more than

**2.** If you promise __________ angry with me, I'll tell you what I broke.
(*a*) get not (*b*) not to get
(*c*) not getting (*d*) not get

**3.** They always give the available seats to __________ comes first.
(*a*) whomever (*b*) whoever
(*c*) whom (*d*) whichever

**4.** A thief does not __________ the door.
(*a*) knock (*b*) knock at
(*c*) knock on (*d*) knock to

**5.** It's unfortunate that he died__________ cancer.
(*a*) by (*b*) of
(*c*) with (*d*) from

**6.** The method and practice of teaching is called __________.
(*a*) philately
(*b*) paediatrics
(*c*) training
(*d*) pedagogy

**7.** There is a lot of work __________ hand. Let's cancel __________ picnic.
(*a*) in, the (*b*) in, a
(*c*) upon, the (*d*) on, a

**8.** A fire broke __________ in the neighbourhood.
(*a*) away (*b*) off
(*c*) from (*d*) out

**9.** Professor Ahmed __________ teaching us __________ August, 2012.
(*a*) had been, since
(*b*) has been, since
(*c*) was, for
(*d*) has been, for

**10.** There isn't __________ water in the overhead tank.
(*a*) little (*b*) some
(*c*) lot of (*d*) any

**Direction for questions 11-15:** Complete the sentences with the correct options :

**11.** I can't bear __________ late.
(*a*) been (*b*) to
(*c*) be (*d*) being

**12.** Mani, along with his friends, __________ for basket ball practice every morning.
(*a*) were going (*b*) goes
(*c*) are going (*d*) go

**13.** I have never come __________ any one as rude as him.
(*a*) across (*b*) around
(*c*) to (*d*) at

**14.** Her parents have arrived __________ the airport.
(*a*) at (*b*) on
(*c*) to (*d*) in

**15.** They returned home __________ a taxi.
(*a*) from (*b*) in
(*c*) with (*d*) on

**Direction for Questions 16-19:** Choose the most appropriate option for each of the following questions:

**16.** Choose the correct option
(*a*) Please stop interfering with my romantic life.
(*b*) Please stop interfering for my romantic life.
(*c*) Please stop interfering into my romantic life.
(*d*) Please stop interfering in my romantic life.

**17.** Choose the correct option
(*a*) The Film Star got off the car and smiled at the people.
(*b*) The Film Star come out of the car and smiled at the people.
(*c*) The Film Star got out of the car and smiled at the people.
(*d*) The Film Star climbed off the car and smiled at the people.

**18.** Choose the correct option
(*a*) Your grammar is very good but you need to work on managing your pronunciation.
(*b*) Your grammar is very good, but you need to work on correcting your pronunciation.
(*c*) Your grammar is very good, but you need to work on repairing your pronunciation.
(*d*) Your grammar is very good, but you need to work on modifying your pronunciation.

**19.** Choose the correct option

(*a*) The Titanic did not reach their destination.

(*b*) The Titanic did not reach her destination.

(*c*) The Titanic did not reach his destination.

(*d*) The Titanic did not reach it's destination.

## ANSWERS

| | | | | |
|---|---|---|---|---|
| **1.**(*d*) | **2.**(*b*) | **3.**(*b*) | **4.**(*b*) | **5.**(*b*) |
| **6.**(*d*) | **7.**(*a*) | **8.**(*d*) | **9.**(*b*) | **10.**(*d*) |
| **11.**(*d*) | **12.**(*b*) | **13.**(*a*) | **14.**(*a*) | **15.**(*b*) |
| **16.**(*d*) | **17.**(*c*) | **18.**(*b*) | **19.**(*b*) | |

## EXPLANATIONS

**1.** Option (a) is incorrect because 'the' is redundant. Option (b) is incorrect because 'most' indicates the greatest in number, quantity etc. So, 'most' will not go with 'reading'. Option (c) is also incorrect. 'Best' means excellent. It cannot be used to make comparison between two things. Option (d) is the correct answer. 'More than' is used to compare two things.

**2.** The grammatically correct phrase is 'not to get', rendering option (b) the answer.

**3.** 'Whoever' means whatever person. 'Whomever' is the objective case of 'whoever'. So, 'whoever' fits in the blank, rendering option (b) the answer.

**4.** 'Knock' takes the preposition 'at' after it. Hence, option (b) is the correct answer.

**5.** When someone dies as a result of a disease, we say that they 'die of' the disease. Hence, option (b) is the correct answer.

**6.** 'Pedagogy' is the art, science, or profession of teaching. Hence, option (d) is the correct answer. 'Philately' is the study or collection of postage stamps. 'Paediatrics' is the branch of medicine concerned with children and their diseases.

**7.** 'In hand' means receiving or requiring immediate attention. So, the first blank will take 'in'. The second blank will take 'the' since we are talking about a particular picnic.

**8.** 'Break away' means to leave or to escape from someone who is holding you. 'Break off' means to separate a part from a larger piece, or to become separate. 'Break from' means a time away from work or your regular activity, or a holiday. 'Break out' means to start suddenly. Only option (d) fits in the meaning of the sentence and hence, is the correct answer.

**9.** The sentence suggests that the professor is still teaching. So, the first blank will take 'has been'. The second blank will take 'since' as 'since' is used to refer back to a previous point in time while 'for' is used to refer to the length of a period of time. Hence, option (b) is the correct answer.

**10.** 'Any' means even the smallest amount or number of. Hence, option (d) is the correct answer. Option (c) would have been correct had it been 'a lot of'.

**11.** 'Being' is the present participle of 'be'. Hence, option (d) is the correct answer. The blank can also take 'to be'.

**12.** The phrase introduced by 'along with' modify the earlier word (Mani in this case), but it does not compound the subjects (as the word and would do). So, the blank will take a word that goes with Mani (singular). Hence, option (b), 'goes' is the correct answer.

**13.** 'To come across' means to meet or find by chance. Hence, option (a) is the correct answer. 'Come around' means to agree to do something eventually, after a long wait. 'Come to' means to become conscious. 'Come at' means to make a threatening move toward someone or something.

**14.** 'At' is used to indicate the place where someone or something is. 'On' is used to indicate the part or object by which someone or something is supported. 'To' is used to indicate the direction of something. 'In' is used to indicate location or position within something. Only 'at' fits in the meaning of the sentence, rendering option (a) the answer.

**15.** 'In' is used as a function word to indicate means, medium, or instrumentality. Hence, option (b) is the correct answer. 'From' is used to indicate the starting point of a physical movement or action. 'With' is used to say that people or things are together in one place. 'On' is used as a function word to indicate position in or in contact with an outer surface.

**16.** 'Interfere with something' means to prevent something from happening or developing in the correct way. 'Interfere in' means to deliberately become involved in a situation and try to influence the way that it develops, although you have no right to do this. Hence, option (d) is the correct answer.

**17.** 'Get out' means to come out. Hence, option (c) is the correct answer. 'Get off' means to start, as on a trip.

**18.** Out of the four options, only 'correcting' goes with 'pronunciation'. Hence, option (b) is the correct answer.

**19.** 'Ship' is personified as female. So, option (b) is the correct answer.

## READING COMPREHENSION

**Direction for Questions 1-10:** Read the given passage carefully and answer the questions given after the passage:

1. Often, we passionately pursue matters that in the future appear to be contradictory to our real intention or nature; and triumph is followed by remorse or regret. There are numerous examples of such a trend in the annals of history and contemporary life.
2. Alfred Nobel was the son of Immanuel Nobel, an inventor who experimented extensively with explosives. Alfred too carried out research and experiments with a large range of chemicals; he found new methods to blast rocks for the construction of roads and bridges; he was engaged in the development of technology and different weapons; his life revolved around rockets and cannons and gun powder. The ingenuity of the scientist brought him enough wealth to buy the Bofors armament plant in Sweden.
3. Paradoxically, Nobel's life was a busy one yet he was lonely; and as he grew older, he began suffering from guilt of having invented the dynamite that was being used for destructive purposes. He set aside a huge part of his wealth to institute Nobel Prizes. Besides honouring men and women for their extraordinary achievements in physics, chemistry, medicine and literature, he wished to honour people who worked for the promotion of peace.
4. It's strange that the very man whose name was closely connected with explosives and inventions that helped in waging wars willed a large part of his earnings for the people who work for the promotion of peace and the benefit of mankind. The Nobel Peace Prize is intended for a person who has accomplished the best work for fraternity among nations, for abolition or reduction of war and for promotion of peace.
5. Another example that comes to one's mind is that of Albert Einstein. In 1939, fearing that the Nazis would win the race to build the world's first atomic bomb, Einstein urged President Franklin D Roosevelt to launch an American programme on nuclear research. The matter was considered and a project called the Manhattan Project was initiated. The project involved intense nuclear research the construction of the world's first atomic bomb. All this while, Einstein had the impression that the bomb would be used to protect the world from the Nazis. But in 1945, when Hiroshima was bombed to end World War II, Einstein was deeply grieved and he regretted his endorsement of the need for nuclear research.
6. He also stated that had he known that the Germans would be unsuccessful in making the atomic bomb, he would have probably never recommended making one. In 1947, Einstein began working for the cause of disarmament. But, Einstein's name still continues to be linked with the bomb.

   Man's fluctuating thoughts, changing opinions, varying opportunities keep the mind in a state of flux. Hence, the paradox of life: it's certain that nothing is certain in life.

**1.** The passage is __________.
(*a*) a descriptive essay
(*b*) an argumentative essay
(*c*) an expository essay
(*d*) a process essay.

**2.** Einstein had the impression that the Germans would __________.
(*a*) be successful in making the world's first atomic bomb
(*b*) bomb Hiroshima
(*c*) work for humanity
(*d*) be unsuccessful in making the atomic bomb

**3.** Alfred established the Nobel Prizes to __________.
(*a*) honour only those people who are intelligent.
(*b*) ease his guilt and promote work for the betterment of mankind.
(*c*) use his wealth for hard working people.
(*d*) remind people of his achievements.

**4.** Immanuel's interest in dynamites influenced Alfred's inclination for working __________.
(*a*) with explosives
(*b*) with contradiction
(*c*) for humanity
(*d*) for the Nobel Peace Prize

**5.** In the fifth paragraph, the word 'endorsement' means
(*a*) expressing one's approval or support
(*b*) expressing one's regret.
(*c*) expressing one's opposition
(*d*) making a promise to do something.

**6.** In paragraph 4, the word 'accomplished' means __________.
(*a*) won awards
(*b*) completed successfully
(*c*) worked hard
(*d*) made an effort to do something

7. The paradox, 'it's certain that nothing is certain in life', indicates the writer's
   (*a*) scientific mind
   (*b*) persuasive nature
   (*c*) analytical mind
   (*d*) hatred for scientists

8. One of the paradoxes in Alfred's life was that he was ________.
   (*a*) lonely yet rich
   (*b*) hard working but a failure
   (*c*) intelligent yet lonely
   (*d*) occupied yet lonely

9. The Manhattan Project was initiated ________.
   (*a*) to carry out nuclear research
   (*b*) to protect the Nazis
   (*c*) to bomb Hiroshima
   (*d*) in honour of Einstein

10. Working with arms and ammunition helped Alfred to amass ______.
    (*a*) wealth
    (*b*) intelligence
    (*c*) popularity
    (*d*) enemies

## ANSWERS

| | | | | |
|---|---|---|---|---|
| 1.(*a*) | 2.(*a*) | 3.(*b*) | 4.(*a*) | 5.(*a*) |
| 6.(*b*) | 7.(*c*) | 8.(*d*) | 9.(*a*) | 10.(*a*) |

## EXPLANATIONS

1. The passage is descriptive in nature. It talks about people who invented certain things with a good intention but their inventions were used for negative or destructive purposes. Hence, option (a) is the correct answer.
2. Refer to the line "In 1939, fearing that the Nazis would win…launch an American programme on nuclear research." Hence, option (a) is the correct answer.
3. Refer to the paragraph "Paradoxically, Nobel's life was a busy one…worked for the promotion of peace." Hence, option (b) is the correct answer.
4. We can infer from the second paragraph that Immanuel's interest in dynamites influenced Alfred's inclination for working with explosives. Hence, option (a) is the correct answer.
5. 'Endorsement', as used in paragraph 5, means expressing one's approval or support.
6. 'Accomplished', as used in paragraph 4, means completed successfully.
7. The paradox indicates that the writer has an analytical mind. Hence, option (c) is the correct answer.
8. Refer to the line "Paradoxically, Nobel's life was a busy one yet he was lonely Paradoxically, Nobel's life was a busy one yet he was lonely". Hence, option (d) is the correct answer.
9. Refer to the fifth paragraph. It clearly says that the Manhattan project was initiated to carry out nuclear research.
10. Refer to the line "The ingenuity of the scientist brought him enough wealth…". Hence, option (a) is the correct answer.

# REASONING

## VERBAL LOGIC

**Direction for Questions 1–3 :** Read the following information carefully and choose the most appropriate option:

A and B are good in driving bus and car. C and A are good in driving car and scooter. C, D and E are good in driving scooter and tractor. E and C are good in driving scooter and auto- rickshaw. D and B are good in driving bus and tractor.

1. Who is good in driving scooter, tractor and auto-rickshaw but not good in driving car?
   (*a*) C (*b*) A
   (*c*) D (*d*) E
2. Who is good in driving tractor, scooter, car and auto-rickshaw but not bus?
   (*a*) D (*b*) B
   (*c*) C (*d*) A
3. Who is good in driving scooter, tractor and bus?
   (*a*) D (*b*) C
   (*c*) A (*d*) B
4. Four statements are given below. Group two of them in such a way that one is logically incorrect and the other is verifiable as a matter of fact
   (a) The Sun does not rise in the East
   (b) A straight line is the shortest distance between any two points
   (c) Every circle has a centre
   (d) The maximum duration of a total solar eclipse is about 7.5 minutes
   (*a*) [a, c] (*b*) [c, d]
   (*c*) [a, d] (*d*) [a, b]

**Direction for Questions 5-6 :** Read the following information carefully and choose the most appropriate option:

In each question, there is a statement and two assumptions numbered as I and II. Read the statement and find which of the given assumptions is implicit:

(A) If assumption I is implicit.

(B) If assumption II is implicit.

(C) If neither assumption I nor Assumption II is implicit.

(D) If both Assumption I and Assumption II are implicit.

**5. Statement:** To attend a convocation ceremony scheduled to be held on Thursday at GM University, Chennai, Mr X left for Chennai on Tuesday by train.

**Assumptions:**

I. Mr X may reach home on Saturday

II. Mr X may reach the University on Wednesday

(*a*) Both Assumption I and Assumption II are implicit.

(*b*) Assumption II is implicit.

(*c*) Neither assumption I nor Assumption II is implicit.

(*d*) Assumption I is implicit.

**6. Statement:** In the State of Zuminisia, people prefer to travel by X airline instead of Y airline, as X airline has advanced German security system and 99% on time operations.

**Assumptions:**

I. Airline X with advanced German security system and record on time operation is perceived better than airline Y.

II. Had advanced German security system and on time performance record of Y airline been implemented, it would have been preferred over airline X.

(*a*) Assumption I is implicit.

(*b*) Neither assumption I nor Assumption II is implicit.

(*c*) Both Assumption I and Assumption II are implicit.

(*d*) Assumption II is implicit.

**7. Statement:** The next meeting of the executive board of a company will be held after six months.

**Assumptions:**

I. Existing executive board will be dissolved before six months

II. The company will remain in function after six months

(*a*) Assumption II is implicit.

(*b*) Assumption I is implicit.

(*c*) Neither assumption I nor Assumption II is implicit.

(*d*) Both Assumption I and Assumption II are implicit.

**8.** Assume that both premises, 'No innocent person should be punished' and 'Socrates is innocent' are true. Then which one of the following options is necessarily true?

(*a*) Socrates is not punished

(*b*) Socrates should not be punished.

(*c*) It is not proper to punish Socrates.

(*d*) Socrates may not be punished.

**9.** If it is false that 'Men always pray to God', then which one of the following statements is true?

(*a*) Men always pray to God

(*b*) Some men pray to God

(*c*) All men pray to God

(*d*) Men seldom pray to God.

**10.** From among the given options, identify the statement which means the same as the statement 'The dual nature of light is an enigma'.

(*a*) Two contradictory descriptions of light presuppose a third description.

(*b*) Light has distinct properties which makes it unique.

(*c*) Light is mysterious.

(*d*) The nature of light is an enigma.

**11.** Identify the statement which cannot be true.

(*a*) All bachelors are faithful to their wives

(*b*) Black body radiation is a physical phenomenon

(*c*) Snow is white

(*d*) Every natural number has a successor

**12.** If it is false that 'There is at least one octogenarian in the room', then which one of the following is probable?

(*a*) One person in the room is not an octogenarian

(*b*) All those who are in the room are octogenarians

(*c*) No one in the room is an octogenarian

(*d*) Some people in the room are not octogenarians

**13.** If it is true that 'All humans are imperfect', then which one of the following is necessarily true?

(*a*) Every human is imperfect

(*b*) Some humans are not imperfect

(*c*) All imperfect beings are humans

(*d*) No humans are imperfect

**14.** Identify the argument which cannot be accepted.

(*a*) All rainy days are wet days. Therefore, all wet days are rainy days

(*b*) All unmarried women are spinsters. Therefore, all spinsters are women.

(*c*) All equilateral triangles are equiangular. Therefore, all equiangular triangles are equilateral.

(*d*) All wives are married. Therefore, all married people are wives.

**15.** If it is false that 'Animals are seldom aggressive', then which one of the following statements conveys the same meaning?

(*a*) Sometimes animals are aggressive

(*b*) All animals are aggressive

(*c*) At least one animal is aggressive

(*d*) All animals are always aggressive

**16.** If it is true that 'Religious fundamentalism is dangerous to the society', then which one of the following statements can also be true?

(*a*) Belief in any religion is dangerous to the society.

(*b*) Disrespect for other religions is dangerous to the society.

(*c*) Religious pluralism is dangerous to the society.

(*d*) Religion without reason is dangerous to the society.

**Direction for Questions 17-18 :** Read the following information carefully and choose the most appropriate option:

In each of the questions, two statements are numbered as I and II. There may be a cause and effect relationship between the two statements. The statements may be the effect of the same cause or an independent cause. The statements may be independent causes without having any relationship. Read both the statements and mark your answer as:

(A) If statement I is the cause and statement II is its effect.

(B) If statement II is the cause and statement I is its effect.

(C) If both statements I and II are independent causes.

(D) If both statements I and II are effects of independent causes.

**17. Statement I:** In last two years, there is a considerable reduction in cancellation of flights due to fog in North India.

**Statement II:** In last two years, there is a considerable improvement in passenger amenities on all airports of North India.

(*a*) Statement II is the cause and statement I is its effect.

(*b*) Both statements I and II are effects of independent causes.

(*c*) Both statements I and II are independent causes.

(*d*) Statement I is the cause and statement II is its effect.

**18. Statement I:** The Government, by legislation has decided to make all public information available to general public.

**Statement II:** Before passing of legislation, general public did not have access to public information.

(*a*) Both statements I and II are effects of independent causes.

(*b*) Both statements I and II are independent causes.

(*c*) Statement II is the cause and statement I is its effect.

(*d*) Statement I is the cause and statement II is its effect.

**19.** If it is true that 'Good governance implies law and order in society' then identify the statement which has to be accepted along with the given statement?

(*a*) An able government very effectively uses laws to promote peace.

(*b*) A strong government uses force to impose laws.

(*c*) A healthy society is governed by maximum number of laws.

(*d*) Law is indispensable for the society.

**20.** Identify the statement which cannot be false.

(*a*) Myopia is a congenital disorder.

(*b*) Democracy is the best form of government.

(*c*) Water evaporates at 100° C.

(*d*) All radii of any given circle are of equal length.

## ANSWERS

| | | | | |
|---|---|---|---|---|
| **1.**(*d*) | **2.**(*c*) | **3.**(*a*) | **4.**(*c*) | **5.**(*b*) |
| **6.**(*a*) | **7.**(*a*) | **8.**(*b*) | **9.**(*d*) | **10.**(*d*) |
| **11.**(*a*) | **12.**(*c*) | **13.**(*a*) | **14.**(*d*) | **15.**(*a*) |
| **16.**(*b*) | **17.**(*b*) | **18.**(*c*) | **19.**(*a*) | **20.**(*d*) |

## EXPLANATIONS

**For questions 1 to 3:**

| Person | Bus | Car | Scooter | Tractor | Auto |
|---|---|---|---|---|---|
| A | √ | √ | | | |
| B | √ | √ | | | |
| C | | √ | √ | √ | √ |
| D | √ | | √ | √ | |
| E | | | | √ | √ |

**4.** It is a fact that sun rises in the east. So, a is logically incorrect. We can measure the maximum duration of every solar eclipse. So, it is verifiable. Hence, option (c) is the correct answer. (b) is not verifiable.

Although it is a fact that straight line is the shortest distance between any two points but we cannot verify that for any two given points on planet Earth. Similarly, it is a fact that every circle has a center, but that cannot be verified for any given circle.

**5.** Since the convocation is on Thursday, we can assume that he may reach the university on Wednesday. We cannot assume when he will come back since he might stay in Chennai for some time. Hence, option (b) is the correct answer.

6. Assumption I is implicit because the statement clearly says that people prefer to travel by X airline. Assumption II is not implicit because even if advanced German security system and on time performance record is implemented in airline Y, there still may be other factors that will make airline X more preferable than airline Y. Hence, option (a) is the correct answer.

7. Assumption I is not implicit because there is no need to dissolve a board to hold a meeting. Next meeting can be held even if the previous board is not dissolved. Assumption II is implicit. Since there will be a board meeting after 6 months, we can assume that the company will remain in function after 6 months.

**8.** Since Socrates is an innocent person and no innocent person is punished, Socrates should not be punished. Hence, option (b) is the correct answer.

**9.** If men do not always pray to god, then the correct statement will be that they seldom pray to god. Hence, option (d) is the correct answer.

**10.** Option (d) simply rephrases the given statement. Hence, option (d) is the correct answer.

**11.** Option (a) cannot be true since bachelors do not have wives. Hence, option (a) is the correct answer.

**12.** If it is false that there is at least one octogenarian in the room than it means that there is no octogenarian in the room. Hence, option (c) is the correct answer.

**13.** If all humans are imperfect, then every human has to be imperfect. Hence, option (a) is the correct answer.

**14.** All married people are not wives. So, if all wives are married, we cannot assume that all married people are wives. Hence, option (d) is the correct answer.

**15.** The statement that convey the same meaning as that given in the question is that 'Sometimes animals are aggressive'. Hence, option (a) is the correct answer.

**16.** Fundamentalism has a religious connotation that indicates unwavering attachment to a set of irreducible beliefs. So, if 'religious fundamentalism' is dangerous to society, then disrespecting other religions will also be dangerous to society. Hence, option (b) is the correct answer.

**17.** Both the statements are effects of independent causes. There have been cancellations because of the fog while there has been considerable improvement in passenger amenities because of some unstated reason.

**18.** The government passed a legislation to make public information available to general public because the public did not have access to public information earlier. So, statement II is the cause and statement I is the effect. Hence, option (c) is the correct answer.

**19.** The statement says that good governance conveys that there is law and order in the society. If the statement is true, then we have to agree that an effective government effectively uses laws to promote peace. Hence, option (a) is the correct answer.

**20.** Congenital disorder is a condition existing at or before birth. Myopia does not exist at or on birth. So, option (a) is incorrect. Option (b) is incorrect because it is an opinion that it is the best form of government. Option (c) is incorrect because water boils and not evaporates at 100 degree Celsius. Option (d) is correct. All radii of any given circle are equal.

## ANALYTICAL REASONING

**Direction for Questions 1-7:** Choose the most appropriate option:

**1.** If Oceans are Deserts, then Waves are:

(*a*) Powerful (*b*) Ripples
(*c*) Water (*d*) Sand Dunes

**2.** In certain code MAIL is written as ZNVY then how will FILM be written in that code?

(*a*) MLIF (*b*) SVYZ
(*c*) NORY (*d*) XLMP

**3.** Who among the following is the odd one in the following group of persons?

Chief Justice of India, Attorney General of India, Solicitor General, Advocate General

(*a*) Solicitor General
(*b*) Advocate General
(*c*) Attorney General of India
(*d*) Chief Justice of India

**4.** Choose the pair of words from the options that best represents a similar relationship as the one expressed in the following pair of words.

WAITER: RESTAURANT

(*a*) Driver : Car (*b*) Actor : Acting
(*c*) Author : Book (*d*) Teacher : School

**5.** This question consists of a related pair of words, followed by four pairs of words. Choose the pair that best represents a similar relationship as the one expressed in the given pair of words:

SANDERLING : BIRD

(*a*) Water : Fish

(*b*) Mastiff: Dog

(*c*) Cat : Mare

(*d*) Frog : Toad

**6.** Find the odd one out from the following group.

WINDSHIELD, SPARK PLUG, CLUTCH PEDAL, CAR, ENGINE

(*a*) Car

(*b*) Windshield

(*c*) Spark Plug

(*d*) Engine

**7.** There is some relationship between the figures given in the series. Find out the missing one from the alternatives given below.

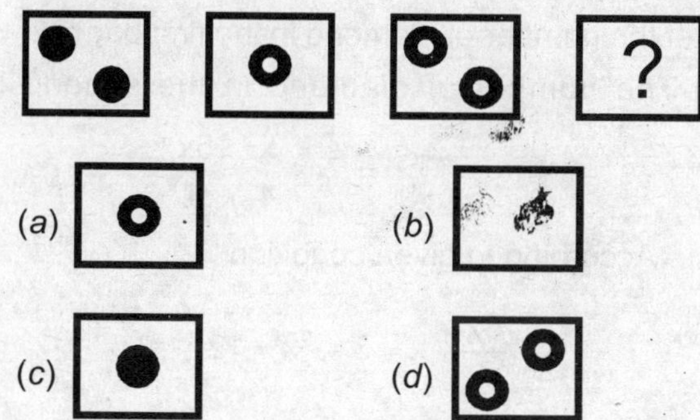

**Direction for Questions 8-9:** Read the following information carefully and choose the most appropriate option:

In a joint family, A, B, C, D, E, and F are the members. B is the son of C. A and C are husband and wife. C is not the mother of B. E is the brother of C. D is the daughter of A and F is the brother of B.

**8.** Which of the following is a pair of females in the family?

(*a*) AD (*b*) DF

(*c*) BD (*d*) AE

**9.** Who is the mother of B?

(*a*) F (*b*) D

(*c*) A (*d*) E

**10.** In a class, student X has 8th position from the top and 84th from the bottom. How many students are there in the class?

(*a*) 88 (*b*) 96

(*c*) 98 (*d*) 91

**11.** In a bag, there are some diamonds. In another bag, there are one fourth the number more than the number of diamonds in the first bag. If the difference in the number of diamonds in the first and second bag is 3, how many diamonds are there in the first bag?

(*a*) 10 (*b*) 16

(*c*) 12 (*d*) 8

**12.** You are given a 60-inch long ribbon, and you are instructed to cut 60 1-inch long strips out of this ribbon. The time taken to cut one strip is one second. So how long will it take to cut 60 strips?

(*a*) 1 minute and 1 second

(*b*) 30 seconds

(*c*) 1 minute

(*d*) 59 seconds

**13.** A, B, C and D have got some money with them. If A gives 8 rupees to B, B will have as much as C has and A will have 3 rupees less than what C has. Also if A takes 6 rupees from C, A will have twice as much money as D. If B and D together have 50 rupees, how much money does A and B have respectively?

(*a*) 29, 32 (*b*) 27, 40

(*c*) 32, 29 (*d*) 40, 27

**14.** Geeta is twice the present age of Seema. If age of Seema is 20 years now, how many years ago Geeta was three times Seema's age?

(*a*) 10 (*b*) 8

(*c*) 12 (*d*) 9

**15.** An old woman decided to divide her gold among her daughter and daughters-in-law. She first kept exactly half of the gold for her daughter. Then she divided the rest of her gold among her daughters-in-law. The eldest one got 26 grams more than the youngest daughter-in-law. The middle one got twice as the youngest one. If the eldest daughter-in-law got 66 grams of gold, how much was received by the daughter?

(*a*) 186 grams

(*b*) 192 grams

(*c*) 172 grams

(*d*) 194 grams

**16.** A 2100 member team consisting of Team Leaders and Athletes is attending a National Athletic Meet. For every 20 Athletes, there is one Team Leader. How many Team Leaders would be there in the team?

(*a*) 100 (*b*) 105

(*c*) 95 (*d*) 110

**17.** Mr. X, the President of a club arrived in a meeting at 10 minutes to 1230 hrs. Mr X came earlier by 20 minutes than the other participating members in the meeting, who arrived late by 30 minutes. At what time was the meeting scheduled?

(*a*) 1240 hrs (*b*) 1220 hrs

(*c*) 1250 hrs (*d*) 1210 hrs

**18.** Examine the series and identify the missing number:

46, 44, 40, 38, 34, â?¦

(*a*) 30 (*b*) 28

(*c*) 32 (*d*) 26

**19.** Examine the following numbers and identify the next number:

45; 43; 40; 36; 31; 25; ....

(*a*) 17 (*b*) 29

(*c*) 18 (*d*) 23

**20.** Which word in the following group DOES NOT belong to the others?

PROSPER, EXCITE, THRIVE, FLOURISH

(*a*) Thrive (*b*) Prosper

(*c*) Flourish (*d*) Excite

## ANSWERS

| | | | | |
|---|---|---|---|---|
| **1.** (*d*) | **2.** (*b*) | **3.** (*d*) | **4.** (*d*) | **5.** (*b*) |
| **6.** (*a*) | **7.** (*c*) | **8.** (*a*) | **9.** (*c*) | **10.** (*d*) |
| **11.** (*c*) | **12.** (*d*) | **13.** (*d*) | **14.** (*a*) | **15.** (*a*) |
| **16.** (*a*) | **17.** (*d*) | **18.** (*c*) | **19.** (*c*) | **20.** (*d*) |

## EXPLANATIONS

**1.** Waves are formed in oceans due to wind. Similarly, sand dunes are formed in deserts due to wind. Hence, option (d) is the correct answer.

**2.** Coding pattern is as follows:

$M \xrightarrow{+13} Z$

$A \xrightarrow{+13} N$

$I \xrightarrow{+13} V$

$L \xrightarrow{+13} Y$

Similarly,

$F \xrightarrow{+13} S$

$I \xrightarrow{+13} V$

$L \xrightarrow{+13} Y$

$M \xrightarrow{+13} Z$

**3.** Chief Justice of India does not act on behalf of government, while the others act on behalf of the government. Chief Justice of India is a part of judiciary.

**4.** Just like a waiter works at a restaurant, a teacher works at a school. Hence, option (d) is the correct answer.

**5.** 'Sanderling' is a type of bird. Similarly, 'mastiff' is a type of a dog. Hence, option (b) is the correct answer.

**6.** All the other options are parts of a car. Hence, option (a) is the correct answer.

**7.** It is clear from the pattern that the required figure must contain one black dot.

**For questions 8 and 9:** The family tree is given below:

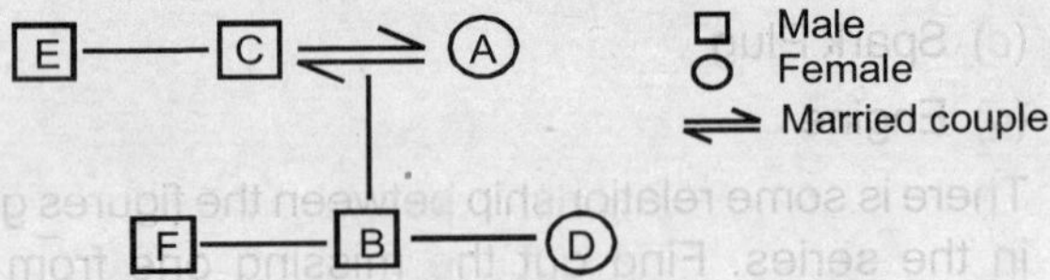


**10.** The required number of students = (84 + 8) – 1 = 91.

**11.** Let the number of diamond in the first bag = x.

∴ The number of diamond in the second bad

$$= x + \frac{x}{4} = \frac{5x}{4}$$

According to given condition

$$\frac{5x}{4} - x = 3 \Rightarrow x = 12.$$

**12.** The number of cut require to cut the ribbon in 60 pieces is 59.

Hence, the required time is 59 seconds.

**13.** Let the amount with B is Rs. x.

So, according to the condition amount with the person is given below:

$A \rightarrow x + 13$

$B \rightarrow x$

$C \rightarrow x + 8$

$D \rightarrow \frac{x+19}{2}$

$$\text{Now } x + \frac{x+19}{2} = 50 \Rightarrow x = 27$$

∴ Amount with A and B are Rs. 40 and Rs. 27 respectively.

**14.** Let the present age of Seema = 20 years

The present age of Geeta = 40 years

10 years ago Geeta will be thrice that of Seema.

**15.** Amont with eldest daughter-in-law = 66 g

Amount with youngest daughter-in-law = 40 g

Amount with middle daughter-in-law = 80 g

Amount with all the daughter-in-law = 186 g

∴ Amount with daughter = 186 g

[As half is given to the daughter and rest half is given to daughters-in-law.]

**16.** Let the member of team leaders be x.

∴ The member of Athletes = 20x.

Now $x + 20x = 2100$

⇒ $x = 100.$

**17.** Mr. X came at 12:20 other members came at 12:40. Since other members were 30 minutes late. So, meeting was scheduled at 12:10.

**18.** Pattern of the sequence is as follows:

48 – 2 = 44, 44 – 4 = 40, 40 – 2 = 38, 38 – 4 = 34

34 – 2 = <u>32</u>

**19.** Patter of the sequence is as follows:

45 – 2 = 43, 43 – 3 = 40, 40 – 4 = 36, 36 – 5 = 31, 31 – 6 = 25, 25 – 7 = <u>18</u>

**20.** 'Prosper', 'thrive' and 'flourish' are synonymous to each other. 'Excite' is the odd one out, rendering option (d) the correct answer.

# QUANTITATIVE APTITUDE

## NUMBER SYSTEM

**Direction for Questions 1-2:** Choose the most appropriate option:

**1.** Two consecutive even positive integers, sum of the squares of which is 1060 are:

(*a*) 20 and 22 (*b*) 12 and 14

(*c*) 22 and 24 (*d*) 16 and 18

**2.** The number of 'three digit numbers' which are multiples of 9 are:

(*a*) 99 (*b*) 101

(*c*) 98 (*d*) 100

## ANSWERS

**1.**(*c*) **2.**(*d*)

## EXPLANATIONS

**1.** $x^2 + (x + 2)^2 = 1060 \quad (x > 0)$

⇒ $x = 22$

So the two numbers are 22 and 24

[Note: use option]

**2.** The required number $= \frac{999}{9} - \frac{99}{9} = 100$

## ARITHMETIC

**Direction for Questions 1-12:** Choose the most appropriate option:

**1.** The value of a machine depreciates every year at the rate of 10% on its value at the beginning of that year. If the present value of the machine is Rs. 729, its worth three years ago was:

(*a*) Rs. 1,000 (*b*) Rs. 947.70

(*c*) Rs. 750.87 (*d*) Rs. 800

**2.** The mean of 72 items was found to be 63. If two of the items were mis-recorded as 27 and 9 instead of 72 and 90 respectively, find the correct mean.

(*a*) 65.75 (*b*) 64.75

(*c*) 66.25 (*d*) 64.25

**3.** A circular park, 42 m in diameter, has a path 3.5 m wide running around it on the outside. Find the cost of gravelling the path at Rs. 4 per m2

(*a*) Rs. 2002 (*b*) Rs. 1652

(*c*) Rs. 2048 (*d*) Rs. 1672

**4.** A man buys Rs. 20 shares paying 9% dividend. The man expects to have an interest of 12% on his money. The market value of each share is:

(*a*) Rs. 12 (*b*) Rs. 18

(*c*) Rs. 21 (*d*) Rs. 15

**5.** A train which is moving at an average speed of 40 kmph, reaches its destination on time. When its average speed reduces to 35 kmph, then it reaches its destination 15 minutes late. The distance travelled by the train is:

(*a*) 30 kms (*b*) 80 kms

(*c*) 40 kms (*d*) 70 kms

**6.** 60 kg of an alloy X is mixed with 100 kg of an alloy Y. If alloy X has lead and tin in the ratio of 3 : 2 and alloy Y has tin and copper in the ratio of 1 : 4, then the amount of tin in the new alloy is

(*a*) 80 kgs. (*b*) 36 kgs.

(*c*) 44 kgs. (*d*) 53 kgs.

**7.** A man earns Rs. 20 on the first day and spends Rs. 15 on the next day. He again earns Rs. 20 on the third day and spends Rs. 15 on the fourth day. If he continues to save in this way, how soon will he have Rs. 60 in hand?

(*a*) on 27th day (*b*) on 12th day

(*c*) on 24th day (*d*) on 17th day

**8.** The traffic lights at three different signal points change after every 45 seconds, 75 seconds and 90 seconds respectively. If all change simultaneously at 7:20:15 hours, then they will change again simultaneously at

(*a*) 7:27:45 hours (*b*) 7:27:30 hours
(*c*) 7:27:50 hours (*d*) 7:28:00 hours

**9.** What is the sum of all the natural numbers from 1 to 100?

(*a*) 5052 (*b*) 5000
(*c*) 6000 (*d*) 5050

**10.** A part of monthly hostel charges is fixed and the remaining depends on the number of days one has taken food in the mess. When a student A takes food for 20 days, she has to pay Rs. 1000 as hostel charges whereas a student B, who takes food for 26 days, pays Rs. 1180 as hostel charges. Find the fixed charges and the cost of food per day.

(*a*) 400, 40
(*b*) 400, 30
(*c*) 300, 30
(*d*) 200, 20

**11.** A shop gives 15% discount on the purchase of a T.V. If paid for in cash immediately, a further discount of 12% is given. If the marked price is Rs. 15,000, what is the price of the T.V if cash purchase is made?

(*a*) Rs. 10,950
(*b*) Rs. 11,220
(*c*) Rs. 11,475
(*d*) Rs. 12,750

**12.** A library has an average of 510 visitors on Sundays and 240 on other days. What is the average number of visitors per day in the month of June beginning with a Sunday?

(*a*) 280 (*b*) 250
(*c*) 276 (*d*) 285

## ANSWERS

| | | | | |
|---|---|---|---|---|
| **1.**(*a*) | **2.**(*b*) | **3.**(*a*) | **4.**(*d*) | **5.**(*d*) |
| **6.**(*c*) | **7.**(*d*) | **8.**(*a*) | **9.**(*d*) | **10.**(*b*) |
| **11.**(*b*) | **12.**(*d*) | | | |

## EXPLANATIONS

**1.** Let the value of machine three years ago was Rs. x.

$$\therefore x\left(1-\frac{10}{100}\right)^3 = 729 \Rightarrow x = 1000.$$

**2.** Error in sum = (77 – 27) + (90 – 9) = 126

$$\therefore \text{Correct mean} = 63 + \frac{126}{72} = 64.75.$$

**3.** Inner radius of that park = 21 m

Outer radius of the park = 21 + 3.5 = 24.5 m

$$\therefore \text{Area of path} = \pi\left((24.5)^2 - (21)^2\right) = 500.5 \text{ m}^2$$

$\therefore$ Cost of gravelling = 500.5 × 4 = Rs. 2002.

**4.** Let the market value of share be x.

$\therefore$ 12% of x = 9% of 20

$$\Rightarrow \frac{12}{100}x = \frac{9}{100} \times 20 \Rightarrow x = 15.$$

**5.** $$\frac{d}{35} - \frac{d}{40} = \frac{15}{60}$$

$\Rightarrow$ d = 70 km.

**6.** Amount of tin in alloy X = $\frac{2}{5} \times 60 = 24$ kg

Amount of tin in alloy Y = $\frac{1}{5} \times 100 = 20$ kg

$\therefore$ Amount of tin in new alloy = 24 + 20 = 44 kg.

**7.** In two days saving = Rs. 5

Saving in 16 days = Rs. 40

Income on 17th day = Rs. 20

In hand on 17th day = Rs. 64.

**8.** LCM of 45, 75 and 90 = 450

i.e. 7 minutes 30 seconds

$\therefore$ The required time = 7:27:45.

**9.** The required sum = $\frac{100 \times 101}{2} = 5050.$

**10.** Let the fixed charge be Rs. x and the cost of food per day be Rs. y.

$\therefore$ x + 20y = 1000 ...(i)

x + 26y = 1180 ...(ii)

Solving the above equations, we get

x = 400 and y = 30.

**11.** Price of TV = $15000\left(1-\frac{15}{100}\right)\left(1-\frac{12}{100}\right)$

= Rs. 11,220.

**12.** The required average = $\frac{5 \times 510 + 240 \times 25}{30} = 285.$

## ALGEBRA

1. If the product of zeroes of the polynomial $ax^2 - 6x - 6$ is 4, find the value of 'a'

(a) $\frac{1}{2}$ (b) $-\frac{3}{2}$

(c) $\frac{3}{2}$ (d) $-\frac{1}{2}$

## ANSWERS

1.(b)

## EXPLANATIONS

1. Product of zeros = 4

$\Rightarrow \frac{-6}{a} = 4$

$\Rightarrow a = \frac{-3}{2}.$

# GENERAL KNOWLEDGE

## CONSTITUTION AND POLITY

1. Who is the Chairperson of NITI Aayog?
   (a) Sh. Narendra Modi
   (b) Ms. Sushmita Mahajan
   (c) Ms. Sushma Swaraj
   (d) Sh. Arun Jately
2. Who was the Constitutional Advisor to the Constituent Assembly in framing the Indian Constitution?
   (a) Sir B.N. Rau
   (b) Dr. B.R. Ambedkar
   (c) Pandit Jawaharlal Nehru
   (d) Dr. Rajendra Prasad
3. Under the Constitution of India the official language of the Union is:
   (a) Hindi in Devanagari Script
   (b) Hindi
   (c) English
   (d) English and Hindi
4. Power to summon the Houses of the Parliament is vested with:
   (a) Prime Minister
   (b) Vice-President
   (c) Speaker and Vice-President
   (d) President
5. Parliament of India consists of:
   (a) President, House of the People and Council of States
   (b) House of the People and Council of States
   (c) Council of States
   (d) House of the People
6. The Constitution (One Hundredth Amendment) Act, 2015 was enacted to give effect to:
   (a) the acquiring of territories by India from Bangladesh.
   (b) transfer of certain territories by India to Bangladesh.
   (c) National Judicial Appointment Commission
   (d) the transfer of certain territories by India to Bangladesh and transfer of certain territories from Bangladesh to India
7. The Parliament of which country became first Parliament in the world to run entirely on Solar Power?
   (a) Japan (b) UK
   (c) India (d) Pakistan
8. In case of death of both the President and Vice-President of India, who shall act as the President of India?
   (a) Prime Minister
   (b) Chief Justice of India
   (c) Attorney General of India
   (d) The Parliament will nominate from among its Members
9. In case the President of India wants to resign, he shall address his resignation to the:
   (a) Vice-President
   (b) Chief Justice of India
   (c) Chief Election Commissioner
   (d) Prime Minister

## ANSWERS

| | | | | |
|---|---|---|---|---|
| 1.(a) | 2.(a) | 3.(a) | 4.(d) | 5.(a) |
| 6.(d) | 7.(d) | 8.(b) | 9.(a) | |

## EXPLANATIONS

1. The Prime Minister is Ex-Officio Chairperson for NITI Aayog.
2. Sir B.N. Rau was the Constitutional Advisor to the Constituent Assembly in framing the Indian Constitution.
3. The official language of the Union shall be Hindi in Devanagari script. The form of numerals to be used for the official purposes of the Union shall be the international form of Indian numerals.

4. The President has the power to summon and prorogue either House of Parliament or to dissolve Lok Sabha.
5. The Indian Parliament comprises of the President and the two Houses-Lok Sabha (House of the People) and Rajya Sabha (Council of States).
6. The Constitution (One Hundredth Amendment) Act, 2015 was enacted to give effect to the transfer of certain territories by India to Bangladesh and transfer of certain territories from Bangladesh to India.
7. Pakistan's parliament became the first in the world to completely run on solar power, a venture supported by close ally China with a whopping $55 million funding.
8. In case of death of both the President and Vice-President of India Chief Justice of India shall act as the President of India.
9. In case the President of India wants to resign, he shall address his resignation to the Vice-President.

## CURRENT AFFAIRS

1. Which State has become the first State to introduce compulsory gender education at the graduate level?
   (*a*) Punjab (*b*) Telangana
   (*c*) Andhra Pradesh (*d*) Kerala
2. A Japanese maglev, which is the fastest passenger train in the world, has broken its own record in 2015. The train reached ____________ kmph in the test run.
   (*a*) 453 (*b*) 603
   (*c*) 503 (*d*) 403
3. The Rajya Sabha in April, 2016 passed two Bills, which had already been passed by the Lok Sabha earlier, repealing certain outdated/old laws. The Bills intended to repeal:
   (*a*) 315 laws (*b*) 1053 laws
   (*c*) 153 laws (*d*) 513 laws
4. Country's first 'visually-challenged friendly' railway station is:
   (*a*) Varanasi (*b*) Tirupathi
   (*c*) Mysuru (*d*) New Delhi
5. Who was crowned as the winner of Femina Miss India 2016 and who will represent India at the Miss World pageant?
   (*a*) Sushruthi Krishna
   (*b*) Pankhuri Gidwani
   (*c*) Sushobita Kapoor
   (*d*) Priyadarshini Chatterjee
6. In April 2016, The Duke and Duchess of Cambridge visited India. Their names are:
   (*a*) Prince Hillery and Victoria.
   (*b*) Prince William and Kate Middleton
   (*c*) Prince Robert and Kateler
   (*d*) Prince Charles and Cathy
7. Name the country that has six Deputy Prime Ministers.
   (*a*) Nigeria
   (*b*) Nicaragua
   (*c*) Maldives
   (*d*) Nepal
8. In 2015, Prime Minister Mr. Narendra Modi launched a new campaign, "Start up India, Stand up India". The campaign is aimed at:
   (*a*) Promoting bank financing for start ups and offer incentives to boost entrepreneurship and job creation.
   (*b*) Promoting free education to all children below the age of 14 years and assuring them jobs after obtaining higher education.
   (*c*) Making India Digital
   (*d*) Promoting Swatch Bharat
9. Which State has the largest number of foreign students in India?
   (*a*) Karnataka
   (*b*) Maharashtra
   (*c*) Uttar Pradesh
   (*d*) Haryana
10. The direction to hold floor test to prove majority in the Legislative Assembly of Uttarakhand , to be held on 10th May, 2016 has been given on 6th May, 2016, by :
   (*a*) The Supreme Court of India
   (*b*) The Governor of Uttarakhand
   (*c*) The President of India
   (*d*) The High Court of Uttarakhand
11. Who lit the torch from the sun's rays reflected in a parabolic mirror during the Olympic flame lighting ceremony for the Rio 2016 Olympic Games at the site of ancient Olympia in Greece on 22nd April, 2016?
   (*a*) Ronaldo
   (*b*) Joanie Laureh aka Chyna
   (*c*) Katerina Lehou
   (*d*) Katerina Kaif

**12.** Prime Minister, Mr. Narendra Modi, in March, 2016, launched an ambitious programme "Setu Bharatam". The programme is aimed at:

(*a*) Providing travel concession to senior citizens throughout India.

(*b*) Making all National Highways railway level crossing free by 2019.

(*c*) Linking all major cities and towns by rail, air and road by 2019.

(*d*) Providing travel concession to women and children throughout India.

**13.** The highest peace time gallantry award Ashok Chakra was awarded posthumously during 2016 to:

(*a*) Mahendra Singh

(*b*) Rajesh Atra

(*c*) Jagdish Chand

(*d*) Mohan Nath Goswami

**14.** The "Paris Agreement" was adopted in the twenty first session of Conference of Parties in the month of:

(*a*) January, 2016

(*b*) December, 2015

(*c*) November, 2015

(*d*) February, 2016

**15.** In an attempt to curb black money, the Government has made PAN mandatory for all financial transactions exceeding Rupees: ______

(*a*) 3 lakhs (*b*) 4 lakhs

(*c*) 2 lakhs (*d*) 1 lakhs

**16.** Name the Indian Gymnast who has become the first female Indian Gymnast to qualify for the Olympics.

(*a*) Bisweshwari Nandi

(*b*) Rupinder Kaur

(*c*) Dipa Karmakar

(*d*) Anjubala

**17.** Which State of India was declared in January, 2016 as the "first organic farming State of India"?

(*a*) Haryana

(*b*) Kerala

(*c*) Sikkim

(*d*) Punjab

**18.** India signed the "Paris Agreement on Climate Change" in April, 2016 at:

(*a*) New York

(*b*) Geneva

(*c*) New Delhi

(*d*) Paris

**19.** In January, 2016, at the first stage, the Union Ministry of Urban Development unveiled the list of ______ cities for smart cities mission out of 98 shortlisted cities:

(*a*) 20 (*b*) 25

(*c*) 30 (*d*) 15

**20.** In which of the following States / Union Territories, the Election Commission has decided to hold election in a single phase on May 16, 2016?

(*a*) West Bengal, Kerala and Assam

(*b*) West Bengal, Kerala and Tamil Nadu

(*c*) Assam, Kerala and Pondicherry

(*d*) Kerala, Tamil Nadu and Pondicherry.

## ANSWERS

| | | | | |
|---|---|---|---|---|
| **1.**(*b*) | **2.**(*b*) | **3.**(*b*) | **4.**(*c*) | **5.**(*d*) |
| **6.**(*b*) | **7.**(*d*) | **8.**(*a*) | **9.**(*a*) | **10.**(*a*) |
| **11.**(*c*) | **12.**(*b*) | **13.**(*d*) | **14.**(*b*) | **15.**(*c*) |
| **16.**(*c*) | **17.**(*c*) | **18.**(*a*) | **19.**(*a*) | **20.**(*d*) |

## EXPLANATIONS

**1.** Telangana has become the first State to introduce compulsory gender education at the graduate level; without repeating gender stereotypes in its bilingual textbook titled, 'Towards a World of Equals.'

**2.** Japan has again demonstrated its prowess in high-speed rail travel with its state-of-the-art maglev train setting a world record of just over 600km/h (373mph), just days after it broke its previous 12-year-old record. The seven-car maglev - short for "magnetic levitation" - reached a top speed of 603km/h during what officials described as a "comfortable" zip along a test track near Mount Fuji.

**3.** Parliament passed two bills to repeal outdated 1053 old laws which had become redundant legislations. The Appropriation Acts (Repeal) Bill 2015 that seeks to repeal 758 old appropriation acts which have lost relevance and The Repealing and Amending (Third) Bill, 2015 to repeal 295 enactments and to amend certain other enactments were passed by the Rajya Sabha on Wednesday by voice vote.

**4.** With a view to facilitating visually impaired train passengers, tactile maps of the railway station and train schedules in Braille were unveiled at the Mysuru Railway station. Speaking to reporters after Mysuru MP Pratap Simha inaugurated the facility; Divisional Railway Manager Rajkumar Lal said Mysuru railway station has become the country's first visually challenged friendly station in India.

5. Delhi girl Priyadarshini Chatterjee has bagged the crown for FBB Femina Miss India World; she will now go on to represent India at the Miss World 2016 pageant.
6. The Duke and Duchess of Cambridge have sat together on the bench at the Taj Mahal in India where Diana, Princess of Wales, was pictured 24 years ago. Prince William and Kate Middleton posed at the mausoleum in Agra on the final day of their tour of India and Bhutan.
7. Council of Minister of Nepal consists of the Prime Minister, six Deputy Prime Ministers, seventeen Ministers and four State Minister. The incumbent Prime Minister is Khadga Prasad Oli.
8. In 2015, Prime Minister Mr. Narendra Modi launched a new campaign, "Start up India, Stand up India". The campaign is aimed at promoting bank financing for start ups and offer incentives to boost entrepreneurship and job creation.
9. Karnataka is the most preferred state by foreign students in India, according to a report prepared by the Confederation of Indian Industry (CII).
10. The direction to hold floor test to prove majority in the Legislative Assembly of Uttarakhand , to be held on 10th May, 2016 has been given on 6th May, 2016 , by the Supreme Court of India.
11. Katerina Lehou lit the torch from the sun's rays reflected in a parabolic mirror during the Olympic flame lighting ceremony for the Rio 2016 Olympic Games at the site of ancient Olympia in Greece on 22nd April, 2016.
12. Prime Minister, Mr. Narendra Modi, in March, 2016, launched an ambitious programme "Setu Bharatam". The programme is aimed at making all National Highways railway level crossing free by 2019.
13. The highest peace time gallantry award Ashok Chakra was awarded posthumously during 2016 to Mohan Nath Goswami.
14. The "Paris Agreement" was adopted in the twenty first session of Conference of Parties in the month of December, 2015.
15. In an attempt to curb black money, the Government has made PAN mandatory for all financial transactions exceeding Rupees 2 lakhs.
16. Dipa Karmakar created history by becoming the first Indian woman gymnast to qualify for Olympics as she booked a berth for the Rio Games after a strong performance at the final qualifying and test event.
17. Sikkim is declared as First Organic State of India. Shri Narendra Modi, Hon'ble Prime Minister, declared Sikkim as first organic state of India. He appreciated Sikkim for its transformation into an eco-friendly farming state. Hon'ble Prime Minister inaugurated a state flower show.
18. India signed the Paris Agreement on climate change, adopted by more than 190 countries in December 2015,in New York in April 2016.
19. The Narendra Modi government has announced the names of the first 20 cities which will be developed into smart cities in 2016. These 20 cities were chosen from 98 cities shortlisted for the 'Smart Cities Mission'.
20. The Election Commission of India announced the schedule for Assembly elections in four States and one Union Territory, which will be conducted in multiple phases from April 4 to May 16. Elections in Tamil Nadu, Kerala and Puducherry will be held in a single phase on May 16, said Chief Election Commissioner Nasim Zaidi.

## EVERYDAY SCIENCE

1. Mars is also known as the:
   (*a*) Red Planet (*b*) Brown Planet
   (*c*) Blue planet (*d*) Green Planet
2. __________ is the fastest planet to revolve around the Sun.
   (*a*) Venus
   (*b*) Mercury
   (*c*) Mars
   (*d*) Jupiter

## ANSWERS

**1.**(*a*) **2.**(*b*)

## EXPLANATIONS

1. Mars is the fourth planet from the Sun and is the second smallest planet in the solar system. Named after the Roman god of war, Mars is also often described as the "Red Planet" due to its reddish appearance. Mars is a terrestrial planet with a thin atmosphere composed primarily of carbon dioxide.
2. Mercury is the fastest planet, which speeds around the sun at 47.87 km/s. In miles per hour this equates to a whopping 107,082 miles per hour.

## MISCELLANEOUS (QUOTES, DAYS, BOOKS TITLES, SPORTS, BASIC LEGAL CONCEPTS)

1. Which organization has the motto 'Be Prepared'?
   (*a*) National Cadet Corps
   (*b*) National Disaster Management Authority
   (*c*) Boys' Scout
   (*d*) National Service Scheme
2. "Beyond the Lines - An Autobiography" is authored by:
   (*a*) Mr. Arun Shourie (*b*) Justice Krishna Iyer
   (*c*) Mr. Kuldip Nayar (*d*) Mr. Soli Sarab Ji
3. The Currency of Thailand is:
   (*a*) Ringgit (*b*) Baht
   (*c*) Peseta (*d*) Rupee
4. Who is the President of Sri Lanka?
   (*a*) Jayavardane
   (*b*) Ranil Wickramasinghe
   (*c*) Maithripala Sirisena
   (*d*) K. Sripavan
5. Who is the author of "Crime & Punishment"?
   (*a*) Geoffrey Chaucer
   (*b*) Karl Marx
   (*c*) Harold Joseph Laski
   (*d*) Fyodor Dostoevsky
6. Who is the Union Finance Minister of India?
   (*a*) Ms. Sushma Swaraj
   (*b*) Mr. D.V. Sadananda Gowda
   (*c*) Mr. Arun Jaitly
   (*d*) Mr. Rajnath Singh
7. Which day is celebrated as "World Consumer Rights Day"?
   (*a*) 5th June (*b*) 15th July
   (*c*) 15th March (*d*) 5th September
8. Who is the Chairperson of National Human Rights Commission?
   (*a*) Justice B.S. Chauhan
   (*b*) Justice Balakrishnan
   (*c*) Justice H.L. Dattu
   (*d*) Justice D.K. Jain
9. Who is the Chairman of National Green Tribunal?
   (*a*) Justice Bhandhari
   (*b*) Justice Balakrishna Reddy
   (*c*) Justice R.C. Lahoti
   (*d*) Justice Swatanter Kumar
10. Punjabi has become the ________ most common language in the Parliament of Canada.
    (*a*) fifth (*b*) fourth
    (*c*) second (*d*) third
11. How many Indian Universities/Institutes figure among the top 200 in BRICS rankings?
    (*a*) 26 (*b*) 6
    (*c*) 20 (*d*) 16
12. The maximum number of 'Smokeless Villages' are found in the State of:
    (*a*) Telangana
    (*b*) Punjab
    (*c*) Karnataka
    (*d*) Rajasthan
13. Who has written the book "Indomitable Spirit"?
    (*a*) Ms. Arundhati Roy
    (*b*) Dr. A.P.J. Abdul Kalam
    (*c*) Justice Krishna Iyer
    (*d*) Sh. Narendra Modi

## ANSWERS

| | | | | |
|---|---|---|---|---|
| 1.(*c*) | 2.(*c*) | 3.(*b*) | 4.(*c*) | 5.(*d*) |
| 6.(*c*) | 7.(*c*) | 8.(*c*) | 9.(*d*) | 10.(*d*) |
| 11.(*d*) | 12.(*c*) | 13.(*b*) | | |

## EXPLANATIONS

1. The Boy Scouts of America (BSA) is one of the largest youth organizations in the United States, with more than 2.4 million youth members and nearly one million adult volunteers. It's motto is 'Be Prepared'.
2. Beyond the Lines - An Autobiography" is authored by Mr. Kuldip Nayar. As a young law graduate in Sialkot (now in Pakistan), Kuldip Nayar witnessed at first hand the collapse of trust between Hindus and Muslims who were living together for generations.
3. The Thai Baht is the currency of Thailand.
4. Maithripala Sirisena is the current and 6th President of the Democratic Socialist Republic of Sri Lanka.
5. The author of "Crime & Punishment" is Fyodor Dostoyevsky
6. The first finance minister of independent India was R. K. Shanmukham Chetty, who also presented its first Budget. The incumbent Arun Jaitley, of the Bharatiya Janata Party, has held office since 26 May 2014.

7. 15 March is World Consumer Rights Day (WCRD), an annual occasion for celebration and solidarity within the international consumer movement. It marks the date in 1962 President John F Kennedy first outlined the definition of Consumer Rights.

8. Former Chief Justice of India HL Dattu took charge as the Chairperson of the National Human Rights Commission (NHRC). He is the seventh Chairperson of the Commission. Justice KG Balakrishnan completed his tenure on May 11, last year following which member of the Commission Justice Cyriac Joseph held charge as the acting Chairperson

9. On 18 October 2010, Justice Lokeshwar Singh Panta became its first Chairman. Currently it is chaired by Justice Swatanter Kumar since 20 Dec 2012. The Tribunal's dedicated jurisdiction in environmental matters shall provide speedy environmental justice and help reduce the burden of litigation in the higher courts.

10. Punjabi is spoken as a minority language in the world and is the third most spoken language in Canada! Recently, Punjabi has become the third most spoken language in Parliament of Canada after English and French.

11. Indian educational institutes occupy 16 places among top 200 universities in Times Higher Education BRICS and Emerging Economies rankings for 2016. At 16th place, Indian Institute of Science, Bangalore is the only Indian institute to feature in the top 20.

12. Around 60 villages in Karnataka have successfully moved away from traditional stoves that use firewood and cow dung cakes to liquefied petroleum gas (LPG) stoves, thereby becoming "smokeless villages". Announcing this on Wednesday, Indrajit Bose, executive director, (Corporate Communications and Branding), IndianOil, said that of the 120 "smokeless villages" in the country, the maximum were in Karnataka. The country's first "smokeless village" was Vychakurahalli of Gauribidanur taluk of Chickballapur district.

13. Indomitable Spirit is an awesome book written by Dr.A.P.J Abdul Kalam. It is the experience from his own life's journey from the shores of Rameswaram to the hallowed portals of Rashtrapati.

# LEGAL APTITUDE

## TORTS

**This section consists of twelve (12) questions.** Follow the instructions carefully and choose the most appropriate option:

The question numbers 1-12 in this section consist of legal proposition(s)/ principle(s) (hereinafter referred to as 'principle') and facts. Such principles may or may not be true in the real and legal sense, yet you have to conclusively assume them to be true for the purposes of this Section. In other words, in answering the following questions, you must not rely on any principle except the principles those are given herein below for every question. Further, you must not assume any facts other than those stated in the question. The objective of this section is to test your interest towards study of law, research aptitude and problem solving ability, even if the "most reasonable conclusion" arrived at may be absurd or unacceptable for any other reason.

To answer a question, the given principle is to be applied to the given facts so as to arrive at most reasonable conclusion. Only one of the options, i.e., (A), (B), (C), or (D) is the most reasonable conclusion.

1. **Principles:** An independent contractor is one who is employed to do some work of his employer. He is engaged under a contract for services. He undertakes to produce a given result, and in the actual execution of the work, he is not under the direct control or following directions of his employer. He may use his own discretion in execution of the work assigned.

In general, an employer is not liable for the torts (wrongful acts) of his independent contractor. But, the employer may be held liable if he directs him to do some careless acts.

**Facts:** Ramesh hired a taxi-cab to go to Delhi Airport. As he started late from his home, he kept on urging the taxi-driver to drive at a high speed and driver followed the directions; and ultimately due to high speed an accident took place causing injuries to a person.

(*a*) Ramesh would not be held liable for damages because the driver was an independent contractor and not his servant.

(*b*) Ramesh would not be held liable for damages because Ramesh did not know the consequences of such rash driving.

(*c*) Ramesh would be held liable for damages as he exercised the control by giving directions to the driver.

(*d*) Ramesh would not be liable as car was not owned by him.

2. **Principle:** Consent is a good defence for civil action in tort. But consent must include both knowledge of risk and assumption of risk, i.e , readiness to bear harm.

**Facts:** A lady passenger was aware that the driver of the cab, in which she opted to travel was little intoxicated. The cab met with an accident and lady got injured.

(*a*) Lady is not entitled to claim compensation as she had knowledge of the risk.

(*b*) Lady can refuse to pay the fare as she had suffered injuries.

(*c*) Driver can take the plea that he was lightly intoxicated.

(*d*) Lady is entitled to claim compensation as she only knew about risk and there was no assumption of risk.

3. **Principles:** A servant is one who is employed to do some work for his employer (master). He is engaged under a contract of service. He works directly under the control and directions of his master.

In general, the master is vicariously liable for those torts (wrongful acts) of his servant which are done by the servant in the course of his employment.

**Facts:** 'M' appointed 'D' exclusively for the purpose of driving his tourist vehicle. 'M' also appointed 'C' exclusively for the purpose of performing the work of a conductor for the tourist vehicle. During one trip, at the end of the journey, 'C', while 'D' was not on the driver's seat, and apparently for the purpose of turning the vehicle in the right direction for the next journey, drove it through the street at high speed, and negligently injured 'P'.

(*a*) 'M' could be made liable for the act of 'C', as 'C' was employed under a contract of service.

(*b*) 'M' could not be made liable for the act of 'C', as his (C's) act of driving the vehicle was not in the course of his employment.

(*c*) 'M' could be made liable for the act of 'C', as his (C's) act of driving the vehicle was within his scope of employment.

(*d*) 'M' is not liable as he was not present at the time of accident.

4. **Principle:** Whoever by words or writing conveys to others any imputation concerning any person's reputation is said to defame that person.

**Facts:** During a marriage ceremony, 'A' circulated a pamphlet saying that 'S', sister of the bride, is a thief, she has stolen the shoes of the bridegroom.

(*a*) A' has defamed 'S'

(*b*) 'A' did not defame 'S' as he never intended it

(*c*) A' has defamed the bridegroom

(*d*) 'A' defamed the bride

5. **Principle:** A person is said to have committed assault when an apprehension is caused in the mind of a person that he is about to use physical force against his body.

**Facts:** 'A' abuses 'B' while he was sitting in a moving train, by aggressively shaking his fists when 'B' was standing on the railway platform at a distance.

(*a*) 'A' has caused fear of assault in the mind of 'B'

(*b*) A has not committed assault against 'B'

(*c*) 'A' has caused apprehension of assault in the mind of 'B'

(*d*) 'A' has committed assault against 'B'

6. **Principle:** In cases where there is an infringement of legal right even without any actual loss or damage, the person whose right is infringed has a cause of action.

**Facts:** 'P' was wrongfully prevented by the Returning Officer from exercising his vote in an assembly election. However, the candidate for whom he wanted to caste his vote won the election. Still, he ('P') brought an action claiming damages. Which of the following derivations is correct?

(*a*) 'P' would not succeed in his action, as the candidate for whom he wanted to give his vote won the election

(*b*) 'P' would not succeed in his action, as he did not suffer any loss in that election

(*c*) 'P' would succeed in his action, as it is mandatory to cast vote

(*d*) 'P' would succeed in his action, as he was wrongfully prevented from exercising his legal right of voting in that election

7. **Principle:** Intentional application of force to another person is actionable in law.

**Facts:** 'P' and 'D' are unknown to each other. When 'P' is about to sit on a chair, 'D' intentionally pulls it away as a result of which 'P' falls on to the floor and is injured.

(*a*) 'D' is liable as he intentionally caused injury to P

(*b*) 'D' is not liable as the injury is not directly caused

(*c*) 'D' is not liable as 'P' is not seriously injured

(*d*) 'D' is not liable as such jokes are common in the society

8. **Principle:** False imprisonment is a tort (wrong) which means the total restraint of a person's liberty without lawful justification.

**Facts:** A part of a public road had been closed for spectators of a boat race. 'P' wanted to enter but he was prevented by 'D' and other policemen because he had not paid the admission fee. 'P' was able to enter the enclosure by other means but was unable to go where he wanted to go. The policemen refused access to where he wanted to go but allowed him to remain where he was or to go back. 'P' remained within the enclosure and refused to leave. Subsequently, 'P' sued 'D' for false imprisonment.

(*a*) 'D' could not be made liable for false imprisonment as he has not touched him.

(*b*) 'D' could not be made liable for false imprisonment, as he did not totally restrict P's movements.

(*c*) It was a case of false imprisonment, but 'D' could not be made liable for it.

(*d*) 'D' could be made liable for false imprisonment, as he did restrict P's movements.

9. **Principle:** Law does not penalise for wrongs which are of trivial nature.

**Facts:** In the course of a discussion, 'A' threw a file of papers at the table which touched the hands of 'B'.

(*a*) 'A' is liable for his act, as the file touched 'B's hand

(*b*) 'A' is liable for his act, as it assaulted 'B'

(*c*) 'A' is not liable for his act, as it was of trivial nature

(*d*) 'A' is liable for insulting 'B'

10. **Principle:** Consent is a good defence in a civil action for tort but the act should be the same for which consent was given.

**Fact:** 'B' was formally invited by 'A' to his house. 'B' after sitting for some time in drawing room, moved to the bed room of the house. 'A' sued 'B' for trespass.

(*a*) 'B' has interfered with privacy of 'A'

(*b*) 'B' has offended 'A' by moving to bed room.

(*c*) 'B' has committed no trespass as he entered the house with 'A's consent

(*d*) 'B' has committed trespass as there was no consent of 'A' for entry in the Bed room

11. **Principle:** There are certain acts which, though harmful, are not wrongful in law; therefore, do not give legal right to bring action in law, to the person who suffers from such acts.

**Facts:** 'Prakash' has a rice mill. His neighbour, Shanti, sets up another rice mill and offers a tough competition to Prakash. As a consequence, Prakash's profits fall down. He brings a suit against Shanti for damages.

(*a*) Prakash can succeed in his claim for damages, as it is a case of damage as a result of infringement of his legal right.

(*b*) Prakash can succeed in his claim as it is a case of actual damages.

(*c*) Prakash may succeed in his claim for damages, as it is a case of loss to his business.

(*d*) Prakash cannot succeed in his claim for damages, as it is a case of damage without infringement of any legal right.

12. **Principle:** Defamation is the publication of a statement which tends to lower reputation of a person in the estimation of other members of the society generally.

**Facts:** 'A' writes a highly offensive and derogatory letter about 'B', and sends it directly to 'B' in a sealed cover.

(*a*) 'A' is liable to 'B' for defamation, as the letter is highly offensive and derogatory and is directly sent to 'B'.

(*b*) 'A' is liable to 'B' for defamation, as the letter is highly offensive and derogatory.

(*c*) 'A' is liable to 'B' for defamation, as it has hurt his (B's) self-esteem.

(*d*) A' is not liable to 'B' for defamation, since there is no publication to any other person in whose estimation the reputation of 'B' could be brought down.

## ANSWERS

| | | | | |
|---|---|---|---|---|
| **1.**(*c*) | **2.**(*d*) | **3.**(*b*) | **4.**(*a*) | **5.**(*b*) |
| **6.**(*d*) | **7.**(*a*) | **8.**(*b*) | **9.**(*c*) | **10.**(*d*) |
| **11.**(*d*) | **12.**(*d*) | | | |

## EXPLANATIONS

1. Ramesh would be held liable as he directed the taxi driver to drive at high speed and basing on his directions taxi driver drove at high speed, which resulted in the accident. Basing on the third Principle, Ramesh would be held liable.

2. Basing on the Principle lady is entitled to claim compensation as she only knew that the driver of the cab was little intoxicated and there was no assumption of risk. Basing on the Principle, consent can be good defence only when there is both knowledge of risk and assumption of risk.

3. 'M' could not be made liable for the act of 'C', as 'C' was appointed for the purpose of performing the work of Conductor and not as driver of the bus. Act of 'C' falls outside the course of employment and hence 'M' cannot be made liable for the act of 'C'.

4. Basing on the Principle, which is talking about defamation, 'A' has defamed 'S', by circulating pamphlet saying that 's' is a thief.

5. Here 'A' cannot be said to have committed assault as there was no apprehension as to use of physical force. 'A' was sitting in a moving train, while 'B' was standing on the railway platform at a distance and it was not possible for 'A' to hit 'B'.

6. The Principle is based on the legal maxim, "Injuria sine damno". Here , Although there is no actual damage to 'P', as the candidate for whom he wanted to vote has won the election, his legal right to cast vote has been violated and hence "P" would succeed in his action.

7. "D" intentionally pulled the chair, when "P" was about to sit and as a result of which 'P' falls on the floor and is injured and hence basing on the Principle, 'D' is liable as he intentionally caused injury to 'P'.

8. Here "D" was totally justified in not allowing "P" to go where he wanted to go as "P" has not paid the required admission fee, and allowed him to stay where he was or to go back. Hence, "d" could not be made liable for false imprisonment, as he did not totally restrict P's movement.

9. Principle states that Law does not penalize for wrongs which are of trivial nature. Here, the act of "A" was of very trivial nature and hence "A" can't be made liable for his act.

10. Here "B" has committed the trespass as there was no consent of "A" for entry in the bedroom. He was formally invited by "A" and hence he cannot take the defence of consent.

11. Principle is based on legal maxim, "Damnum Sine Injuria", which means injury without any legal damage. Here, Prakash cannot succeed in his claim for damages, as it is a case of damage without infringement of any legal right.

12. According to the principle defamation is the publications of statement which tends to lower the reputation of a person in the estimation of other members of the society generally.

Here, A's action can not be made liable under defamation, as there is no publication of the letter to any other person in whose estimation the reputation of B's could be brought down. It was directly send to "b" and hence "A" cannot be made liable.

## LAW OF CONTRACTS

**This section consists of ten (10) questions.** Follow the instructions carefully and choose the most appropriate option:

The question numbers 1-10 in this section consist of legal proposition(s)/ principle(s) (hereinafter referred to as 'principle') and facts. Such principles may or may not be true in the real and legal sense, yet you have to conclusively assume them to be true for the purposes of this Section. In other words, in answering the following questions, you must not rely on any principle except the principles those are given herein below for every question. Further, you must not assume any facts other than those stated in the question. The objective of this section is to test your interest towards study of law, research aptitude and problem solving ability, even if the "most reasonable conclusion" arrived at may be absurd or unacceptable for any other reason.

To answer a question, the given principle is to be applied to the given facts so as to arrive at most reasonable conclusion. Only one of the options, i.e., (A), (B), (C), or (D) is the most reasonable conclusion.

1. **Principle:** Where a person lawfully does anything for another person, or delivers anything to him, not intending to do so or to provide gratuitously, and such other person takes the benefit of that; the latter is bound to compensate the former for something done or thing provided, or to restore, the thing so delivered.

   **Facts:** Trader 'A' delivers certain eatables at B's house by mistake. 'B' consumed the eatables without asking anything. Which of the following derivations is correct?

   (*a*) It is the discretion of 'B' to make payment to 'A'

   (*b*) 'B' is bound to pay 'A' for the eatables.

   (*c*) 'B' can be made liable to pay for the eatables, only if 'A' establishes an express contract between 'A' and 'B'.

   (*d*) 'B' is not bound to pay 'A' for the eatables.

2. **Principle:**

    1. Wagering agreements are void.

    2. Collateral agreements to wagering contracts are valid.

    **Facts:** XYZ Bank lends Rs. 40, 000 to Sabu in order to enable him to award as prize to Randeep who is the winner of horse race. Later Sabu refuses to pay the prize stating that horse racing is wagering agreement. Can XYZ Bank recover money from Sabu?

    (*a*) Bank can recover money from Sabu so that payment of prize money can be made to Randeep.

    (*b*) No, as it is a wagering contract.

    (*c*) Yes, as it is only a collateral agreement to horse racing and therefore the bank can recover the money from Sabu.

    (*d*) Horse racing is illegal and therefore XYZ Bank cannot recover anything from Sabu.

3. **Principle:** Sale of liquor is illegal. All agreements relating to prohibited items do not exist in the eyes of law.

    **Facts:** 'A' entered into an agreement with 'B' for the sale of liquor. 'A' failed to supply the agreed quantity of liquor to 'B'.

    (*a*) 'A' can bring a legal action against 'B'.

    (*b*) 'B' can bring a legal action against 'B'.

    (*c*) 'B' cannot bring any legal action against 'A'.

    (*d*) 'A' and 'B' can initiate appropriate legal proceeding against each other.

4. **Principle:** Mere silence as to facts likely to affect the decision of a person to enter into a contract is not fraud.

    **Facts:** 'A' sells to 'B' (A's daughter who is minor) a horse which 'A' knows to be unsound. 'A' says nothing to 'B' about the unsoundness of the horse.

    (*a*) 'A' has not committed fraud.

    (*b*) 'A' has committed fraud.

    (*c*) 'B' can take plea of fraud because she is minor.

    (*d*) There cannot be a contract between a father and daughter.

5. **Principle:** An agreement may be entered into orally or in writing, or by conduct.

    **Facts:** 'A' went to the shop of 'B' and picked a toothbrush and gave a cheque of Rupees twenty to 'B' and left the shop.

    (*a*) There was an agreement between 'A' and 'B'.

    (*b*) 'A' did not enter into an agreement with 'B'.

    (*c*) Payment of toothbrush cannot be made through a cheque.

    (*d*) 'A' should have carried a currency note of Rupees twenty to make the payment.

6. **Principle:** Law never enforces an impossible promise.

    **Facts:** 'A' made a promise to 'B' to discover treasure by magic

    (*a*) Law will enforce the promise only at the option of 'B'

    (*b*) Law will not enforce the promise

    (*c*) Law will enforce the promise

    (*d*) Law will enforce the promise only at the option of 'A'

7. **Principle:** The communication of a proposal is complete when it comes to the knowledge of the person to whom it is made.

    **Facts:** 'A' sent a letter making a proposal to 'B' to purchase the house of 'B'.

    (*a*) The communication of proposal is complete when B's wife handed over the letter to 'B'.

    (*b*) The communication of proposal is complete when A sent the letter.

    (*c*) The communication of proposal is complete when 'B' reads the letter.

    (*d*) The communication of proposal is complete when B's wife received it.

8. **Principle:** A person, who is usually of unsound mind, but occasionally normal, may make a contract when he is not of unsound mind.

    **Facts:** 'A' generally remains in the state of unsound mind and rarely becomes capable of understanding the things.

    (*a*) 'A' can make a contract only for his own benefit

    (*b*) 'A' can never make a contract

    (*c*) A' can make a contract when normal

    (*d*) 'A' can make a contract at any time whenever he pleases

9. **Principle:** Acceptance of proposal must be the exact mirror image of the proposal.

    **Facts:** 'A' made a proposal to 'B' to sell a chair for Rs. 500. 'B' expressed his desire to buy the said chair for Rs. 400.

    (*a*) 'B' has not accepted the proposal of 'A'

    (*b*) It is not clear whether A made a proposal to 'B'

    (*c*) It is not clear whether 'B' has accepted the proposal of 'A' or not.

    (*d*) 'B' has accepted the proposal of 'A'.

**10. Principle:** A condition to a contract can also be complied with after the happening of the event to which such a condition is attached.

**Facts:** 'A' promises to pay Rs. 5000 to 'B' on the condition that he shall marry with the consent of 'C', 'D' and 'E'. 'B' marries without the consent of 'C', 'D' and 'E', but obtains their consent after the marriage.

(*a*) 'B' has fulfilled the condition

(*b*) 'B' has not fulfilled the condition.

(*c*) The condition is illegal

(*d*) 'B's marriage is not valid.

## ANSWERS

| | | | | |
|---|---|---|---|---|
| **1.**(*b*) | **2.**(*c*) | **3.**(*c*) | **4.**(*a*) | **5.**(*a*) |
| **6.**(*b*) | **7.**(*c*) | **8.**(*c*) | **9.**(*a*) | **10.**(*a*) |

## EXPLANATIONS

1. Since "B" has consumed the eatables, which was delivered by "A", basing on the principle he is bound to pay for the same.
2. The Money which was lend to Sabu, was a collateral agreement between XYZ bank and Sabu and had nothing to do with the horse racing. The money was lend, in order to enable Sabu to award as prize to Randeep, who was winner of Horse Race.
3. The Principle clearly states that sale of liquor is illegal and any agreement related to such prohibited item doesn't exist in the eyes of law, and hence the agreement between 'A' and 'B', with regard to sale of liquor is not a valid agreement in the eyes of law and hence can't be enforced.
4. Basing on the Principle, mere silence does not amount to fraud and hence 'A' has not committed Fraud. Since the Principle is not talking anything about agreement with a minor, or agreement between a father and a daughter, Option 3 and 4 would not be the right answer.
5. Principle states that an agreement can be entered orally, or in writing or by conduct. Here although here is no oral or written agreement but conduct of 'A' and 'B' clearly implies that there was an agreement between them.
6. Principle clearly states that Law never enforces an impossible promises and hence promise between 'A' and 'B' can't be enforced.
7. The Principle states that "Communication of proposal is complete when it comes to the knowledge of the person to whom it is made. The Communication of proposal made by 'A' will be complete, when 'B' reads the letter, sent by 'A" to "B'.
8. A person who is usually of unsound mind, but occasionally of sound mind, may make a contract when he is of sound mind. Basing on the Principle, it can be said that 'A' can make the contract, when is of sound mind
9. Here "B' has not accepted the Proposal of "A" and has made a counter offer to purchase the chair for Rs. 400. A proposal is said to be accepted, when it is accepted in the same form as made by the proposer and there is no change into it.
10. The condition as to getting of consent for marriage from "C", "D", "E" has been complied by "B", after he got married. The Principle clearly states that, the condition to a contract can also be complied with after the happening of event to which such condition is attached. Hence, "B" has fulfilled the condition.

## CRIMINAL LAW

**This section consists of nine (9) questions.** Follow the instructions carefully and choose the most appropriate option:

The question numbers 1-9 in this section consist of legal proposition(s)/ principle(s) (hereinafter referred to as 'principle') and facts. Such principles may or may not be true in the real and legal sense, yet you have to conclusively assume them to be true for the purposes of this Section. In other words, in answering the following questions, you must not rely on any principle except the principles those are given herein below for every question. Further, you must not assume any facts other than those stated in the question. The objective of this section is to test your interest towards study of law, research aptitude and problem solving ability, even if the "most reasonable conclusion" arrived at may be absurd or unacceptable for any other reason.

To answer a question, the given principle is to be applied to the given facts so as to arrive at most reasonable conclusion. Only one of the options, i.e., (A), (B), (C), or (D) is the most reasonable conclusion.

**1. Principle:** Killing is not murder if the offender, whilst deprived of the power of self-control by intense and sudden provocation, causes the death of the person who gave the provocation.

**Facts:** 'A', a man found his girl friend sleeping, in her own bed room, with another man named 'B'. 'A' did not do anything but went to his home, picked a gun and cartridges, returned to the girl friend's bed room with loaded gun but found the place empty. After fifteen days he saw his girl friend dining in a restaurant. Without waiting for even a second, 'A' fired five bullets at his girl friend who died on the spot.

(*a*) 'A' could have killed both 'B' and his girl friend.

(*b*) 'A' killed his girl friend under intense and sudden provocation.

(*c*) 'A' did not kill his girl friend under intense and sudden provocation.

(*d*) 'A' could have killed 'B' instead of his girl friend.

2. **Principle:** Nothing is an offence, which is done by accident or misfortune, and without any criminal intention or knowledge in the doing of a lawful act in a lawful manner by lawful means and with proper care and caution.

**Facts:** 'A' takes up a gun, not knowing whether it is loaded or not, points it playfully at 'B' and pulls the trigger. Consequently, 'B' falls dead.

(*a*) B's death is accidental, as 'A' was just pointing the gun playfully at 'B'.

(*b*) B's death is not accidental, as there was want of proper care and caution on the part of 'A'.

(*c*) B's death is accidental, as 'A' did not have the knowledge that the gun is loaded.

(*d*) B's death is accidental, as 'A' had no intention to kill 'B'.

3. **Principle:** Causing of an effect partly by an act and partly by an omission is an offence.

**Facts:** 'A' confined her daughter 'D' in a room. 'A' also did not provide any food to her daughter 'D'. Consequently, 'D' died of starvation.

(*a*) 'A' committed the offence of not providing food to 'D'.

(*b*) 'A' committed no offence.

(*c*) 'A' committed the offence of confining 'D'.

(*d*) 'A' committed the offence of causing death of 'D'.

4. **Principle:** Whoever takes away any moveable thing from the land of any person without that person's consent, he is said to have committed theft.

**Facts:** During his visit to the house of 'C', 'A' asked 'B', the son of 'C', to accompany 'A' to the forest. Neither 'A' nor 'B' informed 'C' in this regard. 'B' accompanied 'A' to the forest.

(*a*) 'A' has committed theft.

(*b*) 'A' has committed theft as soon as he entered the house of 'C'.

(*c*) 'A' has not committed theft.

(*d*) 'A' has not committed theft till 'B' did not accompany him.

5. **Principle:** Existence of all the alleged facts is relevant, whether they occurred at the same time and place or at different times and places.

**Facts:** 'A', a citizen of England, is accused of committing murder of 'B' in India by taking part in a conspiracy hatched in England.

(*a*) The facts that 'A' citizen of England is accused of commission of murder in India and of conspiracy hatched in England are relevant facts

(*b*) 'A' citizen of England cannot be tried in India

(*c*) Only the fact that 'A' is accused of conspiracy hatched in England is relevant

(*d*) Only the fact that 'A' citizen of England is accused of committing murder of 'B' in India is relevant

6. **Principle:** Nothing is an offence which is done by a child under twelve years of age, who has not attained sufficient maturity of understanding to judge the nature and consequences of his conduct on that occasion.

**Facts:** Himesh, 11 years old boy, picks up a gold ring worth Rs 5000 lying on a table in his friend's house and immediately sells it for Rs 2000, and misappropriates the money.

(*a*) Himesh would be protected under the principle stated above because he is below 12 years of age

(*b*) Himesh would not be protected under the principle stated above because his acts show that he was sufficiently mature to understand the nature and consequences of his conduct

(*c*) Himesh would be protected under the principle stated above because his acts show that he was not sufficiently mature to understand the nature and consequences of his conduct

(*d*) Himesh would not be protected under the principle stated above because, irrespective of the age, stealing is an offence

7. **Principle:** Whoever does not arrest the killer and report the matter to the concerned authorities commits an offence.

**Facts:** 'A', a woman, sees 'B' , another woman, killing a third woman 'C'. 'A' neither attempted to arrest 'B' nor informed the concerned authorities.

(*a*) 'B' has committed an offence

(*b*) 'A' has committed an offence.

(*c*) 'B' has not committed an offence

(*d*) 'A' has not committed an offence

8. **Principle:** One who dishonestly mis-appropriates or converts to his own use or sells any movable property belonging to another, is guilty of the offence of misappropriation.

**Facts:** 'A' takes property belonging to 'Z' out of Z's possession, in good faith, believing when he takes it, that the property belongs to himself. Subsequently, 'A', on discovering his mistake, without disclosing the actual facts, dishonestly sells the property to a stranger.

(*a*) 'A' is not guilty as the property can be recovered from the stranger

(*b*) 'A' may be guilty of theft but not for misappropriation

(*c*) 'A' is not guilty because when he took the property, he believed in good faith that it belonged to him

(*d*) 'A' is guilty of an offence of misappropriation

9. **Principles:**

- A person is said to abet the doing of a thing when he instigates any other person to do that thing.
- Mere acquiescence, however, does not amount to instigation.

**Facts:** 'A' says to 'B': I am going to kill 'C'." And, 'B' replies: "Do as you wish and take the consequences"; whereafter 'A' kills 'C'.

(*a*) 'B' has not abetted 'A' to kill 'C'

(*b*) 'B' abetted 'A' to kill 'C'.

(*c*) B' has abetted 'A' by conspiracy

(*d*) 'B' is jointly liable with 'A' for killing 'C'

## ANSWERS

| | | | | |
|---|---|---|---|---|
| **1.**(*c*) | **2.**(*b*) | **3.**(*d*) | **4.**(*c*) | **5.**(*a*) |
| **6.**(*b*) | **7.**(*b*) | **8.**(*d*) | **9.**(*b*) | |

## EXPLANATIONS

1. This fact is not related to intense and sudden provocation. Killing is not murder, when there is intense and sudden provocation. Here 'A' killed his girlfriend after 15 days, so this can't be the case of intense and sudden provocation.
2. B's death is not accidental, as there was want of proper care and caution on the part of 'A'. It was the duty of 'A' to check the gun, before pointing it on 'B'. There was negligence on the part of 'A'. The last line of Principle clearly says that there must be proper care and caution. If any of the ingredients of the Principle fails, it can't be said that the death was by accident.
3. The Principle says that causing of an effect partly by an act and partly by an omission is an offence. Here 'A' has not only confined his daughter but also did not provide any food to her and because of his act 'D', died of starvation and hence 'A' committed the offence of causing death of 'D'.
4. To constitute an offence of theft, one must takes away any movable thing from the land of any person without that person's consent. Here 'A' just asked 'B' to accompany him to the forest and has not moved any movable things out of 'c' possession without 'c' consent. 'B' is not a thing.
5. Basing on the Principle, option 1 is the correct answer. The fact that "A" citizen of England is accused of commission of murder in India and of conspiracy hatched in England are relevant facts.
6. Principle states that nothing is an offence which is done by a child under 12 years of age, who has not attended sufficient maturity of understanding to judge the nature and consequences of his conduct on that occasion. Here Himesh would not be protected under the principle, because his act shows that he was sufficiently mature to understand the nature and consequences of his conduct.
7. 'A' has failed to arrest 'B', who killed 'C' and neither informed the concerned authorities about the same and hence, basing on the Principle 'A' has committed the offence.
8. The Principle is talking about the offence of "Misappropriation". Here, 'A' even after knowing that property of "Z", does not belongs to "A", dishonestly sells the property to stranger and hence, 'A' is guilty of offence of misappropriation.

9. Here 'B' has not abetted 'A' to kill "C'. Mere acquiescence, does not amount to instigation. Here "B" has not instigated "A" to kill "c".

## CONSTITUTIONAL LAW AND LEGAL FRAMEWORK

1. The object of which one of the following writs is to prevent a person to hold public office which he is not legally entitled to hold?
   (*a*) Quo warranto
   (*b*) Certiorari
   (*c*) Prohibition
   (*d*) Mandamus
2. Which among the following was described by Dr. B. R. Ambedkar as the "heart and soul of the Constitution of India"?
   (*a*) Freedom of Religion
   (*b*) Right to Constitutional Remedies
   (*c*) Right to move throughout the territory of India
   (*d*) Right to equality
3. 'persona non grata' means-
   (*a*) Non-performance of promise
   (*b*) Ungrateful person.
   (*c*) An unacceptable person
   (*d*) Non-person
4. 'alibi' means a plea by an accused person that he-
   (*a*) was facing trial.
   (*b*) underwent preventive detention
   (*c*) remained in judicial custody
   (*d*) was present elsewhere
5. If an authority is holding information about another in a 'fiduciary capacity', the information under the Right to Information Act, 2005 may not be obtainable. 'Fiduciary relationship' is based on:
   (*a*) Trust
   (*b*) Contract
   (*c*) Law
   (*d*) Authority
6. 'audi alteram partem' means-
   (*a*) Following the substantive law
   (*b*) A transferee cannot retransfer.
   (*c*) Giving opportunity of hearing of the other side
   (*d*) Not connected to facts.
7. The Supreme Court of India has struck down the Constitution (Ninety-ninth Amendment) Act, 2014 as unconstitutional. It is related to-
   (*a*) Religious Rights
   (*b*) National Judicial Appointment Commission
   (*c*) Land Exchange between India and Bangladesh
   (*d*) Jallikattu (Bull Fighting)
8. 'lis pendens' means-
   (*a*) Awaited information
   (*b*) Decision awaited.
   (*c*) A pending suit
   (*d*) On the basis of evidence
9. Under the Constitution of India restriction on freedom of religion cannot be placed on the ground of-
   (*a*) Social justice (*b*) Public order
   (*c*) Health (*d*) Morality
10. Which one of the following is not a Directive Principle of State Policy under Part IV of the Constitution of India?
    (*a*) Promotion of International peace and security
    (*b*) Promotion of adult education
    (*c*) Organisation of village panchayats
    (*d*) Provision for just and humane conditions of work and maternity relief.
11. As per law the minimum age for the marriage of a boy and a girl in India is-
    (*a*) 18 years in both cases
    (*b*) 21 years and 18 years respectively
    (*c*) 21 years in both cases
    (*d*) 18 years and 21 years respectively
12. Under the Constitution of India 'Right to Pollution Free Environment' has emerged as a fundamental right from the right to-
    (*a*) Equality under Article 14
    (*b*) Conserve culture under Article 29
    (*c*) Freedom of movement under Article 19
    (*d*) Life and personal liberty under Article 21
13. 'obiter dicta' means-
    (*a*) Direction by a judge.
    (*b*) An opinion given by the court not necessary for the decision.
    (*c*) Judgment of a court in the case before it.
    (*d*) Basis of judicial decision.

**14.** Which among the following does not belong to the 'right to freedom of religion'?

(*a*) Freedom of conscience and free profession, practice and propagation of religion

(*b*) Freedom from payment of taxes for promotion of any particular religion

(*c*) Freedom from attending religious instruction or religious worship in certain educational institutions

(*d*) Freedom of speech and expression

**15.** Which Indian State has prescribed minimum educational qualification for candidates contesting panchayat polls?

(*a*) Punjab

(*b*) Gujarat

(*c*) Haryana

(*d*) Kerala

## ANSWERS

| | | | | |
|---|---|---|---|---|
| **1.**(*a*) | **2.**(*b*) | **3.**(*c*) | **4.**(*d*) | **5.**(*a*) |
| **6.**(*c*) | **7.**(*b*) | **8.**(*c*) | **9.**(*a*) | **10.**(*b*) |
| **11.**(*b*) | **12.**(*d*) | **13.**(*b*) | **14.**(*d*) | **15.**(*c*) |

## MISCELLANEOUS

**This section consists of three (3) questions.** Follow the instructions carefully and choose the most appropriate option:

The question numbers 1-3 in this section consist of legal proposition(s)/ principle(s) (hereinafter referred to as 'principle') and facts. Such principles may or may not be true in the real and legal sense, yet you have to conclusively assume them to be true for the purposes of this Section. In other words, in answering the following questions, you must not rely on any principle except the principles those are given herein below for every question. Further, you must not assume any facts other than those stated in the question. The objective of this section is to test your interest towards study of law, research aptitude and problem solving ability, even if the "most reasonable conclusion" arrived at may be absurd or unacceptable for any other reason.

To answer a question, the given principle is to be applied to the given facts so as to arrive at most reasonable conclusion. Only one of the options, i.e., (A), (B), (C), or (D) is the most reasonable conclusion.

**1. Principle:** Letters or words not describing quality of things can be registered as a trade mark.

**Facts:** Ram made an application for registration of alphabet 'B' written in a fancy style as trade mark to be applied on packets and cartons of shoes manufactured by him.

(*a*) The alphabet 'B' can be registered as trade mark.

(*b*) The alphabet 'B' can be registered as trade mark because it describes the quality of things.

(*c*) The alphabet 'B' cannot be registered as trade mark because it is an English letter.

(*d*) The alphabet 'B' cannot be registered as trade mark because it belongs to humanity.

**2. Principle:** Import means bringing some consignment into India from a foreign country.

**Facts:** A consignment from Sri Lanka entered the territorial waters of India. However, this consignment never crossed the Indian custom barrier nor did it enter into the stream of commerce in India.

(*a*) The consignment will only be imported into India when it enters into the stream of commerce in India

(*b*) The consignment will only be imported into India when it crosses the Indian custom barrier

(*c*) The consignment was imported into India

(*d*) The consignment was not imported into India

**3. Principle:** Copyright law protects only work. 'Work' means cinematographic film but does not include performance by an actor in a cinematographic film.

**Facts:** Alia Bhatt acted in a movie.

(*a*) The acting of Alia Bhatt can be protected under copyright law as professional work.

(*b*) The acting of Alia Bhatt can be protected as film producer's work.

(*c*) The acting of Alia Bhatt can be protected under copyright law only as an artistic work.

(*d*) The acting of Alia Bhatt cannot be protected under copyright law.

## ANSWERS

**1.**(*a*) **2.**(*c*) **3.**(*d*)

## EXPLANATIONS

1. According to the Principle, letters or words not describing the quality of things can be registered as Trademark. The alphabet "B", used by Ram in way describe the quality of Shoes manufactured by him. Hence, the alphabet 'B' can be registered as trademark.

2. Principle clearly states that import means bringing some consignment into India from a foreign country. Here, the consignment from Sri Lanka has entered the territorial waters of India, where India has its jurisdiction and it can be said the the consignment has been imported to India.

3. According to the Principle, Copyright law protects only work and "work' means cinematographic film but does not include performance by an actor in a cinematographic film and hence the acting of Alia Bhatt cannot be protected under copyright law.

■■

# AILET-2016 CHAPTER-WISE

## ENGLISH

### VOCABULARY

**Directions (Q. 1 to 3):** For the word given at the top of each table, match the dictionary definitions on the left (a, b, c, d) with their corresponding usage on the right (e, f, g, h). Out of the four possibilities given below the table select the one that has all the usages correctly matched.

**1.** Run down

| | Dictionary Definition | | Usage |
|---|---|---|---|
| a | Trace | e | My cat was run down by a bus. |
| b | Criticize | f | Have you run down those addresses asked for last week? |
| c | Hit with a car | g | Suraj is running for president of the club. |
| d | Champaign for a government position | h | My father runs everyone down. |

(a) ah, bf, ce, dg (b) ah, be, cf, dg
(c) ag, bf, ce, dh (d) af, bh,ce, dg

**2.** Wind up

| | Dictionary Definition | | Usage |
|---|---|---|---|
| a | Finish | e | She just think it's a big wind-up |
| b | To tighten the spring of (a clockwork mechanism) | f | He wound up the toy top and set it on floor. |
| c | To become nervous, tense, etc; excited | g | If he doesn't get his act together, he is going to wind up in prison. |
| d | An act or instance of teasing | h | The kids always get wound up to when uncle Ronnie comes over. |

(a) ae, bg, cf, dh
(b) ae, bf, cg, dh
(c) ag, bf, ch,de
(d) ah, bg, cf, de

**3.** Run off

| | Dictionary Definition | | Usage |
|---|---|---|---|
| a | Make leave | e | Would you mind running off 20 copies of this document for me? |
| b | Reproduce | f | You shouldn't swim where the dirty water runs off into the ocean. |
| c | Leave quickly | g | Why did you run off after the dinner? |
| d | To flow | h | The new government is trying to run the criminals off. |

(a) ah, be, cg, df
(b) af, bh,cg, de
(c) af, bh,ce, dg
(d) ag, be, ch, df

**4.** In which of the following clusters, all the words mean 'ignoring existence of God' ?
(a) Pantheism, Agnosticism, Secularism
(b) Atheism, Agnosticism, Secularism
(c) Deism, Secularism, Agnosticism
(d) Atheism, Deism, Secularism

**Direction (Q. 5 - 9):** Find the odd-one out.

**5.** (a) wary (b) gullible
(c) credulous (d) naive

**6.** (a) gusto (b) verve
(c) burst (d) zest

**7.** (a) beatific (b) diatribe
(c) blithe (d) ecstatic

**8.** (a) trappings (b) orifice
(c) egress (d) vent

**9.** (a) spectre (b) apparition
(c) hoodlum (d) phantom

### ANSWERS

| | | | | |
|---|---|---|---|---|
| **1.** (d) | **2.** (c) | **3.** (a) | **4.** (b) | **5.** (a) |
| **6.** (c) | **7.** (b) | **8.** (a) | **9.** (c) | |

## EXPLANATIONS

1. 'Run down' as used in (e) means to collide with and knock down someone or something. So, (e) matches with (c), 'hit with a car'. 'Run down' as used in (f) means to hunt for and locate someone or something. So, (f) matches with (a), 'trace'. 'Run for' as used in (g) means to try to be elected to a particular office. So, (g) matches with (d), 'campaign for a government position'. 'Run down' as used in (h) means to criticize or deride someone or something. So, (h) matches with (b), 'criticize'. Hence, option (d) is the correct answer.
2. 'Wind-up' as used in (e) means something done or said in usually a joking way to make someone annoyed or upset. So, (e) matches with (d), 'an act or instance of teasing'. 'Wind up' as used in (f) means to coil something. So, (f) matches with (b), 'to tighten the spring of'. 'Wind-up' as used in (g) means to end up somewhere. So, (g) matches with (a), 'finish'. 'Wind-up' as used in (h) means to get excited. So, (h) matches with (c), 'excited'. Hence, option (c) is the correct answer.
3. 'Run off' as used in (e) means to duplicate something, using a mechanical duplicating machine. So, (e) matches with (b), 'reproduce'. 'Run off' as used in (f) means to drain away from a flat area. So, (f) matches with (d), 'to flow'. 'Run off' as used in (g) means to flee. So, (g) matches with (c), 'leave quickly'. 'Run off' as used in (h) means to force someone to leave suddenly. So, (h) matches with (a), 'make leave'. Hence, option (a) is the correct answer.
4. 'Pantheism' refers to the belief that God is present in all natural things. So, option (a) is negated. 'Deism' refers to belief in God, especially a God that created the universe but does not take part in it. So, options (c) and (d) are also negated. 'Atheism' refers to the belief that God does not exist. 'Agnosticism' refers to the belief that it is not possible to know whether God exists or not. 'Secularism' is the belief that religion should not be involved in the organization of society, education, etc. Hence, option (b) is the correct answer.
5. 'Wary' is used to describe a person who does not have or show complete trust in someone or something that could be dangerous or cause trouble. 'Gullible' is someone who can be easily fooled. 'Credulous' is again someone who can be easily fooled. 'Naive' is used to describe a person who is innocent or simple. So, options (b), (c) and (d) are synonymous to each other, rendering option (a) the correct answer.
6. 'Gusto' means great enjoyment, energy, and enthusiasm. 'Verve' means great energy and enthusiasm. 'Burst' means to break open or into pieces in a sudden and violent way. 'Zest' means lively excitement. Clearly, options (a), (b) and (d) are synonymous to each other. Hence, option (c) is the correct answer.
7. 'Beatific' means showing complete happiness. 'Diatribe' refers to an angry and usually long speech or piece of writing that strongly criticizes someone or something. 'Blithe' means happy and without worry. 'Ecstatic' means very happy or excited. So, options (a), (c) and (d) are synonyms. Hence, option (b) is the correct answer.
8. 'Trappings' is an outward decoration or dress. 'Orifice' is an opening (as a vent, mouth, or hole) through which something may pass. 'Egress' refers to the act of leaving a place. 'Vent' is an opening that allows air, gas or liquid to pass out of or into a room, building, container, etc. Options (b), (c) and (d) are related with leaving and are thus, synonymous. Hence, option (a) is the correct answer.
9. 'Spectre' means a ghost. 'Apparition' is a ghost or an image of a person who is dead. 'Hoodlum' is a violent criminal, especially one who is part of a gang. 'Phantom' is a ghost. All save option (c) are related to ghost. Hence, option (c) is the correct answer.

## GRAMMAR

**Directions (Q. 1 - Q. 5) :** Read the following newspaper report and put the verbs in brackets into the most suitable form. Indicate your choice in the provided box.

A woman______ (1) ______ (take) to hospital after her car collided with a lorry near Noida yesterday. She ______ (2) ______ (allow) home later after treatment. The road ______ (3) ______ (block) for an hour after the accident, and traffic had to ______ (4) ______ (divert). A police inspector said afterwards: The woman was lucky. She could ______ (5) ______ (kiil).

1. (a) is taken (b) took (c) was taken (d) take
2. (a) allow (b) is allowed (c) allowed (d) was allowed
3. (a) was blocked (b) block (c) is blocked (d) be blocked
4. (a) diverted (b) be diverted (c) was diverted (d) is diverted
5. (a) was killed (b) have been killed (c) killed (d) kill

**6.** Which set of words are only nouns?

(a) Pompous, ridiculous, photographic

(b) Penance, science, porous

(c) Analysis, praxis, thesis

(d) Poisonous, vocalize, stupidity

**7.** Which set of words are only adjectives?

(a) Ridiculous, native, psychologise

(b) Astronomy, sympathy, privacy

(c) Nation, action, privacy

(d) Chemical, mathematical, french

**8.** In which set each word is a noun, adjective and verb also?

(a) Delegate, defeat, temporary, tertiary

(b) Chronic, incumbency, parent, proponent

(c) Topic, alacrity, android, auditory

(d) Square, precipitate, collect, free

**Direction (Qs. 9 - 17):** Fill in the blanks with the most appropriate word.

**9.** You_________mad if you think I'm going to lend you any more money.

(a) should be (b) are supposed to be

(c) must be (d) ought to be

**10.** Who_________was coming to see me this morning?

(a) you said (b) did you say

(c) did you say that (d) you did say

**11.** I notified _________ I had changed my address.

(a) with the Bank (b) the Bank that

(c) in the Bank (d) to the Bank that

**12.** If I_________a more reliable car, I_________to Surat rather than fly.

(a) had; would drive

(b) would have; would drive

(c) had; had driven

(d) would have had; would drive

**13.** I first met Sohan on a beach_________Kochi. I later found out that he had been a carpenter and a dustman,_________other things'

(a) by; among (b) near; between

(c) by; between (d) near; among

**14.** 'When did you last hear_________Don?' 'He phoned me just this morning, He's coming to Delhi next week, so we agreed_________a time and place to meet.'

(a) from; on (b) about; on

(c) from; at (d) of; to

**15.** Perhaps because something in us instinctively distrusts such displays of natural fluency, some readers approach John Updike's fiction with_________.

(a) suspicion (b) bewilderment

(c) veneration (d) recklessness

**16.** Despite the mixture's_________nature, we found that by lowering its temperature in the laboratory, we could dramatically reduce its tendency to vaporize.

(a) volatile (b) resilient

(c) insipid (d) acerbic

**17.** I_________you can swim so well and I can't'

(a) hate

(b) hate it that

(c) hate that

(d) hate it

## ANSWERS

| | | | | |
|---|---|---|---|---|
| **1.** (c) | **2.** (d) | **3.** (a) | **4.** (b) | **5.** (b) |
| **6.** (c) | **7.** (d) | **8.** (d) | **9.** (c) | **10.** (b) |
| **11.** (b) | **12.** (a) | **13.** (d) | **14.** (a) | **15.** (b) |
| **16.** (c) | **17.** (b) | | | |

## EXPLANATIONS

**1.** An incident is reported in a newspaper after it has happened. So, the blank will take a word /phrase that suggests that the incident has happened in the past. So, the blank will take 'was taken'. Hence, option (c) is the correct answer.

**2.** The blank will take 'was allowed'. The sentence means that the woman was allowed to go home after the treatment. Hence, option (d) is the correct answer.

**3.** The blank will take 'was blocked'. Hence, option (a) is the correct answer.

**4.** 'had to' suggests that the blank will take 'be diverted'. Hence, option (b) is the correct answer.

**5.** 'could' here will be followed by 'have been'. Hence, option (b) is the correct answer.

**6.** 'Pompous', 'ridiculous' and 'photographic' are all adjectives. So, option (a) is incorrect. While 'penance' and 'science' are nouns, 'porous' is an adjective. So, option (b) is also incorrect. Option (d) is incorrect because only 'stupidity' is a noun. 'Poisonous' is an adjective and 'vocalise' is a verb. 'Analysis', 'praxis' and 'thesis' are all nouns. Hence, the correct answer is option (c).

7. While 'ridiculous' and 'native' are adjectives, 'psychologise' is a verb. This makes option (a) incorrect. 'Astronomy' and 'privacy' are nouns while 'sympathy' is a verb. So, option (b) is incorrect. 'Nation', 'action' and 'privacy' are nouns, rendering option (c) incorrect. 'Chemical', 'mathematical' and 'French' are adjectives. Hence, option (d) is the correct answer.

8. 'Delegate' and 'defeat' are nouns and verbs, but not adjectives. 'Temporary' is only an adjective. 'Tertiary' is only an adjective. So, option (a) is incorrect. 'Chronic' is only an adjective. 'Incumbency', 'parent' and 'proponent' are nouns only. So, option (b) is incorrect. In option (c), while 'topic', 'alacrity' and 'android' are nouns only, 'auditory' is an adjective only. So, option (c) too is incorrect. 'Square', 'precipitate' and 'collect' are nouns, adjectives and verbs. 'Free' is a verb and an 'adjective'; it is not a noun. The noun form of the word is 'freeness'.

9. 'Should' is used to predict that something will probably happen or is expected to be the case, based on logic or a typical situation.'Supposed' means claimed to be true or real.'Must' is used to express the view that something is highly likely because it's a logical conclusion based on something else that the speaker knows, or it's the normal thing to expect. 'Ought' is used to predict that something is fairly likely or expected, based on normal circumstances or logic. The most appropriate phrase to fill in the blank is 'must be', rendering option (c) the correct answer.

10. Option (a) is incorrect because it does not have a verb. Option (c) is incorrect because 'that' is redundant here. Option (d) is incorrect because 'you did say' is assertive, so there is no point of asking a question. Only option (b) is grammatically correct and hence is correct.

11. The word 'notified' will not be followed by an preposition. So, the blank will take 'the bank that', rendering option (b) the correct answer.

12. This is a case of past subjunctive. In such sentences, the 'if' clause is in past simple tense while main clause takes 'would'. So, the first blank will take 'had' while the second blank will take 'would drive'. Hence, option (a) is the correct answer.

13. 'By' means next to something. 'A beach next to Kochi' would be incorrect. So, the first blank will take 'near'. In the phrase 'among other things', 'among' means as well as. 'between other things' is incorrect. Hence, option (d) is the correct answer.

14. The correct phrase is 'hear from someone', which means to get a letter, telephone call, or other message from someone. 'Agree on something' means to agree to the choice of someone or something.Hence, option (a) is the correct answer.

15. 'Distrust' suggests that the blank will take 'suspicion'. Since people do not trust such displays of natural fluency, they approach John Updike's fiction with caution. Hence, option (a) is the correct answer.

16. The sentence says that we can reduce the mixture's tendency to vapourise. 'Despite' suggests that the blank will take a word that suggests that in normal circumstances the mixture does not change. 'Volatile' means likely to change in a very sudden or extreme way. 'Resilient' means able to return to an original shapeafter being pulled, stretched, pressed, bent, etc. 'Resilient' is not used for liquids. 'Insipid' means not interesting or challenging. 'Acerbic' means expressing harsh or sharp criticism in a clever way.Only option (a) fits in the meaning of the sentence and hence, is the answer.

17. The blank will take 'hate it that'. Here 'it' refers to the other person's ability to swim. Hence, option (b) is the correct answer.

## READING COMPREHENSION

**Directions (Qs. 1-9):** Read the following passage carefully and then answer the questions that follow.

Rural manual workers comprise the single largest occupational category in India. In 1991, according to the National Commission on Rural Labour, 60 percent of the workers in rural India were manual workers and they numbered more than 160 million. The changes in the working and living conditions of rural labourers are thus central to changes in the welfare of the rural population and of the country as a whole. The structure and working of rural labour markets in India is complex; as is well known, there is great diversity across regions and across segments of the labour market. This article brings together an interesting body of research that seeks to understand and explain the types of changes that have accrued in the structure of rural labour markets over the last few decades.

The 1980s were characterised by an explosion of the rural labour force, slow employment growth in agriculture and a rise in the share of non-agricultural employment. The decade was also characterized by a growing casualisation of the work force (for a relative rise in casual employment as opposed to regular employment).

At the same time, it was a period when agricultural wages increased in real terms and when income poverty declined. There was what may be called "the tension between the estimated decline in poverty on the one hand, and the slow growth of agricultural employment and increased casualisation of the labour force on the other. Some of the trends in the development of rural labour over for this period are a source of concern. These include, as Radhakrishnan and Sharma note, the continuous widening of the gap between labour productivity in agricultural and non-agricultural occupations, the burgeoning mass of rural casual workers who have no social security safety net, and the increasing number of women employed at very low wages in agriculture. Another matter for concern, one that emerges from a desegregation of data on rural unemployment by age groups, is that the incidence of unemployment is higher for persons in the age group of 15-29 than for any other age group in others words, unemployment is typically high among new entrants to the workforce.

In her review of trends in wages, employment and poverty, Sheila Bhalla shows that the real wages of agricultural labourers stagnated from the time of independence to the mid 1970s and then began to rise in all parts of the country. This was also the period in which the incidence of rural poverty began to decline. The rise in wages was not limited to the more prosperous agricultural zones, and Bhalla argues that the movement in real wages was co-related with the increase in the share of non-agricultural employment in total employment. As wages in non-agricultural work are typically higher than wages in agriculture, the expansion of non-farm work could also explain some of the decline in rural poverty. In the 1990s, the improvement in real wages and the decline in poverty were reversed while agricultural employment expanded. Economic development all over the world has been associated with a rise in the share of employment in the secondary and tertiary sectors of the economy and a fail in the share of the agricultural sector. In India, changes in the composition of the rural workforce in the 1980s points to a "structural retrogression"

**1.** Give an appropriate title to the passage

(a) The complex labour markets in India

(b) Matters of concern in rural agriculture

(c) The agricultural and non- agricultural sectors: Changing perspective

(d) The Changing Structure of Rural labour market

**2.** The author does not say

(a) In 1991, about 3/5 of the workers in rural India were manual workers

(b) The decade of 1980s was characterised by a relative rise in casual employment as opposed to regular employment

(c) There is no gender bias among workers in agriculture sector

(d) Wages in agricultural employment have been lesser than those in non-agricultural employment in the 1990s

**3.** Why is the increasing gap between labour productivity in agricultural and non-agricultural occupations a cause of concern' according to Radhakrishnan and Sharma ?

(a) This would increase the wages of agricultural sector

(b) This would read to pressure on both the agricultural and non-agricultural sectors as whichever sector expands at the expense of the other, there would be increased labour pressure on that sector and lesser economic development in the other

(c) This would indirectly mean a pressure on agricultural sector in terms of higher wages

(d) This would indirectly mean a pressure on non-agricultural sector in terms of higher wages

**4.** How does Bhalla explain the fact that the real wages of agricultural labourers began to rise in all parts of the country after mid-70s ?

(a) Economic development increased for both the sectors across the world

(b) Economic liberalization in India led to the development of the agricultural sector

(c) The agricultural labourers became rich due to successive good crops during the time of Green Revolution

(d) There was a mass outflow of agricultural labourers into the non-agricultural Sectors and the remaining labourers. Who were lesser in number, now apportioned the existing agricultural sector wealth, getting richer individually

**5.** What is the most important problem in understanding the condition of rural labour markets in India ?

(a) The rural labour markets are uneconomic in nature

(b) The rural labour markets are very complex and there exists great diversity across regions and across segments of such markets

(c) The rural labourers are a reticent lot; not forthcoming with their problems, not very open to suggestions on how to improve their lifestyle

(d) They are lazy and want doles from the government without undertaking any viable productive activities

**6.** What sort of tension exists between the decline of poverty and the slow growth of agricultural employment and the increased casualisation of the labour force ?

(a) A decline in rural poverty is only possible when there is increased agricultural employment and lower casualisation of the labour force

(b) The tension exists in the fact that an increased casualisation of the labour force would increase Poverty

(c) When there is a decline in poverty there should be faster growth of agricultural employment and the decreased casualisation of the labour force'

(d) Both (b) and (c)

7. What sort of Passage is this ?

(a) Political

(b) Social commentary

(c) Economic

(d) Philosophical

8. The author does not say which of the following statements in the passage?

(a) The National Commission on Rural Labour gives data on the activities of rural labourers in India

(b) Economic development basically means a rise in the share employment in the agricultural sector at the expense of the secondary and the tertiary sectors

(c) In India, employment was higher among the new entrants to the workforce in the 1980s

(d) Real wages of the agricultural labourers started showing an upward trend from the 1970s

9. Why are changes in the working and living conditions of rural manual workers of utmost significance to the country as a whole ?

(a) Rural workers migrate a lot to the cities, adding to the already burgeoning population of these places and so any improvement in their living conditions which would stall this trend would benefit

(b) The rural workers live in abject poverty and a change in their working and living conditions is therefore very crucial

(c) They form the bulk of the rural workers and so any change in their living standards augurs well for the country as a whole

(d) Both (a) and (b)

## ANSWERS

| | | | | |
|---|---|---|---|---|
| 1. (d) | 2. (c) | 3. (b) | 4. (d) | 5. (b) |
| 6. (a) | 7. (c) | 8. (b) | 9. (c) | |

## EXPLANATIONS

1. Refer to the last sentence of the first paragraph. It says that the passage seeks to understand and explain the types of changes that have accrued in the structure of rural labour markets over the last few decades. Hence, option (d) is the correct answer.

2. Option (a) can be inferred from the second sentence of the first paragraph. It says that in 1991, 60% (3/5) workers in rural India were manual workers. Option (b) can be inferred from the second sentence of the second paragraph-the decade was characterized by a growing casualization of work force. Option (d) can also be inferred from the passage. Refer to the fourth sentence of the last paragraph - "wages in non agricultural work are typically higher than wages in agriculture". Option (c) states the opposite of what the author says. Refer to the penultimate sentence of the third paragraph. It clearly says that there is gender bias among workers from agricultural sector. Hence, option (c) is the correct answer.

3. None of the given options is correct. The passage does not say why the increasing gap is a concern.

4. Refer to the last paragraph. It says that the increase in real wages was co-related with the increase in share of non agricultural employment. From this we can say that there was a mass outflow of agricultural laborers to non-agricultural sectors and the wealth generated by the agricultural sector was now distributed among the existing laborers of agricultural sector. Hence, option (d) is the correct answer.

5. Options (a), (c) and (d) are not stated anywhere in the passage. Option (b) is directly stated in the first paragraph. Refer to the line "The structure and...of the labour market."

6. None of the given options is correct. Options(a) and (c) are incorrect because according to the passage, when agricultural employment increases, casualization of labour force also increases. Option (b) is incorrect because the passage says that at the time casualization of labour force was increasing, poverty was declining.

7. The passage deals with structure of rural labour market. So, it is an economic passage.

8. Option (a) can be inferred from the second sentence of the first paragraph. Option (c) can be inferred from the last sentence of the third paragraph. It says that unemployment was high among new entrants to the workforce. Option (d) is stated in the first sentence of the last paragraph. It says that real wages stagnated till 1970s and then then began to rise. Option (b) is not stated by the author. Hence, option (b) is the correct answer.

9. Refer to the first three sentences of the passage. It can be inferred that the changes in working and living conditions of rural manual workers are of utmost importance because they form a bulk of rural workers. Hence, option (c) is the correct answer.

# REASONING

## VERBAL LOGIC

**Directions (Qs. 1 to 6):** Read the following short passages and answer the questions that follow each passage.

**1.** For some women, the cost of giving birth can be an unexpectedly a large burden. The average normal birth now costs Rs. 3,200 and a birth with complications can cost thousands of rupees more. Of women in the primary child-bearing age range of eighteen to twenty-four, who account for about 40 percent of all births in this country annually, more than 25 percent have no health care insurance to pay maternity costs.

If the above statements are true, which one of the following must also be true ?

(a) Each year, about 75 percent of all births in this country are to women who have health care coverage of maternity costs.

(b) Each year, about 60 percent of all births in this country are to women who are younger than eighteen or older than twenty-four.

(c) For an average birth, health care insurance pays about 75 percent of Rs. 3,200.

(d) In this country, about 75 percent of the women who do not have health care coverage of maternity costs are younger than eighteen or older than twenty-four.

**2.** Products sold under a brand name used to command premium prices because, in general, they were superior to non-brand rival products. Technical expertise in product development has become so widespread, however, that special quality advantages are very hard to obtain these days and even harder to maintain. As a consequence, brand-name products generally neither offer higher quality nor sell at higher prices' Paradoxically, brand names are a bigger marketing advantage than ever.

Which of the following, if true, most helps to resolve the paradox outlined above?

(a) Brand names are taken by consumers as a guarantee of getting a product as good as the best rival product.

(b) Consumers recognised that the quality of products sold under invariant brand names can drift over time

(c) In the acquisition of one corporation by another, the acquiring corporation is interested more in acquiring the right to use certain brand names than in acquiring existing production facilities.

(d) In the earlier days when special quality advantages were easier to obtain than are now, it was also easier to get new brand names established.

**3.** The extent to which a society is really free can be gauged by its attitude towards artistic expression. Freedom of expression can easily be violated in even most outwardly democratic of societies. When a government's Arts Council withholds funding from a dance performance that its members deem "obscene", the voice of a few bureaucrats have in fact censored the work of the choreographer, thereby committing the real obscenity of repression.

Which of the following, if true, would most seriously weaken the argument above?

(a) Members of government Arts Council are screened to ensure that their beliefs reflect those of the majority,

(b) The term obscenity has several different definitions that should not be used interchangeably, for rhetorical effect.

(c) Withholding financial support for a performance is not the same as actively preventing or inhibiting it.

(d) The Council's decision could be reversed if the performance were altered to conform to public standards of appropriateness.

**4.** It is not generally realised that when a court upholds or invalidates legislation or executive action, it neither approves nor condemns any legislative policy, nor is if concerned with the wisdom or expediency of the administrative action. It merely determines whether the legislation or executive action is in conformity with or contrary to the provisions of the Constitution. It discharges the function of guarding the Constitution, no more, no less. Judicial activism is to be properly understood in the context of the extent and the vigour and the readiness with which the courts exercise their power of judicial review. When courts actively perform an interventionist role, we witness the phenomenon of judicial activism. When the judiciary exercises self-restraint in exercising the power of judicial review and limits its role, there is absence of judicial activism. But the pendulum of judicial review is never static and judicial activism, or lack of it, is a variable phenomenon.

Which one of the following, if true, would defeat the case presented above ?

(a) The judiciary is plagued with the Public Interest Litigations against some or the other forms of administrative action.

(b) Often, the judiciary is seen to be making disparaging remarks about the executive, pulling up officials for lapses in conduct, many a time condemning them.

(c) The judicial review exercises that the judiciary often undertakes is what comprises judicial activism.

(d) Judicial activism is not mandatory under the Constitution. It is for the judiciary to decide whether it wants to intervene in a certain issue or not.

**5.** Traditionally, decision-making by managers that is reasoned and step-by-step has been considered preferable to intuitive decision-making. However, a recent study found that top managers used intuition significantly more than did most middle or lower-level managers. This confirms the alternative view that intuition is actually more effective than careful, methodical reasoning.

The conclusion above is based on which of the following assumptions ?

(a) Methodical, step-by-step reasoning is inappropriate for making many real-life management decisions.

(b) Top managers have the ability to use either intuitive reasoning or methodical, step-by-step reasoning in making decisions.

(c) The decisions made by middle and lower-level managers can be made as easily by using methodical reasoning as by using intuitive reasoning.

(d) Top managers are more effective at decision-making than middle or lower-level managers.

**6. Banker:** By transferring income to a retirement account at our bank, people can save money by delaying payment of taxes.

**Accountant:** That plan won't actually save money because the taxes will have to be paid sometime in the future when the money is withdrawn.

Which one of the following best explains the conflict between the Banker and the Accountant ?

(a) The Banker is primarily concerned with recruiting new customers for the bank but the Accountant is not.

(b) The Accountant misunderstands the application of the tax laws.

(c) The Banker and the Accountant disagree on the application of the term "save".

(d) Retirement accounts are nothing more than a tax shelter, which the Parliament intends to cut out of next year's tax amendment.

**Directions (Qs. 7 to 10) :** A passage is given below followed by several inferences. You have to examine each inference separately in the context of the passage and decide upon its degree of truth or falsity. Mark your answer as:

(a) If the inference is 'definitely true'

(b) If the inference is 'probably true'

(c) If the 'data provide in inadequate'

(d) If the inference is 'probably false'

Investors today have more investment options than were available just a few years ago. Choice in any decision-making is good in so far it provides variety, differentiation and benchmarking. It could also, however, at times lead to clutter and "noise" if the options are mostly similar and undifferentiated. To make sense of this choice conundrum, it is imperative for an investor to define objective - both returns and digestible risk and then identify the possible options. The investor also needs to select the mix and regularly monitor that objectives and investment outcomes remain aligned. Sounds simple, but can present the most confounding situation which multiplies with the quantum of wealth.

**7.** Investors need to critically evaluate the risk of each investment option.

**8.** Present day investors need to use their judgement more critically before investing.

**9.** Multiple investment options of similar types helps in making better investment decisions.

**10.** In the past, investors were generally guided by the fund managers.

**Directions (Qs. 11 to 15):** A fact situation and result is presented. Numbered statements follow the result. Each statement has to be separately evaluated in relation to the fact-situation and result' Evaluate these statements with the following sequences of decisions in the order of a, b, c and d. The first of these that you cannot eliminate is the correct answer.

(a) If the statement is inconsistent with, or contradicts, the fact situation, the result, or both together. If so Choose (a).

(b) If the statement present a possible adequate explanation of the result.

(c) If the statement is deducible from something in the fact-situation, or the result, or both together.

(d) If the statement either supports or weakens a possible explanation of the result.

**Situation :**Major X, an able officer in the Kapistan Army, failed to receive a promotion for eight years. Then he had been reassigned to a military supply depot in Khawalpindi, despite his university training in engineering and electronics, and his remarkably high performance ratings from his commanding officers. X had never been an active member of any political party as a youth nor as an adult, yet neither had he given the party or his superiors any cause to doubt his absolute loyalty to Kapistan. X's brother-in-law had been a diplomat in the Kapistan government until his death in 1971 in a plane crash on Koviet soil while he was working in the Kapistan Embassy in Kosco. X had always assumed that the mishap was indeed an accident, until his friend Y, a middle-level officer in the Interior Ministry, broadly hinted that the plane crash had been an act of sabotage. Soon after the talk with Y, X visited his sister, the diplomat's widow, in her Kosco apartment. During the visit she asked X several questions that struck him as strange and inappropriate. As he was leaving her apartment, she asked X to wear her late husband's scarf and to return to his hotel by way of a certain park. Bewildered, but not wishing to offend his sister, X obeyed her odd instructions.

**Result:** Two months later, X received a promotion and was made Commander of the Kapistan missile division in Kahore.

**11.** X's sister had arranged for her husband's fatal accident.

**12.** X's sister was an operative in the Kapistan Secret Police, and her husband had been acting as a spy before his death.

**13.** X's promotion and reassignment to the Kosco Army Headquarters came as a result of Y's recommendations.

**14.** For X, a missile base is a more highly prized assignment than a supply depot.

**15.** X's failure to win a promotion for eight years was the result of the clerical error in his records.

## ANSWERS

| | | | | |
|---|---|---|---|---|
| **1.** (b) | **2.** (a) | **3.** (c) | **4.** (b) | **5.** (d) |
| **6.** (c) | **7.** (a) | **8.** (a) | **9.** (d) | **10.** (c) |
| **11.** (d) | **12.** (b) | **13.** (a) | **14.** (c) | **15.** (b) |

## EXPLANATIONS

**1.** Option (a) is incorrect because the passage says that 'more than 25%' women do not have health care insurance. This means that less than 75% women have health care insurance. Option (b) is correct. Refer to the second sentence. It says that about 40% women in our country bear children between the age of 18 and 24. This means that about 60% women in our country bear children either before attaining 18 years of age or after attaining 24 years of age. Option (c) is incorrect because the passage is silent on the share paid by insurance companies to cover maternity cost. Option (d) is incorrect because the passage does not give any data to support the claim made in option (d). Hence, option (b) is the correct answer.

**2.** The passage says that these days brand-name products neither offer higher quality nor sell at higher prices.Still, brand names provide a bigger marketing advantage. This is because brand names guarantee to provide products that are as good as their rival's products. Hence, option (a) is the correct answer.

**3.** The passage suggests that withholding funds from a dance performance that is deemed obscene and censoring works of choreographers are the real obscenity. Option (c) states the opposite of this, thereby weakening the argument. Hence, option (c) is the correct answer.

**4.** The passage says that courts only guard the constitution; they check if the legislation or executive actions are in conformity with the provisions of the constitution. They neither approve nor condemn any legislative policy. Option (b) says that judiciary makes critical remarks about executives and condemns them. This clearly defeat the case presented. Hence, option (b) is the correct answer.

**5.** The passage says that top managers use intuition more than middle level or lower level managers and this this confirms that intuition is more effective than careful, methodical reasoning. This conclusion can only be drawn if we assume that top managers are more effective at decision making than middle level or lower level managers. This is given in option (d), rendering it the correct answer.

**6.** The passage presents a conflict over tax savings. A banker says that by transferring money to retirement account, people can save money as it will delay payment of tax. On the other hand an accountant says that this is not actually saving money as one will have to pay tax when one withdraws money from account. Clearly, the disagreement is over the application of the term 'save'. Hence, option (c) is the correct answer.

**7.** Refer to the line "To make sense of this choice... then identify possible options." Hence, the inference is definitely true, rendering option (a) the correct answer.

**8.** The inference is definitely true. Look at the first sentence. It says that investors 'today have more investment options' and then later in the paragraph says that investors need to evaluate risk. This means that investors today need to use their judgment more critically. Hence, option (a) is the correct answer.

**9.** The inference is probably false. Refer to the second and the third sentences of the passage. They say that choice is good, but they lead to clutter and noise if the products are similar. Hence, option (d) is the correct answer.

**10.** Nothing has been said about the investors in the past. Hence, option (c) is the correct answer.

**11.** The passage says that X's sister asked him to wear her husband's scarf and return to hishotel through an alternate route. A possible explanation for her doing this could be that she wanted the people, who had a hand in the murder of her husband, to think that her husband is still alive. Now if the criminals see him alive, they would try to kill the brother too, which the sister wouldn't want. This weakens the statement that she arranged for her husband's death. Hence, option (d) is the correct answer.

**12.** The statement is a possible explanation of the result. It is possible that X's sister was in the secret police and she wanted the people who killed her husband to think that the spy is still alive so that she catches them red handed when they try to kill him. So by making him wear the scarf and giving him a promotion, she probably wanted to make the murders believe that the spy is still alive. Hence, option (b) is the correct answer.

**13.** The passage says that Y informs X that his brother-in-law's plane crash was an act of sabotage. No other reference of Y has been made in the passage. So, Y recommending X for a promotion is inconsistent with the fact situation and result. Hence, option (a) is the correct answer.

**14.** Fact situation says that despite X's training in engineering and electronics, he was reassigned to military supply and the result says that he was promoted and made commander of missile division. Since missile division is related to the field in which he received his training, we can say that to X, a missile base is a more highly prized assignment than a supply depot. Hence, option (c) is the correct answer.

**15.** X had high performance ratings from his commanding officers. So, his failure to win a promotion could be a result of a clerical error. Hence, option (b) is the correct answer.

## ANALYTICAL REASONING

**Direction (Qs. 1 - 4):** Find the missing numbers/letters in following series.

**1.** 3, 20, 63, 144, 275, ?

(a) 468 (b) 461

(c) 467 (d) 469

**2.** 113, ?,164, 215, 283, 368

(a) 132 (b) 130

(c) 129 (d) 128

**3.** AYBZC, DWEXF, GUHVI, ?, MQNRO

(a) LSJTL (b) JSKLT

(c) JSKTL (d) LTSKY

**4.** 21 A, X2D, V6G, T21J, R88M, ?

(a) P440P (b) N2670S

(c) N2676S (d) P445P

**Direction (Qs. 5 - 9) :** Read the following information carefully and answer the questions given below.

i. Five friends A, B, C, D and E travelled to five different cities of Chennai, Kolkata, Delhi, Bengaluru and Hyderabad by different modes of transport viz. bus, train, aeroplane, car and boat from Mumbai.

ii. The person who travelled to Delhi did not travel by boat.

iii. C went to Bengaluru by car and B went to Kolkata by aeroplane.

iv. D travelled by boat whereas E travelled by train.

v. Mumbai is not connected by bus to Delhi and Chennai.

**5.** Which of the following combinations of person and mode is not correct ?

(a) A - Bus (b) D - Boat

(c) C - Car (d) E - Aeroplane

**6.** Which of the following combination is true for A ?

(a) Delhi - Bus (b) Chennai - Bus

(c) Hyderabad - Bus (d) Hyderabad - Car

**7.** Which of the following combinations of place and mode is not correct ?

(a) Hyderabad - Train (b) Hyderabad - Bus

(c) Chennai - Boat (d) Delhi - Train

**8.** The person travelling to Hyderabad went by which of the following modes ?

(a) Train (b) Bus

(c) Boat (d) None of these

**9.** Who among the following travelled to Delhi ?

(a) D (b) A

(c) E (d) None of these

**Direction (Qs. 10 - 14) :** Read the following information carefully and answer the questions given below.

All the streets of a city are either perpendicular or parallel to one another. The streets are all straight. Streets N, O, P, Q and R are parallel to one another. Streets S, T, U, V, W, X and Y are horizontally parallel to one another,

i. Street N is 1 km east of Street O.

ii. Street O is % km west of Street p.

iii. Street Q is 1 km west of Street R.

iv. Street S is 1/2 km south of Street T.

v. Street U is 1 km north of Street V.

vi. Street W is 1/2 km north of Street X.

vii. Street W is 1 km south of Street Y.

**10.** If W is parallel to U and W is 1/2 km south of V and 1 km north of T, then which two streets would be 1 & 1/2 km apart ?

(a) U and W (b) V and S

(c) V and T (d) W and V

**11.** Which of the following possibilities would make two streets coincide ?

(a) X is 1/2 km north of U

(b) P is 1 km west of E

(c) O is 1/2 km east of N

(d) R is 1/2 km east of O

**12.** Street R is between O and P, then the distance between p and e is

(a) 1/2 km (b) 1 km

(c) 1.5 km (d) 1.25 km

**13.** R is between O and P, then which of the following is false ?

(a) Q is 1.75 km west of N

(b) P is less than 1 km km from Q

(c) R is less than 1 km km from N

(d) Q is less than 1 km km from O

**14.** Which of the following is necessarily true ?

(a) R and O intersect

(b) Q is 2 km west of O

(c) Y is 1.5 km north of X

(d) O is at least 2 km west of N

**Direction (Qs. 15-18) :** Study the following information carefully and answer the questions given below.

A family consists of six members H, I, J, K, L and M. There are two married couples. I is a doctor and father of L. M is grandfather of J and is a contractor. K is grandmother of L and is a housewife. There is one doctor, one contractor, one nurse, one housewife and two students in the family.

**15.** What is the profession of H ?

(a) Doctor (b) Student

(c) Doctor or Nurse (d) Nurse

**16.** Who is the husband of H ?

(a) I (b) M .

(c) J (d) None of these

**17.** Which of the following are two married couples ?

(a) LK, JM (b) MK, IH

(c) MK, JH (d) MK, IL

**18.** Who is the sister of L ?

(a) J

(b) H

(c) K

(d) Information insufficient

**19.** If Saturday falls four days after today, which is 6th January, on what day did the 1st of December of previous year fall ?

(a) Sunday (b) Monday

(c) Tuesday (d) Wednesday

**20.** At what angle the hands of a clock are inclined when it is half past 8 ?

(a) 70° (b) 80°

(c) 75° (d) 60°

## ANSWERS

| | | | | |
|---|---|---|---|---|
| **1.** (a) | **2.** (b) | **3.** (c) | **4.** (d) | **5.** (d) |
| **6.** (c) | **7.** (a) | **8.** (b) | **9.** (c) | **10.** (a) |
| **11.** (d) | **12.** (d) | **13.** (b) | **14.** (c) | **15.** (d) |
| **16.** (a) | **17.** (b) | **18.** (d) | **19.** (b) | **20.** (c) |

## EXPLANATIONS

**1.** Pattern of the sequence is as follows:

**2.** Pattern of the sequence is as follows:

113 + 17 = 130

130 + 2 × 7 = 164

164 + 3 × 13 = 215

2.5 + 4 × 17 = 283

283 + 5 × 17 = 368.

**3.** Patter of the sequene is as follows:

$A \xrightarrow{+3} D \xrightarrow{+3} G \xrightarrow{+3} J \xrightarrow{+3} M$

$Y \xrightarrow{-2} W \xrightarrow{-2} U \xrightarrow{-2} S \xrightarrow{-2} Q$

$B \xrightarrow{+3} E \xrightarrow{+3} H \xrightarrow{+3} K \xrightarrow{+3} N$

$Z \xrightarrow{-2} X \xrightarrow{-2} V \xrightarrow{-2} T \xrightarrow{-2} R$

$C \xrightarrow{+3} F \xrightarrow{+3} I \xrightarrow{+3} L \xrightarrow{+3} O$

**4.** Pattern of the sequence is as follows:

$Z \xrightarrow{-2} X \xrightarrow{-2} V \xrightarrow{-2} T \xrightarrow{-2} R \xrightarrow{-2} P$

Number

(1 + 1) × 2 = 2

(2 + 1) × 2 = 6

(6 + 1) × 3 = 21

$(21 + 1) \times 4 = 88$

$(88 + 1) \times 5 = 445$

and

$A \xrightarrow{+3} D \xrightarrow{+3} G \xrightarrow{+3} J \xrightarrow{+3} M \xrightarrow{+3} P$

**Solutions for questions 5 to 9:** The information is summarised below:

| Person | City | Mode |
|---|---|---|
| P | Hyderabad | Bus |
| Q | Calcutta | Aeroplane |
| R | Banglore | Car |
| S | Chennai | Boat |
| T | Delhi | Train |

**Solutions for questions 10 to 14 :** The vertical North South streets are N, O, P, Q, R. From the basic information we have two relative positions are available – one between O, P and N and the other between Q and R.

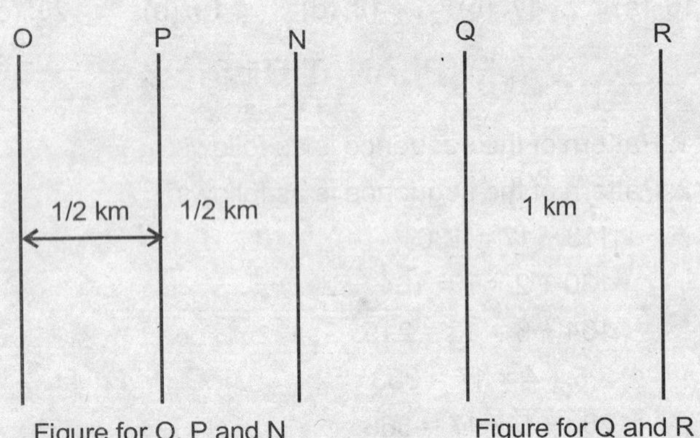


Figure for O, P and N

Figure for Q and R

The horizontal eastwest sxtreets are: S, T, U, V, W, X, Y. Of these seven streets the relative positioning is given in 3 distinct part as shown here:

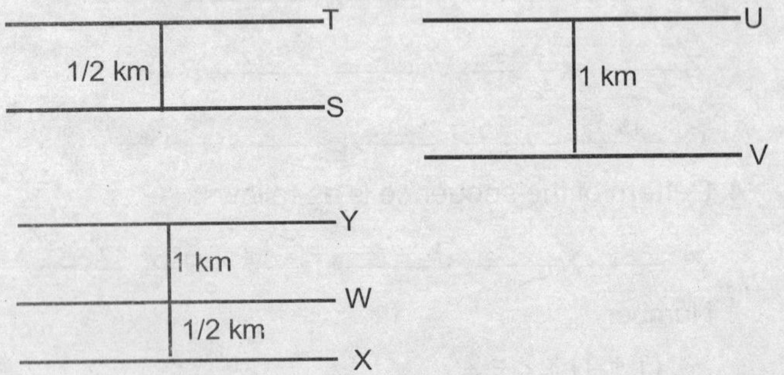


**10.** The solution is visible from the figure below. Option (a) is correct.

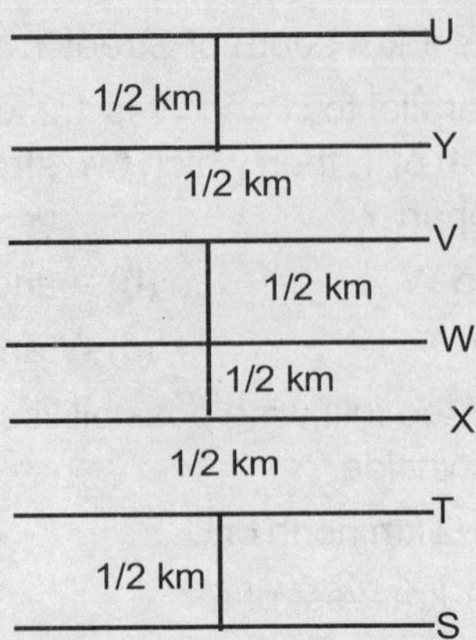


**11.** If R is 1/2 km east of O, then R and P would coincide. Option (d) makes two streets coincide.

**12.** If R is placed between O and P, Q to N would be a minimum of 1.5 and a maximum of 2 kms. Option (d) correct.

**13.** If R is between O and P, then Q being 1 km to the west of R, would be more than 1 km to the west of P. Option (b) is false.

**14.** Y is 1.5 km north of X is correct in all cases as the figure between X, W and Y shows. Option (d) is correct.

**Solutions for questions 15 to 18:** The family relation is presented below.

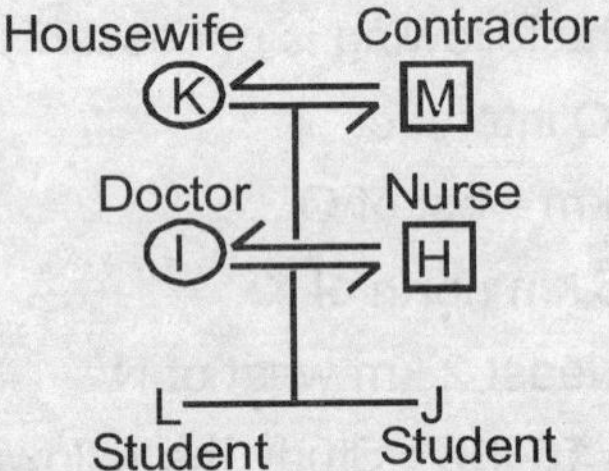


**15.** H is nurse.

**16.** I is the husband of H.

**17.** M, K and I, H are married couple.

**18.** As gender of JJ is not known, so the data is insufficient.

**19.** Number of odd days from 1st December to 10 January next year is 40 i.e. 5 days.

Hence, 1st December will eb 5 days earlier that Saturday i.e. Monday.

**20.** The required angle $= |30h - \frac{11}{2}M|$

$$= |30 \times 8 - \frac{11}{2} \times 30|$$

$$= 75°.$$

# QUANTITATIVE APTITUDE

## ARITHMETIC

**1.** Twenty five workers were employed to complete a compound wall in 12 days. Five workers left after working for 4 days. The remaining 20 workers completed the work. In how many days the total job was completed ?

(a) 15 days
(b) 16 days
(c) 14 days
(d) 18 days

**2.** In a garden, there are B rows and 10 columns of papaya trees. The distance between the two trees is 2 metres and a distance of one metre is left from all sides of the boundary of the garden. The length of the garden is

(a) 24 metres (b) 14 metres
(c) 20 metres (d) 18 metres

**3.** A man can row 14 km/h in still water. In the stream flowing with the speed of 10 km/h he takes 4 hours to move with the stream and come back. Find the distance he rowed the boat.

(a) 11.71 km (b) 13.71 km
(c) 14.71 km (d) 12.71 km

**4.** What will be the difference in simple and compound interest on Rs. 2, 000 after three years at the rate of 10 percent per annum ?

(a) Rs. 60 (b) Rs. 42
(c) Rs. 62 (d) Rs. 40

**5.** A man covers a certain distance between his house and office on a Scooter. Having an average speed of 30 km/hr, he reaches office late by 10 minutes. However, with a speed of 40 km/hr, he reaches his office 5 minutes earlier. The distance between his house and office is

(a) 30 km (b) 10km
(c) 20 km (d) 40 km

**6.** A box contains Rs, 56 in the form of coins of one rupee, 50 paisa and 25 paisa' The number of 50 paisa coins is double the number of 25 paisa coins and four times the number of one rupee coins. The number of 50 paisa coin in the box is

(a) 14 (b) 16
(c) 32 (d) 64

**7.** The price of 7 bananas is equal to the cost of 3 kiwis The price of 2 kiwis is equal to the cost of 1 banana and 5 chikoos. If Rambo has just enough money to buy 30 chikoos, then how many bananas Rambo could buy with the same amount ?

(a) 22 (b) 20
(c) 2s (d) 11

**8.** In a certain class, 72% of the students prefer cold coffee and 44% prefer fruit juice' If each of them prefers cold coffee or fruit juice and 48 likes both, the total number of students in the class is

(a) 240 (b) 200
(c) 300 (d) 250

**9.** The average price of 10 pens is Rs. 12 while the average price of 8 of these pens is Rs. 11.75. Of the remaining two pens, if the price of one pen is 60% more than the price of the other, what is the price of each of these two pens ?

(a) Rs. 12, Rs. 14 (b) Rs. 5, Rs. 7.50
(c) Rs. 8, Rs. 12 (d) Rs. 10, Rs. 16

## ANSWERS

| | | | | |
|---|---|---|---|---|
| **1.** (c) | **2.** (d) | **3.** (b) | **4.** (c) | **5.** (a) |
| **6.** (d) | **7.** (a) | **8.** (c) | **9.** (d) | |

## EXPLANATIONS

**1.** Let the amount of work be 300 units.

Work done by 25 worker in 4 days = 100 units

Remaining work = 200 units

The required number of days = $4 + \frac{200}{20} = 14$.

**2.** The distance between 1st and 10th tree is a row

$= 2 \times 9 = 18$ m

$\therefore$ Length = (18 + 1 + 1) = 20 m.

**3.** Let the required distance be 'D'.

$$\frac{D}{14-10} + \frac{D}{14+10} = 4$$

$\Rightarrow$ D = 13.71 km

**4.** $$CI = 2000\left(1+\frac{10}{100}\right)^3 - 2000$$

$= 662$

$$SI = \frac{2000 \times 3 \times 10}{100} = 600$$

The required difference = 62.

**5.** $$\frac{D}{30} - \frac{D}{40} = \frac{1}{4}$$

$\Rightarrow$ D = 30 km.

**6.** Let the number of Rs. 1 coin be n.

Number of 50 paisa coin be = 4n

Number of 25 paisa coin be = 2n

Now $n+\frac{4n}{2}+\frac{2n}{4}=56$

$\Rightarrow$ n = 16

$\therefore$ Number of 50 paisa coin = 4 × 16 = 64.

**7.** 7B = 3K and 2K = B + 5C

$\Rightarrow \frac{2\times7}{3}B = B+5C$

$\frac{14}{3}B - B = 5C$

$\frac{11}{3}B = 5C$

$\Rightarrow$ 22B = 30C.

**8.** Percentage of students who likes both

= (72 + 44) – 100 = 16

If the number of students be x, then

16% of x = 48

$\Rightarrow$ x = 300.

**9.** Price of the xema two pens = 12 × 10 – 8 × 11.75 = 26

Now x + 1.6x = 26

$\Rightarrow$ x = 10

$\therefore$ Price of the pens are 10 and 16

Note: Among the given ?? only option (d) have value which satisfy the condition.

# GENERAL KNOWLEDGE

## CURRENT AFFAIRS

**1.** Which e-commerce company has made its maiden entry in the Thomson Reuters top 100 Global Innovators list 2015 ?

(a) Amazon (b) Snapdeal

(c) ebay (d) Alibaba

**2.** Tunisian mediators of the so called National Dialogue Quartet won the Nobel Peace Prize 20l5. Which of the following is/are part of Quartet?

I. The Tunisian General Labour Union (UGTT)

II. The Tunisian Confederation of Industry, Trade and Handicrafts (UTICA)

III. The Tunisian Human Rights League (LTDH)

IV. The Tunisian Order of Lawyers

The correct answer is

(a) I and II (b) II and III

(c) I, II and IV (d) I, II, III and IV

**3.** The Employee's Provident Fund organisation has won the National Award on e-governance 2015-16 for launching

(a) Unique Identification Number

(b) Universal Account Number

(c) Online Pension scheme

(d) Online complaint portal

**4.** Which is the World,s first airport to fully run on solar power ?

(a) Vancouver (US) (b) Dubai (UAE)

(c) Kochi (India) (d) Zurich (Switzerland)

**5.** Government has introduced Start-up Scheme to promote new enterprises' Such enterprises has been awarded__________years tax holiday.

(a) 1 (b) 2

(c) 3 (d) 5

**6.** Consider the following statements in respect of PAN (effective from January 1,2016)

I. Quoting PAN is mandatory for cash payments made to settle hotel bills or for buying foreign travel tickets of an amount above Rs 50,000

II. The PAN requirement for non-luxury cash transactions is Rs 2 lakh

III. PAN for making post office deposit of over Rs 50,000 has been dispensed with.

IV. PAN is mandatory on purchase of immovable property of Rs 10 lakh

The correct answer is

(a) I and II (b) I, II and IV

(c) II, III and IV (d) I, II, III and IV

**7.** How many firms, recently, have got licence from RBI for establishing Payment Banks ?

(a) 10 (b) 11

(c) 12 (d) 13

**8.** Government has allowed__________FDI in operations of white level ATMs.

(a) 100% (b) 74%

(c) 51% (d) 4e%

**9.** An Indian car maker recently changed the name of its newly launched car because the name was similar to an epidemic

(a) Tata Motors (b) Maruti Suzuki

(c) Mahindra & Mahindra (d) Honda Motors

**10.** The first telecommunication company to launch pan India 4G mobile services

(a) BSNL (b) Vodafone

(c) Reliance Jio (d) Bharti Airtel

**11.** WTO has recently approved membership of which country ?

(a) Zimbabwe (b) Sweden

(c) Afghanistan (d) Sri Lanka

**12.** Which country recently allowed women to vote in local elections for the first time ?

(a) Iran (b) Iraq

(c) Indonesia (d) Saudi Arabia

**13.** Who has been honoured by the Rajiv Gandhi Khel Ratna Award 2015 ?

(a) Rohit Sharma (b) Jitu Rai

(c) Sania Mirza (d) Deepika Pallikal

**14.** Which of the following countries has recently declared a 'state of economic emergency' ?

(a) Bangladesh (b) Germany

(c) Burundi (d) France

**15.** MNREGA program provides 100 days employment in rural areas. The Government during September 2015 decided to provide additional__________days employment in drought affected areas'

(a) 20 (b) 25

(c) 40 (d) 50

**16.** United Nations has appointed Anupam Kher as the ambassador of

(a) 'Let the Girl Live' campaign

(b) 'He for She' campaign

(c) 'Share Humanity' campaign

(d) 'Youth Now' campaign

## ANSWERS

| | | | | |
|---|---|---|---|---|
| **1.** (a) | **2.** (d) | **3.** (b) | **4.** (c) | **5.** (c) |
| **6.** (d) | **7.** (b) | **8.** (a) | **9.** (a) | **10.** (d) |
| **11.** (c) | **12.** (d) | **13.** (c) | **14.** (d) | **15.** (d) |
| **16.** (b) | | | | |

## EXPLANATIONS

**1.** E-commerce Company Amazon.com Inc has made its maiden entry in the Thomson Reuters Top 100 global innovators list 2015 by dropping International Business Machines Corp (IBM) from the list. The Thomson Reuters Top 100 global innovators program identifies innovators annually through an in-depth analysis based on a series of patent-related metrics that analyze what it means to be truly innovative.

**2.** The National Dialogue Quartet was formed in the summer of 2013.The quartet was awarded the 2015 Nobel Peace Prize on 9th October 2015.The National Dialogue Quartet comprises the following organizations in Tunisian civil society:

- The Tunisian General Labour Union (UGTT, Union Générale Tunisienne du Travail)
- The Tunisian Confederation of Industry, Trade and Handicrafts (UTICA, Union Tunisienne de l'Industrie, du Commerce et de l'Artisanat)
- The Tunisian Human Rights League (LTDH, La Ligue Tunisienne pour la Défense des Droits de l'Homme)
- The Tunisian Order of Lawyers (Ordre National des Avocats de Tunisie)

**3.** 'The Employees' Provident Fund Organisation has won the National Award on e-Governance 2015-16 for launching the Universal Account Number (UAN). The UAN facility enables workers to transfer their provident fund deposits while switching jobs anywhere in India easily.

**4.** Cochin International airport, the country's first airport built under PPP model has scripted another chapter in aviation history by becoming the first airport in the world that completely operates on solar power.

**5.** Prime Minister Narendra Modi unveiled a slew of incentives to boost start-up businesses, offering them a tax holiday and inspector raj-free regime for three years, capital gains tax exemption and Rs 10,000 crore corpus to fund them.

**6.** Very recently, the Government in its move to curb the circulation of black money and widening its tax base decided that quoting of PAN is essential for any form of transaction exceeding Rs.2 lakh, regardless of the mode of payment. Apart from trigger value of Rs 2 lakh, there are several other transactions where quoting of PAN is mandatory. Given below are the details:

1. During purchase/ sale of immovable property exceeding Rs 10 lakh.
2. For payment of hotel or restaurant bills exceeding Rs 50,000 at any one point through any mode of payment.
3. While making a time deposit with any financial institution like Co-op banks, Post Office, Nidhi and NBFC.

**7.** Paving the way for revolutionising cashless payments services in the country, the Reserve Bank of India granted payment bank licences to 11 firms.

**8.** The government has approved 100% foreign direct investment (FDI) under the automatic route for non-bank entities that operate cash machines subject to certain conditions in a bid to boost financial inclusion in the country.

9. The Indian carmaker Tata Motors has decided to change the name of its heavily promoted new car, the Zica, to avoid association with alarm about the spread of the Zika virus.
10. Bharti Airtel, about one-third owned by Singapore Telecom, steals a march over Mukesh Ambani's Reliance Jio by becoming the first to offer fourth generation mobile services across India.
11. The World Trade Organisation (WTO) formally approved Afghanistan's membership at its 10th ministerial conference in the Kenyan capital Nairobi.
12. Women are registering to vote for the first time in Saudi Arabia in a long overdue move towards equality for the nation. Voting registration for the December elections starts today and on August 30, they will even be allowed to register as candidates.
13. Tennis ace Sania Mirza was conferred the Rajiv Gandhi Khel Ratna Award even as the Karnataka High Court sought clarifications from the Union Sports Ministry following a petition from Paralympian H.N. Girisha challenging the Ministry's decision.
14. French President Francois Hollande pledged to redefine France's business model and declared what he called "a state of economic and social emergency," unveiling a 2-billion-euro ($3.19 billion Cdn) plan to revive hiring and catch up with a fast-moving world economy.
15. The Union Cabinet chaired by the Prime Minister Shri Narendra Modi, has given its ex-post facto approval to provide an additional 50 days of unskilled manual work in the financial year over and above the 100 days assured to job card holders, in such rural areas where drought or natural calamities have been notified.
16. Veteran actor Anupam Kher has been appointed as the UN ambassador of the 'HeForShe' campaign for gender equality. The 'HeForShe' campaign has been initiated by UN Women. Its goal is to engage men as agents of change for the achievement of gender equality and women's rights, by encouraging them to take action against inequalities faced by women and girls.

## EVERYDAY SCIENCE

1. FM broadcast band lies in_________.

   (a) HF (b) SHF

   (c) UHF (d) VHF

2. Liquid crystals are used In

   (a) Pocket Calculator (b) Display Devices

   (c) Wrist watches (d) All of the above

## ANSWERS

1. (d) 2. (d)

## EXPLANATIONS

1. FM broadcasting is radio broadcasting using frequency modulation (FM) technology. eting radio broadcasting technology, so it is used for most music broadcasts. FM radio stations use the VHF frequencies. The term "FM band" describes the frequency band in a given country which is dedicated to FM broadcasting.
2. Liquid crystal technology has had a major effect many areas of science and engineering, as well as device technology. Applications for this special kind of material are still being discovered and continue to provide effective solutions to many different problems.

## GEOGRAPHY

1. Which of the following pairs of rivers have been interlinked formally for the first time in India ?

   (a) Betwa - Ken

   (b) Son - Ken

   (c) Ganga - Jhelum

   (d) Godavari - Krishna

2. Why the sidereal day is 4 minutes shorter than the solar day ?

   (a) The Earth is round in shape.

   (b) The Earth revolves around the Sun'

   (c) The Earth rotates on its axis.

   (d) The Earth has an atmosphere'

## ANSWERS

1. (d) 2. (c)

## EXPLANATIONS

1. In an historic step in the mission to inter-link rivers, the Godavari was formally connected with the Krishna in Andhra Pradesh.
2. A solar day is the time taken for the Sun to move from its highest point in the sky back to its highest point the following day. This is exactly 24 hours. A sidereal day is the time it takes for the Earth to actually rotate once on its axis. A sidereal day is four minutes shorter than a solar day. The sidereal day is shorter than the solar day because as well as rotating on its axis, the Earth also orbits the Sun.

## ECONOMICS

**1.** Which of the following variables is not part of the 'Impossible Trinity' conundrum ?

(a) Capital Control (b) Exchange Rate

(c) Fiscal Policy (d) Monetary Policy

**2.** The measurement of poverty-line in India is based on the criteria of

(a) Nature of employment (b) Dwelling houses

(c) Level of education (d) Calorie consumption

**3.** Which is the only industrialised country of the world that did not ratify the Kyoto Protocol?

(a) Russia (b) United States

(c) Japan (d) France

**4.** Which of the following statements is incorrect about foreign investment in India ?

(a) Foreign Portfolio Investment (FPIs) can invest up to 5.1% in multi-brand retail

(b) FPI up to 49% through automatic route is permissible across sectors

(c) 49% FPI in Brownfield pharma projects is allowed

(d) Foreign retailers are not able to have direct management control of an Indian venture

**5.** What percentage of Employees Provident Fund can be invested in equity shares?

(a) 0%

(b) 5%

(c) 10%

(d) Minimum 5% and maximum 15%

**6.** Section 80 TTA of the Income Tax Act pertains to interest earned on

(a) Saving Bank Accounts

(b) Fixed Deposits

(c) Recurring deposit

(d) Government saving schemes

## ANSWERS

**1.** (c) **2.** (d) **3.** (b) **4.** (a) **5.** (d)
**6.** (a)

## EXPLANATIONS

**1.** The Impossible trinity (also known as the Trilemma) is a trilemma in international economics which states that it is impossible to have all three of the following at the same time:

- A stable foreign exchange rate
- Free capital movement (absence of capital controls)
- An independent monetary policy

**2.** The measurement of poverty-|ine in India is based on the criteria of Calorie consumption.

**3.** United States is the signatory and only industria'sed country of the world that did not ratify the Kyoto Protocol.

**4.** In a major turnaround, the BJP-led government, so far opposed to foreign investments in multi-brand retail, has decided to allow FPI up to 49 per cent or up to the sectoral cap (whichever is lower) through the automatic route."This means that foreign investors in multi-brand retail can bring in investments in the form of FPI up to 49 per cent without government approval," a Department of Industrial Policy & Promotion official clarified.

**5.** Union Labour Secretary Shankar Aggarwal said the EPFO investment into the stock market can go up to 15 per cent of the incremental deposit every year. As the EPFO gets around Rs 1,00,000-1,20,000 crore as incremental deposits every year, ETF investment can go up to Rs 15,000-20,000 crore. "It (investment) depends upon the market. The Finance Ministry norms allow me to invest up to 15 per cent (of incremental deposits) but CBT (Central Board of Trustees) allows me to invest 5 per cent in ETFs to start with," Jalan said.

**6.** Section 80TTA is introduced with effect from April 01, 2013 and will apply from AY 2013-14 and onwards. Section is introduced to provide deduction to an individual or a Hindu undivided family in respect of interest received on deposits (not being time deposits) in a savings account held with banks, cooperative banks and post office. The deduction is restricted to Rs 10,000 or actual interest whichever is lower.

## MISCELLANEOUS (QUOTES, DAYS, BOOKS TITLES, SPORTS, BASIC LEGAL CONCEPTS)

**1.** Which folk dance India has made it to the Guinness Book of World Records as the largest folk dance in the world ?

(a) Bihu (Assam)

(b) Garba (Gujarat)

(c) Nati (Himachal Pradesh)

(d) Bhangra (Punjab)

**2.** Who termed Paris deal on climate change as 'Climate Justice' ?

(a) Ban-Ki-Moon (b) Barack Obama

(c) Narendra Modi (d) Francois Hollande

**3.** What is R2 - D2 ?

(a) It is an astromech droid that extinguishes fires' repairs spaceships and assists the lead characters in the Star Wars film

(b) It is a new atomic particle discovered

(c) It is vaccine against Ebola

(d) It is a video game

## ANSWERS

**1.** (c) **2.** (c) **3.** (a)

## EXPLANATIONS

**1.** The Nati folk dance of Kullu district of Himachal Pradesh in second week of January 2016 was listed in the Guinness Book of World Records as the largest folk dance in the world.

**2.** Prime Minister Narendra Modi described the landmark climate change deal reached in Paris last night as the victory of "climate justice" and said there were no winners or losers in the outcome.

**3.** R2 - D2 is an astromechdroid that extinguishes fires',repairs spaceships and assists the lead characters in the Star Wars film.

# LEGAL APTITUDE

## TORTS

**Directions (Qs. 1 - 2):** Given below is a statement of legal principle followed by a factual situation. Apply the principle to the facts given below and select the most appropriate answer.

**1. LEGAL PRINCIPLE :** In the employer - employee relationship, the employer is held liable for all the wrongs committed by his employees in the course of employment.

**FACTUAL SITUATION :** David was employed as a Driver in ABC & Co over the past 15 years and has been appreciated by the General Manager for his hard work and sincerity. He has been rewarded by the company for his accident free record. David's younger brother wanted to join the same company as a driver. He obtained a Learner's Licence, joined a Driving School and was learning driving during the last three months. He was on the verge of completion of the training and appear for the Driving test. He wanted to have more practice before the test and requested his brother David for using the Company's car for two days. David also allowed him to use the office car for the practice. While he was practising driving, a truck came from the wrong side, hit the company's car driven by David's brother, which in turn hit a pedestrian and injured him. The pedestrian sues the company for damages.

**DECISION :**

(a) The Company is not liable as it was driven by David's brother

(b) The Company is liable as David allowed his brother to drive the car

(c) David's brother is personally liable

(d) The Company can shift the responsibility on to the truck driver

**2. LEGAL PRINCIPLE :** When a person unlawfully intervenes in the chattel of another person by which the latter is deprived of its use, the former commits the tort of conversion. And nobody shall enrich himself at other's cost.

**FACTUAL SITUATION :** X, a patient suffering from fibroids in her uterus approached KLM Medical Institute. X was suggested to undergo surgery to remove the fibroids from her uterus. The operation was successfully performed and X was discharged after few days. one of the researchers of the KLM Institute discovered some rare and unique cells in the fibroids of x and using these cells, the laboratory of KLM developed some life-saving drugs and earned rupees twenty crore from a leading International Pharma Company. When X came to know about it, she claimed five crore from the Institute.

**DECISION :**

(a) KLM Institute need not share its income with X because X far from being deprived of the use of her fibroids was actually benefitted by its removal.

(b) KLM Institute need not share its income with X because the medical institute instead of destroying the waste fibroids of X conducted research on its own and invented new life-saving drugs.

(c) KLM Institute must share its income with X because KLM could not have achieved its success without the fibroids of X.

(d) KLM Institute must share its income with X on moral grounds.

**Direction :** The following question consist of two statements, one labelled as, Assertion' and the other as 'Reason'. Read both the statements carefully and answer using the codes given below.

(a) Both A and R are true and R is the correct explanation of A

(b) Both A and R are true but R is not the true explanation of A

(c) A is true but R is false

(d) A is false but R is true

3. **Assertion (A) :** No action lies for mere damage caused by some act which does not violate a legal right.

   **Reason (R) :** An action lies for interference with another's legal right even where it causes no actual damage.

## ANSWERS

**1.** (b) **2.** (b) **3.** (b)

## EXPLANATIONS

1. The company is liable as David allowed his brother to drive the car. David allowed him to use the office car for practice. The employer is liable for the act of employee for all the wrongs committed by his employees in the course of employment.
2. Here the KLM institute has not unlawfully intervened in the chattel of 'X'. The Surgery was to remove the fibroids from the uterus and it was of no use to Mrs. X. KLM institute need not share its income with X because the medical institute instead of destroying the waste fibroids of X conducted research on its own and invented the new life saving drugs.
3. Both A and R are true but R is not correct explanation of A

## LAW OF CONTRACTS

**Direction :** Given below is a statement of legal principle followed by a factual situation. Apply the principle to the facts given below and select the most appropriate answer.

1. **LEGAL PRINCIPLE :** The acceptance of an offer will be valid only if it is made in the way it was expected to be made.

   **FACTUAL SITUATION :** There was a telephonic discussion between 'J' and 'K' for negotiating the sale of the shop of former to the latter. Upon reaching an agreement as to the price of the shop of 'J' at Rs 20 lakh, 'J' told 'K' to send a letter to him within two weeks confirming that she wishes to buy the shop for the price finalized. Two days thereafter, 'K' gave her acceptance to 'J' over telephone but sent the letter of confirmation after lapse of one month. Is 'J' bound by acceptance of 'K' ?

   **DECISION :**

   (a) Yes, because the acceptance was conveyed within two weeks over telephone and it was followed by a letter of acceptance as stipulated.

   (b) No, because although the acceptance over telephone was conveyed in time but not in the mode specified and the letter of acceptance was also not sent within two weeks.

   (c) No, because sale of immovable property cannot be finalized online; neither any acceptance can be given over phone. Hence, the entire negotiation is invalid.

   (d) Yes, because no law can compel the purchaser to give his acceptance through the mode prescribed by the vendor.

**Direction :** The following questions consist of two statements, one labelled as, Assertion' and the other as 'Reason'. Read both the statements carefully and answer using the codes given below.

2. **Assertion (A) :** The parties to the contract must be competent to contract othenrvise it will be a void contract.

   **Reason (R) :** All wagering agreements are void.

## ANSWERS

**1.** (b) **2.** (b)

## EXPLANATIONS

1. Principle says that the acceptance of an offer will be valid only if it is made in the way it was expected to be made. Here, according to the factual situation 'K' was supposed to send a letter within two weeks confirming that she wishes to buy the shop for the price finalized. 'K' although conveyed the acceptance over phone, but failed to make in the way she was supposed to and hence 'J' is not bound by the acceptance of 'K'.
2. Both A and R are true but R is not correct explanation of A

## CRIMINAL LAW

**Direction :** The following questions consist of two statements, one labelled as, Assertion' and the other as 'Reason'. Read both the statements carefully and answer using the codes given below.

1. **Assertion (A) :** An accused person cannot be forced to give his thumb impression.

   **Reason (R) :** An accused person cannot be compelled to be a witness against himself.

## ANSWERS

**1.** (d)

## EXPLANATIONS

1. A is false but R is true.

## CONSTITUTIONAL LAW AND LEGAL FRAMEWORK

**Directions (Qs. 1 - 6):** Given below is a statement of legal principle followed by a factual situation. Apply the principle to the facts given below and select the most appropriate answer.

1. **LEGAL PRINCIPLE :** A reasonable classification having nexus with the object sought to be achieved is not violative of Article 14 or Article 16 of the Constitution of India.

**FACTUAL SITUATION :** 'X' is a male teacher in a Women's college, who applied for the post of principal of that College. His candidature was rejected on the basis of the Government's policy of appointing only women as Principal of a women's college. 'X' challenges the policy on the ground of discrimination. Whether the challenge is sustainable?

**DECISION :**

(a) Yes, because rejection of X's candidature amounts to sexual discrimination and deprivation of opportunity.

(b) No, the rejection does not amount to discrimination since it is a reasonable classification permissible under the Constitution.

(c) No, because the policy of appointment of only lady Principal in a women's college is a reasonable classification having a nexus with the object sought to be achieved.

(d) Yes, because the policy is violative of the guarantee of equality before law under Article 14 of the Constitution.

2. **LEGAL PRINCIPLE :** Any institution or body can be a 'State' if it is created under the Constitution or a statute; or if it is substantially financed by the Government; or the Government holds its share capital.

**FACTUAL SITUATION :** K approached the High court by filing a writ petition against the Board for Control of Cricket in India (BCCI). The argument advanced was that BCCI is a 'State' within the meaning of Article 12 of the constitution of India. The question is whether the argument is acceptable ?

**DECISION :**

(a) Yes, because the Board has monopoly on cricket in India.

(b) No, because the monopoly on cricket is neither State conferred nor State protected.

(c) No, because the control of the government on BCCI, if any, is only regulatory.

(d) No, because neither the Board is created under a statute nor any part of share capital of the Board is held by the government and no financial assistance is given by the government to the Board.

3. **LEGAL PRINCIPLE :** Clause (1) of Article 15 of the Constitution of India prohibits the State from discriminating between citizens on the ground only of religion, race, caste, sex, place of birth or any of them.

**FACTUAL SITUATION :** The admission Rules of an Engineering College located in XYZ State of India provided that no capitation fee shall be charged from the residents of the XYZ State but the non-residents shall be required to pay capitation fee. Whether the Rules are violative of Article 15 (1) of the Constitution ?

**DECISION :**

(a) yes, because Article 15 (1) prohibits discrimination between citizens on the ground only of religion, race, caste, Sex, place of birth or any of them.

(b) yes, because Article 15(1) prohibits discrimination on the basis of place of birth which impliedly includes place of residence.

(c) yes, because Article 15 (1) prohibits discrimination between citizens on the ground only of religion, race, caste, sex, place of birth and the provision suffers from causus omissus and "place of residence" is inadvertently omitted.

(d) No, because Article 15 (1) does not prohibit discrimination based on the place of residence.

4. **LEGAL PRINCIPLE :** No person shall be deprived of his life or personal liberty except according to procedure established by law and Civil Courts have coercive powers to compel attendance of witness only within its local territory.

**FACTUAL SITUATION :** Puchu, a resident of Faridabad was summoned by the Delhi High Court as a witness in a civil case regarding wrongful possession of immovable property filed by Amu against Kichu. He refused to appear before the court due to his office job. He was prosecuted by the court. Is he liable ?

**DECISION :**

(a) He is not liable because he is not the resident of Delhi.

(b) He is not liable because he has fundamental right under Article 21 of personal liberty.

(c) He is liable because he is called as a witness in a civil trial and it is a procedure established by law.

(d) He is not liable because he has no interest in the suit property.

**5. LEGAL PRINCIPLE :** Article 19(1) (g) of the Constitution of India guarantees to all citizens the right to practice any profession, or to carry on any trade, occupation and business but Article 19 (6) empowers the State to impose reasonable restrictions on this right in the interest of public.

**FACTUAL SITUATION :** Having experienced acute shortage of labour for agricultural purpose due to engagement of agricultural labourer in manufacture of Bidis, the state Government enacted a law to prohibit such engagement of agricultural labour in the manufacture of Bidis. Whether the law violates the constitutional provisions ?

**DECISION :**

(a) No, because the law in a reasonable restriction in the interest of public as if labourers would not be available for agricultural purposes there can be shortage of food grains and wastage of crops.

(b) No, because Bidis are harmful for health of people so any law preventing people from engaging in manufacture of Bidis is in the interest of public.

(c) Yes, because the law imposes an unreasonable restriction as it indirectly makes the two sectors (manufacture of Bidis and agriculture) alternative options for the labourers where as some people would like to work in both of these.

(d) Yes, because the object sought to be achieved by this law is to keep sufficient labour supply for agricultural purpose, which could have been easily achieved by restraining the employment of agricultural labour in Bidi manufacturing during the agricultural season only. Absolute restriction amounts to withdrawal of the right. Hence, the law is unconstitutional.

**6. LEGAL PRINCIPLE :** According to Article 20 (1) of the Constitution, no person shall be convicted of any offence except for violation of the law in force at the time of the commission of the act charged as an offence, nor be subjected to a penalty greater than that which might have been inflicted under the law in force at the time of the commission of the offence.

**FACTUAL SITUATION :** 'P' was charged with an offence punishable with imprisonment for a term of one year. The Magistrate convicted him and awarded him a punishment of one year imprisonment. While 'P' was undergoing the sentence, the law under which 'P' was convicted came to be amended and the punishment for the offence of which 'P' was convicted was reduced to six months. The defense filed an application to the Magistrate for review of sentence and to commute it to six months. Can the application be allowed ?

**DECISION :**

(a) No, because penal laws only have prospective application.

(b) No, because a penal statute cannot be given retrospective effect.

(c) No, since at the time of coming into force of the amended law, 'P' was already suffering the sentence and had not completed the full term. Hence, his case should not be dealt under the new law.

(d) Yes, because retrospective application of criminal law if it is beneficial to the accused is not against Article 20 (1) of the Constitution.

**Directions (Qs. 7 - 8) :** The following questions consist of two statements, one labelled as, Assertion' and the other as 'Reason'. Read both the statements carefully and answer using the codes given below.

(a) Both A and R are true and R is the correct explanation of A

(b) Both A and R are true but R is not the true explanation of A

(c) A is true but R is false

(d) A is false but R is true

**7. Assertion (A) :** The entries in the three legislative lists are not always set out with scientific precision.

**Reason (R) :** The entries are not powers but are only fields of legislation.

**8. Assertion (A) :** In federalism, there is division of powers between the centre and the States.

**Reason (R) :** The legislation is not invalid merely because it incidentally encroaches upon matters which have been assigned to another organ.

**9.** The constitution (One hundredth Amendment) Act, 2015 amended the________ Schedule of the Constitution to give effect to an agreement entered into by India and________on acquiring and transferring of territories between the two countries.

(a) Ninth; Pakistan (b) Second; Pakistan

(c) First; Bangladesh (d) First; China

**10.** Who is the CEO of NITI Aayog ?

(a) Sindhushree Khullar (b) Arvind Panagariya

(c) Bikesh Debroy (d) Amitabh Kant

**11.** Allahabad High Court has held that the__________of deceased Government employees are eligible for appointment on compassionate ground.

(a) wife

(b) daughter

(c) mother

(d) married daughter

12. Which party has won the general elections of Spain in spite of its worst result since 1989 ?
(a) People's Party
(b) Pedro Sanchez's Socialist party
(c) Popular Union
(d) Ciudadanos Party

13. Pension Fund Regulatory and Development Authority has started using________ for online registration under the National pension system scheme.
(a) PAN Card (b) passport
(c) Aadhar Card (d) Driving License

14. When a vehicle is financed by a bank, what kind of charge does the bank have over the primary security ?
(a) Pledge (b) Hypothecation
(c) Assignment (d) Lien

15. Under which Act can action be taken against wilful defaulters of banking loans ?
(a) Under Section 420 of IPC
(b) SEBI Act
(c) Banking Regulation Act
(d) Securitisation and Reconstruction of Financial Assets and Enforcement of Security Interest Act (SARFAESI Act)

16. Which of the following court / tribunal ordered levy of an environment compensatory charge on commercial vehicles not bound for the capital yet passing through Delhi ?
(a) Supreme Court of India
(b) Delhi High Court
(c) National Green Tribunal
(d) None of these

17. Parliament has enacted which of the following Legislation in 2015 - 16 ?
I. The Juvenile Justice (Care and Protection of Children) Act
II. The Election Laws (Amendment) Act
III. The Scheduled Caste and Scheduled Tribes (Prevention of Atrocities) Amendment Act
IV. Commercial Courts, Commercial Division and Commercial Appellate Division of High Courts Act
(a) I and III
(b) IV only
(c) I and IV
(d) I, II, III and IV

18. In the following Sates more than 60% seats are in reserved category in educational institutions against 50% cap as fixed by the Supreme Court of India
I. Karnataka II. Tamil Nadu
III. Odisha IV. Bihar
The correct answer is :
(a) only II (b) I and II
(c) II and IV (d) I' II and III

19. According to SEBI norms, a person found guilty of indulging in unfair trade practices shall be liable to a penalty of
I. Rs. 25 crore
II. Three times the amount of profits made out of such practices,.....
The correct answer is :
(a) only I (b) only II
(c) either I or II (d) neither I nor II

20. The minimum wages in________are the highest in the northern region.
(a) Rajasthan (b) Dethi
(c) Punjab (d) Haryana

21. The correct sequence in ascending order of their creation of the following international institution is :
I. WTO II. GATT
III. UNCTAD IV. NAFTA
(a) II, III, I, IV
(b) III, II, I, IV
(c) IV, II, I, III
(d) I, II, III, IV

22. Government of India has decided to establish________in selected High Courts.
(a) Tax Division
(b) SC/ST Division
(c) Commercial Division
(d) Economic Offence Division

23. 'Zero Rating' is a recent term used in
(a) Insurance (b) Credit Rating
(c) Energy Efficiency (d) Net Neutrality

24. Which Article of the Constitution of India was used to impose President Rule in Uttarakhand and placing the Assembly under suspended animation in March 2016 ?
(a) Article 102
(b) Articte 143
(c) Article 356
(d) Arricle 365

## ANSWERS

| | | | | |
|---|---|---|---|---|
| 1. (c) | 2. (d) | 3. (d) | 4. (a) | 5. (d) |
| 6. (d) | 7. (b) | 8. (b) | 9. (c) | 10. (d) |
| 11. (d) | 12. (a) | 13. (a) | 14. (b) | 15. (d) |
| 16. (a) | 17. (d) | 18. (d) | 19. (c) | 20. (b) |
| 21. (a) | 22. (c) | 23. (d) | 24. (c) | |

## EXPLANATIONS

1. The Principle clearly states that a reasonable classification having nexus with the object sought to be achieved is not violative of Article 14 and Article 16 of the Constitution of India and the policy of the government to appoint only lady principal in a women's college is a reasonable classification having a nexus with the object sought to be achieved. Hence the challenge of Mr. X is not sustainable.
2. To constitute State, the institution must be created under the Constitution or a statute, or is financed by the state or government holds the share capital in the institution. BCCI is neither create under statue nor any part of share of the Board is held by the government and no financial assistant is given by the government to the Board and hence it doesn't fulfill the criteria of being a State under Article 12 of the Constitution.
3. According to Clause (1) of Article 15, discrimination cannot be done on the basis of religion, race, caste, sex , place of birth or any of them. It is not talking about resident as one of the criteria and hence the rules are not violative of Article 15(1) of the Constitution.
4. The principle states that civil courts have coercive powers to compel attendance of witness only within its local territory and Faridabad, doesn't comes within the local territory of Delhi High Court and hence Puchu is not liable.
5. basing on the principle the most suitable answer is d. The objective of the government was to keep sufficient labour supply for agricultural purpose and this could have been easily achieved by restraining the employment of agricultural labour in Bidi manufacturing during agricultural season only. Government can impose reasonable restrictions. Absolute restrictions amount to violation of right and hence the law is unconstitutional.
6. Here the principle says that person cannot be subject to penalty greater than that which might have been inflicted under the law in force at the time of the commission of the offence and it does not talk about reduction in the sentence and retrospective application of criminal law if it is beneficial to the accused is not against Article 20(1) of the Constitution.
7. Both A and R are true but R is not correct explanation of A.
8. Both A and R are true but R is not correct explanation of A

## MISCELLANEOUS

**Directions (Qs. 1 - 3):** Given below is a statement of legal principle followed by a factual situation. Apply the principle to the facts given below and select the most appropriate answer.

1. **LEGAL PRINCIPLE :** A suit shall be instituted in the court within whose jurisdiction the cause of action arises; or the defendant actually and voluntarily resides or carries on business, or personally works for gain.

   **FACTUAL SITUATION :** 'Y' carries on business in Mumbai. 'Z' carries on business in Delhi. 'Z' buys goods of 'Y' in Mumbai through his agent and request 'Y' to deliver them at Delhi. Accordingly, 'Y' delivered the goods at Delhi. But he did not get the price of the goods delivered in Delhi. Therefore, he intends to move the Civil Court for recovery of amount from 'Z'. Which court may 'Y' approach ?

   **DECISION :**

   (a) 'Y' may institute the suit either at Delhi where Z carries on business or at Mumbai where the cause of action arose.
   (b) 'Y' may institute the suit at Delhi where 'Z' carries on business.
   (c) 'Y' may institute the suit simultaneously at Delhi where 'Z' caries on business and at Mumbai where the cause of action arose.
   (d) 'Y' may institute the suit at Mumbai where the cause of action arose.

2. **LEGAL PRINCIPLE :** A power conferred by a statute cannot be withdrawn by a subordinate legislation.

   **FACTUAL SITUATION :** The Cinematograph Act conferred powers upon the District Magistrate (DM) to grant license subject to the control of the government. The government framed Rules under the said Act. The effect of these Rules was that the licensing power stood transferred to the Government itself and the District Magistrate was rendered powerless. Whether such Rules are valid ?

   **DECISION :**

   (a) The licensing power was granted by the Cinematograph Act. Any withdrawal or transfer thereof was possible only through an Amending Act and not by any Rules made under the Parent Act.

(b) Although the legislature has conferred power upon the DM to grant license but the government being the implementing agency might find it unfeasible. Therefore, the government rightly withdrew it from the DM.

(c) The Rules are valid since these are framed under the Parent Act in order to better implement it.

(d) The Rules are valid since the DM under the Parent Act was not independent but subject to the control of Government'

3. **LEGAL PRINCIPLE:** A judgment which binds only the parties to a suit in which the judgment was passed is called judgment in personam; whereas a judgment which binds all men irrespective of whether they were party to suit or not is known as judgment in rem.

**FACTUAL SITUATION :** "Judgment of a competent court determining contractual obligations of the parties to a contract is an example of judgment in personam; but a judgment of a competent court declaring a party to be insolvent is an example of judgment in rem." Comment on the correctness of this statement.

**DECISION :**

(a) The statement is incorrect because a judgment relating to contract is a judgment in rem as it binds both the parties to the suit as well as the strangers. But a judgment relating to insolvency applies only to the person who has been adjudged to be an insolvent; hence it is a judgment in personam.

(b) The Statement is wrong as both the judgments are judgments in rem as both bind not only the parties to thesuit but also others.

(c) The Statement is wrong as both the judgments are judgments in personam as both the judgments bind not only the parties to the suit but not the others.

(d) The statement is correct.

**Directions (Qs. 4 - 5) :** The following questions consist of two statements, one labelled as, Assertion' and the other as 'Reason'. Read both the statements carefully and answer using the codes given below.

(a) Both A and R are true and R is the correct explanation of A

(b) Both A and R are true but R is not the true explanation of A

(c) A is true but R is false

(d) A is false but R is true

4. **Assertion (A) :** Custom to have force of law must be followed from time immemorial.

**Reason (R) :** Custom represents common consciousness of the people.

5. **Assertion (A) :** International law is not law at all.

**Reason (R) :** International law has no judicial system to enforce the law by applying sanctions.

## ANSWERS

| **1.** (a) | **2.** (a) | **3.** (d) | **4.** (b) | **5.** (d) |
|---|---|---|---|---|

## EXPLANATIONS

1. The Principle clearly states that a suit shall be instituted where the defendant actually and voluntarily resides or carry on business, or personally works for gain or in whose jurisdiction the cause of action arises and hence 'Y' may institute the suit either at Delhi, where Z carries on business or at Mumbai where the cause of action arose.

2. The Principle states that the power conferred by a statute cannot be withdrawn by a subordinate legislation. The Licensing power was granted by the Cinematographic Act and hence these power cannot be taken away by any rule framed under the same act. Any change in the licensing power can be made only by amending the cinematographic Act and not by any rules made under the parent act.

3. The statement is correct. The judgment related to a contractual obligations, binds only the parties between whom the contract was entered and it is judgment in personam as it does not bind the person who are not party to the contract. But if a party is declared insolvent, it binds everyone not to enter into any contract with him and hence is right in rem.

4. Both A and R are true but R is not correct explanation of A

5. A is false but R is true.

# CLAT-2017
# CHAPTER-WISE

## ENGLISH

### VOCABULARY

**Direction for questions 1-4:** Choose the correct spelling in questions given below.

1. (*a*) Accommedation (*b*) Accommodation
   (*c*) Accomedation (*d*) Accomadation
2. (*a*) Renumaration (*b*) Remunaration
   (*c*) Remuneration (*d*) Renumeration
3. (*a*) Blasphamy (*b*) Blashphemy
   (*c*) Bleshphemy (*d*) Blasphemy
4. (*a*) Gallows (*b*) Ghellows
   (*c*) Gellows (*d*) Ghallows

**Direction for Questions 5-8:** Choose the correct spellings in questions given below.

5. (*a*) Hyphothecation (*b*) Hypthacation
   (*c*) Hypathecation (*d*) Hypothecation
6. (*a*) Gratuitous (*b*) Gratitious
   (*c*) Gratuitus (*d*) Gratetious
7. (*a*) Interrogation (*b*) Interagation
   (*c*) Interogetion (*d*) Interogation
8. (*a*) Annulment (*b*) Annulmant
   (*c*) Annulement (*d*) Anulment

**Direction for questions 9 and 10:** Choose the correct spellings in questions given below.

9. (*a*) Abhayence (*b*) Abeyance
   (*c*) Abeyence (*d*) Abheyance
10. (*a*) Maratorium (*b*) Moratorium
    (*c*) Moratarium (*d*) Moretorium

### ANSWERS

| | | | | |
|---|---|---|---|---|
| 1. (*b*) | 2. (*c*) | 3. (*d*) | 4. (*a*) | 5. (*d*) |
| 6. (*a*) | 7. (*a*) | 8. (*a*) | 9. (*b*) | 10. (*b*) |

### EXPLANATIONS

1. 'Accommodation' is the correct spelling.
2. 'Remuneration' is the correct spelling.
3. 'Blasphemy' is the correct spelling.
4. 'Gallows' is the correct spelling.
5. 'Hypothecation' is the correct spelling.
6. 'Gratuitous' is the correct spelling.
7. 'Interrogation' is the correct spelling.
8. 'Annulment' is the correct spelling.
9. 'Abeyance' is the correct spelling.
10. 'Moratorium' is the correct spelling.

### GRAMMAR

**Direction for Questions 1 -10:** Fill in the blank by choosing the most appropriate option.

1. Sunita decided to set _______ some time every day for prayers.
   (*a*) up (*b*) aside
   (*c*) on (*d*) in
2. We shall fail _______ we are industrious.
   (*a*) until (*b*) though
   (*c*) unless (*d*) whether
3. The doctor advised him to go _______ several medical tests.
   (*a*) through (*b*) under
   (*c*) about (*d*) into
4. Kanak is endowed _______ many great qualities
   (*a*) of (*b*) with
   (*c*) by (*d*) in
5. The minister flew _______ the flooded areas in a helicopter.
   (*a*) in (*b*) over
   (*c*) along (*d*) about
6. If they want to succeed, they _______ have to work very hard.
   (*a*) must (*b*) ought
   (*c*) should (*d*) will
7. You have played a great role, for _______ your help I possibly would have landed myself into a problem.
   (*a*) despite (*b*) without
   (*c*) after (*d*) although
8. She stood _______ Amit, but could not utter a single word for quite so me time.
   (*a*) for (*b*) about
   (*c*) before (*d*) to
9. The passengers were very happy _______ the friendly and warm treatment.
   (*a*) to (*b*) from
   (*c*) by (*d*) about

10. Would anybody _______ a mother have risked her life for the baby?

(a) but (b) rather
(c) however (d) than

**Directions for questions 11-20:** In each of the following sentences four words or phrases are underlined. If there is any mistake with regard to grammar or usage, it is in the underlined part only. Identify the incorrect part.

11. After being finished the last chapter of the
A B
book, return it to me.
C D

(a) C (b) A
(c) B (d) D

12. The hope to go through the book today I have
A B C
almost read half of it.
D

(a) B (b) A
(c) C (d) D

13. Evidently our product is the most unique in
A B C
the market.
D

(a) D (b) B
(c) A (d) C

14. Five gallons of petrol are not enough to cover
A B C
the distance.
D

(a) B (b) C
(c) D (d) D

15. On listening to the confession of love she
A B
blushed until she was purple.
C D

(a) B (b) D
(c) A (d) C

16. The officer asked that the report be submitted
A B C
immediately.
D

(a) B (b) D
(c) A (d) C

17. The most difficult job is to bend and then lifting
A B C
the weight.
D

(a) D (b) A
(c) B (d) C

18. He gave me a ticket so that I may visit the
A B C D
book fair.

(a) C (b) D
(c) A (d) B

19. Out boss always asks us to pay full attention
A B C
to the work at hand.
D

(a) D (b) B
(c) C (d) A

20. Since I have forgotten all the equations I
A B
will have to start from the scratch.
C D

(a) C (b) A
(c) D (d) B

## ANSWERS

| | | | | |
|---|---|---|---|---|
| 1. (b) | 2. (c) | 3. (a) | 4. (b) | 5. (b) |
| 6. (d) | 7. (b) | 8. (c) | 9. (d) | 10. (a) |
| 11. (b) | 12. (d)* | 13. (b) | 14. (a) | 15. (b) |
| 16. (d)* | 17. (d) | 18. (a) | 19. (a) | 20. (c) |

## EXPLANATIONS

1. 'Aside' is the most appropriate answer as 'to set aside something' is a phrase which means to reserve something for someone or for some purpose. None of the other options fit in the blank.
2. 'Unless' is the most appropriate answer as the given sentence presents a condition. It is just like saying that one would fail if one isn't industrious. None of the other options fit in the blank.
3. 'Through' is the most appropriate answer as 'to go through' is a phrasal verb, which means to undergo a period of experience or to be examined thoroughly. Option 2 would have been correct if 'under' had appeared before 'go'. One cannot 'go about' or 'go into' medical tests.
4. 'With' is the most appropriate answer as 'endowed with' is a phrasal verb, which means having been given a gift or having been born with a gift or some quality. None of the other options fit in the blank.
5. 'Over' is the most appropriate answer. One cannot 'fly in' the flooded areas in a helicopter. Accordingly, 'fly about' and 'fly along' are also incorrect. 'Flew over' fits best as helicopters, being aerial mode of transport, fly over and above.

6. 'Will' is the most appropriate answer. With 'have to' only 'will' can appear. Other options will make the sentence incorrect.
7. 'Without' is the correct answer. In the given sentence, the help by the other person is given utmost importance and therefore 'without' his help anything wrong might have occurred. None of the other options fit in the blank.
8. 'Before' is the most appropriate answer. 'To stand before' is to stand in front of someone. Other options will make the sentence incorrect.
9. 'About' is the correct answer. 'From' and 'by' might seem correct but they are not. The correct way is to say 'happy about something'.
10. 'But' is the correct answer. It is just like saying that "nobody other than a mother----". 'Than' and 'rather' can't be used in isolation. 'However' is a total misfit.
11. 'A' is the correct answer. Instead of 'being finished', 'finishing' should have been there in the sentence.
12. This question was cancelled by CLAT as both A and D are incorrect. The correct sentence would have been "Hoping to go through the book today, I have read almost half of it."
13. 'B' is the correct answer. With adjectives like 'unique', 'perfect', 'flawless' etc, there can't be a superlative or comparative degree. 'Unique' in itself will make it stand out. Use of 'most' will lead to error of redundancy.
14. 'B' is the correct answer as 'is' should have been used instead of 'are'. "Five gallons" refers to a singular idea in this sentence.
15. 'D' is the correct answer as the correct phrase is 'to turn red'. There is no phrase as 'turning purple'.
16. CLAT cancelled this question as the sentence is in subjunctive mood and is correct.
17. 'C' is the correct answer. Instead of 'lifting', 'lift' should have been used.
18. 'C' is the correct answer. Instead of 'may visit, 'can visit' should have been used.
19. 'D' is the correct answer. Instead of 'at hand', 'in hand' should have been used.
20. 'D' is the correct answer. The correct phrase is 'to start from scratch' and not 'to start from the scratch'.

## READING COMPREHENSION

**Direction for Questions 1-5:** Read the given passage carefully and choose the most appropriate option to the questions given below. The World Trade Organisation (WTO) was created in the early 1990s as a component of the Uruguay Round negotiation. However, it could have been negotiated as part of the Tokyo Round of the 1970s, since negotiation was an attempt at a 'constitutional reform' of the General Agreement on Tariffs and Trade (GATT). Or it could have been put off to the future, as the US government wanted. What factors led to the creation of the WTO in the early 1990s?

One factor was the pattern of multilateral bargaining that developed late in the Uruguay Round. Like all complex international agreements, the WTO was a product of a series of trade offs between principal actors and groups. For the United States, which did not want a new organization, the disputed settlement part of the WTO package achieved its long standing goal of a more effective and more legal dispute settlement system. For the Europeans, who by the 1990s had come to view GATT dispute settlement less in political terms add more as a regime of legal obligations, the WTO package was acceptable as a means to discipline the resort to unilateral measures by the United States. Countries like Canada and other middle and smaller trading partners were attracted by the expansion of a rule-based system and by the symbolic value of a trade organization, both of which inherently support the weak against the strong. The developing countries were attracted due to the provisions banning unilateral measures. Finally, and perhaps most important, many countries at the Uruguay Round came to put a higher priority on the export gains than on the import losses that the negotiation would produce, and they came to associate the WTO and a rule-based system with those gains. This reasoning - replicated in many countries -was contained in U. S. Ambassador Kantor's defence of the WTO, and it announced to a recognition that international trade and its benefits cannot be enjoyed unless trading nations accept the discipline of a negotiated rule-based environment.

A second factor in the creation of the WTO was pressure from lawyers and the legal process. The dispute settlement system of the WTO was seen as a victory of legalists but the matter went deeper than that. The GATT, and the WTO, are contract organizations based on rules, and it is inevitable that an organization creating a further rule will in turn be influenced by legal process. Robert Hudee has written of the 'momentum of legal development', but what is this precisely? Legal development can be defined as promotion of the technical legal values of consistency, clarity (or certainty) and effectiveness these are values that those responsible for administering any legal system will seek to maximize. As it played out in the WTO, consistency meant integrating under one roof the whole lot of separate agreements signed under GATT auspices clarity meant removing ambiguities about the powers of contracting parties to make certain decisions or to undertake waivers and effectiveness meant eliminating exceptions arising out of grandfather-rights and resolving defects in dispute settlement procedures and institutional provisions.

Concern for these values is inherent in any rule-based system of co -operation, since without these value rules would be meaningless in the first place, therefore, create their own incentive for fulfilment.

The moment of legal development has occurred in other institutions besides the GATT, most notably in the European Union (EU). Over the past two decades the European Court of Justice (ECJ) has consistently rendered decisions that have expanded incrementally the EU' s internal market, in which the doctrine of' mutual recognition 'handed down in Cassis de Dijon ca se in 1979 was a key turning point. The court is now widely recognized as a major player in European integration, even though arguably such a strong role was not originally envisaged in the Treaty of Rome, which initiated the current European Union. One means the Court used to expand integration was the' teleological method of interpretation', whereby the actions of member states were evaluated against' the accomplishment of the most elementary goals set forth in the Preamble to the (Rome) treaty. The teleological method represents an effort to keep current policies consistent with slated goals, and it is analogous to the effort in GATT to keep contracting party trade practices consistent with slated rules. In both cases legal concerns and procedures are an independent force for further co-operation.

In the large part the WTO was an exercise in consolidation. In the context of a trade negotiation that created a near-revolutionary expansion of international trade rules, the formation of the WTO was a deeply conservative act needed to ensure that the benefits of the new rules would not be lost. The WTO was all about institutional structure and dispute settlement: these are the concerns of conservatives and not revolutionaries, that is why lawyers and legalists took the lead on these issues. The WTO codified the GATT institutional practice that had developed by custom over three decades, and it incorporated a new dispute settlement system that was necessary to keep both old and new rules from becoming a sham. Both the international structure and the dispute settlement system were necessary to preserve and enhance the integrity of the multilateral trade regime that had been built incrementally from the 1940s to the 1990s.

1. In the statement ' ... it amounted to a recognition that international trade and its benefits cannot be enjoyed unless trading nations accept the discipline of a negotiated rule-based environment', it refers to:
   (*a*) The higher priority on export gains placed by many countries at s the Uruguay Round.
   (*b*) The provision of a rule-based system by the WTO.
   (*c*) Ambassador Kantor's defence of the WTO.
   (*d*) The export gains many countries ca me to associate with a rule-based system.

2. The most likely reason for the acceptance of the WTO package by nations was that:
   (*a*) They recognized the need for a rule-based environment to protect the benefits of increased trade.
   (*b*) Its rule-based system leads to export gains.
   (*c*) It settles disputes more legally and more effectively.
   (*d*) It has the means to prevent the US from taking unilateral measures.

3. In the method of interpretation of the European Court of Justice:
   (*a*) Enunciation of the most elementary community goals needed to be emphasized.
   (*b*) Actions against member states needed to be evaluated against the said community goals.
   (*c*) Current policies need to be consistent with stated goals.
   (*d*) Contracting party trade practices need to be consistent with stated rules.

4. What would be the closest reason why WTO was not formed in 1970s?
   (*a*) The US government did not like it.
   (*b*) Important players did not find it in their best interest to do so.
   (*c*) Lawyers did not work fo r the dispute settlement system.
   (*d*) The Tokyo Round negotiations was an attempt at constitutional reform.

5. According to the passage, WTO promoted the technical legal values partly through.
   (*a*) Rules that create their own incentive for fulfilment.
   (*b*) Integrating under one roof the agreements signed under GATT.
   (*c*) Ambiguities about the powers of contracting parties to make certain decisions.
   (*d*) Grandfather-rights exceptions and defects in dispute settlement procedures.

## ANSWERS

**1.** (*d*) **2.** (*a*) **3.** (*b*) **4.** (*b*) **5.** (*b*)

## EXPLANATIONS

1. The answer can be found towards the end of paragraph 2- "-----and they came to associate the WTO and a rule based system with those gains." Option 1 is a close answer but it is half complete and therefore incorrect.

**2.** The answer can be seen in the following sentence of paragraph 2- "Countries like Canada and other middle and smaller trading partners were attracted by the expansion of a rule based system and by the symbolic value of a trade organization, both of which inherently support the weak against the strong." This sentence is immediately followed by the idea of WTO package being accepted by several nations and clearly points towards a system that will protect the advantages and benefits of trade.

**3.** It is the correct answer as can be seen in the following sentence of paragraph 4 - "------Countries like Canada and other middle and smaller trading partners were attracted by the expansion of a rule based system and by the symbolic value of a trade organization, both of which inherently support the weak against the strong. The given option in the question is nothing but a paraphrasing of the given option.

**4.** It is the correct answer can be seen in the opening paragraph of the given passage. Important is the term 'negotiated', which can be linked to option 2.

**5.** It is the correct answer as can be seen in the following sentence in paragraph 3- "As it played out in the WTO, consistency meant integrating under one roof the whole lot of separate agreements signed under GATT."

# REASONING

## VERBAL LOGIC

**Direction for Question Numbers 1 & 2 :** Which alternative applies to the following Statement or Assumptions? Choose the most appropriate option.

**1.** 'There is no man that is not naturally good' is equivalent to the proposition:

(*a*) Some men are naturally good.

(*b*) All men are naturally good.

(*c*) No men are good.

(*d*) Some men are not naturally good.

**2.** 'Only ignorant people believe in witchcraft' is equivalent to:

(*a*) There is no link between ignorance and witchcraft.

(*b*) Some ignorant persons are not those who believe in witchcraft.

(*c*) All persons who believe in witchcraft are ignorant.

(*d*) No ignorant persons are those who do not believe in witchcraft.

**Direction for Question Numbers 3 & 4 :** Find the odd one out from the following:

**3.** Find the odd one out from the following:

(*a*) Crusade (*b*) Cruise

(*c*) Campaign (*d*) Expedition

**4.** Find the odd one out from the following:

(*a*) Clearly visible (*b*) Only choice

(*c*) Open secret (*d*) Exact estimate

**Direction for Question Numbers 5 to 6 :** Choose the most appropriate option for each of the following questions.

**5.** Identify the statement which cannot be accepted

(*a*) The earth revolves around the sun in 366 days

(*b*) Odyssey is an ancient epic

(*c*) Fluman race will become extinct sooner or later

(*d*) Almost one third of the human body is made up of water

**6.** What is meant by 'Alliteration'?

(*a*) Act of literary modification,

(*b*) The occurrence of the same letter or sound at the beginning of adjacent or closely connected words.

(*c*) Words which sound alike but have different meanings.

(*d*) Acts of an environmentally conscious person.

## ANSWERS

**1.** (*b*) **2.** (*c*) **3.** (*b*) **4.** (*a*) **5.** (*d*)* **6.** (*b*)

## EXPLANATIONS

**1.** There is no man means who is not means "All men are". This is from clear deduction. The two negatives cancel each other. Hence, 2 is the answer.

**2.**

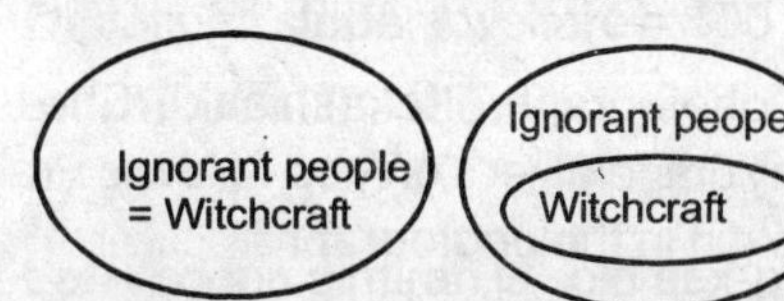


Only ignorant people believe in witchcraft means all those who believe in witchcraft are ignorant people. It doesn't mean all ignorant people believe in witchcraft.

**3.** All other words are synonyms. Cruise is the odd one out.

**4.** All other phrases are examples of oxymoron i.e. two contradictory ideas juxtaposed together. Clearly visible is not an example of oxymoron.

**5.** Even 1 cannot be accepted as the Earth revolves around the Sun in 365 days and 6 hours. It can't be 366 days. Similarly, 3 is an opinion which may be accepted. 4 is wrong as 3/4th of the human body is made up of water.

**6.** It is the correct definition of alliteration which is a figure of speech.

## ANALYTICAL REASONING

**Direction for Question Numbers 1 to 16 :** Choose the most appropriate option for each of the following questions.

1. In the series of alphabets given below, which is the missing alphabet series?
   AX, DU,GR, _____, ML
   (*a*) IK (*b*) JO
   (*c*) JN (*d*) HQ
2. If in a code language, 'ABANDON' is written as 'aramoim'; 'BQRE' is written as 'rits' and 'BASIL' is written as 'rabut', then what is the original word for the code: 'bituo'?
   (*a*) NASIA (*b*) SOFIA
   (*c*) SOMAD (*d*) SOLID
3. If in a certain code, the word MILITARY is written as 12324567, then in the same code, the word TAIL will be written as:
   (*a*) 3254 (*b*) 5432
   (*c*) 2345 (*d*) 4523
4. Coding and decoding 9 : 72 : : 8 : ?
   (*a*) 34 (*b*) 64
   (*c*) 43 (*d*) 18
5. Pointing to a girl in the photograph. Ram said, 'Her mother's brother is the only son of my mother's father'. How is the girl's mother related to Ram?
   (*a*) Grandmother (*b*) Mother
   (*c*) Sister (*d*) Aunt
6. Pointing to a photograph, Prakash said, 'She is the daughter of my grandfather's only son' How is Prakash related to the girl in the photograph?
   (*a*) Cousin (*b*) Father
   (*c*) Brother (*d*) Uncle
7. Ravi was showing a photograph to his friend, Gopi. Pointing at a boy in the photograph, Ravi said: 'The boy sitting at the left is the son of the wife of the only son of the grand-mother of my younger brother'.
   What is the relation between the boy in the photograph and Ravi?
   (*a*) Brothers
   (*b*) First Cousins
   (*c*) Ravi's brother-in-law
   (*d*) Nephew and uncle
8. A girl introduced a boy as the son of the daughter of the father of her uncle. The boy is girl's:
   (*a*) Son (*b*) Uncle
   (*c*) Brother (*d*) Son-in-law
9. When Ravi saw Ramesh, he recalled, 'He is the son of the father of my daughter'. Who is Ramesh?
   (*a*) Brother-in-law (*b*) Brother
   (*c*) Uncle (*d*) Cousin
10. Two ladies and two men are playing bridge and seated at North, East, South and West of a table. No lady is facing East. Persons sitting opposite to each other are not of the same sex. One man is facing South. Which direction are the ladies facing to?
    (*a*) South and East. (*b*) None of these.
    (*c*) East and West. (*d*) North and West.
11. Sunil's school bus is facing North when it reaches his school. After starting from Sunil's house, it turned right twice and then left before reaching the school. What direction the bus was facing when it left the bus stop in front of Sunil's house?
    (*a*) West (*b*) North
    (*c*) South (*d*) East
12. John wants to go the university. He starts from his house which is in the East and comes to a crossing. The road to his left ends in a theatre, straight ahead is the hospital. In which direction is the University?
    (*a*) West (*b*) South
    (*c*) North (*d*) East
13. If South-East becomes North, North-East becomes West and so on, what will West become?
    (*a*) South-East (*b*) North-V\fest
    (*c*) North (*d*) East
14. In a military secret service map, South-East is shown as North, North-East as West and so on. What will West become?
    (*a*) South-West (*b*) North-East
    (*c*) North-West (*d*) South-East
15. A man walks 1 km. towards East and then he turns to South and walk 5 kms. Again he turns to East and walks 2 kms. After this he turns to North and walks 9 kms. Now, how far is he from his starting point?
    (*a*) 4 kms. (*b*) 9 kms.
    (*c*) 10 kms. (*d*) 5 kms.
16. No parrots are black.
    All crows are black.
    From the above premises which one of the following conclusions is true?
    (*a*) No crows are parrots.
    (*b*) No conclusion can be drawn.
    (*c*) Some parrots are not crows.
    (*d*) Some crows are not parrots.

**Direction for Question Numbers 17 - 19:** Read the following information carefully and choose the appropriate option in the questions given below.

i. There is a group of five persons - A, B, C, D and E.

ii. One of them is a Singer, one is a Dancer, one is a Painter, one is a Teacher and one is a Doctor.

iii. Three of them - A, C and Doctor prefer rice to chapatti and two of them - B and the Painter prefer chapatti to rice.

iv. The Teacher, D and A are friends to one another but two of these prefer chapatti to rice.

v. The Singer is C's brother.

**17.** Who is a Dancer?

(*a*) A (*b*) D

(*c*) C (*d*) E

**18.** Who is a Singer?

(*a*) C (*b*) D

(*c*) B (*d*) A

**19.** Who is a Teacher?

(*a*) E (*b*) B

(*c*) C (*d*) D

**Direction for Question Numbers 20 - 22:** Read the following information carefully and choose the most appropriate option in the questions given below

i. Six flats on a floor in two rows facing North and South are allotted to P, Q, R, S, T and U.

ii. Q gets a North-feeing flat and is not next to S.

iii. S and U get diagonally opposite flats.

iv. R, next to U gets a South-facing flat and T gets a North-feeing flat.

**20.** Which of the following combination gets South-facing flats?

(*a*) U, P ,T (*b*) data inadequate

(*c*) Q. T, S (*d*) U,R, P

**21.** If the flats of T and P are interchanged, who's flat will be next to that of U?

(*a*) R (*b*) T

(*c*) Q (*d*) P

**22.** Whose flat is between Q and S?

(*a*) P (*b*) T

(*c*) U (*d*) R

**Direction for Question Numbers 23 to 33 :** Choose the most appropriate option for each of the following questions.

**23.** Vaishnavi prefers Economics to Maths, English to Social science, and Political Science to History. If she prefers Maths to History, and Sociai science to Maths, which is Vaishnavi's least preferred subject?

(*a*) Social science (*b*) Economics

(*c*) Maths (*d*) History

**24.** The birthday of Ms. Y was celebrated six days before Ms. X, who was born on 4th October 1999. The independence day of that year fell on Sunday. On which day did Ms. Y celebrate her birthday, if it was not a leap year?

(*a*) Wednesday (*b*) Sunday

(*c*) Tuesday (*d*) Monday

**25.** If 27th March, 2011 was Sunday, what was the day on 27th June, 2011?

(*a*) Monday (*b*) Tuesday

(*c*) Saturday (*d*) Sunday

**26.** How many times from 4 pm to 10 pm, the hands of a clock are at right angles?

(*a*) 11 (*b*) 6

(*c*) 10 (*d*) 9

**27.** ____________ is a hater of knowledge and learning.

(*a*) Moroccan (*b*) Misogynist

(*c*) Mystique (*d*) Misologist

**28.** A person who renounces religious or political belief or principle is call

(*a*) Apostle (*b*) apostate

(*c*) Ascetic (*d*) Antiquarian

**29.** There were twelve dozens of chocolates with a shopkeeper. Ten chocolates were distributed by the shopkeeper to the children of his colony. The shopkeeper then added two more dozens of chocolates in his stock. If the shopkeeper divided the total chocolates equally in two different packets, then how many chocolates were there in each packet?

(*a*) 158 (*b*) 89

(*c*) 152 (*d*) 79

**30.** wave : crest as ______ : peak.

(*a*) Water (*b*) Land

(*c*) River (*d*) Mountain

**31.** Crumb : Bread is as

(*a*) Inch : Unit (*b*) Water : Vessel

(*c*) Splinter : Wood (*d*) Powder : Face

**32.** What is meant by 'Alliteration'?

(*a*) Act of literary modification,

(*b*) The occurrence of the same letter or sound at the beginning of adjacent or closely connected words.

(*c*) Words which sound alike but have different meanings.

(*d*) Acts of an environmentally conscious person.

33. In a company, 60 % workers are males. If the number of female workers in the company is 800, what is the number of male workers in the company?

(*a*) 1900 (*b*) 1400

(*c*) 1200 (*d*) 1600

## ANSWERS

| | | | | |
|---|---|---|---|---|
| **1.** (*b*) | **2.** (*d*) | **3.** (*d*) | **4.** (*b*) | **5.** (*) |
| **6.** (*c*) | **7.** (*a*) | **8.** (*c*)* | **9.** (*) | **10.** (*d*) |
| **11.** (*a*) | **12.** (*) | **13.** (*a*) | **14.** (*d*) | **15.** (*d*) |
| **16.** (*a*) | **17.** (*c*)* | **18.** (*d*) | **19.** (*b*)* | **20.** (*d*) |
| **21.** (*a*) | **22.** (*b*) | **23.** (*d*) | **24.** (*c*) | **25.** (*a*) |
| **26.** (*a*) | **27.** (*d*) | **28.** (*b*) | **29.** (*d*) | **30.** (*d*) |
| **31.** (*c*) | **32.** (*b*) | **33.** (*c*) | | |

## EXPLANATIONS

1. A + 3 = D + 3 = G + 3 = J

   X – 3 = U – 3 = R – 3 = O

   Thus, missing term = JO

2. This is a type of ordered coding. A is coded as a, B is coded as r, N is coded as m and so on. Thus, bituo will be the code for SOLID.

   (Note: Although 't' was the code for R and L both, however, none of the options had R for the same).

3. This is a type of ordered coding i.e. M is coded as 1, I as 2, L as 3 and so on. Thus, TAIL will be coded as 4523

4. 9 : 9 × 8

   Thus, 8 : 8 × 8 = 64.

5. Now, Ram's maternal uncle is girls mother's brother i.e. Ram's maternal uncle is also the girl's maternal uncle. This means, Ram and girl could be siblings (or) cousins. Thus, girl's mother could be related to Ram as his mother (or) aunt.

6. Grandfather's only son = Father (Assuming grandfather as paternal)

   Thus, Prakash'sgrandfather's only son's daughter will be Prakash's sister. This means Prakash (considering him to be a male) will be the brother of the girl.

7. Ravi's younger brother's grandmother = Ravi's grandmother

   Ravi's grandmother's only son = Ravi's father

   Ravi's grandmother's only son's wife = Ravi's mother

   The boy in the photograph is the son of Ravi's mother i.e. Ravi and the boy in photograph are siblings i.e. brothers.

8. Girl's uncle's father = Girl's grandfather (paternal or maternal)

   Girl's uncle's father's daughter = Girl's grandfather's daughter = Girl's aunt or girl's mother

   The boy is the son of the girl's aunt or girl's mother.

   The boy and girl could be cousins or brother.

9. Ravi's daughter's father = Ravi himself (in case Ravi is a male)

   Now, Ramesh is the son of his daughter's father i.e. of Ravi

   i.e. Ramesh is Ravi's son.

   Even if we consider Ravi to be a female, Ramesh is the son of Ravi.

   (Note: This question is not clear in sense that Ramesh is who's who. Also if we talk w.r.t to Ravi, then Ramesh is Ravi's son, which is not available in options)

10. One man is facing south, thus one lady will be facing north (as persons opposite to each other are of opposite sex.) Further, as no lady is facing east, another lady will face west and another man will face east. Thus, the ladies are facing north & west.

11. From, school if we go back to home. We first turn the bus south. Now, turn right i.e. west, then turn left i.e. south and again turn left i.e. east. This means initially the bus must have been facing west (as it faces east when it enters his house).

12. This question is incomplete as it was no where mentioned that house, theatre, hospital and university were all in different directions, and, also that we are not sure John walks in which direction from his house.

    The correct answer for same should have been cannot be determined.

13. South-east becomes north, north-east becomes west, thus, west will become south-east.

14. Repeated Question. Q. 18.

15. Distance moved in horizontal direction = 1 + 2 = 3 kms

    Distance moved in vertical direction = 9 – 5 = 4 kms

    The shortest distance = 5 kms

16. 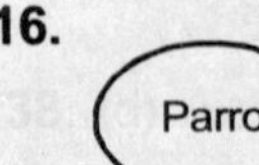

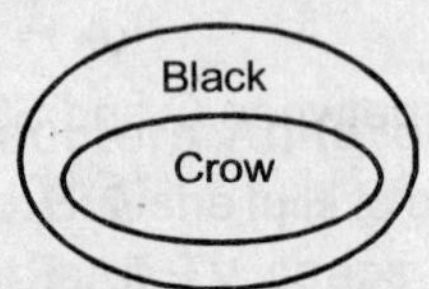


    From clear deduction, 1 is the best answer.

**For questions 17 to 19:** The final arrangement is given below:

| **Name** | A | B | C | D | E |
|---|---|---|---|---|---|
| **Profession** | Singer | Teacher | Dancer | Painter | Doctor |
| **Preference** | Rice | Chapatti | Rice | Chapatti | Rice |

(**Note:** Two questions Q1 and Q3 of the above set had wrong answers in official answer key)

**For questions 20 to 22:** As it is not given that there are equal flats in each row. So, there are two possible cases, as T gets a North–facing flat, therefore P will get a south facing flat.

The possible arrangements are given below:

| South Facing | U | R | P |
|---|---|---|---|
| North Facing | Q | T | S |

OR

| South Facing | P | R | U |
|---|---|---|---|
| North Facing | S | T | Q |

**23.** The answer is History. Just check options. Economics is preferred over Maths. Maths is preferred over History and also Social is preferred over Maths.

**24.** Ms. X birthday = $4^{th}$ October

Ms. Y birthday = $28^{th}$ September

Given, 15 August was on Sunday

Now, calculating odd days Aug (16 days left) = 2 odd days, Sept (till $28^{th}$) = 0 odd day

i.e. 2 odd days

i.e. Ms. Y was born 2 days after Sunday = Tuesday

(Note: Leap year had nothing to do with the question)

**25.** $27^{th}$ March 2011 → Sunday

Now, finding odd days

March (4 days left) = 4 odd days; April (full month) = 2 odd days, May (full month) = 3 odd days; June (till 27) = 6 odd days

Now, total odd days = 4 + 2 + 3 + 6 = 15 i.e. 1 odd day

i.e. $27^{th}$ June 2011 is 1 day after Sunday i.e. on Monday

**26.** Every hour the hands of a clock are at right angles twice i.e. in 6 hours (4 to 10) they would be right angles to each other 12 times. However, since 3 o'clock is the common time in time range 2 to 3 and 3 to 4, thus we subtract this once due to repetition in counting. Thus, from 4 pm to 10 pm the two hands of a clock will be perpendicular to each other 11 times.

**27.** Misologist refers to someone who hates knowledge or learning. Moroccan refers to a native of Morocco. A misogynist hates women.

**28.** Apostate is someone who renounces his/her belief-primarily religious or political. Apostle is a messenger or disciple. Ascetic is a hermit.

**29.** Total chocolates before distributing to children = 12 × 12 = 144

10 chocolates were given to children, then number of chocolates left = 144 – 10 = 134

However, two more dozens of chocolates were added, then total chocolates = 134 + 24 = 158

Number of chocolates per packet = $\frac{158}{2} = 79$

**30.** Waves have a crest and mountains have a peak.

**31.** Crumb is fragment of bread. Similarly, a fragment of wood is called splinter.

**32.** It is the correct definition of alliteration which is a figure of speech.

**33.** If 60% workers are males, thus 40% workers are females.

Now, 40% of total = 800

Thus, 60% of total = $\left(\frac{800}{0.4}\right) \times 0.6 = 1200$

# QUANTITATIVE APTITUDE

## ARITHMETIC

**1.** A piece of cloth costs rupees 75. If the piece is four meters longer and each meter costs rupees 5 less, the cost remains unchanged. What is the length of the piece?

(*a*) 8 meters (*b*) 6 meters
(*c*) 12 meters (*d*) 10 meters

**2.** The Banker' s discount on a sum of money for 18 months is Rs. 600 and the true discount on the same sum for 3 years is Rs. 750/-. The rate percentage is:

(*a*) 12% (*b*) 10%
(*c*) 15% (*d*) 20%

**3.** Two men and seven boys can do a work in 14 days. Three men and eight boys can do the same work in 11 days. Further eight men and six boys can do three times the amount of this work in:

(*a*) 21 days (*b*) 24 days
(*c*) 30 days (*d*) 18 days

**4.** There are two urns. One contains two white balls and four red balls, the other contains three white and nine red balls. All balls are of the same shape and size. From each urn, one ball is drawn. What is the probability of getting both the balls of the same colour?

(*a*) 7/12 (*b*) 1/2
(*c*) 1/12 (*d*) 1 /24

**5.** A clock was set correct at 12 O'clock. It loses 10 minutes per hour. What will be the angle between the hour and minute hands of the clock after one hour?

(*a*) 85° (*b*) 90°
(*c*) 75° (*d*) 105°

6. Keerthi's father gave him some money to buy books. He spent half of the money equally to buy books and entertaining his friends. Whatever amount left with him, he deposited half in his savings account and gave Rs. 5 to a poor person as charity. Finally, Keerthi was left with Rs. 20 which he returned to his father. What amount did his father give him initially?

(a) Rs. 200 (b) Rs. 120
(c) Rs. 100 (d) Rs. 160

7. A vessel contains a mixture of milk and water in the ratio of 5 : 3 respectively. How much of the mixture must be siphoned off and replaced with water, so that the mixture may be half milk and half water?

(a) 1/5 (b) 1/7
(c) 1/3 (d) 1/4

8. A man rows to a place 45 kms distant and back in 12 hours. He realises that he can row 5 kms downstream in the same time as 3 kms against the stream. The velocity of the stream is:

(a) 1 km/hr (b) 4 kms/hr
3.1.5 kms/hr (d) 2 kms/hr

9. A can do a piece of work in 8 days and B alone can do the same work in 10 days. A and B agreed to do the work together for Rs. 720. With the help of C, they finished the work in 4 days. How much C is to be paid?

(a) Rs. 80 (b) Rs.72
(c) Rs.82 (d) Rs.70

10. Gold and copper are as heavy as water by 19 and 9 times respectively. The ratio in which these two metals be mixed so that the mixture is 17 times as heavy as water is:

(a) 4 : 1 (b) 3 : 2
(c) 2 : 3 (d) 3 : 4

11. A trader sells rice at a profit of 20% and uses weights which are 10% less than the correct weight. The total gain earned by him is:

(a) 33 1/3% (b) 30%
(c) 35% (d) 22 2/9%

12. The difference between simple interest and compound interest at the same rate for rupees 5,000 for two years is rupees 98. The rate of interest is:

(a) 10 1/2% (b) 10%
(c) 14% (d) 12%

13. Praveen has Rs. 4,662 in the form of 2,5 and 10 rupee notes. If these notes are in the ratio of 3 : 5 : 8, the number of five rupees notes with him is:

(a) 336 (b) 84
(c) 210 (d) 250

14. 'A' and 'B' complete a work in 12 days, 'B' and 'C' in 8 days and 'C' and 'A' in 16 days. 'A' left after working for 3 days. In how many days more will 'B' and 'C' finish the remaining work?

(a) 7 3/4 (b) 6 5/6
(c) 3 3/4 (d) 4 5/6

15. Taps 'A' and 'B' can fill a tank in 37 1/2 minutes and 45 minutes respectively. Both taps are opened and after some time tap 'B' is turned off. The tank is filled completely in exactly 30 minutes, if tap 'B' is turned off after:

(a) 15 minutes
(b) 12 minutes
(c) 10 minutes
(d) 9 minutes

16. A boat travels upstream from A to B and back from B to A in 5 hours. The speed of the boat in still water is 8 km/hour and the speed of the current is 4 km/hour. Then, the distance from A to B is:

(a) 10 kms. (b) 12 kms.
(c) 15 kms (d) 9 kms.

17. The average weight of three men 'X', 'Y' and 'Z' is 75 kgs. Another man 'A' joins the group and the average weight now becomes 80 kgs. If another person 'B' whose weight is 5 kgs more than 'A' replaces 'X', then the average weight of 'Y', 'Z', 'A' and 'B' will be 85 kgs. What is the weight of 'X'?

(a) 84 kgs. (b) 80 kgs.
(c) 82 kgs. (d) 78 kgs.

18. A train 'X' leaves station 'A' at 3 p.m and reaches station 'B' at 4.30 p.m., while another train 'Y' leaves station 'B' at 3.00 p.m and reaches station 'A' at 4.00 p.m. These two trains cross each other at:

(a) 3.40 p.m. (b) 3.30 p.m.
(c) 3.36 p.m. (d) 3.20 p.m.

19. Age of father 10 years agc was three times the age of his son. After 10 years, father's age is twice that of his son. The ratio of their present ages is:

(a) 7 : 3 (b) 7 :4
(c) 11 : 7 (d) 9 : 5

20. In an office, 1/3 of the workers are Men, 1/2 of the men are married and 1/3 of the married men have children. If 3/4 of the women are married and 2/3 of the 2/3 of the married women have children, then the part of workers without children are:

(a) 11/18 (b) 17/36
(c) 4/9 (d) 5/18

## ANSWERS

| | | | | |
|---|---|---|---|---|
| 1. (b) | 2. (d) | 3. (a) | 4. (a) | 5. (a) |
| 6. (c) | 7. (a) | 8. (d) | 9. (b) | 10. (a) |
| 11. (a) | 12. (c) | 13. (c) | 14. (d) | 15. (d) |
| 16. (c) | 17. (b) | 18. (c) | 19. (a) | 20. (a) |

## EXPLANATIONS

1. Let cost be Rs. x per metre

Then, length of piece in 1st case $= \frac{75}{x}$

Also, in 2nd case: length of piece is $\left(\frac{75}{x}\right) + 4$ and cost per piece = (x – 5)

But as total cost is same, thus,

$\left[\left(\frac{75}{x}\right) + 4\right] \times (x - 5) = 75$

$\Rightarrow \frac{375}{x} + 4x - 20 = 0$

$\Rightarrow 4x^2 - 20x + 375 = 0$

$\Rightarrow 4x^2 - 50x + 30x + 375 = 0$

$\Rightarrow 2x(2x - 25) + 15(2x - 25) = 0$

$\Rightarrow (2x + 15)(2x - 25) = 0$

$\Rightarrow$ x = Rs 12.5 (x cannot be negative)

The required length $= \frac{75}{12.5} = 6$ metres

2. Banker's discount (BD) for 1.5 years = Rs. 600

i.e. BD for 3 years = Rs. 1200

True Discount (TD) for 3 years = Rs. 750

Sum $= \frac{(BD \times TD)}{(BD - TD)} = \frac{(1200 \times 750)}{450} =$ Rs. 2000

Thus, Rs. 1200 is the SI on Rs. 2000 for 3 years

Or, Rs. 400 is the SI on Rs. 2000 for 1 year

i.e. Rate $= \left(\frac{400}{2000}\right) \times 100 = 20\%$

3. 2 men + 7 boys → 14 days ⇒ 28 men + 98 boys → 1 day ...(1)

3 men + 8 boys → 11 days ⇒ 33 men + 88 boys → 1 day ...(2)

Thus, from (1) and (2), we get: 1 man = 2 boys

Now, 8 men + 6 boys = 22 boys

Also, we know from (1): 154 boys can do the work in 1 day.

i.e. 1 boy can do the work in 154 days

i.e. 22 boys can do the work in $\frac{154}{22} = 7$ days

Thus, 22 boys can do thrice the work in

7 × 3 = 21 days.

4. Required probability

$= \frac{2}{6} \times \frac{3}{12} + \frac{4}{6} \times \frac{9}{12} = \frac{42}{72} = \frac{7}{12}$

5. Since the clock loses 10 minutes per hour, the time shown by it after an hour after 12 O'clock will be 12 : 50

Now, Angle (between minute and hour hand at 12:50)

$= \left|\frac{11}{2} \times 50 - 30 \times 12\right| = 85° \quad \left(\theta = \left|30h - \frac{11}{2}m\right|\right)$

6. Using the backward approach.

Total money will be = [(20 + 5) × 2] × 2 = Rs. 100.

7. Final fraction of milk = initial fraction of milk × (1 – fraction of mixture taken out)$^n$

Where 'n' is the number of times process is done

Thus, $\frac{1}{2} = \frac{5}{8} \times (1 - f)^1$

i.e. $1 - f = \frac{4}{5}$

i.e. $f = \frac{1}{5}$

8. Let speed of the man in still water = x km/hr and

Speed of stream = y km/hr

Upstream speed = (x – y) km/hr

Downstream speed = (x + y) km/hr

Given, $\frac{5}{(x + y)} = \frac{3}{(x - y)}$

i.e. 5x – 5y = 3x + 3y ⇒ 2x = 8y ⇒ x = 4y

i.e. Also, $\frac{45}{(x - y)} + \frac{45}{(x + y)} = 12$

i.e. $\frac{45}{3y} + \frac{45}{5y} = 12$

i.e. y = 2

9. Let total units of work = 40 units

A's 1 day work = 5 units

B's 1 day work = 4 units

(A + B + C)'s 1 day work = 10 units

i.e. C's 1 day work = 1 unit

Now, money is distributed in ratio of 1 day's work.

Thus, A : B : C = 5 : 4 : 1

C is paid $= \frac{1}{10} \times 720 =$ Rs. 72

**10.** Using alligation:

The required ratio = 8 : 2 = 4 : 1.

**11.** Let CP of 1 gram = Rs. 1.

Now, 1 kg costs = Rs. 1000 but as he sells only 900 gm, thus, CP = Rs. 900

Further, he sells at markup of 20%, thus SP = Rs. 1200

So, profit% $= \frac{300}{900} \times 100 = 33.33\%$.

**12.** $P\left(\frac{R}{100}\right)^2$ = Difference between CI and SI for 2 years

i.e. $5000 \times \left(\frac{R}{100}\right)^2 = 98$

i.e. $\left(\frac{R}{100}\right)^2 = \frac{98}{5000}$

i.e. $\left(\frac{R}{100}\right)^2 = \frac{49}{2500}$

i.e. $\left(\frac{R}{100}\right) = \frac{7}{50}$

i.e. R = 14%

**13.** Let the number of notes of Rs. 2, Rs. 5 and Rs. 10 be 3x, 5x and 8x respectively.

$\therefore$ $3x \times 2 + 5x \times 5 + 10x \times 8 = 4662$

$\Rightarrow$ $111x = 4662$

$\Rightarrow$ $x = 42$

Then, number of Rs 5 notes = 5 × 42 = 210.

**14.** Let total units of work = 48 units

Then, A + B = 4 units per day

B + C = 6 units per day

C + A = 3 units per day

Now, 2(A + B + C) = 13 units per day

Or, A + B + C = 6.5 units per day

This means A + B + C will do 19.5 units in 3 days

Work left = 48 – 19.5 = 28.5 units, which has to be done by B and C

Time taken by B and C to finish remaining work

$= \frac{28.5}{6} = 4.75$ days

**15.** Let total amount to be filled = LCM (37.5, 45)

= 900 units.

Now, A can fill $= \frac{900}{37.5} = 24$ unit in a minute

B can fill $= \frac{900}{45} = 20$ units in a minute

Since, A fills for entire 30 units, it must have filled

= 24 × 30 = 720 units

This, means B fills 900 – 720 = 180 units

To fill 180 units, B will take $\frac{180}{20} = 9$ minutes.

**16.** Let distance = D

$\therefore \quad \frac{D}{4} + \frac{D}{12} = 5$

D = 15 kms

**17.** Total weight of X, Y and Z = 75 × 3 = 225

Total weight of X, Y, Z and A = 80 × 4 = 320

Therefore, weight of A = 320 – 225 = 95

Now, weight of B = 95 + 5 = 100 kgs

Total weight of Y, Z, A and B = 85 × 4 = 340

Therefore, total weight of Y, Z and A = 340 – 100 = 240

Weight of X = 320 – 240 = 80 kgs

**18.** Train A takes = 1.5 hours to go from A to B

Train B takes = 1 hour to go from A to B

Let distance between AB = 3 kms

Speed of train from A = 2 km/hr

Speed of train from B = 3 km/hr

Time taken by trains to meet $= \frac{3}{(2+3)} = 0.6$ hrs

i.e. 36 minutes after 3 p.m. i.e. at 3:36 p.m.

**19.** Let 10 years ago, age of father = 3x and that of son = x

Now, present age of father = 3x + 10 and present age of son = x + 10

10 years later, age of father = 3x + 20 and son = x + 20

Also, 3x + 20 = 2 × (x + 20)

i.e. x = 20

Thus, present ages of father and son = 70 and 30 respectively.

$\therefore$ The required ratio = 7 : 3

**20.** The question has a typo error i.e. instead of 2/3 of the 2/3 of married women should be 2/3 of the married women.

Let total number of workers be 900.

Then, number of males $= \frac{1}{3} \times 900 = 300$

Now, married men $= \frac{1}{2} \times 300 = 150$

Married men with children $= \frac{1}{3} \times 150 = 50$

Now, number of females = 900 – 300 = 600

Number of married women $= \frac{3}{4} \times 600 = 450$

Number of married women with children

$$= \frac{2}{3} \text{ of } 450 = 300$$

Total married worker with children = 50 + 300 = 350

Now, number of workers without children

= 900 – 350 = 550

Thus, fraction of workers without children

$$= \frac{550}{900} = \frac{11}{18}.$$

# GENERAL KNOWLEDGE

## CURRENT AFFAIRS

**1.** The Happiness Index Department or a Wing has been established in the states of:

(*a*) Madhya Pradesh and Tamil Nadu
(*b*) Madhya Pradesh and Goa
(*c*) Andhra Pradesh and Madhya Pradesh
(*d*) Andhra Pradesh and Sikkim

**2.** The first Commercial Court and Commercial Disputes Resolution Centre was inaugurated at

(*a*) Ahmedabad, Gujarat s
(*b*) Visakapatinam, Andhra Pradesh
(*c*) Raipur, Chattisgarh
(*d*) Mumbai, Maharastra Comprehension:

**3.** Name the President elect of France who is likely to take the oath on 14 May 2017.

(*a*) Emmanuel Macron (*b*) Francois Fillon
(*c*) Francois Holland (*d*) Marine Le Pen

**4.** Among the following M.L.As, who was disqualified by the Governor during January 2017 under Article 192 of the Constitution for undertaking government contracts?

(*a*) Jayalalithaa of Tamil Nadu
(*b*) Srinivas Prasad of Karnataka
(*c*) Uma Shankar Singh of Bihar
(*d*) P.C. George of Kerala

**5.** Volvo has launched the world's largest bus that can carry upto:

(*a*) 320 passengers
(*b*) 300 passengers
(*c*) 260 passengers
(*d*) 150 passengers

**6.** Among the following who was crowned as 'Miss Supernational' during 2016?

(*a*) Srinidhi Shetty (*b*) Aishwarya Rai
(*c*) Shilpa Shetty (*d*) Alia Bhat

**7.** During 2017, which SAARC country has notified the Right to Information Act?

(*a*) Sri Lanka (*b*) Afghanistan
(*c*) Bhutan (*d*) Nepal

**8.** How many billionaires India has lost since demonetization on November 8, 2016?

(*a*) Eight (*b*) Eighteen
(*c*) Eleven (*d*) Two

**9.** Who has been selected for 2016 BC Roy Award?

(*a*) Dr. N. Bhaskaran (*b*) Dr. J. Rajendra
(*c*) Dr. Jagat Ram (*d*) Dr. P. Raghu Ram

**10.** The top destination for domestic tourists in India for the past three consecutive years has been:

(*a*) Orissa (*b*) Rajasthan
(*c*) Kerala (*d*) Tamil Nadu

**11.** According to the Survey Report released by Transparency International during March 2017 on India, the most corrupt are

(*a*) Government officials (*b*) Police
(*c*) Local Councillors (*d*) Business executives

**12.** Who called the immigration the 'Trojan horse of Terrorism'?

(*a*) Theresa May, Prime Minister of U.K
(*b*) Donald Trump, President of the U.S
(*c*) Viktor Orban, Prime Minister of Hungary
(*d*) Angela Merkel, Chancellor of Germany

**13.** The first country in the world to have begun shutting down the entire Frequency Modulation (FM) radio network to be replaced by Digital Audio Broadcasting is:

(*a*) China
(*b*) Norway
(*c*) Switzerland
(*d*) United States of America

**14.** The World Bank had cut India' s GDP growth for 2016-2017 to:

(*a*) 7.6% (*b*) 2.8%
(*c*) 3.7% (*d*) 8.6%

**15.** The first country to have announced euthanasia of a child is:

(*a*) Belgium (*b*) Norway
(*c*) Finland (*d*) Denmark

**16.** The bowler who has claimed the fastest 250 wickets in Cricket test matches is:
(*a*) Rangana Herath (*b*) Ravichandran Ashwin
(*c*) Anil Kumble (*d*) Dennis Lillee

**17.** Highest number of open prisons in India as on 2015 are in
(*a*) Rajasthan (*b*) Maharastra
(*c*) Tamil Nadu (*d*) Kerala

**18.** The Japanese Prime Minister who offered 'sincere and everlasting condolences' to the people of the United States for killing more than 2,400 soldiers in the attack on Pearl harbour was:
(*a*) Hayato Ikeda (*b*) Juniciro Koizumi
(*c*) Kakuei Tanaka (*d*) Shinzo Abe

**19.** Which of the following country enacted a law during August 2016 providing for the right to register the marriages of Hindus?
(*a*) Saudi Arabia (*b*) Afghanistan
(*c*) Pakistan (*d*) Iran

**20.** As on 31st January 2016, the highest number of law colleges were present in:
(*a*) Uttar Pradesh (*b*) Maharashtra
(*c*) Madhya Pradesh (*d*) Andhra Pradesh

**21.** India emerged as ________ largest holder of the U.S Government Securities at the end of 2016:
(*a*) Twelfth (*b*) Twenty eighth
(*c*) Twenty fourth (*d*) Fifteenth

**22.** Donald Trump is _____President of the United States.
(*a*) 46th (*b*) 45th
(*c*) 43rd (*d*) 44th

**23.** Which shoe company in the United States of America has won an IPR dispute against China recently for using their logo?
(*a*) Nike (*b*) Reebok
(*c*) Adidas (*d*) New Balance

**24.** Japan is threatening to drag India to W.T.O on issues relating to the export of its:
(*a*) Small ships (*b*) Steel
(*c*) Tea (*d*) Electronic goods

**25.** Till the end of 2016, the total number of UNESCO's World Heritage Sites in India is:
(*a*) 35 (*b*) 42
(*c*) 18 (*d*) 21

**26.** The 2016 Nobel Peace Prize was won by the President of:
(*a*) Columbia
(*b*) South Africa
(*c*) United States of America
(*d*) Sri Lanka

**27.** Immediately before Antonio Guterres was appointed the U.N Secretary General in October 2016, he was:
(*a*) United Nations High Commissioner for Refugees
(*b*) United Nations High Commissioner for Human Rights
(*c*) The Prime Minister of Portuguese
(*d*) Commissioner General of UNRWA

**28.** The first elected civilian President in Myanmar is:
(*a*) Aung San Suu Kyi (*b*) Khin Ayi
(*c*) Aung San (*d*) Htin Kyaw

**29.** The world's first artificial intelligence lawyer, a robot, is named as:
(*a*) Boss (*b*) Watson
(*c*) Ross (*d*) IBM-LaBrain

**30.** Which of the following individuals was called a 'deceptive actor' by China's foreign ministry during March 2017?
(*a*) Sirisena (*b*) Dalai Lama
(*c*) Narendra Modi (*d*) Donald Trump

**31.** NASA rediscovered India's lunar spacecraft that was lost in the space during the past eight years known as:
(*a*) Chandrayan-I (*b*) Mangalayaan -II
(*c*) Chandrayan -II (*d*) Mangalayaan -I

**32.** The Union Cabinet has recently approved the setting up of a Permanent Tribunal for resolving:
(*a*) Inter-state water disputes
(*b*) Complaints from three services
(*c*) Inter-state boundary disputes
(*d*) Election disputes

**33.** In terms of steel production in the world during 2015-2016, India stood at:
(*a*) Second (*b*) Third
(*c*) Fourth (*d*) Fifth

**34.** Which country 3D-Printed a home of 37 sq. mts?
(*a*) Russia (*b*) South Korea
(*c*) Spain (*d*) Taiwan

**35.** The first statue of a woman in Parliament Square in England is that of:
(*a*) Mother Theresa (*b*) Millicent Fawcett
(*c*) Queen Elizabeth -II (*d*) Margaret Thatcher

**36.** 'World's longest-all women Non-stop flight' from New Delhi to San Francisco covering 14,500 kms was operated by:
(*a*) Jet Airways (*b*) American Airlines
(*c*) United Airlines (*d*) Air India

**37.** India' s third largest trading partner during 2016 is
(*a*) Saudi Arabia (*b*) U.A.E.
(*c*) Kuwait (*d*) Dubai

## ANSWERS

| | | | | |
|---|---|---|---|---|
| **1.** (*c*) | **2.** (*c*) | **3.** (*a*) | **4.** (*c*) | **5.** (*b*) |
| **6.** (*a*) | **7.** (*a*) | **8.** (*c*) | **9.** (*d*) | **10.** (*d*) |
| **11.** (*b*) | **12.** (*c*) | **13.** (*b*) | **14.** (*c*) | **15.** (*a*) |
| **16.** (*b*) | **17.** (*a*) | **18.** (*d*) | **19.** (*c*) | **20.** (*a*) |
| **21.** (*a*) | **22.** (*b*) | **23.** (*d*) | **24.** (*b*) | **25.** (*a*) |
| **26.** (*a*) | **27.** (*a*) | **28.** (*d*) | **29.** (*c*) | **30.** (*b*) |
| **31.** (*a*) | **32.** (*a*) | **33.** (*b*) | **34.** (*a*) | **35.** (*b*) |
| **36.** (*d*) | **37.** (*b*) | | | |

## EXPLANATIONS

**1.** Madhya Pradesh and Andhra Pradesh have become the first and second state in the country to set up 'Happiness Index Department or a Wing'.

**2.** The first Commercial Court and Commercial Disputes Resolution Centre was inaugurated at Raipur, Chattisgarh.

**3.** After a resounding victory in runoff, Emmanuel Macron was sworn in as France President at the Elysee palace on May 14.

**4.** Uttar Pradesh Governor Ram Naik disqualified BSP's Rasra MLA Uma Shankar Singh from Assembly membership for violation of Representation of the People Act.

**5.** Volvo has launched the world's largest bus that can carry upto 300 passengers.

**6.** Srinidhi Shetty- India's representative, has been crowned Miss Supranational 2016, an international beauty pageant. This marks the second time that India has won the pageant following the win by Asha Bhat in 2014.

**7.** In Sri Lanka, the historic Right to Information (RTI) Act has come into force from 3rd Feb 2017. The act marks the culmination of a movement of over 20 years to ensure transparency in governance and easy availability of information.

**8.** According to the Hurun Global Rich List India, the report says that since demonetisation, India has lost 11 billionaires. E-commerce poster boys Sachin and Binny Bansal are no longer part of the billionaires list.

**9.** Dr. P. Raghu Ram, President of Association of Breast Surgeons of India was awarded prestigious Dr. B. C. Roy national award for outstanding service in the field of socio-medical relief for 2016.

**10.** Tamil Nadu and Uttar Pradesh received most number of domestic tourists in 2016. As per the data released by the Ministry, a total of 344.3 million domestic tourists visited Tamil Nadu in 2016 while 229.6 million in Uttar Pradesh. The domestic tourism sector continued its growth momentum with recording a jump of 15.5 % in tourists' visits to various states and Union Territories during 2016.

**11.** India had the highest bribery rate among the 16 Asia Pacific countries surveyed by Transparency International. Nearly seven in 10 Indians who had accessed public services had paid a bribe. Contrast this with the least corrupt country - Japan, where only 0.2% of the respondents reported paying a bribe. The TI report stated that across the region, nearly two in five said that they thought most or all police officers were corrupt, which was the highest of any group.

**12.** Prime Minister Viktor Orban justified the move, saying that Hungary had to act to defend itself. "Migration is the Trojan wooden horse of terrorism," Orban said at a swearing-in ceremony for a new group of border guards, called "border hunters" by the government.

**13.** Norway has become the first country in the world to have begun shutting down the entire Frequency Modulation (FM) radio network to be replaced by Digital Audio Broadcasting.

**14.** According to the World Bank's Global Economic Prospects - January 2017 report, economic growth forecast for India decelerated to 7% from 7.6%. A slowdown in consumption and manufacturing due to demonetization, an ongoing decline in private investment and credit constraints due to impaired bank balance sheets are the major reasons.

**15.** A terminally-ill minor has become the first to be helped to die by doctors in Belgium since age restrictions on euthanasia were lifted two years ago. Belgium is the only country that allows children of all ages to choose euthanasia, provided parental consent is granted.

**16.** Ravichandran Ashwin has become the fastest bowler to take 250 Test wickets in Test Cricket history.

**17.** The highest number of open prisons in India as on 2015 are in Rajasthan.

**18.** Prime Minister Shinzo Abe became the first Japanese leader to visit Pearl Harbour, Hawaii. Pearl Harbour is a site of sneak attack by Japan that provoked America into entering World War II, to reinforce "the power of reconciliation".

**19.** A landmark bill to regulate marriages of Pakistan's Hindu minority has been unanimously passed by the lower house of Parliament, paving the way for adoption of a comprehensive and widely acceptable family law for Hindus.The Hindu Marriage Bill 2016 is the first personal law for the minority community and will help Hindu women get documentary proof of their marriage, which is needed while applying for passports and other official documents.

20. As on 31st January 2016, the highest numbers of law colleges were present in Uttar Pradesh.
21. India emerged as twelfth largest holder of the U.S Government Securities at the end of 2016.
22. Donald Trump pulled off a stunning upset and secured his spot as the 45th president of the United States. When he'sinaugurated this upcoming January, he'll become the oldest elected president in US history.
23. New Balance has won a rare legal victory in China in an intellectual property dispute: A court has ordered five shoe manufacturers and sellers to pay the state $250,000 for using the American shoemaker's signature slanting "N" logo.
24. The WTO's dispute settlement set up a panel to resolve the dispute between Japan and India over imposition of safeguard import duty on iron and steel products.
25. Till the end of 2016, the total number of UNESCO's World Heritage Sites in India is 35.
26. Juan Manuel Santos Calderon is the 32nd and current President of Colombia and sole recipient of the 2016 Nobel Peace Prize.
27. Immediately before Antonio Guterres was appointed the U.N Secretary General in October 2016, he was a United Nations High Commissioner for Refugees.
28. The first elected civilian President in Myanmar is Htin Kyaw.
29. The world's first artificial intelligence lawyer has been employed by a law firm in the US, which will use the robot to assist its various teams in legal research. The robot called 'ROSS' is built upon Watson, IBM's cognitive computer. With the support of Watson's cognitive computing and natural language processing capabilities, lawyers can ask ROSS their research question and the robot reads through the law, gathers evidence, draws inferences and returns highly relevant, evidence-based answers.
30. China's Foreign Ministry called the Dalai Lama a "deceptive actor" , after the exiled Tibetan spiritual leader said in an interview that Chinese hardliners have parts of their brains missing.
31. India's first lunar mission -- the Chandrayaan-1 spacecraft, which was generally considered lost -- is still orbiting the moon, NASA scientists have found with new technological application of interplanetary radar. Chandrayaan-1 is still circling some 200 kilometers above the lunar surface, the scientists determined.
32. The Union Cabinet has recently approved the setting up of a Permanent Tribunal for resolving the Inter-State River Water Disputes.
33. The three-day International Conference and Exhibition on Steel Industry 'India Steel 2017' (3rdedition) held at Mumbai Exhibition center in Mumbai. India is the third largest producer of crude steel in the world.
34. While 3D-printing may have been faded away in recent years from the spotlight of core "disruptive" technologies, that may soon change again after a company managed to 3D-print an entire house in just 24 hours. Located in Russia, the following 400-square-foot home, or 37 square meters, was built in just a day, at a cost of slightly over $10,000.
35. The suffragist Dame Millicent Fawcett is to be the first woman to be honoured with a statue in Parliament Square, the UK prime minister has announced.
36. Air India said it flew the "world's longest" all-women-operated flight from Delhi to San Francisco. The flight, which travelled a distance of around 14,500 kilometre in close to 17 hours, was operated as part of International Women's Day celebrations. The non-stop Delhi-San Francisco flight took off from the national capital on March 6.
37. The UAE and India are making tremendous efforts to scale their economic, investment and trade cooperation to new heights, given the fact that India is today emerging as one of the world's fastest growing economies. Forecasts predict that the South Asian country will rise as the world's third largest economy by 2030 after the United States and China. The UAE was the third key trade partner to India after China and the US in 2013 and 2014.

## EVERYDAY SCIENCE

1. Solar Impulse-2 is:
   (*a*) Solar powered ship
   (*b*) Hybrid airplane
   (*c*) Solar powered airplane that completed the first around the world
   (*d*) Impact of climate change for overall increase of 2°C a year
2. Juno is the name of a:
   (*a*) Solar powered space craft
   (*b*) Hydrogen fuelled spacecraft
   (*c*) Hydrogen fuelled submarine
   (*d*) Atomic powered submarine

## ANSWERS

**1.** (*c*) **2.** (*a*)

## EXPLANATIONS

1. The world's first round-the-world flight to be powered solely by the sun's energy made history as it landed in Abu Dhabi, where it first took off on an epic 25,000-mile journey that began more than a year ago. Since its March 2015 take off, the Swiss-engineered Solar Impulse 2 has made 16 stops across the world without using a drop of fuel to demonstrate that using the plane's clean technologies on the ground can halve the world's energy consumption, save natural resources and improve quality of life.
2. NASA's Juno mission to Jupiter has broken the record to become humanity's most distant solar-powered emissary.

## GEOGRAPHY

1. World' s longest rail tunnel is about:
   (*a*) 47 kms (*b*) 32 kms
   (*c*) 23 kms (*d*) 57 kms

## ANSWER

1. (*d*)

## EXPLANATIONS

1. The world's longest and deepest rail tunnel has officially opened in Switzerland, after almost two decades of construction work. The 57km (35-mile) twin-bore Gotthard base tunnel will provide a high-speed rail link under the Swiss Alps between northern and southern Europe.

## MISCELLANEOUS (QUOTES, DAYS, BOOKS TITLES, SPORTS, BASIC LEGAL CONCEPTS)

1. COIN, a software programme developed by J. P. Morgan supports:
   (*a*) Bitcoin
   (*b*) Robotic surgery
   (*c*) Interpreting commercial documents
   (*d*) Financial accounting
2. The Hubble telescope of NASA is located in
   (*a*) Canada (*b*) Iceland
   (*c*) NASA headquarters (*d*) Space
3. Among the following, who has won the maximum number of titles?
   (*a*) Srikant (*b*) P. V. Sindhu
   (*c*) Gopichand (*d*) Saina Nehwal
4. 'Scorpion kick' is a phrase used in
   (*a*) Kalari Fight
   (*b*) Kung Fu
   (*c*) Kick Boxing
   (*d*) Kabaddi

## ANSWERS

1. (*c*) 2. (*d*) 3. (*d*) 4. (*d*)

## EXPLANATIONS

1. At JP Morgan, a programme called COIN is rounding off the tedious task of analysing financial deals within seconds, something that consumed thousands of hours of legal teams. The software, called COIN for Contract Intelligence, is revolutionary software that does the herculean task of interpreting commercial loan agreements which accounted for about 3,60,000 hours of lawyers' time annually.
2. Astronomers using NASA's Hubble Space Telescope has imaged what may be water vapor plumes erupting off the surface of Jupiter's moon Europa. This finding bolsters other Hubble observations suggesting the icy moon erupts with high altitude water vapor plumes. The observation increases the possibility that missions to Europa may be able to sample Europa's ocean without having to drill through miles of ice.
3. Saina Nehwal has won the maximum number of titles.
4. 'Scorpion kick' is a phrase used in kabaddi

# LEGAL APTITUDE

## TORTS

**Question numbers 1 - 7 :** consists of legal proposition(s)/ principle(s) (hereinafter referred to as 'principle') and facts. Such principles may or may not be true in the real and legal sense, yet you have to conclusively assume them to be true for the purposes of this Section, in other words, in answering these questions, you must not rely on any principle except the principles those are given herein below for every question. Further, you must not assume any facts other than those stated in the question. The objective of this section is to test your interest towards study of law, research aptitude and problem solving ability, even if the 'most reasonable conclusion' arrived at may be absurd or unacceptable for any other reason. It is not the objective of this section to test your knowledge of law. Therefore, to answer a question, principle is to be applied to the given facts and to choose the most appropriate option.

1. **Principle :** A master shall be liable for the fraudulent acts of his servants committed in the course of employment. However, the master and third parties must exercise reasonable care in this regard.

**Facts :** Rahul was a door to door salesman with United Manufacturing Company (the Company). The Company was manufacturing Water Purifiers. Rahul, along with the Company's products, used to carry Water Purifiers manufactured by his Cousin in a local Industrial Estate. He used to sell the local product at a lower rate giving the impression to the buyers that he is offering a discount on the Company's product. The Company Management detected the fraudulent activity of Rahul and dismissed him from service. Rahul still continued to carry on with his activity of selling the local product pretending that he was still a salesman of the Company. Several customers got cheated in this process. The fraud was noticed by the Company when the customers began to complain about the product. The customers demanded the Company to compensate their loss.

(*a*) The Company is liable to the customers who purchased the local product from Rahul only till he remained as a salesman of the Company.

(*b*) The Company is liable to compensate all the customers as it did not inform the public about Rahul's fraudulent conduct and the subsequent dismissal.

(*c*) The Company is not liable as Rahul was dismissed by the Company.

(*d*) The liability rests with the local manufacturer as it was a defective product.

2. **Principle :** Under the Employees Compensation Act, 1923, an employer is liable to pay compensation to his workmen for injuries sustained by them by an accident arising out of and in the course of employment.

**Facts :** M, the Manager of SRK Industries asked his secretary S to submit a report at the Government Labour Office. 'S' submitted the report as directed. On his way back S met one of his class mates. He then decided to have a cup of tea together on a way side restaurant. Some time later, 'S' got a message from his office to report back as it was long time since he left the office. 'S' rushed back on his Motor Cycle. On his way back a Truck which was coming from a side road hit 'S'. He was admitted in a nearby hospital with multiple injuries. He claims compensation under the Employees Compensation Act from his employer.

(*a*) The Employer is not liable as the truck driver was negligent.

(*b*) The Employer is not liable as he was admitted in a private hospital and not a Government Hospital.

(*c*) The Employer is liable to pay compensation as the accident took place arising out of and in the course of employment.

(*d*) The Employer is liable as S had to rush back to the office, because of the message from the office.

3. **Principle :** A violation of a legal right of someone, whether results in a legal injury or not, gives rise to an action in tort for compensation. At the same time, an action by someone, which results in some loss or damage to somebody else is not actionable, if there is no violation of a right of that somebody.

**Facts :** AB Coaching Centre was a popular CLAT coaching academy with several good trainers. A lot of aspirants used to attend its coaching classes from all over and was making good profit. This was going on for the past several years. During a session, T, one of the very good and popular trainers of ABCC, had some difference of opinion with the owner of ABCC and left the coaching centre. In August 2016, T started another Entrance Coaching Centre closer to ABCC which resulted in a substantial drop in its students and huge financial loss. The owner of ABCC wants to file a case against T for the loss sustained by ABCC. What do you think is the right legal position?

(*a*) T has not violated any of ABCC's legal right though they sustained some financial loss, and not legally bound to compensate ABCC.

(*b*) T started the new coaching centre near ABCC intentionally, and shall be liable to compensate the loss of ABCC.

(*c*) T will be liable to compensate the loss to ABCC.

(*d*) 'T should have consulted ABCC before starting his coaching centre.

4. **Principle :** Negligence is actionable in law. In simple terms, negligence is the failure to take proper care over something.

**Facts :** A, a doctor, conducted a hysterectomy sincerely on B and left a small cotton swab inside the abdomen. As a consequence of which B developed some medical problems and had to undergo another surgery. Is A liable?

(*a*) As only a small swab was left In the abdomen, there was no negligence.

(*b*) Liability for negligence does not arise here as A performed the operation sincerely

(*c*) A Is liable for the negligence as he failed to take proper care during the surgery.

(*d*) A is not liable as he did not foresee any consequences at the time of surgery.

5. **Principle :** Assault is causing bodily injury to another person by use of physical force.

   **Facts:** Rustum while entering into compartment of a train raised his fist in anger towards a person Sheetal, Just in front of him in the row, to get way to enter into the train first, but did not hit him. Rustum has:

   (*a*) insulted Sheetal

   (*b*) not committed an assault on Sheetal

   (*c*) committed an assault on Sheetal

   (*d*) Rightly showed his anger

6. **Principle :** When a person makes such a statement which lowers other person's reputation in the estimation of other persons, is liable for committing defamation.

   **Facts :** 'A' writes a letter to 'B' in which he uses abusive language against 'B' and also states that 'B' is a dishonest person. 'A' put the letter in a sealed envelope and delivered it to 'B'.

   (*a*) 'A' has committed defamation

   (*b*) 'A' has not committed defamation

   (*c*) 'A' has not committed moral wrong

   (*d*) 'A' has committed a moral wrong

7. **Principle :** When a person interferes with peaceful possession of another person without the permission of the person in possession of those premises, commits trespass to land.

   **Facts :** 'T just walked over the land of 'P' to reach his house as it was a short cut. 'P' had displayed a notice that it is not a thoroughfare. 'P' did not cause any damage to the land.

   (*a*) 'T' has violated privacy of 'P'

   (*b*) 'T' has not committed any trespass on the land of 'P'.

   (*c*) 'T' has committed trespass to land

   (*d*) 'T' has created nuisance for 'P'

## ANSWERS

**1.** (*b*) **2.** (*c*) **3.** (*a*) **4.** (*c*) **5.** (*b*)

**6.** (*b*) **7.** (*c*)

## EXPLANATIONS

1. A master shall be laible for the fraudulent act of his servant and the Company is liable to compensate all the customers as it did not inform the public about Rahul's fraudulent conduct and the subsequent dismissal.
2. The Employer is liable to pay compensation as the accident took place arising out of and in the course of employment.
3. T has not violated any of ABCC's legal right though they sustained some financial loss, and not legally bound to compensate ABCC.
4. A is liable for the negligence as he failed to take proper care during the surgery.
5. Rustam has not committed an assault on Sheetal as there was no bodily injury.
6. The letter was delivered to B and was not known by any other person and hence A has not commited defamation.
7. When a person interferes with peaceful possession of another person without the permission of the person in possession of those premises, commits trespass to land and here "T' has committed the trespass to the Land.

## LAW OF CONTRACTS

**Question numbers 1 -16 :** consists of legal proposition(s)/principle(s) (hereinafter referred to as 'principle') and facts. Such principles may or may not be true in the real and legal sense, yet you have to conclusively assume them to be true for the purposes of this Section, in other words, in answering these questions, you must not rely on any principle except the principles those are given herein below for every question. Further, you must not assume any facts other than those stated in the question. The objective of this section is to test your interest towards study of law, research aptitude and problem solving ability, even if the 'most reasonable conclusion' arrived at may be absurd or unacceptable for any other reason. It is not the objective of this section to test your knowledge of law. Therefore, to answer a question, principle is to be applied to the given facts and to choose the most appropriate option.

1. **Principle :** If a party to a contract agrees to it under undue influence of any other party then the party under the undue influence may refuse to perform in accordance with the agreement.

   **Facts :** A, a rich youngster became a member of a religious group and soon he was appointed by P the head of the group as his personal secretary. As per the rules of the group, all officials and staff of the group were supposed to stay in the group's official premises itself. Some days later, A was asked by P to execute a Gift deed in favour of P, in which it was mentioned that all immovable properties in his name are being gifted to P. A was unwilling to execute the deed, but he was forcefully restrained by P and his body guards in P's office and made A sign the gift deed. Soon after this A left the group and refused to hand over the property as agreed to in the gift deed. Is A's action valid?

(*a*) As the gift deed was executed by A, he cannot refuse.

(*b*) A executed the deed, under compulsion and undue influence, and was right in withdrawing from the contract.

(*c*) As Gift is also a contract, the consent of A was not obtained by P while executing the deed.

(*d*) It is illegal for religious groups acquire property from its members

2. **Principle :** It is a case of fraud where a party to a contract knows or believes a fact to be true, but conceals it actively from the other party with a view to induce that person to enter into the contract.

**Facts :** While taking a life insurance policy, in reply to questions by the insurance company during the inquiry into his proposal, Zameer deliberately concealed the fact of his medical treatment for a serious ailment, which he had undergone only a few weeks ago.

(*a*) The act of Zameer did not amount to fraud, as disclosing the fact would have resulted in exposure of his privacy.

(*b*) The concealment of fact by Zameer amounted to fraud.

(*c*) The act of Zameer amounted to innocent misrepresentation.

(*d*) The act of Zameer did not amount to any misrepresentation.

3. **Principle :** According to law, a person is deemed to have attained the age of majority when he completes the age of 18 years, except in the case of a person where a guardian of a minor's person or property has been appointed under the Guardians and Wards Act, 1890 or where the superintendence of a minor's property is assumed by a Court of Wards. Indian law expressly forbids a minor from entering into a contract. Hence, any contract entered into by a minor is void-ab-initio regardless of whether the other party was aware of his minority or not. Further, though a minor is not competent to contract, nothing in the Contract Act prevents him from making the other party bound to the minor.

**Facts :** Lal executed a promissory note in favour of Gurudutt, aged 16 years stating that he would pay Gurudutt a sum of Rs. 2 Lakhs when he attains the age of majority. On attaining the age of 18, Gurudutt demanded the amount from Lal, who refused to pay. Gurudutt wants to take legal action against Lal. Identify the most appropriate legal position from the following:

(*a*) Gurudutt should not have entered into a contract with Lal when he was a minor.

(*b*) A promissory note duly executed in favour of a minor is not void and can be sued upon by him, because he though incompetent to contract, may yet accept a benefit.

(*c*) Lal argues that as per the Guardians and Wards Act, 1890, Gurudutt can claim the money only after he attains the age of 21.

(*d*) Lal was not aware of the feet that Gurudutt was a minor.

4. **Principle :** When a person consented to an act to be done by another, he cannot claim any damages resulting from doing that act, provided the act done is the same for which consent is given.

**Facts :** 'P' submitted a written consent to a surgeon 'S' for undergoing a surgical operation for removal of appendicitis. The surgeon while doing surgery also removed the gall bladder of 'A':

(*a*) 'P' is required to pay expenses for surgery for Appendicitis but not for Gall Bladder

(*b*) 'P' cannot claim damages from 'S'

(*c*) 'P' can claim damages from 'S'

(*d*) 'P' is not bound to pay expenses of the surgery

5. **Principle :** When a person who has made a promise to another person to do something does not fulfill his promise, the other person becomes entitled to receive, from the person who did not fulfill his promise, compensation in the form of money.

**Facts :** 'X' made a promise to 'Y' to repair his car engine. 'Y' made the payment for repair. After the repair, 'Y' went for a drive in the same car. While driving the car, 'Y' met with an accident due to bursting of a tyre.

(*a*) 'X' will be entitled to receive compensation from 'Y' in the form of money.

(*b*) 'Y' will not be entitled to receive compensation from 'X'.

(*c*) 'Y' will be entitled to receive compensation from 'X' in the form of money.

(*d*) 'X' will not be entitled to receive compensation.

6. **Principle :** Contract is a written or spoken agreement, with specific terms between two or more persons or entities in which there is a promise to do something in return for a valuable benefit known as consideration. Such an agreement is intended to be enforceable by law. A unilateral contract is one in which there is a promise to pay or give other consideration in return for actual performance.

**Facts :** A Toilet Soap Manufacturing Company in India in order to promote the sale of their product, published an advertisement in all the Newspapers on January 1,2017 that the Company has kept a model ignition key of an Audi A3 Car. The advertisement also stated that whoever gets the said key before December 31,2017 from a soap bar will be gifted with the Audi

A3 Car. Mr. Martin, a foreigner who came to India as a Tourist who was staying in a Hotel found a Key similar to same Car Ignition Key. Mr. Martin brought this matter to the notice of the Hotel Manager. The Manager informed Mr. Martin about the Company's advertisement on January 1,2017. Mr. Martin wants to claim the Car.

Will he succeed?

(*a*) No. The Soap Company has not entered into a contract with Mr. Martin as he was not in India on January 1,2017 when the advertisement was published.

(*b*) No. Actual intention of the Company was to promote the sale of the Soap.

(*c*) The Hotel Manager who could legally claim the Car as he was the one actually purchased the soap for the use in the Hotel.

(*d*) Mr. Martin obtained the Key before the stipulated date from the Soap Bar. So he is covered by the offer of the Soap Company and can claim the car.

**7. Principle :** An offer made by one party when accepted by another makes it a contract.

**Transactions :**

1. P offered to sell his house for Rs. 20 lakhs to R; R told P that he was interested to buy a house for 15 lakhs only.
2. C was looking for a house for not more than 25 lakhs; P informed C that his house was available for 20 lakhs.
3. K wanted to buy some old furniture; L told K that he would sell his furniture for Rs. 10,000.
4. R advertised to sell his old car for a price of Rs. Three lakhs; S found the advertisement and offered to buy it for Rs. 2 lakhs 50 thousand; R agrees to sell it to S.

Which among the above is actually a contract?

(*a*) Situation 4 only is a contract

(*b*) Situations 2 and 4 are contracts

(*c*) Situation 3 only is a contract

(*d*) Situations 1 and 2 are contracts

**8. Principle :** Every agreement, of which the object or consideration is opposed to public policy, is void. An agreement which has the tendency to injure public interest or public welfare is one against public policy. What constitutes an injury to public interest or public welfare would depend upon the times and the circumstances.

**Facts :** 'A' promises to obtain for 'B' an employment in the public service, and 'B' promises to pay rupees 5,00,000/-to 'A'.

(*a*) The agreement is valid, as it is a contract between two parties with their free consent.

(*b*) The agreement is void, as the object and consideration for it is opposed to public policy.

(*c*) The agreement is valid, as it is with consideration for public service.

(*d*) The agreement is void because rupees 5,00,000/- is excessive.

**9. Principle :** A contract would be invalid and unlawful, if the contract is for an immoral or illegal purpose.

**Facts :** P, was a young and helpless widow, living on the pavement. R, a neighbour gave her a house, registered in her name, on the condition that she should allow R to keep his smuggled goods and drugs in her house. After the registration was done, according to the condition in the contract, R's agents went to keep some packets in her house, she refused. R told her the condition under which the house was given to her. She still refused. Is P Justified in her action?

(*a*) P is right as she did not like smuggled goods to be kept in her house.

(*b*) P is not justified as she did not have the right to deny R's request.

(*c*) As R was making the contract for illegal activities. P's stand is valid in law.

(*d*) R can take back the house by canceling the transfer deed.

**10. Principle :** A person is said to do a thing fraudulently, if he does that thing with intent to defraud, but not otherwise.

**Facts :** 'A' occasionally hands over his ATM card to 'B' to withdraw money for 'A'. Qn one occasion 'B' without the knowledge of 'A', uses 'A's ATM card to find out the balance in 'A's account, but does not withdraw any money.

(*a*) 'B' has committed breach of faith

(*b*) 'B' has committed the act fraudulently

(*c*) 'B' has committed misappropriation

(*d*) 'B' has not committed the act fraudulently

**11. Principle :** Every agreement, by which any party is restricted absolutely from enforcing his right in respect of any contract, by the usual legal proceedings in the ordinary Tribunals, is void to that extent. The law also provides that nobody can confer jurisdiction to a civil court by an agreement between parties.

**Facts :** A and B entered into a valid contract for rendering certain service. A clause in the contract was that in case of any dispute arose out of the contract; it shall be referred to for Arbitration only. Is the contract valid?

(*a*) Arbitration is also a valid dispute settlement machinery recognized by law and hence the entire contract is valid.

(*b*) Arbitrator cannot be termed as an ordinary Tribunal. Flence, the agreement is void and would be unenforceable.

(*c*) The parties were trying to confer jurisdiction to some authority to decide a dispute and hence the clause would be invalid.

(*d*) The contract is valid but the clause regarding Arbitration is void.

**12. Principle :** An agreement, the terms of which are not certain, or capable of being made certain, is void.

**Facts :** Sunder agreed to take Bhola's penthouse on rent for three years at the rate of rupees 12,00,000/- per annum provided the house was put to thorough repairs and the living rooms were decorated according to contemporary style.

(*a*) There is a valid contract because there is an offer from Sunder and acceptance from Bhola

(*b*) There is no valid contract because it has vague and uncertain terms, as the term 'present style' may mean one thing to Sunder and another to Bhola.

(*c*) There is a valid contract because all the terms of contract are certain and not vague as the rent is fixed by both of them and the term 'present style' only can be interpreted to mean the latest style.

(*d*) It is voidable contract at the option of Bhola.

**13. Principle :** Acceptance of a proposal must be absolute and unqualified.

**Facts :** 'A' made a proposal to sell his motorcycle to 'B' for rupees 25,000/-. 'B' agreed to buy it for rupees 24,000/-. 'A' sold his motorcycle to 'C' for 26,000/- the next day. 'B' sues 'A' for damages.

(*a*) 'B' will get damages from 'A'

(*b*) 'B' will not get any damages from 'A

(*c*) 'B' can proceed against 'C'

(*d*) 'B' will get the difference of rupees 1,000/- only

**14. Principle :** According to law, a person who find goods belonging to another and takes them into his custody, is subject to the same responsibility as a bailee. Bailee is a person or party to whom goods are delivered for a purpose, such as custody or repair, without transfer of ownership. The finder of the goods legally can sell the goods found by him under certain circumstances including the situation that the owner refuses to pay the lawful charges of the finder.

**Facts :** P, a college student, while coming out of a Cricket stadium found a necklace, studded with apparently precious diamonds. P kept it for two days thinking that the owner would notify it in a local newspaper. Since he did not notice any such notification, P published a small classified advertisement in a local newspaper. In two days' time, P was contacted by a film actor claiming that it was her Necklace and requested P to return it to her. P told her that she should compensate him for the advertisement charges then only he would return it otherwise he will sell it and make good his expenses. The film star told P that she had advertised in a national newspaper about her lost Necklace which was lost somewhere in the Cricket Stadium. The advertisement was published for three consecutive days incurring a large expenditure for her. Mentioning all this she refuses to pay P and claims the Necklace back. Which among the following is the most appropriate answer to this?

(*a*) The film star was right in refusing P, as she did not offer any reward for anyone who would return the Necklace.

(*b*) P was requesting the film star for the actual expenditure incurred by him before returning the Necklace. This request is legally sustainable.

(*c*) As the film star had notified in the newspaper, P ought to have read it and contacted her instead of publishing another notification. So he cannot claim any compensation.

(*d*) As it was wrong on the part of P to bargain over a property belonging to a celebrity and he should have accepted some gift which might have been given t3y the film star and returned the Necklace instead of threatening her that he would sell it.

**15. Principle :** When a person falsifies something with the intent to deceive another person or entity is forgery and is a criminal act. Changing or adding the signature on a document, deleting it, using or possessing the false writing is also considered forgery. In the case of writing/painting to fall under the definition, the material included must have been fabricated or altered significantly in order to represent something it is actually not.

**Facts :** David made a living traveling from city to city, selling paintings that he claimed were done by great artists. Since the artists' signatures were in place, many people fell for them and purchased the paintings. One of these artists saw three of his alleged paintings in a City gallery containing his name. He knew these were not his works and he complained to the police. Police traced David and initiated legal proceedings. Is David guilty of any offence?

(*a*) David is guilty of forgery as the addition of the signature was with an intention to make people believe that those were the paintings of the great artists.

(*b*) David is not guilty of any offence as he was selling the art pieces for his living.

(*c*) Those who buy the art pieces from David ought to have been careful in checking it and ensuring that they were originals before purchasing it.

(*d*) There is no point in taking legal action against David as the signature has not done any alteration to the art work.

**16. Principle :** Where one of the parties to a contract was in a position to dominate the decision of the other party, the contract is enforceable only at the option of the party who was in a position to dominate the decision of the other party.

**Facts :** A doctor asked his patient to make a payment of rupees Ten Lakh for treatment of his fever. The patient paid an amount of rupees Five Lakh and promised to pay the remaining amount after the treatment. After treatment the patient recovered from fever. The doctor demanded the remaining amount from the patient. The patient refused to pay.

(*a*) The contract is not enforceable as doctor was in dominating position.

(*b*) The contract is enforceable against the patient by the doctor.

(*c*) The contract is enforceable against the doctor.

(*d*) The contract is not enforceable without the consent of the patient.

## ANSWERS

| | | | | |
|---|---|---|---|---|
| **1.** (*b*) | **2.** (*b*) | **3.** (*b*) | **4.** (*c*) | **5.** (*b*) |
| **6.** (*d*) | **7.** (*a*) | **8.** (*b*) | **9.** (*c*) | **10.** (*d*) |
| **11.** (*a*) | **12.** (*b*) | **13.** (*b*) | **14.** (*b*) | |
| **15.** (*a*) | **16.** (*b*) | | | |

## EXPLANATIONS

**1.** If a party enters into a Contract under undue influence of the party, the party under undue influence can declare the contract to be voidable. A executed the deed under compulsion and force and hence was right in withdrawing the contract.

**2.** Zameer deliberately concealed the fact of his medical treatment for a serious ailment, which he had undergone only a few weeks ago and hence the concealment of fact amounts to fraud.

**3.** Though a minor is not competent to Contract, nothing in the Indian Contract act prevents him from making other party bound to the minor and hence the promissory note executed in the favor of minor is valid and Gurudutt can claim the benefit.

**4.** 'P' can claim damages from 'S' because he has consented only for the removal of appendices and not gall bladder.

**5.** Y' will not be entitled to receive compensation from 'X', because he had made the payment for repairing of Car and it was done and after that he met with an accident.

**6.** Mr. Martin obtained the Key before the stipulated date from the Soap Bar. So he is covered by the offer of the Soap Company and can claim the car.

**7.** Situation 4 only is a contract. Here R made an offer and S made a counter offer to which R agreed to sell his Car and hence it is a contract.

**8.** The Principle clearly states that every agreement of which the object or consideration is opposed to public policy is void and the agreement between A and B is opposed to public policy and hence would be Void.

**9.** A contract will be invalid or unlawful, if the contract is for illegal or immoral purpose. As R was making the contract for illegal activities, P's stand is valid in law.

**10.** 'B' has not committed the act fraudulently because he never intended to defraud and had just checked the balance and did not withdrew money.

**11.** Arbitration is also a valid dispute settlement machinery recognized by law and hence the entire contract is valid and party is not restricted absolutely to enforce his legal right.

**12.** There is no valid contract because it has vague and uncertain terms, as the term 'present style' may mean one thing to Sunder and another to Bhola.

**13.** B will not get any damages form A, as the acceptance was not complete and was not absolute and unqualified. A offered to sell his motorcycle for rupees 25,000/-, while B offered to purchase it for 24,000/-, so there was no acceptance of the proposal.

**14.** The Principle clearly states that the finder of the goods legally can sell the goods found by him under certain circumstances including the situation that the owner refuses to pay the lawful charges of the finder and P was requesting the film star for the actual expenditure incurred by him before returning the necklace and this request is legally sustainable

**15.** David is guilty of forgery as the addition of the signature was with an intention to make people believe that those were the paintings of the great artists.

**16.** The doctor was in a position to dominate his patient and contract is enforceable only at the option of party who was in the position to dominate the will of the other party and hence the contract is enforceable against the patient

## CRIMINAL LAW

**Question numbers 1 -7 :** consists of legal proposition(s)/ principle(s) (hereinafter referred to as 'principle') and facts. Such principles may or may not be true in the real and legal sense, yet you have to conclusively assume them to be true for the purposes of this Section, in other words, in answering these questions, you must not rely on any principle except the principles those are given herein below for every question. Further, you must not assume any facts other than those stated in the question. The objective of this section is to test your interest towards study of law, research aptitude and problem solving ability, even if the 'most reasonable conclusion' arrived at may be absurd or unacceptable for any other reason. It is not the objective of this section to test your knowledge of law. Therefore, to answer a question, principle is to be applied to the given facts and to choose the most appropriate option.

1. **Principle :** Penal laws provide that whoever voluntarily has carnal intercourse against the order of nature with any man or woman, shall be punished for rape.

   **Facts :** A Police Officer found a man engaged in carnal intercourse with an animal. The Police Officer arrested the man and produced him before the Court.

   (*a*) Court will not punish the police officer.

   (*b*) Court will punish the man for rape.

   (*c*) Court will punish the police officer.

   (*d*) Court will not punish the man for rape.

2. **Principle :** Section 34 of Indian Penal Code provides that 'When a criminal act is done by several persons in furtherance of the common intention of all, each of such persons is liable for that act in the same manner as if it were done by him alone.'

   **Facts :** Three vagabonds, Sanju, Dilbag and Sushil decided to commit burglary. In the night, Sushil opened the lock and they broke into a rich man's house when the entire family was on a pilgrimage. Sanju had gone to that house earlier in connection with some cleaning Job. There was only a servant lady in the house. Hearing some sounds from the master bed room, the servant switched on the lights and went up to the room from where she heard the sound. Noticing that the servant was going to cry for help, Sanju grabbed her and covered her mouth with his hands and dragged her into the nearby room. The other two were collecting whatever they could from the room. When they were ready to go out of the house, they looked for Sanju and found him committing rape on the servant. They all left the house and the servant reported the matter to the police and identified Sanju. Subsequently, all three were arrested in connection with the offences of house breaking, burglary and rape. Identify the legal liability of the three.

   (*a*) All three are liable for all the offences as there was common Intention to commit the crimes.

   (*b*) Sanju will be liable only for housebreaking and rape as he did not participate In the burglary.

   (*c*) Only Dilbag and Sushil are liable for burglary In looting the house, and all three will be liable for housebreaking and rape as they did not stop Sanju from committing the offence and hence were accomplice to the offence.

   (*d*) Only Sanju will be liable for rape as he was the one who actually committed the offence.

3. **Principle :** When a person falsifies something with the intent to deceive another person or entity is forgery and is a criminal act. Changing or adding the signature on a document, deleting it, using or possessing the false writing is also considered forgery. In the case of writing to fall under the definition, the material included must have been fabricated or altered significantly in order to represent something it is actually not.

   **Facts :** John was a publisher of ancient books and papers. In one of his books on the World Wars, he gave photograph of some letters written by famous historic personalities. A researcher in history noted that in the pictures of some of the letters printed in the book, John had added some words or sentences in his own handwriting to give completeness to the sentences, so that the readers will get a clear picture of the writer's intention. The researcher challenges the originality of those pictures and claims that the book containing the forged letters should be banned. Examine the validity of the researcher's demand.

   (*a*) Allowing forged publications to be circulated among the public is as good as committing fraud on the public, so the publication should be banned.

   (*b*) The additions were made to give clarity to the original document and did not in any sense change the contents of the documents and hence there is no forgery as alleged by the researcher.

   (*c*) As forgery amounts to adding or deleting anything from an original document, the demand of the researcher is valid.

   (*d*) The additions in the letters were made by the publisher in his own handwriting would have made material alteration to the original meaning and hence amounted to forgery.

4. **Principle :** There are legal provisions to give authority to a person to use necessary force against an assailant or wrong-doer for the purpose of protecting one's own body and property as also another's body and property when immediate aid from the state

machinery is not readily available; and in so doing he is not answerable in law for his deeds.

**Facts :** X, a rich man was taking his morning walk. Due to the threat of robbers in the locality, he was carrying his pistol also. From the opposite direction, another person was coming with a ferocious looking dog. All of a sudden, the dog which was on a chain held by the owner, started barking at X. The owner of the dog called the dog to be calm. They crossed each other without any problem. But suddenly, the dog started barking again from a distance. X immediately took out his pistol. By seeing the pistol the dog stopped barking and started walking with the owner. However, X shot at the dog which died instantly. The owner of the dog files a complaint against X, which in due course reached the Magistrate Court. X pleads the right of private defence. Decide.

(*a*) Shooting a fierce dog is not to be brought under the criminal law. So the case should be dismissed.

(*b*) The right of private defence is available to persons against assailants or wrong-doers only and a dog does not fell in this category.

(*c*) As there was no guarantee that the dog would not bark again, shooting it was a precautionary measure and hence within the right available to X under law.

(*d*) There was no imminent danger to X as the dog stopped barking and was walking with the owner. Hence, shooting it amounted to excessive use of the right of private defence and hence liable for killing the dog.

5. **Principle :** In criminal law, misappropriation is the intentional, illegal use of the property or funds of another person for one's own use or other unauthorized purpose, particularly by a public official, a trustee of a trust, an executor or administrator of a dead person's estate or by any person with a responsibility to care for and protect another's assets. Embezzlement is misappropriation when the funds involved have been lawfully entrusted to the embezzler. On the contrary, theft is the illegal taking of another person's property or services without that person's permission or consent with the intent to deprive the rightful owner of it.

**Facts :** A went for swimming at the Municipal Swimming Pool. A handed over all his valuables, including some cash to X, the guard on duty for safe custody, as notified by the Municipality. After swimming for an hour, A came out and searched for X. He found another guard on duty and that guard informed A that X had gone home after completing his shift and did not hand over anything to be given to A. A registered a complaint with the police. X was traced but he told the police that he sold all the valuables and the entire cash was used for drinking liquor. What offence, if any, was/were committed by X?

(*a*) X is not guilty of criminal misappropriation as he did not make any personal gain out of those items with him.

(*b*) X is liable for theft as he took A's property without X's permission.

(*c*) X is liable for criminal misappropriation and embezzlement.

(*d*) If at all X is liable, it is for criminal misappropriation only.

6. **Principle :** Nothing is an offence which is done in the exercise of the right of private defence.

**Facts :** 'A', under the influence of madness, attempts to kill 'B'. 'B' to save his life kills 'A'.

(*a*) A has committed the offence of attempt to murder.

(*b*) 'B' has committed an offence.

(*c*) 'A' has not committed an offence because he was mad.

(*d*) 'B' has not committed any offence.

7. **Principle :** Whoever takes away with him any minor less than sixteen years of age if a male, or less than eighteen years of age if a female, out of the custody of parents of such minor without the consent of such parents, is said to commit no offence.

**Facts :** 'A', a man, took away a girl below sixteen years to Mumbai without informing the parents of the girl.

(*a*) 'A' committed an offence against the girl.

(*b*) 'A committed no offence against the parents of the girl.

(*c*) 'A committed an offence against the girl as well as her parents.

(*d*) 'A committed no offence against the girl as well as her parents.

## ANSWERS

| | | | | |
|---|---|---|---|---|
| **1.** (*d*) | **2.** (*d*) | **3.** (*b*) | **4.** (*d*) | **5.** (*c*) |
| **6.** (*d*) | **7.** (*d*) | | | |

## EXPLANATIONS

1. The Principle states that Penal laws provide that whoever voluntarily has carnal intercourse against the order of nature with any man or woman, shall be punished for rape and here man was engaged in carnal intercourse with an animal and hence court will not punish the man for rape.

2. Only Sanju will be liable for rape as he was the one who actually committed the offence
3. The additions were made to give clarity to the original document and did not in any sense change the contents of the documents and hence there is no forgery as alleged by the researcher
4. There was no imminent danger to X as the dog stopped barking and was walking with the owner. Hence, shooting it amounted to excessive use of the right of private defence and hence liable for killing the dog.
5. In criminal law, misappropriation is the intentional, illegal use of the property or funds of another person for one's own use or other unauthorized purpose, particularly by a public official, a trustee of a trust, an executor or administrator of a dead person's estate or by any person with a responsibility to care for and protect another's assets. Embezzlement is misappropriation when the funds involved have been lawfully entrusted to the embezzler. X who was traced by the police told the police that he sold all the valuables and the entire cash was used for drinking liquor and X is liable for criminal misappropriation and embezzlement.
6. B' has not committed any offence as he acted in his private defence.
7. Whoever takes away with him any minor less than sixteen years of age if a male, or less than eighteen years of age if a female, out of the custody of parents of such minor without the consent of such parents, is said to commit no offence 'A' committed no offence against the girl as well as her parent as she was below sixteen years.

## CONSTITUTIONAL LAW AND LEGAL FRAMEWORK

**Question number 1:** consists of legal proposition(s)/ principle(s) (hereinafter referred to as 'principle') and facts. Such principles may or may not be true in the real and legal sense, yet you have to conclusively assume them to be true for the purposes of this Section, in other words, in answering these questions, you must not rely on any principle except the principles those are given herein below for every question. Further, you must not assume any facts other than those stated in the question. The objective of this section is to test your interest towards study of law, research aptitude and problem solving ability, even if the 'most reasonable conclusion' arrived at may be absurd or unacceptable for any other reason. It is not the objective of this section to test your knowledge of law. Therefore, to answer a question, principle is to be applied to the given facts and to choose the most appropriate option.

1. **Principle :** The Constitution of India guarantees certain fundamental rights to its citizens. The Constitution also provides that these rights cannot be taken away by state even by a law. For violation of this, the person adversely affected by the law may approach the High Court or the Supreme Court for the issuance of an appropriate writ. One of these rights includes the freedom to form association that implies the right to join an association or not to Join such an association.

   **Facts :** Owing to some industrial disturbances created by XATU, one of the several trade unions in AB Chemicals (Pvt) Ltd., the Company issued a circular to all its employees that as far as possible the employees may disassociate with XATU. Navin is an employee of AB Chemicals and the current General Secretary of XATU. Aggrieved by this circular, which affected the fundamental rights of his and other members of the Union, approaches the High Court of the state for a relief. Identify the most reasonable legal proposition.

   (*a*) The circular interferes with the freedom guaranteed by the Constitution and hence the High Court can issue an appropriate writ.

   (*b*) The prohibition against any imposition of restriction against a fundamental right is not applicable to anybody other than the state and hence Navin will not get any relief from the High Court.

   (*c*) The Company's circular is illegal and has to be quashed by the Court.

   (*d*) Circular issued by a Company amounts to law in the constitutional sense and hence the High Court can issue a writ as pleaded for by Navin.

**Direction for questions 2 - 6 :** Legal phrases are followed by four meanings. Choose the most appropriate option:

2. Lex loci

   (*a*) Law of a place (*b*) Latin regualtions
   (*c*) Italian laws (*d*) Domestic laws

3. 'Sine die' means:

   (*a*) Adjourned without fixing any date for the next meeting.
   (*b*) Adjourned for the day and scheduled to meet next day again.
   (*c*) Adjourned for the day and meet after one month.
   (*d*) Adjourned for the day and meet after one week.

4. Animus posssidendi' means:

   (*a*) Intention to possess (*b*) Intent to contract
   (*c*) Intention to harm (*d*) Intention to return

5. Autrefois convict
   (*a*) To be convicted (*b*) Failed prosecution
   (*c*) Formerly convicted (*d*) Doubtful conviction
6. Turpis arbiter' means:
   (*a*) Corrupt prosecutor (*b*) inefficient judge
   (*c*) Corrupt judge (*d*) inefficient lawyer

## ANSWERS

**1.** (*b*) **2.** (*a*) **3.** (*a*) **4.** (*a*) **5.** (*c*)
**6.** (*c*)

## EXPLANATIONS

1. The prohibition against any imposition of restriction against a fundamental right is not applicable to anybody other than the state and hence Navin will not get any relief from the High Court.

## MISCELLANEOUS

**Question numbers 1 -4 :** consists of legal proposition(s)/ principle(s) (hereinafter referred to as 'principle') and facts. Such principles may or may not be true in the real and legal sense, yet you have to conclusively assume them to be true for the purposes of this Section, in other words, in answering these questions, you must not rely on any principle except the principles those are given herein below for every question. Further, you must not assume any facts other than those stated in the question. The objective of this section is to test your interest

towards study of law, research aptitude and problem solving ability, even if the 'most reasonable conclusion' arrived at may be absurd or unacceptable for any other reason. It is not the objective of this section to test your knowledge of law. Therefore, to answer a question, principle is to be applied to the given facts and to choose the most appropriate option.

1. **Principle :** Ownership in property consists of right to possess, right to use, right to alienate and right to exclude others. Sale is complete when property gets transferred from the seller to the buyer on sale.

   **Facts :** 'A' sold his car to 'B'. After this, 'B' requested 'A' to keep the car in his care on behalf 'B' for one month. 'A' agreed.
   (*a*) Sale will be completed when 'B' will take the delivery of the car.
   (*b*) Sale will be automatically completed after the expiry of one men
   (*c*) Sale of car is not complete
   (*d*) Sale of car is complete.
2. **Principle :** According to the law of trade unions in India, no suit or other legal proceeding shall be maintainable in any civil court against any registered trade union or any officer or member thereof in respect of any act done in contemplation or in furtherance of a trade dispute.

   **Facts :** Soloman, the Secretary of a registered Trade Union took a loan from a Bank for the higher education of his daughter. Soon after completing the course she was married to an NRI Engineer. Solomon did not repay the loan. The Bank demanded the payments from Soloman and warned him that the Bank will take suitable legal action against him. Identify the legal position in this regard.
   (*a*) The Bank can file a suit for recovery of the loan amount against Soloman as he took the loan for a personal purpose and in such case no
   (*b*) As Soloman did not use the loan amount for his use and hence, no action can be initiated against him.
   (*c*) The Bank cannot initiate any action against Soloman as he is the Secretary of a Registered Trade Union.
   (*d*) The Bank can recover the loan amount from the Trade Union as Soloman is the Secretary of the Union.
3. **Principle :** The concept of natural justice is against bias and for the right to a fair hearing. While the term natural Justice is often retained as a general concept, and it has largely been replaced and extended by the general 'duty to act fairly'.

   **Fact :** 'X', a male employee of a company was dismissed by the employer Just on the basis of a complaint by 'Y', a female employee of the company that 'X' was trying to be too friendly with her and often requested her to accompany him to the canteen. Is the dismissal of 'X' valid?
   (*a*) Yes, because men are not supposed to behave improperly with women and hence there is no violation of any principles of law
   (*b*) No, because in the modern times this type of behaviour is common
   (*c*) Yes, moral law is antique and therefore, not applicable in modern times, therefore the termination is valid and no violations of the principles of natural justice occurred
   (*d*) No, because the employer did not give a chance to 'X' to explain his side, thereby violated the principles of natural justice.
4. **Principle :** According to Sec. 2 of the Industrial Disputes Act, 1947, 'Industrial dispute means any dispute or difference between employers and employers or between employers and workmen or between workmen and workmen, which is connected with the employment or non-employment or the terms

of employment or with the conditions of labour of any person'.

**Facts :** The employees of DK Enterprises met the management and requested half a day leave to allow them to celebrate a lunar eclipse, which was going to happen two days later. The management refused the request. Does this situation amount to an 'industrial dispute'?

(*a*) Yes, because there is some difference of opinion it would be an industrial dispute.

(*b*) No as declaring holidays is a prerogative of the employer. So no industrial dispute.

(*c*) No as Lunar eclipse is unconnected with employment.

(*d*) As the difference of opinion between the employees and employer is on declaration of holiday it amounts to an issue connected with employment or with the terms of employment and hence, an industrial dispute.

## ANSWERS

**1.** (*d*) **2.** (*a*) **3.** (*d*) **4.** (*d*)

## EXPLANATIONS

1. Sale of Car is complete the moment A sold his car to B and B who is having the ownership of the Car has requested A to keep the Car for one month. Ownership in a property consists of Right to Posses, right to use, alienate and exclude others.
2. The Bank can file a suit for recovery of the loan amount against Soloman as he took the loan for a personal purpose and in such case no immunity will work.
3. The Principle of Natural justice means right to fair hearing and , because the employer did not give a chance to 'X' to explain his side, thereby violated the principles of natural justice and his dismissal is not valid.
4. As the difference of opinion between the employees and employer is on declaration of holiday it amounts to an issue connected with employment or with the terms of employment and hence, an industrial dispute.

# AILET-2017 CHAPTER-WISE

## ENGLISH

### VOCABULARY

1. Cashed up, aspirational and a marketer's dream, the hoi polloi are on the march, writes Bridie Smith.

   Choose the antonym of the word **hoi polloi**.

   (*a*) Middle class (*b*) Aristocracy
   (*c*) Masses (*d*) Working class

2. There's a lot in life that can leave you nonplussed.

   Choose the antonym of the word **nonplussed**.

   (*a*) dumbfound (*b*) disconcert
   (*c*) astound (*d*) unperturbed

3. Stay away from the touristy Pioneer Square historic district and most of its cheeseball clubs, at least on nights and weekends.

   Choose the meaning of the word **cheeseball**.

   (*a*) Expensive (*b*) Notorious
   (*c*) Inferior in quality (*d*) Stylish

4. It was marvellous to see how gingerly, the little beasts footed it in such places.

   Choose the synonym of the word **gingerly**.

   (*a*) roughly
   (*b*) assiduously
   (*c*) rashly
   (*d*) carelessly

5. She's also an up-and-coming fiction writer with a penchant for the dark and surreal.

   Choose the meaning of the word **surreal**.

   (*a*) Bizarre
   (*b*) Haunting
   (*c*) Edgy
   (*d*) Satanic

**Direction for questions 6 to 8:** Choose the alternative which best expresses the meaning of the idiom/phrase in the question.

6. Pell-mell

   (*a*) In hurried disorder
   (*b*) Gaiety and excitement
   (*c*) Extremely worried
   (*d*) None of these

7. To have one's heart in one's boots

   (*a*) To get angry
   (*b*) To be deeply depressed
   (*c*) To be frightened
   (*d*) To keep a secret

8. To give one's ears

   (*a*) To listen carefully
   (*b*) To act in a foolish way
   (*c*) To make a guess
   (*d*) To make almost any sacrifice

**Direction for questions 9 to 19:** Fill in the blanks with appropriate words.

Under a zero-hour contract, a party described as a 'casual worker' has a contract with an employer, but the contract may be of little benefit as its provisions do not (9) _____ any obligation upon the employer to offer work, and similarly, there is no obligation for the worker to accept it. A 'casual worker' is the correct term to define workers who do not have (10) _____ hours of work but instead supply services on an irregular, flexible basis when the employer needs them. A 'worker' is not, therefore, an 'employee'. This is an important distinction, as employees enjoy significantly better protection under the law.

Although workers do have basic rights, for example, the right to a national minimum (11) _____, the right not to be unlawfully discriminated against and the right to sick pay, but they are denied other important rights. For example, casual workers do not have the same rights when it comes to issues such as maternity or paternity pay, (12) _____ pay in the event that there is not enough work available and the right not to be unfairly (13) _____. These contracts are very unpopular with trade unions, who argue that employers are using this type of contract as a way of denying workers the benefits which they would otherwise be entitled to under current employment (14) _____.

As a result of public criticism, the Eurona government held an independent review to analyse the use of these contracts. In June 2016, Eurona Business Secretary, Zoro, concluded that zero-hour contracts were not to be declared (15) _____, as he considered that many groups of people benefited from them. However, he did change the law in order to prevent employers from banning casual workers from working elsewhere when bound by a zero-hour contract. This is not the end of the story, however. The use of zero-hour contracts is extremely popular in the food and retail (16) _____ of the Eurona economy.

For example, McDonald's and Burger King have recently disclosed that they use this type of contract for over 80% of their workers in the Eurona and another high-street giant, Sports Direct, has admitted that 90% of its workers are under this type of contract. However, the latter (17) _____ a legal challenge in November 2016 when Tera Phera filed a claim against the company in a Eurona Employment Tribunal. Tera Phera claimed that although she was contracted as a casual worker for Sports Direct, she had the same responsibilities and duties as an employee but without receiving the benefits of an employee. A (18) _____ was reached according to which Sports Direct is now required at the time of advertising for future zero-hours staff to expressly state that the role does not (19) _____ work. The company must also produce clear written policies setting out what sick pay and paid holiday their zero-hours staff are entitled to.

9. (*a*) impose (*b*) compel
   (*c*) force (*d*) impress
10. (*a*) fixed (*b*) secure
    (*c*) firm (*d*) stable
11. (*a*) salary (*b*) wage
    (*c*) earnings (*d*) remuneration
12. (*a*) let go (*b*) redundancy
    (*c*) termination (*d*) release
13. (*a*) dismissed (*b*) discharged
    (*c*) terminated (*d*) laid off
14. (*a*) statutes (*b*) codes
    (*c*) legislations (*d*) acts
15. (*a*) unlawful (*b*) illegal
    (*c*) illegitimate (*d*) felonious
16. (*a*) zones (*b*) regions
    (*c*) sectors (*d*) areas
17. (*a*) suffered (*b*) bore
    (*c*) endured (*d*) faced
18. (*a*) agreement (*b*) settlement
    (*c*) Deal (*d*) Decision
19. (*a*) provide (*b*) entitle
    (*c*) guarantee (*d*) offer

## ANSWERS

| | | | | |
|---|---|---|---|---|
| 1. (*b*) | 2. (*d*) | 3. (*c*) | 4. (*b*) | 5. (*a*) |
| 6. (*a*) | 7. (*b*) | 8. (*a*)* | 9. (*a*) | 10. (*a*) |
| 11. (*b*) | 12. (*b*) | 13. (*a*) | 14. (*c*) | 15. (*a*) |
| 16. (*c*) | 17. (*d*) | 18. (*b*) | 19. (*c*) | |

## EXPLANATIONS

1. Hoi polloi means the common masses; hence the antonym should be aristocracy.
2. Nonplussed means surprised; hence the antonym should be unperturbed.
3. Cheeseball means inferior in taste or quality.
4. Gingerly means to be extra careful. Assiduously is its synonym.
5. Surreal means bizarre or weird.
6. 'Pell-mell' means in a confused, rushed, or disorderly manner.
7. 'To have one's heart in one's boots' means to be depressed.
8. NLU-D has given the answer as (*d*). It is incorrect. The correct option is (*a*). 'To give one's ears' means to listen carefully.
9. Obligations are imposed.
10. "fixed work hours" best fits the context as casual workers don't have these.
11. "National minimum wage" is the correct phrase. There is no legal term called "National minimum salary or earnings or remuneration".
12. "Redundancy pay" fits the blank. Other options are grammatically not suitable.
13. Thematically "laid off, terminated, or dismissed" also fit the blank. However, unfairly dismissed is the common usage.
14. "Legislations" best suits the blank as it correctly matches the theme of the paragraph.
15. The paragraph talks about a legal issue. Hence, illegal best fits the blank.
16. Food and retail refers to a "sector".
17. A company "faces" a challenge.
18. The context refers to a compromise. Hence, "settlement" (which refers to a legal compromise" best suits the blank.
19. As the paragraph talks about a lack of certainty or promise, "guarantee" best fits the blank.

## GRAMMAR

**Directions for questions 1 and 2:** Match the ideas in (i) and (ii) by using the words in the brackets.

1. I. (even though)
   II. (with)
   III. (seeing that)
   IV. (even if)

| | (i) | | (ii) |
|---|---|---|---|
| 1 | I took my raincoat and umbrella ____ | a. | ____ because Davies is its captain. |
| 2 | I still won't be able to get to a meeting at 8.30 ____ | b. | ____ despite a problem in digging the foundations. |
| 3 | The team is likely to do well in this season ____ | c. | ____ as weather forecast was so bad. |
| 4 | The building work is still on schedule ____ | d. | ____ whether or not I natch an earlier train. |

(*a*) III-1-C, IV-2-d, II-3-a, I-4-b (*b*) 1-1-c, II-2-d, III-3-a, IV-4-b

(*c*) I-2-d, III-4-b, II-3-a, iV-1-c (*d*) IV-3-a, III-2-b, II-4-c, 1-1-d

**2.** I. (due to) II. (in order to) III. (in order that) IV. (so as to)

| | (i) | | (ii) |
|---|---|---|---|
| 1 | We have decided not to go on holiday this year ____ | a. | ____ because there had recently been a strike by postal workers. |
| 2 | The council have planted trees at the side of the road ____ | b. | ____ to aive Dave somewhere private to study before his exams. |
| 3 | The parcel has been delayed ____ | c. | ____ because we want to save money for a new car. |
| 4 | We've put a table and chair in the spare bedroom ____ | d. | ____ in an attempt to reduce traffic noise. |

(*a*) I-1-a, II-2-b, III-3-c,IV-4-d (*b*) IV-1-a, III-2-b, II-3-C, I-4-d

(*c*) I-4-a, II-3-C, III-2-b, I-1-a (*d*) II-1-C, IV-2-d, I-3-a, III-4-b

**Directions for questions 3 and 4:** Complete the sentences on the right with appropriate compound nouns related to the two-word verbs used in the sentences on the left.

**3.** I. flashbacks II. Telling off III. hideout IV. downpour

| | (i) | | (ii) |
|---|---|---|---|
| 1 | The teacher told me off for handing in my homework late. | a. | The children have a secret ____ at the bottom of the garden. |
| 2 | My mind flashed back to the time when I was living in Stockholm. | b. | I was caught in a sudden ____ and got soaked through. |
| 3 | The escaped prisoners crept into an old barn and hid out until it got dark. | c. | My father gave me a good ____ for knocking down his prize roses. |
| 4 | The rain was pouring down as we got out of the taxi. | d. | There are a number of ____ in the film to the time before the robbery. |

(*a*) I-1-a, II-2-b, III-3-C, IV-4-d (*b*) II-1-c, I-2-d, III-3-a, IV-4-b

(*c*) II-1-c, I-2-d, IV-3-a, III-4-b (*d*) I-4-d, II-3-C, III-2-b, IV-1-a

**4.** I. setbacks II. Tip-offs III. passers-by IV. Upbringing

| | (i) | | (ii) |
|---|---|---|---|
| 1 | The police were waiting for the thieves. Someone must have tipped them off. | a. | Harry had a verv strict ____ and was glad to move away from his parents. |
| 2 | As I passed by her house, I could see people dancing in the front room. | b. | The engine fault was the latest of several ____ in the development of the car. |
| 3 | She was born and brought up in central London. | c. | We received several ____ that there would be an attempted break-out at the prison. |
| 4 | The injury has set back his chances of being fit to play in the final. | d. | The man was leaning out of the window, shoutinq at ____ in the street below. |

(*a*) I-4-b, II-1-c, III-2-d, IV-3-a (*b*) II-3-c, III-2-b, IV-1-a, I-4-d

(*c*) II-1-C, I-2-d, IV-3-a, III-4-b (*d*) I-3-b, II-4-c, III-1-d, IV-2-a

**Directions for questions 5 to 6:** Observe the following sentences where same word in different form is used keeping the sense of the sentence same. In the following questions, the sentences have some element of similarity. You have to find out the similarity and choose the option which is odd one out.

**5.** (*a*) Such jokes do not give me any amusement.
Such jokes do not amuse me.
(*b*) He put up a brave fight.
He fought bravely.
(*c*) Her failure disappointed her.
She failed and it disappointed her.
(*d*) The boy gave a prompt answer.
The boy answered promptly.

**6.** (*a*) Getting up he walked away.
He got up and walked away.
(*b*) Fortunately, nothing has happened.
It was fortunate that nothing has happened.
(*c*) You must take rest to get well.
You must take some rest otherwise you can't get well.
(*d*) He made a promise. He kept it.
He not only made a promise but also kept it.

**7.** (*a*) Mother said to Geeta, "Where are you going ?"
Mother asked Geeta where she was going.
(*b*) Radhika said, "Can you tell me how to reach there ?" "Yes", said Ram.
Radhika asked if he could tell her how to reach there. Ram replied that he could.
(*c*) All could hear the mournful wails of his wife.
The mournful wails of his wife could be heard by all.
(*d*) She said to her husband, "Did you like my dance yesterday ?"
She asked her husband if he had liked her dance the last day.

**Direction for questions 8 and 9:** Choose the sentence which is incorrect grammatically.

**8.** (*a*) Sita is more intelligent and wise than Rita.
(*b*) The wisest man that ever lived made mistakes.
(*c*) I doubt if Ravi will come.
(*d*) The flowers smelt sweet.

**9.** (*a*) I am looking forward to receiving your reply.
(*b*) Each boy and every girl was given rewards.
(*c*) i can run as fast, if not faster, than you.
(*d*) I can reproduce this lesson word for word.

**Direction for questions 10 to 13 :** Find out the sentence/s which is/are written correctly.

a. Charles is a gifted footballer, but up to now he didn't play well in international matches.
b. We've been staying with Paul and Jenny until last weekend.
c. He just heard the news and was rushing home to tell his family.
d. When I grow up I'm going to be an astronaut.

**10.** a. (*a*), (*d*) b. (*c*)
c. (*d*) d. (*b*), (*c*)

(*a*) Have you ever been to the opera when you lived in Milan ?
(*b*) The man who broke the window wants to see you.
(*c*) I won't be able to meet you next week. I will stay in London for a few days.
(*d*) My mother who is in her seventies enjoys hill walking.

**11.** a. (*b*), (*d*) b. (*a*), (*b*), (*c*)
c. (*b*) d. (*d*)

(*a*) Applications have risen this year by as much as 50%.
(*b*) There are a number of reasons I don't like him, but his meanness is the main.
(*c*) I felt confident to pass my driving test.
(*d*) I haven't got enough cash on me for paying the bill.

**12.** a. (*a*), (*d*) b. (*b*), (*c*)
c. (*d*) d. (*a*)

(*a*) Although they played well, but they never looked like winning.
(*b*) Despite the snow was still falling heavily, she went out.
(*c*) If Schumacher were to win today he would become world champion.
(*d*) She got low grades for her exams, therefore she had to retake them to get into college.

**13.** (*a*) b, d (*b*) c
(*c*) c, d (*d*) d

## ANSWERS

| | | | | |
|---|---|---|---|---|
| **1.** (*a*) | **2.** (*d*) | **3.** (*b*) | **4.** (*a*) | **5.** (*d*) |
| **6.** (*b*) | **7.** (*c*) | **8.** (*a*) | **9.** (*c*) | **10.** (*c*) |
| **11.** (*c*) | **12.** (*d*)* | **13.** (*b*) | | |

## EXPLANATIONS

1. For (1), 'Seeing that' connects the action of taking the rain coat and umbrella with bad forecast. For (2), 'Even if' connects the two sentences. For (3), 'With' connects the two sentences. For (4), 'Even though' connects the two sentences.
2. For (1), 'In order to' connects the two sentences. For (2), 'So as to' connects the two sentences. For (3), 'Due to' connects the two sentences. For (4), 'in order to' connects the two sentences.
3. Telling off means to mildly scold or rebuke or reprimand. B shows the correct match.
4. Only (*a*) correctly matches the given definitions. Tip-off means to warn someone in advance or give information in advance.
5. In (*a*), (*b*) and (*c*) the given word is used as adjectives and adverbs. The meanings remain the same. However, "prompt answer" and "answered promptly" have different meanings. The first one means "timely or on time" and the second one means "swiftly or fast".
6. This sentence has an inconsistence tense structure. The correct sentence will be "It is fortunate that nothing has happened". The other sentences are grammatically correct.
7. Option (*c*) deals with voice change whereas the other options deal with speech change.
8. The correct sentence will be "Sita is more intelligent and wiser than Rita is".
9. The correct sentence will be "I can run as fast, if not faster, as you can".
10. (*a*) is incorrect because of "didn't". It should be "hasn't". (*b*) is incorrect because of "We've". It should be "We had been". In (*c*), 'was rushing' should be replaced with "rushed" to maintain parallelism in the sentence.
11. (*a*) is incorrect because it breaks the parallelism of tense. "Did you ever go to the Opera when you live in Milan" is the correct sentence. (*b*) is correct. (*c*) is wrong. "Will stay" should be replaced with "will be staying". (*d*) is incorrect because of the use of 'hill walking'. It should be "walking in the hills".
12. In (*b*), there should be a connector, 'for which'. (*c*) has a part of speech error. "To pass" is not correct because we need a gerund (in passing) here. In (*d*), instead of 'for paying the bill' it should be 'to pay the bill'. Though A is given as the correct sentence, as per accepted usage, "The number of applications has risen" is the correct construct.
13. In (*a*), 'but' is redundant. In (*b*), 'was still' should be removed. In (*d*), 'in' should be there instead of 'for'.

## READING COMPREHENSION

**Direction for questions 1 to 3:** Rearrange the given six sentences K, L, M, N, O and P in the proper sequence so as to form a meaningful paragraph and then answer the questions that follows.

(K) The subjugation or enslavement of the people and countries is fast becoming a thing of the past.

(L) Since then the progress in science and technology and in other branches of knowledge has resulted in the betterment of the conditions of life in many countries.

(M) The Industrial Revolution in England about the middle of the eighteenth century was history's great leap forward.

(N) All this is on credit of modern civilisation.

(O) Society has been progressing and improving for thousands of years.

(P) The span of human life has been enlarged, the condition of the labouring classes in many countries has improved, knowledge and education have made great strides, the treatment of children has become more humane, feats of engineering have done wonders, democracy and freedom have been granted to most countries of the world, and a very much larger percentage of people have become entitled to the good things of life.

1. Which sentence should come fifth in the paragraph?
   (*a*) P (*b*) K
   (*c*) N (*d*) L
2. Which sentence should come first in the paragraph?
   (*a*) O (*b*) M
   (*c*) P (*d*) K
3. Which sentence should come third in the paragraph?
   (*a*) N (*b*) M
   (*c*) P (*d*) L

## ANSWERS

**1.** (*b*) **2.** (*a*) **3.** (*d*)

## EXPLANATIONS

1. The correct order of the passage is OMLPKN. O opens the paragraph as it is the best topic sentence. ML make a mandatory pair as "since then" in L refers to "Industrial Revolution" in M. P expands the idea expressed in L. N is the closing sentence as it summarizes the achievements of the Industrial era. Hence, 'K' is the fifth sentence.
2. The correct order of the passage is OMLPKN. O opens the paragraph as it is the best topic sentence. ML make a mandatory pair as "since then" in L refers to "Industrial Revolution" in M. P expands the idea

expressed in L. N is the closing sentence as it summarizes the achievements of the Industrial era. Hence, 'O' is the first sentence.

3. The correct order of the passage is OMLPKN. O opens the paragraph as it is the best topic sentence. ML make a mandatory pair as "since then" in L refers to "Industrial Revolution" in M. P expands the idea expressed in L. N is the closing sentence as it summarizes the achievements of the Industrial era. Hence, 'L' is the third sentence.

# REASONING

## VERBAL LOGIC

**Direction for questions 1 and 2:** Select the odd one out.

1. (*a*) ZYAB (*b*) TSGH
   (*c*) ONLM (*d*) UTFH
2. (*a*) JIHG (*b*) RQPO
   (*c*) WXUV (*d*) UTSR

## ANSWERS

1. (*d*) 2. (*c*)

## EXPLANATIONS

1. Difference in last two letters is 2 in (*d*) instead of 1.

| | | | | |
|---|---|---|---|---|
| (*a*) | Z | Y | A | B |
| | 26 | 25 | 1 | 2 |
| (*b*) | T | S | G | H |
| | 20 | 19 | 7 | 8 |
| (C) | O | N | L | M |
| | 15 | 14 | 12 | 13 |
| (*d*) | U | T | F | H |
| | 21 | 20 | 6 | 8 |

2. Except (*c*), all others have terms in decreasing order.

| | | | | |
|---|---|---|---|---|
| (*a*) | J | I | H | G |
| | 10 | 9 | 8 | 7 |
| (*b*) | R | Q | P | O |
| | 18 | 17 | 16 | 15 |
| (*c*) | W | X | U | V |
| | 23 | 24 | 21 | 22 |
| (*d*) | U | T | S | R |
| | 20 | 20 | 19 | 18 |

## ANALYTICAL REASONING

**Direction for questions 1 and 2:** Find out the wrong number.

1. 5, 7.5, 11.25, 17.5, 29.75, 50, 91.25
   (*a*) 29.75 (*b*) 17.5
   (*c*) 91.25 (*d*) 50
2. 10, 13, 26, 37, 51, 85, 154
   (*a*) 154 (*b*) 51
   (*c*) 26 (*d*) 13

**Direction for questions 3 and 4:** Find out the missing number/words.

3. 13 (168) 13, 14 (181) 13, 15 (?) 13
   (*a*) 196 (*b*) 195
   (*c*) 190 (*d*) 194
4. ST39, UV43, WX47, ?
   (*a*) YZ47 (*b*) YZ52
   (*c*) YZ51 (*d*) YZ50

**Direction for questions 5 to 9:** Read the following information carefully and answer the questions given below.

Nine players – G, H, I, J, K, L, M, N and O – have to be put in three teams. Each team will consist of three players and each player will appear only once in a team. The teams must be arranged according to the following conditions.

i. I and N must be in the same team.
ii. K and L must be in the same team.
iii. O and J cannot be in the same team.
iv. M must be in the second team.
v. Either J or M or both must be in the team with H.

5. Which of the following cannot be true?
   (*a*) M is in 1st team and H is in the 3rd
   (*b*) O is in 3rd team
   (*c*) I is in 2nd team
   (*d*) H is in the 3rd team
6. All of the following could be in the same team as K, except
   (*a*) G (*b*) J
   (*c*) I (*d*) M
7. If J and K are in the 3rd team, which of the following players must be in 2nd?
   (*a*) L (*b*) I
   (*c*) G (*d*) H
8. Which of the following players could be in a team together?
   (*a*) K, I, M (*b*) N, I, J
   (*c*) G, J, M (*d*) G, L, O

**9.** The 3rd team could consist of the following except

(*a*) G, H, J (*b*) K, L, J

(*c*) K, L, O (*d*) G, I, J

**Direction for questions 10 to 13:** Read the following information carefully and answer the questions given below.

A couple decided to organize a party and invited a few of their friends. Only the host and hostess were sitting at the opposite ends of a rectangular table with three persons on each side. The pre-requisite of the sitting arrangement was that each person must be seated so that at least on one side he/she has a person of the opposite sex. Romeo is opposite to Sonakshi, who is not the hostess. Ruchir has a woman on his right and is sitting opposite to a woman. Jia is sitting to the hostess's right, next to Vikram. One person is seated between Mahima and Rajni, who is not the hostess. The men were Romeo, Ruchir, Vikram and Rajnikant while the women were Mahima, Rajni, Sonakshi and Jia.

**10.** The eighth person present, Rajnikant must be

I. The host

II. Seated to Sonakshi's right

III. Seated opposite to Rajni

(*a*) Only III (*b*) I and II

(*c*) Only I (*d*) Only II

**11.** If each person is placed directly opposite to his/her spouse, which of the following pairs must be married?

(*a*) Ruchir and Mahima (*b*) Rajni and Rajnikant

(*c*) Mahima and Vikram (*d*) Ruchir and Jia

**12.** Which of the following persons is definitely not seated next to a person of same sex ?

(*a*) Mahima (*b*) Sonakshi

(*c*) Rajnikant (*d*) Romeo

**13.** If Ruchir would have exchanged his seat with a person sitting four places to his left, which of the following would have been true after the exchange?

I. No person of the opposite sex was seated between two persons of same sex

II. One side of the table consisted entirely of persons of the same sex

III. Either the host or the hostess changed their seats

(*a*) Only I (*b*) Only II

(*c*) I and II (*d*) II and III

**Directions for questions 14 to 16:** Read the following case and answer the questions.

Sakshi is the Vice-President in an electrical equipment company in Delhi. One day, her subordinate Bhaskar requested that Kishen, a project manager, be transferred to the Mumbai office from the Delhi office. In Mumbai, Kishen would work alone as a researcher. Bhaskar gave the following reasons for his request "Kishen is known for fighting frequently with colleagues of his team. He cannot accept criticism and feels rejected and get hostile. He is overbearing and is generally a bad influence on the team."

Sakshi called upon Samir, another project manager and sought further information on Kishen. Samir recalled that a former colleague, Lalit (who was also Kishen's former boss) has made few remarks on Kishen in his appraisal report. In his opinion, Kishen was not fit for further promotion as he was emotionally unstable to work in groups in spite of the fact that he had seven years of work experience. Lalit has described Kishen as too authoritative to work under anyone. Lalit has further told Samir that Kishen had an ailing wife and an old mother, who does not want to stay with his wife.

Consider the following solutions to the problem mentioned above

I. Sakshi should transfer Kishen to Mumbai office.

II. Sakshi should try and verify the facts from other sources as well.

III. Kishen should be sacked.

IV. Kishen should be demoted.

V. Sakshi should suggest Kishen to visit a family counsellor.

**14.** Which of the following would be the most appropriate sequence of decisions in terms of immediacy starting from immediate to a long term solution ?

(*a*) II, V, I (*b*) II, III, IV

(*c*) II, V, IV (*d*) II, I, V

**15.** Sakshi sought an appointment with Lalit to find out ways to help Kishen. Lalit is of the view that the company's responsibility is restricted to the workplace and it should not try to address the personal problems of employees. If Sakshi has to agree to Lalit's view, which of the solutions presented in the previous question would be weakened ?

(*a*) Only III (*b*) Only IV

(*c*) Only V (*d*) Only II

**16.** Which of the following statements, if true would weaken the decision to sack Kishen the most?

(*a*) Another article published in the magazine, Caventers Quaterly, highlighted that employee's problem at home affect their performance at work.

(*b*) In the latest issue of a reputed Journal, Xanders Business Review, it was published that most top managers, find it difficult to work In a group.

(c) It was published in Banters Management Review, another reputed Journal that individuals who cannot work in teams find it difficult to adjust to a new location.

(d) Bhaskar was of the opinion that emotionally unstable persons, find it difficult to get back to normal working life.

**Directions for questions 17 to 21:** Read the following information carefully and answer the questions. A word arrangement machine, when given an input line of words, rearranges them following a particular rule in each step. The following is the illustration of the input and the steps of arrangement.

**Input :** Diksha cannot but feel happy for him

**Step I :** but cannot Diksha happy feel him for

**Step II :** cannot but feel happy Diksha for him

**Step III :** but cannot happy feel him for Diksha

**Step IV :** happy cannot but him feel Diksha for

and so on for subsequent steps. You have to find out the logic and answer the questions given below.

**17.** If Step V read "weeks of tepid slothful and weak ideas", then what would be Step IV read?

(a) ideas and tepid weeks of weak slothful

(b) of weeks and slothful tepid ideas weak

(c) ideas weeks and tepid of weak slothful

(d) none of these

**18.** If Step I read "it was the name bestowed upon him", then what would be the arrangement for Step VII?

(a) it was him the name bestowed upon

(b) upon the him was it bestowed name

(c) bestowed it was the name upon him

(d) none of these

**19.** If Step VI reads "workers must take a stand against working", then what will be the last word of Step III?

(a) must

(b) take

(c) a

(d) none of these

**20.** If Step III reads "the best way of promoting our sports", then what will be the arrangement of the input?

(a) best the sports way of our promoting

(b) our promoting the best sports way of

(c) sports best the of way our promoting

(d) of our best the way sports promoting

**21.** If the given input is "it is good approach with care", then what will be Step IV?

(a) care with a good approach is it

(b) approach is a care good it with

(c) a good approach it is with care

(d) with approach it is a good care

**Directions for questions 22 to 26 :** Read the following short passages and choose the best answers to the questions that follow each passage.

**22. Columnist :** Senators who are not firmly committed to a core set of beliefs will formulate new campaign strategies and moot points before each upcoming election. Senators are elected to serve multiple terms in office only if they formulate new campaign strategies and moot points before each upcoming election. Therefore, senators who are not firmly committed to a core set of beliefs are elected to serve multiple terms in office.

Which one of the following displays a flawed pattern of reasoning most closely parallel to that in the columnist's argument?

(a) Nuclear proliferation will accelerate only if there is widespread access to fissile material. Widespread access to fissile material goes hand in glove with increased regional instability. Therefore, nuclear proliferation will not accelerate unless there is an increase in regional instability.

(b) If health care costs continue to rise, foreign currency markets will devalue the Euro. But health care costs will not continue to rise. Therefore, foreign currency markets will not devalue the Euro.

(c) A loyal person is a likeable person, for a loyal person always stands by her friends and a likeable person also always stands by her friends.

(d) A well-constructed house includes code-compliant framing, wiring, and insulation. A house is marketable only if it is well-constructed. Therefore, a marketable house includes code-coitipliant framing, wiring, and insulation.

**23.** Cuisine from the north of China is one of the most popular kinds of food in India. But this is not the case for Southern Chinese cuisine. In fact, in a recent survey. Southern Chinese cuisine was voted one of the least popular styles of cooking in the country.

Which one of the following, if true, most helps to resolve the apparent paradox described above?

(*a*) Southern Chinese cuisine frequently incorporates obscure ingredients that are difficult to locate, while the ingredients necessary to prepare Northern Chinese cuisine are easily found in most Indian grocery stores.

(*b*) Immigrants from all parts of China brought their local cuisines with them when they came to India in great numbers in the seventeenth and eighteenth centuries.

(*c*) Northern Chinese cuisine has recently become more popular in India than the Italian cuisine, which for many years was this country's favourite international food.

(*d*) Northern Chinese cuisine is more time consuming and labour intensive to prepare than Southern Chinese cuisine.

**24.** A growing number of ecologists have begun to recommend lifting the ban on the hunting of leopards, which are not an endangered species, and on the international trade of leopard's skin. Why, then, do I continue to support the protection of leopards ? For the same reason, that I oppose the hunting of people. Admittedly, there are far too many human beings on this planet to qualify us for inclusion on the list of endangered species. Still, I doubt the same ecologists endorsing the resumption of leopard hunting would use that fact to recommend the hunting of human beings.

Which one of the following, if true, would most weaken the author's argument?

(*a*) Human being might, in fact, be placed on the list of endangered species.

(*b*) Despite the growing number of ecologists supporting a repeal of the ban on leopard hunting, most will still support it.

(*c*) The international ban on leopard hunting was instituted before leopards became an endangered species.

(*d*) Leopards, now dangerously overpopulated, cannot be supported by their ecosystems.

**25.** Experts musicologists believe that Beethoven wrote his last piano sonata in 1824, three years before his death. However, the manuscript of a piano sonata was recently discovered that bears Beethoven's name and dates from 1825. Clearly, the experts are mistaken because not every piece that Beethoven wrote was catalogued in his lifetime, and it is known that Beethoven continued to compose until just weeks before his death.

The reasoning in the argument is most vulnerable to which of the following criticisms?

(*a*) That either of two things could have occurred independently is taken to show that those two things could not have occurred simultaneously.

(*b*) An inconsistency that, as presented, has more than one possible resolution is treated as though only one resolution is possible.

(*c*) Establishing that a certain event occurred is confused with having established the cause of that event.

(*d*) A claim that has a very general application is based entirely on evidence from a narrowly restricted range of cases.

**26.** Some people fear that our first extra-terrestrial visitors will not be the friendly aliens envisaged in popular science fiction movies, but rather hostile invaders bent on global domination. This fear is groundless. Any alien civilisation that makes it to our planet must have acquired the wisdom to control war, or it would have destroyed itself long before contacting us.

The author bases the argument above on which of the following assumptions?

(*a*) Our planet will have contact with extra-terrestrial visitors at some time in the future.

(*b*) Interstellar travel is unworkable except in a society much more technologically advanced than ours.

(*c*) A civilisation that has learned to control war on its own planet will not wage war on another.

(*d*) Alien civilisations are more morally advanced than those on Earth.

## ANSWERS

| | | | | |
|---|---|---|---|---|
| **1.** (*a*) | **2.** (*b*) | **3.** (*d*) | **4.** (*c*) | **5.** (*a*) |
| **6.** (*c*) | **7.** (*d*) | **8.** (*b*) | **9.** (*d*) | **10.** (*b*) |
| **11.** (*d*) | **12.** (*b*) | **13.** (*a*) | **14.** (*a*)* | **15.** (*c*) |
| **16.** (*d*)* | **17.** (*b*) | **18.** (*d*) | **19.** (*d*) | **20.** (*c*) |
| **21.** (*b*) | **22.** (*c*) | **23.** (*a*) | **24.** (*d*) | **25.** (*b*) |
| **26.** (*c*) | | | | |

## EXPLANATIONS

**1.** 5, 7.5, 11.25, 17.5, 29.75, 50, 91.25

Instead of 29.75 , it should be 28.75.

1.25 × 2, 1.25 × 3 , 1.25 × 5, 1.25 × 9, 1.25 × 17, 1.25 × 33

Difference in multiples 2,3,5,9,17,33, are 1 , 2, 4, 8, 16.

2. 10, 13, 26, 37 , 51, 85, 154

10+ 16 = 26

13 + 24 = 37

26 + 32 = 58 ( instead of 51)

37 + 48 = 85

58 + 96 = 154

3. 13 × 13 = 169 : 169 – 1 =168

14 ×13 = 182 : 182 – 1 = 181

15 × 13 = 195 : 195 – 1 = 194

4. ST 39 = 19 + 20 IS 39

UV43 = 21+ 22 IS 43

WX47 = 23 + 24 IS 47

So Next Term Should be

YZ51 = 25 +26 IS 51

**For questions 5 to 9 :**

5. M has to be in Team 2 as per statement (iv)
6. As per the below valid combinations K can be with G, J and M

   Some of the valid combination that can be formed are–

   Combination 1 - Team 1- I, N

   Team 2 - M, H

   Team 3 - K, L (This team can have J or G or O)

   Combination 2 - Team 1 - I, N, O

   Team 2 - M, K, L

   Team 3 - J, H, G
7. As per the above combination 1, we can see that H has to be in Team 2
8. (*a*) and (*d*) are incorrect as K and L has to be together (*c*) is incorrect as per statement (v) of the question.
9. I and N has to be together so this is not a valid combination.

**For questions 10 to 13 :** Seating Arrangement as below

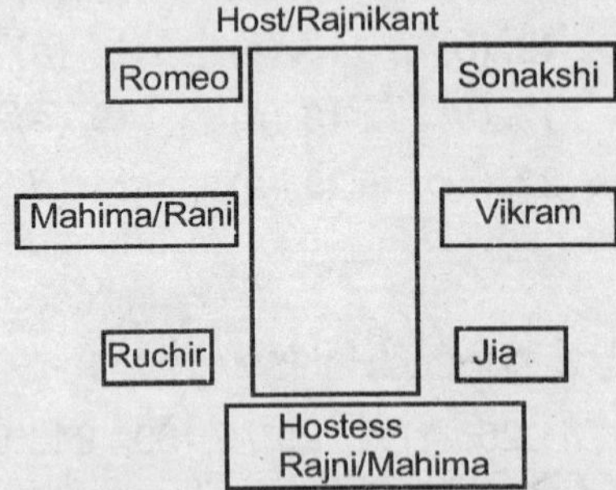


14. Technically, I is a short term solution and V is a long term solution. Hence, (*d*) should have been the answer. Visiting a counselor is a good step but its efficacy can be tested only in the long run. II is obviously the best and most effective step.
15. V talks about a personal problem. As per Lalit, the company should not take any step outside the workplace. Hence, V will become weakened. II, III, and IV are justified actions as they are restricted to the workplace.
16. This is a wrong answer. (*d*) will strengthen the decision to sack Kishen. (*a*) and (*c*) will also strengthen. Only (*b*) will weaken the option. Hence, (*b*) should have been the answer.

**For questions 17 to 21:** Numbering each word with a number

**Input :** Diksha (1) cannot (2) but (3) feel (4) happy (5) for (6) him (7)

**Step 1 :** 3, 2, 1, 5, 4, 7, 6

It has divided these words into 3 sets of 3,2 and 2. Then each set is written in reversed order

**Step 2 :** 2, 3, 4, 5, 1, 6, 7

It has divided words in Step 1 in sets of 2, 3 and 2. Then each set is written in reversed order.

**Step 3 :** 3, 2, 5, 4, 7, 6, 1

It has divided words in Step 2 in sets of 2, 2 and 3. Then each set is written in reversed order.

**Step 4 :** 5, 2, 3, 7, 4, 1, 6

It has divided words again in sets of 3, 2 and 2. Then each set is written in reversed order.

17. **Step 5 :** 2, 5, 4, 7, 3, 6, 1

    Dividing words in step 4 into sets of 2, 3 and 2. Number each word in the set given in this order and then calculate step 4 using the order given in Step 4.
18. **Step 7:** 7, 2, 5, 1, 4, 3, 6

    Number the words given in the question using Step 1 given above and then find Step 7
19. **Step 6** : 5, 2, 7, 4, 1, 6, 3

    Number words given in the question, Last word in step 3 is word numbered 1. Thus answer should be "stand"
20. Number words using step 3 output given above and then arrange them as an input.
21. Question is incorrect as there are only 6 words in the question.
22. The paragraph compares Senators without core values with those senators who are elected. It follows an "if" and "only if" clause structure. (*c*) shows this kind of a re7asoning process. However, (*d*) also shows a similar structure. But (*d*) is a valid argument. Hence, (*c*) is the answer as we have to find a flawed argument.
23. It gives the most plausible reason for the lack of popularity of the Southern Chinese Cuisine. The other options give superficial or out of scope reasons. Hence, (*a*) is the answer.

**24.** (*a*), (*b*), and (*c*) either strengthen the author's argument or are out of scope. (*d*) weakens the argument by showing that there is a justifiable reason for hunting leopards.

**25.** Only (*b*) weakens the argument as the author has assumed the dates on the manuscript to be correct. He has assumed this to be the only possible explanation which is flawed.

**26.** Only (*c*) is a valid assumption as it bridges the logical gap between the fact (intelligence of the aliens) and the conclusion (because of intelligence they will not destroy themselves or others) given in the paragraph.

# QUANTITATIVE APTITUDE

## ARITHMETIC

**1.** A garden is rectangular in shape. A sum of Rs. 1,000 was spent to make the land usable at the rate of 25 paisa per $m^2$. The breadth of the garden is 50 m. If the length of the garden is increased by 20 m, what will be the expenditure in rupees for making the land usable, at the same rate per $m^2$?

(*a*) Rs. 1,250 (*b*) Rs. 1,220
(*c*) Rs. 1,400 (*d*) Rs. 2,250

**2.** The sum of ages of a mother and daughter is 45 years. Five years ago, the product of their ages was four times the mother's age at that time. The present age of the mother is

(*a*) 38 years (*b*) 37 years
(*c*) 36 years (*d*) 39 years

**3.** A streamer goes downstream from one port to another in 4 hours. It covers the same ' distance upstream in 5 hours. If the speed of stream is 2 km/h, the distance between the two ports is

(*a*) 80 km (*b*) 81 km
(*c*) 70 km (*d*) 71 km

**4.** A train running at the rate of 40 km/hr passes a man riding parallel to the railway line in the same direction at 25 km/hr in 48 seconds. Find the length of the train in metres.

(*a*) 100 m (*b*) 200 m
(*c*) 150 m (*d*) 250 m

**5.** Reema, Ruchi and Richa can make a painting in 15, 20 and 30 days, respectively. They undertake to make a painting for Rs. 810. The share of Reema exceeds that of Ruchi by

(*a*) Rs. 91 (*b*) Rs. 92
(*c*) Rs. 90 (*d*) Rs. 89

**6.** Population of a city is 2,96,000 out of which 1,66,000 are males 50% population is literate. If 70% males are literate, then the number of women who are literate is

(*a*) 48,000 (*b*) 66,400
(*c*) 32,200 (*d*) 31,800

**7.** The average weight of 14 students was calculated as 71. But it was later found that the weight of one student had been wrongly entered as 42 instead of 56 and of another as 74 instead of 32. The correct average is

(*a*) 75 (*b*) 80
(*c*) 68 (*d*) 69

**8.** Four years ago, the ages of Ritu and Reena were in the ratio 5 : 6 respectively. Eight years from now the respective ratio of their ages will be 8:9. What is the sum of their ages at present?

(*a*) 52 years (*b*) 50 years
(*c*) 60 years (*d*) 62 years

**9.** A shirt was sold at a profit of 15%. If its cost had been 5% less and it had been sold for Rs. 21 less, then the profit would have been 10%. Find the cost of the shirt.

(*a*) Rs. 210 (*b*) Rs. 220
(*c*) Rs. 100 (*d*) Rs. 200

## ANSWERS

| | | | | |
|---|---|---|---|---|
| **1.** (*a*) | **2.** (*c*) | **3.** (*a*) | **4.** (*b*) | **5.** (*c*) |
| **6.** (*d*) | **7.** (*d*) | **8.** (*a*) | **9.** (*d*) | |

## EXPLANATIONS

**1.**

Length

Breadth = 50 m

$$R = \text{Rs. } 0.25/m^2$$

$\therefore$ Amount = Rs. 1,000

$\therefore$ R × Area = Amount

$\Rightarrow$ 0.25 × Area = 1000 or Area = 4000 $m^2$

$$\therefore \quad \text{Length} = \frac{\text{Area}}{\text{Breadth}} = \frac{4000}{50} = 80$$

If length is increased by 20 m, then area

= (80 + 20) × 50

= Rs. 5000

$\therefore$ Amount = Rs. 5000 × 0.25 = Rs. 1,250.

**2.** Let M and D be the ages (in years) of mother and that of daughter respectively.

$$M + D = 45$$

$(M-5)(D-5) = 4(M-5)$

$\Rightarrow \quad D-5 = 4$ or $D = 9$

$\therefore \quad M = 45-9 = \mathbf{36}$

**3.** Let speed of steamer be S and distance between the ports be D.

Downstream : $(S+2)4 = D$ ... (1)

Upstream : $(S-2)5 = D$ ... (2)

Subtracting (1) from (2)

$S-8-10 = 0$

or $S = 18$

$\therefore \quad D = (18+2)4 = 80$ km.

**4.** Speed of train = 40 km/hr

Speed of man = 25 km/hr

Relative speed = $(40-25) = 15$ km/hr $= 15 \times \frac{5}{18}$ m/s

Distance covered by train in passing the man

= Length of train = speed × time

$= \frac{15 \times 5}{18} \times 48 = 200$ m

**5.**

| | Reema | Ruchi | Richa |
|---|---|---|---|
| Effort proportion | $\frac{1}{15}$ | $\frac{1}{20}$ | $\frac{1}{30}$ |
| Share proportion | $\frac{1}{15}$ | $\frac{1}{20}$ | $\frac{1}{30}$ |
| or | $\frac{60}{15} = 4$ | $\frac{60}{20} = 3$ | $\frac{60}{30} = 2$ |
| ∴ Amount share | $\frac{810 \times 4}{(4+3+2)}$ | $\frac{810 \times 3}{(4+3+2)}$ | $\frac{810 \times 2}{(4+3+2)}$ |

= 360 = 270 =180

Reema's share exceeds Ruchi by (360 – 270) = Rs. 90.

**6.**

| | M | F | Total |
|---|---|---|---|
| Illeterate | | | |
| Literate | 70% | | 50% |
| **Total** | 166000 | | 296000 |

Filling the totals:

| | M | F | Total |
|---|---|---|---|
| Illeterate | | | 148000 |
| Literate | 116200 | 31800 | 148000 |
| **Total** | 166000 | 130000 | 296000 |

**7.** $Avg_{14} = 71$

$\therefore$ Total weight $= 71 \times 14 = 994$

Wrong weights 42 instead of 56, and 74 instead of 32

$\therefore$ Correct total $= 994 - 42 + 56 - 74 + 32$

$= 994 + 88 - 116 = 966$

$\therefore$ Avg weight $= \frac{966}{14} = 69$

**8.** Let '4' years ago ages (in years) be a, b

'8' years from now, ages (in years) will be a + 4 + 8, b + 4 + 8

Givena : b = 5 : 6

a + 12 : b + 12 = 8 : 9

$\frac{a}{b} = \frac{5}{6}$ and $\frac{a+12}{b+12} = \frac{8}{9}$

$6a = 5b$ ... (1)

$9a + 108 = 8b + 96$

or $9a - 8b = -12$ ... (2)

$\therefore \ 3 \times (1) - 2(2)$

$\Rightarrow 18a - 15b - 18a + 16b = 24$

$b = 24$

$\therefore \quad a = \frac{24 \times 5}{6} = 20$

Current ages are 20 + 4, 24 + 4 or 24, 28

Sum = 52 years.

**9.** Let cost of shirt be Rs. 'C'.

Sold at 15% profit.

$\therefore$ Selling price = Rs. $\frac{115}{100}$C

If cost was 5% less or $\frac{95}{100}$C and selling price was $\frac{115C}{100} - 21$, then profit = 10%.

$\Rightarrow \frac{95}{100}C \times \frac{110}{100} = \frac{115C}{100} - 21$

or $1.045C = 1.15C - 21$

or $C = \frac{21}{1.15 - 1.045} = \frac{21}{0.0105} = 200$.

# GENERAL KNOWLEDGE

## CONSTITUTION AND POLITY

**1.** ____ for States and ____ for Union Territories is the new limit of flexible fund decided by the government in the Centrally Sponsored Schemes in order to give more freedom of operation in these schemes.

(*a*) 25%, 30% (*b*) 20%,30%
(*c*)10%,35% (*d*) 50%, 20%

### ANSWER

**1.** (*a*)

## EXPLANATION

1. To meet local developmental requirements, government has issued fresh flexi-fund guidelines that will give more freedom to states in spending money under the Centrally Sponsored Schemes (CSS). Under the new norms, flexi-funds in each CSS have been increased from the current 10 per cent to 25 per cent for states and 30 per cent for Union Territories.

## CURRENT AFFAIRS

1. Which country recently decided to quit Commonwealth group?
(*a*) Maldives (*b*) Fiji
(*c*) Nigeria (*d*) Zimbabwe
2. The official mascot of the 2018 FIFA World Cup is _____ who wears _____.
(*a*) Zabivaka, glasses
(*b*) Willie, glasses
(*c*) Zaumi, Russia's kit
(*d*) Zabivaka, flag of Russia
3. _____ World's largest refugee camp, which was in news recently, is located in _____.
(*a*) Dadaab, Kenya (*b*) Zaatari, Syria
(*c*) Yida, Sudan (*d*) Katumba, Tanzania
4. Train travel insurance in India is available at a premium of _____ with effect from October 7,2016.
(*a*) 1 rupee (*b*) 2 rupees
(*c*) 92 paisa (*d*) 1 paisa
5. Which of the following banks overtook Wells Fargo as the most valuable bank in USA?
(*a*) J.S. Morgan Chase (*b*) HSBC
(*c*) Citigroup (*d*) Bank of America
6. Nobel Prize in Economics for 2016 has been given to Oliver Hart and Bengt Holmstrom for their contribution to
(*a*) Contract Theory
(*b*) Imperfect Competition
(*c*) Game theory
(*d*) Limitations on state intervention in market economy
7. The Union Government has decided to withdraw the benefit of subsidised LPG to the customers having income above
(*a*) Rs. 7.5 lakh (*b*) Rs. 10 lakh
(*c*) Rs. 12.5 lakh (*d*) Rs. 15 lakh
8. Navtej Sarna who is recently appointed as an Ambassador of _____ was Ambassador of _____ earlier.
(*a*) Canada, Israel (*b*) USA, Israel
(*c*) USA, Canada (*d*) USA, France
9. Which of the following banks recently designated P. V. Sindhu and K. Srikanth as brand ambassadors?
(*a*) Canara Bank (*b*) SBI
(*c*) PNB (*d*) Bank of Baroda
10. Which of the following companies has hired World's first robot lawyer ROSS to assist its various teams in legal research?
(*a*) Davis Polk and Wardwell
(*b*) Cravath, Swaine and Moore
(*c*) Baker Hostetler
(*d*) Latham and Watkins
11. _____ has invited India to join in developing next-generation nuclear reactors and also to participate in its fast reactor research project known as MBIR.
(*a*) Russia (*b*) US
(*c*) China (*d*) UK
12. India has launched its latest communication satellite GSAT – 18 from
(*a*) Turkey (*b*) French Guiana
(*c*) Russia (*d*) Japan
13. In which country the World's first baby was born from a new procedure that combines the DNA of three people?
(*a*) Canada (*b*) England
(*c*) Australia (*d*) US
14. Ms. _____ from _____ has been crowned Miss international 2016.
(*a*) Kylie Verzosa, Venezuela
(*b*) Kylie Verzosa, Philippines
(*c*) Edymar Martinez, Venezuela
(*d*) Edymar Martinez, Australia
15. India won _____ medals in 2017 Special Olympics World Winter Games held in Austria.
(*a*) 73 (*b*) 10
(*c*) 12 (*d*) 63
16. Recently a huge Dead Zone is discovered in
(*a*) Gulf of Mexico (*b*) Bay of Bengal
(*c*) Coasts of Namibia (*d*) Baltic Sea

## ANSWERS

| | | | | |
|---|---|---|---|---|
| **1.** (*a*) | **2.** (*a*) | **3.** (*a*) | **4.** (*c*) | **5.** (*a*) |
| **6.** (*a*) | **7.** (*b*) | **8.** (*b*) | **9.** (*d*) | **10.** (*c*) |
| **11.** (*a*) | **12.** (*b*) | **13.** (*d*) | **14.** (*b*) | **15.** (*a*) |
| **16.** (*b*) | | | | |

## EXPLANATIONS

1. The Maldives has announced that it will quit the Commonwealth following criticism from the organisation over political suppression and corruption in the island nation.
2. Zabivaka is the official mascot of the 2018 FIFA World Cup, which will be held in Russia. Representing an anthropomorphic wolf with brown and white wool T-shirt with the words RUSSIA 2018 with put on and removed orange sport glasses. The combination of white, blue and red T-shirt and shorts are the national colors of the Russian team. The student designer is Ekaterina Bocharova, and the mascot was selected by Internet voting.
3. The World's largest refugee camp is located in the Dadaab, Kenya. The Kenyan government has decided to close World's biggest refugee camp in Dadaab.
4. Train passengers booking their tickets online through the IRCTC website is being able to opt for travel insurance cover with effect from October 7, 2016 for a premium of just 92 paisa. The scheme offers travellers or their families' compensation of up to Rs. 10 lakh in the event of death or permanent total disability, Rs. 7.5 lakh for permanent partial disability, up to Rs. 2 lakh for hospitalization expenses
5. The recent drop in Wells Fargo's share price means that it no longer has a larger market capitalization than JPMorgan Chase.Wells Fargo's current market cap is $237 billion. That's down from just under $300 billion in August of last year. JPMorgan Chase, meanwhile, has seen its own market cap temporarily settle at just over $240 billion.
6. Two economists Oliver Hart and Bengt Holmstrom have won the 2016 Nobel Memorial Prize in Economic Sciences. Royal Swedish Academy of Sciences has selected them for their contributions to contract theory which tells how contracts help people deal with conflicting interests.
7. The Union Government has decided to withdraw the benefit of subsidised LPG to the customers having income above Rs.10 lakh. Consumers in Tier-I and II cities will have to submit affidavits to their LPG distributors stating that their annual income is below Rs.10 lakh to continue to receive cooking gas subsidy.
8. Navtej Sarna who is recently appointed as an Ambassador of USA was Ambassador of Israel Earlier.
9. Public sector bank Bank of Baroda has signed a principal sponsorship contract with badminton Olympians P V Sindhu and K Srikanth. The three year deal with the two players was agreed in principle before they represented and made India proud on the International stage at the Rio 2016 Olympics.
10. The world's first artificial intelligence lawyer has been employed by a law firm in the US, which will use the robot to assist its various teams in legal research. The robot called 'ROSS' is built upon Watson, IBM's cognitive computer. BakerHostetler, a US-based law firm, will licence ROSS for use in its Bankruptcy, Restructuring and Creditors' Rights team.
11. Russia has invited India to join in developing next-generation nuclear reactors and to participate in its fast-reactor research project, an official of Rosatom, the country's state atomic energy corporation, has said. The multipurpose fast research reactor project, known by the Russian acronym MBIR, is coming up as the International Research Center in Dimitrovgrad located in the Ulyanovsk region.
12. GSAT-18 is an Indian communications satellite. Built by ISRO and operated by INSAT, it carries 24 C-band, 12 extended C-band, and 12 Ku-band transponders. The satellite was launched on 5 October 2016 from the Guiana Space Centre in Kourou, French Guiana.
13. The world's first baby to be born from a new procedure that combines the DNA of three people appears to be healthy, according to doctors in the US who oversaw the treatment. The baby was born on 6 April after his Jordanian parents travelled to Mexico where they were cared for by US fertility specialists.
14. Ms. Kylie Verzosa from Philippines has been crowned Miss international 2016.
15. India's special athletes gave an impressive performance and won 73 medals in the recently concluded 2017 Special Olympics World Winter Games held in Austria.
16. A 'dead zone' of an estimated 60,000 square kilometres discovered in the Bay of Bengal. It was also found that the Bay of Bengal hosts microbial communities that can remove nitrogen but at very slow rates.

## EVERYDAY SCIENCE

1. Why a small pouch containing silica gel is often found in bottles of medicine in tablet or powder form?

   (*a*) It kills bacteria

   (*b*) It kills germs and spores

   (*c*) It absorbs moisture

   (*d*) It acts as a preservative

2. What is beaufort Scale ?

   (*a*) Scale to measure wind speed

   (*b*) Scale to measure ocean waves

   (*c*) Scale to measure sound waves

   (*d*) Scale to measure depth

3. Which of the following are optical illusions?
   (*a*) Twinkle of stars in the sky
   (*b*) Rainbow
   (*c*) Auroras
   (*d*) All of these

4. Wi-Fi uses _____ in order to transmit data whereas Li - Fi uses _____ in order to transmit data.
   (*a*) radio waves, laser
   (*b*) radio waves, visible light
   (*c*) electromagnetic waves, laser
   (*d*) infrared rays, radio waves

5. _____ is used for constructing filament of the Worlds thinnest light bulb?
   (*a*) Graphite (*b*) Graphene
   (*c*) Carbon (*d*) Tungsten

## ANSWERS

**1.** (*c*) **2.** (*a*) **3.** (*d*) **4.** (*b*) **5.** (*b*)

## EXPLANATIONS

1. A small pouch containing silica gel is often found in bottles of medicine in tablet or powder Forms, as it absorbs the moisture from the surroundings.
2. The Beaufort scale is an empirical measure that relates wind speed to observed conditions at sea or on land. Its full name is the Beaufort wind force scale.
3. Twinkle of stars in the sky, Rainbow and Auroras are optical illusions.
4. Wi-Fi uses radio waves in order to transmit data whereas Li - Fi uses visible light in order to transmit data.
5. A collaboration between mechanical engineers from the US and Korea has resulted in the creation of the world's thinnest light bulb, which is made from wonder material graphene. While we've seen graphene LED bulbs before, this is the first time ever graphene has been used to create a filament for an on-chip visible light source.

## GEOGRAPHY

1. Which of the following seas of Antarctica has been declared as world's largest marine protected area?
   (*a*) Amundsen Sea
   (*b*) Bellingshausen Sea
   (*c*) Weddell Sea
   (*d*) Ross Sea

2. The position of the Earth in its orbit, when it is at its greatest distance from the Sun causing summer in the Northern Hemisphere is
   (*a*) Apogee (*b*) Perigee
   (*c*) Aphelion (*d*) Perihelion

## ANSWERS

**1.** (*d*) **2.** (*c*)

## EXPLANATIONS

1. Antarctica's, Ross Sea has been declared as the world's largest marine protected area.
2. The position of the Earth in its orbit, when it is at its greatest distance from the Sun causing Summer in the Northern Hemisphere is called Aphelion.

## ECONOMICS

1. "Greenmail" is a type of
   (*a*) Currency Manipulation
   (*b*) Takeover Defence
   (*c*) Corporate Communication
   (*d*) Eco- friendly device

2. _____ has become the first bank in India to introduce software robotics in power banking.
   (*a*) HDFC (*b*) ICICI
   (*c*) SBI (*d*) Yes Bank

3. _____ is not a component of the Li Keqiang Index.
   (*a*) Bank Loans
   (*b*) Export
   (*c*) Electricity Consumption
   (*d*) Railway freight

4. What is the primary objective of the Governments in opting for deliberate devaluation of currency?
   (*a*) Boosts import (*b*) Boosts Internal Trade
   (*c*) Boosts exports (*d*) Increase gold reserves

## ANSWERS

**1.** (*b*) **2.** (*b*) **3.** (*b*) **4.** (*c*)

## EXPLANATIONS

1. Greenmail is a defensive maneuver aimed at thwarting a potential takeover in which the target firm purchases shares of its own stock from a raider at a price above that available to other stockholders, who are ordinarily excluded from the transaction.

2. ICICI Bank, India's largest private sector bank announced the deployment of 'Software Robotics' in over 200 business processes across various functions of the bank. The bank is the first in the country and among few, globally, to deploy 'Software Robotics' that emulates human actions to automate and perform repetitive, high volume and time consuming business tasks cutting across multiple applications.
3. Chinese Premier Li Keqiang was quoted as saying that he preferred to use a range of direct indicators of economic activity (as opposed to GDP) when assessing economic growth. His top three were electricity consumption, rail cargo volume and bank lending.
4. The primary objective of the Governments in opting for deliberate devaluation of currency is to boost the exports.

## MISCELLANEOUS (QUOTES, DAYS, BOOKS TITLES, SPORTS, BASIC LEGAL CONCEPTS)

1. In India, three women had held the post of Deputy Governor of RBI. Which of the following is not amongst them ?
   (*a*) K.J. Udeshi (*b*) Usha Thorat
   (*c*) Dr. Isher J. Ahluwalia (*d*) Shyamala Gopinath
2. _____ is the World's lightest material developed by ISRO scientists.
   (*a*) Silica Aerogel (*b*) Carbon Aerogel
   (*c*) Graphite Aerogel (*d*) Fiberol
3. The scientists from _____ have developed a catalyst to render the drinking water E. Coli free.
   (*a*) Indian Institute of Science Education and Research
   (*b*) Tata Institute of Fundamental Research
   (*c*) National Chemical Laboratory
   (*d*) Indian Institute of Sciences
4. International Day of Happiness is observed on _____ and _____ is adjudged as the happiest country in the World in World Happiness Report 2017 released by UN.
   (*a*) February 20, Denmark
   (*b*) March 20, Norway
   (*c*) February 21, Norway
   (*d*) March 21, India

## ANSWERS

**1.** (*c*) **2.** (*a*) **3.** (*d*) **4.** (*b*)

## EXPLANATIONS

1. Dr. Isher J. Ahluwalia has never held the post of Deputy Governor of RBI, while remaining all have held the post of Deputy Governor of RBI.
2. Indian scientists have claimed that they have developed the world's lightest material ever made by man, called Silica Aerogel, also referred to as "frozen smoke" or "blue air."
3. Drinking water can now be made completely free of E. coli in about 30 minutes by exposing it to sunlight, thanks to a catalyst developed by researchers at the Indian Institute of Science (IISc), Bengaluru. The bacterium E. coli is responsible for most of the water-borne bacterial infections.
4. International Day of Happiness is observed on March 20 and Norway is adjudged as the happiest country in the World in World Happiness Report 2017 released by UN.

# LEGAL APTITUDE

## TORTS

**Directions for questions 1 to 5:** Given below is a statement of legal principle followed by a factual situation. Apply the principle to the facts given below and select the most appropriate answer.

1. **Legal Principle :** Employers/Principles are vicariously liable, under the *respondeat superior* doctrine, for negligent acts or omissions by their employees/agents in the course of employment/agency. A servant/agent may be defined as any person employed by another to do work for him on the terms that he, the servant/agent, is to be subject to the control and directions of his employer/principal in respect of the manner in which his work is to be done.

   **Factual Situation :** A motor car was owned by and registered and insured in the name of A (wife) but was regarded by her and her husband (B) as "our car." B used it to go to work, and A for shopping at the weekends. B told A that if ever he was drunk and unfit to drive through, he would get a sober friend to drive him or else telephone her to come and fetch him. On the day in question the husband telephoned the wife after work and told her that he was going out with friends. He visited a number of public houses and had drinks. At some stage, he realised that he was unable to drive safely and asked a friend, C, to drive. C drove them to other public houses. After the last had been visited C offered the three friends (X, Y and Z) a lift and they got in, together with B who was in a soporific condition. C then proceeded, at his own suggestion, to drive in a direction away from the

B's home to have a meal. On the way, due to C's negligent driving, an accident occurred in which both B and C were killed and the other friends got injured. X, Y and Z brought an action against the wife both in her personal capacity and as administratrix of the husband's estate. Decide whether A is liable.

**Decision:**

(*a*) Yes, she was vicariously liable for the negligent driving of C as the principle of vicarious liability was to put responsibility on to the person, namely, in the case of a motor car, the owner, who ought in justice to bear it, and that in the case of a "family car" the owner was responsible for the use of it by the other spouse.

(*b*) No, C had not been the wife's agent in driving the husband about as he had been doing at the time of the accident. To fix vicarious liability on the owner of a motor car in a case such as the present, it must be shown that the driver was using it for the owner's purposes under delegation of a task or duty.

(*c*) No, because this is a case of *volenti non fit injuria* as X, Y and Z voluntarily took the lift knowing that C was also drunk.

(*d*) No, because C was not employed by A to drive her husband back to the home on the day of accident.

**2. Legal Principle :**

1. Battery is the intentional causation of harmful or offensive contact with another's person without that person's consent.
2. When lawfully exercising power of arrest or some other statutory power a police officer had greater rights than an ordinary citizen to restrain another.

**Factual Situation :** Two police officers on duty in a police car observed two women in the street who appeared to be soliciting for the purpose of prostitution. One of the women was known to the police as a prostitute but the other, X, was not a known prostitute. When the police officers requested X to get into the car for questioning she refused to do so and instead walked away from the car. One of the officers, a policewoman, got out of the car and followed X in order to question her regarding her identity and conduct and to caution her, if she was suspected of being a prostitute, in accordance with the approved police procedure for administering cautions for suspicious behaviour before charging a woman with being a prostitute. X refused to speak to the policewoman and walked away, whereupon the policewoman took hold of X's arm to detain her. X then swore at the policewoman and scratched the officer's arm with her fingernails. X was convicted of assaulting a police officer in the execution of her duty. She appealed against the conviction, contending that when the assault occurred the officer was not exercising her power of arrest and was acting beyond the scope of her duty in detaining X by taking hold of her arm. The police contended that the officer was acting in the execution of her duty when the assault occurred because the officer had good cause to detain X for the purpose of questioning her to see whether a caution for suspicious behaviour should be administered. Decide whether the police officer is liable for battery.

**Decision:**

(*a*) X is liable for trespass on the person of a police officer while performing her official duty.

(*b*) The policewoman had not been exercising her power of arrest when she detained X, and since in taking hold of the appellant's arm to detain her the policewoman's conduct went beyond acceptable lawful physical contact between two citizens, hence the officer's act constituted a battery on X and that she had not been acting in the execution of her duty when the assault occurred.

(*c*) The fact that the reason the police officer detained X was to caution her regarding her suspicious behaviour render the officer's conduct lawful if in detaining her she used a degree of physical contact that went beyond lawful physical contact as between two ordinary citizens.

(*d*) The police officer was on duty and performing her duty in the regular course of the work so is not liable for battery.

**3. Legal Principle :**

1. A careless person becomes liable for his negligence when he owed a duty of care to others.
2. *Volenti non fit injure* is defence to negligence.

**Factual Situation :** K was a friend of L and was teaching her to drive. Prior to such an arrangement K had sought assurances from L that appropriate insurance had been purchased in the event of accident. On the third day, L was executing a simple manoeuvre at slow speed when she panicked which resulted in the car crashing into a lamp-post injuring K. L was subsequently convicted of driving without due care and attention. L denied liability to pay compensation to K on the ground of *volenti non fit injuria* and also that she was just learning to drive and was not in complete control of the vehicle. Decide.

**Decision:**

(*a*) L is liable as the defence of volenti non fit injure was not applicable. Secondly, that the duty of care owed by a learner driver to the public (including passengers) was to be measured against the same standard that would be applied to any other driver.

(*b*) L is not liable as K voluntarily accompanied her.

(*c*) L is not liable as she is just learning to drive and duty of care rests upon the instructor.

(*d*) L is not liable as a learner driver do not owe a duty of care towards public in general and towards the passenger in specific.

4. **Legal Principle :** An unlawful interference with a person's use or enjoyment of land or some right over or in connection with it is a nuisance in tort. The fact that the plaintiff "came to the nuisance" by knowingly acquiring property in the vicinity of the defendant's premises is not a defense to nuisance. However, an act cannot be a nuisance if it is imperatively demanded by public convenience. Thus, when the public welfare requires it, a nuisance may be permitted for special purposes.

**Factual Situation:** D owned and occupied an estate about two miles from RAF Wittering, an operational and training base for Harrier Jump Jets. D claimed that they suffered severe noise disturbance every time the Harrier pilots carried out training circuits: an average of 70 times a day. D alleged that the noise nuisance constituted a very serious interference with their enjoyment of their land. D instituted judicial proceedings against the defendants, the Ministry of Defence (MoD), damages amounting to Rs. 1,00,00,000. The MoD denied liability and raised defence that the Harrier training was undertaken for the public benefit and that they had prescriptive right over the land as D had bought their property at a time when RAF Wittering was already established so he cannot claim compensation as he already knew about existence of RAF Wittering near his property.

**Decision:**

(*a*) D is not entitled to compensation as the training of pilots is a public welfare activity.

(*b*) The Harrier training is not an ordinary use of land and that although there was a public benefit to the continued training of Harrier pilots, D should not be required to bear the cost of the public benefit.

(*c*) D is not entitled to compensation as his property is two miles away from the training base.

(*d*) D will not get compensation as the training activity does not amount to nuisance and D had full knowledge about the training activities when he purchased the land.

5. **Legal Principle :**

1. Negligence is the absence of care on the part of one party which results in some damage to the other party.
2. Generally, a person is under no duty to control another to prevent his doing damage to a third party.
3. The foreseeability test basically asks whether the person causing the injury should have reasonably foreseen the general consequences that would result because of his or her conduct.
4. Statutory authority implies that an act is done by a person to fulfil his duty imposed by the State. Statutory authority is a valid defence under the law of torts.

**Factual Situation :** Ten borstal trainees were working on an island in a harbour in the custody and under the control of three officers. During the night, seven of them escaped. It was claimed that at the time of the escape the officers had retired to bed. The seven got on board a yacht, moored off the island and set it in motion. They collided with another yacht, the property of X and damaged it. X sued the Home office for the amount of the damage. Decide whether on the facts pleaded in the statement of claim the Home Office, its servants or agents owed any duty of care to X capable of giving rise to a liability in damages with respect to the detention of persons undergoing sentences of borstal training or with respect to the manner in which such persons were treated, employed, disciplined, controlled or supervised whilst undergoing such sentences.

**Decision :**

(*a*) The Home office is not liable as they are performing statutory duty and has immunity from liability in negligence.

(*b*) The trainees are liable and not the Home Officers as the injury to X's property could not be reasonably foreseen by the officers.

(*c*) The fact that the immediate damage to the property of X was caused by the acts of third persons, the trainees, prevent the existence of a duty on the part of the officers towards X.

(*d*) The taking by the trainees of the nearby yacht and the causing of damage to the other yacht which belonged to X ought to have been foreseen by the borstal officers as likely to occur if they failed to exercise proper control or supervision; in the particular circumstances, the officers prima facie owed a duty of care to X.

**Directions for question :** The following questions consist of two statements, one labelled as 'Assertion' and the other as 'Reason'. Read both the statements carefully and answer using the codes given below.

(*a*) Both A and R are true and R is the correct explanation of A

(*b*) Both A and R are true but R is not the true explanation of A

(*c*) A is true but R is false

(*d*) A is false but R is true

6. **Assertion (A) :** A files a false and frivolous civil suit against B and B wins the case, he cannot file another civil suit for damages and costs.

   **Reason (R) :** In a civil suit, damage of reputation is absent because the action is tried in public and if person wins his case then his reputation will be re-established.

## ANSWERS

**1.** (*b*) **2.** (*b*) **3.** (*a*) **4.** (*b*) **5.** (*d*) **6.** (*b*)

## EXPLANATIONS

1. No, C had not been the wife's agent in driving the husband about as he had been doing at the time of the accident. To fix vicarious liability on the owner of a motor car in a case such as the present, it must be shown that the driver was using it for the owner's purposes under delegation of a task or duty.
2. The policewoman had not been exercising her power of arrest when she detained X, and since in taking hold of the appellant's arm to detain her the policewoman's conduct went beyond acceptable lawful physical contact between two citizens, hence the officer's act constituted a battery on X and that she had not been acting in the execution of her duty when the assault occurred.
3. L is liable as the defence of volenti non fit injuria was not applicable. Secondly, that the duty of care owed by a learner driver to the public (including passengers) was to be measured against the same standard that would be applied to any other driver.
4. The Harrier training is not an ordinary use of land and that although there was public benefit to the continued training of Harrier pilots, D should not be required to bear the cost of the public benefit.
5. The taking by the trainees of the nearby yacht and the causing of damage to the other yacht which belonged to X ought to have been foreseen by the borstal officers as likely to occur if they failed to exercise proper control or supervision; in the particular circumstances, the officers prima facie owed a duty of care to X.

## LAW OF CONTRACTS

**Directions for questions 1 to 2:** Given below is a statement of legal principle followed by a factual situation. Apply the principle to the facts given below and select the most appropriate answer.

1. Irrespective of your answer to Q. 71, assume it is a case of undue influence. Decide whether the bank has done enough to allay concerns of undue influence.

   (*a*) The bank had not made all reasonable steps to allay themselves of the concerns regarding undue influence. The fact that, on advice from the bank, the defendant did not seek independent advice, should have been taken as confirmation of undue influence.

   (*b*) Yes, the Bank has advised Pragya that she should take independent legal advice before putting her property up as security for the debt.

   (*c*) Pragya has a duty to be aware of the consequences of her act.

   (*d*) Bank has done enough as it had notified Pragya that the guarantee was unlimited in both time and financial amount.

2. **Legal Principle :** The acceptance must be absolute and unqualified, leaving no ground for doubt or uncertainty. If the acceptance is conditional, no valid contract is formed, and the offer can be withdrawn at any moment till the absolute acceptance has taken place within reasonable time of such offer.

   **Factual Situation :** Delhi Government conducted an auction for the sale of license of wine shop. X offered the highest bid which was provisionally accepted "...subject to the confirmation of Chief Commissioner who may reject any bid without assigning any reasons." Since X failed to deposit the required amount. Chief Commissioner rejected the bid. The government held X liable for the difference between the bid offered by him and the highest bid accepted in re-auction, and commenced proceedings for the recovery of the sum. It was contended on behalf of the government of Delhi that X was under a legal obligation to pay the difference as it was due to his default that a resale of the excise shop was ordered and hence X was liable for the deficiency in price and all expenses of such resale which was caused by his default.

   **Decide, giving reason, whether X is liable to make payment to the Delhi Government.**

   (*a*) No, X is not liable to make payment as the shop was sold to the highest bidder.

   (*b*) X is liable to pay because the Government of Delhi has to conduct re-auction and also suffered loss in the sale of the shop.

   (*c*) X is liable because his bid was accepted but he failed to deposit the required amount on time.

   (*d*) No, contract for sale was not complete till the bid was confirmed by the Chief Commissioner and till such confirmation ; the bidder was entitled to withdraw the bid.

## ANSWERS

**1.** (*a*) **2.** (*d*)

## EXPLANATIONS

1. The bank had not made all reasonable steps to allay themselves of the concerns regarding undue influence. The fact that; on advice from the bank, the defendant did not seek independent advice, should, have been taken as confirmation of undue influence'
2. No, contract for sale was not complete till the bid was confirmed by the Chief Commissioner and till such confirmation the bidder was entitled to withdraw the bid.

## CRIMINAL LAW

**Direction :** The following questions consist of two statements, one labelled as 'Assertion' and the other as 'Reason'. Read both the statements carefully and answer using the codes given below.

(*a*) Both A and R are true and R is the correct explanation of A

(*b*) Both A and R are true but R is not the true explanation of A

(*c*) A is true but R is false

(*d*) A is false but R is true

1. **Assertion (A) :** If a convict is prepared to give an interview to journalists and video-graphers, the facility should be allowed to the latter.

   **Reason (R) :** Position of a person sentenced to death is not inferior to that of a citizen.

## ANSWER

1. (*a*)

## CONSTITUTIONAL LAW AND LEGAL FRAMEWORK

**Directions for question :** Given below is a statement of legal principle followed by a factual situation. Apply the principle to the facts given below and select the most appropriate answer.

1. **Legal Principle :** Article 19(1) (*d*)ofthe Constitution of India guarantees to all citizens the right to move freely throughout the territory of India. But at the same time, Article 19(5) empowers the State to impose reasonable restrictions on the freedom of movement on the ground of interest of general public.

   **Factual Situation :** Wearing of helmet is made compulsory for all two-wheeler riders by a law enacted by the State. The constitutionality of the law is questioned before the High Court on the ground that it violates Article 19(1 )(*d*) of the petitioner. Will the petitioner succeed ?

   **Decision :**

   (*a*) Yes, because the restriction is not reasonable and no interest of general public is protected by this law.

   (*b*) No, because the restriction is reasonable as it intends to protect interest of general public by preventing loss of lives of citizen of India.

   (*c*) Yes, because freedom of movement is a fundamental right of every citizen of India and the State cannot take it away by way of legislation but has to amend the Constitution to take away the fundamental rights.

   (*d*) No, because the freedom of movement will not be violated by the impugned legislation.

**Directions for questions 2 to 6:** The following questions consist of two statements, one labelled as 'Assertion' and the other as 'Reason'. Read both the statements carefully and answer using the codes given below.

(*a*) Both A and R are true and R is the correct explanation of A

(*b*) Both A and R are true but R is not the true explanation of A

(*c*) A is true but R is false

(*d*) A is false but R is true

2. **Assertion (A) :** The framers of the Indian Constitution were keen to preserve the democratic values to which Indians had attached the highest importance in their struggle for freedom.

   **Reason (R) :** The Constitution describes India as a Union of States, thereby implying the indestructible nature of its unity.

3. **Assertion (A) :** The "basic features" of the Constitution cannot be amended by exercising the power of Amendment under Article 368.

   **Reason (R) :** Though Fundamental Rights, as such are not immune from Amendment *en bloc*, particular Rights or Parts thereof may be held as "basic feature."

4. **Assertion (A) :** Legislations which gives a wide power to the executive to select cases for special treatment, without indicating the policy, may be set aside as violative of equality.

   **Reason (R) :** Article 14 of the Constitution provides that the State shall not deny to any person equality before law or equal protection of laws within the territory of India.

5. **Assertion (A) :** If the Constitution is flexible it may be playing at the whims and caprices of the ruling party.

   **Reason (R) :** The framers of the Indian Constitution were keen to avoid excessive rigidity.

**6. Assertion (A) :** A person suffering from AIDS can be restricted in his movements by law.

**Reason (R) :** Where policy is laid down, discretion is not of reasonableness.

**7.** A minority community may reserve upto _____ seats for members of its own community in an educational institution established and administered by it even if the institution receives aid from the State.

(*a*) 50% (*b*) 40%
(*c*) 33% (*d*) 27%

**8.** After Delhi and Goa, which is the third Indian State to have child - friendly court?

(*a*) West Bengal (*b*) Karnataka
(*c*) Telangana (*d*) Tamil Nadu

**9.** Which of the following statements are true regarding the Constitution (One Hundred and First Amendment) Act, 2016?

I. GST Act is a comprehensive direct tax on manufacture, sale and consumption of goods and services throughout India.

II. The Act will transform India into a common market, harmonising myriads of State and Central levies into a national goods and services tax which is expected to boost manufacturing and reduce corruption.

III. It provides for Constitution of a Goods and Services Tax Council by inserting Article 297A in the Constitution.

IV. GST will be based on input tax credit method.

(*a*) I, II and III (*b*) II, III and IV
(*c*) I, II and IV (*d*) All of the above

**10.** Central Vigilance Commissioner shall hold office for a term of ____ years from the date on which he enters upon his office.

(*a*) 4 (*b*) 3
(*c*) 2 (*d*) 1

**11.** In *Youth Bar Association V. Union of India*, the Supreme Court directed to upload copies of FIR within _____ hours on police website.

(*a*) 48 (*b*) 12
(*c*) 24 (*d*) 48 – 72

**12.** India's first court-annexed mediation centre was established in

(*a*) Delhi (*b*) Tamil Nadu
(*c*) Chennai (*d*) Karnataka

**13.** Which is the first country to allow voting through mobile phones?

(*a*) Estonia (*b*) Finland
(*c*) France (*d*) Germany

**14.** All students graduating from academic year _____ onwards need to clear the All India Bar Examination in order to practice law in India.

(*a*) 2007-08 (*b*) 2009-10
(*c*) 2008-09 (*d*) 2010-11

**15.** "The people have a right, an inalienable, indisputable, indefeasible, divine right to that most dreaded and envied kind of knowledge – I mean, of the character and conduct of their rulers." Who said this?

(*a*) Abraham Lincoln
(*b*) John Adams
(*c*) Martin Luther
(*d*) Mahatma Gandhi

**16.** *John Doe* order in India is known as

(*a*) Ashok Kumar Order
(*b*) DMCA Order
(*c*) Take Down Order
(*d*) Injunction

**17.** In 2016, the Supreme Court has clarified that the "Third Gender" will include(s)

(*a*) Transgender (*b*) Gays and Lesbians
(*c*) Bisexuals (*d*) All of these

**18.** New Zealand Government has granted legal status of a person to a ____ after a legal battle of 140 years.

(*a*) National Park (*b*) Tree
(*c*) Mountain (*d*) River

**19.** Which of the following Articles of the Constitution of India authorize the Chief Justice of India to request a retired Judge to join the Supreme Court?

(*a*) 129 (*b*) 128
(*c*) 127 (*d*) 126

**20.** The 'Public Trust' the doctrine is related to

(*a*) Charitable Institution (*b*) Environment
(*c*) Journalism (*d*) Public Offices

**21.** The Delhi High Court has asked Facebook to ban children below ______ years of age from creating an account.

(*a*) 10 (*b*) 13
(*c*) 16 (*d*) 18

**22.** Which one of the following decided to set up a website, which will compare the World's Constitutions by themes online "to arm drafters with a better tool for Constitution design and writing"?

(*a*) UN (*b*) Google
(*c*) Microsoft (*d*) Amnesty

**23.** Mental Health Care Bill 2016 seeks to

1. Decriminalise suicide
2. Prohibit electro-convulsive therapy
3. Provide right to make Advance Directives
4. Provide for seclusion and solitary confinement in few cases

(*a*) 1, 2 and 4 (*b*) 2, 3 and 4

(*c*) 1, 2 and 3 (*d*) All of the above

**24.** What is the new minimum wage of non-agricultural, unskilled workers of the Central Government as announced by the Union Government on August 30, 2016 ?

(*a*) Rs. 350 per day (*b*) Rs. 250 per day

(*c*) Rs. 246 per day (*d*) Rs. 400 per day

**25.** Maternity Benefits (Amendment) Bill, 2016 provides _____ weeks of full paid maternity leave to women who work in organised sector.

(*a*) 12 (*b*) 26

(*c*) 24 (*d*) 32

## ANSWERS

| | | | | |
|---|---|---|---|---|
| **1.** (*b*) | **2.** (*b*) | **3.** (*b*) | **4.** (*a*) | **5.** (*b*) |
| **6.** (*b*) | **7.** (*a*) | **8.** (*c*) | **9.** (*b*)* | **10.** (*a*) |
| **11.** (*c*) | **12.** (*b*) | **13.** (*a*) | **14.** (*b*) | **15.** (*b*) |
| **16.** (*a*) | **17.** (*a*) | **18.** (*d*) | **19.** (*b*) | **20.** (*b*) |
| **21.** (*b*) | **22.** (*b*) | **23.** (*c*) | **24.** (*a*) | **25.** (*b*) |

## EXPLANATIONS

**1.** No, because the restriction is reasonable as it intends to protect interest of general public by preventing loss of lives of citizen of India.

**9.** Point III is not correct. It would be article 279A and then correct answer would be (*b*).

# MODEL PAPERS

# AILET PATTERN

## MODEL PAPER-I

**INSTRUCTIONS:**

**Time: 90 Minutes**

1. This Model Paper will give you an insight into the pattern of the **AILET (All India Law Etrance Test)**. Undertaking this model test under the mentioned stipulated time frame will allow you to understand real test scenario.
2. This Question Paper consists of five sections viz. A(English), B(General Knowledge), C(Legal Aptitude),D(Logical Reasoning) and E (Mathematics).The total number of questions are 150.
3. Each Question contains one mark. There is NO NEGATIVE MARKING

## SECTION – A: ENGLISH

**Directions for questions 1 to 6:** Read the following passage carefully and answer the questions that follow. Please note that for some of the questions, more than one choice could answer the question. However, you need to select the choice that most appropriately and completely answers the question.

One of Kannabiran's formulations that had a profound impact on demystifying the relationship between the state, citizen and law enforcement, concerned with the centrality of the state in the administration of criminal justice. While it is in the course of crime detection, investigation and apprehension of the accused that human rights violations ordinarily take place, it is in the realm of state violence that the fault lines underlying existing criminal jurisprudence surface. Stressing that there is no permanence about any definition of a crime and criminal law, he pointed to the absolute power accorded to the state to implement the law and the real context of abuse, misuse and vindictive administration of the laws. We have used this particular dictum in innumerable cases involving political challenges to the state particularly in major TADA cases involving minorities and dalits. In May 2009 at the height of the war against Tamils in Sri Lanka, a peaceful protest took place in Coimbatore against army convoys suspected to be taking arms and explosives to help the Sri Lankan army. Two PUCL observers were also arrested and charged with sedition! We used Kannabiran's classic definition in arguments inside courts and in public meetings. Citizens at large clearly understood the message. The simplicity of the formulation masked the profundity of its understanding of criminal law.

Kannabiran forever urged us, as also other lawyers, to never take for granted any audience; he exhorted us to address all fora – from the lowest court to a meeting of jurists – as though we were taking a class. In our 17 years of close interaction we never once heard him use an expletive or speak ill of any person. While he was caustic in his comments, he maintained a dignity and decorum in his political and legal criticism. He was by no means a "soft" person and could be as hard-hitting as anyone when presenting his analysis. But to many of us young activists and lawyers, he offered a different role model – of a person who through personal example became the embodiment of the ethical and political values he advocated.

Kannabiran's contribution to human rights was not only in the field of criminal law. Actually he played a very direct, proactive and catalytic role on many issues of major social and political import. From social justice issues to environmental rights, from issues of election rights to the right of sexual minorities there were no taboo issues for Kannabiran.

1. Which of the following cannot be inferred from the passage?
   - (*a*) Kannabiran believes that definitions of crime and criminal laws are prone to changes.
   - (*b*) Kannabiran contributed to human rights.
   - (*c*) The process of crime detection usually leads to violation of human rights.
   - (*d*) None of these
2. As per your understanding of the passage, the attitude of the author towards Kannabiran appears to be
   - (*a*) smitten
   - (*b*) eulogistic
   - (*c*) complaisant
   - (*d*) ambivalent
3. "The simplicity of the formulation masked the profundity of its understanding of criminal law" pertains to which of the following?
   - (*a*) There being no permanence about any definition of crime and criminal law.
   - (*b*) The absolute power accorded to the state to implement the law.
   - (*c*) The real context of abuse, misuse and vindictive administration of the laws.
   - (*d*) The centrality of the state in the administration of criminal justice.

**4.** The excerpt is most likely a part of

(*a*) a legal report (*b*) a biography

(*c*) an obituary (*d*) a paean

**5.** "There were no taboo issues for Kannabiran" by this, the author means to say

(*a*) that Kannabiran did not have any reservation in deliberating any kind of issues.

(*b*) that Kannabiran played a very important role in major social justice issues and ones pertaining to environmental rights.

(*c*) that Kannabiran played a very proactive role in many issues of election rights and the rights of sexual minorities.

(*d*) that's Kannibaran played a very direct, proactive and catalytic role in issues falling under the umbrella of human rights as a whole.

**6.** In the context of the passage, which of the following words cannot be used as a substitute of the word PROFOUND?

(*a*) deep (*b*) great

(*c*) recondite (*d*) strong

**For questions 7 and 8:** Each question consists of two capitalized words that have a certain relationship to each other, followed by four pairs of words. Select the pair that is related to each other in the same way as the capitalized pair.

**7.** CONCERNED : OBSESSED

(*a*) malleable : tractable (*b*) faithful : resolute

(*c*) firm : unyielding (*d*) critic : quizzical

**8.** SIMPER : SMILE

(*a*) babble : talk (*b*) look : kink

(*c*) wink : eye (*d*) leer : ogle

**Directions for questions 9 to 25:** Complete the sentences by filling the blanks with the grammatically correct option.

**9.** Amit Khurana ______ heavily in the telecom industry before the Recession.

(*a*) has invested (*b*) have been investing

(*c*) had invested (*d*) invested

**10.** By the time he finishes this semester, Vinod ______ nothing but mosquitoes for two years.

(*a*) will have been studying

(*b*) will study

(*c*) studied

(*d*) studies

**11.** Sumit __________ through the entire class.

(*a*) is sleeping (*b*) slept

(*c*) will have slept (*d*) had slept

**12.** For the last 30 years the proceeds of rising prosperity __________ increasingly colonised by big business and a small rich elite.

(*a*) has been (*b*) have been

(*c*) are (*d*) is

**13.** We would have passed if we __________ harder.

(*a*) studied (*b*) study

(*c*) had studied (*d*) will have studied

**14.** It is time we __________.

(*a*) start (*b*) shall start

(*c*) started (*d*) can start

**15.** One of the most ____________, near the river's mouth, is now in danger of being shut down.

(*a*) successful diversion

(*b*) successful diversions

(*c*) unsuccessful diversion

(*d*) successful diversification

**16.** Each of the answers ______ worth 20 points.

(*a*) are (*b*) is

(*c*) were (*d*) have

**17.** Neither of the two washing machines ____ working.

(*a*) is (*b*) are

(*c*) were (*d*) have been

**18.** The politician as well as his brothers _______ going to prison.

(*a*) is (*b*) are

(*c*) were (*d*) have been

**19.** Neither my sisters nor my mother _______ going to sell the car.

(*a*) is (*b*) are

(*c*) were (*d*) has

**20.** Mumps _____ a dangerous disease for pregnant women.

(*a*) is (*b*) are

(*c*) were (*d*) have been

**21.** It is not the faculty members but the Principal who ________ about the issue of holidays.

(*a*) decide (*b*) decides

(*c*) have been deciding (*d*) are deciding

**22.** The patient eventually pulled _________ after having had a close brush with death.

(*a*) out (*b*) away

(*c*) down (*d*) through

**23.** My wife brought ___________ my peccadilloes in front of my boss again.

(*a*) around (*b*) up

(*c*) about (*d*) in

**24.** Ritu and Rashi have been quarreling ________ forty minutes.

(*a*) until (*b*) throughout

(*c*) since (*d*) for

**25.** When Nina went to buy the movie tickets, there was nobody ________ the ticket window.

(*a*) on (*b*) at

(*c*) under (*d*) next to

**Directions for questions 26 to 33:** Select the option that is closest in meaning to the word/ phrase given in bold in the given sentences.

**26.** The newspaper launched a **vitriolic** attack on the president.

(*a*) invective (*b*) temperate

(*c*) moderate (*d*) belligerent

**27.** The movie is a **pallid** version of the classic novel.

(*a*) florid (*b*) dull

(*c*) better (*d*) modern

**28.** The coach **despised** the new player.

(*a*) deplored (*b*) adored

(*c*) abhorred (*d*) protected

**29.** The party appeared **oblivious** to the mounting pressures for political reform.

(*a*) unmindful (*b*) forgetful

(*c*) insensible (*d*) cognizant

**30.** The incident ruined an otherwise **immaculate** safety record.

(*a*) pure (*b*) perfect

(*c*) decorous (*d*) modest

**31.** According to Neha's mother, she has a very **comely** personality.

(*a*) serene (*b*) gratifying

(*c*) attractive (*d*) bold

**32.** Her resources were limited but she **kept up** the good work.

(*a*) persevered in (*b*) adhered to

(*c*) labored (*d*) complied to

**33.** He was told to **discard** all the negative thoughts.

(*a*) retain

(*b*) put away

(*c*) put by

(*d*) embrace

**Directions for questions 34 and 35:** In the following questions, four alternatives are given for the idiom/phrase marked in bold in the sentence. Select the alternative that best expresses the meaning of the idiom/ phrase.

**34.** I'd love to have lunch with you but we're **rushed off our feet** at the moment.

(*a*) in a very difficult situation

(*b*) injured

(*c*) having no money

(*d*) extremely busy

**35.** The refugees are living **cheek by jowl** in a temporary camp.

(*a*) depressed and unhappy

(*b*) crammed uncomfortably close together

(*c*) full of optimism and hope

(*d*) in harmony

## SECTION – B: GENERAL KNOWLEDGE

**36.** Who among the following Indian-origin-boy won 'National Geographic Bee prize 2012'?

(*a*) Rahul Nagvekar (*b*) Vansh Jain

(*c*) Varun Mahadevan (*d*) Rohit Goswami

**37.** The Lok Sabha recently passed the Anand Marriage Act, meeting a long-standing demand of which one of the following communities, for a law allowing them to register their marriages under a separate Act, instead of the Hindu Marriage Act?

(*a*) Parsis (*b*) Sikh

(*c*) Jain (*d*) Buddhists

**38.** Recently, which among the following States has imposed a ban on the manufacture, storage and sale of gutkha, pan masala, and their variants in the State?

(*a*) Kerala (*b*) Tamil Nadu

(*c*) Bihar (*d*) Uttar Pradesh

**39.** Khesari Dal, also known as Grass pea, was banned for consumption in 1961 as it was believed that Beta-N-Oxalyl-aminoalanine, a neuro-toxic amino-acid in the legume, caused neurolathyrim or a paralysis of the lower limbs. Which among the following States where the sale for human consumption was not banned?

(*a*) West Bengal (*b*) Madhya Pradesh

(*c*) Bihar (*d*) Odisha

**40.** Kudumbasree Mission experiment, involving 3.5 million women, is becoming a replicable model for the nation for the abolition of poverty. The mission is introduced in which one of the following states?

(*a*) Kerala

(*b*) Tamil Nadu

(*c*) Andhra Pradesh

(*d*) Karnataka

**41.** The Princess Tower, which the Guinness World Records website has declared the world's tallest residential building, is situated in which one of the following countries?

(*a*) United Arab Emirates

(*b*) USA

(*c*) Malaysia

(*d*) China

**42.** The Union government has set up an expert technical group to review the Tendulkar Committee methodology for estimating poverty and overhaul the norms in keeping with the present-day prices. The committee has been established under the chairmanship of:

(*a*) C. Rangarajan (*b*) Ram Nandan Prasad

(*c*) V. Kelkar (*d*) Tarvinder Singh Bhasin

**43.** Who among the following is the first Indian to qualify for marathon in 36 years for Olympic 2012?

(*a*) Arun Bhardwaj (*b*) Ram Singh Yadav

(*c*) Sandeep Kumar (*d*) Kashinath

**44.** Who among the following tennis players won the Italian Open women's tennis tournament 2012?

(*a*) Li Na (*b*) Serena Williams

(*c*) Maria Sharapova (*d*) Kim Clijsters

**45.** A seven-year-old boy has become the youngest mountaineer to successfully trek to the Everest Base Camp (EBC) in Nepal, at a height of 5,364 metres, and scale Mount Kalapattar at an altitude of 5,554 metres. What is the name of the boy?

(*a*) Arjun Vishnuvardhan

(*b*) Shyam Sundar

(*c*) M. Aditya

(*d*) Aaryan Balaji

**46.** The TAPI pipeline will have a capacity to carry 90 million metric standard cubic metres a day (mmscmd) of gas for a 30-year period and is likely to become operational by 2018.Which among the following countries is not associated with TAPI project?

(*a*) Tajikistan (*b*) Turkmenistan

(*c*) Afghanistan (*d*) Pakistan

**47.** Who among the following tennis players won the Italian Open men's tennis tournament 2012?

(*a*) Novak Djokovic (*b*) Carlos Moyà

(*c*) Roger Federer (*d*) Rafael Nadal

**48.** The Union Government has recently accepted 69 recommendations of the committee to ensure transparency in allocation and pricing of natural resources like land, coal, petroleum and natural gas. The Committee was headed by:

(*a*) Ashok Chawla (*b*) C. Rangrajan

(*c*) N. Bhagawati (*d*) Vijay Kelkar

**49.** Sachin Tendulkar remained the highest-ranked Indian batsman at the 12th spot in the latest ICC Test charts. The batsmen's chart is headed by:

(*a*) Shivnarain Chanderpaul

(*b*) Azhar Ali

(*c*) Jacques Kallis

(*d*) AB de Villiers

**50.** Under the Rani Lakshmibai Pension Yojana women living below the poverty line would be paid Rs.400 per month. Which among the following State governments launched Rani Lakshmibai Pension Yojana?

(*a*) Madhya Pradesh (*b*) Uttar Pradesh

(*c*) Rajasthan (*d*) Maharashtra

**51.** What is AAHAR?

(*a*) Mid-day meal scheme

(*b*) Food Security Mission

(*c*) National Mission for Sustainable Agriculture

(*d*) International Food & Hospitality Fair

**52.** __________ is a military award of India awarded in recognition to peace-time service of the most exceptional order.

(*a*) Param Vishist Seva Medal

(*b*) Ati Vishist Seva Medal

(*c*) Uttam Yudh Seva Medal

(*d*) None of the above

**53.** What is XBRL?

(*a*) Language for electronic communication

(*b*) Technology for electronic communication

(*c*) Device for electronic communication

(*d*) None of the above

**54.** 'Nowcasting' is a term relevant to

(*a*) Web based broadcasting

(*b*) Weather forecasting

(*c*) Television broadcasting

(*d*) None of the above

**55.** The National Science Day (NSD) is celebrated on __________.

(*a*) February 28 (*b*) March 28

(*c*) January 28 (*d*) None of the above

**56.** WHO has taken India's name off the list of polio endemic countries in view of the remarkable progress that India achieved by being polio free for the past one full year. Following this Polio remains endemic in only three countries including all but one of the following:

(*a*) Nigeria (*b*) Pakistan

(*c*) Afghanistan (*d*) Nepal

**57.** Prime Minister of India recently constituted an Expert Committee under the Chairmanship of ____, to examine issues relating to the sugar sector.

(a) Kaushik Basu (b) C. Rangarajan

(c) Ashok Gulati (d) None of the above

**58.** National Bravery Awards for Indian children are given yearly by Government of India together with ________.

(a) UNICEF

(b) CRY

(c) Indian Council for Child Welfare (ICCW)

(d) None of the above

**59.** The Bharatendu Harishchandra Awards are given to encourage original and creative writing in Hindi on the subjects related to various disciplines of_____.

(a) Law (b) Mass Communication

(c) Theatre (d) None of the above

**60.** The Committee to suggest measures to curb ragging was chaired by ________.

(a) Prof. S.G. Dhande (b) Prof. A.K. Agrawal

(c) Dr. R.K. Raghavan (d) None of the above

**61.** National Energy Conservation Day is observed on __________.

(a) December 14 (b) November 14

(c) October 14 (d) None of the above

**62.** What is 'Lakshya'?

(a) Pilotless Target Aircraft

(b) Ballistic Missile

(c) Unmanned Aerial Combat Vehicle

(d) None of the above

**63.** "The Collaborator" book is authored by

(a) Mirza Waheed (b) Basharat Peer

(c) Salman Rashdie (d) None of the above

**64.** GLONASS is a satellite system operated by

(a) USA (b) Russia

(c) UK (d) China

**65.** World Post Day is celebrated on _____ every year.

(a) October 9 (b) November 9

(c) December 9 (d) January 9

**66.** The train covering longest route on Indian Railways network is

(a) Vivek Express

(b) Himsagar Express

(c) Akhand Express

(d) None of the above

**67.** Which UN Agency has granted full membership to Palestine?

(a) United Nations Educational, Scientific and Cultural Organization (UNESCO)

(b) United Nations Industrial Development Organisation (UNIDO)

(c) United Nations Fund for Population Activites (UNFPA)

(d) None of the above

**68.** The Red Ribbon Express Train is part of an initiative to raise awareness about

(a) Cardiovascular Diseases

(b) AIDS

(c) Tuberculosis

(d) Lung Cancer

**69.** National Voters' Day is observed on

(a) January 25 (b) January 26

(c) December 26 (d) December 25

**70.** What is CERT-In ?

(a) Agency to tackle cyber security threats

(b) Authority that grants certificates of recognition to companies

(c) Agency for assessment of risk of epidemics

(d) None of the above

## SECTION – C: LEGAL APTITUDE

**71. Principle:** A negligent act is one where a person commits an act which is normal in the usual course of events but commits it in such a manner as to endanger the personal safety or property of those around him.

**Explanation:** A certain amount of carelessness is of essence in negligence.

**Facts:** Mahabali was agitated because of a business deal one morning, in which he had given away three plots of land to the dwarf's society. At that time he had a heated argument with his adviser Shukracharya, and in the fit of rage he threw a paperweight at him. The paperweight hit Shukracharya in his left eye and was left blinded in that eye.

(a) Mahabali has committed an act of negligence as throwing a paperweight on your advisor is morally wrong under law of tort.

(b) Mahabali has not committed an act of negligence.

(c) Shukracharya can sue him for negligence, but should also simultaneously make a criminal complaint.

(d) Mahabali has committed negligence. This is evident from the damage he has caused.

**72. Principle:** Every person owes a duty of care to his neighbor.

**Explanation:** Duty of care implies an obligation upon one person to take reasonable precautions to ensure harm isn't caused to the other person by that first person.

**Facts:** Ben Ten Co. sends a bus across Dilli for its employees. Usually the driver stops the bus at various points in the city and employees of the company get on at different stops. On one such stop, Billu who is not an employee of the company wrongfully gets on to the bus. The driver does not notice this and carries on. Subsequently the bus meets an accident due to the negligence of the driver and Billu is severely injured.

(*a*) Billu cannot claim damages because he was a trespasser.

(*b*) The driver and the company owe a duty of care to Billu.

(*c*) Billu is not the neighbor of the driver or the company so he cannot claim damages.

(*d*) If Billu can prove that he got on to the bus by mistake and not with fraudulent intent, then he can claim damages.

**73. Principle:** Every person is responsible for the direct and indirect effects of his actions; provided it can be proved that the indirect effects were reasonably foreseeable.

**Explanation:** A person is only responsible for his own acts.

**Facts:** Berlusconi is driving his BMW car and hits the rear bumper of a large truck which is parked on a slope. This sets the truck in motion and it in turn knocks down a pedestrian, killing him immediately. The body of the pedestrian is severely mangled in blood which is seen by Antonia, the wife of the pedestrian. Seeing her husband dead, she faints and suffers mental trauma. Antonia wants to sue Berlusconi on the grounds of mental trauma suffered by her.

(*a*) Antonia can sue in the capacity of a bystander who watched the horrific accident as well as in her capacity as wife of deceased.

(*b*) Antonia can sue only in the capacity of a bystander.

(*c*) Antonia can sue in her capacity as wife of deceased.

(*d*) Antonia cannot sue.

**74. Principle:** An event which cannot be avoided in spite of reasonable precaution taken by a reasonable person does not give rise to any liability.

**Explanation**: The person alleged of the act need not specially prove all the precautions he has taken.

**Facts:** Arjuna was hunting animals in Khandava Vana forest. A bullet shot by him at a cliff swallow unfortunately deflected off a rock face and hit Duryodhana who was also out hunting in the same forest. Duryodhana wants to sue Arjuna.

(*a*) Arjuna is not liable as shooting off swallow is a legal activity and therefore any accident occurring in the process of doing it legally does not amount to a wrong.

(*b*) Arjuna is not liable as the shot was fired towards a swallow only and the deflection was an accident.

(*c*) Arjuna is liable as he should have taken greater care while shooting and should have shot the gun only when he had a clear shot at the swallow.

(*d*) Arjuna is liable as his shot was not during his conduct as a reasonable man, but was an act of carelessness.

**75. Principle:** When a person voluntarily undertakes an activity, he accepts all the risks that may normally be associated with that activity.

**Explanation**: It is no defence to claim that one did not know of the associated risks.

**Facts:** Bheema is giving a display of his strength against Jarasandha, who had challenged him to a wrestling match. One of the people watching is Vrushabhaketu, who has been ordered to stand guard by Jarasandha. When Bheema finally defeats Jarasandha, he throws him into the crowd. He falls on Vrushabhaketu and injures him. Vrushabhaketu wants to sue Jarasandha as it was Jarasandha who had organized the fight.

(*a*) Vrushabhaketu cannot sue Jarasandha as this is a risk associated with wrestling matches.

(*b*) Vrushabhaketu can sue Jarasandha because he wasn't standing there voluntarily but rather on Jarasandha's orders.

(*c*) Vrushabhaketu should sue Bheema instead.

(*d*) Vrushabhaketu cannot sue.

**76. Principle:** Contributory negligence can be a ground for defence when the behavior of the plaintiff has been such that his own actions have also played a part in the tortious act.

**Explanation**: The plaintiff is the person who approaches the court claiming that some wrong has been done to him. And that he has suffered legal injury and sustained damage for which he should be compensated.

**Facts:** Manmohan is driving his car at high speed on Race Course Road. Pranab is driving his motorcycle at high speed on Sansad Marg which meets Race Course road perpendicularly at Gandhi Chowk. At Gandhi Chowk the two are about to crash into each other but Manmohan manages to swerve and narrowly avoid crashing into Pranab. But in this process Manmohan runs over a pedestrian Mr. Aamadmi who is permanently disabled as a result. Mr. Aamadmi sues Manmohan in a court of law. Manmohan pleads that while it is true that he was driving rashly and did not take care to slow down before a junction, the same was true of Pranab also who was also driving rashly. Therefore, he pleads, contributory negligence should be invoked and his liability reduced.

(*a*) Manmohan is not asking for a complete letting off. He is merely asking for reduction in liability which is permissible, given the facts.

(*b*) It was Manmohan's car which hit the pedestrian, so negligence of Pranab doesn't come into question.

(*c*) Contributory Negligence is not applicable here.

(*d*) Pranab and Manmohan should share the liability.

**77. Principle:** Defamation is reducing the worth of a person in the eyes of right thinking members of society. Defamation can be either through written word or through verbal and other transient gestures. A statement is defamatory only if it is communicated to a person other than the one about whom the statement is made.

**Facts:** At the end of a particularly embarrassing day for Duryodhana, he receives an SMS from Draupadi saying "You are the blind son of a blind father, and hence you commit the blunders that you do". Duryodhana is enraged and wants to sue Draupadi for defamation.

(*a*) Draupadi is not liable because she has communicated it directly to Duryodhana and in a manner that no one can know of it.

(*b*) Draupadi is not liable because she has told the truth.

(*c*) Draupadi is liable because she has defamed Duryodhana's father by saying such a thing.

(*d*) Draupadi should not make fun of disabled people.

**78. Principle:** Defamation is reducing the worth of a person in the eyes of right thinking members of society. A statement is defamatory only if it is communicated to a person other than the one about whom the statement is made.

**Explanation:** No statement made in a strictly domestic setting shall be defamatory.

**Facts:** A dhobi D, tells his wife "Go away, I am not Ram that I may accept a woman of loose character such as Seeta even after she has lived with another man". This was said within the confines of their house but a spy deputed by Ram to bring back reports of what people feel about him heard it and reported it to Ram. Ram wants to sue D now for defamation.

(*a*) Ram cannot sue because it is not him rather Seeta who has been defamed.

(*b*) Ram can sue because the statement was made to a person other than the one whom it's about.

(*c*) Ram can sue because though the statement was intended to be made in a domestic setting, it ceased to a domestic setting when the spy started overhearing.

(*d*) Ram cannot sue because the statement was made in a strictly domestic setting.

**79. Principle:** A person is said to have defamed another when he publishes a statement in any form which can potentially lower the status of the subject in the minds of the right thinking members of society who have heard him.

**Explanation:** Truth is a complete defence for the tort of defamation. Defence means a state of affairs which would render an otherwise wrong act innocent. 'Truth' means all such statements which are or were believed to be true by the maker of the statement.

**Facts:** Yudhishtira tells Dronacharya – "One among the dead is Ashwathama the elephant". However, his last two words are obscured by the sound of drums playing loudly. Ashwathama is also the name of Dronacharya's son. He is devastated because he thinks his son is dead and suffers a lot of mental trauma. When he realizes what had actually happened, he sues Yudhishtira for defamation.

(*a*) Yudhishtira has uttered a true statement therefore he is not liable.

(*b*) Yudhishtira's statement, though true, is designed to be falsely believed therefore the truth defence does not apply and hence he is liable.

(*c*) Yudhishtira's statement is not defamatory.

(*d*) Yudhishtira is making this statement in wartime and all is fair in love and war.

**80. Principle:** If a dangerous thing is brought on to the land for non-natural use of the land, and the dangerous thing escapes, then the person who brought it on to the land is strictly liable for any damage caused by the dangerous thing.

**Explanation:** Strict liability means the person will be liable and no special negligence on his part needs to be proved by the person who is complaining against him.

**Facts:** Vikram has a very old house for which proper provisions were not made for electricity at the time of construction as they did not know of electricity. The house is also declared as a heritage building and so no permanent alterations can be made. The wiring for the electricity has to be made externally. Once, unfortunately the wire falls on to grill of the compound wall of the property which is in turn connected to the neighbour's gate. The neighbor, Ram Charan, touches the gate and gets an electric shock and suffers physical damage. He sues Vikram.

(*a*) Ram Charan will succeed because Vikram is strictly.liable.

(*b*) Vikram is not liable because his house is a heritage building and the maintenance responsibility is with the government.

(*c*) Vikram is not liable under strict liability because electric wiring is natural use of land.

(*d*) Vikram is liable only if there was no contributory negligence on part of Ram Charan.

**81. Principle:** The Constitution of Gandhara guarantees that all citizens of Gandhara shall have the right to freedom of speech and expression.

**Explanation:** State may by law impose reasonable restrictions on freedom of speech in the interests of sovereignty and integrity of Gandhara, friendly relations with foreign states, decency or morality, or incitement to offence.

**Facts:** The anti-establishment mood is simmering in Gandhara. The Government of Gandhara has passed a law that allows it to restrict any newspaper from publishing material which directly criticizes the Government. The *Amu Darya Times,* a radical newspaper registered in Gandhara but actually owned by Dost Mohammed who is a resident of Prussia, is particularly affected. The legal officer of the *Amu Darya Publishing Company,* which publishes the newspaper, approaches you.

(*a*) You will advise him that this is a reasonable restriction as criticism of the Government could lead to loss of integrity and security of the country.

(*b*) You advise him that as the owner is not a citizen of Gandhara, Amu Darya Times cannot sue.

(*c*) You advise him that Dost Mohammed as the owner of the paper should sue.

(*d*) You tell him that Amu Darya can sue in its own name because though it says citizen, here it is to be constructively interpreted as including entities.

**82. Principle:** All citizens shall have the right to freedom of speech and expression.

**Explanation:** State may by law impose reasonable restrictions on freedom of speech in the interests of sovereignty and integrity of India, friendly relations with foreign states, decency or morality, or incitement to offence.

**Facts:** Baba Gramdev is a very popular Swamiji who has decided to rouse the people against corruption. He says he will raise armed force of 11000 people who will fight the corrupt Government and thus invites people to join this army. He is promptly arrested by police. He approaches the court.

(*a*) Gramdev is fighting against corruption and it is a justified call.

(*b*) Gramdev will not succeed because the arrest by police is in line with reasonable restriction.

(*c*) Police must have asked him to explain himself first.

(*d*) Gramdev will succeed because he is very popular.

**83.** The first Lokpal Bill was presented in the Parliament in -

(*a*) 1968 (*b*) 1967

(*c*) 1971 (*d*) 1972

**84.** Right to Equality in the Indian Constitution is provided in the article(s):

(*a*) 23, 24

(*b*) 19, 20, 21, 22

(*c*) 14, 15, 16, 17, 18

(*d*) 21

**85.** The right to education at elementary level has been made one of the fundamental rights under the ____amendment of ____year:

(*a*) $86^{th}$, 2002 (*b*) $86^{th}$, 2003

(*c*) $92^{nd}$, 2006 (*d*) $92^{nd}$, 2003

**86.** Which of the following statements is defamatory?

(*a*) All lawyers are scoundrels

(*b*) Abuses hurled in anger in a playground

(*c*) Vulgar statements made about female actresses in a movie

(*d*) X, a maidservant, is the keep of her master, Y

**87.** Which among the following statements is not true of the $42^{nd}$ amendment to the Indian constitution?

(*a*) It changed the preamble

(*b*) It introduced the concept of Fundamental Rights

(*c*) It introduced the concept of Fundamental Duties

(*d*) All are true

**88.** Justice Leela Seth was the first woman Chief Justice of a High Court in India. Name the High Court.

(*a*) Allahabad High Court

(*b*) Calcutta High Court

(*c*) Himachal Pradesh High Court

(*d*) Rajasthan High Court

**89.** Who is the only Chief Justice of India to have held the office of the President of India?

(*a*) Justice A.N. Ray

(*b*) Justice A.M. Ahmadi

(*c*) Justice M. Hidayatullah

(*d*) Justice J.S. Verma

**90.** Which Article of the Constitution provides for equal justice and free legal aid?

(*a*) Article 39 A (*b*) Article 32

(*c*) Article 39 (*d*) Article 42

**91.** The Indian constituent assembly adopted and enacted the Indian constitution on

(*a*) $26^{th}$ November 1949

(*b*) $26^{th}$ January 1949

(*c*) $26^{th}$ November 1950

(*d*) $26^{th}$ November 1947

**92.** The Supreme Court has special advisory jurisdiction in matters which may specifically be referred to it by the President of India under

(*a*) Article 141 of the Constitution

(*b*) Article 226 of the Constitution

(*c*) Article 32 of the Constitution

(*d*) Article 143 of the Constitution

**93.** What does 'ad valorem' literally mean?

(*a*) according to value

(*b*) added to value

(*c*) added percentage to the value

(*d*) a type of a vaseline

**94.** When did the Indian Penal Code come into force?

(*a*) 1861 (*b*) 1860

(*c*) 1862 (*d*) 1947

**95.** The word 'life' in the Indian Penal Code means:

(*a*) life of a human being

(*b*) life of a human being and an animal

(*c*) life of any living being

(*d*) life of a man and a woman

**96.** Who appoints the Attorney-General for India?

(*a*) Prime Minister

(*b*) President of India

(*c*) Speaker of Lok Sabha

(*d*) Chief Minister of Delhi

**97.** The exclusive privilege granted to an inventor to make, use or sell an invention is called ________

(*a*) Copy right

(*b*) Patent

(*c*) Geographical Indication

(*d*) Trademark

**98.** The Constitution of India today has

(*a*) 444 Articles and 11 schedules

(*b*) 432 Articles and 8 schedules

(*c*) 444 Articles and 12 schedules

(*d*) 424 Articles and 12 schedules

**99.** Agreement becomes contract when some conditions are fulfilled. Which of the following is not one such condition?

(*a*) free consent of the parties

(*b*) lawful consideration

(*c*) lawful agreement

(*d*) parties competent to contract

**100.** The term "SOVEREIGN DEMOCRATIC REPUBLIC" was inserted in the Indian constitution by the

(*a*) Constitution (Forty-first Amendment)

(*b*) Constitution (Forty-fourth Amendment)

(*c*) Constitution (Forty-second Amendment)

(*d*) Constitution (Forty-seventh Amendment)

**101.** Where is the International Court of Justice located?

(*a*) The Hague, Netherlands

(*b*) New York City

(*c*) Geneva, Switzerland

(*d*) Luxembourg

**102.** Mark the correct statement –

(*a*) A servant can delegate his authority if so authorised by the master

(*b*) A servant can delegate his authority whenever he likes

(*c*) A servant cannot delegate his authority in any circumstances

(*d*) A servant can delegate his authority even when he is not so authorised by the master

**103.** The first Chief Justice of India who was born after India's Independence is:

(*a*) R. C. Lahoti (*b*) K. G. Balakrishnan

(*c*) S. H. Kapadia (*d*) Y. K. Sabharwal

**104.** Which practicing advocate of the Supreme Court of India authored a book on Keshvananda Bharti Case?

(*a*) F. S. Nariman (*b*) T. R. Andhyarujina

(*c*) Gopal Subramaniam (*d*) Ram Jethmalani

**105.** (A) Law Day in India is celebrated on 26 November.

(R) The Constitution of India was adopted on 26 November, 1949.

(*a*) Both A and R is true and R is the correct explanation of A.

(*b*) Both A and R is true but R is not the correct explanation of A.

(*c*) A is true, but R is false.

(*d*) A is false, but R is true.

## SECTION – D: LOGICAL REASONING

**106.** If it is true that lawyers are seldom sad, which of the following statements is correct?

(*a*) Lawyers are never sad.

(*b*) At least on one occasion lawyers are not sad.

(*c*) Sometimes lawyers are sad.

(*d*) At least one lawyer is not sad.

**107.** If it is false that 'teachers always teach well', which of the following statements is most doubtful?

(*a*) Some teachers do not teach well.

(*b*) Some teachers teach well.

(*c*) All teachers always teach well.

(*d*) Teachers never teach well.

**108.** If it is false that 'all students study hard for all the exams', which of the following statements is true beyond doubt?

(*a*) There are students who do not study hard for exams.

(*b*) There are students who study hard for some exams.

(*c*) All students study hard for some exams.

(*d*) Students never study hard for any exam.

**109.** From among the given alternatives, identify the conclusion of the following argument.

If Asha is Lata, then Rekha is not Helen.

If Rekha is not Helen, then Salman is not Amir.

If Salman is not Amir, then Priyanka is not Rani.

Therefore,

(*a*) if Priyanka is not Rani, then Asha is Lata.

(*b*) if Asha is Lata then Priyanka is not Rani.

(*c*) if Priyanka is Rani, then Asha is Lata.

(*d*) if Asha is not Lata then Priyanka is Rani.

**110.** Given below are premises that lead to the conclusion. One of the premises is missing. On the basis of the given premises and conclusion identify the missing premise from the given alternatives.

1st Premiss: If satisfaction is possible, then happiness is possible.

2nd Premiss: If there is happiness there is prosperity.

3rd Premiss:

4th Premiss: But world peace is a myth.

Conclusion: Therefore satisfaction is not possible.

(*a*) If there is satisfaction, there is prosperity.

(*b*) World peace is a myth if there is satisfaction.

(*c*) If there is happiness there is peace in the world.

(*d*) If there is prosperity world peace is not a myth.

**111.** From among the given alternatives, identify the conclusion of the following argument.

One cannot receive love unless one gives love.

One cannot be contended unless one receives love.

Therefore,

(*a*) one cannot be contended unless one gives love.

(*b*) one can be contended if one gives love.

(*c*) one cannot give love unless one is contended.

(*d*) one who gives love always receives love.

**112.** Identify the statement that can be neither proved nor disproved.

(*a*) Revelations about this secret funding network have brought down a cabinet minister.

(*b*) The Labour government weakened the rules on lobbying transparency.

(*c*) This is a protest at the gross injustice of bailed-out banks and company CEOs still pouring bonuses into their pockets while everyone else pays the price in cuts and lost jobs.

(*d*) Last night, Angelena Joile looked pretty in her red gown.

**113.** If it is true that 'jingoism is detrimental to the establishment of peace in the world' which one of the following statements is also true?

(*a*) The belief that my country is good and the rest of the countries are also good promotes peace in the world.

(*b*) The belief that my country is always right and the favor towards aggressive acts against other countries hampers peace in the world.

(*c*) Fighting with other country/countries is detrimental to peace in the world.

(*d*) Disrespect for other countries defies peace in the world.

**114.** How do you evaluate "She came on stage to receive a posthumous award for her philanthropy"?

(*a*) False (*b*) True
(*c*) Probable (*d*) Absurd

**115.** Identify the argument that has to be accepted when the premiss is accepted as true.

(*a*) John and Milton are good in English.
Therefore, they are good in learning foreign languages.

(*b*) Mike loves painting.
Therefore, the paintings of Mike are generally good.

(*c*) Life is tough when you are poor.
Therefore, money affects our lives.

(*d*) Interest and motivation are connected.
Therefore, when one is interested, he is motivated.

**116.** Identify the argument that cannot be accepted.

(*a*) All plants are living. All living require oxygen. All plants require oxygen.

(*b*) All stationary are moving. Some moving are stagnant. Some stagnant may be stationary.

(*c*) All is well that ends well. All that ends well is predetermined. All that is predetermined is well.

(*d*) Honesty is the best policy. Some best policies are ethical. Honesty may be ethical.

**117.** Which of the following having the same form contradicts the statement 'Indecent students should be rusticated'?

(*a*) Indecent students should be counseled.
(*b*) Indecent students need more attention.
(*c*) Discipline is not a must for a school.
(*d*) Indecent students should be granted amnesty.

**118.** If it is true that 'no clever student should fail' and' Smita is a clever student', which of the following is the correct conclusion?

(*a*) Smita cannot fail.
(*b*) Smita should not fail.
(*c*) Smita will score good marks.
(*d*) Smita will not fail.

**119.** Which of the following alternatives comes very close to the statement, 'Success eludes the weak-hearted'?

(*a*) Weak hearted people can succeed if they work hard.
(*b*) A strong heart is needed to succeed in life.
(*c*) Weak hearted are not able to succeed.
(*d*) Circumstances and luck fail to help the weak-hearted.

**120.** Which of the following alternatives contradicts the statement 'People were dying of starvation while governments procrastinated'.

(*a*) Government has generally been ignorant towards a lot of problems faced by commoners.
(*b*) Sense of duty has always been lacking in the government.
(*c*) People need to work hard and be aware of their rights.
(*d*) Lack of effort on the part of people was responsible for their plight.

**121.** Identify the alternative which gives true picture of the relation between the arguments listed below.

1. Ultrasound is the gold standard used to determine miscarriage. It's assumed — at least by expectant mothers — to be exceptionally accurate. Yet one of the studies, which analyzed the existence or size of the gestational sac, found that the presence or absence of a gestational sac, as well as its size, were not foolproof indicators of miscarriage, casting doubt on the effectiveness of ultrasound.
2. The intake of fruits, green vegetables and milk is considered very good for health. But sometimes, because of extensive used of insecticides, pesticides and adulterants, their original goodness is lost and their consumption can be hazardous.

(*a*) These two are incompatible
(*b*) They are interdependent
(*c*) They are analogous
(*d*) They are compatible

**122.** When the division of labour has been once thoroughly established, it is but a very small part of the man's wants which the produce of his own labour can supply. He supplies the far greater part of them by exchanging that surplus part of the produce of his own labour, which is over and above his own consumption, for such parts of the produce of other men's labour as he has occasion for.

Which of the following assertions, if true, is the summary of the given passage?

(*a*) Man lives by exchanging goods/things with other men.
(*b*) The growth of society is facilitated by exchange of goods among men.
(*c*) Man is generally unsatisfied with what he himself produces.
(*d*) The growth of man will be stymied if he stops socializing.

**123.** Strong nations and hegemonic research universities have a gravitational power of attraction, pulling towards them cross-border flows of faculty talent and doctoral students, tuition fees and research and philanthropic funding. In weaker systems global brain circulation becomes a brain drain transferring long-term academic capacity to the strong nations.

Which of the following statements, if true, is the essence of the passage mentioned above?

(*a*) Cross-border flows are continually undergoing and generating change.

(*b*) Global traffic often flows in a fashion, benefiting some nations and institutions more than others.

(*c*) The capacity of nations and institutions to operate globally depends on both their absolute potential to do so, and their voluntary decisions.

(*d*) Raw national and institutional *potential* in higher education is framed by such elements as the size and wealth of the economy; the systems, resources.

**124.** The tradition prevalent among social scientists of predicting gloom and doom on the evidence of perpetual crises or the deficiencies of human nature overlooks a self-fulfilling danger: such predictions can promote the very conditions so deplored. This defeatist stance also evades the basic fact that people learn and adapt. Radicals may deliver witty, cynical, despairing commentary, but in so doing they reveal how far they have reconciled themselves to their marginality in influencing the course of events. Equally trapped, however, are the perpetual optimists who naively claim linear progress by ignoring its obstacles, who substitute mere exhortation for sober evaluation.

Which one of the following assertions, if true, contradicts the passage mentioned above?

(*a*) The process of prediction regarding bad events is far from perfect.

(*b*) Perpetual optimists ignore the things that stymie growth and progress.

(*c*) The defeatists believe that people are flexible, adaptable and open to learning.

(*d*) None of these

**125.** Despite input costs gnawing at the profit margins of consumer durable companies, they are postponing their decision to hike prices till after the festive season.

Which of the following, if true, underpins the above argument?

(*a*) People have a tendency to spend more during the festive season.

(*b*) Increase in price deters the buyers from buying goods.

(*c*) The decrease in profit margins of company may affect the employees in the long run.

(*d*) None of these

**126.** While on the one hand the Maoist tag is used to persecute and torture those who speak out against the excesses and illegalities of the State, on the other there is a growing trend where the institutions of the State are used to push the vested interests of one section of the population – those who consume high energy and high cost industrial products and profit out of its investment, production and distribution.

From among the alternatives, identify the statement that can be inferred from the given paragraph.

(*a*) The State is using its institutions in a partisan manner.

(*b*) The people of the state are unhappy.

(*c*) The legitimacy of the institutions and of the State itself stands hollowed out.

(*d*) None of these

**127.** Identify the alternative that gives true picture of the relation between the arguments listed below:

1. Whilst abortion has been accepted by the American state since the land-mark Roe v/s. Wade case in the early 1970s, this is by no means a reflection of universal agreement – either international or within America itself – as many Western countries still have considerable restrictions on abortion. For example, the Irish position has softened only recently, and the Catholic Church steadfastly refuses to change its resolutely pro-life stance in the face of criticism from Women's and other lobby-groups.
2. Teenage pregnancy is a stressful experience, and many people would agree that it would be sensible for a pregnant unmarried teenage girl to seek advice from a responsible adult. Parental involvement laws would make notification of pregnancy and consent for abortion from one or both parents mandatory. Such laws exist in 43 US states. Most of the statutes apply to young women under 18 and provide for a court bypass procedure should a young woman be unable to involve her parents. Most of them include exceptions for medical emergencies.

(*a*) These two are related but independent

(*b*) They are neither related nor Interdependent

(*c*) One is conclusion and the other is a premise

(*d*) These two are related and interdependent

**128.** Identify the alternative that gives true picture of the relation between the arguments listed below:

1. Free speech is an inherently ambiguous concept that requires definition and interpretation; Government is the obvious place for such clarifications to be made.
2. An independent judiciary, or politically-independent body for assessing circumstances is the only place that can effectively guarantee freedom of speech.

(*a*) These two are related but independent.

(*b*) One of them is a counter argument to the other.

(*c*) One is conclusion and the other is a premise.

(*d*) They support each other.

**129.** Four statements are given below. Group two of them in such a way that one is logically possible and the other is empirically (factually) possible.

(*a*) A Right angled triangle will always have one angle equal to 90 degree.

(*b*) Velocity of sound in vacuum accelerates.

(*c*) Destruction of forests at this rate can result in shortage of clean breathable air.

(*d*) Colour yellow is yellow only because of the light we see it in.

(*a*) a, b (*b*) b, d

(*c*) c, a (*d*) a, c

**130.** Four statements are given. Group two of them in such a way that one is logically impossible and the other is empirically (factually) correct.

(*a*) Theories of science can explain the existence of God.

(*b*) If earth rotates when there is wind, then wind is necessary for earth to rotate.

(*c*) The colour red is a primary colour.

(*d*) If earth rotates when there is wind, then wind is not necessary for earth to rotate.

(*a*) a, b (*b*) b, c

(*c*) c, d (*d*) a, d

**131.** Four statements are given below. One of them can be demonstrated with the help of reason, while another requires sense experience to ascertain the truth, identify them.

(*a*) Area of rectangle is given by the formula length multiplied by breath.

(*b*) If all X is Y, then some Y is X.

(*c*) Oxygen is poisonous.

(*d*) We do not need religion to know our moral absolutes.

(*a*) a, b (*b*) b, d

(*c*) c, d (*d*) a, d

**132.** Tia: Many readers cannot understand my views and hence leave critical remarks on my blog. They do so because they are jealous and stupid.

Sia: If majority of readers are writing critical remarks on your blog they may be voicing their genuine opinion.

Which of the following is a valid assumption?

(*a*) Readers write critical comments on the blog because they are jealous.

(*b*) Readers are stupid and that is why they cannot understand the views expressed on the blog.

(*c*) If the same response is being given by majority of readers then that response is genuine.

(*d*) None of the above

**133.** Saket: Any form of addiction, in the long run, definitely hurts the society as a whole. Hence, there should be a ban on marijuana.

Deepak: I don't think a ban will work. The prohibition against alcohol was a failure and so the prohibition against marijuana will be a failure as well.

Which of the following is the most serious flaw in the argument above?

(*a*) Deepak assumes that because prohibition against alcohol failed, the same will be the consequences of a ban on marijuana.

(*b*) Saket is trying to relate two totally unrelated things- addiction and society.

(*c*) Deepak and Saket are discussing two separate issues.

(*d*) A failure of ban on alcohol does not necessarily mean that the same will be the consequences of a ban on marijuana.

**134.** The recent spurt in the prices of gold is caused by a prediction of the sluggish stock market. This prediction would not have had an effect on the prices of gold, had the property market not been overvalued.

Which of the following can be a valid conclusion?

(*a*) Price of gold is dependent on the property and stock markets.

(*b*) Price of gold is independent of the property market but dependent on the stock market.

(*c*) Price of gold increase when stock market declines and the property market increases.

(*d*) Price of gold increases when property market declines and stock market increases.

**135.** Dr. Wishwanathan, a financial expert, noticed that many students have been financing their education, since in a sour economy, parents seem to be having troubles obtaining their home equity loans- a key financial instrument for higher education. When a large number of students are graduating with a debt, and without a job in hand - thanks to the economic downturn, it is not surprising that they will default.

Which of the following is a valid conclusion?

(*a*) The default rate for educational loans is likely to be influenced by the sour economy.

(*b*) Parents are unable to fulfill their responsibilities due to the downturn in the economy.

(*c*) Education sector has suffered a setback due to the economic downturn.

(*d*) Educational loans have increased due to the economic downturn.

**136.** Powerful evidence has poured in over decades, showing the 'greenhouse effect' is real and is happening. And yet resistance to the idea among many in the U.S. appears to have hardened. Economist-ethicist Clive Hamilton says' 'Denialism' in America, has taken on a more partisan, ideological tone. The solution: 'Eventually it'll become damned clear that the Earth is warming and the warming is beyond anything we have experienced in millions of years, and people will have to admit...' But then he stops and laughs. 'Well, I suppose they could say God is burning us up.'

Which of the following is a valid inference?

(*a*) The desire to disbelieve deepens as the scale of the threat grows.

(*b*) The 'greenhouse effect' is a real threat.

(*c*) The reluctance to rein in greenhouse effect is widespread.

(*d*) It is surprising how the scientific findings are being rejected in an unscientific manner.

**137.** A lawsuit against a fast food chain for causing obesity was dismissed by the judge. The reason cited was that the food chain gave out nutritional information regarding its products but the consumers continued to eat there.

The argument above depends on which of the following assumptions?

(*a*) People are responsible for the choices that they make.

(*b*) The fast food chain was offering healthy food that could not have caused obesity.

(*c*) The information given by the fast food chain indicated the impact that consumption of their products could have.

(*d*) The consumers indulged in excess consumption.

**138.** Each year the amount of aid country X receives from international agencies to alleviate poverty increases. However, at the same time the level of poverty in the country also increases.

Which of the following, if true, best resolves these conflicting trends?

(*a*) Only ten percent of the amount promised is actually received.

(*b*) The population of country X is increasing every year.

(*c*) The bureaucratic procedures in country X are inefficient and it takes a long time to implement programs.

(*d*) The funds are simply distributed among the poverty stricken instead of being utilized to build capabilities and generate income.

**139.** Most Indian political leaders guard news of their health as if it were a state secret. This may stem from the fear that if the public gets to know of their ill health they might be seen as being incapable of doing their jobs and perhaps replaced. After all, a primal political instinct is the desire to retain power.

Which of the following, if true, weakens the argument above?

(*a*) Several politicians in other countries have been candid about their illnesses and yet continued to hold positions of power.

(*b*) Increasing media coverage is making it difficult for politicians to hide the facts related to their ill health.

(*c*) Politicians have a responsibility to the public and should not conceal their illnesses.

(*d*) A politician's ill heath can make him/her seem more human and might generate more support for him/her among the people.

**140.** You never come in physical contact with anything. Your contact with everything is through your mind, through your nerve fibers, nerve cells, and your entire objective mind. When you feel you see, it is an internal projection with the help of your nerves. It is a mystery that whatever you perceive or whatever you conceive - everything is within you, nothing is outside of you. Hence it is said that the entire universe is within you in miniature form.

Which of the following conclusions is best supported by the information above?

(*a*) Perception is a myth.

(*b*) Perception is controlled by the mind and is thus fallible.

(*c*) The universe is experienced through the senses and thus becomes a part of the human mind.

(*d*) Whatever we experience of the universe is filtered through the mind and is thus a part of it.

## SECTION – E: MATHEMATICS

**141.** January 1, 2006 was a Sunday. What day of the week was January 1, 2010?

(*a*) Sunday (*b*) Saturday
(*c*) Friday (*d*) Monday

**142.** A clock gains 4 seconds every minute. Find the angle traversed by the minute hand in one hour.

(*a*) 360° (*b*) 364°
(*c*) 374° (*d*) 384°

**143.** The total surface areas of two spheres A and B are 100 $cm^3$ and 400 $cm^3$ respectively. The ratio of the volume of the sphere A to the volume of the sphere B is:

(*a*) 1 : 4 (*b*) 1 : 8
(*c*) 8 : 1 (*d*) 3 : 5

**144.** The speed of a train when its stoppages are excluded is 72 km/hr and its speed when stoppages are included is 63 km/hr. For how many minutes does the train stop every hour?

(*a*) 8 minutes (*b*) 8.5 minutes
(*c*) 7.5 minutes (*d*) 9.5 minutes

**145.** A student reads 2/3rd of a book and finds that the read part is 90 pages more than the unread part. How many pages are there in the whole book?

(*a*) 360 (*b*) 270
(*c*) 370 (*d*) 450

**146.** A and B together can complete a work in 20 days. If B alone can complete the work in 60 days, then in how many days A alone can complete the work?

(*a*) 30 days (*b*) 40 days
(*c*) 45 days (*d*) 60 days

**147.** Eight years ago, Himani was 8 times as old as her daughter. After 16 years Himani will be twice as old as her daughter. What is the present age of Himani?

(*a*) 30 years (*b*) 40 years
(*c*) 45 years (*d*) 50 years

**148.** x is twice of y and thrice of z. If the average of x, y and z is 22, then find the value of y.

(*a*) 36 (*b*) 11
(*c*) 12 (*d*) 18

**149.** If $\frac{x}{y} = \frac{2}{3}$ and $\frac{y}{z} = \frac{4}{5}$, then the value of $\left(\frac{5x + 3y - 4z}{5x - 3y + 4z}\right)$ is:

(*a*) $\frac{2}{3}$ (*b*) $\frac{5}{3}$
(*c*) $\frac{3}{4}$ (*d*) $\frac{1}{4}$

**150.** Which of the following is equal to 60% of 25% of 960?

(*a*) 30% of 90% of 600 (*b*) 16% of 900
(*c*) 40% of 80% of 400 (*d*) 18% of 750

## ANSWERS

| 1. (*d*) | 2. (*b*) | 3. (*d*) | 4. (*b*) | 5. (*a*) | 6. (*c*) | 7. (*c*) | 8. (*a*) | 9. (*c*) | 10. (*a*) |
|---|---|---|---|---|---|---|---|---|---|
| 11. (*b*) | 12. (*b*) | 13. (*c*) | 14. (*c*) | 15. (*b*) | 16. (*b*) | 17. (*a*) | 18. (*a*) | 19. (*a*) | 20. (*a*) |
| 21. (*b*) | 22. (*d*) | 23. (*b*) | 24. (*d*) | 25. (*b*) | 26. (*a*) | 27. (*b*) | 28. (*c*) | 29. (*a*) | 30. (*b*) |
| 31. (*c*) | 32. (*a*) | 33. (*b*) | 34. (*d*) | 35. (*b*) | 36. (*a*) | 37. (*b*) | 38. (*a*) | 39. (*a*) | 40. (*a*) |
| 41. (*a*) | 42. (*a*) | 43. (*b*) | 44. (*c*) | 45. (*d*) | 46. (*a*) | 47. (*d*) | 48. (*a*) | 49. (*a*) | 50. (*b*) |
| 51. (*d*) | 52. (*a*) | 53. (*a*) | 54. (*b*) | 55. (*a*) | 56. (*d*) | 57. (*b*) | 58. (*c*) | 59. (*b*) | 60. (*c*) |
| 61. (*a*) | 62. (*a*) | 63. (*a*) | 64. (*b*) | 65. (*a*) | 66. (*a*) | 67. (*a*) | 68. (*b*) | 69. (*a*) | 70. (*a*) |
| 71. (*d*) | 72. (*b*) | 73. (*d*) | 74. (*b*) | 75. (*b*) | 76. (*c*) | 77. (*a*) | 78. (*d*) | 79. (*c*) | 80. (*c*) |
| 81. (*b*) | 82. (*b*) | 83. (*a*) | 84. (*c*) | 85. (*a*) | 86. (*d*) | 87. (*c*) | 88. (*c*) | 89. (*c*) | 90. (*a*) |
| 91. (*a*) | 92. (*d*) | 93. (*a*) | 94. (*c*) | 95. (*a*) | 96. (*b*) | 97. (*b*) | 98. (*c*) | 99. (*c*) | 100. (*c*) |
| 101. (*a*) | 102. (*a*) | 103. (*c*) | 104. (*b*) | 105. (*a*) | 106. (*b*) | 107. (*c*) | 108. (*a*) | 109. (*b*) | 110. (*d*) |
| 111. (*a*) | 112. (*d*) | 113. (*b*) | 114. (*d*) | 115. (*c*) | 116. (*c*) | 117. (*d*) | 118. (*b*) | 119. (*c*) | 120. (*d*) |
| 121. (*c*) | 122. (*a*) | 123. (*b*) | 124. (*c*) | 125. (*b*) | 126. (*a*) | 127. (*b*) | 128. (*b*) | 129. (*c*) | 130. (*b*) |
| 131. (*b*) | 132. (*c*) | 133. (*d*) | 134. (*a*) | 135. (*a*) | 136. (*b*) | 137. (*c*) | 138. (*d*) | 139. (*d*) | 140. (*c*) |
| 141. (*c*) | 142. (*d*) | 143. (*b*) | 144. (*c*) | 145. (*b*) | 146. (*a*) | 147. (*b*) | 148. (*d*) | 149. (*d*) | 150. (*b*) |

# EXPLANATIONS

**1.** Option (*a*) can be inferred from the lines "Stressing that there is no permanence about any definition of a crime and criminal law, he pointed to the absolute power accorded to the state to implement the law and the real context of abuse, misuse and vindictive administration of the laws". Option (*b*) can be inferred from the lines "Kannabiran's contribution to human rights was not only in the field of criminal law". Option (*c*) can be inferred from the lines "While it is in the course of crime detection, investigation and apprehension of the accused that human rights violations ordinarily take place". Thus, the correct answer is option (*d*).

**2.** The author is formally praising Kannabiran in the passage, citing him as a "role model – of a person who through personal example became the embodiment of the ethical and political values he advocated." Thus, the author's attitude towards Kannabiran is eulogistic.

**3.** The formulation refers to the Kannabiran's formulation mentioned in the first sentence of the passage. Thus "The simplicity of the formulation masked the profundity of its understanding of criminal law" pertains to the centrality of the state in the administration of criminal justice.

**4.** The excerpt, it appears, is a part of a biography. Option (*b*) is correct. Option (*a*) is obviously incorrect since the author expresses his admiration for Kinnabiran at length in the passage, which would be quite inappropriate if included in a legal report. Option (*c*) is incorrect since nowhere in the passage is Kinnabiran referred to as Late Kinnabiran. A paean, is a song of praise and hence, (*d*) is incorrect.

**5.** The word 'taboo' refers to any prohibition resulting from social or other conventions. "There were no taboo issues for Kannabiran" by this, the author means to say that Kannabiran did not have any reservation in deliberating any kind of issue. Hence, option (*a*) is correct.

**6.** *Recondite* means 1: hidden from sight : concealed 2 : difficult or impossible for one of ordinary understanding or knowledge to comprehend : deep <a *recondite* subject> 3 : of, relating to, or dealing with something little known or obscure. Thus, recondite is inapt in the context of the line "One of Kannabiran's formulations that had a profound impact on demystifying the relationship between the state, citizen and law enforcement, concerned with the centrality of the state in the administration of criminal justice."

**7.** The second word in the given pair is an undesirable extent of the first one. 'Concerned' and 'obsessed' are synonyms but obsessed is an undesirable extent of being concerned. 'Firm' and 'unyielding' have similar relation. Option (*c*) is analogous to the given pair.

**8.** The first word in the given pair is an undesirable form of the second one. 'Simper' is a silly smile. 'Babble' is a meaningless talk. Option (*a*) is analogous to the given pair.

**9.** The Past Perfect Tense is appropriate in this case. It is used to indicate that an action that was completed (finished or "perfected") at some point in the past <u>before something else happened</u>. This tense is formed with the past tense form of "to have" (had) plus the past participle of the verb. For example: I <u>had walked</u> two miles by dinner time. I <u>had run</u> three other marathons before entering the Delhi Marathon.

**10.** The Future Perfect Continuous Tense is apt for this sentence. This tense indicates a continuous action that will be completed at some point in the future. This tense is formed with the modal 'will' plus the modal 'have' plus 'been' plus the present participle of the verb (with an *-ing* ending): "Next Thursday, I <u>will have been working</u> on this project for five months."

**11.** The Simple Past Tense is apt in this case. It indicates that an action is in the past relative to the speaker or writer. It is used 1. when the time period has finished: "We <u>went</u> to Australia last Christmas." 2. When the time period is definite: "We <u>visited</u> dad last week." 3. with *for*, when the action is finished: "I <u>worked</u> with the SBI for two years."

**12.** Since the subject is proceeds (Plural subject), the verb should be have. Present Perfect Tense is apt here. It is used to denote an action that began at some time in the past and is continuing up to the present moment (it is often used with *since* and *for* phrases).

**13.** In the given sentence, had studied is correct (past subjunctive).

The **subjunctive mood** is used in dependent clauses that do the following: 1) express a wish; 2) begin with *if* and express a condition that does not exist (is contrary to fact); 3) begin with *as if* and *as though* when such clauses describe a speculation or condition contrary to fact; and 4) begin with *that* and express a demand, requirement, request, or suggestion.

**14.** Past subjunctive is apt here. It is used after the phrase *It is time.* The syntax is: It is time + subject+ past subjunctive. It is time we started implies that it is late, we should start.

**15.** The correct phrase is one of the [plural number]. For example: One of the books, one of the students etc. here the subject is one (singular) and a singular verb is needed. Thus, the complete sentence would be 'One of the books is costly'.

**16.** The pronouns *each, everyone, every one, everybody, anyone, anybody, someone,* and *somebody* are singular and require singular verbs. Do not be misled by what follows *of*. ***Examples:** Each of the girls sings well. Every one of the cakes is gone.*

**17.** The pronouns *neither* and *either* are singular and require singular verbs even though they seem to be referring, in a sense, to two things.

**18.** When two subjects are joined with the conjunctions *with, together with, along with, as well as,* the verb should be in accordance with the first subject. If the first subject is singular in number, the verb should be singular. If the first subject is plural in number, the verb should be plural.

**19.** When two subjects are connected with the co-relative conjunction pairs *either-or, neither-nor,* the verb should follow the second (proximal) subject. If the second subject is singular, the verb is singular. If the second subject is plural, verb is plural. For example: Neither my sisters nor my mother is going to sell the car or Neither my mother nor my sisters are going to sell the car.

**20.** Mumps is a name of a disease and is singular in number. Therefore, the verb should be singular.

**21.** The verb should agree in number with its proper subject. The subject who decides upon the issue of holidays is the Principal (singular subject) and not the faculty members. Thus, the verb should be singular.

**22.** 'Pull through' is phrasal verb which means to come safely through (a crisis, illness, etc.); survive.

**23.** 'to bring up' is a phrasal verb which means to mention a topic.

**24.** We use *for* when we talk about a period of time. A period is a duration of time, for example: 5 minutes, 2 weeks, 6 years. **For** means "from the beginning of the period until the end of the period."

**25.** We require a preposition of location here and 'at' is the best possible option.

**26.** 'Vitriolic' means marked by harsh insulting language and 'invective' is its synonym. 'Temperate' and 'moderate' mean mild and are negated. 'Belligerent' means inclined to or exhibiting assertiveness, hostility, or combativeness.

**27.** 'Pallid' means lacking sparkle or liveliness; dull.

**28.** 'Despise' someone means to dislike and have no respect for him and abhorred is its synonym.

**29.** 'Oblivious' means not aware of something; unmindful.

**30.** 'Immaculate' means containing no flaw or error; spotless. In the given context, the word means perfect.

**31.** 'Comely' means pleasing in appearance; attractive. Hence, the correct option is (*c*).

**32.** *Keep up* means to persist in a state, enterprise, or undertaking in spite of counterinfluences, opposition, or discouragement. Thus, persevere in is the correct meaning.

**33.** 'Discard' means to cast aside or dispose of. Put away means to renounce; discard and thus is the apt synonym of the underlined phrase.

**34.** 'Rushed off one's feet' means to be very busy.

**35.** 'Cheek by jowl' means inconveniently close together.

**36.** 14-year-old Rahul Nagvekar took the top prize at the National Geographic Bee.

**37.** Anand Marriage Act has been amended to enable Sikh couple to register their marriages as per this Act.

**38.** Bihar is the third State, after Madhya Pradesh and Kerala, to impose a ban on the manufacture, sale, distribution of gutka, pan masala and its variants, utilising the provisions in the Food Safety and Standards (Prohibition and Restriction on Sale) Regulation 2011.

**39.** Khesari dal, also known as Grass pea, was banned for consumption in 1961 citing health reasons. Khesari Dal is cultivated extensively in central and western India for cattle fodder. Chhattisgarh, Maharashtra and West Bengal are the only States where the sale for human consumption was not banned.

Recently Government decided to withdraw the ban on Khesari dal in order to solve the shortage of pulses, as it is believed that the harmful effects of the same depends on the amount consumed, its toxin content, the method of cooking and the nutritional status of individuals. Furthermore, the amount of neurotoxin varies from variety to variety and is inversely proportional to the moisture content in the soil, with the toxin content increasing in drought conditions.

**40.** The mission aims at the empowerment of women, through forming self help groups and encouraging their entrepreneurial or other wide range of activities. The purpose of the mission is to ensure that the women should no longer remain as passive recipients of public assistance, but active leaders in women involved development initiatives.

**41.** Guinness World Records has recognised Tameer's Princess Tower in Dubai as the world's tallest residential building. Located in the Dubai Marina, a man-made canal overlooking the Gulf, it measures 414 meters from base to tip.

**42.** The move to set up an expert technical group follows all-round criticism of the Planning Commission's estimates on poverty released in this March and the controversy it generated in and outside Parliament on capping the poverty line at a daily consumption of Rs 28.65 per capita in cities and at Rs 22.42 in rural areas.

As per the terms of reference, the panel has been asked to comprehensively review the existing methodology of poverty estimation and examine whether the poverty line should be fixed solely in terms of a consumption basket or whether other criteria are also relevant. If so, it should suggest if they can be effectively combined to evolve a basis for estimation of poverty in rural and urban areas and also recommend how its estimates of poverty should be linked to eligibility and entitlements for the Central government's schemes and programmes.

**43.** Ram Singh Yadav is the first Indian to qualify for marathon at the Olympics in 36 years.

**44.** Maria Sharapova defeated Li Na (China).

**45.** Aryan Balaji, a seven year-old boy-son of an Indian Navy officer has become the youngest mountaineer to successfully trek to the Everest Base Camp (EBC) in Nepal at an height of 5,364 meters and scale Mount Kalapattar at 5,554 meter altitude.

**46.** Tajikistan is not associated with TAPI Pipeline Project.

**47.** Rafael Nadal won the Italian Open men's tennis tournament 2012.

**48.** Ashok Chawla headed the committee to ensure transparency in allocation and pricing of natural resources like land, coal, petroleum and natural gas.

**49.** With 749 points to his kitty, Tendulkar shares the 12th spot with Azhar Ali of Pakistan in the batsmen's chart which is headed by West Indian Shivnarine Chanderpaul.

**50.** Uttar Pradesh Chief Minister Akhilesh Yadav introduced a pension scheme for poor families that are deprived of BPL facilities and are not beneficiary of any other scheme announced by the State or the Central Governments for the poor. The scheme, named Rani Laxmi Bai Pension Yojana, will benefit 25.75 lakh families in the financial year 2012-13 and put an additional burden of Rs 1,289 crore on the state exchequer.

**51.** (*a*) Mid-day meal scheme involves provision of lunch free of cost to school-children on all working days.

(*b*) National Food Security Bill 2011 was recently introduced in the Lok Sabha. The Bill specifies that up to 75 percent of the rural population and 50 percent of the urban population shall be entitled to foodgrains. Of these, at least 46 percent and 28 percent, respectively, shall be categorised as priority groups (the rest are "general").

(*c*) National Mission for Sustainable Agriculture involves adaptation and mitigation measures in order to answer the challenge of climate change to agricultural production.

(*d*) Aahar is an international food and hospitality fair. Recently 27$^{th}$ edition of this fair was inaugurated in New Delhi.

**52.** This award was recently conferred on 8 serving and 4 retired servicemen by President (and Supreme Commander of the Indian Armed Forces) Smt Pratibha Devisingh Patil.

**53.** XBRL is a language for the electronic communication of business and financial data. XBRL stands for eXten sible Business Reporting Language.

**54.** The forecasting of the weather within the next six hours is often referred to as nowcasting. Recently, a workshop-cum-seminar on this topic was held in New Delhi.

**55.** It is the celebration of excellence in Indian Science, in memory of acceptance of "Raman Effects" Sir C.V. Raman who got the Nobel Prize in Physics later.

The NSD is celebrated around a focal theme. The focal theme this year is "Clean Energy Options and Nuclear Safety". This year the National Science Day Lecture was delivered by Dr. Baldev Raj, a distinguished scientist and former Director of Indira Gandhi Centre for Atomic Research, Kalapakkam on February 28, 2012 at Indian Institute of Technology, Delhi.

**56.** The number of polio cases has fallen by over 99% since the Global Polio Eradication Initiative was launched in 1988. In 2012, only three countries (Afghanistan, Nigeria and Pakistan) in the world remain polio-endemic.

**57.** (*a*) Kaushik Basu is the Chief Economic Adviser, Ministry of Finance

(*b*) C. Rangarajan is the Chairman of the Economic Advisory Council to the Prime Minister

(*c*) Ashok Gulati is the Chairperson of the Commission for Agricultural Costs & Prices (CACP)

**58.** Smt. Gita Siddhartha is the President of ICCW. ICCW's mandate is to initiate, undertake or aid directly or through its State/Union Territory Councils or affiliated bodies, schemes for furtherance of child welfare/development in India.

**59.** The Ministry of Information & Broadcasting gives these awards.

**60.** This committee was constituted by the Supreme Court of India.

**61.** Energy conservation means using less energy and avoiding excessive or wasteful uses. India has launched several steps in this regard like raising consciousness through celebrating National Energy Conservation Day on 14th December each year.

**62.** Rustom is the name of an Unmanned Aerial Combat Vehicle developed by Defence RDO

**63.** Mirza Waheed is the author of 'The Collaborator' and Basharat Peer is the author of 'The Curfewed Night'.

**64.** GLONASS stands for Global Navigation Satellite System. Russia has agreed to share civilian as well as military data obtained by this system, with India.

**65.** World Post day falls each year on October 9, remembering this date for the establishment of Universal Postal Union (UPU) in 1874 in Bern, Switzerland.

**66.** (*a*) Dibrugarh Town – Kanyakumari Vivek Express travels a distance of 4287 km in 82:30 hours

(*b*) Himsagar Express runs from Kanyakumari to Jammu Tawi. In 71 hours, the train covers a distance of 3715 km.

**67.** In 2011, Palestine became a UNESCO member following a vote in which 107 member states supported and 14 opposed.

**68.** The Red Ribbon Express Train was launched in India on World AIDS Day, December 1, 2007. The Train seeks to spread awareness about HIV/AIDS, promote safe sex and reduce discrimination against AIDS victims in India, especially those in rural regions.

**69.** In order to encourage more young voters to take part in the political process, Government of India has decided to celebrate January 25 every year as 'National Voters' Day'

**70.** This agency has been in news in connection with many instances of hacking of government websites.

**71.** In this case throwing a paperweight at Shukracharya amounts to negligence as it endangered the safety of the victim.

**72.** Here the driver and company owe a duty of care to Billu as they would to any other person who would get on to the bus. The fact whether Billu is an employee or not is irrelevant.

**73.** Antonia cannot sue Berlusconi as mental trauma suffered by her could not have been reasonably foreseen by Berlusconi.

**74.** The shot was fired at the swallow in a reasonable manner, and therefore, a person being hit by a deflected bullet is an accident.

**75.** Jarasandha had ordered him to stand there. So Vrushabhaketu becomes an employee rather than a spectator.

**76.** Contributory negligence would have come into play only if there was some negligence on the part of the plaintiff i.e. the pedestrian. That is not the case here and Pranab's negligence has nothing to do with contributory negligence.

**77.** SMS is sent directly from the person sending it to the person receiving it. In the usual course, no one else would come to know of it.

**78.** The statement was made between husband and wife within the confines of their house. So it was made in a strictly domestic setting. They were not aware that the spy is overhearing them.

**79.** The statement does not meet the requirement of defamation. It in no way lowers the status of any person.

**80.** Electric wiring is a natural use of land. In this case, Vikram has done the wiring in the best possible way he can.

**81.** The right is conferred only upon citizens by the Constitution.

**82.** Raising an army puts the sovereignty and integrity of the nation in threat.

**83.** The first Jan Lokpal Bill was proposed by Shanti Bhushan in 1968 and passed in the 4th Lok Sabha in 1969, but did not pass through the Rajya Sabha. Subsequently, 'lokpal bills' were introduced in 1971, 1977, 1985, again by Ashoke Kumar Sen, while serving as Law Minister in the Rajiv Gandhi cabinet, and again in 1989, 1996, 1998, 2001, 2005 and in 2008, yet they were never passed. Forty-four years after its first introduction, the Lokpal Bill is still not enacted in India.

**84.** The Right to Equality is one of the six Fundamental Rights that has been guaranteed by the Constitution.

**85.** With the Constitution (Eighty-Sixth) Amendment Act passed on 12th December 2002, Article 21A was amended in order to introduce Right to Education as a Fundamental Right. The Act aims to provide free and compulsory education to all children in the age group of six to fourteen years. The Act notifies that it is a legally enforceable duty of the Centre and the States to provide free and compulsory education.

**86.** In defamation cases a plaintiff must prove that the defamatory statement refers to him or her. Thus when a statement refers to entire group, no individual of such group can have cause of action in such case unless it is proved that the defamatory statement specifically applies to the plaintiff.

Mere vulgar abuses are not considered defamatory as these are not factual in nature and can't constitute falsehood. Since such linguistic assault can't be false, they can't be defamatory as well.

The fourth statement that "X, a maidservant, is the keep of her master, Y" clearly bring disrepute to X, thus constitutes defamatory statement.

**87.** 42nd Constitutional Amendment was enacted during the period of emergency in 1975. It was one of the most controversial Amendments of all which established beyond doubt the supremacy of Parliament over the other wings of Government; gave the Directive Principles precedence over the Fundamental Rights; enumerated for the first time a set of ten Fundamental Duties. It further amended preamble at two places and laid down that no Constitutional Amendment could be questioned in any court of law. However the Act did not introduce Fundamental Rights as it is enshrined in the Constitution already.

**88.** Justice Leila Seth was the first woman judge of the Delhi High Court and the first woman to become the Chief Justice of a State High Court in India.

**89.** During his term as the Chief Justice of India, the then President of India, Dr Zakir Hussain died suddenly, in harness, on May 3, 1969. Then Vice President of India Mr.V V Giri became the acting President. V V Giri resigned to take part in Presidential elections. Justice Hidayatullah then served as the President of India being ex-officio Chief Justice of India for a short period from 20 July to 24 August.

**90.** Article 39A provides that "The State shall secure that the operation of the legal system promotes justice, on a basis of equal opportunity, and shall, in particular, provide free legal aid, by suitable legislation or schemes or in any other way, to ensure that opportunities for securing justice are not denied to any citizen by reason of economic or other disabilities."

**91.** The task of framing the Constitution of India was given to the Constituent Assembly, formed under the Cabinet Mission Plan of 1946. The Constituent Assembly took two years, eleven months and seventeen days to complete its historic task of drafting the Constitution for Independent India. Finally, the Constitution of India was enacted, signed and adopted by the Constituent Assembly on November 26, 1949. On January 26, 1950, the Constitution of India came into force on which date India also became a Republic.

**92.** Article 143(1) of the Constitution of India, 1950, provides that if at any time it appears to the President that a question of law or fact has arisen, or is likely to arise, which is of such a nature and of such public importance that it is expedient to obtain the opinion of the Supreme Court upon it, he may refer the question to that Court for consideration and the Court may, after such hearing as it thinks fit, report to the President, its opinion thereon.

**93.** Ad valorem literally means value added. It is generally used to refer to a tax (an ad-valorem tax) that is a percentage of the price of the product. An example of an ad valorem tax would be VAT. Ad valorem rates, which have come into increased use, have the important advantage of adjusting the tax burden according to the amount the consumer spends on the taxed items. They thus avoid the serious discrimination of specific rates against the low-priced varieties of the commodities.

**94.** The draft of the Indian Penal Code was prepared by the First Law Commission, chaired by Thomas Babington Macaulay. Its basis is the law of England freed from superfluities, technicalities and local peculiarities. The first final draft of the Indian Penal Code was submitted to the Governor-General in Council in 1837, but the draft was again revised. The drafting was completed in 1850 and it was presented to the Legislative Council in 1856 but it did not take its place on the Indian statute book until a generation later, following the Indian Rebellion of 1857. The draft then underwent a very careful revision at the hands of Sir Barnes Peacock, Chief Justice, and the puisne Judges of the Calcutta Supreme Court who were members of the Legislative Council, and was passed into law on 6 October 1860. The Code finally came into operation on 1 January 1862.

**95.** According to section 45 of Indian Penal Code, the word "life" denotes the life of a human being, unless the contrary appears from the context.

**96.** The Attorney General of India is the Indian government's Chief Legal Advisor, and its primary lawyer in the Supreme Court of India. He is appointed by the President of India under Article 76(1) of the Constitution and holds office during the pleasure of the President. He must be a person qualified to be appointed as a Judge of the Supreme Court. The current Attorney General is Goolam Essaji Vahanvati, who was appointed by the government in 2009.

**97.** Patent is a set of exclusive rights granted by a government to an applicant for a limited period of time in which such patent can be exclusively exploited subject to certain exceptions. Indian Patent Act, 1970 fixes this time for 20 years from the date of filing.

**98.** Indian Constitution originally consisted of 395 articles, 22 parts and 8 schedules. With number of amendments in the following years the same has been raised to 448 articles, 22 parts and 12 schedules.

**99.** According to section 10 of the Indian Contract Act, "all agreements are contracts if they are made by the free consent of parties competent to contract, for a lawful consideration and with a lawful object, and are not hereby expressly declared to be void."

**100.** As originally enacted, the preamble described the state as a "sovereign democratic republic". However, in 1976 the Forty-second Amendment substituted "sovereign democratic republic" with "Sovereign Socialist Secular Democratic Republic".

**101.** The International Court of Justice (commonly referred to as the World Court or ICJ) is primary judicial organ of the United Nations which is situated in the Peace Palace in The Hague, Netherlands. Its main functions are to settle legal disputes submitted to it by states and to provide advisory opinions on legal questions submitted to it by duly authorized international organs, agencies, and the UN General Assembly.

**102.** As an appointment of an agent is due to the trust and confidence his principal has in him, usually the agent cannot delegate his authority to another person. He may however appoint another and delegate his authority if it is normal in the trade that he is placed, or if his master permits it.

**103.** Justice S. H. Kapadia is the first CJI born after India gained independence. To be exact, he was born 45 days after India became independent.

**104.** The book *"The Kesavananda Bharati Case: The Untold Story of Struggle for Supremacy by Supreme Court and Parliament"* written by T. R. Andhyarujina has been in news for its controversial comments on the Kesavananda Bharati Case. The book recounts the tensions and conflicts in the Kesavananda Bharati case not only between the rival sides but also amongst the judges some of whom had preconceived views because of being judges in the earliest cases and others by reason of their selection by Government. It also reveals the stratagem of the Chief Justice S M Sikri on the date of the judgments by which he fortuned on a paper hurriedly prepared by him. It also shows how later cases of the Supreme Court have distilled the concept of the basic structure of the Constitution and how it has been considered in other jurisdictions.

**105.** Law Day is celebrated on November 26 because on this very day our constitution was adopted by constitution assembly in 1949. Thus both A and R is true and R is the correct explanation of A.

**106.** Seldom means rarely or at a few instances. Thus, lawyers are seldom sad conveys that at least on one occasion, lawyers are not sad.

**107.** All teachers always teach well is the most doubtful statement.

**108.** There are students who do not study hard for exams contradicts the question statement 'all students study hard for all the exams'. Thus, option (*a*) is correct.

**109.** If Asha is lata then Rekha is not Helen; Salman is not Amir and Priyanka is not Rani. Therefore, if Asha is Lata then Priyanka is not Rani. Hence, option (*b*) is correct. Option (*c*) is incorrect because we do not know whether the reverse is true or not. So option (*c*) is beyond the scope of the information. Similarly, the conclusion when Asha is not Lata is beyond the scope of the information.

**110.** The missing premise should show the connection between prosperity and world peace. Option (*d*) presents the missing premise in the most logical manner. Option (*b*) is incorrect because the premise fails to present the logical connection. Options (*a*) and (*c*) are irrelevant.

**111.** Option (*b*) appears to be close but is incorrect as there is a possibility that one is not contended even when he gives and receives love. But one who is not giving love cannot be contended is true beyond doubt. Thus, option (*a*) is correct.

**112.** The appearance of a lady being pleasing is a subjective issue. The opinion may vary from subject to subject. Some may find her pretty but some may not. Thus, Angelena Jolie looked pretty in her red gown can neither be proved nor disproved.

**113.** 'Jingoism' refers to a strong belief that your own country is best, especially when this is expressed in support of war with another country. It denotes extreme nationalism marked especially by a belligerent foreign policy. Option (*b*) paraphrases the given statement correctly and is the correct answer.

**114.** The given statement is absurd because posthumous award means the award given after the death of the individual. So *the dead individual came on stage to receive her award* is absurd.

**115.** The argument in option (*c*) is correct if the premise is correct. If life is tough when one is poor leads to the conclusion that the presence of money affects our lives. Option (*a*) is incorrect as we have no knowledge of the native countries of John and Milton and we do not know whether English is a foreign language for them. The quality of paintings of Mike cannot be determined on the basis of his love for painting. Thus, (*b*) is incorrect. The premise talks about a connection between interest and motivation, but we do not know what is the connection. So the conclusion in (*d*) is incorrect.

**116.**

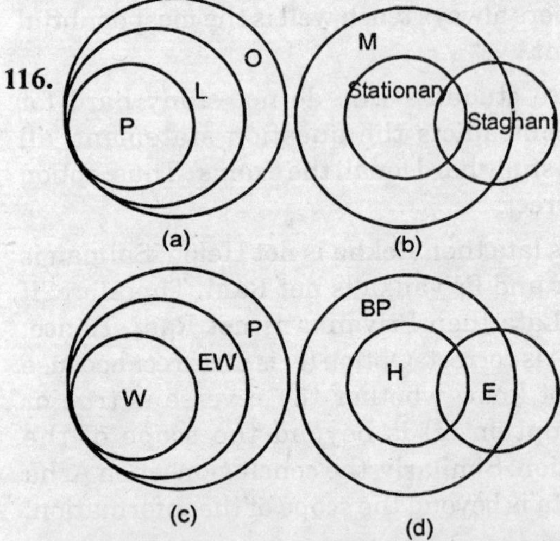


As plants is a subset of living and living require Oxygen therefore, plants require Oxygen. Thus, (*a*) can be accepted. Stationary is a subset of moving and some moving are stagnant. Thus, there is a possibility that some stagnant may be stationary. Since, (*b*) talks about possibility, it can be accepted. On similar grounds, (*d*) which talks about possibility of honesty being ethical can be accepted. All is well is a subset of predetermined and not vice versa. Thus, (*c*) cannot be accepted.

**117.** Grant of amnesty (pardon) to indecent students contradicts the given statement. Option (*c*) fails to address the issue mentioned and deals with discipline which is a broad term. Thus, option (*c*) is incorrect. Options (*a*) and (B) are irrelevant.

**118.** As Smita is a clever student and clever students should not fail. Therefore, Smita should not fail.

**119.** If something eludes you, you are not able to achieve it. Thus option (*c*) paraphrases the statement 'Success eludes the weak-hearted' most accurately.

**120.** The given statement talks about the helplessness of the people and the lack of concern on the part of the government. Option (*d*) contradicts the statement by stating that it's the people who are responsible for their plight. They had failed to put any effort.

**121.** Argument (1) talks about the limitation and inadequacy of the ultrasound technique in determining miscarriage at times. Argument (2) talks about the intake of fruits and vegetables being harmful at times. Thus, both the arguments are analogous.

**122.** Option (*a*) summarizes the passage accurately. Option (*b*) is incorrect because it introduces a new concept (society). Option (*c*) can neither be inferred from the passage nor does it summarize the passage. It is incorrect. Option (*d*) talks about socializing which is beyond the scope of the passage.

**123.** The passage deals with brain drain and the flow of good students and faculties from weaker countries to stronger countries. Option (*b*) is closest in capturing the essence. Option (*d*) is an inference but not the essence. Option (*c*) is irrelevant.

**124.** The passage mentions that the defeatist stance evades the basic fact that people learn and adapt. Thus, option (*c*) contradicts the passage. Option (*a*) and (*b*) can be inferred from the passage.

**125.** If people have a tendency to spend more then the companies will not postpone the decision of increasing the price. Thus (*a*) contradicts and weakens the argument. Option (*b*), if true, supports and justifies the decision of the consumer durable companies to postpone the decision to increase the price of their goods. Thus, option (*b*) underpins the given argument. Option (*c*) is a far-fetched assumption.

**126.** Option (*a*) talks about the biased behavior of the state and can be inferred from the paragraph. Options (*b*) and (*c*) are assumptions and cannot be inferred from the given passage.

**127.** The first argument discusses acceptance of the idea of abortion, while the second argument deals with parental/judicial council in pregnancy. The two arguments are neither related nor interdependent.

**128.** The first argument argues that government should have some role in the practise of the right to freedom of speech , while the second argument counters this opinion. Hence (B) is the correct answer.

**129.** Statement (*a*) is factually correct. Statement (*b*) is factually incorrect. Statement (*c*) is logically possible. Statement (*d*) is factually incorrect

**130.** It is not possible to determine if Statement (*a*) is factually correct or incorrect. Statement (*b*) is logically incorrect. Statement (*c*) is factually correct. Statement (*d*) is logically incorrect.

**131.** Statement (*a*) is factually correct .Statement (*b*) is logically correct. Statement (*c*) is factually incorrect. In Statement (*d*) we requires experience to ascertain its veracity.

**132.** Option (*a*) and (*b*) can easily be eliminated as they are already stated in the arguments given by Tanvi. Hence they are the premises on which Tanvi bases her argument. Option (*c*) is the correct answer choice as Sia assumes that if the same opinion is being voiced by a majority of readers then they must be genuinely feeling so.

**133.** The idea central to the argument is 'should' there be a ban on marijuana. Option (*b*) and (*c*) can be eliminated as they are not related to the core issue. Option (*a*) can be eliminated as it is what Deepak assumes where as the question is asking about the flaw in the argument. Option (*d*) is correct as it mentions the flaw in the reasoning.

**134.** The passage clearly links a sluggish stock market and an overvalued property market to the price of gold. Hence, options (*b*) and (*d*) are incorrect. Option (*c*) can be ruled out because overvalued property market does not mean that the property market is on an increase. The property market may be overvalued and the price/value may have been constant for the given time. Hence, option (*a*) is the most appropriate option.

**135.** The core issue of the passage relates default rate of educational loans to the economic downturn. Hence, only option (*a*) is correct.

**136.** Option (*b*) can be inferred from the lines the 'greenhouse effect is real and is happening' and 'eventually it'll become damned clear that the Earth is warming and the warming is beyond anything we have experienced in millions of years'. The denial and resistance is quoted in relation to greenhouse effect and this cannot be concluded as a general response towards threats. Moreover, the last line of the passage ends on a hilarious note. Thus, option (*a*) is incorrect. Since the argument talks only about the response of America, option (*c*) cannot be deduced. Option (*d*) talks about the general rejection of scientific findings and is beyond the scope of the passage.

**137.** The judgement depends on the underlying assumption that the consumers were aware of the impact that the food would have on them when they were eating it. Thus, the fast food chain was not culpable. This makes (c) the answer.

**138.** Option (*d*) best explains why there is little progress despite increasing amounts of aid being provided. Options (*a*) and (*c*) are inappropriate. Even if only 10 percent of the aid is received and it takes longer to implement programs, the fact remains that each year the country is receiving increasing amounts. Option (*b*) alone also cannot help explain the increase in poverty.

**139.** Option (*d*) weakens the argument as it explains how disclosing an illness might also help a politician to retain power. Option (*a*) brings in the aspect of other countries which may notbe relevant to India. Options (*b*) and (*c*) do not affect the reasoning presented in the argument.

**140.** Option (*a*) is too general. Option (*b*) is incorrect as the aspect of perception being fallible is not mentioned in the paragraph. Option (*c*) is correct as the paragraph suggests that the universe is experienced through the senses and mind and becomes a part of it. Option (*d*) is close but talks about filtering and fails to talk about the role of our nerve fibers. This makes it less appropriate than (c).

**141.** On 31st December 2005 it was Saturday.

Number of odd days from the year 2006 to the year 2009 = (1 + 1 + 2 + 1) = 5 days.

[$\because$ 2008 is a leap year]

$\therefore$ On 31st December 2009, it was Thursday.

Hence, on 1st January, 2010 it is Friday.

**142.** Gain in 60 mintues = 240 seconds i.e. 4 minutes

Angle traversed by minute hand in one hour

$$= 360° + \frac{4}{60} \times 360° = 384°.$$

**143.** Let $r_1$ and $r_2$ (in cm) be the radius of sphere A and B respectively.

$$\therefore \quad \frac{4\pi r_1^2}{4\pi r_2^2} = \frac{100}{400}$$

$$\Rightarrow \quad \frac{r_1}{r_2} = \frac{1}{2}$$

$$\therefore \quad \frac{\text{Volume of sphere (A)}}{\text{Volume of sphere (B)}} = \frac{\frac{4}{3}\pi r_1^3}{\frac{4}{3}\pi r_2^3} = \frac{r_1^3}{r_2^3} = \left(\frac{1}{2}\right)^3$$

$$= \frac{1}{8} \text{ i.e. } 1 : 8.$$

**144.** Due to stoppages train travells 9 km less distance every hour.

Time taken to travell 9 km

$$= \frac{9}{72} \times 60 = 7.5 \text{ minutes.}$$

**145.** Let x be the total number of pages in the book.

Pages read by the student $= \frac{2}{3}x$

Pages left $= \frac{1}{3}x$

$$\therefore \quad \frac{2}{3}x - \frac{1}{3}x = 90$$

$$\Rightarrow \quad \frac{x}{3} = 90$$

$$\Rightarrow \quad x = 270.$$

**146.** Total work units = LCM of (20, 60) = 60 units

Work done by A and B together in a day = 3 units

Work done by B alone in a day = 1 unit

∴ Work done by A alone in a day = 3 – 1 = 2 units

Hence, A alone can complete the whole work in

$$\frac{60}{2} = 30 \text{ days.}$$

**147.** Let x and y (in years) be the present ages of Himani and her daughter respectively.

8 years ago, Himani's age

= x – 8 and her daughter's age = y – 8

$$\therefore \quad x - 8 = 8(y - 8)$$

$$\Rightarrow \quad y = \frac{x + 56}{8} \quad \text{...(i)}$$

After 16 years, Himani's age

= x + 16 and her daughter's age = y + 16

$$\therefore \quad x + 16 = 2(y + 16)$$

$$\Rightarrow \quad y = \frac{x - 16}{2} \quad \text{...(ii)}$$

From (i) and (ii),

$$\frac{x + 56}{8} = \frac{x - 16}{2}$$

$$\Rightarrow \quad x = 40 \text{ years.}$$

**148.** $x = 2y = 3z$

$$\Rightarrow \quad x = 2y \text{ and } z = \frac{2}{3}y$$

$$\frac{x + y + z}{3} = 22$$

$$\Rightarrow \quad \frac{2y + y + \frac{2}{3}y}{3} = 22$$

$$\Rightarrow \quad y = 18.$$

**149.** $\frac{x}{y} = \frac{2}{3}$ and $\frac{y}{z} = \frac{4}{5}$

$$\Rightarrow \quad x : y : z = 8 : 12 : 15$$

$$\therefore \quad \left(\frac{5x + 3y - 4z}{5x - 3y + 4z}\right) = \frac{40 + 36 - 60}{40 - 36 + 60} = \frac{1}{4}.$$

**150.** 60% of 25% of 960

$$= \frac{60}{100} \times \frac{25}{100} \times 960 = 144$$

**Option *a*:**

30% of 90% of 600

$$= \frac{30}{100} \times \frac{90}{100} \times 600 = 162$$

**Option *b*:**

$$16\% \text{ of } 900 = \frac{16}{100} \times 900 = 144$$

**Option *c*:**

$$40\% \text{ of } 80\% \text{ of } 400 = \frac{40}{100} \times \frac{80}{100} \times 400 = 128$$

**Option *d*:**

$$18\% \text{ of } 750 = \frac{18}{100} \times 750 = 135.$$

■■

# AILET PATTERN

## MODEL PAPER-II

**INSTRUCTIONS:**

**Time: 90 Minutes**

1. This Model Paper will give you an insight into the pattern of the **AILET (All India Law Etrance Test)**.. Undertaking this model test under the mentioned stipulated time frame will allow you to understand real test scenario.
2. This Question Paper consists of five sections viz. A(English), B(General Knowledge), C(Legal Aptitude),D(Logical Reasoning) and E (Mathematics).The total number of questions are 150
3. Each Question contains one mark. There is NO NEGATIVE MARKING

## SECTION – A: ENGLISH

**Directions for questions 1 to 6:** Read the given passage and answer the questions that follow.

The book bears the imprint of the Nandkarni's extensive knowledge of ancient philosophical texts like the Upanishads further enriched by his knowledge of Sanskrit. Every page is witness to his enormous erudition. His citations number a hundred, drawn from multiple sources – the west and east, from the Greek to Indian, from Aristotle, Scruton, Russell and Kant to Thirukural (Tamil). The book is almost a condensed encyclopedia on several themes with the result that where perhaps one wanted more elaboration of seminal ideas, one is taken quickly to other domains. It is a very eclectic enterprise drawing from a wide variety of sources and perspectives – epistemology, epics, scriptures, political philosophy, philosophical debates, ecology, and feminism and so on. It is several books rolled into one – a veritable library. There is no logical structure and nor is it necessary. When one draws from diverse sources to buttress one's argument, there is danger in selecting only those sources which favor one's argument. Countervailing texts get ignored. There is much in our tradition which is worth preserving and drawing from and this in fact belongs to the genre of "perennial philosophy".

Nadkarni bases his exposition staunchly on "Hinduism". Unfortunately the word Hinduism is an aberration thrust on us by Semitic religions which are "isms". Hindus were people who lived around the river Sindhu so named by the Greek invaders in our hoary past. Hinduism does not have the trademarks of religion. It has no church, no prophet, no congregation and no one Book. It is the repository of speculative thinking over the centuries and has no unifying dogma and as such provides a wide variety of ideas from Advaita at one end to materialism at the other. What unifies Hindu society is the caste system in its day-to-day life and the life cycle rituals and forms of worship.

Nadkarni reads from Gandhi's ideas and actions to illustrate how his adherence to truth and non-violence was employed in his personal life and in his approach to social problems. Decades after him, we are confronted by precisely the environmental crisis and continuing poverty amidst consumerism and profit-oriented development that he had foreseen. Nadkarni's exposition of Gandhi's prescience, his emphasis on ethics as a fundamental to guide human action is very well written. This is the best part of the book. In many ways there is a resurgent interest in Gandhi's ideas today. His advocacy of village self-sufficiency and revival of crafts to create employment makes sense today but one can accept this as an approach and not as a literal plan because a lot more is needed if we wish to reinvigorate crafts in terms of alternate technology, markets and skill development. Within a globalized world and in an open economy these are difficult to implement unless we eschew international trade and revert to autarky.

To my mind, while the principle behind such an approach cannot be faulted, practice in the present context is not easy. How do we turn back the clock? Personally I am sympathetic to crafts as India has one of the richest craft traditions in the world. Some attempts have been made but not with vigour. The author agrees that while moral principles per se or taken in isolation are independent of facts or situations, in implementation and actual situation conflicts arise and trade-offs become necessary. Here the author could have given some examples from real life.

Nadkarni provides an interesting link between economics and ethics. Both deal with choice. In issues related to human development he points out how ethics and economics overlap because both are subject to ethical evaluation. He argues that ethics is meaningful only in the context of choice – not just between what is good and bad but between different moral principles.

What kind of development will promote overall human welfare? How do we subject it to ethical evaluation? The answer is mutual obligation so as to ensure that our choice is conducive to all sections of society. What is conducive should not be in utilitarian terms of the individual's freedom to choose to maximize his or her satisfaction. Here the relevance of what Nadkarni drives home is well illustrated according to me by the feminist demand of the right to "reproductive choice" which was articulated at a time when a coercive population control programme was unleashed.

However, how can it be an individual choice when the consequences of one's actions impinge on society – the number of children one has in turn affects the number of schools, doctors, and social provisions that would be needed. If economics holds self-interest as the motivating factor in human decisions, it misconstrues the plurality of motivations. Moral dilemmas arise when we follow a single moral principle irrespective of consequences.

**1.** Which of the following correctly depicts/depict the shortcomings of Nandkarni's Book?

1. Less elaborate discussion on some topics that demand elaboration
2. Condensed encyclopedia on several themes
3. Lack of logical structure
4. Text countervailing Nandkarni's argument is ignored.

(*a*) Only 1 (*b*) 1 and 2
(*c*) 1, 2 and 3 (*d*) 1, 2,3 and 4

**2.** According to the passage, which of the following is incorrect about Hindus/Hinduism?

1. People who lived around the river Sindhu.
2. Absence of trademarks of religion and a unifying dogma.
3. Absence of a single book.
4. Caste system and rituals help in unifying Hinduism.

(*a*) 1 and 2 (*b*) 2 and 3
(*c*) 1, 3 and 4 (*d*) None of these

**3.** The author of the passage would be least likely to agree with which of the following?

(*a*) India has one of the richest craft traditions in the world.
(*b*) Our choices should take into account the welfare of the community.
(*c*) Though Gandhi's principles were good, the practical application of many principles is not easy.
(*d*) None of these

**4.** From the following options, which does the author make use of while discussing the Nandkarni' book?

(*a*) Rhetorical questions
(*b*) Comparison and contrast
(*c*) Specific illustrations
(*d*) Connecting links

**5.** Which of the following is correct?

1. The author knows Sanskrit.
2. Nandkarni feels that in practical situations, some aspects of moral principles need to be sidelined and demand compromise.
3. Nandkarni feels that with respect to human development, ethics and economics hardly overlap.

(*a*) 1, 2 and 3
(*b*) 2 and 3
(*c*) 1 and 3
(*d*) only 2

**6.** The author's review of Nadkarni's book can be best described as

(*a*) pedantic and practical
(*b*) pejorative and critical
(*c*) analytical and pragmatic
(*d*) admiring and focused

**Directions for questions 7 to 13:** In each of the following questions, a sentence that is divided into parts is given. One of the parts may be erroneous. Identify the part that is erroneous. If the sentence is grammatically correct, mark *no error* as your answer.

**7.** Over the past 20 years, countries divided (*a*)/ by ethnicity and political turmoil had brought (*b*)/ together through reconciliation (c)./ No error (*d*)

**8.** But the pursuit of justice should (*a*) / not replace or undermine (*b*) / ongoing reconciliation effort. (*c*) / No error (*d*)

**9.** Reconciliation is not an easy option, (*a*) / because it does allow people to move forward with the hope (*b*) / of unity, and the potential for justice in the future.(c)/ No error (*d*)

**10.** The cyclists were (*a*)/ neck to neck as they (*b*)/ approached the final lap.(c)/ No error (*d*)

**11.** She turned (*a*)/ the car around (*b*)/ and drove off.(c)/ No error (*d*)

**12.** From the outside, (*a*) / the one increasingly (*b*) / eclipse the other.(c)/ No error (*d*)

**13.** Nobody likes to say (*a*) / that someone's service was (*b*) / for a misguided cause. (c)/ No error (*d*)

**Directions for questions 14 to 18:** In the following passage there are blanks, each of which has been numbered. These numbers are printed below the passage and against each, four words are suggested, one of which fits the blank appropriately. Find out the appropriate word in each case.

Over the past few decades, with the executive unable to play its role properly and the legislature in a regular logjam, the courts have come forward to ____(14)____ relief to the citizenry and order the government to carry out the tasks which it had failed to. The judiciary has ____(15)____ come to exercise some powers that ideally should have never been its remit. ____(16)____, given the extra responsibility that has been ____(17)____ on the courts due to the acts of omission and commission of the other two legs of the republic, it is even more necessary for the judiciary to act with caution and ____(18)____. However, it is distressing to find that in a number of cases the judges of the higher courts have been slipping into policy making and implementation.

**14.** (*a*) oblige (*b*) mend (*c*) create (*d*) grant

**15.** (*a*) de facto (*b*) prima facie (*c*) sine qua non (*d*) de jure

**16.** (*a*) Therefore (*b*) Although (*c*) However (*d*) Notwithstanding

**17.** (*a*) thrust (*b*) thrown (*c*) ordered (*d*) mane

**18.** (*a*) despair (*b*) enthusiasm (*c*) authority (*d*) restraint

**Directions for questions 19 to 23:** Read the given sentences carefully and identify the most appropriate synonym of the word given in italics.

**19.** She's a *niggardly* woman, so don't expect a favor from her.
(*a*) mean (*b*) charitable (*c*) bounteous (*d*) noxious

**20.** She was very *profligate* in her spending.
(*a*) economical (*b*) frugal (*c*) penny-pinching (*d*) extravagant

**21.** She has heard stories about pirates and *renegades* on the high seas.
(*a*) disciples (*b*) deserters (*c*) loyalists (*d*) followers

**22.** Because he was *indigent*, the court appointed a lawyer to defend him.
(*a*) affluent (*b*) opulent (*c*) broke (*d*) rich

**23.** The *acquisitive* developers are trying to tear down the historic home and build a shopping mall.
(*a*) avaricious (*b*) benignant (*c*) munificent (*d*) propitious

**Directions for questions 24 to 33:** In each of the following questions, a sentence with a blank is given. From the given options, select the one that completes the given sentence in the grammatically correct way.

**24.** Most companies ________ fifty million dollars by the time they quit this business.
(*a*) would made (*b*) would had made (*c*) will make (*d*) will have made

**25.** We ________ for a picnic tomorrow.
(*a*) were going (*b*) will going (*c*) are going (*d*) was going

**26.** This solution is technically superior ______ its competitors.
(*a*) than (*b*) to (*c*) by (*d*) from

**27.** I don't believe ______ nepotism.
(*a*) about (*b*) in (*c*) on (*d*) at

**28.** I would like to talk to you ______ person.
(*a*) on (*b*) in (*c*) with (*d*) by

**29.** The meeting is due ______ 12:15 p.m.
(*a*) on (*b*) at (*c*) in (*d*) for

**30.** Registering an Indian presence ______ finally become easier for all.
(*a*) has (*b*) have been (*c*) have (*d*) had been

**31.** It would be a lot easier when we have the database ________.
(*a*) running along (*b*) run for it (*c*) running off (*d*) up and running

**32.** My father or my sisters _____ arriving by train today.
(*a*) are (*b*) will (*c*) is (*d*) should

**33.** He held this post ________ seven years.
(*a*) since
(*b*) for
(*c*) to
(*d*) around

**Directions for questions 34 and 35:** Read the given sentences carefully and identify the correct meaning of the idiom/phrase that has been underlined.

**34.** Before you conclude that I have become a raging Europhile, let me say that there is a fly in the ointment.

(*a*) factor that spoils a situation

(*b*) test of an opinion

(*c*) variance with the expected

(*d*) relic of the past

**35.** "I am sure you are walking on air," my mother said to Paul at his wedding.

(*a*) acting pretentiously

(*b*) acting snobbishly

(*c*) manner of behaving designed to impress

(*d*) feeling elated

## SECTION – B: GENERAL KNOWLEDGE

**36.** The West Bengal Forest Department recently has decided to reintroduce which one of the following animal, that is listed as critically endangered by the International Union of Conservation of Nature (IUCN), in the grasslands of the Gorumara National Park in north Bengal?

(*a*) Black Deer (*b*) White Tiger

(*c*) Pygmy Hog (*d*) Montane Mouse Shrew

**37.** Templeton Prize established in 1972, to honour a living person who affirms life's spiritual dimension be it through insight, or practical works, was recently conferred to whom among the following?

(*a*) Desmond Tutu (*b*) Sri Sri Ravishankar

(*c*) Aung San Suu Kyi (*d*) Dalai Lama

**38.** Which of the following countries won Uber Cup 2012?

(*a*) India (*b*) China

(*c*) South Korea (*d*) Japan

**39.** India-born Suma Chakrabarti recently has been selected as the President of which one of the following organisations?

(*a*) Asian Development Bank

(*b*) European Bank for Reconstruction and Development

(*c*) International Bank for Reconstruction and Development

(*d*) United Nations Conference on Trade and Development

**40.** Recently Moody's downgraded three top private sector banks in India. Which one of the following is not among them?

(*a*) ICICI Bank (*b*) HDFC Bank

(*c*) Axis Bank (*d*) ING Vysya Bank

**41.** One of the oldest living ancient sports seen in the modern era, Jallikattu or Eruthazhuvuthal or Manju Virattu, a bull taming sport, is played in which one of the following states?

(*a*) Andhra Pradesh (*b*) Karnataka

(*c*) Tamil Nadu (*d*) Kerala

**42.** Which of the following companies is/are the principal sponsors for the Indian squad for the Olympics in London?

(*a*) Indo Nissin Foods Limited (INFL)

(*b*) Samsung

(*c*) Amul

(*d*) Both (*a*) and (*b*)

**43.** Which of the following countries is the world's largest producer and exporter of uranium?

(*a*) Australia (*b*) Kazakhstan

(*c*) Canada (*d*) France

**44.** "Shoor Veer," the war games and military training exercise termed the biggest-ever war games in the Thar Desert, was conducted in which of the following district of Rajasthan?

(*a*) Bikaner (*b*) Hanumangarh

(*c*) Barmer (*d*) Jaisalmer

**45.** Which one of the following Tamil writers won 6th NTR National Literary Award for his novel 'Thanneer'?

(*a*) Ashokamitran (*b*) S.Ramakrishnan

(*c*) Balakumaran (*d*) Jeyamohan

**46.** Gujarat government has refused to impose a total ban on distribution of the Monsanto hybrid seed named "Prabal" to the farmers in the State, particularly the tribal agriculturists. Prabal is the seed of:

(*a*) Wheat (*b*) Maize

(*b*) Rice (*d*) Sorghum

**47.** A U.S. treasure hunter claims to have found the exact spot where al-Qaeda leader Osama bin Laden's body was dumped by U.S. forces in the waters about 320 km west of Surat in Gujarat. Name the treasure hunter.

(*a*) Bill Warren (*b*) Van Zeck

(*c*) Jayson Wechter (*d*) Andrew Lewis

**48.** The empowered committee appointed by the Supreme Court to examine the safety of the 116-year-old Mullaperiyar dam has concluded that it is hydrologically, structurally and seismically safe. Committee was headed by:

(*a*) Justice B.P. Saraf (*b*) Justice A.S. Anand

(*c*) Justice J. C. Shah (*d*) Justice B.N.Kirpal

**49.** Who among the following has been selected for the C.N.R Rao national prize for chemical sciences for the year 2012-13?

(*a*) Srivari Chandrasekhar

(*b*) V Surya Prakasa Rao

(*c*) J. K. Bera

(*d*) A.K.Sood

**50.** 'BeiDou-2' or Compass Navigation Satellite System (CNSS) is capable of providing continuous, real-time passive 3D geo-spatial positioning and speed measurement and is second-generation satellite navigation system of:

(*a*) USA (*b*) Russia

(*c*) China (*d*) UK

**51.** What is 'Jugnu'?

(*a*) Solar Lantern

(*b*) Nano-Satellite

(*c*) Technique for operating cataract patients

(*d*) None of the above

**52.** 'Megha-Tropiques' is a satellite mission to study climate change set up by ISRO in collaboration with space agency of which country?

(*a*) France (*b*) USA

(*c*) Russia (*d*) China

**53.** The Horn of ________ is a term used to describe the easternmost projection of Somalia.

(*a*) Africa (*b*) South America

(*c*) Asia (*d*) Europe

**54.** The Aakash is an Android based tablet computer produced by the company________.

(*a*) Get Jar (*b*) Data Wind

(*c*) Quad (*d*) None of the above

**55.** The Jaitapur nuclear power plant is being set up with cooperation from________

(*a*) France (*b*) UK

(*c*) USA (*d*) Russia

**56.** Right to Education (RTE) pertains to which age-group?

(*a*) 6-14 years

(*b*) 0-6 years

(*c*) 4- 16 years

(*d*) None of the above

**57.** The Emperor of All Maladies: A Biography of Cancer is a book written by

(*a*) Siddhartha Mukherjee

(*b*) Jennifer Egan

(*c*) Robert Wright

(*d*) None of the above

**58.** First private airport in India for both International and Domestic operations is proposed to be established at

(*a*) Karaikal (*b*) Mahe

(*c*) Yanam (*d*) Pondichery

**59.** The North Atlantic Treaty Organisation (NATO) is headquartered at

(*a*) Amsterdam (*b*) London

(*c*) Brussels (*d*) Madrid

**60.** World Book and Copyright Day is observed on ________by UNESCO.

(*a*) April 23 (*b*) May 23

(*c*) April 13 (*d*) March 23

**61.** What is SAGA-220?

(*a*) Combat Aircraft (*b*) Supercomputer

(*c*) Operating System (*d*) None of the above

**62.** Indira Gandhi Centre for Atomic Research (IGCAR) is situated at

(*a*) Trombay (*b*) Kalpakkam

(*c*) Rawatbhata (*d*) Narora

**63.** The ____________ has been set up to facilitate sharing of information by security agencies and law enforcement agencies.

(*a*) NATGRID (*b*) TERRORGRID

(*c*) CRIMEGRID (*d*) None of the above

**64.** Santosh Trophy pertains to which sport?

(*a*) Football (*b*) Cricket

(*c*) Lawn Tennis (*d*) Badminton

**65.** What is C-17 Globemaster?

(*a*) Combat Aircraft

(*b*) Millitary Transport Aircraft

(*c*) Combat Helicopter

(*d*) Luxury Car

**66.** The fastest supercomputer in the world is called____.

(*a*) K (*b*) Tianhe-1A

(*c*) SAGA-220 (*d*) None of the above

**67.** Dadaab in ______ hosts the world's biggest refugee camp.

(*a*) Kenya (*b*) Sudan

(*c*) Somalia (*d*) Egypt

**68.** World Population Day is observed annually on

(*a*) July 11 (*b*) July 21

(*c*) July 1 (*d*) None of the above

**69.** What is 'Prahaar'?

(*a*) Anti-tank missile (*b*) Tactical missile

(*c*) Light Machinegun (*d*) None of the above

**70.** The current system followed for appointment to higher judiciary is called the ______ system.

(*a*) Electoral College (*b*) Collegium

(*c*) Collegiate (*d*) None of the above

## SECTION –C: LEGAL APTITUDE

**71.** The theory of "basic structure" of the Constitution was propounded in....?

(*a*) Indira Nehru Gandhi vs. Raj Narain

(*b*) I.C. Golaknath vs. State of Punjab

(*c*) Kesavanand Bharti vs. State of Kerala

(*d*) Menaka Gandhi vs. Union of India

**72.** International Criminal Court is located in.....

(*a*) Rome (*b*) New York

(*c*) Geneva (*d*) Hague

**73.** Which among the following is directly related to Child Welfare?

(*a*) UNESCO (*b*) ILO

(*c*) UNICEF (*d*) WTO

**74.** The first Secretary General of United Nations was .........?

(*a*) Dag Hammarskjold (*b*) Kurt Waldheim

(*c*) U. Thant (*d*) Trigvi Lie

**75.** An agreement which is not legally enforceable is called.........?

(*a*) Voidable agreement

(*b*) Void Agreement

(*c*) Illegal agreement

(*d*) Valid Contract.

**76.** A person who files a suit in a court of law is called .........?

(*a*) Applicant (*b*) Complainant

(*c*) Defendant (*d*) Plaintiff

**77.** Who is the head of the State as per the Constitution of India ?

(*a*) Prime Minister of India

(*b*) President of India

(*c*) Parliament of India

(*d*) All of the above

**78.** Which of the following is not the principal organ of U.N. Organisation?

(*a*) Trusteeship Council

(*b*) Economic and Social Council

(*c*) International Court of Justice

(*d*) Human Rights Commission

**79.** To whom does the President of India submits his resignation?

(*a*) Prime Minister of India

(*b*) Chief Justice of India

(*c*) Vice President of India

(*d*) Speaker of Lok Sabha.

**80.** Name the first woman Chief Justice of a High Court.

(*a*) Leila Seith (*b*) Leila Mukherjee

(*c*) Lalita Basu (*d*) Sarojni Naidu

**81.** The rule of Evidence law that a person cannot deny the statement which he had previously made is called.........?

(*a*) Waiver (*b*) Denial

(*c*) Estoppel (*d*) None of the above

**82.** A person who may of considerable help to the Court is called.........?

(*a*) Legal Advisor (*b*) Attorney

(*c*) Amicus Curiae (*d*) Legal Representative

**83.** Equality before Law and Equal Protection of Laws is available to.........?

(*a*) Citizens

(*b*) All persons

(*c*) Both *a* & b above

(*d*) Only to the Citizens of India

**84.** Who can file a Public Interest Litigation?

(*a*) Any person (*b*) Lawyers only

(*c*) Company (*d*) None of the above.

**85.** What kind of emergency is not envisaged by the Constitution of India?

(*a*) Threat to security of India

(*b*) Failure of constitutional machinery of a State

(*c*) Natural calamity or epidemics threatening the health and well-being of the people of India

(*d*) Threat to financial stability or credit of India

**86. Principle:** Every person is under an obligation to exercise reasonable care, so as not to cause damage to other person or property of others.

**Explanation:** No person can bring a suit for negligence if his act has directly contributed to the damage caused to him.

**Facts:** X was driving his new car at the speed of 80 kmph. Suddenly he saw Y crossing the road without zebra crossing. X attempted to apply the emergency break but failed. Y suffered multiple fractures and sued X for negligently driving his car. Decide. Whether the suit filed by Y is maintainable?

(*a*) Yes, as X was driving at an excessively high speed despite his duty to exercise reasonable care towards pedestrians.

(*b*) No, as Y contributed to the damage by attempting to cross without zebra crossing in disregard of traffic rules.

(*c*) No, as Y also owed duty to cautiously cross roads.

(*d*) Yes, as X's act caused serious damage to Y.

**87. Principle:** An acceptance where the offeree does not abide by the mode of acceptance stipulated in the offer is not binding.

**Explanation**: Departure from the usual and suggested method of communication throw upon the risk that acceptance would get delayed.

**Facts**: A offered B to convey his acceptance for making hundred pair of military boots by registered post within seven days. B reached A's place within five days with the hundred pair of military boots ready to be delivered. A rejects the consignment which caused B a loss of $500. B sued A for the loss of income and damages. Decide?

(*a*) A is liable to pay as B accepted the offered and prepared hundred pair of military boots.

(*b*) A is not liable as there was no valid acceptance.

(*c*) A is not liable as he was not ready to accept delivery of military shoes.

(*d*) A is liable as he clearly stipulated requirement for hundred pair of military boots.

**88. Principle:** When two or more persons, by fighting, disturb the public peace, they are said to commit an affray.

**Explanation:** Public peace is the usual working environment or atmosphere in which activities are conducted in a public place.

**Facts:** X and Y owned adjoining shops in a busy market place. Y parked his truck in front of X's shops throughout the day. X objected to this but to no avail. Later, after closing of the shop around midnight X and Y start hurling abuses at each other in front of the shop. Whether X and Y are jointly liable for an affray. Decide.

(*a*) Yes, as X and Y have disturbed public peace by abusing each other.

(*b*) No, as there was no disturbance to public peace considering the abusing took place around midnight.

(*c*) No, as X and Y were merely abusing and not fighting with each other.

(*d*) Yes, as X and Y were abusing each other at a public place.

**89. Principle:** Whoever by words, signs or other representation brings contempt or hatred or disaffection towards the Government established commits sedition.

**Explanation:** Exercise of freedom of speech cannot be termed as sedition if it falls short of violence or armed attack.

**Facts:** In a public meeting, X, a popular civil society leader announces that "this government is a bunch of scamsters, scoundrels and thieves and deserve to be chased away from power." X adds that, it is time to teach the government a lesson. Government decides to prosecute X for sedition. Decide.

(*a*) X is guilty for utterances meant to bring contempt or hatred to the duly elected government.

(*b*) X is not guilty as sedition is an archaic law.

(*c*) X is not guilty as he is exercising his freedom to speech and expression.

(*d*) X is for having made irresponsible and contemptuous speech.

**90. Principle:** Malicious intent is said to exist if the prosecution is instituted with a wish to injure the party rather than to vindicate law and justice.

**Explanation:** Malice is not to be inferred merely from the acquittal of the plaintiff.

**Facts:** James saw Jerry misbehave with a girl on a highway. He complained to the police and Jerry was arrested. Later, on the request made by the girl who was Jerry's wife all the charges against him were dropped. Jerry filed action for malicious prosecution against James. Decide.

(*a*) Yes, as he ought to have rechecked the facts before filing a complaint.

(*b*) No, as Jerry was merely fighting with his wife.

(*c*) No, as James did not intend to cause injury but to actually protect the girl.

(*d*) Yes, as Jerry was arrested on compliant by James.

**91. Principle:** Whoever causes death by doing an act with an intention of causing death commits culpable homicide amounting to murder.

**Explanation:** Intention of causing death means and includes the clear mens rea of ending the life of another person.

**Facts:** Siraj, a poacher entered Bandhavgarh tiger reserve despite the statutory warning of not targeting tigers. He saw movement behind the bush and shot there. He found that a forest guard was killed by the bullet. Currently Siraj is being tried in the court for culpable homicide amounting to murder. Decide whether Siraj is guilty of culpable homicide amounting to murder?

(*a*) Yes, as he tried poaching in a reserve area where tiger hunting was a punishable offence.

(*b*) No, as he did not shoot with an intention of causing death of forest guard.

(*c*) No, as provisions of criminal law cannot be applied for an attack essentially directed towards animals.

(*d*) Yes, as he caused death of forest guard and intention to kill is immaterial.

**92. Principle**: An agreement where the parties are under a mistake as to a matter of fact essential to the agreement, the agreement is void.

**Explanation**: An erroneous opinion as to the value of the thing which forms the subject-matter of an agreement is not to be deemed a mistake as to a matter of fact.

**Facts:** X agrees to buy from Y a certain horse. It turns out that the horse was dead at the time of the bargain, though neither party was aware of this material fact. The parties signed a contract but at the time of performance Y declined the performance of the contract citing mistake of fact. X files a suit against Y. Whether there was a valid contract between X and Y?

(*a*) Yes, death of horse was not a mistake of fact.

(*b*) No, as a mistake of fact renders the contract void.

(*c*) No, as Y had not received any consideration from X for performance of contract.

(*d*) Yes, both the parties signed a contract for sale of horse.

**93. Principle**: An agreement under a mistake as to a matter of fact, which is essential to the agreement, is void.

**Explanation**: An erroneous opinion as to the value of the thing which forms the subject-matter of an agreement is not to be deemed a mistake as to a matter of fact.

**Facts:** A decided to buy from B, a consignment of wooden planks, which was on its way from Italy. Both A and B were unaware that the consignment had perished due to cyclone on the date of signing the contract. A sues B for non-performance of contract. Decide whether the contract between B and A can be enforced?

(*a*) Yes, as A had legitimate expectation to buy the designated wooden planks from B.

(*b*) No, as the both A and B were under mistake of fact on the date of execution of the agreement.

(*c*) No, as the consignment had not perished due to B's act.

(*d*) Yes, as Italian timber is a rare commodity.

**94. Principle:** A libel is defamation in some permanent form. It is said to be committed if there is a publication of a false or defamatory statement, which tends to injure the reputation of another person without lawful excuse.

**Explanation:** A libelous statement must be published in a permanent form such as effigy, writing, painting etc.

**Facts:** Sadat, a famous wax statue maker made a statue of the famous actress Madhumati Dixit. The said wax statue portrayed the actress with a long nose and an ugly face. Madhumati sued Sadat for libel. Decide whether there was a publication in the aforesaid facts of the case?

(*a*) Yes, as wax statue was a permanent form of statement.

(*b*) No, as there was no statement made by Sadat much less in writing.

(*c*) No, as Sadat exercised his freedom of expression as per constitution of India.

(*d*) Yes, as Madhumati was wrongly depicted in the wax-statue.

**95. Principle**: Whoever intentionally insults or provokes any person which leads to cause disturbance of public peace, is liable to be punished with an imprisonment of two years.

**Explanation**: Intentional insult or provocation shall be caused only if the person causing the same believes or has reason to believe that it would hurt the sentiment of others.

**Facts**: Robert calls Rando a 'nigger' during university lunch-break. Rando was offended and decided to sit on a hunger strike in the University mess itself. Can Rando be held guilty for his act?

(*a*) No, as Robert spoke the truth.

(*b*) Yes, as Rando was seriously offended and decided to go on a hunger strike.

(*c*) Yes, as Robert had reason to believe that Rando would feel offended.

(*d*) No, as disturbance of peace is an essential element of the offence which could not be satisfied as hunger strike was by peaceful means.

**96. Principle:** Any person who obstructs the other person to move in a direction in which he has a right to proceed causes wrongful restraint.

**Explanation:** Right to proceed can be duly regulated in the interest of public order, health and safety.

**Facts**: A was running late for college examination. He encountered a traffic signal which was red for a long time. A decided to jump the traffic signal and was caught by traffic inspector B. A missed his examination and decided to lodge a complaint against B. Decide was B liable for causing wrongful restraint of A?

(*a*) No, as A jumped the traffic signal.

(*b*) Yes, as B ought to have allowed A to proceed considering that the traffic signal Red for a very long time.

(*c*) Yes, as B was prevented from moving in a direction in which he had right to proceed and he missed his exam.

(*d*) No, as A's right to proceed in a direction was duly regulated by B in interest of public order.

**97. Principle:** Fraud includes an active concealment of a fact by one having knowledge or belief of the fact.

**Explanation:** Mere silence of the facts likely to affect the willingness of a person is not fraud unless the person is under a duty bound to speak.

**Facts:** X sells by auction to Y a horse which X knows to be of unsound mind. X says nothing regarding unsoundness of the horse. After, six months, Y sues X for defrauding him. Decide whether Y can sustain a legal action for fraud against X?

(*a*) Yes, as X is liable for active concealment in this case.

(*b*) No, as X was not duty bound to speak in order to affect willingness of Y to purchase the horse.

(*c*) No, as X never prompted Y to buy the horse.

(*d*) Yes, as X ought to have announced that the horse is insane before auctioning it.

**98. Principle:** Every person is under the obligation to exercise reasonable care so as not to cause damage to the person or property of others.

**Explanation:** No person can bring a suit for negligence if his act has directly contributed to the damage caused to him.

**Facts:** A merchant named Golu was infamous for selling stale food items in Karol Bagh. Once Sanjay bought snacks from Golu's shop. Sanjay had the snacks along with alcohol. Next morning, he was admitted in the city hospital for stomach infection. Doctors told him that the mixture of alcohol and stale food caused the stomach infection. Sanjay sued Golu for selling stale food item to him. Decide whether Golu can be held liable for negligence in the present case?

(*a*) No, as the act of Sanjay directly contributed to his stomach infection.

(*b*) Yes, as Golu owed a responsibility to sell only fresh food items.

(*c*) Yes, as selling stale food item amounted to negligence.

(*d*) No, as Sanjay ought to have known that Golu was infamous for selling stale food items.

**99. Principle:** Agreements, the meaning of which is not certain, or capable of being made certain, are void.

**Explanation:** Uncertainty of a contract exposes the promisee the risk of inability to understand the binding terms and conditions.

**Facts:** X and Y entered into a tenancy agreement. The said agreement provided that Y would have an option to have the tenancy renewed on similar terms after the expiry of one year. Next year, X refused to renew the tenancy on similar terms. Y filed a suit against X. Decide whether the tenancy agreement between X and Y valid?

(*a*) Yes, as the terms of the proposed tenancy agreement was able to be made certain.

(*b*) No, as the terms of agreement were uncertain and hence unenforceable.

(*c*) No, as the agreement was contingent in nature.

(*d*) Yes, as agreement had nothing to do with a future event.

**100. Principle:** No person can claim damages for an injury caused in an act to which he has expressed his consent.

**Explanation**: An act of negligence is an exception to the defence of consent for a tort.

**Facts**: 'X' asked 'Y', a surgeon, to perform surgery on him for ear infection. 'B' performed the surgery but it did not help the ear infection of 'A'. 'A' sued 'B' for recovery of damages. Decide whether X can maintain a suit against Y for recovery of damages?

(*a*) No, as Y enjoys medical immunity being a surgeon.

(*b*) Yes, as Y could not cure X even after the painful ear surgery.

(*c*) Yes, to the extent of recovering the medical expenses and interest thereon.

(*d*) No, as X consented to Y for performing surgery to cure ear infection and no damage was caused in the surgery.

**101. Principle:** A person, who by force compels or deceitfully induces another person to go from any place, is said to commit abduction.

**Explanation**: Usage of force shall mean moving body of a person unless it is done for his benefit.

**Facts:** A was working in his laboratory on an advanced tissue culture research and the breakthrough was imminent. Suddenly B informs him about a fire which had broken out inside the laboratory. A refuses to move until the completion of the research. B drags A out of the laboratory and the research collapsed. Whether B can be held liable for abduction?

(*a*) No, as B did not move A from the laboratory permanently.

(*b*) Yes, as B by force compelled A to leave the laboratory which caused end of his tissue culture research.

(*c*) Yes, as use of force by B proved detrimental of A's interest.

(*d*) No, as B used force to drag out A for his benefit and to protect his life.

**102. Principle**: Any person shall be liable for the loss and injury caused to a servant in the course of employment.

**Explanation**: No person can claim damages for loss or injury caused due to lack of precaution taken by the person suffering it.

**Facts**: Ajit, a construction worker, was working in Delhi Metro Railway Construction site. He was asked by his supervisor to go in basement joint section to perform some welding work. Ajit rushed to the basement without even taking his helmet and boot. He met with an accident causing permanent disability and filed a suit for damages. Whether Delhi Metro Railway is liable to pay damages to Ajit?

(*a*) Yes, as Ajit went to the basement in the course of his employment and under instruction from his supervisor.

(*b*) No, as injury caused to Ajit was due to lack of precaution taken by him.

(*c*) No, as Ajit was a contract labour and not a permanent employee.

(*d*) Yes, as Ajit is permanently disabled now.

**103. Principle:** Agreements, the meaning of which is not certain, or capable of being made certain, are void.

**Explanation:** Uncertainty of a contract exposes the promisee the risk of inability to understand the binding terms and conditions.

**Facts:** Sameer decided to buy one hundred gallon of oil from Sheikh Rehman for Rs 10,000. As promised, Sheikh Rehman sent one hundred gallon of sunflower oil to Sameer on the due date. Sameer refused to take the consignment stating that he had intended to buy hundred gallons of mustard oil. Decide whether the contract between Sameer and Sheikh Rehman was valid and enforceable in the eyes of law?

(*a*) Yes, as the consideration amount was clearly stipulated.

(*b*) No, as the terms were not certain and were incapable of being made certain.

(*c*) No, as Sheikh Rehman ought to have delivered mustard oil instead of sunflower oil.

(*d*) Yes, as Sheikh Rehman delivered oil and his liability was not beyond this.

**104. Principle:** An agreement executed under undue influence of other party is not enforceable in the eyes of law.

**Explanation:** Undue influence is said to be established when one of the parties is in a position to dominate the will of the other and uses that position to obtain an unfair advantage.

**Facts**: Megha and Mithun were the best of friends since school time. Mithun belonged to a very rich family and inherited a lot of his father's wealth. One day Megha asked Mithun to transfer his bungalow in New Delhi to her. On not receiving any reply, Megha decided not to speak to Mithun anymore. Finally, Mithun decided to transfer the property to Megha. After two years, Mithun challenged the transfer as null and void due to undue influence. Decide was the agreement for transfer of bunglow vitiated due to undue influence?

(*a*) Yes, as Mithun transferred the property under alleged undue influence.

(*b*) No, as not speaking to a friend cannot qualify as undue influence as it was not sufficient to dominate will of other person.

(*c*) No, as transfer was voluntarily made by Mithun.

(*d*) Yes, as Mithun initially declined to transfer his bungalow.

**105. Principle:** Nothing is a wrong of which a person of ordinary sense and temper would not complain.

**Explanation**: Act causing even a slight harm is punishable if it causes injury to a legal right.

**Facts:** A casts and draws a net in water where B usually casts his net. Luck disfavoured him and he did not catch any fish. B sued A for damages. Decide. Did 'A' commit any wrong to 'B' for which he is liable to pay damages?

(*a*) Yes, as A casted his net in the usual fishing area of B.

(*b*) No, as no injury much less an injury to a legal right was caused, of which no ordinary person would complain.

(*c*) No, as A couldn't catch even a single fish.

(*d*) Yes, as B is free to exercise his right to seek legal remedy.

## SECTION – D : LOGICAL REASONING

106. If it is true that 'we do not come across dedicated teachers', which one of the following is false beyond doubt?

(*a*) We can never come across dedicated teachers.

(*b*) No teacher is dedicated.

(*c*) All teachers are dedicated, but we can never meet them.

(*d*) None of the above

**Directions for questions 107 to 117:** Read the following arguments/passages carefully and answer the questions that follow.

107. Representation of People's Act empowers every Indian citizen who is more than eighteen years old to cast his vote in elections. Citizens vote to exercise their choice and empowerment. Which of the following has the same logic?

(*a*) Jobs provide money and financial security to people. People do jobs to get money and security.

(*b*) Poaching is the illegal hunting of birds, animals or fish on somebody else's property or without permission. People indulge in poaching to satisfy their greed for money.

(*c*) People want to live and experience pleasures. But death is inevitable.

(*d*) All of these

**108.** Aristotle suggested that the *ethos* of a speaker plays a crucial role in determining whether an argument is persuasive or not. In keeping with this, an *ad hominem* argument may be understood as an attack on the *ethos* of an arguer which is in principle acceptable. This does not mean that every *ad hominem* is acceptable, but only those which convincingly undermine the credibility of the arguer who is criticized.

Which of the following is definitely not implied by the argument?

(*a*) An ad hominem cannot be accepted simply because it attacks the ethos of the arguer.

(*b*) Some arguments are critical in nature.

(*c*) Ad hominem is a type of criticism-based argument.

(*d*) None of these

**109.** The Federal Reserve tried to stir interest among policy makers in the problems afflicting the housing market by sending a white paper to Congress outlining suggestions for easing those problems. The Reserve is concerned that the collapse of mortgage lending during the financial crisis is hardening into "a potentially long-term downshift in the supply of mortgage credit." One reason for this, the paper says, is that Fannie and Freddie, which provide the money for most mortgage loans, are scaring lenders by aggressively seeking refunds on defaulted loans.

Which of the following, if true, justifies the concerns of The Federal Reserve?

1. The ways employed by Fannie and Freddie are discouraging lenders from originating new loans.
2. The methods used by Fannie and Freddie are helping them in maximizing their profits on old business.

(*a*) Both 1 and 2 (*b*) Only 2

(*c*) Only 1 (*d*) Neither 1 nor 2

**110.** A psychological scientist wanted to measure a subjective emotion- happiness. He wanted a rating scale with ratings from 1 to 6 to measure happiness by asking people question about their well-being. But this was difficult as somebody's five might be six for the other. He thought of a solution to this problem. He started thinking of his training days when some cheap thermometers that were not well calibrated were used to measure temperature. A few people with normal temperatures got readings other than 98.6, and occasionally two people with the same temperature used to get different readings. These inaccuracies caused people to seek medical treatment they didn't need or to miss getting treatment they needed. So buggy thermometers were sometimes a problem—but not always. Some thermometers would underestimate, some would overestimate, but as long as enough people were measured, the inaccuracies would cancel themselves out. Even with poorly calibrated instruments, large groups of people could be compared. He thought rating scale is like a buggy thermometer. Its inaccuracies make it inappropriate for some exact measurements (for example, saying exactly how happy John was at 10:42 AM on July 3, 2010), but it's appropriate for most of the measurements needed to measure happiness in a large group of people.

What is the method of reasoning used by the psychological scientist?

(*a*) group study

(*b*) thought and observation

(*c*) analogy

(*d*) inductive logic

**111.** Blogs compete with mainstream media every day. In some cases, they have become more trustworthy as sources of information than some old school practitioners. Oregon's shield law does not recognize the blog as a "medium of communication" worthy of special protection. Such a narrow definition of journalism is archaic. It shouldn't matter whether the person calls himself a journalist or not, nor where he publishes a story. The quality of the story and the integrity of the method of reporting should count. By that standard, some bloggers would qualify as journalists while some deadwood reporters at newspapers would fail.

Which of the following summarizes the argument?

(*a*) Instead of focusing on who is doing the publishing, it is more important to look at how they are doing it.

(*b*) The quality of the story and the integrity of the method of reporting are more important criteria than whether the person who has done it is a journalist or a blogger.

(*c*) Bloggers and journalists are no different from each other.

(*d*) Journalism needs to broaden its line of thought.

**112. Tom:** Within democracies voters are entitled to know the 'down-side' to a candidate – and the other side is obviously well placed to voice it. To stifle one's ability to voice negative things about a candidate would be to obstruct democracy and limit free speech.

**Riddle:** Negative ads produce the politics of the personal, since the easiest ad is an attack-ad which focuses on the personality or personal qualities of one's opponent.

A negative advertisement is one that focuses upon a rival product, in this case a rival election candidate or party, in order to point out its flaws and to persuade the public not to buy it (or vote for it). On the basis of the given debate between Tom and Riddle, identify the main issue of debate.

(*a*) Whether negative advertisement strengthen democratic governance.

(*b*) Whether the practice of negative advertisements is good for democracy and politics.

(*c*) Whether negative advertising needs to be banned.

(*d*) Whether negative advertising produces the politics of the personal.

**113.** "Most cancer cells rely almost exclusively on glucose to fuel their growth," says Guy Perkins of the University of California at San Diego. With the researcher Rudy Yamaguchi of Kyushu University in Fukuoka, Japan, Perkins found the cells would take up a similar sugar called 2-deoxyglucose. But this sugar physically dislodges a protein within the cell that guards a suicide switch. Once exposed, the switch can be activated by a drug called ABT-263. This kills the cell by liberating proteins that order it to commit suicide.

Which of the following summarizes the above argument?

(*a*) Researchers have tricked glucose-eating cancer cells which leaves a "suicide" switch within the cells open to attack.

(*b*) Cancer can now be treated by using a sugar to dislodge proteins.

(*c*) Researchers have tricked glucose-eating cancer cells into consuming a sugar that essentially poisons them - it leaves a "suicide" switch within the cells open to attack.

(*d*) The treatment for cancer has been discovered.

**114.** Eamon McCrory at University College London used fMRI to scan the brains of 20 outwardly healthy children who had been maltreated and 23 "controls" from safe environments. During the scans, the children, aged 12 on average, viewed a mixture of sad, neutral and angry faces. When they saw angry faces, the maltreated children showed extra activity in the areas of brain known to be involved in threat detection and anticipation of pain. Combat soldiers show similar heightened activity.

The argument can be best summarized in which of the following ways?

(*a*) Minds of children respond to some situations in a pattern similar to that found in adults.

(*b*) The brains of children from violent homes function like those of soldiers when it comes to detecting threats.

(*c*) The ability to adapt to threats in present in children as well as adults.

(*d*) Certain areas of the human brain show heightened activity in response to threats.

**115. Reema:** Teenage pregnancy is a stressful experience, it would be sensible for a pregnant unmarried teenage girl to seek advice from a responsible adult. Parental involvement laws would make notification of pregnancy and consent for abortion from one or both parents mandatory.

**Reeta:** Obtaining parental consent necessarily imposes a delay in the abortion process, which increases the likelihood of complications: generally speaking, the earlier in pregnancy an abortion takes place, the safer it is. Necessary safeguards such as judicial waivers introduce even more delays - at least 22 days in the US.

Which of the following best depicts the way in which Reeta responds to Reema's argument?

(*a*) She opposes Reeta's idea by suggesting some complications.

(*b*) She defends the practice by citing evidence to show the time delay.

(*c*) She justifies her opposition to the idea on the premise that delay due to consent may endanger mother's health.

(*d*) She agrees to Reema's idea but introduces evidence to show that it is harmful for the pregnant teenager.

**116. Doctor X:** Anorexia Nervosa is an eating disorder defined as severe, self- inflicted starvation and loss in body weight to at least 15% below that expected for the individual's sex and height. Anorexia is typically associated with women and body image and is thought to be made worse by unrealistic media portrayals of the female body. Mortality varies between 5% and 18%. Patients who are dangerously thin need to be force-fed through a naso-gastric (through the nose) tube.

**Doctor Y:** Force-feeding has negative consequences. If the patient is dangerously thin and is then force-fed, it can led to Hypophosphataemia (reduction of phosphates in the blood) which causes heart failure. Anorexics are characterized by self-denial and often do not come forward voluntarily. They are even less likely to do so if they are faced with the possibility of force- feeding.

Which of the following most accurately expresses the issue between Doctor X and Doctor Y?

(*a*) Whether anorexia nervosa leads to other potentially fatal diseases.

(*b*) Should dangerously thin anorexia nervosa patients be force-fed.

(*c*) Is force-feeding dangerous for the health of patients.

(*d*) Whether self-abnegation is a big problem in patients of anorexia nervosa.

**117. Anjana:** The world is divided in two: those who are taking psychotherapy and those who need to take it.

**Preetam:** I don't subscribe to that view. Some people can manage very well without it. Some people might be able to manage without self-awareness as well.

What is/are the point/points on which both Anjana and Preetam agree?

1. Everybody is suffering from a mental or emotional disorder.
2. Psychotherapy may help those who are not taking it.
3. Everyone is not taking psychotherapy.

(*a*) 2 and 3 (*b*) 1 and 2

(*c*) Only 1 (*d*) Only 3

**118.** Necessity is the mother of inventions. Which of the following supports the above statement?

(*a*) Invention is related to needs.

(*b*) The need of a thing is the driving force to look for ways to create it.

(*c*) People invent new things because outdated things impair growth and stymie progress.

(*d*) All of the above

**119.** Consider a set of premises like this: if spiritualism and materialism clash, then peace and luxury will clash. Luxury is not acceptable and hence materialism. But peace is not sufficient for survival.

Identify the conclusion that follows from the premises.

(*a*) If spiritualism is not accepted, then survival is ensured.

(*b*) If luxury is accepted, survival is certain.

(*c*) If spiritualism is accepted, then something other than peace is also needed to survive.

(*d*) Spiritualism is acceptable as it is sufficient to ensure survival.

**120.** If Rakesh likes Physics more than Geography, Mathematics more than Biology, and Biology more than Physics then which one of the following is not true?

(*a*) He likes Geography more than Mathematics.

(*b*) He likes Mathematics more than Geography.

(*c*) He likes Biology more than Geography.

(*d*) He likes Mathematics more than Biology.

**121.** If you don't study hard, you will not be able to get a good rank.

If you don't get a good rank, will not get into a great college.

If you don't get into a great college, you will not be able to earn handsomely.

Therefore,

(*a*) if you are not able to earn handsomely, you don't study hard.

(*b*) you study hard only to earn handsomely.

(*c*) if you don't study hard, you will not be able to earn handsomely.

(*d*) if you study hard, you will be able to earn handsomely.

**122.** In the following question, four premises lead to a conclusion. Three premises and the conclusion, derived from four, are given. From among the given alternatives, identify the missing premise.

1st Premise : If an art is good, then the artist is good.

2nd Premise : If the artist is good, he is content with life and its challenges.

3rd Premise :

4th Premise : But the artist John is not happy.

**Conclusion:** Therefore, John's art may not be good.

(*a*) If John is happy, he is a good artist.

(*b*) If the artist is good, then his art is good .

(*c*) If an artist is happy, he is content with life and its challenges.

(*d*) If an artist is content with life and its challenges, he is happy.

**123.** Identify the statement that can be neither proved nor disproved.

(*a*) I have pain in my joints.

(*b*) My teacher gave me a book to read.

(*c*) When the algorithm started its frenetic buying spree, the measures designed to shut it down did not work.

(*d*) Although it was not directly triggered by high-frequency traders, the official reports suggested they helped fuel the uncontrolled selling.

**124.** Many cabbies pay a dispatcher to keep the fares coming. The dispatchers are an information clearing-house, offering customers a central point of contact and offering on-the-move drivers directions to the nearest prospective passenger. But location-enabled smart phones in the pockets of more customers, and on the dashboards of more drivers, offer a tempting way to skip the middleman.

If the given passage is true, which of the following is most likely to be true?

(*a*) When a customer requests a taxi, the applications ping the nearest available driver.

(*b*) Customers and drivers may find a handy way to share their locations.

(*c*) Location technology is not new for taxis.

(*d*) Some taxi-booking applications allow users to rate drivers and decide whether or not to hail a particular taxi based on that drivers' rating.

**125.** Fewer than a quarter of the people with severe mental illness in low- and middle-income countries receive any treatment. Psychiatrists are scarce and often concentrated in overcrowded urban hospitals, where human-rights abuses are all too common. Now, thanks to efforts started in the wake of the devastating 2004 earthquake and tsunami, provincial health authorities in Indonesia, aided by foreign advisers, are creating a community mental health program that shifts much of the work traditionally done by psychiatrists to general practitioners, nurses, and even village volunteers.

Which of the following statements, if true, is the essence of the passage mentioned above?

(*a*) A program to cater the needs of mentally ill people is needed on an urgent basis and is being started in Indonesia.

(*b*) In Indonesia, a community mental health program that does not depend upon psychiatrists is being launched to help the people suffering from mental illness.

(*c*) Mental illness is rampant in Indonesia and a program has been launched to help its citizens.

(*d*) General practitioners, nurses and village volunteers are capable of handling and treating mentally ill patients.

**126.** If there is sunshine, there is no darkness. If the given statement is true, which of the following is definitely correct?

(*a*) In presence of sunshine, darkness is not possible.

(*b*) If there is no sunshine, there is darkness.

(*c*) If there is no darkness, sun must be shining.

(*d*) Darkness and sunshine may co-exist.

**127.** Only if a lawyer is talented, he can win the case. If the given statement is true, which of the following is definitely correct?

I. Lawyer X is not talented, he cannot win the case.

II. Lawyer Y wins the case, he is talented.

(*a*) Only I (*b*) Only II

(*c*) Both I and II (*d*) Neither I nor II

**128.** Research shows that when people work with a positive mind-set, performance on nearly every level—productivity, creativity, engagement—improves. Yet happiness is perhaps the most misunderstood driver of performance. For one, most people believe that success precedes happiness. "Once I get a promotion, I'll be happy," they think. Or, "Once I hit my sales target, I'll feel great." But because success is a moving target—as soon as you hit your target, you raise it again.

Which of the following inferences can be drawn from the given argument?

(*a*) The happiness that results from success is fleeting.

(*b*) The habits you cultivate, the way you interact with coworkers, how you think about stress—all these can be managed to increase your happiness and your chances of success.

(*c*) Every business outcome shows improvement when the brain is positive.

(*d*) None of these

**Directions for questions 129 and 130:** In each of the following questions, words in the first pair are related to each other in a certain manner. The second pair is incomplete. Complete the second pair such that the second pair depicts the same relation as depicted by the first pair.

**129.** claustrophobia : closed spaces : : acrophobia : ?

(*a*) river (*b*) height

(*c*) bats (*d*) hair

**130.** satire : mock : : eulogy : ?

(*a*) command (*b*) commend

(*c*) comment (*d*) chastise

**131.** Find out the missing term in the series: IYD, LVG, OSJ, RPM, ?

(*a*) TNP (*b*) UMP

(*c*) UNQ (*d*) TMQ

**132.** Find out the missing term in the series: 132, 126, 114, 96, 72, ?

(*a*) 54 (*b*) 36

(*c*) 48 (*d*) 42

**133.** Six years ago, mother's age was six times the age of her son. Sum of the present ages of the mother and her son is 54 years. After a year, mother's age will be:

(*a*) 42 years (*b*) 45 years

(*c*) 43 years (*d*) 41 years

**134.** A train takes 2 hours 30 minutes to complete its journey from Mumbai to Pune. Four such trains, from Mumbai to Pune everyday are scheduled at 07:40, 11:55, 15:20 and 20:05. A passenger who left for the Mumbai station missed the train by 40 minutes and hence took the next train to Pune and reached at 17:50. When did the passenger reach the Mumbai station?

(*a*) 12:35 (*b*) 14:40
(*c*) 15:10 (*d*) 13:35

**135.** Find out the missing term in the series: X, S, N, K, ?

(*a*) I (*b*) F
(*c*) H (*d*) G

**136.** Find out the missing term in the series: 13, 17, 25, 41, 73, ?

(*a*) 133 (*b*) 137
(*c*) 123 (*d*) 127

**137.** If DEAR is written as EDFEBASR, then MUST can be written as:

(*a*) MNUVSTTU (*b*) MNVUTSTU
(*c*) NMVUTSUT (*d*) NMVTUUST

**138.** In a certain code language, 456417 is written as 638235. How is 322859 written in that language?

(*a*) 504677 (*b*) 140677
(*c*) 504031 (*d*) 544071

**139.** If the second day after tomorrow is Tuesday, then which of the following was the day before yesterday?

(*a*) Saturday (*b*) Friday
(*c*) Thursday (*d*) Wednesday

**140.** Jai turns 135° anticlockwise, then he turns 225° clockwise. Now he turns to his right and is facing South-West. Which direction was he facing initially?

(*a*) South-West (*b*) North-East
(*c*) East (*d*) North-West

## SECTION –E : MATHEMATICS

**141.** A sum of ₹ 470 amounts to ₹ 611 in 5 years at simple interest. What is the rate of interest per annum?

(*a*) 4% (*b*) 5%
(*c*) 6% (*d*) 7%

**142.** While working alone, Ajay and Vijay can do a piece of work in 16 days and 12 days respectively. Vijay started the work alone and after 5 days Ajay joined him till the completion of the work. How long did the work last?

(*a*) 8 days (*b*) 9 days
(*c*) 10 days (*d*) 7.5 days

**143.** Number of people in a group increases by 20% at the beginning of every month. The group has 432 people at the end of the fourth month. How many people were there in the group initially?

(*a*) 200 (*b*) 250
(*c*) 300 (*d*) 350

**144.** Mr. A takes three hours more than the time taken by Mr. B to cover a distance of 40 km. If Mr. A doubles his speed, then he would take one hour less than the time taken by Mr. B to cover the same distance. Speed of Mr. A is:

(*a*) 7.5 km/hr (*b*) 7 km/hr
(*c*) 6 km/hr (*d*) 5 km/hr

**145.** ₹ 363 is divided between three friends A, B and C so that 2a = 3b and 4b = 5c where a, b and c are amounts (in ₹) received by A, B and C respectively. Find the difference between the share of C and A.

(*a*) ₹ 165 (*b*) ₹ 110
(*c*) ₹ 88 (*d*) ₹ 77

**146.** Out of 150 people present in a party, 25 people had neither apple juice nor orange juice, 96 people had apple juice and 36 people had both apple juice as well as orange juice. How many people had orange juice?

(*a*) 29 (*b*) 60
(*c*) 65 (*c*) 101

**147.** A man invested ₹ 1,620 in stocks, of face value ₹ 100, at ₹ 90 to obtain an income of ₹ 162. The dividend (in percentage) from the stock is:

(*a*) 7% (*b*) 8%
(*c*) 9% (*c*) 10%

**148.** Weight of Khali is reduced by 12%. By what percentage must he increase his weight so as to get back to his original weight?

(*a*) 12% (*b*) 10%
(*c*) 13.64% (*d*) 14.28%

**149.** In what ratio must a grocer mix two varieties of tea costing ₹ 180/kg and ₹ 220/kg so that by selling the mixture at Rs. 214.20/kg he gains 5%?

(*a*) 2 : 3 (*b*) 3 : 5
(*c*) 3 : 4 (*d*) 2 : 5

**150.** Population of a village increases at the rate of 20% per year for the first two years and then it increases by 10% per year. If population of the village at the end of the fifth year is 26136, then find its population at the beginning of the first year.

(*a*) 11000 (*b*) 12000
(*c*) 15000 (*d*) 18000

## ANSWERS

| | | | | | | | | | |
|---|---|---|---|---|---|---|---|---|---|
| **1.** (*a*) | **2.** (*d*) | **3.** (*d*) | **4.** (*a*) | **5.** (*d*) | **6.** (*c*) | **7.** (*b*) | **8.** (*c*) | **9.** (*b*) | **10.** (*b*) |
| **11.** (*d*) | **12.** (*c*) | **13.** (*d*) | **14.** (*d*) | **15.** (*a*) | **16.** (*a*) | **17.** (*a*) | **18.** (*d*) | **19.** (*a*) | **20.** (*d*) |
| **21.** (*b*) | **22.** (*c*) | **23.** (*a*) | **24.** (*d*) | **25.** (*c*) | **26.** (*b*) | **27.** (*b*) | **28.** (*b*) | **29.** (*b*) | **30.** (*a*) |
| **31.** (*d*) | **32.** (*a*) | **33.** (*b*) | **34.** (*a*) | **35.** (*d*) | **36.** (*c*) | **37.** (*d*) | **38.** (*b*) | **39.** (*b*) | **40.**(*d*) |
| **41.** (*c*) | **42.** (*d*) | **43.** (*b*) | **44.** (*b*) | **45.** (*a*) | **46.** (*b*) | **47.** (*a*) | **48.** (*b*) | **49.** (*a*) | **50.** (*c*) |
| **51.** (*b*) | **52.** (*a*) | **53.** (*a*) | **54.** (*b*) | **55.** (*a*) | **56.** (*a*) | **57.** (*a*) | **58.** (*a*) | **59.** (*c*) | **60.** (*a*) |
| **61.** (*b*) | **62.** (*b*) | **63.** (*a*) | **64.** (*a*) | **65.** (*b*) | **66.** (*a*) | **67.** (*a*) | **68.** (*a*) | **69.** (*b*) | **70.** (*b*) |
| **71.** (*c*) | **72.** (*d*) | **73.** (*c*) | **74.** (*d*) | **75.** (*b*) | **76.** (*d*) | **77.** (*b*) | **78.** (*d*) | **79.** (*c*) | **80.** (*a*) |
| **81.** (*c*) | **82.** (*c*) | **83.** (*c*) | **84.** (*a*) | **85.** (*c*) | **86.** (*b*) | **87.** (*b*) | **88.** (*c*) | **89.** (*c*) | **90.** (*c*) |
| **91.** (*b*) | **92.** (*b*) | **93.** (*b*) | **94.** (*a*) | **95.** (*d*) | **96.** (*d*) | **97.** (*b*) | **98.** (*c*) | **99.** (*a*) | **100.** (*d*) |
| **101.** (*d*) | **102.** (*b*) | **103.** (*b*) | **104.** (*b*) | **105.** (*b*) | **106.** (*d*) | **107.** (*a*) | **108.** (*d*) | **109.** (*c*) | **110.** (*c*) |
| **111.** (*b*) | **112.** (*b*) | **113** . (*c*) | **114.** (*b*) | **115.** (*c*) | **116.** (*b*) | **117.** (*d*) | **118** .(*d*) | **119.** (*c*) | **120.** (*a*) |
| **121.** (*c*) | **122.** (*d*) | **123.** (*a*) | **124.** (*b*) | **125.** (*b*) | **126.** (*a*) | **127.** (*c*) | **128.** (*a*) | **129.** (*b*) | **130.** (*b*) |
| **131.** (*b*) | **132.** (*d*) | **133.** (*c*) | **134.** (*a*) | **135.** (*c*) | **136.** (*b*) | **137** (*c*) | **138.** (*a*) | **139.** (*c*) | **140.** (*b*) |
| **141.** (*c*) | **142.** (*b*) | **143.** (*b*) | **144.** (*d*) | **145.** (*d*) | **146.** (*c*) | **147.** (*c*) | **148.** (*c*) | **149.** (*a*) | **150.** (*c*) |

## EXPLANATIONS

**1.** Refer to the lines "The book is almost a condensed encyclopedia on several themes with the result that where perhaps one wanted more elaboration of seminal ideas, one is taken quickly to other domains." Thus, 1 is correct. 'Condensed encyclopedia on several themes' is not a problem per se. Refer to the line "There is no logical structure and nor is it necessary." Thus, 3 is not a shortcoming. Refer to the lines "When one draws from diverse sources to buttress one's argument, there is danger in selecting only those sources which favour one's argument. Countervailing texts get ignored. There is much in our tradition which is worth preserving and drawing from and this in fact belongs to the genre of "perennial philosophy"." So, the passage does not state or imply that Nandkarni has ignored the text that contradicted his arguments/ideas. Thus, 4 is beyond the scope of the passage. Hence, option (*a*) is the correct choice.

**2.** All the statements are correct. Refer to the lines "Nadkarni bases his exposition staunchly on "Hinduism". Unfortunately the word Hinduism is an aberration thrust on us by Semitic religions which are "isms". Hindus were people who lived around the river Sindhu so named by the Greek invaders in our hoary past. Hinduism does not have the trademarks of religion. It has no church, no prophet, no congregation and no one Book. It is the repository of speculative thinking over the centuries and has no unifying dogma and as such provides a wide variety of ideas from Advaita at one end to materialism at the other. What unifies Hindu society is the caste system in its day-to-day life and the life cycle rituals and forms of worship."

**3.** Option (*a*) can be inferred from the line "Personally I am sympathetic to crafts as India has one of the richest craft traditions in the world." Option (*b*) can be inferred from the lines "The answer is mutual obligation so as to ensure that our choice is conducive to all sections of society. What is conducive should not be in utilitarian terms of the individual's freedom to choose to maximize his or her satisfaction. Here the relevance of what Nadkarni drives home is well illustrated according to me by the feminist demand of the right to "reproductive choice" which was articulated at a time when a coercive population control programme was unleashed. However, how can it be an individual choice when the consequences of one's actions impinge on society – the number of children one has in turn affects the number of schools, doctors, a social provisions that would be needed. If economics holds self-interest as the motivating factor in human decisions, it misconstrues the plurality of motivations. Moral dilemmas arise when we follow a single moral principle irrespective of consequences." Option (*c*) can be inferred from the line "To my mind, while the principle behind such an approach cannot be faulted, practice in the present context is not easy." Thus, the author agrees to options (*a*), (*b*) and (*c*). Hence, option (*d*) is the correct choice.

**4.** Paragraph four and five mention the various rhetorical questions that have been used by the author while discussing Nandkarni's book.

**5.** 1 is ambiguous as we do not know whether it pertains to the author of the passage or the author of the book. So, options (*a*) and (*c*) are negated. Refer to the lines "Nadkarni provides an interesting link between economics and ethics. Both deal with choice. In issues related to human development he points out how ethics and economics overlap because both are subject to ethical evaluation." Thus, 3 is incorrect. 2 can be inferred from the lines "The author agrees that while moral principles per se or taken in isolation are independent of facts or situations, in implementation and actual situation conflicts arise and trade-offs become necessary. Here the author could have given some examples from real life."

**6.** The author's review is analytical and realistic in nature.

**7.** 'Have been brought' (present perfect progressive tense) should be used in place of 'had brought'. The Present Perfect Progressive Tense indicates a continuous action that has been finished at some point in the past or that was initiated in the past and continues to happen. The action is usually of limited duration and has some current relevance: "She has been running and her heart is still beating fast." The present perfect progressive frequently is used to describe an event of the recent past; it is often accompanied by *just* in this usage: "It has just been raining."

This tense is formed with the modal "HAVE" or "HAS" (for third-person singular subjects) plus "BEEN," plus the present participle of the verb (with an *-ing* ending): "I have been working in the garden all morning. George has been painting that house for as long as I can remember.

**8.** Effort is a countable noun and it has been used in singular form in the given sentence. So, it should be preceded by an article.

**9.** The part (*a*) talks mentions some problems with reconciliation. But, part (*b*) and (*c*) state its advantages. So, we need a conjunction that can highlight the contrast. 'Because' is used to present a reason and not a contrast. 'But' is the correct conjunction. So, option (*b*) is incorrect.

**10.** The correct idiom is 'neck and neck' (with somebody/something). It means close or just even in a race or comparison or competition.

**11.** The given sentence is grammatically correct. 'Around', in the given context, means in a circle or curve to face another way or the opposite way.

**12.** The subject of the sentence is 'one'. It being singular in number, a singular verb (eclipses) is required to make the sentence grammatically correct.

**13.** The given sentence is grammatically correct.

**14.** 'Grant' is the only option that is grammatically and logically fit in the given case.

**15.** 'De facto' which means existing as a fact although it may not be legally accepted as existing matches best with the context of exercise of some powers that ideally should have never been its remit.

**16.** 'Therefore' which is used to introduce the logical result of something that has just been mentioned is the apt choice. Other options are used to show some kind of contrast and are negated.

**17.** 'Thrust' is the grammatically and logically correct choice.

**18.** As the context is of exercise of caution, 'restraint' is the logically correct choice.

**19.** Niggardly means giving or sharing as little as possible .Bounteous means giving or sharing in abundance and without hesitation.

**20.** Profligate means extravagant.

**21.** Renegade means a person who abandons a cause or organization usually without right.

**22.** Indigent means lacking money or material possessions. 'Opulent' means having goods, property, or money in abundance.

**23.** Acquisitive and avaricious both mean having or marked by an eager and selfish desire for material possessions.

**24.** The sentence requires a future perfect tense. The future perfect tense indicates that an action will have been completed at some particular point in the future. This tense is formed with "will" plus "have" plus 'the third form of verb'.

**25.** The sentence requires present continuous tense as it talks about an action that has already been arranged to take place in the near future. Hence, option (*c*) is the correct choice.

**26.** With the words 'anterior', 'posterior', 'superior' and 'inferior', the preposition that is required is "to".

**27.** The correct phrase is 'believe in something'. Hence, the correct preposition is 'in'.

**28.** 'In person' is the correct phrase and it means in one's physical presence. Hence, option (*b*) is the correct choice.

**29.** We use 'at' to designate specific times. For example: The train is due at 11:25 p.m. We use 'on' to designate days and dates. For example: My brother is coming on Monday. We're having a party on the Fourth of July. We use 'in' for nonspecific times during a day, a month, a season, or a year. She likes to jog in the morning.

**30.** The subject is singular in number so, the verb should be singular. 'Has' is the correct choice.

**31.** The correct idiom is 'up and running' it means working fully and correctly.

**32.** As the second subject is plural in number (sisters), the verb should be plural.

**33.** 'For' is used for a period of time. 'Since' is used with a specific date or time. For example: He's worked here since 1970.

**34.** A 'fly in the ointment' refers to a person or thing that spoils a situation.

**35.** 'Walking on air' means feeling very happy.

**36.** IUCN is an international organization dedicated to finding "pragmatic solutions to our most pressing environment and development challenges". The organization publishes the IUCN Red List, which compiles information of species that are most endangered.

**37.** The Dalai Lama is a high lama in the Gelug or "Yellow Hat" branch of Tibetan Buddhism.

**38.** The Uber Cup, sometimes called the World Team Championships for Women, is a major international badminton competition contested by women's national badminton teams.

**39.** Founded in 1991, the European Bank for Reconstruction and Development (EBRD) uses the tools of investment to help build market economies and democracies in 30 countries from central Europe to central Asia. Its mission was to support the formerly communist countries in the process of establishing their private sectors.

**40.** Moody is a credit rating agency that ranks the creditworthiness of borrowers using a standardized ratings scale which measures expected investor loss in the event of default. Investors use Moody's ratings to help price the credit risk of fixed-income securities they may buy or sell.

**41.** Jallikattu is based on the simple concept of "flight or fight or sometimes freeze".

**42.** Both Amul and Samsung were the principal sponsors for the Indian squad for the Olympics in London.

**43.** Kazakhstan has 15% of the world's uranium resources and an expanding mining sector.

**44.** The "Shoor Veer" exercise focused on synergy of the Army and the Air Force in launching air-land battle and the capability to orchestrate battle in a network-centric environment with integration of reconnaissance, surveillance and electronic warfare and communication assets to provide commanders real-time battle situational awareness.

**45.** The NTR National Award is an annual award to recognize people for their lifetime achievements and contributions to the Indian film industry.

**46.** Gujarat government refused "Parbal"'s distribution to the farmers of the state.

**47.** Willam Warren is a film critic and historian of American Origin and he also been involved in production of many science fiction, horror and fantasy films.

**48.** The Mullaperiyar Dam is masonry gravity on the Periyar River in the Kerala state of India. Though located in Kerala, it is operated by TN under 999 years lease. Since 1978, Kerala has been demanding the construction of a new dam. As a reaction to these demands, the TN government brought the water level down from 152ft to 132ft to allay the fears. TN has objection on the idea of Kerala constructing a new dam, because it would mean it that the 999-year lease would be void, and it would have to surrender the 8,000 acres of land under its control to Kerala.

**49.** SrivariChandrashekar, is Head of the Division of Natural Products at Indian Institute of Chemical Technology IICT.

**50.** BeiDou-2is second-generation satellite navigation system of country China.

**51.** Jugnu will be used to provide data for agriculture and disaster monitoring. It will be operated by IIT Kanpur. It was recently launched by PSLV-18.

**52.** The Megha-Tropiques satellite was successfully placed in orbit by PSLV-18

**53.** This area has been in news for variety of reasons viz. famine in Somalia, repeated acts of piracy by groups based in Somalia.

**54.** Aakash is reportedly world's cheapest tablet computer. This tablet will be provided to students in India for use as a learning tool.

**55.** Jaitapur Nuclear Power Plant is a proposed 9900 MW power project of Nuclear Power Corporation of India (NPCIL) in Ratnagiri district in Maharashtra. French company Areva has been roped in to install reactors and France has agreed to supply nuclear fuel for next 25 years.

**56.** RTE is provided in Article 21A of the Constitution of India.

**57.** This book won the 2011 Pulitzer Prize for General Non-Fiction. Siddhartha Mukherjee is an Indian-born American physician, scientist and writer. Currently he is an Assistant Professor of Medicine at Columbia University.

**58.** Karaikal is a major port city of east coast of India and a municipality in Karaikal district in the Union Territory of Pondicherry, India.

**59.** NATO was in news in connection with its decision to impose a no-fly zone over Libya in course of the conflict between forces loyal to Col. Qaddafi and forces loyal to NationalTransitional Council.

**60.** World Book and Copyright Day (also known as International Day of the Book or World Book Days) is a yearly event on 23 April, organized by UNESCO to promote reading, publishing and copyright.

**61.** The name SAGA-220 stands for Supercomputer for Aerospace with GPU Architecture-220 teraflops. It has been developed by ISRO and is India's fastest supercomputer.

**62.** (*a*) The Bhabha Atomic Research Centre is situated at Trombay

(*b*) Indira Gandhi Center for Atomic Research (IGCAR) in Kalpakkam (Kancheepuram district of Tamilnadu) is designing the Prototype Fast Breeder Reactor.

(*c*) & (*d*) Narora in Bulandshahr district of Uttar Pradesh and Rawatbhata in Chittorgarh district of Rajasthan are home to nuclear power plants.

**63.** National Intelligence Grid (NATGRID) was recently set up with P. Raghu Raman as its head.

**64.** Santosh Trophy is an annual Indian football tournament which is contested by states and government institutions. The 65th National Football Championship for Santosh Trophy 2010-11 was held in Assam and Bengal won the tournament defeating Manipur in the final match.

**65.** India recently acquired 17 of these aircrafts from USA.

**66.** 'K' produced by Fujitsu, is currently installed at the RIKEN Advanced Institute for Computational Science campus in Kobe, Japan. Before this supercomputer was produced Chinese Tianhe -1A was the fastest supercomputer.

**67.** Most of the refugees at this camp are from Somalia who are forced to leave their country due to a prolonged famine and armed conflict among various groups.

**68.** World Population Day is an annual event, observed on July 11, which seeks to raise awareness of global population issues. The event was established by the Governing Council of the United Nations Development Programme in 1989.

**69.** Prahaar is a tactical missile that can be deployed quickly. It was successfully test-fired recently.

**70.** Collegium system refers to a system under which appointments and transfers of judges are decided by a forum of the Chief Justice of India and the four senior-most judges of the Supreme Court. A petition seeking to review the judgment on the basis of which this system is being followed is pending in the Supreme Court of India.

**71.** The 13-judge Constitutional bench of the Supreme Court gave verdict on Kesavanand Bharti vs. State of Kerala.

**72.** International Criminal Court is located in Hague, Netherlands.

**73.** UNICEF stands for The United Nations Children's Fund.

**74.** Trygve Halvdan Lie was from Norway.

**75.** A void agreement is not legally enforceable.

**76.** Plaintiff is the one who files the Plaint which initiates the suit.

**77.** President is the executive head of the state and exercises executive powers under the aid and advice of the council of ministers.

**78.** Human Rights Commission is not one of the principal organs of U.N. Organization. .

**79.** According to article 56-1(*a*) of the Constitution of India the President of India submits his resignation to the Vice -President of India.

**80.** Leila Seith was born in Lucknow and she was also the first woman to top the London Bar exams in 1958.

**81.** Estoppel refers to a legal principle that bars a party from denying or alleging a certain fact owing to that party's previous conduct, allegation, or denial.

**82.** 'Amicus *Curiae*' is a Latin term meaning "Friend of the Court".

**83.** Article 14 of Indian Constitution confers the equal protection of law and equal protection of law to every Individual.

**84.** Public Interest Litigation or Social Interest Litigation is a concept under which a person who can approach court due to specific reasons such as his economic and social backwardness and his fundamental rights are violated then in such a case any person on his behalf can approach the court even by writing a letter to the court.

**85.** The Constitution of India only envisages three types of emergencies and there is no emergency based on Natural calamity or epidemics threatening the health and well-being of the people of India.

**86.** The fact that X attempted to apply the emergency break but failed, shows to prove that X had exercised reasonable care to stop the injury. Again Y was crossing the road without zebra crossing which also attributed to the injury. Thus he cannot be held responsible for the same.

**87.** As failure to abide by the mode of acceptance makes the contract voidable at the option of offeror

**88.** As the act did not amount to fighting in itself.

**89.** As X's act was a mere exercise of freedom of speech

**90.** As compliant by James was not motivated by malice

**91.** As there was no intention on part of Siraj to kill a human being.

**92.** As the agreement suffered from a mistake of fact

**93.** As contract was vitiated due to mistake of fact.

**94.** In the instant case, wax statue which is a permanent form of publication depicted the wrong image of actress. The statue maker Saddat would be liable even though it may appear that defamation happen in cases of verbal and written forms of communication that is through slander and libel but here form of expression is a wax statue which will suffice legal requirement of mode of expression.

**95.** In the present case scernario, Robert insulted Rando and would have been liable if Rando had opted to oppose him through indulging any act which entailed disturbance of public peace. Since, sitting on a hunger strike is a peaceful method of protest which does n't jepordize public peace Randò can not be found guilty.

**96.** As traffic signals are legally recognized method to regulate public movement.

**97.** As X was not under obligation to speak as he had made no claim regarding soundness of his horse.

**98.** Golu in the present case is negligent as selling stale food shows him not undertaking reasoable care which if observed by him would not causes damage to another person. The fact that Sanjay had stale snacks with alcohol does not directly contributes to him being ill.

**99.** As terms of the agreement were capable of being made certain by a mere clarification

**100.** Consent and absence of damage would disentitle X to maintain the present suit

**101.** As the usage of force was for benefit of A.

**102.** Ajit waived his right by moving to basement without safety precaution

**103.** As the terms of the agreement were uncertain

**104.** Undue Influence is a circumstance which is compelling enough for a reasonable person 's will to be dominated by another person's will. In the present case, the circumstances no where warrents that Mithuan should necessarily transfer his bungalow considering his relationship with Megha.

**105.** As A caused no injury to legal right of B.

**106.** All the options present possibilities which may be true. No option can be conclusively considered as a false inference.

**107.** The act gives power to vote and job gives money and security. One exercises his power by casting one's vote and one does a job to make money. Here, job is playing the same role as the act was playing. Thus, these two arguments are analogous and have a similar pattern of reasoning.

**108.** (*a*) is in sync with the spirit of the passage because the passage states that only that ad hominem which considerably undermines the credibility of the arguer is acceptable. According to the passage, an ad hominem is a type of argument that is based on criticism. So, (*b*) is implied. (*c*) is also implied. Thus, (*a*), (*b*) and (*c*) can be inferred. Option (*d*) is the correct choice. An Ad Hominem is a general category of failacies in which a claim or argument is rejected on the basis of some irrelevant fact about the author of or the person presenting the claim or argument. Typically, this fallacy involves two steps. First, an attack against the character of person making the claim, her circumstances, or her actions is made (or the character, circumstances, or actions of the person reporting the claim). Second, this attack is taken to be evidence against the claim or argument the person in question is making (or presenting). This type of "argument" has the following form: Person A makes claim X. Person B makes an attack on person A. Therefore A's claim is false.

The reason why an Ad Hominem (of any kind) is a fallacy is that the character, circumstances, or actions of a person do not (in most cases) have a bearing on the truth or falsity of the claim being made (or the quality of the argument being made).

**109.** The Federal Reserve is concerned about the lenders and the effect on the housing market. The argument does not imply that the Reserve is concerned about the profits made by Fannie and Freddie. Thus, (1) strengthens the concerns of the Reserve and (2) does not.

**110.** The psychological scientist considered his rating method to be analogous to a buggy thermometer where inaccuracies get adjusted to yield a fairly correct result.

**111.** Option (*a*) is generic in nature and is negated. (*c*) and (*d*) are inferences that can be drawn from the passage and express the ideas that the author is most likely to agree with. But they do not capture the full meaning of the passage. Option (*b*) is the most appropriate choice.

**112.** The scope of the term democratic governance has not been defined in the given debate. Thus, (*a*) cannot be correct. A clear hint about putting a ban on negative advertising is also not reflected in the debate. Thus, (*c*) is incorrect. (*d*) gives justice to the issue expressed by Riddle but fails to incorporate the opinion of Tom. Thus, (*d*) is negated. (*b*) expresses the issue most effectively.

**113.** Option (*c*) presents the best possible summary of the given passage. It includes the mention of researchers who have succeeded in using the fuel used by most cancer cells to act as their weakness. Option (*a*) is close but is incomplete in expressing the full idea.

**114.** (*a*) lacks the specificity presented in the passage and is generic in nature. (*c*) and (*d*) are conclusions that can be drawn from the passage but fail to capture its full message. (*b*) captures the essence effectively.

**115.** Option (*a*) is incomplete and vague. Option (*b*) is incorrect because it is unclear that which practice is being defended by Reeta. (*d*) is incorrect because Reeta does not agree to Reema's argument. (*c*) expresses the response of Reeta most appropriately.

**116.** The issue between Doctor X and Doctor Y is about the management and treatment of dangerously thin anorexia nervosa patients. Doctor X prescribes the method of force feeding whereas doctor Y opposes it by citing the risks and complications involved. (*b*) captures the issue most effectively. (*c*) is close but deals with patients in general (the scope of the argument is limited to anorexia nervosa patients). Thus, it is negated.

**117.** Preetam does not agree with 1. So, 1 is negated. Preetam does not agree with 2. 3 is the point on which both Anjana and Preetam agree. Anjana says that there are people who are not taking psychotherapy but need it. Preetam states that some people can manage without psychotherapy. This statement is possible only when some people are not taking psychotherapy. Thus, 3 is correct.

**118.** All the given options support the question statement.

**119.** The given premises suggest that spiritualism and materialism clash with each other. This results in peace and luxury clashing with each other. But we cannot accept luxury, so materialism which begets luxury is also unacceptable. Peace is acceptable but it is not sufficient for survival. So, spiritualism which begets peace is acceptable but not sufficient for survival. Hence, the correct option is (*c*).

**120.** M > B > P > G. So, option (*a*) is incorrect.

**121.** If not X, then not Y. If not Y, then not Z. If not Z then not A. So, If not X, then not A. Thus, option (*c*) is the correct choice.

**122.** Option (*d*) states the missing premise.

**123.** Pain is a subjective symptom that cannot be proved or disproved.

**124.** The argument states that the provision of location enabled smart phones in the pockets of the customers and of the dash boards of the drivers offer a way to skip the dispatcher. Thus, this provision is most likely to enable the customer and the cabbie to share their location and thus avoid the dispatcher. Option (*b*) is the most apt choice as it is supported by the argument. Rest of the options are beyond the scope of the argument.

**125.** Only option (*b*) captures the essence of the passage. Option (*a*) is incomplete as it misses the important information about non psychiatrists helping in the program. (*c*) is incorrect. (*d*) is an inference but fails to express the essence of the passage.

**126.** If A then B. Here A is the cause and B is the effect. Valid conclusion 1: If A occurs then B definitely occurs. This conclusion is valid and can be easily derived. It means that A is sufficient to cause B. But A is not the only cause and B may occur even is the absence of A. Thus A is sufficient but not necessary for B. For example: I eat if when I am hungry. So, being hungry is the cause and eating is the effect. But I can eat even without being hungry, like when I go for parties etc. So being hungry is the sufficient condition for eating but not the only condition. So, option (*a*) is correct. Here, presence of sunshine is the cause and absence of darkness is the effect. Valid conclusion 2: If not B, then not A. This means that if B has not occurred I can safely deduce that A has also not occurred. This means that 'If I am not eating, then I am not hungry. The statement If not B, then not A is the contrapositive of If A then B.

**127.** Only if a lawyer is talented, he can win the case means that the cause-lawyer being talented is necessary for the effect-winning the case. But this does not mean that the cause is sufficient for effect to take place. I is correct as in the absence of cause, effect cannot take place (cause is necessary). II is correct because if the effect has happened, cause must have happened. Thus, option (*c*) is the correct choice.

**128.** The given passage suggests that if success precedes happiness, then success being a moving target will affect the happiness. Thus, such happiness will last for a short while. Option (*b*) is beyond the scope of the passage. (*c*) talks about every business outcome, so it cannot be inferred.

**129.** Claustrophobia refers to the fear of closed spaces. Acrophobia refers to the fear of heights.

**130.** Satire is used to mock just as eulogy is used to commend or praise.

**131.** In each subsequent step, position number of middle letter is decreasing by 3 whereas position number of rest of the letters (i.e. first and the third letters) is increasing by 3. Hence, required missing term is 'UMP'.

**132.** 132 → 126 → 114 → 96 → 72 → **42**

−6, −12, −18, −24, −30

**133.** Let the present ages of the mother and her son be 'x' years and '54 – x' years respectively.

Then, $(x - 6) = 6((54 - x) - 6)$

$\Rightarrow \quad 7x = 6 \times (48 + 1)$

$\Rightarrow \quad x = 42$

Mother's age after a year = x + 1 = 43 years.

**134.** Passenger reached Pune at 17:50, it means he went by train which is scheduled at Mumbai at 15:20. Thus he missed the train, which is scheduled at 11:15 by 40 minutes. Hence, he reached Mumbai station at 12:35.

**135.**

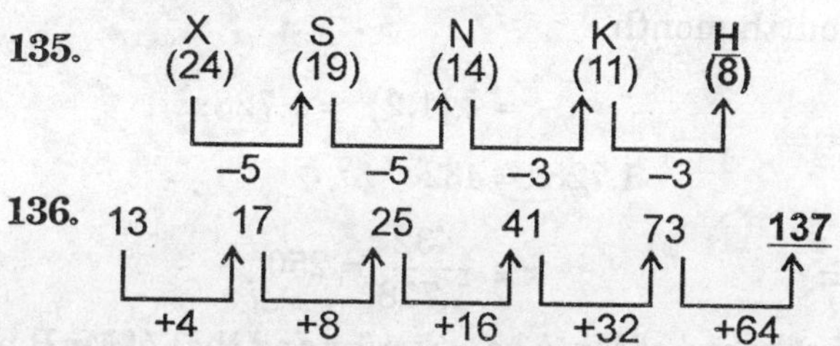


**137.** The next letter in the English alphabet is added before each letter of DEAR i.e. E is added before D, F is added before E and so on.

Therefore, MUST can be written as NMVUTSUT.

**138.** The code follows the following pattern:

4 + 2 = 6

5 – 2 = 3

6 + 2 = 8

4 – 2 = 2

1 + 2 = 3

7 – 2 = 5

Therefore, code for 322859 is 504677 in the same code language.

**139.** The second day after tomorrow is Tuesday, i.e. tomorrow is Sunday.

Therefore, today is Saturday and hence, the day before yesterday was Thursday.

140.

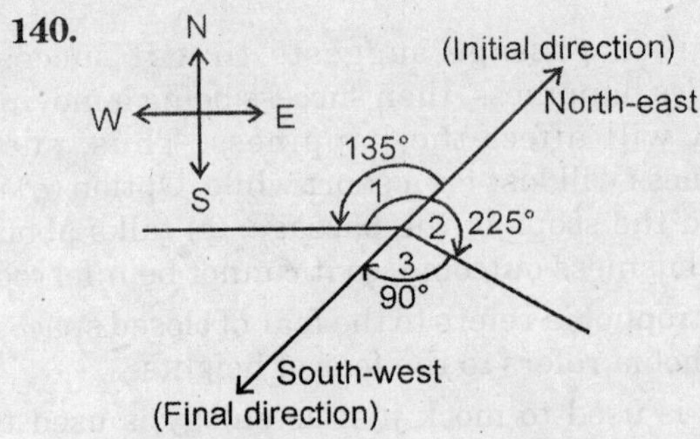


141. Let R be the rate of interest per annum, P be the principle amount invested and T be the time period for which it is invested.

$$\text{S.I.} = 611 - 470 = ₹\ 141$$

$$\text{S.I.} = \frac{P \times R \times T}{100}$$

$$141 = \frac{470 \times R \times 5}{100} \Rightarrow R = 6\%.$$

142. Let the total work to be done be 48 units. Then, the work done by Ajay and Vijay alone in a day will be 3 units and 4 units respectively.

Work done by Vijay in 5 days = 4 × 5 = 20 units

Number of days in which remaining work will be done

$$= \frac{48-20}{3+4} = \frac{28}{7} = 4 \text{ days}$$

Hence, required number of days = 5 + 4 = 9 days.

143. Let initial number of people in the group be 'x'.

Number of people in the group at the end of the fourth month

$$= x(1.2)^3 = 1.728x$$

$$1.728x = 432$$

$$\Rightarrow \quad x = \frac{432}{1.728} = 250.$$

144. Let speed of Mr. A be 'x' km/hr and that of Mr.B be 'y' km/hr. Then,

$$\frac{40}{x} - \frac{40}{y} = 3 \quad \text{...(i)}$$

$$\frac{40}{y} - \frac{40}{2x} = 1 \quad \text{...(ii)}$$

Adding (i) and (ii), we get

$$\frac{40}{x} - \frac{40}{2x} = 4 \Rightarrow x = 5 \text{ km/hr.}$$

145. As per the given information,

$$2a = 3b \text{ and } 4b = 5c$$

$$\Rightarrow \quad a : b : c = 15 : 10 : 8$$

Difference between share of A and C

$$= \frac{15-8}{33} \times 363 = ₹\ 77.$$

146.

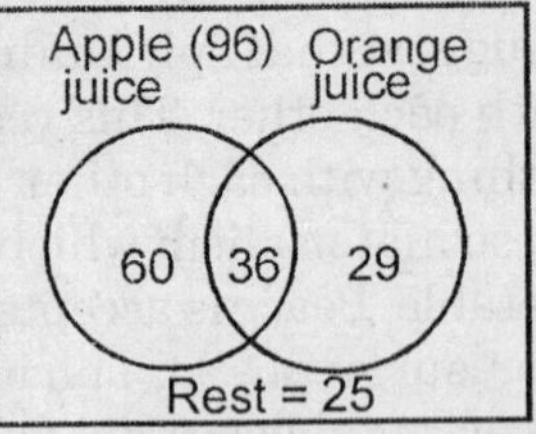


As total number of people is 150, out of which 125 people had at least one of the two drinks.

Number of people who had orange juice

$$= 150 - (60 + 25) = 65.$$

147. Investment = ₹ 1,620

$$\text{Number of shares purchased} = \frac{1620}{90} = 18$$

and income = ₹ 162

$$\text{Income per share} = \frac{162}{18} = ₹\ 9$$

$$\text{Hence, dividend percentage} = \frac{9}{100} \times 100 = 9\%.$$

148. Let the initial weight of Khali be 100 kg, then his new weight will be 100 –12 = 88 kg.

$$\text{Required percentage} = \frac{12}{88} \times 100 = \frac{150}{11} \approx 13.64\%$$

149. Cost price of 1 kg of the mixture

$$= \frac{214.20}{1 + \frac{5}{100}} = ₹\ 204$$

Let the required ratio be a : b. Then,

$$\frac{180 \,.\, a + 220 \,.\, b}{a+b} = 204 \Rightarrow 16b = 24a$$

$$\Rightarrow \quad a : b = 2 : 3.$$

**Alternate Method:**

$$\text{Cost price of 1kg of the mixture} = \frac{214.20}{1 + \frac{5}{100}} = ₹\ 204$$

By alligation:

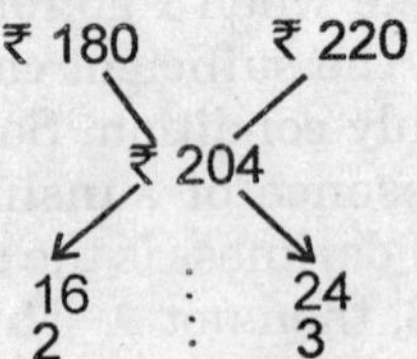


Hence, required ratio = 2 : 3.

150. Let population of the village at the beginning of the first year be p.

Population of the village after 5 years

$$= (1.2)^2 \times (1.1)^2 \times p = 26136$$

$$\Rightarrow \quad p = \frac{26136}{1.7424} = 15000$$

Therefore, population of the village at the beginning of the first year is 15000.

# CLAT PATTERN

## MODEL PAPER-I

**INSTRUCTIONS:** **Time: 2 Hours**

1. This Model Paper will give you an insight into the pattern of the **CLAT (Common Law Admission Test)**Undertaking this model test under the mentioned stipulated time frame will allow you to understand real test scenario.
2. This Question Paper consists of five sections viz. I (English), II (General Knowledge), III (Mathematics), IV (Logical Reasoning) and V (Legal Aptitude).The total number of questions are 200.
3. Each Question contains one mark. There is NO NEGATIVE MARKING

## SECTION –I: ENGLISH

**Directions for questions 1 to 10:** Read the given passage carefully and answer the questions that follow.

"Luminous Modernism" celebrates the "Exhibition of Contemporary Scandinavian Art" that caused a sensation in America 100 years ago. When that show toured New York, Buffalo, Toledo, Chicago and Boston, visitors were astonished by the works of artists many had never heard of or seen. Viewers were moved by the caressing light that enveloped the landscapes and interiors of Vilhem Hammershoi, a Danish painter; they were shocked by the eerie and sometimes painful solitude of people portrayed by Edvard Munch, an artist from Norway. The 160 works had an impact as powerful as it was short lived. Within months, the "Armory Show" opened in New York, featuring 1,300 works that introduced droves of goggle-eyed Americans to everybody who was to become anybody in the history of 20th-century art, from Paul Cezanne to Marcel Duchamp.

Paris was the capital of the international art world, and little more was heard about artists from the frozen north—except for Munch. Nordic art was so little known that when John V. Loeb, a financier, became America's ambassador to Denmark in 1981, he was amazed to discover the "unusual and fascinating" work of its artists. Mr Loeb was no art neophyte. His parents collected French and Italian pictures, and he already had a collection of German Expressionists. Impressed by Danish art, he started buying. The four paintings by Hammershoi in "Luminous Modernism" are from the important Danish art collection he built. Decades after he started, he says the paintings "are so warm and peaceful, they help to calm me down."

Munch became so famous that Andy Warhol, given to capitalizing on icons from Mao to Marilyn, produced his own rendering of "The Scream". Now Hammershoi's star is on the rise; last month one of his interiors sold at Sotheby's London for £577,250. Yet there are many paintings in "Luminous Modernism" by artists as little known in America today as they were a century ago. In fact, some of the countries represented in the show didn't exist at the time of the original exhibition. Finland and Iceland only subsequently gained independence, joining Sweden, Norway and Denmark in the Nordic group.

This reporter's weakness for animals led to special attention being paid to a schmaltzy sunset scene, "Horse by the Beach", a 1902 work by Sweden's Nils Kreuger. "Flower Meadow in the North", an animal-free 1905 painting by Norway's Harald Sohlberg, may sound sentimental, but it isn't. A band of white daisies, like a large handkerchief, stretches out into the distance, cut across by a Silver River beyond which rises a dark forest. The sky is an icy blue. This is a poetic work to stand before and slowly enjoy.

The exhibition is staged by the American-Scandinavian Foundation, established in 1911. The creation of the foundation and the travelling show of Nordic art were both responses to events that are as little known nowadays as some of the art on view. Back then the mass migration of Nordic native sons to the new world was causing alarm. From the early 19th century to the outbreak of the First World War, more than a million Swedes settled in America, many in the prairie land of the Midwest. Swedish commissions studied how to stop the farmer drain. At the same time, bridges were built between the old world, the émigrés and the people they lived among. Happily, this spirit of relationship-building continues. The Kings and Queens of Sweden and Norway, the Crown Prince and Princess of Denmark, and the presidents of Iceland and Finland flew to New York for the official opening of "Luminous Modernism". The next night, at the gala fundraising ball, they were joined by hundreds of Nordic-Americans who seemed delightfully comfortable straddling their new and ancestral homes. May this show will do the same for Nordic artists.

1. Which of the following can be inferred from the phrase "bridges were built between the old world, the émigrés and the people they lived among "?

(*a*) Fight between old and new world had ended and a peaceful and cordial relationship was restored.

(*b*) A mutual relationship developed between the emigrant's native country, emigrants and America.

(*b*) A massive construction was going on at the place.

(*c*) Natives had now allowed the outsiders to live in their country.

2. Choose a word from the given passage that is an antonym of 'Veteran'.

(*a*) Straddling (*b*) Caressing

(*c*) Solitude (*d*) Neophyte

3. What is the meaning of the word 'schmaltzy'?

(*a*) strange (*b*) beautiful

(*c*) sentimental (*d*) avid

4. What does the term "capital" mean in the phrase "capital of international art"?

(*a*) The word capital is used to signify the place that is famous for its art.

(*b*) The word is used to signify a place where artists learn tricks of their trade.

(*c*) This word here signifies the place where art is bought and sold the most in the world.

(*d*) Cannot be determined from the passage.

5. What led to the formation of American-Scandinavian Foundation?

(*a*) The American-Scandinavian foundation was formed primarily due to the mass migration of Nordics to the Americas and the efforts of the Kings, Queens, Prince and Princess of these countries who visited America.

(*b*) The prime factors leading to formation of the American-Scandinavian foundation are mass migration of Nordics to the Americas and also the cordial relationship between the people of old world and the Americans.

(*c*) The foundation was primarily formed because of the radical and open views of the people of new world who were progressive and wanted all the people to move forward.

(*d*) The migrants from Nordic countries was influenced a lot by the open and progressive culture of the Americans, so they decided to incorporate their culture into their own and hence formed a foundation for themselves.

6. The last line of the passage "May this show will do the same for Nordic artists" raises which of the following questions?

(*a*) Whether Nordic artists will be accepted by the Americans with an open heart as was the case with their forefathers.

(*b*) Whether it is possible for the artists from Nordic countries to migrate to America in the same way as the people from their country did 100 years ago.

(*c*) Whether Nordic artists will be able to organize their exhibitions at a regular basis in America.

(*d*) None of these

7. Which of the following is correct?

(*a*) Edward Munch was a Danish painter.

(*b*) Nils Kreuger is from Norway.

(*c*) Hammershoi's paintings are famous for their intensity and colour contrast.

(*d*) None of these

8. Which of the following is incorrect?

I. Andy Warhol produced his own rendering of "The Scream".

II. Leob was a Nordic artist.

III. Hearald Sholberg painted a "Flower Meadow in the North".

(*a*) I and II (*b*) II and III

(*c*) Only II (*d*) I and III

9. According to the passage which of the following event has happened 100 years ago?

(*a*) Luminous Modernism

(*b*) Exhibition of Contemporary Scandinavian Art

(*c*) Migration of Nordics to the America

(*d*) Hammershoi's painting being sold for a huge sum in London

10. What is the most appropriate antonym of the word 'eerie'?

(*a*) bizarre (*b*) quirky

(*c*) outlandish (*d*) vapid

**Directions for questions 11 to 15:** In each of the following questions, a word has been spelt in four different ways. Identify the correct spelling of the given word.

11. (*a*) oppurtunity (*b*) opportunity

(*c*) oppurtunety (*d*) opurtunity

12. (*a*) mendicity (*b*) mendacity

(*c*) mendecity (*d*) mindicity

13. (*a*) sequestration (*b*) siquastration

(*c*) sicuastration (*d*) seqestration

14. (*a*) vacum (*b*) vaccum
(*c*) vacuum (*d*) vaccuum

15. (*a*) felecity (*b*) filicity
(*c*) felicity (*d*) phelicity

**Directions for questions 16 to 20:** Identify the correct meaning of the given idioms.

16. Back seat driver
(*a*) Someone who criticizes
(*b*) Someone who is unaware
(*c*) Someone who is jealous
(*d*) Someone who is unprepared

17. Can't cut the mustard
(*a*) Someone who isn't adequate enough to compete or participate
(*b*) Someone who lacks culinary skills
(*c*) Someone who is frugal and money minded
(*d*) Someone who is brave but dishonest

18. Dead Ringer
(*a*) Horrifying (*b*) Duplicate
(*c*) Original (*d*) Ugly

19. Dry Run
(*a*) Review (*b*) Rehearsal
(*c*) Final Stage (*d*) Lacking Promotions

20. Jaywalk
(*a*) Crossing the street (from the middle) without using the crosswalk
(*b*) A competition where the outcome is difficult to predict or judge
(*c*) To do something in the exactly correct manner
(*d*) Doing above and beyond what is required for the task at hand.

**Directions for questions 21 to 28:** In each of the following questions, a sentence with a blank is given. Fill the blank with the grammatically correct option.

21. Rajiv is older ________ me.
(*a*) to (*b*) than
(*c*) for (*d*) from

22. It is imperative that the session ______ at once.
(*a*) begins (*b*) begin
(*c*) began (*d*) will begin

23. If the team had won, the coach _______happy.
(*a*) would be (*b*) would have been
(*c*) will be (*d*) will have been

24. The flower _________ sweet.
(*a*) smell (*b*) smells
(*c*) is smelling (*d*) will smell

25. Next month, I ____________with the organization for twenty years.
(*a*) will have (*b*) will have been
(*c*) had been (*d*) have been

26. You should reach ______ 9.30. Anyone who comes at or after 9.30 will not be allowed to enter the hall.
(*a*) till (*b*) by
(*c*) on (*d*) at

27. Let you and ________ get ready for the exam.
(*a*) I (*b*) me
(*c*) my (*d*) we

28. Give the book to ________ you please.
(*a*) whomever (*b*) whoever
(*c*) who (*d*) which

**Directions for questions 29 and 30:** In each of the following questions, a sentence with two blank is given. Fill the blanks with the grammatically correct option (the first word in an option is for the first blank).

29. The bridge ______ spans the Nile, ________ flows into Mediterranean Sea, is falling down.
(*a*) which, which (*b*) that, that
(*c*) that, which (*d*) which, that

30. This is a daunting prospect for prison officials ________ difficulties in keeping pace with the present dementia caseload _______ underscored in a recent report by The Times's Pam Belluck.
(*a*) that, are (*b*) who, are
(*c*) which, were (*d*) whose, were

**Directions for questions 31 to 35:** Identify the correct meaning of the given Latin terms.

31. *ex gratia*
(*a*) by legal action (*b*) by force
(*c*) by favour (*d*) by demand

32. *cui bono*
(*a*) as a reward for whom?
(*b*) as a benefit to whom?
(*c*) as a bond with whom?
(*d*) as a duty for whom?

33. *lex lata*
(*a*) future law
(*b*) the current law
(*c*) the law that needs amendment
(*d*) a flaw in the law

34. *male fide*
(*a*) good faith
(*b*) bad faith
(*c*) a working language
(*d*) whose realm his religion

35. *per se*

(*a*) it is not certain

(*b*) by itself

(*c*) not for ourselves alone

(*d*) not for self

**Directions for questions 36 to 38:** The constituent phrases of a sentence have been jumbled. Arrange the given constituents in the correct order so as to form a meaningful sentence.

36. i. the inmate population and prison costs

ii. the get-tough-on-crime and mandatory

iii. beginning in the 1970s did more than drive up

iv. sentencing policies that swept America

(*a*) i ii iii iv (*b*) i iii ii iv

(*c*) ii iv iii i (*d*) iii i ii iv

37. i. we are almost invariably surprised when it turns out that

ii. since we suppose that characters are unified in these ways

iii. stand in tension with one another

iv. the different aspects of someone's personality

(*a*) i iv iii ii (*b*) iv iii ii i

(*c*) iii iv i ii (*d*) ii i iv iii

38. i. since much of art depends on either reaffirming or frustrating

ii. those expectations, and thus, on their very existence

iii. in the context of art, it is surely a good thing

iv. that we expect unity of character and uniformity of behavior

(*a*) i ii iv iii (*b*) ii iv iii i

(*c*) i ii iii iv (*d*) iii iv i ii

**Directions for questions 39 and 40:** Given below is a list of words followed by some choices. In each case, choose the alternative that you can combine with every word in that particular list to form a familiar word phrase.

39. back, away, in, off

(*a*) sit (*b*) ask

(*c*) copy (*d*) give

40. along, after, down, over

(*a*) run

(*b*) walk

(*c*) drop

(*d*) bail

## SECTION –II: GENERAL KNOWLEDGE

41. International Workers' Day, also known as 'May Day' or Labor Day, is observed on:

(*a*) May 27 (*b*) May 2

(*c*) May 14 (*d*) May 1

42. Who among the following has been conferred 'The Grand Cordon of the Order of the Rising Sun' title by Japan for his contribution in strengthening economic relations between Japan and India?

(*a*) Laxmi Nivas Mittal (*b*) Ratan Tata

(*c*) Mukesh Ambani (*d*) Rahul Bajaj

43. Steel tower structure in the form of five rings, for the London Olympic, has been designed by:

(*a*) Shekhar Kapoor (*b*) Sukhdev Malhotra

(*c*) Vikash Kumar Jha (*d*) Anish Kapoor

44. The first 'zero waste toilet system' (ZWTS) in India was inaugurated at which of the following villages?

(*a*) Evoor, Kerala

(*b*) Tundlam, Tamil Nadu

(*c*) Mattur, Karnataka

(*d*) Kunkalamarru, Andhra Pradesh

45. Phu Khanh Basin is situated in:

(*a*) Java Sea (*b*) South China Sea

(*c*) Bay of Bengal (*d*) Yellow sea

46. P. Kunhumohammed is a player associated with:

(*a*) Cricket (*b*) Athletics

(*c*) Football (*d*) Lawn Tennis

47. Who is the current director of the Vikram Sarabhai Space Centre (VSSC)?

(*a*) P.S. Veeraraghavan

(*b*) K Radhakrishnan

(*c*) B. N. Suresh

(*d*) Vijayasekar Subramaniam

48. Who among the following won the World snooker championship, 2012 ?

(*a*) Ronnie O'Sullivan (*b*) Ali Carter

(*c*) Dennis Taylor (*d*) John Higgins

49. A major university centre dedicated to the life and works of Rabindranath Tagore has been opened in:

(*a*) Scotland (*b*) France

(*c*) Germany (*d*) Poland

50. Vladimir Putin was recently sworn as Russia's President for a:

(*a*) third term (*b*) second term

(*c*) fourth term (*d*) None of the above

**51.** "Fortune at the Bottom of the Pyramid" is a book written by:

(*a*) C. K. Prahlad (*b*) Amartya Sen
(*c*) Stephen J. Dubner (*d*) Sudeep Reddy

**52.** Which State governments have banned the use of the expression, 'handicapped'?

(*a*) Haryana (*b*) New Delhi
(*c*) Kerala (*d*) West Bengal

**53.** After successfully launching Agni-V missile, India became the country, which has Inter- Continental Ballistic Missile (ICBM) technology. Which of the following countries has not the ICBM technology?

(*a*) U.S (*b*) Russia
(*c*) China (*d*) Germany

**54.** Ace tennis player and Rajiv Gandhi Khel Ratna awardee, Leander Paes, will be the Sports Ambassador of:

(*a*) Andhra Pradesh (*b*) Kerala
(*c*) Haryana (*d*) Gujarat

**55.** Chief Minister of which of the following States has been recently named as one of the 100 most influential people of the world by the 'Time magazine'?

(*a*) Gujarat (*b*) New Delhi
(*c*) Bihar (*d*) West Bengal

**56.** Recently, in which of the following states Atomic Energy Commission of India has commissioned a uranium ore mine and processing plant set up by Uranium Corporation of India?

(*a*) Karnataka (*b*) Andhra Pradesh
(*c*) Madhya Pradesh (*d*) Jharkhand

**57.** "How to fight Islamist terror from a missionary position" is a book written by:

(*a*) Shashi Tharoor (*b*) Urvashi Butalia
(*c*) Tabish Khair (*d*) Salman Rushdie

**58.** Pobitora Wildlife Sanctuary has the highest density of rhinoceros population in the world. Pobitora Wildlife Sanctuary is located in:

(*a*) Assam (*b*) West Bengal
(*c*) Meghalaya (*d*) Arunachal Pradesh

**59.** Who among the following has been awarded the prestigious 'Dadasaheb Phalke award' for the year 2012?

(*a*) Manna Dey
(*b*) Soumitra Chatterjee
(*c*) VK Murthy
(*d*) K. Balachander

**60.** Who among the following politicians has been declared winner for the prestigious 'International Jurists Award-2012.'?

(*a*) Sheila Dixit (*b*) Mulayam Singh Yadav
(*c*) Narendra Modi (*d*) Nitish Kumar

**61.** What does 'Bio-remediation' mean?

(*a*) Use of microorganism metabolism to remove pollutants
(*b*) Use of micro-organism metabolism to degrade pollutants
(*c*) Use of bacterial metabolism to remove pollutants
(*d*) None of the above

**62.** What is 'Nag'?

(*a*) Anti-tank missile
(*b*) Torpedo
(*c*) Unmanned Aerial Vehicle
(*d*) None of the above

**63.** Which of the following places is famous for its Crafts *Mela* (Fair)?

(*a*) Faridabad (*b*) Surajkund
(*c*) Pushkar (*d*) None of the above

**64.** The Col. C.K. Naidu Lifetime Achievement Award is given for contribution to ________.

(*a*) Cricket (*b*) Football
(*c*) Hockey (*d*) None of the above

**65.** The first indigenous (Indian) nuclear submarine (under development) is known as INS ________.

(*a*) Arihant (*b*) Nishant
(*c*) Rustom (*d*) None of the above

**66.** The Tandon Committee report pertains to

(*a*) Deemed Universities
(*b*) Central Universities
(*c*) Minority Educational Institutions
(*d*) None of the above

**67.** The Satish Dhawan Space Centre (SDSC) is situated at

(*a*) Trivandrum (*b*) Bengaluru
(*c*) Sri Harikota (*d*) None of the above

**68.** Three Gorges, Dam considered to be world's largest hydroelectric project is situated in which of the following countries?

(*a*) India (*b*) USA
(*c*) China (*d*) None of the above

**69.** Recently, the Supreme Court of India appointed a Special Investigation Team (SIT) for Black Money under the Chairmanship of ______.

(*a*) B.P. Jeevan Reddy (*b*) M.B. Shah
(*c*) V.K. Shunglu (*d*) None of the above

70. 'Juno' is the name given to NASA's mission aimed at studying which of the following planets?

(a) Jupiter (b) Saturn
(c) Mars (d) None of the above

71. Recently, an Empowered-Committee headed by _________ was appointed by the Supreme Court of India to enquire into the Mullaperiyar Dam issue.

(a) A.S. Anand (b) K.T. Thomas
(c) A.R. Lakshmanan (d) None of the above

72. The combat version of 'Rudra' was recently inducted in the Indian Army. It is a/an _______

(a) Aircraft
(b) Helicopter
(c) Unmanned Aerial Vehicle
(d) None of the above

73. Usain Bolt is related to which sport?

(a) Athletics (b) Basketball
(c) Football (d) None of the above

74. What is 'New Water'?

(a) Heavy Water (b) Treated Sewage Water
(c) Desalinated Water (d) None of the above

75. 'Time Guerilla' is a two-volume memoir authored by which of the following present or former Head of State?

(a) Fidel Castro (b) S. Berlusconi
(c) Colonel Qadafi (d) George W. Bush

76. Salwa Judum refers to a force consisting of Special Police Officers in the state of

(a) Chattisgarh (b) Madhya Pradesh
(c) Odisha (d) None of the above

77. The Maheshwar Hydroelectric Project is situated in which state?

(a) Uttar Pradesh (b) Madhya Pradesh
(c) Uttarakhand (d) None of the above

78. The Abel Prize for Mathematics is awarded by the King of

(a) Norway (b) Sweden
(c) Denmark (d) None of these

79. What is 'NDX-1'?

(a) Space-suit (b) Space-shuttle
(c) Satellite (d) None of these

80. Change in the name of a State of India requires

(a) Law made by Parliament
(b) Amendment of the Constitution of India
(c) Law made by Parliament with the consent of the Legislature of the concerned state
(d) None of these

81. Change in the name of a Scheduled Language requires

(a) Law made by Parliament
(b) Amendment of the Constitution of India
(c) Law made by Parliament with the consent of the Legislature of the concerned state
(d) None of these

82. Formation of a new state by separation of territory of another state requires

(a) Law made by Parliament
(b) Amendment of the Constitution of India
(c) Law made by Parliament with the consent of the Legislature of the concerned state
(d) None of these

83. Youth-sat is the name of a satellite for atmospheric studies developed jointly by ____ and Russia.

(a) India (b) USA
(c) France (d) None of these

84. DTAA stands for

(a) Direct Taxation Avoidance Agreement
(b) Double Taxation Avoidance Agreement
(c) Doubtful Taxation Avoidance Agreement
(d) None of these

85. M.C. Mary Kom is related to which sport?

(a) Boxing (b) Wrestling
(c) Table Tennis (d) None of these

86. The G. D. Birla Award is given for

(a) Theatre (b) Journalism
(c) Scientific Research (d) None of these

87. India's first Bio-Culture park is proposed to be set up in

(a) Kolkata (b) Ranchi
(c) Bhubaneswar (d) None of these

88. The International Merlin Award is considered to be the Oscar award of

(a) Theatre (b) Magic
(c) Documentaries (d) None of these

89. _______ became the first airline to use a biofuel generated from used cooking oil to power many commercial flights.

(a) Ryan Air (b) KLM
(c) Lufthansa (d) None of these

90. What is 'MediAngels'?

(a) Medical Transcription Service
(b) e-Hospital
(c) Ambulance service
(d) None of these

## SECTION –III: MATHEMATICS

**91.** Three years ago, Isha's age was thrice that of Meshan's age. Five years hence, Meshan' age will be half that of Isha's age. What is Meshan's present age?

(a) 27 years (b) 8 years
(c) 11 years (d) 14 years

**92.** A liquor vendor used to recover cost of 11 cans of bear by selling 8 cans. If now he wants to realize a profit of 50% on each can, by what percent must he mark up his earlier selling price in order to achieve the new profit percentage?

(a) 11.11% (b) 9.09%
(c) 18.18% (d) 22.22%

**93.** In an entrance exam there were two sections – QA and EU. Among the students who took the exam:

(i) 29% of them cleared the cutoff only in EU and 38% of them cleared the cutoff only in QA.
(ii) Number of students who cleared the cutoff in none of the sections is 220033, which is half of the number of students who cleared the cutoff in both the sections.

How many students cleared the cutoff only in EU?

(a) 58087 (b) 560087
(c) 46097 (d) 580087

**94.** When the sum of the digits of a two-digit number is subtracted from the sum of the number and the number formed by reversing the order of its digits, the resultant number is always divisible by

(a) 3 (b) 11
(c) 10 (d) 9

**95.** Ratio of the marks scored by A and B is 10 : 9 and that of the marks scored by A and C is 6 : 5 respectively. If the difference between the marks scored by B and C is 36, find the marks scored by A.

(a) 540 (b) 450
(c) 496 (d) 500

**96.** Ratio of savings of P, Q and R is 5 : 3 : 2 and ratio of expenditure of P and R is 4 : 5 respectively. Q saves 50% of his income which is in turn 150% of income of R. What is the ratio of savings of P to the expenditure of R?

(a) 5 : 3 (b) 5 : 2
(c) 3 : 2 (d) 5 : 1

**97.** The price of 5 mangoes is 25% more than the price of 4 apples, and is 33.33% less than the price of 3 water-melons. If the price of 9 apples is ₹ 225, then find the price of 7 mangoes and 8 watermelons.

(a) ₹ 650 (b) ₹ 675
(c) ₹ 875 (d) ₹ 750

**98.** Average runs scored by Sachin Tendulkar in last 20 ODIs is 20.5. If his career average is 44.5 runs after playing 460 matches, find the average runs scored (approximately) by him in his first 440 ODIs?

$$\left\{\text{Average} = \frac{\text{Total runs scored}}{\text{Number of matches played}}\right\}$$

(a) 44.70 (b) 44.59
(c) 45.59 (d) 44.57

**99.** Susan took on an average 45 classes per month for the first 7 months of a year. He was paid ₹ 1,000 per class throughout the year and his total earnings for the year is ₹ 6,00,000. Find the average number of classes taken per month during the last 5 months.

(a) 59 (b) 57
(c) 49 (d) 47

**100.** Find the sum of the first 18 terms of the sequence: 4, 9, 14, 19, 24, ...

(a) 873 (b) 737
(c) 837 (d) 437

**101.** A basket contains 5 red balls, 6 blue balls and 8 yellow balls. If three balls are picked at random, find the probability that all the three are of the same colour.

(a) $\frac{86}{969}$ (b) $\frac{24}{323}$
(c) $\frac{883}{969}$ (d) $\frac{48}{323}$

**102.** Evaluate: $99^2 + 33 \div 11 \times 31 - 97^2$

(a) 496 (b) 395
(c) 392 (d) 485

**103.** A pole of height 48 m casts a shadow of length 36 m at some time during a day. Find the distance between the top of the pole and the far end of the shadow.

(a) 72 m (b) 60 m
(c) 42 m (d) 80 m

**104.** Two coins and one dice are thrown simultaneously. What is the probability of getting a composite number on the dice and at least one tail?

(a) $\frac{1}{2}$ (b) $\frac{1}{4}$
(c) $\frac{3}{8}$ (d) $\frac{3}{4}$

**105.** Three numbers are selected at random from the first 32 natural numbers. What is the probability that the numbers are either divisible by 2 or 3?

(a) $\frac{^{21}C_3}{^{32}C_3}$ (b) $\frac{^{26}C_3}{^{32}C_3}$
(c) $\frac{^{16}C_3}{^{32}C_3}$ (d) $\frac{^{22}C_3}{^{32}C_3}$

**106.** A alone can do a work in 15 days whereas B and C together can do the same work in 9 days. If C alone start the work and joined by A and B from the 6th day onwards, the work is completed in 10 days. In how many days B alone can complete the work?

(*a*) 12 days (*b*) $11\frac{1}{4}$ days

(*c*) 22 days (*d*) $12\frac{3}{4}$ days

**107.** In an institute, there are 31 faculty members. Among them, 15 faculty teach QA; 17 faculty teach VA; 9 faculty teach LR and 3 faculty teach all the three subjects. If each of them teaches at least on among the three subjects, how many of them teach at least two subjects?

(*a*) 3 (*b*) 7

(*c*) 4 (*d*) 6

**108.** Volume of a cone is $\frac{2}{3}$rd of the volume of a cylinder with the same base radius as that of the cone. If radius of a sphere is twice that of the slant height of the cone, find the ratio of the total surface area of the cylinder to the total surface area of the sphere?

(*a*) 1 : 2 (*b*) 3 : 2

(*c*) 2 : 3 (*d*) Cannot be determined

**109.** A man covers the distance between his office and his home in 30 minutes by his car and in 45 minutes by public transport. One day while traveling by his car from office to his home, due to some technical problem he took public transport exactly from the mid way to his home. Find the time taken to reach his home.

(*a*) 32.50 minutes (*b*) 40 minutes

(*c*) 37.5 minutes (*d*) 50 minutes

**110.** A bike running on a highway parallel to a railway track crosses a train of length 500 m running in the opposite direction with speed 72 km/hr in 20 seconds. Find the speed of the bike.

(*a*) 7.5 m/s (*b*) 4.5 m/s

(*c*) 5 m/s (*d*) 6 m/s

## SECTION –IV: LOGICAL REASONING

**Directions for questions 111 to 116:** In each of the following series find the missing term.

**111.** PP, QN, SK, VG, ZB, ____

(*a*) FV (*b*) EW

(*c*) QW (*d*) EV

**112.** A, B, D, H, P, _____

(*a*) F (*b*) X

(*c*) Q (*d*) S

**113.** BX, DS, GO, KL, PJ, _____

(*a*) JP (*b*) VI

(*c*) QS (*d*) GH

**114.** 9, 20, 35, 54, 77, ____

(*a*) 81 (*b*) 104

(*c*) 117 (*d*) 132

**115.** 421, 300, 381, 332, 357, 348, ___

(*a*) 352 (*b*) 341

(*c*) 343 (*d*) 349

**116.** 2, 2, 12, 12, 30, 30, 56, 56, ____

(*a*) 110 (*b*) 70

(*c*) 90 (*d*) 100

**117.** In an examination, no two students scored the same marks. Names of the students are written on a notice board in an ascending order of their scores. Raju is 3rd from the top and 21st from the bottom. If Satyam is 9th from the top, find his position from the bottom.

(*a*) 14th (*b*) 9th

(*c*) 23rd (*d*) 15th

**118.** Spaceship, Rickshaw, Tractor, ______, Cycle

Which of the following words best fits the blank?

(*a*) Ritz (*b*) Corolla

(*c*) Lancer (*d*) Scorpio

**119.** Complete the sequence: A, Air, Area, Audio, Abstemious, ?

(*a*) Autocratic (*b*) Automation

(*c*) Auction (*d*) Autumn

**120.** Find the odd man out.

24, 360, 54, 48, 120, 168

(*a*) 24 (*b*) 54

(*c*) 168 (*d*) 360

**Directions for questions 121 to 124:** In each of the following questions, two statements are given. There may or may not be a cause and effect relationship between the two statements. Mark your answer using this code.

(*a*) Statement I is the cause and statement II is the effect

(*b*) Statement II is the cause and statement I is the effect

(*c*) Both the statements are effects of a common cause

(*d*) Both the statements are independent effects

**121. Statement I:** In the 33 states and UTs study, milk was found adulterated with detergent, fat and even urea, besides the age-old dilution with water.

**Statement II:** Only in Goa and Pondicherry did 100% of the samples tested conform to required standards.

**122. Statement I:** While Gurgaon (Haryana) has emerged as the major BPO hub in north India, the manpower requirement is met from either Delhi or its adjoining cities.

**Statement II:** The State Government has been discussing the possibility of designing the college syllabus in such a manner that it makes the state's (Haryana) youngsters more employable.

**123. Statement I:** Hungary's political reforms have sparked angry unrest within the nation.

**Statement II:** European Union is facing some very serious problems.

**124. Statement I:** India will allow individual foreign investors direct access to its stock market from January 15, the government said on Sunday.

**Statement II:** India wants foreign investors to directly invest in (the) Indian equity market in order to widen the class of investors, attract more foreign funds, and reduce market volatility

**Directions for questions 125 to 128:** In each of the following questions, a statement/argument followed by two assumptions is given. Read the given statement/argument carefully and identify whether the given assumptions are implicit in the statement/argument. Select

(*a*) If only assumption I is implicit

(*b*) If only assumption II is implicit

(*c*) If both assumptions I and II are implicit

(*d*) If neither assumption I nor II is implicit

**125. Statement:** Cheating in entrance exams has become sadly commonplace, but this gang took technological sophistication to another level.

**Assumptions:**

I. The moral values of students appearing for entrance exams have declined.

II. Advances in technology have made tackling corruption in entrance exams difficult.

**126. Statement:** 'Shudh ke liye yudh' campaign has become a kind of seasonal affair; during the festive season, the government officials show great enthusiasm in raiding shops to collect impure product samples but when the festive season gets over, the campaign, too, loses steam.

**Assumptions:**

I. During festive season the demand for milk products increases and chances of adulteration are high.

II. Government officials work actively for only a short duration.

**127. Statement:** With several adoption centers in the city, cases of abandoning a child have increased these days.

**Assumptions:**

I. Parents who abandon their children think that the children will be picked up by these centers.

II. Most of the parents do not want children.

**128. Argument:** All this time, quiet diplomacy rather than grandstanding has been New Delhi's preferred path in prodding Sri Lanka towards reconciliation with the island's Tamil minority. That this has not produced the desired outcome, especially in the matter of a forward-looking political solution to the Tamil question, is evident.

**Assumptions:**

I. New Delhi expected diplomacy to provide a political solution to the problem with Sri Lanka with respect to the issue of Tamils.

II. Sri Lankans are mavericks and to solve this problem New Delhi needs to adopt non-diplomatic ways.

**Directions for questions 129 to 134:** Each question below contains a statement and two courses of action I and II. Assuming the statement to be true, decide which of the two suggested courses of action logically follows/follow and mark your answer using the code given below. Select:

(*a*) If only I follows

(*b*) If only II follows

(*c*) If both I and II follow

(*d*) If neither I nor II follows

**129.** A lot of male employees of company X have issues with the new female HR who is rude and arrogant.

I. As a lot of male employees have problems, the new HR should be asked to resign.

II. The boss of the new HR should discuss the problems of the employees with her and ask her to behave well.

**130.** A lot of dissatisfied customers of the XYZ Bank complained that the bank opens at 10 am and closes its financial activity for the customers by 3.30 pm. Moreover it has a lunch time of 1 hour during which no customer is attended.

I. The bank manager should expedite the banking operations done between 10 am to 3 .30 pm so that the customers are satisfied with the bank.

II. The bank manager should ask the staff to go for lunch in two shifts of half an hour each so that the banking activities continue during the lunch time.

**131.** A senior member of the team is creating problems for the new recruits by assigning them tasks they are not familiar with and proving them inefficient in front of the manager.

I. The new recruits should first discuss their problem with the senior member of the team and then with the manager and inform about their strengths and weaknesses.

II. The new recruits should put some extra effort from their side and try to improve on their weaknesses and communicate the same to the manager.

**132.** The Drugs Control officials conducted raids on licensed drugs outlets of retailers and wholesalers spread across all districts and found several violations of the provisions of the Drugs and Cosmetics Act, including improper storage conditions of drugs, non-maintenance of sale and purchase records, lack of supervision by qualified and competent persons and sale of Schedule H drugs without proper purchase records.

I. Departmental action, including suspension of license should be initiated against offenders based on the gravity of the violations.

II. Amnesty should be granted to the offenders.

**133.** The cold wave and the unusual snowfall in some States like Jammu & Kashmir, Himachal Pradesh, Uttarakhand and Punjab too has added to the trouble for the homeless who are dying from cold.

I. Some temporary night shelters with basic facilities should be erected on urgent basis to help the homeless people.

II. Food items at subsidized price should be provided to the people in the night shelters.

**134.** Mr Padam Singh a middle aged serviceman felt duped by the insurance company Y when it refused to provide medical insurance in case of accident with minor bone injuries as per its terms and conditions mentioned at the time of signing the documents. Mr Padam Singh had bought the insurance on advice of an experienced banker.

I. As the insurance provider is acting as per the terms of the contract, Mr Padam should learn from his mistake and should read the terms and conditions of the insurance carefully before opting for it in future.

II. He should send a request to the company Y and ask them to help him this time.

**Directions for questions 135 to 140:** In making decisions about important questions, it is desirable to be able to distinguish between 'strong' arguments and 'weak' arguments. 'Strong' arguments are those that are both important and directly related to the question. 'Weak' arguments are those that are of minor importance and also may not be directly related to the question or may be related to a trivial aspect of the question. Each question below is followed by two arguments numbered II and I. You have to decide which of the arguments is/are a 'strong' argument. Select:

(*a*) If argument I is strong

(*b*) If argument II is strong

(*c*) If both I and II are strong

(*d*) If neither I nor II is strong

**135.** Should ragging in colleges be banned?

**Argument I:** No, ragging helps in breaking the ice between the seniors and freshers. It helps in their interaction and development of friendship between them.

**Argument II:** Yes, most cases of ragging involve human rights abuse and physical or psychological trauma.

**136.** Do we need to conserve our palm leaf manuscripts that carry priceless information?

**Argument I:** Yes, because they carry useful information on curing several diseases that affect human beings and animals. These manuscripts given in detail the various herbs that can be used to cure these diseases.

**Argument II:** No, we need to create a digital copy of the manuscripts and chemically treat them with lemon grass oil to kill the fungus that grows on these palm leaves.

**137.** Does it has to be mandatory for individuals to reveal their PAN for purchase of any jewellery worth rupees five lakh or more?

**Argument I:** Yes, a high-value jewellery purchase is one of the simpler routes for black money circulation. PAN identification will help the taxmen in tracking such transactions.

**Argument II:** No, one will have to face discomfort while spending his own money.

**138.** Is understanding the livelihood systems of the poor crucial to effective poverty reduction?

**Argument I:** Yes, such an approach takes into consideration all that the poor are vulnerable to, how they respond to threats and opportunities, and how policies can address their needs.

**Argument II:** No, ensuring employment is closely bound up with notions of entitlement and citizenship irrespective of livelihood systems.

**139.** Does the U.S. stand to gain by implementing energy efficiency measures?

**Argument I:** Yes, developed countries need to take the lead in spreading awareness about energy efficiency measures.

**Argument II:** No, due to its very high per capita energy consumption, the U.S. can forego energy efficiency measures.

**140.** So far, people using swanky and expensive SUVs (Sport Utility Vehicle) for pleasure driving and those who are using buses or trucks for essential services, both are getting equal subsidy on diesel. Should diesel passenger cars be given the fuel subsidizes as those given to trucks and buses?

**Argument I:** No, fuel subsidy on diesel passenger cars hardly goes to the needy sections of the society.

**Argument II:** No, fuel subsidy on diesel should be removed and diesel should be decontrolled.

**Directions for questions 141 to 148:** Each question below consists of one Assertion (A) and one Reason (R). Examine the given assertion and reason carefully and select your answer using the following code:

(*a*) If both A and R are individually true and R is the correct explanation of A

(*b*) If both A and R are individually true but R is not the correct explanation of A

(*c*) If A is true but R is false

(*d*) If A is false but R is true

**141. Assertion:** Women are not responsible for the gender of the fetus.

**Reason:** Women do not have sex chromosomes.

**142. Assertion:** Some inflation is good for the economy.

**Reason:** Inflation leads to stability in prices of goods and thus promotes growth.

**143. Assertion:** Snowfall can occur even when the ground temperature is above the freezing point of water.

**Reason:** Snow forms when the atmospheric temperature is at or below freezing and there is some amount of moisture in the air.

**144. Assertion:** Infants and old people are more likely to acquire fungal infections.

**Reason:** Immune system of infants and old people is weak.

**145. Assertion:** In India, CRR is a central bank regulation that sets the minimum reserves each commercial bank must hold (rather than lend out) of customer deposits and notes.

**Reason:** Central Bank wants to control the amount that banks can lend.

**146. Assertion:** Petrol is costlier in India than in its neighboring countries.

**Reason:** Taxes of petrol are higher in India than in its neighboring countries.

**147. Assertion:** Virus can neither be categorized as living nor non-living.

**Reason:** Virus is living when it is inside the body of a host but when it is not inside a host, it is dormant/non-living.

**148. Assertion:** Ancient civilization grew near rivers.

**Reason:** Rivers provide predictable floods and a stable food resource.

**Directions for questions 149 and 150:** In each of the following questions, words in the first pair are related to each other in a certain manner. The second pair is incomplete. Complete the second pair such that words in the second pair depict the same relation as depicted by words of the first pair.

**149.** Chisel : Shaping and Cutting :: Trowel : ?

(*a*) Cutting and Thrusting

(*b*) Biting and Digging

(*c*) Punching and Pressing

(*d*) Spreading and Shaping

**150.** Blood: Red :: Chlorophyll : ?

(*a*) Blue (*b*) Pink

(*c*) White (*d*) Green

## SECTION –V: LEGAL APTITUDE

**(Question No. 151 to 155 has common applicable principle and facts. Apply the specified principles and answer the questions.)**

**Principle 1:** In an action for the tort of malicious prosecution, the plaintiff must establish four essential conditions for successfully claiming damages.

**Principle 2:** The first condition to establish malicious prosecution is that the plaintiff was prosecuted by the defendant. Prosecution is said to occur when the defendant sets in motion the law by making an application to a person empowered with judicial authority.

**Principle 3:** The second condition to establish malicious prosecution is that the prosecution should be terminated in favour of the plaintiff, if it is so capable to be terminated, or the plaintiff is exonerated of any charge.

**Principle 4:** The third condition to establish malicious prosecution is that there must be an absence of a reasonable and probable cause. A reasonable and probable cause is an honest belief in the guilt of the accused founded on reasonable grounds.

**Principle 5:** The fourth condition to establish malicious prosecution is the existence of a malicious intention on the part of the defendant. Malicious intent is said to exist if the prosecution is instituted with a wish to injure the party rather than to vindicate law and justice.

**Facts:** Sarita was very upset with her boss Rajan due to his high handed attitude. Rajan at various occasions in the past had rejected Sarita's leave application on very flimsy grounds. Once Sarita told her friends that she would teach Rajan a lesson of his life. One day,

Rajan called Sarita to her cabin and told her that she needs to perform as per his expectations otherwise she would not be promoted. Sarita filed a FIR against Rajan for sexual harassment. The police authorities started an investigation and questioned Rajan in his office premises causing immense embarrassment and mental agony to him. Rajan was also taken in remand by the police authorities for interrogation but at last the charges were dropped against him, because of the lack of any evidence. Rajan filed a suit complaining malicious prosecution against Sarita and also for recovering damages. Decide.

**151.** Was there malicious intent on the part of Sarita?

(*a*) Yes, as she intended to get her leave applications sanctioned.

(*b*) No, as Sarita complained about the harassment based on the statement as understood by her.

(*c*) No, as used legal measures to redress her grievance.

(*d*) Yes, as Sarita instituted the proceedings with the intent to injure the reputation of Rajan and teach him a lesson.

**152.** Was there absence of any reasonable or probable cause on the part of Sarita against Rajan?

(*a*) No, as Sarita complained about the harassment based on the statement made by Rajan.

(*b*) Yes, as Sarita's actual grievance was high handed behavior of Rajan.

(*c*) Yes, as Sarita acted on pre-meditated basis without having any reasonable consideration to the guilt of Rajan.

(*d*) No, as Sarita merely filed a FIR by legal means.

**153.** Were the proceedings against Rajan terminated in his favor?

(*a*) No, as the prosecution caused mental agony and irreparable damage to Rajan's reputation.

(*b*) Yes, as the charges of sexual harassment were dropped against him and he was exonerated.

(*c*) Yes, Rajan was supported by his family and office during the investigation.

(*d*) No, as no court of law acquitted Rajan of the allegations leveled against him.

**154.** Was there any prosecution of Rajan by Sarita?

(*a*) No, as no judicial authority issued process against Rajan and the case was closed by police authorities.

(*b*) Yes, as Sarita's acts caused mental agony and irreparable damage to Rajan's reputation.

(*c*) Yes, as Rajan was interrogated by the police authorities.

(*d*) No, as Rajan had no *mens rea* for committing any offence of sexual harassment.

**155.** Whether the suit, which was filed by Rajan against Sarita succeed for the claim of damages?

(*a*) Yes, as all the elements of malicious prosecution stand satisfied.

(*b*) No, as none of the conditions for malicious prosecution stand satisfied.

(*c*) No, as there was no prosecution and the proceedings terminated in favour of Rajan.

(*d*) Yes, as mental agony and irreparable damage to Rajan's reputation must be duly compensated.

**156. Principle:** When a person from is accused of a crime in one country and is found in another country, the process of transferring such person from the country where he is found to the country where he is accused of the crime is known as extradition.

**Explanation:** Diplomatic embassies and consulates of a country are considered to be part of the territory of the country they represent wherever they may be. Extradition is possible only when they are free from any legal proceedings in the country they are found in.

**Facts:** A Pakistani man is found to have planted listening devices in the Indian Embassy at Washington D.C. He is arrested by the American police in a Washington suburb.

(*a*) India should ask for his extradition. The crime was committed on Indian soil.

(*b*) India cannot ask for his extradition.

(*c*) India should prosecute him in USA.

(*d*) India should ask Pakistan to prosecute him.

**157. Principle:** Nothing is an offence which is done in the exercise of the right of private defence.

**Explanation:** Every person has a right to defend his own body, and the body of any other person, against any offence affecting the human body or; property, whether movable or immovable, of himself or of any other person, against any act which is an offence falling under the definition of theft, robbery, mischief etc.

**Facts:** A hears some sounds at night and wakes up. He realizes that a burglar B is trying to break into his neighbor C's house. He takes his gun and starts searching for the burglar. When A finds B he shoots him. A is booked for murder.

(*a*) A is liable for murder, there was no danger to his or C's person.

(*b*) A is not liable for murder there was danger to his or C's person.

(*c*) A is liable for murder, there was no danger to his property as such.

(*d*) A is not liable for murder as he was trying to protect his neighbor's property.

**158. Principle:** A treaty could be invalid if (i) The representative lacks proper authority, (ii) there is a fraud committed by another party, (iii) corruption of the representative (iv) coercion of the representative, (v) coercion of the state.

**Explanation:** The representative is any person who has been deputed by the state to enter into agreements on its behalf.

**Facts:** Xhamster is a person who arrived by a state plane from Libya. He is introduced by a servant of his as "His Excellency, the Empowered Envoy from Libya". He presents his credentials and they begin negotiations. At this point of time the Al Mazeera channel shows breaks news that Muammar Gaddafi, the leader of Libya has been killed by the rebels and the rebels have now formed Government in Libya. Xhamster enters into a treaty with NATO powers. Libya later disclaims any obligations under the treaty.

(*a*) The treaty is invalid because the representative lacks authority.

(*b*) The treaty is valid.

(*c*) The validity of the treaty depends on its contents.

(*d*) The treaty is invalid because of fraud by another party.

**(Question No.159 and 160 has common applicable principle and explanation with different set of facts.)**

**Principle:** Mere attempt to commit an act which is impossible would be no offence, as law treats it as merely a preparation.

**Explanation:** Attempt to commit theft shall be a crime only if it is complimented by an overt act in furtherance to the object.

**159. Facts:** Nishit decided to steal the famous sword of Tipu Sultan from the National Museum. He planned for the theft for more than two months which included collecting necessary weaponry, movement chart and camouflaging gas. One day when the sword was being moved from the National Museum to the Presidents House, Nishit chased the vehicle carrying the sword but failed as his car was impounded for jumping traffic signal. Whether Nishit can be held guilty for attempt to theft?

(*a*) No, as there was no covert act to commit theft.

(*b*) Yes, as preparation for theft and chasing the vehicle carrying the sword amounts to overt act to commit theft.

(*c*) Yes, as Nishit had *mens rea* to commit the offence.

(*d*) No, as it was impossible to steal the famous Sword of Tipu Sultan.

**160. Facts:** Siraj decided to steal Kohinoor diamond from the museum of Nawab of Hyderabad. He invited his friends to plan the theft and also collected money required for the operation. However, Siraj's friends picked up a fight and the group was dismantled. One of the disgruntled members of the group filed a complaint. Decide whether Siraj can be held guilty for attempt to commit theft?

(*a*) Yes, as Siraj invited his friends to plan theft.

(*b*) No, as it was impossible to commit theft and no overt act was committed in the abovementioned case.

(*c*) No, as the group did not succeed in its efforts to steal Kohinoor diamond.

(*d*) Yes, as Siraj had the *mens rea* and collected his friends to commit theft.

**161. Principle:** Only states may be parties to the International Criminal Court.

**Explanation:** ICC has jurisdiction over everyone. But only member countries have an obligation to cooperate with ICC.

**Facts:** The international terrorist brotherhood has been charged with genocide by the ICC. A few of its members are arrested in various places. They plead that they cannot be charged as they are not part of any country, member or non-member as such.

(*a*) They can be charged.

(*b*) They cannot be charged.

(*c*) Only such members of the brotherhood as are citizens of member countries can be charged.

(*d*) None of the above.

**162. Principle:** Nuisance means an unlawful interference with a person's enjoyment of land.

**Explanation:** Acts interfering with health, safety, comfort may be some examples of it. The interference has to be indirect. If it is direct, it becomes trespass.

**Facts:** Babulal installed a brick grinding machine adjacent to the premises of a doctor Dr. Ram Raj Singh. The brick grinding machine generated duct which polluted the atmosphere. Dust entered the consulting chamber of the doctor and caused physical inconvenience to him and his patients and their red coating on clothes etc. could be visible. The land on which the clinic is situated belongs to Babulal and has been leased out to Dr. Ramraj Singh. Can Dr. Ramraj Singh still sue?

(*a*) No, this is not interference with a residential place so it doesn't amount to nuisance.

(*b*) Doctor can sue even if he is not the owner. But he cannot sue the owner himself. Owner has primary rights over the land.

(*c*) Doctor can sue the owner also.

(*d*) None of the above.

**(Instructions: Questions 163 to 166 has common set of principles and facts. Apply the specified principles and answer the questions)**

**Principle 1:** Standard form of contract shall be valid only if it provides reasonable notice and opportunity to the parties to make a reasoned decision.

**Principle 2:** Consent is said to be accorded when two or more persons agree upon the same thing in the same sense with free consent.

**Principle 3:** Any person of sound mind above the age of majority prescribed by law shall be competent to enter into a contract.

**Principle 4**: Freedom to contract is the cardinal principle of law of contract, which presupposes equal bargaining power between the parties.

**Facts:** Raj employed a minor named Ravi as a household help after shifting into his new bungalow. One day Raj sent Ravi to give his clothes for dry-cleaning. Ravi gave the clothes for dry wash and handed over the customer copy to Raj. After three days, when Raj went to the dry-cleaning store to collect his clothes, he found that one of his Sherwani was burnt due to hot ironing. Frantically, Raj complained to the shop owner who apologized for the same. Raj was devastated as it was his wedding Sherwani. Next morning when Raj demanded Rs 75,000 for his Sherwani, the shop owner brought to the attention of Raj the terms and condition on the back of the slip limiting the liability of the shop for any damage to ten rupees only, which was not visible clearly. Raj filed a suit for losses suffered and claimed damages. Decide.

**163.** Can it be said that both the parties had equal bargaining power in the above facts and circumstances?

(*a*) Yes, as Ravi was free to choose any dry-cleaning store.

(*b*) No, as the standard terms regarding limitation of liability was in fine print and it was not possible for Ravi to read it in order to form a reasoned opinion.

(*c*) No, as Ravi was a poor domestic help and shop owner was rich

(*d*) Yes, as Ravi being the consumer is supposed to have a equal bargaining power.

**164.** Whether the parties were competent to enter into the contract?

(*a*) Yes, as both Ravi and the dry-cleaner were persons of sound mind.

(*b*) No, as Ravi was a minor.

(*c*) No, as Ravi ought to have read the terms and conditions regarding limitation of liability before handing over the clothes.

(*d*) Yes, as it was not Ravi had discharged his part if duty without any delinquency.

**165.** Was there a consent which was accorded by the parties for entering into the contract?

(*a*) Yes, the parties agreed for the same thing in the same sense.

(*b*) No, as Ravi was a minor, he was incapable of expressing consent.

(*c*) No, as Ravi was incapable to read the terms and conditions of contract hence there was no valid consent.

(*d*) Yes, as Ravi was acting under the instructions of Raj.

**166.** Whether the standard form contract in the given case is valid or not?

(*a*) No, as Ravi neither had the competence, nor the reasonable notice of the terms to make a reasoned decision.

(*b*) Yes, as Ravi was not under not under any compulsion to hand over the clothes for dry-cleaning.

(*c*) Yes, as the terms regarding limitation of liability was written in the the customer copy.

(*d*) No, as the act of using minor children for domestic work is an offence.

**167. Principle:** The doctrine of *Res Ipsa Loquitur* says - When an event has taken place that could not have taken place but for the negligence of the defendant, the plaintiff just has to prove the accident and need not prove the negligence of the defendant separately. But the defendant can escape liability if he proves that there were factors beyond his control.

**Explanation:** The plaintiff is a person who complains against another person in court. The defendant is the person against whom a complaint is made. Usually when a person brings a claim for negligence, the plaintiff has to prove that the defendant was negligent.

**Facts:** On a day in the monsoon season, there is 7 inches of rain which is 2 inches higher than the previous record which was set in 1905. A wall of a building owned by M collapses killing P, Q and R. The families of the deceased sue M. M pleads that there was no negligence on his part as the rain which is beyond his control caused the collapse.

(*a*) M is liable.

(*b*) M is not liable.

(*c*) M could be liable if it is proved that his was the only building that collapsed.

(*d*) None of the above.

**168. Principle:** An agreement made without consideration is void, unless it is expressed in writing and registered and is made on account of natural love and affection between parties standing in a near relation to each other.

**Explanation:** An agreement without consideration can also be allowed if it is a promise to compensate a person who has already done something for the promisor, or something which the promisor was legally compellable to do.

**Facts:** Raju promises to give Rs.1000 to Reddy. Reddy agrees to accept the Rs.1000 from Raju.

(*a*) There is no consideration here.

(*b*) There is consideration here.

(*c*) The contract is void because it is unlawful.

(*d*) None of the above.

**169. Principle:** A person shall not be qualified for appointment as a Judge of the Supreme Court unless he is a citizen of India and (*a*) has been for at least five years a Judge of a High Court or of two or more such Courts in succession; or (*b*) has been for at least ten years an advocate of a High Court or of two or more such Courts in succession; or (*c*) is, in the opinion of the President, a distinguished jurist.

**Explanation:** In computing for the purpose of this clause the period during which a person has been an advocate, any period during which a person has held judicial office not inferior to that of a district judge after he became an advocate shall be included.

**Facts:** The Registrar of the High Court is a senior district judge. In Karnataka, to be eligible to be appointed as district judge, one must have practiced as an advocate for at least 3 years at the High Court. Ramesh has been the Registrar at Karnataka High Court for 7 years. Is he eligible for appointment to the Supreme Court?

(*a*) Ramesh is eligible.

(*b*) Ramesh is not eligible.

(*c*) Ramesh is eligible only if prior to becoming registrar he has officiated as district judge for 7 years.

(*d*) None of the above.

**170. Principle**: Nothing is an offence which is done by any person who is justified by law, or who by reason of a mistake of fact and not by reason of a mistake of law in good faith, believes himself to be justified by law, in doing it.

**Explanation**: Mistake of fact is an honest and reasonable belief in the existence of circumstances, which, if true would make the act for which a person is indicted an innocent act.

**Facts**: A, a police constable saw B early one morning, holding in his hand three pieces of cloth. Suspecting that he had stolen the cloth, he went up to B and began questioning him. B did not give accurate answers and refused the constable to inspect the cloth material. As a result, the police constable A arrested B after much resistance, however B was released by the Inspector of Police after adequate enquiries were made. B filed a complaint against A for wrongful confinement.

(*a*) A is liable for the wrongful arrest and confinement of B.

(*b*) A is liable since he did not check the particulars of the cloth before arresting B.

(*c*) A is liable since he caused harm to the reputation of B.

(*d*) A is not liable since he acted under the *bona fide* belief that he was legally justified in detaining B as he suspected him of possessing stolen property, and thus committed a mere mistake of fact.

**171. Principle:** All citizens shall have the right to freedom of speech and expression.

**Explanation:** Nothing in the above clause shall prevent the State from making any law relating to, libel, slander, defamation, contempt of court or any matter which offends against decency or morality or which undermines the security of, or tends to overthrow, the State.

**Facts:** The Government makes rules that all wireless conversations in border areas will be monitored.

(*a*) These rules violate the principle.

(*b*) These rules don't violate the principle.

(*c*) The rules violate the principle but since it is for national security, they have to be tolerated.

(*d*) None of the above.

**(Instructions: Questions 172 to 175 has common set of principles and facts. Apply the specified principles and answer the questions).**

**Principle 1:** Libel is an actionable tort punishable with an imprisonment of seven years. Three necessary conditions must be established to sustain an action for libel.

**Principle 2:** The first condition is that there must be false statement on part of the person committing libel. False statement is such statement which is based on events not known to anyone but the person who is accused of making libelous statement.

**Principle 3:** The second condition is that there must be publication of false statement. Publication is said to occur if a statement is made in a permanent form such as effigy, painting, writing, painting etc.

**Principle 4:** The third condition is that such statement should be defamatory. A statement is said to be defamatory if it lowers the plaintiff in the estimation of right thinking members of the society generally.

**Facts:** X produced a movie titled *'the last leader'* which received immense critical appraisal. The movie revolved around the degenerating and abysmal moral standards in politics. In one of the scenes, the protagonist said that the leading coalition of brotherhood party is a bunch a criminals, bootleggers and goons ready to sell the country. Leader of the brotherhood party, Mr. Y, objected to such direct comment on his party. The movie was screened despite public unrest and few incident of burning effigy of X. However, in the elections immediately after the release, the brotherhood party lost the elections. Psephologists blamed the results on *the last leader*. Y sued X for libel. Decide.

**172.** Were the statements made in the last leader defamatory?

(*a*) Yes, as the statement was a direct indictment to the character of Y and his party men.

(*b*) No, as X stated the truth.

(*c*) No, as there was no statement in the present case.

(*d*) Yes, as the statement regarding brotherhood party would lower the dignity of party in the view of public at large.

**173.** Was there any publication in the abovementioned case?

(*a*) No, as depiction of something in the form of a movie, cannot be termed as a publication.

(*b*) Yes, as the false statement was made in a permanent form in the movie which was capable of being understood by others.

(*c*) Yes, as brotherhood party lost elections as result of movie titled *the last leader*.

(*d*) No, as there was no direct communication from X to public at large.

**174.** Were there any false words used by X against Y and his party?

(*a*) No, as the statement made in the movie about members of brotherhood party was corroborated by election results.

(*b*) Yes, as the statement made in the movie was not known to anyone but the person who is accused of making libelous statement.

(*c*) Yes, as nobody can blame the democratically elected government.

(*d*) No, as the statement made in the movie were truth.

**175.** Whether the actions for libel filed by Y against X succeed?

(*a*) Yes, as all the necessary conditions for a libel are satisfied.

(*b*) No, as there was no publication in the aforementioned case.

(*c*) Yes, as the statement in the movie resulted in downfall of the government and public unrest.

(*d*) No, as all the condition for libel are not satisfied.

**176. Principle**: The state shall not deny to any individual equality before the law or equal protection of laws.

**Explanation**: Equality before law means that no man is above the law. Equal protection of laws means equality of treatment in equal circumstances.

**Facts:** Ruby Airlines, owned by the Government, had come up with a policy of termination of service of airhostesses, within four years of marriage of the airhostesses or at the time of the first pregnancy. Furious at the injustice, the Airhostess Fliers Association decided to challenge the rule based on the principle stated below.

(*a*) The policy is not violative of the principle since Ruby Airlines has acted in good faith and in interest of the airhostesses.

(*b*) The Government can make such policies and regulations, which should not be subject to any challenge.

(*c*) The policy has angered the airhostess association and should be done away with.

(*d*) The policy is arbitrary and violates the above stated principle. There should be no differential treatment of air hostesses.

**177. Principle:** An offer need not be made to an ascertained person, but no contract can arise until it has been accepted by an ascertained person.

**Explanation**: Acceptance is completed when the same is conveyed to the person making the offer.

**Facts:** A pharmaceutical company advertised to pay Rs 10,000 to anyone who contracts dengue after having there vaccine called *'dengimonozín'*. It further added that as a sign of their sincerity they have already deposited Rs 1,00,000 with a National Bank. X takes the vaccine *'dengimonozín'*. He suffered from dengue after two months and thereafter communicated the pharmaceutical company claiming Rs 10,000 along with the relevant treatment charges. Whether the pharmaceutical company is liable to pay X?

(*a*) No, as the claim was exaggerated.

(*b*) Yes, as the offer made was duly accepted and acceptance was communicated by X to the pharmaceutical company. However only Rs 10,000 would be payable.

(*c*) Yes, as the offer was duly accepted. However, Rs 10,000 along with treatment charges would be payable.

(*d*) No, as the offer was never made to any specific person.

**178. Principle:** An agreement by way of a wager is void and unenforceable unless specifically provided and regulated by law.

**Explanation**: Wagering contract is said to occur when the parties stakes something of value upon the result of some future uncertain event.

**Facts:** Employees of ABC Corporation decided to float a chit fund which is regulated under Chit Fund Act, 1982. In the said fund, every employee was supposed to contribute Rs 500 per month and the winner of chit every month was supposed to get Rs 50,000. In the month of June 2011, Ram won the chit lottery and was expected to get the Rs 50,000. However, all the fellow employees decided not to give the aforementioned sum considering the bad behaviour of Ram. Ram filed a suit against all the employees participating in the fund. Whether Ram would succeed in the suit filed against employees?

(*a*) Yes, as Ram had duly paid his contribution and abided by the terms of chit fund.

(*b*) No, as the chit fund contract is wager in nature.

(*c*) No, as Ram had behaved badly to all fellow employees.

(*d*) Yes, as the contract for chit fund is not a wager being regulated under Chit Fund Act, 1982.

**(Instructions: Questions 179 to 181 has common set of principles and facts. Apply the specified principles and answer the questions)**

**Principle 1**: If a person commits suicide, whosoever abets the commission of such suicide shall be liable for the offence of abetment of suicide.

**Principle 2:** Abetment means assisting, aiding or advising a person by direct or indirect means.

**Principle 3:** Suicide means an act aimed to end the life of oneself and does not include a failed attempt to commit suicide.

**Facts:** X is suffering from terminal illness and undergoing treatment under Y. One day X requests Y, to give him an injection of Potassium Cyanide to end his agony. Y after much persuasion agrees to design a machine through which Potassium Cyanide can be injected inside the body. Y sets up the machine besides X but leaves the opening nozzle in X's hand. X opens injection nozzle. Due to some design defects administration of potassium cyanide remains incomplete. X slips into Coma. Decide.

**179.** Whether the act of X constitutes suicide?

(*a*) Yes, as X open the nozzle with the intent to end his life.

(*b*) No, as X was not sure if administration of potassium cyanide would be sufficient to end his life.

(*c*) No, as X failed in attempt to commit suicide due to design defect.

(*d*) Yes, as X persuaded Y to specifically design a machine to cause his death.

**180.** Was there abetment by Y in the given set of facts and circumstances?

(*a*) No, as Y left the opening nozzle in X's hand.

(*b*) Yes, as Y aided in designing a machine which was meant to end the life of X.

(*c*) Yes, as Y installed the machine next to X and gave the opening nozzle to be opened.

(*d*) No, as the design itself was defective.

**181.** Whether Y can be held guilty for abetment to suicide?

(*a*) No, as the very ingredient of suicide remains unsatisfied considering that X slipped into Coma.

(*b*) Yes, as Y designed the machine with intent to aid and assist X to commit suicide.

(*c*) Yes, as slipping in coma is as bad as being dead.

(*d*) No, as Y acted after being persuaded by X and in good faith.

**182. Principle:** The consideration or object of an agreement is lawful, unless it is forbidden by law; or is of such a nature that, if permitted, it would defeat the provisions of any law; or is fraudulent; or involves or implies injury to the person or property of another; or the Court regards it as immoral, or opposed to public policy.

**Explanation:** In each of the above cases, the consideration or object of an agreement is said to be unlawful. Every agreement of which the object or consideration is unlawful is void.

**Facts:** Aneeta agrees to let her daughter Champa to hire to Bondamal for concubinage. What is wrong with this contract?

(*a*) The consideration is illegal.

(*b*) The contract has an unlawful object.

(*c*) The contract is immoral.

(*d*) None of the above.

**183. Principle:** An acceptance must be absolute and unconditional to convert a proposal into a promise.

**Explanation**: When the promisee places a condition before accepting the promise, the promise cannot be said to be complete unless promisor accepts the condition.

**Facts:** Steve decided to sell his Oxford dictionary to Sam for Rs 300. Sam proposed to pay Rs 100 in three instalments to Steve. Steve sold the book. After a week, Steve sued Sam to return his Oxford dictionary as he never accepted the condition of payment in three instalments. Decide. Whether Sam is liable to return the book in this case?

(*a*) Yes, as acceptance was conditional and the same was not accepted by Steve.

(*b*) No, as Steve sold the book to Sam, which implies that he accepted the condition regarding instalment.

(*c*) Yes, as Steve had not received full consideration till the date of filing the suit.

(*d*) No, Sam had already paid the first instalment of Rs 100.

**184. Principle:** Fraud includes an active concealment of a fact by one having knowledge or belief of the fact.

**Explanation:** Mere silence of the facts likely to affect the willingness of a person is not fraud unless the person is duty bound to speak. It is duty of a person keeping silence to speak, if his silence is capable to mislead someone.

**Facts:** X sells by auction to Y a cow which X knows to be unhealthy. Before concluding the sale Y asks X that '*If you do not deny it I would assume that the cow is healthy*'. X says nothing. After, six months, Y sues X for committing fraud. Decide. Whether Y can sustain a legal action for fraud against X?

(*a*) Yes, as X was liable for committing fraud by active concealment when he was duty bound to speak.

(*b*) No, as X was not duty bound to speak.

(*c*) No, as X never expressly mislead Y regarding health condition of the cow.

(*d*) Yes, as X ought to have announced that health condition of cow before auctioning it.

**185. Principle:** An agreement executed under undue influence of other party is not enforceable in the eyes of law.

**Explanation:** Undue influence is said to be established when one of the parties is in a position to dominate the will of the other and uses that position to obtain an unfair advantage.

**Facts:** Sanjay's son Sudeep was keen to start his new electronics store but was short of money for capital investment. Sudeep failed in all his efforts to raise a loan of Rs two lakhs. Sudeep requested Sanjay to lend him two lakhs rupees which he declined. Sudeep asked Sanjay that he should either lend him money or prepare for his funeral. Sanjay decided to give a loan to Sudeep but rescinded his promise at the last moment. Sudeep filed a suit against his father Sanjay. Decide. Whether Sanjay was liable to extend the loan to Sudeep?

(*a*) No, as Sudeep did not specify the terms and conditions of the loan and the agreement was without consideration.

(*b*) Yes, as Sudeep had legitimate expectation to receive loan from Sanjay.

(*c*) Yes, as parents ought to help their children in their efforts.

(*d*) No, as the agreement was vitiated due to Sudeep's threat to commit suicide.

**186. Principle:** In any transaction where the order in which reciprocal promises are to be performed is expressly fixed by the contract, they shall be performed in that order.

**Explanation:** Order of performance of reciprocal promises is meant to ensure certainty of contract.

**Facts:** X promised to build Y's house and accept payment of Rs 50,000 thereafter. However, considering hike in the cement prices in between, X demanded Y to pay a initial sum of Rs 10,000. Y refused to make the payment upfront. X stopped the construction and sued Y for recovery of damages. Decide whether the suit filed by X maintainable in the aforementioned case?

(*a*) Yes, as X was ready to adjust ten thousand in final payment.

(*b*) No, as the order of performance of reciprocal promise was breached by X.

(*c*) No, as X should have accounted for hike in cement prices before entering into contract.

(*d*) Yes, as X couldn't have reasonable foreseen hike in cement prices.

**187. Principle:** There can be no wrong without a legal remedy.

**Explanation**: No remedy for an injury caused can be claimed by a person who voluntarily consents to the same.

**Facts:** X, an avid bullfight fan, decided to visit Spain to see a bullfight. The organisers duly issued warnings about the probable damages that may be caused to spectators during a bullfight. In the last round, Bull named 'Gary' charged inside the spectator box causing knee fracture to X. X sued organisers for claiming ticket money as well as damages. Whether bullfight organisers are liable to pay X?

(*a*) No, as X was injured due to act of god.

(*b*) Yes, organisers must pay ticket money and damages as X was injured due to ill performance of bullfighters.

(*c*) Yes, as organisers ought to have made higher boundary walls to ensure that bull did not enter spectator box.

(*d*) No, as X voluntarily consented to the injury by accepting the tickets which displayed the warnings.

**188. Principle**: Fundamental Rights include the right to form associations for peaceful purposes, right to strike as well as the right to free speech and expression.

**Explanation**: The Fundamental Rights are subject to reasonable restrictions which connote a limitation imposed on a person in the enjoyment of a right which should not be arbitrary or of an excessive nature beyond what is actually required.

**Facts**: During a strike of worker employees of DALCO, which included slogans and songs, by people who were claiming their rights, a few people got drunk and in rage threw stones at the office buildings damaging property and injuring some people. Can they avail the benefit of the principle stated above?

(*a*) Yes, since the employees on strike have the freedom to free speech and expression and they have just expressed their anger towards the managements.

(*b*) Yes, because they have the right to strike and enjoy all such rights which may be encompassed therein.

(*c*) No, because as employees they should behave properly.

(*d*) None of the above.

**(Instructions: Questions 189 to 191 has common set of principles and facts. Apply the specified principles and answer the questions).**

**Principle 1:** A servant can claim damages from his master for the negligence of a fellow servant under the doctrine of common employment.

**Principle 2:** Common employment is said to occur if more than one servant is working in furtherance of the benefit or instructions of common master and are engaged in a common work.

**Principle 3:** Negligence in common employment shall mean and include any act or omission which causes harm to a fellow servant.

**Facts:** Anand asked his servant Hemant to clean his rifle. In order to quickly complete the exercise, Anand requested his brother Ashish to hold the rifle while Hemant was cleaning the same. By mistake, Ashish touched the trigger and caused grievous hurt to Hemant. Hemant has filed a suit against Anand. Decide.

**189.** Whether Ashish was negligent in the common employment?

(*a*) Yes, as he touched the trigger that caused grievous hurt.

(*b*) No, as Ashish cannot be termed as a fellow servant as he was not paid for his service being Anand's brother.

(*c*) Yes, as Ashish ought to have checked the rifle before pulling the trigger.

(*d*) No, as Ashish was merely helping Hemant.

**190.** Whether Hemant and Ashish can be termed to be in common employment of Anand?

(*a*) Yes, as both of them were cleaning the rifle together.

(*b*) No, as Ashish cannot be termed as a fellow servant as he was never paid by Anand for his assistance.

(*c*) No, as Ashish was merely holding the rifle while Hemant while engaged in cleaning the rifle singlehandedly.

(*d*) Yes, as Anand requested both of them to perform common task.

**191.** Is Anand vicariously liable to pay Hemant under the doctrine of common employment?

(*a*) No, as Ashish and Hemant were not co-servants in this case.

(*b*) Yes, as both of them were cleaning the rifle together under instructions of a common master.

(*c*) Yes, as Hemant started to work with Ashish only under instructions of his master.

(*d*) No, as causing grievous hurt is a criminal offence.

**192. Principle:** Consideration is the reasonable equivalent of some valuable benefit that is passed on from the promisor to the promisee.

**Explanation:** Consideration would not be invalid merely because it is insufficient, but provided it is certain.

**Facts**: A agreed to sell his horse worth \$500 to B. After negotiation he agreed to sell it for either \$10 or \$ 50. Whether there was valid consideration in the aforementioned case?

(*a*) Yes, as B was not getting the horse free of cost and was required to pay A in lieu of purchase of horse.

(*b*) No, as A was selling his horse for a very insufficient consideration.

(*c*) No, as the consideration was uncertain.

(*d*) Yes, as A agreed to sell his horse after negotiation.

**193. Principle:** A master is not vicariously responsible for the wrongful act done by his servant, unless it is either authorized by him or is done in the course of employment.

**Explanation:** Vicarious liability shall be strictly applied in case the servant causes grave damage to others in course of employment.

**Facts**: X, a driver of petrol lorry was responsible to transport fuel tankers from place to place and had to further ensure the safe unloading of the fuel.. Once during fuel unloading, X lit a cigarette at the petrol pump which caused massive damage and injured many people. The Petrol pump sued the owner of lorry service. Can the owner of the lorry service be held vicariously liable for act of X?

(*a*) Yes, as the vicarious liability is to be strictly applied if the act of the servant has caused grave damage.

(*b*) No, as the lorry Service Company never authorized X to smoke during working hours.

(*c*) No, as the personal wrong of the driver cannot be attributed to the owner of the lorry service.

(*d*) Yes, as the accident was caused during the official working hours.

**194. Principle**: Fundamental Rights include the right to move freely throughout the territory of India and the right to reside and settle in any part of the territory of India.

**Explanation**: The Fundamental Rights are subject to reasonable restrictions which connote a limitation imposed on a person in the enjoyment of a right which should not be arbitrary or of an excessive nature beyond what is actually required.

**Facts**: The Government imposed a new road regulation that all persons driving two wheelers should compulsorily wear helmets. The Free Voice of the Youth Association voiced their opinion against this rule. Does this regulation violate the principle stated below?

(*a*) Yes, because it prevents the two wheeler riders from travelling the way that they choose to.

(*b*) No, because the Government can impose restrictions and requirement as may be necessary.

(*c*) No, because the stated regulation is passed in the best interest of the public.

(*d*) Both (*b*) and (*c*)

**195. Principle:** An agreement made without consideration is void, unless it is expressed in writing and registered and is made on account of natural love and affection between parties standing in a near relation to each other.

**Explanation:** An agreement without consideration can also be allowed if it is a promise to compensate a person who has already done something for the promisor, or something which the promisor was legally compellable to do.

**Facts:** Raju promises to give Rs.1000 to Reddy towards a fund Reddy is raising to provide food to needy people in the locality. Reddy agrees to accept the Rs.1000 from Raju.

(*a*) There is no consideration here.

(*b*) There is consideration here.

(*c*) The contract is void because it is unlawful.

(*d*) None of the above.

**196. Principle:** Recognition of one state by another signifies that the recognizer is now willing to treat the recognized state as a sovereign entity and all that it entails. It means that the recognizer acknowledges the authority of the legal Government of the recognized state over the territory of that recognized state and its subjects.

**Explanation:** India has a policy of granting recognition to regimes that have come to power either by a popular mandate or at least by other constitutional means.

**Facts:** The People's Republic of Ragnarok is ruled by a clique who has no respect for constitutional values. They are driven out in a coup by a faction who brings in a new autocracy known as Democratic Republic of Ragnarok. The PRR also functions as a Government in exile. i.e., it has no power in the country anymore. Both Governments are equally autocratic. A resolution is moved in UN General Assembly saying that DRR is the true representative of Ragnarok. How should India vote?

(*a*) India should vote for the resolution because DRR has control.

(*b*) India should vote against the resolution because PRR has a constitution.

(*c*) India should abstain because both sides have one plus point.

(*d*) None of the above.

**(Instructions: Questions 197 to 200 has common set of principles and facts. Apply the specified principles and answer the questions)**

**Principle 1:** Theft is an offence punishable with imprisonment of 7 years or more, wherein three necessary conditions are required to be established.

**Principle 2:** The first condition to establish theft is that the person committing theft must take away a movable property. Movable property is one that can be taken from one place to other or can be moved after severing the same from earth.

**Principle 3:** The second condition to establish theft is that there must be dishonest intention. Dishonest intention is established if the act is performed with a motive to wrongfully deny a person of benefits which in reasonable course would accrue to him.

**Principle 4:** The third condition to establish theft is that the act must be done without the owner's consent. Consent is established if the granted by meeting of minds unless vitiated by fraud or duress.

**Facts:** Azmal hires Rashid for gardening work. One day in Azmal's absence Rashid decides to take away his mango tree as he was in dire need of timber for building his house. Rashid cuts down the tree. Before Rashid could take out the tree from the premises, Azmal returned. Azmal files a complaint for theft. Decide.

**197.** Did Azmal grant consent to Rashid for the act?

(*a*) Yes, as he there was meeting of mind for the purpose of hiring Rashid for gardening.

(*b*) Yes, as Azmal voluntarily hired Rashid.

(*c*) No, as Rashid committed fraud by taking the tree away.

(*d*) No, as there was no meeting of mind for the purpose of taking tree away from the premises.

**198.** Did Rashid take away the mango tree with dishonest intention?

(*a*) No, as Rashid was in dire necessity of timber.

(*b*) Yes, as Rashid intended to deny the reasonable benefits of mango tree that would have accrued to Azmal.

(*c*) Yes, as Rashid was hired only for gardening work.

(*d*) No, as Rashid intended to take timber in lieu of his remuneration.

**199.** Would the timber classify as movable property in the given facts and circumstances?

(*a*) Yes, as soon as Rashid severed the tree, it became a movable property.

(*b*) No, as tree is an immovable property.

(*c*) No, as Rashid could not move the tree out of Azmal's premises.

(*d*) Cannot be determined on the basis of facts given.

**200.** Would the compliant for theft by Azmal succeed against Rashid?

(*a*) Yes, as all the conditions for the offence of theft are satisfied.

(*b*) No, as all the conditions for the offence of theft are not satisfied.

(*c*) No, as Rashid could not take the timber out of Azmal's premises.

(*d*) Yes, as Rashid was caught red handed.

## ANSWERS

| | | | | | | | | | |
|---|---|---|---|---|---|---|---|---|---|
| **1.** (*b*) | **2.** (*d*) | **3.** (*c*) | **4.** (*d*) | **5.** (*b*) | **6.** (*a*) | **7.** (*d*) | **8.** (*c*) | **9.** (*b*) | **10.** (*d*) |
| **11.** (*b*) | **12.** (*b*) | **13.** (*a*) | **14.** (*c*) | **15.** (*c*) | **16.** (*a*) | **17.** (*a*) | **18.** (*b*) | **19.** (*b*) | **20.** (*a*) |
| **21.** (*b*) | **22.** (*b*) | **23.** (*b*) | **24.** (*b*) | **25.** (*b*) | **26.** (*b*) | **27.** (*b*) | **28.** (*a*) | **29.** (*c*) | **30.** (*d*) |
| **31.** (*c*) | **32.** (*b*) | **33.** (*b*) | **34.** (*b*) | **35.** (*b*) | **36.** (*c*) | **37.** (*d*) | **38.** (*d*) | **39.** (*d*) | **40.** (*a*) |
| **41.** (*d*) | **42.** (*b*) | **43.** (*d*) | **44.** (*a*) | **45.** (*b*) | **46.** (*b*) | **47.** (*a*) | **48.** (*a*) | **49.** (*a*) | **50.** (*a*) |
| **51.** (*a*) | **52.** (*a*) | **53.** (*d*) | **54.** (*c*) | **55.** (*d*) | **56.** (*a*) | **57.** (*c*) | **58.** (*a*) | **59.** (*b*) | **60.** (*b*) |
| **61.** (*a*) | **62.** (*a*) | **63.** (*b*) | **64.** (*a*) | **65.** (*a*) | **66.** (*a*) | **67.** (*c*) | **68.** (*c*) | **69.** (*a*) | **70.** (*a*) |
| **71.** (*a*) | **72.** (*b*) | **73.** (*a*) | **74.** (*b*) | **75.** (*a*) | **76.** (*a*) | **77.** (*b*) | **78.** (*a*) | **79.** (*a*) | **80.** (*a*) |
| **81.** (*b*) | **82.** (*a*) | **83.** (*a*) | **84.** (*b*) | **85.** (*a*) | **86.** (*c*) | **87.** (*c*) | **88.** (*b*) | **89.** (*b*) | **90.** (*b*) |
| **91.** (*c*) | **92.** (*b*) | **93.** (*d*) | **94.** (*c*) | **95.** (*a*) | **96.** (*b*) | **97.** (*b*) | **98.** (*c*) | **99.** (*b*) | **100.** (*c*) |
| **101.** (*a*) | **102.** (*d*) | **103.** (*b*) | **104.** (*b*) | **105.** (*a*) | **106.** (*b*) | **107.** (*b*) | **108.** (*d*) | **109.** (*c*) | **110.** (*c*) |
| **111.** (*d*) | **112.** (*a*) | **113.** (*b*) | **114.** (*b*) | **115.** (*d*) | **116.** (*c*) | **117.** (*d*) | **118.** (*c*) | **119.** (*b*) | **120.** (*b*) |
| **121.** (*d*) | **122.** (*c*) | **123.** (*d*) | **124.** (*b*) | **125.** (*d*) | **126.** (*d*) | **127.** (*a*) | **128.** (*a*) | **129.** (*b*) | **130.** (*a*) |
| **131.** (*c*) | **132.** (*a*) | **133.** (*a*) | **134.** (*a*) | **135.** (*c*) | **136.** (*c*) | **137.** (*a*) | **138.** (*a*) | **139.** (*d*) | **140.** (*a*) |
| **141.** (*c*) | **142.** (*c*) | **143.** (*a*) | **144.** (*a*) | **145.** (*a*) | **146.** (*a*) | **147.** (*a*) | **148.** (*c*) | **149.** (*d*) | **150.** (*d*) |
| **151.** (*d*) | **152.** (*c*) | **153.** (*b*) | **154.** (*a*) | **155.** (*c*) | **156.** (*a*) | **157.** (*d*) | **158.** (*a*) | **159.** (*b*) | **160.** (*b*) |
| **161.** (*a*) | **162.** (*c*) | **163.** (*b*) | **164.** (*b*) | **165.** (*c*) | **166.** (*a*) | **167.** (*b*) | **168.** (*a*) | **169.** (*c*) | **170.** (*d*) |
| **171.** (*b*) | **172.** (*d*) | **173.** (*b*) | **174.** (*b*) | **175.** (*a*) | **176.** (*d*) | **177.** (*b*) | **178.** (*d*) | **179.** (*c*) | **180.** (*b*) |
| **181.** (*a*) | **182.** (*c*) | **183.** (*b*) | **184.** (*a*) | **185.** (*d*) | **186.** (*b*) | **187.** (*d*) | **188.** (*d*) | **189.** (*b*) | **190.** (*b*) |
| **191.** (*a*) | **192.** (*c*) | **193.** (*a*) | **194.** (*b*) | **195.** (*b*) | **196.** (*a*) | **197.** (*d*) | **198.** (*b*) | **199.** (*a*) | **200.** (*a*) |

# EXPLANATIONS

**1.** Option (*c*) and (*d*) are beyond the scope of the passage. (*a*) talks about fight which has neither been mentioned nor implied. Option (*b*) which talks about mutual relationships fits aptly in the given context.

**2.** 'Veteran' refers to person who has a lot of experience in a particular area or activity. 'Neophyte' means a novice.

**3.** Schmaltzy means sentimental.

**4.** This cannot be determined from the passage. The passage does not comment on the nature of work done in Paris, it only tells us that this place was important for art.

**5.** Refer to the lines "The exhibition is staged by the American-Scandinavian Foundation, established in 1911. The creation of the foundation and the travelling show of Nordic art were both responses to events that are as little known nowadays as some of the art on view. Back then the mass migration of Nordic native sons to the new world was causing alarm. From the early 19th century to the outbreak of the First World War, more than a million Swedes settled in America, many in the prairie land of the Midwest. Swedish commissions studied how to stop the farmer drain. At the same time, bridges were built between the old world, the émigrés and the people they lived among."

**6.** Option (*a*) is the correct choice.

**7.** Edward Munch is from Norway. Nils Kreuger is from Sweden. Hammershoi's paintings are famous for the caressing light that envelopes the landscapes and for their soothing and calming effect. Thus, none of the given options are correct.

**8.** Refer to the lines "Munch became so famous that Andy Warhol, given to capitalising on icons from Mao to Marilyn, produced his own rendering of "The Scream". " So, I is correct. Refer to the lines "Nordic art was so little known that when John V. Loeb, a financier, became America's ambassador to Denmark in 1981, he was amazed to discover the "unusual and fascinating" work of its artists." So, II is incorrect. Refer to the lines "Flower Meadow in the North", an animal-free 1905 painting by Norway's Harald Sohlberg, may sound sentimental, but it isn't." So, III is correct. Thus, option (*c*) is the correct choice.

**9.** Refer to the line ""Luminous Modernism" celebrates the "Exhibition of Contemporary Scandinavian Art" that caused a sensation in America 100 years ago."

**10.** Eerie means fearfully and mysteriously strange or fantastic. Thus, bizarre, quirky and outlandish are its synonyms. Vapid which means dull, boring or flat is the most appropriate choice.

**11.** Opportunity

**12.** mendacity

**13.** sequestration

**14.** vacuum

**15.** felicity

**16.** Back seat driver refers to people who criticize from the sidelines, much like someone giving unwanted advice from the back seat of a vehicle to a driver.

**17.** Can't cut the mustard refers to someone who is not adequate enough to compete or participate.

**18.** Dead Ringer refers to something that is 100 % identical or duplicate.

**19.** Dry run refers to rehearsal or trial.

**20.** Jaywalk refers to crossing the street (from the middle) without using the crosswalk.

**21.** With the word 'older', the preposition 'than' is used. With 'elder', the preposition 'to' is used.

**22.** The subjunctive mood is used in dependent clauses that do the following: 1) express a wish; 2) begin with *if* and express a condition that does not exist (is contrary to fact); 3) begin with *as if* and *as though* when such clauses describe a speculation or condition contrary to fact; and 4) begin with *that* and express a demand, requirement, request, or suggestion. The present tense of the subjunctive uses only the base form of the verb. Examples: He demanded that his students *use* two-inch margins. She suggested that we *be* on time tomorrow. The past tense of the subjunctive has the same forms as the indicative except (unfortunately) for the verb *to be*, which uses *were* regardless of the number of the subject. If I *were* seven feet tall, I'd be a great basketball player.

**23.** For past unreal events (things that didn't happen, but we can imagine) we put the verb in the condition clause a further step back — into the Past Perfect.

**24.** A linking verb connects a subject and its complement. Sometimes called *copulas*, linking verbs are often forms of the verb *to be*, but are sometimes verbs related to the five senses (*look, sound, smell, feel, taste*) and sometimes verbs that somehow reflect a state of being (*appear, seem, become, grow, turn, prove, remain*). What follows the linking verb will be either a noun complement or an adjective complement. Continuous tense is not used for linking verbs. In the given sentence, smell is a linking verb and the subject (flower) is singular in number. So, option (*b*) is the correct choice.

**25.** Future Perfect Tense should be used.

**26.** 'By' means not later than the time mentioned; before.

**27.** The verb 'let' needs to be followed by an object. So, the pronoun should be in objective case.

**28.** Objective case is required because the blank needs to be filled by a receiver (of the book).

**29.** The word 'which' is used to non-restrictive clauses; the word 'that' can be used to introduce only restrictive clauses. Think of the difference between "The garage that my uncle built is falling down." And "The garage, which my uncle built, is falling down." I can say the first sentence anywhere and the listener will know exactly which garage I'm talking about — the one my uncle built. In other words, the "that clause" has introduced information that you need or you wouldn't know what garage I'm talking about.

**30.** The first blank needs a possessive pronoun. Thus, option (*d*) is the correct choice.

**31.** *Ex gratia* is Latin for "by favour", and is most often used in a legal context. When something has been done *ex gratia*, it has been done voluntarily, out of kindness or grace. In law, an *ex gratia payment* is a payment made without the giver recognizing any liability or legal obligation.

**32.** *Cui bono* ("To whose benefit?", literally "as a benefit to whom?", also rendered as *Cui prodest,* is a Latin adage that is used either to suggest a hidden motive or to indicate that the party responsible for something may not be who it appears at first to be. Commonly the phrase is used to suggest that the person or people guilty of committing a crime may be found among those who have something to gain, chiefly with an eye toward financial gain.

**33.** *Lex lata* means "the law as it exists" or the current law. *Lex ferenda* refers to the future law.

**34.** *Male fide* means bad faith.

**35.** *Per se* means "by itself", "through itself", or "in itself".

**36.** ii iv iii i: 'The get-tough-on-crime and mandatory' modifies sentencing policies so, (ii) and (iv) form a mandatory pair. Population and prison cost is the object of the phrasal verb 'drive up'. Thus, (iii) and (i) form a pair. So, option (*c*) is the correct choice.

**37.** ii i iv iii: (ii) states what is supposed by us and (i) mentions why we are surprised. So, (ii) should be the opener and (ii) and (i) form a pair. (iv) and (iii) form another mandatory pair as one in (iii) refers to aspect of personality.

**38.** iii iv i ii: The subject is 'art', so (iii) should be the opening phrase. (iv) states what is a good thing. So, (iii) and (iv) form a mandatory pair. Similarly, (ii) states what art depends upon. Thus, (i) and (ii) form a mandatory pair.

**39.** 'Give something back' (to somebody) means: (1) to return something to its owner (2) to allow somebody to have something again. 'Give something away' means: (1) to give something as a (2) to present something (3) to carelessly allow somebody to have an advantage. 'Give in' (to somebody/something) means: (1) to admit that you have been defeated by somebody/something. The rebels were forced to give in. (2) to agree to do something that you do not want to do. 'Give off' something means to produce something such as a smell, heat, light, etc.

**40.** 'Run along' is used in orders to tell somebody, especially a child, to go away. 'Run after somebody' means to try to have a relationship with somebody (synonym - pursue). 'Run after somebody/something' means to run to try to catch somebody/something. 'Run down' means (1) to lose power or stop working (2) to gradually stop functioning or become smaller in size or number. If a container or its contents 'run over', the contents come over the edge of the container (synonym - overflow).

**41.** International Workers' Day (also known as May Day) is a celebration of the international labour movement. May 1 is a national holiday in more than 80 countries and celebrated unofficially in many other countries.

**42.** The order is awarded to those who have made distinguished achievements in international relations, promotion of Japanese culture, advancements in their field, development in social/occupational welfare or preservation of the environment.

**43.** The ArcelorMittal Orbit is a 115-metre-high (377 ft) sculpture and observation tower in the Olympic Park in Stratford, London. It is Britain's largest piece of public art, and is intended to be a permanent lasting legacy of London's hosting of the 2012 Summer Olympics. Orbit was designed by Anish Kapoor and Cecil Balmond of engineering Group Arup.

**44.** Aiming to encourage public to follow environment-friendly solid waste management practices and end open defecation, a Zero Waste Toilet System (ZWTS), claiming to be the first in the country was established.

**45.** The Phu Khanh Basin, offshore central Vietnam, is the only undrilled basin on the Vietnam margin of the South China Sea.

**46.** P Kunhumohammed is amongst India's top athletes (400m).

**47.** Parivakkam Subramaniam Veeraraghavan (born on 24 December 1948) space scientist and rocket technologist. He is presently the Director of Vikram Sarabhai Space Centre (VSSC), Thiruvananthapuram, Kerala. One of the most senior scientists at Indian Space Research Organization (ISRO), Veeraraghavan is known for his contributions to launch vehicle technology. He is a recipient of the ASI Award of the Astronautical Society of India.

**48.** The World Snooker Championship is the leading professional snooker tournament in terms of both prize money and ranking points. It is one of the Triple Crown events.

**49.** A major university Centre dedicated to the life and works of Rabindranath Tagore has opened in Edinburgh, Scotland, to mark the Nobel Laureate's 150th birth anniversary.

Professor Indra Nath Choudhuri, Academic Director of the Indira Gandhi Institute, will be Scotland's first Chair man in Tagore Studies.

**50.** Vladimir Putin has taken the oath of office for a third term as Russia's president.

Putin was president from 2000 to 2008 and then Prime Minister for the past four years. The new, six-year term will keep him in power until 2018 – with the option of running for a fourth term.

**51.** The author C. K. Prahalad argues that companies must revolutionize how they do business in developing countries if both sides of that economic equation are to prosper. Drawing on a wealth of case studies, his compelling new book offers an intriguing blueprint for how to fight poverty with profitability.

**52.** In order to bring disable persons in the mainstream of the society, Haryana Social Justice and Empowerment Department has banned the use of word 'handicapped' as the word "prods" the dignity of disabled persons.

**53.** Intercontinental Ballistic Missiles (ICBMs) have ranges of greater than 5,500 km. ICBMs create a problem because they enable a country to break out of a regional context and move toward potential global impact. Regardless of the origin of a conflict, a country may involve the entire world simply by threatening to spread the war with an ICBM.

**54.** Leander Paes will be the new Sports Ambassador of Haryana. Paes, a Rajiv Gandhi Khel Ratna awardee, will motivate the youth of the state to take up sports as a career. Not just this, the Indian tennis legend would be given a land around Delhi to set up a sports centre on Public Private Partnership Model.

**55.** West Bengal Chief Minister Mamata Banerjee has been named among the 100 most influential people in the world by the Time magazine in its 2012 list which also includes U.S. President Barack Obama, Secretary of State Hillary Clinton and billionaire investor Warren Buffet.

**56.** Atomic Energy Commission Chairman Srikumar Banerjee commissioned the Rs. 1,106 crore plant developed by the Uranium Corporation of India Limited (UCIL) at Thummalapalle in YSR Kadapa district in Andhra Pradesh which is estimated to have world's largest uranium reserves.

**57.** Tabish Khair is a writer. The book reflects contemporary cosmopolitan responses to what they believe to be religious fundamentalism.

**58.** Pobitora or Pabitora Wildlife Sanctuary is a Wildlife Reserve in the Marigaon district of the State of Assam in India. The Pobitora Wildlife Sanctuary is about 48 km by road from Guwahati.

**59.** The Dadasaheb Phalke Award is India's highest award in cinema given annually by the Government of India for lifetime contribution to Indian cinema. The Award is given to a prominent personality from the Indian film industry, noted and respected for significant contributions to Indian cinema.

**60.** Samajwadi Party Chief Mulayam Singh Yadav have been awarded the prestigious International Jurists Award 2012.

**61.** Recently the (former) Union Minister of Environment & Forests Jairam Ramesh launched a bio-remediation technology project in Ludhiana.

**62.** Nag was in news in connection with delayed induction of a special missile-carrier (for this missile) called NAMICA.

**63.** This fair was organised recently in the first week of February and Thailand was the 'Partner Country' for this event. Surajkund is in Haryana. Pushkar is famous for the Pushkar Fair and a reservoir of mythological importance.

**64.** This award is given by the Board of Control of Cricket in India (BCCI) and its named after India's first Test Cricket Captain.

**65.** This submarine is expected to go for sea trials in the next few months. Nishant and Rustom are names of an Unmanned Aerial Vehicle developed for the Indian Air Force.

**66.** This committee had been set up on the issue of de-recognition of about 40 deemed universities.

**67.** SDSC is the satellite launch station of Indian Space Research Organisation (ISRO). Reecently, PSLV-C16 was launched from this centre.

**68.** This dam was in news in connection with a period of drought in Southern provinces of China which was linked with this dam.

**69.** M.B. Shah will be the Vice-Chairman of this team. Shunglu was the head of a committee set up to investigate the Commonwealth Games Scam.

**70.** This mission involves studying the core and atmosphere of Jupiter.

**71.** Kerala and Tamilnadu are involved in a dispute with respect to this dam.

**72.** Rudra is an Advanced Light Helicopter.

**73.** Bolt recently set up a world record in relay at the World Athletic Championships held at Daegu.

**74.** Singapore and Delhi recently signed an agreement whereby the former would share its expertise on treatment of sewage water.

**75.** Fidel Castro is the former Head of State of Cuba. He recently made way for his brother Raul Castro. George W. Bush has recently written a book titled 'Decision Points'.

**76.** The Supreme Court of India recently ordered the Centre and Chattisgarh state to cease and desist using SPOs in the fight against Naxals.

**77.** This project was in news in connection with an order by the Ministry of Environment & Forests lifting its earlier stop-work order.

**78.** This prize is awarded for contribution in the field of Mathematics.

**79.** This is a space-suit developed by NASA for a prospective mission to planet Mars.

**82.** Such a proposal cannot be introduced in either House of Parliament except on the recommendation of the President. Also, the President is required to refers the proposal to the Legislature of the State concerned to know the views of the State Legislature. Note that consent of the State Legislature is not a pre-requisite.

**83.** This satellite was launched by PSLV-18.

**84.** DTAA are signed between countries so as to avoid double taxation of same transaction(s).

**85.** Mary Kom won the Janjatiya award recently.

**86.** Professor Subhasis Chaudhuri of Indian Institute of Technology-Mumbai was recently selected for the prestigious G. D. Birla Award for Scientific Research.

**88.** Gopinath Muthukad, an Indian magician recently won this award.

**91.** Let the present age of Isha and Meshan be 'x' and 'y' years respectively. Therefore,

$$x - 3 = 3(y - 3) \quad ...(i)$$

$$y + 5 = \frac{1}{2} \times (x + 5) \quad ...(ii)$$

On solving (i) and (ii), we get x = 27 and y = 11

Hence, present age of Meshan is 11 years.

**92.** $11CP = 8SP \Rightarrow \frac{CP}{SP} = \frac{8}{11}$

Now, let the cost (in ₹) and selling price (in ₹) of one can of beer be 8k and 11k respectively.

Selling price after 50% profit = 8k × 1.5 = 12k

Required mark up percentage over earlier selling price

$$= \frac{12k - 11k}{11k} \times 100 = 9.09\%.$$

**93.** The given information can be shown with the help of venn diagram below.

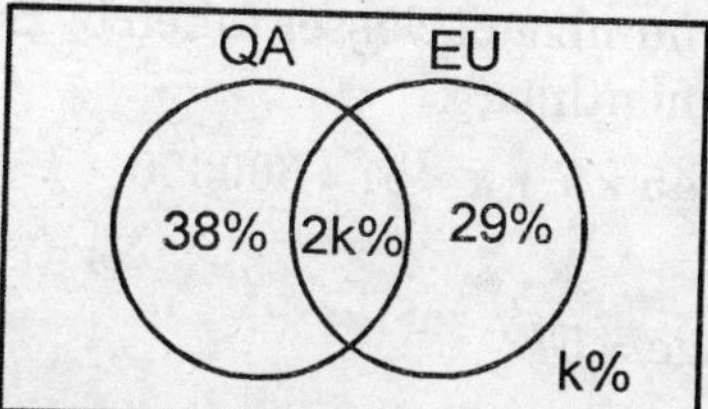


Total = 100%

Let the percentage of students who cleared cut off in none of the subjects be k%.

According to the question,

k + 2k = 100 – (38 + 29) or k = 11

11% = 220033 or 29% = 580087.

**94.** Let the two digit number be 10x +y.

Number formed by reversing its digits = 10y + x

Sum of the two numbers

$$= (10x + y) + (10y + x) = 11(x + y)$$

Required difference = 11(x + y) – (x + y) = 10(x + y)

Hence, the difference is always divisible by 10.

**95.** A : B = 10 : 9 and A : C = 6 : 5

Therefore, A : B : C = 30 : 27 : 25

Let A, B and C equal to 30x, 27x and 25x respectively.

Therefore, 27x – 25x = 36 ⇒ x = 18

Marks scored by A = 30x = 540.

**96.** Let the saving (in ₹) of P, Q and R be 5x, 3x and 2x respectively.

According to the question,

Income (in ₹) of Q = 6x

Income (in ₹) of R $= \frac{100}{150} \times 6x = 4x$

Required ratio = 5x : (4x – 2x) = 5 : 2.

**97.** Let the price (in ₹) of one mango, one apple and one watermelon be m, a and w respectively.

$$\therefore \quad 5m = \frac{5}{4} \times 4a = \frac{2}{3} \times 3w$$

$$\Rightarrow \quad m : a : w = 2 : 2 : 5$$

According to the question,

$$9a = 225 \text{ or } a = 25$$

$$\therefore \quad 7m + 8w = 7 \times 25 + 8 \times \frac{5}{2} \times 25 = 675.$$

Hence, price of 7 mangoes and 8 watermelons is ₹ 675.

**98.** Let average run scored by Sachin in his first 440 ODIs be x.

$$\therefore \quad \frac{440x + 20 \times 20.5}{460} = 44.50$$

$$\Rightarrow \quad x \approx 45.59.$$

**99.** Let the average number of classes taken by Susan in the last five month be x.

$$1000 \times (45 \times 7 + x \times 5) = 600000$$

$$\Rightarrow \quad x = 57$$

Required average = 57.

**100.** Sum of 'n' terms of an A.P. is given as:

$$S_n = \frac{n}{2}\{2a + (n-1)d\},$$

where 'a' is the first term and 'd' is common difference.

$$S_{18} = \frac{18}{2}\{2 \times 4 + (18-1) \times 5\} = 837.$$

**101.** Total number of balls

$$= 5(\text{Red}) + 6(\text{Blue}) + 8\ (\text{Yellow}) = 19$$

Total number of ways of picking three ball = $^{19}C_3$

Favourable number of ways (all the three balls are of the same colour)

$$= {}^5C_3 + {}^6C_3 + {}^8C_3$$

Required probability

$$= \frac{{}^5C_3 + {}^6C_3 + {}^8C_3}{{}^{19}C_3} = \frac{86}{969}.$$

**102.** $99^2 + 33 \div 11 \times 31 - 97^2$

$$= 99^2 - 97^2 + \frac{33}{11} \times 31$$

$$= (99 + 97) \times (99 - 97) + 3 \times 31$$

$$= 196 \times 2 + 93 = 485.$$

**103.** Let PQ and QR represent the height and the length of the pole respectively.

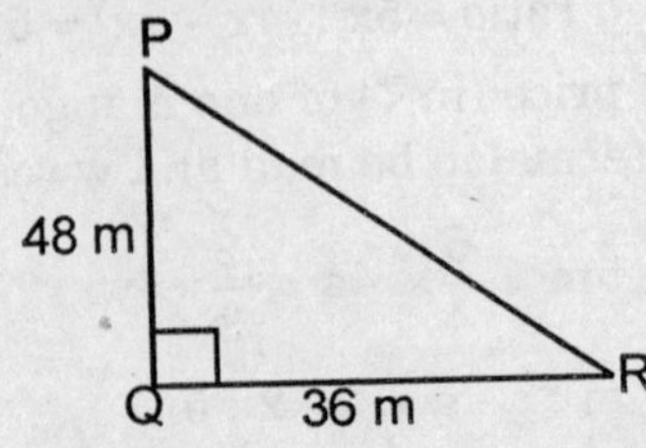


Since triangle PQR is a right angled,

$$PR^2 = PQ^2 + QR^2$$

$$\Rightarrow \quad PR = \sqrt{48^2 + 36^2} = 60 \text{ m}.$$

**104.** Possible outcomes when the two coins are thrown: (H, H); (H, T); (T, H) and (T, T)

Probability of getting at least one tail $= \frac{3}{4}$

Probability of getting a composite number on the dice

$$= \frac{2}{6} = \frac{1}{3}$$

($\because$ 4 and 6 are the only composite numbers)

Required probability $= \frac{1}{3} \times \frac{3}{4} = \frac{1}{4}.$

**105.** Number of numbers among first 32 natural numbers which are divisible by either 2 or 3

$$= 16 + 10 - 5 = 21$$

Required probability $= \frac{{}^{21}C_3}{{}^{32}C_3}.$

**106.** Let the number of days taken by B alone to complete the work be x.

C's one days work $= \left(\frac{1}{9} - \frac{1}{x}\right)$th

and A's one day's work $= \frac{1}{15}$th

According to the question,

$$10 \times \left(\frac{1}{9} - \frac{1}{x}\right) + 5 \times \frac{1}{15} + 5 \times \frac{1}{x} = 1$$

$$\Rightarrow \quad \frac{10x + 3x - 45}{9x} = 1$$

$$\Rightarrow \quad x = 11\frac{1}{4} \text{ days}.$$

**107.** Let the number of faculty members who teach exactly two subjects be x. Therefore,

$$15 + 17 + 9 - x - 2 \times 3 = 31 \text{ or } x = 4$$

Number of faculty members teach two or more subjects = 4 + 3 = 7.

**108.** Let the height (in cm) of cone and the height of the cylinder be $h_1$ and $h_2$ respectively. Let their radius (in cm) be r.

According to the question,

$$\frac{1}{3} \times \pi \times r^2 \times h_1 = \frac{2}{3} \times \pi \times r^2 \times h_2$$

$$\Rightarrow \quad \frac{h_1}{h_2} = \frac{2}{1}$$

In order to compute the required ratio we need to compute slant height of the cone in term of either r or $h_1$ but we cannot correlate them on the basis of the given information.

Hence, unique value of the ratio cannot be determined.

**109.** Required time $= \frac{30}{2} + \frac{45}{2} = 37.5$ minutes

(Since the distance covered through both the modes is same).

**110.** Speed of the train = 72 km/hr = $72 \times \frac{5}{18} = 20$ m/s

Let the speed of the bike be x m/s.

According to the question, $\frac{500}{20+x} = 20$ or $x = 5$

Speed of the bike = 5 m/s.

**111.**

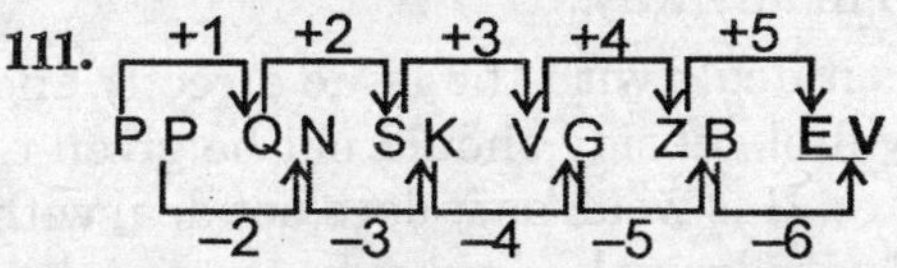


**112.** A $\xrightarrow{+1}$ B $\xrightarrow{+2}$ D $\xrightarrow{+4}$ H $\xrightarrow{+8}$ P $\xrightarrow{+16}$ F

**113.**

**114.** Terms of the series are changing as follows:

$3 \times 3 = 9$

$4 \times 5 = 20$

$5 \times 7 = 35$

$6 \times 9 = 54$

$7 \times 11 = 77$

$8 \times 13 = \underline{104}$.

**Alternate:**

9 20 35 54 77 **104**

+11 +15 +19 +23 +27

**115.** 421 300 381 332 357 348 **349**

$-11^2$ $+9^2$ $-7^2$ $+5^2$ $-3^2$ $+1^2$

**116.** $1^2 + 1 = 2$

$2^2 - 2 = 2$

$3^2 + 3 = 12$

$4^2 - 4 = 12$

$5^2 + 5 = 30$

$6^2 - 6 = 30$

$7^2 + 7 = 56$

$8^2 - 8 = 56$

$9^2 + 9 = \underline{90}$

**Alternate:**

+10 +18 +26

2 2 12 12 30 30 56 56 **90**

+10 +18 +26 +34

**117.** As Raju is 21[st] from the bottom and 3rd from the top, there are 20 more students who scored less than Raju. Hence, total number of students in the class is (3+20) i.e. 23.

In 23 students Satyam is 9[th] from the top so there are 14 students who scored less than Satyam. Therefore, Satyam is 15[th] from bottom.

**118.** Number of letters in the words is decreasing by one in each subsequent term. Hence, Lancer is the most suitable word among the given options.

**119.** Number of vowels is increasing by one in each subsequent word of the sequence from left to right.

**120.** Apart from 54, rest of the numbers are one less than square of a prime number.

**121.** The two statements discuss the findings of the milk samples that were tested for adulteration. They do not bear a cause-effect relation.

**122.** The cause is the shortage of manpower in Gurgaon with respect to its needs. Statement I and II are effects of this cause.

**123.** Both the statements talk about the problems (effects). Statement I talks about internal issues of Hungary while II talks about those of European Union. They are unrelated and are effects of independent causes.

**124.** Statement II states expectations of India and statement I states the efforts made by India to meet its goals. Thus, II is the cause and I is the effect.

**125.** Though cheating has become commonplace, no assumption can be drawn on the percentage of students who cheat in the competitive examinations. Moreover, it is also possible that lethargy on the part of the invigilators encourages students to cheat. Thus, a generic assumption about the morals and values of all students who appear for entrance exams cannot be drawn. II is beyond the scope of the given statement as the statement does not mention the hurdles in tackling the problem of cheating. Also, cheating and corruption are two different things. Hence, neither I nor II follow.

**126.** The statement fails to throw light on the reason for the limited period enthusiasm shown by the officials. Thus, I cannot be assumed. II is generic in nature and cannot be assumed from the specific data given in the statement.

**127.** As the increase in the number of adoption centers has led to increase incidences of abandoning of children (by the parents), it can be safely assumed that such parents think that their abandoned children will be picked up by some or the other adoption center. II is beyond the scope of the given statement.

**128.** I is implicit because New Delhi adopted diplomatic ways assuming that they will help. II is beyond the scope of the argument.

**129.** I is too harsh. II is the logical course of action that needs to be followed in such cases. A discussion of the boss with the HR will help in resolving the issues as she will become aware of the issues and will be able to work on the areas of improvement.

**130.** The main problem of the customers is that banking activities continue from 10 am to 3.30 pm only (minus a gap of one hour for lunch). I fails to address the bone of contention as expedition in the banking activities will not increase the working hours of bank. II is a practical and feasible solution to the interruption of baking activities during the lunch hour.

**131.** Both I and II discuss the logical actions that need to be followed in such cases. The new recruits need to discuss their problem with the senior person and then communicate them to the manager. This should be done in order to follow the hierarchy. Such an action will lead to communication of their issues in a professionally correct manner. II also follows as the new recruits should identify their weaknesses and should work on them. They should also inform about this effort to the manager so that he is certain of their sincerity.

**132.** The violations have been confirmed and departmental action should follow. Thus, I is correct and II is incorrect.

**133.** The problem is regarding cold weather and lack of proper shelter so, I follows. Provision of food at subsidized rates is impractical.

**134.** Only I follows. Nothing can be done as the insurance provider is acting as per the terms and conditions of the initial contract. So II does not follow.

**135.** Argument I states the advantages of ragging and is a strong argument. Argument II states its disadvantages and is thus a strong argument. Though both the arguments are contradictory in nature but both of them are strong as they are important and deal with the question directly.

**136.** If the information is priceless and useful, the efforts to use these manuscripts should be put. Since both the arguments stress retaining priceless information, both are strong.

**137.** Argument I is strong as it states the reason for need of revealing PAN while purchasing jewellery worth five lakhs or more and the advantage of such a move. II deals with a trivial aspect of discomfort which makes it weak.

**138.** Argument I is strong because it provides concrete reasons for understanding livelihood systems of the poor and how the approach can be instrumental in poverty reduction measures. Argument II is weak as it does not address poverty reduction, instead it goes on to discuss why employment must be ensured.

**139.** Both arguments are weak. Argument I makes a general statement about developed countries, but does not explain how the U.S. will gain from energy efficiency measures. Argument II talks about high per capita energy consumption, but does not link energy efficiency to per capita energy consumption in any way.

**140.** I is strong as it deals with the issue directly and justifies why fuel subsidy should not be given to passenger cars. II is weak as it does not deal with the issue of withdrawal of subsidy on diesel to passenger cars but deals with a larger issue of removal on subsidy on diesel irrespective of it being used for trucks, buses or cars. This is beyond the scope of the given question statement and deals with another question.

**141.** The assertion is true but R is not the correct reason. The XX/XY sex-determination system is found in human beings. In this system, females have two of the same kind of sex chromosome (XX), while males have two distinct sex chromosomes (XY). Humans have a gene SRY on the Y chromosome that determines maleness. Human gender is determined by containing SRY or not. As women do not have the Y chromosome (SRY gene), they play no role in the determination of the gender of the fetus.

**142.** Assertion is true but the reason is incorrect as inflation leads to increase in the price of commodities.

**143.** Both A and R are true and R is the correct explanation.

**144.** Both A and R are correct and R is the correct reason for A. Infants and older people have weaker immune systems. In case of infants, the immune system is not well developed and in case of old, the immune system has become weak with age. If the immune system is weak, the chances of acquiring fungal infections are higher. So, R is the correct explanation of A.

**145.** Both A and R are correct and R is the correct reason for A. The central bank in question is the Reserve Bank of India.

**146.** Both A and R are correct and R is the correct reason for A. In comparison to its neighboring countries, India charges higher taxes on petrol which lead to it being costlier.

**147.** Both A and R are correct and R is the correct reason for A.

**148.** A is true but R is incorrect. The various River Valley Civilizations are as follows:

Nile Valley Civilization (present-day Egypt), Tigris-Euphrates River Valley Civilization (present-day Iraq),Yellow River Valley Civilization (present-day China), Indus Valley Civilization (present-day India). The Nile River provided predictable floods and a stable food source. The other rivers used to flood and make the soil fertile which lead to a sustainable food resource. But these floods were not always predictable. So, R is incorrect.

**149.** Chisel is a metal tool with a cutting edge at the end of a blade. It is used for cutting and shaping/ carving. Trowel is the tool used by a mason and is used for spreading, applying, shaping and smoothening.

**150.** Blood appears red in color whereas chlorophyll appears green in color.

**151.** Sarita had initiated the case with a malafide intention to injure the reputation of Rajan.

**152.** Sarita acted against Rajan, purely because of personal considerations and without having any reasonable consideration to the guilt of Rajan.

**153.** The answer is self-explanatory.

**154.** There was no prosecution of Rajan by Sarita as the matter was dropped by police and no judicial proceedings were initiated against Rajan.

**155.** No case was filed by Rajan in any court of law and no proceedings were initiated against him, so Rajan cannot succeed in his claims.

**156.** He has committed a crime on Indian soil.

**157.** Right of Private Defence extends to another's property also.

**158.** The new Government in Libya might not have named him as Envoy.

**159.** Nishit is guilty as he had chased the vehicle with an intention to commit the theft

**160.** In the instant case, Siraj had only planned to commit the theft and there was no overt act done in furtherance of committing the theft.

**161.** In ICC, if an individual is being charged with a crime, then it has to do nothing with his nationality. ICC has jurisdiction over everyone.

**162.** Doctor Ram Raj here has a right to enjoy that land through lease. Anyone who interferes, even if it is the owner, can be sued. Further, here the owner is acting in his capacity as a neighbor and not an owner.

**163.** Ravi could not clearly understand the terms and conditions set out in the back paper of the bill, as the print was not clear and he was in no position to clearly understand the terms and conditions of the contract.

**164.** In the instant case, Ravi was a minor and according to Principle No.3, he was not eligible to enter into a contract.

**165.** The answer is self-explanatory.

**166.** As Ravi was a minor and further the terms and conditions in the contract were not clearly visible, so standard form of contract is not valid in the instant case.

**167.** Record rain which is substantially higher than anything seen before is something that can't be foreseen and cannot be prepared for.

**168.** There is no consideration here.

**169.** In calculation of requirement for eligibility for the post of Supreme Court Judge Ramesh's experience as an advocate of at least 10 years standing will be reckoned by reading the explanation in conjunction with principle supplied which will include years served as an advocate (3 years) and apart from that, years served as a Registrar of the High Court (7 years) which as given in facts is equivalent to a post of senior district judge when counted adds up to 10 years making him eligible.

**170.** A has acted under the *bona fide* belief that he was legally justified in detaining B as he suspected him of possessing stolen property. Thus, he has committed a mere mistake of fact.

**171.** This is a reasonable rule, which has been obviously brought into effect to safeguard the sovereignty and security of the country.

**172.** The answer is self-explanatory

**173.** The statement was made in a permanent form; i.e. through a movie, which could be seen by a large number of people and was further permanent in nature.

**174.** The statements made against Y by X , and no one knew about its authenticity or truthfulness, except X, and neither were these statements been proved before any competent court or forum.

**175.** All the 3 prerequisites have been clearly fulfilled in the instant case.

**176.** The policy is arbitrary and violates the above stated principle. Furthermore there is not rational nexus for differential treatment of airhostesses.

**177.** According to the relevant advertisement, the pharmaceutical company's liability is paying Rs.10,000 only.

**178.** The contract here is clearly not a case of a wagering contract as the chit fund was being regulated under the Chit Fund Act, 1982.

**179.** Carefully read Principle No.3.

**180.** Y had specifically built the machine in an attempt to end X's life and had aided X in ending his life by building the machine.

**181.** X had slipped into a coma and therefore the most important parameter or ingredient for suicide was not fulfilled in the instant case.

**182.** There is no law against such letting, but it is immoral.

**183.** As soon as Steve sold the book to Sam, it could be reasonably implied that Steve understood the terms and conditions of the contract, and therefore Sam is not liable to return the book to Steve in the instant case.

**184.** X clearly knew that the cow was unhealthy and when he was asked by Y, he did not utter a word and therefore he actively concealed this material fact.

**185.** d This is a clear case of undue influence and coercion, as Sanjay had decided to give a loan to Sudeep, only because Sudeep had threatened to commit suicide.

**186.** X had promised to build Y's house for which he had already been paid Rs.50,000 upfront, after which any other demand of X for money would vitiate the reciprocal promise which had been made by him.

**187.** X had himself voluntarily consented to the danger and therefore he had no right to ask compensation from the organizers.

**188.** The employees have the right to exercise their freedom of speech and expression as long as they do so within defined limits and do not resort to violence as in the given fact situation.

**189.** The answer is self-explanatory

**190.** Anand never paid Ashish for his work. Infact, Ashish was doing this out of personal reasons.

**191.** The answer is self-explanatory.

**192.** There was no fixed consideration in this instant case.

**193.** The owner of the lorry owner can be held vicariously liable as he his servant had caused grave damage to others in the course of employment.

**194.** Such a rule is validly imposed by the Government in public interest.

**195.** There is consideration here. The consideration is as follows. Reddy agrees to provide food to needy people if Raju (and other good Samaritans) give money for the same.

**196.** The policy of India is clear about recognizing the regimes coming in power. The current autocratic government in People's Republic of Ragnarok neither has been chosen by public mandate (as it is a faction) nor is made through any constitutional means (as came in power through a coup) so it would not be recognized. Since all answers do not contain any correct reasoning that's why it will be option D.

**197.** Azmal had hired Rashid for gardening purposes and not for any other purpose.

**198.** The answer is self-explanatory.

**199.** As soon as the tree was severed and detached from the ground, it became a movable property.

**200.** The answer is self-explanatory.

■■

# CLAT PATTERN

## MODEL PAPER-II

**INSTRUCTIONS:** **Time: 2 Hours**

1. This Model Paper will give you an insight into the pattern of the **CLAT (Common Law Admission Test)** Undertaking this model test under the mentioned stipulated time frame will allow you to understand real test scenario.
2. This Question Paper consists of five sections viz. I (English), II (General Knowledge), III (Mathematics), IV (Logical Reasoning) and V (Legal Aptitude).The total number of questions are 200.
3. Each Question contains one mark. There is NO NEGATIVE MARKING

## SECTION – I : ENGLISH

**Directions for questions 1 to 5:** Read the given passage carefully and answer the questions that follow.

The Writ Jurisdiction of Supreme Court can be invoked under Article 32 of the Constitution for the violation of fundamental rights guaranteed under Part – III of the Constitution. Any provision in any Constitution for Fundamental Rights is meaningless unless there are adequate safeguards to ensure enforcement of such provisions. Since the reality of such rights is tested only through the judiciary, the safeguards assume even more importance. In addition, enforcement also depends upon the degree of independence of the Judiciary and the availability of relevant instruments with the executive authority. Indian Constitution, like most of Western Constitutions, lays down certain provisions to ensure the enforcement of Fundamental Rights.

However, Article 32 is referred to as the "Constitutional Remedy" for enforcement of Fundamental Rights. This provision itself has been included in the Fundamental Rights and hence it cannot be denied to any person. Dr. B.R.Ambedkar described Article 32 as the most important one, without which the Constitution would be reduced to nullity. It is also referred to as the heart and soul of the Constitution. By including Article 32 in the Fundamental Rights, the Supreme Court has been made the protector and guarantor of these Rights. An application made under Article 32 of the Constitution before the Supreme Court, cannot be refused on technical grounds. In addition to the prescribed five types of writs, the Supreme Court may pass any other appropriate order. Moreover, only the questions pertaining to the Fundamental Rights can be determined in proceedings against Article 32. Under Article 32, the Supreme Court may issue a Writ against any person or government within the territory of India. Where the infringement of a Fundamental Right has been established, the Supreme Court cannot refuse relief on the ground that the aggrieved person may have remedy before some other court or under the ordinary law

The relief can also not be denied on the ground that the disputed facts have to be investigated or some evidence has to be collected. Even if an aggrieved person has not asked for a particular Writ, the Supreme Court, after considering the facts and circumstances, may grant the appropriate Writ and may even modify it to suit the exigencies of the case. Normally, only the aggrieved person is allowed to move the Court. But it has been held by the Supreme Court that in social or public interest matters, any one may move the Court. A Public Interest Litigation can be filed before the Supreme Court under Article 32 of the Constitution or before the High Court of a State under Article 226 of the Constitution under their respective Writ Jurisdictions.

**1.** The main purpose of the passage is to

(*a*) educate the reader about the importance of article 32 in the Indian constitution.

(*b*) educate the reader about the importance of the Supreme court in the country

(*c*) inform the reader about the safeguards regarding Fundamental Rights

(*d*) educate the reader about his rights as a citizen of the country.

**2.** All of the following can be inferred from the passage except :-

(*a*) An application made under Article 32 of the Constitution before the Supreme Court, cannot be refused.

(*b*) The Supreme Court, after considering the facts and circumstances, may modify the appropriate writ to suit the exigencies of a case.

(*c*) The relevance of article 32, without an independent judicial system, is questionable.

(*d*) In proceedings against article 32, the questions pertaining to, but not limited to, fundamental rights are considered.

3. According to the passage, article 32 has which of the following characteristics?

(A) it is used for enforcement of fundamental rights.

(B) The Supreme Court may issue a writ against any person or government of India.

(C) Article 32 defines a fundamental right.

(*a*) B and C (*b*) Only A

(*c*) Only B (*d*) All of the above

4. What is the tone of the author?

(*a*) critical (*b*) analytical

(*c*) mendacious (*d*) objective

5. What is the correct meaning of the word 'infringement'?

(*a*) provision

(*b*) infarction

(*c*) observance

(*d*) violation

**Directions for questions 6 to 10:** In each of the following questions, four sentences are given. Three sentences are grammatically incorrect and only one sentence is correct. Identify the grammatically correct sentence.

6. (*a*) We are behind schedule.

(*b*) He likes to sing and dancing.

(*c*) Either Richa or her friends is affected by the new policy.

(*d*) Information further is available on request.

7. (*a*) I met him in the party.

(*b*) Rajiv as well as his friends are ready for the presentation.

(*c*) Hardly had I reached the station when the train left.

(*d*) It is me.

8. (*a*) This is a grand spectacle.

(*b*) My spectacle needs to be repaired.

(*c*) I was carrying lots of baggages.

(*d*) I need to buy furnitures for my office.

9. (*a*) I like poems of Tagore which are good.

(*b*) This is best that I can do.

(*c*) Harpreet is enough strong to play cricket.

(*d*) A grin spread across her face.

10. (*a*) He sat besides her all night.

(*b*) Wages are paid on Fridays.

(*c*) I am loving it.

(*d*) Standing in a line, the teacher took us inside the seminar hall.

**Directions for questions 11 to 17:** Read the given passage carefully and answer the questions that follow.

When it comes to travel, popular imagination can sometimes be as misleading as tourism over-drive. Nothing can be truer than the case of the archipelago of Indonesia which many view as a one-stop destination. In an attempt to dispel the stereotype, the Indonesian Tourism Board invited some of us to explore the idea that there is more to Indonesia than Bali and that, indeed, there is more to Bali than sun-bleached beaches and a hectic night life. Perhaps, it is taking a cue from Thailand — the Big Daddy of tourism in South Asia — which keeps unleashing newer and newer tourist destinations upon an insatiable world. Beach-combers and back-packers flock to lesser-known travel hot-spots in this part of the world along with high-end tourists seeking nirvana in exclusive spas and resorts and rambunctious families on a jolly good outing. Increasingly, the focus of the travel industry is shifting towards inclusiveness rather than exclusiveness, towards affordable luxury rather than en masse shoestring budget travellers. The idea, everywhere, seems to be to promote a place where a good time can be had by people of different age groups and diverse interests.

11. What makes Thailand a "Big Daddy" of tourism in South Asia?

(*a*) Apart from scenic beauty, it offers a lot of other advantages to tourists like night clubs, massage parlours and gems factories.

(*b*) Its currency provides maximum value for Aussies who are the major tourists of the place.

(*c*) It keeps on unleashing new destinations for all kind of tourists.

(*d*) It offers a wide range of beaches and spas.

12. What do you infer by "When it comes to travel, popular imagination can sometimes be as misleading as tourism over-drive?"

(*a*) Popular imagination that runs in a tourist's mind can sometimes be exaggerated and over hyped in comparison to the reality.

(*b*) In context of travel, the general perception of people might not always be true.

(*c*) The truth might not be always what one thinks it to be.

(*d*) None of these

13. What is the tone of the author?

(*a*) Descriptive (*b*) Sanguine

(*c*) Satiric (*d*) Didactic

**14.** Complete the following sentence by selecting the grammatically correct option. "Thailand is not only famous for its lesser known travel spots ________."

(*a*) but it also famous for its exclusive spa and resorts

(*b*) but also for its exclusive spa and resorts

(*c*) but the fact is that it is also known for its exclusive spa and resorts

(*d*) but for its exclusive spa and resorts too

**15.** Identify the most appropriate synonym of the word 'rambunctious'?

(*a*) coarse (*b*) boisterous

(*c*) peace-loving (*d*) bovine

**16.** Identify the most appropriate antonym of the word 'stereotype'?

(*a*) proposition (*b*) atypical

(*c*) mature (*d*) archaic

**17.** What is the meaning of the word 'shoestring'?

(*a*) one that uses very little money

(*b*) one that spends reasonably

(*c*) one that spends lavishly

(*d*) one who is a broke

**Directions for questions 18 to 22:** In each of the following questions, two blank are given. Fill the given blanks with the correct option (the first word in an option is for the first blank).

**18.** The rule would seem ________ any new coal-fired power that lacks the costly technology to trap carbon dioxide before _________ leaves the smokestack and bury it.

(*a*) doom, it (*b*) dooming, them

(*c*) to doom, it (*d*) dooming, it

**19.** The plant was closed ________ years later after ______________ to military contracts, but the thousands of people who lost their jobs didn't forget.

(*a*) few, converted

(*b*) a few, being converted

(*c*) few, being converted

(*d*) the few, its conversion

**20.** States that use sodium thiopental ___________ prisoners unconscious as part of their execution protocols ______________ foreign suppliers when the sole domestic manufacturer stopped producing the drug.

(*a*) render, reach out

(*b*) to render, reached out to

(*c*) rendering, reaching out to

(*d*) rendered, reached out to

**21.** Many Indian companies have entered into cash-rich deals with pharmaceutical MNCs _______ which they either manufacture medicines for them or the __________ market their products outside India.

(*a*) by, later (*b*) through, latter

(*c*) because of, later (*d*) because, latter

**22.** Instead of a possible negotiated settlement which could have ________ thousands of lives and would have made a political solution within the ________ of a united Sri Lanka likely, India's silence during the war has only encouraged continued triumphalism by the Rajapaksa regime.

(*a*) benefited, reach (*b*) improvised, backdrop

(*c*) saved, resolution (*d*) spared, framework

**Directions for questions 23 to 29:** In the following passage there are blanks, each of which has been numbered. These numbers are printed below the passage and against each, four words are suggested, one of which fits the blank appropriately. Find out the appropriate word in each case.

The ideological nature of the health care case___(23)____ obvious on the last day of oral argument. By the time the proceedings were over, much of what the conservative justices said in court seemed like part of a ___(24)_____ driven exercise — especially because the issues addressed on Wednesday were not largely _______(25)________ in nature. In fact, they were the kinds of policy questions that are properly left to Congress and state governments to answer, not the Supreme Court.

On Wednesday morning, the court heard_______(26)_______ on the issue of "severability" — the question of what should happen with the rest of the 2,700-page statute if the requirement that most Americans obtain health insurance is struck down. The insurance mandate was effectively ______(27)______ to a bumper sticker by the opponents in their constitutional challenge, and the entire law reduced to little more than an _____(28)_____ to the mandate. "My approach would be to say that if you take the heart out of the statute, the statute's gone", Justice Antonin Scalia said, a position held by the law's opponents, who want to _____ (29)_______ the whole thing.

**23.** (*a*) were (*b*) are

(*c*) is (*d*) was

**24.** (*a*) constitutionally (*b*) spiritually

(*c*) politically (*d*) mutually

**25.** (*a*) political (*b*) constitutional

(*c*) deliberate (*d*) promotional

26. (*a*) arguments (*b*) debacle
(*c*) pleas (*d*) petitions

27. (*a*) increased (*b*) enlarged
(*c*) reduced (*d*) minimized

28. (*a*) appendage (*b*) adaptor
(*c*) appliance (*d*) adage

29. (*a*) exacerbate (*b*) restore
(*c*) conciliate (*d*) demolish

**Directions for questions 30 to 32:** Each question is based on arrangement of parts of legal phrases in one sentence/paragraph, providing the most appropriate meaning. One or more parts of the sentence/paragraph is given in the question, remaining parts of the sentence/paragraph are to be sequentially selected from the remaining four parts of the sentence/paragraph (P, Q, R, S) given under each question. The most suitable sequence is required to be selected from the four choices (a, b, c, d) given for each question.

30. *Quo warranto* (Medieval Latin for "by what warrant?") ______ requiring ______ to show ______ exercising ______ (or "franchise") they claim to hold.

(P) what authority they have for
(Q) the person to whom it is directed
(R) some right or power
(S) is a prerogative writ

(*a*) PQRS (*b*) SQPR
(*c*) QSRP (*d*) RPSQ

31. *Nihil dicit* is Latin for "he says nothing"; ________. It refers to the name of a judgment which a judge may render against a defendant who ________ within the prescribed time limit. The defendant failed to say why the court ____________. The failure to say constitutes ____________; it does so more strongly than a mere default.

(P) should not issue the judgment against him
(Q) failed to plead and failed to answer a plaintiff's declaration or complaint
(R) a judgement for want of a plea
(S) an admission of the justice of the cause of action against the defendant

(*a*) PQRS (*b*) QPSR
(*c*) SQPR (*d*) RQPS

32. *Restitutio in integrum* means ______. It is one of the primary guiding principles ______ claims. The general rule, as the principle implies, is that the ______ in the position he or she would have been had the ______.

(P) behind the awarding of damages in common law negligence
(Q) tortious action not been committed
(R) restoration to original condition
(S) amount of compensation awarded should put the successful plaintiff

(*a*) RSPQ (*b*) PQRS
(*c*) PSRQ (*d*) RPSQ

**Directions for questions 33 to 40:** Read the given passage and answer the questions that follow.

While virtually anyone who wants to do so can train his or her brain to the habits of long-form reading, in any given culture, few people will want to. And that's to be expected. Serious "deep attention" reading has always been and will always be a minority pursuit, a fact that has been obscured in the past half-century.

I don't think of the distinction between readers and non-readers—better, those who love reading and those who don't so much—in terms of class, which may be a function of my profession, but may also be a function of my knowledge that readers can be found at all social stations.

The extreme reader, to coin a phrase, is a rare bird indeed. ("I have done what people do, my life makes a reasonable showing," Lynne Sharon Schwartz writes. "Can I go back to my books now?") Such people are born, not made, I think; or mostly born and only a little made. They come out of the woodwork when Clay Shirky says that War and Peace isn't interesting to reply that, to the contrary, it's immensely interesting, fascinating, absorbing, and by the way, Mr. Shirky, have you ever tried reading it or are you speaking out of ignorance?—and then back to their books they go.

Those are my tribe, but they are few. It is more common to come across the person who has known the joys of reading but who can be distracted from them. But even those folks are a small percentage of the population.

For lovers of books and reading, and especially for those who become teachers, this fact can be painful and frustrating. We love reading, we think it's wonderful, and we want other people to think so, too. "What we have loved,/Others will love," wrote Wordsworth, "and we will teach them how." A noble sentiment! Inspiring! But what if, after great labor, we discover—this often happens—that we can't teach them how? Whose fault is that?

Perhaps it isn't anyone's fault. Steven Pinker once said that "Children are wired for sound, but print is an optional accessory that must be painstakingly bolted on." The key here is "painstakingly": There can be many pains, in multiple senses of the word, for all parties involved, and it cannot be surprising that many of the recipients of the bolting aren't overly appreciative, and that even those who are appreciative don't find the procedure notably pleasant. So it's important to dissociate reading from academic life, not just because teachers and professors make reading so much more dutiful and good-for-you than it ought to be, but also because the whole environment of school is simply alien to what long-form reading has been for almost all of its history.

Rarely has education been about teaching children, adolescents, or young adults how to read lengthy and complicated texts with sustained, deep, appreciative attention—at least, not since the invention of the printing press. When books were scarce, the situation was different: The North African boy who later became known to history as St. Augustine spent countless hours of his education poring over, analyzing word by word, and memorizing a handful of books, most of them by Virgil and Cicero; this model was followed largely because no one had many books, so each one was treated as precious. Augustine's biographer Peter Brown has commented that some of Augustine's intellectual eccentricities are the product of "a mind steeped too long in too few books"—something that can be said of almost nobody today.

Rarely have young people been expected to have truly deep knowledge of particular texts. Instead, education, especially in its "liberal arts" embodiments, has been devoted to providing students with navigational tools—with enough knowledge to find their way through situations that they might confront later in life. (Even the old English public schools flogged their students through years of Latin and Greek not because Latin and Greek were intrinsically valuable, still less useful, but because the discipline of such study would have a salutary effect on young men's characters. And these are the terms in which survivors of that system typically praise it.) This is one of the ways in which the artes liberales are supposed to be "liberal," that is, "liberating": They free you to make your own way through the challenges of life without requiring external props.

**33.** In the context of the passage, what can be inferred from the phrase "such people are born, not made?"

(*a*) You cannot make someone learn to be an extreme reader, it is an attribute that one is born with.

(*b*) You cannot make people behave and think in a particular manner.

(*c*) Great people like Lynne Sharon Schwartz are born and not made.

(*d*) Those who love reading are born with the desire to read which gets polished with age.

**34.** The author of the passage is most likely

(*a*) a philosopher

(*b*) a writer

(*c*) a human psychology teacher

(*d*) a language teacher

**35.** Why does the author say "it's important to dissociate reading from academic life?"

(*a*) To express his belief that great academicians make worst readers.

(*b*) To imply that one need not be academically oriented to be a good reader.

(*c*) To highlight the importance of making reading pleasurable and less dutiful.

(*d*) To give more importance to reading for self development.

**36.** According to the passage, the author is most likely to agree with which of the following?

(*a*) Extreme and voracious readers are not tough to find.

(*b*) A number of people like to read but easily get distracted from it.

(*c*) People can be trained to become a reader.

(*d*) One should know what a joy of reading is.

**37.** In the context of the passage, what do you infer from the phrase "They free you to make your own way through the challenges of life without requiring external props?"

(*a*) 'Liberal Arts' make one liberal.

(*b*) 'Liberal Arts' teaches one to support liberty and avoid subjugation.

(*c*) 'Liberal Arts' liberates one to learn with the experiences and challenges of life.

(*d*) None of these

**38.** What does the phrase "Can I go back to my books now?" imply about the speaker?

(*a*) It implies that the person referred to is a bookworm.

(*b*) It implies that the person referred to is a librarian.

(*c*) It implies that the person referred to is a student.

(*d*) It implies that the person referred to is a voracious reader.

**39.** Last line of fifth paragraph throws up a question "whose fault is that?" What does 'that' refer to?

(*a*) Reader's assume that since they like a piece of literature others will like it too.

(*b*) Not being able to make someone learn how to love reading.

(*c*) Forcefully teaching people how to love reading.

(*d*) Great labour spent on teaching someone a thing which you know that they can't learn.

**40.** Identify the most appropriate antonym of the word 'embodiment'?

(*a*) Structure (*b*) Expression

(*c*) Epitome (*d*) Exclusion

## SECTION – II : GENERAL KNOWLEDGE

41. Which of the following Indian states won the best state award for strengthening its panchayati raj institutions?
(*a*) Rajasthan (*b*) Maharashtra
(*c*) Goa (*d*) Sikkim

**42.** India hosted the BRICS (Brazil, Russia, India, China and South Africa) summit for the first time on 29 March 2012. It was:
(*a*) Fourth BRICS summit
(*b*) Fifth BRICS summit
(*c*) Sixth BRICS summit
(*d*) Seventh BRICS summit

**43.** Who among the following won the French Open Final 2012?
(*a*) Rafael Nadal (*b*) Novak Djokovic
(*c*) Roger Federer (*d*) Robin Söderling

**44.** Kaladan project is related to which of the following countries:
(*a*) Nepal (*b*) Bhutan
(*c*) Myanmar (*d*) Sri Lanka

**45.** Kalesar National Park is located in:
(*a*) Chhattisgarh (*b*) Haryana
(*c*) Himachal Pradesh (*d*) Assam

**46.** Chairperson of the Central Sangeet Natak Akademi Leela Samson is associated with:
(*a*) Kuchipudi (*b*) Bharatanatyam
(*c*) Kathak (*d*) Odissi

**47.** Which among the following former Presidents was elected unopposed in independent India?
(*a*) V.V. Giri
(*b*) Giani Zail Singh
(*c*) Neelam Sanjiva Reddy
(*d*) S Radhakrishnan

**48.** The book, 'Barack Obama: The Story' written by:
(*a*) Mick Jagger (*b*) David Maraniss
(*c*) Mark Parsons (*d*) Ismat Tahseen

**49.** 'Surface' is a tablet manufactured by:
(*a*) Apple (*b*) Microsoft
(*c*) Amazon (*d*) Samsung

**50.** Bandipur Tiger Sanctuary is located in which of the following district of Karnataka?
(*a*) Chamarajanagar
(*b*) Ramanagara
(*c*) Chikamagalur
(*d*) Shimoga

**51.** Which of the following states area-wise is the largest in India?
(*a*) Uttar Pradesh (*b*) Madhya Pradesh
(*c*) Rajasthan (*d*) Maharashtra

**52.** Tirupati is located in which of the following states?
(*a*) Kerala (*b*) Tamilnadu
(*c*) Andhra Pradesh (*d*) Karnataka

**53.** The southern-most point of India is:
(*a*) Indira Col (*b*) Indira Point
(*c*) Kanyakumari (*d*) Nancowry Island

**54.** Which is the second largest river of India:
(*a*) Ganga (*b*) Brahmputra
(*c*) Godavari (*d*) Narmada

**55.** Indian Standard Time is ahead of Greenwich Mean Time by:
(*a*) 4 hours 30 minutes. (*b*) 5 hours 30 minutes.
(*c*) 5 hours (*d*) 6 hours

**56.** Through which of the following Indian states the Tropic of Cancer does not pass?
(*a*) Rajasthan (*b*) West Bengal
(*c*) Bihar (*d*) Mizoram

**57.** Srinagar is located on the bank of :
(*a*) Ravi (*b*) Shyok
(*c*) Jhelum (*d*) Indus

**58.** Bihu is the festival of:
(*a*) Assam (*b*) West Bengal
(*c*) Uttrakhand (*d*) Bihar

**59.** Rajgir, a Buddhist pilgrim place is situated in which of the following states?
(*a*) Madhya Pradesh (*b*) Uttar Pradesh
(*c*) West Bengal (*d*) Bihar

**60.** The Salim Ali Bird Sanctuary is located in:
(*a*) Goa (*b*) Maharashtra
(*c*) Tamilnadu (*d*) Odisha

**61.** The 'Bagh Mitra' (Friend of Tiger) Awards have been instituted by
(*a*) Ministry of Environment & Forests
(*b*) World Wildlife Fund
(*c*) International Union for Conservation of Nature (IUCN)
(*d*) None of the above

**62.** Which of the following anti-inflammatory drug is considered responsible for near extinction of three vulture species in India?
(*a*) Endosulfan (*b*) Diclofenac
(*c*) Gatifloxacin (*d*) None of the above

**63.** As of now there are ___ woman judges in the Supreme Court of India.

(*a*) One (*b*) Two
(*c*) Three (*d*) None of the above

**64.** The capital of India (then British India) was shifted from Calcutta (now Kolkata) to Delhi during the reign of

(*a*) King George V (*b*) Queen Victoria
(*c*) Queen Elizabeth I (*d*) None of the above

**65.** Akhlaq Mohammed Khan was known for contribution to

(*a*) Literature (*b*) Painting
(*c*) Photography (*d*) None of the above

**66.** The Prime Minister of which of the following countries was recently charged with contempt of the Supreme Court of that country?

(*a*) Pakistan (*b*) Bangladesh
(*c*) Maldives (*d*) None of the above

**67.** Rail _____ the first onboard magazine of Indian Railways was launched recently.

(*a*) Bandhu (*b*) Path
(*c*) Saathi (*d*) None of the above

**68.** What is Rustom 1?

(*a*) Unmanned Aerial Vehicle
(*b*) Main Battle Tank
(*c*) Nuclear Submarine
(*d*) None of the above

**69.** 'Operation Atlanta' is a joint millitary operation of India and _______ aimed at countering piracy in the Indian Ocean.

(*a*) China (*b*) USA
(*c*) European Union (*d*) None of the above

**70.** Tour de France is an international competitive sports event related to which of the following sport?

(*a*) Table Tennis (*b*) Steeple Chase
(*c*) Cycling (*d*) None of the above

**71.** Which of the following was named the Chairman of Tata Sons?

(*a*) Ratan Tata (*b*) Cyrus Mistry
(*c*) Noel Tata (*d*) None of the above

**72.** ____________ is the first metro and rail based system in the world to be allotted carbon credits.

(*a*) Delhi Metro (*b*) London Metro
(*c*) Moscow Metro (*d*) None of the above

**73.** 57th National School Games were recently held in

(*a*) Bengaluru (*b*) Delhi
(*c*) Kolkata (*d*) None of the above

**74.** Gini Rometty was recently appointed the first woman Chief Executive Officer (CEO) of which of the following companies?

(*a*) Microsoft Inc. (*b*) Apple Inc.
(*c*) IBM Inc. (*d*) None of the above

**75.** 'A Shot at History' is the autobiography of

(*a*) Gagan Narang (*b*) R.S. Rathore
(*c*) Abhinav Bindra (*d*) None of the above

**76.** What is ca-MRSA?

(*a*) Supercomputer (*b*) Bacterium
(*c*) Satellite (*d*) None of the above

**77.** The movie .Jashn-e-Azadi' has been directed by

(*a*) Sanjay Kak (*b*) Nila Madhab Panda
(*c*) Mira Nair (*d*) None of the above

**78.** 'Sanjeevani' is a life-detection kit used to trace people buried under debris. It has been developed by

(*a*) Defence Research & Development Organisation
(*b*) Indian Space Research Organisation
(*c*) Indian Institute of Science
(*d*) None of the above

**79.** Hay Festival is an international ______ event.

(*a*) Cinema (*b*) Arts
(*c*) Literary (*d*) None of the above

**80.** Sudirman Cup is related to which sport?

(*a*) Badminton (*b*) Table Tennis
(*c*) Lawn Tennis (*d*) None of the above

**81.** In which of the following countries, the right to vote in municipal elections was recently granted to women?

(*a*) Oman (*b*) Saudi Arabia
(*c*) Kuwait (*d*) None of the above

**82.** Which of the following cities hosts an Indian Film Festival annually?

(*a*) London (*b*) New York
(*c*) San Francisco (*d*) None of the above

**83.** The Palace of Great Happiness is situated in which of the following countries?

(*a*) Nepal (*b*) Bhutan
(*c*) Tibet (China) (*d*) None of the above

**84.** Currently, nuclear waste is being stored at

(*a*) Tarapur (*b*) Kalpakkam
(*c*) Narora (*d*) None of the above

**85.** The ______ spacecraft of NASA became the first spacecraft to enter into an asteroid's orbit.

(*a*) Dawn (*b*) Dusk
(*c*) Sunrise (*d*) None of the above

**86.** The Union Government recently notified Section _____ of the Advocates Act, 1961 and this has enabled advocates to practice in all courts and quasi-judicial authorities.

(*a*) 20 (*b*) 30

(*c*) 40 (*d*) None of the above

**87.** 'The First Class Man' is an in-production movie based on the life of

(*a*) Mahatma Gandhi (*b*) S. Ramanujam

(*c*) C.V. Raman (*d*) None of the above

**88.** Centres of Excellence for Fruits and Vegetables were recently set up in _______ with cooperation of Israel.

(*a*) Uttar Pradesh (*b*) Karnataka

(*c*) Haryana (*d*) None of the above

**89.** 'Hamza' is the name given to a recently discovered river that flows 13,000 feet beneath _______.

(*a*) Nile (*b*) Mississipi

(*c*) Amazon (*d*) None of the above

**90.** The Prem Bhatia award is given for excellence in which of the following fields?

(*a*) Journalism (*b*) Cinema

(*c*) Literature (*d*) None of the above

## SECTION – III : MATHEMATICS

**91.** A girl can buy 7 apples and 12 mangoes in ₹ 150 while her brother can purchase 16 apples and 6 mangoes in ₹ 150. Find the price of an apple and two mangoes.

(*a*) ₹ 24 (*b*) ₹ 30

(*c*) ₹ 15 (*d*) ₹ 21

**92.** Mr. Niraj had dinner at a restaurant and paid ₹ 240 for food. He also paid 12.5% sales tax and 10% tip. How much did he pay for the dinner?

(*a*) ₹ 297 (*b*) ₹ 286

(*c*) ₹ 292 (*d*) ₹ 294

**93.** A total of ₹ 918 is divided among A, B and C, such that for every rupee that A gets, B gets 75 paise and for every rupee that B gets, C gets 50 paise. Find the amount received by C.

(*a*) ₹ 432 (*b*) ₹ 324

(*c*) ₹ 162 (*d*) ₹ 225

**94.** Ajay makes 19% profit by selling an article. If he had bought the same article at 10% less than the initial cost price and sold it for ₹ 5 less than the initial selling price, he would have made 10% profit. Find the initial cost price of the article.

(*a*) ₹ 20 (*b*) ₹ 16

(*c*) ₹ 25 (*d*) ₹ 30

**95.** A trader while buying uses a weight balance that shows 1000 gm instead of 1100 gm and while selling he uses a weight balance that shows 1000 gm instead of 900 gm. If he sells at the cost price, then find his approximate profit percentage.

(*a*) 12% (*b*) 18%

(*c*) 22% (*d*) 30%

**96.** Two persons A and B start running at 12 p.m. and 3 p.m. from points P and Q for Q and P respectively. They meet at a point R at 4 p.m. and after that they both reached their respective destinations at the same time. What is the ratio of speeds of A and B?

(*a*) 1 : 3 (*b*) 1 : 4

(*c*) 2 : 3 (*d*) 1 : 2

**97.** Which of the following cannot be the product of two prime numbers?

(*a*) Even number (*b*) Odd number

(*c*) Integer (*d*) Prime number

**98.** If sum of the squares of two numbers is 85 and sum of these two numbers is 13. Then, find the absolute difference of these two numbers.

(*a*) 1 (*b*) 2

(*c*) 3 (*d*) 4

**99.** The average age of 'n' students of a class is 12 years. The average age of the class increased by 0.1 year after admission of a new 14 years old student in the class. Find the value of 'n'.

(*a*) 18 (*b*) 19

(*c*) 20 (*d*) 21

**100.** If the average marks of 10 students in a class is 'a', the average marks of 3 of these 10 students in the class is 'b' and the average marks of the remaining 7 students is 'c', then

(*a*) a = 3b + 7c (*b*) 7a = 3b + 10c

(*c*) 10a = 7b + 3c (*d*) 10a = 3b + 7c

**101.** A train travels 20 km in 15 minutes, 16 km in next 11 minutes and 24 km in next 10 minutes. Find the average speed of the train per hour over the entire journey.

(*a*) 116 km/hr (*b*) 100 km/hr

(*c*) 120 km/hr (*d*) 36 km/hr

**102.** In a group of 80 people, 30 people like tea, 50 people like coffee and 40 people like lassi. What is the maximum number of people who like all the three beverages?

(*a*) 20 (*b*) 30

(*c*) 40 (*d*) 60

**103.** From a bag containing 10 white balls, 6 green balls and 8 blue balls, two balls are drawn at random. What is the probability that both the balls drawn are of the same colour?

(*a*) $\frac{1}{23}$ (*b*) $\frac{22}{69}$

(*c*) $\frac{20}{23}$ (*d*) $\frac{1}{8}$

**104. A person going from home to office has to cross 5 traffic lights – 1, 2, 3, 4 and 5. The probabilities of all the traffic lights 1 to 5 being green when he reaches that traffic light are 0.2, 0.5, 0.3, 0.9 and 0.4 respectively. What is the probability that all the lights will be green?**

(*a*) 0.0108 (*b*) 0.000023

(*c*) 0.23 (*d*) 0.108

**105. If the first and the second terms of an arithmetic progression are 2 and –2 respectively, find the sum of the first n terms of the arithmetic progression.**

(*a*) 2(3 – 2n) (*b*) 3n(2 – n)

(*c*) 2n(3 – 2n) (*d*) 2n(2 – n)

**106. A right circular cone is cut by a plane parallel to its base such that the height of the upper part and lower part is in the ratio of 2 : 1. Find the ratio of the volume of the upper part to the lower part of the cone.**

(*a*) 4 : 5 (*b*) 19 : 27

(*c*) 8 : 19 (*d*) 8 : 27

**107. Mr. X borrows ₹ 350 from Tolaram at the rate of 15% per annum simple interest. He pays the total amount after 16 months. What is the total amount he pays back to Tolaram?**

(*a*) ₹ 400 (*b*) ₹ 420

(*c*) ₹ 436 (*d*) ₹ 484

**108. Ten women work 10 hours a day to complete a work in 10 days. How many women can complete half of the same work by working 5 hours a day for 5 days?**

(*a*) 10 (*b*) 40

(*c*) 15 (*d*) 20

**109. In a 60 litres mixture of milk and water, 25 litres of water is added such that the percentage of water becomes 40%. Find the milk percentage in the initial mixture.**

(*a*) 15%

(*b*) 60%

(*c*) 85%

(*d*) 65%

**110.** A group of 20 men is employed to complete a work in 24 days. After 18 days, 16 more men are employed and the work is finished 1 day earlier. If 16 more men were not employed, how many more days would it have taken beyond the expected period?

(*a*) 4 days (*b*) 3 days

(*c*) 2 days (*d*) 1 day

## SECTION – IV : LOGICAL REASONING

**Directions for questions 111 to 115:** Read the given arguments carefully and answer the questions that follow.

**111. Productive capacity varies from person to person. The price to purchase it varies with the capacity of the employer. The employer keeps buying units of a person's potential/capacity, or not buying it, depending on the money he pays to encourage/ discourage it. The use of money, aka financial incentive, permits two things that the absence of it does not. It allows the employer to recruit people from a more valuable talent pool, and it motivates the people that have been recruited to produce more value than they would without it.**

**Which of the following must be true if the given argument is true?**

1. The employer does not "buy" a person's full productive capacity with the initial salary he offers him.
2. Productive capacity of a person is not fixed.

(*a*) Both 1 and 2 (*b*) Only 1

(*c*) Only 2 (*d*) Neither 1 nor 2

**112. Ratings agencies were one of the major culprits of the financial crisis — bestowing top-notch, triple-A ratings on thousands of mortgage-backed securities that proved to be worth less than junk when the housing bubble burst. It has taken three years, but the nation's banking regulators have now made a good proposal to remove the raters as the official arbiters of financial reliability and replace them with a set of objective, transparent criteria to determine the riskiness of assets in the trading portfolios of the nation's 30 biggest banks**

**Which of the following strengthens the argument?**

1. Ratings agencies were paid millions by the companies and banks whose securities they rate.
2. Regulators — and the financial system — need a more objective way to assess risk.

(*a*) Only 1 (*b*) Only 2

(*c*) Both 1 and 2 (*d*) Neither 1 nor 2

**113.** The sight of already very well paid bankers being given six-figure bonus payments has been criticized from the left for some time, but these criticisms became much more widespread during the financial crisis. Not only were large bonus pay-outs contrasted with the reduced pay or unemployment being experienced by many people in the rest of the economy, but bankers were widely held to blame for the recession and its impact on society as a whole. The greatest criticism has tended to be reserved for bonus pay-outs at companies that received government bail-outs.

Which of the following, if true, underpins the criticism?

1. Bankers are less socially useful than nurses, doctors, teachers or engineers.
2. Taxpayers, without having any say, have indirectly poured tens of billions into firms that took irresponsible risks and tax payers hard-earned money has gone to banker's pockets.
3. Even mediocre performers are given large bonuses, when their performance is the result of wider economic trends, not of their own skill.

(*a*) Only 2 (*b*) 1 and 2
(*c*) 1 and 3 (*d*) only 3

**114.** Women in beauty contests are judged on their physical appearance, which depicts the ideal femininity, rather than on any other qualities they may possess, despite the talent round in such contests. Judging women, but not men, primarily on their looks contributes to the subjugation of women. Ideal masculinity, while in itself potentially damaging to men, tends to be construed in much wider and less restrictive terms.

Which of the following inference/inferences can be drawn from the argument?

1. Qualities such as intelligence are not seen as part of ideal femininity.
2. Ugly women never win the beauty contests.
3. Beauty is all that matters in a beauty contest.

(*a*) 2 and 3 (*b*) 1 and 3
(*c*) 1 and 2 (*d*) only 2

**115.** The district authorities' decision to strike off names of about 55,000 families from Below the Poverty Line (BPL) list has raked up a controversy and prompted those affected to launch an agitation. Hundreds of agitated people held a demonstration in Sonipat on Monday, to protest against the cancellation of BPL cards.

Which of the following, if true, will strengthen the cause of protest against cancellation?

1. Eligibility for BPL families in 2011 is being determined on the basis of guidelines of 2001 without taking any account of the inflation that has taken place.
2. A lot of people have lost the privileges they used to enjoy.
3. Corruption is rampant and most of the affected people had managed to bribe the officials and get their names registered in the BPL list.

(*a*) 1 and 2 (*b*) 2 and 3
(*c*) only 2 (*d*) none of these

**116.** Read the given debate and answer the question that follows.

**Anita:** Some people say that introducing identity cards would help prevent terrorism. But, identity cards are an attack by governments on privacy and basic freedoms. Why should we be required to prove who we are all the time? Don't we have the right to be left alone by the government? Making everyone carry such a card suggests that we are in some way owned by the state. Identity cards are a tool of suspicious dictatorships, not of modern liberal democracies.

**Prashant:** Even if the cards could not be faked, criminals and illegal migrants will carry on hiding from authority. If they do not come to the attention of the police, then they can't be asked to identify themselves.

Prashant responds to Anita's argument in which one of the following ways?

(*a*) He supports the Anita's argument by pointing out the flaw in the identity cards.

(*b*) He defends Anita's argument by producing an evidence to support her argument.

(*c*) He draws attention to one of the flaws that makes the benefit of identity cards questionable.

(*d*) He points out the Anita's reasoning is flawed and is based on assumptions.

**117.** Read the given debate and answer the question that follows.

**Jimmy:** At any firm there are always a limited number of senior jobs. If these are taken up by older workers staying on indefinitely, firms may find it hard to recruit, motivate and retain younger workers looking to replace them, leading to high turnover among younger staff.

**Robert:** The belief that the economy has only a limited number of jobs and presence of existing employees will deny job opportunities to younger employees, or push down wages, is the well-known 'lump of labour' fallacy. Wages are especially unlikely to drop in industries with existing or projected shortages, such as in teaching, and nursing.

How does Robert respond to Jimmy's argument?

(*a*) He refutes Jimmy's argument by giving an example.

(*b*) He states his opinion which is generic in nature and un-related to Jimmy's argument.

(*c*) He supports Jimmy's argument but explains that the argument may not be valid under some circumstances.

(*d*) He criticizes Jimmy's argument and mentions one of its flaws.

**Directions for questions 118 and 119:** Read the given argument and answer the questions that follow.

The central argument for deconstruction depends on relativism, by which I mean the view that truth itself is always relative to the differing standpoints and predisposing intellectual frameworks of the judging subject. Indeed, to attempt to define deconstruction is to defy another of its main principles – which is to deny that final or true definitions are possible, because even the most plausible candidates will always invite a further defining move, or 'play', with language. For the deconstructor, the relationship of language to reality is not given, or even reliable.

**118.** Which of the following, if true, lends greatest support to the opinion of the deconstructor?

(*a*) All languages have some words that are similar and show little if any change.

(*b*) All language systems are based on logically relevant theories of their time.

(*c*) All language systems are inherently unreliable cultural constructs.

(*d*) Language has essentially evolved due to the need to humans to communicate their deepest thoughts.

**119.** Which of the following if true weakens the opinion of the deconstructor?

1. The meaning of a word has its origin in the structure of reality itself.
2. Words attain new meanings with time due to changes in their relevance.

(*a*) Only 1 (*b*) Only 2

(*c*) Both 1 and 2 (*d*) Neither 1 nor 2

**Directions for questions 120 and 121:** Read the given argument and answer the questions that follow.

**120.** It may seem counterintuitive that in film, where there's so much more money at stake, producers are more inclined to invest in new properties, while TV viewers have to make do with dusty reruns and the likes of *Merry Madagascar*. It's all about supply and demand. Over the long winter break, parents willing to take the kids to the multiplex will see anything with Santa in it, so there's no shortage of demand for something new. But when it comes to TV they are content with old TV shows.

Which of the following, if true, strengthens the argument?

1. Most parents feel more comfortable with the TV shows they remember from when they grew up.
2. Parents fear that the content of the new serials will produce a negative effect on the minds of their children.

(*a*) Only 2 (*b*) Only 1

(*c*) Neither 1 nor 2 (*d*) Both 1 and 2

**121.** Which of the following is a valid assumption?

(*a*) Old TV shows are as popular as new films.

(*b*) Investing in TV shows is pragmatic.

(*c*) Old TV shows are as good as new films.

(*d*) None of these

**Directions for questions 122 and 123:** Read the given debate and answer the questions that follow.

**Rajiv:** Child soldiers are no different from child criminals. Child soldiers have been responsible for some of the most brutal and violent acts in wartime. In Sierra Leone child soldiers committed acts of rape, mutilation and mass killings of civilians. Under most domestic laws the age of criminal responsibility is much lower than 18, in the USA criminal responsibility can be as low as age 8. If a child can be convicted for murder under national law they should also be held responsible for international crimes. There should be no exception simply because the crimes occurred in wartime.

**Ranjeet:** Child soldiers are often victims of war themselves. Prosecutions do not allow the opportunity to rehabilitate child soldiers and instead prioritize the rights of victims over the rights of the child, even though the child himself will probably have suffered abuse as well.

**122.** Which of the following most accurately expresses the point of issue between Rajiv and Ranjeet?

(*a*) Instead of prosecuting child criminals should they be rehabilitated?

(*b*) Should there be an international minimum age of criminal responsibility for war crimes and crimes against humanity?

(*c*) Are child soldiers actually guilty of wartime crimes?

(*d*) Should child soldiers be prosecuted for the crimes they commit during wartime?

**123.** Ranjeet responds to Rajiv's argument in which of the following ways?

(*a*) He argues that Rajiv's logic is based on false premises.

(*b*) He disapproves Rajiv's argument by weakening its premises.

(*c*) He agrees to Rajiv's argument but advocates the need to look at the situation from a different angle.

(*d*) He empathizes with the child soldiers and supports their cause.

**Directions for questions 124 and 125:** Read the given debate and answer the questions that follow.

**Beth:** Anti-Social Behaviour Orders (ASBOs) are explicitly intended to deal with bad juvenile behaviour. But, they push people that could be helped by social work or proper attention into an unenviable category of 'offender' – they criminalize people for behavior that isn't criminal.

**Judith:** Something meaningful has to exist to punish actions that don't merit criminal punishment, but damage the quality of life of others, especially through constant repetition. The ASBO is such a tool as it allows communities to take back their streets and estates from intimidating and out of control youths, and to establish proper norms of behavior thus preventing a slide into more serious lawlessness and criminality.

**124.** Judith response to Beth's argument is based on which of the following premises?

1. Bad behaviour on the part of the youth has a damaging effect of the communities.
2. Lawlessness can be kept under control by ASBO's.
3. The youth need to exercise proper behaviour.
4. Those actions that do not merit criminal punishments deserve at least a milder punishment.

(*a*) 1,2, and 3 (*b*) only 4

(*c*) 1 and 3 (*d*) 2 and 4

**125.** Which of the following strengthens Judith's argument most effectively?

(*a*) ASBO's are a form of restraint to prevent future misbehaviour.

(*b*) ASBOs are more likely to be abused because (unlike prison) the offender remains in his own environment.

(*c*) ASBOs are one way to punish offenders while still ensuring they have continuing access to education, family support, job opportunities, etc.,

(*d*) Whilst ASBOs are civil orders, criminal penalties can result from breaching them.

**Directions for question 126:** In making decisions about important questions, it is desirable to be able to distinguish between 'strong' arguments and 'weak' arguments. 'Strong' arguments are those that are both important and directly related to the question. 'Weak' arguments are those that are of minor importance and also may not be directly related to the question or may be related to a trivial aspect of the question. Each question below is followed by two arguments numbered II and I. You have to decide which of the arguments is/are a 'strong' argument. Select:

(*a*) If argument I is strong

(*b*) If argument Il is strong

(*c*) If both I and II are strong

(*d*) If neither I nor II is strong

**126.** Should colleges open a second campus in some other city?

Argument I: No, the second campus will dilute their brand value and eliminate exclusivity.

Argument II: Yes, students should be given more options and opportunities in order to dilute the effect of competition.

**127.** Read the given premises carefully and identify the conclusion that definitely does not follow.

If we do not spend any time watching television, then we will score well in exams. Scoring well in exams is desirable. Therefore,

(*a*) not spending time on watching television is desirable.

(*b*) not spending time on watching television leads to desirable results.

(*c*) we will score well only when we avoid watching television.

(*d*) All of these

**128.** Read the given premises carefully and identify the conclusion that follows.

Justice leads to harmony. Harmony leads to peace. Peace makes life mundane. Therefore,

(*a*) mundanity is equivalent to justice.

(*b*) justice makes life mundane.

(*c*) a mundane existence is always characterized by justice.

(*d*) justice is undesirable.

**129.** Only if A attends the meeting, B goes to the party. But B does not go to the party.

Which of the following is the correct conclusion?

(*a*) A attended the meeting.

(*b*) A did not attend the meeting.

(*c*) A may have or may not have attended the meeting.

(*d*) B goes to party.

**Directions for questions 130 to 133:** In each of the following questions, words in the first pair are related to each other in a certain manner. The second pair is incomplete. Complete the second pair such that words of the second pair depict the same relation as depicted by the first pair.

**130.** abrupt : brusque :: content : ?
(*a*) blue (*b*) doleful
(*c*) enraptured (*d*) crestfallen

**131.** parricide: close relative :: regicide : ?
(*a*) friend (*b*) sister
(*c*) king (*d*) business partner

**132.** theocracy: priest :: plutocracy : ?
(*a*) books (*b*) rich people
(*c*) demagogue (*d*) atheist

**133.** cat : kitten :: deer : ?
(*a*) nymph (*b*) fawn
(*c*) shoal (*d*) cub

**134.** Identify the odd word.
(*a*) sobriquet (*b*) nickname
(*c*) moniker (*d*) tirade

**135.** Identify the odd word.
(*a*) besmirch (*b*) soil
(*c*) sully (*d*) sand

**Directions for questions 136 to 140:** In each of the questions below are given three statements followed by three conclusions numbered I, II and III. You have to take the given statements to be true even if they seem to be at variance with commonly known facts. Read all the conclusions and then decide which of the given conclusions logically follow/follows from the given statements disregarding commonly known facts.

**136. Statements:**
All good are bad. All bad are ugly. Some ugly are smart.
**Conclusions:**
I. Some smart are bad.
II. No good is smart.
III. Some ugly are bad.
(*a*) I and II (*b*) II and III
(*c*) Only III (*d*) None of these

**137. Statements:**
No brick is clay. Some clay is curtain. All curtains are curved.
**Conclusions:**
I. No brick is curved.
II. Some clay is curved.
III. Some curtain is curved.
(*a*) Only II (*b*) Only III
(*c*) Both II and III (*d*) I, II and III

**138. Statements:**
All sailors are experienced. Some experienced are bold. Some bold are bankrupt.
**Conclusions:**
I. Some sailors are bankrupt.
II. Some bold are sailors.
III. All experienced are bold.
(*a*) Only II (*b*) I and III
(*c*) Both II and III (*d*) None of these

**139. Statements:**
Some monkeys are rats. All rats are cats. No cat is a kitten.
**Conclusions:**
I. No rat is a kitten.
II. Some cats are monkeys.
III. Some monkeys are not kittens.
(*a*) Only I (*b*) I and II
(*c*) Only III (*d*) I, II and III

**140. Statements:**
Some pens are pencils. Some pencils are erasers. Some erasers are brushes.
**Conclusions:**
I. Some pens are brushes.
II. Some pencils are brushes.
III. Some pens are erasers.
(*a*) only I (*b*) Only II
(*c*) I and III (*d*) None of these

**141.** 7, 4, 5, 9, 20, ____________
What is the next number in this sequence?
(*a*) 33 (*b*) 39.5
(*c*) 43 (*d*) 52.5

**142.** O, R, V, B, K, X, ____________
What is the next letter in this sequence?
(*a*) D (*b*) E
(*c*) P (*d*) S

**143.** Mayank is the brother of Vinita and Amar is the brother of Suman. Vinita is the daughter of Suman and Kundan is the father of Amar. Who is the father of Mayank?
(*a*) Amar (*b*) Suman
(*c*) Kundan (*d*) Data inadequate

**144.** Abhishek's mother is the only sister of Swati's father. How is Abhishek's father related to Swati's father?
(*a*) Brother (*b*) Brother-in-law
(*c*) Son-in-law (*d*) Father

**145.** EXCAVATION is coded as CZTRERLBUJ and INEQUALITY is coded as BJCZFRDBLA, then how will EQUIVALENT be coded in the same code language?

(*a*) CQFBERTCJL (*b*) CUWEBRXCJL

(*c*) CZFBERDCJL (*d*) CUWEBRPCJL

**146.** KJU, MIR, PKO, TIL, YMI, _____

What is the next term in this sequence?

(*a*) EOG (*b*) FJG

(*c*) FOF (*d*) EJF

**147.** Nakul walked 50 m from his house towards North, then he turned to the left and walked 20 m. He then again turned to the left and walked 30 m. After this he turned to the left at 135° and started walking. In which direction was he walking in the end?

(*a*) North (*b*) East

(*c*) North-East (*d*) North-West

**148.** Five girls – A, B, C, D and E – live in five different cities namely Banda, Gwalior, Sasaram, Jaunpur and Asansol (not necessarily in this order). D lives in Banda.

(i) If E lives in Asansol, then A lives in Sasaram. Otherwise, A lives in Gwalior.

(ii) B does not live in Sasaram or Gwalior.

(iii) Jaunpur is the city where A or C lives.

In which city does E live?

(*a*) Gwalior (*b*) Sasaram

(*c*) Asansol (*d*) Cannot be determined

**149.** 1, 4, 15, 78, 549, _____

What is the next number in this sequence?

(*a*) 4580 (*b*) 4944

(*c*) 3248 (*d*) 5888

**150.** June, September, November, April, _____

Which of the following best fits in the blank?

(*a*) September (*b*) December

(*c*) June (*d*) May

## SECTION – V : LEGAL APTITUDE

**(Instructions: Question 151 to 155 has common set of principles and facts. Apply the specified principles to the set of facts and answer the questions.)**

**Principle 1**: Whoever intending to take dishonestly any moveable property out of the possession of any person without that person's consent, moves that property in order to such taking, is said to commit theft.

**Principle 2:** A moving affected by the same act which affects the severance may be a theft.

**Principle 3:** A person is said to cause a thing to move by removing an obstacle which prevented it from moving or by separating it from any other thing, as well as by actually moving it.

**Principle 4:** A person, who by any means causes an animal to move, is said to move that animal, and to move everything which, in consequence of the motion so caused, is moved by that animal.

**Principle 5:** The consent mentioned in the definition may be express or implied, and may be given either by the person in possession, or by any person having for that purpose authority either express or implied.

**Facts:** Durjan Singh, a notorious thief plans to commit theft and did various acts to accomplish his plans.

**151.** Durjan Singh cuts down a tree in the garden of Sher Singh, with the intention of dishonestly taking the tree out of Sher Singh's possession without Sher Singh's consent. Will Durjan Singh be liable for committing theft? [Refer to Principles 1 and 2].

(*a*) No, Durjan Singh will not be liable since he has only severed the tree from the roots and has not moved it out of Sher Singh's garden.

(*b*) No, Durjan Singh will not be liable since the tree being large in size, it is not possible to take away a huge tree alone.

(*c*) Yes, Durjan Singh will be liable for theft since the offence of theft is completed as soon as he severed the tree from the roots.

(*d*) Yes, Durjan Singh will be liable for theft since cutting down a tree is a punishable offence.

**152.** Durjan Singh entered the garden of Sher Singh to dishonestly cut the tree but by his good fortune he found a box full of jewellery which was kept as a safe hide under the shade of a tree by the garden owner Sher Singh. Amazed by this, Durjan dropped the idea of cutting down the tree but took out the box of treasure and instead of taking it away in the same instance, hides it at some other place in the same garden thereby making it highly improbable that the box will ever be found by Sher Singh. Does this act of Durjan Singh amounts to theft? [Refer to principle 1 and 3]

(*a*) No, Durjan Singh will not be liable since his intention was to cut the tree and not to steal the box.

(*b*) Yes, Durjan Singh will be liable for theft since the offence of theft is completed as soon as he took the box out of the place where Sher Singh had hidden the box thereby making it highly improbable that it will ever be found by Sher Singh.

(*c*) No, Durjan will not be liable since he did not take the box out of the garden of Sher Singh.

(*d*) Yes, Durjan will be liable since he dishonestly entered the garden of Sher Singh and it is immaterial whether he cuts the tree or finds a treasure box.

**153.** Durjan Singh, while on his way back home finds a ring lying on the highroad, not in the possession of any person. Durjan Singh picks it up and takes it along with. Is he liable for theft? [Refer to principle 1and 5]

(*a*) No. Durjan is not liable because even if his intention was dishonest he did not move it out of any one's possession.

(*b*) Yes, he is liable since the ring is a movable property and can be subject to theft.

(*c*) No, he is not liable because theft of a small ring is not a penal offence under Indian Penal Code and law does not take trivial acts into account.

(*d*) Yes, Durjan Singh will be liable because he did not inquire about the ownership of the gold ring.

**154.** While still on his way, Durjan Singh saw a bullock standing on Nikhil's property carrying a box of treasure. Instead of running away with the box, he drives the bullock in a certain direction, in order that he may dishonestly take the treasure. Whether he is liable for committing theft of treasure box? [Refer to principle 1 and 4]

(*a*) No, Durjan is not liable because he did not even touch the treasure box.

(*b*) Yes, he is liable because as soon as the bullock begins to move, the offence of theft is constituted.

(*c*) The liability of theft will be for the bullocks only and not for the box of treasure.

(*d*) No penultimate act was committed hence Durjan Singh will not be held liable for theft.

**155.** One fine day, Durjan Singh gave his watch for repair to Moolchand but Moolchand did not repair it in time. Durjan being a furious man went to Moolchand's shop and took it out of Moolchand's possession without Moolchand's consent without paying what was due on repair of the watch. Is Durjan Singh liable for theft? [Refer to principle 5]

(*a*) No, Durjan is not liable because the watch was his own property and he is free to take it back.

(*b*) Yes, he commits theft, even though the watch is his own property in as much as he takes it dishonestly.

(*c*) Such acts are common business practice and can not be categorized as theft.

(*d*) Yes he is liable, the act being morally wrong.

**156.** **Principle**: Right of hot pursuit - A coastal state cannot be expected to allow a foreign ship evade its jurisdiction by escaping into the high seas. Hot pursuit of a foreign ship may be undertaken when the competent authorities of the state have good reason to believe that the ship has violated the laws and regulations of the State.

**Explanation:** Hot pursuit cannot be taken into the territorial waters of another state. It is recognized only when continuous pursuit takes place beginning from within the territorial waters of the pursuing country.

**Facts**: Indian coast guard suspects that a murder has been committed on MV Malinga which is docked in Bombay. As they make preparations to arrest the captain, they get to know that it has silently taken off. The coast guard pursues it in one of their frigates and it goes beyond the territorial waters of India into the high seas. The coast guard frigate transmits a message to a gun boat patrolling the territorial waters. The coast guard gunboat captures it in the Indian Ocean. The captain of Malinga contends that the arrest is illegal.

(*a*) The arrest is illegal.

(*b*) The arrest is legal.

(*c*) There was no continuous chase. The chase was taken over by another ship midway.

(*d*) None of the above.

**(Instructions: Question 157 to 159 has common set of principles and facts. Apply the specified principles to the set of facts and answer the questions.)**

**Principle 1:** When both parties to the agreement are under a mistake as to the matter of fact essential to the agreement, the agreement is said to be caused by a mistake of fact.

**Principle 2:** When one party incorrectly states a fact material to the agreement the agreement is said to be caused by misrepresentation.

**Principle 3:** When one party intentionally incorrectly states a fact material to the agreement the agreement is said to be caused by fraud.

**Principle 4:** Any agreement that is a result of misrepresentation, fraud or mistake is no agreement in eyes of law and is unenforceable.

**Facts:** X had a very old vintage car. He auctioned the car on the internet and sold it to Y. Z got to know of this transaction. So one day Z approached X and introduced himself as Y and offered to pay the amount in cash and take the car. X believing Z to be Y, takes the cash and hands over the car as well as its papers. Later on X finds out that the person who took the car was actually Z and not Y. The matter goes to the court. What would you decide as a judge?

**157.** Which amongst the following most correctly explains what has been done by Z to X?

(*a*) Z defrauded X by intentionally misrepresenting himself as Y

(*b*) X was mistaken as to the true identity of Z and thus the agreement is a result of mistake

(*c*) Z caused a factual misrepresentation that voided the agreement

(*d*) There is nothing wrong done by Z as all essentials of a valid contract are satisfied

**158.** In the facts given above, assume that Z is absent. Now further assume that after taking delivery of car from X, Y finds out that the car was not a vintage. What would be your decision as per the above stated principles?

(*a*) This is a misrepresentation of facts by X and thus the agreement is void.

(*b*) This is a fraudulent misrepresentation of facts and thus the agreement is void.

(*c*) This is a mistaken representation of facts and thus the agreement is void.

(*d*) The only material fact here is that Y really liked the car thus the agreement is void.

**159.** In the facts given above, assume that Z never got to know of the online auction sale transaction. Assume further that he purchased a vintage car himself from A. Believing X to be A he approaches him to take his car and X believing Z to be Y hands him over the car. What is the status of this agreement as per the principles given above?

(*a*) This is a clear case of misrepresentation on part of X thus it is a void agreement

(*b*) This is a case of a mistake on part of Z thus it is a voidable agreement

(*c*) This is of bilateral mistake on part of Z and X making it a void agreement

(*d*) This is a case of bilateral fraud

**160.** **Principle 1:** When a person is accused of a crime in one country and is found in another country, the process of transferring such person from the country where he is found to the country where he is accused of the crime is known as extradition.

**Principle 2:** If a person commits murder, he shall be punished for imprisonment or death penalty.

**Explanation**: Extradition is possible only when a treaty of extradition exists between the country where he is found and the country to which he is extradited. Countries that are members of the European Union have an obligation to not extradite persons if there is a possibility that they will be given the death penalty.

**Facts**: Bhullar is accused of separatist activities in India. Specifically, he is said to have had a hand in the assassination of a chief minister. He has since fled to Germany. India and Germany have an extradition treaty. India is prosecuting him under a provision under which the highest sentence that may be awarded is death.

(*a*) Bhullar should be extradited to India.

(*b*) Bhullar should not be extradited to India.

(*c*) Bhullar should be tried in Germany under Indian laws.

(*d*) None of the above.

**161.** **Principle**: In so far as the proposal or acceptance of any promise is made in words, the promise is said to be express. In so far as such proposal or acceptance is made otherwise than in words, the promise is said to be implied.

**Explanation:** Valid proposal can be made in the form of an express or an implied offer.

**Facts**: A fire broke out in Shyam's House and he contacted the Golden Brown Fire brigade believing that he was entitled to their free service. However, since his house was not located within the free service zone, the fire brigade claimed compensation for their services. Has a valid proposal been made?

(*a*) Yes, by Shyam's conduct it is implied that he was aware of the conditions governing functioning of the services and he would be liable to pay them.

(*b*) No, since Shyam was under the mistaken belief that the free zone rule was applicable to him.

(*c*) Yes, since Shyam should have checked regarding the rules applicable to him before calling the fire brigade.

(*d*) None of the above statements is correct.

**(Instructions: Question 162 and 163 has common set of principles and facts. Apply the specified principles to the set of facts and answer the questions.)**

**Principle 1:** Any assembly of five or more persons is designated an 'unlawful assembly', if the common object of the persons composing that assembly is to commit any offence.

**Principle 2:** Whenever force or violence is used by an unlawful assembly, or by any member thereof, in prosecution of the common object of such assembly, every member of such assembly is guilty of the offence of rioting.

**Facts**: A, B, C, D, E and F often used to assemble in a local town park and discuss issues of contemporary politics. One day they assembled and concluded that the local MLA was a super corrupt person and something had to be done to replace him. A suggested they will go back to their respective houses and gather whatever weapons that they can and meet again at the park to figure out further course of action. Accordingly they all dispersed to their respective houses.

**162.** As per the principles provided below has any offence been committed yet?

(*a*) Yes they have committed the offence of unlawful assembly.

(*b*) Yes they have committed the offence of unlawful assembly and conspiracy.

(*c*) Yes they have committed the offence of attempting to rioting.

(*d*) No they have committed no offence.

**163.** Presume that A suggested they will go back to their respective houses and gather whatever weapons that they can and meet again at the park and together march on to the MLA's house to forcibly remove him from his house and make him resign by publicly humiliating them. Accordingly they all dispersed to their respective houses. What offence have they committed now?

(*a*) They have committed the offence of unlawful assembly.

(*b*) They have committed the offence of unlawful assembly and rioting.

(*c*) They have committed no offence yet as they are yet to do anything illegal.

(*d*) They have committed the offence of rioting.

**164. Principle**: Nuisance means an unlawful interference with a person's enjoyment of land

**Explanation**: Acts interfering with health, safety, comfort may be some examples of it. The interference has to be indirect. If it is direct, it becomes trespass.

**Facts**: Babulal has installed a brick grinding machine, his machine is causing loss of business to the stone cutter nearby as many people who would have wanted stones cut are opting for buying bricks and having them grinded instead. The stone cutter sues him for nuisance.

(*a*) There is no nuisance caused.

(*b*) Babulal has caused nuisance.

(*c*) Babulal has caused Private nuisance.

(*d*) None of the above.

**(Instructions: Question 165 to 167 has common set of principles and facts. Apply the specified principles to the set of facts and answer the questions.)**

**Principle 1:** Whoever, intending to take dishonestly any moveable property out of the possession of any person without that person's consent, moves that property in order to such taking, is said to commit theft.

**Principle 2:** Whoever dishonestly receives or retains any stolen property, knowing or having reason to believe the same to be stolen, commits the offence of possession of stolen property.

**Principle 3:** Whoever intentionally puts a person in fear of any injury to that person or to any other and thereby dishonestly induces the person so put in fear to deliver to any person any moveable property commits extortion.

**Facts:** P, Q and R went to see a movie. In the movie theatre P saw a rich lady L wearing an expensive diamond necklace. He decided to steal it. He asked Q to help him out and he agreed. After one hour they slowly started moving towards the seat where L was seated. Q diverted L's attention by spilling some pop-corn on her dress while P removed the necklace and pocketed it. During the intermission they convinced R that the movie was boring and they should instead leave and go for some drinks. R agreed and they all left the theatre. While having drinks P and Q told R of their recent exploit in the movie theatre and gave the necklace to R for safe keeping. Later on L realized that her necklace has been stolen and approached the police. P, Q and R were arrested and the matter went to a court of law.

**165.** P, Q and R are all facing criminal charges. By application of principle 1 alone what of the following would the correct decision?

(*a*) P, Q and R are all guilty of theft.

(*b*) P, Q and R are all guilty of theft and possession of stolen property.

(*c*) P and Q are guilty of theft and R is guilty of possession of stolen property.

(*d*) Only P and Q are guilty of theft.

**166.** In the facts, assume that R was heading to his place after having the drinks. In the middle he was stopped by X who put a knife to his throat and asked him to deliver all the valuables that he might have. R hands over the necklace, his wallet and his watch to X. Which of the above given three principles most adequately explains the offence committed by X?

(*a*) Principle 1 as the requirement of taking the property with a dishonest intention and moving the property in order to take it with such intention is satisfied.

(*b*) Principle 2 and 3 X clearly committed extortion as he took the property from R by putting him into fear of injury and X is also in possession of property that was stolen by P and Q.

(*c*) Principle 3 X has committed only extortion.

(*d*) None of the above.

**167.** In the facts, assume that while having drinks P handed over the necklace to R saying that it was his (i.e. P's) wife's necklace which he wants R to keep safe. Later on R finds out that the necklace was stolen. He wanted to return it immediately but was able to locate P only after two days whereupon he immediately handed over the stolen necklace back to P. In this case, which of the following would be most appropriate as per application of principles 1 and 2?

(*a*) R would not be guilty as he had neither knowledge nor reason to believe that the necklace was stolen and did not retain it upon getting to know that it was.

(*b*) R would be guilty of possession of stolen property as he was in possession of the same for several days before he returned it to P.

(*c*) R would be guilty of possession of stolen property as he retained the property for two days after getting to know that the property was stolen.

(*d*) R would be guilty as R's intent is irrelevant as per the principle 2.

**168. Principle**: The doctrine of Res Ipsa Loquitur says - When an event has taken place that could not have taken place but for the negligence of the defendant, the plaintiff just has to prove the accident and need not prove the negligence of the defendant separately.

**Explanation**: The plaintiff is a person who complains against another person in court. The defendant is the person against whom a complaint is made. Usually when a person brings a claim for negligence, the plaintiff has to prove that the defendant was negligent.

**Facts**: Manju is a cycle rickshaw operator. A bus dashes against him from behind at such great speed that he is thrown 15 feet from the spot. Manju sues the bus company.

(*a*) An accident can happen anytime. Negligence has to be proved.

(*b*) Contributory negligence from Manju has to be taken into account.

(*c*) Res ipsa loquitur applies.

(*d*) None of the above.

**(Instructions: Question 169 and 170 has common set of facts. Apply the specified principles to the set of facts and answer the questions.)**

**Facts**: X was a card carrying member of the Communist Society of India and he was disgusted at the recent news stories exposing corruption in India. Accordingly he organized a group of like minded people who started a web-site to record and organize activities to counter corruption. One day he was invited to give a speech at a local community college. He gave a strong speech and over night 100 students from the college joined his group. When his group reached the 1000 members mark, he organized a public rally and openly suggested that they should march together towards the Parliament House and stop the MPs from entering the house thereby restrict the proceedings as a mark of the their protest. He was arrested immediately thereafter. He challenged his arrest as a violation of his right to freedom of speech and expression. Decide this case on the basis of the principles as provided in following problems.

**169. Principle**: All persons have the right to freedom of speech and expression subject to reasonable restrictions that may be imposed by the State on activities that have a reasonable tendency to disrupt public order.

(*a*) X's right has been violated as his activities are only a mark of protest and have not disrupted any public order.

(*b*) Police action is justified as his activities have a very high tendency to disrupt public order.

(*c*) Police action is not justified as this restriction can be only be enforced when there is genuine threat to public order and public protests are not threats to public order since public is a part of such protests.

(*d*) The police is clearly acting politically and in a democratic society this cannot be tolerated.

**170. Principle**: All persons have the right to freedom of speech and expression subject to reasonable restrictions that may be imposed by the State for maintenance of public order.

(*a*) X's right has been violated as his activities are only a mark of protest and have not disrupted any public order.

(*b*) Police action is justified as his activities have a very high tendency to disrupt public order.

(*c*) Police action is not justified as this restriction can be only be enforced when there is genuine threat to public order and public protests are not threats to public order since public is a part of such protests.

(*d*) The police is clearly acting politically and in a democratic society this cannot be tolerated.

**171. Principle 1**: A person is said to be of sound mind for the purpose of making a contract if, at the time when he makes it, he is capable of understanding it and of forming a rational judgment as to its effect upon his interests.

**Principle 2:** A person, who is usually of unsound mind, but occasionally of sound mind, may make a contract when he is of sound mind. A person, who is usually of sound mind, but occasionally of unsound mind, may not make a contract when he is of unsound mind.

**Explanation**: A person, who is usually of unsound mind, but occasionally of sound mind, may make a contract when he is of sound mind. A person, who is usually of sound mind, but occasionally of unsound mind, may not make a contract when he is of unsound mind.

**Facts**: Indrajit contracted with Sonapati to sell his house worth Rs. 30000 for Rs. 5000. His mother however refused to honor the contract since her son was of unsound mind and incapable of understanding the nature of the transaction. Can such an agreement be held to be valid?

(*a*) Yes, since Sonapati has contracted with Indrajit for the sale of property, for a specific consideration.

(*b*) No, since Indrajit is of unsound mind.

(*c*) No, the consideration amount to be paid was insufficient.

(*d*) None of the above statements are correct.

**172. Principle**: No person shall be deprived of life or personal liberty, except in accordance with procedure established by law.

**Explanation:** Procedure established by law includes only such statutes and law which may be enacted by the state only. Right to life includes the right to privacy.

**Facts:** The police had been permitted to carry on surveillance activities to keep a check on rowdies. One day a police officer tried to enter with force the house of an aged couple and forced them to open their treasury, without sufficient cause to suspect them of wrong. Can it be stated that their basic right to life has been infringed upon?

(*a*) No, since the police had full authorisation to carry out surveillance activities.

(*b*) No, since the object of the police was only to check and not to take anything away from the couple or to harm them.

(*c*) Yes, since the surveillance activities infringed upon the right of privacy of the couple.

(*d*) Both a and b are true.

**173. Principle:** Every agreement in restraint of the marriage of any person, other than a minor, is void.

**Explanation:** The restraint may be partial, that is a person is forbidden to marry within a specified period or absolute that is a person is forbidden to marry at all.

**Facts**: Ritu and Anju enter into an agreement that Anju's daughter will marry Ritu's son and in case she fails to marry Ritu's son Anju will pay Ritu, Rs. 10000. Can such an agreement be enforced?

(*a*) No, the agreement cannot be enforced since it does not create a restriction on marriage for anyone.

(*b*) Yes, the agreement can be enforced since it does not create a restraint on marriage, but merely places a condition before Anju.

(*c*) Yes, it can be enforced since it is a friendly agreement between friends.

(*d*) None of the above statements are correct.

**(Instructions: Question 174 and 175 has common set of principles and facts. Apply the specified principles to the set of facts and answer the questions.)**

**Principle 1:** Unintentionally causing the death of any person by doing any rash or negligent act is a punishable offence.

**Principle 2:** Criminal negligence is gross and culpable neglect or failure to exercise reasonable and proper care that one is duty bound to take to guard against injury to one and all.

**Principle 3:** Criminal rashness is doing an act with the knowledge of the consequences or indifference as to the consequences.

**174. Facts**: P was driving a SUV. Suddenly a pedestrian came in front of his car. P was unable to stop the car in time and the car collided with the pedestrian breaking his leg who had to spend three months in the hospital to totally recover. What among the following options is the most appropriate situation that captures P's liability based on the principles given below?

(*a*) P is not guilty under principle 1 for the pedestrian suddenly came in front of the car leaving P very little time to respond and control the vehicle.

(*b*) P is guilty of criminal rashness as he was driving very fast which is evident from the fact that car collided with the pedestrian.

(*c*) P is guilty of criminal negligence as he ought to make sure that his brakes are working property and it is evident from the fact of collision that they were not.

(*d*) All of the above are correct.

**175. Facts**: H was a registered Homeopath. A patient P came to him who was showing general symptoms of headache, high temperature and shivering. H started treating P for viral fever and prescribed allopathic medicine. H did not order any pathological tests. P's condition deteriorated after a few days at which time P prescribed medicine for typhoid fever. P's condition further deteriorated and he was thereafter shifted to the Government Medical Hospital where he died after three days. P's son approaches a criminal court for justice. What would you decide in this case?

(*a*) H is guilty of criminal rashness as he prescribed medicine from an area of medicine that he does not practice.

(*b*) H is guilty of criminal negligence as he prescribed medicine from an area of medicine that he is not authorized to practice.

(*c*) H is not guilty as he is a doctor and his first duty is to help the patient by using all means possible.

(*d*) H must be held guilty of murder.

**176. Principle**: Criminal negligence is gross and culpable neglect or failure to exercise reasonable and proper care that one is duty bound to take to guard against injury to one and all. Unintentionally causing the death of any person by doing a criminally negligent act is a punishable offence.

**Facts**: X was admitted into a hospital in a critical state with respiratory problems. He was stabilized by the doctors and put under observation. One day X complained of difficulty in breathing. D was doctor in charge who immediately rushed to X's bed. D assessed that an oxygen cylinder was immediately required. The only oxygen cylinder in the hospital was not working as it was found empty. Another cylinder was immediately ordered. But it took 15 minutes for the cylinder to get there. Meanwhile X died of respiratory complications. Relatives of X filed a case of criminal negligence against D in a criminal court. Can D be held guilty?

(*a*) Yes he can as he failed to observe the duties of a doctor by failing to ensure that a working oxygen cylinder was in the hospital.

(*b*) Yes he can as he failed to assess the situation and acted too late.

(*c*) No he cannot be as the non availability of the oxygen cylinder is not a case of a doctor acting negligently or incompetently, the duty to provide oxygen cylinder rest with the hospital authority.

(*d*) No he cannot as the non availability of the oxygen cylinder is not the doctor's fault rather it is fault of hospital management.

**177. Principle:** In order to convert a proposal into a promise, the acceptance must be absolute and unqualified. To make an agreement valid there has to be consensus ad idem, meaning same thing in the same sense.

**Explanation**: Three components of offer and acceptance are certainty, communication and commitment.

**Facts**: A offered to sell B his black horse for 10000 rupees and wrote a letter to him to this effect. B offered to purchase the black horse for 8000 rupees and wrote a reply to A. A did not reply back but sought to enforce the contract. Has a valid contract been entered into between A and B?

(*a*) Yes, A has made an offer to sell his horse and B has accepted the same.

(*b*) Yes, since A has not replied back to B so it is assumed that he has accepted the new terms.

(*c*) No, as there is no meeting of minds between the parties.

(*d*) None of the above statements is correct.

**178. Principle**: No liability of the accused can arise in a situation of grave and sudden provocation.

**Explanation**: The test of grave and sudden provocation arises when a reasonable man belonging to the same class of society as the accused, placed in the situation in which the accused was placed would be so provoked as to lose his self control.

**Facts**: Seema threatened to leave Guru her husband and in a fit took off her mangalsutra and threw it at his face. He became furious and in a fit of rage he shot her in the stomach. Can Guru claim the exception of grave and sudden provocation?

(*a*) No, because Guru has shot his wife and thus committed the act of murder.

(*b*) Yes, because Guru loved his wife very much to actually kill her.

(*c*) Yes, because Guru has reacted in a sudden rage, thus the defence of grave and sudden provocation would be available to him.

(*d*) Can't say, the information is inadequate.

**179. Principle:** Unlawful agreements are void.

**Explanation**: Seeking to avert the processes of law by conniving is an unlawful act, unless supported by grave and immediate necessity.

**Facts**: The estate of A was sold for arrears of revenue under the provisions of an Act of the legislature according to which the defaulter would be prohibited from purchasing the estate. B, upon entering into an understanding with A, purchases the property and agrees to convey the estate to A upon receiving from him, the price which B had agreed to pay. Is such an agreement valid?

(*a*) A has purchased the estate from B, which is not prevented by law, and also A was in grave and immediate necessity of the estate.

(*b*) A is a defaulter and is prevented from purchasing his own estate.

(*c*) A has entered into a contract with B, the object of which is contrary to law and thus the agreement is void.

(*d*) B has only done a favour for A and as such the agreement should not be rendered void.

**180. Principle:** A person abets the doing of a thing, who (1) Instigates any person to do that thing; or (2) Engages with one or more other person or persons in any conspiracy for the doing of that thing, if an act or illegal omission takes place in pursuance of that conspiracy, and in order to the doing of that thing.

**Explanation**: A person who, by willful misrepresentation, or by willful concealment of a material fact which he is bound to disclose, voluntarily causes or procures, or attempts to cause or procure, a thing to be done, is said to instigate the doing of that thing.

**Facts**: Gangu concerts with Ramu for a plan to poison Rajeesh. It was agreed that Gangu would administer the poison. Ramu then explains to Manju the entire plan without mentioning the fact that a third person is administering the poison. Manju procures and delivers the poison to Ramu for the purpose of it being used in the explained manner. Would Manju be held liable for abetment of the crime?

(*a*) Manju is not liable since he had merely delivered the poison without actually participating in the commission of the crime.

(*b*) Intention on the part of Manju cannot be made out, thus he will not be held liable.

(*c*) Manju is not liable since he has acted without knowing the complete facts of the case, thus knowledge of the crime cannot be attributed to him.

(*d*) Manju is liable since he has actively engaged in the conspiracy in pursuance of which the death of Rajeesh has taken place.

**181. Principle**: When a party to a contract has refused to perform, or disabled himself from performing, his promise in its entirety, the promisee may put an end to the contract, unless he has signified, by words or conduct, his acquiescence in its continuance.

**Explanation**: When a party who is supposed to perform a contract disables himself from doing so, the other party may exercise discretion in actually putting an end to such a contract

**Facts**: A who is a singer, willingly enters into a contract with B, who was the Manager of Dreams for All Theatre, to sing at his theatre for two nights in every week for 3 months and it was agreed that she would be paid ₹ 100 per night for the performance. On the 8th night, A willfully absented herself and she did not inform the reason for her sudden absence. However, on the 9th night A returns and sings with the consent of B. B thereafter seeks to avoid the contract. Can he do so?

(*a*) B can do so, since A has willfully absented herself from the show.

(*b*) Since A has disabled herself from performing the contract, B can choose to avoid it.

(*c*) B cannot avoid the contract since he has signified his acquiescence by allowing A to perform on the 9th night.

(*d*) None of the above statements are true.

**(Instructions: Question 182 to 184 has common set of principles and facts. Apply the specified principles to the set of facts and answer the questions.)**

**Principle 1:** Anyone who dishonestly misappropriates or converts to his own use any moveable property is said to have committed the offence of 'dishonest misappropriation'.

**Principle 2:** Anyone who intending to take dishonestly any moveable property out of the possession of any person without that person's consent, moves that property in order to such taking is said to have committed the offence of 'theft'.

**182. Facts**: A and B were good friends. They decided to purchase identical sets of the recently launched mobile phones. One day A and B were hanging out at B's house. A decided to leave as it was getting late, got up and went to the coffee table, picked up his phone and left. When he reached his house he realized that he had his own phone in his left pocket already and has mistakenly taken B's phone. Sensing an opportunity to make a quick buck, he removed the sim card and sold the phone. When B realized this he filed a criminal complaint against A for theft and dishonest misappropriation of property. You are the judge. What will you decide as per the principles provided above?

(*a*) A is guilty of theft alone as he intentionally took B's phone.

(*b*) A is guilty of dishonest misappropriation alone as he sold B's phone for his own benefit.

(*c*) A is guilty of both theft and dishonest misappropriation as he intentionally took the phone and dishonestly sold the phone for his own benefit.

(*d*) A is not guilty of anything.

**183. Facts**: X and Y were good friends. X had a huge collection of DVDs. One day when he was showing his collection to Y he told Y that he had full authorization to take whichever DVD he wanted, view it and return it provided he took good care of the same. Accordingly one day Y came and took a DVD in X's absence and did not return it for a period of 15 days. Realizing one of his DVDs is missing he filed a criminal complaint with the police. The police investigated and recovered the DVD from Y's house. They arrested Y and took him to a criminal court on charges of theft and criminal misappropriation of property. Decide on the basis of principles given above?

(*a*) Y is not guilty of anything.

(*b*) Y is guilty of criminal misappropriation alone as he was not authorized to keep the DVD for such a long period of time with him.

(*c*) Y is guilty of theft alone as though he was authorized to take the DVD he was not authorized to do so on his own and should have sought X's permission first.

(*d*) Y is guilty of both as he took the DVD without permission of X and retained it for 15 days.

**184. Facts**: X and Y were good friends. X had a huge collection of DVDs. One day when he was showing his collection to Y he told Y that he had full authorization to take whichever DVD he wanted, view it and return it provided he took good care of the same. Accordingly one day Y came and took a DVD in X's absence and did not return it for a period of 15 days. It turns out that X had further rented the DVD out to his friend P with full intention of giving the DVD back to X as soon as P returns it. X filed a criminal complaint with the police. The police investigated and recovered the DVD from P's house. They arrested Y and P took them to a criminal court on charges of theft and criminal misappropriation of property. Decide on the basis of principle 1 given above?

(*a*) Y is not guilty of dishonest misappropriation as he had every intention to return the DVD to X.

(*b*) Y and P are both guilty of dishonest misappropriation as they are both complicit in commission of this offence.

(*c*) Y and P are not guilty of anything as they P took the DVD out on rent and Y had the full authorization to use the DVD in any way he wanted.

(*d*) Y alone is guilty of dishonest misappropriation as he used X's DVD for personal benefit.

**185. Principle 1**: Free Consent is a necessary element to enter into a contract. Without it the contract would be rendered invalid. Two or more persons are said to consent when they agree upon the same thing in the same sense.

**Principle 2**: Amount of compensation paid should be real and illusory.

**Explanation**: Consent is said to be free when it is not caused by Undue Influence. A contract is said to be induced by undue influence where the relations subsisting between the parties are such that one of the parties is in a position to dominate the will of the other and uses that position to obtain an unfair advantage over the other.

**Facts**: Anand was enfeebled by old age and disease, and was influenced by his medical attendant to pay him an unreasonably large sum of money for the services offered by him. Can such an agreement be held to be valid?

(*a*) Yes, the agreement can be enforced since Anand has consented to signing the agreement.

(*b*) Yes, the agreement can be enforced since the medical attendant is providing the necessary services to Anand.

(*c*) No, the agreement cannot be enforced since the medical attendant has used exercised undue influence on Anand, who is dependent on him to get him to sign the agreement.

(*d*) None of the above statements is correct.

**186. Principle:** Even if no damage occurs, if a legal right is violated, compensation must be awarded.

**Explanation:** Legal rights include all rights which are available to a person under the legal system.

**Facts:** A member of the legislative assembly was proceeding to participate in a vote on a legislative proposal. While he was going, he was apprehended by the police, and taken in custody for interrogation. Due to this, he could not cast his vote in the assembly. The legislation however passed through the legislature with a resounding majority which the member aggrieved supported. He filed a suit against the state for damages. Will the member get any damages?

(*a*) No, because no damage occurred to his objective.

(*b*) Yes, because his right to vote was infringed

(*c*) No, because he was apprehended by the law enforcing authorities.

(*d*) Yes, because the members reputation was damaged due to the arrest.

**(Instructions: Question 187 and 188 has common set of principles and facts. Apply the specified principles to the set of facts and answer the questions.)**

**Principle 1:** Every person is entitled to the freedom of speech and expression.

**Principle 2:** The State is authorized to impose taxes on commercial and business activities.

**Principle 3:** The State shall not deny to any person equality before the law or the equal protection of the laws. The State however may create reasonable classifications for purposes of creation of law.

**187. Facts**: X was a cable television operator. He used to transmit several television channels that included educational and news channels as well as religious and entertainment channels. The State imposed a tax on the services provided by all cable television operators. X challenged this imposition on the grounds that the tax imposed is a violation of the freedom of speech and expression to which he is fully entitled. What would be fate of this tax based on the first two principles given above?

(a) The tax violates the freedom of speech and expression as it restricts the extent to which views can be transmitted on cable television.

(b) The tax violates the freedom of speech and expression as it restricts the number of people who can have access to cable television.

(c) The tax does not violate the freedom as no freedom is absolute and every freedom is subject to reasonable restrictions.

(d) The tax does not violate the freedom as cable television operation is a commercial and business activity on which the State is authorized to impose taxes.

**188. Facts**: X was a cable television operator in state of Punjab. He used to transmit several television channels that included educational and news channels as well as religious and entertainment channels. Government of India imposed a tax on the services provided by all cable television operators in state of Punjab alone. X challenged this imposition on the grounds that the tax imposed is a violation of the freedom of speech and expression and right to equality to which he is fully entitled. What would be fate of this tax based on the principle 1 and 3 given above?

(a) X will fail because the State has the full authority to impose taxes on commercial and business activities.

(b) X will fail because the State has the full authority to impose tax based on a reasonable classification.

(c) X will succeed because the State while has the authority to impose tax is not authorized to do so in an arbitrary manner.

(d) X will succeed because the tax has been imposed only on state of Punjab thus creating a class of people who have to pay such tax while there is no reason given to create such a class.

**189. Principle**: The communication of proposals the acceptance of proposals, and the revocation of proposals and acceptances, respectively, are deemed to be made by any act or omission of the party proposing, accepting or revoking by which he intends to communicate such proposal acceptance or revocation, or which has the effect of communicating it.

**Explanation**: The, communication of a proposal is complete when it comes to the knowledge of the person to whom it is made. The communication of an acceptance is complete, as against the proposer, when it is put in a course of transmission to him, so as to be out of the power of the acceptor; as against the acceptor, when it comes to the, knowledge, of the proposer.

**Facts**: A proposes by a letter to sell a house to B for a certain amount. In accordance with the principle stated below, when is the communication of the proposal complete?

(a) When the letter is typed by A.

(b) When the letter is stamped and posted to B.

(c) When the intention to sell the house for a certain amount to B arises in the mind of A.

(d) When the letter is received by B.

**(Instructions: Question 190 and 191 has common set of principles and facts. Apply the specified principles to the set of facts and answer the questions.)**

**Principle**: Subject to public order, every religious denomination or any section thereof shall have the right to manage its own affairs in matters of religion. Provided that, the State can make any law providing for social welfare and reform by throwing open religious institutions of a public character to all classes and sections.

**Facts**: R was the majority religion in State X. R had two castes A and B, A being the pure caste and B being the impure caste. As per the tenets of R religion only A's were allowed to perform the religious rituals and functions. B's were not allowed to perform any rituals and they were not even allowed to attend such functions. Though they were allowed to stand outside the temples and listen to the religious chanting. State X passed the Temple Act that provided that Bs have the right to go inside the temple and perform religious rituals. The validity of this law was challenged on the grounds of being in violation of the principles given above. Examine the validity of this law as per the questions given below.

**190.** Is the provision of the Temple Act that provides Bs a right to enter into the temples in violation of the principles?

(a) The Act shall be struck down as it violates the right of to manage their one's own affairs in matters of religion.

(b) No it is not as it is only a piece of social welfare legislation.

(c) The Act may or may not be okay but it is an unnecessary consideration as the Temple Act is not applicable to the temples in question

(d) The Act must be struck down as excessively interfering.

191. Is the provision of the Temple Act that provides Bs a right to perform religious rituals in the temples in violation of the principles?

(*a*) Yes it is as performance of religious rituals by a certain caste of people in a religion can be said to be an essential tenet of the religion.

(*b*) Yes it is as only A's have the right to perform religious rituals as per religion R.

(*c*) No it is not as only body can perform a religious ritual.

(*d*) No it is not as Bs must be allowed to perform religious rituals.

**(Instructions: Question 192 and 194 has common set of principles and facts. Apply the specified principles to the set of facts and answer the questions.)**

**Principle 1:** No person can be convicted for a wrong/tort which happened in the natural course of events, happened suddenly and without any warning or indication and no prudent person could predict it in the natural course of events.

**Principle 2:** An aggrieved party in such a case can claim compensation from the defendant/accused party, if he/she was well aware of the forth coming of the incident and was lax and negligent in acting properly.

**Facts:** The city of Mallapuram in Tamil Nadu lying along the picturesque Bay of Bengal is suddenly struck by a devastating tsunami. The high tides result in the collapse of Iyer Apartments, situated along the beach killing many residents. The remaining survivors file a case against Iyer builders, the constructors of the building claiming compensation.

192. Will they succeed?

(*a*) Yes, because they were living in the building which was constructed by Iyer Builders so the builders owed them a duty of care;

(*b*) Yes, because the collapse of the building clearly proves that inferior quality of construction material was used in the construction purpose;

(*c*) No, because the apartment collapsed as a result of the tsunami, which is a natural calamity and whose arrival or windfall cannot be predicted by anyone.

(*d*) No, because the inhabitants should have immediately moved out once the tsunami had struck. They were per se negligent.

193. Suppose, the Government of India was very well aware of the approaching tsunami as its satellites had caught the occurrence of the tsunami, but the Govt. had just 10 minutes to warn the citizens. In this case, can the survivors sue the Govt. of India?

(*a*) Yes, because the Government was lax in protecting the lives of its citizens.

(*b*) No, because 10 minutes is too less a time to do anything and the Government was totally helpless because of the paucity of time;

(*c*) Yes, because the Government of India should have used better satellites which could have tracked the tsunamimuch earlier;

(*d*) They should rather sue the apartment builders for compensation.

194. Suppose, the residents of Iyer society were warned about the approaching tsunami 3 hours before by the Government of Tamil Nadu and were asked to move to safer places, but the residents did not pay any heed and refused to move out. Who would be responsible for damages in the instant case?

(*a*) The Government of Tamil Nadu;

(*b*) The residents of the society

(*c*) Both (*a*) and (*b*).

(*d*) None

**(Instructions: Question 195 to 197 has common set of principles and facts. Apply the specified principles to the set of facts and answer the questions.)**

**Principle 1:** A person has every right to defend his/her property from encroachers or trespassers, provided that his actions are not excessive or dangerous to the lives and safety of others.

**Principle 2:** A sovereign body or Government installations carrying out the task of guarding the safety and security of the country/officials/agencies can take any measure to prevent encroachment or trespass into their property, provided they do it within the prescribed vicinity or boundary.

**Facts:** The Nuclear Power Corporation of India built a huge nuclear power plant in Kaiga, Karnataka. This nuclear plant was then taken over by Indian Army, which was responsible for its safety and security of the nuclear plant. The plant is considered as a high security zone and fool-proof measures are put in place for its security. The outer walls of the compound of the plant are barbed and electric fences had been put up, with adequate sign boards in English and Kannada to warn people about the electric fences. Raju a 5 year old boy, whose family were traditional shepherds, came into the contact with the live wires one day, while trying to fetch is cricket ball, while playing near the walls of the plant.

**195.** Can Raju's parents sue the Indian army?

(*a*) Yes, because the army officers should not have used live wires to protect the plant;

(*b*) No, because the Army had done with electrification work with the sole aim of protecting the nuclear plant and it was carrying out its sovereign functions.

(*c*) No, because they should not have allowed Raju to play so closely to the nuclear plant;

(*d*) Yes, because they had lost their son, and therefore the Army should pay them compensation.

**196.** Suppose, Raju was gunned down by one of the sentries of the watch tower, who mistook Raju for a child suicide bomber. Can Raju's parents still sue the Indian Army?

(*a*) No, because a civilian has not right to bring a case against the Indian army and the local courts do not have power to try army officials;

(*b*) Yes, because the sentry should have first verified the antecedents of Raju before shooting him;

(*c*) Yes, because the purported action took place outside the vicinity of the plant.

(*d*) No, because the Indian Army had every right to protect vital national installations and carrying out its sovereign functions.

**197.** Suppose, the Indian Army decided to set up secret booby traps in an area of 500 meters adjoining the nuclear plant to trap and arrest possible encroachers. Is this action legal and justified?

(*a*) No, because the booby traps were being set up beyond the territory of the power plant;

(*b*) No, because setting up booby traps may hurt innocent civilians;

(*c*) Yes, because they were doing this while discharging their sovereign functions;

(*d*) Yes, because the Indian Army is not accountable for its actions in any court of law;

**(Instructions: Question 198 to 200 has common set of principles and facts. Apply the specified principles to the set of facts and answer the questions.)**

**Principle:** No person shall be liable to be compensated for a wrong, in which he had voluntarily taken part.

**Facts:** Ruben de La Red, a promising footballer playing with Spanish football club Real Madrid was diagnosed with a serious heart ailment. The hospital authorities asked him to quit soccer for a year and undergo medication. He did not report about his condition to his club fearing that he would be removed from the club. In the next subsequent match, De la Red while playing suffered serious pain and collapsed. He filed a case for compensation against Real Madrid.

**198.** Will he succeed in his claims?

(*a*) Yes, because he was a contracted footballer of Real Madrid, and the club must take care of him;

(*b*) No, because he had voluntarily accepted the danger, by playing even though he knew about his health condition very well;

(*c*) Yes, because Real Madrid should have conducted their own medical tests on every player and ensured their medical fitness;

(*d*) No, because he is not an employee of Real Madrid, but only a football player playing for them.

**199.** Suppose, the test was carried out by doctors of Real Madrid and they did not disclose this fact to Ruben de la Red. Who would be held liable in that case?

(*a*) The club would be held liable as Ruben de la red was their footballer;

(*b*) Ruben de la red would be held liable as he should have himself undergone periodic medical tests to ascertain his fitness;

(*c*) The club would be liable because they had hidden this medical fact from Ruben de la red and had thus brought the danger on him;

(*d*) Partly the club and Ruben would share the onus and liability.

**200.** Suppose, Jose Mourinho, the coach of Real Madrid threatens Ruben de la Red that if he did not play the next match against Barcelona, their arch rivals, he would immediately suspend the player and stop all his salary and benefits. Ruben de la red had to play in the mach and he died because of a heart stroke. Can his family sue Real Madrid?

(*a*) Yes, because Ruben was forced to play because of the coercion and threat of Jose Mourinho and he did not voluntarily consent to the danger;

(*b*) Yes, because they were dependent upon Ruben for their survival and now Real Madrid must take care of them;

(*c*) No, because Ruben should have flatly refused to play in the match, come what may;

(*d*) No, because such incidents are a part of the game and Ruben very well knew about the hazards.

## ANSWERS

| | | | | | | | | | |
|---|---|---|---|---|---|---|---|---|---|
| **1.** (*a*) | **2.** (*d*) | **3.** (*d*) | **4.** (*d*) | **5.** (*d*) | **6.** (*a*) | **7.** (*c*) | **8.** (*a*) | **9.** (*d*) | **10.** (*b*) |
| **11.** (*c*) | **12.** (*b*) | **13.** (*a*) | **14.** (*b*) | **15.** (*b*) | **16.** (*b*) | **17.** (*a*) | **18.** (*c*) | **19.** (*b*) | **20.** (*b*) |
| **21.** (*b*) | **22.** (*d*) | **23.** (*d*) | **24.** (*c*) | **25.** (*b*) | **26.** (*a*) | **27.** (*c*) | **28.** (*a*) | **29.** (*d*) | **30.** (*b*) |
| **31.** (*d*) | **32.** (*d*) | **33.** (*a*) | **34.** (*d*) | **35.** (*c*) | **36.** (*d*) | **37.** (*c*) | **38.** (*d*) | **39.** (*b*) | **40.** (*d*) |
| **41.** (*d*) | **42.** (*a*) | **43.** (*a*) | **44.** (*c*) | **45.** (*b*) | **46.** (*b*) | **47.** (*c*) | **48.** (*b*) | **49.** (*b*) | **50.** (*a*) |
| **51.** (*c*) | **52.** (*c*) | **53.** (*b*) | **54.** (*c*) | **55.** (*b*) | **56.** (*c*) | **57.** (*c*) | **57.** (*a*) | **59.** (*d*) | **60.** (*a*) |
| **61.** (*b*) | **62.** (*b*) | **63.** (*b*) | **64.** (*a*) | **65.** (*a*) | **66.** (*a*) | **67.** (*a*) | **68.** (*a*) | **69.** (*c*) | **70.** (*c*) |
| **71.** (*b*) | **72.** (*a*) | **73.** (*d*) | **74.** (*c*) | **75.** (*c*) | **76.** (*b*) | **77.** (*a*) | **78.** (*a*) | **79.** (*c*) | **80.** (*a*) |
| **81.** (*b*) | **82.** (*b*) | **83.** (*b*) | **84.** (*a*) | **85.** (*a*) | **86.** (*b*) | **87.** (*b*) | **88.** (*c*) | **89.** (*c*) | **90.** (*a*) |
| **91.** (*a*) | **92.** (*d*) | **93.** (*c*) | **94.** (*c*) | **95.** (*c*) | **96.** (*d*) | **97.** (*d*) | **98.** (*a*) | **99.** (*b*) | **100.** (*) |
| **101.** (*) | **102.** (*b*) | **103.** (*b*) | **104.** (*a*) | **105.** (*d*) | **106.** (*c*) | **107.** (*b*) | **108.** (*d*) | **109.** (*c*) | **110.** (*b*) |
| **111.** (*c*) | **112.** (*a*) | **113.** (*a*) | **114.** (*b*) | **115.** (*d*) | **116.** (*c*) | **117.** (*b*) | **118.** (*c*) | **119.** (*a*) | **120.** (*d*) |
| **121.** (*d*) | **122.** (*d*) | **123.** (*b*) | **124.** (*d*) | **125.** (*a*) | **126.** (*a*) | **127.** (*d*) | **128.** (*b*) | **129.** (*c*) | **130.** (*c*) |
| **131.** (*c*) | **132.** (*b*) | **133.** (*b*) | **134.** (*d*) | **135.** (*d*) | **136.** (*c*) | **137.** (*c*) | **138.** (*d*) | **139.** (*d*) | **140.** (*d*) |
| **141.** (*d*) | **142.** (*c*) | **143.** (*d*) | **144.** (*b*) | **145.** (*c*) | **146.** (*d*) | **147.** (*c*) | **148.** (*b*) | **149.** (*b*) | **150.** (*c*) |
| **151.** (*c*) | **152.** (*b*) | **153.** (*a*) | **154.** (*b*) | **155.** (*b*) | **156.** (*b*) | **157.** (*a*) | **158.** (*b*) | **159.** (*c*) | **160.** (*b*) |
| **161.** (*a*) | **162.** (*d*) | **163.** (*a*) | **164.** (*a*) | **165.** (*d*) | **166.** (*c*) | **167.** (*a*) | **168.** (*c*) | **169.** (*b*) | **170.** (*a*) |
| **171.** (*b*) | **172.** (*c*) | **173.** (*b*) | **174.** (*a*) | **175.** (*b*) | **176.** (*c*) | **177.** (*c*) | **178.** (*c*) | **179.** (*c*) | **180.** (*d*) |
| **181.** (*c*) | **182.** (*b*) | **183.** (*b*) | **184.** (*d*) | **185.** (*c*) | **186.** (*b*) | **187.** (*d*) | **188.** (*d*) | **189.** (*d*) | **190.** (*b*) |
| **191.** (*d*) | **192.** (*c*) | **193.** (*b*) | **194.** (*d*) | **195.** (*b*) | **196.** (*c*) | **197.** (*a*) | **198.** (*b*) | **199.** (*c*) | **200.** (*a*) |

## EXPLANATIONS

**1.** The passage is primarily concerned with telling us about article 32. It does talk about the Supreme Court and Fundamental Rights, but the primary emphasis is on article 32. Hence, option (*a*) is the correct choice.

**2.** Refer to the following line in para 2, "Moreover, only the questions pertaining to the Fundamental Rights can be determined in proceedings against Article 32". Hence, option (*d*) is incorrect. All other options can be deduced from the passage.

**3.** A and B are mentioned in the passage. It is mentioned that article 32 refers to the "Constitutional Remedy" for the enforcement of the Fundamental Rights and is in itself a Fundamental Right. Hence, option (*d*) is correct.

**4.** The author has stated various facts and figures in a factual/objective tone. He neither expresses his opinions nor analyzes the issue. Thus, option (*d*) is the correct choice.

**5.** Violation means a failure to uphold the requirements of law, duty, or obligation. Thus, violation is the correct word.

**6.** Option (*a*) is correct. Option (*b*) has error of parallelism (correct sentence: He likes singing and dancing or He likes to sing and to dance). Option (*c*) has subject-verb agreement error (correct sentence: Either Richa or her friends **are** affected by the new policy). Option (*d*) has error of modifier placement (correct sentence: **Further information** is available on request).

**7.** Preposition 'at' is used with 'party'. When two subjects are connected with 'as well as', the verb follows the number of the first subject. 'It is I.' is the correct sentence. Option (*c*) is grammatically correct.

**8.** In option (*a*), spectacle refers to a sight or view that is very impressive to look at. Thus, option (*a*) is correct. In option (*b*), spectacle has been used incorrectly. 'Spectacles' is the correct word. Plural forms like baggages and furnitures are grammatically incorrect. Furniture and baggage remain the same in their singular and plural constructions.

**9.** Option (*a*) has pronoun antecedent error. The correct sentence would be "I like poems of Tagore who is a good poet." Adjectives of superlative degree are preceded by the definite article 'the'. In case of the modifier 'enough', the modifier follows the adjective. The correct sentence would be "Harpreet is strong enough to play cricket". Option (*d*) is correct.

**10.** In option (*a*), 'besides' need to be replaced by 'beside'. Love is not used in progressive tense. Option (*d*) has dangling modifier error (correct sentence: Standing in a line, we were taken inside the seminar hall by the teacher). Option (*b*) is correct.

**11.** Refer to the lines "Thailand — the Big Daddy of tourism in South Asia — which keeps unleashing newer and newer tourist destinations upon an insatiable world." Thus, option (*c*) is the correct choice.

**12.** Refer to the lines "When it comes to travel, popular imagination can sometimes be as misleading as tourism over-drive. Nothing can be truer than the case of the archipelago of Indonesia which many view as a one-stop destination." "there is more to Indonesia than Bali and that, indeed, there is more to Bali than sun-bleached beaches and a hectic night life." Thus, option (*b*) is the correct choice.

**13.** The tone of the author is descriptive as he is describing tourism in context of Indonesia, Thailand and Bali.

**14.** Not only-but also form a co-ordinating conjunction pair.

**15.** 'Rambunctious' means full of energy in a cheerful and noisy way. Thus, boisterous is its synonym.

**16.** 'Stereotype' refers to a fixed idea or image that many people have of a particular type of person or thing,

**17.** Shoestring means one that uses very little money. Example: The club exists on a shoestring budget.

**18.** With the verb 'seem', infinitive is used instead of gerund. So, option (*b*) and (*d*) are negated. Option (*b*) presents the correct infinitive form. For the second blank, the antecedent of the pronoun is carbon dioxide (singular in number). So, the pronoun 'it' is appropriate.

**19.** We use **a few** and **a little** to mean "not very much" or "not very many". Whether you use **a few** or **a little** depends on what type of noun you are describing. For example, "A few people came to the party." We use **a few** with plural, countable nouns. "There's a little coffee left, if you would like some." We use **a little** with uncountable nouns. We can also use **few** and **little** (without "a") for a more negative meaning. For example, "there's little point in calling" (= there's not much point calling). "Few people understand" (not many people understand), compared to "a few people understand" (some people understand). When we make comparisons, we use **fewer** for plural nouns and **less** for uncountable nouns. For example, "There are fewer people here than last year" or "he drinks less coffee than I do". 'The few' is also correct. It refers to the limited quantity of a thing being referred to. Example: A class has ten students. On a rainy day, three students came to attend the class. The teacher asked the monitor about the number of students. She replied that a few (three) students have come. The teacher wanted to meet the few students. Note: few means negligible or equivalent to zero. Plant has been converted. It is the receiver of action and not the doer. Thus, option (*b*) is the correct choice.

**20.** The infinitive form of verb is appropriate for the first as well as the second blank.

**21.** For the second blank, the word 'latter' which means being the second of two things, people or groups that have just been mentioned, or the last in a list. The second thing mentioned in the sentence is pharmaceutical MNC. Thus, latter which refers to pharmaceutical MNCs is the correct fit for the second blank. In option (*d*), 'because' is incorrect due to absence of the preposition 'of'. 'Through' which means 'by the means of' or 'because of' is the correct choice.

**22.** For the first blank, three words can be used: benefited, saved and spared. Framework means a set of beliefs, ideas or rules that is used as the basis for making judgements, decisions, etc. Resolution means a formal statement of an opinion agreed on by a committee or a council, especially by means of a vote. So, for the second blank, framework is the apt word. Thus, option (*d*) is the best choice.

**23.** The line "By the time the proceedings were over.", suggests the use of past tense. Since the subject 'health care case' is singular in number, "was" is the appropriate word for the first blank.

**24.** The line "In fact, they were the kinds of policy questions that are properly left to Congress and state governments to answer, not the Supreme Court" suggests that the issues were political and not constitutional. So, option (*c*) is the correct choice.

**25.** The line "In fact, they were the kinds of policy questions that are properly left to Congress and state governments to answer, not the Supreme Court" suggests that the issues were political and not constitutional. So, option (*b*) is the correct choice.

**26.** The lines "the question of what should happen with the rest of the 2,700-page statute if the requirement that most Americans obtain health insurance is struck down" suggest that arguments and not pleas or petitions were presented.

**27.** The line "and the entire law reduced to little more than" suggests that the law has been reduced to a bumper sticker.

**28.** The word appendage which means an adjunct to something larger or more important is the correct word for the given blank.

**29.** The line, 'the entire law reduced to little more than an appendage to the mandate' suggests that the law's opponents wanted to 'demolish' the whole thing. Thus, option (*d*) is correct.

**30.** As the subject is quo warranto, the first phrase should describe what it is. So, S should come first. The correct sentence would be "*Quo warranto* (Medieval Latin for "by what warrant?") is a prerogative writ requiring the person to whom it is directed to show what authority they have for exercising some right or power (or "franchise") they claim to hold."

**31.** Q is the best fit for the second blank as it mentions the case when *nihil dicit* is applicable. As judgements can only be issued by a court, P is fit for the third blank. Hence, option (*a*) and (*b*) are negated. S is fit for the fourth blank because it mentions that when one does not plead he admits that an action should be taken against him to punish him. Thus, option (*d*) is the correct choice.

**32.** Only P is fit for the second blank as a preposition is required after the noun 'principles'. (S) and (Q) logically fit for the third and fourth blank respectively. The correct sequence would be "Restitutio in integrum means restoration to original condition. It is one of the primary guiding principles behind the awarding of damages in common law negligence claims. The general rule, as the principle implies, is that the amount of compensation awarded should put the successful plaintiff in the position he or she would have been had the tortious action not been committed."

**33.** Refer to the lines "The extreme reader, to coin a phrase, is a rare bird indeed. ("I have done what people do, my life makes a reasonable showing," Lynne Sharon Schwartz writes. "Can I go back to my books now?") Such people are born, not made, I think; or mostly born and only a little made. They come out of the woodwork when Clay Shirky says that War and Peace isn't interesting to reply that, to the contrary, it's immensely interesting, fascinating, absorbing, and by the way, Mr. Shirky, have you ever tried reading it or are you speaking out of ignorance?—and then back to their books they go." Thus, option (*a*) is the correct choice.

**34.** The passage expresses a teacher's point of view. The tone of the passage is instructive. It is implied that the author is a teacher. The author's main concern is reading habits and not human psychology behind it. Thus, option (*d*) is the correct choice.

**35.** Refer to the lines "Perhaps it isn't anyone's fault...... what long-form reading has been for almost all of its years. Only option (*c*) states the purpose of the author correctly.

**36.** Option (*d*) can be inferred from the lines ""For lovers of books and reading, and especially for those who become teachers, this fact can be painful and frustrating. We love reading, we think it's wonderful, and we want other people to think so, too. "What we have loved,/Others will love," wrote Wordsworth, "and we will teach them how." A noble sentiment! Inspiring! But what if, after great labor, we discover—this often happens—that we can't teach them how? Whose fault is that?"" Options (*a*), (*b*) and (*c*) are factually incorrect.

**37.** Refer to the last paragraph of the passage. Option (*c*) is the correct inference.

**38.** Refer to the lines "The extreme reader, to coin a phrase, is a rare bird indeed. ("I have done what people do, my life makes a reasonable showing," Lynne Sharon Schwartz writes. "Can I go back to my books now?")." These lines suggest that the speaker loves and is keenly interested in reading.

**39.** Refer to the lines ""We love reading, we think it's wonderful, and we want other people to think so, too. "What we have loved,/Others will love," wrote Wordsworth, "and we will teach them how." A noble sentiment! Inspiring! But what if, after great labor, we discover—this often happens—that we can't teach them how? Whose fault is that?"" Thus, option (*b*) is the correct choice.

**40.** Embodiment in the given context refers to something that has been incorporated or included. Thus, option (*d*) is the correct choice.

**41.** Union Goverment has ranked the Sikkim state as the best state in the country in the category of smaller states for its outstanding performance in strengthening and developing the Panchayati Raj institutions in the state.

**42.** India hosted the BRICS(Brazil, Russia, India, China, South Africa) summit for the first time on 29 March 2012. It was the fourth BRICS summit. It was held in Indian capital New Delhi. The summit was participated by Brazil, Russia, India, China and South Africa. The theme of the Summit was BRICS Partnership for Global Stability, Security and Prosperity.

**43.** Rafael Nadal won a record seventh French Open 2012 title after defeating Novak Djokovic.

**44.** The governments of India and Myanmar are working on Kaladan Multi-modal Transit Transport Project that will facilitate trade between the two nations.The project includes the construction of the deepwater Sittwe Port at the mouth of the river, dredging of the Kaladan river to enable cargo vessels to navigate the river from Sittwe to Mizoram.

**45.** Kalesar National Park is a protected area located in eastern Haryana, India, 150 km from Chandigarh. It is a popular destination for bird-watching.

**46.** Leela Samson (born 1951) is a Bharatanatyam dancer, choreographer, instructor and writer. As a soloist she is known for her technical virtuosity and has taught Bharatanatyam at Shriram Bhartiya Kala Kendra in Delhi for many years; presently she is the chairperson of the Central Board of Film Certification (1 April 2011); director of Kalakshetra (April 2005); and chairperson of the Sangeet Natak Akademi (2010– ).

**47.** As uncertainty prevails over the candidature for the July 19 presidential poll, history shows there has been only one President — the late Neelam Sanjiva Reddy — who was elected unopposed in independent India.

**48.** Barack Obama; The Story By David Maraniss. It is a story starting from "what happened" and working backward, constructing a chronological narration from the evidence that is available to them.

**49.** The much awaited and hyped tablet 'Surface' has been manufactured by Microsoft.

**50.** Bandipur National Park is one of India's best known protected areas and is an important Project Tiger reserve. It is located in the Chamarajanagar district of southern Karnataka in South India.

**51.** Top five, largest states of India (Areawise in Sq.Kms) Rajasthan 342,236, Madhya Pradesh 308,144, Maharashtra 307,713, Andhra Pradesh 275,068, Uttar Pradesh 238,566

**52.** Tirupati is a major pilgrimage and Cultural City located in the Chittoor district.It is the largest city in Rayalaseema region. It is located at the foothills of the Eastern Ghats at a distance of 550 kilometres (340 mi) south of Hyderabad, the capital of the state.

**53.** Kanniyakumari in Kerala is the southernmost point of Indian mainland and Indira Point in the Andaman and Nicobar Islands is the southernmost point of India.

**54.** The second largest river flowing through the Indian sub-continent is the river Godavari.

**55.** IST is 5.5 hours ahead of GMT.

**56.** It passes through: Gujarat, Rajasthan, Madhya Pradesh, Chattisgarh, Jharkhand, West Bengal, Tripura and Mizoram.

**57.** Srinagar is the summer capital of the Indian state of Jammu and Kashmir. It is situated in the Kashmir Valley and lies on the banks of the Jhelum River, a tributary of the Indus. The city is famous for its gardens, lakes and houseboats. It is also known for traditional Kashmiri handicrafts and dry fruits.

**58.** Bihu denotes a set of three different cultural festivals of Assam and celebrated by the Assamese diaspora around the world. The most important festivals of Assam are the Bihus, celebrated with fun and abundance by all Assamese people irrespective of caste, creed, religion, faith and belief.

**59.** Rajgir is a city and a notified area in Nalanda district in the Indian state of Bihar. The city of Rajgir was the first capital of the kingdom of Magadha, a state that would eventually evolve into the Mauryan Empire. Its date of origin is unknown, although ceramics dating to about 1000 BC have been found in the city. This area also notable in Buddhism, as one of the favorite places for Gautama Buddha and the well known "Atanatiya" conference was held at Vulture's Peak mountain.

**60.** The Salim Ali Bird Sanctuary is a bird sanctuary located on western tip of the Island of Chorao along the river Mandovi, Goa, in India. The sanctuary is named after Salim Ali, the eminent Indian ornithologist. Away from the beaches of Goa this is truly a paradise for nature lovers and bird watchers where you can see a variety of species of birds and plants.

**61.** This award was recently given to R.S. Murthy, the Chief Conservator of Forests and Field Director, Panna Tiger Reserve and Tana Tapi, Divisional Forest Officer, Pakke Wildlife Sanctuary, Assam. IUCN compiles the Red List of Endangered Species.

**62.** Endosulfan is a pesticide and Gatifloxacin was recently banned in India. Use of Diclofenac on cattle is supposed to be responsible for threat to three species of Vulture in India.

**63.** Justice Ranjana Desai and Justice Gyan Sudha Mishra are two woman judges.

**64.** The proclamation of transfer of capital from Calcutta to Delhi was made on December 12, 1911. $100^{th}$ anniversary of this event was observed recently.

**65.** Also known as .Shahryar' Akhlaq Khan was a Jnanpith awardee who expired recently.

**66.** Gilani, the Prime Minister of Pakistan was charged with contempt of court by the Supreme Court of Pakistan.

**67.** This magazine was launched during the tenure of Ms. Mamta Bannerjee as the Minister of Railways. It will be distributed free of cost in Shatabdi Express, Rajdhani Express and AC coaches of Duronto Express trains.

**68.** This UAV was recently tested by the Aeronautical Defence Estalishment (ADE), a division of the Defence Research & Development Organisation (DRDO).

**69.** Joao Cravinho Ambassador and Head of EU Delegation to India recently gave information about this operation.

**70.** Evans recently won the Tour de France.

**71.** Mistry is the Chairman of Shapoorji Pallonji (SP).

**72.** It is the first railway network to earn carbon credits under the UN-run Clean Development Mechanism (CDM). **Carbon Credit** is tradable certificate or permit representing the right to emit one tonne of carbon dioxide or the mass of another greenhouse gas with a carbon dioxide equivalent ($tCO_2e$) equivalent to one tonne of carbon dioxide.

**73.** It was held at Guru Nanak Stadium, in Ludhiana, for a period of six days from January 19, 2012

**74.** Steve Balmer is the CEO of Microsoft. Tim Cook became the CEO of Apple after the demise of Steve Jobs.

**75.** This book has been co-authored by sports journalist Rohit Brijnath.

**76.** ca-MRSA stands for Community Acquired-Methicillin Resistant Staphylococcus Aureus is a bacterium which is drug resistant to many antibiotics.

**77.** This movie was recently in news in connection with a students' organisation affiliated to a political party stopping its screening.

**79.** This event was recently held in Thiruvananthapuram.

**80.** Sudirman Cup is the world mixed team badminton championship which takes place every two years.. China defeated Denmark to win its fourth consecutive Sudirman Cup.

**81.** A decree to this effect was issued by the King of Saudi Arabia.

**82.** The 11th New York Indian Film Festival was held recently. The mother-daughter duo of Aparna Sen and Konkona Sen won the award for Best Director and Best Actress respectively.

**83.** This palace is situated at Phunaka, the old capital of Bhutan. The King of Bhutan got married at this palace recently. Gross National Happiness is a term coined by the King of Bhutan.

**84.** Solid Storage Surveillance Facility at Tarapur is used to store nuclear waste. Kalpakkam is the site for Indira Gandhi Centre for Atomic Research (IGCAR).

**85.** This spacecraft entered into the orbit of an asteroid called Vesta.

**87.** Ramanujam was a renowned Mathematician.

**90.** Deceased reporter J. Dey (of Mid Day) and Josy Joseph (of Times of India) recently won this award.

**91.** Let the price of an apple and a mango be ₹ a and ₹ m, respectively. Then,

$$7a + 12m = 150 \text{ and } 16a + 6m = 150.$$

On solving, we get, $a = 6$ and $m = 9$.

Hence, price of an apple and two mangoes

$$= 6 + 2 \times 9 = ₹\,24.$$

**92.** Total amount paid for dinner

$$= \text{Food} + \text{Sales tax} + \text{Tip}$$

$$= 240 + \frac{12.5}{100}\times 240 + \frac{10}{100}\times 240$$

$$= 240 + 30 + 24 = ₹\,294.$$

**93.** Let the amounts received by A, B and C be a, b and c, respectively.

It is given that $b = \frac{3a}{4}$ and $c = \frac{b}{2}$

$\Rightarrow \quad 3a = 4b = 8c$

Also, $\quad a + b + c = 918$

$\Rightarrow \quad \frac{8c}{3} + 2c + c = 918$

$\Rightarrow \quad c = 918 \times \frac{3}{17} = ₹\,162.$

**94.** Let the initial cost price of the article be ₹ x. Then, selling price = ₹ 1.19x.

Now, cost price (in ₹) in second case

= 0.9x and selling price (in ₹) = 1.19x – 5

According to the question,

$1.19x - 5 = 1.1 \times 0.9x$

$\Rightarrow \quad (1.19 - 0.99)x = 5$

$\Rightarrow \quad 0.2x = 5$

$\Rightarrow \quad x = 25$

Hence, the initial cost price is ₹ 25.

**95.** Let the price of 1000 gm be ₹ 1,000 when the trader buys. When he purchases 1000 gm, he actually gets 1100 gm.

$\therefore$ His cost price $= \frac{1000}{1100} = ₹\,0.909/\text{gm}$

While selling, he sells 1000 gm but actually he sells only 900 gm.

$\therefore$ His selling price $= \frac{1000}{900} = ₹\,1.111/\text{gm}$

$$\text{His profit \%} = \frac{\text{Selling price} - \text{Cost price}}{\text{Cost price}} \times 100$$

$$= \frac{1.111 - 0.909}{0.909} \times 100$$

$$= \frac{0.202}{0.909} \times 100 \approx 22.22\%.$$

**96.**

12 p.m. 4 p.m. 3 p.m.
A→ ←B
P R Q
u→ ←v

Let 't' be the time taken by A and B to reached their respective destinations after meeting at R at 4 p.m. and let u and v be the speeds of A and B, respectively.

$$PR = 4u = tv \Rightarrow t = \frac{4u}{v} \quad \text{... (i)}$$

$$PQ = 1 \times v = tu \Rightarrow t = \frac{v}{u} \quad \text{... (ii)}$$

From (i) and (ii), we get

$$\frac{4u}{v} = \frac{v}{u} \Rightarrow \left(\frac{u}{v}\right)^2 = \frac{1}{4} \Rightarrow \frac{u}{v} = \frac{1}{2}$$

i.e. 1 : 2.

**97.** Product of two prime numbers can be even number when one of the numbers is 2. Product of two prime numbers can be an odd number when both of the numbers are odd. Product of two prime numbes is always an integer. Product of the two prime numbers can never be a prime number.

**98.** Let the two numbers be a and b.

Then, $(a - b)^2 = 2(a^2 + b^2) - (a + b)^2$

$\Rightarrow (a - b)^2 = 2 \times 85 - 13^2 = 170 - 169 = 1$

$\Rightarrow$ Absolute difference of a and b = 1.

**99.** The sum of the ages of 'n' students after admission of a new student of aged 14 years

$= 12 \times n + 14 = 12.1 \times (n + 1)$

$\Rightarrow \quad 1.9 = 0.1 \times n$

$\Rightarrow \quad n = 19.$

**100.** Sum of the marks of all the 10 students in the class

$= 10 \times a$

$\Rightarrow \quad 10a = 3b + 7c.$

**101.** Average speed $= \dfrac{\text{Total distance travelled}}{\text{Total time taken}}$

$= \dfrac{20 + 16 + 24}{15 + 11 + 10} \times 60$

$= \dfrac{60}{36} \times 60 = 100 \text{ km/hr.}$

**102.**

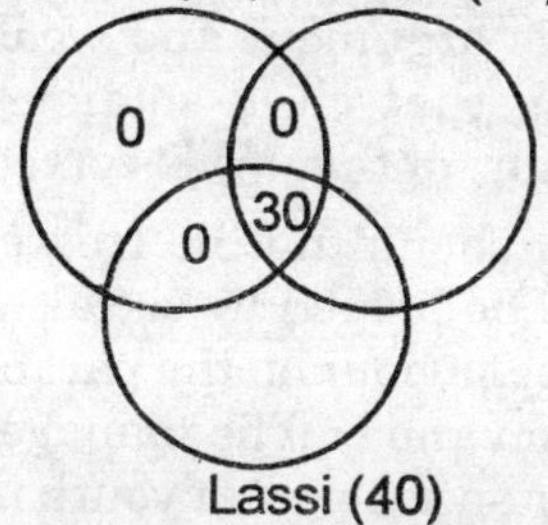


Hence, the maximum number of people who like all the three beverages is 30.

**103.** P(w) = Probability of drawing 2 white balls $= \dfrac{^{10}C_2}{^{24}C_2}$

P(g) = Probability of drawing 2 green balls $= \dfrac{^{6}C_2}{^{24}C_2}$

P(*b*) = Probability of drawing 2 blue balls $= \dfrac{^{8}C_2}{^{24}C_2}$

$\therefore$ P(E) = Probability of drawing 2 balls of the same colour = P(w) + P(g) + P(*b*)

$= \dfrac{^{10}C_2}{^{24}C_2} + \dfrac{^{6}C_2}{^{24}C_2} + \dfrac{^{8}C_2}{^{24}C_2} = \dfrac{45 + 15 + 28}{23 \times 12} = \dfrac{22}{69}.$

**104.** Probability that all the 5 traffic lights will be green

$= 0.2 \times 0.5 \times 0.3 \times 0.9 \times 0.4 = 0.0108.$

**105.** Let the common difference of the A.P. be d.

It is given,

First term = a = 2 and second term = a + d = –2

$\Rightarrow \quad d = (a + d) - a = -2 - 2 = -4$

$\therefore \quad S_n$ = Sum of first n terms

$= \dfrac{n}{2}\{2a + (n-1)d\}$

$= \dfrac{n}{2}\{2 \times 2 + (n-1)(-4)\} = \dfrac{n}{2}[4 - 4(n-1)]$

$= \dfrac{n}{2}(8 - 4n) = 2n(2 - n).$

**106.** Let height and radius of the cone be 3h and 3r respectively.

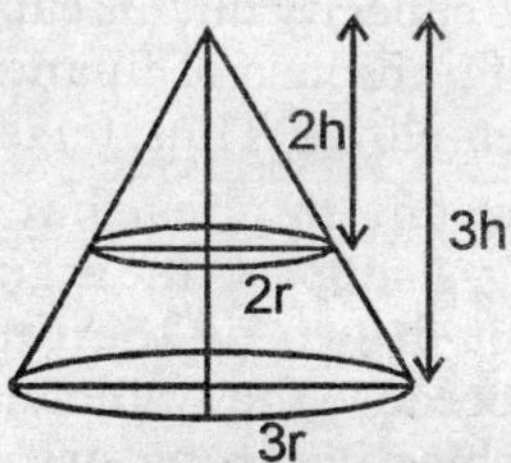


$\because$ Height of upper part : Height of lower part = 2 : 1

Therefore, height and radius of the upper part of the cone will be 2h and 2r respectively.

$\therefore$ Required ratio $= \dfrac{\frac{1}{3}\pi(2r)^2 \times 2h}{\frac{1}{3}\pi(3r)^2 \times 3h - \frac{1}{3}\pi(2r)^2 \times 2h}$

$= \dfrac{2^3}{3^3 - 2^3} = \dfrac{8}{19}$ i.e. 8 : 19.

**107.** Interest $= \dfrac{P \times n \times r}{100}$, (where P = Principal, n = Number of years and r = Rate of interest)

Interest $= \dfrac{350 \times 16 \times 15}{12 \times 100} = ₹\,70$

Total amount Mr. X pays to Tolaram

= Amount + Interest = 350 + 70 = ₹ 420.

**108.** Let half of the same work be completed by x women working 5 hours a day in 5 days. Then,

$x \times 5 \times 5 = \dfrac{10 \times 10 \times 10}{2} \Rightarrow x = 20.$

**109.** Let the percentage of water in initial mixture be x%.

Volume of water in initial mixture = 0.6x liter

Volume of water in new mixture

$= (60 + 25) \times \dfrac{40}{100} = 34$ liter

$\therefore \quad 0.6x + 25 = 34$

$\Rightarrow \quad x = 15\%$

Hence, the percentage of milk in initial mixture

= (100 – 15)% = 85%.

**110.** Let a man do a unit of work in a day.

Total units of work = $20 \times 18 + (20 + 16) \times 5 = 540$

$\therefore$ 20 men will take to complete the whole work

$$= \frac{540}{20} = 27 \text{ days.}$$

Hence, required number of days will be $(27 - 24) = 3$.

**111.** 2 can be inferred from the line "The employer keeps buying units of a person's potential, or not buying it, depending on the money he pays to encourage it." As the productive capacity can be increased or decreased on the basis of financial encouragement, it is not fixed and can vary. 1 cannot be inferred because a case is possible when an employee joined a firm with his highest productive capacity but his capacity declined with time due to absence of financial encouragement from the employer. Thus, (*c*) is the correct choice.

**112.** The argument implies that the ratings were misleading. 1 supports the argument by discussing the benefit drawn by the rating agencies. 2 is incorrect because the system used by the agencies was not objective in nature so the question of making it more objective does not arise.

**113.** 3 underpins the criticism but becomes directionless because of its generic nature. 2 is specific and strengthens the criticism. 1 is a weak argument as it talks about social usefulness whereas the argument focuses on economic issues. Thus, option (*a*) is the correct choice.

**114.** 2 is beyond the scope of the argument. 1 can be inferred from the lines "physical appearance depicts ideal femininity". 3 is an inference that can be drawn from the complete argument. Thus, option b is correct.

**115.** Only 1 strengthens the cause of protest as it is wrong to determine the eligibility of BPL families in 2011 on the basis of 2001 guidelines, when inflation might have occurred.

**116.** It is unclear whether Prashant is supporting or defending Anita's argument or not. Moreover, he neither mentions a flaw in the identity cards nor produces an evidence. So, (*a*) and (*b*) are incorrect. (*d*) is irrelevant. Prashant states a flaw that makes the usefulness of identity cards questionable. Thus, option (*c*) is the most appropriate choice.

**117.** Jimmy's argument specifically deals with senior level jobs whereas Robert talks about the 'lump of labour fallacy' for jobs in general. Thus, option (*b*) is the correct choice.

**118.** Refer to the line "For the deconstructor, the relationship of language to reality is not given, or even reliable." A deconstructor doubts that language is based on reality. Thus, option (*c*) which states that all language systems are unreliable and are based on the culture of the time they were developed supports the view point of the deconstructor.

**119.** 1 is contradictory to the opinion of the deconstructor. 2 supports his opinion.

**120.** The logic, expressed in the argument, behind the practice of investing huge sums on making new films and not on serials is that of demand and supply. Both 1 and 2 suggest reasons to affect the demand and supply. Thus, both of them strengthen the argument.

**121.** None of the given assumptions is implicit in the argument because no comparison between the popularity or goodness of old TV shows and new films has been presented. Thus, (*a*) and (*c*) are beyond the scope of the argument. (*b*) contradicts the spirit of the argument and is thus negated.

**122.** a is incorrect because it lacks the main ingredient 'crimes done by child soldiers during war times'. b is incorrect because Ranjeet does not comment on the issue of age. He raises the issue that child soldiers who commit crimes during wartime are also victims of the same abuse. c becomes vague as it talks about being actually guilty or not whereas the idea is of prosecuting them or not. d captures the point of issue most effectively as it includes the argument of Rajiv to prosecute child soldiers of war time crimes and Ranjeet's idea of such children themselves being victims of the same abuses and deserve help rather than prosecution.

**123.** Rajiv's argument is based on the premise that child soldiers are criminals, so they should be convicted. Ranjeet disapproves his argument and weakens his premise by stating that child soldiers are themselves victims. Thus, option (*b*) is correct.

**124.** Beth states that youth should not be treated as criminals and they can be helped by social work. Judith states that bad behaviour on the part of the youth deserves attention and can be managed by ASBO. If bad behaviour on the part of youth is not managed and kept under control, it can graduate to the level of criminality. Thus, option (*d*) is the correct choice.

**125.** Option (*a*) highlights the specific advantage and positive role of ASBO in context of the argument. Option (*c*) is close but is beyond the scope of the argument.

**126.** Argument I justifies the reason for disapproval. It states that the image and brand value of the college will be affected. Thus, it is a strong argument. Argument II is weak as it deals with a trivial aspect of diluting the competition.

**127.** Deriving "X is desirable" from the premises "If X then Y" and "Y is desirable" is incorrect and fallacious. So, (*a*) is incorrect. (*b*) talks about desirable results and is generic in nature. (*c*) states that it is necessary to avoid watching television to score well whereas the premises only talk of it being a sufficient and not necessary cause.

**128.** A leads to B. B leads to C. C leads to D. Thus, A leads to D. So, option (*b*) is the correct choice.

**129.** The cause is necessary but not sufficient for the effect. So, if the effect has not taken place, the cause may or may not have occurred.

**130.** Abrupt is a synonym of brusque. Similarly, content is a synonym of enraptured.

**131.** Parricide refers to the crime of killing one's father, mother or a close relative. Regicide refers to killing a king, ruler or monarch.

**132.** Theocracy refers to the government of a country by religious leaders or priests. Plutocracy refers to the government of a country by rich people.

**133.** The young one of cat is kitten. Similarly, the young one of deer is fawn.

**134.** Sobriquet, nickname and moniker are synonyms. 'Tirade' refers to an angry speech.

**135.** Besmirch means to damage the opinion that people have of somebody/something. Sully and soil are its synonyms. Sand is the odd word.

**136.**

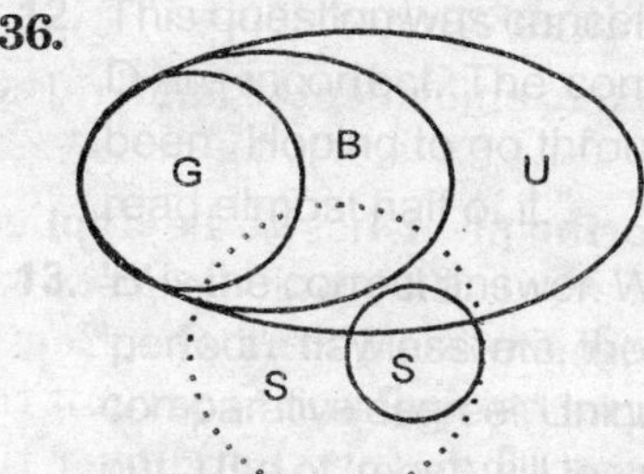


Only III follows.

**137.**

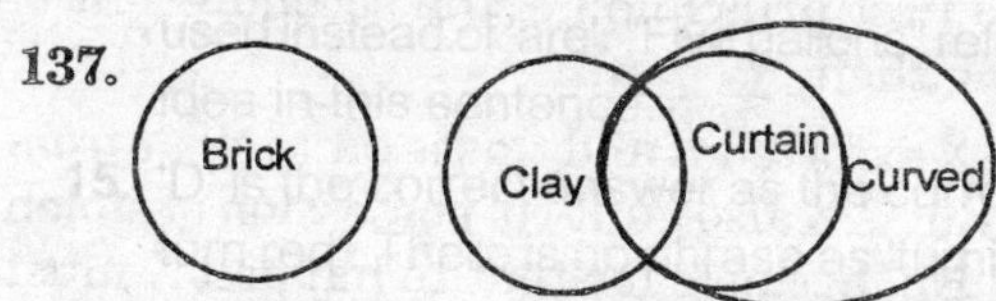


Both II and III follow.

**138.**

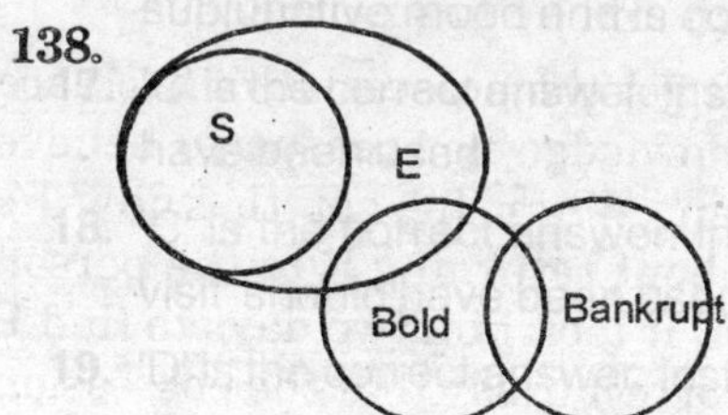


None follows.

**139.**

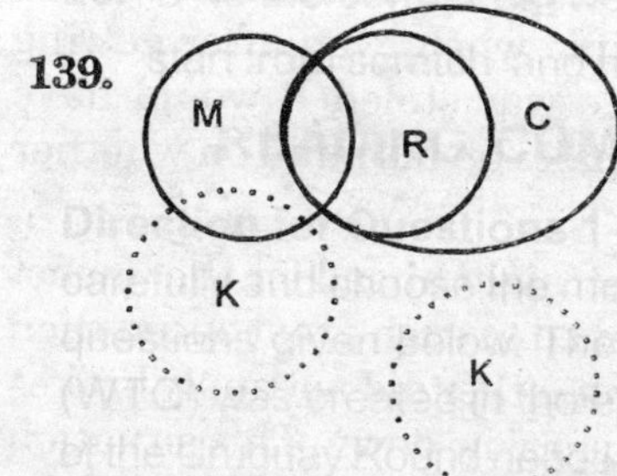


I, II and III follow.

**140.**

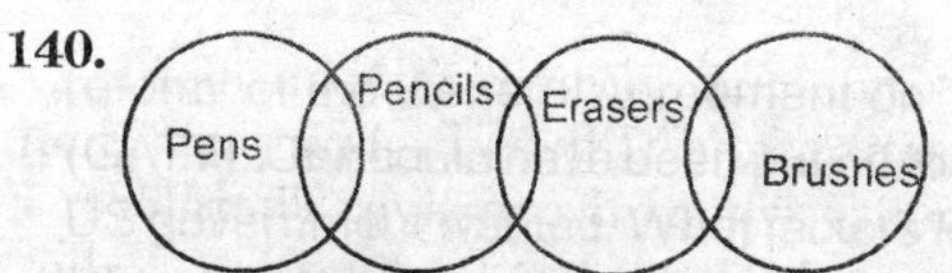


**None of these follow.**

**141.** The series is moving as:

$(7 + 1) \times 0.5 = 4$

$(4 + 1) \times 1.0 = 5$

$(5 + 1) \times 1.5 = 9$

$(9+ 1) \times 2 = 20$

$(20 + 1) \times 2.5 = \underline{\mathbf{52.5}}$.

**142.** The sereis is moving as:

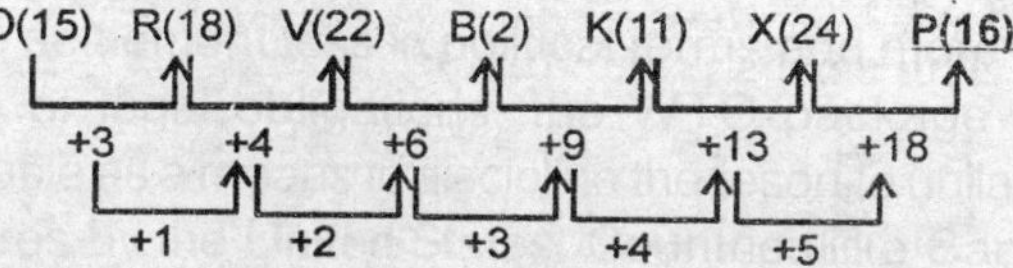


**143.** Mayank is the brother of Vinita and Vinita is the daughter of Suman, therefore, Mayank is the son of Suman. But, gender of Suman is not known. Therefore, Suman can be either mother or father.

Hence, data is inadequate to answer the question.

**144.** Abhishek's father is the brother-in-law of Swati's father.

**145.** Given letters are coded as follow:

| | | |
|---|---|---|
| E → C | | I → B |
| X → Z | | N → J |
| C → T | | E → C |
| A → R | | Q → Z |
| V → E | | U → F |
| A → R | and | A → R |
| T → L | | L → D |
| I → B | | I → B |
| O → U | | T → L |
| N → J | | Y → A |

∴ Coding of EQUIVALENT will be CZFBERDCJL.

**146.** The sereis is moving as:

−3 −3 −3 −3 −3

KJU MIR PKO TIL YMI EJF

+2 +3 +4 +5 +6

−1 +2 −2 +4 −3

**147.**

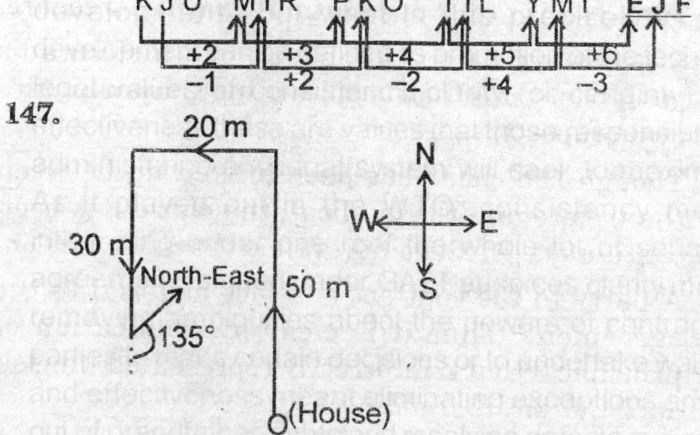


Hence, he was walking in the North-East direction.

**148.** D lives in Banda and if E lives in Asansol, then A lives in Sasaram and C lives in Jaunpur. Then, there is no city where B can live. Therefore, E does not live in Asansol. Then A lives in Gwalior, D lives in Banda, C lives in Jaunpur and B lives in Asansol.

Hence, E lives in Sasaram.

| City | Girl |
|---|---|
| Banda | B |
| Gwalior | A |
| Sesaram | E |
| Jaunpur | C |
| Asansol | B |

**149.** The sereis is moving as:

1 → 4 → 15 → 78 → 549 → <u>4944</u>

1×1+3  4×3+3  15×5+3  78×7+3  549×9+3

**150.** All months are of 30 days starting from June.

Hence, the next month will be June.

**151.** Under principle 3, moving a property out of someone's possession would include an action whereby a property is moved by way of separating it from any other property. Thus when Durjan Singh cuts down the tree in order to take it out of the possession of Sher Singh, the offence of theft was committed.

**152.** The offence of theft was committed at the very moment when Durjan Singh took out the box of treasure in order to hide it at another place. Here it doesn't matter that he hid it in the same garden again because a mere moving of the property with the intention to take it later had constituted theft.

**153.** According to principle 1, the essential element in the offence of theft is to move the property out of one's possession. However, in the present case since the ring was not in anyone's possession, it would not constitute the offence of theft.

**154.** By applying principles 1 & 4, the offence of theft was committed as soon as the bullock began to move, because box of treasure is considered being moved when the bullock carrying the same is moved so as to dishonestly take away the treasure.

**155.** Since watch was taken out of Moolchand's possession , it is theft despite being Durjan Singh's own property.

**156.** Though the chase has been broken up between the frigate and the gunboat, the chase has been continuous. At all points of time the chase was on.

**157.** A party to the contract is a fact material to the agreement. Thus it is clear by application of principle 3 that Z incorrectly represented himself as Y, thereby defrauding X.

**158.** In the given case, X displayed a vintage car on internet and sold a car other than the one agreed to. Thus, it is clear that he intentionally misrepresented the facts material to the agreement, thereby rendering it void by way of fraudulent misrepresentation.

**159.** In the given circumstances both the parties had mistaken each other's identities. Thus because of this bilateral mistake the agreement is void.

**160.** There is likelihood that he will be given the death penalty.

**161.** Shyam has ordered for the services of Golden Brown, it is implied that he was aware of the conditions and he would be liable to pay them.

**162.** They have certainly not committed any rioting as they have not used any force or violence yet. They have also not committed the offence of unlawful assembly as the common purpose of their assembly was to go back to the houses, gather weapons and meet again. None of these purposes is an offence.

**163.** They have clearly committed the offence of unlawful assembly and the purpose of their assembly is to commit an offence.

**164.** Here loss is not caused to enjoyment of land, rather to the business.

**165.** d remember only principle 1 has to be applied. Out of the three legal events that could be described as criminal (first being when P and Q agree to commit a crime; second being P and Q commit the crime; and third being when they hand over the stolen property to R) only one becomes an offence as per the first principle i.e. the second event of committing theft.

**166.** Option (*c*) X extorted R and this is quite clear from the facts. But is X also guilty of possession of stolen property? No, because for that to happen X must either know or have reason to believe that the necklace was stolen and he has neither.

**167.** Option (*a*) When R got the possession of necklace he had neither knowledge nor reason to believe that it was stolen. When he got to know he immediately set about returning it to the person who gave it to him. It took him two days to find P but it would be incorrect to say that the possession of the necklace for those days was the same as laid down in the principle 2. Such a situation might be covered by the principle when even after getting to know that necklace was stolen R would have waited a few days to make up his mind on whether to return it or not.

**168.** The bus was moving straight ahead for the impact to happen. If it happened at such great speed then it means that the driver either did not apply brakes or wasn't in a position to slow down. This situation wouldn't have arisen without the negligence of the driver.

**169.** The principle provides for the right to restrict freedom of speech and expression on the ground of a reasonable tendency of disruption of public order. This basically means that if the State has reasonably believes that a certain action is likely to disrupt public order they are authorized to act to prevent it. Logically, this equation puts public order on a higher pedestal than the freedom of speech and expression. If such is the case then the police was totally justified in arresting X as his actions would have clearly disrupted the peace in society.

**170.** The police had a right to restrict any exercise of freedom of speech and expression that had a reasonable tendency to disrupt public order in question 81. However, here the police have a power to restrict any exercise of the freedom only in order to maintain public order. The ambit in which the police can exercise their power is wider in question 81 and narrower in 82. In this case, the police can take an action only if a certain exercise of the freedom actually disrupts the public order as the necessity to take action warrants itself only when public order is actually being disrupted (hence the power to maintain it). Though in question 81 the power could be exercise if it was reasonably likely that public order would be disrupted while any actual disruption taking place. Thus the right option becomes (*a*) as no such disruption has yet taken place.

Note: Do note that the options and facts in questions 81 and 82 are exactly the same. These two problems are a good case study in understanding that a minor change in a principle can totally alter the conclusion, thus the stress in your LA classes to read the principle very carefully.

**171.** Indrajit is of unsound mind and was thus rendered incapable of understanding the nature of the transaction. He was incapable of forming a rational judgment as to its effect upon his interest.

**172.** The surveillance activities carried out by the police was excessive and this infringing upon their right to privacy.

**173.** Since the agreement does not create a restraint in marriage for Anju and Ritu's daughter and son respectively, it is a valid agreement.

**174.** The fact of collision is being used to infer two things that either the driver was driving rashly or that the driver was negligent in properly maintaining his vehicle (options (*b*) and (*c*) respectively). Both of these inferences are unwarranted. There is no fact to establish either of them in the facts. Though, we do have the fact that the pedestrian 'suddenly' came in front of the car. Though the correct reasoning ought to be that we cannot hold P guilty under principle 1 for there are not facts that warrant such a conclusion, option (*a*) presents us the best reasoning of all and thus is the right option.

**175.** Medical negligence of a criminal nature comprises of an error of the sort that would not have been made by a reasonably competent professional man professing to have standards and type of skill he holds himself out as having. H was not a competent professional to prescribe allopathic medicine and thus he was under a duty not to enter that field of medicine. By prescribing allopathic medicine, without being qualified in that system he committed the offence of criminal negligence.

**176.** Medical negligence of a criminal nature comprises of an error of the sort that would not have been made by a reasonably competent professional man professing to have standards and type of skill he holds himself out as having. In this case, there is no fact to establish that D while discharging his professional duties as a doctor was negligent or incompetent in any way. Absence of a working oxygen cylinder cannot be used to hold D guilty except in a case where we know that D was also the manager of the hospital. There is no such fact present and presence of the same can neither be presumed nor is warranted. The answer therefore is option (*c*).

**177.** Since there is no certainty regarding the terms of the offer such as price and the new offer made by B should be treated as a counter offer. The facts show that there is a lack of meeting of the minds between the parties.

**178.** Yes, because Guru has reacted in a sudden rage, responding to the actions of his wife and thus the defence of grave and sudden provocation would be available to him.

**179.** A has convinced B to buy the estate and sell it to him, thus the object of the agreement is not permitted by law and this agreement would be rendered void.

**180.** Manju has actively participated in the conspiracy in pursuance of the death of Rajeesh, thus he should be held liable.

**181.** B has signified his acquiescence in the continuance of the contract, and cannot now put an end to it.

**182.** A got the possession of the phone under a mistaken belief that it was his phone. Thus there was no dishonest intention when he took the phone. But his intention changed subsequently when he realized that it was not his phone and he sold the same to make a quick buck thus committing the offence of dishonest misappropriation of property.

**183.** Despite the fact that X had fully authorized Y to take any DVD from his collection, Y was never authorized to keep the DVD for such a long time. Thus he is guilty of misappropriation.

**184.** Y did not have authorization to use the DVD that he took in 'any way he wanted'. He only had authorization to 'view it' and return it. Thus the moment he rents the DVD out to P for personal benefit he dishonestly misappropriates the property for personal benefit. Y's intention to return the DVD to X is irrelevant as the only thing that matters is that he must appropriate the property for his personal benefit with a dishonest intent and this requirement is totally satisfied. For this reason Y must be held guilty of the same. P however is not guilty of anything.

**185.** Anand has exercised undue influence and abused his position as the medical attendant of Anand to get him to sign the agreement.

**186.** Even if no harm occurs, if a legal right is infringed, damages would be awarded.

**187.** This problem raises a conflict between a freedom to be exercised by the citizens and a power to be exercised by the State. The State has the power to impose taxes on commercial and business activities and cable television is a commercial activity thus the tax can be validly imposed. The freedom of speech and expression has no restriction in principle 1 but an implied restriction automatically comes into play when such freedom becomes a commercial and business activity. That said, of course, the tax cannot be an unreasonable burden. In this problem there is no fact to suggest that any such unreasonable burden is being imposed. The decision therefore must go in favour of the State.

**188.** This is a problem that raises a conflict between the powers that has to be exercised with the manner of exercise of such power. The power of taxation can be exercised on a commercial activity and cable television service is such an activity. However there is a restriction imposed on such a power now which is that the Government of India cannot pick and chose people upon whom they will impose the tax. If they do pick and chose the classification so created must be reasonable i.e. supported by reasons that are sound and logical. In this problem there is no reason why only state of Punjab has been singled out for the levy of this tax. In absence of any such reason, the decision must go in favour of X.

**189.** Communication of proposal is complete when the letter is received by B.

**190.** The test of whether a given activity is an essential part of a religion is that such activity must be an essential tenet of the religion. The Temple Act essentially provides for two things. Firstly, it provides B's a right to enter into temples and secondly performance of religious rituals. Only the validity of the first part is being examined in this question. Clearly, the part under examination is a valid law as it removes a disability that is based on a class/caste discrimination and cannot be said to be an essential tenet of the religion.

**191.** The State can make any law providing for social welfare and reform, thereby allowing Bs to perform religious rituals.

**192.** c As tsunami is something, which is a natural tragedy and calamity. Its path or windfall is very difficult to predict, so. Iyer builders are not responsible for the act.

**193.** b Because clearly the Government of India had very less time at its disposal and even if it wanted to do something, it was not at all possible for it to do anything.

**194.** The government was not lax and negligent in the given situation since it released warning as soon as possible. Residents are aggrieved party themselves and no liability can be attached to them in the given case. Thus neither government nor residents are liable in the given circumstances.

**195.** Since the nuclear power plant was high security zone, electrocution of fences can't be considered as an excessive action. Thus by applying principles 1 and 2, it is correct to conclude that army was right in protecting its property.

**196.** Read Principle 2 very carefully. The act took place outside the compound of the building, and the army was not supposed to take proactive measures outside its boundary or vicinity.

**197.** a Read Principle 2 very carefully. Notwithstanding anything, the Indian army cannot do anything beyond the boundary of the power plant.

**198.** Because Ruben had himself accepted the danger, while he very well knew his medical condition, which did not permit him to play soccer for a year. Even though Option (*c*) is also close, but we have to go by the principle given.

**199.** As the club had willfully hidden this fact from him and had put Ruben de la Red in great risk. They should have immediately intimated this fact to him, and placed him under proper medication and care.

**200.** As Ruben was forced to play with the threat of punitive retribution, and therefore Real Madrid has to compensate the family of Ruben de la red.

■■

## ANSWERS

| | | | | |
|---|---|---|---|---|
| 1. (b) | 2. (d) | 3. (a) | 4. (a) | 5. (a) |
| 6. (c) | 7. (a) | 8. (d) | 9. (b) | 10. (a) |
| 11. (a) | 12. (c) | 13. (c) | 14. (d) | 15. (d) |
| 16. (b) | 17. (b) | 18. (c) | 19. (a) | 20. (a) |

## EXPLANATIONS

1. Let cost be Rs. x per metre.

   Then, length of piece in 1st case $= \frac{75}{x}$

   Also, in 2nd case, length of piece is $\left(\frac{75}{x}\right) + 4$ and cost per piece $= (x - 5)$

   But as total cost is same, thus,

   $\left[\left(\frac{75}{x}\right) + 4\right] \times (x - 5) = 75$

   $\Rightarrow -\frac{375}{x} + 4x - 20 = 0$

   $\Rightarrow 4x^2 - 20x + 375 = 0$

   $\Rightarrow 4x^2 - 50x + 30x + 375 = 0$

   $\Rightarrow 2x(2x - 25) + 15(2x - 25) = 0$

   $\Rightarrow (2x + 15)(2x - 25) = 0$

   $\Rightarrow x =$ Rs 12.5 (x cannot be negative)

   The required length $= \frac{75}{12.5} = 6$ metres

2. Banker's discount (BD) for 1.5 years = Rs. 600

   i.e. BD for 3 years = Rs. 1200

   True Discount (TD) for 3 years = Rs. 750

   Sum $= \frac{(BD \times TD)}{(BD - TD)} = \frac{(1200 \times 750)}{450} =$ Rs. 2000

   Thus, Rs. 1200 is the SI on Rs. 2000 for 3 years.

   Or Rs. 400 is the SI on Rs. 2000 for 1 year

   i.e. Rate $= \left(\frac{400}{2000}\right) \times 100 = 20\%$

3. 2 men + 7 boys → 14 days ⇒ 28 men + 98 boys → 1 day (1)

   3 men + 8 boys → 11 days ⇒ 33 men + 88 boys → 1 day (2)

   Thus, from (1) and (2), we get 1 man = 2 boys

   Now, 8 men + 6 boys = 22 boys

   Also, we know from (1), 154 boys can do the work in 1 day

   i.e. 1 boy can do the work in 154 days

   i.e. 22 boys can do the work in $\frac{154}{22} = 7$ days

   Thus, 22 boys can do thrice the work in

   $7 \times 3 = 21$ days

4. Required probability

   $\frac{2}{6} \times \frac{5}{12} + \frac{4}{6} \times \frac{3}{12} = \frac{42}{72} = \frac{7}{12}$

5. Since the clock loses 10 minutes per hour, the time shown by it after an hour after 12 O'clock will be 12 : 50.

   Now, Angle (between minute and hour hand at 12:50)

   $= \left|\frac{11}{2} \times 50 - 30 \times 12\right| = 85^\circ \quad \left[\theta = \left|30h - \frac{11}{2}m\right|\right]$

6. Using the backward approach

   Total money will be = [(20 + 5) × 2] × 2 = Rs. 100

7. Final fraction of milk = Initial fraction of milk × (1 − fraction of mixture taken out)$^n$

   Where n is the number of times process is done

   Thus, $\frac{1}{2} = \frac{5}{8} \times (1 - f)^1$

   i.e. $1 - f = \frac{4}{5}$

   i.e. $f = \frac{1}{5}$

8. Let speed of the man in still water = x km/hr and Speed of stream = y km/hr

   Upstream speed = (x − y) km/hr

   Downstream speed = (x + y) km/hr

   Given, $\frac{5}{(x + y)} = \frac{3}{(x - y)}$

   i.e. $5x - 5y = 3x + 3y \Rightarrow 2x = 8y \Rightarrow x = 4y$

   i.e. Also, $\frac{45}{(x - y)} + \frac{45}{(x + y)} = 12$

   i.e. $\frac{45}{3y} + \frac{45}{5y} = 12$

   i.e. $y = 2$

9. Let total units of work = 40 units

   A's 1 day work = 5 units

   B's 1 day work = 4 units

   (A + B + C)'s 1 day work = 10 units

   i.e. C's 1 day work = 1 unit

   Now, money is distributed in ratio of 1 day's work.

   Thus, A : B : C = 5 : 4 : 1

   C is paid $= \frac{1}{10} \times 720 =$ Rs. 72

# Solved Papers

# CLAT-2018

## ENGLISH INCLUDING COMPREHENSION

**Directions for questions 1 to 3:** In the paragraph below there are five sentences. In each sentence there are pairs fo highlighted words (A, B). Select the most apropriate words to form correct sentences. Then from the options given select the correct option.

1. Internationally high rise walls serve as street **A) paintings B) canvasses.** In Delhi and Gurgaon artists have **A) earmarked B) earmark** a district and after civic authority **A) compliance, B) grant** transformed it into a throbing art district. A walk through the **A) instalment B) installations** for public interaction is **A) instituted B) envisaged.** It is hoped that this will discourage defiling city's public places.

   The correct sequence should be:

   (1) ABABB (2) BABAB

   (3) BAABB (4) ABABA

2. Pie charts are another extremely effective **A) visual B) graph** presentation of data. They show what proportions make up a whole. Each segment should be **A) cleared B) differentiated** by shading, cross -hatching or colour and should be **A) labelled B) articulated** horizontally. **A) Initially B) Conventionally,** the largest slice begins at the 12 o' clock position then slices are sequenced clockwise in **A) desçending B) clarified** positions.

   The correct sequence should be:

   (1) ABABA (2) BBABA

   (3) BABBA (4) BAABA

3. One of the predictable difficulties you can expect to **A) encounter B) counter** when you go to a different country to study or work is language. But difficulties may also result from **A) culture B) cultural** differences, which are often less **A) conscious B) obvious** at first and can be unexpected. A Dutch academic was one of the first persons to propose an **A) influential B) dire** theory of cultural **A) diversity B) division.**

   The correct sequence should be:

   (1) ABABA (2) ABBAA

   (3) AABBA (4) ABABB

**Directions for questions 4 to 6:** Identify the incorrect sentence/sentences.

4. A) It is important to monitor the groups.

   B) Check that the instructions are clear, and tell the students to begin.

   C) Inefficient bus service are a hazard.

   D) Traffic in the city has reached unsustainable levels.

   (1) A (2) B

   (3) C (4) D

5. A) The college has organized a science fare

   B) This is to notify that a leather wallet has been lost

   C) Shortly blood donation will begin a camp

   D) The agenda of the meeting is available on the website.

   (1) B (2) C

   (3) D (4) A

6. A) It is vastly reading is significant

   B) Reading for pleasure is linked to parental support at an early age.

   C) We can read intensively and extensively.

   D) Basic literacy among the prison population is insignificant.

   (1) C (2) D

   (3) B (4) A

**Directions for questions 7 to 12:** Fill up the blanks numbered (a) (b) (c) (d) (e) (f) in the passage given below with the most appropriate word from the options given for each blank.

7. The main objective of art and (a) living is to develop (b) sensibilities and skills of healthful living besides providing a (c) ground for love of labour, (d) social attitudes and moral values so as to enable the child to be (e) to the ideas of others with humility and sincerity in thought, word and deed. Love for mankind and helping the needy would (f) at this stage and its culmination would be in terms of attainment of selfless service. 'a' is

   (1) profitable (2) promising

   (3) productive (4) praise

**8.** The main objective of art and (a) living is to develop (b) sensibilities and skills of healthful living besides providing a (c) ground for love of labour, (d) social attitudes and moral values so as to enable the child to be (e) to the ideas of others with humility and sincerity in thought, word and deed. Love for mankind and helping the needy would (f) at this stage and its culmination would be in terms of attainment of selfless service. 'b' is

(1) nature (2) healthy
(3) aesthetic (4) genuine

**9.** The main objective of art and (a) living is to develop (b) sensibilities and skills of healthful living besides providing a (c) ground for love of labour, (d) social attitudes and moral values so as to enable the child to be (e) to the ideas of others with humility and sincerity in thought, word and deed. Love for mankind and helping the needy would (f) at this stage and its culmination would be in terms of attainment of selfless service. 'c' is

(1) nurturing (2) fruitful
(3) attractive (4) interesting

**10.** The main objective of art and (a) living is to develop (b) sensibilities and skills of healthful living besides providing a (c) ground for love of labour, (d) social attitudes and moral values so as to enable the child to be (e) to the ideas of others with humility and sincerity in thought, word and deed. Love for mankind and helping the needy would (f) at this stage and its culmination would be in terms of attainment of selfless service. 'd' is

(1) clear (2) positive
(3) growing (4) negative

**11.** The main objective of art and (a) living is to develop (b) sensibilities and skills of healthful living besides providing a (c) ground for love of labour, (d) social attitudes and moral values so as to enable the child to be (e) to the ideas of others with humility and sincerity in thought, word and deed. Love for mankind and helping the needy would (f) at this stage and its culmination would be in terms of attainment of selfless service. 'e' is

(1) welcome (2) clear
(3) receptive (4) illegal

**12.** The main objective of art and (a) living is to develop (b) sensibilities and skills of healthful living besides providing a (c) ground for love of labour, (d) social attitudes and moral values so as to enable the child to be (e) to the ideas of others with humility and sincerity in thought, word and deed. Love for mankind and helping the needy would (f) at this stage and its culmination would be in terms of attainment of selfless service. 'f' is

(1) disappear
(2) reveal
(3) link
(4) germinate

**13.** Four alternative summaries are given in the text: Choose the option that best captures the essence of the text.

Develop Critical Thinking

The way we see the world and relate to others is intrinsically connected to our own set of values that govern the way we decide to live. However, the influence of fashion, consumerism, pop culture, broken homes, social unrest, and the media is all-pervasive. For many people, teachers and students alike, this influence goes unquestioned. Critical thinking, if successfully taught at this level, becomes the antidote for individual and social illiteracy. For the authors, critical thinking should constitute an indivisible part of the overall educational process. Facione (1995) comments: 'Critical thinking lies at the root of civilisation. It is a cornerstone in the journey humankind is taking from beastly savagery to global sensitivity'.

Supporting the development of these skills involves reflective teaching and learning, which is highly complex and which some students may find difficult, or interpret as weakness on the part of the teacher. But in the long run, with patience on the part of the teacher, it will develop students who can view old or new material, from a variety of sources, through new eyes, using their skills to define their own stance and express it, often better in their second language, with an open-minded confidence.

(1) The world view of the human being today is influenced by a lot of things. Critical thinking cannot be taught as it involves reflective teaching and could be misunderstood.

(2) Critical thinking must be part of an individual's education but it is a difficult concept because it very often reflects a teacher as a dominating individual.

(3) Critical thinking is an important aspect of an individual's literacy level and his social knowhow. It is part of civilization and eventually leads to global sensitivity. Students can look at information in a variety of ways.

(4) Reflective teaching is another aspect of initial thinking and it could lead to individual and social illiteracy.

**14.** Four alternative summaries are given in the text: Choose the option that best captures the essence of the text.

The construct of democracy rests on informed choice and governance on informed policy. Answers to critical questions are stranded in the arena of claims and counter claims. Measures of progress are simply not known or available. The debate to job creation is a mystery of sorts. The public are not aware that the Center and States spend crores on education, health and social services. Take education. Barely a few of Class V students can read a Class II text, the poor are switching to private schools and over 33% of million-plus schools do not maintain a feasible pupil teacher ratio.

(1) Being informed is an important aspect of any democracy. This information is not available especially in the area of education, health and social services.

(2) Answers are often given but they need to be deciphered accurately. Job clarity is available but sometimes it is a mystery. There is confusion about information.

(3) Health and social services is clearly communicated but education remains an area of ignorance. Claims and counter claims create even more confusion.

(4) Crores are spent on many areas of growth but there is no accountability for information. Parents are switching to private schools as the information on education is available there.

**Directions for questions 15 to 19:** The word given in each of the sentences is used contextually. Pick the word from the alternatives given that is most inappropriate in the given context.

**15.** VENERATE - We venerate aged priests and martyrs.

(1) respect (2) revere
(3) spurn (4) honor

**16.** PRUDENCE - Prudence and sacrifice help us in meeting the future.

(1) caution (2) reckless
(3) foresight (4) judgement

**17.** OSTENTATION - Ostentation in wealth and living styles can sometimes turn vulgar.

(1) pageantry (2) display
(3) modesty (4) flourish

**18.** DOCTRINE - A doctrine is often refined by reasoning.

(1) offense (2) dogma
(3) precept (4) principle

**19.** BENEVOLENCE : Every religion believes in the concept of benevolence.

(1) generosity
(2) malignity
(3) liberality
(4) benignity

**Directions for questions 20 and 21:** Answer the questions, based on the following information. Indicate which of the statements given with that particular question, is consistent with the information given in the passage below.

**A Holistic Viewpoint**

It is now recognised by modern science that the universe at the subatomic level does not have solid material objects, but consists of only wavelike patterns which represent probabilities of interconnections between other interconnections, all of which together constitute an inseparable web of inter-relationships constituting the entire universe. Fritj of Capra therefore, views the universe not as "an assemblage of independent parts" but as "a dynamic web of inter-related events" in which each part of the web determines the structure of the whole. Geoffrey Chew views such inter-penetrating and interdependent relationships in the universe in terms of a "bootstrap" theory which implies that all forces in the universe are inseparably linked together, every part affects every other part, and the whole world is held together so to say, by bootstraps. David Bohm refers to a holographic concept which implies not only that every part is connected with every other part within the whole but also that, in a sense, each part contains the whole. This, according to David Bohm, recognises the "Undivided wholeness" of the entire universe instead of the classical idea of analysability of the world into separately and independently existent parts. Choose the appropriate option

**20.** (1) there are many solid material objects in the universe

(2) the entire universe has a web of inter-relationships

(3) the universe comprises of a number of independent parts

(4) these independent parts determine the structure of the web

**21.** (1) the holographic theory speaks of the exclusiveness of each part.

(2) the world can be analysed into separate independent parts.

(3) the classical idea recognizes the concept of wholeness.

(4) the boot strap theory speaks of interdependent relationships

**Directions for questions 22 to 24:** In the following sentences a part of the sentence is underlined. Beneath each sentence four different ways of paraphrasing the underlined part are indicated. Choose the best alternative among the four options.

**22.** The police searched everywhere but they drew a blank.

(1) upset

(2) did not find any information

(3) came to an end

(4) drew a line

**23.** She was accused of being close-minded and intolerant.

(1) did not agree

(2) kept to herself

(3) not open to new ideas

(4) unwilling to discuss

**24.** Rehman likes to have a finger in every pie.

(1) likes cooking (2) wants to do everything

(3) object to everything (4) cannot take decisions

**Directions for questions 25 to 27:** In the questions below, a related phrase is followed by a group of words. Select the group of words that best expresses a relationship similar to the one expressed in the original phrase.

**25.** At one's wits end

(1) cannot say anything funny

(2) not able to think logically

(3) not able to work

(4) clarity of thought

**26.** Gift of the gab

(1) clever at work (2) flatter someone

(3) promise blatantly (4) fluent at speaking

**27.** Die in harness

(1) die while riding

(2) die at the height of one's success

(3) die with help

(4) die when the work has been completed

**Directions for questions 28 to 37:** Read the passage given below. Choose the best options for the Question.

IOT has had an impact across all fields, be it industries, government, small or large businesses and even for Personal Consumption.

What is IOT (Internet of things) you might ask. It's been a growing topic of conversation for some time now. Put in the simplest term it means anything that has an on and off button and is connected to the internet for receiving, analyzing, storing or sending data. This could mean anything, from the watch that you wear to airplanes that can be controlled from a remote location. According to the analyst firm Gartner, by the year 2020 we'll have over 26 billion connected devices. That could mean people to people, people connected to things and things connected to things. The new rule of the future is going to be "Anything that can be connected will be connected". Take for example that when you set an alarm to wake up and that alarm goes off it not only wakes you up but also brews your coffee, sets the right temperature of water for your bath, puts on the television to bring you the latest updates from around the globe and all this before you even put a foot out of your bed. This is all done by simply getting the network of interconnected things/devices that have embedded sensors, network connectivity, software and necessary electronics that collect and exchange data.

To show how far we have come with technology and connectivity, we have smart watches such as Fitbit Garmin to name a few that have changed the way we look at time. We have one device that not only tells us the time but also tracks the number of steps, calories and our heart rate. This watch is actually connected to our phone so with just one turn of the wrist one can tell who is calling or what messages have been received without having to dig through pockets or handbags.

IOT is making its presence felt in health care as well. Doctors can now remotely monitor and communicate with their patients and health care providers can benefit from this. Whether data comes from foetal monitors, electrocardiograms, temperature monitors or blood glucose levels, tracking this information is vital for some patients. Many of this requires follow up interaction with healthcare professionals. With smarter devices that deliver more valuable data it can reduce the need for direct patient-physician interaction.

Take for instance in the sporting field, minute chips are being attached to balls and bats which will transmit information of how fast the ball is travelling and a batsman's moves, the time, the angles, the pressure on the bat at different positions, data of the muscle stretch if he's hit a six so on and so forth. Formula one cars are also being fitted with these sensors which relay information on the minute moves being made by the driver. Chips are also being put into wearable devices of sportsmen to detect sub-optimal action of any body part to show signs of stress or strain which will help in the early detection of injuries and take preventive measures.

IOT has had an impact across all fields, be it industries, government, small or large business and even for personal consumption. IBM, Google, Intel, Microsoft and Cisco are some of the top players in the IOT spectrum.

With billions of devices connected security becomes a big issue. How can people make sure that their data is safe and secure? This is one of the major concerns in the IOT that becomes a hot topic. Another issue is with all these billions of devices sharing data companies will be faced with the problem of how to store, track, analyse and make vast sense of the information being generated. Companies are monitoring the network segment to identify anomalous traffic and to take action if necessary.

Now that we have a fair understanding of IOT let's see what impact it's had on the education sector. The only constant in our lives is change and learning. From the get go we learn, be it to the walk, talk or run. We adapt to the changing times and constantly learn from it. Education or learning as we know it in the broader sense is the most important of all and the one that decides which way we handle those changes to impact us and the world.

Today's world is fast paced and to keep up with this we need an infusion of speed with learning. From the classroom assignments, lectures, blackboards and chalk we have come a long way to what is now known as e-learning (electronic learning) or m-learning (mobile learning). With the GenNext it is imperative to provide the right kind of education.

The rise of technology and IOT allows schools to improve the safety of their campuses, keep track of resources and enhance access to information. It ensures data quality being the top priority but also facilitates development of content allowing teachers to use this technology to create smart lesson plans and ensuring the reach of this content to any corner of the world.

**28.** How is IOT a concept of connecting?

(1) It is the internet in a different form.

(2) It is the internet but connected to anything.

(3) It is an analysing machine.

(4) It is a data collection term.

**29.** It is said that we look at time differently now, why?

(1) It is connected to different devices.

(2) It is in a different format.

(3) It is connected to the aeroplane

(4) It connects people.

**30.** IOT will help in simplifying patient - physician interaction because:

(1) It helps reduce data.

(2) Doctors can remotely connect to patients

(3) It improves connectivity.

(4) It is a simple process.

**31.** How will IOT work in the sporting field?

(1) Through sport fields with chips.

(2) Through special machine.

(3) Through minute wearable chips which are connected.

(4) Through special moves by the sportsmen.

**32.** Preventive measure is imperative because:

(1) It can detect anything.

(2) It identifies treatment needed.

(3) It keeps them in touch.

(4) It helps to identify stress and strain.

**33.** One of the major concerns of IOT is:

(1) Security and privacy, data loss and tracking data

(2) Only security and privacy.

(3) Only data loss.

(4) Only tracking data.

**34.** Technology and IOT has benefited education considerably because it has:

(1) Helped in improving the lesson.

(2) Helped keep track of all resources.

(3) Helped teachers to track.

(4) Helped with keeping up with the change in learning.

**35.** Teachers can use this data:

(1) Only to teach with more resources.

(2) Only to create a smart classroom.

(3) Only to reach out to the world.

(4) To teach with more resources, create a smart classroom and reach out to the world

**36.** Select a title that is most suitable for the passage

(1) IOT curse or boon

(2) IOT and our life tomorrow

(3) IOT is changing the way we learn

(4) IOT is all pervading

**37.** To conclude, IOT has an impact on:

(1) Education, sports, medicine and our daily lives

(2) Education, sports only

(3) Education only

(4) Education and medicine only

**Directions for questions 38 to 40:** Choose the option closest to the Capitalized word.

**38.** ANNIHILATE

(1) devastate (2) delay

(3) investigate (4) retaliate

39. FACILITATE
(1) lend (2) share
(3) support (4) serve

40. CAMPAIGN
(1) lobby (2) run
(3) agree (4) work

## GENERAL KNOWLEDGE AND CURRENT AFFAIRS

41. Who wrote the memoir book "My Brief History"?
(1) Dr. G. Madhavan Nair
(2) Stephen Hawking
(3) Angeline Merkel
(4) Rosalind Franklin

42. What is the Motto of the Commonwealth Games 2018?
(1) People, Place, Passion
(2) Share the Dream
(3) Come out and play
(4) United by the moment

43. The 2024 Summer Olympics will be held in Paris, France for a third time. How many years before that, did the city host the Summer Olympics for the second time?
(1) 100 YEARS (2) 96 YEARS
(3) 92 YEARS (4) 88 YEARS

44. Who won the Men's Singles title in Australian Open 2018?
(1) Dylan Alcott (2) R. Nadal
(3) Roger Federer (4) Marin Cilic

45. In which election was the Electronic Voting Machines tried out on an experimental basis in India?
(1) The 1982 Kerala Legislative Assembly Elections.
(2) The Karnataka State for the 1984, Legislative Assembly Elections.
(3) The U.P State for the 1989, Lok Sabha Elections.
(4) The 1987, Delhi Corporation Election in Karol Bagh constituency.

46. Recently a star, Icarus was seen by NASA's Hubble Space Telescope. What was the approximate time taken by Icarus' light to reach the Earth?
(1) Nine billion years (2) Ten million years
(3) Seven trillion years (4) One hundred years

47. Who won the first Gold Medal for India at the Commonwealth Games 2018?
(1) Punam Yadav (2) Mirabai Chanu
(3) Jitu Rai (4) Sanjita Chanu

48. Who is the first Indian to hold the post of Deputy Director General for Programmes at the World Health Organisation?
(1) Rasha Omar
(2) Vijayalakshmi Pandit
(3) Soumya Swaminathan
(4) Kiran Bedi

49. Who is the first female fighter pilot of India?
(1) Punit Arora (2) Avani Chaturvedi
(3) Mitali Madhumita (4) Priya Jhingan

50. The Reserve Bank of India issued the 100 rupee coin to mark the birth centenary of which Carnatic Music Legend?
(1) Dr. Balamurali Krishna
(2) Dr. M.S. Subbulakshmi
(3) Muthuswami Deekshithar
(4) Chembai Vaidynatha Bhagavathar

51. Which type of mango from Andhra Pradesh received a Geographical Indication (GI) Tag in 2017?
(1) Alphonso (2) Banganapalle
(3) Totapuri (4) Himsagar

52. The International Day of the Girl Child is observed by the UN on
(1) March 8 (2) August 12
(3) October 16 (4) October 11

53. Where is the temple of Angkor Wat located?
(1) Singapore (2) Cambodia
(3) Thailand (4) Indonesia

54. Which one of the following States lifted the Santosh Trophy Football title 2018?
(1) Kerala (2) Punjab
(3) Karnataka (4) Utter Pradesh

55. IRDA stands for
(1) Insurance Regulatory and Development Authority
(2) International Resources Development Agency
(3) Indian Roads Development Authority
(4) Indian Rural Development Authority

56. The first Defence Minister of India was
(1) K.M. Cariappa (2) V.K. Krishna Menon
(3) Baldev Singh (4) Kailash Nath Katju

57. Who is the legendary figure who won both a Nobel Prize and an Oscar?
(1) Satyajit Ray
(2) William Goldman
(3) Gabriel Garcia Marquez
(4) George Bernard Shaw

**58.** The discipline that deals with map making is known as

(1) Cryptography (2) Carpology
(3) Cartography (4) Lithography

**59.** The prize established, based on a donation from the Sveriges Riksbank in memory of Alfred Nobel, is the

(1) Prize in Medicine
(2) Prize in Economic Sciences
(3) Peace Prize
(4) Prize in Literature

**60.** What is the significance of May 13, 1952 with regard to Indian polity?

(1) First sitting of the Lok Sabha
(2) First sitting of the Rajya Sabha
(3) First sitting of the Supreme Court of India
(4) Formation of the Election Commission of India

**61.** Which among the following is the earliest literary work in Tamil language?

(1) Manimegalai (2) Silappadikaram
(3) Thirukkural (4) Tolkappiyam

**62.** Who has been appointed in 2018 as the Principal Scientific Advisor to the Government of India?

(1) S.N. Joshi (2) Rakesh Aggarwal
(3) K Vijay Raghavan (4) Vinod Kumar

**63.** Escape velocity of a rocket fired from the earth towards the moon is a velocity to get rid of the:

(1) Centripetal force due to Earth's revolution
(2) Earth's gravitational pull
(3) Centripetal force due to Earth's rotation
(4) Moons gravitational pull

**64.** From which animal is catgut usually made of?

(1) Sheep (2) Camel
(3) Cat (4) Rabbit

**65.** Who wrote the book *Der Ursprung der Familie, des Privateigenthums und des Staats I The Origin of the Family, Private Property, and the State?*

(1) Friedrich Engels
(2) Lewis H. Morgan
(3) Karl Marx
(4) Friedrich Carl von *Savigny*

**66.** Name the part of the human body reclassified as an organ due to research conducted in the past decade.

(1) Alimentary
(2) Mesentery
(3) Epithelium
(4) Spleen

**67.** The World's first 'negative emissions' power plant has been built in

(1) Iceland (2) Poland
(3) Finland (4) China

**68.** Which platform has been launched by the Union Government on the occasion of the 2018 International Women's Day?

(1) Women Entrepreneurship Platform
(2) Women Combat Platform
(3) Women Power Platform
(4) Women Literacy Platform

**69.** Who is the author of' *The Coalition Years 1996-2012'?*

(1) Manmohan Singh (2) Pratibha Patil
(3) Sharad Pawar (4) Pranab Mukherjee

**70.** What does 'NITI' in *Niti Ayog* stand for?

(1) National Invitation To Invest in India
(2) New India Transformation Initiative
(3) National Institution for Transforming India
(4) *Nayi India Turant India*

**71.** In commemoration of which of the following events, is May 1 celebrated in many places as the International Workers' Day?

(1) The Haymarket affair, Chicago
(2) Foundation Day of International Labour Organisation
(3) Commencement of the First International Labour Conference
(4) Concluding Day of the Russian Revolution

**72.** The National Social Security Board functioning under the Ministry of Labour and Employment is meant for recommending formulation of social security schemes for

(1) Industrial workers
(2) Women and Children
(3) Government employees
(4) Unorganised workers

**73.** The scarcity definition of economics is credited to

(1) Alfred Marshall (2) Lionel Robbins
(3) Adam Smith (4) Dennis Robertson

**74.** Name the digital payment app introduced by Google in 2017 for India.

(1) BHIM (2) Tez
(3) Citrus Pay (4) MobiKwik

**75.** Which of the following countries runs bullet trains with the highest operational speed?

(1) China (2) Germany
(3) South Korea (4) USA

**76.** Who became the Chief Justice of the Federal Court of India on 14 August, 1947?

(1) Maurice Gwyer (2) Patanjali Shastri
(3) H.J. Kania (4) Srinivas Varadachariar

**77.** In which country outside India has the Energy Efficiency Services Limited, under the Ministry of Power, Government of India, launched the UJALA scheme in 2017?

(1) Malaysia (2) Srilanka
(3) Indonesia (4) Maldives

**78.** Which is the organisation that initiates and presents the National Film Awards in India?

(1) Film and Television Institute of India
(2) Central Board of Film Certification
(3) Directorate of Film Festivals
(4) Prasar Bharati

**79.** In 2017, eBay India was merged with which of the following Companies?

(1) Flipkart (2) Alibaba
(3) Naaptol (4) Snapdeal

**80.** The world's first fully Solar-powered Airport is

(1) Cochin International Airport
(2) Shanghai Pudong International Airport
(3) Dubai International Airport
(4) Singapore Changi Airport

**81.** The winner of the Jnanpith Award 2017 is

(1) G. Sankara Kurup (2) Shankha Ghosh
(3) Raghuvir Chaudhari (4) Krishna Sobti

**82.** What do the paintings of Ajanta caves primarily depict?

(1) Ramayana (2) Panchatantra
(3) Jataka Tales (4) Mahabharata

**83.** Which country joined as the eighth member of the South Asia Sub-regional Economic Cooperation (SASEC) in February 2017?

(1) Myanmar (2) Nepal
(3) Bhutan (4) Bangladesh

**84.** What is the theme of the 2018 World Wildlife Day?

(1) Stop wildlife crime
(2) Listen to the young voices
(3) Big cats: predators under threat
(4) The future of wildlife is in our hands

**85.** In which athletics event did Bob Beamon hold the world record for 23 years?

(1) Triple Jump (2) High Jump
(3) Long Jump (4) Steeple Chase

**86.** Which State government has come up with a Wate ATM Policy in April 2018?

(1) Haryana (2) Maharashtra
(3) Utter Pradesh (4) Madhya Pradesh

**87.** The military operation which annexed Hyderabad int the Indian Union was code named as:

(1) Operation Meghdoot
(2) Operation Polo
(3) Operation Viraat
(4) Operation Vijay

**88.** Which of the following movies won the Best Movi Oscar Award 2018?

(1) The Shape of Water
(2) Call Me by Your Name
(3) Darkest Hour
(4) Dunkirk

**89.** Who is the first woman Defence Minister o Independent India:

(1) Nirmala Sitharaman
(2) Indira Gandhi
(3) Sushma Swaraj
(4) Sheela Dixit

**90.** What is the motto of the Supreme Court of India?

(1) Satyameva Jayate
(2) Dharmo Rakshati Rakshitah
(3) Sarve Jana Sukhino Bhavanthu
(4) Yato Dharmastato Jayah

## LOGICAL REASONING

**91.** Find the missing group in the sequence:

X7D, V11G, T13J, ______, P19P

(1) Q15M (2) R17M
(3) Q17L (4) R15M

**92.** Find the missing number in the sequence:

9, 3, ___, 1/3, 1/9

(1) 2 (2) 6
(3) 1/2 (4) 1

**93.** Which word does not belong with the others?

(1) Flute (2) Clarinet
(3) Saxophone (4) Violin

**94.** Find the next group of alphabets:

CFI, DHL, ILO, LPT, _____ ?

(1) ORU
(2) RUW
(3) OQT
(4) OSV

**95.** If "VOLKSWAGEN" is written as "UQKMRYZIDP" then "SWITZERLAND" is written as ?

(1) RVHSYDFPMOD (2) TXJUAFSMBOE

(3) RYHYVGQNZPE (4) RYHVYGQNZPC

**96.** In an archery match, Suresh's team got more scores than Mahesh's team but not as many as Yogesh's team. Yogesh's team got more scores than Mukesh's team. Mukesh's team got less score than Mahesh's team.

Which team is in second place in the descending order of scores?

(1) Yogesh's team (2) Mukesh's team

(3) Suresh's team (4) Mahesh's team

**97.** Choose the word that is not a necessary part of the underlined word. <u>Movie</u>

(1) Scene (2) Video

(3) Duration (4) Dialogue

**98.** The doctor is a person who looks after the sick people and prescribes medicines so that the patient recovers fast. In order to become a doctor, a person has to study medicine. Doctors lead a hard life. Their life is very busy. They get up early in the morning and go to the hospital. They work without taking a break. They always remain polite so that patients feel comfortable with them. Since doctors work so hard we must realise their value.

Based on the above paragraph, who among the following is/are doctor(s)?

i. Kumar Sharma wakes up early in the morning everyday and treats everyone with patience. He usually gives emergency aid to the persons who are injured in accidents.

ii. Rakesh studied medicine in Russia and practiced medicine there for 2 years. Later, stopped medical practice and turned into some business.

iii. Shalini works in Apollo Hospitals. She always remains polite so that patients feel comfortable.

She is a specialist in providing quality care for the cancer patients.

(1) All are doctors

(2) Rakesh and Shalini are the doctors

(3) Kumar Sharma and Rakesh are doctors

(4) Only Rakesh is a doctor

**Directions for questions 99 to 103:** Read the passage given below and answer the Question.

Ten friends attended a marriage, five of them Venkat, Manohar, Ravi, Prasanth and Tilak are sitting in a row facing North and other five friends Vidya, Maya, Divya, Keerthi and Anu are sitting in a row facing south not exactly in the same order. Each friend in a row is facing exactly one from the other row. One of them is using a Skoda Car. Manohar sits opposite to his friend who is using a Ford Car and sits at one of the extremes. The friend who uses a Honda car, is not Ravi who sits second to the right of Manohar. Venkat sits exactly in the middle of Ravi and the friend who uses a Nissan car is not Manohar. Keerthi does not sit at the extreme end but uses a Tata car and sits opposite the friend who uses a Fiat Car. The one who uses a Maruthi car sits opposite to the friend who is to the immediate left of Keerthi. The friend who uses a Toyota Car but not Anu, sits opposite Prasanth. Tilak does not sit at any of the extremes, but sits opposite the friend who uses a Chevrolet car, and is sitting adjacent to Divya and the friend who uses a Mahindra car. Vidya neither uses Chevrolet nor Toyota cars.

**99.** Who uses the Mahindra Car?

(1) Venkat (2) Anu

(3) Vidya (4) Divya

**100.** Keerthi is how many places away from the one who uses the Ford car?

(1) One (2) Three

(3) Four (4) Two

**101.** Who sits third to the left of the one who uses the Chevrolet?

(1) Anu (2) Maya

(3) Divya (4) Vidya

**102.** Which one does not belong to the group?

(1) Maruthi (2) Skoda

(3) Honda (4) Mahindra

**103.** Which is the car used by Maya?

(1) Toyota (2) Chevrolet

(3) Mahindra (4) Ford

**104.** In a queue, I am the last person while my friend is seventh from the front. If the person exactly between me and my friend is on the 23rd position from the front, what is my position in the queue?

(1) 37 (2) 36

(3) 38 (4) 39

**Directions for questions 105 and 106:** Read the statement and on the basis of that, choose the most appropriate course of action(s) given below the statement.

**105. Statement:** Most of those who study in premier Medical colleges in India migrate to developed nations for better prospects in their professional pursuits.

**Courses of Action:**

I. All the students joining these colleges should be asked to sign a bond at the time of admission to the effect that they will remain in India at least for ten years after they complete their medical education.

II. All those students who desire to settle in the developed nations should be asked to pay the entire cost of their education which the government subsidised.

(1) Only I follows
(2) Only II follows
(3) Both I and II follow
(4) Neither I nor II follows

**106. Statement:** Official data show more people died on Indian roads in 2016 than in 2015; UP and Tamil Nadu accounted for the largest numbers of fatalities.

**Courses of Action:**

I. Government should make a policy regulating the manufacturing of automobiles for private use.

II. Government should take steps to create awareness among the public about road safety.

III. Accidents can be avoided if the Government takes steps to make good roads.

IV. To eliminate accidents completely the Government should impose stringent punishments for traffic violations.

(1) Only II and IV follow
(2) Only II follows
(3) Only III and IV follow
(4) Only IV follows

**Directions for questions 107 and 108:** Read the statements and presume that whatever statements given are true. On the basis of that, choose the most appropriate conclusion(s) given below.

**107. Statements:** Some rats are cows. All cows are animals.

**Conclusions:**

I. All rats are animals

II. Some animals are rats

(1) Only Conclusion I follows
(2) Only Conclusion II follows
(3) Both Conclusions I and II follow
(4) Neither Conclusion I nor Conclusion II follows.

**108. Statements:** All the students are young. All the teens are young. Some men are teens.

**Conclusions:**

I. Some students are teens.

II. Some young are students.

III. Some young are men.

(1) Only (I) follows
(2) Only (II) and (III) follow
(3) Only (I) and (II) follow
(4) Only (I) and (III) follow

**109.** 'X' started walking towards the west, after travelling 5 kilometres turned exactly to his right and walked 3 kms. Then he decided to walk exactly to his left. On reaching 2 kilometres, he heard a voice and walked back. Then he noticed that, his friend 'Y' was walking towards him from his right side. In which direction is 'Y' walking?

(1) East (2) West
(3) North (4) South

**110.** If 'DECEMBER' is 'AUGUST, 'MARCH' is 'MAY', 'SEPTEMBER' is 'SEPTEMBER' and 'OCTOBER' is 'JULY', then 'JUNE1 is?

(1) February (2) April
(3) January (4) November

**Directions for questions 111 and 112:** Read the information below and answer the questions.

A neurosurgeon, an orthopaedist, a plastic surgeon and an ophthalmologist visited the patient after a surgery.

The time of each visit is mentioned below:

Neurosurgeon at 7:45

Orthopaedist 8:30

Plastic surgeon 9:15

Ophthalmologist 9:50

Each time mentioned above may be either A.M. or P.M.

**111.** If the ophthalmologist generally goes for his rounds before the surgeons, but not unless any other doctor does, and the neurosurgeon is not the last to go for his rounds, what is the correct sequence of their visit?

(1) Orthopaedist, Neurosurgeon, Plastic surgeon, Ophthalmologist
(2) Neurosurgeon .Orthopaedist, Plastic surgeon, Ophthalmologist
(3) Orthopaedist, Ophthalmologist, Neurosurgeon, Plastic surgeon
(4) Ophthalmologist, Orthopaedist, Neurosurgeon, Plastic surgeon

**112.** Who were the doctors to visit the patient in the evening?

(1) Neurosurgeon and Plastic surgeon
(2) Plastic surgeon Ophthalmologist and Neurosurgeon
(3) Orthopaedist and Neurosurgeon
(4) Ophthalmologist and Orthopaedist and Plastic surgeon

**113.** Samantha is your father's mother's grandson's daughter. Therefore, Samantha is your

(1) niece (2) sister
(3) uncle (4) brother

**114.** Look at this series: 7, 10, 8, 11, 9, 12, ... What number should come next?

(1) 7 (2) 10
(3) 12 (4) 13

**115.** In an interview for selection of two District Judges, four candidates, P, Q, R and S were shortlisted. All of them had 10 years standing as Lawyers.

Who among them are most suitable?

I. P - Very academic not much interested in litigation practice, very honest and impatient.
II. Q -A patient listener, average in academics, thorough with Laws and sharp.
III. R-Jovial, Patient, good academic records and actively involved in politics.
IV S-Shrewd, Quick tempered, punctual and Published several Legal articles

(1) P and Q (2) Q and S
(3) R and S (4) P and S

**116.** Find the odd one out

(1) Bat (2) Vulture
(3) Eagle (4) Owl

**Directions for questions 117 and 118:** Read the information below and answer the questions.

On the farewell day five best friends, namely, Vishal, Anirudh, Gaurav, Mansi and Sapna, clicked their photo, facing the photographer who is on the west.

They were standing as per the following conditions:

i. Sapna stands to the right of Mansi and Gaurav
ii. Gaurav stands to the left of Vishal and Sapna
iii. Mansi stands between Vishal and Anirudh
iv. There are two people between Anirudh and Gaurav

**117.** Who will be standing at the 2nd position from the right in the photograph?

(1) Vishal (2) Mansi
(3) Gaurav (4) Anirudh

**118.** Who stands to the left of Anirudh?

(1) Sapna (2) Gaurav
(3) Mansi (4) Vishal

**119.** Find the equivalent for' ?

'Sphygmomanometer: Blood Pressure :: Pyrometer: ?

(1) Temperature (2) Blood Flow
(3) Urine Flow (4) Atmospheric Pressure

**120.** From morning 11 O' clock to Evening 7 O' clock, how many times the hour hand and minutes hand will overlap each other?

(1) 9 (2) 8
(3) 7 (4) 6

**121.** Find the odd one out

(1) Police station (2) Railway station
(3) Supermarket (4) Airport

**122.** Read the following carefully and answer the question given below

Although women now constitute 30 percent of the global industrial force, legal hurdles and traditional barriers still hinder the vast majority of women in their efforts to achieve parity with men.

The paragraph best supports the statement

(1) The Author claims that Feminism rules.
(2) Equality of men and women is still a myth.
(3) Women should surpass men in all the fields.
(4) The Author claims that women have to take more efforts.

**123.** If TEACHER is coded as CAHEETR and STUDENT is coded as DUETNST, then what is the code for SUCCESS?

(1) CECSUSS (2) CCEUSSS
(3) SCUSCES (4) UCSECSS

**Directions for questions 124 and 129:** Read the following and answer the questions.

Chetan invited five of his friends, namely Ritwik, Avantika, Darshan, Parul and Shweta to his birthday party. Each of the five friends gifted Chetan a different article - a jacket, a watch, a shirt, a video game and a headphone. As a return gift, Chetan gifted each of them a different article -goggles, a bag, a pen, a mobile case and a diary. The following is additional information about the gifts given by the friends and the return gifts they received.

i. Avantika gifted the shirt but did not receive a bag in return.
ii. Shweta did not gift the headphone but received the mobile case in return.
iii. Neither Ritwik nor Darshan gifted the jacket but the person who did gift it, received the goggles in return.
iv. The person who gifted the video game received a diary or a bag.
v. Darshan did not gift a watch but received a pen in return.
vi. Neither Shweta gifted a video game nor did Ritwik received a diary in return.

**124.** Who gifted the watch?

(1) Shweta (2) Darshan
(3) Ritwik (4) Parul

**125.** Who received goggles as a return gift?

(1) Avantika (2) Ritwik
(3) Parul (4) Darshan

**126.** Which among the following combination is correct?

(1) Avantika- Bag (2) Ritwik-Video Game
(3) Ritwik-Diary (4) Parul-Watch

**127.** Who gifted the headphones?

(1) Shweta (2) Ritwik
(3) Darshan (4) Parul

**128.** Which among the following combination is correct?

(1) Avantika- Diary
(2) Headphones - Diary
(3) Ritwik-Goggles
(4) Watch - Bag

**129.** The one who received the bag in return, gifted which among the following items?

(1) Watch (2) Video game
(3) Headphones (4) Jackets

**130.** Examine the following expressions/activities/ processes, and arrange them in the most logical sequence

1. Design, 2. Need,
3. Launching, 4. Research,
5. Testing, 6. Identify

(1) 4, 1, 6, 2, 3, 5 (2) 2, 6, 4, 1, 5, 3
(3) 3, 5, 4, 1, 6, 2 (4) 2, 4, 1, 5, 6, 3

## ELEMENTARY MATHEMATICS (NUMERICAL ABILITY)

**131.** The value of the expression

$$\frac{\left(1\frac{29}{36}+4\frac{1}{8}\times1\frac{7}{11}\right)\div\left(5\frac{1}{9}-7\frac{7}{8}\div9\frac{9}{20}\right)}{3\frac{1}{5}\div\frac{9}{2}\text{ of }5\frac{1}{3}}$$ is

(1) $\frac{2}{15}$ (2) 2
(3) $7\frac{1}{2}$ (4) 15

**132.** The fractions $\frac{42}{491}$, $\frac{30}{313}$ and $\frac{35}{367}$ are arranged in ascending order of magnitude as

(1) $\frac{35}{367}, \frac{30}{313}, \frac{42}{491}$ (2) $\frac{42}{491}, \frac{35}{367}, \frac{30}{313}$
(3) $\frac{30}{313}, \frac{35}{367}, \frac{42}{491}$ (4) $\frac{42}{491}, \frac{30}{313}, \frac{35}{367}$

**133.** Let x be the greatest number of 4 digits, which when divided by 15, 20 and 28 leaves in each case the remainder 2. The sum of digits of x is

(1) 19 (2) 21
(3) 23 (4) 25

**134.** A student was asked to simplify the expression: $\frac{0.1216\times0.105\times0.0002}{0.625\times0.08512\times0.039\times0.16}$ his answer was $\frac{1}{65}$. What is the difference between his answer and the correct answer?

(1) $\frac{1}{65}$ (2) $\frac{1}{130}$
(3) $\frac{1}{26}$ (4) $\frac{1}{13}$

**135.** When 13511, 13903 and 14589 are divided by the greatest number 'n', the remainder in each case is 'm'. The value of (n + m) is

(1) 183 (2) 182
(3) 181 (4) 179

**136.** ABCD is a quadrilateral in which measures of angle D and angle C are 60 degree, and 100 degree respectively. If the internal bisectors of angle A and angle B meet at P, then measure of angle APB is

(1) 80° (2) 90°
(3) 100° (4) 110°

**137.** Suman saves 10% of her monthly salary. Now her expenditure increases by 30% and savings increases by 50%. The present increase in her salary is

(1) 25% (2) 30%
(3) 32% (4) 40%

**138.** A sum amounts to Rs. 9680 in 2 years and to Rs. 10648 in 3 years respectively at compound interest. What will be the amount if the same sum is invested for $1\frac{2}{5}$ years at the same rate of compound interest?

(1) Rs. 9025 (2) Rs. 9152
(3) Rs 9215 (4) Rs. 9251

**139.** The marked price of an article is 20% more than the cost price. If the article is sold at a discount of 15% on its marked price, then the gain percent is

(1) 5 (2) $4\frac{1}{2}$
(3) $2\frac{1}{2}$ (4) 2

**140.** Reshma sells an article to Rekha at 37.5% profit, Rekha sells it to Madhu at $9\frac{1}{11}$% profit. Again Madhu sells it to Mitu at 25% loss. If Mitu pays Rs. 342 for the article, then what is the cost price of the article to Reshma?

(1) Rs.304 (2) Rs.266.50
(3) Rs.380 (4) Rs.384.75

41. The number of children in a camp is x and their average weight is 20 kg. If 5 children each weighing 12 kg, join the camp or if 10 children each weighing 21 kg leave the camp, the average weight in both the cases remain the same. The value of x is

(1) 18 (2) 16
(3) 15 (4) 14

42. In a 120 litre of solution of Acid and water, acid is 75%. A person takes out 20 litres of this solution and added 16.2 litres of acid and 3.8 litres of water in the remaining solution. What is the percentage of water in the final solution?

(1) 22 (2) 24
(3) 25 (4) 28

43. Twelve men and 5 women can complete a work in 2 days whereas 4 men and 3 women can complete the same work in 5 days. In how many days can 8 men complete the work?

(1) 3 (2) 4
(3) 5 (4) 6

44. a and b are inversely proportional to each other and are positive. If a increases by 100%, then b decreases by

(1) 50% (2) 75%
(3) 100% (4) 200%

45. Four pipes A, B, C and D can fill a tank with water in 15, 20, 30 and 60 hours respectively. Pipe A is opened at 4 a.m., B at 5 a.m., C at 6 a.m. and D at 7 a.m. When is the tank filled up completely?

(1) 9:30 a.m.
(2) 10:00 a.m.
(3) 10:30 a.m.
(4) 11:00 a.m.

6. If a person travels at a speed of 40 km/h he will reach his destination on time. He covered half the journey in $\frac{2}{3}$ of the time, At what speed (in km/h) should he travel to cover the remaining journey to reach the destination on time?

(1) 48 (2) 50
(3) 60 (4) 72

7. The parallel sides of a trapezium shaped field are 25 m and 10 m and non parallel sides are 14 m and 13 m. What is the area (in m$^2$) of the field?

(1) 204 (2) 196
(3) 156 (4) 144

148. $-x^2(a-b) + a^2(b-x) + b^2(x-a)$ is factored as

(1) $(a-b)(x-a)(x-b)$
(2) $(a-b)(x-a)(x+b)$
(3) $(b-a)(x+a)(x-b)$
(4) $(a+b)(x-a)(x+b)$

149. Three fair dice are thrown simultaneously. What is the probability that the sum of numbers on their tops, is at least 6?

(1) $\frac{5}{108}$ (2) $\frac{1}{24}$
(3) $\frac{103}{108}$ (4) $\frac{17}{18}$

150. Six dice are stacked on the floor as shown in the figure below. On each dice, the sum of numbers on opposite faces is 7, i.e., if 1 is written on one face then 6 is written on the face opposite it and so on.

What is the maximum possible sum of numbers on the 21 visible faces?

(1) 88 (2) 89
(3) 96 (4) 147

## LEGAL APTITUDE

151. Article 51-A on Fundamental Duties was inserted into the Constitution of India through the

(1) 41st Constitution (Amendment) Act, 1976
(2) 44th Constitution (Amendment) Act, 1978
(3) 40th Constitution (Amendment) Act, 1976
(4) 42nd Constitution (Amendment) Act, 1976

152. The highest law officer in India is the

(1) Attorney General
(2) Advocate General
(3) Solicitor General
(4) Chief Justice of the Supreme Court of India

153. How many languages are there in the Eighth Schedule of the Constitution of India?

(1) 21 (2) 22
(3) 19 (4) 18

154. A Panchayat Samiti at the block level in India is only a/an:

(1) Administrative authority
(2) Co-ordinating and Supervisory authority
(3) Consultative Committee
(4) Advisory body

**155.** Which of the following is NOT a fundamental duty as per the provisions of the Constitution of India?

(1) To uphold and protect the sovereignty, unity and integrity of India

(2) To join the Defence Forces of India

(3) To defend the country and render national service when called upon to do so

(4) To value and preserve the rich heritage of our composite culture

**156.** The Right to Education Act, 2009 (RTE) provides for free and compulsory education to:

(1) All illiterate children of India

(2) All citizens of India

(3) Children aged between 6 and 14 years

(4) All children up to the age of 10 years

**157.** The question below consists of two statements, one labeled as 'Assertion' (A) and another as 'Reason' (R). Examine these two statements carefully and select the answers to these items from the codes given below.

**Assertion (A):** It is the legal and constitutional duty of the State to provide legal aid to the poor.

**Reason (R):** No one should be denied justice by reason of his poverty.

**Codes:**

(1) Both A and R are individually true and R is the correct explanation to A

(2) Both A and R are individually true but R is not the correct explanation to A

(3) A is true but R is false

(4) A is false but R is true

**158.** Which was the law introduced by Sir William Bentinck to prohibit the practice of Sati?

(1) Bengal Sati Regulation, 1829

(2) U.P. Sati Prohibition Act, 1828

(3) Indian Sati Prohibition Act, 1827

(4) Rajasthan Sati (Prevention) Act, 1830

**159. Legal Principle:** Nothing is an 'offence', if committed by a child below seven years of age.

**Fact Situation:** Adil, aged six years, is a student of class one. He placed his sharpened pencil on the bench with its pointed end up when his classmate Ajay stood up to answer a question from the teacher. Ajay gets hurt when he sits on the pencil and Adil and his friends have a good laugh. Ajay's father, on seeing his son injured when he returns home, wants action against Adil.

Which of the following statements is the most appropriate in relation to the legal principle stated above?

(1) Adil has committed an 'offence'.

(2) Adil has not committed any 'offence'.

(3) Childish pranks cannot be investigated by the police.

(4) The class teacher must be arrested.

**160. Legal Principle:** The doctrine of basic structure in Constitutional jurisprudence means that the Constitution of India has certain basic features that cannot be taken away through amendments by the Parliament. The power of judicial review is a part of the basic structure and it helps the constitutional Courts to determine whether an amendment is against the basic structure or not.

**Fact Situation:** Parliament proposes an amendment to limit the power of appeal against conviction for the offence of Sedition, to be exercised only by the Supreme Court of India.

Which of the following statements is the most appropriate in relation to the legal principle stated above?

(1) The proposed amendment is against the doctrine of basic structure.

(2) The proposed amendment is unconnected to the doctrine of basic structure.

(3) The proposed amendment can be reviewed and struck down by the Constitutional Courts.

(4) The proposed amendment is beyond the power of the Parliament.

**161.** Who among the following was the first Chairman of the Constituent Assembly in India?

(1) Dr. Rajendra Prasad

(2) Dr. Sachchidananda Sinha

(3) Harendra Coomar Mookerjee

(4) Dr. B.R. Ambedkar

**162. Legal Principle:** It is an offence to obstruct a public servant in the due discharge of his duty. Right of private defence is available to protect one's person and property.

**Fact Situation:** Sidhu comes to the rescue of his uncle who is sought to be taken into a car by some men. In the process, he causes injury to some of them. Later, it turns out that the men were police persons in plain clothes trying to enforce a warrant against his uncle.

Which of the following statements is the most appropriate in relation to the legal principle stated above?

(1) Sidhu has committed the offence of obstructing a public servant in due discharge of his duty.

(2) Sidhu has not committed an offence since he did not know that the men were from the police.

(3) Sidhu's uncle has resisted arrest and should be proceeded against.

(4) Sidhu should not have tried to help his uncle without ascertaining the fact

**163. Legal Principle:** An employer is liable for the act of his servant performed during the course of employment.

**Fact Situation:** While working as a driver for Verma, Alok sometimes used to earn some side income by carrying parcels for others in Verma's car without his knowledge or permission. While going to pick Verma from the airport one day, Alok stopped to deliver a parcel he was carrying with him. While he was delivering the parcel, which unknown to him was one of contraband goods, the police arrested Alok.

Which of the following statements is the most appropriate in relation to the legal principle stated above?

(1) Verma is liable for the act of Alok since he is Verma's driver.

(2) Verma is liable for the act of Alok since he had gone to pick Verma from the airport.

(3) Verma is not liable for the act of Alok since Alok himself did not know that he was carrying contraband goods.

(4) Verma is not liable for the act of Alok since carrying the parcel was not in the course of his employment.

**164.** Which law introduced the system of dyarchy in India during the British reign?

(1) The Government of India Act, 1858

(2) The Government of India Act, 1909

(3) The Government of India Act, 1919

(4) The Government of India Act, 1935

**165. Legal Principle:** The Latin maxim *nemo bis punitur pro eodem delicto* means that nobody can be punished twice for the same offence.

**Fact Situation:** Sajan, a petty thief, is caught and thrashed thoroughly by the people before being handed over to the police. Sajan pleads before the magistrate that since he was already thrashed by the people he should not be again punished by the State.

Which of the following statements is the most appropriate in relation to the legal principle stated above?

(1) Sajan is right since nobody should be punished for the same offence twice.

(2) Thrashing given by the people does not amount to legal punishment and so Sajan can be punished by the State.

(3) Giving a good thrashing to the thief is the best form of punishment to prevent future theft.

(4) The Magistrate should take into consideration the thrashing received by Sajan while fixing his punishment.

**166. Legal Principle:** The Latin maxim *qui facit per alium, facit per se* means that he who acts through another, acts himself.

**Fact Situation:** Heema requests her minor sister Harika to purchase a bag for her from the local shop. Harika purchases the bag on credit telling the shop keeper that her sister will pay for it. Afterwards, Heema refuses to pay for the bag.

Which of the following statements is the most appropriate in relation to the legal principle stated above?

(1) Since Heema has not purchased the bag herself she is not liable to pay for it.

(2) Harika being a minor the shop keeper should not have sold the bag to her.

(3) Since she purchased the bag through her sister, Heema is liable to pay for it.

(4) Harika being a minor should not have been entrusted by Heema for the purchase of the bag.

**167. Legal Principle:** Negligence is the absence of care by one party which results in some damage to another. Damage is an essential ingredient to constitute a tort of negligence.

**Fact Situation:** Mistry left his ladder on the public road while unloading it from a truck when he went to open the shutters of his shop. Saini who was riding his motorcycle had to swerve hard to avoid hitting the ladder as he came with speed on the road. Saini fell down but was miraculously not injured.

Which of the following statements is the most appropriate in relation to the legal principle stated above?

(1) Mistry is not liable for the tort of negligence since Saini was not injured though he fell down.

(2) Mistry is liable for the tort of negligence since Saini fell down due to the presence of the ladder.

(3) Mistry is not liable for the tort of negligence since Saini was speeding on the road.

(4) Mistry is liable for the tort of negligence since he was careless in leaving the ladder on the road.

**168. Legal Principle:** Every partner is liable alone and jointly with other partners for the debts of a partnership firm incurred for the business. Every partner is an agent of every other partner while being a principal in his own right in the business of the partnership.

**Fact Situation:** Varun is a partner in a firm with Chinmoy and Jaffar. Jaffar purchases a car for his personal purpose and obtains credit for the same in the name of the partnership behind the back of the other partners. He fails to pay the due amount on the expiry of the period of credit.

Which of the following statements is the most appropriate in relation to the legal principle stated above?

(1) Varun, Chinmoy and Jaffar are liable to pay for the car since they are partners and the credit was obtained in the name of the firm.

(2) Varun and Chinmoy are not liable to pay for the car since Jaffar purchased it for his personal purpose.

(3) Varun, Chinmoy and Jaffar are liable as partners for all credit obtained in the name of the firm even if it is for the personal purpose of a partner.

(4) Jaffar can use the credit of the firm to make purchases even for personal purposes since he is a partner in the partnership.

**169. Legal Principle:** Parents are not liable for wrongs committed by their children unless they provide the opportunity for such wrongful acts to be committed by their children.

**Fact Situation:** Sunil, a minor, takes the keys to his father's car from the table top where his father keeps it, drives the car on the public road and hits a pedestrian who gets injured.

Which of the following statements is the most appropriate in relation to the legal principle stated above?

(1) Since Sunil took the car without his father's permission, his father is not liable for Sunil's act resulting in the accident.

(2) Sunil's father is liable for the conduct of Sunil resulting in the accident since he left the car keys where his son could easily take it without permission.

(3) Accidents happen despite utmost care and hence neither Sunil nor his father is liable in the instant case.

(4) Sunil's father is not liable since he had kept his car locked and securely deposited its keys without negligence on his table top.

**170. Legal Principle:** No remedy lies in law where an injury is caused to a person without any infringement of his legal right.

**Fact Situation:** Ashutosh started a tuition Centre right next to the one being run for the past twenty years by Gulshan. After Ashutosh started his Centre, a large number of students shifted from Gulshan's tuition Centre to Ashutosh's Centre forcing Gulshan to close down his establishment suffering huge losses. Can Gulshan initiate legal action against Ashutosh?

Which of the following statements is the most appropriate in relation to the legal principle stated above?

(1) Ashutosh must compensate Gulshan for his loss consequent to the start of the new tuition centre.

(2) Gulshan cannot blame Ashutosh if he cannot retain his students.

(3) Ashutosh has not violated any legal right of Gulshan, though students shifted to Ashutosh's Centre and though Gulshan suffered loss, after he shut down his tuition Centre.

(4) Gulshan should have improved his quality with lower fees to retain his students in the light of competition brought in by Ashutosh.

**171. Legal Principle:** Article 20(3) of the Constitution of India states that no person accused of any offence shall be compelled to be a witness against himself.

**Fact Situation:** Ubaid refuses to give a sample of his blood after he is stopped by the police for driving over the speed limit. The police suspect him to be driving under the influence of alcohol, which is prohibited under the law.

Which of the following statements is the most appropriate in relation to the legal principle stated above?

(1) Ubaid is protected by Article 20(3) in his refusal to give a blood sample.

(2) Ubaid is not protected by Article 20(3) as he was under the influence of alcohol.

(3) Ubaid is not protected by Article 20(3) in his refusal to give a blood sample since he is not accused of any offence yet.

(4) Refusal to give a blood sample is a crime and Ubaid must be punished for the same.

**172.** The law which provides special powers to the Armed Forces in India is popularly known as:

(1) AFSPA (2) POTA

(3) TADA (4) SARFAESI

**173. Legal Principle:** The law states that a food business operator must be registered with or licensed by the Food Safety and Standards Authority of India (FSSAI) to run a food business.

**Fact Situation:** Kavita's neighbours suffer food poisoning after consuming sweets gifted by her on the occasion of a celebration at her home. Kavita does not have a registration or license from the FSSAI.

Which of the following statements is the most appropriate in relation to the legal principle stated above?

(1) Kavita is in violation of the law since she does not have a FSSAI registration or license.

(2) Kavita is not in violation of the law since she did not make the sweets she gave by way of gift.

(3) Law does not apply in cases like this where transactions happen between neighbours.

(4) Kavita need not take a license or register with FSSAI since she is not running a food business.

**174. Legal Principle:** An agreement entered into by way of a wager/bet is unenforceable in law.

**Fact Situation:** Thomas is very good at predicting outcomes of cricket matches. Raja and Hoja give him rupees thousand each to enable him to bet with others about the outcome of a cricket match. Thomas wins rupees three lakh after betting three thousand rupees.

Which of the following statements is the most appropriate in relation to the legal principle stated above?

(1) Thomas must share rupees three lakh with Raja and Hoja equally.

(2) Thomas must return rupees thousand each to Raja and Hoja.

(3) Thomas need not share the three lakh with Raja and Hoja since it is the outcome of an unenforceable agreement.

(4) If Thomas does not pay them rupees two lakh each, Raja and Hoja can sue him to recover their share.

**175. Legal Principle:** *'Audi alteram partem'* is a Latin phrase which means 'hear the other side'. It is the principle that no person should be judged without a fair hearing.

**Fact Situation:** Sanjay, in Delhi, is accused of theft and brought before the Court. The magistrate discovers that Sanjay is mute.

Which of the following statements is the most appropriate in relation to the legal principle stated above?

(1) The principle is not applicable to Sanjay since he is mute.

(2) The principle is applicable to Sanjay even though he cannot speak since he can be asked to write down his defence.

(3) The Magistrate has to take all measures to understand what Sanjay has to convey about the accusation against him.

(4) Since it is a Latin principle it is not applicable in India.

**176. Legal Principle:** An essential condition in a contract for sale of goods is that the seller has title over the goods sold.

**Fact Situation:** Ranjan pays rupees two thousand and buys a watch from Mohit who runs a watch showroom and a repair shop. Jatin sees the watch with Ranjan and tells him that it is his watch and was only given to Mohit for repairs. If what Jatin says is true

Which of the following statements is the most appropriate in relation to the legal principle stated above?

(1) Ranjan is now the owner of the watch since he paid rupees two thousand for it.

(2) Ranjan is not the owner of the watch since Mohit did not have a title to it.

(3) Mohit must pay Jatin rupees two thousand since he sold Jatin's watch.

(4) Mohit is the owner of the watch since he sold it to Ranjan.

**177. Legal Principle:** The insurer agrees to pay no more than the actual amount of the loss.

**Fact Situation:** Sunny insures his car worth rupees five lakh with X, an insurance company, for its value. He again insures the same car with Y, another insurance company, on the same terms. There is an accident and the car suffers a total loss. In his separate suits against X and Y, if Sunny recovers rupees five lakh from X, how much can he recover from Y?

Which of the following statements is the most appropriate in relation to the legal principle stated above?

(1) Sunny can recover rupees five lakhs from Y.

(2) Sunny cannot recover any amount from Y

(3) Sunny must pay Y, the rupees five lakhs he received from X.

(4) Sunny cannot insure his car with both X and Y at the same time.

**178. Legal Principle:** When there is an infringement of the legal right of a person, he gets a right to sue the wrongdoer for remedy irrespective of any actual loss caused.

**Fact Situation:** Saroj is prevented from voting at an election. The candidate she intended to vote for, wins the election.

Which of the following statements is the most appropriate in relation to the legal principle stated above?

(1) Saroj's legal right has been violated and she can sue the persons who prevented her from voting

(2) Since Saroj's candidate has won the election, her rights are not violated and she cannot sue.

(3) Since Saroj is not the candidate, her rights are not violated if she is prevented from voting.

(4) This principle is not at all applicable in this case.

**179.** Which of the following is the oldest law code in India?

(1) Hammurabi's code

(2) Prasarsmriti

(3) Manusmriti

(4) Naradasmriti

**180. Legal Principle:** A product cannot be sold in shops to consumers after its date of expiry.

**Fact Situation:** Lata, while shopping, notices that the milk packets on the shelves are due for expiry on that day. She objects to this to the shopkeeper, saying that since she was there to buy milk for the next day, keeping the milk on its date of expiry was against the law.

Which of the following statements is the most appropriate in relation to the legal principle stated above?

(1) Lata is right and the shopkeeper should take the milk packets off his shelves.

(2) The shopkeeper should not sell the milk packets after the date of expiry is over.

(3) The shopkeeper must remove the milk packets from the shelves and keep it refrigerated.

(4) Milk is not a product and hence the principle is not applicable in this case.

**181. Legal Principle:** Nuisance is the unlawful interference with a person's enjoyment of his land or some rights over or in connection with it.

**Fact Situation:** Ashok, in his nineties, is hard of hearing and plays the radio very loudly throughout the day and on a daily basis. Raju, his neighbour, complaints that he cannot listen to his favourite TV show in his home due to the radio of Ashok.

Which of the following statements is the most appropriate in relation to the legal principle stated above?

(1) Listening to the radio is Ashok's freedom.

(2) Ashok is creating nuisance to his neighbour by playing the radio loud perpetually and disturbing Raju in being able to listen to the TV in his home.

(3) Raju is creating nuisance by complaining about Ashok's enjoyment of hearing his radio.

(4) Raju should appreciate that Ashok is aged and hard of hearing.

**182. Legal Principle:** Agreements in restraint of trade are void and unenforceable.

**Fact Situation:** Manu has been working as a blacksmith in his village for many decades. Somu has been undergoing training with him for the past three years. After his training is over, Somu enters into an agreement with Manu that he will not start a competing business in the same village while Manu is alive.

Which of the following statements is the most appropriate in relation to the legal principle stated above?

(1) This agreement is void and unenforceable since it is a restraint on trade.

(2) This agreement is valid and enforceable since Manu is Somu's teacher.

(3) This agreement is valid but not enforceable after Manu's death.

(4) This agreement is valid and enforceable since it is to protect Manu's interest in consideration for teaching Somu to be a blacksmith.

**183.** What does FIR stand for under the Criminal Law?

(1) Forensic Investigation Report

(2) First Investigation Report

(3) First Information Report

(4) Formal Interrogation Record

**184.** Under which of the following enactments, is the use of mobile phone while driving made punishable?

(1) The Information Technology Act

(2) The Indian Penal Code

(3) The Motor Vehicles Act

(4) The Criminal Procedure Code

**185. Legal Principle:** A person is liable to compensate others for harm caused by the escape of any inherently dangerous material that he keeps on his land.

**Fact Situation:** Ankit lights a bonfire in his courtyard to warm himself up during a cold winter evening.

A strong wind suddenly blows some sparks from the fire, on to his neighbour's house which catches fire and gets completely destroyed.

Which of the following statements is the most appropriate in relation to the legal principle stated above?

(1) Ankit's neighbour is liable to Ankit for distress caused by keeping a house that catches fire so quickly.

(2) Ankit is not liable because nobody could foresee that the sudden wind will blow the sparks to cause afire.

(3) Ankit's neighbour cannot make Ankit liable for the loss of his house since it was an accidental fire that destroyed it.

(4) Ankit is liable to compensate because the fire escaped from his premises to burn down his neighbour's house.

**186. Legal Principle:** A characteristic feature of partnerships is the principle of mutual agency, i.e., every partner is an agent for every other partner and will hence be able to bind them by his act, within the business of partnership.

**Fact Situation :** Ram and Shyam are partners of M/s R & S Trading Company which trades in rice varieties. Ram agrees to purchase ten tons of rice from Govind. Ram dies after the rice is delivered to the premises of M/s R & S Trading Company but before the payment of price is made. Is the agreement binding on Shyam?

Which of the following statements is the most appropriate in relation to the legal principle stated above?

(1) Being partners, Ram's agreement to purchase rice for their partnership, is not binding on Shyam.

(2) Since Ram is no more, the agreement is not binding on Shyam.

(3) Being partners, Ram's agreement to purchase rice for their partnership, is binding on Shyam.

(4) The agreement is binding on Ram and not on Shyam since the rice is delivered only to M/s R & S Trading Company and not to Shyam.

**187.** Who is an Ombudsman?

(1) A judicial officer designated to receive complaints against the violation of rights of citizens.

(2) An official who is charged with representing the interests of the public by investigating and addressing complaints of maladministration or a violation of rights.

(3) An elected representative of the people to investigate and address the complaints of maladministration or a violation of rights.

(4) A specially designated police officer assigned with the power to investigate and address the complaints of maladministration or a violation of rights.

**188.** Which authority in India notified the guidelines for the protection of persons assisting accident victims on Indian roads based on the Supreme Court direction?

(1) Ministry of Surface Transport, Govt. of India

(2) Ministry of Social Justice, Govt. of India

(3) Ministry of Road Transport and Highways, Govt. of India

(4) National Human Rights Commission

**189.** Article 1 of a legal instrument reads: "All human beings are born free and equal in dignity and rights. They are endowed with reason and conscience and should act towards one another in a spirit of brotherhood".

Which is the legal instrument being referred to above?

(1) National Human Rights Act, 1995

(2) Constitution of India, 1951

(3) Universal Declaration of Human Rights, 1948

(4) Philadelphia Declaration, 1944

**190.** Examine the Statement and Conclusions given below and choose a suitable answer from the options given:

**Statement:** It is a fundamental duty, which is unenforceable in a Court of Law that every citizen shall renounce practices derogatory to the dignity of women.

**Conclusions:**

1. Reservation of seats for women in employment is violative of the principle stated.
2. Asking a lady inappropriate questions about her personal life is violative of the principle stated.

(1) Only Conclusion 1 follows.

(2) Only Conclusion 2 follows.

(3) Conclusions 1 and 2 follow.

(4) Neither Conclusion 1 nor 2 follows.

**191.** Examine the Statement and Conclusions given below and choose a suitable answer from the options given:

**Statement:** A punishment is the imposition of an undesirable or unpleasant outcome upon a group or individual, meted out by an authority.

**Conclusions:**

1. Eye for an eye and tooth for a tooth is an example of punishment.
2. Imposition of fine on someone who inflicted bodily injury on another is justified by the statement.

(1) Only Conclusion 1 follows.
(2) Only Conclusion 2 follows.
(3) Conclusions 1 and 2 follow.
(4) Neither Conclusion 1 nor 2 follows.

**192.** Examine the Statement and Conclusions given below and choose a suitable answer from the options given:

**Statement:** Necessity knows no law.

**Conclusions:**

1. The act of a captain throwing some cargo into the ocean to save the ship from sinking is justified by the principle.
2. The act of a man out of poverty and starvation stealing some food from a hotel is justified by the principle.
3. The act of a tourist killing a tiger when it was attacking a villager is justified by the principle.

(1) Only Conclusion 1 follows.
(2) Only Conclusion 2 follows.
(3) Only Conclusion 1 and 3 follow.
(4) All Conclusions follow.

**193.** Examine the Statement and Conclusions given below and choose a suitable answer from the options given:

**Statements:**

1. Justice delayed is justice denied. Justice hurried is justice buried.
2. More than 3 crore cases are pending in the Indian Courts.

**Conclusions:**

1. People are not getting justice in India.
2. Disposal of cases by 'Fast track courts' results in injustice.
3. Cases must be disposed off within a reasonable time.

(1) Only Conclusion 1 follows.
(2) Only Conclusion 2 follows.
(3) Only Conclusion 3 follows.
(4) No Conclusion follows.

**194. Legal Principle:** One of the principles of' Natural Justice' states that, "No person shall be a judge in his own cause".

**Facts:** A, a driver of B, a Branch Manager of ABC Bank was caught, suspecting theft, in the bank premises. The Bank management instituted an enquiry and made B the enquiry officer.

Which of the following statements is correct?

(1) As B is a Bank Manager and not a judge, this principle is inapplicable.
(2) Since the suspected theft was in the bank premises, the manager is the only competent person to enquire. Hence, the principle is not applicable.
(3) Since B is the employer of A, B should not be conducting the enquiry on the basis of the given principle.
(4) The principle will be applicable, only if the theft committed by A was in relation to the car.

**195. Legal Principle:** Justice should not only be done, but also seen to be done.

**Facts:** L, an honest Lawyer had 200 shares in Company X. Later, L was elevated to the High Court as a Judge and had to deal with Company matters. A dispute between Company X and its creditors came before L for decision.

Which among the following proposition is true?

(1) L, as an honest person will definitely judge the matter on the merits only. So, the principle cannot apply.
(2) A judge cannot excuse himself from taking up a case posted before him by the Court Registry.
(3) L should refrain from hearing the matter as he holds shares of the Company X.
(4) Since, L has only 200 shares he has no substantial interest in the company and hence can decide the matter.

**196. Legal Principle:** A person who keeps hazardous substances in his premises, is responsible for the fault if that substance escapes in any manner and causes damage.

**Facts:** A, an industrialist stored 1000 litres of liquid ammonia in a tank in his premises for his industrial use. There was a leakage from the tank due to which there was ammonia vapour in the surroundings. Many workers in other industries as well as his own industry and some members from the public suffered serious health hazards.

Examine the liability of A, if any.

(1) A may be liable for the injury sustained by his workers only and not others.
(2) A is liable as he is responsible for the injury caused by the leakage of ammonia from his premises.
(3) A is not liable because there was no fault on his part for the escape of the dangerous substance.
(4) A is not liable because he did not expect a leakage from the tank.

**197. Legal Principle:** In the law of evidence, a person missing for long and not heard of, for over seven years is presumed to have died.

**Facts:** A, B and C are children of F and M. At the age of 20, A went out in search of a job and was not contacting the family. All attempts to trace A by the family failed. Eight years after the death of the parents, B and C entered into a partition and took equal share in the property of F and M. One year after this, A returned home with his wife and two children and claimed his share in the property.

Whether A's claim is legally sustainable?

(1) Since A was not heard of, for more than eight years, the legal presumption of death will apply and hence, he cannot claim a share in the property.

(2) It was A's duty to be in touch with the family at least once in a year. The failure of this duty will disentitle him from claiming property.

(3) A will succeed because he is a legitimate son of F and M.

(4) B and C are legally bound to give 1/3rd share of the property to A.

**198. Legal Principle:** 'Gift' means transfer of certain existing property made voluntarily and without consideration, by a donor, to a donee, and accepted by or on behalf of the donee during the lifetime of the donor.

**Facts:** Amit executed a gift deed for property 'X' in favour of Sooraj, who happened to be Amit's loyal servant's son settled in the U.S. Two months thereafter, Amit died without leaving a will regarding his assets. Amit's children initiated steps to partition his entire property, including property 'X' among themselves. At that time, Sooraj came to India, and learning about the gift, claimed the property 'X'.

(1) Sooraj can legally get the property 'X', as soon as he gets to know about the gift.

(2) Sooraj cannot legally claim the property 'X' because, the children of Amit have already initiated steps for partition.

(3) Sooraj can claim the property 'X', because, his acceptance of the gift is implicit by his conduct of claiming the property as soon as he came to know about the gift.

(4) Sooraj apparently did not comply with the essential requirements of a gift and hence, the entire property including property 'X', can be partitioned among the children of Amit.

**199.** The right to information under the Right to Information Act, 2005 is a:

(1) Legal Right

(2) Fundamental Right

(3) Human Right

(4) Constitutional Right

**200.** The primary legislation relating to organ donation and transplantation, aimed at regulation of removal, storage and transplantation of human organs for therapeutic purposes and for prevention of commercial dealings in human organs in India, namely, the Transplantation of Human Organs Act, was passed in the year

(1) 1994

(2) 1998

(3) 2004

(4) 2014

## ANSWERS

**1.** (3) **2.** (1) **3.** (2) **4.** (3) **5.** (2) **6.** (4) **7.** (3) **8.** (3) **9.** (1) **10.** (2)
**11.** (3) **12.** (4) **13.** (3) **14.** (1) **15.** (3) **16.** (2) **17.** (3) **18.** (1) **19.** (2) **20.** (2)
**21.** (4) **22.** (2) **23.** (3) **24.** (2) **25.** (2) **26.** (4) **27.** (2) **28.** (2) **29.** (1) **30.** (2)
**31.** (3) **32.** (4) **33.** (1) **34.** (4) **35.** (4) **36.** (2) **37.** (1) **38.** (1) **39.** (3) **40.** (1)
**41.** (2) **42.** (2) **43.** (1) **44.** (3) **45.** (1) **46.** (1) **47.** (2) **48.** (3) **49.** (2) **50.** (2)
**51.** (2) **52.** (4) **53.** (2) **54.** (1) **55.** (1) **56.** (3) **57.** (4) **58.** (3) **59.** (2) **60.** (2)
**61.** (4) **62.** (3) **63.** (2) **64.** (1) **65.** (1) **66.** (2) **67.** (1) **68.** (1) **69.** (4) **70.** (3)
**71.** (1) **72.** (4) **73.** (2) **74.** (2) **75.** (1) **76.** (3) **77.** (1) **78.** (3) **79.** (1) **80.** (1)
**81.** (4) **82.** (3) **83.** (1) **84.** (3) **85.** (3) **86.** (1) **87.** (2) **88.** (1) **89.** (2) **90.** (4)
**91.** (2) **92.** (4) **93.** (4) **94.** (1) **95.** (4) **96.** (3) **97.** (4) **98.** (4) **99.** (3) **100.** (2)
**101.** (2) **102.** (4) **103.** (1) **104.** (4) **105.** (2) **106.** (2) **107.** (2) **108.** (2) **109.** (3) **110.** (2)
**111.** (3) **112.** (1) **113.** (1) **114.** (2) **115.** (2) **116.** (1) **117.** (1) **118.** (3) **119.** (1) **120.** (3)
**121.** (1) **122.** (2) **123.** (2) **124.** (1) **125.** (3) **126.** (2) **127.** (3) **128.** (1) **129.** (2) **130.** (2)
**131.** (4) **132.** (2) **133.** (3) **134.** (2) **135.** (1) **136.** (1) **137.** (3) **138.** (2) **139.** (4) **140.** (1)
**141.** (3) **142.** (2) **143.** (2) **144.** (1) **145.** (4) **146.** (3) **147.** (2) **148.** (1) **149.** (3) **150.** (2)
**151.** (4) **152.** (1) **153.** (2) **154.** (2) **155.** (2) **156.** (3) **157.** (1) **158.** (1) **159.** (2) **160.** (3)
**161.** (2) **162.** (2) **163.** (4) **164.** (3) **165.** (2) **166.** (3) **167.** (2) **168.** (2) **169.** (2) **170.** (3)
**171.** (3) **172.** (1) **173.** (4) **174.** (3) **175.** (3) **176.** (2) **177.** (2) **178.** (1) **179.** (3) **180.** (2)
**181.** (2) **182.** (1) **183.** (3) **184.** (3) **185.** (4) **186.** (3) **187.** (2) **188.** (3) **189.** (3) **190.** (2)
**191.** (3) **192.** (3) **193.** (3) **194.** (3) **195.** (3) **196.** (2) **197.** (1) **198.** (4) **199.** (1) **200.** (1)

## EXPLANATIONS

**1.** (3) BAABB Walls can be used as canvasses. It should be followed by earmarked because the participle form should be used. For the fourth option, "a walk through the installations" makes sense.

**2.** (1) ABABA For the first option, it should be "visual." An adjective is required there. For the second blank, "differentiated" makes sense. For the third option, "labeled" is appropriate because the passage wants to say that the segments are defined or named.

**3.** (2) ABBAA Only "encounter" makes sense for the first blank. "Cultural" is correct because an adjective is required for the said blank. "Less obvious" means "less pronounced". So, it is making sense.

**4.** (3) Error in subject verb agreement. The verb should be "is."

**5.** (2/4)Both sentences are incorrect. It should be 'science FAIR, not fare'. Fare is a verb. Sentence C is like a jumbled sentence. There is a clear modifier error. So, both 2/4 can be the answer. Also, except D, no other sentence has a full stop. In that way, A, B, and C are all incorrect.

**6.** (4) The adverb is misplaced.

**7.** (3) "Productive living" makes sense in the context of the sentence. An adjective is required for the said blank.

**8.** (3) Since we are talking about sensibilities, "aesthetic" is most appropriate.

**9.** (1) "Nurture" means to nourish. "Nurturing" is making sense in the context of the sentence.

**10.** (2) Since we are talking about social attitudes and moral values, "positive" is the most appropriate.

**11.** (3) "Receptive to the ideas of others" makes sense. The other options are not feasible.

**12.** (4) The blank requires a word related to "culmination." Hence, "germination" is the most appropriate. "Germination" here refers to a beginning.

**13.** (3) The passage emphasizes critical thinking and asserts that critical thinking is a parameter of an individual's literacy level.

**14.** (1) The key sentence of the passage is "The public are not aware that the Center and States spend crores on education, health and social services." Hence, the correct summary of the passage is "Being informed is an important aspect of any democracy. This information is not available especially in the area of education, health and social services."

**15.** (3) "Venerate" means "to respect." "Spurn" means "to reject."

**16.** (2) "Reckless" is the most inappropriate word among the given options.

**17.** (3) "Modesty" is the most inappropriate word. Ostentation refers to "showiness."

**18.** (1) Other than offence, the other options are more or less synonyms.

**19.** (2) "Malignity" is an inappropriate word in the context of the sentence. The word refers to "malevolence."

**20.** (2) Refer to the sentence, "Fritj of Capra therefore, views the universe not as "an assemblage of independent parts" but as "a dynamic web of inter-related events" in which each part of the web determines the structure of the whole."

**21.** (4) In the given passage it is stated that, "bootstrap" theory which implies that all forces in the universe are inseparably linked together, every part affects every other part, and the whole world is held together so to say, by bootstraps. This makes 4 the correct choice.

**22.** (2) 'Drew a blank' means when one attempts to recall something and fail, or when one tries to come up with a solution to a problem and can't think of one.

**23.** (3) 'Close-minded' means narrow restricted worldview and refusing to change that.

**24.** (2) The given idiom means to have an interest in or be involved in everything.

**25.** (2) The given idiom means to be at the end of one's ideas or mental resources.

**26.** (4) 'Gift of the gab' means the ability to speak with eloquence and fluency.

**27.** (2) The given idiom means to die while still working or active, prior to retirement.

**28.** (2) According to the passage IOT, 'Put in the simplest term it means anything that has an on and off button and is connected to the internet'. This makes 2 the correct choice out of the given options.

**29.** (1) The passage mentions how devices meant to measure time are various now and each have a unique function. The other options cannot be verified from the data provided.

**30.** (2) In the passage it is stated that, 'With smarter devices that deliver more valuable data it can reduce the need for direct patient- physician interaction.' The other options cannot be verified from the data provided.

**31.** (3) In the passage it is mentioned that, 'Chips are also being put into wearable devices of sportsmen to detect sub-optimal action of any body parts to show signs of stress or strain which will help in the early detection of injuries and take preventive measures.' From the options provided, 3 is the moist concrete choice.

**32.** (4) In the passage it is mentioned that chips are being used to monitor body parts so that preventive measures can be taken with respect to injuries and stress and strain. The other options cannot be verified from the given passage.

**33.** (1) In the passage it is mentioned that, 'With billions of devices connected security becomes a big issue. How can people make sure that their data is safe and secure? This is one of the major concerns in the IOT that becomes a hot topic.' The other options cannot be verified from the data provided.

**34.** (4) In the passage it has been stated that, 'Today's world is fast paced and to keep up with this we need an infusion of speed with learning.' It also mentions how change and learning are the constant factors in life. This makes 4 the correct choice.

**35.** (4) In the final paragraph it has been mentioned that, 'It ensures data quality being the top priority but also facilitates development of content allowing teachers to use this technology to create smart lesson plans and ensuring the reach of this content to any corner of the world.' This makes 4 the only correct option.

**36.** (2) Since the passage mentions how much IOT will influence life in the future according to analysts and then goes on to enumerate the ways it has already impacted us, Option 2 is the correct choice.

**37.** (1) Only 1 mentions all the fields discussed in the given passage.

**38.** (1) Annihilation means 'complete destruction or obliteration.' This makes 1 the correct choice.

**39.** (3) Facilitate means 'make (an action or process) easy or easier.' This makes 3 the correct choice.

**40.** (1) Campaign means work in an organized and active way towards a goal. Lobby means an organized attempt by members of the public to influence legislators.

**41.** (2) Stephen Hawking wrote the memoir book "My Brief History". Hawking's memoir, My Brief History, is a skip across the surface of the Cambridge cosmologist's life, from his quirky upbringing in London and St Albans to his latest work on the beginning of time and the evolution of the universe.

**42.** (2) The official motto for the 2018 Commonwealth Games is "Share the Dream". It was chosen to highlight the dreams and experience at the games that were shared by participants of the games, ranging from athletes to volunteers and the host country Australia to the world including the Commonwealth nations.

**43.** (1) The 2024 Summer Olympics will be held in Paris, France for a third time. The city last held the Olympics in 1924, meaning 2024 will mark the 100-year anniversary of its previous hosting.

**44.** (3) Roger Federer was the defending champion and successfully defended his title, defeating Marin Cilic in the final, 6–2, 6–7, 6–3, 3–6, 6–1. It was Federer's 20th Grand Slam singles title and record-equalling sixth Australian Open men's singles title (tied with Roy Emerson and Novak Djokovic).With the win, Federer became the first male player to win at least six titles at two Grand Slam tournaments (six at the Australian Open and eight at Wimbledon). Federer became the oldest man to win a Grand Slam singles title in the Open era since Ken Rosewall in 1972.

**45.** (1) The election was the Electronic Voting Machines tried out on an experimental basis in1982 Kerala Legislative Assembly Elections.

**46.** (1) Nasa's Hubble Space Telescope has discovered the farthest individual star ever seen - an enormous blue stellar body nicknamed Icarus located over halfway across the universe. The star, harboured in a very distant spiral galaxy, is so far away that its light has taken nine billion years to reach Earth. It appears to us as it did when the universe was about 30 per cent of its current age. Normally, the star would be too faint to view, even with the world's largest telescopes.

**47.** (2) Mirabai Chanu won the first Gold Medal for India at the Commonwealth Games 2018.

**48.** (3) Soumya Swaminathan is the first Indian to hold the post of Deputy Director General for Programmes at the World Health Organisation.

**49.** (2) Avani Chaturvedi is one of the first female fighter pilots of India. She is from Satna district in Madhya Pradesh. She was declared as the first combat pilot along with two of her cohort, Mohana Singh, and Bhawana Kanth. The trio was inducted into the Indian Air Force fighter squadron in June 2016.

**50.** (2) The Reserve Bank of India issued the 100 rupee coin to mark the birth centenary of Carnatic Music Legend M S Subbulakshmi.

**51.** (2) Banganapalle mango from Andhra Pradesh received a Geographical Indication (GI) Tag in 2017

**52.** (4) International Day of the Girl Child is an international observance day declared by the United Nations; it is also called the Day of the Girl and the International Day of the Girl. October 11, 2012, was the first Day of the Girl.

**53.** (2) Angkor Wat is a temple complex in Cambodia and the largest religious monument in the world

**54.** (1) Kerala has lifted the Santosh Trophy Football title 2018 by defeating West Bengal.

**55.** (1) The Insurance Regulatory and Development Authority of India (IRDAI) is an autonomous, statutory body tasked with regulating and promoting the insurance and re-insurance industries in India.

**56.** (3) The first defence minister of independent India was Baldev Singh, who served in Prime Minister Jawaharlal Nehru's cabinet during 1947–52. Nirmala Sitharaman, the current defence minister of India is the second woman since Indira Gandhi to hold this major post.

**57.** (4) George Bernard Shaw is the legendary figure who won both a Nobel Prize and an Oscar.

**58.** (3) The discipline that deals with map making is known as Cartography

**59.** (2) The Prize is based on a donation received by the Nobel Foundation in 1968 from Sveriges Riksbank on the occasion of the Bank's 300th anniversary. The first Prize in Economic Sciences was awarded to Ragnar Frisch and Jan Tinbergen in 1969.

**60.** (2) The significance of May 13, 1952 with regard to Indian polity is, Rajya Sabha held its first sitting on 13 May 1952.

**61.** (4) Tolkappiyam is the earliest literary work in Tamil language.

**62.** (3) K Vijay Raghavan has been appointed in 2018 as the Principal Scientific Advisor to the Government of India.

**63.** (2) Escape velocity of a rocket fired from the earth towards the moon is a velocity to get rid of the Earth's gravitational pull.

**64.** (1) The animal is catgut usually made from Sheep.

**65.** (1) Friedrich Engels wrote the book *Der Ursprung der Familie, des Privateigenthums und des Staats I The Origin of the Family, Private Property, and the State*

**66.** (2) Mesentery the part of the human body reclassified as an organ due to research conducted in the past decade

**67.** (1) The World's first 'negative emissions' power plant has been built in Iceland.

**68.** (1) Women Entrepreneurship Platform has been launched by the Union Government on the occasion of the 2018 International Women's Day.

**69.** (4) Pranab Mukherjee is the author of 'The Coalition Years 1996-2012'.

**70.** (3) The National Institution for Transforming India, also called NITI Aayog, was formed via a resolution of the Union Cabinet on January 1, 2015. NITI Aayog is the premier policy 'Think Tank' of the Government of India, providing both directional and policy inputs.

**71.** (1) May 1 is marked as International Labour Day, also referred as May Day. The day celebrates labourers and the working class. Labour Day is an annual public holiday in many countries. In India, Labour Day is referred as *Antarrashtriya Shramik Diwas or Kamgar Din*. It is also referred as International Workers' Day or just Worker's Day. May 1 was chosen to be International Workers' Day to commemorate the 1886 Haymarket affair in Chicago. In that year, on May 1, there was a general strike for the eight-hour workday.

**72.** (4) The National Social Security Board functioning under the Ministry of Labour and Employment is meant for recommending formulation of social security schemes for unorganised workers.

**73.** (2) The scarcity definition of economics is credited to Lionel Robbins.

**74.** (2) Tez is the digital payment app introduced by Google in 2017 for India.

**75.** (1) China runs bullet trains with the highest operational speed.

**76.** (3) H.J. Kania became the Chief Justice of the Federal Court of India on 14 August, 1947.

**77.** (1) Energy Efficiency Services Limited ( EESL) , under Ministry of Power, Government of India has launched UJALA (Unnat Jyoti by Affordable Lighting for All) Scheme in the State of Melaka, Malaysia . The Scheme was launched by Chief Minister of Melaka Datuk Seri Utama Ir. Hj. Idris Bin Hj. Haron. In due course of time, the successful Indian model of UJALA scheme has become a sought-after example for the different nations of the world and will now be implemented in Melaka to extend programme benefits to people of the region.

**78.** (3) Directorate of Film Festivals is the organisation that initiates and presents the National Film Awards in India.

**79.** (1) In 2017, eBay India was merged with Flipkart.

**80.** (1) The world's first fully Solar-powered Airport is Cochin International Airport.

**81.** (4) The winner of the Jnanpith Award 2017 is Krishna Sobti.

**82.** (3) The paintings of Ajanta caves primarily depict Jataka Tales.

**83.** (1) Myanmar became the seventh member of the SASEC partnership in March 2017, but not as eighth member. Myanmar became the seventh member of the SASEC partnership in March 2017. Its participation in SASEC is expected to further promote and accelerate inter-subregional cooperation between South Asia and Southeast Asia and beyond, and will contribute significantly to achieving the future development goals of both subregions.

**84.** (3) 'Big cats: predators under threat' is the theme of the 2018 World Wildlife Day.

**85.** (3) Robert Beamon or Bob Beamon is an American former track and field athlete, best known for his world record in the long jump at the Mexico City Olympics in 1968. He broke the existing record by a margin of 55 cm (21¾ in.) and his world record stood for almost 23 years until it was broken in 1991 by Mike Powell. Beamon's Olympic record stands to this day.

**86.** (1) Haryana State government has come up with a Water ATM Policy in April 2018.

**87.** (2) Operation Polo is the code name of the Hyderabad "police action" in September 1948, by the newly independent India against the Hyderabad State. It was a military operation in which the Indian Armed Forces invaded the Nizam-ruled princely state, annexing it into the Indian Union.

**88.** (1) The Shape of Water movie has won the Best Movie Oscar Award 2018.

**89.** (2) Indira Gandhi was the first woman Defence Minister of Independent India.

**90.** (4) Yato Dharmastato Jayah is the motto of the Supreme Court of India.

**91.** (2) The pattern of the series is as follows:

X 7 D, V 11 G, T 13 J, [R 17 M], P 19 P

24 ↑ 4 22 ↑ 7 20 ↑ 10 18 ↑ 13 16 ↑ 16

+4 +2 +4 +2

**92.** (4) The pattern of the series is as follows:

$9, 3, \boxed{1}, \frac{1}{3}, \frac{1}{9}$

$9 \div 3 = 3$

$3 \div 3 = \boxed{1}$

$1 \div 3 = \frac{1}{3}$

$\frac{1}{3} \div 3 = \frac{1}{9}$

**93.** (4) Flute and Clarinet and Saxophone all are played using mouth whereas in Violin there is a stick which is used to play it with the help of the hand.

**94.** (1) The pattern of the series is as follows:

C F I, D H L, I L O, L P T, O R U,
3 6 9 4 8 12 9 12 15 12 16 20 15 18 21
+3 +3 +4 +4 +3 +3 +4 +4 +3 +3

**95.** (4) The pattern of the coding is as follows:

V O L K S W A G E N
22 15 12 11 19 23 1 7 5 14
–1 +2 –1 +2
U Q K M R Y Z I D P
21 17 11 13 18 25 26 9 4 16

Following the above pattern:

19 23 9 20 26 5 18 12 1 14 4
S W I T Z E R L A N D
R Y H V Y G Q N Z P C
18 25 8 22 25 7 17 14 26 16 3

**96.** (3) Yogesh > Suresh > Mahesh

Yogesh > Mukesh

Mahesh > Mukesh

$\Rightarrow$ Yogesh > Suresh > Mahesh > Mukesh

Suresh's team is in second place in the descending order of scores.

**97.** (4) Dialogue is not a necessary part of the word "Movie" whereas rest are.

**98.** (4) The paragraph talks about two main criteria for being called a doctor – Prescribes medicine, study medicine. Only Rakesh fits the criteria. Kumar and Shalini might be doctor's aids. They have neither studied medicine nor do they prescribe medicine.

**For questions 99 to 103:**

**Note:** Actual question was wrong. Fourth last and second last statements should be this.

The one who uses a Maruthi car sits opposite to the friend who is to the

IMMEDIATE RIGHT of Keerthi.

Tilak does not sit at any of the extremes, but sits opposite the friend who uses a Chevrolet car, WHO IS sitting adjacent to Divya and the friend who uses a Mahindra car

After making the above corrections, we will get the following arrangement:

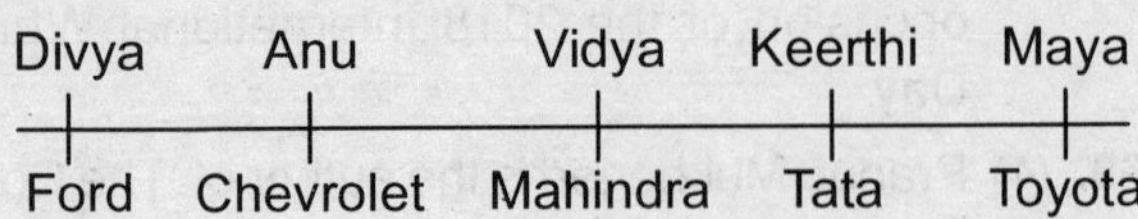


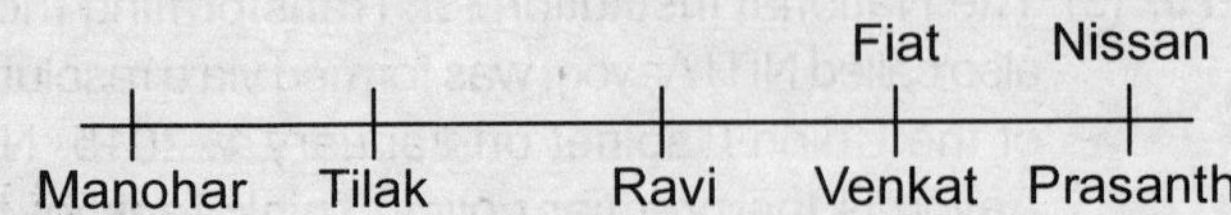


Now after the corrections, we can see that Ravi is the one who has Maruthi car.

**99.** (3) Vidya

**100.** (2) Three

**101.** (2) Maya

**102.** (4) Mahindra

**103.** (1) Toyota

**104.** (4) 7L 23L

Friend Person I

Number of persons in between me and my friend is 23 – 7 – 1 = 15

Similarly 15 persons will be in between the person who is 23rd from front and me.

$\therefore$ My position in the queue is 23 + 15 + 1 = 39

**105.** (2) Though it looks extreme, it's practically feasible. The government has subsidized means it can ask for the money back. Making them sign a bond is against their fundamental rights.

**106.** (2) Silly question. The wordings make them look like conclusion questions. II and III would have been the correct answer.

**107.** (2) **Case I:**

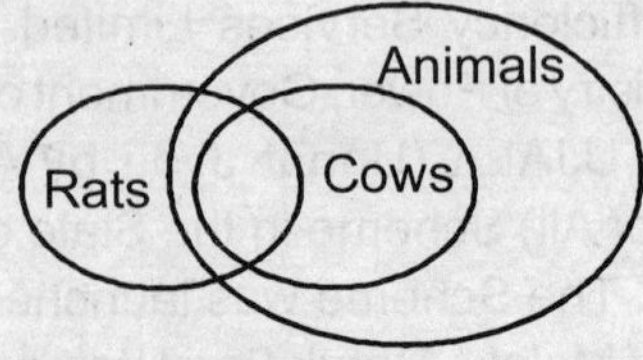


**Case II:**

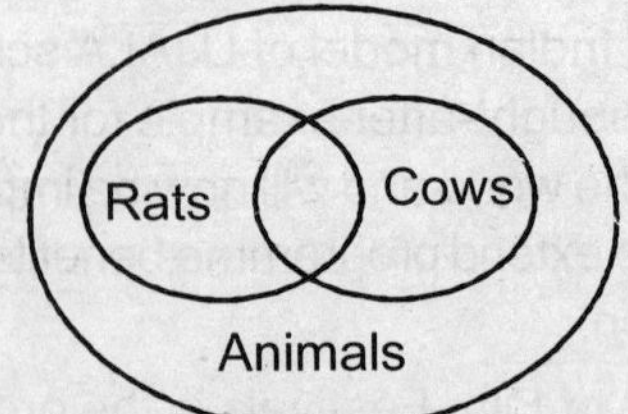


Only II follows. Clear deduction.

**108.** (2) **Case I:**

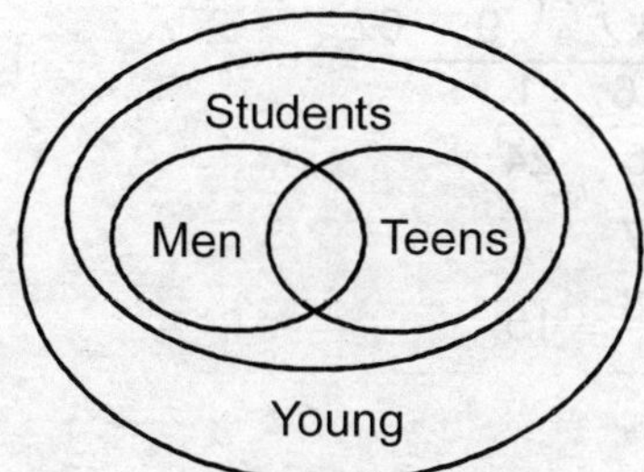


**Case II:**

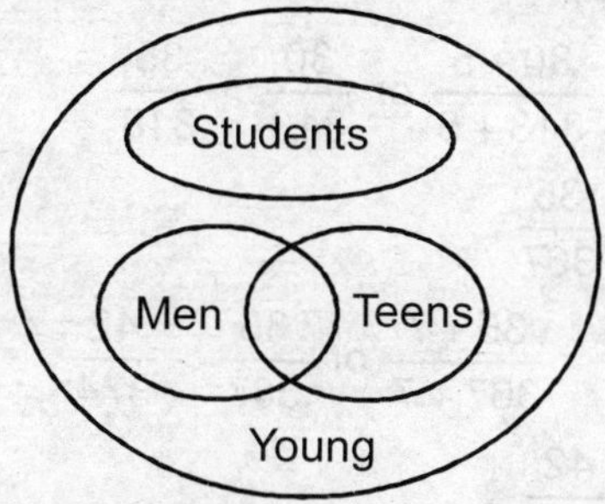


Both II and III follow. Clear deduction.

**109.** (3)

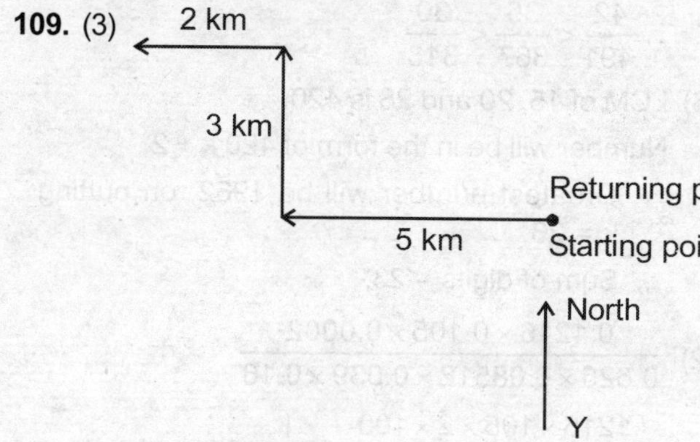


When he walked back, he was facing East direction and his friend Y was walking towards him from his right side, so Y was facing towards North.

**110.** (2) The pattern of these months is as follows:

In DECEMBER, total letters = 8

In a year, the 8th month is AUGUST

∴ code of DECEMBER is AUGUST

Similarly,

MARCH = 5 means 5th month i.e. MAY

SEPTEMBER = 9 means 9th month i.e. SEPTEMBER

∴ JUNE = 4 means 4th month i.e. APRIL

The code of JUNE is APRIL.

**111.** (3) The only possibility among the given options is that first orthopaedist visit the patient 8:30 am, then Ophthalmologist at 9:50 am, then Neurosurgeon at 7:45 pm and finally Plastic surgeon at 9:15 pm.

**112.** (1) Neurosurgeon at 7:45 pm and plastic surgeon at 9:15 pm(The condition given in the previous question also applies here)

**113.** (1)

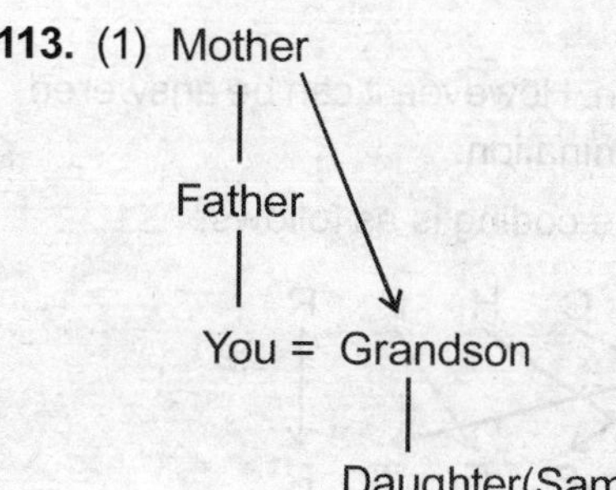


∴ Samantha is your niece.

**114.** (2) The pattern of this series is as follows:

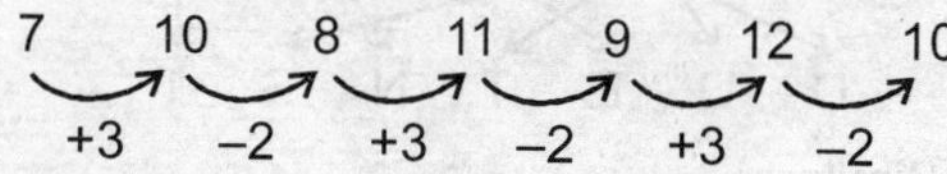


**115.** (2) P and R are rejected because both of them are not interested in legal practice.

**116.** (1) Bat is a mammal whereas vulture, eagle and owl are birds.

**For questions 117 and 118:**

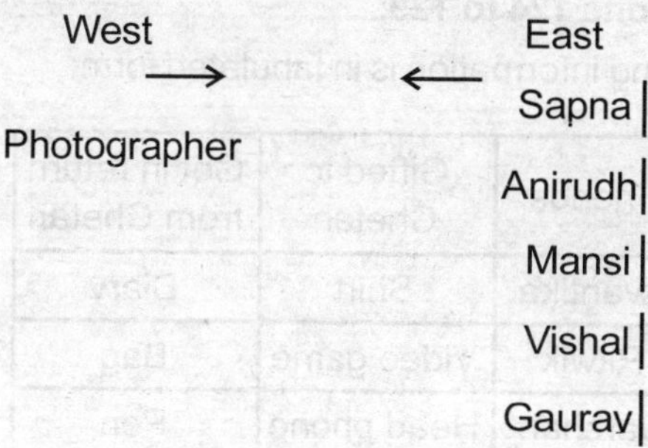


**117.** (1) Vishal will be standing at the 2nd position from the right in the photograph.

**118.** (3) Mansi is to the left of Anirudh.

**119.** (1) Sphygmomanometer is used to measure blood pressure similarly pyrometer is used to measure temperature.

**120.** (3) Between 11 O'clock and 12 O'clock, the minute hand will start moving from the right hand side of the hour hand and it will overlap the hour hand when both point towards 12.

Then between 12 O'clock and 1 O'clock, they will not overlap.

Between 10 O'clock and 2 O'clock, they will overlap once.

Similarly, between 2 O'clock and 3 O'clock, between 3 O'clock and 4 O'clock, 4 O'clock and 5 O'clock, 5 O'clock and 6 O'clock, 6 O'clock and 7 O'clock each, the minute hand will overlap with the hour hand once.

∴ They will overlap 7 times

**121.** (1) Police station is a government office where criminals are kept behind the bars whereas railway station, supermarket, and airport are public places.

**122.** (2) Very silly question. However, it can be answered by the rule of elimination.

**123.** (2) The pattern of the coding is as follows:

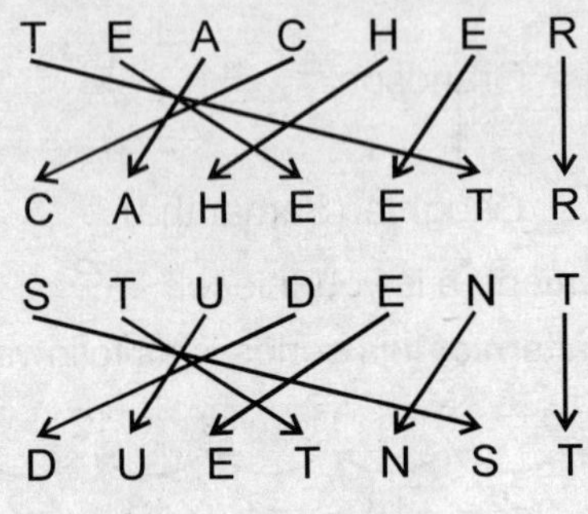


Similarly,

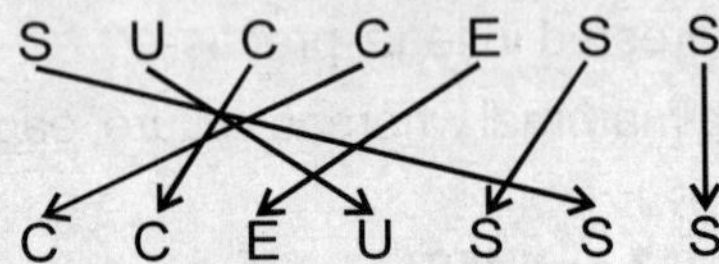


**For questions 124 to 129:**

The following information is in tabulated form:

| Friends | Gifted to Chetan | Got in return from Chetan |
|---|---|---|
| Avantika | Shirt | Diary |
| Ritwik | Video game | Bag |
| Darshan | Head phone | Pen |
| Parul | Jacket | Goggles |
| Shweta | Watch | Mobile case |

**124.** (1) Shweta gifted the watch.

**125.** (3) Parul received goggles as a return gift.

**126.** (2) Ritwik – Videogame is the correct combination.

**127.** (3) Darshan gifted the headphones.

**128.** (1) Avantika – Diary is the correct combination.

**129.** (2) Ritwik who got the bag in return, gifted the video game.

**130.** (2) The proper sequence is as follows:-

Need, Identity, Research, Design, Testing, Launching.

2, 6, 4, 1, 5, 3

**131.** (4) $$\frac{\left(\frac{65}{36}+\frac{33}{8}\times\frac{18}{11}\right)\div\left(\frac{46}{9}-\frac{63}{8}\div\frac{181}{20}\right)}{\frac{16}{5}\div 24}$$

$$=\frac{\left(\frac{65}{36}+\frac{27}{4}\right)\div\left(\frac{46}{9}-\frac{5}{6}\right)}{\frac{16}{5}\times\frac{1}{24}}$$

$$=\frac{\frac{308}{36}\div\frac{77}{18}}{\frac{2}{15}}=15.$$

**132.** (2) As $\frac{a}{b}>\frac{a+k}{b+k}$

So, $\frac{30}{313}>\frac{30+5}{313+5}$ or $\frac{30}{313}>\frac{35}{318}$

$\Rightarrow \frac{30}{313}>\frac{35}{367}$

Now, $\frac{35}{367}>\frac{35+7}{367+7}$ or $\frac{35}{367}>\frac{42}{374}$

$\Rightarrow \frac{35}{367}>\frac{42}{491}$

$\therefore \frac{42}{491}<\frac{35}{367}<\frac{30}{313}$

**133.** (3) LCM of 15, 20 and 28 is 420

Number will be in the form of 420 k + 2

$\Rightarrow$ Greatest number will be 1962, on putting k = 23.

$\therefore$ Sum of digits = 23.

**134.** (2) $$\frac{0.1216\times0.105\times0.0002}{0.625\times0.08512\times0.039\times0.16}$$

$$=\frac{1216\times105\times2\times100}{625\times8512\times39\times16}=\frac{1}{130}$$

$\therefore$ Correct answer is $\frac{1}{130}$

His answer was $\frac{1}{165}$

$\therefore$ Difference $=\frac{1}{65}-\frac{1}{130}=\frac{2-1}{130}=\frac{1}{130}$

**135.** (1) 13511 13903 14589

First take the difference between every two numbers

13903 – 13511 = 392

14589 – 13903 = 686

14589 – 13511 = 1078

Now HCF of 392, 686 and 1078 = 98 which is the value of m.

So, on dividing 13511, 13903 and 14589 by 98, we get 85 as remainder in each case

$\therefore$ n = 85

m + n = 98 + 85 = 183

**136.** (1)

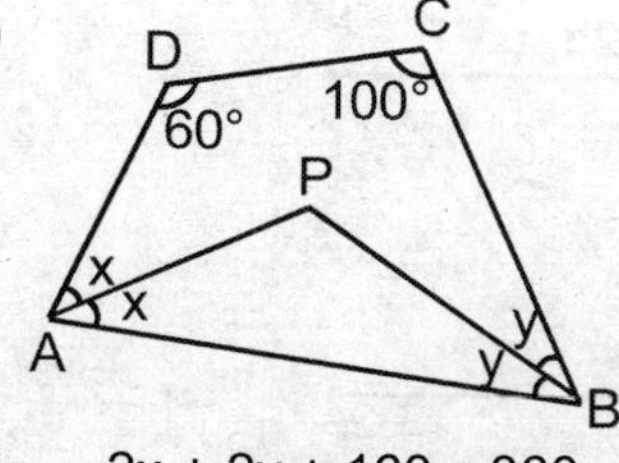


$$2x + 2y + 160 = 360$$
$$2x + 2y = 200$$
$$x + y = 100$$
$$\angle APB = 80°$$

**137.** (3) Let salary be Rs.100

Savings = Rs.10, Expenditure = Rs.90

New savings $= \frac{150}{100} \times 10 = \text{Rs.}15$

New expenditure $= \frac{130}{100} \times 90 = \text{Rs.}117$

$\therefore$ New salary is Rs.132

% increase in her salary is 32%

**138.** (2) Interest of 1 year = 10648 – 9680 = Rs. 968

So, rate % $= \frac{968}{9680} \times 100 = 10\%$

$$\therefore 9680 = P\left(1 + \frac{10}{100}\right)^2$$

P = Rs.8000

So, amount will become after 1 year

$= 8000 \times \frac{11}{10} = \text{Rs.}8800$

So, now interest at 10% for next year

$= \frac{10}{100} \times 8800 = \text{Rs.}880$

So, for $\frac{2}{5}$ year only, $I = \frac{2}{5} \times 880 = \text{Rs. } 352$

$\therefore$ Amount after $1\frac{2}{5}$ years

= 8800 + 352

= Rs.9152

**139.** (4) Let CP be Rs. 100

$\therefore$ M.P. Rs. 120

D = 15%

SP $= \frac{85}{100} \times 120 = \text{Rs.}102.$

P% $= \frac{2}{100} \times 100 = 2\%.$

**140.** (1) Let C.P. of Reshma be Rs.x

$$x \times \left(1 + \frac{3}{8}\right) \times \left(1 + \frac{1}{11}\right) \times \left(1 - \frac{1}{4}\right) = 342$$

$$x \times \frac{11}{8} \times \frac{12}{11} \times \frac{3}{4} = 342$$

x = Rs.304

**141.** (3) Let the average after 5 children join or 10 children leave be y.

| $\therefore$ No. | Sum | Average |
|---|---|---|
| x | 20x | 20 |
| ↓ +5 | ↓ +60 | |
| x + 5 | 20x + 60 | y |

$$\therefore y = \frac{20x + 60}{x + 5}$$

| No. | Sum | Average |
|---|---|---|
| x | 20x | 20 |
| ↓ –10 | ↓ –210 | |
| x – 10 | 20x – 210 | y |

$$\therefore y = \frac{20x - 210}{x - 10}$$

$$\frac{20x + 60}{x + 5} = \frac{20x - 210}{x - 10}$$

$\Rightarrow$ x = 15.

**142.** (2) Acid $= \frac{75}{100} \times 120 = 90$ litre

Water = 30 litre

| Acid | Water |
|---|---|
| 90 | 30 |
| –20 | –20 |
| +16.2 | +3.8 |
| 86.2 | 13.8 |

So, percentage of water in the final solution

$= \frac{13.8}{100} \times 100 = 13.8$ litre

20 litres of the solution is taken out so remaining solution is 120 – 20 = 100 litres

Now,

| Acid | Water |
|---|---|
| 75 | 25 |
| +16.2 | +3.8 |
| 91.2 | 28.8 |

Percentage of water in the final solution is

$$\frac{28.8}{120} \times 100 = 24\%$$

**143.** (2) 2(12 men + 5 women ) = 5(4 men + 3 women)

24 men + 10 women = 20 men + 15 women

4 men = 5 women

$$\frac{\text{Men}}{\text{Women}} = \frac{5}{4}$$

⇒ 1 woman is equivalent to $\frac{4}{5}$ man

Total 12 men + 5 × $\frac{4 \text{ men}}{5}$ = 16 men complete the work in 2 days.

∴ 8 men will complete the same work in 2 × 2 = 4 days.

**144.** (1) $a \propto \frac{1}{b}$

$$a = \frac{k}{b}$$

$$\Rightarrow b = \frac{k}{a}$$

Now, $2a = \frac{k}{b'}$

$$b' = \frac{k}{2a}$$

$$\text{\% decrease in } b = \frac{\frac{k}{a} - \frac{k}{2a}}{\frac{k}{a}} \times 100 = 50\%$$

**145.** (4) A can fill the tank in 15 hours

B can fill the tank in 20 hours

C can fill the tank in 30 hours

D can fill the tank in 60 hours

So total capacity of the tank is LCM of 15, 20, 30 and 60 = 120

So, in 1 hour, A fills = 8 litres

in 1 hour, B fills = 6 litres

in 1 hour, C fills = 4 litres

in 1 hour, D fills = 2 litres

From 4 am to 5 am, only pipe A fills = 8 litres

From 5 am to 6 am, A and B together fills = 14 litres

From 6 am to 7 am, A, B and C together fill = 18 litres

At 7 am, all pipes fill the remaining volume = 120 – (8 + 14 + 18) = 80 litres

20 litres is filled by them in 1 hour

80 litres is filled by them in 4 hour

∴ Tank is filled completely at 11 am.

**146.** (3) 2d, t

S = 40 km/hr

2d = 40 × t

d = 20 t

$d, \frac{2}{3}t$ $\quad$ $d, \frac{1}{3}t$

Now speed to cover remaining half distance

$$= s = \frac{d}{t} \times 3$$

$$= \frac{20t \times 3}{t} = 60 \text{ km/hr}$$

**147.** (2)

(Figure: trapezium with A, B on top (AB = 10), AF = 14, AG = 13, BE = 13, F 7.5 D, G 10, C 7.5 E)

Draw AG || BE

∴ ABEG is a || gm

⇒ FG = 15 m

Let AD = BC = h

$$\therefore \text{ Area of } \Delta AFG = \frac{1}{2} \times 15 \times h$$

or

$$\therefore \text{ Area of } \Delta AFG = \sqrt{s(s-a)(s-b)(s-c)}$$

$$\therefore \frac{1}{2} \times 15 \times h = \sqrt{21(21-14)(21-13)(21-15)}$$

$$\frac{1}{2} \times 15 \times h = 84$$

$$h = \frac{56}{5} m$$

$$\text{Area of the field} = \frac{1}{2} \times 35 \times \frac{56}{5} = 196 \text{ m}^2$$

**148.** (1) $x^2(a-b) + a^2(b-x) + b^2(x-a)$

$x^2(a-b) + a^2b - a^2x + b^2x - ab^2$

$(a-b)x^2 - (a^2 - b^2)x + ab(a-b)$

$(a-b)[x^2 - (a+b)x + ab]$

This equation $x^2 - (a+b)x + ab$ can be factorised as $(x-a)(x-b)$

∴ $(a-b)(x-a)(x-b)$ will be the answer

**149.** (3) Total outcomes = 216

Total numbers whose sum of the digits is less than 6 are 111, 112, 113, 121, 122, 131, 211, 212, 221 and 311

So, favourable outcomes $= \frac{216-10}{216}$

$= \frac{206}{216} = \frac{103}{108}$

**150.** (2) If we number the dice from left most side and from top to bottom.

Then Dice I will have numbers on the visible face = 6, 5, 2, 4, 3

Dice 2 = 6, 4, 3

Dice 3 = 6, 4, 3

Dice 4 = 6, 5, 4, 3

Dice 5 = 6, 1

Dice 6 = 6, 5, 4, 3

∴ Maximum possible sum of these numbers = 89.

**151.** (4) 42[ND] AMENDMENT(CONSTITUTION) ACT,1976

**152.** (1) AG

**153.** (2) 22 LANGUAGES

**159.** (2) As per principle 'nothing is an offence ',if committed by a child below 7years,Therefore Adil who is only 6 years cannot be punished for any offence.

**160.** (3) Judicial review is a part of 'basic structure' and hence cannot be removed. Therefore any such amendment can be reviewed and struck down by constitutional courts such as Supreme court and HIGH courts.

**161.** (2) Dr.Sachidanand Sinha was the first Chairman for temporary period and later on Dr.Rajendra Prasad was made permanent chairman of constituent of Assembly.

**162.** (2) Since Sidhu was not aware of the identity of men who were taking his uncle forcibly who later turned out to be policemen in plainclothes therefore he cannot be held liable for any offence as in order to constitute an offence either knowledge or intention is required .Had he known about the identity and then resisted then the above principle would have applied and he would have been held guilty.

**163.** (4) An employer's liability for the act of his servant is not 'unlimited'. He cannot be held liable for every act of his employees. He can be held liable for acts done by an employee during the 'course of employment' .The course of employment will include authorized work given to employee.Here clearly the employee was engaged in something which was not authorized.

**164.** (3) Also known as Montague Chelmsford Reforms.

**165.** (2) In order to invoke defence of 'double jeopardy' the punishment must be given by some judicial authority twice for the same offence.Even administrative action like sacking employees will not qualify as punishment as far as double jeopardy is concerned forget about thrashing by public.

**166.** (3) As per the principle 'he who acts through another,acts himself ' therefore heema will be liable to pay as she purchased through her sister.

**167.** (2) In tort of negligence damage must be suffered in order to claim compensation.In this case even though he was not injured(physically) but still a fall from speeding vehicle will cause damage atleast to his vehicle.

**168.** (2) As per principle every partner is liable jointly with other partners for the debts of a partnership firm incurred for 'business'.Here Jaffer bought the car for his personal purposes and not for 'business' purposes of partnership firm.

**169.** (2) Sunil's father will be liable as he gave 'opportunity' to his son by keeping car keys at his table top.

**170.** (3) A direct application of principle will lead to this option as there was no violation of legal right by Ashutosh even though Sunil did suffer damages.( Damnum Sine Injuria).As per this principle there must be violation of legal right in to claim any compensation.

**171.** (3) The critical word here is 'accused'.As per the principle an 'accused' cannot be forced to be witness against himself.In order to be an 'accused' a person must be charged with some offence like an FIR registered against him which was not the case here.

**172.** (1) AFSPA.(ARMED FORCES SPECIAL POWERS ACT).This law is normally applied in insurgency/ militancy hit areas like J&K ,North East etc.

**173.** (4) As per the principle only' food business operators' are required to take FSSAI permission/licence. Clearly kavita only gifted sweets and was not engaged in food business as such.

**174.** (3) Thomas need not share the three lakh with Raja and Hoja since it is an outcome of an unenforceable agreement.

**175.** (3) The principle says you must hear the other side before pronouncing any judgement.What it means is that both the parties should be given adequate opportunity to present their side of story.Even though Sanjay is 'mute' still it is the duty of Magistrate to take all measures to understand what Sanjay has to convey about accusation against him.

**176.** (2) As per the principle in order to be a 'seller' you must 'own' that goods or must have 'title' over the goods to sold. Here Mohit never had title over the watch he sold to Ranjan.It was given to him only for repairs .Hence he can't sell something which he never owned.As a result Ranjan can't be the owner of watch even though he might have paid for it.

**177.** (2) As per the principle the insurer will pay only for the actual loss suffered by the insured.Since Sunny has already recovered his entire loss of 5lakh from X therefore he cannot recover from Y.

**178.** (1) Simple application of principle will lead us to choice 1 as what is important is that legal right must be violated which in this was violated as she was not allowed to vote even though she may not have suffered any damage(her candidate winning).Saroj had the legal right to vote.

**179.** (3) Manusmriti.

**180.** (2) The shopkeeper should not sell milk 'after' the date of expiry is over.

**181.** (2) In order to constitute tort of nuisance there must be unlawful interference and an element of continuity in the wrongful act .In this case both the elements are present.It is not the case of Ashok that since he is hard of hearing therefore he can play music loudly. Ashok is clearly a 'sensitive' client here and law only takes in its ambit reasonable person .If he is hard of hearing he should better get himself treated.

**182.** (1) By not letting Somu to start a competing business till he is "alive" there is clear restraint of trade.

**183.** (3) FIR

**184.** (3) MOTOR VEHICLES ACT.

**185.** (4) As per the principle a person is liable to compensate others for harm caused by the escape of any "inherently" dangerous material that is kept there.Fire is an "inherently" dangerous material and it did escape from Ankit's place to his neighbor's house resulting in complete destruction of that house.

**186.** (3) In a partnership every partner is an agent of other partner and therefore responsible for act of other partners.In this case Since Ram and Shyam are partners therefore Ram's agreement with Govind will be binding on Shyam .

**187.** (2) Like incase of banking there is an ombudsman to look into the complaints and grievances of public.

**192.** (3) "necessity" generally applies when there is question of life and death.clearly in option 2 question of life and death is not there.

**194.** (3) The essence of the principle is that justice should not only be done but also seen to be done .Since B is the employer of A ,B should not be conducting the enquiry on the basis of above principle.

**195.** (3) This is a clear case of 'conflict of interest'.Judge was an interested party as he was holding shares of company X therefore he must refrain/recuse himself from hearing this matter as justice should not only be done but also seen to be done.

**196.** (2) Simple application of principle will lead us option 2.

**197.** (1) Again direct application of principle .

**198.** (4) One of essential element for transfer of gift is that it must be 'accepted' by the donee or his agent. But in this case since the donee was in US and there is no way he could have accepted this gift therefore Sooraj did not comply with essential requirements of gift.

**199.** (1) LEGAL RIGHT

**200.** (1) 1994

# AILET-2018

## SECTION - A : ENGLISH

**Directions (Q. 1 - Q. 4):** For each question, choose the correct sentence/s.

**1.** I. Due to the amicable nature of the new neighbours in the locality, we could come to an amiable settlement of the dispute that had taken place.

II. Edmund Hillary and Tenzing Norgay gave ascent that they will assent the Mt. Everest and conquer it together.

III. His immanent literary qualities made him an eminent writer and hence fame became imminent for him.

IV. Kamal is very obedient, agreeable and gracious: a complaisant child. His mother feels complacent of her percentage.

(a) I, IV (b) III, IV
(c) II, IV (d) I, III

**2.** I. The Music Director ingeniously told the media that the song was his ingenuous work.

II. If you are mendacious in life most of the times, you will have to be mendicant later to win their trust back again.

III. Being venal is not a venial crime under the court of law.

IV. The leader abjured his followers to adjure violence as a means to demand their rights.

(a) II, III (b) I, IV
(c) II, IV (d) I, III

**3.** (a) Ketan has to be more discreet or he'll literally drive his wife up the wall.

(b) Ketan has to be more discrete or he'll literally drive his wife up the wall.

(c) Ketan has to be more discrete or he'll drive his wife up the wall.

(d) Katan has to be more discreet or he'll drive his wife up the wall.

**4.** (a) Hema prophesized that if Ratna kept dancing that way, she'd get her just desserts.

(b) Hema prophesized that if Ratna kept dancing that way, she'd get her just deserts.

(c) Hema prophesied that if Ratna kept dancing that way, she'd get her just deserts.

(d) Hema prophesied that if Ratna kept dancing that way, she'd get her just desserts.

**Directions (Q. 5 - Q. 6):** Following are the questions based on the same words used as different parts of speech. Choose the correct matches.

**5. Well**

| | |
|---|---|
| 1. Noun | a. Well begun is half done. |
| 2. Adjective | b. Let well alone. |
| 3. Adverb | c. Well, who would have thought it? |
| 4. Interjection | d. I hope you are now well. |

(a) 1-a, 2-b, 3-c, 4-d (b) 1-b, 2-d, 3-a, 4-c
(c) 1-c, 2-d, 3-a, 4-b (d) 4-a, 3-b, 2-c, 1-b

**6. What**

| | |
|---|---|
| 1. Interjection Adjective | a. Give me what you can. What happened then, I do not know. |
| 2. Interjection | b. What does he want? |
| 3. Interjection Pronoun | c. What! You don't mean to say so? |
| 4. Relative Pronoun | d. What evidence have you got ? |

(a) 4-b, 1-c, 2-d, 3-a (b) 3-c, 2-b, 1-a, 4-d
(c) 1-c, 2-b, 3-d, 4-a (d) 1-d, 2-c, 3-b, 4-a

**Directions (Q. 7 - Q. 12):** Name the various Figures of Speech in the following.

**7.** He was a learned man among lords, and a lord among learned men.

(a) Epigram (b) Metonymy
(c) Oxymoron (d) Antithesis

**8.** Sceptre and crown
Must tumble down,
And in dust be equal made
With the poor crooked scythe and spade.

(a) Irony (b) Apostrophe
(c) Metonymy (d) Synecdoche

**9.** Brave Macbeth, with his brandished steel, carved out his passage.

(a) Metaphor (b) Litotes
(c) Climax (d) Synecdoche

**10.** We had nothing to do, and we did it very well.
(a) Antithesis (b) Paradox
(c) Anticlimax (d) Litotes

**11.** And thou, Dalhousie, the great god of war Lieutenant-Colonel to the Earl of Mar:
(a) Apostrophe (b) Epigram
(c) Anticlimax (d) Paradox

**12.** The Puritan had been rescued by no common deliverer from the gasp of no common foe.
(a) Hyperbole (b) Epigram
(c) Metaphor (d) Litotes

**Directions (Q. 13 - Q. 19):** Choose the sentence (s) which is/are punctuated correctly.

**13.** I. Our daughter will be three years old next week.
II. Our son will be two-years-old next week.
III. Our two-year-old is starting to talk.
IV. Our two year old is starting to talk.
(a) I, III (b) I & IV
(c) II, III (d) III

**14.** I. Jan asked; "What did Joe mean when he said, 'I will see you later.' "
II. Jan asked, "What did Joe mean when he said, 'I will see you later?' "
III. Jan asked, "What did Joe mean when he said, 'I will see you later'?"
IV. Jan asked, "What did Joe mean when he said, 'I will see you later' "?
(a) II (b) I
(c) IV (d) III

**15.** I. You are my friend; however, I cannot afford to lend you any more money.
II. Truly, a popular error has as many lives as a cat: it comes walking in, long after you have imagined it effectually strangled.
III. There is only one cure for the evils which newly acquired freedom produces, and that cure is freedom,
IV. There is a slavery that no legislation can abolish; the slavery of caste.
(a) I, II, III (b) II, IV
(c) I, II, III, IV (d) II, III

**16.** I. Yes, Jagrit, you were right about that answer.
II. Yes Jagrit, you were right about that answer.
III. I saw our town's ex-Mayor Prakash Kumar in the mall.
IV. I saw our town's ex-mayor in the market.
(a) I, III (b) I, III, IV
(c) I, IV (d) II, III

**17.** I. As Caesar loved me, I wept for him; as he was fortunate, I rejoice at it; as he was valiant, I honour him; but as he was ambitious, I slew him.
II. Danish, my friend from Chandigarh, Punjab, will join us.
III. Danish, my friend, from Chandigarh, Punjab will join us.
IV. As Caesar loved me, I wept for him; as he was fortunate, I rejoice at it; as he was valiant, I honour him: but as he was ambitious I slew him.
(a) II (b) II, IV
(c) I, III (d) I, II

**18.** I. A liberally sprinkled dose of humour was very much appreciated.
II. Right now I want two things: peace and quiet.
III. Our liberal-minded clergyman managed to unite the entire congregation.
IV. Right now I want two things; peace and quiet.
(a) II, III (b) I, IV
(c) I, II, III (d) III, IV

**19.** I. It may not be the correct part, but I bet that it works.
II. It may not be the correct part but: I bet that it works.
III. O father! I hear the sound of guns.
IV. O Hamlet, speak no more!
(a) I, III (b) I, III, IV
(c) II, III (d) I, IV

**Directions (Q. 20 - Q. 26):** For each question, identify the correct subjects and verbs. The subjects are in bold and the verbs are underlined.

**20.** (a) Every environmental **regulation** has been undermined *by* that industry.
(b) **Every** environmental regulation *has been* undermined by that industry.
(c) Every environmental **regulation** *has been undermined* by that industry.
(d) Every environmental **regulation** has been *undermined* by that **industry**.

**21.** (a) My **gift** for singing and dancing simultaneously did *not fail to attract* attention.
(b) **My** gift for *singing* and *dancing* simultaneously did not fail to attract attention.
(c) My **gift** for *singing and dancing* simultaneously did not fail to attract attention.
(d) My **gift** for singing and dancing simultaneously *did* not *fail* to attract attention.

22. (a) **Every** attempt to flatter her <u>failed miserably</u>.
(b) Every **attempt** <u>to flatter</u> her failed miserably.
(c) Every **attempt** to flatter her <u>failed</u> miserably.
(d) Every attempt to flatter **her** <u>failed</u> miserably.

23. (a) If **all** <u>is</u> lost, why <u>am</u> I still <u>playing</u> cricket ?
(b) If **all** <u>is lost</u>, why am I still playing cricket ?
(c) If all is lost, why am **I** still <u>playing</u> cricket?
(d) If **all** is lost, why am I <u>still playing</u> cricket?

24. (a) "Buses" has only one **s** <u>in</u> the middle of it.
(b) **"Buses"** has only one s <u>in the middle</u> of it.
(c) "Buses" <u>has</u> only **one s** in the middle of it.
(d) **"Buses"** <u>has</u> only one s in the middle of it.

25. (a) <u>Have</u> **you** <u>memorized</u> all the chemical symbols on the chart ?
(b) Have you <u>memorized</u> all the chemical **symbols** on the chart?
(c) <u>Have</u> **you** memorized all the chemical symbols on the chart?
(d) <u>Have</u> you <u>memorized</u> all the chemical symbols on the **chart**?

26. (a) This gorgeous grand **sitar** is tuned to <u>perfection</u>.
(b) This gorgeous grand **sitar** <u>is tuned</u> to perfection.
(c) This gorgeous **grand** sitar <u>is</u> tuned to perfection.
(d) This <u>gorgeous</u> grand **sitar** is tuned to perfection.

**Directions (Q. 27 - Q. 30):** Find out the sentence/s which is/are written correctly.

I. Some of the desserts was left by the end of the birthday party.
II. Your brilliant excuses almost makes up for your tardiness.
III. Neither Jackson nor Jenna have played hooky.
IV. Either of us is capable of winning.

27. (a) I, II, III (b) II, III
(c) II (d) IV

I. Here's the paper clips you requested.
II. A limousine and driver are in the driveway.
III. One-fourth of the voters tend not to cast its ballots in national elections.
IV. Either of the classic cars are for sale.

28. (a) I, II (b) I, II, III
(c) II (d) II, IV

I. Ten dollars are too much to pay for a pen.
II. The water polo team have won the state championship for the second time.
III. That skier is one of those who competes nationally.
IV. I can not be calm on roller coasters.

29. (a) I, II, III (b) II, III, IV
(c) I, III, IV (d) None of these

I. The sexy, slim, Indian superstar.
II. The Indian, slim, sexy superstar.
III. My yellow, old, Ferrari sports car.
IV. My old, yellow, Ferrari sports car.

30. (a) I, IV (b) I, III
(c) II, IV (d) II, III

**Directions (Q. 31 - Q. 35):** Choose the alternative which best expresses the meaning of the idiom/ phrase in the question.

31. Find your feet
(a) desire to escape from a situation
(b) adapting and attuning to something
(c) finding one's own space
(d) ready to fight a war

32. (To be) On the ball
(a) another thing coming
(b) having fun
(c) being alert or well prepared
(d) raise the roof

33. (To) Go cold turkey
(a) speaking truth
(b) getting down to business
(c) gradually cutting down
(d) withdraw abruptly and completely

34. Break a leg
(a) good luck (b) take a break
(c) bad luck (d) trying hard to succeed

35. White-knuckled handshake
(a) sign of stressful situation
(b) friendly handshake
(c) sign of peace
(d) holding hands very lightly

## SECTION - B : GENERAL KNOWLEDGE

36. Voter Verifiable Paper Audit Trail (VVPAT) is an independent verification system for EVM designed to
I. allow voters to verify that their votes are cast correctly.
II. detect possible election fraud or malfunction.
III. Provide a means to audit the stored electronic results.
IV. Voter can see printout and take it out too.
(a) I and II (b) I, III and IV
(c) I, II and III (d) All of the above

37. The Film Federation of India (FFI) has selected the Hindi film ____________ to represent India in Best Foreign Language category at the 90th Academy Awards (Oscars).

(a) Padmavat (b) Dangal
(c) Bahubali (d) Newton

38. Who is awarded the Person of the Year for 2017 by Times magazine?

(a) The Silence Breakers
(b) Crown Prince Mohammed bin Salman
(c) The Dreamers
(d) Colin Kaepernick

39. How many banks have merged with SBI with effect from October 2017?

(a) 4 (b) 5
(c) 6 (d) 7

40. According to a recent report by NASA, the El Nino led to excessive carbon dioxide releases in which of the following ways ?

I. Hot weather and drought caused extensive wildfires in south-east Asia.

II. Drought in the Amazon rainforest stunted plant growth, reducing the amount of carbon they absorb while growing.

III. Warmer weather and near normal rainfall in Africa caused forests to exhale more $CO_2$.

(a) I only (b) II only
(c) II and III (d) I, II and III

41. Scientists from which of the following countries have developed the world's first artificial intelligence politician named SAM ?

(a) New Zealand (b) Japan
(c) China (d) Korea

42. Which State became the first State in India to operate electric bus services?

(a) Assam (b) Himachal Pradesh
(c) Karnataka (d) Maharashtra

43. ____________ officially launched its own oil-backed cryptocurrency called Petro.

(a) China (b) Senegal
(c) Venezuela (d) Singapore

44. ____________ is the first Indian woman pilot of Indian Air Force who created history by completing a solo flight on a MiG-21 Bison fighter aircraft.

(a) Bhawana Kanth (b) Mohana Singh
(c) Anny Divya (d) Avani Chaturvedi

45. ____________ is first city in India to get World Heritage City status by United Nations Educational, Scientific and Cultural Organization (UNESCO).

(a) Delhi (b) Mumbai
(c) Ahmadabad (d) Jaipur

46. Which of these digital payment mechanisms does not require an internet connection ?

(a) USSD (b) UPI
(c) e- wallets (d) IMPS 24X7

47. ____________ is a popular statistical simulation named after a city.

(a) Bristol (b) Vienna
(c) Berlin (d) Monte Carlo

48. BookMyShow and PayTM are examples of ____________ and ____________ wallets respectively.

(a) Open, Closed
(b) Closed, Semi-closed
(c) Semi-open, Semi-closed
(d) Semi-closed, closed

49. Which of the following Indian companies had become one of the top three most- valuable brands in the information technology (IT) service sector of the world?

(a) Wipro
(b) Infosys
(c) HCL Technologies
(d) Tata Consultancy Services

50. ICC Under-19 World Cup Trophy 2018 was won by India defeating Australia. What is special about this tournament ?

(a) Shubman Gill of India was declared the 'Man of the Tournament'.
(b) Team Afghanistan defeated three high profile teams namely Pakistan, Sri Lanka and New Zealand.
(c) India now holds the most wins record in Under-19 World Cup.
(d) All of the above

51. When ghee is kept in open air/sunlight for 30 minutes, the loss of Vitamin 'A' is

(a) 100% (b) 75%
(c) 34% (d) None of the above

52. Which one of the following has been appointed first female independent Director of International Cricket Council in 2018?

(a) Naina Lal Kidwai (b) Indra Nooyi
(c) Nita Ambani (d) Chitra Ramkrishna

**53.** Light waves can be polarised because they
(a) have high frequency
(b) have short wavelength
(c) are compressive
(d) are transverse

**54.** As per NITI Aayog's Health Index, 2018, which of the following States is the healthiest State in India ?
(a) Punjab (b) Haryana
(c) Kerala (d) Tamil Nadu

**55.** Which one of the following has been described as a 'Frozen Moment in History' ?
(a) Fatehpur Sikri
(b) Jallianwala Bagh
(c) Gol Gumbas Bijapur
(d) Kutub Minar

**56.** In a coastal city, a high tide occurs every
(a) 24 hours
(b) 12 hours and 25 minutes
(c) 12 hours
(d) 24 hours and 25 minutes

**57.** Which of the followings are the exclusive powers of Rajya Sabha under the Constitution of India?
I. Creation of new All India Services.
II. Enable Parliament to enact law on a subject in State List.
III. Enforcing proclamation of emergency when Lok Sabha is dissolved.
(a) I, II (b) II, III
(c) I, III (d) I, II, III

**58.** India and China jointly submitted a proposal to the World Trade Organisation (WTO) calling for the elimination - by developed countries - of the most trade-distorting form of farm subsidies, known in WTO parlance as ________ support as a prerequisite for consideration of other reforms in domestic support negotiations.
(a) Amber Box (b) Green Box
(c) Blue Box (d) Orange Box

**59.** Which of the following statements is correct as per the announcement of Union Budget 2018-19?
(a) 24 new Medical Colleges will be established as green field projects.
(b) 24 new Medical Colleges to be established by upgrading leading district hospitals.
(c) 24 new Medical Colleges to be established in tribal areas.
(d) 24 new Medical Colleges to be established for girl students.

**60.** Which has been termed as the 'Green Gold' by the Finance Minister ?
(a) Shell Gas
(b) CNG
(c) Bamboo
(d) Medicinal and Aromatic plants

**61.** Which of the following statements is not true about UNAIDS' target 90: 90: 90?
(a) 90% control of HIV infection by the year 2020.
(b) 90% of all people living with HIV will know their HIV status.
(c) 90% of all people with diagnosed HIV infection will receive sustained anti-retroviral therapy.
(d) 90% of all people receiving anti-retroviral therapy will have viral suppression.

**62.** According to John Templeton - Bull markets are born on pessimism, grow on scepticism, mature on optimism and die on ____________
(a) Excitement
(b) Euphoria
(c) Ebullition
(d) Ravishment

**63.** If RBI lowers the Cash Reserve Ratio (CRR), then
I. supply of money in the economy may increase.
II. banks will increase the interest rates.
III. exports will become cheaper.
(a) I (b) I, II
(c) I, III (d) I, II, III

**64.** GST has a ____________-tier structure for taxation of goods and services.
(a) Two (b) Three
(c) Four (d) Five

**65.** Which of the following statements is correct about FDI in India ?
(a) 100% FDI is allowed in single brand retail via automatic route
(b) 100% FDI is admissible in construction sector via automatic route
(c) Foreign airlines are allowed to invest upto 49% in Air India through approval route
(d) All of the above

**66.** 'Diopter' is the unit of measurement of ____________
(a) Heat
(b) Sound
(c) Energy
(d) power of a lens

**67.** If the election of the President of India is declared void by the Supreme Court, the acts performed by the President incumbent before the date of such decision of court are

(a) valid but subject to judicial review

(b) invalid

(c) valid

(d) valid but subject to the approval of the Parliament

**68.** In 2018, scientists have discovered a new organ which could also be the biggest organ in human body. What is the name of the organ?

(a) Interstitium (b) Mesentery

(c) Langerhans (d) Myeloid

**69.** World's longest sandstone cave has been discovered in which of the following States?

(a) Assam (b) Meghalaya

(c) Jammu & Kashmir (d) Nagaland

**70.** Which is the first Indian city to have its own logo for promoting tourism ?

(a) Goa (b) Agra

(c) Jaipur (d) Bengaluru

## SECTION - C : LEGAL APTITUDE

**Directions :** Apply the legal principles to the facts given below and select the most appropriate answer.

**71. Legal Principle :**

1. A person is liable for his negligence when he owed a duty of care to others and commits a breach of that duty causing injury thereby.
2. Valenti non fit injuria is defence to negligence.

**Factual Situation :** Anil and his wife, Reena, were in a shop as customers, where a skylight in the roof of the shop was broken, owing to the negligence of the contractors engaged in repairing the roof, and a portion of the glass fell and struck Anil causing him a severe shock. Reena, who was standing close to him, was not touched by the falling glass, but, reasonably believing her husband to be in danger, she instinctively clutched his arm, and tried to pull him from the spot. In doing this, she strained her-leg in such a way as to bring about a recurrence of thrombosis. Anil and Reena are claiming compensation for their injuries which were caused due to the negligence of the shop owners. The shop owners are denying liability on the grounds of volenti non fit injuria. The defence of volenti non fit injuria

(a) is available in respect of husband

(b) is available in respect of wife

(c) is available in respect of both husband and wife

(d) is not available in respect of both husband and wife

**Directions (Q. 72 - Q. 73):** Apply the legal principles to the facts given below and select the most appropriate answer.

**Legal Principles :**

1. Private nuisance is a continuous, unlawful and indirect interference with the use or enjoyment of land, or of some right over or in connection with it.
2. The person who for his own purposes brings on his lands and collects and keeps there anything likely to do mischief if it escapes, must keep it at his peril, and, if he does not do so, is prima facie answerable for all the damage which is the natural consequence of its escape.
3. A person is liable if he can reasonably foresee that his acts would likely to injure his neighbour.
4. The foreseeability of the type of damage is a pre-requisite of liability in actions of nuisance.

**72. Factual Situation :** During 2011, a European Directive was issued requiring nations of the European Community to establish standards on the presence of Perchloroethene (PCE) in water, which the Kingsland did in 2013. Alfa Water Co. purchased a borehole in 2007 to extract water to supply to the public in Kingsland.In 2014, it tested the water to ensure that it met minimum standards for human consumption and discovered that it was contaminated with an organochlorine solvent (PCE). On investigation, it emerged that the solvent seeped into the soil through the building floor of the Light & Soft Leather Tannery, about 3 miles from the borehole that eventually contaminated the Alfa's borehole.

Since the tannery opened in 1910, until 2007, the solvent it used had been delivered in 40-gallon drums which were transported by fork lift truck and then tipped into a sump. Since 2007, solvents had been delivered in bulk and stored in tanks. It was then piped to the tanning machinery. There was no evidence of any spills from the tanks or pipes, and it was concluded that the water had been contaminated by frequent spills under the earlier system. Alfa Water brought a claim against the Tannery on the grounds of nuisance. Whether the Tannery owners are liable?

(a) Yes, the escape of the solvent which contaminated the water is sufficient for making them liable.

(b) No, the damage is too remote as it was not possible for the Tannery owners to reasonably foresee a spillage which would eventually lead to contamination of a water borehole so far away.

(c) No, because Alfa Water Co. should have been careful in using good purifying mechanisms to ensure that the water is fit for human consumption. They cannot shift the blame on the Tannery owners.

(d) Yes, the damage is not remote as it was possible for the Tannery owners to reasonably foresee a spillage which would eventually lead to contamination of a water borehole just 3 miles away.

**73. Factual Situation :** MG Ltd. was constructing Crystal Heights, a posh state-of-the-art tower for commercial and residential purposes, in Gurugram. During construction, hundreds of claimants alleged that, in addition to dust and noise caused by the erection of the building, their television signals had been interrupted by the tower. The claimants, some of whom were absolute owners, and many others who were renting, sued in both negligence and in nuisance for the harm done to their amenity by the loss of their television signals. Whether the respondent's action in causing the appellant's television signals to be interrupted with the construction of their tower could constitute a private nuisance ?

(a) The interference with the television signal caused by the construction of the tower could not amount to a private nuisance at law. Effective town planning can sort this matter, instead.

(b) Yes, the large tower had interrupted their television reception, and caused private nuisance - for loss of enjoyment - and remuneration for their wasted television license fee, from the time their signal had been impaired.

(c) No, it cannot constitute private nuisance but the claimants can claim damages for loss of television signals.

(d) Yes, the respondent's conduct was unreasonable because the act of building the tower caused impairment of enjoyment of the land.

**74. Legal Principle :**

1. Any intentional false communication, either written or spoken, that harms a person's reputation; decreases the respect, regard, or confidence in which a person is held; or induces disparaging, hostile, or disagreeable opinions or feelings against a person.
2. The statement must tend to lower the claimant in the estimation of right-thinking members of society.
3. A mere vulgar abuse is not defamation.
4. Sometimes a statement may not be defamatory on the face of it but contain an innuendo, which has a defamatory meaning.
5. Defamation encompasses both written statements, known as libel, and spoken statements, called slander.

**Factual Situation :** In May 2017, a memorial commemorating the women of World War II was vandalized during an anti-government demonstration following the General Election. An offensive political slogan was spray painted across the plinth of the memorial. This act caused public outrage and widespread condemnation.

On Twitter, a political writer, Asha Mehta said that she did not have a problem with the vandalism of the memorial building. Chandna reacted to this negatively, suggesting that Asha should be sent to join Terrorist Organization. Asha's comments and Chandna's reactions both received national media coverage.

A few days later, Chandna published a tweet asking the question "Scrawled on any war memorials recently?" to Anshika Chauhan, another political activist. Anshika Chauhan responded stating that they had never vandalised any memorial building, and moreover had family members serving in the armed forces. Chandna followed with a second tweet, in which she asked if someone could explain the difference between Mehta (an "irritant") and Anshika Chauhan (whom she described as "social anthrax").

Anshika Chauhan asked for a retraction via Twitter and was promptly blocked by Chandna. Anshika Chauhan asked Chandna to make a public apology and claimed compensation for libel alleging that the First Tweet suggested that she had either vandalised a war memorial, which was a criminal act; and the Second Tweet suggested that she approved or condoned that vandalisation. What is the meaning of the Tweets and whether those meanings had defamatory tendency?

(a) Both the tweets were defamatory to Anshika Chauhan as the hypothetical ordinary reader can be expected to understand defamatory tendency of the tweet in the context of the situation.

(b) Second tweet was not defamatory as it was not referring directly to Anshika Chauhan. So, she cannot claim compensation.

(c) Natural and ordinary meaning of the tweets are not defamatory. So, she cannot claim compensation.

(d) First tweet was not defamatory because the natural and ordinary meaning of the statement which is conveyed to a hypothetical ordinary reader is not defamatory.

**75. Legal Principle :**

1. An assault is an act which intentionally causes another person to apprehend the infliction of immediate, unlawful force on a person.
2. A battery consists of an intentional application of force to another person without any lawful justification.

**Factual Situation :** Jagan was in his car when he was approached by a police officer who told him to move the vehicle. Jagan did so, reversed his car and rolled it on to the foot of the police officer. The officer forcefully told him to move the car off his foot at which point Jagan swore at him and refused to move his vehicle and turned the engine off. Jagan was convicted for assaulting a police officer in the execution of his duty. Is he liable for battery or assault?

(a) He is not liable because there cannot be an assault in omitting to act and that driving on to the officer's foot was accidental, meaning that he was lacking mens rea when the act causing damage had occurred.

(b) He is not liable as the act neither amount to an attempt nor a threat to commit a battery that amounts to an actionable tort of assault.

(c) Jagan's crime was not the refusal to move the car but that of having driven on to the foot of the officer and decided not to cease the act, he had established a continual act of battery.

(d) He is neither liable for assault nor battery as he accidently drove his car on the police officer's foot.

**Directions (Q. 76 - Q. 78):** Apply the legal principles to the facts given below and select the most appropriate answer.

**Legal Principles:**

1. Consideration is something that moves from the promisee to the promisor, at the implied or express request of the latter, in return for his promise. The item that moves can be a right, interest, profit, loss, responsibility given or suffered, forbearance or a benefit which is of some value in the eyes of law.
2. An offer may be revoked at any time before the communication of its acceptance is complete as against the proposer, but not afterwards.

**76. Factual Situation :** The defendant, Mr. Dhawan, wrote to the complainant, Mr. Chaman, with an offer to sell his house to him fort ₹ 8,00,000. He promised that he would keep this offer open to him until Friday. However, on the Thursday Mr. Dhawan accepted an offer from a third party and sold his house. According to Mr. Chaman, he was going to accept this offer but had not said anything to Mr. Dhawan because he understood that he had time until Friday. Mr. Dhawan communicated to Mr. Chaman that the offer had been withdrawn, through a friend to the complainant. After hearing this, Mr. Chaman went to find the defendant, informing of his acceptance to the offer. Thereafter, the complainant brought an action for specific performance and breach of contract against the defendant. Whether the defendant's promise to keep the offer open until Friday morning was a binding contract between the parties and whether he was allowed to revoke this offer and sell to a third party?

(a) The statement made by Mr. Dhawan amounts to a valid contract and he has committed a breach by selling the house before Friday.

(b) The statement made by Mr. Dhawan was nothing more than a promise; there was no binding contract formed. He had communicated an offer for buying his house to the complainant and this offer can be revoked any time before there is acceptance.

(c) The communication by a friend or other party that an offer had been withdrawn is invalid and could not be treated as if it came from the person himself.

(d) Promises to keep an offer open until a certain time is a binding agreement as it is accepted by the other party.

**77. Factual Situation:** MXM Co. is a building contractor who entered into an agreement with Star Heights Housing Association to refurbish a block of 27 flats. This contract was subject to a liquidated damages clause if they did not complete the contract on time. The MXM Co. engaged Hasan to do the carpentry work for an agreed price of ₹ 20,000. After six months of commencing the work, Hasan realised he had priced the job too low and would be unable to complete at the originally agreed price. He approached MXM Co. who recognised that the price was particularly low and was concerned about completing the contract on time. MXM Co. agreed to make additional payments to Hasan in return for his promise to carry out his existing obligations.

MXM Co. agreed to pay Hasan an additional ₹ 575 per flat. Hasan continued work on the flats for a further period of 6 weeks but only received an additional ₹ 5,000. He then ran out of money and refused to continue unless payment was made. MXM Co. engaged another carpenter to complete the contract and refused to pay Hasan any further sums. Hasan sued for payment under the original agreement and the subsequent agreement. MXM Co. argued that the agreement to make additional payments was unenforceable as Hasan has not provided any consideration to make this agreement a valid contract. Decide.

(a) The agreement to pay extra was unenforceable as Hasan had provided no consideration as he was already under an existing contractual duty to complete the work.

(b) Consideration was provided by Hasan in the form of conferring a benefit on the MXM Co. by helping them to avoid the penalty clause. Therefore, MXM Co. was liable to make the extra payments promised.

(c) There was no consideration provided by Hasan as to avoid the penalty clause was the main object of the contract. Therefore, MXM Co. was not liable to make the extra payments promised.

(d) MXM Co. is liable to pay compensation to Hasan as they have committed a breach of contract by employing another carpenter.

**78. Factual Situation:** Bournville ran a sales promotion whereby if persons sent in 3 chocolate bar wrappers and a postal order for ₹ 100 they would be sent a record. Big Beats owned the copyright in one of the records offered and disputed the right of Bournville to offer the records and sought an injunction to prevent the sale of the records which normally retailed at ₹ 1,000. Under the Copyright Act, retailers are protected from breach of copyright if they gave notice to the copyright holders of the ordinary retail selling price and paid them 6.25% of this. Bournville gave notice stating the ordinary selling price was ₹ 100 and three chocolate bar wrappers. The issue is whether the chocolate bar wrappers formed part of the consideration?

(a) The wrappers were a mere token or condition of sale and not consideration.

(b) The wrappers did form part of the consideration for the sale of records despite the fact that they had no intrinsic economic value in themselves.

(c) The wrappers did not form part of the consideration for the sale of records as they had no intrinsic economic value in themselves.

(d) There was consideration for the sale of records in the form of postal order for ₹ 100.

**Directions (Q. 79 - Q. 80):** Apply the legal principles to the facts given below and select the most appropriate answer.

**Legal Principles :**

1. Offer is a proposal made by one person to another to do an act or abstain from doing it. The person who makes the offer is known as the promisor or offeror and the person to whom an offer is made is known as the promisee or the offeree.
2. A contract comes into being by the acceptance of an offer. When the person to whom the offer is made signifies his consent thereto, the proposal is said to be accepted and the parties are at consensus ad idem regarding the terms of the agreement.

**79. Factual Situation :** Tejas drove his car to a car park named Super Car Park (SCP).Outside the car park, the prices were displayed and a notice stated cars were parked at the owner's risk. An automatic ticket vending machine provided a ticket, a barrier was raised and Tejas parked his car. In small print on the ticket it was stated that the ticket is issued subject to conditions displayed on the premises. On a pillar opposite to the machine was a notice stating the owners would not be liable for any injuries occurring on their premises. Tejas met with an accident and sought damages from SCP. SCP denied any liability on the basis of the exclusion clause which was mentioned in the notice on the pillar. Whether there is an offer and acceptance of the exclusion clause?

(a) There is a valid contract between Tejas and SCP as SCP had taken reasonable steps to bring exclusion clause to Tejas's attention at the time of making the contract.

(b) The contract was made when Tejas received the ticket and parked his car. The ticket amounted to a contractual document which effectively referred to the terms which were clearly visible on the premises.

(c) The machine itself constituted the offer. The acceptance was by putting the money into the machine. The ticket was dispensed after the acceptance took place and therefore the exclusion clause was not incorporated into the contract.

(d) The machine itself constituted the offer. The acceptance was by putting the money into the machine and acceptance of the offer mean acceptance of all the terms of the offer and hence SCP is not liable.

**80. Factual Situation :** The plaintiffs offered to provide delivery of a machine tool for a price of ₹ 75,535. The delivery of the tool was set for 10 months, with the condition that orders only qualified as accepted once the terms in the quotation were met and prevailed over any of the buyer's terms. The buyer responded to the offer with their own terms and conditions, which did not include the 'price variation clause' listed in the seller's terms. This included a response section which required a signature and to be returned in order to accept the order. The sellers returned this response slip with a cover letter signaling that delivery would be in accordance with their original quotation.

The tool was ready for delivery but the buyers could not accept delivery, for which the sellers increased the price which was in line with their initial terms. This was denied by the buyer and an action was brought by the seller to claim the cost of delay and interest. Was a contract made with or without a price variation clause?

(a) The buyer's order was not an acceptance of the initial offer from the seller but a counter-offer which the sellers had accepted by returning the signature section of the buyer's letter and so the contract was completed without the price variation clause and therefore the seller could not increase the cost of the tool.

(b) The buyer's order was an acceptance of the initial offer from the seller and so the contract was completed with the price variation clause and therefore the seller can increase the cost of the tool.

(c) The contract was made with price variation clause due to the condition that orders only qualified as accepted once the terms in the quotation were met and prevailed over any of the buyer's terms.

(d) The contract between the buyer and seller is not valid as both the parties are not agreeing to the same thing in the same sense.

**81. Legal Principle :**

1. 'Misrepresentation' means and includes-the positive assertion, in a manner not warranted by the information of the person making it, of that which is not true, though he believes it to be true;any breach of duty which, without an intent to deceive, gains an advantage of the person committing it, or any one claiming under him, by misleading another to his prejudice, or to the prejudice of any one claiming under him;causing, however innocently, a party to an agreement, to make a mistake as to the substance of the thing which is the subject of the agreement.
2. The tort of negligent misstatement is defined as an inaccurate statement made honestly but carelessly usually in the form of advice given by a party with special skill/knowledge to a party that doesn't possess this skill or knowledge.

**Factual Situation :** The plaintiff, Mr. Madan, entered into a tenancy agreement with the defendant, Esso Petroleum, in respect of a petrol station owned by the latter. During the course of the negotiation of the agreement, 'expert' advisers employed by the defendant had provided an estimate of the sales which the petrol station could expect which was based on inaccurate information and consequently was significantly inflated. The value of the rent on the agreement had been calculated based on this inflated figure. As a result, it was impossible for the plaintiff to operate the petrol station profitably. Whether the plaintiff could have any action for negligent misrepresentation ?

(a) The contract could not be held void for misrepresentation as the defendants presented the inflated figure as an estimate rather than as a hard fact.

(b) The defendant has no obligation to disclose as the parties contracting should obtain the necessary information themselves without relying upon the other party.

(c) As the defendant had taken it upon themselves to employ experts for the purpose of providing an estimate of sales, they owed a duty of care to the plaintiff to ensure that this was done on the basis of accurate information. Hence, the plaintiff can recover the losses which he had suffered as a result of the defendant's negligent misstatement.

(d) Both (a) and (c)

**Directions (Q. 82 - Q. 83):** Apply the legal principles to the facts given below and select the most appropriate answer.

**Legal Principles :**

1. The Tort of Negligence is a legal wrong that is suffered by someone at the hands of another who fails to take proper care to avoid what a reasonable person would regard as a foreseeable risk.
2. The test of liability requires that the harm must be a reasonably foreseeable result of the defendant's conduct, a relationship of proximity must exist and it must be fair, just and reasonable to impose liability.
3. The claimant must prove that harm would not have occurred 'but for' the negligence of the defendant. The claimant must prove, on the balance of probabilities, that the defendant's breach of duty caused the harm.

**82. Factual Situation:** Amar worked for an iron works, Luxmi Mills & Co. Ltd. operating a remotely controlled crane, Amar galvanized items by dipping them into a large tank of molten metal. In order to protect its crane operators, whose controls were located just a few feet from the tank, Luxmi Mills erected a low wall around the tank and also provided a sheet of corrugated iron that crane operators placed between themselves and the wall. The operators were not facing the tank while operting the crane. Thus, they could not see the operation of the crane and therefore relied upon signals from another worker located farther from the tank. Many other galvanizers at the time situated their operators in enclosed, windowed spaces from which they could safely see and perform their work. Luxmi Mills eventually adopted that practice as well. One day, Amar was working on the crane. At one point, he either turned toward the tank or leaned out to see the worker giving him instructions, thereby placing his head outside the iron sheet. A spray of molten metal burned Amar's lip. When it failed to heal and began to ulcerate, he consulted a doctor who diagnosed the wound as cancerous. Amar ultimately died from the spread of cancer after three years. His widow sued Luxmi Mills for negligence. Whether the employers would be liable for the full extent of the burn and cancer that had developed as a result?

(a) The employers are liable for all of the consequences of their negligence; thus, liable for the employee's death. His predisposition to cancer did not matter, nor did the results of the injury. The question of liability was, whether the defendant could reasonable foresee the injury.

(b) The employers are not liable because the duty of care towards Amar was not breached by them as they were using the same practices which were used by other companies at that time.

(c) The employers are not liable because Amar suffered injury due to his own negligence in stepping out of the protective shield.

(d) The employers are liable for burns and not for the death which happened due to Amar's cancerous condition which could not have been known to the employers.

**83. Factual Situation:** A 13-year-old boy fell from a tree. He went to a hospital where his hip was examined, but an incorrect diagnosis was made. After 5 days it was found that he was suffering from avascular necrosis. This was more advanced and serious than if it had been spotted straight away. Despite receiving treatment, it was determined that he had suffered from a muscular condition (avascular necrosis) which left the boy with a permanent disability and further left a strong probability that he would develop severe osteoarthritis later in life. The expert medical testimony indicated that had his fractured hip been identified on his initial hospital visit, there was a 25% chance of his condition having been successfully treated. He is claiming compensation for the negligence of hospital. Whether the hospital's negligence on his initial visit had caused his injury ?

(a) No, because there are very less chances that correct diagnosis and treatment would have prevented the disability from occurring.

(b) Where there are a number of possible causes, the claimant must still prove the defendant's breach of duty caused the harm or was a material contribution.

(c) Yes, because there are some chances that correct diagnosis and treatment would have prevented the disability from occurring.

(d) Both (a) and (b)

**84. Legal Principle :** Vicarious liability is when employers are held liable for the torts committed by their employees during the course of employment.

**Factual Situation :** New Vision School opened a boarding house (Shivaji House) for boys in the year 2000 for the students having behavioural and emotional difficulties. The claimants in the instant case had resided there between 2000 to 2003, being aged 12 to 15 during that time, under the care of a warden, who was in charge of maintaining discipline and the running of the house. The warden lived in the House, with his disabled wife, and together they were the only two members of staff in the House. His duties were ensuring order, in making sure the children went to bed, went to school, engaged in evening activities, and supervising other staff. It had been alleged by some of the boys that the warden had sexually abused them, including inappropriate advances and taking trips alone with them. A criminal investigation took place some ten years later, resulting in the warden being sentenced to seven years imprisonment. Following this, the victims brought an action for personal injury against the employers, alleging that they were vicariously liable. Whether the employers of the warden may be held vicariously liable for their employee's intentional sexual abuse of school boys placed under his care?

(a) No, vicarious liability could only arise when the employee is acting during the course of his employment and for his employer's benefit.

(b) No, the employers cannot be made liable for acts which are not authorised by them.

(c) Yes, there was a sufficient connection between the work that the warden was employed to do and the abuse that he committed to render it within the scope of employment. The abuse was committed at the time, premises and during the course of the warden's care of the boys.

(d) Yes, because the employers should be made liable in cases of sexual abuse of differently abled children.

**85.** In 2017, Special Leave Petition for re-investigation in the Mahatma Gandhi murder case was filed by ________

(a) Amrendra Sharan

(b) Pankaj K. Phadnis

(c) Tushar Gandhi

(d) Raju Ramachandran

**86.** Who is the first Indian woman to be elected as the Judge of the International Tribunal for the Law of Sea?

(a) Dr. Neeru Chadha

(b) Justice Gita Mittal

(c) Vijaya Lakshmi Pandit

(d) Dr. Menaka Guruswamy

**87.** Which of the following river(s) is/are declared as a legal entity by an Act of Parliament?

(a) Ganga (b) Whanganui

(c) Yamuna (d) All of the above

**88.** Which of the following lawyers approached the Supreme Court challenging the existing system of 'designation of Senior Advocates' ?

(a) Meenakashi Lekhi (b) Vrinda Grover

(c) Indira Jaisingh (d) Meenakshi Arora

**89.** 'Drunken Driving' is punishable under ____________.

(a) Indian Penal Code

(b) Motor Vehicles Act

(c) Road Safety Standards Act

(d) National Highways Act

**90.** The Supreme Court on 12 December 2017, had directed that _____________special criminal courts, to be set up to exclusively deal with cases involving _____________, should start functioning from March 1, 2018.

(a) 12, MPs/MLAs

(b) 12, Rape Accused

(c) 24, child-sexual abuser

(d) 24, Terrorism related offences

**91.** Which State Government, in India, has recently sanctioned stipend for junior lawyers practicing in the courts?

(a) Delhi (b) Punjab

(c) Kerala (d) Maharashtra

**92.** From the field of Law and Justice, who is awarded the Nari Shakti Puraskar 2018 on the International Women's Day?

(a) Geeta Mittal (b) Sudha Bharadwaj

(c) Flavia Agnes (d) Indira Jaisingh

**93.** Recently, the Supreme Court allowed ____________ euthanasia and right to give advance medical directives ____________, stating that human beings have the right to die with dignity as part of fundamental right to life.

(a) active, dying will (b) passive, living will

(c) active, living will (d) passive, dying will

**94.** Local self-governance is an example of

(a) federalism

(b) democratic decentralisation

(c) direct democracy

(d) administrative delegation

**95.** The institutional infrastructure under the Insolvency and Bankruptcy Code, 2016, rests on certain pillars:

I. Insolvency Professionals

II. Information Utilities

III. Adjudication

IV. The Insolvency and Bankruptcy Board of India

V. Asset Construction Companies

Correct code is :

(a) I, II and III

(b) II, III and IV

(c) I, II, III and IV

(d) All of the above

**96.** In 2017, the Supreme Court held that right to privacy is protected under Article 21 of the Constitution of India in the context of ____________

(a) State Surveillance

(b) Power of search & seizure

(c) Homosexuality

(d) Indian Biometric Identification Scheme

**97.** The age of consent for sexual intercourse between a husband and wife has been made ____________from ____________ years by the Supreme Court of India.

(a) 18, 16 (b) 16, 15

(c) 21, 18 (d) 18, 15

**98.** An accused is entitled to statutory bail (default bail) if the police failed to file the charge-sheet within ____________of his arrest for the offence punishable with 'imprisonment up to 10 years'.

(a) 30 days (b) 60 days

(c) 90 days (d) 180 days

**99.** Nelson Mandela Rules deals with ____________

(a) Apartheid

(b) Truth and Reconciliation

(c) Prison Management

(d) Global Peace-making

**100.** The Lok Sabha passed the Muslim Women (Protection of Rights on Marriages) Bill 2017. Which of the following are true about it?

I. It declares instant triple talaq illegal and criminalizes it.

II. It makes declaration of talaq a bailable offence.

III. A husband declaring talaq can be imprisoned for up to two years along with a fine.

IV. It entitles Muslim woman against whom triple talaq has been declared to seek subsistence allowance from her husband for herself and for her dependent children.

(a) I and IV (b) I, III and IV
(c) I, II and IV (d) All of the above

**101.** In August 2017, the Union Ministry of Law & Justice in association with the National Legal Service Authority (NALSA) launched 'Tele-Law' scheme in ______ to provide legal aid services to marginalised communities and citizens living in rural areas through digital technology.

(a) Andhra Pradesh (b) Bihar
(c) Madhya Pradesh (d) Rajasthan

**102.** In March 2018, the Supreme Court of India has held that there cannot be a stay of more than ______ on trial of ______

(a) 6 months, civil and criminal cases
(b) 6 months, criminal cases
(c) 3 months, rape cases
(d) 3 months, civil and criminal cases

**103.** Which country has withdrawn from the International Criminal Court (ICC) citing reasons of international bias in March, 2018 ?

(a) Burundi (b) Russia
(c) South Africa (d) Philippines

**104.** Regarding foreign law firms, the Supreme Court held

I. That foreign law firms can set up offices in India.

II. Foreign lawyers can practice in India.

III. Foreign lawyers can visit India for a temporary period on a fly in and fly out basis.

IV. Foreign lawyers can give advice to their clients on Indian laws.

(a) I, II, III (b) II, IV
(c) III (d) III, IV

**105.** Which is the world's first country to enact a law under which companies and government agencies that employ at least 25 people will be fined if they can't prove they pay men and women equally?

(a) Iceland (b) India
(c) Sweden (d) France

## SECTION - D : REASONING

**Directions (Q. 106 - Q. 110):** Read the following information carefully and answer the questions given below.

Eight friends Akash, Bunty, Chandan, Deepak, Esha, Fiza, Gazal and Hema are sitting around a circle facing the centre. Deepak is between Akash and Esha only, Fiza is second to the left of Esha. Bunty is between Chandan and Gazal only. Fiza is between Gazal and Hema only.

**106.** Who is fourth to the right of Bunty ?

(a) Esha (b) Hema
(c) Gazal (d) Deepak

**107.** In which of the following pairs, second person is to the immediate left of the first person?

(a) Deepak, Akash (b) Bunty, Gazal
(c) Bunty, Chandan (d) Hema, Esha

**108.** Which of the following is definitely true ?

(a) Chandan is to the immediate right of Bunty.
(b) Esha is to the immediate left of Chandan.
(c) Deepak is second to the left of Hema.
(d) Akash is second to the right of Esha.

**109.** Who is sitting in the immediate left of Esha?

(a) Fiza (b) Hema
(c) Gazal (d) Deepak

**110.** Who is third to the right of Gazal ?

(a) Fiza (b) Akash
(c) Hema (d) Esha

**111.** Harsh moves 15 kms in East direction, then turns towards North and moves 4 kms. From there he turns West and travels 12 kms. How far and in which direction is he from his starting point ?

(a) 5 kms, North-East (b) 5 kms, South-West
(c) 27 kms, North-East (d) 19 kms, North-East

**112.** Pratham travels 10 metres in North direction, he turns right and travels 20 metres. Again, he turns towards right and travels 25 metres. Then, he turns towards left and travels 15 metres. In which direction and how far is Pratham from his original position?

(a) 35 metres, East
(b) 38. 07 metres, South-East
(c) 25. 08 metres, West
(d) 25 metres, North-East

**Directions (Q. 113 - Q. 119):** Read the following information carefully and answer the questions given below.

Seven film buffs -Aamna, Archana, Aradhana, Anu, Aahana, Anuja and Aashna - attend a showing of classic movies. Three films are shown, one directed by Satyajit Ray, one by Stanley Kubrick, and one by Steven Spielberg. Each of the film buff see only one of the three films. The films are shown only once, one film at a time. The following restrictions must apply:

i. Exactly twice as many of the film buffs see the Stanley Kubrick film as the Satyajit Ray film.

ii. Aamna and Aahana do not see the same film as each other.

iii. Archana and Anu do not see the same film as each other.

iv. Anuja and Aashna see the same film as each other.

v. Aradhana sees the Stanley Kubrick film.

vi. Aamna sees either the Satyajit Ray film or the Steven Spielberg film.

**113.** Which one of the following could be an accurate matching of film buffs to films?

(a) Aamna: the Steven Spielberg film; Archana: the Satyajit Ray film; Anuja: the Satyajit Ray film

(b) Anu: the Steven Spielberg film; Aahana: the Steven Spielberg film; Anuja: the Steven Spielberg film

(c) Anu: the Stanley Kubrick film; Aahana: the Stanley Kubrick film; Aashna: the Stanley Kubrick film

(d) Archana: the Stanley Kubrick film; Aahana: the Steven Spielberg film; Anuja: the Satyajit Ray film

**114.** Each of the following must be false EXCEPT

(a) Aahana is the only film buff to see the Satyajit Ray film.

(b) Aahana is the only film buff to see Stanley Kubrick film.

(c) Aashna is the only film buff to see the Steven Spielberg film.

(d) Exactly three film buffs see the Stanley Kubrick film.

**115.** Which one of the following could be a complete and accurate list of the film buffs who do Not see the Stanley Kubrick film ?

(a) Aamna, Aahana

(b) Aamna, Archana, Aahana

(c) Aamna, Anu, Aashna

(d) Aamna, Anuja, Aashna

**116.** If exactly one film buff sees the Steven Spielberg film, then which one of the following must be true ?

(a) Aamna sees the Satyajit Ray film.

(b) Anu sees the Satyajit Ray film.

(c) Anuja sees the Stanley Kubrick film.

(d) Archana sees the Satyajit Ray film.

**117.** Which of the following must be true ?

(a) Archana, Aradhana and Anuja do not all see the same film.

(b) Archana sees a different film than Anuja does.

(c) Aamna sees a different film than Archana does.

(d) Aamna, Aradhana and Anu do not all see the same film.

**118.** If Anuja sees the same film as Aamna does, then which one of the following could be true?

(a) Aahana sees the Stanley Kubrick film.

(b) Aashna sees the Satyajit Ray film.

(c) Archana sees the Stanley Kubrick film.

(d) Aamna sees the Satyajit Ray film.

**119.** Each of the following could be a complete and accurate list of the film buffs who see the Satyajit Ray film EXCEPT

(a) Aamna, Archana (b) Anuja, Aashna

(c) Anu, Aahana (d) Aamna, Anu

**Directions (Q. 120 - Q. 121):** In each of the following questions, there are two statements labelled as Assertion (S) and Reason (R). Give answer

(a) if both 'S' & 'R' are true and 'R' is the correct explanation of 'S'.

(b) if 'S' is true but 'R' is false

(c) if 'S' is false and 'A' is true

(d) if both 'S' &'R' are false

**120. Assertion (S) -** Bulb filament is made of titanium.

**Reason (R) -** The filament should have low melting point.

**121. Assertion (S) -** Moon cannot be used as a satellite for communication.

**Reason (R) -** Moon does not move in the equatorial plane of the Earth.

**Directions (Q. 122 - Q. 126) :** Given below is a passage followed by few statements about that passage. You must select one of the following answers:

**Definitely True:** The statement follows logically from the information contained in the passage.

**Definitely False:** The statement is logically false from the information contained in the passage.

**Probably False:** The statement is more likely to be false than true, but not definitely false beyond a reasonable doubt, based solely on the information in the passage.

**Data Inadequate:** It is not possible to determine whether the statement is true or false without further information.

Mediators recognize that the law is generally in place to uphold mediator - client confidentiality, however, there are situations that may occur where the mediator is under obligation to break that confidence. This obligation can vary depending upon where the mediator is practicing and it may occur as a result of their employment contract or of the law. Where such an issue does occur, the mediator is expected to firstly try and discuss the presenting issue with their client; however, in situations where the factors under consideration are particularly urgent, it is accepted that this cannot always be the case.

Legitimate breaches of confidentiality relate to circumstances where the information the client has shared relates to anti-national activities; information of this nature must be reported. There are other circumstances where breaching confidentiality may be considered legitimate, for example, in the case of serious crime or suspected child abuse. Mediation service providers and mediators practicing independently have their own boundaries but must agree this contractually with their client at the outset of the client-counsel relationship.

**122.** Being obliged to break confidentiality in a mediator-client relationship is always a direct result of the law.

(a) Definitely True (b) Definitely False
(c) Data Inadequate (d) Probably False

**123.** When a client reports their involvement in a serious crime, their Mediators is legally obliged to report this ?

(a) Definitely True (b) Probably True
(c) Definitely False (d) Data Inadequate

**124.** Mediators have some flexibility regarding what they deem serious enough to lead them to breach confidentiality.

(a) Definitely True (b) Definitely False
(c) Probably False (d) Data Inadequate

**125.** Most Mediators agree with the conditions that the law places on them relating to breaching client confidentiality.

(a) Definitely True (b) Definitely False
(c) Probably False (d) Data Inadequate

**126.** If a mediator breaches his client's confidence about a serious issue without first informing their client of their intentions, they are breaking the law.

(a) Definitely True (b) Probably False
(c) Definitely False (d) Data Inadequate

**Directions (Q. 127 - Q. 128):** Find out the wrong number in the series.

**127.** 1, 2, 8, 33, 148, 760, 4626

(a) 760 (b) 148
(c) 4626 (d) 2

**128.** 888,440,216, 104,48,22, 6

(a) 440 (b) 216
(c) 22 (d) 6

**Directions (Q. 129 - Q. 130):** Find the one that does not belong to the group.

**129.** (a) 1 : 0 (b) 7 : 50
(c) 6 : 35 (d) 3 : 8

**130.** (a) LO (b) HS
(c) DW (d) JR

**131.** If in a certain code language 'BETTER' is written as 'EHWQBO', then how will 'LAWYER' be written in that language ?

(a) ODZVBO (b) OBZVDO
(c) DOZVBO (d) OVZOBD

**132.** If in a certain code language 'PERFECT' is written as '116', then how will 'DIVORCE' be written in that code ?

(a) 111 (b) 120
(c) 113 (d) 117

**133.** Which is the largest fraction ?

(a) 3/4 (b) 7/8
(c) 4/5 (d) 7/9

**134.** How many degrees are there between clock hands at 3.15 ?

(a) 0 (b) 5.5
(c) 7.5 (d) 10

**Directions (Q. 135 - Q. 140):** Read the following short passages and choose the best answer to the questions that follow each passage.

**135.** Modern science is built on the process of posing hypotheses and testing them against observations - in essence, attempting to show that the hypotheses are incorrect. Nothing brings more recognition than overthrowing conventional wisdom. It is accordingly not surprising that some scientists are sceptical of the widely accepted predictions of global warming. What is instead remarkable is that with hundreds of researchers striving to make breakthroughs in climatology, very few find evidence that global warming is unlikely.

The information above provides the most support for which one of the following statements?

(a) Most researchers in climatology have substantial motive to find evidence that would discredit the global warming hypothesis.
(b) There is evidence that conclusively shows that the global warming hypothesis is true.
(c) Most scientists who are reluctant to accept the global warming hypothesis are not acting in accordance with the accepted standards of scientific debate.
(d) Research in global warming is primarily driven by a desire for recognition in the scientific community.

**136.** The indigenous people of Tago are clearly related to the indigenous people of Taminia, but were separated from them when the land bridge between Taminia and Tago disappeared approximately 10,000 years ago. Two thousand years after the disappearance of the land bridge, however, there were major differences between the culture and technology of the indigenous Tagoians and those of the indigenous Taminians. The indigenous Tagoian unlike their Taminian relatives, had no domesticated dogs, fishing nets, polished stone tools, or hunting implements like the boomerang and the spear-thrower.

Each of the following, if true, would contribute to an explanation of differences described above EXCEPT

(a) Although the technological and cultural innovations were developed in Taminia more than 10,000 years ago, they were developed by groups in Northern Taminia with whom the indigenous Tagoian had no contact prior to the disappearance of the land bridge.

(b) Devices such as the spear-thrower and the boomerang were developed by the indigenous Tagoian more than 10,000 years ago.

(c) After the disappearance of the land bridge the indigenous Tagoian simply abandoned certain practices and technologies that they had originally shared with their Taminian relatives.

(d) Indigenous people of Taminia developed hunting implements like boomerang and the spear-thrower after the disappearance of the land bridge.

**137. Arbitrator:** The shipping manager admits that he decided to close the old facility on October 14 and to schedule the new facility's opening for October 17, the following Monday. But he also claims that he is not responsible for the business that was lost due to new facility's failing to open as scheduled. He blames the contractor for not finishing on time, but he too, is to blame, for he was aware of the contractor's typical delays and should have planned for this contingency.

Which one of the following principles underlies the arbitrator's argument ?

(a) A manager should see to it that contractors do their job promptly.

(b) A manager should be held responsible for mistakes by those whom the manager directly supervises.

(c) A manager should take foreseeable problems into account when making decisions.

(d) A manager, and only a manager, should be held responsible for a project's failure.

**138. Anita:** Television programs and movies that depict violence among teenagers are extremely popular. Given how influential these media are, we have good reason to believe that these depictions cause young people to engage in violent behaviour. Hence, depictions of violence among teenagers should be prohibited from movies and television programs.

**Amrita :** But you are recommending nothing short of censorship! Besides which, your claim that television and movie depictions of violence causes violence is mistaken: violence among young people predates movies and television by centuries.

Amrita's attempted refutation of Anita's argument is vulnerable to criticism on which one of the following grounds ?

(a) It confuses a subjective judgment of private moral permissibility with an objective description of social fact.

(b) It presupposes that an unpopular policy cannot possibly achieve its intended purpose.

(c) It cite purported historical facts that cannot possibly be verified.

(d) It rules out something as a cause of a current phenomenon solely on the ground that the phenomenon used to occur without that thing.

**139.** Most people feel that they are being confused by the information from the broadcast news. This could be the effect of the information's being delivered too quickly or of its being poorly organized. Analysis of the information content of a typical broadcast news story shows that news stories are far lower in information density than the maximum information density with which most people can cope at any one point of time. So, the information in typical broadcast news stories is poorly organised.

Which one of the following is an assumption that the argument requires in order for its conclusion to be properly drawn ?

(a) It is not the number of broadcast news stories to which a person is exposed that is the source of the feeling of confusion.

(b) Poor organisation of information in a news story makes it impossible to understand the information.

(c) Being exposed to more broadcast news stories within a given day would help a person to better understand the news.

(d) Most people can cope with a very high information density.

**140.** Cafe's Coffee Emporium stocks only two decaffeinated coffees: English Roast and German Mocha. Ratan only serves decaffeinated coffee, and the coffee he served after dinner last night was far too smooth and mellow to have been English Roast. So, if Ratan still gets all his coffee from Cafe's, what he served last night was German Mocha.

The argument above is most similar in its logical structure to which one of the following?

(a) Sunny wants to take three friends to the beach. His mother owns both a sedan and a convertible. The convertible can accommodate four people. Although the sedan has a more powerful engine, if Sunny borrows a vehicle from his mother, he will borrow the convertible.

(b) Ruchi can either take a two-week vacation in July or wait until October and take a three-week vacation. The trail she had planned to hike requires three weeks to complete but is closed by October, so if Ruchi takes a vacation, it will not be the one she had planned.

(c) If Tamanna does not fire her assistant, her staff will rebel and her department's efficiency will decline. Losing her assistant would also reduce its efficiency, so, if no alternative solution can be found, Tamanna's department will become less efficient.

(d) Wikro, Inc. has offered Arshit a choice between a job in sales and a job in research. Arshit would like to work at Wikro but he would never take a job in sales when another job is available, so if he accepts one of these jobs, it will be the one in research.

## SECTION - E : MATHEMATICS

**141.** Two cards are drawn together from a pack of 52 cards. The probability that one is a club and one is a diamond, is

(a) $\frac{13}{102}$ (b) $\frac{46}{104}$

(c) $\frac{12}{21}$ (d) $\frac{13}{200}$

**142.** Sanju has two watches with a 12-hour cycle. One of these watches, gains one minute a day and the other loses 1 and $\frac{1}{2}$ minutes per day. If Sanju sets both the watches at the correct time, how long will it be before they again show the correct time together ?

(a) 482 days (b) 290 days

(c) 1440 days (d) 730 days

**143.** To display 500 Wax Statuettes in a Museum, it is required to construct a big rectangular hall, allowing 22.5 $m^3$ space per statuette. The height of the hall is to be kept at 7.5 m, while the total inner surface area of the walls must be 1,200 sq.m.

Then the length and breadth of the hall, respectively, are

(a) 62 m and 22 m

(b) 50 m and 30 m

(c) 46 m and 35 m

(d) 40 m and 32 m

**144.** The ratio between the length and the breadth of a rectangular Jogging Park is 3 : 2. If Ashish cycling along the boundary of the park at the speed of 12 km/hr completes one round in 8 minutes, then the area of the park (in sq. m) is

(a) 3,07,200 sq. m

(b) 30,720 sq. m

(c) 1,53,600 sq. m

(d) 15,360 sq. m

**145.** A certain sum of money amounts to ₹ 1,008 in 2 years and to ₹ 1,164 in $3\frac{1}{2}$ years. Find the sum and the rate of interest.

(a) ₹ 900 and 12% (b) ₹ 800 and 12%

(c) ₹ 700 and 13% (d) ₹ 800 and 13%

**146.** Azhar can row 9.333 kmph in still waters and finds that it takes him thrice as much time to row up than as to row down the same distance in the river. The speed of the current of the river is

(a) 3. 333 km/hr (b) 3.111 km/hr

(c) 4.666 km/hr (d) 4.5 km/hr

**147.** A wheel that has 6 cogs is meshed with a larger wheel of 14 cogs. When the smaller wheel has made 21 revolutions, then the number of revolutions made by the larger wheel is

(a) 7 (b) 9

(c) 14 (d) 42

**148.** In a University, for each ₹ 200 spent by the Cultural Committee, Debating Committee spends ₹ 20 and for every ₹ 400 spent by the Debating Committee, the Student Welfare Committee spends ₹ 150. The triple ratio of the money spent by the Cultural Committee to the money spent by the Debating Committee to the money spent by the Student Welfare Committee can be expressed as

(a) 80 : 8 : 3 (b) 60 : 8 : 3

(c) 40: 4: 3 (d) 20: 4: 3

**149.** A wooden almirah is sold at a certain price. By selling it at $\frac{2}{3}$ of that price one loses 10%. Find the profit per cent at the original price.

(a) 15%

(b) 25%

(c) 35%

(d) 45%

**150.** The ratio between the present ages of Anu and Balbir is 5 : 3, respectively. The ratio between Anu's age 4 years ago and Balbir's 4 years hence is 1 : 1. What is the ratio between Anu's age 4 years hence and Balbir's age 4 years ago ?

(a) 4 : 1

(b) 2 : 4

(c) 3 : 2

(d) 3 : 1

## ANSWERS

| | | | | | | | | | |
|---|---|---|---|---|---|---|---|---|---|
| **1.** (b) | **2.** (a) | **3.** (d) | **4.** (c) | **5.** (b) | **6.** (d) | **7.** (a) | **8.** (c) | **9.** (d) | **10.** (b) |
| **11.** (c) | **12.** (d) | **13.** (a) | **14.** (d) | **15.** (a) | **16.** (d) | **17.** (d) | **18.** (c) | **19.** (b) | **20.** (c) |
| **21.** (d) | **22.** (c) | **23.** (a) | **24.** (d) | **25.** (a) | **26.** (b) | **27.** (d) | **28.** (c) | **29.** (d) | **30.** (a) |
| **31.** (b) | **32.** (c) | **33.** (d) | **34.** (a) | **35.** (a) | **36.** (c) | **37.** (d) | **38.** (a) | **39.** (c) | **40.** (d) |
| **41.** (a) | **42.** (b) | **43.** (c) | **44.** (d) | **45.** (c) | **46.** (a) | **47.** (d) | **48.** (b) | **49.** (d) | **50.** (d) |
| **51.** (a) | **52.** (b) | **53.** (d) | **54.** (c) | **55.** (a) | **56.** (b) | **57.** (d) | **58.** (a) | **59.** (b) | **60.** (c) |
| **61.** (a) | **62.** (b) | **63.** (a) | **64.** (c) | **65.** (d) | **66.** (d) | **67.** (c) | **68.** (a) | **69.** (b) | **70.** (d) |
| **71.** (d) | **72.** (b) | **73.** (a) | **74.** (a) | **75.** (c) | **76.** (b) | **77.** (b) | **78.** (b) | **79.** (c) | **80.** (d) |
| **81.** (c) | **82.** (a) | **83.** (d) | **84.** (c) | **85.** (b) | **86.** (a) | **87.** (b) | **88.** (c) | **89.** (b) | **90.** (a) |
| **91.** (c) | **92.** (a) | **93.** (b) | **94.** (b) | **95.** (c) | **96.** (d) | **97.** (d) | **98.** (b) | **99.** (c) | **100.** (a) |
| **101.** (b) | **102.** (a) | **103.** (d) | **104.** (c) | **105.** (a) | **106.** (a) | **107.** (c) | **108.** (d) | **109.** (b) | **110.** (d) |
| **111.** (a) | **112.** (b) | **113.** (b) | **114.** (a) | **115.** (b) | **116.** (c) | **117.** (d) | **118.** (c) | **119.** (b) | **120.** (d) |
| **121.** (a) | **122.** (b) | **123.** (c) | **124.** (a) | **125.** (d) | **126.** (c) | **127.** (a) | **128.** (c) | **129.** (b) | **130.** (d) |
| **131.** (a) | **132.** (c) | **133.** (b) | **134.** (c) | **135.** (a) | **136.** (b) | **137.** (c) | **138.** (d) | **139.** (a) | **140.** (d) |
| **141.** (a) | **142.** (c) | **143.** (b) | **144.** (c) | **145.** (d) | **146.** (c) | **147.** (b) | **148.** (a) | **149.** (c) | **150.** (d) |

# EXPLANATIONS

1. (b) In I, use of amicable and amiable are incorrect. Similarly in II, use of assent and ascent are incorrect.
2. (a) In I, it should be 'indigenous' in the 1st case and not ingenious. In IV, use of adjure and abjure are incorrect.
3. (d) Except IV, all other sentences are grammatically incorrect.
4. (c) It should be 'prophesied' and not prophesized. It should desert and not dessert. Correct usage of these two words make (c), the correct option.
5. (b) Sentence b in the 2nd column, portrays the use of 'well' as a noun. Out of the given options, only (b) represents this correct match. Hence (b) is the answer.
6. (d) In sentence (d) of the 2nd column, 'evidence' has been used as an interjection adjective. Out of the given options, only (d) represents this correct match. Hence (d) is the answer.
7. (a) The given sentence is an example of an epigram. An epigram is a pithy saying or remark expressing an idea in a clever and amusing way.
8. (c) Metonymy is a figure of speech which depicts substitution of the name of an attribute or adjunct for that of the thing meant. Here 'Sceptre and crown' stands for the kingship.
9. (d) "Steel" stands for sword.
10. (b) It is an example of paradox. A paradox is a statement or proposition which, despite sound (or apparently sound) reasoning from acceptable premises, leads to a conclusion that seems logically unacceptable or self-contradictory.
11. (c) It is an example of anticlimax. In the 1st line, It describes Dalhousie as a God. In the second line he is called the Lieutenant Colonel which provides a disappointing ending to an exciting event.
12. (d) Litotes is a figure of speech which means "Ironic understatement in which an affirmative is expressed by the negative of its contrary." The given statement is therefore an example of litotes.
13. (a) In II, it should have been, 'two years old'. And in IV, there is a hyphen missing. It should be 'two-year-old'.
14. (d) In I, there is a semicolon after 'asked' which makes it incorrect. The question mark at the end should cater to 'What did Joe mean.. .'. This makes II incorrect. In IV, the location of the question mark is incorrect.
15. (a) In IV, there should be a hyphen instead of a semicolon after abolish. Other sentences are correct.
16. (d) Statement IV is incorrect because the 'M' in Mayor should have been in Capital. Too many commas in statement I. The flow is interrupted.
17. (d) In III, the comma after 'friend' is redundant. In IV, the ':' after 'honour him' is incorrect.
18. (c) The use of semicolon after 'two things' makes IV incorrect. Statement II represents the correct sentence.
19. (b) The use of colon after 'but' makes II incorrect.
20. (c) 'regulation' is the subject here and 'has been undermined' is the verb. Here 'environmental' is an adjective.
21. (d) Only option (d) represents the correct pair of subject and verb.
22. (c) 'attempt' is the subject and 'failed' is the verb.
23. (a) (a) represents the correct set of subjects and verbs.
24. (d) 'Buses' is the subject and 'has' is the verb.
25. (a) Only option (a) represents the correct pair of subject and verb.
26. (b) 'sitar' is the subject and 'is tuned' is the verb.
27. (d) Except (d), all other options have subject-verb agreement errors.
28. *doubt. Here II is incorrect. It should be 'A limousine and a driver' or 'its driver'. Since driver is a countable noun, there should be a determiner before it.
29. (d) All the sentences have errors in them. In I, it should be 'Ten dollars is' and not 'are'. In II, 'state championship' should be in capitals. In, III, 'That skier' is incorrect. In IV, it should be 'cannot'.
30. (a) I and IV represent the correct order of words. Hence, II and III are incorrect.
31. (b) Find your feet means 'adapting or attuning to something'.
32. (c) On the ball means to be prepared for something.
33. (d) Go cold turkey means to quit something abruptly or suddenly.
34. (a) Break e leg means wishing someone good luck.

**35.** (a) White knuckled handshake refers to someone who is under lot of stress.

**36.** (c) Voter Verifiable Paper Audit Trail (VVPAT) is an independent verification system for EVM designed to allow voters to verify that their votes are cast correctly and detect possible election fraud or malfunction as well as to provide a means to audit the stored electronic results, but Voter can see printout and cannot take it out too. After the voter views the slip, seven seconds later, that slip will be dropped inside a sealed box linked to the EVM. It can only be authorised by authorised persons.

**37.** (d) Newton was India's official entry to the Best Foreign Film category at the Oscars 2018, according to a Film Federation of India official. The Oscars was held on March 4, 2018, in Los Angeles.

**38.** (a) Time magazine has named 'The Silence Breakers' – featuring the men and women who spoke up with the #MeToo movement – as the 2017 Person of the Year. Time's parameters of ranking were based on the magazine editors' reckoning of who or what had most influenced the news in the past year, for good or bad. US President Donald Trump was second, while Chinese Premier Xi Jinping came in the third spot.

**39.** (c) The State Bank of India, which was India's largest bank, merged with five of its associate banks (State Bank of Bikaner & Jaipur, State Bank of Hyderabad, State Bank of Mysore, State Bank of Patiala and State Bank of Travancore), and with the Bharatiya Mahila Bank.

**40.** (d) According to a recent report by NASA, the El Nino led to excessive carbon dioxide releases in hot weather and drought caused extensive wildfires in south-east Asia and drought in the Amazon rainforest stunted plant growth, reducing the amount of carbon they absorb while growing as well as warmer weather and near normal rainfall in Africa caused forests to exhale more $CO_2$.

**41.** (a) Scientists from New Zealand have developed the world's first artificial intelligence politician that can answer a person's queries regarding local issues such as policies around housing, education and immigration. The virtual politician, called SAM, was created by Nick Gerritsen, a 49-year-old entrepreneur in New Zealand.

**42.** (b) Goldstone Infratech Limited announced that its electric bus - Goldstone eBuzz K7, has been commercially launched for public transport in the state of Himachal Pradesh. The eBuzz K7 is the country's first electric bus to enter the public transport sector started running under Himachal Pradesh Transport Corporation.

**43.** (c) Venezuela's government opened the pre-sale of its contentious petro cryptocurrency, making 82.4 million of the blockade-busting virtual coins available for purchase. Venezuela became the first country to launch its own Petro cryptocurrency.

**44.** (d) Avani Chaturvedi is the first Indian woman pilot of Indian Air Force who created history by completing a solo flight on a MiG-21 Bison fighter aircraft.

**45.** (c) In July 2017, the Historic City of Ahmadabad or Old Ahmadabad was declared as India's first UNESCO World Heritage City.

**46.** (a) USSD digital payment mechanism does not require an internet connection.

**47.** (d) Monte Carlo simulation is named after the city of Monte Carlo in Monaco, which is famous for gambling such as roulette, dice, and slot machines.

**48.** (b) BookMyShow and PayTM are examples of closed and semi-closed wallets respectively.

**49.** (d) Tata Consultancy Services has become one of the top three most- valuable brands in the information technology (IT) service sector of the world.

**50.** (d) India pulled off a sensational eight-wicket win over Australia in the big final of the ICC Under-19 Cricket World Cup to become the only side in history to lift the coveted title for a record fourth time, 2000, 2008, 2012 and now 2018. During this tournament, team Afghanistan defeated three high profile teams namely Pakistan, Sri Lanka and New Zealand.

**51.** (a) When ghee is kept in open air/sunlight for 30 minutes, the loss of Vitamin 'A' is 100%.

**52.** (b) PepsiCo Chairman and CEO Indra Nooyi has been appointed to the International Cricket Council (ICC) Board as the governing body's first independent female director.

**53.** (d) Light waves can be polarised because they are transverse.

**54.** (c) According to the health index report, prepared by NITI Aayog, among the larger states (21), Kerala has topped the list, followed by Punjab and Tamil Nadu.

**55.** (a) Fatehpur Sikri has been described as a 'Frozen Moment in History'.

**56.** (b) In a coastal city, a high tide occurs every12 hours and 25 minutes.

**57.** (d) The exclusive powers of Rajya Sabha under the Constitution of India are creation of new All India Services and enable Parliament to enact law on a subject in State List as well as enforcing proclamation of emergency when Lok Sabha is dissolved.

**58.** (a) India and China jointly submitted a proposal to the World Trade Organisation (WTO) calling for the elimination - by developed countries - of the most trade-distorting form of farm subsidies, known in WTO parlance as Amber Box support as a prerequisite for consideration of other reforms in domestic support negotiations.

**59.** (b) As per the announcement of Union Budget 2018-19, 24 new Medical Colleges to be established by upgrading leading district hospitals.

**60.** (c) Bamboo has been termed as the 'Green Gold' by the Finance Minister.

**61.** (a) By 2020, 90% of all people living with HIV will know their HIV status. By 2020, 90% of all people with diagnosed HIV infection will receive sustained antiretroviral therapy. By 2020, 90% of all people receiving antiretroviral therapy will have viral suppression.

**62.** (b) According to John Templeton - Bull markets are born on pessimism, grow on scepticism, mature on optimism and die on Euphoria.

**63.** (a) If RBI lowers the Cash Reserve Ratio (CRR), then supply of money in the economy may increase.

**64.** (c) GST has a four tier structure for taxation of goods and services.

**65.** (d) 100% FDI is allowed in single brand retail via automatic route and 100% FDI is admissible in construction sector via automatic route as well as Foreign airlines are allowed to invest upto 49% in Air India through approval route.

**66.** (d) 'Diopter' is the unit of measurement of power of a lens.

**67.** (c) If the election of the President of India is declared void by the Supreme Court, the acts performed by the President incumbent before the date of such decision of court are valid.

**68.** (a) Scientists have identified a new human organ hiding in plain sight; in a discovery they hope could help them understand the spread of cancer within the body. Layers long thought to be dense, connective tissue are actually a series of fluidfilled compartments researchers have termed the "interstitium".

**69.** (b) World's longest sandstone cave discovered in Meghalaya. near Laitsohum village in Mawsynram area in East Khasi Hills. The cave is 24,583 metres (24.5 km) in length and 6,000 metres longer than previous world record-holder Cueva Del Saman in Edo Zulia, Venezuela.

**70.** (d) Bengaluru is the first Indian city to have its own logo for promoting tourism.

**71.** (d) The defence of VNFI is not available in respect of both husband and wife as it clearly shows that contractors were NEGLIGENT in their work due to which husband got injured and incase of wife she 'instinctively' pulled her husband aside which led to her injuries. Once it is proven that a person is negligent then he will be made responsible for all the natural consequences which results from such act.Also wife's act could be regarded as a 'rescue' act which again is an exception to VNFI.

**72.** (b) Clearly tannery owners are not liable because since 2007 they employed a new system of transporting and storing solvents and it is proven that spillage occurred due to earlier system of storage and transportation i.e,prior to 2007. The water was tested in 2014 which is 7 years later which is a pretty long time for anyone to foresee such a damage.Also the tannery was located a good 3 miles away from the borewell.

**73.** (a) The question asked is whether it is a 'PRIVATE' nuisance. It is clearly a 'PUBLIC' nuisance since there are number of people who have been affected and not just one single individual in order to constitute 'private' nuisance.

**74.** (a) Principle 1 is clearly applicable as both the tweets were intentional and since it received wide publicity therefore publication also happened which lowered the reputation in the eyes of public resulting in defamation. Moreover it was a false imputation made on Anshika as she never made such defamatory statemets in the first place.

**75.** (c) Clearly principle 2 is applicable as the moment Jagan refused to move to his vehicle off the foot of policeman there was intentional application of force and it had no lawful justification.

**76.** (b) Consideration is the price paid by the promisee for the promise of the promisor.In this case no consideration passed from promisee to promisor.

Also as per principle 2 offer can be revoked before acceptance.Since there was no acceptance given before he revoked his offer therefore the promisor is not held liable for breach of contract as there was no binding contract that came into being between the two.

**77.** (b) First,MXM agreed to increase the amount after acknowledging the amount payable to Hasan for work was inadequate. Secondly MXM also wanted to avoid penalty clause for not completing work on time. Both are sufficient consideration from promisee to the promisor. Hence to claim that no consideration passed from Hasan to MXM for second promise of increasing the remuneration does not hold ground.

**78.** (b) The question asked is whether chocolate bar wrappers formed part of consideration or not. The answer is clearly YES as even though wrappers may not have intrinsic value of their own yet the chocolates do come at a price and that is the consideration as one needs to purchase chocolates in order to have those wrappers. The wrappers don't come on their own they always come along with chocolates for which consideration must be paid.

**79.** (c) Since the ticket was issued after the acceptance took place therefore exclusion clause will not apply as the exclusion clause came only after the ticket was dispensed.It is imperative that all the conditions should be told before the contract comes into place. Here the contract came into being the moment money was put into the machine and was accepted by the machine.

**80.** (d) The buyer's order was not an acceptance of seller's initial offer as he gave his own terms and conditions which amounted to counter offer and this was accepted by seller by signing on the counter slip but it also attached a cover letter reiterating its original price variation clause therefore there doesn't seem to be meeting of minds as far as crucial part of agreement is concerned i.e,price. Therefore even though option (a) seems inviting but it is option (d) which is the correct option

**81.** (c) Clearly the answer is (c) in this case as per principle 2. An estimate given by 'experts' will tantamount to hard fact for a commoner who has very little knowledge of the subject and thereby goes by advice of such experts.It is for the defendant to be careful when they dish out any advice to anyone and they cannot be allowed to escape from their liabilities by taking such technical defence by saying that it was only an 'estimate' rather than a statement of fact.

**82.** (a) The question asked is whether the employers would be liable for 'full extent of burn and cancer that followed' which means that we don't have to establish whether the employers are liable for the tort of negligence or not it is **implied** that they are guilty of negligence only thing that is to be decided is as to what extent they are liable.Therefore option (a) is best option which tells about to what extent employers could be held liable for their negligence.

**83.** (d) An incorrect diagnosis does not mean a negligent act. It is nowhere given that hospital or its doctors were negligent in treating the boy.Nobody can ensure correct diagnosis for every patient all the time.Also there was only 25% chance that a correct diagnosis would have prevented the disability from occurring.hence if option (a) and (b) are read together it gives clear picture.

**84.** (c) Ordinarily an employer cannot be held liable for the 'criminal' acts of their employees but there are exceptions in cases where there is close connection between the work the employee was employed to do and the crime that was committed.Clearly here the employers will be vicariously liable for sexual abuse committed by the warden as his job was closely and intricately linked with the crime that committed.

**85.** (b) PANKAJ K PHADNIS

**86.** (a) DR.NEERU CHADHA

**87.** (b) WHANGANUI..river in New Zealand given status of living entity by act Parliament in 2014.

**88.** (c) INDIRA JAISINGH

**89.** (b) MOTOR VEHICLES ACT

**91.** (c) (KERALA)

**92.** (a) GEETA MITTAL..Acting Chief Justice of Delhi High Court

**98.** (b) 60 DAYS

**99.** (c) PRISON MANAGEMENT

**100.** (a) its cognizable and non bailable and imprisonment upto 3 years

**101.** (b) BIHAR

**103.** (d) PHILIPINES

**105.** (a) ICELAND

**For questions 106 to 110:**

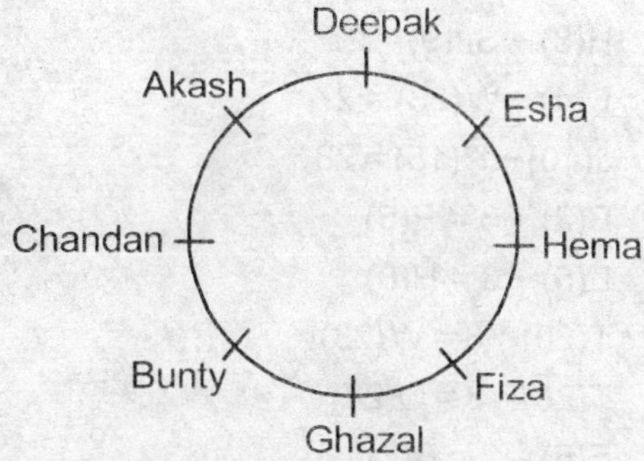


**106.** (a) Esha is fourth to the right of Bunty

**107.** (c) Chandan is sitting immediate left of the Bunty.

**108.** (d) Akash is second to the right of Esha.

**109.** (b) Hema

**110.** (d) Esha

**111.** (a)

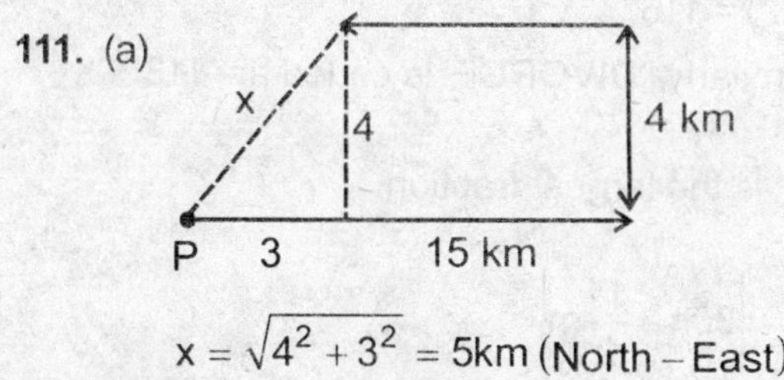


$x = \sqrt{4^2 + 3^2} = 5\text{km (North – East)}$

**112.** (b)

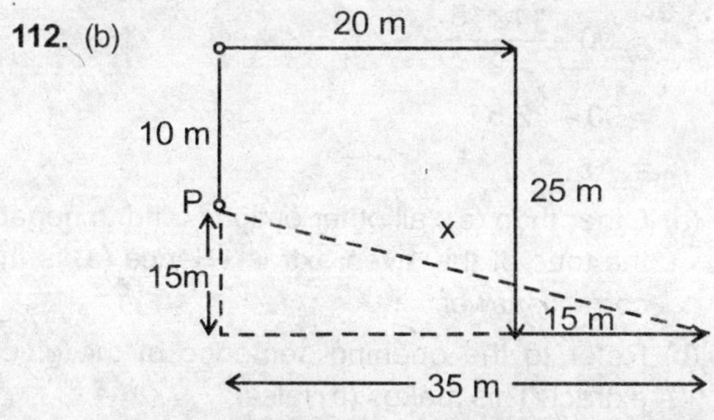


$x = \sqrt{15^2 + 35^2}$

$= \sqrt{225 + 1225}$

$= \sqrt{1450}$

= 38.07 m [South-East]

**For questions 113 to 119:**

By first statement, since twice as many of the film buffs see the Stanley Kubrick film as the Satyajit Ray film, therefore two cases our possible when:

| SK | 2 |
|---|---|
| SR | 1 |
| SS | 4 |

or

| SK | 4 |
|---|---|
| SR | 2 |
| SS | 1 |

where SK - Stanley Kubrick, SR - Satyajit Ray, SS- Steven Spielberg

**113.** (b)

| Satyajit Ray | Stanley Kubrick | Steven Spiclberg |
|---|---|---|
| Aamna | Aradhna<br>Archana | Anuja<br>Aashna<br>Aahana<br>Anu |

**114.** (a)

| Satyajit Ray | Stanley Kubrick | Steven Spiclberg |
|---|---|---|
| Aahana | Aradhna<br>Anu | Aamna<br>Anuja<br>Aashna<br>Archana |

or

| Satyajit Ray | Stanley Kubrick | Steven Spiclberg |
|---|---|---|
| Aahana | Aradhna<br>Archana | Aamna<br>Anuja<br>Aashna<br>Anu |

**115.** (b)

| Satyajit Ray | Stanley Kubrick | Steven Spiclberg |
|---|---|---|
| Aamna<br>Archana | Aradhna<br>Aashna<br>Anuja<br>Anu | Aahana |

**116.** (c)

| Satyajit Ray | Stanley Kubrick | Steven Spiclberg |
|---|---|---|
| Aamna<br>Archana / Anu | Aradhna<br>Aashna<br>Anuja<br>Anu / Aahana /<br>Archana | Aahana / Anu |

or

| Satyajit Ray | Stanley Kubrick | Steven Spiclberg |
|---|---|---|
| Archana / Anu<br>Aahana | Aradhna<br>Aashna<br>Anuja<br>Archana / Anu | Aamna |

Anuja sees the Satyajit Ray film is a must be true statement.

**117.** (d) Since, Aradhna saw stanley Kubrick film and Aamna saw either Satyajit Ray or Steven Spiclkerg.

**118.** (c) There are two possible answers option (a) and (c)

| Satyajit Ray | Stanley Kubrick | Steven Spiclberg |
|---|---|---|
| Anu /<br>Archana | Aahana<br>Aradhna | Aamna<br>Anuja<br>Aashna<br>Archana / Anu |

| Satyajit Ray | Stanley Kubrick | Steven Spiclberg |
|---|---|---|
| Aahana | Aradhna<br>Archana | Aamna<br>Anuja<br>Aashna<br>Anu |

But according to the official answer key, the answer is option (c).

**119.** (b) Anuja & Aashna

**120.** (d) In this case both the assertion and the reason are incorrect. Bulb filament is made of tungsten and it should have high melting point.

**121.** (a) In this case both the assertion and the reason are correct.

**122.** (b) The use of 'always' in the given inference makes it definitely false. The given passage instead have used the word 'may be' top describe the same condition.

**123.** *doubt. The answer should be "probably true" because it is stated in the passage that 'breaching confidentiality may be considered legitimate'. This clearly rejects option (c).

**124.** (a) Refer to the last sentence of the passage. This makes the given inference definitely true.

**125.** (d) Although the given inference may seem true as far as the given passage is concerned but because of lack of sufficient date we cannot conclude.

**126.** (c) The sentence-"...however, in situations where the...cannot always be the case..." makes the given inference definitely false.

**127.** (a) The pattern of the series is as follows:

1, 2, 8, 33, 148, 765, 4626,...

$\times 1+1^2$ $\times 2+2^2$ $\times 3+3^2$ $\times 4+4^2$ $\times 5+5^2$ $\times 6+6^2$

**128.** (c) The pattern of the series is as follows:

888, 440, 216, 104, 48, 20, 6

x2 + 8 x2 + 8 x2 + 8 x2 + 8 x2 + 8 x2 + 8

**129.** (b) The pattern is as follows:

1 : 0

0 = (1 – 0) × (1 + 1)

6 : 35

35 (6 – 1) (6 + 1) = 5 × 7

3 : 8

8 = (3 – 1) (3 + 1) = 4 × 2

(7 – 1)(7 + 1) = 6 × 8 = 48

**130.** (d) The pattern is as follows:

L (12) + 0(15) = 27

H(8) + S(19) = 27

D(4) + W(23) = 27

J(10) + R(18) = 28

**131.** (a) B(2) + 3 = E(5)

E(5) + 3 = H(8)

T(20) + 3 = W(23)

T(20) – 3 = Q(23)

E(5) – 3 = B(2)

R(18) – 3 = O(15)

Similarly, 'LAWYER' will be coded as 'ODZVBO'

**132.** (c) Count the position of every alphabet from backwards and add all the numbers.

P(11) + E(22) + R(9) + F(21) + E(22) + C(24) + T(7) = 116.

Similarly, 'DIVORCE' is coded as '113'

**133.** (b) $\frac{7}{8}$ is the largest fraction.

**134.** (c) $d = \left|30h - \frac{11}{2}m\right|$

$= 90 - \frac{11 \times 15}{2}$

$= 90 - 82.5$

$= 7.5$

**135.** (a) Other than (a), all other options tend to negate the tone of the given extract. Hence (a) is the correct answer.

**136.** (b) Refer to the opening sentence of the given extract. This makes (b) false.

**137.** (c) The given extract depicts the decision making problems faced by the shipping manager which means before taking decisions he did not foresee the problems. This makes (c) the correct choice.

**138.** (d) Amrita counters Anita on the ground of censorship. But, she fails to address the primary issue, that is, if TV soaps and films are not responsible then what is responsible for the on growing violence among teenagers. Hence, (d) is the correct option.

**139.** (a) Except option (a), if we negate all other options, they do not affect the given argument. If we negate option (a), the argument falls flat. Hence (a) represents the correct assumption.

**140.** (d) Except option (d), others are logically incorrect when we compare the analogy given with that of the actual argument.

**141.** (a) Let P(A) be the probability that one case is a club and one is diamond.

$$= \frac{^{13}C_1 \times ^{13}C_1}{^{52}C_1} = \frac{13 \times 13 \times 2}{51 \times 52} = \frac{13}{102}$$

**142.** (c) Ratio of gain to lose is 2 : 3

As the time format is of 12 hours so it will display the same time when one will gain $\frac{2}{5} \times 12$ hours

another will lose $\frac{3}{5} \times 12$ hours

To gain $\frac{2}{5} \times 12$ hours, the required time

$$= \frac{2}{5} \times 12 \times 60 \text{ days} = 288 \text{ days}$$

So, the answer must be the multiple of 288 i.e. 1440 days.

**143.** (b) Total volume of the hall = 500 × 22.5 m³

$= 11250 \text{ m}^3.$

$11250 = l \times b \times 7.5$

$lb = 1500 \text{ m}^2$

$1200 = 2[h(l + b)]$

$\frac{600}{7.5} = l + b$

$80 = l + b$

50 m and 30 m are length & breadth respectively.

**144.** (c) $\text{speed} = \frac{\text{distance}}{\text{time}}$

$12 \times \frac{8}{60} = \text{distance} = 2(l + b)$

$\frac{8}{5} = 2[5x]$

$4 = 25x$

$\frac{4}{25} = x \text{ km}$

$l \times b = 3 \times \frac{4}{25} \times 2 \times \frac{4}{25} \times 1000 \times 1000$

$= 153600 \text{ m}^2.$

**145.** (d) $\frac{PRT}{100} = A - P = P\left[\frac{2R}{100} + 1\right] = 1008$

$= P[100 + 2R] = 100800$

$\frac{P[100 + 2R]}{P[100 + 3.5R]} = \frac{100800}{116400}$

$\Rightarrow 116400 + 2328R = 100800 + 3528R$

$\Rightarrow 15600 = 1200R$

$\Rightarrow \boxed{13 = R}$

$\boxed{P = 800₹}$

**146.** (c) $\frac{d}{(9.333 - s)} = 3t$

$\frac{d}{(9.333 + s)} = t$

$\frac{9.333 + 5}{9.333 - 5} = 3$

$9.333 + 5 = 27.999 - 3S$

$4S = 18.666$

$S = 4.6665$

**147.** (b) Let larger wheel made x revolutions then

$x = \frac{21 \times 6}{14} = 9$

**148.** (a) Cultural : Debating = 200 : 20

Debating : student welfare = 400 : 150

$\Rightarrow$ 4000 : 400 : 150

$\Rightarrow$ 80 : 8 : 3

**149.** (c) Let wooden almirah is sold at x-price

If selling price = $\frac{2}{3}x$

$$\frac{CP - \frac{2}{3}x}{CP} \times 100 = 10 \quad ...(1)$$

$$\boxed{\frac{x - CP}{CP} \times 100 = P} \quad ...(2)$$

$$\frac{CP - \frac{2}{3}x}{x - CP} = \frac{10}{P}$$

$$1 - \frac{x}{CP}\frac{2}{3} = \frac{10}{10}$$

$$1-\frac{1}{10}=\frac{x}{CP}\frac{2}{3}$$

$$\frac{9}{10}\times\frac{3}{2}=\frac{x}{CP}$$

$$\frac{27}{20}\ \frac{x}{CP}$$

$$\frac{x}{CP}-61\times100$$

$$\left(\frac{27}{20}-1\right)\times100$$

$$\frac{7}{20}\times100=35$$

**150.** (d) Let x and y be the present ages of Anu & Balbir respectively

$$\frac{x}{y}=\frac{5}{3}\Rightarrow 3x=5y\Rightarrow x=\frac{5}{3}y$$

4 years & 4 years hence

$$\frac{x-4}{y+4}=\frac{1}{1}$$

$$x-4=y+4$$

$$x-y=8$$

$$\Rightarrow\frac{5}{3}y-y=8$$

$$\Rightarrow y=12$$

$$x=\frac{5}{3}\times12=20$$

$$\frac{x+4}{y-4}=\frac{24}{8}=\frac{3}{1}$$